MANAGEMENT INFORMATION SYSTEMS

Tenth Edition

James A. O'Brien

College of Business Administration
Northern Arizona University

George M. Marakas

KU School of Business
University of Kansas

McGraw-Hill
Irwin

MANAGEMENT INFORMATION SYSTEMS: GLOBAL EDITION

Published by McGraw-Hill/Irwin, a business unit of The McGraw-Hill Companies, Inc., 1221 Avenue of the Americas, New York, NY, 10020. Copyright © 2011, 2009, 2008, 2006, 2004, 2002, 1999, 1996, 1993, 1990 by The McGraw-Hill Companies, Inc. All rights reserved. No part of this publication may be reproduced or distributed in any form or by any means, or stored in a database or retrieval system, without the prior written consent of The McGraw-Hill Companies, Inc., including, but not limited to, in any network or other electronic storage or transmission, or broadcast for distance learning.

Some ancillaries, including electronic and print components, may not be available to customers outside the United States.

This book is printed on acid-free paper.

1 2 3 4 5 6 7 8 9 0 DOW/DOW 10 9 8 7 6 5 4 3 2 1

ISBN 978-0-07-122109-2
MHID 0-07-122109-3

Dedicated to our families and our friends. You make everything possible.

The world of information systems presents new and exciting challenges each and every day. Creating a textbook to capture this world is a formidable task, to be sure. This, the 10th edition of *Management Information Systems,* represents the best we have to offer. We take pride in delivering this new edition to you, and we thank all of you for your loyalty to the book and the input you provided that was instrumental in its development. Your continued support fills us with joy and a sense of both accomplishment and contribution.

We are also pleased and excited to welcome a new member to our writing family. Miguel Aguirre-Urreta has joined us in the creation of the materials contained herein. His work and effort on the Real World Cases and blue boxes will be apparent as we bring you new cases in every chapter of the book. Please join us in welcoming Miguel to our family.

On behalf of Jim, Miguel, and myself, please accept our sincere appreciation for your support and loyalty. As always, we hope you enjoy and benefit from this book.

About the Authors

James A. O'Brien was an adjunct professor of Computer Information Systems in the College of Business Administration at Northern Arizona University. He completed his undergraduate studies at the University of Hawaii and Gonzaga University and earned an MS and PhD in Business Administration from the University of Oregon. He was professor and coordinator of the CIS area at Northern Arizona University, professor of Finance and Management Information Systems and chairman of the Department of Management at Eastern Washington University, and a visiting professor at the University of Alberta, the University of Hawaii, and Central Washington University.

Dr. O'Brien's business experience included working in the Marketing Management Program of the IBM Corporation, as well as serving as a financial analyst for the General Electric Company. He is a graduate of General Electric's Financial Management Program. He also served as an information systems consultant to several banks and computer services firms.

Jim's research interests were in developing and testing basic conceptual frameworks used in information systems development and management. He wrote eight books, including several that have been published in multiple editions, as well as in Chinese, Dutch, French, Japanese, and Spanish translations. He also contributed to the field of information systems through the publication of many articles in business and academic journals, as well as through his participation in academic and industry associations in the field of information systems.

George M. Marakas is a professor of Information Systems at the School of Business at the University of Kansas. His teaching expertise includes Systems Analysis and Design, Technology-Assisted Decision Making, Electronic Commerce, Management of IS Resources, Behavioral IS Research Methods, and Data Visualization and Decision Support. In addition, George is an active researcher in the area of Systems Analysis Methods, Data Mining and Visualization, Creativity Enhancement, Conceptual Data Modeling, and Computer Self-Efficacy.

George received his PhD in Information Systems from Florida International University in Miami and his MBA from Colorado State University. Prior to his position at the University of Kansas, he was a member of the faculties at the University of Maryland, Indiana University, and Helsinki School of Economics. Preceding his academic career, he enjoyed a highly successful career in the banking and real estate industries. His corporate experience includes senior management positions with Continental Illinois National Bank and the Federal Deposit Insurance Corporation. In addition, George served as president and CEO for CMC Group Inc., a major RTC management contractor in Miami, Florida, for three years. Throughout his academic career, George has distinguished himself both through his research and in the classroom. He has received numerous national teaching awards, and his research has appeared in the top journals in his field. In addition to this text, he is the author of three best-selling textbooks on information systems: *Decision*

6

Support Systems for the 21st Century; Systems Analysis and Design: An Active Approach; and *Data Warehousing, Mining, and Visualization: Core Concepts.*

Beyond his academic endeavors, George is also an active consultant and has served as an advisor to a number of organizations, including the Central Intelligence Agency, Brown & Williamson, the Department of the Treasury, the Department of Defense, Xavier University, Citibank Asia-Pacific, Nokia Corporation, Professional Records Storage Inc., and United Information Systems. His consulting activities are concentrated primarily on e-commerce strategy, the design and deployment of global IT strategy, workflow reengineering, e-business strategy, and ERP and CASE tool integration.

George is also an active member of a number of professional IS organizations and an avid golfer, a motorcyclist, a second-degree Black Belt in Tae Kwon Do, a PADI master scuba diver trainer and IDC staff instructor, and a member of Pi Kappa Alpha fraternity.

The O'Brien and Marakas Approach

A Business and Managerial Perspective

The Tenth Edition is designed for business students who are or who will soon become business professionals in today's fast-changing business world. The goal of this text is to help business students learn how to use and manage information technologies to revitalize business processes, improve business decision making, and gain competitive advantage. Thus, it places a major emphasis on up-to-date coverage of the essential role of Internet technologies in providing a platform for business, commerce, and collaboration processes among all business stakeholders in today's networked enterprises and global markets. This is the business and managerial perspective that this text brings to the study of information systems. Of course, as in all O'Brien texts, this edition:

- Loads the text with **Real World Cases,** in-depth examples **(Blue Boxes),** and opportunities to learn about real people and companies in the business world **(Real World Activities, Case Study Questions, Discussion Questions,** and **Analysis Exercises).**
- Organizes the text around a simple **Five-Area Information Systems Framework** that emphasizes the IS knowledge a business professional needs to know.
- Places a **major emphasis on the strategic role of information technology** in providing business professionals with tools and resources for managing business operations, supporting decision making, enabling enterprise collaboration, and gaining competitive advantage.

Modular Structure of the Text

The text is organized into modules that reflect the five major areas of the framework for information systems knowledge. Each chapter is then organized into two or more distinct sections to provide the best possible conceptual organization of the text and each chapter. This organization increases instructor flexibility in assigning course material because it structures the text into modular levels (i.e., modules, chapters, and sections) while reducing the number of chapters that need to be covered.

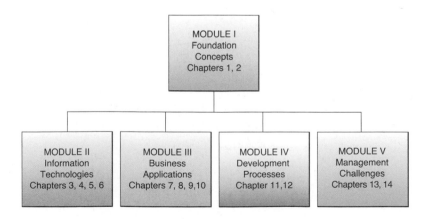

An Information Systems Framework

Business Applications

How businesses use the Internet and other information technologies to support their business processes, e-business and e-commerce initiatives, and business decision making (Chapters 7, 8, 9, and 10).

Management Challenges

The challenges of business/IT technologies and strategies, including security and ethical challenges and global IT management (Chapters 13 and 14).

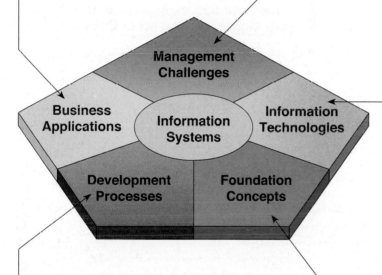

Information Technologies

Includes major concepts, developments, and managerial issues involved in computer hardware, software, telecommunications networks, data resource management technologies, and other technologies (Chapters 3, 4, 5, and 6).

Development Processes

Developing and implementing business/IT strategies and systems using several strategic planning and application development approaches (Chapters 11 and 12).

Foundation Concepts

Fundamental business information systems concepts, including trends, components, and roles of information systems (Chapter 1) and competitive advantage concepts and applications (Chapter 2). Selective coverage of relevant behavioral, managerial, and technical concepts.

Real World Examples

Real World Cases

Each chapter provides four Real World Cases—in-depth examples that illustrate how prominent businesses and organizations have attempted to implement the theoretical concepts students have just learned.

A full list of cases is available on pages 1–2.

REAL WORLD

CASE 1

Enterprise Data Explosion Will Only Get Bigger and That Means Big Risk!

Despite the fanfare over cloud computing and mobile technologies, possibly the most pervasive underlying trend in all of IT is the enterprise data explosion.

Borrowing from Moore's Law (see Chapter 3): Data doubles every 18 months and this explosion shows no sign of abating. New compliance regulations in the wake of the global financial meltdown will likely mandate even more data retention, while the imperative to digitize healthcare records in the United States will prompt a fresh set of storage requirements. With the cost of disk space at an all-time low and the vagaries of compliance laws compelling businesses to "save everything" as a brute force method to reduce risk, enterprises are adding capacity at an astounding rate.

Analysts predict that unstructured data will grow at twice the rate of conventional structured data held in databases. By 2010, this "dark matter," so named due to the challenge of extracting useful information from raw data, will make up the majority of all enterprise data stored.

Most of that dark matter comes in the form of security, network, and system event logs. Almost everything that happens in a business is recorded in a log file, making the search and analysis of that data an essential part of managing, securing, and auditing how a company's technology infrastructure is used. Logs are key to many forms of regulatory compliance and are a source of business intelligence just waiting to be tapped.

FIGURE 5.1

Data may be the single most important asset in an organization.

Source: ThinkStock/PunchStock.

Dark matter is only about half of all enterprise data stored. The structured stuff is ballooning, too: transaction records, e-mail archives, rich media, near-line database backups, and on and on. We all know how low-cost storage systems and virtualization are making it more economical to store this stuff. But managing and securing these huge volumes of data are becoming prohibitively difficult, and the cost of buying and maintaining new hardware without increased efficiencies cannot be sustained forever.

We are still years away from solutions that allow administrators to wrap their arms around the whole, heterogeneous storage mess and manage it from one monster control panel. Meanwhile, some interesting new options for easing the pain are emerging.

Most people have heard of one of them, thanks to the recent bidding war over Data Domain: *data deduplication*. Here, byte- or block-level data reduction techniques shrink the disk requirements (by as much as 80 percent or more) for backups, snapshots, and even virtual server disk files, lowering overall data protection costs while at the same time making more data available on near-line storage.

Some of the new cloud solutions are interesting, too, the most prevalent of which are cloud-based hosting or backup/recovery solutions from the likes of SunGard or RackSpace. In addition, many of the first practical cloud-based applications have been built to store, manage, and process massive data sets, leveraging large clusters of commodity hardware and using programming frameworks (such as MapReduce and Hadoop) for reliable and scalable distributed computing.

These and other technologies can be marshaled to manage the explosive growth of data—and, in some cases, to extract new value from that data. But determining the best practices in each discipline and creating a grand strategy that drives toward an enterprise-wide solution isn't going to be easy.

For example, IT managers in Hong Kong, Singapore, and Australia may be putting company data at risk by underestimating the effect of its loss, according to a recent survey by Kroll Ontrack, a large data recovery tools provider. Only 7 percent of respondents believe data loss has a "high" impact on a business. The survey, conducted in early 2010, asked IT managers from 945 companies of different sizes throughout Hong Kong, Singapore, and Australia about their views and experiences related to data management, said Kroll, adding that under half (49 percent) of all IT managers have reported a data loss situation in the last two years.

While larger companies may not fully appreciate the risks they face with data loss, it is the small business sector that appears to be most at risk. An alarming 49 percent of small companies stated that they fail to backup their data on a daily basis, said Kroll. This is despite the fact that nearly half of all participants had experienced data loss in their workplace in the past two years, and 36 percent felt that

---

Real Life Lessons

Use Your Brain

Traditional case study questions promote and provide opportunity for critical thinking and classroom discussion.

---

reason than to reduce what he calls the "ridiculous cost" of outsourcing the e-discovery function.

"We had to find a way to provide a better IT service to reduce the amount of data to hand over, to see how much more of that review cycle we could pull [in-house] with our legal team before they send it out to outside counsel," he says. "It was an IT initiative to say, 'We've got to do this better to cut this cost.'"

Royer says IT's initial implementation focused on giving the company's in-house legal team the technology to search and hold e-mails. A hold keeps the data from being moved into long-term storage. Now, with that done, IT plans to add features so the legal department can perform e-discovery searches and holds on additional data sources and repositories, such as file servers and backup tapes.

Royer could not disclose actual figures, but he says that bringing some of the e-discovery functions in house immediately reduced the amount of material the company had to send to outside counsel for reviewing. In fact, he says it cut the amount "by well over 75 percent on the next four litigation matters that arose post-implementation. These matters arose within the first six months of go-live, and the cost savings put us into a 300 percent ROI within that same time frame."

The move to bring e-discovery in-house also corresponds with a broadening in how companies define e-discovery, says Jonathan Gossels, president and CEO of SystemExperts Corp., a security consulting firm in Sudbury, Massachusetts. Companies now realize that they need the ability to search electronic records not just in response to legal action, he says. They also need it for regulatory requests and inquiries and for their own internal investigations, such as potential security breaches or personnel violations.

"That's why it makes perfect sense to bring it in-house. It's the recognition that they need it to run their day-to-day business," Gossels says, noting that customers are increasingly defining the function as "discovery and investigations."

In fact, many companies still need to get a good handle on information governance before they can determine how much of the e-discovery capability they should have under their own purview, adds Gossels. Governance refers to the process, procedures and policies that are in place that dictate what information the company stores, where and how it is stored, and when it should be deleted. Gartner analyst Debra Logan says probably fewer than 10 percent of companies do a really good job at information governance—and even those companies aren't as comprehensive as they could be.

Case in point: Microsoft. Joe Banks, litigation program manager at Microsoft, says the company started to look more closely at litigation costs over the past two years and found that "discovery just leaps off the page. It was exorbitantly expensive, and the trend was just going up. So we wanted to figure out ways to cut those costs."

As a result, Banks says, Microsoft invested in e-discovery software. (Banks declines to name the product for publication but says it's not a tool from Microsoft.) He says that although he hasn't seen a product that provides an end-to-end solution, technology improvements in recent years have made bringing e-discovery in-house even more advantageous for companies such as his.

Banks says Microsoft has started to perform pieces of the e-discovery process internally. The company does its own data minimization, which culls through the raw data using specific search parameters; that reduced volume of data can then be handed over to attorneys for review. Banks says he expects Microsoft to increase the percentage of the culling it does internally and, as the technology improves, possibly bringing some of the review process in-house, too.

Advances in technology have helped make it more cost-effective to perform many searches in-house, Banks says, for Microsoft and for just about everyone else. "And when you combine that with the economic factors of the past two years, where people were forced to find ways to cut costs, it was just a natural inflection point for corporations to re-examine the old model."

Source: Adapted from Mary K. Pratt, "e-Discovery Moves In-House," *Computerworld*, Fairfax Media Business Group, October 1, 2010.

CASE STUDY QUESTIONS

1. What does the move from outsourced e-discovery to an enterprise solution mean to the organization? What qualifications or experiences would you think an IT professional should have to create enterprise solutions? Support your answer with examples from the case.

2. Consider the different companies mentioned in the case and their experiences with enterprise architecture. Does this approach seem to work better in certain types of companies or industries than in others? Why or why not?

3. What is the value derived from companies that adopt enterprise-wide solutions? Can you see any disadvantages? Discuss.

REAL WORLD ACTIVITIES

1. e-Discovery is a relatively new approach to litigation. Go online and research the various ways in which it is used. Prepare a report to summarize your work.

2. Have you considered a career as an IT professional? What bundle of courses would you put together to design a major or a track specializing in enterprise solutions? Break into small groups with your classmates to outline the major areas that should be covered.

Use Your Hands

The Real World Activities section offers possibilities for hands-on exploration and learning.

Strategy, Ethics . . .

Competitive Advantage

Chapter 2 focuses on the use of IT as a way to surpass your competitor's performance.

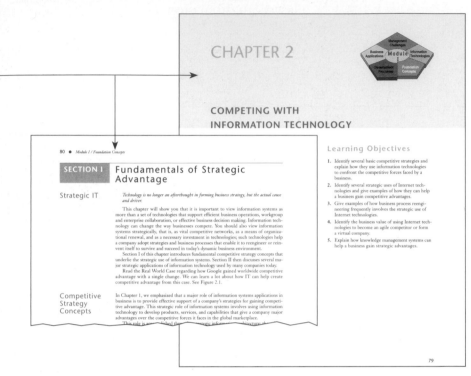

Ethics & Security

Chapter 13 discusses the issues surrounding these topics and the challenges IT faces.

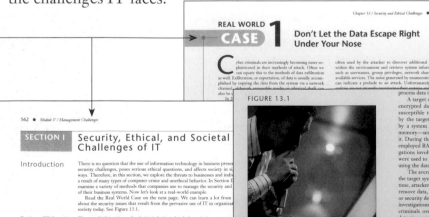

. . . and Beyond

Go Global with IT

This text closes with Chapter 14, an in-depth look at IT across borders.

[Embedded sample page]

SECTION II   Managing Global IT

The International Dimension

Whether they are in Berlin or Bombay, Kuala Lumpur or Kansas, San Francisco or Seoul, companies around the globe are developing new models to operate competitively in a digital economy. These models are structured, yet agile; global, yet local; and they concentrate on maximizing the risk-adjusted return from both knowledge and technology assets.

International dimensions have become a vital part of managing a business enterprise in the inter-networked global economies and markets of today. Whether you become a manager in a large corporation or the owner of a small business, you will be affected by international business developments and deal in some way with people, products, or services whose origin is not your home country.

Read the Real World Case on the next page. We can learn a lot about the challenges facing senior IT executives who operate in a globalized world. See Figure 14.11.

Global IT Management

Figure 14.12 illustrates the major dimensions of the job of managing global information technology that we cover in this section. Notice that all global IT activities must be adjusted to take into account the cultural, political, and geoeconomic challenges that exist in the international business community. Developing appropriate business and IT strategies for the global marketplace should be the first step in global information technology management. Once that is done, end users and IS managers can move on to developing the portfolio of business applications needed to support business/IT strategies; the hardware, software, and Internet-based technology platforms to support those applications; the data resource management methods to provide necessary databases; and finally the systems development projects that will produce the global information systems required.

Global Teams: It's Still a Small World

We seem to have reached a point where virtually every CIO is a global CIO—a leader whose sphere of influence (and headaches) spans continents. The global CIO's most common challenge, according to CIO Executive Council members, is managing global virtual teams. In an ideal world, HR policies across the global IT team should be consistent, fair, and responsive. Titles and reporting structures (if not compensation) should be equalized.

The council's European members, representing Royal Dutch Shell, Galderma, Olympus, and others, commissioned a globalization playbook that collects and codifies best practices in this and other globalization challenges.

Obtain local HR expertise. Companies must have a local HR person in each country to deal with local laws. "Hiring, firing, and training obligations must be managed very differently in each location, and you need someone with local expertise on the laws and processes," says Michael Pilkington, former chief information officer of Euroclear, the Brussels-based provider of domestic and cross-border settlement for bond, equity, and fund transactions.

Create job grade consistency across regions. Euroclear is moving toward a job evaluation methodology that organizes job types into vertical categories, such as managing people/process, product development, business support, and project management. This provides a basis for comparing and managing roles and people across locations. Grade level is not the same thing as a title; people's titles are much more subject to local conventions.

FIGURE 14.11

Emerging economies are increasingly demanding—and getting—IT executives' attention.

Source: © Getty Images.

It's an extreme example, but supporting business in oping regions rarely lends itself to cookie-cutter IT. Mor the importance of emerging markets today means IT l can't fob off secondhand technology to non-Western loc

"The strategy of many corporations was basically velop things in major markets then hand down those tions to the emerging markets," Shurts says. "Hey, this is two years old, maybe we pass that down, too."

That's not the case at Cadbury, explains Shurts. " to deliver strategies that address the specific needs of e ing markets. It requires some creativity and new think

Understanding your company's business model f veloping markets is critical. "Will there be manufact Will you distribute from this market? How will your force engage customers and what is their role whi gagedl" says Ed Holmes, vice president of Global I Stiefel, an $812 million dollar skin care company, acc by GlaxoSmithKline, that operates in 28 countries.

You may end up providing technology and services lar to those you supply in established markets, Holmes "but you must challenge the baseline assumptions in to ensure that your solution will fit the market both nomically and culturally."

Expand Your Knowledge

Blue boxes in each chapter provide brief, in-depth examples of how corporations apply IS concepts and theories.

[Embedded sample boxes]

The Paperless Office Is Not a Reality

The dream of every environmentally conscious organization—the paperless office—has been "somewhat of a fallacy" according to Bruce Dahlgren, HP's senior vice president of managed enterprise solutions, imaging, and printing group. "It's unrealistic to think that printing is just going to go away," he told *Computerworld Australia*. "However, I think the way people print and copy is changing."

Data collected from HP's 2600 managed print service clients worldwide showed that 84 percent of print and copy jobs were three pages or less. "We're able to distribute so much more of the information electronically, and people are printing off what they need," he said.

The trend is likely to continue too, as more information is distributed online rather than printed and mailed. However, Dahlgren said he didn't think companies would reach a completely paperless office anytime soon.

HP's managed print service division is worth $US5.5 billion worldwide, and accounts for 18.5 billion printed pages per year. The market is particularly lucrative

Whole Body Area Network: Human Cellular Towers Maybe?

A team of Irish researchers is studying how humans can become the next wireless infrastructure, by wearing sensors, radios, and gateways linked together in "body-to-body" networks. With redesigned antennas, low-power radios, and new network protocols, potentially huge, constantly shifting body networks could create an "ultra-high-bandwidth" mobile infrastructure." Such networks could offload even large file transfers from cellular networks, by making use of parallel transmission and routing through a mesh of body nodes. The body node can link to fixed access points, gateways, or cellular networks when needed. Small sensor nodes would be worn on the head, shoulders, chest, arms, and ankles and a signal collector for them would be worn on the hip.

The work on "body-centric" communications has been a focus of the Institute of Electronics, Communications and Information Technology at Queen's University, Belfast, Northern Ireland. The researchers were awarded a grant in 2010 of about $800,000 from the Royal Academy of Engineering and the Engineering and Physical Research Council. This new work is a five-year exploration of the challenges of body-to-body wireless communications, including how human bodies and movement affect radio signal propagation, according to Dr. Simon Cotton, a research fellow with the Institute.

The concept of body networks is an extension of the work that's being done with wireless medical sensors that are placed on, or implanted in, a patient's body and

Listen to the Users: It's All About the Interface

Four years after its debut, the "ribbon" interface in Microsoft's Office suite still gives businesses the shudders, a research firm said recently.

The interface first appeared in Office 2007 to catcalls as users struggled with the massive redesign, which substituted a wide ribbon-like display at the top for the traditional drop-down menus, small icons, and toolbars that epitomized Windows applications' look-and-feel for decades.

Months after the release of Office 2010, which also relies on the ribbon, enterprise IT professionals still think the interface is a headache, said Diane Hagglund, a senior analyst at Dimensional Research.

After polling more than 950 business IT executives, managers, and staffers, Hagglund found that the ribbon and its impact on worker training led all worries about deploying Office 2010. Nearly half of the IT pros—45 percent—pegged user training on the ribbon as a concern, more than double that of worries about the new software's stability and reliability, and significantly higher than the next-most expressed anxieties, including nonribbon training issues and add-in compatibility problems.

In the past, Microsoft has argued that training problems stemming from the ribbon interface have been overblown. Users, however, have continued to knock the ribbon, whether in Office on Windows or in the just-shipped Office for Mac 2011, which features a variant on the interface.

Dimensional also noted a slow uptake of Office 2010 so far, with just 20 percent of organizations

---

Expand Your Horizons

Globe icons indicate examples with an international focus so that your knowledge makes you truly worldly.

[Embedded sample box]

Global e-Commerce Sees New Highs in India

The Internet has transformed many aspects of life, but perhaps none more so than how we shop for goods and services. More than 8 out of 10 Indian online consumers plan to shop online in the next 12 months and more than a quarter indicate they spend upward of 11 percent of their monthly shopping expenditure on online purchases, according to a recent Nielsen global online shopping report. The report found that Asia-Pacific consumers spend the most on online purchases—as a percentage of total shopping expenditure—compared to any other region globally.

Twenty-three percent of Indians surveyed said that they had never shopped online. Globally, 16 percent of consumers have never shopped online and the percentage is even less in Asia-Pacific, with only 13 percent of consumers indicating that they had never shopped online.

"Low Internet penetration and lack of confidence in using credit card credentials are the biggest challenges for online shopping in India, though high adoption for online travel sites is changing this. The medium to heavy users have always been quite comfortable buying stuff online," says Karthik Nagarajan, director, Online Division at The Nielsen Company.

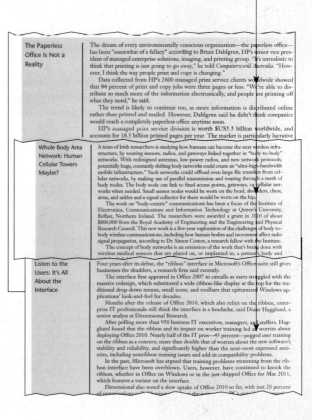

What's New?

The Tenth Edition includes significant changes to the Ninth Edition's content that update and improve its coverage, many of them suggested by an extensive faculty review process. Highlights of key changes for this edition include the following:

- Real World Cases provide current, relevant, and in-depth examples of IS theory applications. A combination of *Case Study Questions* and *Real World Activities* allows you to engage students on a variety of levels.
- More new Real World Cases: More than two-thirds of the cases are new to the Tenth Edition. These up-to-date cases provide students with in-depth business examples of the successes and challenges that companies are experiencing in implementing the information technology concepts covered in each chapter.
- Chapter 1: *Foundations of Information Systems in Business* provides an expanded discussion of IS careers and the job market outlook.
- Chapter 2: *Competing with Information Technology* has added coverage of the strategic uses of IS/IT.
- Chapter 3: *Computer Hardware* provides an expanded history of computing section and updated coverage of the iPhone.
- Chapter 4: *Computer Software* includes two brand-new sections that cover cloud computing and application virtualization. It also includes added coverage of Windows Server 2008 and an updated Java discussion to reflect the most recent version, Java EE 5.
- Chapter 5: *Data Resource Management* expands the discussions of Facebook, YouTube, and strategic data management.
- Chapter 6: *Telecommunications and Networks* updates the discussions of Internet2, the number of Internet users, and metropolitan area networks.
- Chapter 7: *e-Business Systems* includes a new discussion on the relationship between SCM, CRM, and ERP with regard to supporting corporate strategy. There is also an expanded discussion of SCM as a top strategic objective of modern enterprises and a new discussion of the use of digital billboards in targeted marketing.
- Chapter 9: *e-Commerce Systems* provides a new section and discussion of search engine optimization, new data relating to top retail web sites and online sales volume, and increased coverage and discussion of e-commerce success factors.
- Chapter 10: *Decision Support Systems* includes an additional discussion with regard to the strategic value of business intelligence activities in the modern organization.
- Chapter 11: *Developing Business/IT Strategies* has added coverage of system implementation challenges, user resistance, end-user development, and logical versus physical models.
- Chapter 12: *Developing Business/IT Solutions* has increased coverage of system implementation challenges, user resistance, and end-user development.
- Chapter 13: *Security and Ethical Challenges* includes a new section on cyberterrorism. Additionally, it provides updated coverage of software piracy economic impacts, increased coverage of HIPAA, and a significant increase in discussion of current state of cyber law.
- Chapter 14: *Enterprise and Global Management of Information Technology* provides expanded in-depth coverage of COBIT and IT governance structures in organizations, as well as an added section on trends in outsourcing and offshoring.

Student Support

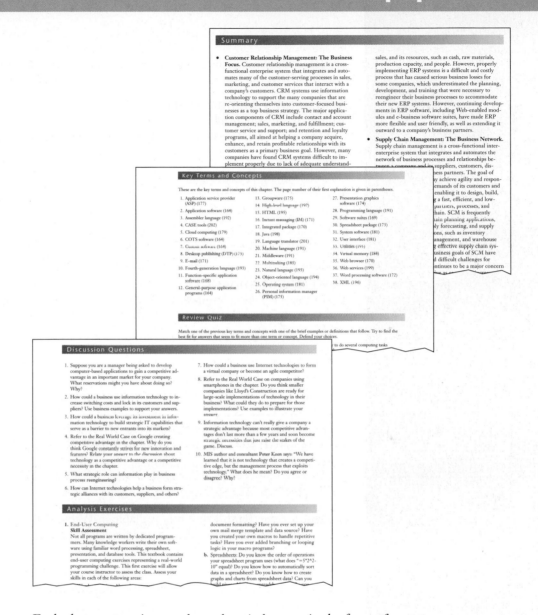

Each chapter contains *complete pedagogical support* in the form of:

- **Summary.** Revisiting key chapter concepts in a bullet-point summary.
- **Key Terms and Concepts.** Using page numbers to reference where terms are discussed in the text.
- **Review Quiz.** Providing a self-assessment for your students. Great for review before an important exam.
- **Discussion Questions.** Whether assigned as homework or used for in-class discussion, these complex questions will help your students develop critical thinking skills.
- **Analysis Exercises.** Each innovative scenario presents a business problem and asks students to use and test their IS knowledge through analytical, Web-based, spreadsheet, and/or database skills.
- **Closing Case Studies.** Reinforcing important concepts with prominent examples from businesses and organizations. Discussion questions follow each case study.

Instructor Support

Online Learning Center

Available to adopting faculty, the Online Learning Center provides one convenient place to access the Instructor's Manual, PowerPoint slides, and videos.

Instructor's Manual (IM)

To help ease your teaching burden, each chapter is supported by solutions to Real World Case questions, Discussion Questions, and Analysis Exercises.

Test Bank

Choose from more than 1,200 true/false, multiple-choice, and fill-in-the-blank questions of varying levels of difficulty. Complete answers are provided for all test questions. By using the **EZ Test Computerized Test Bank,** instructors can design, save, and generate custom tests. EZ Test also enables instructors to edit, add, or delete questions from the test bank; analyze test results; and organize a database of tests and student results.

PowerPoint Slides

A set of visually stimulating PowerPoint slides accompanies each chapter, providing a lecture outline and key figures and tables from the text. Slides can be edited to fit the needs of your course.

Videos

Videos will be downloadable from the instructor side of the OLC.

MBA MIS Cases

Developed by Richard Perle of Loyola Marymount University, these 14 cases allow you to add MBA-level analysis to your course. See your McGraw-Hill Irwin sales representative for more information.

Online Course Formats

Content for the Tenth Edition is available in WebCT, Blackboard, and PageOut formats to accommodate virtually any online delivery platform.

Online Learning Center

Visit www.mhhe.com/obrien for additional instructor and student resources.

Use our EZ Test Online to help your students prepare to succeed with Apple iPod® iQuiz.

Using our EZ Test Online, you can make test and quiz content available for a student's Apple iPod®.

Students must purchase the iQuiz game application from Apple for 99¢ in order to use the iQuiz content. It works on fifth-generation iPods and better.

Instructors only need EZ Test Online to produce iQuiz-ready content. Instructors take their existing tests and quizzes and export them to a file that can then be made available to the student to take as a self-quiz on their iPods. It's as simple as that.

Empower Your Students

Mastery of Skills and Concepts

This student supplement provides animated tutorials and simulated practice of the core skills in Microsoft Office 2007 Excel, Access, and PowerPoint, as well as animation of 47 important computer concepts.

With MISource's three-pronged **Teach Me–Show Me–Let Me Try** approach, students of all learning styles can quickly master core MS Office skills—leaving you more classroom time to cover more important and more complex topics.

For those students who need it, MISource for Office 2007 is delivered online at www.mhhe.com/misource.

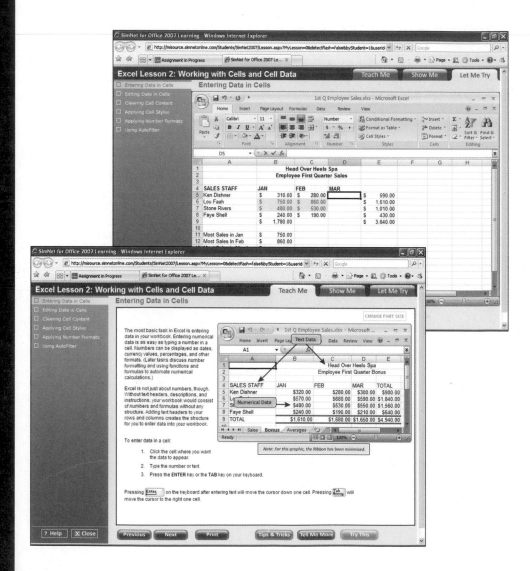

Empower Your Classroom

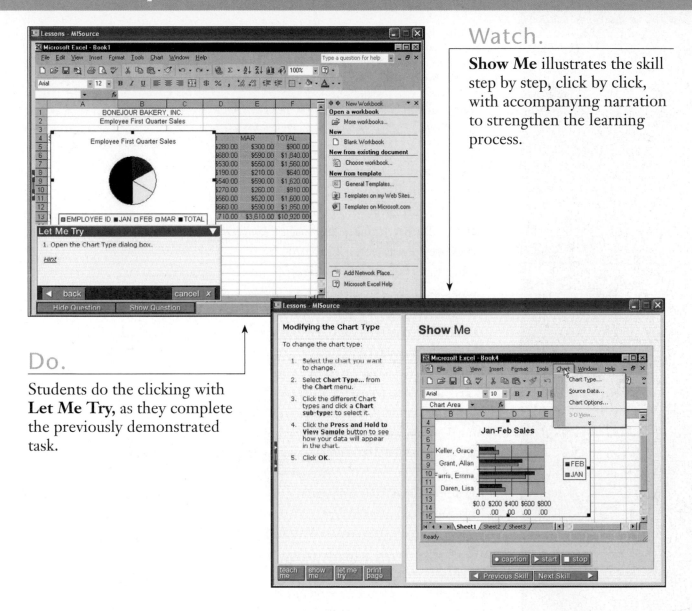

Watch.

Show Me illustrates the skill step by step, click by click, with accompanying narration to strengthen the learning process.

Do.

Students do the clicking with **Let Me Try,** as they complete the previously demonstrated task.

Acknowledgments

The Tenth Edition represents an ongoing effort to improve and adapt this text to meet the needs of students and instructors. For this revision, we received the guidance of more than 80 reviewers over the course of several months of review work. We thank all of them for their insight and advice

Hans-Joachim Adler, *University of Texas at Dallas*
Beni Asllani, *University of Tennessee—Chattanooga*
Michel Benaroch, *Syracuse University*
James P. Borden, *Villanova University*
Kevin Brennan, *University of Rochester*
Richard L. Brozovic, *McMurry University*
Mari W. Buche, *Michigan Technological University*
Jane Carey, *Arizona State University*
Arthur E. Carter, *Radford University*
Steve Casarow, *Clearwater Christian College*
Carl J. Case, *St. Bonaventure University*
David Chao, *San Francisco State University*
Edward J. Cherian, *George Washington University*
Robert Chi, *California State University—Long Beach*
Dale Chisamore, *University of Texas at Dallas*
Michael Cummings, *Georgia Institute of Technology*
Andy Curran, *University of Cincinnati—Clermont*
Joanna DeFranco-Tommarello, *New Jersey Institute of Technology*
Robin L. Dillon-Merrill, *Georgetown University*
Kevin Lee Elder, *Ohio University*
Kurt Engemann, *Iona College*
Roger Finnegan, *Metropolitan State University*
Gary Fisher, *Angelo State University*
Thomas Franza, *Dowling College*
Carl Friedman, *University of the District of Columbia*
Zbigniew J Gackowski, *California State University—Stanislaus*
Maria R. Garcia, *Franklin Pierce University*
Leo Gemoets, *University of Texas at El Paso*
Richard T. Grenci, *John Carroll University*
Bernard Han, *Western Michigan University—Kalamazoo*
Joseph T. Harder, *Indiana State University*
David Harris, *University of New Mexico—Albuquerque*
Nik Hassan, *University of Minnesota—Duluth*
James He, *Fairfield University*
Jun He, *University of Pittsburgh*
Fred Hughes, *Faulkner University*
Lynn Isvik, *Upper Iowa University*

A. T. "Tom" Jarmoszko, *Central Connecticut State University*

Jeanne Johnson, *Culver-Stockton University*

Surinder Kahai, *Binghamton University*

Rex Karsten, *University of Northern Iowa*

Ranjan B. Kini, *Indiana University Northwest*

Ronald Kizior, *Loyola University—Chicago*

Rebecca Berens Koop, *University of Dayton*

Linda Lau, *Longwood University*

Al Lederer, *University of Kentucky*

Anita Lee-Post, *University of Kentucky*

John D. "Skip" Lees, *California State University—Chico*

David Lewis, *University of Massachusetts—Lowell*

Dahui Li, *University of Minnesota—Duluth*

Shin-jeng Lin, *Le Moyne College*

Celia Romm Livermore, *Wayne State University*

John Lundin, *San Jose State University*

Sharad K. Maheshwari, *Hampton University*

Yogish Malhotra, *Syracuse University*

Victor Mbarika, *Louisiana State University*

Denise McManus, *University of Alabama—Tuscaloosa*

William A. McMillan, *Madonna University*

Patricia McQuaid, *California State Polytechnic University—San Luis Obispo*

Janet T. Nilsen, *Metropolitan State University*

Peter Otto, *Dowling College*

Shailendra C. Palvia, *Long Island University*

Panagiotis Petratos, *California State University—Stanislaus*

William Pritchard, *Wayne State University*

Mahesh S. Raisinghani, *University of Dallas*

Frederick Rodammer, *Michigan State University*

Paula Ruby, *Arkansas State University*

Mark B. Schmidt, *Mississippi State University*

Roy Schmidt, *Bradley University*

Ganesan Shankar, *Boston University*

Betsy Page Sigman, *Georgetown University*

K. David Smith, *Cameron University*

Marion Smith, *Texas Southern University*

Bill Sodeman, *Hawaii Pacific University*

Toni M. Somers, *Wayne State University*

Richard W. Srch, *DeVry University*

Godwin Udo, *University of Texas at El Paso*

Gregory W. Ulferts, *University of Detroit Mercy*

David A. Vance, *Mississippi State University*
Sameer Verma, *San Francisco State University*
Padmal Vitharana, *Syracuse University*
Anita Whitehill, *Foothill College*
G. W. Willis, *Baylor University*
Wita Wojtkowski, *Boise State University*
Robert Wurm, *Nassau Community College*
Yue "Jeff" Zhang, *California State University—Northridge*
Robert Zwick, *Baruch College (CUNY)*

Our thanks also go to Robert Lawton of Western Illinois University for his contribution to the analysis exercises and to Richard Perle of Loyola Marymount University for his MBA cases that so many instructors use in conjunction with this text.

Much credit should go to several individuals who played significant roles in this project. Thus, special thanks go to the editorial and production team at McGraw-Hill/ Irwin: Paul Ducham, editorial director; Trina Hauger, senior developmental editor; Sarah Schuessler, marketing manager; Jill Eccher, freelance project editor; Jeremy Chesharek, photo coordinator; and Mary Sander, designer. Their ideas and hard work were invaluable contributions to the successful completion of the project. The contributions of many authors, publishers, and firms in the computer industry that contributed case material, ideas, illustrations, and photographs used in this text are also thankfully acknowledged.

Acknowledging the Real World of Business

The unique contribution of the hundreds of business firms and other computer-using organizations that are the subjects of the Real World Cases, exercises, and examples in this text is gratefully acknowledged. The real-life situations faced by these firms and organizations provide readers of this text with valuable demonstrations of the benefits and limitations of using the Internet and other information technologies to enable electronic business and commerce, as well as enterprise communications and collaboration in support of the business processes, managerial decision making, and strategic advantage of the modern business enterprise.

George M. Marakas
James A. O'Brien
Miguel Aguirre-Urreta

Assurance of Learning Ready

Many educational institutions today are focused on the notion of assurance of learning, an important element of some accreditation standards. *Management Information Systems* is designed specifically to support your assurance of learning initiatives with a simple, yet powerful, solution.

Each test bank question for *Management Information Systems* maps to a specific chapter learning outcome/objective listed in the text. You can use our test bank software, *EZ Test*, to query about learning outcomes/objectives that directly relate to the learning objectives for your course. You can then use the reporting features of *EZ Test* to aggregate student results in similar fashion, making the collection and presentation of assurance of learning data simple and easy.

AACSB Statement

McGraw-Hill Companies is a proud corporate member of AACSB International. Recognizing the importance and value of AACSB accreditation, the authors of *Management Information Systems* 10e have sought to recognize the curricula guidelines detailed in AACSB standards for business accreditation by connecting selected questions in *Management Information Systems* or its test bank with the general knowledge and skill guidelines found in the AACSB standards. It is important to note that the statements contained in *Management Information Systems* 10e are provided only as a guide for the users of this text.

The statements contained in *Management Information Systems* 10e are provided only a guide for the users of this text. The AACSB leaves content coverage and assessment clearly within the realm and control of individual schools, the mission of the school, and the faculty. The AACSB charges schools with the obligation of doing assessments against their own content and learning goals. Although *Management Information Systems* 10e and its teaching package make no claim of any specific AACSB qualification or evaluation, we have, within *Management Information Systems* 10e, labeled selected questions according to the six general knowledge and skills areas. The labels or tags within *Management Information Systems* 10e are as indicated. There are, of course, many more within the test bank, the text, and the teaching package, which might be used as a "standard" for your course. However, the labeled questions are suggested for your consideration.

Brief Contents

Module I Foundation Concepts

Module II Information Technologies

Module III Business Applications

Module IV Development Processes

Module V Management Challenges

Contents

Module II Information Technologies

Chapter 5

Data Resource Management   211

Chapter 6

Telecommunications and Networks   251

Module IV Development Processes

Chapter 11

Developing Business/IT Strategies   481

Chapter 12

Developing Business/IT Solutions   515

Module V   Management Challenges

Chapter 13

Security and Ethical Challenges   561

Chapter 14

Enterprise and Global Management of Information Technology 613

MANAGEMENT
INFORMATION
SYSTEMS

MODULE I

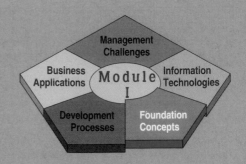

FOUNDATION CONCEPTS

Why study information systems? Why do businesses need information technology? What do you need to know about the use and management of information technologies in business? The introductory chapters of Module I are designed to answer these fundamental questions about the role of information systems in business.

- **Chapter 1: Foundations of Information Systems in Business** presents an overview of the five basic areas of information systems knowledge needed by business professionals, including the conceptual system components and major types of information systems. In addition, trends in information systems and an overview of the managerial challenges associated with information systems are presented.

- **Chapter 2: Competing with Information Technology** introduces fundamental concepts of competitive advantage through information technology and illustrates major strategic applications of information systems.

Completing these chapters will prepare you to move on to study chapters on information technologies (Module II), business applications (Module III), systems development processes (Module IV), and the management challenges of information systems (Module V).

CHAPTER 1

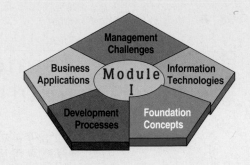

FOUNDATIONS OF INFORMATION SYSTEMS IN BUSINESS

Chapter Highlights

Learning Objectives

1. Understand the concept of a system and how it relates to information systems.

2. Explain why knowledge of information systems is important for business professionals, and identify five areas of information systems knowledge that they need.

3. Give examples to illustrate how the business applications of information systems can support a firm's business processes, managerial decision making, and strategies for competitive advantage.

4. Provide examples of several major types of information systems from your experiences with business organizations in the real world.

5. Identify several challenges that a business manager might face in managing the successful and ethical development and use of information technology in a business.

6. Provide examples of the components of real world information systems. Illustrate that in an information system, people use hardware, software, data, and networks as resources to perform input, processing, output, storage, and control activities that transform data resources into information products.

7. Demonstrate familiarity with the myriad of career opportunities in information systems.

SECTION I	# Foundation Concepts: Information Systems in Business

The question of why we need to study information systems and information technology has evolved into a moot issue. Information systems have become as integrated into our daily business activities as accounting, finance, operations management, marketing, human resource management, or any other major business function. Information systems and technologies are vital components of successful businesses and organizations—some would say they are business imperatives. They thus constitute an essential field of study in business administration and management, which is why most business majors include a course in information systems. Since you probably intend to be a manager, entrepreneur, or business professional, it is just as important to have a basic understanding of information systems as it is to understand any other functional area in business.

Information technologies, including Internet-based information systems, are playing vital and expanding roles in business. Information technology can help all kinds of businesses improve the efficiency and effectiveness of their business processes, managerial decision making, and workgroup collaboration, which strengthens their competitive positions in rapidly changing marketplaces. This benefit occurs irrespective of whether the information technology is used to support product development teams, customer support processes, e-commerce transactions, or any other business activity. Information technologies and systems are, quite simply, an essential ingredient for business success in today's dynamic global environment.

The Real World of Information Systems

Let's take a moment to bring the real world into our discussion of the importance of information systems (IS) and information technology (IT). See Figure 1.1, and read the Real World Case about using information technology to leverage business value and advanced global organizational strategy.

If we are to understand information systems and their functions, we first need to be clear on the concept of a system. In its simplest form, a system is a set of interrelated components, with a clearly defined boundary, working together to achieve a common set of objectives. Using this definition, it becomes easy to see that virtually everything you can think of is a system, and one system can be made up of other systems or be part of a bigger system. We will expand on this concept later in the next section, but for now, this definition gives us a good foundation for understanding the focus of this textbook: information systems.

What Is an Information System?

We begin with a simple definition that we can expand upon later in the chapter. An information system (IS) can be any organized combination of people, hardware, software, communications networks, data resources, and policies and procedures that stores, retrieves, transforms, and disseminates information in an organization. People rely on modern information systems to communicate with one another using a variety of physical devices *(hardware)*, information processing instructions and procedures *(software)*, communications channels *(networks)*, and stored data *(data resources)*. Although today's information systems are typically thought of as having something to do with computers, we have been using information systems since the dawn of civilization. Even today we make regular use of information systems that have nothing to do with a computer. Consider some of the following examples of information systems:

- **Smoke signals for communication** were used as early as recorded history and can account for the human discovery of fire. The pattern of smoke transmitted valuable information to others who were too far to see or hear the sender.

- **Card catalogs in a library** are designed to store data about the books in an organized manner that allows readers to locate a particular book by its title, author name, subject, or a variety of other approaches.

REAL WORLD CASE 1

The Global Innovation Revolution and IT's Indispensable Role

MIT's Erik Brynjolfsson has a new theory on how leading companies around the globe are leveraging IT to unlock unprecedented waves of innovation—and are reinventing research and development (R&D).

For all of its faults and shortcomings—its complexity, its cost, its fragility, and its runaway variability—strategically applied information technology has become the primary tool with which leading companies in many industries have begun to separate themselves from competitors, says MIT professor and global IT expert Erik Brynjolfsson. And that momentous achievement might be only a hint of the IT-driven business value still to be realized.

As Brynjolfsson (brin-YOLF-son) sees it, in addition to the surface-level operational and financial improvements IT has helped to create are some less-obvious but extremely valuable enhancements to the sought-after process every CEO wants to master: innovation. "IT is setting off a global revolution in innovation on four dimensions simultaneously: measurement, experimentation, sharing and replication. Each of these is important in and of itself, but, more profoundly, they reinforce each other. They magnify the impact of each other . . . By doing all four of these changes together, companies are, in essence, creating a new kind of R&D."

This is exactly the type of finding that needs to be more widely disseminated in today's challenging economic times as the hunt for scapegoats intensifies: Why do we have to spend so much on IT? We can't measure ROI, so how do we know what we're getting? Shouldn't all those systems have been able to tell us that a downturn was coming? IT is just a cost center—why don't we just get rid of the whole headache and outsource it to somebody who'll do a far better job for half the cost?

FIGURE 1.1

Access to quality information about customers helps companies succeed at delivering value to shareholders.

So let's look at this from the opposite perspective, which is one that Brynjolfsson takes: how can companies leverage their IT assets and the output from those assets for maximum value? Brynjolfsson suggests four important approaches:

1) Measurement. "It's more like radically improved measurement, through the use of nano data. That includes clickstream data, Google trends, detailed e-mail data, the billions and trillions of bits of information that are thrown off by enterprise planning systems. Even without any conscious effort on the part of the designers, this information is just generated. But by studying these data very carefully, companies can have much better knowledge of their customers, of their business processes, of their product quality, and of defects of their supply chains. The field of business intelligence has been tapping into this explosion of data."

2) Experimentation. "IT-based experimentation is most obvious in companies like Amazon, which regularly conducts what it calls "A/B experiments," tests of its Web pages that deliver different versions of the same page at the same time to different visitors, monitoring customer experience and follow-through. Google, similarly, does 200 to 300 experiments on any given day. But it's also quite common in catalog companies, like credit card companies and direct mail companies, and even in mainstream brick and mortar companies like the casino chain Harrah's . . . And that, of course, is the gold standard for being able to have actionable knowledge about what's really happening in your business, what innovations are paying off and which ones aren't."

3) Sharing. "We often think of grand innovations, like the invention of the light bulb, as what drives economic growth. But equally important, and perhaps more important, are the 1,001 small innovations that regular business managers and line workers do every day at their jobs. If we can find more effective ways of sharing those micro-innovations with one another so that each person doesn't have to reinvent the wheel or reinvent the printer routine, then we're much more likely to be able to get a faster, more steady pace of economic growth—and improved competitive advantage for the companies that make that easy."

4) Replication. "However, what we also see is that *business processes themselves* can be replicated by leveraging information technology. A nice example is what Andrew McAfee at the MIT Center for Digital Business described in his study of CVS (a US-based retail pharmacy chain). The company implemented an improved business process for prescription drug ordering at one of its pharmacies, which improved customer satisfaction significantly. But what happened next is what's really important. Managers took that business process and embedded it in an enterprise information technology system, and then they replicated it to 4,000 other pharmacies in 4,000 other CVS stores within a year. We're seeing that not just in retailing but also in manufacturing, in banking, in industry after industry."

Brynjolfsson's arguments are compelling in several respects but primarily for his unabashed contentions that IT has not only been carrying its own weight for the past decade but that it's been delivering far more value and improvements and capabilities than most companies are willing or able to grasp—and that trend, he says, will continue: "What we're going to see in the coming decade are companies whose whole culture is based on continuous improvement and experimentation—not just of specific processes, but of the entire way the company runs," Brynjolfsson says. "I think this revolution can be fairly compared to the scientific revolution that happened centuries ago. Great revolutions in science have almost always been preceded by great revolutions in

measurement. Management historically has not had that kind of careful measurement or experimentation. But it's time that we catch up."

Indeed—time for many companies not only to catch up but to push ahead. For CIOs, that means leveraging the full thought leadership Brynjolfsson is advocating here: driving the idea that the IT systems and processes for which the CIOs are responsible are not just linear and mechanistic devices that can handle lots of transactions, but instead can help create ideas and insights that enhance customer engagements and then increase revenue.

As Brynjolfsson says in his concluding comment: "And when historians look back on this era, I think many people will call it not just The Great Recession, but perhaps The Great Restructuring because of the way that businesses are changing how they're working and because of the central role that IT has in driving some of those changes."

Source: Adapted from Bob Evans, "Global CIO: The Innovation Revolution and IT's Indispensable Role," *InformationWeek*, May 26, 2010.

CASE STUDY QUESTIONS

1. How do information technologies contribute to the business success of the companies depicted in the case? Provide an example from each company explaining how the technology implemented led to improved performance.

2. CVS used IT to improve business processes, which resulted in improved customer satisfaction. What other professions could benefit from a similar use of these technologies, and how? Develop two different possibilities.

3. Brynjolfsson lists four ways in which companies can leverage their IT assets. What other ways can global firms use their IT assets for strategic advantage?

REAL WORLD ACTIVITIES

1. Use the Internet to research examples of global companies using one or more of the four strategies offered by Brynjolfsson. What differences can you find with those reviewed in the case? Prepare a report to summarize your findings and highlight new and innovative uses of these technologies.

2. Why do some companies in a given industry, like Google above, adopt and deploy innovative technologies while others in the same line of business do not? Break into small groups with your classmates to discuss what characteristics of companies could influence their decision to innovate with the use of information technologies.

- **Your book bag, day planner, notebooks, and file folders** are all part of an information system designed to help you organize the inputs provided to you via handouts, lectures, presentations, and discussions. They also help you process these inputs into useful outputs: homework and good exam grades.

- **The cash register at your favorite fast-food restaurant** is part of a large information system that tracks the products sold, the time of a sale, inventory levels, and the amount of money in the cash drawer; it also contributes to the analysis of product sales in any combination of locations anywhere in the world.

- **A paper-based accounting ledger** as used before the advent of computer-based accounting systems is an iconic example of an information system. Businesses used this type of system for centuries to record the daily transactions and to keep a record of the balances in their various business and customer accounts.

Figure 1.2 illustrates a useful conceptual framework that organizes the knowledge presented in this text and outlines areas of knowledge you need about information systems. It emphasizes that you should concentrate your efforts in the following five areas of IS knowledge:

- **Foundation Concepts.** Fundamental behavioral, technical, business, and managerial concepts about the components and roles of information systems. Examples include basic information system concepts derived from general systems theory or competitive strategy concepts used to develop business applications of information technology for competitive advantage. Chapters 1 and 2 and other chapters of the text support this area of IS knowledge.

- **Information Technologies.** Major concepts, developments, and management issues in information technology—that is, hardware, software, networks, data management, and many Internet-based technologies. Chapters 3 and 4 provide an overview of computer hardware and software technologies, and Chapters 5 and 6 cover key data resource management and telecommunications network technologies for business.

- **Business Applications.** The major uses of information systems for the operations, management, and competitive advantage of a business. Chapters 7 and 8 cover applications of information technology in functional areas of business such as marketing, manufacturing, and accounting. Chapter 9 focuses on e-business applications that most companies use to buy and sell products on the Internet, and Chapter 10 covers the use of information systems and technologies to support decision making in business.

- **Development Processes.** How business professionals and information specialists plan, develop, and implement information systems to meet business opportunities. Several developmental methodologies are explored in Chapters 11 and 12, including

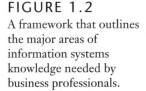

FIGURE 1.2

A framework that outlines the major areas of information systems knowledge needed by business professionals.

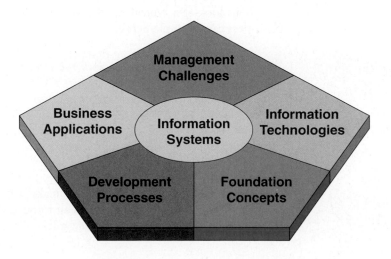

FIGURE 1.3

The three fundamental roles of the business applications of information systems. Information systems provide an organization with support for business processes and operations, decision making, and competitive advantage.

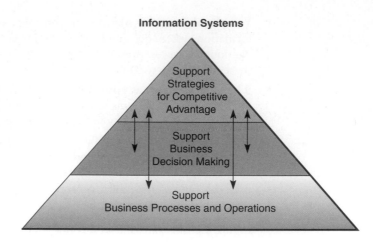

Information Systems

Support Strategies for Competitive Advantage

Support Business Decision Making

Support Business Processes and Operations

the systems development life cycle and prototyping approaches to business application development.

- **Management Challenges.** The challenges of effectively and ethically managing information technology at the end-user, enterprise, and global levels of a business. Thus, Chapter 13 focuses on security challenges and security management issues in the use of information technology, while Chapter 14 covers some of the key methods business managers can use to manage the information systems function in a company with global business operations.

The Fundamental Roles of IS in Business

Although there are a seemingly endless number of software applications, there are three fundamental reasons for all business applications of information technology. They are found in the three vital roles that information systems can perform for a business enterprise:

- Support of business processes and operations.
- Support of decision making by employees and managers.
- Support of strategies for competitive advantage.

Figure 1.3 illustrates how the fundamental roles interact in a typical organization. At any moment, information systems designed to support business processes and operations may also be providing data to, or accepting data from, systems focused on business decision making or achieving competitive advantage. The same is true for the other two fundamental roles of IS. Today's organizations are constantly striving to achieve integration of their systems to allow information to flow freely through them, which adds even greater flexibility and business support than any of the individual system roles could provide.

Let's look at a typical retail store as a good example of how these roles of IS in business can be implemented.

The Fundamental Roles of IS in Business

Support of Business Processes and Operations. As a consumer, you regularly encounter information systems that support the business processes and operations at the many retail stores where you shop. For example, most retail stores now use computer-based information systems to help their employees record customer purchases, keep track of inventory, pay employees, buy new merchandise, and evaluate sales trends. Store operations would grind to a halt without the support of such information systems.

Support of Business Decision Making. Information systems also help store managers and other business professionals make better decisions. For example, decisions about what lines of merchandise need to be added or discontinued and what kind of investments they require are typically made after an analysis provided by computer-based information systems. This function not only supports the decision making of store managers, buyers, and others, but also helps them look for ways to gain an advantage over other retailers in the competition for customers.

Support of Strategies for Competitive Advantage. Gaining a strategic advantage over competitors requires the innovative application of information technologies. For example, store management might make a decision to install touch-screen kiosks in all stores, with links to the e-commerce Web site for online shopping. This offering might attract new customers and build customer loyalty because of the ease of shopping and buying merchandise provided by such information systems. Thus, strategic information systems can help provide products and services that give a business a comparative advantage over its competitors.

Welch's: Balancing Truckloads with Business Intelligence

Given dramatic fluctuations in gas prices, it's no surprise that companies want to find ways to rein in transportation costs. One company finding success in that endeavor is Welch's, a well-known purveyor of food and packaged consumer goods. The company is tapping the power of business intelligence for better insight into its supply-chain operations, which in turn can help keep transportation expenses lower. Welch's, the $654 million manufacturer known for its jams, jellies, and juices, recently installed an on-demand BI application from Oco.

One way Welch's is leveraging the Oco BI application is to ensure that truckloads delivered by its carriers go out full.

The idea is that customers are already paying for the full truck when it delivers goods, even if it's only halfway or three-quarters loaded. With the BI system, Welch's can tell if a buyer's shipment is coming up short of full capacity and help them figure out what else they can order to max it out, thus saving on future shipping costs.

"Welch's can go to the customer and say, 'You're only ordering this much. Why not round out the load with other things you need? It will be a lot cheaper for you,'" says Bill Copacino, president and CEO of Oco. "If you're able to put 4,000 more pounds on the 36,000-pound shipment, you're getting a 10 percent discount on transportation costs," he adds.

"We're essentially capturing every element—from the customer orders we receive, to bills of lading on every shipment we make, as well as every data element on every freight bill we pay," says Bill Coyne, director of purchasing and logistics for Welch's. "We dump them all into one data warehouse [maintained by Oco], and we can mix-and-match and slice-and-dice any way we want." Coyne says that Welch's tries to ship its products five days a week out of its distribution center. "But we found ourselves just totally overwhelmed on Fridays," he says. "We would complain, 'How come there are so many orders on Friday?'"

Now, the new system helps Welch's balance its daily deliveries so that it uses about the same number of trucks, rather than hiring seven trucks on a Monday, five on a Tuesday, eight on a Wednesday, and so forth.

The company reaps transportation savings by using a stable number of trucks daily—"as capacity is not jumping all over the place," Copacino says.

"We are gaining greater visibility into cost-savings opportunities, which is especially important in light of rising fuel and transportation costs," says Coyne. Welch's spends more than $50 million each year on transportation expenses, and the Oco BI application and reporting features have become critical in a very short period of time. "We literally can't go any amount of time without knowing this stuff," Coyne says.

Source: Adapted from Ted Samson, "Welch's Leverages BI to Reduce Transport Costs," *InfoWorld*, October 16, 2008; and Thomas Wailgum, "Business Intelligence and On-Demand: The Perfect Marriage?" *CIO Magazine*, March 27, 2008.

Trends in Information Systems

The business applications of information systems have expanded significantly over the years. Figure 1.4 summarizes these changes.

Until the 1960s, the role of most information systems was simple: transaction processing, record keeping, accounting, and other *electronic data processing* (EDP) applications. Then another role was added, namely, the processing of all these data into useful, informative reports. Thus, the concept of *management information systems* (MIS) was born. This new role focused on developing business applications that provided managerial end users with predefined management reports that would give managers the information they needed for decision-making purposes.

By the 1970s, it was evident that the prespecified information products produced by such management information systems were not adequately meeting the decision-making needs of management, so the concept of *decision support systems* (DSS) was born. The new role for information systems was to provide managerial end users with ad hoc, interactive support of their decision-making processes. This support would be tailored to the unique decisions and decision-making styles of managers as they confronted specific types of problems in the real world.

In the 1980s, several new roles for information systems appeared. First, the rapid development of microcomputer processing power, application software packages, and telecommunications networks gave birth to the phenomenon of *end-user computing*.

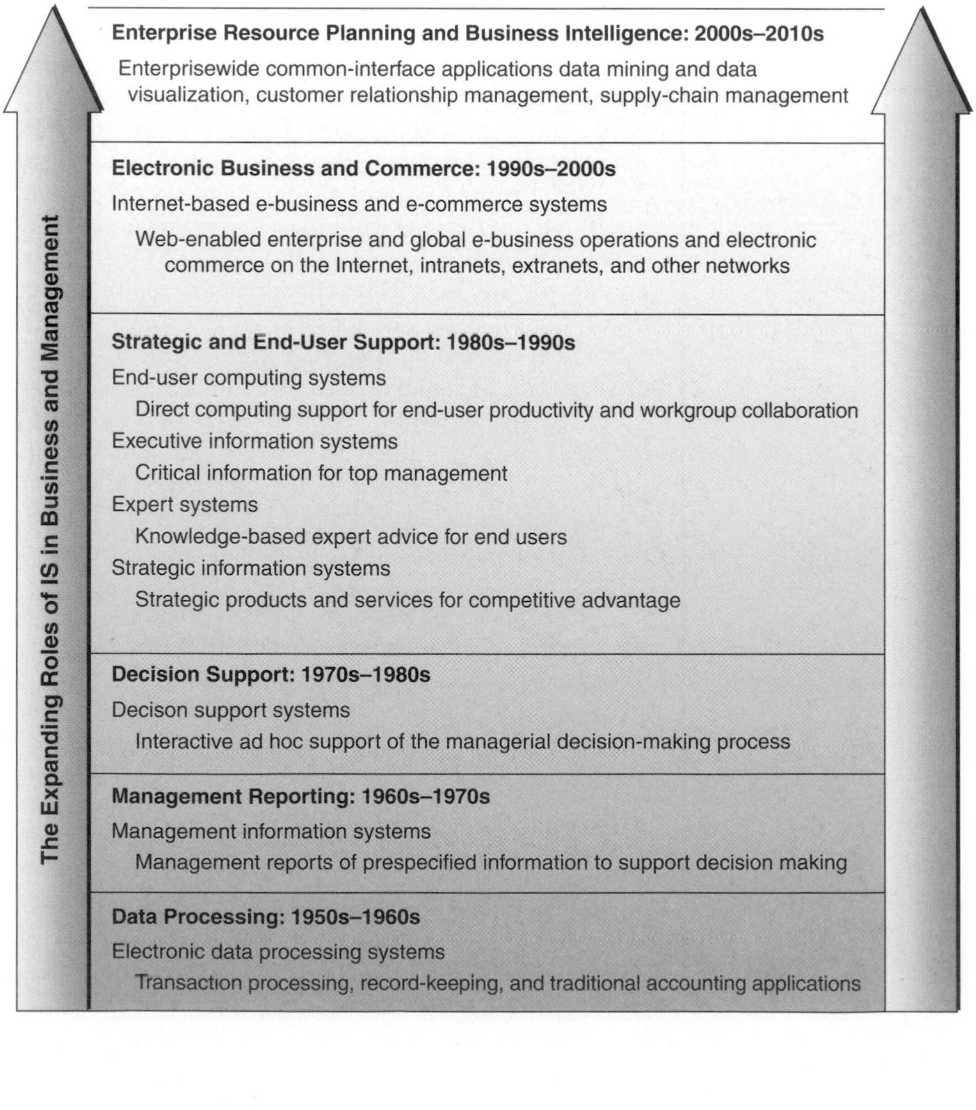

FIGURE 1.4

The expanding roles of the business applications of information systems. Note how the roles of computer-based information systems have expanded over time. Also, note the impact of these changes on the end users and managers of an organization.

The Expanding Roles of IS in Business and Management

Enterprise Resource Planning and Business Intelligence: 2000s–2010s
Enterprisewide common-interface applications data mining and data visualization, customer relationship management, supply-chain management

Electronic Business and Commerce: 1990s–2000s
Internet-based e-business and e-commerce systems
Web-enabled enterprise and global e-business operations and electronic commerce on the Internet, intranets, extranets, and other networks

Strategic and End-User Support: 1980s–1990s
End-user computing systems
Direct computing support for end-user productivity and workgroup collaboration
Executive information systems
Critical information for top management
Expert systems
Knowledge-based expert advice for end users
Strategic information systems
Strategic products and services for competitive advantage

Decision Support: 1970s–1980s
Decison support systems
Interactive ad hoc support of the managerial decision-making process

Management Reporting: 1960s–1970s
Management information systems
Management reports of prespecified information to support decision making

Data Processing: 1950s–1960s
Electronic data processing systems
Transaction processing, record-keeping, and traditional accounting applications

End users could now use their own computing resources to support their job requirements instead of waiting for the indirect support of centralized corporate information services departments.

Second, it became evident that most top corporate executives did not directly use either the reports of management information systems or the analytical modeling capabilities of decision support systems, so the concept of *executive information systems* (EIS) developed. These information systems were created to give top executives an easy way to get the critical information they wanted, when they wanted it, and tailored to the formats they preferred.

Third, breakthroughs occurred in the development and application of artificial intelligence (AI) techniques to business information systems. Today's systems include intelligent software agents that can be programmed and deployed inside a system to act on behalf of their owner, system functions that can adapt themselves on the basis of the immediate needs of the user, virtual reality applications, advanced robotics, natural language processing, and a variety of applications for which artificial intelligence can replace the need for human intervention, thus freeing up knowledge workers for more complex tasks. *Expert systems* (ES) and other *knowledge-based systems* also forged a new role for information systems. Today, expert systems can serve as consultants to users by providing expert advice in limited subject areas.

An important new role for information systems appeared in the 1980s and continued through the 1990s: the concept of a strategic role for information systems, sometimes called *strategic information systems* (SIS). In this concept, information technology becomes an integral component of business processes, products, and services that help a company gain a competitive advantage in the global marketplace.

The mid- to late 1990s saw the revolutionary emergence of *enterprise resource planning* (ERP) systems. This organization-specific form of a strategic information system integrates all facets of a firm, including its planning, manufacturing, sales, resource management, customer relations, inventory control, order tracking, financial management, human resources, and marketing—virtually every business function. The primary advantage of these ERP systems lies in their common interface for all computer-based organizational functions and their tight integration and data sharing, necessary for flexible strategic decision making. We explore ERP and its associated functions in greater detail in Chapter 8.

We are also entering an era where a fundamental role for IS is *business intelligence* (BI). BI refers to all applications and technologies in the organization that are focused on the gathering and analysis of data and information that can be used to drive strategic business decisions. Through the use of BI technologies and processes, organizations can gain valuable insight into the key elements and factors—both internal and external—that affect their business and competitiveness in the marketplace. BI relies on sophisticated metrics and analytics to "see into the data" and find relationships and opportunities that can be turned into profits. We'll look closer at BI in Chapter 10.

Finally, the rapid growth of the Internet, intranets, extranets, and other interconnected global networks in the 1990s dramatically changed the capabilities of information systems in business at the beginning of the 21st century. Further, a fundamental shift in the role of information systems occurred. Internet-based and Web-enabled enterprises and global e-business and e-commerce systems are becoming commonplace in the operations and management of today's business enterprises. Information systems is now solidly entrenched as a strategic resource in the modern organization.

A closer look at Figure 1.4 suggests that though we have expanded our abilities with regard to using information systems for conducting business, today's information systems are still doing the same basic things that they began doing more than 50 years ago. We still need to process transactions, keep records, provide management with useful and informative reports, and support the foundational accounting systems and processes of the organization. What has changed, however, is that we now enjoy a much higher level of integration of system functions across applications, greater connectivity across both similar and dissimilar system components, and the ability to reallocate critical computing tasks such as data storage, processing, and presentation to take maximum advantage of business and strategic opportunities. Because of these increased capabilities, the systems of tomorrow will be focused on increasing both the speed and reach of our systems to provide even tighter integration, combined with greater flexibility.

The Role of e-Business in Business

The Internet and related technologies and applications have changed the ways businesses operate and people work, as well as how information systems support business processes, decision making, and competitive advantage. Thus, many businesses today are using Internet technologies to Web-enable their business processes and create innovative e-business applications. See Figure 1.5.

In this text, we define e-business as the use of Internet technologies to work and empower business processes, e-commerce, and enterprise collaboration within a company and with its customers, suppliers, and other business stakeholders. In essence, e-business can be more generally considered an *online exchange of value*. Any online exchange of information, money, resources, services, or any combination thereof falls under the e-business umbrella. The Internet and Internet-like networks—those inside the enterprise (intranet) and between an enterprise and its trading partners (extranet)—have become the primary information technology infrastructure that supports the e-business applications of many companies. These companies rely on e-business applications to (1) reengineer internal business processes, (2) implement e-commerce systems with their customers and suppliers, and (3) promote enterprise collaboration among business teams and workgroups.

FIGURE 1.5

Businesses today depend on the Internet, intranets, and extranets to implement and manage innovative e-business applications.

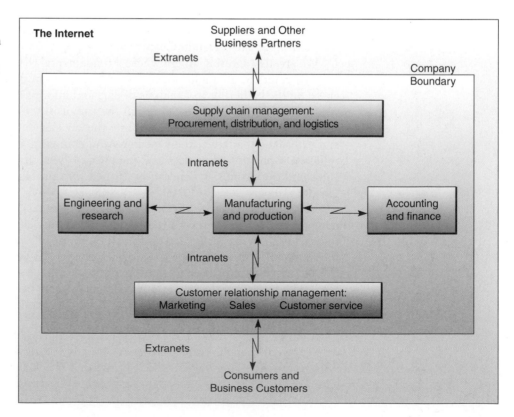

Enterprise collaboration systems involve the use of software tools to support communication, coordination, and collaboration among the members of networked teams and workgroups. A business may use intranets, the Internet, extranets, and other networks to implement such systems. For example, employees and external consultants may form a *virtual team* that uses a corporate intranet and the Internet for e-mail, videoconferencing, e-discussion groups, and Web pages of work-in-progress information to collaborate on business projects.

E-commerce is the buying, selling, marketing, and servicing of products, services, and information over a variety of computer networks. Many businesses now use the Internet, intranets, extranets, and other networks to support every step of the commercial process, including everything from advertising, sales, and customer support on the World Wide Web to Internet security and payment mechanisms that ensure completion of delivery and payment processes. For example, e-commerce systems include Internet Web sites for online sales, extranet access to inventory databases by large customers, and the use of corporate intranets by sales reps to access customer records for customer relationship management.

Types of Information Systems

Conceptually, the applications of information systems that are implemented in today's business world can be classified in several different ways. For example, several types of information systems can be classified as either operations or management information systems. Figure 1.6 illustrates this conceptual classification of information systems applications. Information systems are categorized this way to spotlight the major roles each plays in the operations and management of a business. Let's look briefly at some examples of such information systems categories.

Operations Support Systems

Information systems have always been needed to process data generated by, and used in, business operations. Such operations support systems produce a variety of information products for internal and external use; however, they do not emphasize the

FIGURE 1.6 Operations and management classifications of information systems. Note how this conceptual overview emphasizes the main purposes of information systems that support business operations and managerial decision making.

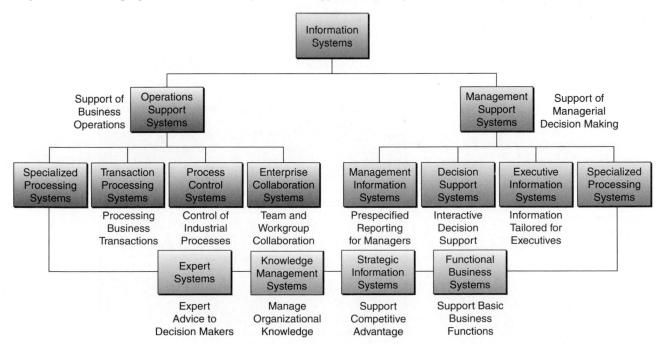

FIGURE 1.7 A summary of operations support systems with examples.

Operations Support Systems
• **Transaction processing systems.** Process data resulting from business transactions, update operational databases, and produce business documents. Examples: sales and inventory processing and accounting systems.
• **Process control systems.** Monitor and control industrial processes. Examples: petroleum refining, power generation, and steel production systems.
• **Enterprise collaboration systems.** Support team, workgroup, and enterprise communications and collaborations. Examples: e-mail, chat, and videoconferencing groupware systems.

specific information products that can best be used by managers. Further processing by management information systems is usually required. The role of a business firm's operations support systems is to process business transactions, control industrial processes, support enterprise communications and collaborations, and update corporate databases efficiently. See Figure 1.7.

Transaction processing systems are important examples of operations support systems that record and process the data resulting from business transactions. They process transactions in two basic ways. In *batch processing*, transactions data are accumulated over a period of time and processed periodically. In *real-time* (or *online*) processing, data are processed immediately after a transaction occurs. For example, point-of-sale (POS) systems at many retail stores use electronic cash register terminals to capture and transmit sales data electronically over telecommunications links to regional computer centers for immediate (real-time) or nightly (batch) processing. Figure 1.8 is an example of software that automates accounting transaction processing.

Process control systems monitor and control physical processes. For example, a petroleum refinery uses electronic sensors linked to computers to monitor chemical processes continually and make instant (real-time) adjustments that control the refinery process. Enterprise collaboration systems enhance team and workgroup communications and productivity and include applications that are sometimes called *office automation systems*. For example, knowledge workers in a project team may use e-mail to send and receive e-messages or use videoconferencing to hold electronic meetings to coordinate their activities.

Management Support Systems

When information system applications focus on providing information and support for effective decision making by managers, they are called management support systems. Providing information and support for decision making by all types of managers

FIGURE 1.8

QuickBooks is a popular accounting package that automates small office or home office (SOHO) accounting transaction processing while providing business owners with management reports.

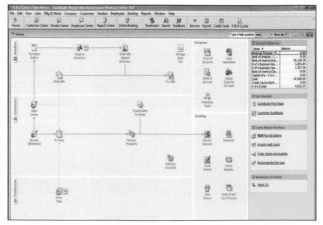

Source: Courtesy of Quickbooks.

FIGURE 1.9   A summary of management support systems with examples.

Management Support Systems
● **Management information systems.** Provide information in the form of prespecified reports and displays to support business decision making. Examples: sales analysis, production performance, and cost trend reporting systems.
● **Decision support systems.** Provide interactive ad hoc support for the decision-making processes of managers and other business professionals. Examples: product pricing, profitability forecasting, and risk analysis systems.
● **Executive information systems.** Provide critical information from MIS, DSS, and other sources tailored to the information needs of executives. Examples: systems for easy access to analyses of business performance, actions of competitors, and economic developments to support strategic planning.

and business professionals is a complex task. Conceptually, several major types of information systems support a variety of decision-making responsibilities: (1) management information systems, (2) decision support systems, and (3) executive information systems. See Figure 1.9.

Management information systems (MIS) provide information in the form of reports and displays to managers and many business professionals. For example, sales managers may use their networked computers and Web browsers to receive instantaneous displays about the sales results of their products and access their corporate intranet for daily sales analysis reports that evaluate sales made by each salesperson. **Decision support systems** (DSS) give direct computer support to managers during the decision-making process. For example, an advertising manager may use a DSS to perform a what-if analysis as part of the decision to determine how to spend advertising dollars. A production manager may use a DSS to decide how much product to manufacture, based on the expected sales associated with a future promotion and the location and availability of the raw materials necessary to manufacture the product. **Executive information systems** (EIS) provide critical information from a wide variety of internal and external sources in easy-to-use displays to executives and managers. For example, top executives may use touch-screen terminals to view instantly text and graphics displays that highlight key areas of organizational and competitive performance. Figure 1.10 is an example of an MIS report display.

Other Classifications of Information Systems

Several other categories of information systems can support either operations or management applications. For example, **expert systems** can provide expert advice for operational chores like equipment diagnostics or managerial decisions such as loan portfolio management. **Knowledge management systems** are knowledge-based information systems that support the creation, organization, and dissemination of business knowledge to employees and managers throughout a company. Information systems that focus on operational and managerial applications in support of basic business functions such as accounting or marketing are known as functional business systems. Finally, **strategic information systems** apply information technology to a firm's products, services, or business processes to help it gain a strategic advantage over its competitors. See Figure 1.11.

It is also important to realize that business applications of information systems in the real world are typically integrated combinations of the several types of information systems just mentioned. That is because conceptual classifications of information systems are designed to emphasize the many different roles of information systems. In practice, these roles are combined into integrated or cross-functional informational systems that provide a variety of functions. Thus, most information systems are designed to produce information and support decision making for various levels of management and business functions, as well as perform record-keeping and transaction-processing chores. Whenever you analyze an information system,

FIGURE 1.10

Management information systems provide information to business professionals in a variety of easy-to-use formats.

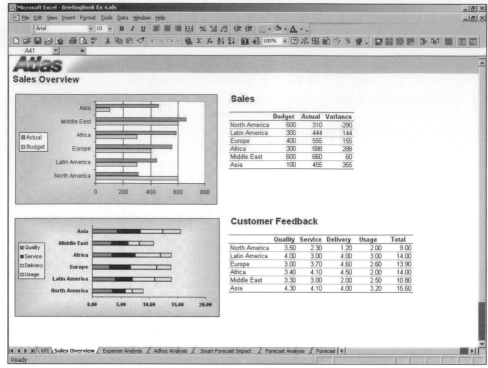

Source: Courtesy of Infor.

FIGURE 1.11

A summary of other categories of information systems with examples.

Other Categories of Information Systems

- **Expert systems.** Knowledge-based systems that provide expert advice and act as expert consultants to users. Examples: credit application advisor, process monitor, and diagnostic maintenance systems.

- **Knowledge management systems.** Knowledge-based systems that support the creation, organization, and dissemination of business knowledge within the enterprise. Examples: intranet access to best business practices, sales proposal strategies, and customer problem resolution systems.

- **Strategic information systems.** Support operations or management processes that provide a firm with strategic products, services, and capabilities for competitive advantage. Examples: online stock trading, shipment tracking, and e-commerce Web systems.

- **Functional business systems.** Support a variety of operational and managerial applications of the basic business functions of a company. Examples: information systems that support applications in accounting, finance, marketing, operations management, and human resource management.

you probably see that it provides information for a variety of managerial levels and business functions.

Managerial Challenges of Information Technology

Figure 1.12 illustrates the scope of the challenges and opportunities facing business managers and professionals in effectively managing information systems and technologies. Success in today's dynamic business environment depends heavily on maximizing the use of Internet-based technologies and Web-enabled information systems to meet the competitive requirements of customers, suppliers, and other business partners in a global marketplace. Figure 1.12 also emphasizes that information systems

FIGURE 1.12   Examples of the challenges and opportunities that business managers face in managing information systems and technologies to meet business goals.

Business / IT Challenges

- Speed and flexibility requirements of product development, manufacturing, and delivery cycles.
- Reengineering and cross-functional integration of business processes using Internet technologies.
- Integration of e-business and e-commerce into the organization's strategies, processes, structure, and culture.

Business / IT Developments

- Use of the Internet, intranets, extranets, and the Web as the primary IT infrastructure.
- Diffusion of Web technology to internetwork employees, customers, and suppliers.
- Global networked computing, collaboration, and decision support systems.

Business / IT Goals

- Give customers what they want, when and how they want it, at the lowest cost.
- Coordination of manufacturing and business processes with suppliers and customers.
- Marketing channel partnerships with suppliers and distributors.

and their technologies must be managed to support the business strategies, business processes, and organizational structures and culture of a business enterprise. That is because computer-based information systems, though heavily dependent on information technologies, are designed, operated, and used by people in a variety of organizational settings and business environments. The goal of many companies today is to maximize their customer and business value by using information technology to help their employees implement cooperative business processes with customers, suppliers, and others.

Success and Failure with IT

By now you should be able to see that the success of an information system should not be measured only by its *efficiency* in terms of minimizing costs, time, and the use of information resources. Success should also be measured by the *effectiveness* of the information technology in supporting an organization's business strategies, enabling its business processes, enhancing its organizational structures and culture, and increasing the customer and business value of the enterprise.

It is important to realize, however, that information technology and information systems can be mismanaged and misapplied in such a way that IS performance problems create both technological and business failures. Let's look at an example of what happens after these failures occur, as well as what can be done to avoid them.

Responsibility and Accountability for Project Success (and Failure)

Your department—information technology—has just played a starring role in blowing a multimillion-dollar enterprise software project. The intense glare from the CEO, CFO and other business leaders is squarely focused on the CIO, VP of applications, project managers and business analysts charged with making sure that this didn't happen. Of course, IT is never 100 percent at fault for any massive project—whether an ERP or CRM implementation, mainframe migration, or networking upgrade. The business side usually plays its part.

But the unfortunate and unfair fact is that because these initiatives are considered "technology projects," the business will almost always look in IT's direction when there's blame to be tossed around. "That's just a fact of life in IT," says Chris Curran, who's both a consulting partner at Diamond Management & Techonology Consultants and its Chief Technology Offer.

No sane executive would dismiss the strategic importance of IT today. And most don't: An IT Governance Institute study, consisting of more than 250 interviews with executives of both large and small companies in a variety of industry sectors, found that half of the respondents said that IT is "very important to the enterprise," and three-quarters stated that they align IT and business strategies.

When it came to IT project accountability, "executive management" was identified as the group held accountable for IT governance in 71 percent of the enterprises. That's all well and good, but when it comes to walking the walk with technology projects, non-IT executives appear to fall back on familiar rhetoric. In a similar 2009 survey of more than 500 IT professionals by ISACA, a nonprofit trade group focusing on corporate governance, almost half of respondents said "the CIO is responsible for ensuring that stakeholder returns on IT-related investments are optimized," notes the survey report.

Curran takes those results a step further. "Business investments need to have business accountability," Curran says. "But when a project goes south, especially high-profile ERP implementations, IT gets blamed—but it's not an IT project."

Curran's advice for such massive undertakings, which CIOs and analysts talk up but many don't follow, is practical: Think bite-sized project chunks and set proper expectations. He also advises his clients and their IT shops to embrace change and transparency—even if it hurts at first. "The corporate culture—the status quo—tends to be: 'Everything's good. We don't talk about problems until they are near unrecoverable, because we know people don't like bad news,'" Curran says.

But there are always going to be problems. That, also, is "just a fact of life in IT."

Source: Adapted from Thomas Wailgum, "After a Massive Tech Project Failure: What IT Can Expect," CIO.com, August 5, 2009.

Developing IS Solutions

Developing successful information system solutions to business problems is a major challenge for business managers and professionals today. As a business professional, you will be responsible for proposing or developing new or improved uses of information technologies for your company. As a business manager, you will frequently manage the development efforts of information systems specialists and other business end users.

Most computer-based information systems are conceived, designed, and implemented using some form of systematic development process. Figure 1.13 shows that several major activities must be accomplished and managed in a complete IS development cycle. In this development process, end users and information specialists *design* information system applications on the basis of an *analysis* of the business requirements of an organization. Examples of other activities include *investigating* the economic or technical feasibility of a proposed application, acquiring and learning how to use any software necessary to *implement* the new system, and making improvements to *maintain* the business value of a system.

We discuss the details of the information systems development process in Chapters 11 and 12. We will explore many of the business and managerial challenges that arise in developing and implementing new uses of information technology in Chapters 13 and 14. Now let's look at how a company changed its development practices to deliver the

FIGURE 1.13

Developing information
systems solutions to
business problems can be
implemented and managed
as a multistep process or
cycle.

right functionality to users and become more responsive to their needs. This example
emphasizes the importance of tailoring systems development practices to the needs of
a business.

Agile Systems Development at Con-Way, Inc.

In the old days, companies could spend months planning a technology project and
then months or even years implementing it. Not anymore. Strategies are far more
dynamic these days, especially as companies respond to challenging economic
times.

When someone has a good idea, it's nice to see it come to fruition right away.
At transportation company Con-Way—founded in 1929, with more than 26,000 employees and 2008 revenue of more than $5 billion—almost all good ideas require
technology to implement. Yet historically, ideas became cold by the time they
made it through IT steering committees, project planning, and design reviews.
Then, Con-Way became agile—that is, it adopted Agile development practices.

Using Agile, software development is no longer accomplished through lengthy
projects.

Instead, the overall concept of the desired system is defined at a high level up
front and then developed in short iterations. An iteration is typically no longer than
one month, and the software is released for use after each iteration. As people use the
software, they determine which features should be built next, providing a feedback
loop that results in building the highest priority functionality. One big change for
IT is that with Agile, an implementation date is always impending; team members
never feel they are able to relax on a project. Meanwhile, developers, used to having
private space, can feel that space is violated resulting from "pair programming,"
which has two developers constructing the same piece of code at the same time, and
colocation, which has team members sitting as close together as humanly possible.
As for the business users, Agile requires them to take a much more active role
throughout the entire process. They must work jointly with IT to determine the
priorities for each iteration, and they must provide daily direction to IT on the
needs for the functionality being built.

"I made the case for change in IT by explaining how the business would benefit
if we delivered the highest priority functionality faster. I also kept reiterating what
was in it for them—and there was a lot," says Jackie Barretta, vice president and CIO
of Con-Way, Inc. "At the same time, I made the case for change to the business by
preparing a solid ROI that quantified the benefits of increasing the efficiency of

development processes, delivering the right functionality more quickly and reducing the overall amount of work in progress."

The change effort has been worth it: After nine months, Agile is delivering on its promises. The iterative approach to software development is providing a feedback loop that results in building the right functionality. "We no longer have the waste problem that was inherent in the old waterfall method. Agile is creating greater alignment between IT and the business because of the constant, daily interaction and because Agile techniques help IT personnel understand the business better," says Barretta. "However, like anything that's really going to pay off, Agile is a huge change for IT and the user community."

Source: Adapted from Jackie Barretta, "How to Instill Agile Development Practices Among Your IT Team," *CIO Magazine*, January 14, 2009.

Challenges and Ethics of IT

As a prospective manager, business professional, or knowledge worker, you will be challenged by the **ethical responsibilities** generated by the use of information technology. For example, what uses of information technology might be considered improper, irresponsible, or harmful to other people or to society? What is the proper business use of the Internet and an organization's IT resources? What does it take to be a **responsible end user** of information technology? How can you protect yourself from computer crime and other risks of information technology? These are some of the questions that outline the ethical dimensions of information systems that we will discuss and illustrate with real world cases throughout this text. Figure 1.14 outlines some of the ethical risks that may arise in the use of several major applications of information technology. The following example illustrates some of the security challenges associated with conducting business over the Internet.

Hannaford Bros.: The Importance of Securing Customer Data

Hannaford Bros. may have started as a fruit and vegetable stand in 1883, but it has expanded from its Maine roots to become an upscale grocer with more than 160 stores throughout Maine, Massachusetts, New Hampshire, upstate New York, and Vermont. In March 2008, the supermarket chain disclosed a data security breach; Hannaford said in a notice to customers posted on its Web site that unknown intruders had accessed its systems and stolen about 4.2 million credit and debit card numbers between December 7 and March 10. The breach affected all of Hannaford's

FIGURE 1.14 Examples of some of the ethical challenges that must be faced by business managers who implement major applications of information technology.

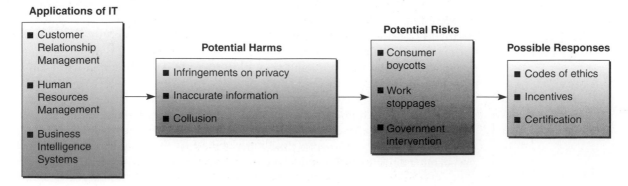

165 supermarkets in New England and New York, as well as 106 stores operated under the Sweetbay name in Florida and 23 independently owned markets that sell Hannaford products.

In a likely precursor of what was yet to come, two class-action lawsuits were filed against the company within the week. The filers argued that inadequate data security at Hannaford had resulted in the compromise of the personal financial data of consumers, thereby exposing them to the risk of fraud. They also claimed the grocer also appeared not to have disclosed the breach to the public quickly enough after discovering it.

Even though the Hannaford breach is relatively small compared with some other corporate security problems, it is likely to result in renewed calls for stricter regulations to be imposed on companies that fail to protect consumer data. In addition to facing the likelihood of consumer lawsuits, retailers who suffer breaches have to deal with banks and credit unions, which are getting increasingly anxious about having to shell out tens of thousands of dollars to pay for the cost of notifying their customers and reissuing credit and debit cards.

Retailers, on the other hand, have argued that the commissions they pay to card companies on each transaction are supposed to cover fraud-related costs, making any additional payments a double penalty. They also have said that the only reason they store payment card data is because of requirements imposed on them by the major credit card companies.

While the ultimate impact of these and other security breaches may be hard to quantify, it represents one of the most important challenges resulting from the ubiquitous use of electronic transaction processing and telecommunication networks in the modern networked enterprise, and one that is likely to keep growing every day. The security of customer and other sensitive data also represents one of the primary concerns of IT professionals.

Source: Adapted from Jaikumar Vijayan, "Hannaford Hit by Class-Action Lawsuits in Wake of Data-Breach Disclosure," *Computerworld*, March 20, 2008.

Challenges of IT Careers

Both information technology and the myriad of information systems it supports have created interesting, challenging, and lucrative career opportunities for millions of men and women all over the globe. At this point in your life you may still be uncertain about the career path you wish to follow, so learning more about information technology may help you decide if you want to pursue an IT-related career. In recent years, economic downturns have affected all job sectors, including IT. Further, rising labor costs in North America, Canada, and Europe have resulted in a large-scale movement to outsource basic software programming functions to India, the Middle East, and Asia-Pacific countries. Despite this move, employment opportunities in the information systems field are strong, with more new and exciting jobs emerging each day as organizations continue to expand their use of information technology. In addition, these new jobs pose constant human resource management challenges to all organizations because shortages of qualified information systems personnel frequently occur. Dynamic developments in business and information technologies cause constantly changing job requirements in information systems, which will ensure that the long-term job outlook in IT remains both positive and exciting.

Along with the myth that there are no jobs for IS professionals (we will dispel this one below!), another common myth is that IS professionals are computer geeks who live in a cubicle. Once again, nothing could be further from the truth! Today's IS professional must be highly skilled in communication, dealing with people, and, most of all, articulate in the fundamentals of business. The marketplace is demanding a *business technologist* with a big "B" and a big "T." The world of the IS professional is filled with constant challenge, variety, social interaction, and cutting-edge decision making. No desks and cubicles here. If action is what you are after, then you have found it here.

One major recruiter of IS professionals is the IT industry itself. Thousands of companies develop, manufacture, market, and service computer hardware, software, data, and network products and services. The industry can also provide e-business and e-commerce applications and services, end-user training, or business systems consulting. The biggest need for qualified people, however, comes from the millions of businesses, government agencies, and other organizations that use information technology. They need many types of IS professionals, such as systems analysts, software developers, and network managers to help them plan, develop, implement, and manage today's Internet-based and Web-enabled business/IT applications.

The accounting industry is a more recent major recruiter of IS professionals. Recent legislation, entitled the Sarbanes-Oxley Act of 2002, required major changes with regard to auditing practices by public accounting firms and internal control processes within publicly held organizations of all sizes and industries. Many of these changes directly affect the IT/IS practices of all parties involved. To facilitate the execution of the covenants of Sarbanes-Oxley, the accounting industry is actively recruiting graduates from accounting programs that have a significant emphasis on IS education. In addition, they are spending equal energy to recruit IS/IT professionals to work within the accounting industry. In either case, the result is a significant increase in demand for graduates with an IS/IT background or emphasis. Figure 1.15 lists just a few of the many career roles available to the modern IT professional.

According to recent reports by the U.S. Department of Labor, computer systems analysts, database administrators, and other managerial-level IS positions are expected to be among the fastest-growing occupations through 2012. Employment of IS professionals is expected to grow more than 36 percent (much higher than average) for all occupations as organizations continue to adopt and integrate increasingly sophisticated technologies. Job increases will be driven by very rapid growth in computer system design and related services, which is projected to be one of the fastest-growing

FIGURE 1.15

Careers in IS are as diverse and exciting as the technologies used in them; IS professionals have career opportunities in every business environment and activity throughout the world.

Systems Analyst	System Consultant	Business Applications Consultant
Chief Information Officer	Computer Operator	Computer Serviceperson
Network Administrator	Data Dictionary Specialist	Network Manager
Database Administrator	Database Analyst	Documentation Specialist
IS Auditor	End-User Computer Manager	Equipment Manufacturer Representative
PC Sales Representative	Programmer	Program Librarian
Project Manager	Records Manager	Hardware Sales Representative
Scheduling and Control Person	Security Officer	Office Automation Specialist
Senior Project Leader	Service Sales Representative	Software Sales Representative
Technical Analyst	Software Quality Evaluator	Technical Writer
Telecommunications Specialist	Training & Standards Manager	User Interface Specialist

industries in the U.S. economy. In addition, many job openings will arise annually from the need to replace workers who move into managerial positions or other occupations or who leave the labor force. Most important to you, IS/IT graduates generally receive one of the highest starting salaries in the school.

Despite the recent economic downturn among information technology firms, IS professionals still enjoy favorable job prospects. The demand for networking to facilitate sharing information, expanding client/server environments, and the need for specialists to use their knowledge and skills in a problem-solving capacity will be major factors in the rising demand for computer systems analysts, database administrators, and other IS professionals. Moreover, falling prices of computer hardware and software should continue to induce more businesses to expand their computerized operations and integrate new technologies. To maintain a competitive edge and operate more efficiently, firms will keep demanding the services of professionals who are knowledgeable about the latest technologies and can apply them to meet the needs of businesses.

Perhaps the time has come to put a sharper edge on this message: The field of information systems is growing at an increasingly rapid pace, and there is no risk of being unemployed upon graduation! I believe that the concern over a lack of IT/IS-related jobs was fueled by the news media and is now, quite simply, unfounded. Headlines proclaimed the death of IS and the lack of jobs in the United States due to massive outsourcing and offshoring. The jobs that were being sent overseas were real ones, to be sure. They were, however, not the jobs that you or your fellow students were ever going to train for during your stay in college—unless, of course, you aspire to being a faceless voice in a call center. These jobs are service-related jobs that, while vital to the big picture, are not the management level, creative business technologist positions that colleges and universities typically train their students to obtain. The real problem facing the IS field today is the lack of graduates! Students are choosing other professions because they fear low pay and unemployment, whereas recruiters are simultaneously begging for more graduates to feed their voracious appetites for more IS professionals. If you choose to avoid a career in information systems, it should not be because you think there are no jobs, that it does not have to do with people, or that it is no fun. Over the course of this book, we will dispel, with strong evidence, all of these rumors and myths. Let's start with some facts related to the first one.

The Bureau of Labor Statistics has some compelling evidence in favor of a career in information systems:

> *Prospects for qualified computer and information systems managers should be* **excellent.** Fast-paced occupational growth and the limited supply of technical workers will lead to a wealth of opportunities for qualified individuals. While technical workers remain relatively scarce in the United States, the demand for them continues to rise. This situation was exacerbated by the economic downturn in the early 2000s, when many technical professionals lost their jobs. Since then, many workers have chosen to avoid this work since it is **perceived** to have poor prospects.

> *People with management skills and an understanding of business practices and principles will have excellent opportunities, as companies are increasingly looking to technology to drive their revenue. (Bureau of Labor Statistics Occupational Outlook Handbook, 2008–2009)*

Increasingly, more sophisticated and complex technology is being implemented across all organizations, which will continue to fuel the demand for these computer occupations. The demand for systems analysts continues to grow to help firms maximize their efficiency with available technology. Expansion of e-commerce—doing business on the Internet—and the continuing need to build and maintain databases that store critical information about customers, inventory, and projects are fueling demand for database administrators familiar with the latest technology. Finally, the increasing importance placed on "cybersecurity"—the protection of electronic information—will result in a need for workers skilled in information security. Let's take a look at the ever-increasing problems with worldwide network security threats.

The Worldwide Network Security Threat	IT managers say mounting security risks combined with insufficient budgeting and staffing put their organizations in danger. According to a study conducted by net-Forensics, an international security information and event management provider, 80 percent of IT managers expect network-borne threats to increase throughout 2010 and 2011, and 85 percent see their security environment becoming more complex. But more than half said that their organization wasn't budgeting sufficiently, or recruiting enough new talent, to counter the added threats or complexity. The study of about 100 IT managers also found changes in security staff size over the past year, with it increasing for 15 percent of responding organizations, decreasing for 24 percent, and remaining static for 54 percent. Going forward, 20 percent of organizations planned to hire more security personnel, 15 percent planned to downsize, and 51 percent expected to stay the same.

According to Dale Cline, CEO of netForensics, "with security staff [size] remaining static or decreasing, and budgets not being allocated to put security processes in place, organizations are going to face greater challenges than ever to their security posture."

The study also found that just over half of the respondents stated that their organization was more secure today, versus 12 months ago. Yet 65 percent don't think their organization has "complete visibility" into its security posture at any given time. Based on the survey results, "security professionals are being asked to do more with less, while at the same time, the organization is being put at a higher risk," said Tracy Hulver, executive VP of products and marketing at netForensics, in a statement.

Her recommendation is that organizations should look at using tools and technologies that can scale up their response, without adding staff or budget. Examples of such tools include "outsourcing to cloud security, deploying technologies that maximize existing security infrastructure without having to invest in new, big-budget items [and] acquiring technology via SaaS [software as a service—see Chapter 4] pricing models." Interestingly, even with the majority of organizations seeing increasing numbers of threats, but little or no increase in their security budget, 70 percent of respondents said they wouldn't outsource their organization's security. Then again, such a move might risk making study respondents redundant.

Source: Adapted from Mathew J. Schwartz, "Network Security Threats Increasing," *InformationWeek*, June 25, 2010.

The IS Function

The successful management of information systems and technologies presents major challenges to business managers and professionals. Thus, the information systems function represents:

- A major functional area of business equally as important to business success as the functions of accounting, finance, operations management, marketing, and human resource management.
- An important contributor to operational efficiency, employee productivity and morale, and customer service and satisfaction.

- A recognized source of value to the firm.
- A major source of information and support needed to promote effective decision making by managers and business professionals.
- A vital ingredient in developing competitive products and services that give an organization a strategic advantage in the global marketplace.
- A dynamic, rewarding, and challenging career opportunity for millions of men and women.
- A key component of the resources, infrastructure, and capabilities of today's networked business enterprises.
- A strategic resource.

Foundation Concepts: The Components of Information Systems

System Concepts: A Foundation

System concepts underlie all business processes, as well as our understanding of information systems and technologies. That's why we need to discuss how generic system concepts apply to business firms and the components and activities of information systems. Understanding system concepts will help you understand many other concepts in the technology, applications, development, and management of information systems that we cover in this text. For example, system concepts help us understand:

- **Technology.** Computer networks are systems of information processing components that use a variety of hardware, software, data management, and telecommunications network technologies.

- **Applications.** E-business and e-commerce applications involve interconnected business information systems.

- **Development.** Developing ways to use information technology in business includes designing the basic components of information systems.

- **Management.** Managing information technology emphasizes the quality, strategic business value, and security of an organization's information systems.

Read the Real World Case about how some companies are turning to IT to help them develop new products and services. We can learn a lot from this case regarding the various ways in which IT can be used to foster innovation. See Figure 1.16.

What Is a System?

We have used the term *system* more than 100 times already and will use it thousands more before we are done. It therefore seems reasonable that we focus our attention on exactly what a system is. As we discussed at the beginning of the chapter, a system is defined as *a set of interrelated components, with a clearly defined boundary, working together to achieve a common set of objectives by accepting inputs and producing outputs in an organized transformation process.* Many examples of systems can be found in the physical and biological sciences, in modern technology, and in human society. Thus, we can talk of the physical system of the sun and its planets, the biological system of the human body, the technological system of an oil refinery, and the socioeconomic system of a business organization.

Systems have three basic functions:

- **Input** involves capturing and assembling elements that enter the system to be processed. For example, raw materials, energy, data, and human effort must be secured and organized for processing.

- **Processing** involves transformation processes that convert input into output. Examples are manufacturing processes, the human breathing process, or mathematical calculations.

- **Output** involves transferring elements that have been produced by a transformation process to their ultimate destination. For example, finished products, human services, and management information must be transmitted to their human users.

Example. A manufacturing system accepts raw materials as input and produces finished goods as output. An information system is a system that accepts resources (data) as input and processes them into products (information) as output. A business organization is a system in which human and economic resources are transformed by various business processes into goods and services.

REAL WORLD CASE 2

The New York Times and Boston Scientific: Two Different Ways of Innovating with Information Technology

Almost everybody has a theory about how to save the U.S. newspaper industry. The only consensus, it seems, is that it needs to change fundamentally or it could all but disappear. At *The New York Times*, tough times have elevated IT-enabled innovation to the top of the agenda.

A research and development group, created in 2006, operates as a shared service across nearly two dozen newspapers, a radio station, and more than 50 Web sites.

"Our role is to accelerate our entry onto new platforms by identifying opportunities, conceptualizing, and prototyping ideas," explains Michael Zimbalist, the company's vice president of R&D.

Zimbalist's staff of 12 includes experts in rapid prototyping, specialists in areas like mobile or cloud computing and data miners who probe Web site data for insight into what visitors do. They work within a common framework based on idea generation, development, and diffusion throughout the business. Recent projects included prototypes for new display ad concepts, as well as BlackBerry applications for Boston.com and the expert site About.com. The team's work is intended to supplement and support innovation taking place within the business units. For example, the team is prototyping E-Ink, an emerging display technology; some business units can't spare the resources to investigate it.

At NYTimes.com, the design and product development group of Marc Frons, CTO of Digital Operations, worked with Zimbalist's team and Adobe developers on the Times Reader 2.0 application, the next generation, on-screen reading system it developed on the Adobe AIR platform. Frons further encourages forward thinking among his 120-person team with twice-annual innovation contests. Winners receive cash, recognition

FIGURE 1.16

IT can enable innovation initiatives as companies seek to develop new products and services.

Source: © Stockbyte/Getty Images.

and the resources to turn their ideas into reality. Typical projects are measured against criteria like revenue potential or journalistic value. R&D projects aren't. "Since we build software, there's no huge capital investment up front," Frons says, "which allows us to experiment. The emphasis is on rapid development."

Times Widgets, a widget-making platform, was a contest winner, as was the recently launched Times Wire, a near real-time customizable interface for online content. "We're trying to solve specific problems and think about where the business is going," Frons says. Frons is focused on enhancing revenue, cutting costs, and increasing efficiency through process improvements and automation.

The New York Times has launched a cool interactive map that shows the most popular Netflix rentals across 12 U.S. metropolitan areas: New York, San Francisco/Bay Area, Boston, Chicago, Washington, Los Angeles, Seattle, Minneapolis, Denver, Atlanta, Dallas, and Miami. If you're a Netflix junkie and a closet *Twilight* fan (and you live in a major U.S. city), your rental habits are now on display. To create the map, *The New York Times* partnered with Netflix. The map is a graphical database of the top 100 most-rented Netflix films of 2009 laid on top of maps. With it you can graphically explore top 2009 Netflix movies based on three criteria: films that were hated or loved by critics, an alphabetical list, and most rented. For example, select most rented, and when you place the mouse over a zip code, a window pops up showing you what the top Netflix rentals are for that specific region.

Some trends are not surprising: The most popular Netflix movie of 2009 was *The Curious Case of Benjamin Button*, although *Slumdog Millionaire* and *Twilight* were both in the top 10. *Milk*, the story of San Franciscan activist Harvey Milk, was popular in San Francisco and other city centers, but not so much in the suburbs of southern cities (such as Dallas and Atlanta). *Mad Men*, the 1960s-set drama about advertising execs, was hot in parts of Manhattan and Brooklyn, but not in any other major cities. It barely got mention in Denver and Dallas, and not at all in Miami.

The map does show some interesting trends: Big blockbusters were not as popular in city centers (*Wanted* and *Transformers: Revenge of the Fallen*, barely made a splash in the city centers of Manhattan and San Francisco), although this could be due to the fact that a lot of people see blockbusters in movie theaters. *Last Chance Harvey*, a romantic comedy starring Dustin Hoffman and Emma Thompson, was enjoyed in wealthier suburbs (such as Scarsdale), but not in city centers (such as Manhattan). Tyler Perry's movies (Tyler Perry's *Madea Goes to Jail* and Tyler Perry's *The Family That Preys*) were popular in predominantly black neighborhoods.

Much of what has been innovative thus far at *The New York Times* can be classified as process or product innovation. Typically, a healthy and growing company should be content with focusing 90 to 95 percent of its innovation dollars on such core business innovation and 5 percent or 10 percent on new business models, says Mark Johnson, chairman of strategic innovation consultancy Innosight. However, he adds, "The newspaper industry is in so much trouble that business model innovation is more important than ever."

Now is a good—and bad—time for fostering such innovation. "You've got the leadership's attention you need," says Johnson. "But it's harder in the sense that there's an urgency to fix the financials, and being patient in the way you need to be for a new business model to unfold is a very difficult thing to do."

The New York Times is focused on experimenting with a number of different initiatives, but Boston Scientific faces a much different challenge: how to foster innovation without risking the disclosure and leakage of very valuable intellectual property. And the company has turned to technology to help find the right mix of access and security.

Boston Scientific wants to tear down barriers that prevent product developers from accessing the research that went into its successful medical devices so that they can create new products faster. But making data too easily accessible could open the way to theft of information potentially worth millions or billions of dollars. It's a classic corporate data privacy problem.

"The more info you give knowledge workers, the more effective they can be in creating a lot of value for the company," says Boris Evelson, a principal analyst at Forrester. "This creates disclosure risks—that someone's going to walk away with the data and give it to a competitor."

This tension compels the $8 billion company to seek out software that allows the broader engineering community to share knowledge while managing access to product development data, says Jude Currier, cardiovascular knowledge management and innovation practices lead at Boston Scientific. "Active security is the way to address this problem," Currier says.

That is, regularly monitor who's accessing what, and adjust permissions as business conditions change.

Keeping the pipeline of new stents, pacemakers, and catheters fresh is especially important because heart-related items account for 80 percent of Boston Scientific's sales. Over the past few years, engineers have been focused on

quality system improvements, Currier says. Boston Scientific had inherited regulatory problems from acquisitions it made during that time. Now that those situations are addressed, the company is ready to reinvigorate internal innovation.

Boston Scientific is piloting Invention Machine's Goldfire software, which, Currier says, provides the right mix of openness and security for data. Before, Boston Scientific's product developers worked in silos with limited access to research by colleagues on different product lines. Information was so locked down that even if scientists found something useful from a past project, they often didn't have access to it. "We're changing that," Currier says.

Goldfire makes an automated workflow out of such tasks as analyzing markets and milking a company's intellectual property. It combines internal company data with information from public sources, such as federal government databases.

Researchers can use the software to find connections among different sources, for instance by highlighting similar ideas. Engineers can use such analysis to get ideas for new products and begin to study their feasibility. The goal is to have any engineer be able to access any other engineer's research.

"The people in the trenches can't wait for that day to arrive," he says.

Although the goal is more openness, not all data stay open forever. For example, as a project gets closer to the patent application stage, access to the data about it is clipped to fewer people, Currier says.

He adds that since installing Goldfire, patent applications are up compared to similar engineering groups that do not use the Goldfire tool. "We have had to educate people that we aren't throwing security out the window but making valuable knowledge available to the organization," he says.

Source: Adapted from Stephanie Overby, "Rapid Prototyping Provides Innovation that Fits at the New York Times," *CIO.com*, June 24, 2009; Sarah Jacobson, "Netflix Map Shows What's Hot in Your Neighborhood," *PCWorld.com*, January 11, 2010; and Kim S. Nash, "Innovation: How Boston Scientific Shares Data Securely to Foster Product Development," *CIO.com*, November 23, 2009.

CASE STUDY QUESTIONS

1. As stated in the case, *The New York Times* chose to deploy their innovation support group as a shared service across business units. What do you think this means? What are the advantages of choosing this approach? Are there any disadvantages?

2. Boston Scientific faced the challenge of balancing openness and sharing with security and the need for restricting access to information. How did the use of technology allow the company to achieve both objectives at the same time? What kind of cultural changes were required for this to be possible? Are these more important than the technology-related issues? Develop a few examples to justify your answer.

3. The video rental map developed by *The New York Times* and Netflix graphically displays movie popularity across neighborhoods from major U.S. cities. How would Netflix use this information to improve their business? Could other companies also take advantage of these data? How? Provide some examples.

REAL WORLD ACTIVITIES

1. The newspaper industry has been facing serious challenges to its viability ever since the Internet made news available online. In addition to those initiatives described in the case, how are *The New York Times* and other leading newspapers coping with these challenges? What do you think the industry will look like 5 or 10 years from now? Go online to research these issues and prepare a report to share your findings.

2. Go online and search the Internet for other examples of companies using technology to help them innovate and develop new products or services. Break into small groups with your classmates to share your findings and discuss any trends or patterns you see in current uses of technology in this regard.

Feedback and Control

The system concept becomes even more useful by including two additional elements: feedback and control. A system with feedback and control functions is sometimes called a *cybernetic* system, that is, a self-monitoring, self-regulating system.

- **Feedback** is data about the performance of a system. For example, data about sales performance are feedback to a sales manager. Data about the speed, altitude, attitude, and direction of an aircraft are feedback to the aircraft's pilot or autopilot.

- **Control** involves monitoring and evaluating feedback to determine whether a system is moving toward the achievement of its goal. The control function then makes the necessary adjustments to a system's input and processing components to ensure that it produces proper output. For example, a sales manager exercises control when reassigning salespersons to new sales territories after evaluating feedback about their sales performance. An airline pilot, or the aircraft's autopilot, makes minute adjustments after evaluating the feedback from the instruments to ensure that the plane is exactly where the pilot wants it to be.

Example. Figure 1.17 illustrates a familiar example of a self-monitoring, self-regulating, thermostat-controlled heating system found in many homes; it automatically monitors and regulates itself to maintain a desired temperature. Another example is the human body, which can be regarded as a cybernetic system that automatically monitors and adjusts many of its functions, such as temperature, heartbeat, and breathing. A business also has many control activities. For example, computers may monitor and control manufacturing processes, accounting procedures help control financial systems, data entry displays provide control of data entry activities, and sales quotas and sales bonuses attempt to control sales performance.

Other System Characteristics

Figure 1.18 uses a business organization to illustrate the fundamental components of a system, as well as several other system characteristics. Note that a system does not exist in a vacuum; rather, it exists and functions in an *environment* containing other systems. If a system is one of the components of a larger system, it is a *subsystem*, and the larger system is its environment.

Several systems may share the same environment. Some of these systems may be connected to one another by means of a shared boundary, or *interface*. Figure 1.18 also illustrates the concept of an *open system*, that is, a system that interacts with other systems in its environment. In this diagram, the system exchanges inputs and outputs with its environment. Thus, we could say that it is connected to its environment by input and output interfaces. Finally, a system that has the ability to change itself or its environment to survive is an *adaptive system*.

FIGURE 1.17   A common cybernetic system is a home temperature control system. The thermostat accepts the desired room temperature as input and sends voltage to open the gas valve, which fires the furnace. The resulting hot air goes into the room, and the thermometer in the thermostat provides feedback to shut the system down when the desired temperature is reached.

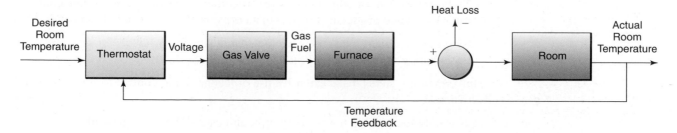

FIGURE 1.18

A business is an example of an organizational system in which economic resources (input) are transformed by various business processes (processing) into goods and services (output). Information systems provide information (feedback) about the operations of the system to management for the direction and maintenance of the system (control) as it exchanges inputs and outputs with its environment.

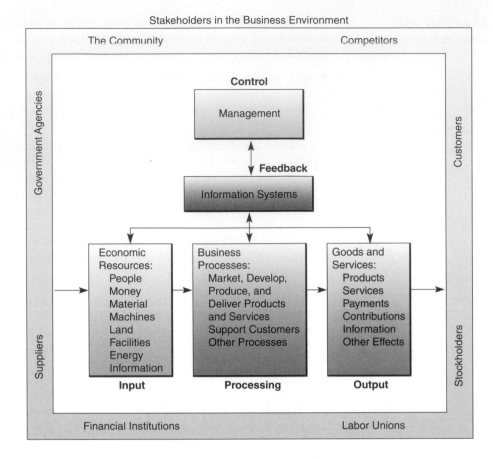

Example. Organizations such as businesses and government agencies are good examples of the systems in society, which is their environment. Society contains a multitude of such systems, including individuals and their social, political, and economic institutions. Organizations themselves consist of many subsystems, such as departments, divisions, process teams, and other workgroups. Organizations are examples of open systems because they interface and interact with other systems in their environment. Finally, organizations are examples of adaptive systems because they can modify themselves to meet the demands of a changing environment.

If we apply our understanding of general system concepts to information systems, it should be easy to see the parallels.

Information systems are made up of interrelated components:

- People, hardware, software, peripherals, and networks.

  They have clearly defined boundaries:

- Functions, modules, type of application, department, or end-user group.

  All the interrelated components work together to achieve a common goal by accepting inputs and producing outputs in an organized transformation process:

- Using raw materials, hiring new people, manufacturing products for sale, and disseminating information to others.

  Information systems make extensive use of feedback and control to improve their effectiveness:

- Error messages, dialog boxes, passwords, and user rights management.

Many information systems are designed to change in relation to their environments and are adaptive:

- Intelligent software agents, expert systems, and highly specialized decision support systems.

Information systems are systems just like any other system. Their value to the modern organization, however, is unlike any other system ever created.

Components of Information Systems

We have noted that an information system is a system that accepts data resources as input and processes them into information products as output. How does an information system accomplish this task? What system components and activities are involved?

Figure 1.19 illustrates an information system model that expresses a fundamental conceptual framework for the major components and activities of information systems. An information system depends on the resources of people (end users and IS specialists), hardware (machines and media), software (programs and procedures), data (data and knowledge bases), and networks (communications media and network support) to perform input, processing, output, storage, and control activities that transform data resources into information products.

This information system model highlights the relationships among the components and activities of information systems. It also provides a framework that emphasizes four major concepts that can be applied to all types of information systems:

- People, hardware, software, data, and networks are the five basic resources of information systems.

- People resources include end users and IS specialists, hardware resources consist of machines and media, software resources include both programs and procedures, data resources include data and knowledge bases, and network resources include communications media and networks.

FIGURE 1.19

The components of an information system. All information systems use people, hardware, software, data, and network resources to perform input, processing, output, storage, and control activities that transform data resources into information products.

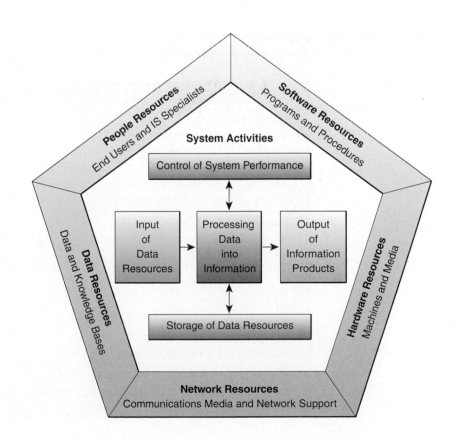

- Data resources are transformed by information processing activities into a variety of information products for end users.
- Information processing consists of the system activities of input, processing, output, storage, and control.

Information System Resources

Our basic IS model shows that an information system consists of five major resources: people, hardware, software, data, and networks. Let's briefly discuss several basic concepts and examples of the roles these resources play as the fundamental components of information systems. You should be able to recognize these five components at work in any type of information system you encounter in the real world. Figure 1.20 outlines several examples of typical information system resources and products.

People Resources

People are the essential ingredient for the successful operation of all information systems. These people resources include end users and IS specialists.

- End users (also called users or clients) are people who use an information system or the information it produces. They can be customers, salespersons, engineers, clerks, accountants, or managers and are found at all levels of an organization. In fact, most of us are information system end users. Most end users in business are knowledge workers, that is, people who spend most of their time communicating and collaborating in teams and workgroups and creating, using, and distributing information.

- IS specialists are people who develop and operate information systems. They include systems analysts, software developers, system operators, and other managerial, technical, and clerical IS personnel. Briefly, systems analysts design information systems based on the information requirements of end users, software developers create computer programs based on the specifications of systems analysts, and system operators help monitor and operate large computer systems and networks.

Hardware Resources

The concept of hardware resources includes all physical devices and materials used in information processing. Specifically, it includes not only machines, such as computers

FIGURE 1.20

Examples of information system resources and products.

Information System Resources and Products
People Resources
Specialists—systems analysts, software developers, systems operators.
End Users—anyone else who uses information systems.
Hardware Resources
Machines—computers, video monitors, magnetic disk drives, printers, optical scanners.
Media—floppy disks, magnetic tape, optical disks, plastic cards, paper forms.
Software Resources
Programs—operating system programs, spreadsheet programs, word processing programs, payroll programs.
Procedures—data entry procedures, error correction procedures, paycheck distribution procedures.
Data Resources
Product descriptions, customer records, employee files, inventory databases.
Network Resources
Communications media, communications processors, network access, control software.
Information Products
Management reports and business documents using text and graphics displays, audio responses, and paper forms.

and other equipment, but also all data media, that is, tangible objects on which data are recorded, from sheets of paper to magnetic or optical disks. Examples of hardware in computer-based information systems are:

- **Computer systems,** which consist of central processing units containing microprocessors and a variety of interconnected peripheral devices such as printers, scanners, monitors, and so on. Examples are handheld, laptop, tablet, or desktop microcomputer systems, midrange computer systems, and large mainframe computer systems.

- **Computer peripherals,** which are devices such as a keyboard, electronic mouse, trackball, or stylus for the input of data and commands, a video screen or printer for the output of information, and magnetic or optical disk drives for the storage of data resources.

Software Resources

The concept of software resources includes all sets of information processing instructions. This generic concept of software includes not only the sets of operating instructions called programs, which direct and control computer hardware, but also the sets of information processing instructions called procedures that people need.

It is important to understand that even information systems that do not use computers have a software resource component. This claim is true even for the information systems of ancient times or the manual and machine-supported information systems still used in the world today. They all require software resources in the form of information processing instructions and procedures to properly capture, process, and disseminate information to their users.

The following are examples of software resources:

- **System software,** such as an operating system program, which controls and supports the operations of a computer system. Microsoft Windows and Unix are two examples of popular computer operating systems.

- **Application software,** which are programs that direct processing for a particular use of computers by end users. Examples are sales analysis, payroll, and word processing programs.

- **Procedures,** which are operating instructions for the people who will use an information system. Examples are instructions for filling out a paper form or using a software package.

Data Resources

Data are more than the raw material of information systems. The concept of data resources has been broadened by managers and information systems professionals. They realize that data constitute valuable organizational resources. Thus, you should view data just as you would any organizational resource that must be managed effectively to benefit all stakeholders in an organization.

The concept of data as an organizational resource has resulted in a variety of changes in the modern organization. Data that previously were captured as a result of a common transaction are now stored, processed, and analyzed using sophisticated software applications that can reveal complex relationships among sales, customers, competitors, and markets. In today's wired world, the data to create a simple list of an organization's customers are protected with the same energy as the cash in a bank vault. Data are the lifeblood of today's organizations, and the effective and efficient management of data is considered an integral part of organizational strategy.

Data can take many forms, including traditional alphanumeric data, composed of numbers, letters, and other characters that describe business transactions and other events and entities; text data, consisting of sentences and paragraphs used in written communications; image data, such as graphic shapes and figures or photographic and video images; and audio data, including the human voice and other sounds.

The data resources of information systems are typically organized, stored, and accessed by a variety of data resource management technologies into:

- Databases that hold processed and organized data.
- Knowledge bases that hold knowledge in a variety of forms, such as facts, rules, and case examples about successful business practices.

For example, data about sales transactions may be accumulated, processed, and stored in a Web-enabled sales database that can be accessed for sales analysis reports by managers and marketing professionals. Knowledge bases are used by knowledge management systems and expert systems to share knowledge or give expert advice on specific subjects. We explore these concepts further in subsequent chapters.

Data versus Information. The word data is the plural of *datum*, though *data* commonly represents both singular and plural forms. Data are raw facts or observations, typically about physical phenomena or business transactions. For example, a spacecraft launch or the sale of an automobile would generate a lot of data describing those events. More specifically, data are objective measurements of the *attributes* (the characteristics) of *entities* (e.g., people, places, things, events).

Example. Business transactions, such as buying a car or an airline ticket, can produce a lot of data. Just think of the hundreds of facts needed to describe the characteristics of the car you want and its financing or the intricate details for even the simplest airline reservation.

People often use the terms *data* and *information* interchangeably. However, it is better to view data as raw material resources that are processed into finished information products. Then we can define information as data that have been converted into a meaningful and useful context for specific end users. Thus, data are usually subjected to a value-added process (*data processing* or *information processing*) during which (1) their form is aggregated, manipulated, and organized; (2) their content is analyzed and evaluated; and (3) they are placed in a proper context for a human user.

The issue of context is really at the heart of understanding the difference between information and data. Data can be thought of as context independent: A list of numbers or names, by itself, does not provide any understanding of the context in which it was recorded. In fact, the same list could be recorded in a variety of contexts. In contrast, for data to become information, both the context of the data and the perspective of the person accessing the data become essential. The same data may be considered valuable information to one person and completely irrelevant to the next. Just think of data as potentially valuable to all and information as valuable relative to its user.

Example. Names, quantities, and dollar amounts recorded on sales forms represent data about sales transactions. However, a sales manager may not regard these as information. Only after such facts are properly organized and manipulated can meaningful sales information be furnished and specify, for example, the amount of sales by product type, sales territory, or salesperson.

Network Resources

Telecommunications technologies and networks like the Internet, intranets, and extranets are essential to the successful e-business and e-commerce operations of all types of organizations and their computer-based information systems. Telecommunications networks consist of computers, communications processors, and other devices interconnected by communications media and controlled by communications software. The concept of network resources emphasizes that communications technologies and networks are fundamental resource components of all information systems. Network resources include:

- **Communications media.** Examples include twisted-pair wire, coaxial and fiber-optic cables, and microwave, cellular, and satellite wireless technologies.

FIGURE 1.21

Business examples of the basic activities of information systems.

Information System Activities
● **Input.** Optical scanning of bar-coded tags on merchandise.
● **Processing.** Calculating employee pay, taxes, and other payroll deductions.
● **Output.** Producing reports and displays about sales performance.
● **Storage.** Maintaining records on customers, employees, and products.
● **Control.** Generating audible signals to indicate proper entry of sales data.

● **Network infrastructure.** This generic category emphasizes that many hardware, software, and data technologies are needed to support the operation and use of a communications network. Examples include communications processors, such as modems and inter-network processors, and communications control software, such as network operating systems and Internet browser packages.

Information System Activities

Regardless of the type of information system, the same basic information system activities occur. Let's take a closer look now at each of the basic data or information processing activities. You should be able to recognize input, processing, output, storage, and control activities taking place in any information system you are studying. Figure 1.21 lists business examples that illustrate each of these information system activities.

Input of Data Resources

Data about business transactions and other events must be captured and prepared for processing by the input activity. Input typically takes the form of *data entry* activities such as recording and editing. End users usually enter data directly into a computer system or record data about transactions on some type of physical medium such as a paper form. This entry includes a variety of editing activities to ensure that they have recorded the data correctly. Once entered, data may be transferred onto a machine-readable medium, such as a magnetic disk, until needed for processing.

For example, data about sales transactions may be recorded on source documents such as paper order forms. (A **source document** is the original, formal record of a transaction.) Alternatively, salespersons might capture sales data using computer keyboards or optical scanning devices; they are visually prompted to enter data correctly by video displays. This method provides them with a more convenient and efficient **user interface,** that is, methods of end-user input and output with a computer system. Methods such as optical scanning and displays of menus, prompts, and fill-in-the-blank formats make it easier for end users to enter data correctly into an information system.

Processing of Data into Information

Data are typically subjected to processing activities, such as calculating, comparing, sorting, classifying, and summarizing. These activities organize, analyze, and manipulate data, thus converting them into information for end users. The quality of any data stored in an information system also must be maintained by a continual process of correcting and updating activities.

Example. Data received about a purchase can be (1) *added* to a running total of sales results, (2) *compared* to a standard to determine eligibility for a sales discount, (3) *sorted* in numerical order based on product identification numbers, (4) *classified* into product categories (e.g., food and nonfood items), (5) *summarized* to provide a sales manager with information about various product categories, and finally (6) used to *update* sales records.

Output of Information Products

Information in various forms is transmitted to end users and made available to them in the output activity. The goal of information systems is the production of appropriate information products for end users. Common information products include messages, reports, forms, and graphic images, which may be provided by video displays, audio responses, paper products, and multimedia. We routinely use the information provided by these products as we work in organizations and live in society. For example, a sales manager may view a video display to check on the performance of a salesperson, accept a computer-produced voice message by telephone, and receive a printout of monthly sales results.

Storage of Data Resources

Storage is a basic system component of information systems. Storage is the information system activity in which data are retained in an organized manner for later use. For example, just as written text material gets organized into words, sentences, paragraphs, and documents, stored data are commonly organized into a variety of data elements and databases. This organization facilitates their later use in processing or retrieval as output when needed by users of a system. Such data elements and databases are discussed further in Chapter 5, Data Resource Management.

Control of System Performance

An important information system activity is the control of system performance. An information system should produce feedback about its input, processing, output, and storage activities. This feedback must be monitored and evaluated to determine whether the system is meeting established performance standards. Then appropriate system activities must be adjusted so that proper information products are produced for end users.

For example, a manager may discover that subtotals of sales amounts in a sales report do not add up to total sales. This conflict might mean that data entry or processing procedures need to be corrected. Then changes would have to be made to ensure that all sales transactions would be properly captured and processed by a sales information system.

Recognizing Information Systems

As a business professional, you should be able to recognize the fundamental components of information systems you encounter in the real world. This demand means that you should be able to identify:

- The people, hardware, software, data, and network resources they use.
- The types of information products they produce.
- The way they perform input, processing, output, storage, and control activities.

This kind of understanding will help you be a better user, developer, and manager of information systems. As we have pointed out in this chapter, this is important to your future success as a manager, entrepreneur, business professional, or modern business technologist.

Summary

- **IS Framework for Business Professionals.** The IS knowledge that a business manager or professional needs to know is illustrated in Figure 1.2 and covered in this chapter and text. This knowledge includes (1) *foundation concepts:* fundamental behavioral, technical, business, and managerial concepts like system components and functions, or competitive strategies; (2) *information technologies:* concepts, developments, or management issues regarding hardware, software, data management, networks, and other technologies; (3) *business applications:* major uses of IT for business processes, operations, decision making, and strategic/competitive advantage; (4) *development processes:* how end users and IS specialists develop and implement business/IT solutions to problems and opportunities arising in business; and (5) *management challenges:* how to manage the IS function and IT resources effectively and ethically to achieve top performance and business value in support of the business strategies of the enterprise.

- **Business Roles of Information Systems.** Information systems perform three vital roles in business firms. Business applications of IS support an organization's business processes and operations, business decision making, and strategic competitive advantage. Major application categories of information systems include operations support systems, such as transaction processing systems, process control systems, and enterprise collaboration systems; and management support systems, such as management information systems, decision support systems, and executive information systems. Other major categories are expert systems, knowledge management systems, strategic information systems, and functional business systems. However, in the real world, most application categories are combined into cross-functional information systems that provide information and support for decision making and also performing operational information processing activities. Refer to Figures 1.7, 1.9, and 1.11 for summaries of the major application categories of information systems.

- **System Concepts.** A system is a group of interrelated components, with a clearly defined boundary, working toward the attainment of a common goal by accepting inputs and producing outputs in an organized transformation process. Feedback is data about the performance of a system. Control is the component that monitors and evaluates feedback and makes any necessary adjustments to the input and processing components to ensure that proper output is produced.

- **Information System Model.** An information system uses the resources of people, hardware, software, data, and networks to perform input, processing, output, storage, and control activities that convert data resources into information products. Data are first collected and converted to a form that is suitable for processing (input). Then the data are manipulated and converted into information (processing), stored for future use (storage), or communicated to their ultimate user (output) according to correct processing procedures (control).

- **IS Resources and Products.** Hardware resources include machines and media used in information processing. Software resources include computerized instructions (programs) and instructions for people (procedures). People resources include information systems specialists and users. Data resources include alphanumeric, text, image, video, audio, and other forms of data. Network resources include communications media and network support. Information products produced by an information system can take a variety of forms, including paper reports, visual displays, multimedia documents, e-messages, graphics images, and audio responses.

Key Terms and Concepts

These are the key terms and concepts of this chapter. The page number of their first explanation appears in parentheses.

1. Computer-based information system (42)
2. Control (63)
3. Data (68)
4. Data or information processing (69)
5. Data resources (67)
6. Developing successful information system solutions (52)
7. E-business (46)
8. E-business applications (46)
9. E-commerce (47)
10. Enterprise collaboration systems (47)
11. Extranet (46)
12. Feedback (63)
13. Hardware resources (66)
    a. Machines (66)
    b. Media (66)
14. Information (68)
    a. Information products (69)
15. Information system (38)
16. Information system activities (69)
    a. Input (69)
    b. Processing (69)
    c. Output (69)
    d. Storage (70)
    e. Control (70)
17. Information system model (65)
18. Intranet (46)
19. Knowledge workers (66)
20. Management information systems (49)
21. Network resources (68)
22. People resources (66)
    a. IS specialists (66)
    b. End users (66)
23. Roles of IS in business (42)
    a. Support of business processes and operations (42)
    b. Support of business decision making (42)
    c. Support of strategies for competitive advantage (43)
24. Software resources (67)
    a. Programs (67)
    b. Procedures (67)
25. System (60)
26. Types of information systems (47)
    a. Cross-functional informational systems (49)
    b. Management support systems (48)
    c. Operations support systems (47)
    d. Functional business systems (49)
    e. Transaction processing systems (48)
    f. Process control systems (48)
    g. Enterprise collaboration systems (48)

Review Quiz

Match one of the previous key terms and concepts with one of the following brief examples or definitions. Look for the best fit for answers that seem to fit more than one key term or concept. Defend your choices.

_____ 1. People who spend most of their workday creating, using, and distributing information.

_____ 2. Information systems support an organization's business processes, operations, decision making, and strategies for competitive advantage.

_____ 3. Using IT to reengineer business processes to support e-business operations.

_____ 4. Using Web-based decision support systems to support sales managers.

_____ 5. Using information technology for e-commerce to gain a strategic advantage over competitors.

_____ 6. A system that uses people, hardware, software, and network resources to collect, transform, and disseminate information within an organization.

_____ 7. An information system that uses computers and their hardware and software.

_____ 8. Anyone who uses an information system or the information it produces.

_____ 9. Applications using the Internet, corporate intranets, and interorganizational extranets for e-business operations, e-commerce, and enterprise collaboration.

_____ 10. The buying, selling, marketing, and servicing of products over the Internet and other networks.

_____ 11. Groupware tools to support collaboration among networked teams.

_____ 12. A group of interrelated components with a clearly defined boundary working together toward the attainment of a common goal.

_____ 13. Data about a system's performance.

_____ 14. Making adjustments to a system's components so that it operates properly.

_____ 15. Facts or observations.

_____ 16. Data that have been placed into a meaningful context for an end user.

_____ 17. Converting data into information is a type of this kind of activity.

_____ 18. An information system uses people, hardware, software, network, and data resources to perform input, processing, output, storage, and control activities that transform data resources into information products.

_____ 19. Machines and media.

_____ 20. Computers, disk drives, video monitors, and printers are examples.

_____ 21. Magnetic disks, optical disks, and paper forms are examples.

_____ 22. Programs and procedures.

_____ 23. A set of instructions for a computer.

_____ 24. A set of instructions for people.

_____ 25. End users and information systems professionals.

_____ 26. Using the keyboard of a computer to enter data.

_____ 27. Computing loan payments.

_____ 28. Printing a letter you wrote using a computer.

_____ 29. Saving a copy of the letter on a magnetic disk.

_____ 30. Having a sales receipt as proof of a purchase.

_____ 31. Information systems can be classified into operations, management, and other categories.

_____ 32. Includes transaction processing, process control, and end-user collaboration systems.

_____ 33. Includes management information, decision support, and executive information systems.

_____ 34. Information systems that perform transaction processing and provide information to managers across the boundaries of functional business areas.

_____ 35. Internet-like networks and Web sites inside a company.

_____ 36. Interorganizational Internet-like networks among trading partners.

_____ 37. Using the Internet, intranets, and extranets to empower internal business operations, e-commerce, and enterprise collaboration.

_____ 38. Information systems that focus on operational and managerial applications in support of basic business functions such as accounting or marketing.

_____ 39. Data should be viewed the same way as any organizational resource that must be managed effectively to benefit all stakeholders in an organization.

_____ 40. A major challenge for business managers and professionals today in solving business problems.

_____ 41. Examples include messages, reports, forms, and graphic images, which may be provided by video displays, audio responses, paper products, and multimedia.

_____ 42. These include communications media and network infrastructure.

_____ 43. People who develop and operate information systems.

_____ 44. The execution of a set of activities in order to convert data into information.

_____ 45. Those systems implemented in order to direct physical conversion processes, such as oil refinement.

_____ 46. The second stage of information systems evolution, focused on providing managerial users with information relevant to decision making in the form of predefined reports.

_____ 47. A type of operation support systems geared toward the recording and processing of data captured as a result of business transactions.

_____ 48. A type of operation support systems that enhance team and workgroup communication and productivity.

Discussion Questions

1. How can information technology support a company's business processes and decision making and give it a competitive advantage? Give examples to illustrate your answer.

2. How does the use of the Internet, intranets, and extranets by companies today support their business processes and activities?

3. Refer to the Real World Case on the four ways in which IT can leverage strategy and innovation. To what extent do specific technologies help companies gain an edge over their competitors? How easy or difficult would it be to imitate such advantages?

4. Why do big companies still fail in their use of information technology? What should they be doing differently?

5. How can a manager demonstrate that he or she is a responsible end user of information systems? Give several examples.

6. Refer to the Real World Case on *The New York Times* and Boston Scientific in the chapter, and think about any technology-enabled innovations that you have read about or come across recently. To what extent is innovation about the technology itself, and to what extent is it about changing the underlying ways that companies do business?

7. What are some of the toughest management challenges in developing IT solutions to solve business problems and meet new business opportunities?

8. Why are there so many conceptual classifications of information systems? Why are they typically integrated in the information systems found in the real world?

9. In what major ways have information systems in business changed during the last 40 years? What is one major change you think will happen in the next 10 years? Refer to Figure 1.4 to help you answer.

10. Refer to the real world example about responsibility and accountability for project failures in the chapter. Are these IT projects, or business projects with a significant IT component? Who should be responsible for ensuring their success? Explain.

Analysis Exercises

Complete the following exercises as individual or group projects that apply chapter concepts to real-world business situations.

1. **Understanding the Information System**
   The Library as an Information System
   A library makes an excellent information systems model. It serves as a very large information storage facility with text, audio, and video data archives. Look up the definitions for each term listed below and briefly explain a library's equivalents.

   a. Input
   b. Processing
   c. Output
   d. Storage
   e. Control
   f. Feedback

2. **Career Research on the Web**
   Comparing Information Sources
   Select a job title for a career you would like to pursue as a summer intern or new graduate. Provide a real-world example of each element in Figure 1.19. You may need to interview someone familiar with this position to find the information you require.

3. **Skydive Chicago: Efficiency and Feedback**
   Digital Data
   Skydive Chicago (www.SkydiveChicago.com) is one of the premier skydiving resorts in the United States, serving skydivers ranging in skills from first-time jumpers to internationally competitive freefly teams.

   Each student in Skydive Chicago's training program makes a series of progressive training jumps under the direct supervision of a United States Parachute Association–rated jumpmaster. The training program gears each jump in the series toward teaching one or two new skills. Jumpmasters video their students' jumps. Students use the feedback these videos provide to identify mistakes. They often copy their videos onto a personal tape for future reference.

   Jumpmasters may also copy well-executed student skydives to the facility's tape library. All students are given access to the dropzone's training room and are encouraged to watch video clips in preparation for their next training jump. This step saves jumpmasters, who are paid per jump, considerable time. Jumpmasters also use these videos to evaluate their training method's effectiveness.

a. How can this information system benefit the skydiving student?

b. How can this information system benefit Skydive Chicago?

c. Draw an information systems model (Figure 1.19). Fill in your diagram with the information about people, hardware, software, and other resources from this exercise.

4. Are Textbooks History?
Trends in Information Systems
The wealth of free information available via the Internet continues to grow at incredible rates. Search engines such as Google make locating useful information practical. This textbook often explores the Internet's impact on various industries, and the textbook industry is no exception. Is it possible that free Internet content might one day replace textbooks?

a. Go to www.google.com and use the search box to look up "End user." Were any of Google's first five search results useful with respect to this course?

b. Go to www.wikipedia.com and use the search box to look up "Knowledge worker." Compare Wikipedia's article with the information provided within this textbook. Which source did you find easiest to use?

What advantages did Wikipedia provide? What advantages did this textbook provide?

c. Did Google, Wikipedia, or this textbook provide the most useful information about "Intranets"? Why?

5. Careers in IS
Disaster Recovery
"How important are your data to you?" "What would happen if . . . ?" While business managers focus on solving business problems and determining what their information systems should do, disaster recovery consultants ask what would happen if things go wrong.

With careful advance planning, disaster recovery specialists help their clients prevent calamity. Although this topic covers a wide variety of software issues, installation configuration issues, and security threats, examining common end-user mistakes may also prove enlightening. Common end-user mistakes include:

- Failure to save work in progress frequently.
- Failure to make a backup copy.
- Failure to store original and backup copies in different locations.

For each of the common end-user mistakes listed above, answer the following questions:

a. How might this mistake result in data loss?

b. What procedures could you follow to prevent this risk?

REAL WORLD CASE 3

Sew What? Inc.: The Role of Information Technology in Small Business Success

What do Sting, Elton John, and Madonna have in common? Besides being international rock stars, they all use theatrical backdrops designed and manufactured by custom drapery maker Sew What? Inc. Based in Rancho Dominguez, California, Sew What? provides custom theatrical draperies and fabrics for stages, concerts, fashion shows, and special events worldwide and has become an industry leader in rock-and-roll staging.

Founded in 1992 by Australian-born Megan Duckett, Sew What? has grown from a tiny kitchen-and-garage operation to a multimillion-dollar enterprise, thanks to Duckett's never-say-no approach to customer satisfaction. "When I see a problem, I just don't back down. I find a way to overcome it and I use everybody I know to help me," she says.

What made it possible for a one-woman business that started in a kitchen to evolve and grow into a multimillion-dollar company with 35 employees? Megan Duckett attributes her success to hard work, quality workmanship, and especially information technology.

Sew What? has enjoyed explosive growth in recent years, reaching $4 million per year in sales by the end of 2006. Company president Duckett credits much of her firm's rapid growth to its ability to leverage information technology and the Internet to drive sales. "Before we put up our Web site, sewwhatinc.com, our business was almost all local," says Duckett. "But after launching the Web site three years ago, we now have clients all over the world. In fact, last year our revenue grew 45 percent on the previous year's sales, and this year we are on target to enjoy a 65 percent increase on 2005 sales. And nearly all that growth came from Web-driven sales."

Although the company's Web site may take center stage, managing all the business the site brings in requires a lot of effort behind the scenes. In particular, Duckett relies on a solid IT infrastructure to help keep the company running smoothly. "We are a customer-centric company," notes Duckett. "It's critical that we have excellent back-office information technology to manage the business and deliver outstanding service to our customers."

Sew What? runs most of its business with Intuit's Quick-Books Enterprise Solutions Manufacturing and Wholesale Edition software and Microsoft's Windows Server operating system installed on a Dell PowerEdge 860 server, sporting an Intel Xeon processor and 146 gigabytes of disk storage. According to Duckett, "Running our business requires a lot of storage. In addition to customer information and vital operational and financial QuickBooks files, we need to store thousands of drapery and fabric image files, customer instruction document files, and other types of data." Sew What?'s additional computer support includes an older Dell PowerEdge 500 server dedicated to a few smaller applications and a variety of Dell desktop PC systems for employees.

Sew What? started in 1992 as a part-time endeavor, with Duckett cutting and sewing fabric on her kitchen table. She went full time in 1997 and incorporated in 1998. The important role technology plays in running a successful small business hit home when she lost a big contract. The potential client said that without a Web site, her company "lacked credibility." "Before losing that contract, I thought, 'I run a sewing business, a cottage craft. I don't need a Web site,'" she says. Duckett admits she was rather cocky, mainly because she had grown her business "quite well" by word of mouth alone. "I quickly learned the error of that thought process. You can't have that attitude and stick around," she acknowledges.

Losing the contract also coincided with a period of low growth between 2001 and 2002. That's when Duckett decided to embrace technology. Using Microsoft Publisher, she designed and built her own Web site. "You figure things out and learn how to do it yourself when budgets are thin," she admits.

Duckett kept working to improve the site and make it better for her customers. A year later, feeling that the site needed refreshing, she signed up for a 10-week course in Dreamweaver and again completely rebuilt the site. Yet another Web site reconstruction helped Sew What? grow into a company with customers around the world and a clientele list that includes international rock stars, Gucci, and *Rolling Stone* magazine.

In 2005, Duckett decided she needed to improve the site's navigation because "I wanted it to be sleek and to provide a really good customer experience. That was beyond my abilities, so we hired a Web marketing consulting company to build a custom navigation system for the site."

She worked with the hired guns on branding, search engine optimization, overall design, and site layout. Duckett still provides all the content, including text and images. There's also a Spanish version of the site, and the professionals tuned up the main site's search features to include spelling variants for different English-speaking countries. For example, you can search for the American spelling of theater or the British and Australian version, theatre.

The site also lets potential customers review all kinds of color swatches and teaches them how to calculate accurate measurements for their projects; the differences between a scrim, a tormentor, and a traveler curtain; the proper care and feeding of a variety of drapery materials; and a lot more.

While perusing the Dell Web site one day, Duckett saw a news article about the Dell/NFIB Small Business Excellence Award. The National Federation of Independent Businesses (NFIB) and Dell Inc. present this annual prize to one small business in recognition of its innovative use of technology to improve its customers' experience. The winner receives $30,000 worth of Dell products and services, a lifetime membership to the NFIB, and a day at Dell's headquarters with Michael Dell and other senior executives.

"The description of the kinds of businesses they were looking for perfectly described Sew What?" Duckett realized. "Everything they were looking for, we'd done, so I decided to enter. My husband [and business partner] laughed and reminded me that I never win anything." Writing the essay for the contest caused Duckett to reflect on everything she and her employees had achieved over the years: "We got to sit back and feel really proud of ourselves. Just that process was enough to invigorate everyone in our weekly production meetings."

The contest judges also recognized Megan Duckett's passionate commitment to customer satisfaction and use of information technology for business success, so they awarded Sew What? the Small Business Excellence Award. Winning the award proved to be a very emotional experience. Looking at the caliber and achievements of the nine other finalists, Duckett figured Sew What? would remain just a top-10 finalist: "I could not believe that a big company like Dell—so entrepreneurial and advanced in every way—would look at our little company and recognize it."

Like other small business owners, Duckett puts an enormous amount of physical and emotional energy into her work. "Winning this award is so flattering on a personal level," she says. "This business is ingrained in every cell of my body, and to have someone saying, 'Good job,' well, in small business, nobody ever says that to you."

That may have been true previously, but Sew What?'s technology leadership and business success continue to earn recognition. In March 2007, the company received a Stevie Award for Women in Business for "most innovative company of the year" among those with up to 100 employees. A few months earlier, Sew What? had received an SMB 20 Award from *PC Magazine*, which honors 20 of the most technologically innovative small- and medium-sized businesses (SMBs) each year. "Small and medium businesses drive today's economy. However, they often don't get the attention and recognition they deserve," said *PC Magazine*'s Editor-in-Chief, Jim Louderback. "We want to highlight the hard work, technological leadership, and innovative spirit of thousands of SMB companies throughout the world."

Duckett plans to use her prize winnings to add a bar code system that can track the manufacturing process at the company's warehouse. In the drapery business, fabric is stored on a roll in the warehouse and then moves through different stages: receiving, cutting, sewing, shipping, and so forth. The scanning process will enable Duckett's team to track how long the fabric stays in any given stage. These data will give them a better idea of their costs, which will then help them produce more accurate price lists.

"We don't need to charge an hour and a half for labor if the cutting only takes an hour and 15 minutes," Duckett notes. Currently, the company uses a handwritten system of sign-in and sign-out sheets that, she says, takes too long and introduces too many errors. "The new system will also let us track the progress of individual orders," she promises. "We'll be able to provide better service by keeping the customer updated."

Source: Adapted from Lauren Simonds, "Pay Attention to the Woman Behind the Curtain," *SmallBusinessComputing.com*, July 21, 2006.

CASE STUDY QUESTIONS

1. How do information technologies contribute to the business success of Sew What? Inc.? Give several examples from the case regarding the business value of information technology that demonstrate this conclusion.

2. If you were a management consultant to Sew What? Inc., what would you advise Megan Duckett to do at this point to be even more successful in her business? What role would information technology play in your proposals? Provide several specific recommendations.

3. How could the use of information technology help a small business you know be more successful? Provide several examples to support your answer.

REAL WORLD ACTIVITIES

1. Search the Internet to help you evaluate the business performance of Sew What? Inc. and its competitors at the present time. What conclusions can you draw from your research about Sew What?'s prospects for the future? Report your findings and recommendations for Sew What?'s continued business success to the class.

2. Small businesses have been slower to integrate information technology into their operations than larger companies. Break into small groups with your classmates to discuss the reasons for this state of affairs, identifying several possible IT solutions and their business benefits that could help small businesses become more successful.

REAL WORLD CASE 4

JetBlue and the Veterans Administration: The Critical Importance of IT Processes

When most people think of information technology, software and hardware immediately come to mind. While these are certainly important, good IT processes, particularly those that need to kick in during a disaster situation, are also critical. Most important, these need to be in place before, and not after, they are needed. For an example, go back to February 2007, when JetBlue Airways was forced to cancel more than 1,000 flights after an ice storm.

"For one, we didn't have enough of our home-office employees or crew members trained on our reservation system, so while we were dispatching people to the airports to help, which was great, they weren't trained to actually use the computer system. So we're going through a process now where we're actively training those crew members," says spokesman Eric Brinker. The discount airline is also in the process of expanding the capabilities of its reservation crew members so they can accept more inbound calls. "We basically maxed out," Brinker said. "We're working on a system to be able to automatically notify them better to take phone calls."

In the middle of the crisis, JetBlue's IT department developed a database that allowed the airline's scheduling team to improve multitasking. "They were receiving tons of phone calls from our crew members, and we created a database to enter in the whereabouts of our crew members. Then that information would sync up with the information about the crew members that was in the main system," Brinker said. "Now, during a weather situation, our flight crews and flight hands can call us and give us the location of where they are, and we can start to rebuild the airline immediately using this tool. We do that by cross-referencing where the crew members say they are versus where the computer says they are, which weren't always in sync."

Brinker said the airline had never experienced a full meltdown before, so it hadn't needed to use this type of database. "The system, which was developed in 24 hours and implemented in the middle of JetBlue's crisis, has now been implemented as a full-time system," he said. "It's a real behind-the-scenes improvement for both our crew members and customers," he said. JetBlue is also improving the way it communicates with its customers, including pushing out automated flight alerts to customers via e-mail and mobile devices.

Even seemingly smaller and less critical processes can have ramifications of a large magnitude in the interconnected world in which we live. In September 2007, during a hearing by the House Committee on Veterans' Affairs, lawmakers learned about an unscheduled system failure that took down key applications in 17 Veterans Administration (VA) medical facilities for a day. Dr. Ben Davoren, the director of clinical informatics for the San Francisco VA Medical Center, characterized the outage as "the most significant technological threat to patient safety the VA has ever had." Yet the shutdown grew from a simple change in management procedure that wasn't properly followed. The small, undocumented

change ended up bringing down the primary patient applications at 17 VA medical centers in northern California.

The breakdown exposed just how challenging it is to effect substantial change in a complex organization the size of the VA Office of Information & Technology (OI&T). Begun in October 2005 and originally scheduled to be completed by October 2008, the "reforming" of the IT organization at the VA involved several substantial goals. As part of the reform effort, the VA was to shift local control of IT infrastructure operations to regional data-processing centers.

Historically, each of the 150 or so medical centers run by the VA had its own IT service, its own budget authority, and its own staff, as well as independence with regard to how the IT infrastructure evolved. All of the decisions regarding IT were made between a local IT leadership official and the director of that particular medical center. While that made on-site IT staff responsive to local needs, it made standardization across sites nearly impossible in areas such as security, infrastructure administration and maintenance, and disaster recovery.

On the morning of August 31, 2007, staffers in medical centers around northern California starting their workday quickly discovered that they couldn't log onto their patient systems. The primary patient applications, Vista and CPRS, had suddenly become unavailable. Vista, which stands for Veterans Health Information Systems and Technology Architecture, is the VA's system for maintaining electronic health records. CPRS, the Computerized Patient Record System, is a suite of clinical applications that provides an across-the-board view of each veteran's health record. It includes a real-time order-checking system, a notification system to alert clinicians of significant events, and a clinical reminder system. Without access to Vista, doctors, nurses, and others were unable to pull up patient records.

"There was a lot of attention on the signs and symptoms of the problem and very little attention on what is very often the first step you have in triaging an IT incident, which is, 'What was the last thing that got changed in this environment?'" Director Eric Raffin said.

The affected medical facilities immediately implemented their local contingency plans, which consist of three levels: the first of those is a fail-over from the Sacramento Data Center to the Denver Data Center, according to Bryan D. Volpp, associate chief of staff and clinical informatics. Volpp assumed that the data center in Sacramento would move into the first level of backup—switching over to the Denver data center. It didn't happen.

On that day, the Denver site wasn't touched by the outage at all. The 11 sites running in that region maintained their normal operations throughout the day. So why didn't Raffin's team make the decision to fail over to Denver? "What the team in Sacramento wanted to avoid was putting at risk the remaining 11 sites in the Denver environment, facilities that were still operating with no glitches. The problem could have been software-related," Raffin says. In that case, the problem may have spread to the VA's Denver facilities, as well. Since the Sacramento group couldn't pinpoint the problem, they made a decision not to fail over.

Greg Schulz, senior analyst at The Storage I/O Group, said the main vulnerability with mirroring is exactly what Raffin feared. "If I corrupt my primary copy, then my mirror is corrupted. If I have a copy in St. Louis and a copy in Chicago and they're replicating in real time, they're both corrupted, they're both deleted." That's why a point-in-time copy is necessary, Schulz continued. "I have everything I need to get back to that known state."

According to Volpp, "the disruption severely interfered with our normal operation, particularly with inpatient and outpatient care and pharmacy." The lack of electronic records prevented residents on their rounds from accessing patient charts to review the prior day's results or add orders. Nurses couldn't hand off from one shift to another through Vista, as they were accustomed. Discharges had to be written out by hand, so patients didn't receive the normal lists of instructions or medications, which were usually produced electronically.

Volpp said that within a couple of hours of the outage, "most users began to record their documentation on paper," including prescriptions, lab orders, consent forms, and vital signs and screenings. Cardiologists couldn't read EKGs, since those were usually reviewed online, nor could they order, update, or respond to consultations.

In Sacramento, the group finally got a handle on what had transpired to cause the outage. "One team asked for a change to be made by the other team, and the other team made the change," said Raffin. It involved a network port configuration, but only a small number of people knew about it. More important, said Raffin, "the appropriate change request wasn't completed." A procedural issue was at the heart of the problem. "We didn't have the documentation we should have had," he said. If that documentation for the port change had existed, Raffin noted, "that would have led us to very quickly provide some event correlation: Look at the clock, look at when the system began to degrade, and then stop and realize what we really needed to do was back those changes out, and the system would have likely restored itself in short order."

According to Evelyn Hubbert, an analyst at Forrester Research Inc., the outage that struck the VA isn't uncommon. "They don't make the front page news because it's embarrassing." Then, when something happens, she says, "it's a complete domino effect. Something goes down, something else goes down. That's unfortunately typical for many organizations." Schulz concurred. "You can have all the best software, all the best hardware, the highest availability, you can have the best people," Schulz said. "However, if you don't follow best practices, you can render all of that useless."

Source: Adapted from Linda Rosencrance, "Overwhelmed IT Systems Partly to Blame for JetBlue Meltdown," *Computerworld*, February 20, 2007; and Dian Schaffhauser, "The VA's Computer Systems Meltdown: What Happened and Why," *Computerworld*, November 20, 2007.

CASE STUDY QUESTIONS

1. Eric Brinker of JetBlue noted that the database developed during the crisis had not been needed before because the company had never experienced a meltdown. What are the risks and benefits associated with this approach to IT planning? Provide some examples of each.

2. With hindsight, we now know that the decision made by Eric Raffin of the VA not to fail over to the Denver site was the correct one. However, it involved failing to follow established backup procedures. With the information he had at the time, what other alternatives could he have considered? Develop at least two of them.

3. A small, undocumented change resulted in the collapse of the VA system, largely because of the high interrelationship between its applications. What is the positive side of this high degree of interconnection, and how does this benefit patients? Provide examples from the case to justify your answer.

REAL WORLD ACTIVITIES

1. Go online and search for reports on the aftermath of these two incidents. What consequences, financial and otherwise, did the two organizations face? What changes, if any, were implemented as a result of these problems? Prepare a report and present your findings to the class.

2. Search the Internet for examples of problems that companies have had with their IT processes. Break into small groups with your classmates to discuss your findings and what solutions you can propose to help organizations avoid the problems you discovered.

CHAPTER 2

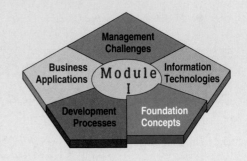

COMPETING WITH INFORMATION TECHNOLOGY

Learning Objectives

1. Identify several basic competitive strategies and explain how they use information technologies to confront the competitive forces faced by a business.

2. Identify several strategic uses of Internet technologies and give examples of how they can help a business gain competitive advantages.

3. Give examples of how business process reengineering frequently involves the strategic use of Internet technologies.

4. Identify the business value of using Internet technologies to become an agile competitor or form a virtual company.

5. Explain how knowledge management systems can help a business gain strategic advantages.

SECTION I   Fundamentals of Strategic Advantage

Strategic IT

Technology is no longer an afterthought in forming business strategy, but the actual cause and driver.

This chapter will show you that it is important to view information systems as more than a set of technologies that support efficient business operations, workgroup and enterprise collaboration, or effective business decision making. Information technology can change the way businesses compete. You should also view information systems strategically, that is, as vital competitive networks, as a means of organizational renewal, and as a necessary investment in technologies; such technologies help a company adopt strategies and business processes that enable it to reengineer or reinvent itself to survive and succeed in today's dynamic business environment.

Section I of this chapter introduces fundamental competitive strategy concepts that underlie the strategic use of information systems. Section II then discusses several major strategic applications of information technology used by many companies today.

Read the Real World Case regarding how Google gained worldwide competitive advantage with a single change. We can learn a lot about how IT can help create competitive advantage from this case. See Figure 2.1.

Competitive Strategy Concepts

In Chapter 1, we emphasized that a major role of information systems applications in business is to provide effective support of a company's strategies for gaining competitive advantage. This strategic role of information systems involves using information technology to develop products, services, and capabilities that give a company major advantages over the competitive forces it faces in the global marketplace.

This role is accomplished through a strategic information architecture: the collection of strategic information systems that supports or shapes the competitive position and strategies of a business enterprise. So a strategic information system can be any kind of information system (e.g., TPS, MIS, and DSS) that uses information technology to help an organization gain a competitive advantage, reduce a competitive disadvantage, or meet other strategic enterprise objectives.

Figure 2.2 illustrates the various competitive forces a business might encounter, as well as the competitive strategies that can be adopted to counteract such forces. It is important to note that the figure suggests that any of the major strategies may be deemed useful against any of the common competitive forces. Although it is rare and unlikely that a single firm would use all strategies simultaneously, each has value in certain circumstances. For now, it is only important that you become familiar with the available strategic approaches. Let us look at several basic concepts that define the role of competitive strategy as it applies to information systems.

Competitive Forces and Strategies

How should a business professional think about competitive strategies? How can a business use information systems to apply competitive strategies? Figure 2.2 illustrates an important conceptual framework for understanding forces of competition and the various competitive strategies employed to balance them.

A company can survive and succeed in the long run only if it successfully develops strategies to confront five competitive forces that shape the structure of competition in its industry. In Michael Porter's classic model of competition, any business that wants to survive and succeed must effectively develop and implement strategies to counter (1) *the rivalry of competitors within its industry*, (2) *the threat of new entrants into an industry and its markets*, (3) *the threat posed by substitute products that might capture market share*, (4) *the bargaining power of customers*, and (5) *the bargaining power of suppliers*.

REAL WORLD CASE 1

Instant Competitive Advantage: Google Pulls Ahead in Worldwide Search Strategy

Microsoft's Bing and Yahoo officially joined forces in 2010, and Google needed to come up with a new, splashy feature that would give them a clear edge over their new and formidable rivals. And that's just what Google did!

In September 2010, the company unveiled Google Instant—a new feature that will speed up searching for things on the Internet. Google Instant is aimed at speeding search results by searching as you type. The new, dynamic feature, which is fully operational worldwide, is about starting the search process before the user even finishes typing in the query. Google is now predicting what people will be asking for. The move is a "dramatic break" from the traditional Google search experience, says Hadley Reynolds, an analyst with IDC.

The intention is to compress the loop of entering queries, scanning the search results, refining the query, and checking the new results, a process that may be repeated multiple times and sometimes leads to frustration. The feature is undeniably a computer engineering tour-de-force, but it remains to be seen how it will be accepted by end users and what impact it will have on ad performance and efficiency, as well as on the visibility of organic search results.

Developing such a groundbreaking and bold feature shows that, at Google, the search business remains king, even when the company plays in a broad range of worldwide markets. "Google is clearly doubling down on its heritage: search, which it does really, really well," said analyst Charlene Li of Altimeter Group.

FIGURE 2.1

Google continues to dominate the worldwide search marketplace.

According to Google, Instant isn't "search as you type" but rather "search before you type" because the engine is anticipating and predicting the most likely query the user intends to key in. As Google rolls out the feature, sophisticated users are more likely to embrace it than are ordinary ones, as the former understand the convenience and time savings while the latter may feel disconcerted, at least initially. "It's an improvement, and represents greater efficiency and convenience for people who are accustomed to using search," said analyst Greg Sterling of Sterling Market Intelligence. "But there is this blinking-light effect, with the way the page changes as you proceed with the character entry, that may be a bit disorienting to more ordinary users."

"While many of the familiar [search] elements are still in place, the speed and streaming aspects of Google's understanding of the user query and presentation of the results will be revolutionary," Reynolds said. "The traditional Google search model was incredibly wasteful of users' time . . . Instant will help show what the right links are more quickly," he said.

Reynolds sees big potential in speeding up the process of refining queries, which he calls the "pogo stick" problem. "Google Instant will help show what the right links are more quickly," he said via e-mail. "Google Instant will take some getting used to. But I think most users will adjust to the changes and come to like Google's tightening up of the search experience and all the guidance that will be presented to them."

Perhaps anticipating some resistance, Google is giving users the option of turning off Google Instant, which for now will be limited to general Web searches on google.com in the United States for all users, and in a few other countries such as France, Germany, and the U.K. for users signed into their Google accounts. It will be launched later for all users worldwide, as well as in mobile devices.

Marissa Mayer, Google's vice president of Search Products, said, "The user benefits of Google Instant are many but the primary one is time saved." Mayer announced the new feature at the company's launch event in San Francisco in September 2010. "Our testing has shown that Google Instant saves the average searcher 2 to 5 seconds per search. That may not seem like a lot at first, but it adds up," she said.

Dan Olds, an analyst with The Gabriel Consulting Group, said he agreed that on first thought, it might not sound like a lot of time saved, but it could be enough to give Google a leg up on its worldwide search competition. "Google did some more math and figured it would save users 3.5 billion seconds per day. I'm not sure what we're all going to do with the extra time, but hopefully we'll think of something," Olds said. "This gives Google something to brag about. I think that this is a feature that Microsoft will have to add to Bing in the near future. It's pretty useful and gives Google a clear competitive advantage." If Microsoft adds this feature to Bing, it will only serve to dilute Google's advantage but will really not provide Microsoft with any significant gain (see the blue box on Competitive Advantage later in this chapter).

Late 2010 was a good time for Google to fire a major shot across the bow of the new Microsoft Bing and Yahoo partnership. In August 2010, Microsoft and Yahoo finished a major integration project, which has Yahoo using Microsoft's Bing search engine to power all searches on the various Yahoo sites. The Microsoft-Yahoo deal was aimed squarely at Google in an effort to gain competitive advantage for Microsoft and Yahoo. Neither company has had much luck tearing away at Google's hefty lead in the worldwide search market. By merging their efforts, they're hoping for better luck. With Google Instant, the search leader is firing back at its rivals.

"While I don't think that Google Instant will move the bar in terms of market share, it does give Google a new feature that will be noticed by every user they have and it'll be another reason to stick with Google for their search needs," Olds said. "We're going to see more innovations along these lines as Google continues to develop its offerings in the face of renewed competition from the combined Microsoft and Yahoo partnership."

Rob Enderle, an analyst with the Enderle Group, noted that despite Microsoft's team-up with Yahoo, Google is still so far ahead of it that the innovations are simply icing on the cake. "Google is the dominant vendor in the space, which means they only need to be seen as 'good enough' and this goes over that admittedly low bar," Enderle said. "But this is exactly what they need to do to hold on to their base and keep [defectors] to a minimum. As long as folks think Google is good enough they won't move and this appears to be a relatively low-risk way to do that."

Source: Adapted from Sharon Gaudin, "In an Instant, Google Pulls Further Ahead of Microsoft, Yahoo," *Computerworld, Inc.*, September 9, 2010; Juan Carlos Perez, "Google Instant: Big Changes for Users, Publishers, and Marketers," *Computerworld, Inc.*, September 8, 2010.

CASE STUDY QUESTIONS

1. By changing the way users see their search queries, Google is trying to change the way the world sees Google as their default search engine. Why do you think this is necessary? Provide some examples of how Google could strengthen their user loyalty even more. How could they be beaten?

2. Hadley Reynolds of IDC sees Google Instant as a "dramatic break" from the traditional search experience. Why does he say this? Would users want the "old" experience back instead?

3. Do you agree with Marissa Mayer that the small savings that Instant provides each search will add up and be noticed by the search community? Would it influence you to either stay with Google or switch to Google?

REAL WORLD ACTIVITIES

1. Do you think Google Instant will be noticeably faster to you than Bing or some other search engine?

2. Can you think of ways in which Microsoft can combat Google's continued quest for search engine dominance? Do you agree with Rob Enderle that Google only needs to be seen as "good enough"?

3. Go online and run some tests on Google Instant versus Microsoft's Bing. Can you tell the difference? Try different search criteria and a multiple set of search terms. Prepare a presentation to share your findings.

FIGURE 2.2

Businesses can develop competitive strategies to counter the actions of the competitive forces they confront in the marketplace.

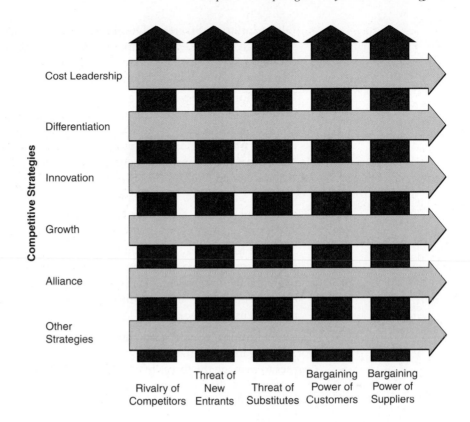

Competition is a positive characteristic in business, and competitors share a natural, and often healthy, rivalry. This rivalry encourages and sometimes requires a constant effort to gain competitive advantage in the marketplace. This ever-present competitive force requires significant resources on the part of a firm.

Guarding against the threat of new entrants also requires the expenditure of significant organizational resources. Not only do firms need to compete with other firms in the marketplace, but they must also work to create significant barriers to the entry of new competition. This competitive force has always been difficult to manage, but it is even more so today. The Internet has created many ways to enter the marketplace quickly and with relatively low cost. In the Internet world, a firm's biggest potential competitor may be one that is not yet in the marketplace but could emerge almost overnight.

The threat of substitutes is another competitive force that confronts a business. The effect of this force is apparent almost daily in a wide variety of industries, often at its strongest during periods of rising costs or inflation. When airline prices get too high, people substitute car travel for their vacations. When the cost of steak gets too high, people eat more hamburger and fish. Most products or services have some sort of substitute available to the consumer.

Finally, a business must guard against the often opposing forces of customer and supplier bargaining powers. If customers' bargaining power gets too strong, they can drive prices to unmanageably low levels or just refuse to buy the product or service. If a key supplier's bargaining power gets too strong, it can force the price of goods and services to unmanageably high levels or just starve a business by controlling the flow of parts or raw materials essential to the manufacture of a product.

Figure 2.2 also illustrates that businesses can counter the threats of competitive forces that they face by implementing one or more of the five basic competitive strategies.

- **Cost Leadership Strategy.** Becoming a low-cost producer of products and services in the industry or finding ways to help suppliers or customers reduce their costs or increase the costs of competitors.

- **Differentiation Strategy.** Developing ways to differentiate a firm's products and services from those of its competitors or reduce the differentiation advantages of competitors. This strategy may allow a firm to focus its products or services to give it an advantage in particular segments or niches of a market.
- **Innovation Strategy.** Finding new ways of doing business. This strategy may involve developing unique products and services or entering unique markets or market niches. It may also involve making radical changes to the business processes for producing or distributing products and services that are so different from the way a business has been conducted that they alter the fundamental structure of an industry.
- **Growth Strategies.** Significantly expanding a company's capacity to produce goods and services, expanding into global markets, diversifying into new products and services, or integrating into related products and services.
- **Alliance Strategies.** Establishing new business linkages and alliances with customers, suppliers, competitors, consultants, and other companies. These linkages may include mergers, acquisitions, joint ventures, formation of virtual companies, or other marketing, manufacturing, or distribution agreements between a business and its trading partners.

One additional point regarding these strategies is that they are not mutually exclusive. An organization may make use of one, some, or all of the strategies in varying degrees to manage the forces of competition. Therefore, a given activity could fall into one or more of the categories of competitive strategy. For example, implementing a system that allows customers to track their orders or shipments online could be considered a form of differentiation if the other competitors in the marketplace do not offer this service. If they do offer the service, however, online order tracking would not serve to differentiate one organization from another.

If an organization offers its online package tracking system in a manner that allows its customers to access shipment information via not only a computer but a mobile phone as well, then such an action could fall into both the differentiation and innovation strategy categories. Think of it this way: Not everything innovative will serve to differentiate one organization from another. Likewise, not everything that serves to differentiate organizations is necessarily viewed as innovative. These types of observations are true for any combination of the competitive strategies, thus making them complementary to each other rather than mutually exclusive.

Strategic Uses of Information Technology

How can business managers use investments in information technology to support a firm's competitive strategies? Figure 2.3 answers this question with a summary of the many ways that information technology can help a business implement the five basic competitive strategies. Figure 2.4 provides examples of how specific companies have used strategic information systems to implement each of these five basic strategies for competitive advantage. Note the major use of Internet technologies for e-business and e-commerce applications. In the rest of this chapter, we discuss and provide examples of many strategic uses of information technology.

Other Strategic Initiatives

There are many strategic initiatives available to a firm in addition to the five basic strategies of cost leadership, differentiation, innovation, growth, and alliance. Let's look at several key strategies that can also be implemented with information technology. They include locking in customers or suppliers, building switching costs, raising barriers to entry, and leveraging investment in information technology.

Investments in information technology can allow a business to lock in customers and suppliers (and lock out competitors) by building valuable new relationships with them. These business relationships can become so valuable to customers or suppliers that they deter them from abandoning a company for its competitors or intimidate

FIGURE 2.3
A summary of how
information technology
can be used to implement
the five basic competitive
strategies. Many companies
are using Internet
technologies as the
foundation for such
strategies.

Basic Strategies in the Business Use of Information Technology
Lower Costs ● Use IT to substantially reduce the cost of business processes. ● Use IT to lower the costs of customers or suppliers.
Differentiate ● Develop new IT features to differentiate products and services. ● Use IT features to reduce the differentiation advantages of competitors. ● Use IT features to focus products and services at selected market niches.
Innovate ● Create new products and services that include IT components. ● Develop unique new markets or market niches with the help of IT. ● Make radical changes to business processes with IT that dramatically cut costs; improve quality, efficiency, or customer service; or shorten time to market.
Promote Growth ● Use IT to manage regional and global business expansion. ● Use IT to diversify and integrate into other products and services.
Develop Alliances ● Use IT to create virtual organizations of business partners. ● Develop interenterprise information systems linked by the Internet and extranets that support strategic business relationships with customers, suppliers, subcontractors, and others.

FIGURE 2.4 Examples of how, over time, companies have used information technology to implement five competitive strategies for strategic advantage.

Strategy	Company	Strategic Use of Information Technology	Business Benefit
Cost Leadership	Dell Computer Priceline.com eBay.com	Online build to order Online seller bidding Online auctions	Lowest-cost producer Buyer-set pricing Auction-set prices
Differentiation	AVNET Marshall Moen Inc. Consolidated Freightways	Customer/supplier of e-commerce Online customer design Customer online shipment tracking	Increase in market share Increase in market share Increase in market share
Innovation	Charles Schwab & Co. Federal Express Amazon.com	Online discount stock trading Online package tracking and flight management Online full-service customer systems	Market leadership Market leadership Market leadership
Growth	Citicorp Walmart Toys 'R' Us Inc.	Global intranet Merchandise ordering by global satellite network POS inventory tracking	Increase in global market Market leadership Market leadership
Alliance	Walmart/Procter & Gamble Cisco Systems Staples Inc. and Partners	Automatic inventory replenishment by supplier Virtual manufacturing alliances Online one-stop shopping with partners	Reduced inventory cost/increased sales Agile market leadership Increase in market share

FIGURE 2.5   Additional ways that information technology can be used to implement competitive strategies.

Other Strategic Uses of Information Technology
• Develop interenterprise information systems whose convenience and efficiency create switching costs that lock in customers or suppliers.
• Make major investments in advanced IT applications that build barriers to entry against industry competitors or outsiders.
• Include IT components in products and services to make substitution of competing products or services more difficult.
• Leverage investment in IS people, hardware, software, databases, and networks from operational uses into strategic applications.

them into accepting less profitable business arrangements. Early attempts to use information systems technology in these relationships focused on significantly improving the quality of service to customers and suppliers in a firm's distribution, marketing, sales, and service activities. More recent projects characterize a move toward more innovative uses of information technology.

A major emphasis in strategic information systems has been to find ways to create switching costs in the relationships between a firm and its customers or suppliers. In other words, investments in information systems technology, such as those mentioned in the Boeing example, can make customers or suppliers dependent on the continued use of innovative, mutually beneficial interenterprise information systems. They then become reluctant to pay the costs in time, money, effort, and inconvenience that it would take to switch to a company's competitors.

By making investments in information technology to improve its operations or promote innovation, a firm could also raise barriers to entry that would discourage or delay other companies from entering a market. Typically, these barriers increase the amount of investment or the complexity of the technology required to compete in an industry or a market segment. Such actions tend to discourage firms already in the industry and deter external firms from entering the industry.

Investing in information technology enables a firm to build strategic IT capabilities so that they can take advantage of opportunities when they arise. In many cases, this happens when a company invests in advanced computer-based information systems to improve the efficiency of its own business processes. Then, armed with this strategic technology platform, the firm can leverage investment in IT by developing new products and services that would not be possible without a strong IT capability. An important current example is the development of corporate intranets and extranets by many companies, which enables them to leverage their previous investments in Internet browsers, PCs, servers, and client/server networks. Figure 2.5 summarizes the additional strategic uses of IT we have just discussed.

Boeing: Saving Big by Cutting Imaging Costs

Hitting "Ctrl+P" can cost your business more than you think. It certainly did at aerospace giant Boeing. Imaging services—which includes production printing, office printing, faxing, scanning, and related supplies—used to cost the company nearly $150 million annually. The problem, says Earl Beauvais, Boeing's director of print, plot, and scan services, was that imaging wasn't centrally controlled, and the company used several vendors. Boeing also owned, operated, and maintained about 32,000 imaging devices. The lack of an enterprisewide solution meant, among other things, that each department was responsible for purchasing its own toner, paper, and other supplies.

To increase efficiency and reduce cost, Beauvais and his team sought a managed services solution to handle everything from print cartridges to printer upkeep across

Boeing's 195 domestic sites and 168 international sites. Beauvais spent 18 months researching and interviewing vendors, who had to show how they would manage the company's imaging technology needs while providing the greatest efficiency at the best price. He and his team chose a partnership comprising Dell (for maintenance and asset management) and Lexmark (for devices). They picked them in part because Dell had infrastructure in place at Boeing.

To prove the concept, a six-month pilot implementation launched at Boeing's St. Louis office in May 2007. The St. Louis system included 47 new Lexmark device categories, including printers, copy machines, and scanners. "We replaced the devices because we didn't want variability of age," says Beauvais.

The beauty of managed services is that Dell owns the devices and handles maintenance, a key goal for Beauvais.

Boeing saw ROI immediately because Dell's service contract cost less than its existing agreements. In the end, Boeing saved about 30 percent of its imaging maintenance and supplies costs, and 27 percent of its overall imaging costs annually at locations with the new system. The initiative began rolling out companywide at the end of 2007.

For Boeing, the benefits couldn't be clearer. Beauvais's staff can now focus more on other business needs, and the company's total imaging spending has been reduced to $110 million annually. Both will aid Boeing as it navigates a turbulent economy.

Source: Adapted from Jarina D'Auria, "Boeing Saves Big by Cutting Imaging Costs," *CIO.com*, March 25, 2009.

Competitive Advantage and Competitive Necessity

The constant struggle to achieve a measurable competitive advantage in an industry or marketplace occupies a significant portion of an organization's time and money. Creative and innovative marketing, research and development, and process reengineering, among many other activities, are used to gain that elusive and sometimes indescribable competitive advantage over rival firms.

The term *competitive advantage* is often used when referring to a firm that is leading an industry in some identifiable way such as sales, revenues, or new products. In fact, the definition of the term suggests a single condition under which competitive advantage can exist: *when a firm sustains profits that exceed the average for its industry, the firm is said to possess competitive advantage over its rivals.* In other words, competitive advantage is all about profits. Of course, sales, revenues, cost management, and new products all contribute in some way to profits, but unless the contribution results in sustained profits above the average for the industry, no measurable competitive advantage has been achieved. The real problem with a competitive advantage, however, is that it normally doesn't last very long and is generally not sustainable over the long term. Figure 2.6 illustrates this cycle. Once a firm figures out how to gain an advantage over its competitors (normally through some form of innovation), the competitors figure out how it was done through a process referred to as organizational learning. To combat the competitive advantage, they adopt the same, or some similar, innovation. Once this occurs, everyone in the industry is doing what everyone else is doing; what was once a competitive advantage is now a competitive necessity. Instead of creating an advantage, the strategy or action becomes necessary to compete and do business in the industry. When this happens, someone has to figure out a new way to gain a competitive edge, and the cycle starts all over again.

Every organization is looking for a way to gain competitive advantage, and many have successfully used strategic information systems to help them achieve it. The important point to remember is that no matter how it is achieved, competitive advantage doesn't last forever. Arie de Geus, head of strategic planning for Royal Dutch Shell, thinks there may be one way to sustain it: "The ability to learn faster than your competitors may be the only sustainable competitive advantage in the future."

FIGURE 2.6
The move from innovation
to competitive advantage
quickly becomes
competitive necessity when
other firms learn how to
respond strategically.

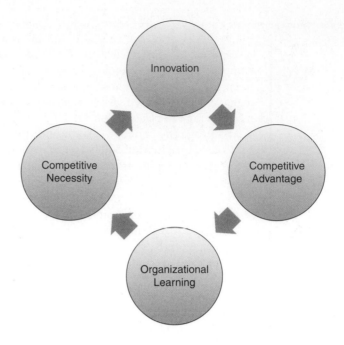

Building a Customer-Focused Business

The driving force behind world economic growth has changed from manufacturing volume to improving customer value. As a result, the key success factor for many firms is maximizing customer value.

For many companies, the chief business value of becoming a customer-focused business lies in its ability to help them keep customers loyal, anticipate their future needs, respond to customer concerns, and provide top-quality customer service. This strategic focus on customer value recognizes that quality, rather than price, has become the primary determinant in a customer's perception of value. Companies that consistently offer the best value from the customer's perspective are those that keep track of their customers' individual preferences; keep up with market trends; supply products, services, and information anytime and anywhere; and provide customer services tailored to individual needs. Thus, Internet technologies have created a strategic opportunity for companies, large and small, to offer fast, responsive, high-quality products and services tailored to individual customer preferences.

Internet technologies can make customers the focal point of customer relationship management (CRM) and other e-business applications. In combination, CRM systems and Internet, intranet, and extranet Web sites create new channels for interactive communications within a company, as well as communication with customers, suppliers, business partners, and others in the external environment. Such communications enable continual interaction with customers by most business functions and encourage cross-functional collaboration with customers in product development, marketing, delivery, service, and technical support. We will discuss CRM systems in Chapter 8.

Typically, customers use the Internet to ask questions, lodge complaints, evaluate products, request support, and make and track their purchases. Using the Internet and corporate intranets, specialists in business functions throughout the enterprise can contribute to an effective response. This ability encourages the creation of cross-functional discussion groups and problem-solving teams dedicated to customer involvement, service, and support. Even the Internet and extranet links to suppliers and business partners can be used to enlist them in a way of doing business that ensures the prompt delivery of quality components and services to meet a company's commitments to its customers. This process is how a business demonstrates its focus on customer value.

Figure 2.7 illustrates the interrelationships in a customer-focused business. Intranets, extranets, e-commerce Web sites, and Web-enabled internal business processes

FIGURE 2.7 How a customer-focused business builds customer value and loyalty using Internet technologies.

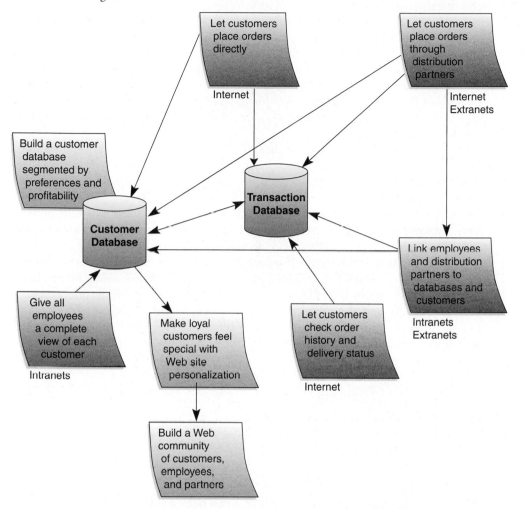

form the invisible IT platform that supports this e-business model. The platform enables the business to focus on targeting the kinds of customers it really wants and "owning" the customer's total business experience with the company. A successful business streamlines all business processes that affect its customers and develops CRM systems that provide its employees with a complete view of each customer, so they have the information they need to offer their customers top-quality personalized service. A customer-focused business helps its e-commerce customers help themselves while also helping them do their jobs. Finally, a successful business nurtures an online community of customers, employees, and business partners that builds great customer loyalty as it fosters cooperation to provide an outstanding customer experience. Let's review a real-world example.

| How Telepresence Is Changing the Way You Go to School | When you were growing up, you probably remember most educational videos as very poor quality productions. But due to the advent of videoconferencing set up by Internet 2 connectivity (a new and faster version of the Internet for education and research—see Chapter 6), schools are now utilizing video services that actually help students learn. Many Boston-area schools have started using such technology this year thanks to the combined efforts of Harvard, Cisco, and BBN |

Technologies, all of whom worked to bring Internet 2 to Boston and Cambridge schools this past year.

In addition to Internet 2 connectivity, both the John D. O'Bryant School of Math and Science and the Cambridge Rindge and Latin School received donated Cisco TelePresence equipment to help them utilize Internet 2 to get high-definition live video streams beamed directly into classrooms. The O'Bryant School has set up its Cisco TelePresence system in a small auditorium that has microphones installed throughout that can pick up where students are talking and can shift the system's cameras on them so that people on the other side of the video call can see who is speaking to them.

Steve Sullivan, the headmaster at the O'Bryant School, says that having the Cisco equipment on hand will help bring students more in-depth learning experiences that will let them watch events live and interact with the people participating in them. "In the case of a medical science class you'll be able to dial into Harvard Medical School, and maybe someone there is giving a lecture on how to perform a certain procedure," he says. "Or it might be that you give a book report and then are able to call up the professor at Stanford who wrote it to talk with him about it."

Donnelly says that teachers will soon have much more video content to choose from since high-definition videoconferencing technology is becoming more ubiquitous throughout the United States. Cisco is selling its at-home telepresence system for $600, and the next generation of Apple iPads is expected to have a front-facing camera that will support high-definition videoconferencing technology. Once more people adopt this technology, Donnelly says, videoconferences in classrooms will become much more of a regular occurrence than what we see today. "The next generation of the iPad will have a camera built into it so it essentially becomes a video phone," he says. "You're going to see this type of technology explode in school systems all over the world."

Source: Adapted from Brad Reed, "How Telepresence and Internet 2 Changed Boston Schools," *Computerworld, Inc.*, October 16, 2010.

The Value Chain and Strategic IS

Let's look at another important concept that can help you identify opportunities for strategic information systems. The value chain concept, developed by Michael Porter, is illustrated in Figure 2.8. It views a firm as a series, chain, or network of basic activities that add value to its products and services and thus add a margin of value to both the firm and its customers. In the value chain conceptual framework, some business activities are primary processes; others are support processes. *Primary processes* are those business activities that are directly related to the manufacture of products or the delivery of services to the customer. In contrast, *support processes* are those business activities that help support the day-to-day operation of the business and that indirectly contribute to the products or services of the organization. This framework can highlight where competitive strategies can best be applied in a business. So managers and business professionals should try to develop a variety of strategic uses of the Internet and other technologies for those basic processes that add the most value to a company's products or services and thus to the overall business value of the company.

Value Chain Examples

Figure 2.8 provides examples of how and where information technologies can be applied to basic business processes using the value chain framework. For example, the figure illustrates that collaborative workflow intranets can increase the communications and collaboration required to improve administrative coordination and support services dramatically. An employee benefits intranet can help the human resources management function provide employees with easy, self-service access to their benefits information. Extranets enable a company and its global business partners to use the

FIGURE 2.8   The value chain of a firm. Note the examples of the variety of strategic information systems that can be applied to a firm's basic business processes for competitive advantage.

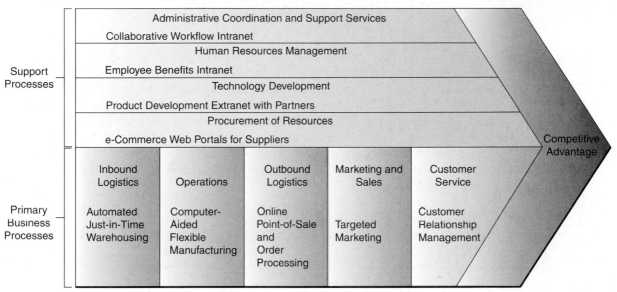

Web to design products and processes jointly. Finally, e-commerce Web portals can dramatically improve procurement of resources by providing online marketplaces for a firm's suppliers.

The value chain model in Figure 2.8 also identifies examples of strategic applications of information systems technology to primary business processes. These include automated just-in-time warehousing systems to support inbound logistic processes that involve inventory storage, computer-aided flexible manufacturing systems, as well as online point-of-sale and order processing systems to improve the outbound logistics processes that handle customer orders. Information systems can also support marketing and sales processes by developing an interactive targeted marketing capability on the Internet and the Web. Finally, a coordinated and integrated customer relationship management system can dramatically improve customer service.

Thus, the value chain concept can help you identify where and how to apply the strategic capabilities of information technology. It shows how various types of information technologies might be applied to specific business processes to help a firm gain competitive advantages in the marketplace.

SECTION II	# Using Information Technology for Strategic Advantage

Strategic Uses of IT

Organizations may view and use information technology in many ways. For example, companies may choose to use information systems strategically, or they may be content to use IT to support efficient everyday operations. If a company emphasized strategic business uses of information technology, its management would view IT as a major competitive differentiator. They would then devise business strategies that use IT to develop products, services, and capabilities that give the company major advantages in the markets in which it competes. In this section, we provide many examples of such strategic business applications of information technology. See Figure 2.9.

Read the Real World Case 2 about using information technology to redesign how a business works. We can learn a lot about the advantages gained through the appropriate use of information technology and mobile communications from this case.

Reengineering Business Processes

One of the most important implementations of competitive strategies is business process reengineering (BPR), often simply called *reengineering*. Reengineering is a fundamental rethinking and radical redesign of business processes to achieve dramatic improvements in cost, quality, speed, and service. BPR combines a strategy of promoting business innovation with a strategy of making major improvements to business processes so that a company can become a much stronger and more successful competitor in the marketplace.

However, Figure 2.10 points out that although the potential payback of reengineering is high, so too is its risk of failure and level of disruption to the organizational environment. Making radical changes to business processes to dramatically improve efficiency and effectiveness is not an easy task. For example, many companies have used cross-functional enterprise resource planning (ERP) software to reengineer, automate, and integrate their manufacturing, distribution, finance, and human resource business processes. Although many companies have reported impressive gains with such ERP reengineering projects, many others either have experienced dramatic failures or did not achieve the improvements they sought.

Many companies have found that *organizational redesign* approaches are an important enabler of reengineering, along with the use of information technology. For example, one common approach is the use of self-directed cross-functional or multidisciplinary *process teams*. Employees from several departments or specialties, including engineering, marketing, customer service, and manufacturing, may work as a team on the product development process. Another example is the use of *case managers*, who handle almost all tasks in a business process instead of splitting tasks among many different specialists.

The Role of Information Technology

Information technology plays a major role in reengineering most business processes. The speed, information-processing capabilities, and connectivity of computers and Internet technologies can substantially increase the efficiency of business processes, as well as communications and collaboration among the people responsible for their operation and management. For example, the order management process illustrated in Figure 2.11 is vital to the success of most companies. Many of them are reengineering this process with ERP software and Web-enabled e-business and e-commerce systems, as outlined in Figure 2.12. Let's take a look at an example.

REAL WORLD CASE 2

For Companies Both Big and Small: Running a Business on Smartphones

In early 2006, San Antonio, Texas-based CPS Energy, the nation's largest municipally owned energy provider, was by all accounts riding the road to riches. The company had the highest bond ratings of any such utility provider. Its workforce and customer base in general expressed satisfaction. And most important, it was profitable. In other words, there were no external signs that the company was about to launch a technology program that would redefine the way it did business and reshape its workforce of roughly 4,000.

There weren't external signs, but for those in the know, including Christopher Barron, CPS Energy's VP and CIO, it couldn't have been more clear that a change was imminent—and that the future of the company might depend on it.

"We had a much larger workforce than a business our size maybe should have," Barron says.

Barron looked at other companies with large mobile workforces like its own, companies like UPS and FedEx, and he saw a huge disparity in the way his business was operating. For instance, specific CPS workers had little or no access to IT systems and resources while they were away from the office or warehouse. They were often required to visit work sites or customer locations to diagnose issues or suggest fixes before reporting to the appropriate departments or parties, which would then initiate the next step of the resolution process. That could mean dispatching additional workers, and the whole ordeal could take days.

"If we kept with the amount of manual labor that it took for us to accomplish that work, we would not be in the position to be competitive in the future," Barron says. From this realization, the company's Magellan Program was born.

FIGURE 2.9

Companies of all sizes can benefit from using smartphones to improve their business processes.

The Magellan Program was envisioned by Barron and his colleagues as a better way to mobilize and connect its traditionally siloed workforce to the people and systems they needed to do their jobs. The goals of the program were to extend CPS's networking infrastructure, build its own secure Wi-Fi networks in offices and warehouses, and deploy smartphones and custom mobile applications to all CPS staffers who didn't currently have a laptop or other mobile device. For Barron, the first and most significant challenge in deploying smartphones to such a large user base was getting executive buy-in.

"One of our biggest headaches has been, and continues to be, the perception that the technology brings little to the table other than e-mail, and it costs a lot," Barron says.

"For a CIO to try to eliminate all the resistance from a senior executive might take forever," Barron says. "So rather than try to get to the execs and mollify all their fears about cost, usage and safety, we've gone to specific groups, engineers, line workers, office workers, and because it's so cheap we've been able to give the devices out on 'experimental basis.' There's so much value in these handheld devices and two or three applications that they prove themselves," he says. "You just have to get them into the hands of the people that actually need to use them in order to demonstrate that."

Three innovative ways CPS staffers use their smartphones are as digital cameras at work sites, as GPS tracking mechanisms, and as emergency notification receivers. In the past, CPS might have had to dispatch a small group of "generalist" workers to a service call to make sure the correct person was there. Today, a single worker can visit a site, take a photo of a damaged piece of equipment or infrastructure, and then send it back to headquarters or the office.

Then an expert diagnoses the issue and sends along instructions to fix the problem or dispatches the appropriate worker, who is available immediately via voice e-mail and SMS text via smartphone.

"The Magellan Program, through the use of smartphones and other technology, has or will empower all employees, no matter what work they perform, to become part of the greater company's 'thought network,'" Barron says. "Each person is now like a node in our network." The company is also seeing significant gains in supply chain efficiency related to Magellan and the smartphone deployment, he says. For instance, smartphones help speed up the purchase order process, because in the past a specific person or group of people needed to be on-site to approve orders. Now the approvers can be practically anywhere with cellular coverage. The company's supply chain buyers can also visit warehouses to work with the people who actually order parts, leading to faster order times and more proactive supply chain management overall. In just one year, the time it took to close purchasing and procurement deals decreased by more than 65 percent. Also, inventory levels were reduced by more than $8 million since the Magellan Program began.

In addition, both employee and customer satisfaction levels are up, Barron notes, because staffers now have more access to corporate systems and information, and they feel closer to the business. Because CPS can now resolve more customer issues with fewer processes, they've reduced the time it takes to complete most service calls, leading to happier customers. In fact, the company received the highest score in J.D. Power and Associates' 2007 Gas Utility Residential Customer Satisfaction Survey.

The technology, however, is no longer the exclusive purview of large companies with significant IT budgets, at least not anymore. Lloyd's Construction in Eagan, Minnesota, might not seem as if it needs flashy phone software. The $9-million-a-year demolition and carting company has been run by the same family for the past 24 years. Lloyd's takes down commercial and residential buildings and then hauls them away. What could be more simple? That is, if wrangling 100 employees, 30 trucks, and more than 400 dumpsters can be called simple. Coordinating those moving parts is crucial to growing the business—and to saving the sanity of Stephanie Lloyd, 41, who has run the company for the past four years. Until recently, Lloyd's used a hodgepodge of spreadsheets, paper ledgers, and accounting software on company PCs to keep track of its workers and equipment. To make matters worse, the company used radios to coordinate with its workers on the job. The more cell phone towers that came online in Minnesota, the worse Lloyd's radio reception got. It was time, the Lloyds decided, to drag their company into the 21st-century world of smartphones.

Lloyd's considered a half-dozen mobile-productivity software suites before settling on eTrace, which happened to come from a company called GearWorks based just across town. Not only was GearWorks local, but its software worked on Sprint Nextel's i560 and i850 phones, which are aimed at the construction industry. Lloyd's had already started buying these push-to-talk phones to wean workers from their dying radios. Immediately, technophobic staff had trouble. Employees had to be guided up a steep learning curve in order to master even basic features on their new phones. For 18 months, the two systems ran side by side: eTrace as it was phased in, and the old paper-and-pencil system as it was phased out. Accounting inconsistencies quickly crept in.

And eTrace gave rise to a delicate labor problem. The software featured integrated mapping and travel data that showed the real-time locations of all company assets. To their chagrin, the Lloyds discovered that those assets were spending too much time parked outside the same lunch spots—ones that were not on prescribed routes. Lloyd was sympathetic to workers' needs for breaks—"we've all worked demolition here," she says—but quickly clamped down on unauthorized ones.

GearWorks' CEO says the challenges Lloyd's faced are to be expected. "All these products operate under the ominous pendulum of challenge and opportunity," says Todd Krautkremer, 47. "But our software does a good job of letting the customer control that rate of change in the business."

Once the deployment dust had settled, the savings became clear. The company employs 12 drivers, 22 foremen, and 7 office workers who use 41 phones running eTrace. The company buys an unlimited data package for each phone, which totals about $4,000 a month. Add other networking charges, and Lloyd's spends about $50,000 a year for a complete business, accounting, and communications solution.

Before eTrace, the company paid an accountant 40 hours a week to do the books. Now that person comes in one day a week for 6 hours, saving roughly $1,000 a week.

Data entry and job logging by the dispatcher and foremen, Lloyd says, is roughly 1½ times faster than paper and radio. More efficient routing has cut fuel costs by about 30 percent. And employees have stopped making unauthorized stops. Lloyd estimates a net improvement in performance of 10–12 percent, or roughly $1 million for 2007—not a bad return on $50,000.

"It really does work," she says.

Source: Adapted from Jonathan Blum, "Running an Entire Business from Smartphones," *FORTUNE Small Business*, March 12, 2008; and Al Sacco, "How Smartphones Help CPS Energy Innovate and Boost the Bottom Line," *CIO Magazine*, July 11, 2008.

CASE STUDY QUESTIONS

1. In which ways do smartphones help these companies be more profitable? To what extent are improvements in performance coming from revenue increases or cost reductions? Provide several examples from the case.

2. The companies described in the case encountered a fair amount of resistance from employees when introducing smartphone technologies. Why do you think this happened? What could companies do to improve the reception of these initiatives? Develop two alternative propositions.

3. CPS Energy and Lloyd's Construction used smartphones to make existing processes more efficient. How could they have used the technology to create new products and services for their customers? Include at least one recommendation for each organization.

REAL WORLD ACTIVITIES

1. In addition to the companies featured in the case, others like FedEx and UPS, which have large mobile workforces, heavily use mobile communication technologies. What other companies could benefit from these innovations?

2. Go online and research uses of smartphones in industries different from the ones reviewed here. Prepare a report to share your findings.

3. Use the Internet to research the latest technological developments in smartphones, and discuss how those could be used by companies to deliver value to customers and shareholders.

FIGURE 2.10

Some of the key ways that business process reengineering differs from business improvement.

	Business Improvement	Business Process Reengineering
Level of Change	Incremental	Radical
Process Change	Improved new version of process	Brand-new process
Starting Point	Existing processes	Clean slate
Frequency of Change	One-time or continuous	Periodic one-time change
Time Required	Short	Long
Typical Scope	Narrow, within functions	Broad, cross-functional
Horizon	Past and present	Future
Participation	Bottom-up	Top-down
Path to Execution	Cultural	Cultural, structural
Primary Enabler	Statistical control	Information technology
Risk	Moderate	High

Source: Adapted from Howard Smith and Peter Fingar, *Business Process Management: The Third Wave* (Tampa, FL: Meghan-Kiffer Press, 2003), p. 118.

FIGURE 2.11 The order management process consists of several business processes and crosses the boundaries of traditional business functions.

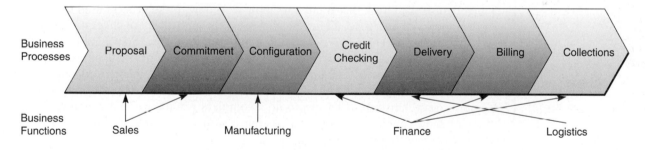

FIGURE 2.12

Examples of information technologies that support reengineering the order management processes.

Reengineering Order Management
● Customer relationship management systems using corporate intranets and the Internet.
● Supplier-managed inventory systems using the Internet and extranets.
● Cross-functional ERP software for integrating manufacturing, distribution, finance, and human resource processes.
● Customer-accessible e-commerce Web sites for order entry, status checking, payment, and service.
● Customer, product, and order status databases accessed via intranets and extranets by employees and suppliers.

Making Workflow Work and Flow: Not Entirely Rocket Science

From a business perspective, workflow is a way to make people, information, and computers work together consistently and efficiently to produce the results the business needs. In effect, workflow applies the equivalent of systems analysis to the entire process, not just to the part done on a machine. From a bottom line perspective, adding workflow to a process saves money, increases customer satisfaction, gets results quicker, and largely eliminates things getting lost in the shuffle. From a manager's perspective, the most important benefits to workflow are saving cost and saving time.

As an example of a typical workflow, Wilhelm Ederyd, a technical project manager at Bonver, a major Scandinavian distributor of home entertainment products, cites building support for individuals and businesses ordering broadband services via the Internet, postal mail, and e-mail. "This can be a rather complex process, with the need for the systems and personnel to interact efficiently in order to make the process slim and pleasant to the customer," Ederyd explains. You can think of workflow as systems analysis that mixes humans, machines, documents, and other information.

In Ederyd's case, he designed the process for ordering and installing the broadband connection for the customer. Given a whole raft of business requirements generated by others, typically that means working out how the process would flow from the customer's initial contact to the actual installation.

Ederyd's example is a classic case: a fairly complex, multistep process where computers and people have to interact as smoothly and efficiently as possible. It's also a process that is exposed to the customer, and delays or mistakes can damage customer relationships. An advantage of a well-designed workflow process is that it can serve as a template that can be applied quickly to similar processes. "Once you're comfortable with workflow in your organization, it will allow you to implement new business models much faster than your competitors," says Ederyd. "The cost and complexity of doing so is now manageable."

Craig Cameron, a workflow consultant based in Melbourne, cites the example of a major Australian bank that wanted to apply workflow to the process used to order large amounts of hardware. "They needed to go through all these checks and make sure that the right people had signed off on it," Cameron says. "So we implemented a system to do that." This was fine until the other divisions of the bank found out about the new process. "We found out later we'd only created a system for three or so of their teams and suddenly another 15 or so teams wanted to be involved," Cameron says. "Instead of having to do a complete restart, we're extracting what we've already done and cutting and pasting it into a new system. Then we hit a button to create the end user interface."

Workflow isn't rocket science, but it isn't magic either. Although workflow can make major improvements in the way an organization runs, it can only do so if the principles are applied correctly. Fundamentally, making workflow work for you comes down to understanding the processes that make your business work.

Source: Adapted from Rick Cook, "Making Workflow Work and Flow for You," *CIO Magazine*, October 23, 2007.

Becoming an Agile Company

We are changing from a competitive environment in which mass-market products and services were standardized, long-lived, information-poor, and exchanged in one-time transactions, to an environment in which companies compete globally with niche market products and services that are individualized, short-lived, information-rich, and exchanged on an ongoing basis with customers.

To be an agile company, a business must use four basic strategies. First, the business must ensure that customers perceive the products or services of an agile company as solutions to their individual problems. Thus, it can price products on the basis of their value as solutions, rather than their cost to produce. Second, an agile company cooperates with customers, suppliers, other companies, and even with its competitors. This cooperation allows a business to bring products to market as rapidly and cost-effectively as possible, no matter where resources are located or who owns them. Third, an agile company organizes so that it thrives on change and uncertainty. It uses flexible organizational structures keyed to the requirements of different and constantly changing customer opportunities. Fourth, an agile company leverages the impact of its people and the knowledge they possess. By nurturing an entrepreneurial spirit, an agile company provides powerful incentives for employee responsibility, adaptability, and innovation.

Figure 2.13 summarizes another useful way to think about agility in business. This framework emphasizes the roles that customers, business partners, and information technology can play in developing and maintaining the strategic agility of a company. Notice how information technology can enable a company to develop relationships with its customers in virtual communities that help it be an agile innovator. As we will see repeatedly throughout this textbook, information technologies enable a company to partner with its suppliers, distributors, contract manufacturers, and others via collaborative portals and other Web-based supply chain systems that significantly improve its agility in exploiting innovative business opportunities.

FIGURE 2.13 How information technology can help a company be an agile competitor, with the help of customers and business partners.

Type of Agility	Description	Role of IT	Example
Customer	Ability to co-opt customers in the exploitation of innovation opportunities • As sources of innovation ideas • As cocreators of innovation • As users in testing ideas or helping other users learn about the idea	Technologies for building and enhancing virtual customer communities for product design, feedback, and testing	eBay customers are its de facto product development team because they post an average of 10,000 messages each week to share tips, point out glitches, and lobby for changes
Partnering	Ability to leverage assets, knowledge, and competencies of suppliers, distributors, contract manufacturers, and logistics providers in the exploration and exploitation of innovation opportunities	Technologies facilitating interfirm collaboration, such as collaborative platforms and portals, supply chain systems	Yahoo! has accomplished a significant transformation of its service from a search engine into a portal by initiating numerous partnerships to provide content and other media-related services from its Web site
Operational	Ability to accomplish speed, accuracy, and cost economy in the exploitation of innovation opportunities	Technologies for modularization and integration of business processes	Ingram Micro, a global wholesaler, has deployed an integrated trading system allowing its customers and suppliers to connect directly to its procurement and ERP systems

Source: Adapted from V. Sambamurthy, Anandhi Bhaharadwaj, and Varun Grover, "Shaping Agility through Digital Options: Reconceptualizing the Role of Information Technology in Contemporary Firms," *MIS Quarterly*, June 2003, p. 246.

FIGURE 2.14   A virtual company uses the Internet, intranets, and extranets to form virtual workgroups and support alliances with business partners.

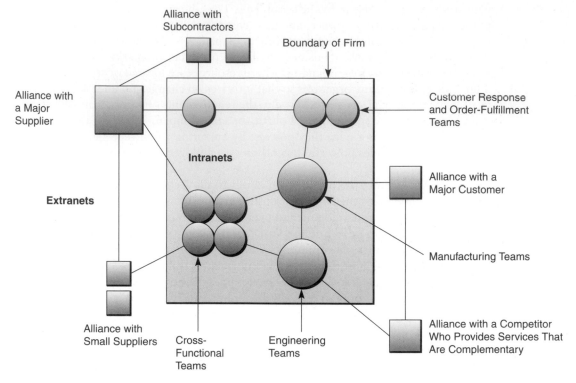

Creating a Virtual Company

In today's dynamic global business environment, forming a virtual company can be one of the most important strategic uses of information technology. A virtual company (also called a *virtual corporation* or *virtual organization*) is an organization that uses information technology to link people, organizations, assets, and ideas.

Figure 2.14 illustrates that virtual companies typically form virtual workgroups and alliances with business partners that are interlinked by the Internet, intranets, and extranets. Notice that this company has organized internally into clusters of process and cross-functional teams linked by intranets. It has also developed alliances and extranet links that form interenterprise information systems with suppliers, customers, subcontractors, and competitors. Thus, virtual companies create flexible and adaptable virtual workgroups and alliances keyed to exploit fast-changing business opportunities.

Virtual Company Strategies

Why do people form virtual companies? It is the best way to implement key business strategies and alliances that promise to ensure success in today's turbulent business climate. Several major reasons for virtual companies stand out and are summarized in Figure 2.15.

For example, a business may not have the time or resources to develop the necessary manufacturing and distribution infrastructure, personnel competencies, and information technologies to take full advantage of a new market opportunity in a timely manner. It can assemble the components it needs to provide a world-class solution for customers and capture the market opportunity only by quickly forming a virtual company through a strategic alliance of all-star partners. Today, of course, the Internet, intranets, extranets, and a variety of other Internet technologies are vital components in creating such successful solutions.

FIGURE 2.15

The basic business
strategies of virtual
companies.

Strategies of Virtual Companies
● Share infrastructure and risk with alliance partners.
● Link complementary core competencies.
● Reduce concept-to-cash time through sharing.
● Increase facilities and market coverage.
● Gain access to new markets and share market or customer loyalty.
● Migrate from selling products to selling solutions.

United Kingdom's National Rail Enquiries: Everything They Do Is Outsourced

In-house technology is no longer an operational prerequisite, thanks to outsourcing. Software, servers, Internet connectivity, and even whole operations like payroll and HR can be sourced from third parties and branded, so neither the customers nor employees of the business need ever know these mechanisms reside outside the company headquarters.

That being said, the fact that the United Kingdom's rail information service, National Rail Enquiries (NRE), served 55 million customers online last year alone—it relies on extensive self-service and contact center service channels, but has a core staff of only 21 people—is no small achievement. "NRE has about 22 suppliers of various services. Everything we do is outsourced. We have 1,500 people in call centers alone, who all work for NRE," says Chris Scoggins, NRE's CEO. The NRE's telephone information service was born of the creation of the organization in 1996 with the privatization of British Rail. Since then, it has expanded to include automated telephone services and a very successful real-time online train time and journey planning service.

Scoggins says NRE has a strategy of maintaining a number of suppliers to play them off against each other and raise the stakes in terms of demonstrating service excellence. "We have the maximum number of suppliers we can manage effectively. But also, and perhaps more importantly, we need the right number of suppliers to maintain a competitive market for the services they run. In some areas, we have a strategy to build up a number of niche players in the market; otherwise we are relying on one supplier."

"What we're trying to do is move toward a number of long-term relationships with partners we trust and give more work to them," Scoggins says. "Contracts are aligned to incentives related to achieving our business objectives, and it's up to the supplier to outperform the minimum standard. If they demonstrate they can deliver over and above that, then they get more work." Despite heading up a vast, virtual company, Scoggins says there is still pressure to drive business improvement and success. "When I joined there was no real self-service provision for the customer. NRE was a very big, outsourced call center with virtually no other provision for finding information. I saw this as a huge opportunity driven by two things. The first was that customer needs should be met by whichever channel is most convenient for them; the second was our call centers, which have the most volatile volumes in Europe."

NRE is always seeking to be proactive and do new things, like the speech recognition technology they use with their telephone TrainTracker service. "It is the most sophisticated mass-market speech recognition service in the world," notes Scoggins. He adds, "I regard our outsourcing suppliers as part of our team, and my job is getting my team excited and encouraged to do the job in hand."

Source: Adapted from Miya Knights, "Everything We Do Is Outsourced," *CIO Magazine*, June 13, 2007.

Building a Knowledge-Creating Company

In an economy where the only certainty is uncertainty, the one sure source of lasting competitive advantage is knowledge. When markets shift, technologies proliferate, competitors multiply, and products become obsolete almost overnight, successful companies are those that consistently create new knowledge, disseminate it widely throughout the organization, and quickly embody it in new technologies and products. These activities define the "knowledge-creating" company, whose sole business is continuous innovation.

Many companies today can only realize lasting competitive advantage if they become knowledge-creating companies or learning organizations. That means consistently creating new business knowledge, disseminating it widely throughout the company, and quickly building the new knowledge into their products and services.

Knowledge-creating companies exploit two kinds of knowledge. One is *explicit knowledge*, which is the data, documents, and things written down or stored on computers. The other kind is *tacit knowledge*, or the "how-tos" of knowledge, which resides in workers. Tacit knowledge can often represent some of the most important information within an organization. Long-time employees of a company often "know" many things about how to manufacture a product, deliver the service, deal with a particular vendor, or operate an essential piece of equipment. This tacit knowledge is not recorded or codified anywhere because it has evolved in the employee's mind through years of experience. Furthermore, much of this tacit knowledge is never shared with anyone who might be in a position to record it in a more formal way because there is often little incentive to do so or simply, "Nobody ever asked."

As illustrated in Figure 2.16, successful knowledge management creates techniques, technologies, systems, and rewards for getting employees to share what they know and make better use of accumulated workplace and enterprise knowledge. In that way, employees of a company are leveraging knowledge as they do their jobs.

Knowledge Management Systems

Making personal knowledge available to others is the central activity of the knowledge-creating company. It takes place continuously and at all levels of the organization.

Knowledge management has thus become one of the major strategic uses of information technology. Many companies are building knowledge management systems (KMS) to manage organizational learning and business know-how. The goal of such systems is to help knowledge workers create, organize, and make available important business knowledge, wherever and whenever it's needed in an organization. This information includes processes, procedures, patents, reference works, formulas, best

FIGURE 2.16
Knowledge management can be viewed as three levels of techniques, technologies, and systems that promote the collection, organization, access, sharing, and use of workplace and enterprise knowledge.

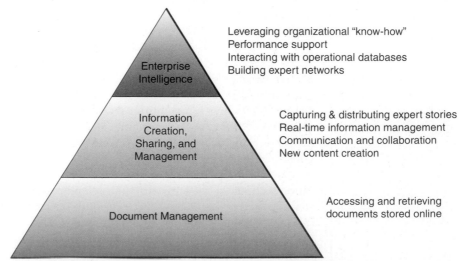

Source: Adapted from Marc Rosenberg, *e-Learning: Strategies for Delivering Knowledge in the Digital Age* (New York: McGraw-Hill, 2001), p. 70.

practices, forecasts, and fixes. As you will see in Chapter 10, Internet and intranet Web sites, groupware, data mining, knowledge bases, and online discussion groups are some of the key technologies that may be used by a KMS.

Knowledge management systems also facilitate organizational learning and knowledge creation. They are designed to provide rapid feedback to knowledge workers, encourage behavior changes by employees, and significantly improve business performance. As the organizational learning process continues and its knowledge base expands, the knowledge-creating company works to integrate its knowledge into its business processes, products, and services. This integration helps the company become a more innovative and agile provider of high-quality products and customer services, as well as a formidable competitor in the marketplace. Now let's close this chapter with an example of knowledge management strategies from the real world.

Goodwin Procter Makes a Strong Case for Knowledge Management

If anyone knows that time is money, it's an attorney. The 850 attorneys and their staff at Goodwin Procter LLP were spending too much time assembling documents and looking up information, which meant cases took more time than they should to proceed.

The $611 million law firm's eight offices used seven different applications to manage more than 2 terabytes of data for Goodwin Procter's more than 60,000 cases—close to 10 million documents. CIO Peter Lane wanted to integrate the data. Using Microsoft SharePoint, his team created the Matter Page System as a hub through which attorneys could access business data and client information.

What's more, the firm has been able to use the platform to share its notes and work in progress. It's now easy for an attorney to find a colleague who can help with a similar case. Matter Pages took a year to implement, but it immediately changed how Goodwin Procter's attorneys work.

When a client called with a question, finding the answer used to mean launching more than one application and looking up the data in different systems. Attorneys needed contact information, documents, billing information, and more.

The process sometimes took hours.

"Now, instead of having to launch the different systems from the desktop, or the web interface, or the document management system, we were able to pull all of this information into a one-stop-shop view for the users in our company," says Andrew Kawa, Goodwin Procter's development manager, who leads its system development efforts.

The system increases efficiency for the attorneys because they can find previous matters that they or others have worked on and gain extra information much more quickly than before. They spend less time researching and more time moving a case forward.

Matter Pages' initial success has Lane investigating new SharePoint features, such as wikis and blogs. He expects to deploy these new capabilities widely over the next few months.

For example, each matter has a wiki that is used to track notes, or other unstructured data that relates to it. These notes are open for editing by all users. Blogs tend to be used for discussions that are not case-specific, although when a matter or set of matters apply to the topic of the blog, users can add links to related cases.

"One of the IT goals is to take advantage of the new technology as it becomes available," Lane adds. With that goal in mind, says Lane, the Matter Page System won't ever truly be completed. Currently, Kawa is looking to integrate Goodwin Procter's patent and trademark information with data about their patent applications from the U.S. Patent and Trademark Office. The integration would allow attorneys to retrieve real-time information on their pending patents and actions they need to take.

"I don't think we will ever declare the project done or say we don't have to put any more time or effort in," he says.

Source: Adapted from Jarina D'Auria, "Goodwin Procter Makes Strong Case for Knowledge Management," *CIO.com*, August 1, 2008.

Summary

- **Strategic Uses of Information Technology.** Information technologies can support many competitive strategies. They can help a business cut costs, differentiate and innovate in its products and services, promote growth, develop alliances, lock in customers and suppliers, create switching costs, raise barriers to entry, and leverage its investment in IT resources. Thus, information technology can help a business gain a competitive advantage in its relationships with customers, suppliers, competitors, new entrants, and producers of substitute products. Refer to Figures 2.3 and 2.5 for summaries of the uses of information technology for strategic advantage.

- **Building a Customer-Focused Business.** A key strategic use of Internet technologies is to build a company that develops its business value by making customer value its strategic focus. Customer-focused companies use Internet, intranet, and extranet e-commerce Web sites and services to keep track of their customers' preferences; to supply products, services, and information anytime or anywhere; and to provide services tailored to the individual needs of the customers.

- **Reengineering Business Processes.** Information technology is a key ingredient in reengineering business operations because it enables radical changes to business processes that dramatically improve their efficiency and effectiveness. Internet technologies can play a major role in supporting innovative changes in the design of workflows, job requirements, and organizational structures in a company.

- **Becoming an Agile Company.** A business can use information technology to help it become an agile

company. Then it can prosper in rapidly changing markets with broad product ranges and short model lifetimes in which it must process orders in arbitrary lot sizes; it can also offer its customers customized products while it maintains high volumes of production. An agile company depends heavily on Internet technologies to help it respond to its customers with customized solutions, and to cooperate with its customers, suppliers, and other businesses to bring products to market as rapidly and cost effectively as possible.

- **Creating a Virtual Company.** Forming virtual companies has become an important competitive strategy in today's dynamic global markets. Internet and other information technologies play a key role in providing computing and telecommunications resources to support the communications, coordination, and information flows needed. Managers of a virtual company depend on IT to help them manage a network of people, knowledge, financial, and physical resources provided by many business partners to take advantage of rapidly changing market opportunities.

- **Building a Knowledge-Creating Company.** Lasting competitive advantage today can only come from the innovative use and management of organizational knowledge by knowledge-creating companies and learning organizations. Internet technologies are widely used in knowledge management systems to support the creation and dissemination of business knowledge and its integration into new products, services, and business processes.

Key Terms and Concepts

These are the key terms and concepts of this chapter. The page number of their first explanation is in parentheses.

1. Agile company (97)
2. Business process reengineering (92)
3. Competitive forces (80)
4. Competitive strategies (83)
5. Create switching costs (86)
6. Customer value (88)
7. Interenterprise information systems (98)
8. Knowledge-creating company (100)
9. Knowledge management system (100)
10. Leverage investment in IT (86)
11. Lock in customers and suppliers (84)
12. Raise barriers to entry (86)
13. Strategic information systems (80)
14. Value chain (90)
15. Virtual company (98)

Review Quiz

Match one of the key terms and concepts listed previously with one of the brief examples or definitions that follow. Try to find the best fit for answers that seem to fit more than one term or concept. Defend your choices.

_____ 1. A business must deal with customers, suppliers, competitors, new entrants, and substitutes.

_____ 2. Cost leadership, differentiation of products, and new product innovation are examples.

_____ 3. Using investments in technology to keep firms out of an industry.

_____ 4. Making it unattractive for a firm's customers or suppliers to switch to its competitors.

_____ 5. Strategies designed to increase the time, money, and effort needed for customers or suppliers to change to a firm's competitors.

_____ 6. Information systems that reengineer business processes or promote business innovation are examples.

_____ 7. This strategic focus recognizes that quality, rather than price, has become the primary determinant in customers choosing a product or service.

_____ 8. Highlights how strategic information systems can be applied to a firm's business processes and support activities for competitive advantage.

_____ 9. A business finding strategic uses for the computing and telecommunications capabilities it has developed to run its operations.

_____ 10. Information technology helping a business make radical improvements in business processes.

_____ 11. A business can prosper in rapidly changing markets while offering its customers individualized solutions to their needs.

_____ 12. A network of business partners formed to take advantage of rapidly changing market opportunities.

_____ 13. Learning organizations that focus on creating, disseminating, and managing business knowledge.

_____ 14. Information systems that manage the creation and dissemination of organizational knowledge.

_____ 15. Using the Internet and extranets to link a company's information systems to those of its customers and suppliers.

Discussion Questions

1. Suppose you are a manager being asked to develop computer-based applications to gain a competitive advantage in an important market for your company. What reservations might you have about doing so? Why?

2. How could a business use information technology to increase switching costs and lock in its customers and suppliers? Use business examples to support your answers.

3. How could a business leverage its investment in information technology to build strategic IT capabilities that serve as a barrier to new entrants into its markets?

4. Refer to the Real World Case on Google creating competitive advantage in the chapter. Why do you think Google constantly strives for new innovation and features? Relate your answer to the discussion about technology as a competitive advantage or a competitive necessity in the chapter.

5. What strategic role can information play in business process reengineering?

6. How can Internet technologies help a business form strategic alliances with its customers, suppliers, and others?

7. How could a business use Internet technologies to form a virtual company or become an agile competitor?

8. Refer to the Real World Case on companies using smartphones in the chapter. Do you think smaller companies like Lloyd's Construction are ready for large-scale implementations of technology in their business? What could they do to prepare for those implementations? Use examples to illustrate your answer.

9. Information technology can't really give a company a strategic advantage because most competitive advantages don't last more than a few years and soon become strategic necessities that just raise the stakes of the game. Discuss.

10. MIS author and consultant Peter Keen says: "We have learned that it is not technology that creates a competitive edge, but the management process that exploits technology." What does he mean? Do you agree or disagree? Why?

Analysis Exercises

1. **End-User Computing**
   Skill Assessment
   Not all programs are written by dedicated programmers. Many knowledge workers write their own software using familiar word processing, spreadsheet, presentation, and database tools. This textbook contains end-user computing exercises representing a real-world programming challenge. This first exercise will allow your course instructor to assess the class. Assess your skills in each of the following areas:

   a. Word processing: About how many words per minute can you type? Do you use styles to manage document formatting? Have you ever set up your own mail merge template and data source? Have you created your own macros to handle repetitive tasks? Have you ever added branching or looping logic in your macro programs?

   b. Spreadsheets: Do you know the order of operations your spreadsheet program uses (what does "=5*2^2-10" equal)? Do you know how to automatically sort data in a spreadsheet? Do you know how to create graphs and charts from spreadsheet data? Can you build pivot tables from spreadsheet data? Do you know the difference between a relative and a fixed cell reference? Do you know how to use functions in your spreadsheet equations? Do you know how to use the IF function? Have you created your own macros to handle repetitive tasks? Have you ever added branching or looping logic in your macro programs?

c. Presentations: Have you ever used presentation software to create presentation outlines? Have you added your own multimedia content to a presentation? Do you know how to add charts and graphs from spreadsheet software into your presentations so that they automatically update when the spreadsheet data change?

d. Database: Have you ever imported data into a database from a text file? Have you ever written queries to sort or filter data stored in a database table? Have you built reports to format your data for output? Have you built forms to aid in manual data entry? Have you built functions or programs to manipulate data stored in database tables?

2. **Marketing: Competitive Intelligence**
Strategic Marketing
Marketing professionals use information systems to gather and analyze information about their competitors. They use this information to assess their product's position relative to the competition and make strategic marketing decisions about the product, its price, its distribution (place), and the best way to manage its promotion. Michael Bloomberg, founder of Bloomberg (www.bloomberg.com), and others have made their fortunes gathering and selling data about businesses. Marketing professionals find information about a business's industry, location, employees, products, technologies, revenues, and market share useful when planning marketing initiatives.

During your senior year, you will find yourself in close competition for jobs. You can take the same intelligence-gathering approach used by professional marketers when planning how to sell your own skills. Use the following questions to help you prepare for your job search:

a. Product: Which business majors are presently in greatest demand by employers? Use entry-level salaries as the primary indicator for demand.

b. Product: Which colleges or universities in your region pose the greatest competitive threat to students with your major?

c. Price: What is the average salary for entry-level employees in your major and geographic region? Is salary your top concern? Why or why not?

d. Place: Which areas of the country are currently experiencing the greatest employment growth?

e. Promotion: What is your marketing plan? Describe how you plan to get your name and qualifications in front of prospective employers. How can the Internet help you get noticed?

3. **Competing against Free**
Wikipedia Faces Down Encyclopedia Britannica
The record and movie industries are not the only industries to find themselves affected by free access to their products. Encyclopedia Britannica faces challenges by a nonprofit competitor that provides its services without charge or advertising, Wikipedia.org. Wikipedia depends on volunteers to create and edit original content under the condition that contributors provide their work without copyright.

Who would work for free? During the creation of the *Oxford English Dictionary* in the 19th century, the editors solicited word articles and references from the general public. In the 20th century, AOL.com found thousands of volunteers to monitor its chat rooms. Amazon.com coaxed more than 100,000 readers to post book reviews on its retail Web site. Outdoing them all in the 21st century, Wikipedia published its one-millionth English language article in March 2006. Wikipedia includes more than two million articles in more than 200 languages, all created and edited by more than one million users.

Can Wikipedia compete on quality? Wikipedia provides its users both editing and monitoring tools, which allows users to self-police. Wikipedia also uses voluntary administrators who block vandals, temporarily protect articles, and manage arbitration processes when disputes arise. A paper published by *Nature* in December 2005 evaluated 50 Wikipedia articles and found an average of four factual errors per Wikipedia article compared with an average of three errors per article in the Encyclopedia Britannica. More significantly, Wikipedians (as the volunteers call themselves) corrected each error by January 2006. Alexa.com rated Wikipedia.org as the 17th most visited Web site on the Internet, while Britannica.com came in 2,858th place (Yahoo and Google ranked in the 1st and 2nd places).

Wikipedia has already built on its success. In addition to offering foreign language encyclopedias, it also provides a common media archive (commons.wikimedia.org), a multilingual dictionary (www.wiktionary.org), and a news service (www.wikinews.org).

a. How does the Wikimedia Foundation meet the criteria for an agile company?

b. How does the Wikimedia Foundation meet the criteria for a virtual company?

c. How does the Wikimedia Foundation meet the criteria for a knowledge-creating organization?

d. How would you recommend that Encyclopedia Britannica adapt to this new threat?

4. **Knowledge Management**
Knowing What You Know
Employees often receive a great deal of unstructured information in the form of e-mails. For example, employees may receive policies, announcements, and daily operational information via e-mail. However, e-mail systems typically make poor enterprisewide knowledge

management systems. New employees don't have access to e-mails predating their start date. Employees typically aren't permitted to search others' e-mail files for needed information. Organizations lose productivity when each employee spends time reviewing and organizing his or her e-mail files. Lastly, the same information may find itself saved across thousands of different e-mail files, thereby ballooning e-mail file storage space requirements.

Microsoft's Exchange server, IBM's Domino server, and Interwoven's WorkSite, along with a wide variety of open-standard Web-based products, aim to address an organization's need to share unstructured information. These products provide common repositories for various categories of information. For example, management may use a "Policy" folder in Microsoft Exchange to store all their policy decisions. Likewise, sales representatives may use a "Competitive Intelligence" database in IBM's Domino server to store information obtained during the sales process about competing products, prices, or marketplace rumors. WorkSite users categorize and store all their electronic documents in a large, searchable, secured common repository. Organizations using these systems can secure them,

manage them, and make them available to the appropriate personnel. Managers can also appoint a few specific employees requiring little technical experience to manage the content.

However, these systems cannot benefit an organization if its employees fail to contribute their knowledge, if they fail to use the system to retrieve information, or if the system simply isn't available where and when needed. To help managers better understand how employees use these systems, knowledge management systems include usage statistics such as date/time, user name, reads, writes, and even specific document access information.

Research each of the products mentioned above and answer the following questions:

a. What steps might a manager take to encourage his or her employees to use the organization's knowledge management system?

b. Should managers set minimum quotas for system usage for each employee? Why or why not?

c. Aside from setting employee usage quotas, how might an organization benefit from knowledge management system usage statistics?

REAL WORLD

CASE 3

Wachovia and Others: Trading Securities at the Speed of Light

Securities trading is one of the few business activities where a one-second processing delay can cost a company big bucks. Wachovia Corporate and Investment Bank is addressing the growing competitive push toward instantaneous trading with a comprehensive systems overhaul. In a project that has cost more than $10 million so far, Wachovia is tearing down its systems silos and replacing them with an infrastructure that stretches seamlessly across the firm's many investment products and business functions.

"Competitive advantage comes from your math, your workflow and your processes through your systems. Straight-through processing is the utopian challenge for Wall Street firms," says Tony Bishop, senior vice president and head of architecture and engineering. The first step in the project, according to Bishop, was to prepare a matrix that cross-referenced every major function (such as research, risk management, selling, trading, clearing, settlement, payment, and reporting) to each major product (debt and equity products, asset-backed finance, derivatives, and so on). The project team then had to take a hard look at the existing systems in each cell. "We looked at the current systems and said, 'Where can we build standardized frameworks, components and services that would allow us to, instead of building it four different times in silos, build it once and extend it into one common sales platform, one common trading platform and so on?'"

The resulting Service Oriented Enterprise Platform is connected to a 10,000-processor grid using GridServer and FabricServer from DataSynapse Inc.

In its data centers, Wachovia brought in Verari Systems Inc.'s BladeRacks with quad-core Intel processors. Bishop says he's creating a "data center in a box" because Verari also makes storage blades that can be tightly coupled with processing blades in the same rack. The processing load at the bank involves a great deal of reading and writing to temporary files, and the intimate linkage of computing and storage nodes makes that extremely efficient.

"We now do pricing in milliseconds, not seconds, for either revenue protection or revenue gain," says Bishop. The advanced infrastructure has tripled processing capacity at one-third the cost, for a ninefold financial return, Bishop adds. Report generation that used to take 16 hours is now done in 15 minutes. "This is where IT becomes the enabler to new business capabilities," he says.

Executing complex strategies based on arcane mathematical formulas, algorithmic trading systems generate thousands of buy and sell orders every second, many of which are canceled and overridden by subsequent orders, sometimes only a few seconds apart. The goal of these computer traders is to profit from minute, fleeting price anomalies and to mask their intentions via "time slicing," or carving huge orders into smaller batches so as not to move the market. A one-millisecond advantage in trading applications can be worth $100 million a year to a major brokerage firm, by one estimate.

The fastest systems, running from traders' desks to exchange data centers, can execute transactions in a few milliseconds—so fast, in fact, that the physical distance between two computers processing a transaction can slow down how fast it happens. This problem is called data latency—delays measured in split seconds. To overcome it, many high-frequency algorithmic traders are moving their systems as close to the Wall Street exchanges as possible.

Wall Street's quest for speed is not only putting floor traders out of work but also opening up space for new alternative exchanges and e-communications networks that compete with the established stock markets. E-trading has reduced overall volatility in the equities markets, because volatility is a product of herd buying or selling, and e-trading—responding instantaneously to tiny price fluctuations—tends to smooth out such mass behavior. It has also provided established exchanges with new revenue opportunities, such as co-location services for companies that wish to place their servers in direct physical proximity to the exchanges' systems. E-trading has also created opportunities for a new class of vendors—execution services firms and systems integrators promising the fastest possible transaction times.

At its most abstract level, the data-latency race represents the spear point of the global movement to eradicate barriers—geographic, technical, psychological—to fair and transparent markets. "Any fair market is going to select the best price from the buyer or seller who gets their [*sic*] order in there first," says Alistair Brown, founder of Lime Brokerage, one of the new-school broker-dealers, which uses customized Linux servers to trade some 200 million shares a day. "At that point, speed definitely becomes an issue. If everyone has access to the same information, when the market moves, you want to be first. The people who are too slow are going to get left behind."

Value in Milliseconds

On the New Jersey side of the Lincoln Tunnel, in an anonymous three-story building, is one of the financial world's most important data centers. Pushing the doorbell at the unmarked main entrance won't get you inside. It's merely a facade; the real entrance is harder to find.

The servers for five electronic exchanges are located in this data center, along with computers belonging to dozens of trading firms. Run by hosting company Savvis, the Weehawken facility is home to some of the most advanced trading technology anywhere. Much of Savvis's growth can be traced to the spread of what's known as direct market access. In the past, traders used consolidated feeds, which are market data updates such as those provided by Reuters and Thomson. Distributing those feeds, however, could take up to 500 milliseconds, far too long for today's automated trading.

"Now you're seeing a lot of the market data providers and vendors who have direct exchange-feed connectivity," says Varghese Thomas, Savvis's vice president of financial markets. Savvis provides connectivity from the exchange directly to the client without having to go through a consolidated system. The exchanges themselves are also profiting from the demand for server space in physical proximity to the markets. Even on the fastest networks, it takes 7 milliseconds for data to travel between the New York markets and Chicago-based servers and 35 milliseconds between the West and East coasts.

Many broker-dealers and execution-services firms are paying premiums to place their servers inside the data centers of the National Association of Securities Dealers (NASDAQ) and the New York Stock Exchange (NYSE).

About 100 firms now co-locate their servers with NASDAQ's, says Brian Hyndman, NASDAQ's senior vice president of transaction services, at a going rate of about $3,500 per rack per month. NASDAQ has seen 25 percent annual increases in co-location in the last two years.

Physical co-location eliminates the unavoidable time lags inherent in even the fastest wide area networks. Servers in shared data centers typically are connected via Gigabit Ethernet, with the ultra-highspeed switching fabric called InfiniBand increasingly used for the same purpose, says Yaron Haviv, CTO at Voltaire, a supplier of systems that can achieve latencies of less than a microsecond, or one-millionth of a second. Later this year, NASDAQ will shut down its data center in Trumbull, Connecticut, and move all operations to one opened last year in New Jersey, with a backup in the mid-Atlantic region, Hyndman says. (Trading firms and exchanges are reluctant to disclose the exact locations of their data centers.)

The NYSE will begin to reduce its 10 data centers to two in the next couple of years, says CTO Steve Rubinow. Co-location, Rubinow says, not only guarantees fast transactions, but also predictable ones. "If you've got some trades going through at 10 milliseconds and some at 1 millisecond, that's a problem" he says. "Our customers don't like variance."

One of the biggest co-location customers is Credit Suisse, which handles about 10 percent of all U.S. equity trades daily and which helped pioneer black-box trading systems with exotic algorithms that go by monikers like Sniper, Guerrilla, and Inline. Credit Suisse maintains Sun and Egenera blade servers, some running Linux and some Windows, in all the major U.S. markets, says Guy Cirillo, manager of global sales channels for Credit Suisse's Advanced Execution Services (AES) unit, which serves major hedge funds and other buy-side clients.

The AES trading engine in Credit Suisse's Manhattan headquarters is replicated in London, Hong Kong, and Tokyo.

Guaranteed transaction times for AES clients—from the time the order is received on the Credit Suisse system until it gets an acknowledgment from the exchange, e-communications network or "crossing network"—has dropped from 15 milliseconds to 8 in the last year, Cirillo says. Total execution time also includes any delays within the exchange or "liquidity point" itself, a latency variable over which Credit Suisse has no control.

"That response time is something the ECNs [electronic communications networks] and the exchanges compete on as well," Cirillo says. "Their latency, their turnaround time, and their infrastructure are all part of the electronic game."

Source: Adapted from Gary Anthes, "Split Second Securities Trading at Wachovia," *Computerworld*, May 21, 2007; and Richard Martin, "Wall Street's Quest to Process Data at the Speed of Light," *InformationWeek*, April 21, 2007.

CASE STUDY QUESTIONS

1. What competitive advantages can the companies described in the case derive from the use of faster technology and co-location of servers with the exchanges? Which would you say are sustainable, and which ones temporary or easily imitable? Justify your answer.

2. Tony Bishop of Wachovia stated that "Competitive advantage comes from your math, your workflow and your processes through your systems." Referring to what you have learned in this chapter, develop opposing viewpoints as to the role of IT, if any, in the development of competitive advantage. Use examples from the case to support your positions.

3. What companies in industries other than securities trading could benefit from technologies that focus on reducing transaction processing times? Provide several examples.

REAL WORLD ACTIVITIES

1. Most of the discussion in the case was done from the perspective of the trading firms and the value that these technologies add to them and their customer. However, the case also mentions actions taken by stock exchanges to improve their transaction processing and turn these needs into a revenue-generating asset. Research what recent technologies have been implemented by major stock exchanges such as NYSE and NASDAQ and prepare a report detailing what benefits have occurred as a result.

2. The technologies described in the case represent an example of how different barriers to the flow of goods and information are being overcome by the use of IT. Break into small groups and select an industry other than the one described in the case ; brainstorm what barriers to commerce you see there and how IT may help to do away with them.

REAL WORLD

CASE 4

IT Leaders: Reinventing IT as a Strategic Business Partner

CIO Steve Olive isn't handing out any gold stars to IT for providing good PC support or networking service at Raytheon Integrated Defense Systems. "Consistently reliable and excellent IT service should be a given," he says. "What businesses need and IT should be providing are innovative solutions to business challenges." That means creatively applying technology to produce goods more efficiently and at a lower cost, to sell and service more of them, and to do so at the highest possible profit margins.

It also means using IT to create new products and services and even whole new business models, says Darryl Lemecha, CIO at ChoicePoint Inc. Because technology is embedded in just about everything a company does, "technology strategy and business strategy are now one." Kathleen McNulty, CIO at The Schwan Food Co., puts it this way: "It's not about IT automating the business anymore. It's about innovating it, improving it." So forget about IT supporting the business. IT leaders are focused on reinventing the business, starting with the IT organization.

Their timing couldn't be better. According to Gartner Inc., within five years, 60 percent of chief executives will make their CIOs responsible for using information as a strategic (read: revenue-generating) asset. Gartner also predicts that 40 percent of CEOs will make CIOs responsible for business model innovation.

IT executives such as John Hinkle at Trans World Entertainment Corp., Patrick Bennett at E! Entertainment Television Inc., and Filippo Passerini at the Procter & Gamble Co. are all over this trend already. They are completely transforming their IT organizations, and everything is up for radical change, from how and where IT is housed within their companies to IT job titles. IT duties increasingly involve responsibility for business processes, as well as the technology that supports them. Also up for reinvention is how IT value is measured.

"If you want to drive a significant amount of behavioral change in an organization, it takes some big swings," says Hinkle. "Maybe that means dramatic structural change or changing what people do." At Trans World, it involved all of the above.

One of the first things Hinkle did when he came to Trans World from General Electric was abolish the title of analyst and move people in that role into the project management office (PMO), which oversees all technology and business projects, as well as all business process changes for the company's 800 music stores. Project managers have developed expertise and a special rapport with the specific business functions to which they are dedicated. New projects and even systems changes go through the PMO, which uses Six Sigma project management processes.

As CIO, Hinkle oversees the PMO, is a member of the company's executive board, and is deeply entrenched in all business decisions. "I'm involved in merchandising, store planning and in every other core strategic meeting at the company," Hinkle says. "I'm expected to be very well versed in these things, and I'm also expected to answer more than the IT questions. I'm part of the strategy brainstorming."

Hinkle expects his IT team to be equally well versed in business processes, which is why every IT staffer spends a minimum of three days in the field every year, working in a store, a warehouse, or a department such as finance or payroll. "That way, they know what the business really needs and how to help," he says. "You don't have a supply chain system or financial system that works in a box or a point-of-sale system that just takes money. Now we have highly integrated data flows, so every project requires an understanding of all systems and all business areas." By knowing the business, "they better understand why they might get a call for support at 1:00 in the morning," he adds.

At ChoicePoint, Lemecha created a federated structure with two bands of IT positions: one for technical workers, who hold the title of IT architect; and one for managers, who hold the title of business information officer (BIO). "We believe in two independent career paths. Just because you don't manage people doesn't mean you should be limited in how far you go in the company," he says.

The BIOs are embedded in each of ChoicePoint's businesses and act as local CIOs. "They understand the operational issues, they know all of the people, and they spend 100 percent of their time in the business units," where they can directly affect business–IT alignment, Lemecha says. "They know and understand the business because they live in the business," he says. The chief benefit of this arrangement is "when you fix the alignment problems, you do the right IT projects and, ultimately, impact revenue and get better customer service," Lemecha says. ChoicePoint's consistent revenue growth, ranging between 5 percent and 15 percent annually for the past several years, is no coincidence.

At Cincinnati-based Procter & Gamble (P&G), the company's top IT project over the past three years has been to reinvent IT itself according to a four-year strategic alignment plan. "In the last year, we reshaped, renamed, refocused and began retraining our 2,500-person IT team," says Passerini, who is global business services officer in addition to CIO. The IT department was renamed Information & Decision Solutions (IDS). The new IDS group was then merged into P&G's Global Business Services shared-services organization, which is also home to the human resources, finance, strategic planning, and relocation functions. IDS staffers focus on high-level, IT-enabled business projects exclusively; routine IT tasks are outsourced to Hewlett-Packard Co. under a 10-year, $3 billion agreement signed in 2003.

Passerini has charged IDS with the same three business goals of every other P&G business unit: to increase profits, market share, and volume. To accomplish this, IDS focuses on three key tactics: getting and distributing data faster, innovating and speeding the ways in which P&G gets products to market, and applying consumer-friendly techniques to delivering new IT products and services to P&G's internal user base. For example, IDS has developed a virtual modeling process and simulation techniques that allow package design, consumer testing, product testing, and even new manufacturing techniques to be developed and tested in a fully virtual environment, dramatically accelerating the cycle time for new products.

"When we have new products, we can build virtual retail shelves and even show our competitors' products on them. More importantly, we can build our products to the scale of different retailers' shelves. This is all about building business capabilities for P&G," Passerini says. "The whole idea is running IT as a business, but not necessarily using [traditional return-on-investment] financial measures to quantify IT's value," he says. "In the end, no one believes those numbers anyhow. The numbers you want are higher profits, market share, and volumes. In reality, it's all about the relevancy of IT's contribution to the business," Passerini adds. That is how IT's value is measured at P&G.

E! Entertainment Television in Los Angeles has radically departed from its traditional model of separate IT and television broadcast operations. The change coincides with the broadcast side's shift from tape to digital technology. Before, separate vice presidents oversaw online, television network, and IT operations. Now there is a single senior vice president of technology and operations ; ideas, designs, technology, and projects are shared among all three operations.

For example, IT personnel were involved in the design of E! Online content from the time the site was first launched in October 2006, notes Bennett, executive director of business applications. "Before, we would have gotten the specs and built it much like a contractor," he says. "But now, IT was in on branding discussions and audience focus groups from the beginning. "What we've done is flatten the more formal [software development] processes and made them

more person-to-person" as a way to develop products and services faster across all media, Bennett says. "As we interact with executives and users and release software iteratively, we're also gaining greater domain knowledge about the business," he notes.

Just recently, IT participated in a discussion about offering an online feature that would let Web viewers of E! Online vote on whether celebrities on the red carpet at the Golden Globe and Oscar celebrations are hot or not. "Now that's not a traditional discussion or conversation you would have in IT," Bennett notes wryly, "but now we're thinking about these kinds of things across all media." Under the new organizational structure, "there's constant interaction and exchange of information and ideas through human contact. As opposed to being assigned to a user department, IT is constantly interacting across media," he says. "You're more of a partner with the business. You're creating products together. IT is definitely stepping out from behind the shadows of backoffice corporate systems."

"It's very much a different mind-set," says Raytheon's Olive, whose overhauled IT organization now includes customer relationship managers who are embedded in the business, plus 10 teams of technical workers who support IT frameworks such as infrastructure, application support, and desktop services. The vast majority of those technical workers are "home-roomed" in cross-business teams that work on projects that the customer relationship managers bring to them, he notes.

"It took two years for this model to really jell. At first, there was a little bit of tension while the clarity of roles and responsibilities was a little confusing," Olive acknowledges. "But once we defined roles and responsibilities, it improved morale and worked to create a highly motivated workforce because we were making higher-level contributions to the business."

Source: Adapted from Julia King, "How IT Is Reinventing Itself as a Strategic Business Partner," *Computerworld*, February 19, 2007.

CASE STUDY QUESTIONS

1. What are the business and political challenges that are likely to occur as a result of the transformation of IT from a support activity to a partner role? Use examples from the case to illustrate your answer.

2. What implications does this shift in the strategic outlook of IT have for traditional IT workers and for the educational institutions that train them? How does this change the emphasis on what knowledge and skills the IT person of the future should have?

3. To what extent do you agree with the idea that technology is embedded in just about everything a company does? Provide examples, other than those included in the case, of recent product introductions that could not have been possible without heavy reliance on IT.

REAL WORLD ACTIVITIES

1. Search the Internet to find information about other firms that have transformed their IT organizations and the role that the CIO plays in the governance structure of the organization. What benefits have they been able to derive from these changes? Prepare a report and present your findings to your class.

2. Consider the virtual reality technologies employed by Procter & Gamble and described in this case. Break into small groups and brainstorm applications of these types of technologies for companies in industries other than those reviewed in the case.

MODULE II

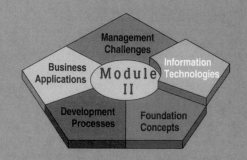

INFORMATION TECHNOLOGIES

What challenges do information system technologies pose for business professionals? What basic knowledge should you possess about information technology? The four chapters of this module give you an overview of the hardware, software, and data resource management and telecommunications network technologies used ian information systems and their implications for business managers and professionals.

- **Chapter 3: Computer Hardware** reviews history, trends, and developments in microcomputer, midrange, and mainframe computer systems; basic computer system concepts; and the major types of technologies used in peripheral devices for computer input, output, and storage.

- **Chapter 4: Computer Software** reviews the basic features and trends in the major types of application software and system software used to support enterprise and end-user computing.

- **Chapter 5: Data Resource Management** emphasizes management of the data resources of computer-using organizations. This chapter reviews key database management concepts and applications in business information systems.

- **Chapter 6: Telecommunications and Networks** presents an overview of the Internet and other telecommunication networks, business applications, and trends and reviews technical telecommunications alternatives.

CHAPTER 3

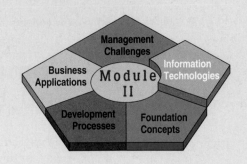

Module II
Management Challenges
Business Applications
Information Technologies
Development Processes
Foundation Concepts

COMPUTER HARDWARE

Chapter Highlights

Section I
Computer Systems: End User and Enterprise Computing
Introduction
A Brief History of Computer Hardware
Real World Case: The Bootless PC and Terabytes on a Small Coin
Types of Computer Systems
Microcomputer Systems
Midrange Systems
Mainframe Computer Systems
Technical Note: The Computer System Concept
Moore's Law: Where Do We Go from Here?

Section II
Computer Peripherals: Input, Output, and Storage Technologies
Peripherals
Input Technologies
Real World Case: IT in Healthcare: Voice Recognition Tools Make Rounds at Hospitals
Output Technologies
Storage Trade-Offs
Semiconductor Memory
Magnetic Disks
Magnetic Tape
Optical Disks
Radio Frequency Identification
Predictions for the Future
Real World Case: IBM, Wachovia, and PayPal: Grid Computing Makes It Easier and Cheaper
Real World Case: Apple, Microsoft, IBM, and Others: The Touch Screen Comes of Age

Learning Objectives

1. Understand the history and evolution of computer hardware.

2. Identify the major types and uses of microcomputer, midrange, and mainframe computer systems.

3. Outline the major technologies and uses of computer peripherals for input, output, and storage.

4. Identify and give examples of the components and functions of a computer system.

5. Identify the computer systems and peripherals you would acquire or recommend for a business of your choice, and explain the reasons for your selections.

SECTION I   Computer Systems: End User and Enterprise Computing

Introduction

All computers are systems of input, processing, output, storage, and control components. In this section, we discuss the history, trends, applications, and some basic concepts of the many types of computer systems in use today. In Section II, we will cover the changing technologies for input, output, and storage that are provided by the peripheral devices that are part of modern computer systems.

Read the Real World Case regarding making technologies smaller. We can learn a lot about how computers that are getting smaller are changing the way we do things from this case. See Figure 3.1.

A Brief History of Computer Hardware

Today we are witnessing rapid technological changes on a broad scale. However, many centuries elapsed before technology was sufficiently advanced to develop computers. Without computers, many technological achievements of the past would not have been possible. To fully appreciate their contribution, we must understand their history and evolution. Although a thorough discussion of computing history is beyond the scope of this text, a brief consideration of the development of the computer is possible. Let's look quickly into the development of computers.

At the dawn of the human concept of numbers, humans used their fingers and toes to perform basic mathematical activities. Then our ancestors realized that by using some objects to represent digits, they could perform computations beyond the limited scope of their own fingers and toes. Can't you just see in your mind a cave full of cavemen performing some group accounting function using their fingers, toes, sticks, and rocks? It creates a comical, yet accurate, picture.

Shells, chicken bones, or any number of objects could have been used, but the fact that the word *calculate* is derived from *calculus*, the Latin word for "small stone," suggests that pebbles or beads were arranged to form the familiar abacus, arguably the first human-made computing device. By manipulating the beads, it was possible with some skill and practice to make rapid calculations.

Blaise Pascal, a French mathematician, invented what is believed to be the first mechanical adding machine in 1642. The machine partially adopted the principles of the abacus but did away with the use of the hand to move the beads or counters. Instead, Pascal used wheels to move counters. The principle of Pascal's machine is still being used today, such as in the counters of tape recorders and odometers. In 1674, Gottfried Wilhelm von Leibniz improved Pascal's machine so that the machine could divide and multiply as easily as it could add and subtract.

When the age of industrialization spread throughout Europe, machines became fixtures in agricultural and production sites. An invention that made profound changes in the history of industrialization, as well as in the history of computing, was the mechanical loom, invented by a Frenchman named Joseph Jacquard. With the use of cards punched with holes, it was possible for the Jacquard loom to weave fabrics in a variety of patterns. Jacquard's loom was controlled by a program encoded into the punched cards. The operator created the program once and was able to duplicate it many times over with consistency and accuracy.

The idea of using punched cards to store a predetermined pattern to be woven by the loom clicked in the mind of Charles Babbage, an English mathematician who lived in the 19th century. He foresaw a machine that could perform all mathematical calculations, store values in its memory, and perform logical comparisons among values. He called it the *Analytical Engine*. Babbage's analytical engine, however, was never built. It lacked one thing: electronics. Herman Hollerith eventually adapted Jacquard's concept of the punched card to record census data in the late 1880s.

REAL WORLD
CASE 1

The Bootless PC and Terabytes on a Small Coin

Imagine a PC with instantaneous boot-up or storing 10TB of data—10,000 gigabytes—on a device the size of a dime with data-transfer rates unhampered by any latency. Those are just two examples of the promises that storage nanotechnologies hold: combining the functions of memory chips and disk drives on a single piece of hardware that is a fraction of the size of devices today.

Nanotechnology, the science of engineering functional systems at the molecular scale, holds the possibility of billions of infinitesimally small machines working together to build products from the ground up using readily available materials. Systems in development today could do away with internal disk drives all together as well as the computer boot-up process, instantaneously bringing applications up when a PC or laptop is turned on. Other nanotechnology hardware may allow data to be stored for more than 100 years without having to refresh media.

Most production applications for nanotechnology are now used in reading and writing from storage media that are many times superior to today's storage products at a fraction of the cost. But these developments are prompting storage vendors of all sizes to examine not only how they will manufacture products in the future, but what their business models may ultimately look like as a result of the disruptive nature of nanotechnology.

Large and small storage vendors are well into developing storage nanotechnology that promises to shrink by tens or hundreds of times the space required to fit today's data.

FIGURE 3.1

Companies are increasingly focusing on ways to make memory and computing resources smaller so rooms of computers become a thing of the past.

Source: © Royalty Free/Corbis.

Physicists at the University of California at Riverside have made a breakthrough in developing a "spin computer," which would combine logic with nonvolatile memory, bypassing the need for computers to boot up. The new transistor technology, which one lead scientist believes could become a reality in about five years, would reduce power consumption to the point where eventually computers, mobile phones, and other electronic devices could remain on all the time.

The breakthrough came when scientists at UC Riverside successfully injected a spinning electron into a resistor material called graphene, which is essentially a very thin layer of graphite, just like you might find in a pencil. The graphene in this case is one-atom thick. The process is known as "tunneling spin injection." It involves laying down an electron in the graphene, which then represents a bit of data. By injecting multiple bits into the graphene, they cannot only be stored in a nonvolatile state (without the need of electricity), but the data can be used for computations in the graphene itself. If successful, the researchers will have created a chip that removes the input/output (I/O) bottleneck created by the system bus between a computer's CPU and a mass storage device such as a hard drive or solid state drive (SSD.

One of the project's lead scientists, Roland Kawakami, an associate professor of physics and astronomy at UC Riverside, said the clock speeds of chips made using tunneling spin injection would be "thousands of times" faster than today's processors. One of the major hurdles that remains involves finding a lower-power method to coax electrons into being flipped by a magnetic field, turning them into bits representing zeros or ones. Currently, the graphene spin technology requires more power than DRAM or SRAM to work, Kawakami said.

"If you can lower the energy needed, then you could lower the size of the supporting circuitry," Kawakami said. "What we're working on is a whole new concept. This will essentially give memory some brains." The researchers also need to build out the circuitry. That will be the job of electrical engineers. Kawakami's team has used a semiconductor laser to essentially free-up electrons so they can be polarized and given a directional orientation, called "spin." The electrons can either "spin up" or "spin down" and allow for more data storage than is possible with current electronics, according to the university. Once the electrons are polarized, they remain in place for the life of the chip, which in the case of graphene is almost practically an eternity.

"So it's the type of memory that can be very fast and it can be very durable. You're moving atoms. There's not a large magnetic field," Kawakami said. "I'm one of those researchers that really cringes at the thought of saying this [new technology] can be useful. I think for us, maybe within five years we can get one device working."

Kawakami's team is working on the electrical spin injection from a ferromagnetic electrode into graphene, which to date has been inefficient, he said. The spin lifetime of the electrons is thousands of times shorter than they should be from a theoretical perspective. "We would like longer spin lifetimes because the longer the lifetime, the more computational operations you can do," he said.

Kawakami's team has been able to lengthen the spin lifetime through the use of a nanometer-thick insulating layer, known as a "tunnel barrier," in between the ferromagnetic electrode and the graphene layer. They found that the spin injection efficiency increased dramatically, he said. "We found a 30-fold increase in the efficiency of how spins were being injected by quantum tunneling across the insulator and into graphene," Kawakami said.

Kawakami said the research on spin computing is at a stage similar to that of the movement from vacuum tubes to transistors in the 1950s. Once one transistor was created, the floodgates to the modern computers were opened. Once a spin-computing transistor has been created, in say about five years, he expects industrial support to ramp up and consumer products to follow in under 10 years. Kawakami's team of three graduate-student researchers has for the first time joined with electrical engineers at the university, who are designing the circuitry that will carry the electrons through the graphene.

Graphene received broad notoriety in late 2010 when the scientists who discovered its properties as the thinnest and strongest material known to mankind received the Nobel Prize in physics. Graphene is made up of carbon atoms and looks like chicken wire or lattice through an electron microscope.

To date, development of spin electronics has been geared entirely toward memory. Two years ago, another group of researchers at Rice University demonstrated a data storage medium made out of a layer of graphite only 10 atoms thick. That technology has the potential to provide many times the capacity of current NAND flash memory and can withstand temperatures of 200 degrees Celsius and radiation that would make solid-state disk memory disintegrate. That technology, for example, would be useful in satellites, which are constantly bombarded by the sun's radiation. But the researchers, focused on combining the memory aspects with the computational capabilities of tunneling spin injection, are hopeful now that the right material is on hand.

"Things that have been missing are that the right material [graphene] hasn't been there on one hand, and on the other hand, the circuit computing design concept hasn't been there. It's like the chicken and the egg. One has to develop to give motivation to the other," Kawakami said.

Source: Adapted from Lucas Mearian, "Researchers One Step Closer to "Bootless' Computer," *Computerworld, Inc.*, October 18, 2010; Jerome Wendt, "The Bootless PC and Terabytes on a Dime," *Computerworld, Inc.*, September 18, 2006.

CASE STUDY QUESTIONS

1. Why are the companies mentioned in the case trying to make PCs smaller and eliminate the entire operating system? What is the problem?

2. What are the business benefits of having an extremely small computing device that uses very little power? In what ways would such technology change the way we use our computing devices? Provide several examples.

3. One of the advantages of nanotechnology as stated in the case is that data could be stored for hundreds of years without refreshing the media. Why is this so important? Justify your answer.

REAL WORLD ACTIVITIES

1. An important point made about nanotechnology is that it could allow PCs and other electronic devices to remain on all the time. This suggests that current technologies use too much energy. Prepare a presentation on the current costs associated with "always on" technologies and share your research with the rest of your class.

2. Break into small groups with your classmates and discuss how nanotechnology could change the way we do everything in the future.

Census data were translated into a series of holes in a punched card to represent the digits and the letters of the alphabet. The card was then passed through a machine with a series of electrical contacts that were either turned off or on, depending on the existence of holes in the punched cards. These different combinations of off/on situations were recorded by the machine and represented a way of tabulating the result of the census. Hollerith's machine was highly successful; it cut the time it took to tabulate the result of the census by two-thirds, and it made money for the company that manufactured it. In 1911, this company merged with its competitor to form International Business Machines (IBM).

The ENIAC (Electronic Numerical Integrator and Computer) was the first electronic digital computer. It was completed in 1946 at the Moore School of Electrical Engineering of the University of Pennsylvania. With no moving parts, ENIAC was programmable and had the capability to store problem calculations using vacuum tubes (about 18,000).

A computer that uses vacuum tube technology is called a first-generation computer. The ENIAC could add in 0.2 of a millisecond, or about 5,000 computations per second. The principal drawback of ENIAC was its size and processing ability. It occupied more than 1,500 square feet of floor space and could process only one program or problem at a time. As an aside, the power requirements for ENIAC were such that adjacent common area lighting dimmed during the power up and calculation cycles. Figure 3.2 shows the ENIAC complex.

In the 1950s, Remington Rand manufactured the UNIVAC I (Universal Automatic Calculator). It could calculate at the rate of 10,000 additions per second. In 1957, IBM developed the IBM 704, which could perform 100,000 calculations per second.

In the late 1950s, transistors were invented and quickly replaced the thousands of vacuum tubes used in electronic computers. A transistor-based computer could perform 200,000–250,000 calculations per second. The transistorized computer represents the second generation of computer. It was not until the mid-1960s that the third generation of computers came into being. These were characterized by solid-state technology and integrated circuitry coupled with extreme miniaturization.

No history of electronic computing would be complete without acknowledging Jack Kilby. Kilby was a Nobel Prize laureate in physics in 2000 for his invention of the integrated circuit in 1958 while working at Texas Instruments (TI). He is also the inventor of the handheld calculator and thermal printer. Without his work that generated a patent for a "Solid Circuit made of Germanium," our worlds, and most certainly our computers, would be much different and less productive than we enjoy today.

FIGURE 3.2
ENIAC was the first digital computer. It is easy to see how far we have come in the evolution of computers.

Source: Photo courtesy of United States Army.

In 1971, the fourth generation of computers was characterized by further miniaturization of circuits, increased multiprogramming, and virtual storage memory. In the 1980s, the fifth generation of computers operated at speeds of 3–5 million calculations per second (for small-scale computers) and 10–15 million instructions per second (for large-scale computers).

The age of microcomputers began in 1975 when a company called MITS introduced the ALTAIR 8800. The computer was programmed by flicking switches on the front. It came as a kit and had to be soldered together. It had no software programs, but it was a personal computer available to the consumer for a few thousand dollars when most computer companies were charging tens of thousands of dollars. In 1977 both Commodore and Radio Shack announced that they were going to make personal computers. They did, and trotting along right beside them were Steve Jobs and Steve Wozniak, who invented their computer in a garage while in college. Mass production of the Apple began in 1979, and by the end of 1981, it was the fastest selling of all the personal computers. In August 1982 the IBM PC was born, and many would argue that the world changed forever as a result.

Following the introduction of the personal computer in the early 1980s, we used our knowledge of computer networks gained in the early days of computing and combined it with new and innovative technologies to create massive networks of people, computers, and data on which anyone can find almost anything: the Internet. Today we continue to see amazing advancements in computing technologies.

Okay, it's time to slow down a bit and begin our discussion of today's computer hardware.

Types of Computer Systems

Today's computer systems come in a variety of sizes, shapes, and computing capabilities. Rapid hardware and software developments and changing end-user needs continue to drive the emergence of new models of computers, from the smallest handheld personal digital assistant/cell phone combinations to the largest multiple-CPU mainframes for enterprises. See Figure 3.3.

FIGURE 3.3   Examples of computer system categories.

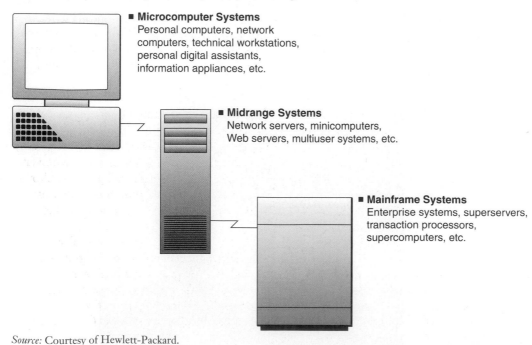

- **Microcomputer Systems**
  Personal computers, network computers, technical workstations, personal digital assistants, information appliances, etc.

- **Midrange Systems**
  Network servers, minicomputers, Web servers, multiuser systems, etc.

- **Mainframe Systems**
  Enterprise systems, superservers, transaction processors, supercomputers, etc.

Source: Courtesy of Hewlett-Packard.

Categories such as *mainframe, midrange,* and *microcomputer* systems are still used to help us express the relative processing power and number of end users that can be supported by different types of computers. These are not precise classifications, and they do overlap each other. Thus, other names are commonly given to highlight the major uses of particular types of computers. Examples include personal computers, network servers, network computers, and technical workstations.

In addition, experts continue to predict the merging or disappearance of several computer categories. They feel, for example, that many midrange and mainframe systems have been made obsolete by the power and versatility of networks composed of microcomputers and servers. Other industry experts have predicted that the emergence of network computers and *information appliances* for applications on the Internet and corporate intranets will replace many personal computers, especially in large organizations and in the home computer market. Still others suggest that the concept of *nanocomputers* (computing devices that are smaller than micro) will eventually pervade our entire understanding of personal computing. Only time will tell whether such predictions will equal the expectations of industry forecasters.

Microcomputer Systems

The entire center of gravity in computing has shifted. For millions of consumers and business users, the main function of desktop PCs is as a window to the Internet. Computers are now communications devices, and consumers want them to be as cheap as possible.

Microcomputers are the most important category of computer systems for both businesspeople and consumers. Although usually called a *personal computer,* or PC, a microcomputer is much more than a small computer for use by an individual as a communication device. The computing power of microcomputers now exceeds that of the mainframes of previous computer generations, at a fraction of their cost. Thus, they have become powerful networked *professional workstations* for business professionals.

Consider the computing power on the *Apollo 11* spacecraft. Most certainly, landing men on the moon and returning them safely to earth was an extraordinary feat. The computer that assisted them in everything from navigation to systems monitoring was equally extraordinary. *Apollo 11* had a 2.048 MHz CPU that was built by MIT. Today's standards can be measured in the 4 GHz in many home PCs (MHz is 1 million computing cycles per second and GHz is 1 billion computing cycles per second). Further, the *Apollo 11* computer weighed 70 pounds versus today's powerful laptops weighing in as little as 1 pound. This is progress, for sure.

Microcomputers come in a variety of sizes and shapes for a variety of purposes, as Figure 3.4 illustrates. For example, PCs are available as handheld, notebook, laptop, tablet, portable, desktop, and floor-standing models. Or, based on their use, they include home, personal, professional, workstation, and multiuser systems. Most microcomputers are *desktops* designed to fit on an office desk or laptops for those who want a small, portable PC. Figure 3.5 offers advice on some of the key features you should consider when acquiring a high-end professional workstation, multimedia PC, or beginner's system. This breakdown should give you some idea of the range of features available in today's microcomputers.

Some microcomputers are powerful workstation computers (technical workstations) that support applications with heavy mathematical computing and graphics display demands, such as computer-aided design (CAD) in engineering or investment and portfolio analysis in the securities industry. Other microcomputers are used as network servers. These are usually more powerful microcomputers that coordinate telecommunications and resource sharing in small local area networks (LANs) and in Internet and intranet Web sites.

FIGURE 3.4   Examples of microcomputer systems:

a. A notebook microcomputer.
Source: Hewlett-Packard.

b. The microcomputer as a professional workstation.
Source: Corbis.

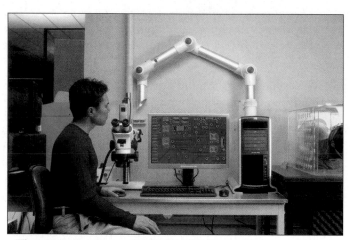

c. The microcomputer as a technical workstation.
Source: Courtesy of Hewlett-Packard.

FIGURE 3.5   Examples of recommended features for the three types of PC users. Note: www.dell.com and www.gateway.com are good sources for the latest PC features available.

Business Pro	Multimedia Heavy or Gamer	Newcomer
To track products, customers, and firm performance, more than just a fast machine is necessary:	Media pros and dedicated gamers will want at least a Mac G4 or a 2–3 GHz Intel dual-core chip, and	Save some money with a Celeron processor in the 2–3 GHz range while looking for
• 3–4 GHz dual-core processor	• 4–8 GB RAM	• 2 GB RAM
• 4–8 GB RAM	• 250$^+$ GB hard drive	• 120–160 GB hard drive
• 500 GB hard drive	• 19-inch or better flat-panel display	• 15- to 17-inch flat panel or wide screen
• Up to 19-inch flat-panel display	• 16× or better DVD+RW	
• CD-RW/DVD+RW	• Video cards (as fast and as powerful as budget permits)	• CD-RW/DVD
• Network interface card	• Sound cards	• USB port
• Color laser printer	• Laser printer (color or B&W)	• Inkjet printer

Corporate PC Criteria

What do you look for in a new PC system? A big, bright screen? Zippy new processor? Capacious hard drive? Acres of RAM? Sorry, none of these is a top concern for corporate PC buyers. Numerous studies have shown that the price of a new computer is only a small part of the total cost of ownership (TCO). Support, maintenance, and other intangibles contribute far more heavily to the sum. Let's take a look at three top criteria.

Solid Performance at a Reasonable Price. Corporate buyers know that their users probably aren't mapping the human genome or plotting trajectories to Saturn. They're doing word processing, order entry, sales contact management, and other essential business tasks. They need a solid, competent machine at a reasonable price, not the latest whizbang.

Many organizations are adopting a laptop, rather than desktop, strategy. Using this approach, the employee uses his or her laptop while in the office and out in the field. With the proliferation of wireless Internet access, this strategy allows employees to take the desktop with them wherever they may be—at their desk, in a conference room, at a meeting off-site, or in a hotel room in another country.

One outcome of this strategy is the development and acquisition of more powerful laptops with larger and higher-quality screens. This demand presents a challenge to laptop manufacturers to provide higher quality while continuing to make the laptop lightweight and portable.

Operating System Ready. A change in the operating system of a computer is the most disruptive upgrade an enterprise has to face. That's why many corporate buyers want their machines to be able to handle current operating systems and anticipate new ones. Although most organizations have adopted Windows XP or Vista, some enterprises still use operating systems of an earlier vintage. Ultimately, they must be able to make the transition to Windows 7 (the newest OS from Microsoft) and even to OS versions expected three to five years from now. Primarily, that demand means deciding what hard disk space and RAM will be sufficient.

Connectivity. Networked machines are a given in corporate life, and Internet-ready machines are becoming a given. Buyers need machines equipped with reliable wireless capabilities. With fewer cables to worry about, wireless networks, especially when combined with laptop PCs, contribute to the flexibility of the workplace and the simplicity of PC deployment. Many organizations are planning for Internet-based applications and need machines ready to make fast, reliable, and secure connections.

Security-Equipped. Most of the data that is processed by networked workstations in a modern corporate environment can be considered proprietary, if not mission-critical. A major criterion for corporate purchase is the degree to which the device can accept or conform to the myriad of security measures in use in that organization. Can it accept a USB dongle, smartcard reader, biometric access device, and so forth? We will cover this aspect in greater detail in Chapter 13.

Computer Terminals

Computer terminals, essentially any device that allows access to a computer, are undergoing a major conversion to networked computer devices. *Dumb terminals*, which are keyboard/video monitor devices with limited processing capabilities, are being replaced by *intelligent terminals*, which are modified networked PCs or network computers. Also included are network terminals, which may be *Windows terminals* that depend on network servers for Windows software, processing power, and storage, or *Internet terminals*, which depend on Internet or intranet Web site servers for their operating systems and application software.

Intelligent terminals take many forms and can perform data entry and some information processing tasks independently. These tasks include the widespread use of **transaction terminals** in banks, retail stores, factories, and other work sites. Examples are automated teller machines (ATMs), factory production recorders, airport check-in kiosks, and retail point-of-sale (POS) terminals. These intelligent terminals use keypads, touch screens, bar code scanners, and other input methods to capture data and interact with end users during a transaction, while relying on servers or other computers in the network for further transaction processing.

Network Computers

Network computers (NCs) are a microcomputer category designed primarily for use with the Internet and corporate intranets by clerical workers, operational employees, and knowledge workers with specialized or limited computing applications. These NCs are low-cost, sealed microcomputers with no or minimal disk storage that are linked to the network. Users of NCs depend primarily on network servers for their operating system and Web browser, application software, and data access and storage.

One of the main attractions of network computers is their lower TCO (total cost of ownership), that is, the total of all costs associated with purchasing, installing, operating, and maintaining a computer. Purchase upgrades, maintenance, and support cost much less than for full-featured PCs. Other benefits to business include the ease of software distribution and licensing, computing platform standardization, reduced end-user support requirements, and improved manageability through centralized management and enterprisewide control of computer network resources.

Information Appliances

PCs aren't the only option: A host of smart gadgets and information appliances—from cellular phones and pagers to handheld PCs and Web-based game machines—promise Internet access and the ability to perform basic computational chores.

Handheld microcomputer devices known as **personal digital assistants** (PDAs) are some of the most popular devices in the information appliance category. Web-enabled PDAs use touch screens, pen-based handwriting recognition, or keypads so that mobile workers can send and receive e-mail, access the Web, and exchange information such as appointments, to-do lists, and sales contacts with their desktop PCs or Web servers.

Now a mainstay of PDA technology is the RIM BlackBerry, a small, pager-sized device that can perform all of the common PDA functions, plus act as a fully functional mobile telephone. What sets this device apart from other wireless PDA solutions is that it is always on and connected. A BlackBerry user doesn't need to retrieve e-mail; the e-mail finds the BlackBerry user. Because of this functionality, there is no need to dial in or initiate a connection. The BlackBerry doesn't even have a visible antenna. When a user wishes to send or reply to an e-mail, the small keyboard on the device allows text entry. Just like a mobile telephone, the BlackBerry is designed to remain on and continuously connected to the wireless network, allowing near real-time transfer of e-mail. Furthermore, because the BlackBerry uses the same network as most mobile telephone services, the unit can be used anywhere that a mobile phone can be used.

A relatively new entrant to this field (although gaining favor in leaps and bounds) is the Apple iPhone (Figure 3.6). The iPhone essentially combines three products—a revolutionary mobile phone, a wide-screen iPod music and video player with touch controls, and a breakthrough Internet communications device with desktop-class e-mail, Web browsing, maps, and searching—into one small and lightweight handheld device. The iPhone also introduces an entirely new user interface based on a large, multitouch display and pioneering new software, letting users control everything with just their fingers.

The genesis of the iPhone began with Apple CEO Steve Jobs's direction that Apple engineers investigate touch screens. Apple created the device during a secretive and unprecedented collaboration with AT&T Mobility—called Cingular Wireless at the time of the phone's inception—at a development cost of $150 million, by one

FIGURE 3.6

The Apple iPhone—a revolutionary player in the information appliance and PDA marketplace.

Source: Lourens Smak/Alamy.

estimate. During development, the iPhone was code-named "Purple 2." The company rejected an early "design by committee" built with Motorola in favor of engineering a custom operating system, interface, and hardware.

The iPhone went on sale on June 29, 2007. Apple closed its stores at 2:00 p.m. local time to prepare for the 6:00 p.m. iPhone launch, while hundreds of customers lined up at stores nationwide. They sold 270,000 iPhones in the first 30 hours on launch weekend.

In Germany, Deutsche Telekom signed up 70,000 iPhone customers during the 11-week period of November 9, 2007, to January 26, 2008. In the United Kingdom, it has been estimated that 190,000 customers signed with O2 during an eight-week period from the November 9, 2007 launch date to January 9, 2008.

The newest generation of iPhone is the 3G. This version accesses data from the much faster 3G network and provides for the download of literally thousands of applications that allow the iPhone to perform tasks ranging from accessing online banking services to acting as a sophisticated leveling device and everything in between.

The iPhone has truly ushered in an era of software power and sophistication never before seen in a mobile device, completely redefining what people can do on a mobile phone. We can expect to see even more sophisticated mobile PDA-type devices in the future as Moore's law continues to prevail and the marketplace continues to demand more functionality (see the discussion on Moore's law at the end of Section I for more details on this concept).

Information appliances may also take the form of video-game consoles and other devices that connect to your home television set. These devices enable people to surf the World Wide Web, send and receive e-mail, and watch television programs or play video games, at the same time. Other information appliances include wireless PDAs and Internet-enabled cellular and PCS phones, as well as wired, telephone-based home appliances that can send and receive e-mail and access the Web.

Midrange Systems

Midrange systems are primarily high-end network servers and other types of servers that can handle the large-scale processing of many business applications. Although not as powerful as mainframe computers, they are less costly to buy, operate, and maintain than mainframe systems and thus meet the computing needs of many organizations. See Figure 3.7.

FIGURE 3.7

Midrange computer systems can handle large-scale processing without the high cost or space considerations of a large-scale mainframe.

Source: China Foto Press/Getty Images.

> *Burgeoning data warehouses and related applications such as data mining and online analytical processing are forcing IT shops into higher and higher levels of server configurations. Similarly, Internet-based applications, such as Web servers and electronic commerce, are forcing IT managers to push the envelope of processing speed and storage capacity and other [business] applications, fueling the growth of high-end servers.*

Midrange systems have become popular as powerful network servers (computers used to coordinate communications and manage resource sharing in network settings) to help manage large Internet Web sites, corporate intranets and extranets, and other networks. Internet functions and other applications are popular high-end server applications, as are integrated enterprisewide manufacturing, distribution, and financial applications. Other applications, like data warehouse management, data mining, and online analytical processing (which we will discuss in Chapters 5 and 10), are contributing to the demand for high-end server systems.

Midrange systems first became popular as minicomputers for scientific research, instrumentation systems, engineering analysis, and industrial process monitoring and control. Minicomputers could easily handle such uses because these applications are narrow in scope and do not demand the processing versatility of mainframe systems. Today, midrange systems include servers used in industrial process-control and manufacturing plants and play major roles in computer-aided manufacturing (CAM). They can also take the form of powerful technical workstations for computer-aided design (CAD) and other computation and graphics-intensive applications. Midrange systems are also used as *front-end servers* to assist mainframe computers in telecommunications processing and network management.

And the Oscar Goes to . . . Penguins and 2,000 Blade Servers	An initial implementation of 500 blade servers soon grew to 2,000 to meet the processing capacity requirements for creating the Oscar-winning animated film *Happy Feet*. The 108-minute computer-generated animated feature, which won an Academy Award in 2006, was put together by digital production company The Animal Logic Group. "We needed huge numbers of processors in a form factor and price level that would work for our business," says Xavier Desdoigts, director of technical operations.

"We had to render 140,000 frames, and each frame could take many hours to render. The photorealistic look of the movie made our computational requirements soar to new heights."

For example, Mumble, the main character in the movie, had up to 6 million feathers. "There were six shots in the movie that had more than 400,000 penguins in them," Desdoigts explained. This added up to more than 17 million CPU hours used throughout the last nine months of *Happy Feet* production. "We were initially concerned about our ability to build and manage a processing capacity of that scale."

Animal Logic and IBM built a rendering server farm using BladeCenter HS20 blade servers, each with two Intel Xeon servers. Rendering was completed in October 2006, and the film was released the following month in the United States. Management tools to deploy and control the servers while in production included an open-source package for administering computing clusters. For Animal Logic, the biggest sign of success from an IT perspective was that the entire server farm was managed by a single person.

"We have to make sure we choose solutions that aren't overly complex to set up or manage, so our focus can stay on realizing the creative visions of our clients," Desdoigts said. *Happy Feet* quickly became one of the Australian film industry's greatest box-office successes, taking the No. 1 spot in the United States for three consecutive weeks. It made more than $41 million (U.S.) on its opening weekend and showed on 3,800 cinema screens.

Source: Adapted from Sandra Rossi, "And the Oscar Goes to . . . Jovial Penguins and 2,000 Blade Servers," *Computerworld Australia*, March 6, 2007.

Mainframe Computer Systems

Several years after dire pronouncements that the mainframe was dead, quite the opposite is true: Mainframe usage is actually on the rise. And it's not just a short-term blip. One factor that's been driving mainframe sales is cost reductions [of 35 percent or more]. Price reductions aren't the only factor fueling mainframe acquisitions. IS organizations are teaching the old dog new tricks by putting mainframes at the center stage of emerging applications such as data mining and warehousing, decision support, and a variety of Internet-based applications, most notably electronic commerce.

Mainframe systems are large, fast, and powerful computer systems. For example, mainframes can process thousands of million instructions per second (MIPS). Mainframes can also have large primary storage capacities. Their main memory capacity can range from hundreds of gigabytes to many terabytes of primary storage. Mainframes have slimmed down drastically in the last few years, dramatically reducing their air-conditioning needs, electrical power consumption, and floor space requirements—and thus their acquisition and operating costs. Most of these improvements are the result of a move from cumbersome water-cooled mainframes to a newer air-cooled technology for mainframe systems. See Figure 3.8.

Thus, mainframe computers continue to handle the information processing needs of major corporations and government agencies with high transaction processing volumes or complex computational problems. For example, major international banks, airlines, oil companies, and other large corporations process millions of sales transactions and customer inquiries each day with the help of large mainframe systems. Mainframes are still used for computation-intensive applications, such as analyzing seismic data from oil field explorations or simulating flight conditions in designing aircraft. Mainframes are also widely used as *superservers* for the large client/server networks and high-volume Internet Web sites of large companies. As previously mentioned, mainframes are becoming a popular business computing platform for data mining and warehousing, as well as electronic commerce applications.

FIGURE 3.8
Mainframe computer systems are the heavy lifters of corporate computing.

Source: © Royalty Free/Corbis.

Supercomputer Systems

Supercomputers have now become "scalable servers" at the top end of the product lines that start with desktop workstations. Market-driven companies, like Silicon Graphics, Hewlett-Packard, and IBM, have a much broader focus than just building the world's fastest computer, and the software of the desktop computer has a much greater overlap with that of the supercomputer than it used to, because both are built from the same cache-based microprocessors.

The term supercomputer describes a category of extremely powerful computer systems specifically designed for scientific, engineering, and business applications requiring extremely high speeds for massive numeric computations. The market for supercomputers includes government research agencies, large universities, and major corporations. They use supercomputers for applications such as global weather forecasting, military defense systems, computational cosmology and astronomy, microprocessor research and design, and large-scale data mining.

Supercomputers use *parallel processing* architectures of interconnected microprocessors (which can execute many instructions at the same time in parallel). They can easily perform arithmetic calculations at speeds of billions of floating-point operations per second (*gigaflops*). Supercomputers that can calculate in *teraflops* (trillions of floating-point operations per second), which use massive parallel processing (MPP) designs of thousands of microprocessors, are now in use. Purchase prices for large supercomputers are in the $5 million to $50 million range.

The use of symmetric multiprocessing (SMP) and distributed shared memory (DSM) designs of smaller numbers of interconnected microprocessors has spawned a breed of *minisupercomputers* with prices that start in the hundreds of thousands of dollars. For example, IBM's RS/6000 SP system starts at $150,000 for a one-processing-node SMP computer. However, it can be expanded to hundreds of processing nodes, which drives its price into the tens of millions of dollars.

The ASCI White supercomputer system, shown in Figure 3.9, consists of three IBM RS/6000 SP systems: White, Frost, and Ice. White, the largest of these systems, is a 512-node, 16-way SMP supercomputer with a peak performance of 12.3 teraflops. Frost is a 68-node, 16-way SMP system; and Ice is a 28-node, 16-way SMP system. Supercomputers like these continue to advance the state of the art for the entire computer industry.

FIGURE 3.9

The ASCI White supercomputer system at Lawrence Livermore National Laboratory in Livermore, California.

Source: Image courtesy of Silicon Graphics, Inc.

China's Internet Connection Comes a Long Way in Two Decades

In 1993, Xu Rongsheng helped drop a bomb on Beijing. That bomb was the Internet. "This bomb is not a nuclear reaction. It's like information exploded," the Chinese scientist said. Xu and physicist Les Cottrell worked to set up the first Internet connection in China. The two were reunited in late 2010, videoconferencing by the very technology that they helped pioneer in the country.

The two scientists, who established the Internet connection during the early 1990s, reminisced about the experience at China 2.0, a technology conference in Beijing that was hosted by Stanford University. "I can see you very clear by Internet now," Xu said to Cottrell, who was viewable through real-time video. "I see you didn't change much. But Beijing has changed very much."

China has the world's largest Internet population, with more than 420 million users, according to the Chinese government. But more than 15 years ago, hardly anyone in the country was using the Internet, except for a group of China's scientists. The initial Internet connection was the result of a partnership between the Institute of High Energy Physics (IHEP) in Beijing and what is now the SLAC National Accelerator Laboratory in Menlo Park, California. The institutions had simply wanted to improve overseas communication to conduct research. Originally, IHEP could communicate to SLAC through a dial-up connection that allowed only one e-mail be exchanged once per day. The connection cost US$100 per hour.

In 1991, the institutions began working to establish a direct link with each other. Cottrell, who works at SLAC, traveled to Beijing, helping to first set up a direct modem connection between IHEP and SLAC. Cottrell recalled initially thinking that the experience would be a "nice tourist trip." But he soon realized it had become a mission. The institutes faced challenges that included IHEP needing to install international phone line connections for the modem, as well as language barriers. Cottrell resorted to writing down all he said to ensure everyone understood his instructions. "It was very easy to make a mistake because you didn't understand," he said. "It was increasingly difficult as we went on, but increasingly rewarding."

In March 1993, the two institutes had managed to establish a faster dedicated link using AT&T's SkyNet satellite service, an action that was approved by the U.S. Department of Energy. The link allowed the institutes to exchange an average of 2,500 e-mail messages per day. But more importantly, certain physicists at IHEP could remotely log into SLAC's computers via the connection to access the Internet. A year later, after the U.S. government gave approval, IHEP would be allowed a direct link to the Internet without the need for remote access.

Source: Adapted from Michael Kan, "Pioneers of China's First Internet Connection Recall Work," *CIO Magazine*, October 18, 2010.

The Next Wave of Computing

Interconnecting microprocessors to create minisupercomputers is a reality, as discussed in the previous section. The next wave is looking at harnessing the virtually infinite amount of unused computing power that exists in the myriad of desktops and laptops within the boundaries of a modern organization.

Distributed or *grid computing* in general is a special type of parallel computing that relies on complete computers (with onboard CPU, storage, power supply, network interface, and so forth) connected to a network (private, public, or the Internet) by a conventional network interface. This is in contrast to the traditional notion of a supercomputer, which has many processors connected together in a single machine. The grid could be formed by harnessing the unused CPU power in all of the desktops and laptops in a single division of a company (or in the entire company, for that matter).

The primary advantage of distributed computing is that each node can be purchased as commodity hardware; when combined, it can produce similar computing resources to a multiprocessor supercomputer, but at a significantly lower cost. This is due to the economies of scale of producing desktops and laptops, compared with the lower efficiency of designing and constructing a small number of custom supercomputers.

One feature of distributed grids is that they can be formed from computing resources belonging to multiple individuals or organizations (known as multiple administrative domains). This can facilitate commercial transactions or make it easier to assemble volunteer computing networks.

A disadvantage of this feature is that the computers that are actually performing the calculations might not be entirely trustworthy. The designers of the system must thus introduce measures to prevent malfunctions or malicious participants from producing false, misleading, or erroneous results, and from using the system as a platform for a hacking attempt. This often involves assigning work randomly to different nodes (presumably with different owners) and checking that at least two different nodes report the same answer for a given work unit. Discrepancies would identify malfunctioning and malicious nodes.

Another challenge is that because of the lack of central control over the hardware, there is no way to guarantee that computers will not drop out of the network at random times. Some nodes (like laptops or dial-up Internet customers) may also be available for computation but not for network communications for unpredictable periods. These variations can be accommodated by assigning large work units (thus reducing the need for continuous network connectivity) and reassigning work units when a given node fails to report its results as expected.

Despite these challenges, grid computing is becoming a popular method of getting the most out of the computing resources of an organization.

Technical Note: The Computer System Concept

As a business professional, you do not need detailed technical knowledge of computers. However, you do need to understand some basic concepts about computer systems, which should help you be an informed and productive user of computer system resources.

A computer is more than a high-powered collection of electronic devices performing a variety of information processing chores. A computer is a *system*, an interrelated combination of components that performs the basic system functions of input, processing, output, storage, and control, thus providing end users with a powerful information processing tool. Understanding the computer as a computer system is

FIGURE 3.10 The computer system concept. A computer is a system of hardware components and functions.

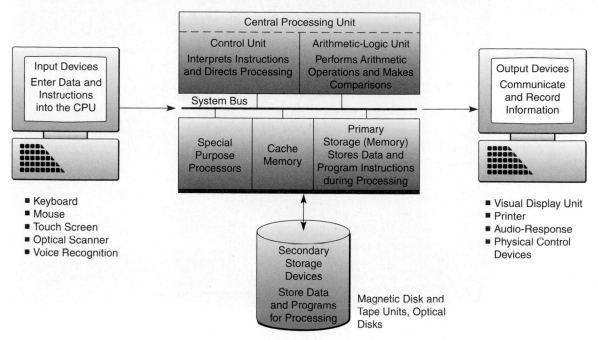

vital to the effective use and management of computers. You should be able to visualize any computer this way, from the smallest microcomputer device to the largest computer networks whose components are interconnected by telecommunications network links throughout a building complex or geographic area.

Figure 3.10 illustrates that a computer is a system of hardware devices organized according to the following system functions:

- **Input.** The input devices of a computer system include computer keyboards, touch screens, pens, electronic mice, and optical scanners. They convert data into electronic form for direct entry or through a telecommunications network into a computer system.

- **Processing.** The central processing unit (CPU) is the main processing component of a computer system. (In microcomputers, it is the main *microprocessor*. See Figure 3.11.) Conceptually, the circuitry of a CPU can be subdivided into two major subunits: the arithmetic-logic unit and the control unit. The electronic circuits (known as *registers*) of the *arithmetic-logic unit* perform the arithmetic and logic functions required to execute software instructions.

- **Output.** The output devices of a computer system include video display units, printers, and audio response units. They convert electronic information produced by the computer system into human-intelligible form for presentation to end users.

- **Storage.** The storage function of a computer system takes place in the storage circuits of the computer's primary storage unit, or *memory*, supported by secondary storage devices such as magnetic disk and optical disk drives. These devices store data and software instructions needed for processing. Computer processors may also include storage circuitry called *cache memory* for high-speed, temporary storage of instruction and data elements.

- **Control.** The control unit of a CPU is the control component of a computer system. Its registers and other circuits interpret software instructions and transmit directions that control the activities of the other components of the computer system.

We will explore the various hardware devices associated with each of these system functions in the next section of this chapter.

FIGURE 3.11
Mobile CPU chips, such as the one shown here, can reach speeds up to 3 Ghz to bring desktop-like power to a mobile setting.

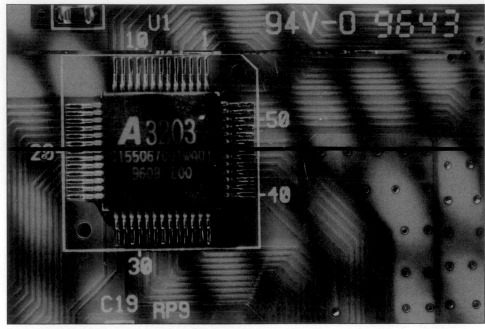

Source: © Getty Images.

Computer Processing Speeds

How fast are computer systems? Early computer processing speeds were measured in milliseconds (thousandths of a second) and microseconds (millionths of a second). Now computers operate in the nanosecond (billionth of a second) range, with picosecond (trillionth of a second) speed being attained by some computers. Such speeds seem almost incomprehensible. For example, an average person taking one step each nanosecond would circle the earth about 20 times in one second!

We have already mentioned the *teraflop* speeds of some supercomputers. However, most computers can now process program instructions at million instructions per second (MIPS) speeds. Another measure of processing speed is *megahertz* (MHz), or millions of cycles per second, and *gigahertz* (GHz), or billions of cycles per second. This rating is commonly called the *clock speed* of a microprocessor because it is used to rate microprocessors by the speed of their timing circuits or internal clock rather than by the number of specific instructions they can process in one second.

However, such ratings can be misleading indicators of the effective processing speed of microprocessors and their *throughput*, or ability to perform useful computation or data processing assignments during a given period. That's because processing speed depends on a variety of factors, including the size of circuitry paths, or *buses*, that interconnect microprocessor components; the capacity of instruction-processing *registers*; the use of high-speed cache memory; and the use of specialized microprocessors such as a math coprocessor to do arithmetic calculations faster.

Moore's Law: Where Do We Go from Here?

Can computers get any faster? Can we afford the computers of the future? Both of these questions can be answered by understanding Moore's law. Gordon Moore, cofounder of Intel Corporation, made his famous observation in 1965, just four years after the first integrated circuit was commercialized. The press called it "Moore's law," and the name has stuck. In its form, Moore observed an exponential growth (doubling every 18 to 24 months) in the number of transistors per integrated circuit and predicted that this trend would continue. Through a number of advances in technology, Moore's law, the doubling of transistors every couple of years, has been maintained and still holds true today. Figure 3.12 illustrates Moore's law as it relates to the evolution of computing power.

FIGURE 3.12

Moore's law suggests that computer power will double every 18 to 24 months. So far, it has.

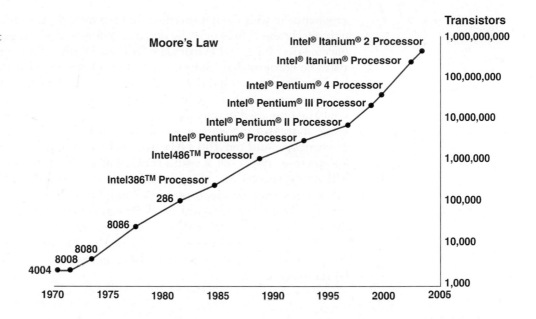

Despite our regular use of exponential growth when predicting the future, particularly the future of technology, humans are often not very good at realizing what exponential growth really looks like. To understand this issue better, let's take a moment to reflect on what Moore's law would mean to us if it applied beyond the number of transistors on a computer chip:

- According to Moore's law, the estimated number of transistors shipped in 2003 was 10^{18}. That's just about 100 times the estimated number of ants in the world.

- In 1978, a commercial flight between New York and Paris cost about $900 and took about seven hours. If Moore's law could be applied to commercial aviation, that same flight today would cost about a penny and would take less than one second.

Over the years, Moore's law has been interpreted and reinterpreted such that it is commonly defined in a much broader sense than it was originally offered. Nonetheless, its application, and its relative accuracy, is useful in understanding where we have been and in predicting where we are going. For example, one common corollary of Moore's law is that the price of a given level of computing power will be cut in half about every 18 to 24 months. Moore didn't specifically predict this effect, but it has been shown to be rather consistently accurate as well. This trend is also true for the cost of storage (we will explore this further in the next section).

Although Moore's law was initially made in the form of an observation and prediction, the more widely it became accepted, the more it served as a goal for an entire industry. This caused both marketing and engineering departments of semiconductor manufacturers to focus enormous energy on the specified increase in processing power that it was presumed one or more of their competitors would soon actually attain. Expressed as "a doubling every 18 to 24 months," Moore's law suggests the phenomenal progress of technology in recent years. Expressed on a shorter timescale, however, Moore's law equates to an average performance improvement in the industry as a whole of more than 1 percent *per week*. For a manufacturer competing in the processor, storage, or memory markets, a new product that is expected to take three years to develop and is just two or three months late is 10–15 percent slower or larger than the directly competing products, thus rendering it harder to sell.

A sometimes misunderstood point is that exponentially improved hardware does not necessarily imply that the performance of the software is also exponentially improved. The productivity of software developers most assuredly does not increase exponentially with the improvement in hardware; by most measures, it has increased only slowly and fitfully over the decades. Software tends to get larger and more complicated over time, and Wirth's law (Niklaus Wirth, a Swiss computer scientist) even states humorously that "Software gets slower faster than hardware gets faster."

Recent computer industry studies predict that Moore's law will continue to hold for the next several chip generations (at least another decade). Depending on the doubling time used in the calculations, this progress could mean up to a 100-fold increase in transistor counts on a chip in the next 10 years. This rapid exponential improvement could put 100 GHz personal computers in every home and 20 GHz devices in every pocket. It seems reasonable to expect that sooner or later computers will meet or exceed any conceivable need for computation. Intel, however, suggests that it can sustain development in line with Moore's law for the next 20 years *without* any significant technological breakthroughs. Given the frequency of such breakthroughs in today's marketplace, it is conceivable that Moore's law can be sustained indefinitely. Regardless of what the end of Moore's law may look like, or when it may arrive, we are still moving along at a phenomenal rate of evolution, and the best may be yet to come.

SECTION II Computer Peripherals: Input, Output, and Storage Technologies

The right peripherals can make all the difference in your computing experience. A top-quality monitor will be easier on your eyes—and may change the way you work. A scanner can edge you closer to that ever-elusive goal: the paperless office. Backup-storage systems can offer bank-vault security against losing your work. CD and DVD drives have become essential for many applications. Thus, the right choice of peripherals can make a big difference.

Read the Real World Case 2 about the use of voice recognition technology in health care settings. We can learn a lot about the future of the human–computer interface and its business applications from this case. See Figure 3.13.

Peripherals

Peripherals is the generic name given to all input, output, and secondary storage devices that are part of a computer system but are not part of the CPU. Peripherals depend on direct connections or telecommunications links to the central processing unit of a computer system. Thus, all peripherals are online devices; that is, they are separate from, but can be electronically connected to and controlled by, a CPU. (This is the opposite of off-line devices that are separate from and not under the control of the CPU.) The major types of peripherals and media that can be part of a computer system are discussed in this section. See Figure 3.14.

Input Technologies

Input technologies now provide a more **natural user interface** for computer users. You can enter data and commands directly and easily into a computer system through pointing devices like electronic mice and touch pads and with technologies like optical scanning, handwriting recognition, and voice recognition. These developments have made it unnecessary to record data on paper *source documents* (e.g., sales order forms) and then keyboard the data into a computer in an additional data-entry step. Further improvements in voice recognition and other technologies should enable an even more natural user interface in the future.

Pointing Devices

Keyboards are still the most widely used devices for entering data and text into computer systems. However, pointing devices are a better alternative for issuing commands, making choices, and responding to prompts displayed on your video screen. They work with your operating system's graphical user interface (GUI), which presents you with icons, menus, windows, buttons, and bars for your selection. For example, pointing devices such as an electronic mouse, trackball, and touch pads allow you to choose easily from menu selections and icon displays using point-and-click or point-and-drag methods. See Figure 3.15.

The **electronic mouse** is the most popular pointing device used to move the cursor on the screen, as well as issue commands and make icon and menu selections. By moving the mouse on a desktop or pad, you can move the cursor onto an icon displayed on the screen. Pressing buttons on the mouse initiates various activities represented by the icon selected.

The trackball, pointing stick, and touch pad are other pointing devices most often used in place of the mouse. A **trackball** is a stationary device related to the mouse. You turn a roller ball with only its top exposed outside its case to move the cursor on the screen. A **pointing stick** (also called a *trackpoint*) is a small button-like device, sometimes likened to the eraser head of a pencil. It is usually centered one row above the space bar of a keyboard. The cursor moves in the direction of the pressure you place on the stick. The **touch pad** is a small rectangular touch-sensitive surface usually placed below the keyboard. The cursor moves in the direction your finger moves on the pad.

REAL WORLD CASE 2

IT in Health Care: Voice Recognition Tools Make Rounds at Hospitals

The infamous doctor's scrawl may finally be on the way out.

Voice technology is the latest tool health care providers are adopting to cut back on time-consuming manual processes, freeing clinicians to spend more time with patients and reduce costs.

At Butler Memorial Hospital, voice-assisted technology has dramatically reduced the amount of time the Butler, Pa., hospital's team of intravenous (IV) nurses spends recording information in patients' charts and on other administrative tasks.

And at the Cleveland Clinic's Fairview Hospital, doctors are using speech recognition to record notes in patients' e-medical records.

Butler recently completed a pilot project where three IV nurses used Vocollect's AccuNurse hands-free, voice-assisted technology along with Boston Software System's workflow automation tools. The nurses were able to cut the time they spent on phone calls and manual processes, including patient record documentation, by at least 75 percent. Now, Butler is rolling out the voice technology for its full IV team of four nurses and seven other clinicians to use for patient care throughout the facility.

The productivity boost from the voice-assisted tools also helps with the hospital's expansion plans, says Dr. Tom McGill. Butler VP of quality and safety.

Butler will soon add about 70 beds—growing from 235 beds now to more than 300—but it won't need to expand the IV nursing team because of the time savings from the voice-assisted technology, McGill says.

In the past, when a patient needed IV care, such as a change in the intravenous medication being administered, an IV nurse would be paged. The nurse would have to call the patient's nursing station or the doctor requesting the IV to obtain details. The nurse then would prioritize the request with all the existing IV orders. Once IV care was completed, nurses would record what they did in the patient's e-medical record.

With the AccuNurse, which combines the use of speech recognition and synthesis for charting and communication, Butler's IV nurses wear lightweight headsets and small pocket-sized wireless devices that enable them to hear personalized care instructions and other information about patients' IV needs.

IV requests are entered into Butler's computer system, which sends them through the Vocollect system to the appropriate headset. IV nurses listen to details about new orders and use the system to prioritize IV orders.

When they finish caring for a patient, nurses record what they did in the patient's e-medical record using voice commands. "The nurses can document as they're walking to the next patient's room," says McGill. Once they finish with one patient, nurses say "next task" to obtain instructions for the next patient, McGill says.

The system has shown itself to be capable of understanding different accents, he said. Butler is evaluating expanding use of the voice-assisted technology to other clinical areas, including surgery. The technology could be used to help ensure that surgical staff complete patient safety checklists.

McGill wouldn't say how much Butler paid for the system, but he expects the ROI will be realized in 12 to 18 months. "It's very affordable," he notes. Meanwhile, Dr. Fred Jorgenson, a faculty physician at Cleveland Clinic's Fairview Hospital, is using Nuance's Dragon Medical speech recognition technology to speak patient notes into the hospital's Epic EMR (electronic medical records) system.

"I'm not a fast typist," Jorgenson says. "Many doctors over a certain age aren't. If I had to type all the time, I'd be dead." And, at 13 cents to 17 cents per line, dictation transcription services are expensive.

"In primary care, patient notes can be 30 to 40 lines. That adds up," he says. Fairview is saving about $2,000 to $3,000 a month that might have otherwise been spent on transcription, Jorgenson said. It cost about $3,500 to get Dragon up and running.

With transcription services, the turnaround time is 24 to 36 hours before information is available in the EMR. Spoken notes are available immediately.

Jorgensen describes the accuracy of Dragon Medical's speech-to-text documentation as "very good," especially with medical terms and prescriptions. "It rarely gets medical words wrong," he says. "If you see a mistake, it's usually with 'he' or 'she,' and you can correct it when you see it."

Mount Carmel St. Ann's hospital in Columbus, Ohio, has been among the early wave of health care providers using electronic clinical systems bolstered with speech recognition capabilities. About seven years ago, emergency department doctors at Mount Carmel St. Ann's hospital began having access to Dragon's speech recognition software

FIGURE 3.13

Smart use of voice recognition technologies allows hospitals to improve the quality of care while keeping costs under control.

Source: ERproductions Ltd./Getty Images.

not long after an e-health record system from Allscripts was rolled out there.

When the e-health record was first rolled out—without the voice capabilities—Mount Carmel St. Ann's doctors didn't necessarily see the kind of productivity boost they had been hoping for, in large part because they found themselves spending a lot of time typing notes, says Dr. Loren Leidheiser, chairman and director of emergency medicine at Mount Carmel St. Ann's emergency department. But as more Mount Carmel St. Ann's ER doctors began incorporating the speech recognition capabilities into their workflow—whether speaking notes into a lapel microphone or into a computer in the patient room or hallway—the efficiency picked up tremendously, says Leidheiser.

Also, before using the Dragon software, the ER department spent about $500,000 annually in traditional dictation transcription costs for the care associated with the hospital's 60,000 to 70,000 patient visits yearly at the time. That was cut down "to zero," he says. The return on investment on the speech recognition, combined with the use of the e-health record system, was "within a year and a half," notes Leidheiser.

Leidheiser also makes use of time stuck in traffic to dictate notes that are later incorporated into patient records or turned into e-mails or letters. Using a Sony digital recorder, Leidheiser can dictate a letter or note while in his car, then later plug the recorder into his desktop computer, where his spoken words are converted to text.

Speech recognition technology is also helping U.S. military doctors keep more detailed patients notes while cutting the time they spend typing on their computers. By 2011, the U.S. Department of Defense expects to have implemented its integrated, interoperable electronic medical record system—AHLTA—at more than 500 military medical facilities and hospitals worldwide.

The system will be used for the care of more than 9 million active military personnel, retirees, and their dependents. Military doctors using the AHLTA system also have access to Dragon NaturallySpeaking Medical speech recognition technology from Nuance Communications' Dictaphone health care division, allowing doctors to speak "notes" into patient records, as an alternative to typing and dictation.

Over the last year, the adoption of Dragon has doubled, with about 6,000 U.S. military doctors using the software at health care facilities of all military branches, including the Air Force, Army, Navy, and Marine Corps.

The use of Dragon Naturally Speaking voice recognition software with the AHLTA e-health record systems is freeing doctors from several hours of typing their various patient notes each week into the AHLTA, he said. Being able to speak notes into an e-health record at the patient beside—rather than staring at a computer screen typing—also helps improves doctors' bedside manner and allows them to narrate more comprehensive notes, either while the patients are there or right after a visit. That cuts down on mistakes caused by memory lapses and boosts the level of details that are included in a patient record, says Dr. Robert Bell Walker, European Regional Medical Command AHLTA consultant and a family practice physician for the military.

The voice capability "saves a lot of time and adds to the thoroughness of notes from a medical and legal aspect," says Dr. Craig Rohan, a U.S. Air Force pediatrician at Peterson Air Force base in Colorado. The ability to speak notes directly into a patient's electronic chart is particularly helpful in complicated cases, where a patient's medical history is complex, he says. Text pops up on the computer screen immediately after words are spoken into the system, so doctors can check the accuracy, make changes, or add other details.

Also, because spoken words are immediately turned into text, the medical record has "a better flow" to document patient visits. Previously, "the notes that had been created by [entering] structured text into the AHLTA system looks more like a ransom note," says Walker, with information seemingly randomly pasted together.

Doctors can speak into a microphone on their lapels to capture notes in tablet PCs during patient visits, or speak into headsets attached to desktop or wall-mounted computers. The storage requirement of voice notes is "small," especially when compared with other records, such as medical images, says Walker. By adding spoken notes to medical records, e-mails, and letters, "it's easier to tell the story," remarks Leidheiser.

Source: Adapted from Marianne Kolbasuk McGee, "Voice Recognition Tools Make Rounds at Hospitals," *InformationWeek*, September 17, 2009; Marianne Kolbasuk McGee, "Doctors Use Speech Recognition Tools to Enhance Patient E-Health Records," *InformationWeek*, May 19, 2008; and Matt Hamblen, "Doctors' Notes Get Clearer with Speech Recognition Software," *Computerworld*, May 16, 2008.

CASE STUDY QUESTIONS

1. What are some of the benefits afforded to organizations implementing voice recognition technologies in these settings? How can you quantify these benefits to assess the value of the investment? Provide several examples from the case.

2. There is no margin for error when working in a health care setting. How would you go about implementing these technologies in this high-risk environment? What precautions or approaches would you take to minimize risks? Develop some recommendations.

3. In what other areas of medicine would you expect technology to make inroads next? Where do you think it would be most beneficial, and how would it change the way doctors and nurses work today? Provide several examples.

REAL WORLD ACTIVITIES

1. The case talks about electronic medical or health records systems. These are slowly becoming standard in many hospitals and clinics, both private and public. Go online and search for reports of these implementations. What are the main benefits derived from their adoption? What have been the major roadblocks preventing their acceptance? Prepare a report to share your findings.

2. The case above was presented from the perspective of practitioners and hospital administrators. How comfortable would you feel, as a patient, knowing that your health care providers are using these technologies? Would you have any concerns? Break into small groups with your classmates to discuss this issue.

FIGURE 3.14
Some advice about
peripherals for a
business PC.

Peripherals Checklist
● **Monitors.** Bigger is better for computer screens. Consider a high-definition 19-inch or 21-inch flat screen CRT monitor, or LCD flat-panel display. That gives you much more room to display spreadsheets, Web pages, lines of text, open windows, and so on. An increasingly popular setup uses two monitors that allow multiple applications to be used simultaneously.
● **Printers.** Your choice is between laser printers and color inkjet printers. Lasers are better suited for high-volume business use. Moderately priced color inkjets provide high-quality images and are well suited for reproducing photographs; per-page costs are higher than for laser printers.
● **Scanners.** You'll have to decide between a compact, sheet-fed scanner and a flatbed model. Sheet-fed scanners will save desktop space, while bulkier flatbed models provide higher speed and resolution.
● **Hard Disk Drives.** Bigger is better; as with closet space, you can always use the extra capacity. So go for 80 gigabytes at the minimum to 160 gigabytes and more.
● **CD and DVD Drives.** CD and DVD drives are a necessity for software installation and multimedia applications. Common today is a built-in CD-RW/DVD drive that both reads and writes CDs and plays DVDs.
● **Backup Systems.** Essential. Don't compute without them. Removable mag disk drives and even CD-RW and DVD-RW drives are convenient and versatile for backing up your hard drive's contents.

Trackballs, pointing sticks, and touch pads are easier to use than a mouse for portable computer users and are thus built into most notebook computer keyboards.

Touch screens are devices that allow you to use a computer by touching the surface of its video display screen. Some touch screens emit a grid of infrared beams, sound waves, or a slight electric current that is broken when the screen is touched. The computer senses the point in the grid where the break occurs and responds with an appropriate action. For example, you can indicate your selection on a menu display just by touching the screen next to that menu item.

**Pen-Based
Computing**

Handwriting-recognition systems convert script into text quickly and are friendly to shaky hands as well as those of block-printing draftsmen. The pen is more powerful than the keyboard in many vertical markets, as evidenced by the popularity of pen-based devices in the utilities, service, and medical trades.

FIGURE 3.15   Many choices exist for pointing devices including the trackball, mouse, pointing stick, and touch screen.

Source: (left to right) Courtesy of Logitech, Microsoft®, International Business Machines Corporation, and © Don Wright/AP Images.

FIGURE 3.16
Many PDAs accept
pen-based input.

Source: © Comstock/PunchStock.

Pen-based computing technologies are still being used in many handheld computers and personal digital assistants. Despite the popularity of touch-screen technologies, many still prefer the use of a stylus rather than their fingertip. *Tablet* PCs and PDAs contain fast processors and software that recognizes and digitizes handwriting, handprinting, and hand drawing. They have a pressure-sensitive layer, similar to that of a touch screen, under their slate-like liquid crystal display (LCD) screen. Instead of writing on a paper form fastened to a clipboard or using a keyboard device, you can use a pen to make selections, send e-mail, and enter handwritten data directly into a computer. See Figure 3.16.

Various pen-like devices are available. One example is the *digitizer pen* and *graphics tablet.* You can use the digitizer pen as a pointing device or to draw or write on the pressure-sensitive surface of the graphics tablet. Your handwriting or drawing is digitized by the computer, accepted as input, displayed on its video screen, and entered into your application.

Speech Recognition Systems

Speech recognition is gaining popularity in the corporate world among nontypists, people with disabilities, and business travelers, and is most frequently used for dictation, screen navigation, and Web browsing.

Speech recognition may be the future of data entry and certainly promises to be the easiest method for word processing, application navigation, and conversational computing because speech is the easiest, most natural means of human communication. Speech input has now become technologically and economically feasible for a variety of applications. Early speech recognition products used *discrete speech recognition,* for which you had to pause between each spoken word. New *continuous speech recognition* software recognizes continuous, conversationally paced speech. See Figure 3.17.

Speech recognition systems digitize, analyze, and classify your speech and its sound patterns. The software compares your speech patterns to a database of sound patterns in its vocabulary and passes recognized words to your application software. Typically, speech recognition systems require training the computer to recognize your voice and its unique sound patterns to achieve a high degree of accuracy.

FIGURE 3.17
Using speech recognition technology for word processing.

Source: © Tim Pannell/Corbis.

Training such systems involves repeating a variety of words and phrases in a training session, as well as using the system extensively.

Continuous speech recognition software products like Dragon Naturally Speaking and ViaVoice by IBM have up to 300,000-word vocabularies. Training to 95 percent accuracy may take several hours. Longer use, faster processors, and more memory make 99 percent accuracy possible. In addition, Microsoft Office Suite 2007 has built-in speech recognition for dictation and voice commands of a variety of software processes.

Speech recognition devices in work situations allow operators to perform data entry without using their hands to key in data or instructions and to provide faster and more accurate input. For example, manufacturers use speech recognition systems for the inspection, inventory, and quality control of a variety of products; airlines and parcel delivery companies use them for voice-directed sorting of baggage and parcels. Speech recognition can also help you operate your computer's operating systems and software packages through voice input of data and commands. For example, such software can be voice-enabled so you can send e-mail and surf the World Wide Web.

Speaker-independent voice recognition systems, which allow a computer to understand a few words from a voice it has never heard before, are being built into products and used in a growing number of applications. Examples include *voice-messaging computers*, which use speech recognition and voice response software to guide an end user verbally through the steps of a task in many kinds of activities. Typically, they enable computers to respond to verbal and Touch-Tone input over the telephone. Examples of applications include computerized telephone call switching, telemarketing surveys, bank pay-by-phone bill-paying services, stock quotation services, university registration systems, and customer credit and account balance inquiries.

One of the newest examples of this technology is Ford SYNC. SYNC is a factory-installed, in-car communications and entertainment system jointly developed by Ford Motor Company and Microsoft. The system was offered on 12 different Ford, Lincoln, and Mercury vehicles in North America for the 2008 model year and is available on most 2009 Ford offerings.

Ford SYNC allows a driver to bring almost any mobile phone or digital media player into a vehicle and operate it using voice commands, the vehicle's steering wheel, or manual radio controls. The system can even receive text messages and read them aloud using a digitized female voice named "Samantha." SYNC can interpret a hundred or so shorthand messages, such as LOL for "laughing out loud," and it will read swear words; it won't, however, decipher obscene acronyms. Speech recognition is now common in your car, home, and workplace.

Optical Scanning

Few people understand how much scanners can improve a computer system and make your work easier. Their function is to get documents into your computer with a minimum of time and hassle, transforming just about anything on paper—a letter, a logo, or a photograph—into the digital format that your PC can read. Scanners can be a big help in getting loads of paper off your desk and into your PC.

Optical scanning devices read text or graphics and convert them into digital input for your computer. Thus, optical scanning enables the direct entry of data from source documents into a computer system. For example, you can use a compact desktop scanner to scan pages of text and graphics into your computer for desktop publishing and Web publishing applications. You can scan documents of all kinds into your system and organize them into folders as part of a *document management* library system for easy reference or retrieval. See Figure 3.18.

There are many types of optical scanners, but all use photoelectric devices to scan the characters being read. Reflected light patterns of the data are converted into electronic impulses that are then accepted as input to the computer system. Compact desktop scanners have become very popular due to their low cost and ease of use with personal computer systems. However, larger, more expensive *flatbed scanners* are faster and provide higher-resolution color scanning.

Another optical scanning technology is called **optical character recognition** (OCR). The OCR scanners can read the characters and codes on merchandise tags, product labels, credit card receipts, utility bills, insurance premiums, airline tickets,

FIGURE 3.18   A modern document management system can serve as an optical scanner, copier, fax, and printer.

Source: Courtesy of Xerox.

FIGURE 3.19
Using an optical scanning wand to read bar coding of inventory data.

Source: © Jeff Smith/Getty Images.

and other documents. In addition, OCR scanners are used to automatically sort mail, score tests, and process a wide variety of forms in business and government.

Devices such as handheld optical scanning **wands** are frequently used to read *bar codes*, codes that use bars to represent characters. One common example is the Universal Product Code (UPC) bar coding that you see on just about every product sold. For example, the automated checkout scanners found in supermarkets read UPC bar coding. Supermarket scanners emit laser beams that are reflected off a code. The reflected image is converted to electronic impulses that are sent to the in-store computer, where they are matched with pricing information. Pricing information is returned to the terminal, visually displayed, and printed on a receipt for the customer. See Figure 3.19.

| Forget the ATM: Deposit Checks Without Leaving Home | First, we didn't need to visit the bank teller anymore. Then we were able to stick our checks right into the ATM without an envelope. Now we won't have to leave the house to make deposits. |

First, we didn't need to visit the bank teller anymore. Then we were able to stick our checks right into the ATM without an envelope. Now we won't have to leave the house to make deposits.

Sacramento, California–based Schools Financial Credit Union is one of the latest banks to allow customers to scan checks at home and deposit them over the Internet. Golden One Credit Union, also from California, had introduced scanner-based check deposits in July 2009. "Banking's not the way it was five or 10 years ago," said Nathan Schmidt, a vice president at Schools Financial. "With any type of technology, it becomes more convenient to self-service."

Even with the widespread use of direct deposit and online banking, people still write and receive millions of paper checks each year. And for the most part, when we have to deposit a paper check, we still need to go to an ATM to do it.

Businesses have been making deposits over the Internet far longer, ever since the passage in 2004 of the federal Check 21 Act, which made a digital image of a check legally acceptable for payment. Businesses quickly saw the benefits of the new law. Sending checks as digital images eliminated courier costs and paperwork.

The extension of the service to consumers has come much more slowly. Cary Whaley, a director at Washington, D.C.-based Independent Community Bankers of America, says financial institutions have been wary about potential fraud.

"For many banks, it remains a business application," Whaley says. "The next step is the consumer side, but a lot of community banks are a little wary. When you're getting into thousands of consumers, the challenge for banks and credit unions is not only monitoring risk, but monitoring for changes in transactions and transaction amounts."

But some bankers say consumers are increasingly demanding the same convenience given to their business counterparts, and it's simply a matter of time before remote deposits become much more widespread.

When Schools Financial Credit Union decided to take the plunge, it included safeguards to prevent abuse. Customers must use their existing secure online banking log-in, and they can't transmit items more than twice a day.

Users have a time limit to scan and deposit the check online, and checks must meet specific requirements before they are deposited. Post-dated, damaged, or lightly printed checks, for instance, will not scan properly and cannot be deposited.

"So many people prefer to do self-service. They choose to go online—maybe they're parents with small kids, or they might not want to go to an ATM at 3 a.m.," says Golden One's chief executive officer, Teresa Halleck.

"People are already online," she says. "They're comfortable with electronic delivery and they're looking for more."

Source: Adapted from Darrell Smith, "Forget the ATM—Some Banks Allow Check Deposits via Scanner, iPhone," *The Sacramento Bee*, October 26, 2009.

Other Input Technologies

Magnetic stripe technology is a familiar form of data entry that helps computers read credit cards. The coating of the magnetic stripe on the back of such cards can hold about 200 bytes of information. Customer account numbers can be recorded on the magnetic stripe so that it can be read by bank ATMs, credit card authorization terminals, and many other types of magnetic stripe readers.

Smart cards that embed a microprocessor chip and several kilobytes of memory into debit, credit, and other cards are popular in Europe and becoming available in the United States. One example is in the Netherlands, where millions of smart debit cards have been issued by Dutch banks. Smart debit cards enable you to store a cash balance on the card and electronically transfer some of it to others to pay for small items and services. The balance on the card can be replenished in ATMs or other terminals. The smart debit cards used in the Netherlands feature a microprocessor and either 8 or 16 kilobytes of memory, plus the usual magnetic stripe. The smart cards are widely used to make payments in parking meters, vending machines, newsstands, pay telephones, and retail stores.

Digital cameras represent another fast-growing set of input technologies. Digital still cameras and digital video cameras (digital camcorders) enable you to shoot, store, and download still photos or full-motion video with audio into your PC. Then you can use image-editing software to edit and enhance the digitized images and include them in newsletters, reports, multimedia presentations, and Web pages. Today's typical mobile phone includes digital camera capabilities as well.

The computer systems of the banking industry can magnetically read checks and deposit slips using **magnetic ink character recognition** (MICR) technology. Computers can thus sort and post checks to the proper checking accounts. Such processing is possible because the identification numbers of the bank and the customer's account are preprinted on the bottom of the checks with an iron oxide-based ink. The first bank receiving a check after it has been written must encode the amount of the check in magnetic ink on the check's lower righthand corner. The MICR system uses 14 characters (the 10 decimal digits and 4 special symbols) of a standardized design. *Reader-sorter* equipment reads a check by first magnetizing the magnetic ink characters and then sensing the signal induced by each character as it passes a reading head. In this way, data are electronically captured by the bank's computer systems.

Output Technologies

Computers provide information in a variety of forms. Video displays and printed documents have been, and still are, the most common forms of output from computer systems. Yet other natural and attractive output technologies, such as **voice response** systems and multimedia output, are increasingly found along with video displays in business applications.

For example, you have probably experienced the voice and audio output generated by speech and audio microprocessors in a variety of consumer products. Voice messaging software enables PCs and servers in voice mail and messaging systems to interact with you through voice responses. Of course, multimedia output is common on the Web sites of the Internet and corporate intranets.

Video Output

Video displays are the most common type of computer output. Many desktop computers still rely on **video monitors** that use a *cathode ray tube* (CRT) technology similar to the picture tubes used in home television sets. Usually, the clarity of the video display depends on the type of video monitor you use and the graphics circuit board installed in your computer. These can provide a variety of graphics modes of increasing capability. A high-resolution, flicker-free monitor is especially important if you spend a lot of time viewing multimedia on CDs, or on the Web, or the complex graphical displays of many software packages.

The biggest use of **liquid crystal displays** (LCDs) has been to provide a visual display capability for portable microcomputers and PDAs. However, the use of "flat panel" LCD video monitors for desktop PC systems has become common as their cost becomes more affordable. See Figure 3.20. These LCD displays need significantly less electric current and provide a thin, flat display. Advances in technology such as *active matrix* and *dual scan* capabilities have improved the color and clarity of LCD displays. In addition, high-clarity flat panel televisions and monitors using *plasma* display technologies are becoming popular for large-screen (42- to 80-inch) viewing.

Printed Output

Printing information on paper is still the most common form of output after video displays. Thus, most personal computer systems rely on an inkjet or laser printer to produce permanent (hard-copy) output in high-quality printed form. Printed output is still a common form of business communications and is frequently required for legal documentation. Computers can produce printed reports and correspondence, documents such as sales invoices, payroll checks, bank statements, and printed versions of graphic displays. See Figure 3.21.

FIGURE 3.20

The flat-panel LCD video monitor is becoming the de facto standard for a desktop PC system.

Source: Courtesy of Hewlett-Packard.

FIGURE 3.21

Modern laser printers produce high-quality color output with high speed.

Source: Courtesy of Xerox.

Inkjet printers, which spray ink onto a page, have become the most popular, low-cost printers for microcomputer systems. They are quiet, produce several pages per minute of high-quality output, and can print both black-and-white and high-quality color graphics. **Laser printers** use an electrostatic process similar to a photocopying machine to produce many pages per minute of high-quality black-and-white output. More expensive color laser printers and multifunction inkjet and laser models that print, fax, scan, and copy are other popular choices for business offices.

Storage Trade-Offs

Data and information must be stored until needed using a variety of storage methods. For example, many people and organizations still rely on paper documents stored in filing cabinets as a major form of storage media. However, you and other computer users are more likely to depend on the memory circuits and secondary storage devices of computer systems to meet your storage requirements. Progress in very-large-scale integration (VLSI), which packs millions of memory circuit elements on tiny semiconductor memory chips, is responsible for continuing increases in the main-memory capacity of computers. Secondary storage capacities are also escalating into the billions and trillions of characters, due to advances in magnetic and optical media.

There are many types of storage media and devices. Figure 3.22 illustrates the speed, capacity, and cost relationships of several alternative primary and secondary storage media. Note the cost/speed/capacity trade-offs as you move from semiconductor memories to magnetic disks to optical disks and to magnetic tape. High-speed storage media cost

FIGURE 3.22

Storage media cost, speed, and capacity trade-offs. Note how cost increases with faster access speeds but decreases with the increased capacity of storage media.

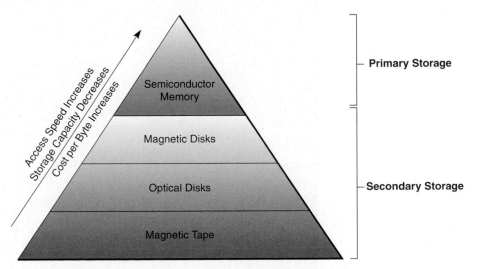

more per byte and provide lower capacities. Large-capacity storage media cost less per byte but are slower. These trade-offs are why we have different kinds of storage media.

However, all storage media, especially memory chips and magnetic disks, continue to increase in speed and capacity and decrease in cost. Developments like automated high-speed cartridge assemblies have given faster access times to magnetic tape, and the speed of optical disk drives continues to increase.

Note in Figure 3.22 that semiconductor memories are used mainly for primary storage, although they are sometimes used as high-speed secondary storage devices. Magnetic disk and tape and optical disk devices, in contrast, are used as secondary storage devices to enlarge the storage capacity of computer systems. Also, because most primary storage circuits use RAM (random-access memory) chips, which lose their contents when electrical power is interrupted, secondary storage devices provide a more permanent type of storage media.

Computer Storage Fundamentals

Data are processed and stored in a computer system through the presence or absence of electronic or magnetic signals in the computer's circuitry or in the media it uses. This character is called "two-state" or binary representation of data because the computer and the media can exhibit only two possible states or conditions, similar to a common light switch: "on" or "off." For example, transistors and other semiconductor circuits are in either a conducting or a nonconducting state. Media such as magnetic disks and tapes indicate these two states by having magnetized spots whose magnetic fields have one of two different directions, or polarities. This binary characteristic of computer circuitry and media is what makes the binary number system the basis for representing data in computers. Thus, for electronic circuits, the conducting ("on") state represents the number 1, whereas the nonconducting ("off") state represents the number 0. For magnetic media, the magnetic field of a magnetized spot in one direction represents a 1, while magnetism in the other direction represents a 0.

The smallest element of data is called a bit, short for *binary digit*, which can have a value of either 0 or 1. The capacity of memory chips is usually expressed in terms of bits. A byte is a basic grouping of bits that the computer operates as a single unit. Typically, it consists of eight bits and represents one character of data in most computer coding schemes. Thus, the capacity of a computer's memory and secondary storage devices is usually expressed in terms of bytes. Computer codes such as ASCII (American Standard Code for Information Interchange) use various arrangements of bits to form bytes that represent the numbers 0 through 9, the letters of the alphabet, and many other characters. See Figure 3.23.

FIGURE 3.23

Examples of the ASCII computer code that computers use to represent numbers and the letters of the alphabet.

Character	ASCII Code	Character	ASCII Code	Character	ASCII Code
0	00110000	A	01000001	N	01001110
1	00110001	B	01000010	O	01001111
2	00110010	C	01000011	P	01010000
3	00110011	D	01000100	Q	01010001
4	00110100	E	01000101	R	01010010
5	00110101	F	01000110	S	01010011
6	00110110	G	01000111	T	01010100
7	00110111	H	01001000	U	01010101
8	00111000	I	01001001	V	01010110
9	00111001	J	01001010	W	01010111
		K	01001011	X	01011000
		L	01001100	Y	01011001
		M	01001101	Z	01011010

FIGURE 3.24

Computers use the binary system to store and compute numbers.

2^7	2^6	2^5	2^4	2^3	2^2	2^1	2^0
128	64	32	16	8	4	2	1
0 or 1	0 or 1	0 or 1	0 or 1	0 or 1	0 or 1	0 or 1	0 or 1

To represent any decimal number using the binary system, each place is simply assigned a value of either 0 or 1. To convert binary to decimal, simply add up the value of each place.

Example:

2^7	2^6	2^5	2^4	2^3	2^2	2^1	2^0	
1	0	0	1	1	0	0	1	
128	0	0	16	8	0	0	1	
128 +	0 +	0 +	16 +	8 +	0 +	0 +	1	= 153

10011001 = 153

Since childhood, we have learned to do our computations using the numbers 0 through 9, the digits of the decimal number system. Although it is fine for us to use 10 digits for our computations, computers do not have this luxury. Every computer processor is made of millions of tiny switches that can be turned off or on. Because these switches have only two states, it makes sense for a computer to perform its computations with a number system that has only two digits: the **binary number system.** These digits (0 and 1) correspond to the off/on positions of the switches in the computer processor. With only these two digits, a computer can perform all the arithmetic that we can with 10 digits. Figure 3.24 illustrates the basic concepts of the binary system.

The binary system is built on an understanding of exponentiation (raising a number to a power). In contrast to the more familiar decimal system, in which each place represents the number 10 raised to a power (ones, tens, hundreds, thousands, and so on), each place in the binary system represents the number 2 raised to successive powers (2^0, 2^1, 2^2, and so on). As shown in Figure 3.24, the binary system can be used to express any integer number by using only 0 and 1.

Storage capacities are frequently measured in kilobytes (KB), megabytes (MB), gigabytes (GB), or terabytes (TB). Although *kilo* means 1,000 in the metric system, the computer industry uses K to represent 1,024 (or 2^{10}) storage positions. For example, a capacity of 10 megabytes is really 10,485,760 storage positions, rather than 10 million positions. However, such differences are frequently disregarded to simplify descriptions of storage capacity. Thus, a megabyte is roughly 1 million bytes of storage, a gigabyte is roughly 1 billion bytes, and a terabyte represents about 1 trillion bytes, while a petabyte is more than 1 quadrillion bytes.

To put these storage capacities in perspective, consider the following: A terabyte is equivalent to about 20 million typed pages, and it has been estimated that the total size of all the books, photographs, video and sound recordings, and maps in the U.S. Library of Congress approximates 3 petabytes (3,000 terabytes).

Direct and Sequential Access

Primary storage media such as semiconductor memory chips are called direct access memory or random-access memory (RAM). Magnetic disk devices are frequently called direct access storage devices (DASDs). In contrast, media such as magnetic tape cartridges are known as sequential access devices.

The terms *direct access* and *random access* describe the same concept. They mean that an element of data or instructions (such as a byte or word) can be directly stored and retrieved by selecting and using any of the locations on the storage media. They also mean that each storage position (1) has a unique address and (2) can be individually accessed in about the same length of time without having to search through other

FIGURE 3.25 Sequential versus direct access storage. Magnetic tape is a typical sequential access medium. Magnetic disks are typical direct access storage devices.

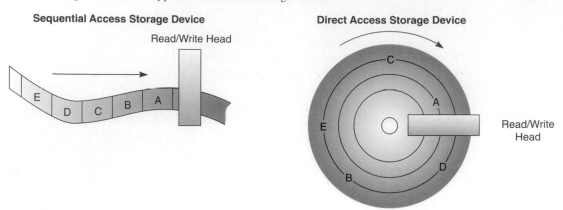

storage positions. For example, each memory cell on a microelectronic semiconductor RAM chip can be individually sensed or changed in the same length of time. Also, any data record stored on a magnetic or optical disk can be accessed directly in about the same period. See Figure 3.25.

Sequential access storage media such as magnetic tape do not have unique storage addresses that can be directly addressed. Instead, data must be stored and retrieved using a sequential or serial process. Data are recorded one after another in a predetermined sequence (e.g., numeric order) on a storage medium. Locating an individual item of data requires searching the recorded data on the tape until the desired item is located.

Semiconductor Memory

Memory is the coalman to the CPU's locomotive: For maximum PC performance, it must keep the processor constantly stoked with instructions. Faster CPUs call for larger and faster memories, both in the cache where data and instructions are stored temporarily and in the main memory.

The primary storage (main memory) of your computer consists of microelectronic semiconductor memory chips. It provides you with the working storage your computer needs to process your applications. Plug-in memory circuit boards containing 256 megabytes or more of memory chips can be added to your PC to increase its memory capacity. Specialized memory can help improve your computer's performance. Examples include external cache memory of 512 kilobytes to help your microprocessor work faster or a video graphics accelerator card with 64 megabytes or more of RAM for faster and clearer video performance. Removable credit-card-size and smaller "flash memory" RAM devices like a jump drive or a memory stick can also provide hundreds of megabytes of erasable direct access storage for PCs, PDAs, or digital cameras.

Some of the major attractions of semiconductor memory are its small size, great speed, and shock and temperature resistance. One major disadvantage of most semiconductor memory is its volatility. Uninterrupted electric power must be supplied, or the contents of memory will be lost. Therefore, either emergency transfer to other devices or standby electrical power (through battery packs or emergency generators) is required if data are to be saved. Another alternative is to permanently "burn in" the contents of semiconductor devices so that they cannot be erased by a loss of power.

Thus, there are two basic types of semiconductor memory: random-access memory (RAM) and read-only memory (ROM).

- **RAM, random-access memory.** These memory chips are the most widely used primary storage medium. Each memory position can be both sensed (read) and changed (written), so it is also called read/write memory. This is a volatile memory.

FIGURE 3.26

A USB flash memory drive.

Source: Courtesy of
Lexar Media.

- **ROM, read-only memory.** Nonvolatile random-access memory chips are used for permanent storage; ROM can be read but not erased or overwritten. Frequently used control instructions in the control unit and programs in primary storage (such as parts of the operating system) can be permanently burned into the storage cells during manufacture, sometimes called *firmware*. Variations include PROM (programmable read-only memory) and EPROM (erasable programmable read-only memory), which can be permanently or temporarily programmed after manufacture.

One of the newest and most innovative forms of storage that uses semiconductor memory is the *flash drive* (sometimes referred to as a *JumpDrive*). Figure 3.26 shows a common flash memory drive.

Flash memory uses a small chip containing thousands of transistors that can be programmed to store data for virtually unlimited periods without power. The small drives can be easily transported in your pocket and are highly durable. Storage capacities currently range as high as 20 gigabytes, but newer flash technologies are making even higher storage capacities a reality. The advent of credit-card-like memory cards and ever-smaller storage technologies puts more data into the user's pocket every day.

Nanochip Inc.: New Memory Process May Overcome Traditional Barriers

A new kind of flash memory technology with potentially greater capacity and durability, lower power requirements, and the same design as flash memory is primed to challenge today's solid-state disk products. Nanochip Inc., based in Fremont, California, said it has made breakthroughs in its array-based memory research that will enable it to deliver working prototypes to potential manufacturing partners by 2009.

Current thinking is that flash memory could hit its limit at around 32–45 nanometers. That describes the smallest possible width of a metal line on the circuit or the amount of space between that line and the next line. The capacity of an integrated circuit is restricted by the ability to print to a smaller and smaller two-dimensional plane, otherwise known as the lithography. That's exactly where Nanochip's technology shines.

"Every two years, you need to buy this new machine that allows you to print something that's smaller and finer," says Stefan Lai of Nanochip. Array-based memory uses a grid of microscopic probes to read and write to a storage material. The storage area isn't defined by the lithography but by the movement of the probes. "If Nanochip can move the probes one-tenth the distance, for example, they can get 100 times the density with no change in the lithography," says Lai. "You don't have to buy all these new machines." IBM has been working on a similar technology for years.

Lai believes that the new memory could herald breakthroughs in mobile devices and biotechnology. "You now need your whole life history stored in your mobile device," he says. "If you want something to store your genome in, it may take a lot of memory, and you'll want to carry it with you." The big question that remains for Nanochip is whether the company can create working prototypes with the cost advantages that array-based technology is supposed to offer over conventional forms of memory.

The challenge for adoption of any new type of memory is that flash itself isn't standing still. "In 2010, it's going to be $1 per gigabyte . . . so hopefully the cost per gigabyte [of probe-based arrays] is going to be low."

Source: Adapted from Dian Schaffhauser, "A Storage Technology That Breaks Moore's Law," *Computerworld*, March 19, 2008.

Magnetic Disks

Multigigabyte magnetic disk drives aren't extravagant, considering that full-motion video files, sound tracks, and photo-quality images can consume colossal amounts of disk space in a blink.

Magnetic disks are the most common form of secondary storage for your computer system. That's because they provide fast access and high storage capacities at a reasonable cost. Magnetic disk drives contain metal disks that are coated on both sides with an iron oxide recording material. Several disks are mounted together on a vertical shaft, which typically rotates the disks at speeds of 3,600 to 7,600 revolutions per minute (rpm). Electromagnetic read/write heads are positioned by access arms between the slightly separated disks to read and write data on concentric, circular tracks. Data are recorded on tracks in the form of tiny magnetized spots to form the binary digits of common computer codes. Thousands of bytes can be recorded on each track, and there are several hundred data tracks on each disk surface, thus providing you with billions of storage positions for your software and data. See Figure 3.27.

Types of Magnetic Disks

There are several types of magnetic disk arrangements, including removable disk cartridges as well as fixed disk units. Removable disk devices are popular because they are transportable and can be used to store backup copies of your data off-line for convenience and security.

- Floppy disks, or magnetic diskettes, consist of polyester film disks covered with an iron oxide compound. A single disk is mounted and rotates freely inside a protective flexible or hard plastic jacket, which has access openings to accommodate the read/write head of a disk drive unit. The 3½-inch floppy disk, with capacities of 1.44 megabytes, was the most widely used version, with a Superdisk technology offering 120 megabytes of storage. Zip drives use a floppy-like technology to provide up to 750 MB of portable disk storage. Today's computers have all but eliminated inclusion of a drive to read floppy disks, but they can be found if necessary.

FIGURE 3.27   Magnetic disk media: a hard magnetic disk drive and a 3½-inch floppy disk.

Source: © Royalty Free/Corbis.

Source: © Stockbyte/PunchStock.

- **Hard disk drives** combine magnetic disks, access arms, and read/write heads into a sealed module. This combination allows higher speeds, greater data recording densities, and closer tolerances within a sealed, more stable environment. Fixed or removable disk cartridge versions are available. Capacities of hard drives range from several hundred megabytes to hundreds of gigabytes of storage.

RAID Storage

RAID computer storage equipment—big, refrigerator-size boxes full of dozens of inter-linked magnetic disk drives that can store the equivalent of 100 million tax returns—hardly gets the blood rushing. But it should. Just as speedy and reliable networking opened the floodgates to cyberspace and e-commerce, ever-more-turbocharged data storage is a key building block of the Internet.

Disk arrays of interconnected microcomputer hard disk drives have replaced large-capacity mainframe disk drives to provide virtually unlimited online storage. Known as **RAID (redundant arrays of independent disks)**, they combine from 6 to more than 100 small hard disk drives and their control microprocessors into a single unit. These RAID units provide large capacities (as high as 1–2 terabytes or more) with high access speeds because data are accessed in parallel over multiple paths from many disks. Also, RAID units provide a *fault-tolerant* capacity, in that their redundant design offers multiple copies of data on several disks. If one disk fails, data can be recovered from backup copies automatically stored on other disks. Storage area networks (SANs) are high-speed *fiber channel* local area networks that can interconnect many RAID units and thus share their combined capacity through network servers with many users.

There are a variety of classifications of RAID, and newer implementations include not only hardware versions, but also software methods. The technical aspects of RAID are beyond the scope of this text and probably beyond the needs of the modern business technologist as well. It is sufficient to note that the storage mechanisms in the modern organization are probably using some type of RAID technology. If you are interested in drilling deeper into this technology and how it works, a wide variety of Internet resources are available.

Magnetic Tape

Tape storage is moving beyond backup. Although disk subsystems provide the fastest response time for mission-critical data, the sheer amount of data that users need to access these days as part of huge enterprise applications, such as data warehouses, requires affordable [magnetic tape] storage.

Magnetic tape is still being used as a secondary storage medium in business applications. The read/write heads of magnetic tape drives record data in the form of magnetized spots on the iron oxide coating of the plastic tape. Magnetic tape devices include tape reels and cartridges in mainframes and midrange systems and small cassettes or cartridges for PCs. Magnetic tape cartridges have replaced tape reels in many applications and can hold more than 200 megabytes.

One growing business application of magnetic tape involves the use of high-speed 36-track magnetic tape cartridges in robotic automated drive assemblies that can directly access hundreds of cartridges. These devices provide lower-cost storage to supplement magnetic disks to meet massive data warehouse and other online business storage requirements. Other major applications for magnetic tape include long-term *archival* storage and backup storage for PCs and other systems.

Optical Disks

Optical disk technology has become a necessity. Most software companies now distribute their elephantine programs on CD-ROMs. Many corporations are now rolling their own CDs to distribute product and corporate information that once filled bookshelves.

FIGURE 3.28

Comparing the capabilities of optical disk drives.

Optical Disk Drive Capabilities
● **CD-ROM** A CD-ROM drive provides a low-cost way to read data files and load software onto your computer, as well as play music CDs.
● **CD-RW** A CD-RW drive allows you to easily create your own custom data CDs for data backup or data transfer purposes. It will also allow you to store and share video files, large data files, digital photos, and other large files with other people that have access to a CD-ROM drive. This drive will also do anything your CD-ROM drive will do. It reads all your existing CD-ROMs, audio CDs, and CDs that you have created with your CD burner.
● **CD-RW/DVD** A CD-RW/DVD combination drive brings all the advantages of CD-RW, CD-ROM, and DVD-ROM to a single drive. With a CD-RW/DVD combo drive, you can read DVD-ROM disks, read CD-ROM disks, and create your own custom CDs.
● **DVD-ROM** A DVD-ROM drive allows you to enjoy the crystal-clear color, picture, and sound clarity of DVD video on your PC. It will also prepare you for future software and large data files that will be released on DVD-ROM. A DVD-ROM drive can also read CD-ROM disks, effectively providing users with full optical read capability in one device.
● **DVD+RW/+R with CD-RW** A DVD+RW/+R with CD-RW drive is a great all-in-one drive, allowing you to burn DVD+RW or DVD+R disks, burn CDs, and read DVDs and CDs. It enables you to create DVDs to back up and archive up to 4.7GB of data files (that's up to 7 times the capacity of a standard 650MB CD) and store up to to 2 hours of MPEG2 digital video.

Source: Adapted from "Learn More—Optical Drives," www.dell.com.

Optical disks, a fast-growing type of storage media, use several major alternative technologies. See Figure 3.28. One version is called **CD-ROM** (compact disk–read-only memory). CD-ROM technology uses 12-centimeter (4.7-inch) compact disks (CDs) similar to those used in stereo music systems. Each disk can store more than 600 megabytes. That's the equivalent of more than 400 1.44-megabyte floppy disks or more than 300,000 double-spaced pages of text. A laser records data by burning permanent microscopic pits in a spiral track on a master disk from which compact disks can be mass produced. Then CD-ROM disk drives use a laser device to read the binary codes formed by those pits.

CD-R (compact disk–recordable) is another popular optical disk technology. CD-R drives or CD *burners* are commonly used to record data permanently on CDs. The major limitation of CD-ROM and CD-R disks is that recorded data cannot be erased. However, **CD-RW** (CD-rewritable) drives record and erase data by using a laser to heat a microscopic point on the disk's surface. In CD-RW versions using magneto-optical technology, a magnetic coil changes the spot's reflective properties from one direction to another, thus recording a binary 1 or 0. A laser device can then read the binary codes on the disk by sensing the direction of reflected light.

DVD technologies have dramatically increased optical disk capacities and capabilities. DVD (digital video disk or digital versatile disk) optical disks can hold from 3.0 to 8.5 gigabytes of multimedia data on each side. The large capacities and high-quality images and sound of DVD technology are expected to replace CD technologies for data storage and promise to accelerate the use of DVD drives for multimedia products that can be used in both computers and home entertainment systems. Thus, **DVD-ROM** disks are increasingly replacing magnetic tape video-cassettes for movies and other multimedia products, while **DVD+RW** disks are being used for backup and archival storage of large data and multimedia files. See Figure 3.29.

FIGURE 3.29
Optical disk storage includes CD and DVD technologies.

Source: Photodisc/Getty Images.

Business Applications

One of the major uses of optical disks in mainframe and midrange systems is in **image processing,** where long-term archival storage of historical files of document images must be maintained. Financial institutions, among others, are using optical scanners to capture digitized document images and store them on optical disks as an alternative to microfilm media.

One of the major business uses of CD-ROM disks for personal computers is to provide a publishing medium for fast access to reference materials in a convenient, compact form. This material includes catalogs, directories, manuals, periodical abstracts, part listings, and statistical databases of business and economic activity. Interactive multimedia applications in business, education, and entertainment are another major use of optical disks. The large storage capacities of CD and DVD disks are a natural choice for computer video games, educational videos, multimedia encyclopedias, and advertising presentations.

Radio Frequency Identification

One of the newest and most rapidly growing storage technologies is radio frequency identification (RFID), a system for tagging and identifying mobile objects such as store merchandise, postal packages, and sometimes even living organisms (like pets). Using a special device called an **RFID reader,** RFID allows objects to be labeled and tracked as they move from place to place.

The RFID technology works using small (sometimes smaller than a grain of sand) pieces of hardware called **RFID chips.** These chips feature an antenna to transmit and receive radio signals. Currently, there are two general types of RFID chips: *passive* and *active*. **Passive RFID** chips do not have a power source and must derive their power from the signal sent from the reader. **Active RFID** chips are self-powered and do not need to be close to the reader to transmit their signal. Any RFID chips may be attached to objects or, in the case of some passive RFID systems, injected into objects. A recent use for RFID chips is the identification of pets such as dogs or cats. By having a tiny RFID chip injected just under their skin, they can be easily identified if they become lost. The RFID chip contains contact information about the owner of the pet. Taking this a step further, the Transportation Security Administration is considering using RFID tags embedded in airline boarding passes to keep track of passengers.

Whenever a reader within range sends appropriate signals to an object, the associated RFID chip responds with the requested information, such as an identification number or product date. The reader, in turn, displays the response data to an operator. Readers may also forward data to a networked central computer system. Such RFID systems generally support storing information on the chips as well as simply reading data.

The RFID systems were created as an alternative to common bar codes. Relative to bar codes, RFID allows objects to be scanned from a greater distance, supports storing of data, and allows more information to be tracked per object.

Recently (as discussed in the next section), RFID has raised some privacy concerns as a result of the invisible nature of the system and its capability to transmit fairly sophisticated messages. As these types of issues are resolved, we can expect to see RFID technology used in just about every way imaginable.

RFID Privacy Issues

How would you like it if, for instance, one day you realized your underwear was reporting on your whereabouts?—California State Senator Debra Bowen, at a 2003 hearing on RFID privacy concerns.

The use of RFID technology has caused considerable controversy and even product boycotts by consumer privacy advocates who refer to RFID tags as *spychips*. The two main privacy concerns regarding RFID are:

- Because the owner of an item will not necessarily be aware of the presence of an RFID tag, and the tag can be read at a distance without the knowledge of the individual, it becomes possible to gather sensitive data about an individual without consent.

- If a customer pays for a tagged item by credit card or in conjunction with a loyalty card, then it would be possible to deduce the identity of the purchaser indirectly by reading the globally unique ID of that item (contained in the RFID tag).

Most concerns revolve around the fact that RFID tags affixed to products remain functional even after the products have been purchased and taken home; thus, they can be used for surveillance and other purposes unrelated to their supply chain inventory functions.

Read range, however, is a function of both the reader and the tag itself. Improvements in technology may increase read ranges for tags. Having readers very close to the tags makes short-range tags readable. Generally, the read range of a tag is limited to the distance from the reader over which the tag can draw enough energy from the reader field to power the tag. Tags may be read at longer ranges by increasing reader power. The limit on read distance then becomes the signal-to-noise ratio of the signal reflected from the tag back to the reader. Researchers at two security conferences have demonstrated that passive UHF RFID tags (not the HF-type used in U.S. passports), normally read at ranges of up to 30 feet, can be read at ranges of 50–69 feet using suitable equipment. Many other types of tag signals can be intercepted from 30–35 feet away under good conditions, and the reader signal can be detected from miles away if there are no obstructions.

The potential for privacy violations with RFID was demonstrated by its use in a pilot program by the Gillette Company, which conducted a "smart shelf" test at a Tesco in Cambridge, England. They automatically photographed shoppers taking RFID-tagged safety razors off the shelf to see if the technology could be used to deter shoplifting. This trial resulted in consumer boycott against Gillette and Tesco. In another incident, uncovered by the *Chicago Sun-Times*, shelves in a Wal-Mart in Broken Arrow, Oklahoma, were equipped with readers to track the Max Factor Lipfinity lipstick containers stacked on them. Webcam images of the shelves were viewed 750 miles away by Procter & Gamble researchers in Cincinnati, Ohio, who could tell when lipsticks were removed from the shelves and observe the shoppers in action.

The controversy surrounding the use of RFID technologies was furthered by the accidental exposure of a proposed Auto-ID consortium public relations campaign that was designed to "neutralize opposition" and get consumers to "resign themselves to the inevitability of it" while merely pretending to address their concerns. During the U.N. World Summit on the Information Society (WSIS) on November 16–18, 2005, Richard Stallman, founder of the free software movement, protested the use of RFID security cards. During the first meeting, it was agreed that future meetings would no longer use RFID cards; upon finding out this assurance was broken, he covered his card in tin foil and would uncover it only at the security stations. This protest caused the security personnel considerable concern. Some did not allow him to leave a conference room in which he had been the main speaker, and then prevented him from entering another conference room, where he was due to speak.

The Food and Drug Administration in the United States has approved the use of RFID chips in humans. Some business establishments have also started to "chip" customers, such as the Baja Beach Nightclub in Barcelona. This has provoked concerns into privacy of individuals, as they can potentially be tracked wherever they go by an identifier unique to them. There are concerns that this could lead to abuse by an authoritarian government or lead to removal of other freedoms.

In July 2006, Reuters reported that Newitz and Westhues, two hackers, showed at a conference in New York City that they could clone the RFID signal from a human-implanted RFID chip, which proved that the chip is not as secure as was previously believed.

All of these examples share a common thread, showing that whatever can be encoded can also be decoded. RFID presents the potential for enormous efficiencies and cost savings. It also presents significant challenges to privacy and security. Until these issues are worked through, much controversy will continue to surround RFID technologies.

RFID: A GPS for Your Data Assets

Vendors are increasingly trying to sell users on the idea that they need to stick RFID tags on IT equipment to keep track of it. Users are interested in this technology because they would much rather automate inventory tracking then go server-to-server with a bar code scanner and clipboard. But the new push for RFID tags in data centers also hints at a larger issue: There may be a significant amount of equipment that can't be located and is, in effect, lost.

Misplaced equipment, particularly "ghost server" systems that may still be drawing power but perform no work and may be difficult to locate, has long been recognized as a problem. Vendors offer estimates, ranging from single to low double digits, on the number of servers either misplaced or working as ghosts. It means that users may be wasting a significant amount of money on electricity, lease, and maintenance fees. At the Afcom data center conference, two vendors released new products with different approaches. Even though the products appear to be relatively inexpensive, some users said they could have trouble justifying the purchase.

Methode Data Solutions Group in Richardson, Texas, uses a passive RFID tag, which is activated by a signal from an RFID reader, for each server in a rack. "Think of it as a GPS for your assets," said Larry Lozon, general manager of the group. The cost is about $200 to $400 per rack.

The approach used by RF Code in Austin is to use an active RFID system that tracks rack locations by sending out a beacon to a reader. Each tag costs about $14. Eric Moore, enterprise data center manager at a regional hospital in Illinois, would like to have RFID tags on his equipment because he needs to know if someone is moving or adding servers in his data center. He just completed an asset inventory but said the inventories have a limited shelf life because of ongoing changes. But justifying the move to RFID is difficult, said Moore. "It's more of 'nice to have' than 'need' right now," he said.

That physical servers fall into disuse is a problem that Dimitri Mundarain, group manager for data center operations at Citrix Systems, discovered when he moved 680 servers to a collocation facility in 2004. He found that about 10 percent of the servers were doing absolutely nothing. Today, Mundarain said, his environment is completely virtualized. The ability to create virtual servers also means creating a logical obsolescence for them as well, which gives him better control of his environment. Previously, his group used to revisit physical servers only when they needed to upgrade the hardware. With this environment, he doesn't see a need for RFID tags.

Security is an issue with Rosner Mehahem, a senior project manager at MSR Engineering and Development Ltd. in Israel. He said some of his government customers don't like the active RFID tags because the information they transmit can be read outside the data center. But Mitch Medford, CEO of RF Code, said the data being transmitted is just a meaningless number that tells nothing about the equipment. The data associated with the number is behind the customer's firewall, he said. "I would love to use RFID, but it's not in the budget," said Scott Nahman, a data center manager with the U.S. federal government. For now, equipment is checked by scanning the bar codes on it. If anything is lost, you "don't go home from work until it's found," he said.

Source: Adapted from Patrick Thibodeau, "Finding Lost IT with RFID," *Computerworld, Inc.*, October 6, 2010.

Predictions for the Future

If Moore's law prevails and technology advancement continues, we can expect to see our lives change in remarkable and unimaginable ways. Although we cannot really predict the future, it is interesting and fun to read the predictions of futurists—people whose job is to think about what the future might bring. Here's one man's perspective on what computing technology might do to change our lives in the decades to come.

Computers Will Enable People to Live Forever

In just 15 years, we'll begin to see the merger of human and computer intelligence that ultimately will enable people to live forever. At least that's the prediction of author and futurist Ray Kurzweil.

Kurzweil suggests that nanobots will roam our bloodstreams, fixing diseased or aging organs, while computers will back up our human memories and rejuvenate our bodies by keeping us young in appearance and health.

The author of the book *The Singularity Is Near*, Kurzweil says that within a quarter of a century, nonbiological intelligence will match the range and subtlety of human intelligence. He predicts that it will then soar past human ability because of the continuing acceleration of information-based technologies, as well as the ability of machines to share their knowledge instantly.

Kurzweil predicts people and computers will intermix with nanobots, blood cell-sized robots, that will be integrated into everything from our clothing to our bodies and brains. People simply need to live long enough—another 15–30 years—to live forever. Think of it as replacing everyone's "human body version 1.0" *with nanotechnology* that will repair or replace ailing or aging tissue, he says. Parts will become easily replaceable.

"A $1,000 worth of computation in the 2020s will be 1,000 times more powerful than the human brain," says Kurzweil, adding that in 25 years we'll have multiplied our computational power by a billion. "Fifteen years from now, it'll be a very different world. We'll have cured cancer and heart disease, or at least rendered them to manageable chronic conditions that aren't life threatening. We'll get to the point where we can stop the aging process and stave off death."

Actually, we'll hit a point where human intelligence simply can't keep up with, or even follow, the progress that computers will make, according to Kurzweil. He expects that nonbiological intelligence will have access to its own design plans and be able to improve itself rapidly. Computer, or nonbiological, intelligence created in the year 2045 will be one billion times more powerful than all human intelligence today.

"Supercomputing is behind the progress in all of these areas," says Kurzweil, adding that a prerequisite for nonbiological intelligence is to reverse-engineer biology and the human brain. That will give scientists a "toolkit of techniques" to apply when developing intelligent computers. In a written report, he said, "We won't experience 100 years of technological advance in the 21st century; we will witness on the order of 20,000 years of progress, or about 1,000 times greater than what was achieved in the 20th century."

According to Kurzweil, here's what we can expect in the not-so-distant future:

- Doctors will be doing a backup of our memories by the late 2030s.
- By the late 2020s, doctors will be sending intelligent bots, or nanobots, into our bloodstreams to keep us healthy, and into our brains to keep us young.

- In 15 years, human longevity will be greatly extended. By the 2020s, we'll be adding a year of longevity or more for every year that passes.

- In the same time frame, we'll routinely be in virtual reality environments. Instead of making a cell call, we could "meet" someone in a virtual world and take a walk on a virtual beach and chat. Business meetings and conference calls will be held in calming or inspiring virtual locations.

- When you're walking down the street and see someone you've met before, background information about that person will pop up on your glasses or in the periphery of your vision.

- Instead of spending hours in front of a desktop machine, computers will be more ingrained in our environment. For instance, computer monitors could be replaced by projections onto our retinas or on a virtual screen hovering in the air.

- Scientists will be able to rejuvenate all of someone's body tissues and organs by transforming their skin cells into youthful versions of other cell types.

- Need a little boost? Kurzweil says scientists will be able to regrow our own cells, tissues, and even whole organs, and then introduce them into our bodies, all without surgery. As part of what he calls the "emerging field of rejuvenation medicine," new tissue and organs will be built out of cells that have been made younger.

- Got heart trouble? No problem, says Kurzweil. "We'll be able to create new heart cells from your skin cells and introduce them into your system through the bloodstream. Over time, your heart cells get replaced with these new cells, and the result is a rejuvenated, young heart with your own DNA."

- One trick we'll have to master is staying ahead of the game. Kurzweil warns that terrorists could obviously use this same technology against us. For example, they could build and spread a bioengineered biological virus that's highly powerful and stealthy.

According to Kurzweil, we're not that far away from solving a medical problem that has plagued scientists and doctors for quite some time now: the common cold. He notes that though nanotechnology could go into our bloodstreams and knock it out, before we even get to that stage, biotechnology should be able to cure the cold in just 10 years.

Source: Adapted from Sharon Gaudin, "Kurzweil: Computers Will Enable People to Live Forever," *InformationWeek*, November 21, 2006.

Summary

- **Computer Systems.** Major types of computer systems are summarized in Figure 3.3. Microcomputers are used as personal computers, network computers, personal digital assistants, technical workstations, and information appliances. Midrange systems are increasingly used as powerful network servers and for many multiuser business data processing and scientific applications. Mainframe computers are larger and more powerful than most midsize systems. They are usually faster, have more memory capacity, and can support more network users and peripheral devices. They are designed to handle the information processing needs of large organizations with high volumes of transaction processing or with complex computational problems. Supercomputers are a special category of extremely powerful mainframe computer systems designed for massive computational assignments.

- **The Computer Systems Concept.** A computer is a system of information processing components that perform input, processing, output, storage, and control functions. Its hardware components include input and output devices, a central processing unit (CPU), and primary and secondary storage devices. The major functions and hardware in a computer system are summarized in Figure 3.10.

- **Peripheral Devices.** Refer to Figures 3.14 and 3.22 to review the capabilities of peripheral devices for input, output, and storage discussed in this chapter.

Key Terms and Concepts

These are the key terms and concepts of this chapter. The page number of their first explanation is given in parentheses.

1. Binary representation (142)
2. Central processing unit (127)
3. Computer system (126)
4. Computer terminal (119)
5. Cycles per second (128)
6. Direct access (143)
7. Graphical user interface (131)
8. Information appliance (120)
9. Magnetic disks (146)
   a. Floppy disk (146)
   b. Hard disk (147)
   c. RAID (redundant array of independent disks) (147)
10. Magnetic stripe (139)
11. Magnetic tape (147)
12. Mainframe system (123)
13. Microcomputer (117)
14. Midrange system (121)
15. Minicomputer (122)

16. MIPS (million instructions per second) (128)
17. Moore's law (128)
18. Network computer (120)
19. Network server (117)
20. Network terminal (119)
21. Off-line (131)
22. Online (131)
23. Optical disks (148)
24. Optical scanning (137)
25. Peripherals (131)
26. Pointing devices (131)
27. Primary storage unit (127)
28. Processing speed (128)
    a. Millisecond (128)
    b. Microsecond (128)
    c. Nanosecond (128)
    d. Picosecond (128)

29. RFID (radio frequency identification) (149)
30. Secondary storage (127)
31. Semiconductor memory (144)
    a. RAM (random-access memory) (144)
    b. ROM (read-only memory) (144)
32. Sequential access (143)
33. Speech recognition (135)
34. Storage capacity (143)
    a. Bit (142)
    b. Byte (142)
    c. Kilobyte (143)
    d. Megabyte (143)
    e. Gigabyte (143)
    f. Terabyte (143)
    g. Petabyte (143)
35. Supercomputer (124)
36. Volatility (144)
37. Workstation computer (117)

Review Quiz

Match one of the previous key terms and concepts with one of the following brief examples or definitions. Try to find the best fit for answers that seem to fit more than one term or concept. Defend your choices.

_____ 1. A computer is a combination of components that perform input, processing, output, storage, and control functions.

_____ 2. The main processing component of a computer system.

_____ 3. A measure of computer speed in terms of processor cycles.

_____ 4. Devices for consumers to access the Internet.

_____ 5. The memory of a computer.

_____ 6. Magnetic disks and tape and optical disks perform this function.

_____ 7. Input/output and secondary storage devices for a computer system.

_____ 8. Connected to and controlled by a CPU.

_____ 9. Separate from and not controlled by a CPU.

_____ 10. Results from the presence or absence or change in direction of electric current, magnetic fields, or light rays in computer circuits and media.

_____ 11. A common computer interface using a desktop metaphor and icons.

_____ 12. Can be a desktop/laptop or handheld computer.

_____ 13. A computer category between microcomputers and mainframes.

_____ 14. A small, portable magnetic disk encased in a thin plastic shell.

_____ 15. A large-capacity disk typically found in computer systems.

_____ 16. Low-cost microcomputers for use with the Internet and corporate intranets.

_____ 17. A redundant array of inexpensive hard drives.

_____ 18. A terminal that depends on network servers for its software and processing power.

_____ 19. A computer that manages network communications and resources.

_____ 20. The most powerful type of computer.

_____ 21. A magnetic tape technology for credit cards.

_____ 22. One-billionth of a second.

_____ 23. Roughly 1 billion characters of storage.

_____ 24. Includes electronic mice, trackballs, pointing sticks, and touch pads.

_____ 25. Early midrange systems used for processing-intensive applications such as scientific research and engineering analysis.

_____ 26. The largest of the three main types of computers.

_____ 27. Processor power measured in terms of number of instructions processed.

_____ 28. Prediction that computer power will double approximately every 18 to 24 months.

_____ 29. Promises to be the easiest, most natural way to communicate with computers.

_____ 30. Capturing data by processing light reflected from images.

_____ 31. The speed of a computer.

_____ 32. One one-thousandth of a second.

_____ 33. 1,024 bytes.

_____ 34. A device with a keyboard and a video display networked to a computer is a typical example.

_____ 35. The amount of data a storage device can hold.

_____ 36. A personal computer used as a technical workstation.

_____ 37. The smallest unit of data storage.

_____ 38. One trillion bytes.

_____ 39. You cannot erase the contents of these storage circuits.

_____ 40. The memory of most computers consists of these storage circuits.

_____ 41. The property that determines whether data are lost or retained when power fails.

_____ 42. Each position of storage can be accessed in approximately the same time.

_____ 43. Each position of storage can be accessed according to a predetermined order.

_____ 44. Microelectronic storage circuits on silicon chips.

_____ 45. Uses magnetic spots on metal or plastic disks.

_____ 46. Uses magnetic spots on plastic tape.

_____ 47. Uses a laser to read microscopic points on plastic disks.

_____ 48. A millionth of a second.

_____ 49. A trillionth of a second.

_____ 50. A grouping of eight bits that represents one alphabetic or special character.

_____ 51. A short-range wireless technology most commonly used to tag, track, and identify objects.

_____ 52. Around a million bytes; more precisely, 2 to the 20th power.

_____ 53. A unit of information or computer storage equal to one quadrillion bytes, or 1,024 terabytes.

Discussion Questions

1. What trends are occurring in the development and use of the major types of computer systems?

2. Will the convergence of PDAs, subnotebook PCs, and cell phones produce an information appliance that will make all of those categories obsolete? Why or why not?

3. Refer to the Real World Case on nanotechnologies in the chapter. What advice would you provide to a growing company to take advantage of, or prepare for, the issues discussed in the case?

4. Do you think that information appliances like PDAs will replace personal computers (PCs) in business applications? Explain.

5. Are networks of PCs and servers making mainframe computers obsolete? Explain.

6. Refer to the Real World Case on speech recognition in health care in the chapter. Although these and other technologies are becoming more prevalent in health care, doctors have traditionally been reluctant to adopt them. Why do you think this is the case? How would these technologies change the way doctors perform their job?

7. What are several trends that are occurring in computer peripheral devices? How do these trends affect business uses of computers?

8. What are several important computer hardware developments that you expect to happen in the next 10 years? How will these affect the business use of computers?

9. What processor, memory, magnetic disk storage, and video display capabilities would you require for a personal computer that you would use for business purposes? Explain your choices.

10. What other peripheral devices and capabilities would you want to have for your business PC? Explain your choices.

Analysis Exercises

1. Hardware Costs
Purchasing Computer Systems for Your Workgroup
You have been asked to get pricing information for a potential purchase of PCs for the members of your workgroup. Go to the Internet to get prices for these units from Dell and Hewlett-Packard. Look for a high-end office desktop model.

The table below shows the specifications for the basic system you have been asked to price and potential upgrades to each feature. You will want to get a price for the basic system described below and a separate price for each of the upgrades shown.

Component	Basic Unit	Upgrade
CPU (gigahertz)	2.8	3.4
Hard drive (gigabytes)	160	500
RAM (gigabytes)	1	2
Removable media	16× DVD+R/W	48× DVD+R/W
Monitor	17-inch flat screen	19-inch flat screen

Select the standard software licenses; your IT department will install the necessary software for your workgroup. Take a two-year warranty and servicing coverage offered by each supplier. If a two-year warranty is not available, simply note any differences in the coverage with the closest match.

a. Prepare a spreadsheet summarizing this pricing information and showing the cost from each supplier of the following options: (1) units with the basic configuration, (2) the incremental cost of each upgrade separately, and (3) the cost of a fully upgraded unit. If you cannot find features that exactly match the requirements, then use the next higher standard for comparison and make a note of the difference.

b. Prepare a set of PowerPoint slides summarizing your results. Include a discussion of the warranty and servicing contract options offered by each supplier.

2. Price and Performance Trends for Computer Hardware
Hardware Analysis
The table below details price and capacity figures for common components of personal computers. Typical prices for microprocessors, random-access memory (RAM), and hard disk storage are displayed.

The performance of typical components has increased substantially over time, so the speed (for the microprocessor) or the capacity (for the storage devices)

is also listed for comparison purposes. Although not all improvements in these components are reflected in these capacity measures, it is interesting to examine trends in these measurable characteristics.

a. Create a spreadsheet based on the figures above and include a new row for each component, showing the price per unit of capacity (cost per megahertz of speed for microprocessors and cost per megabyte of storage for RAM and hard disk devices).

b. Create a set of graphs highlighting your results and illustrating trends in price per unit of performance (speed) or capacity.

c. Write a short paper discussing the trends you found. How long do you expect these trends to continue? Why?

d. Prepare a summary presentation outlining the points from your paper (above). Be sure to *link* your Excel chart into the PowerPoint presentation so that it automatically updates when any data change in the spreadsheet.

3. Can Computers Think Like People?
The Turing Test
The Turing test is a hypothetical test to determine whether a computer system has reached the level of artificial intelligence. If the computer can fool a person into thinking it is another person, then it has artificial intelligence. Except in very narrow areas, no computer has passed the Turing test.

Free e-mail account providers such as Hotmail or Yahoo take advantage of this fact. They need to distinguish between new account registrations generated by a person and registrations generated by spammers' software. Why? Spammers burn through thousands of e-mail accounts to send millions of e-mails. To help them, spammers need automated tools to generate these accounts. Hotmail fights this practice by requiring registrants to enter correctly an alphanumeric code hidden within an image. Spammers' programs have trouble correctly reading the code, but most humans do not. With this reverse Turing test, also called a CAPTCHA, Hotmail can distinguish between a person and a program and allow only humans to register. As a result, spammers must look elsewhere for free accounts.

a. Aside from those mentioned above, in what applications might businesses find it useful to distinguish between a human and a computer?

	1991	1993	1995	1997	1999	2001	2003	2005
Processor: Speed, MHz	25	33	100	125	350	1000	3,000	3,800
Cost	$180	$125	$275	$250	$300	$251	$395	$549
RAM chip: MB per chip	1	4	4	16	64	256	512	2,000
Cost	$55	$140	$120	$97	$125	$90	$59	$149
Hard drive: GB per drive	0.105	0.250	0.540	2.0	8.0	40.0	160.0	320
Cost	$480	$375	$220	$250	$220	$138	$114	$115

b. Describe a Turing test that a visually impaired person, but not a computer, might pass.

c. Search the Internet for the term CAPTCHA and describe its strengths and weaknesses.

3. **Radio Frequency Identification**
Input Device or Invasion of Privacy?
Punch cards, keyboards, bar code scanners—the trend is clear. Input devices have continued to promote faster and more accurate data entry. Key to this advance is capturing data at their source, and no tool does this better than radio frequency identification (RFID) systems. An RFID transmitter sends out a coded radio signal. An RFID tag changes and reflects this signal back to an antenna. The RFID system can read the reflection's unique pattern and record it in a database. Depending on the system, this pattern may be associated with a product line, shipping palette, or even a person. Although an RFID system's range is limited to a few dozen feet, this approach enables remarkable inventory tracking that doesn't rely on a human to keyboard interaction or scan. Except for the presence of a 1-inch-square (5-cm-square) RFID tag, humans may have no idea an RFID system is in operation.

Indeed, that may be part of the problem. Consumers have expressed concern that RFID chips attached to products they purchase may be used to track them. Others fear their government may require embedded RFID chips as a form of personal identification and tracking. What started as a new and improved input device has devolved into a matter of public policy.

a. How would you feel if your university used RFID tags embedded in student IDs to replace the magnetic swipe strip? On a campus, RFID tags might be used to control building access, manage computer access, or even automatically track class attendance.

b. Enter "RFID" into an Internet search engine and summarize the search results. Of the top 20 results, how many were positive, negative, or neutral?

c. Enter "RFID" and "privacy" into an Internet search engine, select a page expressing privacy concerns, and summarize them in a brief essay. Do you find these concerns compelling?

REAL WORLD CASE 3

IBM, Wachovia, and PayPal: Grid Computing Makes It Easier and Cheaper

IBM researchers and a team of doctors are building a database of digital images they hope will enable oncologists to diagnose and treat cancer patients faster and with more success. Researchers at the Cancer Institute of New Jersey have digitized CAT scans, MRIs, and other images using a high-performance system and computational time on the World Community Grid, also known as the world's largest public computing grid.

"Digitizing images should enable doctors to diagnose cancers earlier and detect their growth or shrinkage more accurately during treatment," says Robin Willner, vice president of the global community initiatives at IBM. "Right now, the doctor is basically eyeballing it when he's analyzing tissues and biopsies. They're trying to figure out what type of cancer it is and if there's been progress during treatment. If you digitize the image, you're able to compare numbers because you've turned an image into bits and bytes. Now it's a much more accurate comparison."

Researchers have been using the grid to convert hundreds of thousands of images of cancerous tissues and cells into digital images. Once the images are digitized, the grid can check the accuracy of the digital information to ensure that the bits and bytes are translating into real diagnoses. The World Community Grid acts as a virtual supercomputer that is based on thousands of volunteers donating their unused computer time. "If we can improve treatment and diagnosis for cancer, that's great for everybody," said Willner. "There couldn't be a better use for the grid."

The next phase of the project is to build a database that will hold hundreds of thousands, if not millions, of these images. A $2.5 million grant from the National Institutes of Health (NIH) will enable the Cancer Institute of New Jersey, Rutgers University, and cancer centers around the country to pool their digital images in the database. Willner said the database will enable doctors to compare patients' new images to ones already in the database to help them diagnose the cancer and figure out the best way to treat it. Doctors should be able to use the database to personalize treatments for cancer patients based on how other patients with similar protein expression signatures and cancers have reacted to various treatments.

"The overarching goal of the new NIH grant is to expand the library to include signatures for a wider range of disorders and make it, along with the decision-support technology, available to the research and clinical communities as grid-enabled deployable software," said David J. Foran, a director of the Cancer Institute of New Jersey. "We hope to deploy these technologies to other cancer research centers around the nation."

This isn't IBM's first foray into the medical arena by any means. IBM has also teamed up with the Mayo Clinic to develop a research facility to advance medical imaging. Researchers from both the Mayo Clinic and IBM are working at the new Medical Imaging Informatics Innovation Center in Rochester, Minnesota. Bradley Erickson, chairman of radiology at the Mayo Clinic, said a joint team is already working to find ways to use the Cell chip, mostly known for running inside the PlayStation 3 video-game console, in a medical imaging system. Erickson said that the technology could either reduce work that now takes minutes to a matter of seconds, or work that now takes hours to only minutes.

Grid computing, however, is not limited to nonprofit institutions. Financial services firm Wachovia Corp. has freed some of its Java-based applications from dedicated servers and is allowing these transaction applications to draw computing power from a 10,000-CPU resource pool on servers spread across cities in the United States and in London. Wachovia is tapping into computing power that's available on other systems to perform work. That capability allows companies to avoid dedicated hardware costs and make better use of underutilized hardware.

Tony Bishop, a Wachovia senior vice president and director of product management, said that to use dedicated systems as an alternative would be "three times the cost in terms of capital and people to support it otherwise." Wachovia has eight applications running on its grid that are used in internal transactions, such as order management. The servers are in New York, Philadelphia, London, and at the company's corporate headquarters in Charlotte, North Carolina. Jamie Bernardin, chief technology officer at DataSynapse, the company that developed the technology, said that to improve transaction speeds, the transaction application running on it can grow and contract as needed.

Because the system can provide resources as needed for the applications, Bishop said performance has improved on some transactions fivefold. "This ability to speed processing means decisions and services can be made and delivered more rapidly. As things get more and more automated and more and more real time it will be IT in this business that differentiates," says Bishop.

A Linux grid is the power behind the payment system at PayPal, and it has converted a mainframe believer. Scott Thompson, the former executive VP of technology solutions at Inovant, ran the Visa subsidiary responsible for executing Visa credit card transactions worldwide. The VisaNet system was strictly based on IBM mainframes.

In February 2005, Thompson became chief technology officer at the eBay payments company, PayPal, where he confronted a young Internet organization building its entire transaction processing infrastructure on open-source Linux and low-cost servers. Hmmmm, he thought at the time. "I came from Visa, where I had responsibility for VisaNet. It was a fabulous processing system, very big and very global. I was intrigued by PayPal. How would you use Linux for processing payments and never be wrong, never lose messages, never fall behind the pace of transactions?" he wondered.

He now supervises the PayPal electronic payment processing system, which is smaller than VisaNet in volume and total dollar value of transactions, but it's growing fast. It is currently processing $1,571 worth of transactions per second in 17 different currencies. In 2006, the online payments firm, which started out over a bakery in Palo Alto, processed a total of $37.6 billion in transactions. It's headed toward $50 billion very soon.

Now located in San Jose, PayPal grants its consumer members options in payment methods: credit cards, debit cards, or directly from a bank account. It has 165 million account holders worldwide, and it has recently added such businesses as Northwest Airlines, Southwest Airlines, U.S. Airways, and Overstock.com, which now permit PayPal payments on their Web sites.

Thompson supervises a payment system that operates on about 4,000 servers running Red Hat Linux in the same manner that eBay and Google conduct their business on top of a grid of Linux servers. "I have been pleasantly surprised at how much we've been able to do with this approach. It operates like a mainframe," he says.

As PayPal grows, it's much easier to grow the grid with Intel-based servers than it would be to upgrade a mainframe, according to Thompson. "The cost to increase capacity a planned 15 or 20 percent in a mainframe environment is enormous. It could be in the tens of millions to do a step increase. In PayPal's world, we add hundreds of servers in the course of a couple of nights and the cost is in the thousands, not millions."

PayPal takes Red Hat Enterprise Linux and strips out all features unnecessary to its business, and then adds proprietary extensions around security. Another virtue of the grid is that PayPal's 800 engineers can all get a copy of that customized system on their development desktops, run tests on their raw software as they work, and develop to PayPal's needs faster because they're working in the target environment. That's harder to do when the core of the data center consists of large boxes or mainframes. It's not cheap in either case to install duplicates for developers, says Thompson.

Source: Adapted from Sharon Gaudin, "IBM Uses Grid to Advance Cancer Diagnosis and Treatment," *Computerworld*, January 28, 2008; Patrick Thibodeau, "Wachovia Uses Grid Technology to Speed Up Transaction Apps," *Computerworld*, May 15, 2006; and Charles Babcock, "PayPal Says Linux Grid Can Replace Mainframes," *InformationWeek*, November 28, 2007.

CASE STUDY QUESTIONS

1. Applications for grid computing in this case include medical diagnosis and financial transaction processing. What other areas do you think would be well suited to the use of grid computing and why? Provide several examples from organizations other than those included in the case.

2. The joint effort by IBM and the Cancer Institute of New Jersey works by digitalizing medical diagnoses on the World Community Grid (WCG). What are the advantages and disadvantages of relying on a volunteer-based network such as this? Provide examples of both. Visit the Web site of the WCG to inform your answer.

3. IBM, Wachovia, and PayPal are arguably large organizations. However, several vendors have started offering computing power for rent to smaller companies, using the principles underlying grid computing. How could small and medium companies benefit from these technologies? Search the Internet for these offerings to help you research your answer.

REAL WORLD ACTIVITIES

1. Grid computing technology is becoming increasingly popular and has recently received support from giants such as IBM, Sun, and Oracle. Visit their Web sites (www.ibm.com, www.sun.com, and www.oracle.com) and review their current offerings in this regard. How do their products compare to each other? Prepare a presentation to share your findings with the class.

2. One of the main benefits of grid computing arises from the possibility of replacing expensive hardware, such as mainframes or supercomputers, with commodity-priced servers and even personal computers. What about the cost of administering so many different servers and the power consumption associated with them? Go online to search for information that would allow you to compare grid computing to more traditional, mainframe-based alternatives. Write a report to present your findings.

REAL WORLD

CASE 4 Apple, Microsoft, IBM, and Others: The Touch Screen Comes of Age

The WIMP human–computer interface may have an uninspiring name, but Windows, Icons, Menus, and Pointing (WIMP) devices have dominated computing for some 15 years. The keyboard, mouse, and display screen have served users extraordinarily well.

Now the hegemony of WIMP may be coming to an end, say developers of technologies based on human touch and gesture. For evidence, look no further than Apple's iPhone. From a human-interface point of view, the combined display and input capabilities of the iPhone's screen, which can be manipulated by multiple fingers in a variety of intuitive touches and gestures, is nothing short of revolutionary.

The iPhone isn't the only commercial device to take the human–computer interface to a new level. The Microsoft Surface computer puts input and output devices in a large tabletop device that can accommodate touches and gestures and even recognize physical objects laid on it. In addition, the DiamondTouch Table from Mitsubishi is a touch- and gesture-activated display that supports small-group collaboration. It can even tell who is touching it.

These devices point the way toward an upcoming era of more natural and intuitive interaction between human and machine. Robert Jacob, a computer science professor at Tufts University, says touch is just one component of a booming field of research on post-WIMP interfaces, a broad coalition of technologies he calls reality-based interaction.

Those technologies include virtual reality, context-aware computing, perceptual and affective computing, and tangible interaction, in which physical objects are recognized directly by a computer.

"What's similar about all these interfaces is that they are more like the real world, Jacob says.

For example, the iPhone "uses gestures you know how to do right away, such as touching two fingers to an image or application, then pulling them apart to zoom in or pinching them together to zoom out." These actions have also found their way into the iPod Touch and the track pad of the new MacBook Air. "Just think of the brain cells you don't have to devote to remembering the syntax of the user interface! You can devote those brain cells to the job you are trying to do." In particular, he says, the ability of the iPhone to handle multiple touches at once is a huge leap past the single-touch technology that dominates in traditional touch applications such as ATMs.

Although they have not gotten much traction in the marketplace yet, advanced touch technologies from IBM may point a way to the future. In its Everywhere Displays Project, IBM mounts projectors in one or more parts of an ordinary room and projects images of touch screens onto ordinary surfaces, such as tables, walls, or the floor. Video cameras capture images of users touching various parts of the surfaces and send that information for interpretation by a computer. The touch screens contain no electronics—

indeed, no computer parts at all—so they can be easily moved and reconfigured.

A variation on that concept has been deployed by a wine store in Germany, says Claudio Pinhanez at IBM Research. The METRO Future Store in Rheinberg has a kiosk that enables customers to get information about the wines the store stocks. "But the store's inventory was so vast customers often had trouble finding the particular wine they wanted on the shelf. They often ended up buying a low-margin wine in a nearby bin of sales specials, " Pinhanez says. Now the kiosk contains a "show me" button that, when pressed, shines a spotlight on the floor in front of the chosen item.

IBM is also working on a prototype system for grocery stores that might, for example, illuminate a circle on the floor that asks, Do you want to take the first steps toward more fiber in your diet? If the customer touches "yes" with his foot, the system projects footsteps to the appropriate products, such as high-fiber cereal. "Then you could make the cereal box itself interactive," says Pinhanez. "You touch it, and the system would project information about that box on a panel above the shelf." Asked if interactive cereal boxes might be a solution in search of a problem, Pinhanez says, "The point is, with projection and camera technology you can transform any everyday object into a touch screen." He says alternatives that are often discussed (e.g., a store system that talks to customers through their handheld devices) are hard to implement because of a lack of standards for the technology.

Microsoft is working with several commercial partners, including Starwood Hotels & Resorts, which owns the prestigious Sheraton, W, Westin, and Méridien brands, among others, to introduce Surface. It will initially target leisure, entertainment, and retail applications, says Mark Bolger, director of marketing for Surface Computing. For example, he says, one could imagine a hotel guest using a virtual concierge in a Surface computer in the lobby to manipulate maps, photos, restaurant menus, and theater information.

Some researchers say that a logical extension of touch technology is gesture recognition, by which a system recognizes hand or finger movements across a screen or close to it without requiring an actual touch. "Our technology is halfway there," IBM's Pinhanez says, "because we recognize the gesture of touching rather than the occlusion of a particular area. You can go over buttons without triggering them."

Patrick Baudisch at Microsoft Research says the Microsoft prototypes can already act on finger gestures, with the system recognizing finger motions, as well as positions, and understanding the meaning of different numbers of fingers. For example, the motion of one finger is seen as equivalent to a mouse movement, a finger touch is interpreted as a click, and two fingers touching and moving is seen as a scroll command.

Touch technology in its many variations is an idea whose time has come. "It's been around a long time, but traditionally in niche markets. The technology was more expensive, and there were ergonomic problems," he says. "But it's all kind of coming together right now." The rise of mobile devices is a big catalyst, because the devices are getting smaller and their screens are getting bigger. When a screen covers the entire device, there is no room for conventional buttons, which makes it necessary to have other types of interaction (e.g., voice).

Of course, researchers and inventors have envisioned even larger touch displays, including whole interactive walls. A quick YouTube search for "multitouch wall" shows that a number of these fascinating devices have reached the prototype stage, causing multitudes at technology conferences to be entranced. Experts predict, however, that this is just the beginning.

Pradeep Khosla, professor of electrical and computer engineering and robotics at Carnegie Mellon University in Pittsburgh, says touch technology will proliferate, but not by itself. "When we talk face to face, I make eye gestures, face gestures, hand gestures, and somehow you interpret them all to understand what I am saying. I think that's where we are headed," he says. "There is room for all these things, and multimodal gestures will be the future."

Bill Buxton, a researcher at Microsoft, also anticipates a fusion of different interaction technologies. "Touch now may be where the mouse was in about 1983," Buxton says. "People now understand there is something interesting here that's different. But I don't think we yet know what that difference could lead to. Until just one or two years ago there was a real separation between input devices and output devices. A display was a display and a mouse was a mouse."

"There's been this notion that less is more—you try to get less and less stuff to reduce complexity," he says. "But there's this other view that more is actually less—more of the right stuff in the right place, and complexity disappears." In the office of the future, Buxton predicts, desktop computers might be much the same as they are today. "But you can just throw stuff, with the mouse or a gesture, up onto a wall or whiteboard and then work with it with your hands by touch and gesture standing up. Then you'll just pull things into your mobile and have this surface in your hand. The mobile, the wall, the desktop—they are all suitable for different purposes."

Will that be the end of the WIMP interface? Tufts University's Jacob advises users not to discard their keyboards and mice anytime soon. "They really are extremely good," he says. "WIMP almost completely dislodged the command-line interface. The WIMP interface was such a good invention that people just kind of stopped there, but I can't believe it's the end of the road forever."

Buxton agrees. "WIMP is the standard interface going back 20-plus years, and all the applications have been built around that," he says. "The challenge is, without throwing the baby out with the bath, how do we reap the benefits of these new approaches while preserving the best parts of the things that exist?"

Source: Adapted from Gary Anthes, "Give Your Computer the Finger: Touch-Screen Tech Comes of Age," *Computerworld*, February 1, 2008.

CASE STUDY QUESTIONS

1. What benefits may Starwood Hotels derive from the introduction of touch-screen technology as noted in the case? What possible disruptions may occur as a result. Provide several examples of each.

2. Bill Buxton of Microsoft stated that "[t]ouch now may be where the mouse was in about 1983." What do you make of his comments, and what do you think it would take for touch technology to displace the WIMP interface? Justify your answer.

3. Is advanced touch-screen technology really a solution in search of a problem? Do you agree with this statement? Why or why not?

REAL WORLD ACTIVITIES

1. Most of the fame attached to the iPhone has resulted from individual, end-user applications. How could companies use the iPhone as a platform for commercial use? Break into small groups and brainstorm some possible uses of the technology, as well as what benefits organizations can derive from them. Then prepare a presentation to share your ideas with the class.

2. Information technology advances rapidly, and touch screen is no exception. Go online and search for developments more recent than those mentioned in the case. What new large-scale (i.e., wall-sized) applications could you find? Prepare a report comparing new developments with the examples mentioned here.

CHAPTER 4

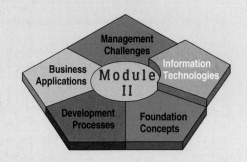

COMPUTER SOFTWARE

Chapter Highlights

Learning Objectives

1. Describe several important trends occurring in computer software.

2. Give examples of several major types of application and system software.

3. Explain the purpose of several popular software packages for end-user productivity and collaborative computing.

4. Define and describe the functions of an operating system.

5. Describe the main uses of computer programming software, tools, and languages.

6. Describe the issues associated with open-source software.

| SECTION I | # Application Software: End-User Applications |

Introduction to Software

This chapter provides an overview of the major types of software you depend on as you work with computers and access computer networks. It discusses their characteristics and purposes and gives examples of their uses. Before we begin, let's look at an example of the changing world of software in business.

Read the Real World Case discussing some costly and embarrassing, yet small, software coding errors. We can learn a lot about the importance of accuracy in software programming from this example. See Figure 4.1.

What Is Software?

To fully appreciate the need for and value of the wide variety of software available, we should be sure we understand what software is. **Software** is the general term for various kinds of programs used to operate and manipulate computers and their peripheral devices. One common way of describing hardware and software is to say that software can be thought of as the variable part of a computer and hardware as the invariable part. There are many types and categories of software. We will focus our attention on the different types of software and its uses in this chapter.

Types of Software

Let's begin our analysis of software by looking at an overview of the major types and functions of **application software** and **system software** available to computer users, shown in Figure 4.2. This figure summarizes the major categories of system and application software we will discuss in this chapter. Of course, this figure is a conceptual illustration. The types of software you will encounter depend primarily on the types of computers and networks you use and on the specific tasks you want to accomplish. We will discuss application software in this section and the major types of system software in Section II.

Application Software for End Users

Figure 4.2 shows that application software includes a variety of programs that can be subdivided into general-purpose and function-specific application categories. General-purpose application programs are programs that perform common information processing jobs for end users. For example, word processing, spreadsheet, database management, and graphics programs are popular with microcomputer users for home, education, business, scientific, and many other purposes. Because they significantly increase the productivity of end users, they are sometimes known as *productivity packages*. Other examples include Web browsers, e-mail, and groupware, which help support communication and collaboration among workgroups and teams.

An additional common way of classifying software is based on how the software was developed. Custom software is the term used to identify software applications that are developed within an organization for use by that organization. In other words, the organization that writes the program code is also the organization that uses the final software application. In contrast, COTS software (an acronym that stands for *commercial off-the-shelf*) is developed with the intention of selling the software in multiple copies (and usually for a profit). In this case, the organization that writes the software is not the intended target audience for its use.

Several characteristics are important when describing COTS software. First, as stated in our definition, COTS software products are sold in many copies with minimal changes beyond scheduled upgrade releases. Purchasers of COTS software generally have no control over the specification, schedule, evolution, or access to either the source code or the internal documentation. A COTS product is sold, leased, or licensed to the general public, but in virtually all cases, the vendor of the product retains the intellectual property rights of the software. Custom software, in contrast,

REAL WORLD CASE 1

Space Bugs and Really Bad PR: Software Coding Errors Can Be Costly

Programming errors that derail high-profile projects like space-exploration missions—especially bugs that cause spectacular explosions—are frightening, expensive, and career-killingly embarrassing for those who let them slip through. They provide extremely vivid reminders for every programmer to check and recheck (and recheck and recheck and recheck) every line of code.

In other cases, some software errors are just plain noisy: They cause explosions that are subtler in their destructiveness. They cause severe embarrassment that turns companies' good names to "Mud" and sometimes threatens the bottom line. Here are some examples of famous software coding errors and their subsequent "explosions."

The Mars Climate Orbiter Doesn't Orbit: Back in physics class, our teachers leaped all over answers that consisted of a number. If the answer was 2.5, they'd take their red pens and write "2.5 what? Weeks? Puppies? Demerits?" And proceed to mark the answer wrong. Back then, we thought that they were just being finicky. But it's the kind of error that can burn up a $327.6 million project in minutes. It did in 1998, when the Mars Climate Orbiter built by NASA's Jet Propulsion Laboratory approached the Red Planet at the wrong angle. At this point, it could easily have been renamed the Mars Climate Bright Light in the Upper Atmosphere, and shortly afterward been renamed the Mars Climate Debris Drifting Through the Sky.

FIGURE 4.1

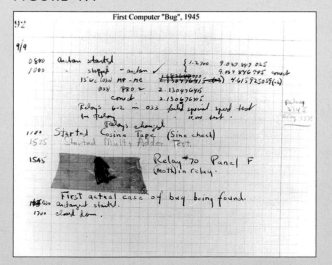

The infamous "first software bug" is attributed to U.S. Navy Rear Admiral Grace Hopper when she found this moth caught in a relay.

There were several problems with this spacecraft—its uneven payload made it twist and turn during flight, and its project managers neglected some important details during several stages of the mission. But the biggest problem was that different parts of the engineering team were using different units of measurement. One group working on the thrusters measured in English units of pounds-force seconds; the others used metric Newton-seconds. And whoever checked the numbers didn't use the red pen like our finicky high school teacher.

The result: The thrusters were 4.45 times more powerful than they should have been. If this goof had been spotted earlier, it could have been compensated for, but it wasn't, and the result of that inattention is now lost in space, possibly in pieces.

Mariner 1's Five-Minute Flight: On July 22, 1962, the first spacecraft of NASA's Mariner program blasted off on a mission to fly by Venus. The booster did its job, taking the spacecraft from its Cape Canaveral launch pad, but after a few minutes, Mariner 1 began to veer off course. The guidance system failed to correct the trajectory, and guidance commands failed to correct it manually. As the rocket veered off toward North Atlantic shipping lanes, the range safety officer did the only thing he could do: blow the thing up. Four minutes and 55 seconds into the mission, the Mariner 1 exploded.

NASA was already suffering from envy over the Russians being first into space with their Sputnik satellite, and the Mariner 1 incident was another international embarrassment for the agency. The postmortem of this debacle revealed what NASA described as "improper operation of the Atlas airborne beacon equipment"—though later it came out that the misplacement of a single punctuation mark by an engineer caused the mission's fatal software error.

In his 1968 book *The Promise of Space*, Arthur C. Clarke described the mission as "wrecked by the most expensive hyphen in history." That may not be strictly accurate. Although NASA did mention a hyphen in some of its reports of the incident, it appears that the agency was simplifying the story for a nontechnical audience.

A more widely accepted account is that the punctuation mark was a superscript bar over a radius symbol, handwritten in a notebook. In rocket science, the overbar signifies a smoothing function, so the formula should have calculated the smoothed value of the time derivative of a radius. Without the smoothing function, even minor variations of speed would trigger the corrective boosters to kick in. The automobile driving equivalent would be to yank the steering wheel in the opposite direction of every obstacle in the driver's field of vision.

But few people know what an overbar is, and since it looks like a hyphen, that's how most people tell the story.

Forty Seconds of Ariane-5: The European Space Agency (ESA) has also suffered embarrassment on the software front. The inaugural flight of its fifth-generation Ariane launcher bested NASA's Mariner 1 score for unmanned spacecraft disaster: It took only 40 seconds to blow up. On June 4, 1996, after the kind of dramatic vertical blastoff you'd expect from a high-profile European vehicle, cameras on the ground barely had time to focus on the Ariane-5 as it turned around and began to fall apart, before it completely exploded. The Ariane Flight 501 disaster began with a loss of guidance and altitude information 30 seconds after liftoff. Once it veered completely off course, it automatically self-destructed.

The problem was that Ariane-5's inertial reference system dealt with 64-bit floating-point data and converted it into 16-bit signed integer values. The result of the data conversion was too large for a 16-bit signed integer, which caused an arithmetic overflow in the hardware. In the ESA's case, a software handler that could have dealt with the problem had been disabled, and so there was no levee to dam the cascade of system failures that led to the destruction. Basically, it was a rounding error.

Pentium Chips Fail Math: As stated previously, not all explosions are big, loud booms. Some are quieter but just as destructive. In 1994, an entire line of CPUs by market leader Intel simply couldn't do their math. The Pentium floating-point flaw ensured that no matter what software you used, your results stood a chance of being inaccurate past the eighth decimal point. The problem lay in a faulty math co-processor, also known as a floating-point unit. The result was a small possibility of tiny errors in hardcore calculations, but it was a costly PR debacle for Intel.

How did the first generation of Pentiums go wrong? Intel's laudable idea was to triple the execution speed of floating-point calculations by ditching the previous-generation 486 processor's clunky shift-and-subtract algorithm and substituting a lookup-table approach in the Pentium. So far, so smart. The lookup table consisted of 1,066 table entries,

downloaded into the programmable logic array of the chip. But only 1,061 entries made it onto the first-generation Pentiums; five got lost on the way.

When the floating-point unit accessed any of the empty cells, it would get a zero response instead of the real answer. A zero response from one cell didn't actually return an answer of zero: A few obscure calculations returned slight errors typically around the 10th decimal digit, so the error passed by quality control and into production.

What did that mean for the lay user? Not much. With this kind of bug, there's a 1-in-360 billion chance that miscalculations could reach as high as the fourth decimal place. More likely, with odds of 1-to-9 billion against, was that any errors would happen in the 9th or 10th decimal digit.

Ask people with calculators or slide rules to multiply 850×77.1, and they'll answer 65,535. But in September 2007, it was discovered that Excel 2007 answered 100,000. According to Microsoft, this bizarre rounding-up occurred only in calculations that resulted in 65,535 or 65,536. What's more, Excel actually calculated the correct answer, but a bug prevented it from displaying properly.

But wouldn't you know it? A Virginia-based math professor named Thomas Nicely needed that level of accuracy, found he wasn't getting it, and figured out why. In October 1994, he alerted Intel, then others, to the problem. Intel retorted with a response only marginally less tactful than "Oh, that thing? Yeah, we noticed that back in June." Thus began an inexorable slide into PR hell and a costly mop-up bill. In January 1995, Intel announced a pretax charge of $475 million against earnings, most of which apparently stemmed from replacing flawed processors.

The bottom line in this arithmetic mess is this: In lookup-table and money calculations, $1,066 - 5 = -\$475,000,000$. Any way you look at it, that's bad math.

Source: Adapted from Matt Lake, "Epic Failures: 11 Infamous Software Bugs," *Computerworld, Inc.*, September 9, 2010.

CASE STUDY QUESTIONS

1. What factors should companies take into consideration when making the decision between developing their own applications or purchasing them from a vendor? Is the chance for error any different? Make a list of factors and discuss their importance to this decision.

2. What could have been done to prevent each of the disasters? Provide several examples.

3. What should companies do when faced with large-scale innovative software challenges? Is there a common theme among the cases discussed above that you can identify? What do you think it is?

REAL WORLD ACTIVITIES

1. The case mentions several software disasters. There are examples of many others on the Internet. Go online and research examples of costly software programming errors and prepare a report for your class.

2. Figure 4.1 shows a famous picture of the first ever-discovered software bug. While this bug has become the subject of quite a widespread urban myth, the actual story is much different than the myth. Go online and see if you can find the true story of Rear Admiral Grace Hopper's famous moth.

FIGURE 4.2 An overview of computer software. Note the major types and examples of application and system software.

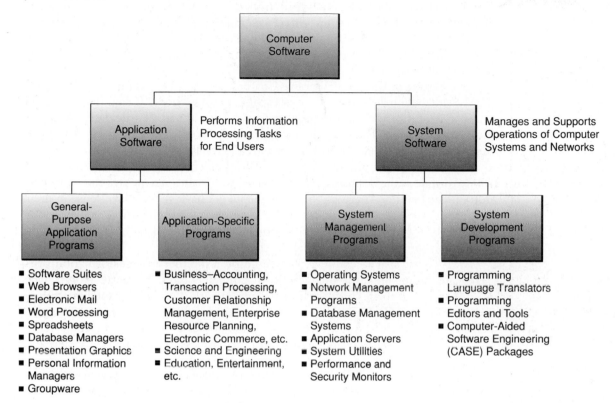

is generally owned by the organization that developed it (or that paid to have it developed), and the specifications, functionality, and ownership of the final product are controlled or retained by the developing organization.

The newest innovation in software development is called **open-source software.** In this approach, developers collaborate on the development of an application using programming standards that allow for anyone to contribute to the software. Furthermore, as each developer completes his or her project, the code for the application becomes available and free to anyone else who wishes to use it. We will discuss this new approach to software development in greater detail in Section II of this chapter.

SAP Business Suite 7: Introducing Modular Scenarios Cutting Across Organizational Functions	Germany-based SAP AG is tackling business processes in a novel way with the newest version of its Business Suite, which embeds analytics acquired from Business Objects SA and introduces industry-specific "value scenarios." Version 7.0 of SAP Business Suite, a library of business processes, adds industry best practices through more than 30 modular value scenarios—like Superior Customer Value, Product Lifecycle Management (PLM)—designed to cross traditional organizational boundaries.

These "pre-defined end-to-end business processes" are intended to be implemented in small steps by organizations as they need it, says Jim Hagemann Snabe, SAP executive board member. The value scenarios basically illustrate interrelationships between SAP product capabilities using graphical guides and business terms, not feature and function lists. The customer can also see the impact on the associated systems, and ultimately, the specific SAP modules that would need to be activated.

Ray Wang, vice president at Cambridge, Massachusetts-based Forrester Research Inc., says customers will find the value scenarios "compelling as they align with the key business drivers users face." But as with all best practices, Wang notes that "SAP will need to make it easy for customers to modify those scenarios, reduce the overall cost of owning SAP, and provide more frequent levels of innovation."

One customer, Colgate-Palmolive Co., has large implementations in CRM and PLM that would benefit from the new capabilities of version 7.0, says the company's senior vice president of IT and business services, Ed Toben. "Particularly when you look at PLM, which is newer, the processes and the enhancement pack concept of turning on pieces should make us move faster," says Toben.

Another customer, pharmaceutical company Roche, requires the flexibility and ability to scale as the business changes in order to remain current, says chief information officer Jennifer Allerton. "IT investments . . . have got to make sense in their own right," she says. "And, the pharmaceuticals business is one where you invest for the long term and when you make investments about IT packages, you're not going to change your mind the next day about them."

IBM Corp., also a customer, is focused on a number of transformation programs, including the area of operational efficiency, says Jeannette Horan, vice president of enterprise business transformation with the office of the chief information officer at IBM. To that end, the company's strategy, says Horan, is to globally integrate the enterprise through common processes, using the Business Suite, she says, to "mix and match components of the business to go to market in new and interesting ways."

But while companies are taking a hard look at spending and reviewing projects, "that does not mean . . . that companies do not spend, they just spend very smartly and very wisely," says Léo Apotheker, co-CEO of SAP AG. There is a need, says Apotheker, "to provide better and faster insight, a higher level of efficiency, a need to introduce a whole new degree of flexibility in the way we do business."

Source: Adapted from Kathleen Lau, "Industry 'Value Scenarios' in SAP Business Suite 7," *Computerworld Canada*, February 12, 2009.

Business Application Software

Thousands of function-specific application software packages are available to support specific applications of end users in business and other fields. For example, business application software supports the reengineering and automation of business processes with strategic e-business applications like customer relationship management, enterprise resource planning, and supply chain management. Other examples are software packages that Web-enable electronic commerce applications or apply to the functional areas of business like human resource management and accounting and finance. Still other software empowers managers and business professionals with decision support tools like data mining, enterprise information portals, or knowledge management systems.

We will discuss these applications in upcoming chapters that go into more detail about these business software tools and applications. For example, data warehousing and data mining are discussed in Chapters 5 and 10; accounting, marketing, manufacturing, human resource management, and financial management applications are covered in Chapters 7 and 8. Customer relationship management, enterprise resource planning, and supply chain management are also covered in Chapter 8. Electronic commerce is the focus of Chapter 9, and decision support and data analysis applications are explored in Chapter 10. Figure 4.3 illustrates some of the many types of business application software that are available today. These particular applications are integrated in the Oracle E-Business Suite software product of Oracle Corp.

FIGURE 4.3   The business applications in Oracle's E-Business Suite software illustrate some of the many types of business application software being used today.

ORACLE E-BUSINESS SUITE

Advanced Planning	Business Intelligence	Contracts
e-Commerce	Enterprise Asset Management	Exchanges
Financials	Human Resources	Interaction Center
Manufacturing	Marketing	Order Fulfillment
Procurement	Product Development	Professional Services Automation
Projects	Sales	Service
Training	Treasury	

Source: Adapted from Oracle Corp., "E-Business Suite: Manage by Fact with Complete Automation and Complete Information," Oracle.com, 2002.

Software Suites and Integrated Packages

Let's begin our discussion of popular general-purpose application software by looking at software suites. The most widely used productivity packages come bundled together as software suites, such as Microsoft Office, Lotus SmartSuite, Corel WordPerfect Office, Sun's StarOffice, and their open-source product, OpenOffice. Examining their components gives us an overview of the important software tools that you can use to increase your productivity.

Figure 4.4 compares the basic programs that make up the top four software suites. Notice that each suite integrates software packages for word processing, spreadsheets, presentation graphics, database management, and personal information management. Microsoft, Lotus, Corel, and Sun bundle several other programs in each suite, depending on the version you select. Examples include programs for Internet access, e-mail, Web publishing, desktop publishing, voice recognition, financial management, and electronic encyclopedias.

A software suite costs a lot less than the total cost of buying its individual packages separately. Another advantage is that all programs use a similar *graphical user interface* (GUI) of icons, tool and status bars, menus, and so on, which gives them the same look and feel and makes them easier to learn and use. Software suites also share common tools such as spell checkers and help wizards to increase their efficiency. Another big advantage of suites is that their programs are designed to work together seamlessly and import each other's files easily, no matter which program you are using at the time. These capabilities make them more efficient and easier to use than a variety of individual package versions.

FIGURE 4.4   The basic program components of the top four software suites. Other programs may be included, depending on the suite edition selected.

Programs	Microsoft Office	Lotus SmartSuite	Corel WordPerfect Office	Sun Open Office
Word Processor	Word	WordPro	WordPerfect	Writer
Spreadsheet	Excel	1–2–3	Quattro Pro	Calc
Presentation Graphics	PowerPoint	Freelance	Presentations	Impress
Database Manager	Access	Approach	Paradox	Base
Personal Information Manager	Outlook	Organizer	Corel Central	Schedule

Of course, putting so many programs and features together in one supersize package does have some disadvantages. Industry critics argue that many software suite features are never used by most end users. The suites take up a lot of disk space (often upward of 250 megabytes), depending on which version or functions you install. Because of their size, software suites are sometimes derisively called *bloatware* by their critics. The cost of suites can vary from as low as $100 for a competitive upgrade to more than $700 for a full version of some editions of the suites.

These drawbacks are one reason for the continued use of integrated packages like Microsoft Works, Lotus eSuite WorkPlace, and AppleWorks. Integrated packages combine some of the functions of several programs—word processing, spreadsheets, presentation graphics, database management, and so on—into one software package.

Because integrated packages leave out many features and functions that are in individual packages and software suites, they are considered less powerful. Their limited functionality, however, requires a lot less disk space (often less than 10 megabytes), costs less than $100, and is frequently preinstalled on many low-end microcomputer systems. Integrated packages offer enough functions and features for many computer users while providing some of the advantages of software suites in a smaller package.

Web Browsers and More

The most important software component for many computer users today is the once simple and limited, but now powerful and feature-rich, Web browser. Browsers such as Microsoft Explorer, Netscape Navigator, Mozilla Firefox, and Opera are software applications designed to support navigation through the point-and-click hyperlinked resources of the World Wide Web and the rest of the Internet, as well as corporate intranets and extranets. Once limited to surfing the Web, browsers are becoming the universal software platform from which end users launch information searches, e-mail, multimedia file transfers, discussion groups, and many other Internet-based applications.

Figure 4.5 illustrates the use of the Microsoft Internet Explorer browser to access search engines on the Netscape.com Web site. Netscape uses top-rated Google as its

FIGURE 4.5

Using the Microsoft Internet Explorer browser to access Google and other search engines on the Netscape.com Web site.

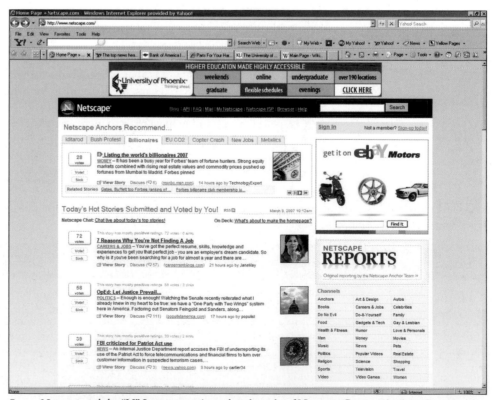

Source: Netscape and the "N" Logo are registered trademarks of Netscape Communications Corporation. Netscape content © 2010. Used with permission.

default search engine but also provides links to other popular search tools including Ask Jeeves, Look Smart, Lycos, and Overture. Using search engines to find information has become an indispensable part of business and personal Internet, intranet, and extranet applications.

Industry experts predict the Web browser will be the model for how most people use networked computers in the future. Even today, whether you want to watch a video, make a phone call, download some software, hold a videoconference, check your e-mail, or work on a spreadsheet of your team's business plan, you can use your browser to launch and host such applications. That's why browsers are sometimes called the *universal client*, that is, the software component installed on all of the networked computing and communications devices of the clients (users) throughout an enterprise. As an aside, this entire book was revised and edited in a browser-based authoring program called PowerXEditor (we will learn more about PowerXEditor later in this chapter).

Electronic Mail, Instant Messaging, and Weblogs

The first thing many people do at work, all over the world, is check their electronic mail. **E-mail** has changed the way people work and communicate. Millions of end users now depend on e mail software to communicate with one another by sending and receiving electronic messages and file attachments via the Internet or their organizations' intranets or extranets. E-mail is stored on networked mail servers until you are ready. Whenever you want to, you can read your e-mail by displaying it on your workstation. So, with only a few minutes of effort (and a few microseconds of transmission time), a message to one or many individuals can be composed, sent, and received.

As we mentioned previously, e-mail software is now a mainstay component of top software suites and Web browsers. Free e-mail packages such as Microsoft HotMail, Yahoo! Mail, and Netscape WebMail are available to Internet users from online services and Internet service providers. Most e-mail software like Microsoft Outlook Express, Windows Mail, or Netscape Messenger can route messages to multiple end users based on predefined mailing lists and provide password security, automatic message forwarding, and remote user access. They also allow you to store messages in folders and make it easy to add documents and Web file attachments to e-mail messages. E-mail packages enable you to edit and send graphics and multimedia files, as well as text, and provide computer conferencing capabilities. In addition, your e-mail software may automatically filter and sort incoming messages (even news items from online services) and route them to appropriate user mailboxes and folders. Finally, many e-mail clients also include calendaring and contact management functions.

Instant messaging (IM) is an e-mail/computer-conferencing hybrid technology that has grown so rapidly that it has become a standard method of electronic messaging for millions of Internet users worldwide. By using instant messaging, groups of business professionals or friends and associates can send and receive electronic messages instantly and thus communicate and collaborate in real time in a near-conversational mode. Messages pop up instantly in an IM window on the computer screens of everyone in your business workgroup or friends on your IM "buddy list," as long as they are online, no matter what other tasks they are working on at that moment. Instant messaging software can be downloaded and IM services implemented by subscribing to many popular IM systems, including AOL's Instant Messenger and ICQ, MSN Messenger, and Yahoo Messenger. See Figure 4.6.

A **Weblog** (usually shortened to **blog** or written as "Web log" or "weblog") is a **Web site** of personal or noncommercial origin that uses a dated log format updated daily or very frequently with new information about a particular subject or range of subjects. The information can be written by the site owner, gleaned from other Web sites or other sources, or contributed by users via e-mail.

A Weblog often has the quality of being a kind of "log of our times" from a particular point of view. Generally, Weblogs are devoted to one or several subjects or themes, usually of topical interest. In general, Weblogs can be thought of as developing

FIGURE 4.6

Using the e-mail features of the Yahoo! instant messaging system.

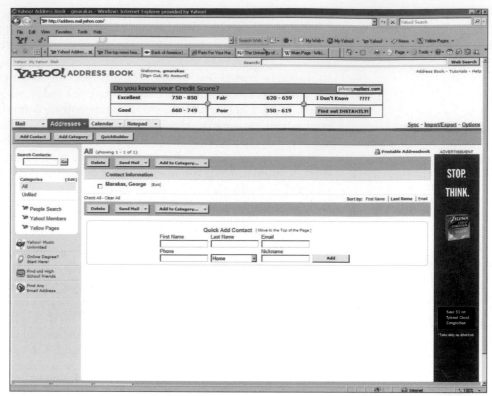

Source: YAHOO! and the YAHOO! logo are trademarks of Yahoo! Inc. Reproduced with permission of Yahoo! Inc.

commentaries, individual or collective, on their particular themes. A Weblog may consist of the recorded ideas of an individual (a sort of diary) or be a complex collaboration open to anyone. Most of the latter are *moderated discussions*.

Because there are a number of variations on this idea and new variations can easily be invented, the meaning of this term is apt to gather additional connotations with time. As a formatting and content approach for a Web site, the Weblog seems popular because the viewer knows that something changes every day, there is a personal (rather than bland commercial) point of view, and, on some sites, there is an opportunity to collaborate with or respond to the Web site and its participants.

Word Processing and Desktop Publishing

Software for word processing has transformed the process of writing just about anything. Word processing packages computerize the creation, editing, revision, and printing of *documents* (e.g., letters, memos, reports) by electronically processing *text data* (words, phrases, sentences, and paragraphs). Top word processing packages like Microsoft Word, Lotus WordPro, Corel WordPerfect, and OpenOffice Writer can provide a wide variety of attractively printed documents with their desktop publishing capabilities. These packages can also convert documents to HTML format for publication as Web pages on corporate intranets or the World Wide Web.

Word processing packages also provide other helpful features. For example, a *spelling checker* capability can identify and correct spelling errors, and a *thesaurus* feature helps you find a better choice of words to express ideas. You can also identify and correct grammar and punctuation errors, as well as suggest possible improvements in your writing style, with grammar and style checker functions. In addition to converting documents to HTML format, you can use the top packages to design and create Web pages from scratch for an Internet or intranet Web site. See Figure 4.7.

FIGURE 4.7
Using the Microsoft Word word processing package. Note the insertion of a table in the document.

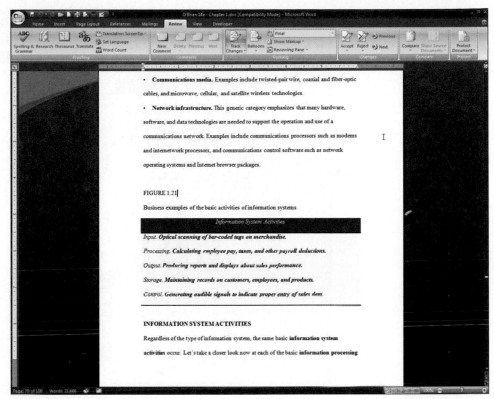

Source: Courtesy of Microsoft®.

End users and organizations can use **desktop publishing (DTP)** software to produce their own printed materials that look professionally published. That is, they can design and print their own newsletters, brochures, manuals, and books with several type styles, graphics, photos, and colors on each page. Word processing packages and desktop publishing packages like Adobe InDesign, Microsoft Publisher, and QuarkXPress are used for desktop publishing. Typically, text material and graphics can be generated by word processing and graphics packages and imported as text and graphics files. Optical scanners may be used to input text and graphics from printed material. You can also use files of *clip art*, which are predrawn graphic illustrations provided by the software package or available from other sources.

Electronic Spreadsheets

Spreadsheet packages like Lotus 1-2-3, Microsoft Excel, OpenOffice Calc, and Corel QuattroPro are used by virtually every business for analysis, planning, and modeling. They help you develop an *electronic spreadsheet*, which is a worksheet of rows and columns that can be stored on your PC or on a network server, or converted to HTML format and stored as a Web page or Web sheet on the World Wide Web. Developing a spreadsheet involves designing its format and developing the relationships (formulas) that will be used in the worksheet. In response to your input, the computer performs necessary calculations according to the formulas you defined in the spreadsheet and displays the results immediately, whether on your workstation or Web site. Most packages also help you develop charts and graphic displays of spreadsheet results. See Figure 4.8.

For example, you could develop a spreadsheet to record and analyze past and present advertising performance for a business. You could also develop hyperlinks to a similar Web sheet on your marketing team's intranet Web site. Now you have a decision support tool to help you answer *what-if questions* you may have about advertising. For example, "What would happen to market share if advertising expenses were to

FIGURE 4.8

Using an electronic spreadsheet package, Microsoft Excel. Note the use of graphics.

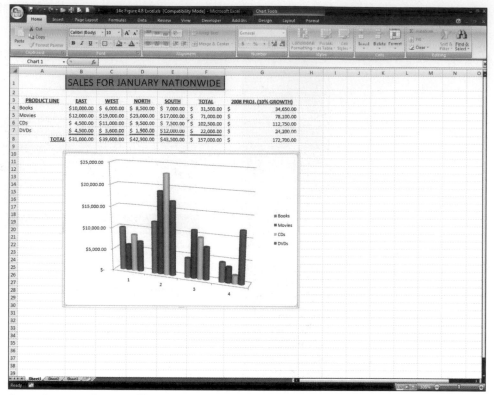

Source: Courtesy of Microsoft®.

increase by 10 percent?" To answer this question, you would simply change the advertising expense formula on the advertising performance worksheet you developed. The computer would recalculate the affected figures, producing new market share figures and graphics. You would then have better insight into the effect of advertising decisions on market share. Then you could share this insight with a note on the Web sheet on your team's intranet Web site.

Presentation Graphics

Presentation graphics software packages help you convert numeric data into graphics displays such as line charts, bar graphs, pie charts, and many other types of graphics. Most of the top packages also help you prepare multimedia presentations of graphics, photos, animation, and video clips, including publishing to the World Wide Web. Not only are graphics and multimedia displays easier to comprehend and communicate than numeric data, but multiple-color and multiple-media displays can more easily emphasize key points, strategic differences, and important trends in the data. Presentation graphics have proved to be much more effective than tabular presentations of numeric data for reporting and communicating in advertising media, management reports, or other business presentations. See Figure 4.9.

Presentation graphics software packages like Microsoft PowerPoint, OpenOffice Impress, Lotus Freelance, or Corel Presentations give you many easy-to-use capabilities that encourage the use of graphics presentations. For example, most packages help you design and manage computer-generated and orchestrated *slide shows* containing many integrated graphics and multimedia displays. You can select from a variety of predesigned *templates* of business presentations, prepare and edit the outline and notes for a presentation, and manage the use of multimedia files of graphics, photos, sounds, and video clips. Of course, the top packages help you tailor your graphics and multimedia presentation for transfer in HTML format to Web sites on corporate intranets or the World Wide Web.

FIGURE 4.9

Using the slide preview feature of a presentation graphics package, Microsoft PowerPoint.

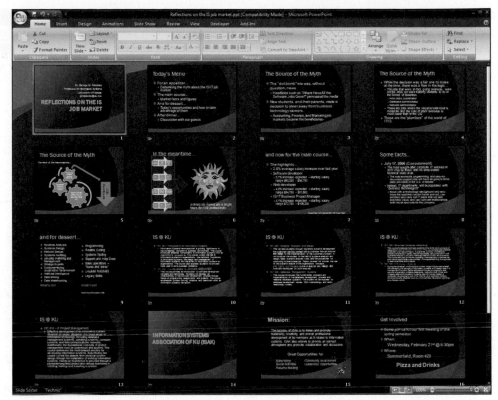

Source: Courtesy of Microsoft®.

Personal Information Managers

The personal information manager (PIM) is a popular software package for end-user productivity and collaboration, as well as a popular application for personal digital assistant (PDA) handheld devices. Various PIMs such as Lotus Organizer and Microsoft Outlook help end users store, organize, and retrieve information about customers, clients, and prospects or schedule and manage appointments, meetings, and tasks. A PIM package will organize data you enter and retrieve information in a variety of forms, depending on the style and structure of the PIM and the information you want. For example, information can be retrieved as an electronic calendar or list of appointments, meetings, or other things to do; as the timetable for a project; or as a display of key facts and financial data about customers, clients, or sales prospects. Most PIMs now include the ability to access the World Wide Web and provide e-mail capability. Also, some PIMs use Internet and e-mail features to support team collaboration by sharing information such as contact lists, task lists, and schedules with other networked PIM users. See Figure 4.10.

Groupware

Groupware is software that helps workgroups and teams collaborate to accomplish group assignments. Groupware is a category of general-purpose application software that combines a variety of software features and functions to facilitate collaboration. For example, groupware products like Lotus Notes, Novell GroupWise, and Microsoft Exchange support collaboration through e-mail, discussion groups and databases, scheduling, task management, data, audio and videoconferencing, and so on.

Groupware products rely on the Internet and corporate intranets and extranets to make collaboration possible on a global scale by *virtual teams* located anywhere in the world. For example, team members might use the Internet for global e-mail, project discussion forums, and joint Web page development. Or they might use corporate intranets to publish project news and progress reports and work jointly on documents stored on Web servers. See Figure 4.11.

Collaborative capabilities are also being added to other software to give it groupware-like features. For example, in the Microsoft Office software suite, Microsoft Word

FIGURE 4.10
Using a personal
information manager
(PIM): Microsoft Outlook.

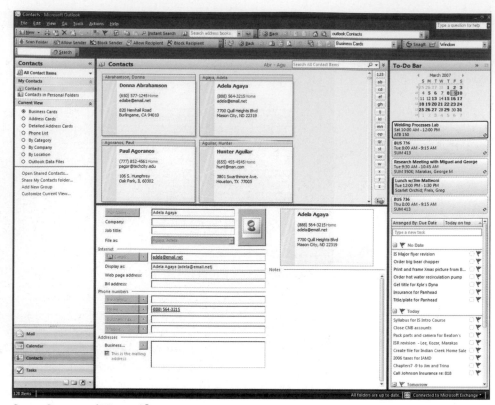

Source: Courtesy of Microsoft®.

FIGURE 4.11
Lotus Sametime enables
workgroups and project
teams to share spreadsheets
and other work documents
in an interactive online
collaboration process.

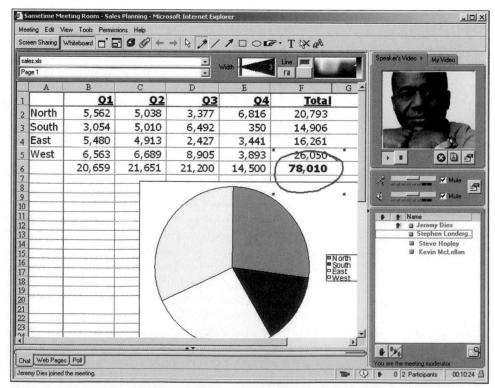

Source: Courtesy of International Business Machines Corporation. Unauthorized use not permitted.

keeps track of who made revisions to each document, Excel tracks all changes made to a spreadsheet, and Outlook lets you keep track of tasks you delegate to other team members. Recently, the Microsoft Office suite has included functions that allow multiple people to work on and edit the same document at the same time. Using this feature, any changes made by one team member will become visible to all team members as they are being made.

Two recent additions to the collaborative software marketplace are Microsoft's Windows SharePoint Services and IBM's WebSphere. Both products allow teams to create sophisticated Web sites for information sharing and document collaboration quickly. Furthermore, businesses can use these products as a platform for application development to facilitate the efficient creation of Web-based business portals and transaction processing applications. Web sites built with collaborative development tools can integrate a wide variety of individual applications that can help increase both individual and team productivity.

Software Alternatives

Many businesses are finding alternatives to acquiring, installing, and maintaining business application software purchased from software vendors or developing and maintaining their own software in-house with their own software developer employees. For example, as we will discuss further in Chapter 14, many large companies are *outsourcing* the development and maintenance of software they need to *contract programming* firms and other software development companies, including the use of *offshore* software developers in foreign countries, and employing the Internet to communicate, collaborate, and manage their software development projects.

Application Service Providers

A large and fast-growing number of companies are turning to application service providers (ASPs), instead of developing or purchasing the application software they need to run their businesses. Application service providers are companies that own, operate, and maintain application software and the computer system resources (servers, system software, networks, and IT personnel) required to offer the use of the application software for a fee as a service over the Internet. The ASP can bill their customers on a per-use basis or on a monthly or annual fee basis.

Businesses are using an ASP instead of owning and maintaining their own software for many reasons. One of the biggest advantages is the low cost of initial investment, and in many cases, the short time needed to get the Web-based application set up and running. The ASP's pay-as-you-go fee structure is usually significantly less expensive than the cost of developing or purchasing, as well as running and maintaining, application software. In addition, using an ASP eliminates or drastically reduces the need for much of the IT infrastructure (servers, system software, and IT personnel) that would be needed to acquire and support application software, including the continual challenges of distributing and managing companywide software patches and upgrades. Consequently, the use of ASPs by businesses and other organizations is expected to accelerate in the coming years. See Figure 4.12.

McAfee Inc.: Security under a Software-as-a-Service Model

Santa Clara, California-based security vendor McAfee Inc. released a software-as-a-service Web security tool for protecting a distributed workforce from Web threats, while rendering IT departments fewer upfront costs in light of current budgetary constraints.

Especially in tough economic times, a SaaS model of software delivery, like the McAfee Web Protection Service, saves cash-strapped organizations money because IT staff don't have to spend valuable time managing on-site equipment, says Mark Campbell, senior product marketing manager with McAfee Inc. "They get the advantages of having a tool that is always on, always up-to-date and with uptime guarantees," says Campbell. One challenge with on-premise tools, he continues, is that when vendors issue a feature update, a period of time can elapse before the enhancements are up and running in the environment, says Campbell. That problem goes away when the software is hosted centrally.

Features of the hosted security offering include reputation-based filtering, based on McAfee's reputation system TrustedSource, to block constantly morphing threats. There's flexible policy manager for setting policies for certain employee groups like access to certain social networking sites by contract employees versus executive management. Users have the ability to run reports and use dashboards to reap insight into an organization's Web usage. "Are employees spending all day on Facebook and does this align with our appropriate usage of Web tools?" says Campbell. Other features include malware protection, remote office and user support, and transparent user authentication.

James Quin, senior research analyst with London, Ontario-based Info-Tech Research Group Ltd., can't yet say if McAfee's SaaS offering will be cheaper in the long run given monthly recurring costs for the service. That said, in this climate of eliminated capital budgets, Quin says "a solution like this offers them value there." Small organizations in particular, says Quin, will benefit from not having to retain as much security expertise.

Offering a SaaS option for malware technology that is "pretty commoditized" is certainly a move by McAfee to differentiate itself in a crowded space, says Quin. "And it puts them out front first because they're not going to be the last ones to offer this kind of service," he says.

Campbell thinks customers' perception of hosted security products has changed for the better, helped along by the successful adoption of hosted CRM tools like salesforce.com. "More and more IT departments are beginning to accept and really realize the benefits of it," says Campbell.

Source: Adapted from Kathleen Lau, "SaaS Web Security a Cheaper Option, McAfee Says," *CIO.com*, April 30, 2009.

FIGURE 4.12

Salesforce.com is a leading application service provider of Web-based sales management and customer relationship management services to both large and small businesses.

Source: Courtesy of Salesforce.com.

Cloud Computing

One of the most recent advances in computing and software delivery is called cloud computing. Cloud computing is a style of computing in which software and, in some cases, virtualized hardware resources are provided as a service over the Internet. Users need not have knowledge of, expertise in, or control over the technology infrastructure "in the cloud" that supports them. The term cloud is used as a metaphor for the Internet, based on how the Internet is often depicted in computer network diagrams.

The concept incorporates technology trends that have the common theme of reliance on the Internet for satisfying the computing needs of the users. Examples of vendors providing cloud services include SAP Business ByDesign, MidlandHR's "iTrent as a Service," Salesforce.com, and Google Apps, which provide common business applications online that are accessed from a Web browser, while the software and data are stored on the servers.

Cloud computing is often confused with grid computing (recall the concept from Chapter 3 where the CPU power of multiple computers is harnessed to act like one big computer when necessary). Indeed, many cloud computing deployments depend on grids, but cloud computing can be seen as a natural next step from the grid model. The majority of cloud computing infrastructure consists of reliable services delivered through data centers and built on servers with different levels of virtualization technologies. The services are accessible anywhere that has access to networking infrastructure. The cloud appears as a single point of access for all the computing needs of consumers.

As many computer software users generally do not own the infrastructure around them, they can avoid capital expenditure and consume resources as a service, paying instead for what they use. If this sounds a lot like how you pay for your electricity or natural gas, it is because the same basic model has been adopted. Many cloud computing offerings have adopted the utility computing model, which is analogous to how traditional utilities like electricity are consumed, while others are billed on a subscription basis. Sharing "perishable and intangible" computing power among multiple users or enterprises can improve utilization rates, as servers are left idle less often because more people are accessing and using the computing resources. Through this approach, significant reductions in costs can be realized while increasing the overall speed of application development. A side effect of this approach is that a given user's or enterprise's computing capacity can be scaled upward almost instantly as needed without having to own an infrastructure that is engineered to be ready for short-term peak loads. Cloud computing has been enabled by large increases in available commercial bandwidth, which makes it possible to receive the same response times from centralized infrastructure at other sites.

The real benefit to the organization comes from the cost savings. Cloud computing users can avoid capital expenditure on hardware, software, and services, by simply paying a provider only for what they use. As stated above, consumption is billed on a utility (e.g. resources consumed, like electricity) or subscription (e.g., time based, like a newspaper) basis, with little or no upfront cost. Other benefits of this time-sharing style approach are low barriers to entry, shared infrastructure and costs, low management overhead, and immediate access to a broad range of applications. Users can generally terminate the contract at any time, and the services are often covered by service level agreements with financial penalties in the event the agreed-upon service levels are not delivered. It is predicted that someday, everyone will compute "in the cloud."

Software Licensing

Regardless of whether a software application is purchased COTS or accessed via an ASP, the software must be licensed for use. Software licensing is a complex topic that involves considerations of the special characteristics of software in the context of the underlying intellectual property rights, including copyright, trademark, and trade secrets, as well as traditional contract law, including the Uniform Commercial Code (UCC).

Contrary to what many believe, when an individual or company buys a software application, they have not purchased rights of ownership. Rather, they have purchased a license to use the software under the terms of the software licensing agreement. Software is generally licensed to better protect the vendor's intellectual property rights. The license often prohibits reverse engineering, modifying, disclosing, or transferring the software. In most cases, the license also gives the purchaser permission to sell or dispose of the rights provided by the license but not to duplicate or resell multiple copies of the software.

The requirement for licensing does not disappear when use of the software is obtained through an ASP. In this case, the license to dispense use of the software is granted to the ASP by the various software vendors, and in return, the ASP agrees to pay the software vendor a royalty based on the number of user accounts to which the ASP resells the rights.

Software vendors are working hard to provide easy licensing and access to their products while simultaneously preventing software piracy, which serves only to raise the ultimate cost of the product.

In the next section, we will learn about an entirely new approach to software licensing: open-source code.

SECTION II	# System Software: Computer System Management

System Software Overview

System software consists of programs that manage and support a computer system and its information processing activities. For example, operating systems and network management programs serve as a vital *software interface* between computer networks and hardware and the application programs of end users.

Read the Real World Case on the use of open-source software by the U.S. Department of Defense. We can learn a lot about new trends regarding the use of open-source applications from this example. See Figure 4.13.

Overview

We can group system software into two major categories (see Figure 4.14):

- **System Management Programs.** Programs that manage the hardware, software, network, and data resources of computer systems during the execution of the various information processing jobs of users. Examples of important system management programs are operating systems, network management programs, database management systems, and system utilities.

- **System Development Programs.** Programs that help users develop information system programs and procedures and prepare user programs for computer processing. Major software development programs are programming language translators and editors, and a variety of CASE (computer-aided software engineering) and other programming tools. We will take a closer look at CASE tools later in this chapter.

Operating Systems

The most important system software package for any computer is its operating system. An operating system is an integrated system of programs that manages the operations of the CPU, controls the input/output and storage resources and activities of the computer system, and provides various support services as the computer executes the application programs of users.

The primary purpose of an operating system is to maximize the productivity of a computer system by operating it in the most efficient manner. An operating system minimizes the amount of human intervention required during processing. It helps your application programs perform common operations such as accessing a network, entering data, saving and retrieving files, and printing or displaying output. If you have any hands-on experience with a computer, you know that the operating system must be loaded and activated before you can accomplish other tasks. This requirement emphasizes that operating systems are the most indispensable components of the software interface between users and the hardware of their computer systems.

Operating Systems Functions

An operating system performs five basic functions in the operation of a computer system: providing a user interface, resource management, task management, file management, and utilities and support services. See Figure 4.15.

The User Interface. The user interface is the part of the operating system that allows you to communicate with it so you can load programs, access files, and accomplish other tasks. Three main types of user interfaces are the *command-driven*, *menu-driven*, and *graphical user interfaces*. The trend in user interfaces for operating systems and other software is moving away from the entry of brief end-user commands, or even the selection of choices from menus of options. Instead, most software provides an easy-to-use graphical user interface (GUI) that uses icons, bars, buttons, boxes, and other images. These GUIs rely on pointing devices like the electronic mouse or touch pad to make selections that help you get things done. Currently, the most common and widely recognized GUI is the Microsoft Windows desktop.

REAL WORLD CASE 2

U.S. Department of Defense: Enlisting Open-Source Applications

The U.S. Defense Department is enlisting an open-source approach to software development, which is an about-face for such a historically top-down organization. The Department of Defense (DoD) says open-source software is equal to commercial software in almost all cases and by law should be considered by the agency when making technology purchase decisions.

In terms of guidance, the DoD says open-source software (OSS) meets the definition of "commercial computer software" and thus executive agencies are required to include open source when evaluating software that meets their computing needs. OSS is defined as "software for which the human-readable source code is available for use, study, re-use, modification, enhancement, and redistribution by the users of that software."

In addition, it lays out a list of open-source positives, including broad peer-review that helps eliminate defects, modification rights that help speed changes when needed, a reduction in the reliance on proprietary vendors, a licensing model that facilitates quick provisioning, cost reduction in some cases, reduction in maintenance and ownership costs, and favorable characteristics for rapid prototyping and experimentation. "The continuous and broad peer-review enabled by publicly available source code supports software reliability and security efforts through the identification and elimination of defects that might otherwise go unrecognized by a more limited core development team," states deputy CIO David Wennergren in a memo to top military officials.

"I would consider this a milestone day," says John Scott, director of open-source software and open integration for Mercury Federal Systems, a technology consultancy to the U.S. government. Scott helped draft some of the open-source guidance contained in the memo, which took about 18 months to draft. "The 2003 policy study was OK to use, but this one goes a bit further in expanding on what open source is and why you would want to use it. But it is not just about usage, it is also about helping create OSS by submitting changes back out to the public."

Scott says he believes this is the first time guidance has been issued about sharing the government's own open-source changes with the public.

Taken together, two developments show how the Defense Department is trying to take advantage of Web-based communities to speed up software development and reduce its costs. Dave Mihelcic, CTO of the Defense Information Systems Agency, says the military believes in the core Web 2.0 philosophy of the power of collaboration.

The military has launched a collaborative platform called Forge.mil for its developers to share software, systems components, and network services. The agency also signed an agreement with the Open Source Software Institute (OSSI) to allow 50 internally developed workforce management applications to be licensed to other government agencies, universities, and companies.

"The Web is a platform for harvesting collective intelligence," Mihelcic says. He points to "remixable data sources, services in perpetual beta and lightweight programming models" as some of the aspects of open-source software development that are applicable to the Defense Department.

One example of the Defense Department's new community-based approach to software development is Forge.mil, which was made generally available for unclassified use within the department in April 2009. Forge.mil is powered by CollabNet Team Forge, a commercial lifecycle management platform for distributed software development teams, and is modeled after the popular SourceForge.net.

The Defense Information Systems Agency (DISA) has issued version two of SoftwareForge (software that runs on the Forge.mil site to enable sharing and collaborative development of open-source software) after a three-month trial that grew to 1,300 users. SoftwareForge provides software version control, bug tracking, requirements management, and release packaging for software developers, along with collaboration tools such as wikis, discussion forums, and document repositories, DISA says.

DISA also says it will deploy a cloud computing-based version of the SoftwareForge tools for classified environments. DISA also plans to add software testing and certification services to Forge.mil. Mihelcic says Forge.mil is similar to the "Web 2.0 paradigm of putting services on the Web and making them accessible to a large number of users to increase the adoption of capabilities. We're using the same collaboration approach to speed the development of DOD systems."

FIGURE 4.13

The U.S. Department of Defense is becoming both an adopter and a provider of open-source software.

Source: Andrea Comas/Reuters/Landov.

Meanwhile, DISA has licensed its Corporate Management Information System (CMIS) to the OSSI to develop an open-source version of the 50-odd applications that DISA uses to manage its workforce. The CMIS applications support human resources, training, payroll, and other personnel management functions that meet federal regulations. DISA, which provides IT services to the Department of Defense, made the decision to share its applications after other agencies expressed interest in them, says Richard Nelson, chief of personnel systems support at DISA's manpower, personnel, and security directorate. "Federal agencies discovered that the applications we have could be of benefit more widely," he says. Interest is coming from states and counties, as well.

DISA worked with the nonprofit OSSI, which promotes the use of open source in government and academia. OSSI copyrighted the software stack and licensed it back to DISA, making it available at no cost to government agencies under the Open Software License 3.0. "It's already paid for because the taxpayer paid for us to build it," Nelson says.

OSSI wanted to create a process that could be repeated with other government-built applications. "The opportunity was more than the product," executive director John Weatherby says. "One of the key things was to set up a system, a process that can be replicated by other government agencies."

CMIS comprises more than 50 Web applications, including workforce management, automated workflow, learning management, balanced scorecard, and telework management. CMIS has 16,000 users, including DISA employees and military contractors. Originally written in 1997, CMIS was revamped in January 2006 using the latest Web-based tools, including an Adobe Cold Fusion front-end and a Microsoft SQL Server 2005 back-end.

Nelson says CMIS is easy to use because it takes advantage of modern Web-based interfaces, including drop-down lists for data input. "We've been able to cut down on help desk support so substantially," Nelson says. "With the old version, we were running anywhere from 75 to 100 help desk calls and e-mails a day. Now our average is less than five e-mails and calls. It's not because people are using it less but because it has fewer problems."

Nelson says a key driver for CMIS is that it needs to be so intuitive that users don't need training. "If the customer requires instruction on the product, we have failed and we will do it over," Nelson says. "The reason that we're able to do that so successfully is that we take a somewhat different approach to the way most software is designed. Most software is designed so that business logic and processes need to follow software logic and process. Therefore it requires substantial training. We do it exactly opposite."

The OSSI will make CMIS available in two different licenses: a regular open-source license for government agencies and companies, and a free license for academia. Nelson says CMIS has a cutting-edge approach to learning management, handling everything from training course sign-up to approvals and payment. Another unusual feature of CMIS is its telework management application.

Nelson says he hopes many organizations will license CMIS and start adding new capabilities so DISA can take advantage of a vibrant CMIS community of developers. Within three years, "I would hope that a number of others inside government and beyond are using it," Nelson says. "I'm hoping we all have ready access to qualified developers. I'm hoping that DISA gets access to a substantial number of additional applications . . . without having to build them ourselves."

Going forward, DISA wants to encourage use of and training in Adobe Cold Fusion, which it used to build OSCMIS, to increase the talent pool of OSCMIS developers. "We would even like to start with kids in high school to get them interested in software development as a career," Nelson says."

Source: Adapted from Carolyn Duffy Marsan, "Military Enlists Open Source Community," *Network World*, April 27, 2009; John Fontana, "DoD: Open Source as Good as Proprietary Software," *Network World*, October 27, 2009; J. Nicholas Hoover, "Defense CIO Touts Benefits of Open Source," *InformationWeek*, October 28, 2009; and J. Nicholas Hoover, "Defense Info Agency Open-Sources Its Web Apps," *InformationWeek*, August 21, 2009.

CASE STUDY QUESTIONS

1. Given the critical nature of defense activities, security in this environment is a primary concern. How do the agencies discussed in the case address this issue? Can you think of anything else they could be doing? Provide some recommendations.

2. The U.S. Department of Defense is arguably one of the largest organizations in the world. Managing technology for such an organization is certainly a major endeavor. Does the shift toward open-source initiatives help in this regard? Does it hurt? Discuss the advantages and disadvantages of adopting open-source applications in large organizations.

3. After reading the case, do you think the shift to open-source software involved a major cultural change for the Department of Defense? Would you expect the same to be the case for large companies? Justify your answer.

REAL WORLD ACTIVITIES

1. Small open-source applications have been around for quite some time, but large-scale open-source systems have begun to emerge. Go online and search the Internet for examples of businesses adopting open-source technologies for major organizational systems. Prepare a presentation to highlight several examples from your research.

2. How does the open-source model of application development and distribution differ from the more common, proprietary approach? Do open-source applications present a legitimate threat to commercial software development, or will they remain niche applications? Break into small groups to discuss various reasons that the companies may or may not want to adopt open-source technologies.

FIGURE 4.14

The system and application software interface between end users and computer hardware.

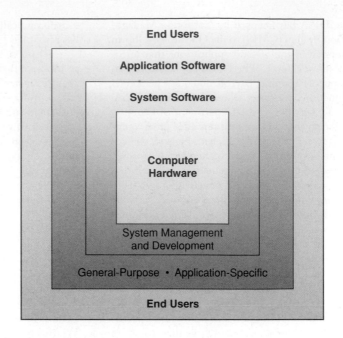

Resource Management. An operating system uses a variety of resource management programs to manage the hardware and networking resources of a computer system, including its CPU, memory, secondary storage devices, telecommunications processors, and input/output peripherals. For example, memory management programs keep track of where data and programs are stored. They may also subdivide memory into a number of sections and swap parts of programs and data between memory and magnetic disks or other secondary storage devices. This process can provide a computer system with a virtual memory capability that is significantly larger than the real memory capacity of its primary storage circuits. So, a computer with a virtual memory capability can process large programs and greater amounts of data than the capacity of its memory chips would normally allow.

File Management. An operating system contains **file management** programs that control the creation, deletion, and access of files of data and programs. File management also involves keeping track of the physical location of files on magnetic disks and other secondary storage devices. So operating systems maintain directories of information about the location and characteristics of files stored on a computer system's secondary storage devices.

Task Management. The **task management** programs of an operating system help accomplish the computing tasks of end users. The programs control which task gets

FIGURE 4.15

The basic functions of an operating system include a user interface, resource management, task management, file management, and utilities and other functions.

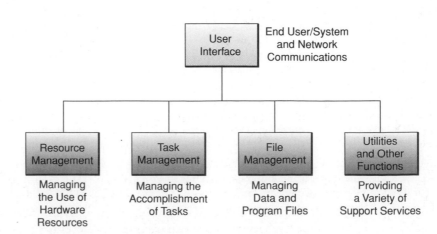

access to the CPU and for how much time. The task management functions can allocate a specific slice of CPU time to a particular task and interrupt the CPU at any time to substitute a higher priority task. Several different approaches to task management may be taken, each with advantages in certain situations.

Multitasking (sometimes referred to as *multiprogramming* or *time-sharing*) is a task management approach that allows for several computing tasks to be performed in a seemingly simultaneous fashion. In reality, multitasking assigns only one task at a time to the CPU, but it switches from one program to another so quickly that it gives the appearance of executing all of the programs at the same time. There are two basic types of multitasking: *preemptive* and *cooperative*. In preemptive multitasking, the task management functions parcel out CPU *time slices* to each program. In contrast, cooperative multitasking allows each program to control the CPU for as long as it needs it. If a program is not using the CPU, however, it can allow another program to use it temporarily. Most Windows and UNIX-based operating systems use the preemptive approach, whereas most Macintosh-style platforms use cooperative multitasking. Although the terms *multitasking* and *multiprocessing* are often used interchangeably, they are actually different concepts based on the number of CPUs being used. In multiprocessing, more than one CPU is being accessed, but in multitasking, only one CPU is in operation.

Most computers make use of some sort of multitasking. On modern microcomputers, multitasking is made possible by the development of powerful processors and their ability to address much larger memory capacities directly. This capability allows primary storage to be subdivided into several large partitions, each of which is used by a different software application.

In effect, a single computer can act as if it were several computers, or *virtual machines*, because each application program runs independently at the same time. The number of programs that can be run concurrently depends on the amount of memory that is available and the amount of processing each job demands. That's because a microprocessor (or CPU) can become overloaded with too many jobs and provide unacceptably slow response times. However, if memory and processing capacities are adequate, multitasking allows end users to switch easily from one application to another, share data files among applications, and process some applications in a *background* mode. Typically, background tasks include large printing jobs, extensive mathematical computations, or unattended telecommunications sessions.

Microsoft Windows

For many years, MS-DOS (Microsoft Disk Operating System) was the most widely used microcomputer operating system. It is a single-user, single-tasking operating system but was given a graphical user interface and limited multitasking capabilities by combining it with Microsoft **Windows.** Microsoft began replacing its DOS/Windows combination in 1995 with the Windows 95 operating system, featuring a graphical user interface, true multitasking, networking, multimedia, and many other capabilities. Microsoft introduced an enhanced Windows 98 version during 1998, and a Windows Me (Millennium Edition) consumer PC system in 2000.

Microsoft introduced its **Windows NT** (New Technology) operating system in 1995. Windows NT is a powerful, multitasking, multiuser operating system that was installed on many network servers to manage PCs with high-performance computing requirements. New Server and Workstation versions were introduced in 1997. Microsoft substantially enhanced its Windows NT products with the **Windows 2000** operating system during the year 2000.

Late in 2001, Microsoft introduced **Windows XP** Home Edition and Professional versions, and thus formally merged its two Windows operating system lines for consumer and business users, uniting them around the Windows NT and Windows 2000 code base. With Windows XP, consumers and home users finally received an enhanced Windows operating system with the performance and stability features that business users had in Windows 2000 and continue to have in Windows XP Professional. Microsoft also introduced four new **Windows Server 2003** versions in 2008, which are summarized and compared in Figure 4.16.

FIGURE 4.16   Comparing the purposes of the four versions of the Microsoft Windows Server 2008 operating system.

Microsoft Windows Server 2008 Comparisons

- **Windows Server 2008, Standard Edition**
  For smaller server applications, including file and print sharing, Internet and intranet connectivity, and centralized desktop application deployment.
- **Windows Server 2008, Enterprise Edition**
  For larger business applications, XML Web services, enterprise collaboration, and enterprise network support.
- **Windows Server 2008, Datacenter Edition**
  For business-critical and mission-critical applications demanding the highest levels of scalability and availability.
- **Windows Server 2008, Web Edition**
  For Web serving and hosting, providing a platform for developing and deploying Web services and applications.

In 2006, Microsoft released their next operating system called Vista. Vista contains hundreds of new features; some of the most significant include an updated graphical user interface and visual style dubbed Windows Aero, improved search features, new multimedia creation tools such as Windows DVD Maker, and completely redesigned networking, audio, print, and display subsystems. Vista also aims to increase the level of communication between machines on a home network using peer-to-peer technology, making it easier to share files and digital media between computers and devices.

For developers, Vista introduced version 3.0 of the .NET Framework, which aims to make it significantly easier for developers to write high-quality applications than with the previous versions of Windows.

Microsoft's primary stated objective with Vista, however, was to improve the state of security in the Windows operating system. One of the most common criticisms of Windows XP and its predecessors has been their commonly exploited security vulnerabilities and overall susceptibility to malware, viruses, and buffer overflows. In light of these complaints, then-Microsoft chairman Bill Gates announced in early 2002 a companywide "Trustworthy Computing Initiative" to incorporate security work into every aspect of software development at the company. Microsoft claimed that it prioritized improving the security of Windows XP and Windows Server 2003 rather than finishing Windows Vista, significantly delaying its completion.

During 2008, a new server product, entitled (appropriately enough) Windows Server 2008, has emerged. Windows Server 2008 is built from the same code base as Windows Vista; therefore, it shares much of the same architecture and functionality. Because the code base is common, it automatically comes with most of the technical, security, management, and administrative features new to Windows Vista such as the rewritten networking processes (native IPv6, native wireless, speed, and security improvements); improved image-based installation, deployment, and recovery; improved diagnostics, monitoring, event logging, and reporting tools; new security features; improved Windows Firewall with secure default configuration; .NET Framework 3.0 technologies; and the core kernel, memory, and file system improvements. Processors and memory devices are modeled as Plug and Play devices, to allow hot-plugging of these devices.

Windows Server 2008 is already in release 2 as several performance and security enhancements required a major upgrade.

In 2009, Microsoft released their newest operating system, Windows 7. Unlike its predecessor, Vista, which introduced a large number of new features, Windows 7 was intended to be a more focused and incremental upgrade with the goal of being fully compatible with applications and hardware with which Vista was already compatible. Windows 7 has been very well received and is rapidly replacing the installed base of Vista without receiving any of the complaints and struggles encountered by Vista adopters and users.

UNIX

Originally developed by AT&T, **UNIX** now is also offered by other vendors, including Solaris by Sun Microsystems and AIX by IBM. UNIX is a multitasking, multiuser, network-managing operating system whose portability allows it to run on mainframes, midrange computers, and microcomputers. UNIX is still a popular choice for Web and other network servers.

Linux

Linux is a low-cost, powerful, and reliable UNIX-like operating system that is rapidly gaining market share from UNIX and Windows servers as a high-performance operating system for network servers and Web servers in both small and large networks. Linux was developed as free or low-cost *shareware* or *open-source software* over the Internet in the 1990s by Linus Torvald of Finland and millions of programmers around the world. Linux is still being enhanced in this way but is sold with extra features and support services by software vendors such as Red Hat, Caldera, and SUSE Linux. PC versions, which support office software suites, Web browsers, and other application software, are also available.

Open-Source Software

The concept of **open-source software** (OSS) is growing far beyond the Linux operating system. The basic idea behind open source is very simple: When programmers can read, redistribute, and modify the source code for a piece of software, the software evolves. People improve it, people adapt it, people fix bugs. This development can happen at a speed that, if one is accustomed to the slow pace of conventional software development, seems astonishing. The open-source community of software developers has learned that this rapid evolutionary process produces better software than the traditional commercial (closed) model, in which only a very few programmers can see the source. The concept of open source, admittedly, runs counter to the highly commercial (and proprietary) world of traditional software development. Nonetheless, an increasingly large number of developers have embraced the open-source concept and come to realize that the proprietary approach to software development has hidden costs that can often outweigh its benefits.

Since 1998, the OSS movement has become a revolution in software development. This revolution, however, can actually trace its roots back more than 30 years. Typically, in the PC era, computer software had been sold only as a finished product, otherwise called a *precompiled binary*, which is installed on a user's computer by copying files to appropriate directories or folders. Moving to a new computer platform (Windows to Macintosh, for example) usually required the purchase of a new license. If the company went out of business or discontinued support of a product, users of that product had no recourse. Bug fixes were completely dependent on the organization that sold the software. In contrast, OSS is software that is licensed to guarantee free access to the programming behind the precompiled binary, otherwise called the *source code*. This access allows the user to install the software on a new platform without an additional purchase and to get support (or create a support consortium with other like-minded users) for a product whose creator no longer supports it. Those who are technically inclined can fix bugs themselves rather than waiting for someone else to do so. Generally, there is a central distribution mechanism that allows users to obtain the source code, as well as precompiled binaries in some cases. There are also mechanisms by which users may pay a fee to obtain the software, such as on a CD-ROM or DVD, which may also include some technical support. A variety of licenses are used to ensure that the source code will remain available, wherever the code is actually used.

To be clear, there are several things open source is not: It is not shareware, public-domain software, freeware, or software viewers and readers made freely available without access to source code. Shareware, whether or not the user registers it and pays the registration fee, typically allows no access to the underlying source code. Unlike freeware and public-domain software, OSS is copyrighted and distributed with license terms designed to ensure that the source code will always be available. Although a fee may be charged for the software's packaging, distribution, or support, the complete package needed to create files is included, not simply a portion needed to view files created elsewhere.

The philosophy of open source is based on a variety of models that sometimes conflict; indeed, it often seems there are as many philosophies and models for developing and managing OSS as there are major products. In 1998, a small group of open-source enthusiasts decided it was time to formalize some things about open source. The newly formed group registered themselves on the Internet as www.open-source.org and began the process of defining exactly what is, and what is not, open-source software. As it stands today, open-source licensing is defined by the following characteristics:

- The license shall not restrict any party from selling or giving away the software as a component of an aggregate software distribution containing programs from several different sources.

- The program must include source code and must allow distribution in source code, as well as compiled form.

- The license must allow modifications and derived works and must allow them to be distributed under the same terms as the license of the original software.

- The license may restrict source code from being distributed in modified form only if the license allows the distribution of patch files with the source code for the purpose of modifying the program at build time.

- The license must not discriminate against any person or group of persons.

- The license must not restrict anyone from making use of the program in a specific field of endeavor.

- The rights attached to the program must apply to all to whom the program is redistributed without the need for execution of an additional license by those parties.

- The license must not be specific to a product.

- The license must not contaminate other software by placing restrictions on any software distributed along with the licensed software.

This radical approach to software development and distribution is not without its detractors—most notably Microsoft. Nonetheless, the open-source movement is flourishing and stands to continue to revolutionize the way we think about software development.

OpenOffice.org 3

A relative newcomer to the open-source arena is an entire office suite offered by Sun Microsystems called OpenOffice.org 3. This product, built under the open-source standards described above, is a complete integrated office suite that provides all the common applications including word processing, spreadsheet, presentation graphics, and database management. It can store and retrieve files in a wide variety of data formats, including all of the file formats associated with the other major office suite applications on the market.

Best of all, OpenOffice.org 3 can be downloaded and used *entirely free of any license fees*. OpenOffice.org 3 is released under the LGPL license. This means you may use it for any purpose: domestic, commercial, educational, or public administration. You may install it on as many computers as you like, and you may make copies and give them away to family, friends, students, employees—anyone you like.

Mac OS X

Actually based on a form of UNIX, the **Mac OS X** (pronounced MAC OS 10) is the latest operating system from Apple for the iMac and other Macintosh microcomputers. The Mac OS X version 10.2 Jaguar has an advanced graphical user interface and multi-tasking and multimedia capabilities, along with an integrated Web browser, e-mail, instant messaging, search engine, digital media player, and many other features.

Mac OS X was a radical departure from previous Macintosh operating systems; its underlying code base is completely different from previous versions. Its core, named Darwin, is an open source, UNIX-like operating system. Apple layered over Darwin a number of proprietary components, including the Aqua interface and the Finder, to complete the GUI-based operating system that is Mac OS X.

Mac OS X also included a number of features intended to make the operating system more stable and reliable than Apple's previous operating systems. Preemptive multitasking and memory protection, for example, improved the ability of the operating system to run multiple applications simultaneously that don't interrupt or corrupt each other.

The most visible change was the Aqua theme. The use of soft edges, translucent colors, and pinstripes—similar to the hardware design of the first iMacs—brought more texture and color to the interface than OS 9's "Platinum" appearance had offered. Numerous users of the older versions of the operating system decried the new look as "cutesy" and lacking in professional polish. However, Aqua also has been called a bold and innovative step forward at a time when user interfaces were seen as "dull and boring." Despite the controversy, the look was instantly recognizable, and even before the first version of Mac OS X was released, third-party developers started producing skins (look-and-feel colors and styles for application interfaces) for customizable applications that mimicked the Aqua appearance.

Mac OS X also includes its own software development tools, most prominently an integrated development environment called Xcode. Xcode provides interfaces to compilers that support several programming languages including C, C++, Objective-C, and Java. For the Apple Intel Transition, it was modified so that developers could easily create an operating system to remain compatible with both the Intel-based and PowerPC-based Macintosh.

Application Virtualization

Consider all of the various types of software applications we discussed in the first section of this chapter along with the multiple operating systems we just discussed. What happens when a user who has a machine running Windows needs to run an application designed specifically for a machine running Mac OS X? The answer used to be "Borrow someone's Mac." Through the development of application virtualization, a much more useful and productive answer exists. *Application virtualization* is an umbrella term that describes software technologies that improve portability, manageability, and compatibility of applications by insulating them from the underlying operating system on which they are executed. A fully virtualized application is not installed in the traditional sense; it is just executed as if it is. The application is fooled into believing that it is directly interfacing with the original operating system and all the resources managed by it, when in reality it is not. Application virtualization is just an extension of operating system virtualization where the same basic concepts fool the whole operating system into thinking it is running on a particular type of hardware when it is, in fact, not.

The concept of virtualization is not a recent development. The use of a virtual machine was a common practice during the mainframe era where extremely large machines were partitioned into smaller, separate virtual machines or domains to allow multiple users to run unique sets of applications and processes simultaneously. Each user constituency used a portion of the total available machine resources and the virtualization approach made it appear that each domain was an entirely separate machine from all the rest. If you have ever set up a new PC and created a partition on the hard drive, you have taken advantage of virtualization. You have taken one physical drive and created two virtual drives—one for each partition.

Application virtualization is a logical next step from these early roots. The benefits to the enterprise range from the cost savings associated with not having to have multiple platforms for multiple applications, to the energy savings associated with not having a multitude of servers running at low capacity while eating up electricity and generating heat.

A thorough discussion of virtualization is well beyond the scope of this text but suffice to say it is rapidly blurring the boundaries between machines and operating systems and operating systems and applications. Add this to the cloud computing concept and we have the makings of an anytime, anywhere, any machine, any application world.

Toronto's Hospital for Sick Children: Challenges in Making Virtualization Work

Toronto's Hospital for Sick Children has learned the hard way that virtualization efforts won't be successful if vendors aren't ready to support you, according to its director of technology, Ana Andreasian. The hospital (usually referred to as "Sick Kids") has already consolidated a considerable amount of its server infrastructure, which now includes 300 physical and 60 virtual machines. Sick Kids employs about 110 IT staff members who serve more than 5,000 employees.

Andreasian said the biggest issue she's experienced so far has come from vendors who do not properly test their applications before offering them to virtualization customers. "They'll say, 'Give me one CPU, one gig of memory, and I'm good,'" she says. "Then you'll find they need four CPUs and four gigs of RAM. You wind up having a never-ending discussion on how to solve the performance problems."

Another challenge has been vendors who say they're willing to support virtual environments, but not fully. "Some vendors have a condition: if you have a problem, you have to move (the application) out of a virtual environment," she says. "That's just not practical."

Sick Kids Hospital is somewhat unusual in that it started its virtualization journey by focusing on storage systems rather than servers. Andreasian explained that the organization currently manages some 150 terabytes of data, which is always on the increase. Devices to handle that data, meanwhile, always end up going out of support. "We were facing the question: How do you migrate that data? It's a huge cost," she says, adding that no one wants to experience any downtime associated with such a migration. And all this has to happen in such a way that's transparent to the user.

The hospital has also turned to Citrix for application virtualization in order to allow remote support, which is important in a hospital situation where many clinicians may need to work from home. Sick Kids is now using VMware to deal with the more common issues around managing server fleets, such as lack of real estate, power costs, and the need to provision (that is, set up) machines more quickly.

"In the physical world, if you have good planning and processes in place, that will help you with virtualization," says Dennis Corning, HP's worldwide senior manager of product marketing for virtualization.

Andreasian agrees. "Provisioning (a virtual server) is easy. De-provisioning once the business user no longer needs it is where it's difficult," she says. "They might not tell you it's no longer necessarily. You need governance and monitoring and process."

Source: Adapted from Shane Schick, "Hospital CTO Identifies Virtualization Gotchas," *CIO.com*, January 28, 2010.

Other System Management Programs

There are many other types of important system management software besides operating systems. These include *database management systems*, which we will cover in Chapter 5, and *network management programs*, which we will cover in Chapter 6. Figure 4.17 compares several types of system software offered by IBM and its competitors.

Several other types of system management software are marketed as separate programs or included as part of an operating system. Utility programs, or utilities, are an important example. Programs like Norton Utilities perform miscellaneous housekeeping and file conversion functions. Examples include data backup, data recovery, virus protection, data compression, and file defragmentation. Most operating systems also provide many utilities that perform a variety of helpful chores for computer users.

FIGURE 4.17   Comparing system software offered by IBM and its main competitors.

Software Category	What It Does	IBM Product	Customers	Main Competitor	Customers
Network management	Monitors networks to keep them up and running.	Tivoli	T. Rowe Price uses it to safeguard customer records.	HP OpenView	Amazon.com uses it to monitor its servers.
Application server	Shuttles data between business apps and the Web.	WebSphere	REI uses it to serve up its Web site and distribute data.	BEA WebLogic	Washingtonpost.com builds news pages with it.
Database manager	Provides digital storehouses for business data.	DB2	Mikasa uses it to help customers find its products online.	Oracle 11g	It runs Southwest Airlines' frequent-flyer program.
Collaboration tools	Powers everything from e-mail to electronic calendars.	Lotus	Retailer Sephora uses it to coordinate store maintenance.	Microsoft Exchange	Time Inc. uses it to provide e-mail to its employees.
Development tools	Allows programmers to craft software code quickly.	Rational	Merrill Lynch used it to build code for online trading.	Microsoft Visual Studio .NET	Used to develop management system.

Other examples of system support programs include performance monitors and security monitors. **Performance monitors** are programs that monitor and adjust the performance and usage of one or more computer systems to keep them running efficiently. **Security monitors** are packages that monitor and control the use of computer systems and provide warning messages and record evidence of unauthorized use of computer resources. A recent trend is to merge both types of programs into operating systems like Microsoft's Windows 2008 Datacenter Server or into system management software like Computer Associates' CA-Unicenter, which can manage both mainframe systems and servers in a data center.

Another important software trend is the use of system software known as **application servers,** which provide a *middleware* interface between an operating system and the application programs of users. Middleware is software that helps diverse software applications and networked computer systems exchange data and work together more efficiently. Examples include application servers, Web servers, and enterprise application integration (EAI) software. Thus, for example, application servers like BEA's WebLogic and IBM's WebSphere help Web-based e-business and e-commerce applications run much faster and more efficiently on computers using Windows, UNIX, and other operating systems.

Programming Languages

To understand computer software, you need a basic knowledge of the role that programming languages play in the development of computer programs. A programming language allows a programmer to develop the sets of instructions that constitute a computer program. Many different programming languages have been developed, each with its own unique vocabulary, grammar, and uses.

Machine Languages

Machine languages (or *first-generation languages*) are the most basic level of programming languages. In the early stages of computer development, all program instructions had to be written using binary codes unique to each computer. This type of programming involves the difficult task of writing instructions in the form of strings of binary digits (ones and zeros) or other number systems. Programmers must have a detailed knowledge of the internal operations of the specific type of CPU they are using. They must write long series of detailed instructions to accomplish even simple processing tasks. Programming in machine language requires specifying the storage

FIGURE 4.18

Examples of four levels of programming languages. These programming language instructions might be used to compute the sum of two numbers as expressed by the formula X = Y + Z.

Four Levels of Programming Languages	
● **Machine Languages:** Use binary coded instructions 1010 11001 1011 11010 1100 11011	● **High-Level Languages:** Use brief statements or arithmetic notations BASIC: X = Y + Z COBOL: COMPUTE X = Y + Z
● **Assembler Languages:** Use symbolic coded instructions LOD Y ADD Z STR X	● **Fourth-Generation Languages:** Use natural and nonprocedural statements SUM THE FOLLOWING NUMBERS

locations for every instruction and item of data used. Instructions must be included for every switch and indicator used by the program. These requirements make machine language programming a difficult and error-prone task. A machine language program to add two numbers together in the CPU of a specific computer and store the result might take the form shown in Figure 4.18.

Assembler Languages

Assembler languages (or *second-generation languages*) are the next level of programming languages. They were developed to reduce the difficulties in writing machine language programs. The use of assembler languages requires language translator programs called *assemblers* that allow a computer to convert the instructions of such language into machine instructions. Assembler languages are frequently called symbolic languages because symbols are used to represent operation codes and storage locations. Convenient alphabetic abbreviations called *mnemonics* (memory aids) and other symbols represent operation codes, storage locations, and data elements. For example, the computation X = Y + Z in an assembler language might take the form shown in Figure 4.18.

Assembler languages are still used as a method of programming a computer in a machine-oriented language. Most computer manufacturers provide an assembler language that reflects the unique machine language instruction set of a particular line of computers. This feature is particularly desirable to *system programmers*, who program system software (as opposed to application programmers, who program application software), because it provides them with greater control and flexibility in designing a program for a particular computer. They can then produce more efficient software—that is, programs that require a minimum of instructions, storage, and CPU time to perform a specific processing assignment.

High-Level Languages

High-level languages (or *third-generation languages*) use instructions, which are called *statements*, that include brief statements or arithmetic expressions. Individual high-level language statements are actually *macroinstructions*; that is, each individual statement generates several machine instructions when translated into machine language by high-level language translator programs called *compilers* or *interpreters*. High-level language statements resemble the phrases or mathematical expressions required to express the problem or procedure being programmed. The *syntax* (vocabulary, punctuation, and grammatical rules) and *semantics* (meanings) of such statements do not reflect the internal code of any particular computer. For example, the computation X = Y + Z would be programmed in the high-level languages of BASIC and COBOL as shown in Figure 4.18.

High-level languages like BASIC, COBOL, and FORTRAN are easier to learn and program than an assembler language because they have less rigid rules, forms, and syntaxes. However, high-level language programs are usually less efficient than assembler language programs and require a greater amount of computer time for translation into machine instructions. Because most high-level languages are machine-independent, programs written in a high-level language do not have to be reprogrammed when a new computer is installed, and programmers do not have to learn a different language for each type of computer.

Fourth-Generation Languages

The term fourth-generation language describes a variety of programming languages that are more nonprocedural and *conversational* than prior languages. These languages are called fourth-generation languages (4GLs) to differentiate them from machine languages (first generation), assembler languages (second generation), and high-level languages (third generation).

Most fourth-generation languages are *nonprocedural languages* that encourage users and programmers to specify the results they want, while the computer determines the sequence of instructions that will accomplish those results. Thus, fourth-generation languages have helped simplify the programming process. Natural languages are sometimes considered *fifth-generation* languages (5GLs) and are very close to English or other human languages. Research and development activity in artificial intelligence (AI) is developing programming languages that are as easy to use as ordinary conversation in one's native tongue. For example, INTELLECT, a natural language, would use a statement like, "What are the average exam scores in MIS 200?" to program a simple average exam score task.

In the early days of 4GLs, results suggested that high-volume transaction processing environments were not in the range of a 4GL's capabilities. Although 4GLs were characterized by their ease of use, they were also viewed as less flexible than their predecessors, primarily due to their increased storage and processing speed requirements. In today's large data volume environment, 4GLs are widely used and no longer viewed as a trade-off between ease of use and flexibility.

Modern (and Automatic?) Code Generation

Twenty years ago, software engineer Fred Brooks famously observed that there was no silver bullet that could slay "the monster of missed schedules, blown budgets and flawed products." Today, the creation of software might seem as expensive, trouble-prone, and difficult as ever—and yet progress is being made. Although no silver bullet is in sight, an array of new techniques promises to further boost a programmer's productivity, at least in some application domains.

The techniques span a broad spectrum of methods and results, but all are aimed at generating software automatically. Typically, they generate code from high-level, machine-readable designs or from domain-specific languages—assisted by advanced compilers—that sometimes can be used by nonprogrammers.

Gordon Novak, a computer science professor at the University of Texas at Austin and a member of the school's Laboratory for Artificial Intelligence, is working on "automatic programming"—using libraries of generic versions of programs, such as algorithms—to sort or find items in a list. Unlike traditional subroutines, which have simple but rigid interfaces and are invoked by other lines of program code, his technique works at a higher level and is therefore more flexible and easier to use.

Novak's users construct "views" that describe application data and principles and then connect the views by arrows in diagrams that show the relationships among the data. The diagrams are, in essence, very high-level flowcharts of the desired program. They get compiled in a way that customizes the stored generic algorithms for the user's specific problem, and the result is ordinary source code such as C, C++, or Java.

Novak says he was able to generate 250 lines of source code for an indexing program in 90 seconds with his system. That's equivalent to a week of productivity for an average programmer using a traditional language. "You are describing your program at a higher level," he says. "And what my program is saying is, 'I can tailor the algorithm for your application for free.'"

Douglas Smith, principal scientist at Kestrel Institute, a nonprofit computer science research firm in Palo Alto, California, is developing tools to "automate knowledge and get it into the computer." A programmer starts with Kestrel's Specware, which is a general-purpose, fifth-generation language that specifies a program's functions without regard to the ultimate programming language, system architecture, algorithms, data structures, and so on. Specware draws on a library of components, but the components aren't code. They are at a higher level and include design knowledge and principles about algorithms, data structures, and so on. Smith calls them "abstract templates."

In addition, Specware can produce proofs that the working code is "correct"—that is, that it conforms to the requirements put in by the user (which, of course, may contain errors). "Some customers want that for very-high-assurance applications, with no security flaws," Smith says. Kestrel does work for NASA and U.S. military and security agencies.

"It's a language for writing down problem requirements, a high-level statement of what a solution should be, without saying how to solve the problem," Smith says. "We think it's the ultimate frontier in software engineering. It's what systems analysts do."

Source: Adapted from Gary Anthes, "In the Labs: Automatic Code Generators," *Computerworld*, March 20, 2006.

Object-Oriented Languages

Object-oriented languages like Visual Basic, C++, and Java are also considered fifth-generation languages and have become major tools of software development. Briefly, whereas most programming languages separate data elements from the procedures or actions that will be performed on them, object-oriented languages tie them together into **objects.** Thus, an object consists of data and the actions that can be performed on the data. For example, an object could be a set of data about a bank customer's savings account and the operations (e.g., interest calculations) that might be performed on the data. An object also could be data in graphic form, such as a video display window plus the display actions that might be used on it. See Figure 4.19.

In procedural languages, a program consists of procedures to perform actions on each data element. However, in object-oriented systems, objects tell other objects to perform actions on themselves. For example, to open a window on a computer video display, a beginning menu object could send a window object a message to open, and

FIGURE 4.19

An example of a bank savings account object. This object consists of data about a customer's account balance and the basic operations that can be performed on those data.

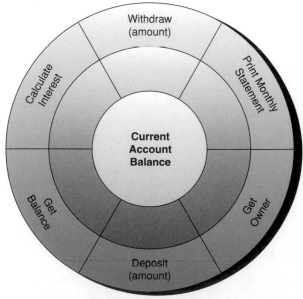

Savings Account Object

FIGURE 4.20 The Visual Basic object-oriented programming environment.

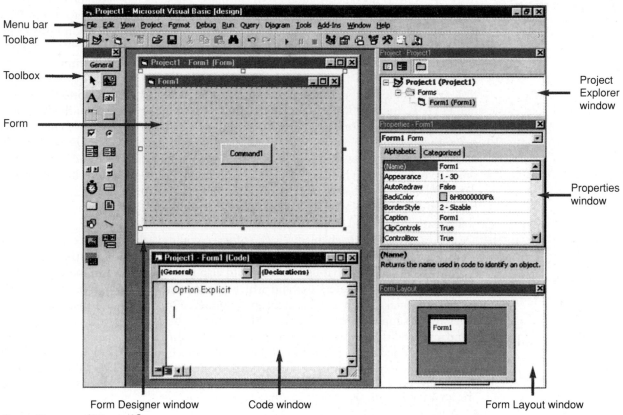

Menu bar

Toolbar

Toolbox

Form

Project Explorer window

Properties window

Form Designer window   Code window   Form Layout window

Source: Courtesy of Microsoft®.

a window would appear on the screen. That's because the window object contains the program code for opening itself.

Object-oriented languages are easier to use and more efficient for programming the graphics-oriented user interfaces required by many applications. Therefore, they are the most widely used programming languages for software development today. Also, once objects are programmed, they are reusable. Therefore, reusability of objects is a major benefit of object-oriented programming. For example, programmers can construct a user interface for a new program by assembling standard objects such as windows, bars, boxes, buttons, and icons. Therefore, most object-oriented programming packages provide a GUI that supports a point-and-click, drag-and-drop visual assembly of objects known as *visual programming*. Figure 4.20 shows a display of the Visual Basic object-oriented programming environment. Object-oriented technology is discussed further in the coverage of object-oriented databases in Chapter 5.

Web Languages and Services

HTML, XML, and Java are three programming languages that are important tools for building multimedia Web pages, Web sites, and Web-based applications. In addition, XML and Java have become strategic components of the software technologies that support many Web services initiatives in business.

HTML

HTML (Hypertext Markup Language) is a page description language that creates hypertext or hypermedia documents. HTML inserts control codes within a document at points you can specify that create links (*hyperlinks*) to other parts of the document or to other documents anywhere on the World Wide Web. HTML embeds control codes in the ASCII text of a document that designate titles, headings, graphics, and multimedia components, as well as hyperlinks within the document.

As we mentioned previously, several of the programs in the top software suites automatically convert documents into HTML formats. These include Web browsers, word processing and spreadsheet programs, database managers, and presentation graphics packages. These and other specialized *Web publishing* programs like Microsoft FrontPage, Lotus FastSite, and Macromedia's DreamWeaver provide a range of features to help you design and create multimedia Web pages without formal HTML programming.

XML

XML (eXtensible Markup Language) is not a Web page format description language like HTML. Instead, XML describes the contents of Web pages (including business documents designed for use on the Web) by applying identifying tags or *contextual labels* to the data in Web documents. For example, a travel agency Web page with airline names and flight times would use hidden XML tags like "airline name" and "flight time" to categorize each of the airline flight times on that page. Or product inventory data available at a Web site could be labeled with tags like "brand," "price," and "size." By classifying data in this way, XML makes Web site information much more searchable, easier to sort, and easier to analyze.

For example, XML-enabled search software could easily find the exact product you specify if the product data on the Web site had been labeled with identifying XML tags. A Web site that uses XML could also more easily determine which Web page features its customers use and which products they investigate. Thus, XML promises to make electronic business and commerce processes a lot easier and more efficient by supporting the automatic electronic exchange of business data between companies and their customers, suppliers, and other business partners.

As mentioned at the beginning of the chapter, this entire textbook was revised and edited for the current edition using an XML-based application called PowerXEditor by Aptara. Let's focus our attention on this unique application of XML intended to create efficiencies in the publishing industry.

Aptara, Inc.: Revolutionizing the Publishing Industry through XML

The publishing industry has experienced an upheaval in the past decade or so. The "long tail" of sales of existing books via Web sellers such as Amazon and the improvement in software and hardware technologies that can replicate the experience of reading a book or magazine means publishing houses are printing and selling fewer new books. As a result, many of these companies are venturing into digital publishing.

"All the publishers are shifting from print to digital," said Dev Ganesan, president and CEO of Aptara, which specializes in content transformation. "That's a huge change. What that means for software companies is that they need to develop platforms for content creation that meet the needs of every customer. At the same time, customers are looking at publishing in terms of handling content in terms of authors, editors, and production employees. On top of that, they're trying to automate parts of the production process. And companies must be willing to market products using traditional and new media to reach the widest possible audience. So there are a lot of challenges, but a lot of opportunities, too."

The upshot of all this is that learning professionals now can deliver content more flexibly and at a lower cost. They can make static content dynamic by taking a body of knowledge in print—such as a book—and converting it to a digital format. They can then chunk that content into smaller sizes and organize those nuggets of information according to learners' needs. Moreover, they can get content published and distributed much more quickly via digital, online media. This is critical in an industry such as health care, which faces rapid changes due to technological innovation and regulation, said another Aptara source.

"In addition to the cost savings, they want to turn it around much faster," he said. "Time to market is becoming paramount because there's so much innovation going on. If they don't have their print products out faster, they fall behind."

A breakthrough product from Aptara is called PowerXEditor (PXE). An XML-based application, PXE allows a publisher to upload an existing book layout; edit or revise all elements of the book, including text look and feel, figures, tables, and other elements unique to that book; and output the book to a paging program that sets the book up for final printing. The important issue is that all of this is done in a digital format instead of the previously common method of tear pages and cut and paste of figures and tables. Because the PXE content is XML-based, the application can be accessed via the Internet using any conventional Web browser. This means all of the contributors to a textbook can have access to the various chapters and elements no matter where they are. Add in the workflow management aspects of PXE, and all phases of the textbook revising, copyediting, and proofing processes can be handled with ease.

Figure 4.21 shows a typical PXE screen. You might notice that it is in the process of editing the page you are currently reading. Figure 4.22 shows the XML code for the same page.

Source: Adapted from Brian Summerfield, "Executive Briefings: Balancing Print and Digital Media," *Chief Learning Officer*, March 2008. http://www.clomedia.com/includes/printcontent.php?aid=2133

FIGURE 4.21

The XML-based PowerXEditor allows all the collaborators on a book project to access the elements of the book via a common Web browser. Here is a screenshot of PXE on the page you are currently reading.

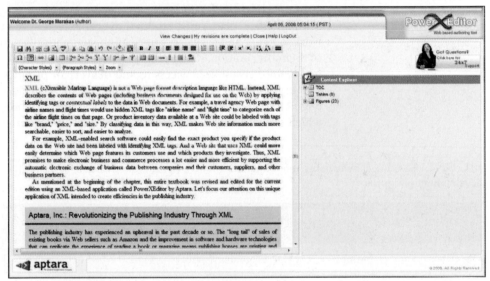

Source: Courtesy of Aptara.

FIGURE 4.22

This is a section of the XML code from the page you are currently reading. While XML looks similar to HTML source code, it is far more powerful and complex.

```
        features to help you design and create multimedia Web pages without formal HTML programming.
    </p>
    <p class="Head3" id="head3_19">XML</p>
  - <p class="Para_FL">
    - <span class="Def_term">
        <b>XML</b>
      </span>
      (eXtensible Markup Language) is not a Web page format description language like HTML. Instead, XML
      describes the contents of Web pages (including business documents designed for use on the Web) by
      applying identifying tags or
      <i>contextual labels</i>
      to the data in Web documents. For example, a travel agency Web page with airline names and flight
      times would use hidden XML tags like "airline name" and "flight time" to categorize each of the airline
      flight times on that page. Or product inventory data available at a Web site could be labeled with tags
      like "brand," "price," and "size." By classifying data in this way, XML makes Web site information much
      more searchable, easier to sort, and easier to analyze.
    </p>
    <p class="Para_indented">For example, XML-enabled search software could easily find the exact product
      you specify if the product data on the Web site had been labeled with identifying XML tags. And a Web
      site that uses XML could more easily determine which Web page features its customers use and which
      products they investigate. Thus, XML promises to make electronic business and commerce processes a
      lot easier and more efficient by supporting the automatic electronic exchange of business data between
      companies and their customers, suppliers, and other business partners.</p>
    <p class="Head3" id="head3_20">Java and .NET</p>
  - <p class="Para_FL">
    - <span class="Def_term">
```

Source: Courtesy of Aptara.

Java and .NET

Java is an object-oriented programming language created by Sun Microsystems that is revolutionizing the programming of applications for the World Wide Web and corporate intranets and extranets. Java is related to the C++ and Objective C programming languages but is much simpler and more secure and is computing-platform independent. Java is also specifically designed for real-time, interactive, Web-based network applications. Java applications consisting of small application programs, called *applets*, can be executed by any computer and any operating system anywhere in a network.

The ease of creating Java applets and distributing them from network servers to client PCs and network computers is one of the major reasons for Java's popularity. Applets can be small, special-purpose application programs or small modules of larger Java application programs. Java programs are platform-independent, too—they can run on Windows, UNIX, and Macintosh systems without modification.

Microsoft's **.NET** is a collection of programming support for what are known as Web services, the ability to use the Web rather than your own computer for various services (see Figure 4.23). .NET is intended to provide individual and business users with a seamlessly interoperable and Web-enabled interface for applications and computing devices and to make computing activities increasingly Web browser–oriented. The .NET platform includes servers, building-block services such as Web-based data storage, and device software. It also includes Passport, Microsoft's fill-in-the-form-only-once identity verification service.

The .NET platform is expected to enable the entire range of computing devices to work together and have user information automatically updated and synchronized on all of them. In addition, it will provide a premium online subscription service. The service will feature customized access to and delivery of products and services from a central starting point for the management of various applications (e.g., e-mail) or software (e.g., Office .NET). For developers, .NET offers the ability to create reusable modules, which should increase productivity and reduce the number of programming errors.

FIGURE 4.23 The benefits and limitations of the Java Enterprise Edition 6 (Java EE 6) and Microsoft .NET software development platforms.

Java EE 5		.NET	
PROS	**CONS**	**PROS**	**CONS**
• Runs on any operating system and application server (may need adjustments). • Handles complex, high-volume, high-transaction applications. • Has more enterprise features for session management, fail-over, load balancing, and application integration. • Is favored by experienced enterprise vendors such as IBM, BEA, SAP, and Oracle. • Offers a wide range of vendor choices for tools and application servers. • Has a proven track record.	• Has a complex application development environment. • Tools can be difficult to use. • Java Swing environment's ability to build graphical user interfaces has limitations. • May cost more to build, deploy, and manage applications. • Lacks built-in support for Web services standards. • Is difficult to use for quick-turnaround, low-cost, and mass-market projects.	• Easy-to-use tools may increase programmer productivity. • Has a strong framework for building rich graphical user interfaces. • Gives developers choice of working in more than 20 programming languages. • Is tightly integrated with Microsoft's operating system and enterprise server software. • May cost less, due in part to built-in application server in Windows, unified management, and less expensive tools. • Has built-in support for Web service standards.	• Framework runs only on Windows, restricting vendor choice. • Users of prior Microsoft tools and technology face a potentially steep learning curve. • New run-time infrastructure lacks maturity. • Questions persist about the scalability and transaction capability of the Windows platform. • Choice of integrated development environments is limited. • Getting older applications to run in new .NET environment may require effort.

Source: Carol Silwa, ".NET vs. Java," *Computerworld*, May 20, 2002, p. 31.

The full release of .NET is expected to take several years to complete, with intermittent releases of products such as a personal security service and new versions of Windows and Office that implement the .NET strategy coming on the market separately. Visual Studio .NET is a development environment that is now available, and Windows XP supports certain .NET capabilities.

The latest version of Java is Java Enterprise Edition 6 (Java EE 6), which has become the primary alternative to Microsoft's .NET software development platform for many organizations intent on capitalizing on the business potential of Web-based applications and Web services. Figure 4.23 compares the pros and cons of using Java EE 6 and .NET for software development.

Web Services

Web services are software components that are based on a framework of Web and object-oriented standards and technologies for using the Web that electronically link the applications of different users and different computing platforms. Thus, Web services can link key business functions for the exchange of data in real time within the Web-based applications that a business might share with its customers, suppliers, and other business partners. For example, Web services would enable the purchasing application of a business to use the Web to check the inventory of a supplier before placing a large order, while the sales application of the supplier could use Web services to automatically check the credit rating of the business with a credit-reporting agency before approving the purchase. Therefore, among both business and IT professionals, the term *Web services* is commonly used to describe the Web-based business and computing functions or services accomplished by Web services software technologies and standards.

Figure 4.24 illustrates how Web services work and identifies some of the key technologies and standards that are involved. The XML language is one of the key technologies that enable Web services to make applications work between different computing

FIGURE 4.24
The basic steps in accomplishing a Web services application.

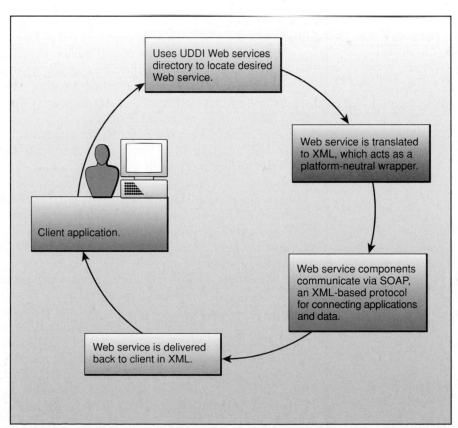

Source: Adapted from Bala Iyer, Jim Freedman, Mark Gaynor, and George Wyner, "Web Services: Enabling Dynamic Business Networks," *Communications of the Association for Information Systems* 11 (2003), p. 543.

platforms. Also important are **UDDI** (Universal Description, Discovery, and Integration), the "yellow pages" directory of all Web services and how to locate and use them, and **SOAP** (Simple Object Access Protocol), an XML-based protocol of specifications for connecting applications to the data that they need.

Web services promise to be the key software technology for automating access to data and application functions between a business and its trading partners. As companies increasingly move to doing business over the Web, Web services will become essential for the development of the easy and efficient e-business and e-commerce applications that will be required. The flexibility and interoperability of Web services will also be essential for coping with the fast-changing relationships between a company and its business partners that are commonplace in today's dynamic global business environment.

Airbus: Flying on SAP and Web Services

European aircraft builder Airbus has implemented a Web services–based travel management application from SAP as a first step in a planned groupwide migration to a service-oriented architecture (SOA). The airplane manufacturer is installing the travel management component of SAP's ERP software, mySAP, which uses SOA technology. "The new system replaces a homegrown system at the company's plant in France, a Lotus-based system in its Spanish operations, and earlier SAP versions at facilities in Germany and the United Kingdom," says James Westgarth, manager of travel technology procurement at Airbus.

"We like the idea of an open architecture, which SOA enables," Westgarth says. "We like the idea of being able to manage everything internally and to cherry-pick for the best solution in every class." "Additional components, such as online booking, could also come from SAP—if the software vendor has a superior product for that application," says Westgarth.

The decision to deploy a new Web services–based travel management system was driven in large part by a need to reduce administration costs and improve business processes.

Airbus has a travel budget of 250 million euros, which is used to help pay for more than 180,000 trips annually. The company aims to reduce costs by eliminating the current paper-based reimbursement process, which consumes time and labor, with a system that enables employees to process their own travel expenses online from their desktops or mobile devices.

A key benefit for employees: Reimbursement time will be reduced to 3 days from about 10 days. In addition, the new system allows Airbus to integrate new service providers more easily into its operations, notes Westgarth. The manufacturer has outsourced its valued-added tax reclaim activities to a third party specializing in this service. With the help of application link enablers, Westgarth and his team are able to link their travel management system into the company's other SAP applications, including finance and human resources. Airbus has a strategy to eventually migrate to the mySAP ERP across multiple systems and countries over a number of years.

"The company chose travel management to pilot mySAP ERP," says Westgarth. There have been some issues with the rollout of the travel management application, Westgarth concedes. "Because we're the first big company to implement this technology, we've had difficulty finding enough skilled people on the market," he said. "And some work was required to integrate the Web interface into our portal."

But Airbus employees, Westgarth said, like the Web-based application's new user interface, the single sign-on and the step-by-step guidance. And the company likes the flexibility. "No one was talking about low-cost carriers five years ago," he said. "We need to adapt to the market and to changing needs."

Source: Adapted from John Blau, "Airbus Flies on Web Services With SAP," *IDG News Service/CIO Magazine*, June 8, 2006.

Programming Software

Various software packages are available to help programmers develop computer programs. For example, *programming language translators* are programs that translate other programs into machine language instruction codes that computers can execute. Other software packages, such as programming language editors, are called *programming tools* because they help programmers write programs by providing a variety of program creation and editing capabilities. See Figure 4.25.

Language Translator Programs

Computer programs consist of sets of instructions written in programming languages that must be translated by a language translator into the computer's own machine language before they can be processed, or executed, by the CPU. Programming language translator programs (or *language processors*) are known by a variety of names. An **assembler** translates the symbolic instruction codes of programs written in an assembler language into machine language instructions, whereas a **compiler** translates high-level language statements.

An **interpreter** is a special type of compiler that translates and executes each statement in a program one at a time, instead of first producing a complete machine language program, as compilers and assemblers do. Java is an example of an interpreted language. Thus, the program instructions in Java applets are interpreted and executed *on the fly* as the applet is being executed by a client PC.

Programming Tools

Software development and the computer programming process have been enhanced by adding *graphical programming interfaces* and a variety of built-in development capabilities. Language translators have always provided some editing and diagnostic capabilities to identify programming errors or *bugs*. However, most software development programs now include powerful graphics-oriented *programming editors* and *debuggers*. These **programming tools** help programmers identify and minimize errors while they are programming. Such programming tools provide a computer-aided programming environment, which decreases the drudgery of programming while increasing the efficiency and productivity of software developers. Other programming tools include diagramming packages, code generators, libraries of reusable objects and program code, and prototyping tools. All of these programming tools are an essential part of widely used programming languages like Visual Basic, C++, and Java.

FIGURE 4.25

Using the graphical programming interface of a Java programming tool, Forte for Java, by Sun Microsystems.

Source: Courtesy of Sun Microsystems.

CASE Tools

Since the early days of programming, software developers have needed automated tools. Initially the concentration was on program support tools such as translators, compilers, assemblers, macroprocessors, and linkers and loaders. However, as computers became more powerful and the software that ran on them grew larger and more complex, the range of support tools began to expand. In particular, the use of interactive time-sharing systems for software development encouraged the development of program editors, debuggers, and code analyzers.

As the range of support tools expanded, manufacturers began to integrate them into a single application using a common interface. Such tools were referred to as CASE tools (computer-aided software engineering).

CASE tools can take a number of forms and be applied at different stages of the software development process. Those CASE tools that support activities early in the life cycle of a software project (e.g., requirements, design support tools) are sometimes called *front-end* or *upper* CASE tools. Those that are used later in the life cycle (e.g., compilers, test support tools) are called *back-end* or *lower* CASE tools.

Exploring the details of CASE tools is beyond the scope of this text, and you will encounter them again when you study systems analysis and design. For now, remember that CASE is an important part of resolving the problems of complex application development and maintenance of software applications.

Summary

- **Software.** Computer software consists of two major types of programs: (1) application software that directs the performance of a particular use, or application, of computers to meet the information processing needs of users and (2) system software that controls and supports the operations of a computer system as it performs various information processing tasks. Refer to Figure 4.2 for an overview of the major types of software.

- **Application Software.** Application software includes a variety of programs that can be segregated into general-purpose and application-specific categories. General-purpose application programs perform common information processing jobs for end users. Examples are word processing, electronic spreadsheet, and presentation graphics programs. Application-specific programs accomplish information processing tasks that support specific business functions or processes, scientific or engineering applications, and other computer applications in society.

- **System Software.** System software can be subdivided into system management programs and system development programs. System management programs manage the hardware, software, network, and data resources of a computer system during its execution of information processing jobs. Examples of system management programs are operating systems, network management programs, database management systems, system utilities, application servers, and performance and security monitors. Network management programs support

and manage telecommunications activities and network performance telecommunications networks. Database management systems control the development, integration, and maintenance of databases. Utilities are programs that perform routine computing functions, such as backing up data or copying files, as part of an operating system or as a separate package. System development programs like language translators and programming editors help IS specialists develop computer programs to support business processes.

- **Operating Systems.** An operating system is an integrated system of programs that supervises the operation of the CPU, controls the input/output storage functions of the computer system, and provides various support services. An operating system performs five basic functions: (1) a user interface for system and network communications with users, (2) resource management for managing the hardware resources of a computer system, (3) file management for managing files of data and programs, (4) task management for managing the tasks a computer must accomplish, and (5) utilities and other functions that provide miscellaneous support services.

- **Programming Languages.** Programming languages are a major category of system software. They require the use of a variety of programming packages to help programmers develop computer programs and language translator programs to convert programming language instructions into machine language instruction codes. The five major levels of programming languages are machine languages, assembler languages, high-level languages, fourth-generation languages, and object–oriented languages. Object-oriented languages like Java and special-purpose languages like HTML and XML are being widely used for Web-based business applications and services.

Key Terms and Concepts

These are the key terms and concepts of this chapter. The page number of their first explanation is given in parentheses.

1. Application service provider (ASP) (177)
2. Application software (164)
3. Assembler language (192)
4. CASE tools (202)
5. Cloud computing (179)
6. COTS software (164)
7. Custom software (164)
8. Desktop publishing (DTP) (173)
9. E-mail (171)
10. Fourth-generation language (193)
11. Function-specific application software (168)
12. General-purpose application programs (164)
13. Groupware (175)
14. High-level language (192)
15. HTML (195)
16. Instant messaging (IM) (171)
17. Integrated package (170)
18. Java (198)
19. Language translator (201)
20. Machine language (191)
21. Middleware (191)
22. Multitasking (185)
23. Natural language (193)
24. Object-oriented language (194)
25. Operating system (181)
26. Personal information manager (PIM) (175)
27. Presentation graphics software (174)
28. Programming language (191)
29. Software suites (169)
30. Spreadsheet package (173)
31. System software (181)
32. User interface (181)
33. Utilities (193)
34. Virtual memory (184)
35. Web browser (170)
36. Web services (199)
37. Word processing software (172)
38. XML (196)

Review Quiz

Match one of the previous key terms and concepts with one of the brief examples or definitions that follow. Try to find the best fit for answers that seem to fit more than one term or concept. Defend your choices.

_____ 1. An approach to computing where tasks are assigned to a combination of connections, software, and services accessed over a network.

_____ 2. Programs that direct the performance of a specific use of computers.

_____ 3. A system of programs that manages the operations of a computer system.

_____ 4. Companies that own, operate, and maintain application software for a fee as a service over the Internet.

_____ 5. Integrated software tool that supports the development of software applications.

_____ 6. Software designed in-house for use by a specific organization or set of users.

_____ 7. The function that provides a means of communication between end users and an operating system.

_____ 8. Acronym meaning commercial off-the-shelf.

_____ 9. Provides a greater memory capability than a computer's actual memory capacity.

_____ 10. The ability to do several computing tasks concurrently.

_____ 11. Converts numeric data into graphic displays.

_____ 12. Translates high-level instructions into machine language instructions.

_____ 13. Performs housekeeping chores for a computer system.

_____ 14. A category of application software that performs common information processing tasks for end users.

_____ 15. Software available for the specific applications of end users in business, science, and other fields.

_____ 16. Helps you surf the Web.

_____ 17. Uses your networked computer to send and receive messages.

_____ 18. Creates and displays a worksheet for analysis.

_____ 19. Allows you to create and edit documents.

_____ 20. Enables you to produce your own brochures and newsletters.

_____ 21. Helps you keep track of appointments and tasks.

_____ 22. A program that performs several general-purpose applications.

_____ 23. A combination of individual general-purpose application packages that work easily together.

_____ 24. Software to support the collaboration of teams and workgroups.

_____ 25. Uses instructions in the form of coded strings of ones and zeros.

_____ 26. Uses instructions consisting of symbols representing operation codes and storage locations.

_____ 27. Uses instructions in the form of brief statements or the standard notation of mathematics.

_____ 28. Might take the form of query languages and report generators.

_____ 29. Languages that tie together data and the actions that will be performed on the data.

_____ 30. As easy to use as one's native tongue.

_____ 31. Includes programming editors, debuggers, and code generators.

_____ 32. Produces hyperlinked multimedia documents for the Web.

_____ 33. A Web document content description language.

_____ 34. A popular object-oriented language for Web-based applications.

_____ 35. Windows, Linux, and Mac OS are common examples.

_____ 36. Software that helps diverse applications work together.

_____ 37. Enables you to communicate and collaborate in real time with the online associates in your workgroup.

_____ 38. Links business functions within applications for the exchange of data between companies via the Web.

Discussion Questions

1. What major trends are occurring in software? What capabilities do you expect to see in future software packages?

2. How do the different roles of system software and application software affect you as a business end user? How do you see this changing in the future?

3. Refer to the Real World case on costly software programming errors. How often do you think small errors occur in commercially available software? How many such errors go undetected by the consumer?

4. Why is an operating system necessary? That is, why can't an end user just load an application program into a computer and start computing?

5. Should a Web browser be integrated into an operating system? Why or why not?

6. Refer to the Real World Case about the U.S. Department of Defense and its adoption of open-source software in the chapter. Would such an approach work for a commercial organization, or is it limited to government entities? What would be the most important differences in each case, if any?

7. Are software suites, Web browsers, and groupware merging together? What are the implications for a business and its end users?

8. How are HTML, XML, and Java affecting business applications on the Web?

9. Do you think Linux will surpass, in adoption and use, other operating systems for network and Web servers? Why or why not?

10. Which application software packages are the most important for a business end user to know how to use? Explain the reasons for your choices.

Analysis Exercises

Complete the following exercises as individual or group projects that apply chapter concepts to real-world business situations.

1. **Desktop Application Recognition**
   Tool Selection
   ABC Department Stores would like to acquire software to do the following tasks. Identify which software packages they need.

   a. Surf the Web and their intranets and extranets.

   b. Send messages to one another's computer workstations.

   c. Help employees work together in teams.

d. Use a group of productivity packages that work together easily.

e. Help sales reps keep track of meetings and sales calls.

f. Type correspondence and reports.

g. Analyze rows and columns of sales figures.

h. Develop a variety of graphical presentations.

2. **Y2K Revisited**
The End of Time
Decades ago, programmers trying to conserve valuable storage space shortened year values to two digits. This shortcut created what became known as the "Y2K" problem or "millennium bug" at the turn of the century. Programmers needed to review billions of lines of code to ensure important programs would continue to operate correctly. The Y2K problem merged with the dot-com boom and created a tremendous demand for information technology employees. Information system users spent billions of dollars fixing or replacing old software. The IT industry is only now beginning to recover from the postboom slump. Could such hysteria happen again? It can and, very likely, it will.

Today, most programs use several different schemes to record dates. One scheme, POSIX time, widely employed on UNIX-based systems, requires a signed 32-bit integer to store a number representing the number of seconds since January 1, 1970. "0" represents midnight on January 1, "10" represents 10 seconds after midnight, and "−10" represents 10 seconds before midnight. A simple program then converts these data into any number of international date formats for display. This scheme works well because it allows programmers to subtract one date/time from another date/time and directly determine the interval between them. It also requires only 4 bytes of storage space. But 32 bits still calculates to a finite number, whereas time is infinite. As a business manager, you will need to be aware of this new threat and steer your organization away from repeating history. The following questions will help you evaluate the situation and learn from history.

a. If 1 represents 1 second and 2 represents 2 seconds, how many seconds can be represented in a binary number 32 bits long? Use a spreadsheet to show your calculations.

b. Given that POSIX time starts at midnight, January 1, 1970, in what year will time "run out"? Remember that half the available numbers represent dates before 1970. Use a spreadsheet to show your calculations.

c. As a business manager, what can you do to minimize this problem for your organization?

3. **Tracking Project Work**
Queries and Reports
You are responsible for managing information systems development projects at AAA Systems. To better track progress in completing projects, you have decided to maintain a simple database table to track the time your employees spend on various tasks and the projects with which they are associated. It will also allow you to keep track of employees' billable hours each week. The table below provides a sample data set.

a. Build a database table to store the data shown and enter the records as a set of sample data.

b. Create a query that will list the hours worked for all workers who worked more than 40 hours during production week 20.

c. Create a report grouped by project that will show the number of hours devoted to each task on the project and the subtotal number of hours devoted to each project, as well as a grand total of all hours worked.

d. Create a report grouped by employee that will show each employee's hours worked on each task and total hours worked. The user should be able to select a production week and find data for just that week presented.

4. **Matching Training to Software Use**
3-D Graphing
You have the responsibility to manage software training for Sales, Accounting, and Operations Department workers in your organization. You have surveyed the workers to get a feel for the amounts of time spent using various packages, and the results are shown below. The values shown are the total number of workers in each department and the total weekly hours the department's workers spend using each software package. You have been asked to prepare a spreadsheet summarizing these data and comparing the use of the various packages across departments.

Department	Employees	Spreadsheet	Database	Presentations
Sales	225	410	1,100	650
Operations	75	710	520	405
Accounting	30	310	405	50

a. Create a spreadsheet illustrating each application's average use per department. To do this, you will first enter the data shown above. Then compute the average weekly spreadsheet use by dividing spreadsheet hours by the number of Sales workers. Do this for each department. Repeat these three calculations for both database and presentation use. Round results to the nearest 1/100th.

b. Create a three-dimensional bar graph illustrating the averages by department and software package.

c. A committee has been formed to plan software training classes at your company. Prepare a slide presentation with four slides illustrating your findings. The first slide should serve as an introduction to the data; the second slide should contain a copy of the original data table (without the averages); the third slide should contain a copy of the three-dimensional bar graph from the previous answer; and the fourth slide should contain your conclusions regarding key applications per department. Use professional labels, formatting, and backgrounds.

Project_Name	Task_Name	Employee_ID	Production_Week	Hours_Worked
Fin-Goods-Inv	App. Devel.	456	21	42
Fin-Goods-Inv	DB Design	345	20	20
Fin-Goods-Inv	UI Design	234	20	16
HR	Analysis	234	21	24
HR	Analysis	456	20	48
HR	UI Design	123	20	8
HR	UI Design	123	21	40
HR	UI Design	234	21	32
Shipmt-Tracking	DB Design	345	20	24
Shipmt-Tracking	DB Design	345	21	16
Shipmt-Tracking	DB Development	345	21	20
Shipmt-Tracking	UI Design	123	20	32
Shipmt-Tracking	UI Design	234	20	24

REAL WORLD CASE 3

Wolf Peak International: Failure and Success in Application Software for the Small-to-Medium Enterprise

One of the hazards of a growing small business is a software upgrade. If you pick the wrong horse, you may find yourself riding in the wrong direction. Correcting your course may mean not only writing off your first upgrade selection but then going through the agonizing process of finding a better software solution for your company. That's what happened to Wolf Peak International of Layton, Utah, which designs and manufactures eyewear for the safety, sporting, driving, and fashion industries. Founded in 1998, the privately held small to midsize enterprise (SME) also specializes in overseas production, sourcing, importing, and promotional distribution services.

In Wolf Peak's early days, founder-owner Kurt Daems was happy using QuickBooks to handle accounting chores. The package is user friendly and allowed him to drill down to view transaction details or combine data in a variety of ways to create desired reports. As the company prospered, however, it quickly outgrew the capabilities of QuickBooks.

"As Wolf Peak got bigger, the owner felt the need to get into a more sophisticated accounting system," says Ron Schwab, CFO at Wolf Peak International. "There were no financial people in-house at the time the decision was made to purchase a replacement for QuickBooks, and the decision was made without a finance person in place to review it."

Wolf Peak selected one of several accounting software packages promoted to growing SMEs. By the time Schwab joined the company, the package had been installed for six months, following an implementation period that lasted a full year. "The biggest difficulty for QuickBooks users is to go from a very friendly user interface and the ability to find information easily to a more sophisticated, secured, batch-oriented accounting system that became an absolute nightmare to get data out of," notes Schwab. "So the company paid a lot of money to have this new accounting system, but nobody knew how to go in and extract financial or operational data used to make critical business decisions."

There were other problems. Developing reusable reports was difficult, time-consuming, and expensive. The company paid IT consultants to develop reports for specific needs, some of which still had not been delivered, months after they were commissioned. Ad hoc reporting was similarly intractable. Furthermore, the company's prior-year history in QuickBooks could not be converted into the new accounting package. A situation like this creates serious problems.

Accustomed to keeping close tabs on the company's operations, Daems found that he simply could not get the information he wanted. He began to lose track of his business. "He got so fed up he finally came to me and said he was ready to look at a SAP software alternative he'd heard about," Schwab recalls. "He wasn't ready to buy it, though, because he'd just sunk a lot of money into the new accounting package."

One year after Wolf Peak had switched over to the new accounting software, Schwab called the offices of JourneyTEAM, a local SAP services partner, and asked their software consultants to demonstrate the SAP Business One software suite.

SAP Business One is an integrated business management software package designed specifically for SMEs like Wolf Peak: The application automates critical operations including sales, finance, purchasing, inventory, and manufacturing and delivers an accurate, up-to-the-minute view of the business. Its relative affordability promises a rapid return on investment, and its simplicity means users have a consistent, intuitive environment that they can learn quickly and use effectively.

"We had a wish list from various company employees asking for a variety of capabilities," recalls Schwab. "The JourneyTEAM people came in and demonstrated all those functionalities and more. They even generated four or five reports that we had spent several thousand dollars and several months trying to get from our other software consultants and had not yet received. Based on our data that they had input into Business One, JourneyTEAM put those reports together in an afternoon."

Daems still had a few reservations: He needed the buy-in of his VP of sales and was concerned about cost. He still wasn't ready to write off the recently installed accounting software.

JourneyTEAM came in and gave another presentation for the Wolf Peak sales team and, following that, came back with an acceptable quote. With some pain, but also considerable relief, Daems wrote off the existing accounting package. "We felt the benefits of SAP Business One far outweighed the costs and time already invested in that software system," Daems says.

Implementation of Business One took just seven weeks from the day of the initial sales presentation. "We implemented SAP Business One during our busiest period of the year with no disruptions," notes Schwab. "It went better than I expected, in particular the cutover and conversion to Business One. JourneyTEAM did an amazing job of getting all our old records converted with no real problems at all. We met our June 30 deadline and cutover during the succeeding long weekend without incident."

Schwab's enthusiasm for SAP Business One is high. "This is the best accounting program I've ever worked with," he says. "I can drill down to anything I want. And with the XL Reporter tool, I can build reports on the fly."

Business One includes a seamlessly integrated reporting and financial analysis tool called XL Reporter that works with Microsoft Excel to provide instant access to financial and operational data. It reports on live data drawn from a variety of sources including general ledger, receivables, payables, sales, purchasing, and inventory software. "Now we're building the reports we want," says Schwab. "To have a program like XL Reporter that lets us build custom reports, preset regular updates, and then work within Microsoft Excel—that's hugely valuable to us. Nobody else offers the ability to do ad hoc queries so easily. Even people who aren't serious programmers can go in and create the documents they need within the limits of their authorizations. So I highly recommend it."

For years, Daems had been running an open receivables report that presents, for example, all the invoices that are 15 days past due and greater than $450. Unfortunately, he simply could not run a report like that with the software package he bought to replace his old QuickBooks program. That situation has now changed.

"With SAP Business One, we can go in there and ask for those parameters and then sort it by oldest, biggest amount, or customer," says Schwab. "And it's paperless. The accounts receivable person doesn't have to print anything out and then write a bunch of notes on it and type them into the system for someone else to find. It's all right there."

Wolf Peak also requires a very complicated commissions report, used to generate the checks that go out to the company's commissioned sales representatives, who receive individualized reports as well. The previous consultants were unable to deliver this set of reports. JourneyTEAM was able to develop it on Business One in an afternoon.

Wolf Peak is already expanding its use of SAP Business One into other areas. The company has applied the software to warehouse management, where it enables Wolf Peak to manage inventory, receiving, warehouse delivery, shipping, and all the other aspects of the warehousing task. Inventory is one of the company's biggest assets, and it has to be managed well. "We have an audit report that lists all of the inventory, the current on-hand quantity, and the demands on it through sales orders or outstanding purchase orders," Schwab says.

This report then lists the value of that inventory and allows Schwab to look at the activity against any inventory item during any period. Beyond that, it enables him to drill down to the actual invoices that affect that inventory item. "We want to minimize what we have on hand," he says, "but we always have to be sure we have enough to meet our customers' needs. Business One lets us do that."

Wolf Peak's management has also begun using the customer relationship management (CRM) functionality within Business One to assist with its collection of receivables. The company's plan is to extend its use of the software to develop and track sales opportunities as well. Three months following its installation, Wolf Peak is quite happy with its decision to go with SAP's Business One software. "Reports that used to take months to create—if we could get them at all—can now be created in minutes," says Schwab.

A less tangible but no less important benefit is the renewed confidence Business One brings to management. "A company's greatest untapped asset is its own financial information," says Schwab. "SAP Business One creates an environment where the decision makers get the information they want on a timely basis, in a format they can use. It's amazing what happens when management begins to see what is really happening inside the enterprise. Business One delivers useful information to help make good business decisions—and that's really the bottom line. This is a business management tool."

Source: Adapted from SAP America, "Wolf Peak: Making the Best Choice to Support Growth," *SAP BusinessInsights*, March 2007; JourneyTEAM, "Wolf Peak Success Story—SAP Business One," ABComputer.com, March 2007.

CASE STUDY QUESTIONS

1. What problems occurred when Wolf Peak upgraded from QuickBooks to a new accounting software package? How could these problems have been avoided?

2. Why did SAP's Business One prove to be a better choice for Wolf Peak's management than the new accounting software? Give several examples to illustrate your answer.

3. Should most SMEs use an integrated business software suite like SAP Business One instead of specialized accounting and other business software packages? Why or why not?

REAL WORLD ACTIVITIES

1. This case demonstrates failure and success in the software research, selection, and installation process, as well as some major differences among business application software packages in capabilities, such as ease of use and information access for employees and management. Search the Internet to find several more examples of such success and failure for software suites like SAP Business One or Oracle E-Business Suite and specialized business packages like QuickBooks or Great Plains Accounting.

2. Break into small groups with your classmates to discuss several key differences you have found on the basis of your Internet research. Then make recommendations to the class for how these differences should shape the business application software selection decision for an SME.

REAL WORLD CASE 4

Power Distribution and Law Enforcement: Reaping the Benefits of Sharing Data through XML

A power consortium that distributes a mix of "green" and conventional electricity is implementing an XML-based settlements system that drives costs out of power distribution. The Northern California Power Agency (NCPA) is one of several state-chartered coordinators in California that schedules that delivery of power to the California power grid and then settles the payment due to suppliers. NCPA sells the power generated by the cities of Palo Alto and Santa Clara, as well as hydro- and geothermal sources farther north.

Power settlements are a highly regulated and complicated process. Each settlement statement contains how much power a particular supplier delivered and how much was used by commercial vs. residential customers, and the two have different rates of payment. The settlements are complicated by the fact that electricity meters are read only once every 90 days; many settlements must be based on an estimate of consumption that gets revised as meter readings come in.

On behalf of a supplier, NCPA can protest that fees for transmission usage weren't calculated correctly, and the dispute requires a review of all relevant data. Getting one or more of these factors wrong is commonplace. "Power settlements are never completely settled," says Bob Caracristi, manager of power settlements for NCPA. "Negotiations over details may still be going on a year or two after the power has been delivered."

Furthermore, "the enormity of the data" has in the past required a specialist vendor that creates software to analyze the massive settlement statements produced by the grid's manager, the California Independent System Operator. NCPA sought these vendor bids three years ago and received quotes that were "several hundred thousand dollars a year in licensing fees and ongoing maintenance," remarks Caracristi. The need for services from these customized systems adds to the cost of power consumption for every California consumer.

Faced with such a large annual expense, NCPA sought instead to develop the in-house expertise to deal with the statements. Senior programmer analyst Carlo Tiu and his team at NCPA used Oracle's XML-handling capabilities to develop a schema to handle the data and a configuration file that contained the rules for determining supplier payment from the data. That file can be regularly updated, without needing to modify the XML data themselves. In doing so, the NCPA gained a step on the rest of the industry, as the California Independent System Operator started requiring all of its vendors to provide power distribution and billing data as XML files. NCPA has already tested its ability to process XML settlement statements automatically and has scaled out its Oracle system to 10 times its needs "without seeing any bottlenecks," says Tiu.

Being able to process the Independent System Operator statements automatically will represent huge cost savings to NCPA, according to IS manager Tom Breckon. "When settlement statements come in," Breckon says, "NCPA has eight working days to determine where mistakes may have been made. If we fail to get back to [the California Independent System Operator], we lose our chance to reclaim the monies from corrections." Yet, he acknowledges, "we can't inspect that volume of data on a manual basis."

Gaining the expertise to deal with settlements as XML data over the past three years has cost NCPA the equivalent of one year's expense of a manager's salary. Meanwhile, NCPA has positioned itself to become its own statement processor and analyzer, submit disputes to the California Independent System Operator for corrections, and collect more of those corrected payments for members on a timely basis. "In my opinion," says Breckon, "everybody will be doing it this way five years from now. It would reduce costs for all rate payers."

In the state of Ohio, almost 1,000 police departments have found critical new crime-fighting tools by gaining access to the digital records kept by neighboring law enforcement agencies. The Ohio Law Enforcement Gateway Search Engine is an Internet-based tool that can securely comb through numerous crime databases using a single log-in and query, making it easier to use than separate crime databases. For police officers, searching for information on a suspect or a rash of crimes used to require manually logging into several separate crime databases, which could take hours. Now, officers in even the smallest communities can log in just once and quickly gain access to criminal information.

The project, which began in 2003, faced a major hurdle: finding a way to get the disparate crime information systems to interoperate with each other. "Everybody wants to share, but nobody wants to use the same product," says Chief Gary Vest of the Powell, Ohio, Police Department, near Columbus. In a major metropolitan area in Ohio, there can be 30 different police departments, each using different products that aren't linked, he says. "That made it difficult for local departments to link suspects and crimes in neighboring jurisdictions."

To make the systems compatible, crime records management vendors rewrote their software so that data from participating departments could be converted into the gateway format for easier data sharing. The vendors used a special object-oriented Global Justice XML Data Model and interoperability standards developed by the U.S. Department of Justice for such purposes. What makes this project different from other fledgling police interoperability programs in the United States is that it's a standards-based system. "You don't have to throw out your vendor to play," notes Vest.

So far, Ohio police can't search on criminal "M.O.'s," but that capability is being worked on. By combing local police records, officers can search for a suspect's name even before it's in the national databases or other larger data repositories, says Vest, "You're a step earlier." Other regional police interoperability projects are in progress around the nation, but this is believed to be the first statewide effort.

In San Diego County, police agencies have been sharing crime data for 25 years using a custom program called the Automated Regional Justice Information System (ARJIS). Barbara Montgomery, project manager for ARJIS, says it differs from the Ohio initiative because it is mainframe-based and all police agencies have to use the same software to access information. Such data-sharing programs are not widespread in the United States because of their cost, especially for smaller police departments, she says. In fact, ARJIS was made possible only after a number of departments pooled their money.

"No single police department could afford to buy [the hardware and the skills of] a bunch of computer programmers so it was truly a 'united we stand, divided we fall' approach," Montgomery says. "The next generation of ARJIS is being planned now, with the system likely to evolve over the next few years from its mainframe roots to a server-based enterprise architecture for more flexibility," says Montgomery.

Along the same lines, the Florida Department of Law Enforcement will begin work on a $15 million project to integrate the back-end systems of 500 law enforcement organizations across the state. In many cases, investigators in Florida law enforcement offices now gather information from other departments in the state via telephone or e-mail. The Florida Law Enforcement Exchange project promises to provide access to statewide law enforcement data with a single query, says state's CIO Brenda Owens, whose IT unit is overseeing the project.

"Our goal is to provide seamless access to data across the state," says Owens. "An operator sitting at a PC in a police department doesn't know or care what the data look like; they can put the inquiry in and get the information back."

Large integration projects such as this often derail because it's difficult to get different groups to agree on metadata types. "The metadata management or understanding the common elements is a huge part of [an integration project]," notes Ken Vollmer, an analyst at Forrester Research. "Trying to combine information from two agencies—that is hard enough. In Florida, you're talking 500 agencies, and they have to have some software to help them determine what the common data elements are."

Source: Adapted from Charles Babcok, "Electricity Costs Attacked through XML," *InformationWeek*, December 26, 2007; Todd Weiss, "Ohio Police Use Specialized Software to Track Data (and Bad Guys)," *Computerworld*, June 23, 2006; and Heather Havenstein, "Florida Begins Linking Its Law Enforcement Agencies," *Computerworld*, February 13, 2006.

CASE STUDY QUESTIONS

1. What is the business value of XML to the organizations described in the case? How are they able to achieve such large returns on investment?

2. What are other ways in which XML could be used by organizations to create value and share data? Look for examples involving for-profit organizations to gain a more complete perspective on the issue.

3. What seem to be important elements in the success of projects relying on extensive use of XML across organizations, and why? Research the concept of metadata to inform your answer.

REAL WORLD ACTIVITIES

1. XBRL stands for eXtensible Business Reporting Language, and it is one of the family of XML languages that is becoming standard for business communication across companies. Among other uses, the Securities and Exchange Commission has run a voluntary XBRL filing program since 2005. Go online and research the current status of XBRL implementation and adoption, including examples of companies that are already using it for business purposes. Prepare a report to share your findings.

2. Investigate other large-scale, systemwide implementations of XML such as the one described in the case involving the California Independent System Operator. Prepare a presentation with the proposed or realized costs and benefits of those efforts and share your findings with the class.

CHAPTER 5

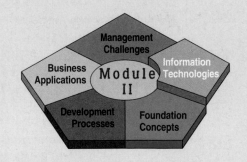

DATA RESOURCE MANAGEMENT

Chapter Highlights

Learning Objectives

1. Explain the business value of implementing data resource management processes and technologies in an organization.

2. Outline the advantages of a database management approach to managing the data resources of a business, compared with a file processing approach.

3. Explain how database management software helps business professionals and supports the operations and management of a business.

4. Provide examples to illustrate each of the following concepts:

   a. Major types of databases.

   b. Data warehouses and data mining.

   c. Logical data elements.

   d. Fundamental database structures.

   e. Database development.

SECTION I	# Technical Foundations of Database Management

Database Management

Just imagine how difficult it would be to get any information from an information system if data were stored in an unorganized way or if there were no systematic way to retrieve them. Therefore, in all information systems, data resources must be organized and structured in some logical manner so that they can be accessed easily, processed efficiently, retrieved quickly, and managed effectively. Data structures and access methods ranging from simple to complex have been devised to organize and access data stored by information systems efficiently. In this chapter, we will explore these concepts, as well as the managerial implications and value of data resource management. See Figure 5.1.

It is important to appreciate from the beginning the value of understanding databases and database management. In today's world, just about every piece of data you would ever want to access is organized and stored in some type of database. The question is not so much "Should I use a database?" but rather "What database should I use?" Although many of you will not choose a career in the design of databases, all of you will spend a large portion of your time—whatever job you choose—accessing data in a myriad of databases. Most database developers consider accessing the data to be the business end of the database world, and understanding how data are structured, stored, and accessed can help business professionals gain greater strategic value from their organization's data resources.

Read the Real World Case 1 on the incredible explosion of data in organizations and the risks of data loss. We can learn a lot about the importance of data in organizations from this case.

Fundamental Data Concepts

Before we go any further, let's discuss some fundamental concepts about how data are organized in information systems. A conceptual framework of several levels of data has been devised that differentiates among different groupings, or elements, of data. Thus, data may be logically organized into *characters, fields, records, files,* and *databases,* just as writing can be organized into letters, words, sentences, paragraphs, and documents. Examples of these logical data elements are shown in Figure 5.2.

Character

The most basic logical data element is the character, which consists of a single alphabetic, numeric, or other symbol. You might argue that the bit or byte is a more elementary data element, but remember that those terms refer to the physical storage elements provided by the computer hardware, as discussed in Chapter 3. Using that understanding, one way to think of a character is that it is a byte used to represent a particular character. From a user's point of view (i.e., from a *logical* as opposed to a physical or hardware view of data), a character is the most basic element of data that can be observed and manipulated.

Field

The next higher level of data is the field, or data item. A field consists of a grouping of related characters. For example, the grouping of alphabetic characters in a person's name may form a name field (or typically, last name, first name, and middle initial fields), and the grouping of numbers in a sales amount forms a sales amount field. Specifically, a data field represents an attribute (a characteristic or quality) of some entity (object, person, place, or event). For example, an employee's salary is an attribute that is a typical data field used to describe an entity who is an employee of a business. Generally speaking, fields are organized such that they represent some logical order, for example, last_name, first_name, address, city, state, and zip code.

Record

All of the fields used to describe the attributes of an entity are grouped to form a record. Thus, a record represents a collection of *attributes* that describe a single instance of an *entity*. An example is a person's payroll record, which consists of data

REAL WORLD
CASE 1

Enterprise Data Explosion Will Only Get Bigger and That Means Big Risk!

Despite the fanfare over cloud computing and mobile technologies, possibly the most pervasive underlying trend in all of IT is the enterprise data explosion.

Borrowing from Moore's Law (see Chapter 3): Data doubles every 18 months and this explosion shows no sign of abating. New compliance regulations in the wake of the global financial meltdown will likely mandate even more data retention, while the imperative to digitize healthcare records in the United States will prompt a fresh set of storage requirements. With the cost of disk space at an all-time low and the vagaries of compliance laws compelling businesses to "save everything" as a brute force method to reduce risk, enterprises are adding capacity at an astounding rate.

Analysts predict that unstructured data will grow at twice the rate of conventional structured data held in databases. By 2010, this "dark matter," so named due to the challenge of extracting useful information from raw data, will make up the majority of all enterprise data stored.

Most of that dark matter comes in the form of security, network, and system event logs. Almost everything that happens in a business is recorded in a log file, making the search and analysis of that data an essential part of managing, securing, and auditing how a company's technology infrastructure is used. Logs are key to many forms of regulatory compliance and are a source of business intelligence just waiting to be tapped.

FIGURE 5.1

Data may be the single most important asset in an organization.

Source: ThinkStock/PunchStock.

Dark matter is only about half of all enterprise data stored. The structured stuff is ballooning, too: transaction records, e-mail archives, rich media, near-line database backups, and on and on. We all know how low-cost storage systems and virtualization are making it more economical to store this stuff. But managing and securing these huge volumes of data are becoming prohibitively difficult, and the cost of buying and maintaining new hardware without increased efficiencies cannot be sustained forever.

We are still years away from solutions that allow administrators to wrap their arms around the whole, heterogeneous storage mess and manage it from one monster control panel. Meanwhile, some interesting new options for easing the pain are emerging.

Most people have heard of one of them, thanks to the recent bidding war over Data Domain: *data deduplication.* Here, byte- or block-level data reduction techniques shrink the disk requirements (by as much as 80 percent or more) for backups, snapshots, and even virtual server disk files, lowering overall data protection costs while at the same time making more data available on near-line storage.

Some of the new cloud solutions are interesting, too, the most prevalent of which are cloud-based hosting or backup/recovery solutions from the likes of SunGard or RackSpace. In addition, many of the first practical cloud-based applications have been built to store, manage, and process massive data sets, leveraging large clusters of commodity hardware and using programming frameworks (such as MapReduce and Hadoop) for reliable and scalable distributed computing.

These and other technologies can be marshaled to manage the explosive growth of data—and, in some cases, to extract new value from that data. But determining the best practices in each discipline and creating a grand strategy that drives toward an enterprise-wide solution isn't going to be easy.

For example, IT managers in Hong Kong, Singapore, and Australia may be putting company data at risk by underestimating the effect of its loss, according to a recent survey by Kroll Ontrack, a large data recovery tools provider. Only 7 percent of respondents believe data loss has a "high" impact on a business. The survey, conducted in early 2010, asked IT managers from 945 companies of different sizes throughout Hong Kong, Singapore, and Australia about their views and experiences related to data management, said Kroll, adding that under half (49 percent) of all IT managers have reported a data loss situation in the last two years.

While larger companies may not fully appreciate the risks they face with data loss, it is the small business sector that appears to be most at risk. An alarming 49 percent of small companies stated that they fail to backup their data on a daily basis, said Kroll. This is despite the fact that nearly half of all participants had experienced data loss in their workplace in the past two years, and 36 percent felt that data loss could have a significant impact on their business, the firm added.

Small businesses were also less likely to test their backup systems on a regular basis, or to have implemented a policy for the preservation of data, Kroll said. While 61 percent of overall respondents reported that their company had a formalized data retention policy, this figure fell to just 45 percent for companies with 50 or fewer employees, the firm added.

Survey results revealed that geography may influence data protection practices, with Singaporean companies appearing to manage their data most effectively, said Kroll, adding that both Hong Kong and Australian respondents were more likely to report having more than five instances of data loss in the last five years.

"The survey exposes a worrying approach to the storage, retention, backup and disposal of organizations' valuable data," said Adrian Briscoe, general manager, Ontrack Data Recovery APAC, Kroll Ontrack. "Data loss and associated challenges can have a devastating effect on business productivity, yet the survey shows that many organizations are ill-equipped to deal with the problem and do not fully understand the importance of implementing simple procedures for protecting their data."

The need to adapt backup procedures to match changes in the IT environment was highlighted as a potential problem area for both large and small organizations, with only 52 percent of companies having reviewed their disaster recovery plans in the last 12 months, said Kroll.

In addition to system failure, data are at risk when end-of-life cycle or unwanted computer hardware is not completely and securely erased, according to Kroll.

This raises the potential for business-critical information to fall into the wrong hands. The survey found that nearly a quarter (24 percent) of companies had no formal policy for erasing sensitive data, which means that they aren't destroying their sensitive information systematically. Just under half the respondents (46 percent) failed to keep a log of equipment that had been erased—an omission that has compliance implications and which can lead to significant legal penalties.

"These results indicate that there may be a lack of understanding of the benefits of using a data service specialist," said Briscoe. "That fact that 39 percent of IT managers still rated their company as doing 'well' or 'very well' even if it took more than three days to recover data, suggests there is a low expectation of what can be achieved."

Source: Adapted from Eric Knorr, "Enterprise Data Explosion Will Only Get Bigger," *Computerworld*, Fairfax Media Group, August 31, 2009 and *Computerworld* Hong Kong staff, "IT Managers Underestimate Data Loss Impact," *Computerworld*, Fairfax Media Group, June 23, 2009.

CASE STUDY QUESTIONS

1. What are some of the reasons for the explosion of data in organizations mentioned in the case? Why are these sources of data so important to an organization? Provide several examples.

2. Why are the risk issues faced by organizations with regard to data loss so important? What can happen? Where do these problems come from? Explain.

3. Imagine that you are in charge of the data in a large organization. How would you go about insuring the data is protected while also being available to those who need it?

REAL WORLD ACTIVITIES

1. The case discusses many issues related to burgeoning data storage needs and risk of loss issues that organizations face. Go online and research how these issues manifest themselves in companies, and some of the approaches used to manage them. Prepare a report to share your findings.

2. The case discusses the large volume of data that is generated simply by keeping detailed logs of all the data-related events in an organization. Are you, as an individual, experiencing the same sort of data explosion? Do know where the event logs are on your computer? Break into small groups with your classmates to discuss these issues and arrive at some recommendations.

FIGURE 5.2   Examples of the logical data elements in information systems. Note especially the examples of how data fields, records, files, and databases relate.

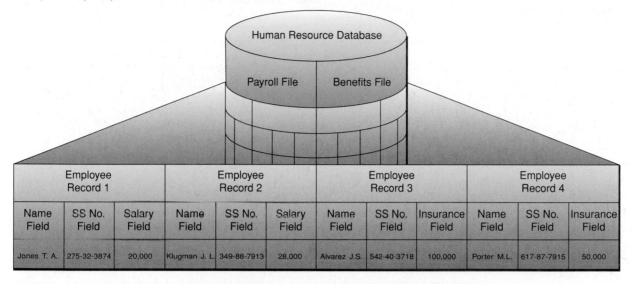

fields describing attributes such as the person's name, Social Security number, and rate of pay. *Fixed-length* records contain a fixed number of fixed-length data fields. *Variable-length* records contain a variable number of fields and field lengths. Another way of looking at a record is that it represents a single *instance* of an entity. Each record in an employee file describes one specific employee.

Normally, the first field in a record is used to store some type of unique identifier for the record. This unique identifier is called the **primary key.** The value of a primary key can be anything that will serve to uniquely identify one instance of an entity, and distinguish it from another. For example, if we wanted to uniquely identify a single student from a group of related students, we could use a student ID number as a primary key. As long as no one shared the same student ID number, we would always be able to identify the record of that student. If no specific data can be found to serve as a primary key for a record, the database designer can simply assign a record a unique sequential number so that no two records will ever have the same primary key.

File

A group of related records is a data file (sometimes referred to as a *table* or *flat file*). When it is independent of any other files related to it, a single *table* may be referred to as a *flat file*. As a point of accuracy, the term *flat file* may be defined either narrowly or more broadly. Strictly speaking, a flat file database should consist of nothing but data and delimiters. More broadly, the term refers to any database that exists in a single file in the form of rows and columns, with no relationships or links between records and fields except the table structure. Regardless of the name used, any grouping of related records in tabular (row-and-column form) is called a *file*. Thus, an employee file would contain the records of the employees of a firm. Files are frequently classified by the application for which they are primarily used, such as a *payroll file* or an *inventory file*, or the type of data they contain, such as a *document file* or a *graphical image file*. Files are also classified by their permanence, for example, a payroll *master file* versus a payroll weekly *transaction file*. A transaction file, therefore, would contain records of all transactions occurring during a period and might be used periodically to update the permanent records contained in a master file. A *history file* is an obsolete transaction or master file retained for backup purposes or for long-term historical storage, called *archival storage*.

Database

A database is an integrated collection of logically related data elements. A database consolidates records previously stored in separate files into a common pool of data

FIGURE 5.3

Some of the entities and relationships in a simplified electric utility database. Note a few of the business applications that access the data in the database.

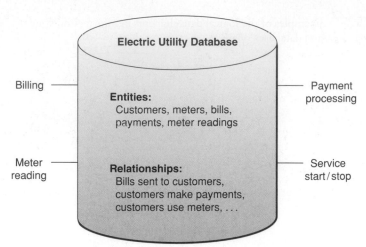

Billing

Meter reading

Electric Utility Database

Entities:
Customers, meters, bills, payments, meter readings

Relationships:
Bills sent to customers, customers make payments, customers use meters, . . .

Payment processing

Service start / stop

Source: Adapted from Michael V. Mannino, *Database Application Development and Design* (Burr Ridge, IL: McGraw-Hill/Irwin, 2001), p. 6.

elements that provides data for many applications. The data stored in a database are independent of the application programs using them and of the type of storage devices on which they are stored.

Thus, databases contain data elements describing entities and relationships among entities. For example, Figure 5.3 outlines some of the entities and relationships in a database for an electric utility. Also shown are some of the business applications (billing, payment processing) that depend on access to the data elements in the database.

As stated in the beginning of the chapter, just about all the data we use are stored in some type of database. A database doesn't need to look complex or technical to be a database; it just needs to provide a logical organization method and easy access to the data stored in it. You probably use one or two rapidly growing databases just about every day: How about Facebook, MySpace, or YouTube?

All of the pictures, videos, songs, messages, chats, icons, e-mail addresses, and everything else stored on each of these popular social networking Web sites are stored as fields, records, files, or objects in large databases. The data are stored in such a way to ensure that there is easy access to it, it can be shared by its respective owners, and it can be protected from unauthorized access or use. When you stop to think about how simple it is to use and enjoy these databases, it is easy to forget how large and complex they are.

For example, in July 2006, YouTube reported that viewers watched more than 100 million videos every day, with 2.5 billion videos in June 2006 alone. In May 2006, users added 50,000 videos per day, and this increased to 65,000 videos by July. In January 2008 alone, almost 79 million users watched more than 3 billion videos on YouTube. In August 2006, *The Wall Street Journal* published an article revealing that YouTube was hosting about 6.1 million videos (requiring about 45 terabytes of storage space), and had about 500 accounts. As of March 2008, a YouTube search turned up about 77.3 million videos and 2.89 million user channels.

Perhaps an even more compelling example of ease of access versus complexity is found in the popular social networking Web site Facebook. Some of the basic statistics are nothing short of amazing! Facebook reports more than 200 million users with more than 100 million logging in at least once each day. The average user has 120 friend relationships established. More than 850 million photos, 8 million videos, 1 billion pieces of content, and 2.5 million events are uploaded or created each month. More than 40 language translations are currently available on the site, with more than 50 more in development. More than 52,000 software applications exist in the Facebook Application Directory, and more than 30 million active users access Facebook through their mobile devices. The size of their databases is best measured in petabytes, which is equal to one quadrillion bytes. All of this from a database and a simple access method launched in 2004 from a dorm room at Harvard University.

The important point here is that all of these videos, user accounts, and information are easily accessed because the data are stored in a database system that organizes it so that a particular item can be found on demand.

Database Structures

The relationships among the many individual data elements stored in databases are based on one of several logical data structures, or models. Database management system (DBMS) packages are designed to use a specific data structure to provide end users with quick, easy access to information stored in databases. Five fundamental database structures are the *hierarchical, network, relational, object-oriented*, and *multidimensional* models. Simplified illustrations of the first three database structures are shown in Figure 5.4.

FIGURE 5.4

Example of three fundamental database structures. They represent three basic ways to develop and express the relationships among the data elements in a database.

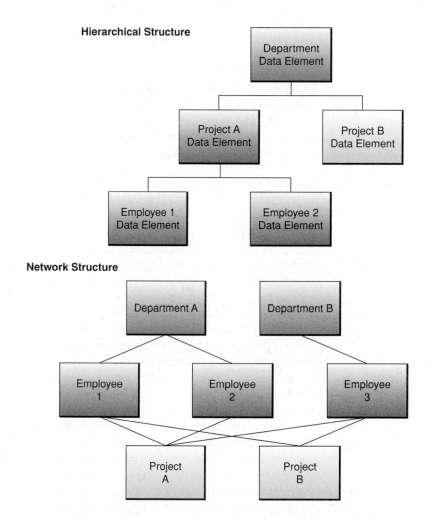

Source: Adapted from Michael V. Mannino, *Database Application Development and Design* (Burr Ridge, IL: McGraw-Hill/Irwin, 2001), p. 6.

Hierarchical Structure

Early mainframe DBMS packages used the hierarchical structure, in which the relationships between records form a hierarchy or treelike structure. In the traditional hierarchical model, all records are dependent and arranged in multilevel structures, consisting of one *root* record and any number of subordinate levels. Thus, all of the relationships among records are *one-to-many* because each data element is related to only one element above it. The data element or record at the highest level of the hierarchy (the department data element in this illustration) is called the root element. Any data element can be accessed by moving progressively downward from a root and along the branches of the tree until the desired record (e.g., the employee data element) is located.

Network Structure

The network structure can represent more complex logical relationships and is still used by some mainframe DBMS packages. It allows *many-to-many* relationships among records; that is, the network model can access a data element by following one of several paths because any data element or record can be related to any number of other data elements. For example, in Figure 5.4, departmental records can be related to more than one employee record, and employee records can be related to more than one project record. Thus, you could locate all employee records for a particular department or all project records related to a particular employee.

It should be noted that neither the hierarchical nor the network data structures are commonly found in the modern organization. The next data structure we discuss, the relational data structure, is the most common of all and serves as the foundation for most modern databases in organizations.

Relational Structure

The relational model is the most widely used of the three database structures. It is used by most microcomputer DBMS packages, as well as by most midrange and mainframe systems. In the relational model, all data elements within the database are viewed as being stored in the form of simple two-dimensional **tables,** sometimes referred to as *relations*. The tables in a relational database are *flat files* that have rows and columns. Each row represents a single record in the file, and each column represents a field. The major difference between a flat file and a database is that a flat file can only have data attributes specified for one file. In contrast, a database can specify data attributes for multiple files simultaneously and can relate the various data elements in one file to those in one or more other files.

Figure 5.4 illustrates the relational database model with two tables representing some of the relationships among departmental and employee records. Other tables, or relations, for this organization's database might represent the data element relationships among projects, divisions, product lines, and so on. Database management system packages based on the relational model can link data elements from various tables to provide information to users. For example, a manager might want to retrieve and display an employee's name and salary from the employee table in Figure 5.4, as well as the name of the employee's department from the department table, by using their common department number field (Deptno) to link or join the two tables. See Figure 5.5. The relational model can relate data in any one file with data in another file if both files share a common data element or field. Because of this, information can be created by retrieving data from multiple files even if they are not all stored in the same physical location.

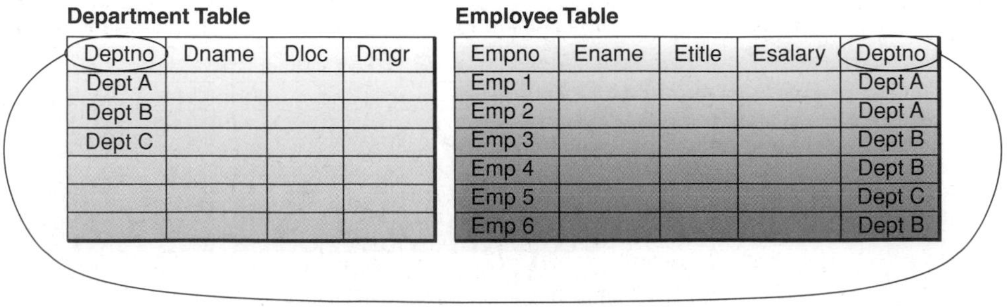

FIGURE 5.5

Joining the employee and department tables in a relational database enables you to access data selectively in both tables at the same time.

Department Table

Deptno	Dname	Dloc	Dmgr
Dept A			
Dept B			
Dept C			

Employee Table

Empno	Ename	Etitle	Esalary	Deptno
Emp 1				Dept A
Emp 2				Dept A
Emp 3				Dept B
Emp 4				Dept B
Emp 5				Dept C
Emp 6				Dept B

Relational Operations

Three basic operations can be performed on a relational database to create useful sets of data. The *select* operation is used to create a subset of records that meet a stated criterion. For example, a select operation might be used on an employee database to create a subset of records that contain all employees who make more than $30,000 per year and who have been with the company more than three years. Another way to think of the select operation is that it temporarily creates a table whose rows have records that meet the selection criteria.

The *join* operation can be used to combine two or more tables temporarily so that a user can see relevant data in a form that looks like it is all in one big table. Using this operation, a user can ask for data to be retrieved from multiple files or databases without having to go to each one separately.

Finally, the *project* operation is used to create a subset of the columns contained in the temporary tables created by the select and join operations. Just as the select operation creates a subset of records that meet stated criteria, the project operation creates a subset of the columns, or fields, that the user wants to see. Using a project operation, the user can decide not to view all of the columns in the table but instead view only those that have the data necessary to answer a particular question or construct a specific report.

Because of the widespread use of relational models, an abundance of commercial products exist to create and manage them. Leading mainframe relational database applications include Oracle 10g from Oracle Corp. and DB2 from IBM. A very popular midrange database application is SQL Server from Microsoft. The most commonly used database application for the PC is Microsoft Access.

Multidimensional Structure

The multidimensional model is a variation of the relational model that uses multidimensional structures to organize data and express the relationships between data. You can visualize multidimensional structures as cubes of data and cubes within cubes of data. Each side of the cube is considered a dimension of the data. Figure 5.6 is an example that shows that each dimension can represent a different category, such as product type, region, sales channel, and time.

Each cell within a multidimensional structure contains aggregated data related to elements along each of its dimensions. For example, a single cell may contain the total sales for a product in a region for a specific sales channel in a single month. A major benefit of multidimensional databases is that they provide a compact and easy-to-understand way to visualize and manipulate data elements that have many interrelationships. So multidimensional databases have become the most popular database structure for the analytical databases that support *online analytical processing* (OLAP) applications, in which fast answers to complex business queries are expected. We discuss OLAP applications in Chapter 10.

Object-Oriented Structure

The object-oriented model is considered one of the key technologies of a new generation of multimedia Web-based applications. As Figure 5.7 illustrates, an **object** consists of data values describing the attributes of an entity, plus the operations that can be performed upon the data. This *encapsulation* capability allows the object-oriented model to handle complex types of data (graphics, pictures, voice, and text) more easily than other database structures.

The object-oriented model also supports *inheritance*; that is, new objects can be automatically created by replicating some or all of the characteristics of one or more *parent* objects. Thus, in Figure 5.7, the checking and savings account objects can inherit both the common attributes and operations of the parent bank account object. Such capabilities have made *object-oriented database management systems* (OODBMS) popular in computer-aided design (CAD) and a growing number of applications. For example, object technology allows designers to develop product designs, store them as objects in an object-oriented database, and replicate and modify them to create new product designs. In addition, multimedia Web-based applications for the Internet and corporate intranets and extranets have become a major application area for object technology.

FIGURE 5.6   An example of the different dimensions of a multidimensional database.

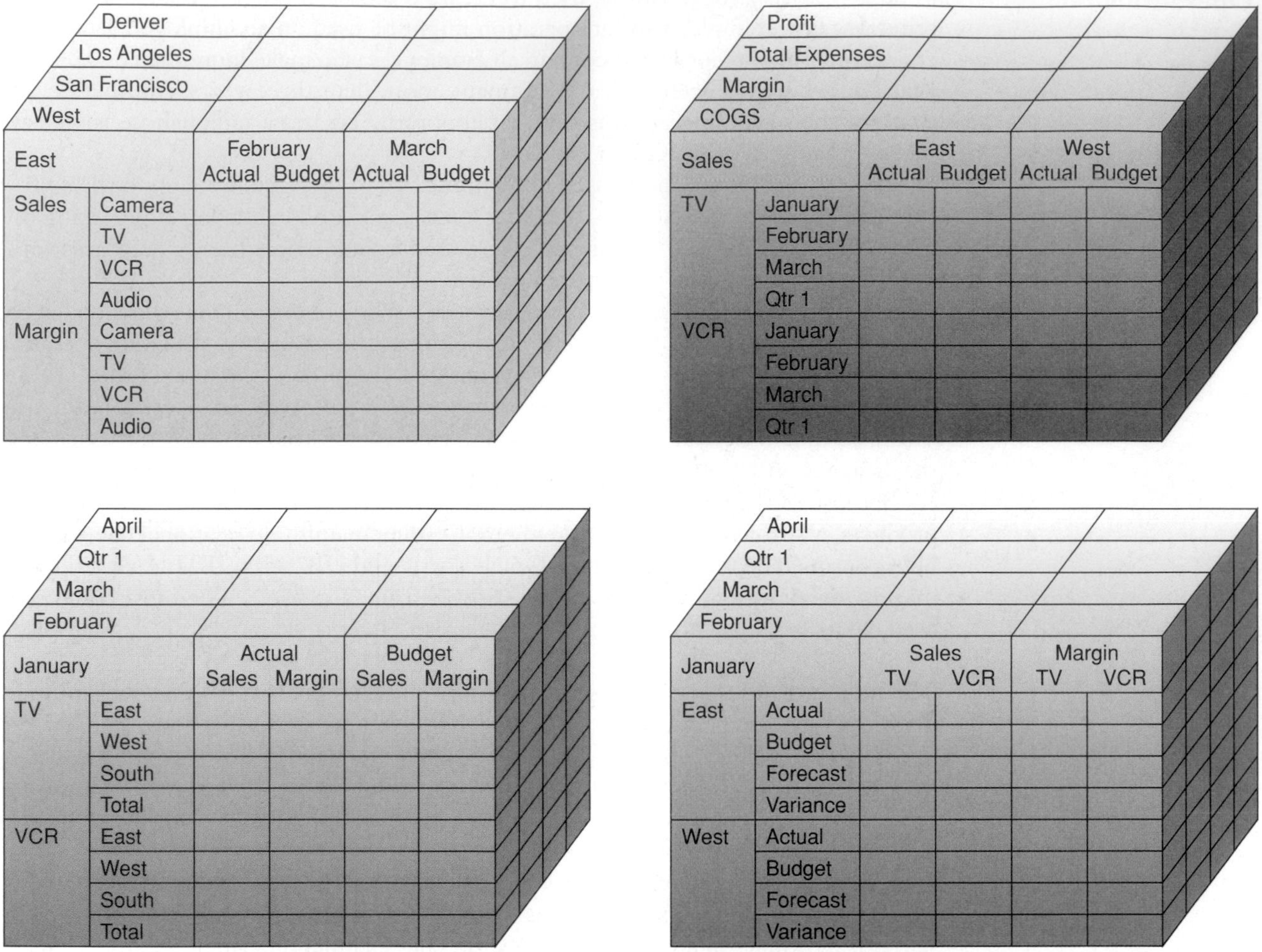

FIGURE 5.7

The checking and savings account objects can inherit common attributes and operations from the bank account object.

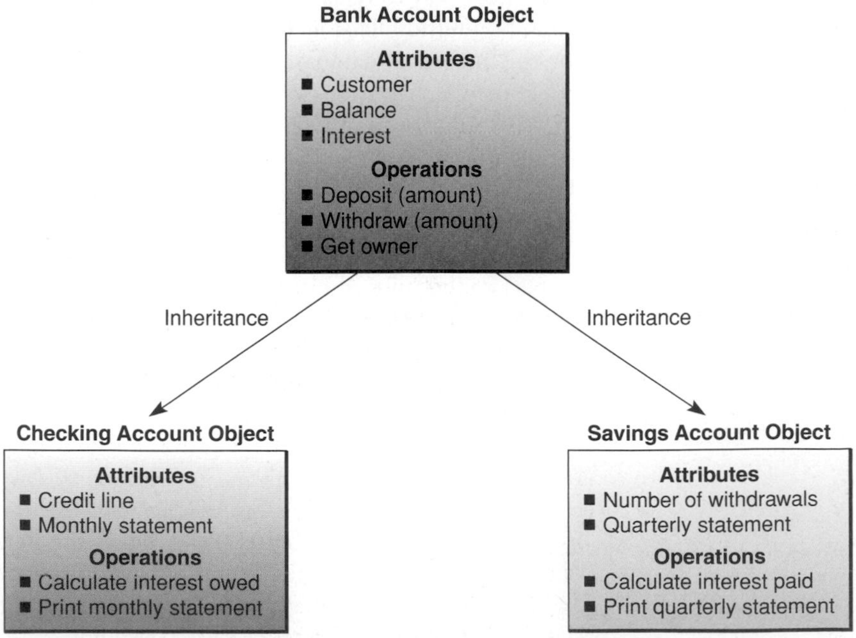

Bank Account Object

Attributes
- Customer
- Balance
- Interest

Operations
- Deposit (amount)
- Withdraw (amount)
- Get owner

Inheritance   Inheritance

Checking Account Object

Attributes
- Credit line
- Monthly statement

Operations
- Calculate interest owed
- Print monthly statement

Savings Account Object

Attributes
- Number of withdrawals
- Quarterly statement

Operations
- Calculate interest paid
- Print quarterly statement

Source: Adapted from Ivar Jacobsen, Maria Ericsson, and Ageneta Jacobsen, *The Object Advantage: Business Process Reengineering with Object Technology* (New York: ACM Press, 1995), p. 65. Copyright © 1995, Association for Computing Machinery. Used by permission.

FIGURE 5.8
Databases can supply data to a wide variety of analysis packages, allowing for data to be displayed in graphical form.

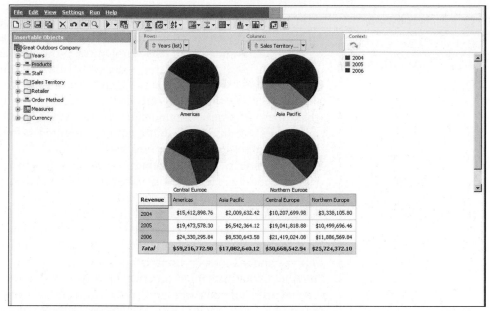

Source: Courtesy of Microsoft®.

Object technology proponents argue that an object-oriented DBMS can work with *complex data types* such as document and graphic images, video clips, audio segments, and other subsets of Web pages much more efficiently than relational database management systems. However, major relational DBMS vendors have countered by adding object-oriented modules to their relational software. Examples include multimedia object extensions to IBM's DB2 and Oracle's object-based "cartridges" for Oracle 10g. See Figure 5.8.

Evaluation of Database Structures

The hierarchical data structure was a natural model for the databases used for the structured, routine types of transaction processing characteristic of many business operations in the early years of data processing and computing. Data for these operations can easily be represented by groups of records in a hierarchical relationship. However, as time progressed, there were many cases in which information was needed about records that did not have hierarchical relationships. For example, in some organizations, employees from more than one department can work on more than one project (refer to Figure 5.4). A network data structure could easily handle this many-to-many relationship, whereas a hierarchical model could not. As such, the more flexible network structure became popular for these types of business operations. Like the hierarchical structure, the network model was unable to handle ad hoc requests for information easily because its relationships must be specified in advance, which pointed to the need for the relational model.

Relational databases enable an end user to receive information easily in response to ad hoc requests. That's because not all of the relationships among the data elements in a relationally organized database need to be specified when the database is created. Database management software (such as Oracle 11g, DB2, Access, and Approach) creates new tables of data relationships by using parts of the data from several tables. Thus, relational databases are easier for programmers to work with and easier to maintain than the hierarchical and network models.

The major limitation of the relational model is that relational database management systems cannot process large amounts of business transactions as quickly and efficiently as those based on the hierarchical and network models; they also cannot process complex, high-volume applications as well as the object-oriented model. This performance gap has narrowed with the development of advanced relational database software with object-oriented extensions. The use of database management software based on the object-oriented and multidimensional models is growing steadily, as these technologies are playing a greater role for OLAP and Web-based applications.

Database Pioneer Rethinks the Best Way to Organize Data

Is there a better way to build a data warehouse? For years, relational databases, which organize data in tables composed of vertical columns and horizontal rows, have served as the foundation of data warehouses. Now database pioneer Michael Stonebraker is promoting a different way to organize them, promising much faster response times. As a scientist at the University of California at Berkeley in the 1970s, Stonebraker was one of the original architects of the Ingres relational database, which spawned several commercial variants. A row-based system like Ingres is great for executing transactions, but a column-oriented system is a more natural fit for data warehouses, Stonebraker now says.

SQL Server, Sybase, and Teradata all have rows as their central design point. Yet in data warehousing, faster performance may be gained through a column layout. Stonebraker says all types of queries on "most data warehouses" will run up to 50 times faster in a column database. The bigger the data warehouse, the greater the performance gain.

Why? Data warehouses frequently store transactional data, and each transaction has many parts. Columns cut across transactions and store an element of information that is standard to each transaction, such as customer name, address, or purchase amount. A row, by comparison, may hold 20–200 different elements of a transaction. A standard relational database would retrieve all the rows that reflect, say, sales for a month, load the data into system memory, and then find all sales records and generate an average from them. The ability to focus on just the "sales" column leads to improved query performance.

There is a second performance benefit in the column approach. Because columns contain similar information from each transaction, it's possible to derive a compression scheme for the data type and then apply it throughout the column. Rows cannot be compressed as easily because the nature of the data (e.g., name, zip code, and account balance) varies from record to record. Each row would require a different compression scheme.

Compressing data in columns makes for faster storage and retrieval and reduces the amount of disk required. "In every data warehouse I see, compression is a good thing," Stonebraker says. "I expect the data warehouse market to become completely column-store based."

Source: Adapted from Charles Babcock, "Database Pioneer Rethinks the Best Way to Organize Data," *InformationWeek*, February 23, 2008.

Database Development

Database management packages like Microsoft Access or Lotus Approach allow end users to develop the databases they need easily. See Figure 5.9. However, large organizations usually place control of enterprisewide database development in the hands of database administrators (DBAs) and other database specialists. This delegation improves the integrity and security of organizational databases. Database developers use the *data definition language* (DDL) in database management systems like Oracle 11g or IBM's DB2 to develop and specify the data contents, relationships, and structure of each database, as well as to modify these database specifications when necessary. Such information is cataloged and stored in a database of data definitions and specifications called a *data dictionary*, or *metadata repository*, which is managed by the database management software and maintained by the DBA.

A data dictionary is a database management catalog or directory containing metadata (i.e., data about data). A data dictionary relies on a specialized database software component to manage a database of data definitions, which is metadata about the structure, data elements, and other characteristics of an organization's databases. For example, it contains the names and descriptions of all types of data records and their interrelationships; information outlining requirements for end users' access and use of application programs; and database maintenance and security.

FIGURE 5.9

Creating a database table using the Table Wizard of Microsoft Access.

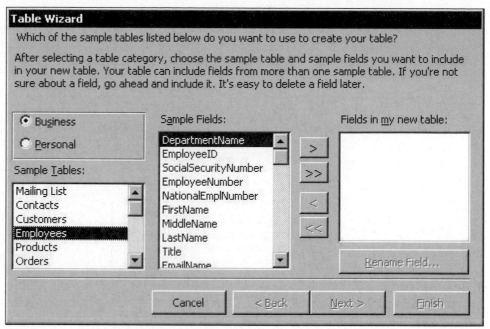

Table Wizard

Which of the sample tables listed below do you want to use to create your table?

After selecting a table category, choose the sample table and sample fields you want to include in your new table. Your table can include fields from more than one sample table. If you're not sure about a field, go ahead and include it. It's easy to delete a field later.

○ Business
○ Personal

Sample Tables:

Mailing List
Contacts
Customers
Employees
Products
Orders

Sample Fields:

DepartmentName
EmployeeID
SocialSecurityNumber
EmployeeNumber
NationalEmplNumber
FirstName
MiddleName
LastName
Title
EmailName

Fields in my new table:

Rename Field...

Cancel   < Back   Next >   Finish

Source: Courtesy of Microsoft®.

The database administrator can query data dictionaries to report the status of any aspect of a firm's metadata. The administrator can then make changes to the definitions of selected data elements. Some *active* (versus *passive*) data dictionaries automatically enforce standard data element definitions whenever end users and application programs access an organization's databases. For example, an active data dictionary would not allow a data entry program to use a nonstandard definition of a customer record, nor would it allow an employee to enter a name of a customer that exceeded the defined size of that data element.

Developing a large database of complex data types can be a complicated task. Database administrators and database design analysts work with end users and systems analysts to model business processes and the data they require. Then they determine (1) what data definitions should be included in the database and (2) what structures or relationships should exist among the data elements.

Data Planning and Database Design

As Figure 5.10 illustrates, database development may start with a top-down **data planning process.** Database administrators and designers work with corporate and end-user management to develop an *enterprise model* that defines the basic business process of the enterprise. They then define the information needs of end users in a business process, such as the purchasing/receiving process that all businesses have.

Next, end users must identify the key data elements that are needed to perform their specific business activities. This step frequently involves developing *entity relationship diagrams* (ERDs) that model the relationships among the many entities involved in business processes. For example, Figure 5.11 illustrates some of the relationships in a purchasing/receiving process. The ERDs are simply graphical models of the various files and their relationships, contained within a database system. End users and database designers could use database management or business modeling software to help them develop ERD models for the purchasing/receiving process. This would help identify the supplier and product data that are required to automate their purchasing/receiving and other business processes using enterprise resource management (ERM) or supply chain management (SCM) software. You will learn about ERDs and other data modeling tools in much greater detail if you ever take a course in systems analysis and design.

FIGURE 5.10

Database development involves data planning and database design activities. Data models that support business processes are used to develop databases that meet the information needs of users.

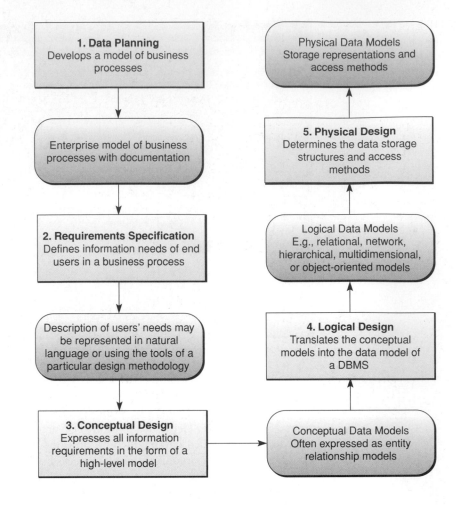

1. Data Planning
Develops a model of business processes

Enterprise model of business processes with documentation

2. Requirements Specification
Defines information needs of end users in a business process

Description of users' needs may be represented in natural language or using the tools of a particular design methodology

3. Conceptual Design
Expresses all information requirements in the form of a high-level model

Conceptual Data Models
Often expressed as entity relationship models

4. Logical Design
Translates the conceptual models into the data model of a DBMS

Logical Data Models
E.g., relational, network, hierarchical, multidimensional, or object-oriented models

5. Physical Design
Determines the data storage structures and access methods

Physical Data Models
Storage representations and access methods

Such user views are a major part of a data modeling process, during which the relationships among data elements are identified. Each data model defines the logical relationships among the data elements needed to support a basic business process. For example, can a supplier provide more than one type of product to us? Can a customer have more than one type of account with us? Can an employee have several pay rates or be assigned to several project workgroups?

Answering such questions will identify data relationships that must be represented in a data model that supports business processes of an organization. These data models then serve as *logical design* frameworks (called *schema* and *subschema*). These frameworks determine the *physical design* of databases and the development of application programs to support the business processes of the organization. A schema is an overall logical view of the relationships among the data elements in a database, whereas the

FIGURE 5.11

This entity relationship diagram illustrates some of the relationships among the entities (product, supplier, warehouse, etc.) in a purchasing/receiving business process.

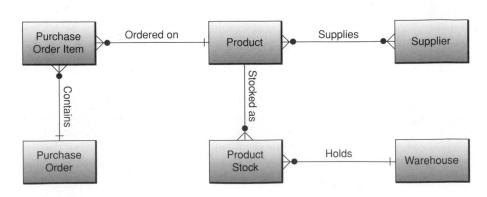

FIGURE 5.12 Example of the logical and physical database views and the software interface of a banking services information system.

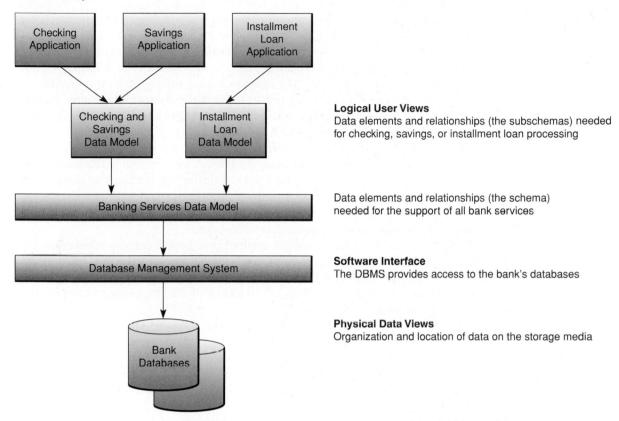

subschema is a logical view of the data relationships needed to support specific end-user application programs that will access that database.

Remember that data models represent logical views of the data and relationships of the database. Physical database design takes a physical view of the data (also called the *internal view*) that describes how data are to be physically stored and accessed on the storage devices of a computer system. For example, Figure 5.12 illustrates these different database views and the software interface of a bank database processing system. This figure focuses on the business processes of checking, savings, and installment lending, which are part of a banking services data model that serves as a logical data framework for all bank services.

Hadoop: Ready for the Large-Scale Data Sets of the Future

Traditional business intelligence solutions can't scale to the degree necessary in today's data environment. One solution getting a lot of attention recently: Hadoop, an open-source product inspired by Google's search architecture. Twenty years ago, most companies' data came from fundamental transaction systems: Payroll, ERP, and so on. The amounts of data seemed large, but they usually were bounded by well-understood limitations: the overall growth of the company and the growth of the general economy.

For those companies that wanted to gain more insight from those systems' data, the related data warehousing systems reflected the underlying systems' structure: regular data schema, smooth growth, and well-understood analysis needs. The typical business intelligence constraint was the amount of processing power that could be applied. Consequently, a great deal of effort went into the data design to restrict the amount of processing required to the available processing power. This led to the now time-honored business intelligence data warehouses: fact tables, dimension tables, and star schemas.

Today, the nature of business intelligence is totally changed. Computing is far more widespread throughout the enterprise, leading to many more systems generating data. Companies are on the Internet, generating huge torrents of unstructured data: searches, click-streams, interactions, and the like. And it's much harder—if not impossible—to forecast what kinds of analytics a company might want to pursue.

Today it might be click-stream patterns through the company Web site. Tomorrow it might be cross-correlating external blog postings with order patterns. The day after it might be something completely different.

And the system bottleneck has shifted. In the past, the problem was how much processing power was available, but today the problem is how much data needs to be analyzed. At Internet-scale, a company might be dealing with dozens or hundreds of terabytes. At that size, the number of drives required to hold the data guarantees frequent drive failures, but attempting to centralize the data imposes too much network traffic to conveniently migrate data to processors.

Hadoop is an open-source product inspired by Google's search architecture. Interestingly, unlike previous open-source products that were usually implementations of previously existing proprietary products, Hadoop has no proprietary predecessor. The innovation in this aspect of big data resides in the open-source community, not in a private company.

Hadoop creates a pool of computers, each with a special Hadoop file system. A central master Hadoop node spreads data across each machine in a file structure designed for large block data reads and writes. It uses a clever hash algorithm to cluster data elements that are similar, making processing data sets extremely efficient. For robustness, three copies of all data are kept to ensure that hardware failures do not halt processing.

The advantage of this approach is that very large sets of data can be managed and processed in parallel across the machine pool managed by Hadoop. The power of Hadoop is clear from the way the New York Times used it to convert a 4-terabyte collection of its pages from one format to another.

Source: Adapted from Bernard Golden, "Large Data Set Analysis in the Cloud: Amazon, Cloudera Improve Hadoop," *CIO.com*, April 9, 2009.

| SECTION II | Managing Data Resources |

Data Resource Management

Data are a vital organizational resource that need to be managed like other important business assets. Today's business enterprises cannot survive or succeed without quality data about their internal operations and external environment.

With each online mouse click, either a fresh bit of data is created or already-stored data are retrieved from all those business Web sites. All that's on top of the heavy demand for industrial-strength data storage already in use by scores of big corporations. What's driving the growth is a crushing imperative for corporations to analyze every bit of information they can extract from their huge data warehouses for competitive advantage. That has turned the data storage and management function into a key strategic role of the information age.

That's why organizations and their managers need to practice data resource management, a managerial activity that applies information systems technologies like *database management*, *data warehousing*, and other data management tools to the task of managing an organization's data resources to meet the information needs of their business stakeholders. This section will show you the managerial implications of using data resource management technologies and methods to manage an organization's data assets to meet business information requirements.

Read the Real World Case 2 on Duke University Health System, Beth Israel Deaconess Medical Center, and others. We can learn a lot from this case about the business value of data analytics in a health care setting. See Figure 5.13.

Types of Databases

Continuing developments in information technology and its business applications have resulted in the evolution of several major types of databases. Figure 5.14 illustrates several major conceptual categories of databases that may be found in many organizations. Let's take a brief look at some of them now.

Operational Databases

Operational databases store detailed data needed to support the business processes and operations of a company. They are also called *subject area databases* (SADB), *transaction databases*, and *production databases*. Examples are a customer database, human resource database, inventory database, and other databases containing data generated by business operations. For example, a human resource database like that shown in Figure 5.2 would include data identifying each employee and his or her time worked, compensation, benefits, performance appraisals, training and development status, and other related human resource data. Figure 5.15 illustrates some of the common operational databases that can be created and managed for a small business using Microsoft Access database management software.

Distributed Databases

Many organizations replicate and distribute copies or parts of databases to network servers at a variety of sites. These distributed databases can reside on network servers on the World Wide Web, on corporate intranets or extranets, or on other company networks. Distributed databases may be copies of operational or analytical databases, hypermedia or discussion databases, or any other type of database. Replication and distribution of databases improve database performance at end-user worksites. Ensuring that the data in an organization's distributed databases are consistently and concurrently updated is a major challenge of distributed database management.

Distributed databases have both advantages and disadvantages. One primary advantage of a distributed database lies with the protection of valuable data. If all of an

CASE 2

Duke University Health System, Beth Israel Deaconess Medical Center, and Others: Medical IT Is Getting Personal

Personalized medicine brings to mind researchers doing complicated analysis of a single patient's genetic makeup and fine-tuning medicine and other treatments to those results. But Duke University Health System is using everyday data from patients' electronic medical records combined with an analytics tool to personalize its approach to treating patients.

County health officials recently asked Duke how many of its patients would need priority access to the H1N1 flu vaccine. Duke used IBM Cognos to sift through information on the more than 20 million patients in its Oracle-based clinical data repository and in an hour was able to identify about 120,000 of them with risk factors, such as age, pregnancy, respiratory, and other conditions that made them vulnerable to complications from swine flu. And now that the H1N1 vaccine is available, Duke is letting those patients know that they're first in line to get it.

"We put an analytics engine on top of our clinical repository and were able to stratify by age and key illnesses millions of records, and streamline who was most at risk," says Asif Ahmed, diagnostics services CIO for the Duke system, which runs three hospitals and about 100 clinics in the Raleigh/Durham, North Carolina, area and treats more than 1 million patients a year.

This is a practical example of how health care IT is being used to personalize medical care in ways that help doctors make smarter decisions about patients' conditions and tailor treatment to an individual's needs. This evolving field covers a broad range of efforts. Beyond analytics systems like Duke's, it includes decision-support tools that help doctors pick the best tests and treatments for patients, remote monitoring tools that provide close to real-time care, as well as software that helps researchers identify the best candidates to participate in trials or experimental treatments.

At Beth Israel Deaconess Medical Center in Boston, helping doctors make better treatment choices and arrive at more accurate diagnoses is a big and growing area of personalized medicine. One example is clinical support software to help its 1,600 staff and affiliated physicians choose the best radiology tests for patients.

When ordering CT scans, MRIs, X-rays, ultrasounds, and other radiology tests, doctors enter a patient's electronic medical record number into the Anvita Health decision support system. Data from Beth Israel's records system, such as recent lab tests and allergies, is automatically loaded into the software. The doctor then adds information on the current complaint, such as symptoms, what area of the body is a concern, and the suspected diagnosis, as well as whether the person has any implants that might interfere with radiology treatment.

The software analyzes the data and rates the best tests for the patient, giving five stars for the top choices and one for the worst ones based on the risks and benefits of each. It can also recommend that the patient forgo radiological testing.

The system can catch details that might otherwise elude a doctor, such as a previous blood test indicating decreased kidney function that could mean the patient can't metabolize the dyes used in certain radiological tests. It also checks how much radiation the patient has already been exposed to.

"Excessive radiation can cause second malignancies," says Dr. Richard Parker, medical director of Beth Israel's physician organization.

"The system takes that into account when ordering a scan." For instance, the software might point out that a patient suspected of having pneumonia has enough symptoms and clinical indicators to make that the most likely diagnosis, and that treating the patient for pneumonia would be better than exposing him or her to a chest X-ray.

During three years in which the hospital system has used the Anvita software, it has cut out about 5 percent of tests as unnecessary or inappropriate, Parker says.

Beth Israel launched a related pilot project six months ago to analyze doctors' thought processes when ordering radiology tests. When a doctor orders a test, the system asks what diagnosis the physician is leaning toward, with what percentage of certainty. After the test, the system follows up with an e-mail asking the doctor whether the test confirmed the original diagnosis. The study aims to gain insight into how doctors decide which tests to use, and in which situations doctors are most likely to prescribe the wrong test for a given set of symptoms.

Information technology isn't just helping doctors choose the right test for a patient; it's also making more personalized medical tests possible. For example, diagnostic testing services provider Quest Diagnostics and Vermillion, a

FIGURE 5.13

IT is starting to have major impacts on both medical research and patient treatment.

Source: © Jose Luis Pelaez Inc/Blend Images/Getty Images.

molecular diagnostic test developer, have developed a test to assess the likelihood that women diagnosed with pelvic masses have ovarian cancer as opposed to benign tumors.

Its use helps those women most at risk for cancer get to specialists faster.

Many of the newest personalized medicine efforts are focused on giving analytics and decision-support tools to doctors and other clinicians. But medical researchers are also still focused on the more complex efforts to analyze genomic data and use the results to create individualized treatments that doctors will use in the future.

One such initiative is Cancer Biomedical Informatics Grid, or caBig, a biomedical informatics network that the National Cancer Institute launched in 2004. Its mission is to develop more personalized cancer treatments and get them into doctors' hands faster.

Researchers at the approximately 100 academic and community-based cancer centers that make up caBig use the network to share data and research results. They can make use of the data in analytics, data-mining, decision-support, and other software tools. Members are using the network's data and software today to identify the best patients to participate in clinical trials of experimental cancer treatments.

Multiple myeloma, a cancer that strikes white blood cells and eventually bone marrow, can be difficult to treat. Now, the Dana-Farber Cancer Institute in Boston is harnessing the dual power of business intelligence and Web 2.0-based scientific search tools to gather complex, scattered data to better treat patients and work toward a cure for this formidable disease.

Dana-Farber is a treatment, research, and teaching facility affiliated with Harvard Medical School. Its physicians and researchers regularly slog through complex calculations to find connections between data gleaned from tumor biopsies and other clinical samples and the vast genetic research housed within the organization or spread among three massive public domain databases.

Dana-Farber officials are working to leverage grant money and other resources to blend data warehousing capabilities with Web-based data-collection tools, since vital connections between patient samples and analytical data will almost certainly prove the crux of both effective patient treatment and any potential breakthroughs tied to the disease, according to researchers.

To make the hunt for precious genetic information easier, Dana-Farber officials have stitched together a system that wraps in Oracle's Healthcare Transaction Base, a service-oriented architecture that supports the medical industry's HL7 standard for the electronic exchange of clinical data.

Increased use of e-medical records should make more patient data available for research, says Ken Buetow, director of the center of bioinformatics and IT at the National Cancer Institute.

Ultimately, Buetow expects the caBig network, combined with doctors' growing use of electronic data. will shorten the time it takes for research findings to show up as clinical treatments. "We think this could be one of those moments for a big shift," he says.

John Glaser, CIO at Partners Healthcare, which operates several Boston-area hospitals, including Massachusetts General. Brigham, and Women's, sees that shift coming. As the use of EMRs become more pervasive and the amount of digitized clinical data increases, it will be easier to provide patients with more personalized care, says Glaser, who also is an adviser on the U.S. Department of Health and Human Services' Health IT Policy Committee. EMRs make data on patients easier to search and analyze. Doctors using them are also more likely to use decision support tools, Glaser says.

"Science is moving rapidly," he says, and health IT helps capture and disseminate to doctors perspective and research findings that are impossible for even the most diligent physicians to keep up with.

Once the use of EMRs is standard practice, the federal government is likely to put greater emphasis on personalized medicine initiatives, Glaser predicts. In the future, health care providers could be rewarded in terms of patient outcomes, and personalized medical treatments are one of the most likely ways to improve outcomes and improve health care across the board.

Source: Adapted from Marianne Kolbasuk McGee, "Medical IT Gets Personal," *InformationWeek*, November 16, 2009; and Jennifer McAdams, "Better BI: Dana-Farber Cancer Institute," *Computerworld*, September 1, 2008.

CASE STUDY QUESTIONS

1. What are the benefits that result from implementing the technologies described in the case? How are those different for hospitals, doctors, insurance companies and patients? Provide examples of each from the case.

2. Many of the technologies described in the case require access to large volumes of data in order to be effective. At the same time, there are privacy considerations involved in the compiling and sharing of such data. How do you balance those?

3. What other industries that manage large volumes of data could benefit from an approach to technology similar to the one described in the case? Develop at least one example with sample applications.

REAL WORLD ACTIVITIES

1. The legal and regulatory environment of the health care industry has changed significantly in recent times. How does this affect technology development and implementation in these organizations. Go online and research new uses of information technology in health care motivated by these developments. Prepare a presentation to share your findings.

2. Some of the technologies described in the case verify the diagnostics made by doctors and can sometimes make recommendations of their own. Does this improve the quality of care, or are these organizations putting too much faith on a computer algorithm that did not attend medical school? Break into small groups to discuss this and provide some recommendations about what organizations should do before deploying these technologies in the field, if anything.

FIGURE 5.14   Examples of some of the major types of databases used by organizations and end users.

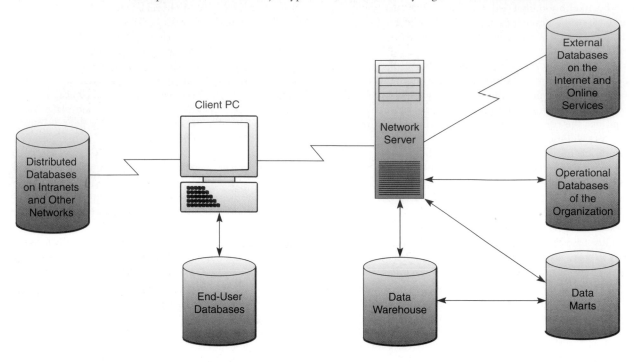

organization's data reside in a single physical location, any catastrophic event like a fire or damage to the media holding the data would result in an equally catastrophic loss of use of that data. By having databases distributed in multiple locations, the negative impact of such an event can be minimized.

Another advantage of distributed databases is found in their storage requirements. Often, a large database system may be distributed into smaller databases based on some logical relationship between the data and the location. For example, a company with several branch operations may distribute its data so that each

FIGURE 5.15

Examples of operational databases that can be created and managed for a small business by microcomputer database management software like Microsoft Access.

Source: Courtesy of Microsoft®.

branch operation location is also the location of its branch database. Because multiple databases in a distributed system can be joined together, each location has control of its local data while all other locations can access any database in the company if so desired.

Distributed databases are not without some challenges, however. The primary challenge is the maintenance of data accuracy. If a company distributes its database to multiple locations, any change to the data in one location must somehow be updated in all other locations. This updating can be accomplished in one of two ways: *replication* or *duplication*.

Updating a distributed database using replication involves using a specialized software application that looks at each distributed database and then finds the changes made to it. Once these changes have been identified, the replication process makes all of the distributed databases look the same by making the appropriate changes to each one. The replication process is very complex and, depending on the number and size of the distributed databases, can consume a lot of time and computer resources.

The duplication process, in contrast, is much less complicated. It basically identifies one database as a master and then duplicates that database at a prescribed time after hours so that each distributed location has the same data. One drawback to the duplication process is that no changes can ever be made to any database other than the master to avoid having local changes overwritten during the duplication process. Nonetheless, properly used, duplication and replication can keep all distributed locations current with the latest data.

One additional challenge associated with distributed databases is the extra computing power and bandwidth necessary to access multiple databases in multiple locations. We will look more closely at the issue of bandwidth in Chapter 6 when we focus on telecommunications and networks.

External Databases

Access to a wealth of information from external databases is available for a fee from commercial online services and with or without charge from many sources on the World Wide Web. Web sites provide an endless variety of hyperlinked pages of multimedia documents in *hypermedia databases* for you to access. Data are available in the form of statistics on economic and demographic activity from *statistical* databanks, or you can view or download abstracts or complete copies of hundreds of newspapers, magazines, newsletters, research papers, and other published material and periodicals from *bibliographic* and *full-text* databases. Whenever you use a search engine like Google or Yahoo to look up something on the Internet, you are using an external database—a very, very large one! Also, if you are using Google, you are using one that averages 112 million searches per day.

Hypermedia Databases

The rapid growth of Web sites on the Internet and corporate intranets and extranets has dramatically increased the use of databases of hypertext and hypermedia documents. A Web site stores such information in a hypermedia database consisting of hyperlinked pages of multimedia (text, graphic and photographic images, video clips, audio segments, and so on). That is, from a database management point of view, the set of interconnected multimedia pages on a Web site is a database of interrelated hypermedia page elements, rather than interrelated data records.

Figure 5.16 shows how you might use a Web browser on your client PC to connect with a Web network server. This server runs Web server software to access and transfer the Web pages you request. The Web site illustrated in Figure 5.16 uses a hypermedia database consisting of Web page content described by HTML (Hypertext Markup Language) code or XML (Extensible Markup Language) labels, image files, video files, and audio. The Web server software acts as a database management system to manage the transfer of hypermedia files for downloading by the multimedia plug-ins of your Web browser.

FIGURE 5.16   The components of a Web-based information system include Web browsers, servers, and hypermedia databases.

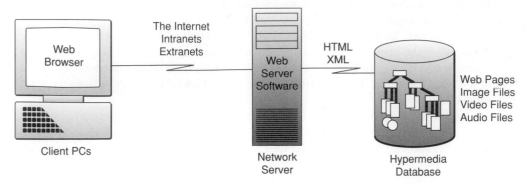

Coty: Using Real-Time Analytics to Track Demand

In the perfume business, new products like the recent launch of Kate, a fragrance Coty branded for supermodel Kate Moss, can make or break a company's year. But big hits can also lead to big problems. When a product takes off, Coty must respond quickly to keep shelves full, but its ability to ramp up is dependent on glass, packaging, and other suppliers. "If we can't meet demand . . . it annoys the retailers, the consumers lose interest, and we lose sales," says Dave Berry, CIO at Coty, whose other brands include Jennifer Lopez, Kenneth Cole, and Vera Wang.

Empty shelves are the scourge of manufacturing and retail. Just look at the annual shortages of the Christmas season's hottest toys or the rain checks stores must write regularly on sale items. At any given time, 7 percent all U.S. retail products are out of stock; goods on promotion are out of stock more than 15 percent of the time. That's why manufacturers and retailers are pushing for the next breakthroughs in demand forecasting, what has emerged as the discipline of "demand-signal management." Instead of just relying on internal data such as order and shipment records, manufacturers are analyzing weekly and even daily point-of-sale data from retailers so that they can better see what's selling where. This sort of timely, detailed data lets manufacturers spot trends much sooner by region, product, retailer, and even by individual store.

Handling demand-signal data presents the same problems that real-time data causes in any industry: how to access and integrate high volumes of data, and then combine and analyze it alongside historical information. With the advent of highly scalable data warehouses, low-latency integration techniques, and faster, deeper query and analysis capabilities, the technology is finally here, at a price most can afford. And with easier-to-use business intelligence tools, manufacturers and retailers are pushing analytic tools into the hands of front-line decision makers, most often field sales and marketing people involved in planning, merchandising, and supply chain management.

Over the last two years, Coty has pushed the responsibility for developing accurate forecasts down to its salespeople. Field-level forecasting makes for more accurate and responsive planning, says CIO Berry, who credits an analytics application from vendor CAS with making it easier for salespeople who are new to business intelligence to analyze point-of-sale data and develop forecasts.

An important obstacle to broad adoption of demand-signal analysis has been the lack of standardization in the data supplied by retailers. Coty gets point-of-sale data from the likes of CVS, Target, and Walgreens, but each uses a different format. "The timeliness, accuracy, and depth of the data also varies from retailer to retailer, so it's tough to bring it into a data warehouse," says Berry.

That being said, the payoff from early efforts by Coty has been more accurate forecasting, higher on-shelf availability, and more effective promotions. With faster and more detailed insight into demand, manufacturers can ratchet up revenue by 2 percent to 7 percent, which more than justifies any data-related headaches.

Source: Adapted from Doug Henschen, "In A Down Economy, Companies Turn to Real-Time Analytics to Track Demand," *InformationWeek*, February 28, 2009.

Data Warehouses and Data Mining

A **data warehouse** stores data that have been extracted from the various operational, external, and other databases of an organization. It is a central source of the data that have been cleaned, transformed, and cataloged so that they can be used by managers and other business professionals for data mining, online analytical processing, and other forms of business analysis, market research, and decision support. (We'll talk in-depth about all of these activities in Chapter 10.) Data warehouses may be subdivided into **data marts,** which hold subsets of data from the warehouse that focus on specific aspects of a company, such as a department or a business process.

Figure 5.17 illustrates the components of a complete data warehouse system. Notice how data from various operational and external databases are captured, cleaned, and transformed into data that can be better used for analysis. This acquisition process might include activities like consolidating data from several sources, filtering out unwanted data, correcting incorrect data, converting data to new data elements, or aggregating data into new data subsets.

These data are then stored in the enterprise data warehouse, from which they can be moved into data marts or to an *analytical data store* that holds data in a more useful form for certain types of analysis. *Metadata* (data that define the data in the data warehouse) are stored in a metadata repository and cataloged by a metadata directory. Finally, a variety of analytical software tools can be provided to query, report, mine, and analyze the data for delivery via Internet and intranet Web systems to business end users. See Figure 5.18.

One important characteristic about the data in a data warehouse is that, unlike a typical database in which changes can occur constantly, data in a data warehouse are

FIGURE 5.17 The components of a complete data warehouse system.

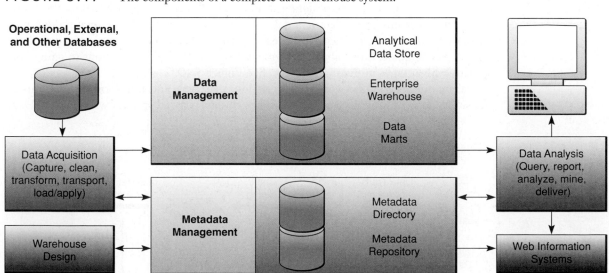

Source: Courtesy of Hewlett-Packard.

FIGURE 5.18

A data warehouse and its data mart subsets hold data that have been extracted from various operational databases for business analysis, market research, decision support, and data mining applications.

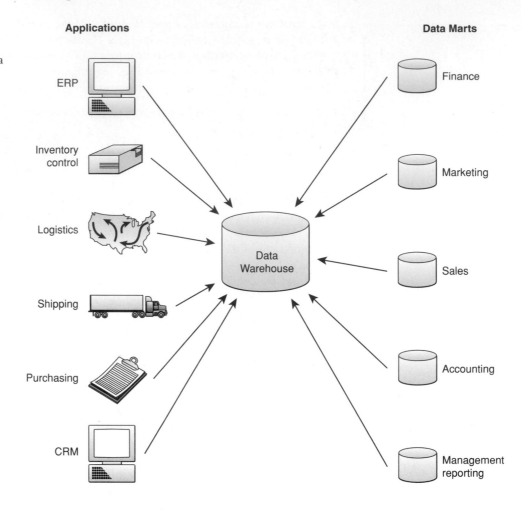

static, which means that once the data are gathered up, formatted for storage, and stored in the data warehouse, they will never change. This restriction is so that queries can be made on the data to look for complex patterns or historical trends that might otherwise go unnoticed with dynamic data that change constantly as a result of new transactions and updates.

Data Mining

Data mining is a major use of data warehouse databases and the static data they contain. In data mining, the data in a data warehouse are analyzed to reveal hidden patterns and trends in historical business activity. This analysis can be used to help managers make decisions about strategic changes in business operations to gain competitive advantages in the marketplace. See Figure 5.19.

Data mining can discover new correlations, patterns, and trends in vast amounts of business data (frequently several terabytes of data) stored in data warehouses. Data

FIGURE 5.19   How data mining extracts business knowledge from a data warehouse.

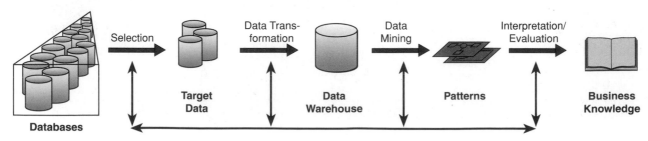

mining software uses advanced pattern recognition algorithms, as well as a variety of mathematical and statistical techniques, to sift through mountains of data to extract previously unknown strategic business information. For example, many companies use data mining to:

- Perform market-basket analysis to identify new product bundles.
- Find root causes of quality or manufacturing problems.
- Prevent customer attrition and acquire new customers.
- Cross-sell to existing customers.
- Profile customers with more accuracy.

We will discuss data mining further, as well as online analytical processing (OLAP) and other technologies that analyze the data in databases and data warehouses to provide vital support for business decisions, in Chapter 10.

R.L. Polk & Co.: Cars Are a Gold Mine of Information

Like a muscle car driving 55 mph on the freeway, R.L. Polk & Co.'s new grid-based data warehouse boasts gobs of untapped power under the hood. In 2006, the Southfield, Michigan–based automotive industry market research company finished moving its main 4TB customer-facing data warehouse to an Oracle 10g grid comprising Dell PowerEdge servers running Linux. The move has helped R.L. Polk save money and improve data redundancy, availability, and access time. It also supports Polk's new service-oriented architecture, which is improving customer service.

"We are getting more bang for our buck," notes Kevin Vasconi, the company's CIO. The data warehouse is doing 10 million transactions a day "without any issues." Encouraged by the experience so far, R.L. Polk is bringing onto the grid other databases, both domestic and overseas, that total 2.5 petabytes of actively managed data.

Founded in 1870—the same year the automobile's predecessor, a motorized handcart, was invented in Germany—R.L. Polk started as a publisher of business directories. It became a car information supplier in 1921 and began to use computer punch cards in 1951. The company is best known to consumers for its Carfax database of car histories.

Only a tiny portion of the grid is apportioned now to the data warehouse. Much of it is devoted to running R.L. Polk's new Web-based applications, which both import data into the data warehouse from 260 discrete sources, such as car dealers or state licensing boards, and stream it out to paying customers, such as carmakers, car dealers, and parts suppliers. The data warehouse serves as R.L. Polk's "single source of truth" on a massive database that includes 500 million individual cars, or almost 85 percent of all cars in the world as of 2002. It also includes data on 250 million households and 3 billion transactions.

R.L. Polk cleanses the names and addresses of all incoming records, adds location data such as latitude and longitude, and, in the case of the 17-digit vehicle identification numbers unique to every car, extrapolates each car's individual features and styling. Looking forward, Vasconi says data already stored on vehicles' on-board computers—such as engine-trouble history, GPS-based location history, and average speeds—will soon also be imported into the data warehouse if privacy issues can be resolved. It's a complicated process, but as his team continues to tweak the Oracle grid engine, he expects to be able to shorten the importation time to less than 24 hours.

"The car is a gold mine of consumer information," notes Vasconi.

Source: Adapted from Eric Lai, "Auto Market Researcher Revs Up Oracle Grid for Massive Data Warehouse," *Computerworld*, October 19, 2006.

Traditional File Processing

How would you feel if you were an executive of a company and were told that some information you wanted about your employees was too difficult and too costly to obtain? Suppose the vice president of information services gave you the following reasons:

- The information you want is in several different files, each organized in a different way.

- Each file has been organized to be used by a different application program, none of which produces the information you want in the form you need.

- No application program is available to help get the information you want from these files.

That's how end users can be frustrated when an organization relies on **file processing** systems in which data are organized, stored, and processed in independent files of data records. In the traditional file processing approach that was used in business data processing for many years, each business application was designed to use one or more specialized data files containing only specific types of data records. For example, a bank's checking account processing application was designed to access and update a data file containing specialized data records for the bank's checking account customers. Similarly, the bank's installment loan-processing application needed to access and update a specialized data file containing data records about the bank's installment loan customers. See Figure 5.20.

FIGURE 5.20

Examples of file processing systems in banking. Note the use of separate computer programs and independent data files in a file processing approach to the savings, installment loan, and checking account applications.

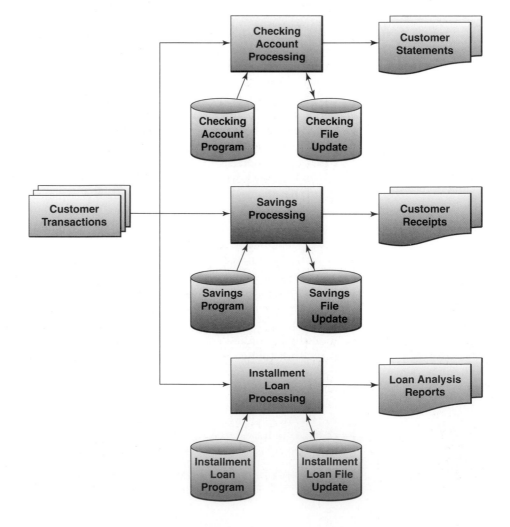

Problems of File Processing

The file processing approach finally became too cumbersome, costly, and inflexible to supply the information needed to manage modern business and, as we shall soon see, was replaced by the *database management approach*. Despite their apparent logic and simplicity, file processing systems had the following major problems:

Data Redundancy. Independent data files included a lot of duplicated data; the same data (such as a customer's name and address) were recorded and stored in several files. This data redundancy caused problems when data had to be updated. Separate *file maintenance* programs had to be developed and coordinated to ensure that each file was properly updated. Of course, this coordination proved difficult in practice, so a lot of inconsistency occurred among data stored in separate files.

Lack of Data Integration. Having data in independent files made it difficult to provide end users with information for ad hoc requests that required accessing data stored in several different files. Special computer programs had to be written to retrieve data from each independent file. This retrieval was so difficult, time-consuming, and costly for some organizations that it was impossible to provide end users or management with such information. End users had to extract the required information manually from the various reports produced by each separate application and then prepare customized reports for management.

Data Dependence. In file processing systems, major components of a system—the organization of files, their physical locations on storage hardware, and the application software used to access those files—depended on one another in significant ways. For example, application programs typically contained references to the specific *format* of the data stored in the files they used. Thus, changes in the format and structure of data and records in a file required that changes be made to all of the programs that used that file. This *program maintenance* effort was a major burden of file processing systems. It proved difficult to do properly, and it resulted in a lot of inconsistency in the data files.

Lack of Data Integrity or Standardization. In file processing systems, it was easy for data elements such as stock numbers and customer addresses to be defined differently by different end users and applications. This divergence caused serious inconsistency problems in the development of programs to access such data. In addition, the *integrity* (i.e., the accuracy and completeness) of the data was suspect because there was no control over their use and maintenance by authorized end users. Thus, a lack of standards caused major problems in application program development and maintenance, as well as in the security and integrity of the data files needed by the organization.

The Paperless Office Is Not a Reality

The dream of every environmentally conscious organization—the paperless office—has been "somewhat of a fallacy" according to Bruce Dahlgren, HP's senior vice president of managed enterprise solutions, imaging, and printing group. "It's unrealistic to think that printing is just going to go away," he told *Computerworld Australia*. "However, I think the way people print and copy is changing."

Data collected from HP's 2600 managed print service clients worldwide showed that 84 percent of print and copy jobs were three pages or less. "We're able to distribute so much more of the information electronically, and people are printing off what they need," he said.

The trend is likely to continue too, as more information is distributed online rather than printed and mailed. However, Dahlgren said he didn't think companies would reach a completely paperless office anytime soon.

HP's managed print service division is worth $US5.5 billion worldwide, and accounts for 18.5 billion printed pages per year. The market is particularly lucrative in Australia, where HP controls over a 40 percent share, despite increasing clues as to the entry of potential rivals like Dell.

The key behind managed print service is typically to reduce unnecessary infrastructure, particularly the size of the printer fleet, as well as the consumables used and pages printed. While many companies still share one printer or multifunction device between two or three workers, Dahlgren said that HP typically saw this change to 15 to 20 people for every device.

However, there are a few who have gotten rid of printers altogether. One company is Kogan Technologies, the online-only store that buys OEM consumer electronics from Chinese manufacturers and sells them at a significant discount over alternatives from better-known brands. Founded by Ruslan Kogan, the business employs 25 people in a Melbourne-based head office and distributes its products through warehouses it does not own.

The company's head office as well as the warehouses it deals with are paperless. Ruslan said that he even made logistics giant DHL implement paperless processes when dealing with the consumer electronics company. "Our business is all about efficiency," he said. "We have to keep costs down in order to compete in the marketplace."

According to its founder, Kogan Technologies' ability to keep overhead costs down through paperless processes is a key factor in running the business. All pertaining documents—including manuals, sales orders as well as all internal and external customer receipts—are indexed and stored in a mix of Google cloud services and hosted data centers with The Planet. "I couldn't imagine doing what we do if there was paper involved," he said.

Kogan Technologies and its affiliate furniture delivery company, Milan Direct, have been paperless from the start, eliminating the need for a resource-heavy transition. However, Kogan said that even for larger companies, the initial outlay would be easily made up through the resulting efficiency savings.

Source: Adapted from James Hutchinson, "Paperless Offices 'a Fallacy': HP Exec," *Computerworld*, Fairfax Media Group, May 10, 2010.

The Database Management Approach

To solve the problems encountered with the file processing approach, the database management approach was conceived as the foundation of modern methods for managing organizational data. The database management approach consolidates data records, formerly held in separate files, into databases that can be accessed by many different application programs. In addition, a *database management system* (DBMS) serves as a software interface between users and databases, which helps users easily access the data in a database. Thus, database management involves the use of database management software to control how databases are created, interrogated, and maintained to provide information that end users need.

For example, customer records and other common types of data are needed for several different applications in banking, such as check processing, automated teller systems, bank credit cards, savings accounts, and installment loan accounting. These data can be consolidated into a common *customer database*, rather than being kept in separate files for each of those applications. See Figure 5.21.

Database Management System

A database management system (DBMS) is the main software tool of the database management approach because it controls the creation, maintenance, and use of the databases of an organization and its end users. As we saw in Figure 5.16, microcomputer database management packages such as Microsoft Access, Lotus Approach, or Corel Paradox allow you to set up and manage databases on your PC, network server, or the World Wide Web. In mainframe and server computer systems, the database management system is an important system software package that controls the development, use, and maintenance of the databases of computer-using organizations.

FIGURE 5.21

An example of a database management approach in a banking information system. Note how the savings, checking, and installment loan programs use a database management system to share a customer database. Note also that the DBMS allows a user to make direct, ad hoc interrogations of the database without using application programs.

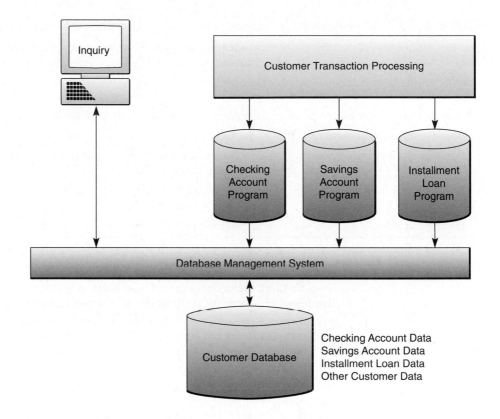

Examples of popular mainframe and server versions of DBMS software are IBM's DB2 Universal Database, Oracle 10g by Oracle Corp., and MySQL, a popular open-source DBMS. See Figure 5.22. Common DBMS components and functions are summarized in Figure 5.23.

FIGURE 5.22

Database management software like MySQL, a popular open-source DBMS, supports the development, maintenance, and use of the databases of an organization.

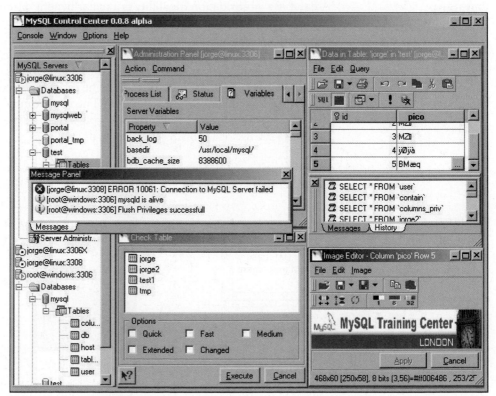

Source: Courtesy of MySQL.com.

FIGURE 5.23   Common software components and functions of a database management system.

Common DBMS Software Components	
● **Database Definition**	Language and graphical tools to define entities, relationships, integrity constraints, and authorization rights.
● **Nonprocedural Access**	Language and graphical tools to access data without complicated coding.
● **Application Development**	Graphical tools to develop menus, data entry forms, and reports.
● **Procedural Language Interface**	Language that combines nonprocedural access with full capabilities of a programming language.
● **Transaction Processing**	Control mechanisms to prevent interference from simultaneous users and recover lost data after a failure.
● **Database Tuning**	Tools to monitor and improve database performance.

Source: Michael V. Mannino, *Database Application Development and Design* (Burr Ridge, IL: McGraw-Hill/Irwin, 2001), p. 7.

The three major functions of a database management system are (1) to *create* new databases and database applications, (2) to *maintain* the quality of the data in an organization's databases, and (3) to *use* the databases of an organization to provide the information that its end users need. See Figure 5.24.

Database development involves defining and organizing the content, relationships, and structure of the data needed to build a database. **Database application development** involves using a DBMS to develop prototypes of queries, forms, reports, and Web pages for a proposed business application. **Database maintenance** involves using transaction processing systems and other tools to add, delete, update, and correct the data in a database. The primary use of a database by end users involves employing the *database interrogation* capabilities of a DBMS to access the data in a database to selectively retrieve and display information and produce reports, forms, and other documents.

Database Interrogation

A database interrogation capability is a major benefit of the database management approach. End users can use a DBMS by asking for information from a database using a *query* feature or a *report generator*. They can receive an immediate response in the form of video displays or printed reports. No difficult programming is required. The **query language** feature lets you easily obtain immediate responses to ad hoc data requests: You merely key in a few short inquiries—in some cases, using common sentence structures just like you would use to ask a question. The **report generator** feature allows you to specify a report format for information you want presented as a report. Figure 5.25 illustrates the use of a DBMS report generator.

SQL Queries. SQL (pronounced "see quill"), or Structured Query Language, is an international standard query language found in many DBMS packages. In most cases,

FIGURE 5.24

The three major uses of DBMS software are to create, maintain, and use the databases of an organization.

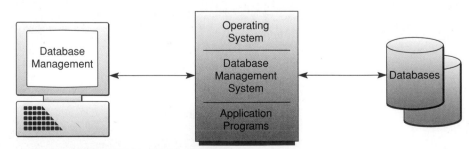

■ Create: Database and Application Development
■ Maintain: Database Maintenance
■ Use: Database Interrogation

FIGURE 5.25

Using the report generator of Microsoft Access to create an employee report.

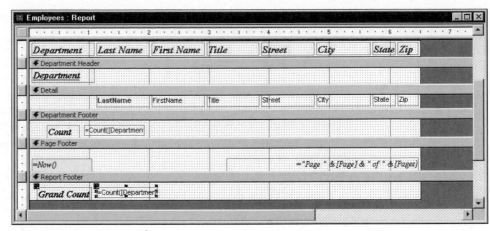

Source: Courtesy of Microsoft®.

SQL is the language structure used to "ask a question" that the DBMS will retrieve the data to answer. The basic form of a SQL query is:

SELECT . . . FROM . . . WHERE . . .

After SELECT, you list the data fields you want retrieved. After FROM, you list the files or tables from which the data must be retrieved. After WHERE, you specify conditions that limit the search to only those data records in which you are interested. Figure 5.26 compares a SQL query to a natural language query for information on customer orders.

Boolean Logic. To fully access the power of SQL, a database user needs to have a basic understanding of the concepts behind **Boolean logic.** Developed by George Boole in the mid-1800s, Boolean logic allows us to refine our searches for specific information such that only the desired information is obtained.

Boolean logic consists of three logical operators: (1) AND, (2) OR, and (3) NOT. Using these operators in conjunction with the syntax of a SQL query, a database user can refine a search to ensure that only the desired data are retrieved. This same set of logical operators can be used to refine searches for information from the Internet (which is really nothing more than the world's largest database). Let's look at an example of how the three logical operators work.

Suppose we are interested in obtaining information about cats from the Internet. We could just search on the word *cats*, and a large number of potentially useful Web sites would be retrieved. The problem is that in addition to the Web sites about cats, we would also retrieve Web sites about cats and dogs, pets in general (if the site includes the word *cats*), and probably even sites about the Broadway musical titled *Cats*.

FIGURE 5.26

Comparing a natural language query with a SQL query.

Operations Support Systems
A Sample Natural Language-to-SQL Translation for Microsoft Access
Natural Language
What customers had no orders last month?
SQL

SELECT [Customers].[Company Name],[Customers].[Contact Name]
FROM [Customers]
WHERE not Exists {SELECT [Ship Name] FROM [Orders]
    WHERE Month {[Order Date]}=1 and Year {[Order Date]}=2004 and [Customers].
    [Customer ID]=[Orders].[Customer ID]}}

To avoid having to sift through all the sites to find what we want, we could use Boolean logic to form a more refined query:

Cats OR felines AND NOT dogs OR Broadway

By using this search query, we would retrieve any Web site with the word *cats* or *felines* but exclude any site that also has the words *dogs* or *Broadway*. Using this approach, we would eliminate any reference to cats and dogs or to the Broadway musical titled *Cats*. This query therefore would result in a more refined search and eliminate the need to look at Web sites that do not pertain to our specific interest.

Graphical and Natural Queries. Many end users (and IS professionals) have difficulty correctly phrasing SQL and other database language search queries. So most end-user database management packages offer GUI (graphical user interface) point-and-click methods, which are easier to use and are translated by the software into SQL commands. See Figure 5.27. Other packages are available that use *natural language* query statements similar to conversational English (or other languages), as illustrated in Figure 5.26.

Database Maintenance

The **database maintenance** process is accomplished by *transaction processing systems* and other end-user applications, with the support of the DBMS. End users and information specialists can also employ various utilities provided by a DBMS for database maintenance. The databases of an organization need to be updated continually to reflect new business transactions (e.g., sales made, products produced, inventory shipped) and other events. Other miscellaneous changes also must be made to update and correct data (e.g., customer or employee name and address changes) to ensure the accuracy of the data in the databases. We introduced transaction processing systems in Chapter 1 and will discuss them in more detail in Chapter 7.

Application Development

In addition, DBMS packages play a major role in **application development.** End users, systems analysts, and other application developers can use the internal 4GL programming language and built-in software development tools provided by many DBMS packages to develop custom application programs. For example, you can use a DBMS to develop the data entry screens, forms, reports, or Web pages of a business application that accesses a company database to find and update the data it needs. A DBMS also makes the job of application software developers easier, because they do not have to develop detailed data-handling procedures using conventional programming languages every time they write a program. Instead, they can include features such as *data manipulation language* (DML) statements in their software that call on the DBMS to perform necessary data-handling activities.

FIGURE 5.27

Using the Query Wizard of the Microsoft Access database management package to develop a query about employee health plan choices.

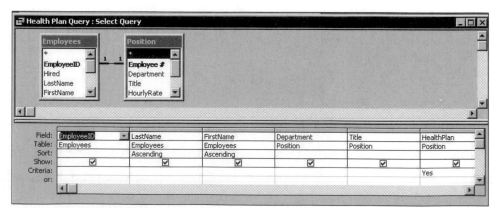

Source: Courtesy of Microsoft®.

Summary

- **Data Resource Management.** Data resource management is a managerial activity that applies information technology and software tools to the task of managing an organization's data resources. Early attempts to manage data resources used a file processing approach in which data were organized and accessible only in specialized files of data records that were designed for processing by specific business application programs. This approach proved too cumbersome, costly, and inflexible to supply the information needed to manage modern business processes and organizations. Thus, the database management approach was developed to solve the problems of file processing systems.

- **Database Management.** The database management approach affects the storage and processing of data. The data needed by different applications are consolidated and integrated into several common databases instead of being stored in many independent data files. Also, the database management approach emphasizes updating and maintaining common databases, having users' application programs share the data in the database, and providing a reporting and an inquiry/response capability so that end users can easily receive reports and quick responses to requests for information.

- **Database Software.** Database management systems are software packages that simplify the creation, use, and maintenance of databases. They provide software tools so that end users, programmers, and database administrators can create and modify databases; interrogate a database; generate reports; do application development; and perform database maintenance.

- **Types of Databases.** Several types of databases are used by business organizations, including operational, distributed, and external databases. Data warehouses are a central source of data from other databases that have been cleaned, transformed, and cataloged for business analysis and decision support applications. That includes data mining, which attempts to find hidden patterns and trends in the warehouse data. Hypermedia databases on the World Wide Web and on corporate intranets and extranets store hyperlinked multimedia pages on a Web site. Web server software can manage such databases for quick access and maintenance of the Web database.

- **Data Access.** Data must be organized in some logical manner on physical storage devices so that they can be efficiently processed. For this reason, data are commonly organized into logical data elements such as characters, fields, records, files, and databases. Database structures, such as the hierarchical, network, relational, and object-oriented models, are used to organize the relationships among the data records stored in databases. Databases and files can be organized in either a sequential or direct manner and can be accessed and maintained by either sequential access or direct access processing methods.

- **Database Development.** The development of databases can be easily accomplished using microcomputer database management packages for small end-user applications. However, the development of large corporate databases requires a top-down data planning effort that may involve developing enterprise and entity relationship models, subject area databases, and data models that reflect the logical data elements and relationships needed to support the operation and management of the basic business processes of the organization.

Key Terms and Concepts

These are the key terms and concepts of this chapter. The page number of their first explanation is in parentheses.

1. Data dependence (237)
2. Data dictionary (222)
3. Data integration (237)
4. Data integrity (237)
5. Data mining (234)
6. Data modeling (224)
7. Data redundancy (237)
8. Data resource management (227)
9. Database administrator (DBA) (222)
10. Database interrogation (240)
11. Database management approach (238)
12. Database management system (DBMS) (238)
13. Database structures (217)
    a. Hierarchical structure (218)
    b. Multidimensional model (219)
    c. Network structure (218)
    d. Object-oriented model (219)
    e. Relational model (218)
14. Duplication (231)
15. File processing (236)
16. Logical data elements (212)
    a. Attribute (212)
    b. Character (212)
    c. Database (215)
    d. Entity (212)
    e. Field (212)
    f. File (215)
    g. Record (212)
17. Metadata (222)
18. Replication (231)
19. Structured Query Language (SQL) (240)
20. Types of databases (227)
    a. Data warehouse (233)
    b. Distributed (227)
    c. External (231)
    d. Hypermedia (231)
    e. Operational (227)

Review Quiz

Match one of the key terms and concepts listed previously with one of the brief examples or definitions that follow. Try to find the best fit for answers that seem to fit more than one term or concept. Defend your choices.

_____ 1. The use of integrated collections of data records and files for data storage and processing.

_____ 2. Data in independent files made it difficult to provide answers to ad hoc requests and required special computer programs to be written to perform this task.

_____ 3. A specialist in charge of the databases of an organization.

_____ 4. A nonprocedural computer language used to interrogate a database.

_____ 5. Defines and catalogs the data elements and data relationships in an organization's database.

_____ 6. A feature of database systems that uses queries or report generators to extract information.

_____ 7. The main software package that supports a database management approach.

_____ 8. Databases that are dispersed over the Internet and corporate intranets and extranets.

_____ 9. Databases that organize and store data as objects.

_____ 10. Databases of hyperlinked multimedia documents on the Web.

_____ 11. The management of all the data resources of an organization.

_____ 12. Processing data in a data warehouse to discover key business factors and trends.

_____ 13. Developing conceptual views of the relationships among data in a database.

_____ 14. A customer's name.

_____ 15. A customer's name, address, and account balance.

_____ 16. The names, addresses, and account balances of all of your customers.

_____ 17. An integrated collection of all of the data about your customers.

_____ 18. Business application programs that use specialized data files.

_____ 19. A treelike structure of records in a database.

_____ 20. A tabular structure of records in a database.

_____ 21. Records organized as cubes within cubes in a database.

_____ 22. Databases that support the major business processes of an organization.

_____ 23. A centralized and integrated database of current and historical data about an organization.

_____ 24. Databases available on the Internet or provided by commercial information services.

_____ 25. A problem in the file processing approach where major components of a system are dependent on each other to a large degree.

_____ 26. Different approaches to the logical organization of individual data elements stored in a database.

_____ 27. The most basic logical data element corresponding to a single letter or number.

_____ 28. A feature of distributed databases that identifies changes in one database and then makes appropriate changes in the others.

_____ 29. A characteristic of data that refers to their accuracy and completeness.

_____ 30. Data that describe the structure and characteristics of databases.

_____ 31. A characteristic or quality of some entity used to describe that entity.

_____ 32. Includes, among others, operational, distributed, and hypermedia databases.

_____ 33. The existence of duplicate data among different files in an organization.

_____ 34. An approach to distributed databases that copies the complete content of a master database to others at a prescribed time of the day.

_____ 35. An object, person, place, event, and so on that is of interest to an organization and thus included in a database.

_____ 36. An approach to database structure that improves on the hierarchical model by allowing many-to-many relationships.

_____ 37. Different levels of data groupings that exist in a database.

Discussion Questions

1. How should a business store, access, and distribute data and information about its internal operations and external environment?

2. What role does database management play in managing data as a business resource?

3. What are the advantages of a database management approach to the file processing approach? Give examples to illustrate your answer.

4. Refer to the Real World Case on Data Explosion and Risk of Data Loss in the chapter. Given the need for

better data security combined with the explosion of organizational data, is there any truly effective solution to protecting data? Should an organization simply assume an inherent risk of loss as a cost of doing business? Explain your position.

5. What is the role of a database management system in a business information system?

6. In the past, databases of information about a firm's internal operations were the only databases that were considered important to a business. What other kinds of databases are important for a business today?

7. Refer to the Real World Case on Medical IT in the chapter. What do these automated or semi-automated technologies spell for the future of medicine? How

much of this discipline can be captured using these algorithms. What about pharmacy?

8. What are the benefits and limitations of the relational database model for business applications today?

9. Why is the object-oriented database model gaining acceptance for developing applications and managing the hypermedia databases on business Web sites?

10. How have the Internet, intranets, and extranets affected the types and uses of data resources available to business professionals? What other database trends are also affecting data resource management in business?

Analysis Exercises

Complete the following exercises as individual or group projects that apply chapter concepts to real-world businesses.

1. **Joining Tables**

You have the responsibility for managing technical training classes within your organization. These classes fall into two general types: highly technical training and end-user training. Software engineers sign up for the former, and administrative staff sign up for the latter. Your supervisor measures your effectiveness in part according to the average cost per training hour and type of training. In short, your supervisor expects the best training for the least cost.

To meet this need, you have negotiated an exclusive on-site training contract with Hands-On Technology Transfer (HOTT) Inc. (www.traininghott.com), a high-quality technical training provider. Your negotiated rates are reproduced below in the pricing table. A separate table contains a sample list of courses you routinely make available for your organization.

a. Using these data, design and populate a table that includes basic training rate information. Designate the "Technical" field type as "Yes/No" (Boolean).

b. Using these data, design and populate a course table. Designate the CourseID field as a "Primary Key" and allow your database to automatically generate a value for this field. Designate the "Technical" field type as "Yes/No" (Boolean).

c. Prepare a query that lists each course name and its cost per day of training.

d. Prepare a query that lists the cost per student for each class. Assume maximum capacity and that you will schedule two half-day classes on the same day to take full advantage of HOTT's per-day pricing schedule.

Course Table

Course ID	Course Name	Duration	Technical
1	ASP Programming	5	Yes
2	XML Programming	5	Yes
3	PHP Programming	4	Yes
4	Microsoft Word–Advanced	.5	No
5	Microsoft Excel–Advanced	.5	No

. . .

2. **Training-Cost Management**

Having determined the cost per student for each of the classes in the previous problem, you now must carefully manage class registration. Because you pay the same flat rates no matter how many students attend (up to capacity), you want to do all you can to ensure maximum attendance. Your training provider, Hands-On Technology Transfer Inc., requires two weeks' notice in the event that you need to reschedule a class. You should make sure your classes are at least two-thirds full before this deadline. You should also make sure you send timely reminders to all attendees so that they do not forget to show up. Use the database you created in Problem 1 to perform the following activities:

a. Using the information provided in the sample below, add a course schedule table to your training database. Designate the ScheduleID field as a "Primary Key" and allow your database program to generate a value for this field automatically. Make the CourseID field a number field and the StartDate field a date field.

b. Using the information provided in the sample below, add a class roster table to your training database. Make the ScheduleID field a number field. Make the Reminder and Confirmed fields both "Yes/No" (Boolean) fields.

Pricing Table

Technical	Price per Day	Capacity
Yes	$2,680	15
No	$2,144	30

c. Because the Class Schedule table relates to the Course Table and the Course Table relates to the Pricing Table, why is it appropriate to record the Price per Day information in the Class Schedule table too?

d. What are the advantages and disadvantages of using the participant's name and e-mail address in the Class Roster table? What other database design might you use to record this information?

e. Write a query that shows how many people have registered for each scheduled class. Include the class name, capacity, date, and count of attendees.

Class Schedule

Schedule ID	Course ID	Location	Start Date	Price per Day
1	1	101-A	7/12/2008	$2,680
2	1	101-A	7/19/2008	$2,680
3	1	101-B	7/19/2008	$2,680
4	4	101-A&B	7/26/2008	$2,144
5	5	101-A . . . B	8/2/2008	$2,144
. . .				

Class Roster

Schedule ID	Participant	e-mail	Reminder	Confirmed
1	Linda Adams	adams.l@ . . .	Yes	Yes?
1	Fatima Ahmad	ahmad.f@ . . .	Yes	No?
1	Adam Alba	alba.a@ . . .	Yes	Yes
4	Denys Alyea	alyea.d@ . . .	No	No
4	Kathy Bara	bara.k@ . . .	Yes	No
. . .				

3. Selling the Sawdust
Selling Information By-Products

Sawmill operators are in the business of turning trees into lumber. Products include boards, plywood, and veneer. For as long as there have been sawmills, there have been sawmill operators who have tried to solve the problem of what to do with their principal by-product: sawdust. Numerous creative examples abound.

Likewise, businesses often generate tremendous amounts of data. The challenge then becomes what to do with this by-product. Can a little additional effort turn it into a valuable product? Research the following:

a. What are your college's or university's policies regarding student directory data?

b. Does your college or university sell any of its student data? If your institution sells student data, what data do they sell, to whom, and for how much?

c. If your institution sells data, calculate the revenue earned per student. Would you be willing to pay this amount per year in exchange for maintaining your privacy?

4. Data Formats and Manipulation
Importing Formatted Data into Excel

Ms. Sapper, a marketing manager in a global accounting firm, was this year's coordinator for her firm's annual partner meeting. With 400 partners from around the world, Sapper faced daunting communications tasks that she wanted to automate as much as possible. Sapper received a file containing all partners' names, as well as additional personal information, from her IT department. The file ended with the extension "CSV." She wondered to herself what to do next.

The CSV, or *comma separated values* format, is a very basic data format that most database applications use to import or export data. As a minimum, the CSV format groups all fields in a record into a single line of text. It then separates each field within a line with a comma or other delimiter. When the text information contains commas, the format requires this text information to be placed within quotes. Sapper needed to get these data into Excel. Given how busy the IT guys appeared, she decided to do this herself.

a. Download and save "partners.csv" from the MIS 10e OLC. Open the file using Microsoft Word. Remember to look for the "csv" file type when searching for the file to open. Describe the data's appearance.

b. Import the "partner.csv" file into Excel. Remember to look for the "csv" file type when searching for the file to open. Does Excel automatically format the data correctly? Save your file as "partner.xls."

c. Describe in your own words why you think database manufacturers use common formats to import and export data from their systems.

Cogent Communications, Intel, and Others: Mergers Go More Smoothly When Your Data Are Ready

When Cogent Communications eyes a company to acquire, it goes into battle mode. Two miles north of the Pentagon, across the Potomac in Washington, Cogent sets up what it calls the War Room, where it marshals eight top executives to evaluate the target company. Among those on the due diligence squad are the IS director and IT infrastructure manager.

Cogent, a midsize Internet service provider, understands what far too many companies do not: Its ability to integrate and, in some cases, adopt an acquired company's IT systems and operations can determine whether a merger flourishes or founders. For one thing, unanticipated IT integration costs can offset merger savings. Imagine the business lost when orders vanish, accounts payable go uncollected, and customer information goes AWOL because the acquiring company gave short shrift to the IT challenge ahead.

As 2006 came to a close, it broke records for the number of mergers and acquisitions, but now IT managers have to step up and make sure their data centers can help make those deals a reality. "A well-run data center with reduced complexity makes mergers and acquisitions much easier," says Andi Mann, senior analyst at Enterprise Management Associates (EMA).

More than 11,700 deals were done. As the dust clears, experts and IT managers agree that companies will feel the full impact of this merger and acquisition (M&A) frenzy directly in their data centers. So they advise organizations to prep now or risk experiencing downtime if they have to merge mission-critical assets. "Today, the most downtime companies can afford for critical data center infrastructure is measured in minutes." Merged and acquired infrastructure "has to be available right away," says Ryan Osborn of AFCOM, a data center industry group.

Observers agree that the key to M&A success from a data center perspective is to focus on virtualization, documentation, and logistics.

Osborn says these three areas will help companies get ahead of the game and turn a time of crisis into one of opportunity. "You won't spend your time just moving infrastructure from one data center to another. You can actually do a technology refresh, get newer equipment and come out ahead," he says.

For John Musilli, data center operations manager at Intel in Santa Clara, California, the most critical piece is knowing about basic logistics. "I don't always have to know what a server does, but I do have to know how to keep it alive," he says. "It's getting something moved from Point A to Point B and it doesn't matter whether the logistics deals with putting servers on a truck or transferring data over a line."

Musilli has been through a handful of acquisitions in his eight years at Intel, and he says that he has it down to a science. "As part of the acquiring company, it's my job to provide the skeletal environment to accept any company's assets

that come to us," he says. As such, he keeps a healthy amount of generic racking, generic cabling, extra bandwidth on the network, and generic power. "I go generic because I probably won't know what servers, how many slots, or what type of power we'll need beforehand. With generic, I can configure whatever I need in minutes," he says.

For instance, he uses a universal busway for power so that he doesn't have to be concerned about the particular electrical needs of the acquired equipment. "We acquired a company and needed to integrate them in a short period of time because their building lease was up and they had to get out of there," Musilli says. One team was sent ahead of time and spent a year trying to identify each server on 30–40 racks. "None of their applications matched our operating systems," he says.

As time dwindled, Musilli told them to pack up all the servers and send them to him. "In the end, it took two man-days to move them intact and get them up and running in our data center," he says.

As companies begin to contemplate future mergers or acquisitions, they must look inward at their own processes and procedures. "Just as important as technology is documentation of processes—you have to know what people are doing with the systems," says EMA's Mann. He warns that one of the first obstacles to having a successful merger or acquisition is the reliance on what he refers to as tribal knowledge. Companies that have data centers where the employees hold all the knowledge suffer greatly when, after a merger or acquisition, those people are let go.

"You have to document the knowledge from those people and figure out how to make the processes work with only a handful of employees," he says. Mann recommends creating a workflow chart that outlines who's responsible for each part of the data center. He suggests considering who handles network management, systems management, application management, and storage. "This will also help you spot redundancies in skill sets or areas where you are lacking in the event of a merger," he says. John Burke, senior analyst at Nemertes Research in Minneapolis, says that in addition to knowing who is responsible, IT groups must know which systems perform which processes.

"You have to have really good information about what goes on in your data center in terms of systems and how they interact with each other and how they interface with the business. You should always know what services you offer and how much it costs to offer them," Burke says. As part of this effort, many organizations employ a configuration management database and asset management tool to help track elements within the data center. "You need a clear and concise view of the data flow within the data center. If you don't know what has to move together, you might disrupt business during a merger or acquisition," he says.

Companies must also develop guidelines for governance to be referenced during a merger. For instance, if two law firms are merging and have competing clients, then IT groups must ensure that data are protected and there is sufficient access control. AFCOM's Osborn says that good documentation helps the discovery process that companies go through before a merger or acquisition.

"If the company you are acquiring has good documentation and good processes in place, the acquisition goes much more smoothly," he says.

"In some cases, you might be able to lower your software costs if you use a more robust server with fewer processors, but if the application license doesn't allow for that, then you can't," Osborn says, and adds: "How much money you're going to have to spend to merge technology can weigh heavily on the decision to acquire a company." Nemertes' Burke suggests that one major step to M&A success is to make sure your data center has virtualization tools running on both servers and storage.

Virtualization is important not only for scaling the data center but also for creating a standardized execution environment. "With a well-virtualized data center, you can hide the fact that things are moving around multiple servers and storage devices," Burke says. Rob Laurie, CEO at virtualization-software provider Dunes Technologies in Stamford, Connecticutt, says that virtualization is useful for companies that want to test application and infrastructure integration before they put their merged or acquired assets into production.

It's also helpful for companies that must integrate assets that can't be physically moved, he says. He warns, however, that for virtualization to be most effective, merging companies must decide on a uniform platform for their virtual environment. "That way, whatever is virtualized in one company could run in the other company's data center without problems," he says. If they don't have the same environment, they must at least have a compatible data format to gain any benefit.

Intel's Musilli suggests that IT's natural attention to detail can sometimes overcomplicate matters. "Mergers and acquisitions aren't always as difficult as people make them. They're simply about the ability to assimilate any two environments," he says. M&As create stress for both acquirer and acquiree, but early involvement by IT can minimize the trauma. Otherwise, you'll need to do too much in too little time. As software engineering guru Frederick Brooks once said, "You can't make a baby in a month using nine women. Plan ahead."

Source: Adapted from Sandra Gittien, "Mergers Go Smoother with a Well-Prepped Data Center," *Computerworld*, July 28, 2007, and Eric Chabrow, "IT Plays Linchpin Role in High-Stake M&As," *InformationWeek*, June 26, 2006.

CASE STUDY QUESTIONS

1. Place yourself in the role of a manager at a company undergoing a merger or acquisition. What would be the most important things customers would expect from you while still in that process? What role would IT play in meeting those expectations? Provide at least three examples.

2. Focus on what Andi Mann in the case calls "tribal knowledge." What do you think is meant by that, and why is it so important to this process? What strategies would you suggest for companies that are faced with the extensive presence of this issue in an acquired organization? Develop some specific recommendations.

3. Most of the discussion on the case focused on hardware and software issues. However, these are essentially enablers for underlying business processes developed by each of the companies involved. What different alternatives do companies have for merging their business processes, and what role would IT play in supporting those activities? Pay particular attention to data management and governance issues.

REAL WORLD ACTIVITIES

1. The case extensively discusses the idea of " virtualization" and the role it plays in the merger process. Go online to research this concept and prepare a report about what it entails, how it works, what are its advantages and disadvantages, and other applications in addition to those noted in the case.

2. Search the Internet for reports of merger and acquisition cases where IT issues played an important role, either positive or negative. How did different organizations handle IT-related matters in the situations you found? What was the ultimate outcome of the process? Prepare a presentation to share your findings with the class.

REAL WORLD CASE 4

Applebee's, Travelocity, and Others: Data Mining for Business Decisions

Randall Parman, database architect at restaurant chain Applebee's International and head of Teradata's user group, opened Teradata's annual user conference in Las Vegas with a warning to those who aren't making the best use of their data. "Data are like gold," Parman noted. "If you don't use the gold, you will have someone else who will come along and take the opportunity," speaking to a room packed with almost 3,900 attendees.

Parman drew an analogy to the story about Isaac Newton's discovery of gravity after he was hit on the head with an apple. "What if Newton had just eaten the apple?" he asked. "What if we failed to use the technology available, or failed to use these insights to take action?" Applebee's, which has 1,900 casual dining restaurants worldwide and grossed $1.34 billion in revenue last year, has a four-node, 4-terabyte data warehouse system. Although the company has a staff of only three database administrators working with the system, "we have leveraged our information to gain insight into the business," he said. "Some of those insights were unexpected, coming out of the blue while we were looking in a completely different direction."

For example, Applebee's had been using the data warehouse to analyze the "back-of-house performance" of restaurants, including how long it took employees to prepare food in the kitchens. "Someone had the unanticipated insight to use back-of-house performance to gauge front-of-house performance," he said. "From looking at the time the order was placed to when it was paid for by credit card and subtracting preparation meal time, we could figure out how long servers were spending time with customers." Parman added that the information is being used to help the company improve customer experiences.

Applebee's has also advanced beyond basic business decisions based on data—such as replenishing food supplies according to how much finished product was sold daily—to developing more sophisticated analyses. His department, for example, came up with a "menu optimization quadrant" that looks at how well items are selling so that the company can make better decisions about not only what to order, but about what products to promote.

Meanwhile, technology vendors see untapped potential for businesses to spend money on software and hardware that lets them use data to make more sophisticated business decisions. "Companies who operate with the greatest speed and intelligence will win," says Teradata CEO Michael Koehler.

Like many companies, Travelocity.com has lots of unstructured data contained in e-mails from customers, call center representative notes, and other sources that contain critical nuggets of information about how customers feel about the travel site. To offset the inability of business intelligence tools to search for unstructured data, Travelocity has launched a new project to help it mine almost 600,000 unstructured comments so that it can better monitor and respond to customer service issues.

The online travel site has begun to install new text analytics software that will be used to scour some 40,000 verbatim comments from customer satisfaction surveys, 40,000 e-mails from customers, and 500,000 interactions with the call center that result in comments to surface potential customer service issues. "The truth is that it is very laborious and extremely expensive to go through all that verbatim customer feedback to try to extract the information we need to have to make business decisions," notes Don Hill, Travelocity's director of customer advocacy.

"The text mining capability . . . gives us the ability to go through all that verbatim feedback from customers and extract meaningful information. We get information on the nature of the comments and if the comments are positive or negative."

Travelocity will use text analytics software from Attensity to automatically identify facts, opinions, requests, trends, and trouble spots from the unstructured data. Travelocity will then link that analysis with structured data from its Teradata data warehouse so the company can identify trends. "We get to take unstructured data and put it into structured data so we can track trends over time," adds Hill. "We can know the frequency of customer comments on issue 'x' and if comments on that topic are going up, going down, or staying the same."

Unlike other text analytics technology, which requires manual tagging, sorting, and classifying of terms before analysis of unstructured data, Attensity's technology has a natural language engine that automatically pulls out important data without a lot of predefining terms, notes Michelle de Haaff, vice president of marketing at the vendor. This allows companies to have an early warning system to tackle issues that need to be addressed, she added.

VistaPrint Ltd., an online retailer based in Lexington, Massachusetts, which provides graphic design services and custom-printed products, has boosted its customer conversion rate with Web analytics technology that drills down into the most minute details about the 22,000 transactions it processes daily at 18 Web sites.

Like many companies that have invested heavily in online sales, VistaPrint found itself drowning, more than a year ago, in Web log data tracked from its online operations. Analyzing online customer behavior and how a new feature might affect that behavior is important, but the retrieval and analysis of those data were taking hours or even days using an old custom-built application, says Dan Malone, senior manager of business intelligence at VistaPrint.

"It wasn't sustainable, and it wasn't scalable," Malone says. "We realized that improving conversion rates by even a few percentage points can have a big impact on the bottom line." So VistaPrint set out to find a Web analytics package that could test new user interfaces to see whether they could increase conversion rates (the percentage of online visitors who become customers), find out why visitors left the site, and determine the exact point where users were dropping off.

The search first identified two vendor camps. One group offered tools that analyzed all available data, without any up-front aggregation. The other offered tools that aggregated everything upfront but required users to foresee all the queries they wanted to run, Malone says. "If you have a question that falls outside the set of questions you aggregated the data for, you have to reprocess the entire data set."

The company finally turned to a third option, selecting the Visual Site application from Visual Sciences Inc. Visual Site uses a sampling method, which means VistaPrint can still query the detailed data. but "it is also fast because you're getting responses as soon as you ask a question. It queries through 1% of the data you have, and based on that . . . it gives you an answer back. It assumes the rest of the 99% [of the data] looks like that. Because the data has been randomized, that is a valid assumption," notes Malone.

VistaPrint, which has been using the tool for just over a year, runs it alongside the 30–40 new features it tests every three weeks. For example, the company was testing a four-page path for a user to upload data to be printed on a busi-ness card. The test showed that the new upload path had the same conversion rate as the control version. "We were a little disappointed because we put in a lot of time to improve this flow," he adds.

When the company added Visual Site to the operation, it found that although the test version was better than the control in three out of four pages, the last page had a big drop-off rate. "We were able to tell the usability team where the problem was," Malone says. VistaPrint also reduced the drop-offs from its sign-in page after the Visual Site tool showed that returning customers were using the new customer-registration process and getting an error notice. The company fixed the problem, and "the sign-in rate improved significantly and led to higher conversions," he says. While Malone concedes that it is hard to measure an exact return on the investment, the company estimates that the tool paid for itself several months after installation.

Source: Adapted from Heather Havenstein, "Use Web Analytics to Turn Online Visitors into Paying Customers," *Computerworld*, September 17, 2007; Mary Hayes Weier, "Applebee's Exec Preaches Data Mining for Business Decisions," *InformationWeek*, October 8, 2007; and Heather Havenstein, "Travelocity.com Dives into Text Analytics to Boost Customer Service," *Computerworld*, November 14, 2007.

CASE STUDY QUESTIONS

1. What are the business benefits of taking the time and effort required to create and operate data warehouses such as those described in the case? Do you see any disadvantages? Is there any reason that all companies shouldn't use data warehousing technology?

2. Applebee's noted some of the unexpected insights obtained from analyzing data about "back-of-house" performance. Using your knowledge of how a restaurant works, what other interesting questions would you suggest to the company? Provide several specific examples.

3. Data mining and warehousing technologies use data about past events to inform better decision making in the future. Do you believe this stifles innovative thinking, causing companies to become too constrained by the data they are already collecting to think about unexplored opportunities? Compare and contrast both viewpoints in your answer.

REAL WORLD ACTIVITIES

1. Go online to the Web site of Attensity (www.attensity.com) and research which other products are offered by the company that complement those discussed in the case. What other examples can you find of companies that have benefited from using these technologies? Prepare a report to summarize your findings.

2. In the opening of the case, Randall Parman of Applebee's International compared data to gold. Although it is easy to figure out the value of gold at any time, valuing data has always been subject to controversy. Search the Internet for alternative methodologies to putting a price tag on the data assets of a company. Contrast different approaches and share your findings with the class.

CHAPTER 6

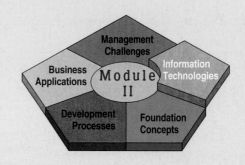

TELECOMMUNICATIONS AND NETWORKS

Chapter Highlights

Learning Objectives

1. Understand the concept of a network.

2. Apply Metcalfe's law in understanding the value of a network.

3. Identify several major developments and trends in the industries, technologies, and business applications of telecommunications and Internet technologies.

4. Provide examples of the business value of Internet, intranet, and extranet applications.

5. Identify the basic components, functions, and types of telecommunications networks used in business.

6. Explain the functions of major components of telecommunications network hardware, software, media, and services.

7. Explain the concept of client/server networking.

8. Understand the two forms of peer-to-peer networking.

9. Explain the difference between digital and analog signals.

10. Identify the various transmission media and topologies used in telecommunications networks.

11. Understand the fundamentals of wireless network technologies.

12. Explain the concepts behind TCP/IP.

13. Understand the seven layers of the OSI network model.

The Networked Enterprise

The Networked Enterprise

When computers are networked, two industries—computing and communications—converge, and the result is vastly more than the sum of the parts. Suddenly, computing applications become available for business-to-business coordination and commerce, and for small as well as large organizations. The global Internet creates a public place without geographic boundaries—cyberspace—where ordinary citizens can interact, publish their ideas, and engage in the purchase of goods and services. In short, the impact of both computing and communications on our society and organizational structures is greatly magnified.

Telecommunications and network technologies are inter-networking and revolutionizing business and society. Businesses have become networked enterprises. The Internet, the Web, and intranets and extranets are networking business processes and employees together and connecting them to their customers, suppliers, and other business stakeholders. Companies and workgroups can thus collaborate more creatively, manage their business operations and resources more effectively, and compete successfully in today's fast-changing global economy. This chapter presents the telecommunications and network foundations for these developments.

Read the Real World Case 1 on the future of virtual business meeting. We can learn a lot about the possibilities offered by new telecommunication developments from this case. See Figure 6.1.

The Concept of a Network

Because of our focus on information systems and technologies, it is easy for us to think of networks in terms of connected computers. To understand the value of connecting computers fully, however, it is important to understand the concept of a network in its broader sense.

By definition, the term network means an interconnected or interrelated chain, group, or system. Using this definition, we can begin to identify all kinds of networks: a chain of hotels, the road system, the names in a person's address book or PDA, the railroad system, the members of a church, club, or organization. The examples of networks in our world are virtually endless, and computer networks, though both valuable and powerful, are just one example of the concept.

The concept of networks can be expressed as a mathematical formula that calculates the number of possible connections or interactions in a one-way communication environment: $N(N-1)$, or $N^2 - N$. In the formula, N refers to the number of *nodes* (points of connection) on the network. If only a few nodes exist on a network, the number of possible connections is quite small. Using the formula, we see that three nodes result in only 6 possible connections. A network of 10 nodes results in a somewhat larger number—90 connections. It's when a large number of nodes are connected that the possible number of connections grows to significant proportions. A network with 100 nodes has 9,900 possible connections, and a network with 1,000 nodes has 999,000 possible connections. This type of mathematical growth is called *exponential*. This term just means that the growth in number of connections is many times greater than the number of nodes. Adding only one more node to a network makes the number of connections grow many times greater. Think of the effect of adding a new entry and exit ramp on a highway system that connects 30,000 cities and towns. How many more connections does that one new ramp create? Maybe more relevant is the effect of adding one additional person as a friend to your Facebook, MySpace, or Plaxo account. If you have 100 unique friends who each have 100 unique friends and the new friend has 100 unique friends—well, you get the picture. That's what the next section is all about.

Metcalfe's Law

Robert Metcalfe founded 3Com Corp. and designed the Ethernet protocol for computer networks. He used his understanding of the concept of networks to express the exponential growth in terms of potential business value. Metcalfe's law states that *the*

REAL WORLD CASE 1

DLA Piper, MetLife, PepsiCo, and Others: Telepresence Is Finally Coming of Age

Sprawling international law firm DLA Piper has upgraded from videoconferencing to telepresence, which will save the firm nearly $1 million per year in reduced travel costs and lost productivity. The conferencing gear that simulates across-the-table meetings has "a provable and achievable return on investment over five years, and may actually pay for itself before then," says Don Jaycox, CIO of DLA Piper U.S.

This involves an "immersive video experience," or technology that provides high-end, high-definition visual and audio communications in a completely integrated environment. The goal is to make anyone involved in these meetings feel as if they're actually in the room with the other meeting participants, regardless of where everyone is physically based.

"Rescheduling half the firm's in-person board meetings as telepresence conferences and relying on at least two attorneys per week to use telepresence rather than travel accounts for significant savings when lost productivity for travel time is factored in," says Jaycox.

"If I look at my total telepresence project cost, which includes equipment, room construction, implementation services, maintenance contract, financing costs, etc., then amortize that over the expected five-year life of the system, it works out to be just a hair under $500,000 per year for our six U.S. sites," he says. "Our early experience suggests that a more accurate number of avoided trips is closer to four or five per week, so the $970,000 projection almost certainly underestimates our actual savings," he notes.

The sites were selected so they put 80 percent of the attorneys within a one-hour drive of a telepresence room.

FIGURE 6.1

Telepresence technology provides a high-definition alternative to business travel.

Source: Courtesy of Hewlett-Packard Company.

Jaycox says he has observed attorneys working together via telepresence conferences, and he was struck to see two workgroups formed at either end of the telepresence table, just as they might be if they were all working around the same physical table. "You had the sense all these people were in the same strategy room," he says.

With the economy in a downturn, it's no surprise that companies have been slashing travel budgets. But at MetLife, officials say the focus is also on employees' quality of life, keeping them home as much as possible. As a result, the insurance giant has recently made a big push into telepresence technology.

MetLife is using Cisco Telepresence in three dedicated conference rooms in Chicago, New York, and New Jersey, and soon plans to expand to other offices nationally and internationally. "Instead of having to take people away from their families, you walk down to the room and turn on the lights and have your three-hour meeting and it's extremely effective," says Anthony Nugent, executive vice president of employee benefits sales. He regularly uses telepresence to communicate with his direct reports in Chicago and Somerset, New Jersey, and the clarity is so good that he says with a laugh, "Everyone jokes around that they can reach a Coke across the table" from one location to another.

MetLife has seen a direct cost savings as well as better employee time efficiency and a way to help the company meet its "green initiative" goal of reducing its carbon emissions by 20 percent this year, says Nugent. The company finished its initial telepresence rollout a year ago and hasn't yet determined an exact savings, but Nugent estimates the use of the systems will provide double-digit ROI in travel savings alone.

At MetLife, the three Cisco telepresence systems cost just under $1 million to install, according to Paul Galvin, vice president of enterprise services in the information technology group. Nugent says he uses both videoconferencing and telepresence, depending on his needs. Videoconferencing is a better choice for one-on-one situations, such as "if someone is going to do a quick presentation to me," he says, but telepresence is ideal for meetings where participants are located in multiple offices.

Telepresence gives him face-to-face contact with a broader group, "So it allows me to get to know people better," Nugent says. He runs an organization with people based all around the country and used to require that his direct reports come to New York for quarterly reviews. Now they can stay in their offices and he can discuss business with a wider range of employees.

"Using telepresence allows me to see and virtually interact with more people on my team instead of just my direct reports," says Nugent. "When we use telepresence for meetings, people who wouldn't normally be asked to travel to New York have the opportunity to make presentations and get valuable exposure to executive management. It really facilitates face-to-face interaction with a broader cross-section of employees on an economically efficient basis."

MetLife is considering putting a telepresence system at a business processing plant in India to avoid having employees fly over to see it. The company is also looking at ways to utilize telepresence with salespeople across the country. The idea is to have as many people using the system as possible, Nugent says.

"Flying out of Boston for a meeting when I was 20 sounded great, but the sales pitch I always give is we're respecting the time of the employee," he says. "So if we can give a person the effectiveness of being there and then be home with his family, it's two wins."

PepsiCo is deploying Cisco Telepresence systems in its major offices worldwide. PepsiCo CIO Robert Dixon says that using telepresence "will reinvent the way we work" while cutting down on travel, which, in turn, improves productivity and reduces the company's environmental footprint. "In this day and age, it's simply a smarter way of going about our business," he adds. PepsiCo sells products from 18 different product lines in 200 countries and employs nearly 200,000 workers.

The law firm of Lathrop & Gage, LLP, is using both high-definition videoconferencing and telepresence. Employees conduct more than 300 meetings every month at the firm's Kansas City, Missouri, headquarters. "It's a more meaningful way to conduct meetings than over the phone," says CEO Joel Voran, who uses the system about three times a week. Although he still tries to make it to all of the firm's offices twice a year, Voran says use of the Polycom systems has significantly reduced the need for lawyers to fly to Kansas City.

"The clarity has been impressive," Voran says. "At one of our very first meetings at one of our offices I could see the brand of the beverage someone was drinking and that made the partner sit up and take notice."

"This is a billable-hour profession," notes Ben Weinberger, CIO at Lathrop & Gage, who adds that one attorney alone can save more than $1,500 in travel expenses and productivity loss by not having to fly somewhere to attend a meeting. Because many lawyers travel monthly, the Polycom system could represent a savings of more than $30,000 in annual travel expenses and productivity loss for a single attorney, he estimates.

Weinberger differentiates between high-end videoconferencing and telepresence by the size of the screens. The rooms that have 50-plus-inch screens and run high-quality, high-definition cameras are utilizing telepresence, he says.

Making it possible for far-flung attorneys to work closely together via telepresence helps emphasize that the firm has offices around the world and should have an international focus—a benefit of the system that can't be quantified in dollars and cents. "When you work in one location, you tend to draw inward. We want people to think globally," says Jaycox.

Source: Adapted from Esther Shein, "Telepresence Catching on, but Hold onto Your Wallet," *Computerworld*, January 22, 2010; Matt Hamblen, "PepsiCo to Deploy Telepresence from Cisco and BT Globally," *Computerworld*, February 2, 2010; and Tim Greene, "Telepresence Cuts Near $1M in Travel Costs for Law Firm," *Network World*, October 7, 2009.

CASE STUDY QUESTIONS

1. Implementing telepresence seems to have other, less tangible, advantages beyond travel cost savings. What are some of those? How do you quantify them to make the case for investing in the technology? Provide at least two fully developed examples.

2. DLA Piper, MetLife, and the other companies featured in the case are very optimistic about the technology. However, other than its cost, what are some potential disadvantages of implementing telepresence in organizations?

3. Do you think meetings conducted through telepresence technology will be similar to face-to-face ones as the technology becomes more pervasive? How would the rules of etiquette change for telepresence meetings? Which type of meeting would you like best?

REAL WORLD ACTIVITIES

1. Telepresence is described in the case as a green technology because it replaces air travel with a more environmentally friendly alternative. Recently, many organizations are looking to IT to help them cut their carbon footprint. What other technologies can be helpful in this regard?

2. Go online and research different ways in which the "green IT" movement is catching on. Prepare a report to share your findings.

3. The organizations featured in the case are not too keen on the future of business travel. Despite the high quality of current and future telepresence systems, do you believe these companies are missing something by not having people meet face to face? Why or why not? Break into small groups with your classmates to discuss this issue.

usefulness, or utility, of a network equals the square of the number of users. In other words, every time you add a new user to a network, the value of the network, in terms of potential connections amongst its members, doubles!

Metcalfe's law becomes easy to understand if you think of a common piece of technology we all use every day: the telephone. The telephone is of very limited use if only you and your best friend have one. If a whole town is on the system, it becomes much more useful. If the whole world is wired, the utility of the system is phenomenal. Add the number of wireless telephone connections, and you have a massive potential for value. To reach this value, however, many people had to have access to a telephone— and they had to have used it. In other words, telephone use had to reach a critical mass of users. So it is with any technology.

Until a critical mass of users is reached, a change in technology affects only the technology. Once critical mass is attained, however, social, political, and economic systems change. The same is true of **digital network technologies.** Consider the Internet. It reached critical mass in 1993, when there were roughly 2.5 million host computers on the network; by November 1997, the vast network contained an estimated 25 million host computers. According to Internet World Stats, the number of users on the Internet in September 2009 topped 1.7 billion! More important, that represents only slightly more than 25 percent of the estimated world population. With computing costs continuing to drop rapidly (remember Moore's law from Chapter 3) and the Internet growing exponentially (Metcalfe's law), we can expect to see more and more value—conceivably for less cost—virtually every time we log on. The Internet is kind of a big deal, and it's getting bigger even as we write.

Trends in Telecommunications

Telecommunications is the exchange of information in any form (voice, data, text, images, audio, video) over networks. The Internet is the most widely visible form of telecommunications in your daily lives. Early telecommunications networks did not use computers to route traffic and, as such, were much slower than today's computer-based networks. Major trends occurring in the field of telecommunications have a significant impact on management decisions in this area. You should thus be aware of major trends in telecommunications industries, technologies, and applications that significantly increase the decision alternatives confronting business managers and professionals. See Figure 6.2.

Industry Trends

The competitive arena for telecommunications service has changed dramatically in recent years. The telecommunications industry has changed from government-regulated

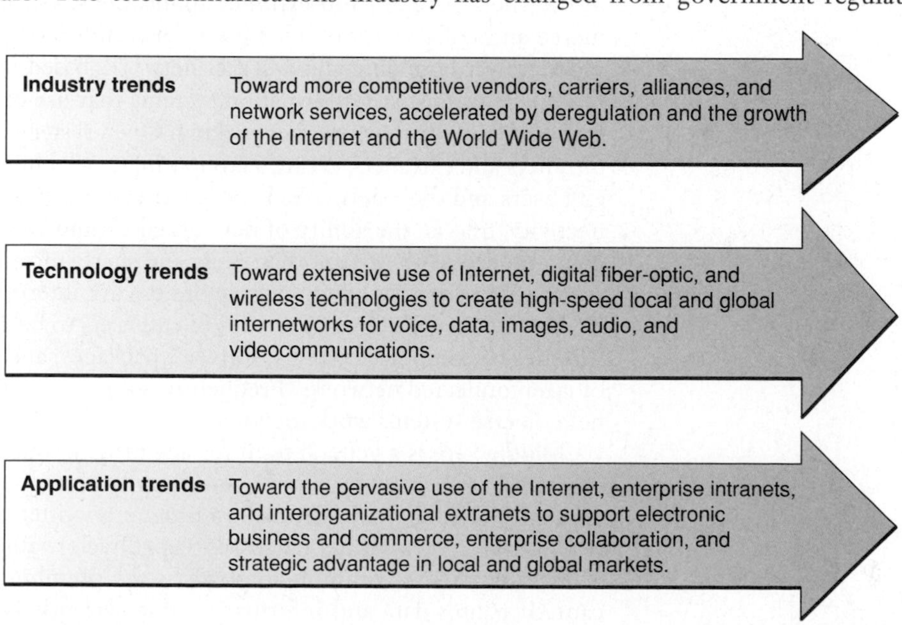

FIGURE 6.2

Major trends in business telecommunications.

Industry trends Toward more competitive vendors, carriers, alliances, and network services, accelerated by deregulation and the growth of the Internet and the World Wide Web.

Technology trends Toward extensive use of Internet, digital fiber-optic, and wireless technologies to create high-speed local and global internetworks for voice, data, images, audio, and videocommunications.

Application trends Toward the pervasive use of the Internet, enterprise intranets, and interorganizational extranets to support electronic business and commerce, enterprise collaboration, and strategic advantage in local and global markets.

FIGURE 6.3

The spectrum of telecommunications-based services available today.

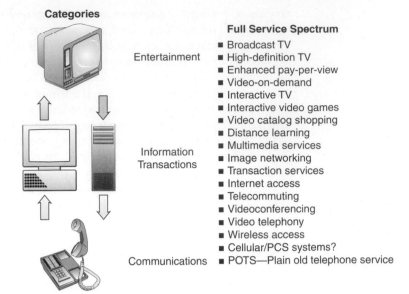

Categories

Entertainment

Information Transactions

Communications

Full Service Spectrum

- Broadcast TV
- High-definition TV
- Enhanced pay-per-view
- Video-on-demand
- Interactive TV
- Interactive video games
- Video catalog shopping
- Distance learning
- Multimedia services
- Image networking
- Transaction services
- Internet access
- Telecommuting
- Videoconferencing
- Video telephony
- Wireless access
- Cellular/PCS systems?
- POTS—Plain old telephone service

monopolies to a deregulated market with fiercely competitive suppliers of telecommunications services. Numerous companies now offer businesses and consumers a choice of everything from local and global telephone services to communications satellite channels, mobile radio, cable television, cellular phone services, and Internet access. See Figure 6.3.

The explosive growth of the Internet and the World Wide Web has spawned a host of new telecommunications products, services, and providers. Driving and responding to this growth, business firms have dramatically increased their use of the Internet and the Web for electronic commerce and collaboration. Thus, the service and vendor options available to meet a company's telecommunications needs have increased significantly, as have a business manager's decision-making alternatives.

Technology Trends

Open systems with unrestricted connectivity, using Internet networking technologies as their technology platform, are today's primary telecommunications technology drivers. Web browser suites, HTML Web page editors, Internet and intranet servers and network management software, TCP/IP Internet networking products, and network security firewalls are just a few examples. These technologies are being applied in Internet, intranet, and extranet applications, especially those for electronic commerce and collaboration. This trend has reinforced previous industry and technical moves toward building client/server networks based on an open-systems architecture.

Open systems are information systems that use common standards for hardware, software, applications, and networking. Open systems, like the Internet and corporate intranets and extranets, create a computing environment that is open to easy access by end users and their networked computer systems. Open systems provide greater connectivity, that is, the ability of networked computers and other devices to access and communicate with one another easily and share information. Any open-systems architecture also provides a high degree of network interoperability. That is, open systems enable the many different activities of end users to be accomplished using the different varieties of computer systems, software packages, and databases provided by a variety of interconnected networks. Frequently, software known as *middleware* may be used to help diverse systems work together.

Middleware is a general term for any programming that serves to glue together or mediate between two separate, and usually already existing, programs. A common application of middleware is to allow programs written for access to a particular database (e.g., DB2) to access other databases (e.g., Oracle) without the need for custom coding.

Middleware is commonly known as the plumbing of an information system because it routes data and information transparently between different back-end data sources and end-user applications. It's not very interesting to look at—it usually doesn't have much, if any, visible "front end" of its own—but it is an essential component of any IT infrastructure because it allows disparate systems to be joined together in a common framework.

Telecommunications is also being revolutionized by the rapid change from analog to digital network technologies. Telecommunications systems have always depended on voice-oriented analog transmission systems designed to transmit the variable electrical frequencies generated by the sound waves of the human voice. However, local and global telecommunications networks are rapidly converting to digital transmission technologies that transmit information in the form of discrete pulses, as computers do. This conversion provides (1) significantly higher transmission speeds, (2) the movement of larger amounts of information, (3) greater economy, and (4) much lower error rates than with analog systems. In addition, digital technologies allow telecommunications networks to carry multiple types of communications (data, voice, video) on the same circuits.

Another major trend in telecommunications technology is a change from reliance on copper wire–based media and land-based microwave relay systems to fiber-optic lines and cellular, communications satellite, and other wireless technologies. Fiber-optic transmission, which uses pulses of laser-generated light, offers significant advantages in terms of reduced size and installation effort, vastly greater communication capacity, much faster transmission speeds, and freedom from electrical interference. Satellite transmission offers significant advantages for organizations that need to transmit massive quantities of data, audio, and video over global networks, especially to isolated areas. Cellular, mobile radio, and other wireless systems are connecting cellular phones, PDAs, and other wireless appliances to the Internet and corporate networks.

Business Application Trends

The changes in telecommunications industries and technologies just mentioned are causing a significant change in the business use of telecommunications. The trend toward more vendors, services, Internet technologies, and open systems, and the rapid growth of the Internet, the World Wide Web, and corporate intranets and extranets, dramatically increases the number of feasible telecommunications applications. Thus, telecommunications networks are now playing vital and pervasive roles in Web-enabled e-business processes, e-commerce, enterprise collaboration, and other business applications that support the operations, management, and strategic objectives of both large and small business enterprises.

Internet2

We cannot leave our overview of trends in telecommunications without reiterating that the Internet sits firmly in the center of the action. Despite its importance and seemingly unexplored boundaries, we are already embarking on the next generation of the "network of networks." Internet2 is a high-performance network that uses an entirely different infrastructure than the public Internet we know today. Already, more than 300 universities and scientific founding institutions and 60,000 member institutions throughout the United States and the rest of the world are part of the Internet2 network. One big misconception about Internet2 is that it's a sequel to the original Internet and will replace it someday. It never will, because it was never intended to replace the Internet. Rather, its purpose is to build a road map that can be followed during the next stage of innovation for the current Internet. The ideas being honed, such as new addressing protocols and satellite-quality streaming video, will likely be deployed to the Internet, but it might take close to 10 years before we see them.

Furthermore, the Internet2 network may never become totally open; it might remain solely in the domain of universities, research centers, and governments. To be sure, the lightning-fast technologies in use by Internet2 right now must eventually be turned over to the public Internet. For now, the Internet2 project lives for the purpose of sharing, collaborating, and trying new high-speed communication ideas—interestingly, many of the same goals that shaped the early history of today's Internet.

Most of the institutions and commercial partners on the Internet2 network are connected via *Abilene*, a network backbone that will soon support throughput of 10 gigabits per second (Gbps). Several international networks are also plugged into Abilene's infrastructure, and as the project grows, more and more networks will be able to connect to the current framework. The one common denominator among all of the Internet2 partners is their active participation in the development and testing of new applications and Internet protocols with an emphasis on research and collaboration, focusing on things such as videoconferencing, multicasting, remote applications, and new protocols that take advantage of the many opportunities megabandwidth provides. In short, Internet2 is all about high-speed telecommunications and infinite bandwidth.

To give you an idea of exactly how fast this network of the future is, an international team of researchers has already used it to set a new landspeed record. At the end of 2002, the team sent 6.7 gigabytes of data across 6,821 miles of fiber-optic network in less than one minute. That's roughly two full-length DVD-quality movies traveling a quarter of the way around the earth in less than one minute at an average speed of 923 million bits per second! It's also approximately 410,000 miles per hour. The same team is already hard at work, attempting to break its own record.

As we are exploring new ways to gain business advantage through the Internet, a significant effort is being made to make the Internet bigger and faster. In 2009, Internet2 celebrated its 13th anniversary and has significantly expanded in breadth, speed, and storage capacity since its inception in 1996. We'll look at Internet2 again later in this chapter when we discuss Internet-addressing protocols.

The Business Value of Telecommunications Networks

What *business value* is created when a company capitalizes on the trends in telecommunications we have just identified? Use of the Internet, intranets, extranets, and other telecommunications networks can dramatically cut costs, shorten business lead times and response times, support e-commerce, improve the collaboration of workgroups, develop online operational processes, share resources, lock in customers and suppliers, and develop new products and services. These benefits make applications of telecommunications more strategic and vital for businesses that must increasingly find new ways to compete in both domestic and global markets.

Figure 6.4 illustrates how telecommunications-based business applications can help a company overcome geographic, time, cost, and structural barriers to business

FIGURE 6.4   Examples of the business value of business applications of telecommunications networks.

Strategic Capabilities	e-Business Examples	Business Value
Overcome geographic barriers: Capture information about business transactions from remote locations.	Use the Internet and extranets to transmit customer orders from traveling salespeople to a corporate data center for order processing and inventory control.	Provide better customer service by reducing delay in filling orders and improves cash flow by speeding up the billing of customers.
Overcome time barriers: Provide information to remote locations immediately after it is requested.	Credit authorization at the point of sale using online POS networks.	Credit inquiries can be made and answered in seconds.
Overcome cost barriers: Reduce the cost of more traditional means of communication.	Desktop videoconferencing between a company and its business partners using the Internet, intranets, and extranets.	Reduce expensive business trips; allow customers, suppliers, and employees to collaborate, thus improving the quality of decisions reached.
Overcome structural barriers: Support linkages for competitive advantage.	Business-to-business electronic commerce Web sites for transactions with suppliers and customers using the Internet and extranets.	Fast, convenient services lock in customers and suppliers.

success. Note the examples of the business value of these four strategic capabilities of telecommunications networks. This figure emphasizes how several e-business applications can help a firm capture and provide information quickly to end users at remote geographic locations at reduced costs, as well as support its strategic organizational objectives.

For example, traveling salespeople and those at regional sales offices can use the Internet, extranets, and other networks to transmit customer orders from their laptops or desktop PCs, thus breaking geographic barriers. Point-of-sale terminals and an online sales transaction processing network can break time barriers by supporting immediate credit authorization and sales processing. Teleconferencing can be used to cut costs by reducing the need for expensive business trips, allowing customers, suppliers, and employees to participate in meetings and collaborate on joint projects without traveling. Finally, business-to-business e-commerce Web sites are used by businesses to establish strategic relationships with their customers and suppliers by making business transactions fast, convenient, and tailored to the needs of the business partners involved.

The Internet Revolution

The explosive growth of the Internet is a revolutionary phenomenon in computing and telecommunications. The Internet has become the largest and most important network of networks today and has evolved into a global *information superhighway*. We can think of the Internet as a network made up of millions of smaller private networks, each with the ability to operate independent of, or in harmony with, all the other millions of networks connected to the Internet. When this network of networks began to grow in December 1991, it had about 10 servers. In January 2004, the Internet was estimated to have more than 46 million connected servers with a sustained growth rate in excess of 1 million servers per month. In January 2007, the Internet was estimated to have more than 1 billion users with Web sites in 34 languages from English to Icelandic. Now that is some growth!

The Internet is constantly expanding as more and more businesses and other organizations and their users, computers, and networks join its global Web. Thousands of business, educational, and research networks now connect millions of computer systems and users in more than 200 countries. Internet users projected for 2010 are expected to top the 2 billion user mark, which still only represents approximately one-third of the worldwide population. Apply these numbers to Metcalfe's law, and you can see that the number of possible connections is extraordinary.

The Net doesn't have a central computer system or telecommunications center. There are, however, 13 servers called *root servers* that are used to handle the bulk of the routing of traffic from one computer to another. Each message sent has a unique address code, so any Internet server in the network can forward it to its destination. Also, the Internet does not have a headquarters or governing body. International advisory and standards groups of individual and corporate members, such as the Internet Society (www.isoc.org) and the World Wide Web Consortium (www.w3.org), promote use of the Internet and the development of new communications standards. These common standards are the key to the free flow of messages among the widely different computers and networks of the many organizations and *Internet service providers* (ISPs) in the system.

Internet Service Providers

One of the unique aspects of the Internet is that nobody really owns it. Anyone who can access the Internet can use it and the services it offers. Because the Internet cannot be accessed directly by individuals, we need to use the services of a company that specializes in providing easy access. An **ISP**, or Internet service provider, is a company that provides access to the Internet to individuals and organizations. For a monthly fee, the service provider gives you a software package, user name, password, and access phone number or access protocol. With this information (and some specialized hardware), you can then log onto the Internet, browse the World Wide Web, and send and receive e-mail.

In addition to serving individuals, ISPs serve large companies, providing a direct connection from the company's networks to the Internet. These ISPs themselves are connected to one another through *network access points*. Through these connections, one ISP can easily connect to another ISP to obtain information about the address of a Web site or user node.

Internet Applications

The most popular Internet applications are e-mail, instant messaging, browsing the sites on the World Wide Web, and participating in *newsgroups* and *chat rooms*. Internet e-mail messages usually arrive in seconds or a few minutes anywhere in the world and can take the form of data, text, fax, and video files. Internet browser software like Netscape Navigator and Internet Explorer enables millions of users to surf the World Wide Web by clicking their way to the multimedia information resources stored on the hyperlinked pages of businesses, government, and other Web sites. Web sites offer information and entertainment and are the launch sites for e-commerce transactions between businesses and their suppliers and customers. As we will discuss in Chapter 9, e-commerce Web sites offer all manner of products and services via online retailers, wholesalers, service providers, and online auctions. See Figure 6.5.

The Internet provides electronic discussion forums and bulletin board systems formed and managed by thousands of special-interest newsgroups. You can participate in discussions or post messages on a myriad of topics for other users with the same interests. Other popular applications include downloading software and information files and accessing databases provided by a variety of business, government, and other organizations. You can conduct online searches for information on Web sites in a variety of ways by using search sites and search engines such as Yahoo!, Google, and Fast Search. Logging on to other computers on the Internet and holding real-time conversations with other Internet users in *chat rooms* are also popular uses of the Internet.

FIGURE 6.5
Popular uses of the Internet.

● **Surf.** Point-and-click your way to thousands of hyperlinked Web sites and resources for multimedia information, entertainment, or electronic commerce.
● **e-Mail.** Use e-mail and instant messaging to exchange electronic messages with colleagues, friends, and other Internet users.
● **Discuss.** Participate in discussion forums of special-interest newsgroups, or hold real-time text conversations in Web site chat rooms.
● **Publish.** Post your opinion, subject matter, or creative work to a Web site or Weblog for others to read.
● **Buy and Sell.** Buy and sell practically anything via e-commerce retailers, wholesalers, service providers, and online auctions.
● **Download.** Transfer data files, software, reports, articles, pictures, music, videos, and other types of files to your computer system.
● **Compute.** Log onto and use thousands of Internet computer systems around the world.
● **Connect.** Find out what friends, acquaintances, and business associates are up to.
● **Other Uses.** Make long-distance phone calls, hold desktop videoconferences, listen to radio programs, watch television, play video games, explore virtual worlds, etc.

Virtual Barmaid Is "Untouchable"

Natasha the "virtual" barmaid is one of a kind, but she has a sporty sister called Emma. Just outside Nelson, New Zealand, at the upmarket Monaco Resort, Natasha serves guests drinks from the hotel bar and even gives some chatter, in addition to weather forecasts and local tourist information. Emma, meanwhile, has worked in the Nelson R&R sports outlet, running a store customer loyalty program, and she too can talk about the weather.

While Natasha is having a short break while the Monaco Resort is refurbished, and Emma has finished her trial at R&R Sports, the pair, created by Stoke-based SHE Technology, represents a new face in retailing. SHE Technology stands for *Systems for Human Engagement*. Company founder and operator Matthew Dodd says making retail systems more animated boosts their acceptance and improves sales and customer loyalty—claims backed by the operators of Natasha and Emma.

With Natasha, hotel guests using their room card can gain entry to the bar fridge and scan an item, say a bottle of beer and, as in *Cheers*, she even knows your name. The cost is charged back to your room account since Natasha is integrated with the hotel's Property Management System. Hidden cameras ensure honesty.

Like any good barmaid, Natasha also has a reply for anyone who gets fresh. If you touch her, she will say "Please leave me alone," "Please stop touching me," "Don't touch what you cannot afford," and "Sorry, I'm just for looking at." Monaco Resort duty manager Helen Saville says, "Guests love Natasha and she's great fun. If she wasn't here, we wouldn't have this bar area. She's very much a novelty and she gives guests extra service."

Natasha was developed locally three years ago by Dodd with resort developer Mike Jepp as "a laugh" and so Monaco Resort could offer 24-hour bar service without needing staff. However, bar workers need not worry about any potential threat to their jobs. Matthew has taken Natasha off the market, as he believes retailing rather than hospitality offers better potential, which is how the equally unique Emma arrived.

Back in 2007, Emma, the "SHE Retail Engine," spent four months in R&R Sports Nelson running a customer rewards program via the store's point of sale system, and gave weather and other local information. "She was excellent, a good system," says store manager Zane Kennedy. "I feel she boosted trade and people still ask if we still have the system. The customers loved her and she was easy to interact with." However, R&R Sports felt Emma was too expensive for the whole chain of eight stores and is working on its own loyalty system.

Undeterred, however, citing success from Emma's RFID (see Real World Case 2 and Chapter 3) customer card system and guerrilla survey technology, SHE Technology is working on follow-up products. Dodd claims "executive level discussions" with two major retailers for a similar system, with advertising and customer directions a greater focus. This follows trials of simpler self-service loyalty programs at a couple of Nelson VideoEzy outlets. "Stores typically display advertising from LCD screens, but that is pushing content to customers. We say that should be pull advertising with the customer in control," he explains. Such interaction with customers gives retailers better information on who is entering stores, so they can better tailor their offerings. Thus, bricks and mortar retailers can learn as much about their customers as online traders, he says.

Systems for Human Engagement, whose "core" technology has a patent pending in the US, also lets stores use digital media for "below the line" advertising aimed at individual customers. However, Dodd adds he needs joint-venture funding with a retailer to help commercialize these products, which will involve making a new "personality" for each retailer.

Source: Adapted from Darren Greenwood, "Untouchable Virtual Barmaid Fills Service Gaps," *Computerworld NZ*, Fairfax New Zealand Ltd., August 8, 2007.

FIGURE 6.6   Examples of how a company can use the Internet for business.

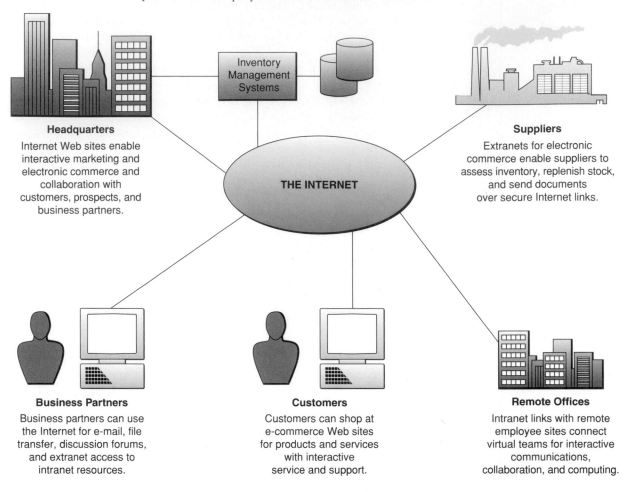

Headquarters
Internet Web sites enable interactive marketing and electronic commerce and collaboration with customers, prospects, and business partners.

Inventory Management Systems

THE INTERNET

Suppliers
Extranets for electronic commerce enable suppliers to assess inventory, replenish stock, and send documents over secure Internet links.

Business Partners
Business partners can use the Internet for e-mail, file transfer, discussion forums, and extranet access to intranet resources.

Customers
Customers can shop at e-commerce Web sites for products and services with interactive service and support.

Remote Offices
Intranet links with remote employee sites connect virtual teams for interactive communications, collaboration, and computing.

Business Use of the Internet

As Figure 6.6 illustrates, business use of the Internet has expanded from an electronic information exchange to a broad platform for strategic business applications. Notice how applications such as collaboration among business partners, providing customer and vendor support, and e-commerce have become major business uses of the Internet. Companies are also using Internet technologies for marketing, sales, and customer relationship management applications, as well as for cross-functional business applications, and applications in engineering, manufacturing, human resources, and accounting. Let's look at a real-world example.

The Business Value of the Internet

The Internet provides a synthesis of computing and communication capabilities that adds value to every part of the business cycle.

What business value do companies derive from their business applications on the Internet? Figure 6.7 summarizes how many companies perceive the business value of the Internet for e-commerce. Substantial cost savings can arise because applications that use the Internet and Internet-based technologies (like intranets and extranets) are typically less expensive to develop, operate, and maintain than traditional systems. For example, an airline saves money every time customers use its Web site instead of its customer support telephone system.

It is estimated that for certain types of transactions, the transaction cost savings are significant for online versus more traditional channels. For example, booking a reservation over the Internet costs about 90 percent less for the airline than booking the same reservation over the telephone. The banking industry has also found significant cost

FIGURE 6.7

How companies are deriving business value from their e-business and e-commerce applications.

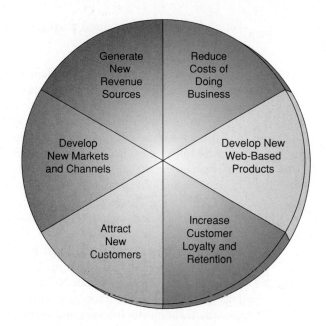

savings via the Internet. A typical online banking transaction (payments, balance inquiry, check payment) is estimated to cost anywhere from 50 percent to 95 percent less than its bricks-and-mortar counterpart. Generally speaking, anytime you convert a business process from a manual one to a software-based version, the transaction costs associated with that process can be expected to go down by the order of several magnitudes.

Other primary sources of business value include attracting new customers with innovative marketing and products, as well as retaining present customers with improved customer service and support. Of course, generating revenue through e-commerce applications is a major source of business value, which we will discuss in Chapter 9. To summarize, most companies are building e-business and e-commerce Web sites to achieve six major business values:

- Generate new revenue from online sales.
- Reduce transaction costs through online sales and customer support.
- Attract new customers via Web marketing and advertising and online sales.
- Increase the loyalty of existing customers via improved Web customer service and support.
- Develop new Web-based markets and distribution channels for existing products.
- Develop new information-based products accessible on the Web.

The Role of Intranets

Many companies have sophisticated and widespread intranets, offering detailed data retrieval, collaboration tools, personalized customer profiles, and links to the Internet. Investing in the intranet, they feel, is as fundamental as supplying employees with a telephone.

Before we go any further, let's redefine the concept of an intranet, to emphasize specifically how intranets are related to the Internet and extranets. An intranet is a network inside an organization that uses Internet technologies (such as Web browsers and servers, TCP/IP network protocols, HTML hypermedia document publishing and databases, and so on) to provide an Internet-like environment within the enterprise for information sharing, communications, collaboration, and the support of business processes. An intranet is protected by security measures such as passwords, encryption, and firewalls, and thus can be accessed by authorized users through the Internet. A company's intranet can also be accessed through the intranets of customers, suppliers, and other business partners via *extranet* links. Just think of an intranet as a private version of the Internet.

The Business Value of Intranets

Organizations of all kinds are implementing a broad range of intranet uses. One way that companies organize intranet applications is to group them conceptually into a few categories of user services that reflect the basic services that intranets offer to their users. These services are provided by the intranet's portal, browser, and server software, as well as by other system and application software and groupware that are part of a company's intranet software environment. Figure 6.8 illustrates how intranets provide an *enterprise information portal* that supports communication and collaboration, Web publishing, business operations and management, and intranet portal management. Notice also how these applications can be integrated with existing IS resources and applications and extended to customers, suppliers, and business partners via the Internet and extranets.

Communications and Collaboration. Intranets can significantly improve communications and collaboration within an enterprise. For example, you can use your intranet browser and your PC or NC workstation to send and receive e-mail, voice mail, pages, and faxes to communicate with others within your organization, as well as externally through the Internet and extranets. You can also use intranet groupware features to improve team and project collaboration with services such as discussion groups, chat rooms, and audio and videoconferencing.

FIGURE 6.8

Intranets can provide an enterprise information portal for applications in communication and collaboration, business operations and management, Web publishing, and intranet portal management.

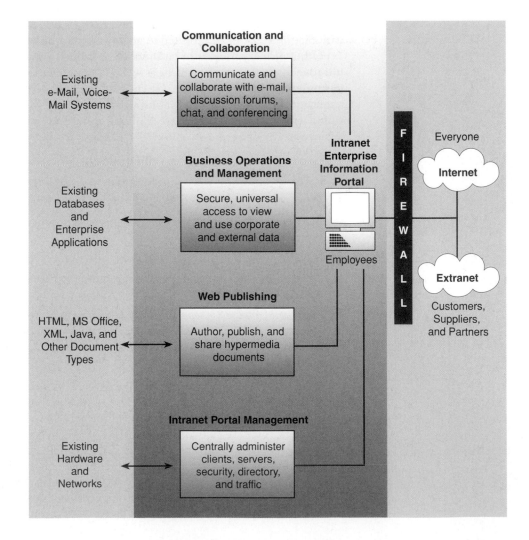

Web Publishing. The advantage of developing and publishing hyperlinked multimedia documents to hypermedia databases accessible on World Wide Web servers has moved to corporate intranets. The comparative ease, attractiveness, and lower cost of publishing and accessing multimedia business information internally via intranet Web sites have been the primary reasons for the explosive growth in the use of intranets in business. For example, information products as varied as company newsletters, technical drawings, and product catalogs can be published in a variety of ways, including hypermedia Web pages, e-mail, and net broadcasting, and as part of in-house business applications. Intranet software browsers, servers, and search engines can help you easily navigate and locate the business information you need.

Business Operations and Management. Intranets have moved beyond merely making hypermedia information available on Web servers or pushing it to users via net broadcasting. Intranets are also being used as the platform for developing and deploying critical business applications to support business operations and managerial decision making across the inter-networked enterprise. For example, many companies are developing custom applications like order processing, inventory control, sales management, and enterprise information portals that can be implemented on intranets, extranets, and the Internet. Many of these applications are designed to interface with and access existing company databases and legacy systems. The software for such business uses is then installed on intranet Web servers. Employees within the company or external business partners can access and run such applications using Web browsers from anywhere on the network whenever needed.

Intranet Portal Management. Organizations must employ IT and IS professionals to manage the functions of the intranet along with maintaining the various hardware and software components necessary for successful operations. For example, a network administrator must manage the access of users via passwords and other security mechanisms to ensure that each user is able to use the intranet productively while simultaneously protecting the integrity of the data resources. Included in this job are issues related to protection against unauthorized access, computer viruses, directory management, and other highly important functions.

Now let's look at one company's use of an intranet in more detail to get a better idea of how intranets are used in business.

Intranet Dashboard Revs Up Audi Australia

Audi is a brand synonymous with sporty, progressive, and sophisticated cars that embody technological perfection. On the back of the company's year-on-year record growth since 2004—including 30 percent growth in Australia in 2008—the company needed to position itself, and its national dealer network, to manage its future growth.

Audi Australia has a network of 30 dealerships across Australia. It needed to communicate with a range of people within its dealer network and ensure that different roles within the dealership were given access to the right information. There was a complex network of stakeholders who required access: the solution needed to cater to 500 users who were broken into 90 different user groups.

Audi had an existing portal solution that has been built on an open-source solution. Audi's business had outgrown this solution which had become unreliable and required a lot of technical management. Audi only has one in-house IT staff member, and it needed a solution that could be administered and maintained by nontechnical staff, without intervention from a third-party supplier.

"The old portal wasn't letting us provide all the information we wanted to the dealers. We just couldn't update it frequently enough," says Wolf-Christian Vaross, IT Specialist for Audi Australia. "Administration of the old site wasn't easy—to make changes we had to get a programmer to do it. The software might have been free initially but we didn't have the expertise to support it in house, and we didn't want to keep paying someone outside the company to maintain it."

Audi chose the iD solution because it was able to deliver all the features they required out of the box. Another important component of the project was that the dealer portal had to meet Audi's scrupulous design standards to match Audi's distinctive branding.

As part of the implementation, Audi involved the general managers from across five key departments including sales, corporate communications, and finance to find out what information they needed to share with dealers. This ensured that the broader business would be involved in creating and maintaining the dealer portal and had buy-in of the project. "The preparation process that iD took us through made it easy—they gave us an understanding of how to structure it," says Vaross.

"Now when someone from a dealership logs in, they'll see the latest news relevant to them, and it will only take one mouse click for them to find what they're looking for. It was important to give them the easiest possible route to the information they need," adds Vaross.

Audi's dealer portal was launched on February 1, 2009, and enjoyed rapid uptake by its dealer users. The number of users increased by 450 percent in the second month of use. "As users have discovered that the new portal is easy to use and offers relevant information, they are already beginning to access more information via the portal," says Vaross. "We have seen the number of pages they visit increase by 300% in the second month of operation."

Source: Adapted from *Intranet Dashboard Case Study*, "Intranet Dashboard Revs Up Audi Australia," *Intranet Journal*, October 22, 2009.

The Role of Extranets

As businesses continue to use open Internet technologies [extranets] to improve communication with customers and partners, they can gain many competitive advantages along the way—in product development, cost savings, marketing, distribution, and leveraging their partnerships.

As we explained previously, **extranets** are network links that use Internet technologies to interconnect the intranet of a business with the intranets of its customers, suppliers, or other business partners. Companies can establish direct private network links among themselves or create private, secure Internet links called *virtual private networks* (VPNs). (We'll look more closely at VPNs later in this chapter.) Or a company can use the unsecured Internet as the extranet link between its intranet and consumers and others but rely on the encryption of sensitive data and its own firewall systems to provide adequate security. Thus, extranets enable customers, suppliers, consultants, subcontractors, business prospects, and others to access selected intranet Web sites and other company databases. See Figure 6.9.

As shown in the figure, an organization's extranet can simultaneously link the organization to a wide variety of external partners. Consultants and contractors can use the extranet to facilitate the design of new systems or provide outsourcing services. The suppliers of the organization can use the extranet to ensure that the raw materials necessary for the organization to function are in stock or delivered in a timely fashion. The customers of an organization can use the extranet to access self-service functions such as ordering, order status checking, and payment. The extranet links the organization to the outside world in a manner that improves the way it does business.

The business value of extranets is derived from several factors. First, the Web browser technology of extranets makes customer and supplier access of intranet resources a lot easier and faster than previous business methods. Second, as you will see

FIGURE 6.9 Extranets connect the inter-networked enterprise to consumers, business customers, suppliers, and other business partners.

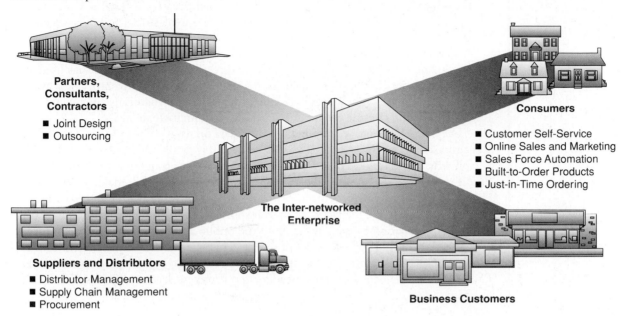

in two upcoming examples, extranets enable a company to offer new kinds of interactive Web-enabled services to their business partners. Thus, extranets are another way that a business can build and strengthen strategic relationships with its customers and suppliers. Also, extranets can enable and improve collaboration by a business with its customers and other business partners. Extranets facilitate an online, interactive product development, marketing, and customer-focused process that can bring better-designed products to market faster.

| Extranets: Collaboration Speeds Information | Highway engineers around the sprawling state of Texas want all the accident data they can get. With 800,000 crashes a year in the state, lives can be saved with a new left-turn lane here or a guardrail there, or perhaps a traffic light over a once-quiet rural intersection. Engineers need to analyze accident patterns to know where to spend limited highway-safety funds. Until 2005, however, engineers in the Department of Transportation's 25 district offices could not get the data. To view accident records, they had to go to Austin and pore through reels of microfilm in the state archives, trying to find reports relevant to particular stretches of highway. Even if they found what they were looking for, the information was at least three years out of date because of the backlog of accident reports awaiting microfilming.
 | |

That all changed in May 2005 when the state fired up its new Crash Records Information System with digitized police and highway patrol accident reports available through a business intelligence extranet. Traffic engineers around the state are now able to access and analyze the data from their offices, equipped with nothing more than a browser and a password. Making reports available over the Web "will help us save lives," says Carol Rawson, deputy director for traffic operations.

Supersol, a 160-store Israeli supermarket chain, has found that sharing business intelligence with suppliers means fresher goods and fewer products sitting in warehouses. Previously, suppliers had to visit stores and eyeball what was sitting on the shelves or call a Supersol purchasing manager to find out what to deliver.

Now 10 key suppliers check stocks by tapping into Supersol's inventory data warehouse to learn what the supermarket chain has in its Tel Aviv distribution center.

The data warehouse is built on NCR's Teradata system with Panorama Software's business intelligence software for accessing and analyzing information. When suppliers can see inventory data, it's easier to eliminate out-of-stocks and overstocking. "The transparency of information is good for both sides," CIO Isaac Shefer says.

Similarly, ArvinMeritor Inc., which manufactures car parts for automakers, service companies such as Midas and Meinke, and retailers like AutoZone, has used an extranet for about 18 months to make production schedules and inventory data available to its suppliers. They check inventory levels of the materials they supply to ArvinMeritor and consult production schedules to anticipate needs.

"They have access to weekly and monthly data on what we plan to produce," says CIO and senior VP Perry Lipe. "That information is extremely key to them. It's one reason why our plants are on schedule and able to meet production forecasts. In addition to helping the just-in-time manufacturing model succeed, making data available to suppliers takes excess inventory out of the supply chain and reduces costs."

"Back in Texas, the Department of Transportation is planning to make the Crash Records Information System available to the public and insurance company representatives who want copies of accident reports," says Catherine Cioffi, Crash Records Information System's project manager. The extranet also will be used to alert local law-enforcement agencies where speeding and drunken-driving offenses occur with greater frequency. Business intelligence extranets, says deputy director for traffic operations Rawson, "help us all do our jobs better."

Source: Adapted from Charles Babcock, "Collaboration Speeds Information," *InformationWeek*, January 24, 2005.

SECTION II	# Telecommunications Network Alternatives

Telecommunications Alternatives

Telecommunications is a highly technical, rapidly changing field of information systems technology. Most business professionals do not need a detailed knowledge of its technical characteristics. However, it is necessary that you understand some of the important characteristics of the basic components of telecommunications networks. This understanding will help you participate effectively in decision making regarding telecommunications alternatives.

Read the Real World Case 2 about the use of wireless RFID (see Chapter 3) technologies in health care. We can learn a lot about the value of wireless applications from this case. See Figure 6.10.

A Telecommunications Network Model

Figure 6.11 outlines key telecommunications component categories and examples. Remember, a basic understanding and appreciation, not a detailed knowledge, is sufficient for most business professionals.

Before we begin our discussion of telecommunications network alternatives, we should understand the basic components of a telecommunications network. Generally, a *communications network* is any arrangement in which a *sender* transmits a message to a receiver over a *channel* consisting of some type of *medium*. Figure 6.12 illustrates a simple conceptual model of a telecommunications network, which shows that it consists of five basic categories of components:

- **Terminals,** such as networked personal computers, network computers, net boxes, or information appliances. Any input/output device that uses telecommunications networks to transmit or receive data is a terminal, including telephones and the various computer terminals that were discussed in Chapter 3.

- **Telecommunications processors,** which support data transmission and reception between terminals and computers. These devices, such as modems, switches, and routers, perform a variety of control and support functions in a telecommunications network. For example, they convert data from digital to analog and back, code and decode data, and control the speed, accuracy, and efficiency of the communications flow between computers and terminals in a network.

- **Telecommunications channels** over which data are transmitted and received. Telecommunications channels may use combinations of **media,** such as copper wires, coaxial cables, or fiber-optic cables, or use wireless systems like microwave, communications satellite, radio, and cellular systems to interconnect the other components of a telecommunications network.

- **Computers** of all sizes and types are interconnected by telecommunications networks so that they can carry out their information processing assignments. For example, a mainframe computer may serve as a *host computer* for a large network, assisted by a midrange computer serving as a *front-end processor,* while a microcomputer may act as a *network server* in a small network.

- **Telecommunications control software** consists of programs that control telecommunications activities and manage the functions of telecommunications networks. Examples include network management programs of all kinds, such as *telecommunications monitors* for mainframe host computers, *network operating systems* for network servers, and *Web browsers* for microcomputers.

No matter how large and complex real-world telecommunications networks may appear to be, these five basic categories of network components must be at work to support an organization's telecommunications activities. This is the conceptual framework you can use to help you understand the various types of telecommunications networks in use today.

REAL WORLD CASE 2

The Body Electric: Wireless Data Can Really Get Under Your Skin

Joseph Krull doesn't have a chip on his shoulder. But he has one in it. The San Antonio security consultant is one of a small but growing number of people who essentially turn themselves into wireless network nodes for the sake of making personal information available to authorized parties with the wave of a radio frequency identification (RFID) scanner.

In Krull's case, the chip was implanted so hospital staff could access his medical information quickly in emergency situations. Others are "getting chipped," as those in the know call it, for everything from entertainment to personal safety. Krull's chip is basically the same kind of RFID-based technology that's been used for years to tag dogs so they can be identified if lost, except the human chip works on a different radio frequency.

Since Applied Digital, on behalf of its subsidiary VeriChip, got authorization from the U.S. Food and Drug Administration (FDA) last October to sell the chips for human implantation, about 1,000 chips have gone live. "I have a blown pupil and a detached retina in my left eye from a skiing accident," says Krull, explaining his decision to have a physician with a syringe stick a chip in him under local anesthetic in what he described as a fairly simple procedure. "I'm supposed to wear a MedAlert bracelet because one of the indicators of a head injury is a blown pupil. One thing they might do in that kind of emergency is drill holes in your skull." The thought of having holes unnecessarily drilled into his head, because of a misdiagnosis during a medical emergency, got Krull thinking about having a chip implanted after he heard about it during a conference in Spain. "I wanted to get chipped," he says.

His family—wife, sisters, nephews and nieces—was wary. "They said, 'Are you nuts?' They had a lot of questions, like will the chip be visible or is there a risk of rejection," Krull says. Now officially human No. 1020000000, Krull can access his personal data stored online at VeriChip's portal and make any changes he wants by using a reader and a PIN code. Krull elected to store his medical information and address, phone numbers, fax, and e-mail at the Web site.

One catch with RFID implants is that emergency technicians won't necessarily know that a patient has a chip under his or her skin. But VeriChip is giving away its RFID scanners to hospitals in the hope of building momentum for use of chips. While Krull's family has grown relaxed about it all, "the biggest opposition is from people in my own field—security," Krull points out. Critics say the chip poses a huge privacy and security threat that will let the government and private-sector snoops get personal information.

Krull says he understands the point of view taken by some privacy advocates but contends there's little value in keeping information such as the condition of his eyeball a secret. "It's entirely up to me what I put on my chip," he says. "I've been involved with authentication for 20 years, working with biometrics, and I was promoting the token. Now I am the token."

Fellow implantees include the attorney general of Mexico City and some of his staff, who were chipped to help identify them in the event that they become crime victims. Some are getting implants just for kicks—a nightclub in Glasgow, Scotland, called Bar Soba, offers to implant chips in its guests so the bar can prepare each patron's favorite drink the minute he walks in.

Also getting a chip shot was John Halamka, the CIO at Beth Israel Deaconess Medical Center in Boston and Harvard Medical School and a practicing physician. Halamka got chipped in an experiment of his own making. The outspoken CIO says he's had "no side effects, no pain, no change in muscle function and no migration of the chip" in the months it's been in him, despite rock and ice climbing where Halamka exposed himself to "extremes of temperature, wind, water."

Halamka decided to be a chip guinea pig as the result of experiences he had while working in emergency medicine at Harbor-UCLA Medical Center in Carson, California. Emergency care often put him in the situation of having to identify patients who were without ID documents and unconscious, nonverbal, or mentally ill. That often involved picking out clues found in their belongings such as a clothing label. "I would inevitably reunite the patients with their loved ones, but not before significant worry and possibly unwanted medical interventions had occurred," Halamka says.

FIGURE 6.10

Implantable microchips can be used for patient identification as well as for access to critical data.

Source: Kevin Maloney/The New York Times/Redux.

In his CIO role, Halamka is responsible for all clinical, financial, educational and research technologies for 3,000 doctors, 12,000 employees, and 2 million patients. After the FDA approved the implantable chip, "I felt I was in a unique position to pilot the technology," Halamka says. "That means that when a scanner is passed within 6 inches of my arm, my medical identifier is displayed and can be used by authorized healthcare workers to retrieve information about my identity and medical history via a secure Web site." Halamka emphasizes his role at present is not that of chip advocate for hospitals but as a real-life test case. Though he says that Alzheimer's patients might benefit from RFID chips one day, as long as it's clear the patients gave informed consent to have a chip implanted.

The chip is expected to last at least 10 years based on pet experience. Halamka says it's safe for MRI scans, and he sees no evidence the chip can be deactivated through magnetic energy. "I have flown to several dozen cities since the implant and have not triggered any airline security systems," he notes. The chip is not a GPS. The unique ID transmitted by the VeriChip human-implantable chip isn't encrypted, so it could be read by a compatible reader. But unauthorized reading of the chip doesn't disclose any specific health information, he adds, because that's on a closed Web site.

However, Halamka says there are privacy concerns that should be addressed. He points out that an RFID scanner theoretically could record his presence while he was making a purchase, and on a repeat visit it would be possible to identify him and his previous purchases using that information for marketing purposes. "Spam, generated by the presence of your body, is theoretically possible," he says. He says there's no legislation to preclude RFID scanning of an individual for anonymous tracking, which could be "analogous to the spyware and adware infecting our computers after surfing Internet sites." The potential for hacker abuse shouldn't be underestimated, he adds. The security issue "must be understood as one of the risks of having an implanted identifier," Halamka says.

Nonetheless, he has listed his identifier as part of his medical record in the Beth Israel Deaconess medical record system, called CareWeb, so that a physician, with his consent, could enter the RFID tag information to retrieve his medical history. "I have no regrets," Halamka says about the whole implant experience, even though removing the chip would require minor surgery. And he would consider upgrading himself with a new chip, too, should a better one come along.

Source: Adapted from Ellen Messmer, "RFID Is Really Getting Under People's Skin," *Network World*, April 4, 2005.

CASE STUDY QUESTIONS

1. From the perspective of a patient, how would you feel about having your medical information on a chip embedded under your skin? What kind of expectations or concerns would you have about that kind of experience?

2. What other professions, aside from health care and education, could benefit from application of some of the technologies discussed in the case? How would they derive business value from these projects? Develop two proposals.

3. The deployment of IT in the health professions is still very much in its infancy. What other uses of technology could potentially improve the quality of health care? Brainstorm several alternatives.

REAL WORLD ACTIVITIES

1. Technology enhances the ability of educational institutes to reach students across geographic boundaries. One recent development in this area is YouTube EDU. Go online to check out the site and prepare a report summarizing its objectives, the kind of content available there, and how it could be used to support traditional modes of education delivery, such as lectures.

2. If widely adopted, these technologies could conceivably lead to a widespread use of human embedded RFIDs for a variety of applications. What could be the positive and negative consequences of this development? Break into small groups with your classmates to discuss these issues.

FIGURE 6.11
Key telecommunications network component categories and examples.

Network Alternative	Examples of Alternatives
Networks	Internet, intranet, extranet, wide area, local area, client/server, network computing, peer-to-peer
Media	Twisted-pair wire, coaxial cable, fiber optics, microwave radio, communications satellites, cellular and PCS systems, wireless mobile and LAN systems
Processors	Modems, multiplexers, switches, routers, hubs, gateways, front-end processors, private branch exchanges
Software	Network operating systems, telecommunications monitors, Web browsers, middleware
Channels	Analog/digital, switched/nonswitched, circuit/message/packet/cell switching, bandwidth alternatives
Topology/Architecture	Star, ring, and bus topologies, OSI and TCP/IP architectures and protocols

FIGURE 6.12 The five basic components in a telecommunications network: (1) terminals, (2) telecommunications processors, (3) tele communications channels, (4) computers, and (5) telecommunications software.

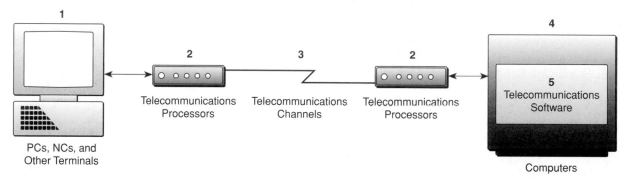

Types of Telecommunications Networks

Many different types of networks serve as the telecommunications infrastructure for the Internet and the intranets and extranets of inter-networked enterprises. However, from an end user's point of view, there are only a few basic types, such as wide area and local area networks and client/server, network computing, and peer-to-peer networks.

Wide Area Networks

Telecommunications networks covering a large geographic area are called wide area networks (WANs). Networks that cover a large city or metropolitan area (*metropolitan area networks*) can also be included in this category. Such large networks have become a necessity for carrying out the day-to-day activities of many business and government organizations and their end users. For example, WANs are used by many multinational companies to transmit and receive information among their employees, customers, suppliers, and other organizations across cities, regions, countries, and the world. Figure 6.13 illustrates an example of a global wide area network for a major multinational corporation.

Metropolitan Area Network

When a wide area network optimized a specific geographical area, it is referred to as a **metropolitan area network** (MAN). Such networks can range from several blocks of buildings to entire cities. MANs can also depend on communications channels of moderate-to-high data rates. A MAN might be owned and operated by a single organization, but it usually will be used by many individuals and organizations. MANs

FIGURE 6.13   A global wide area network (WAN): the Chevron MPI (Multi-Protocol Inter-Network).

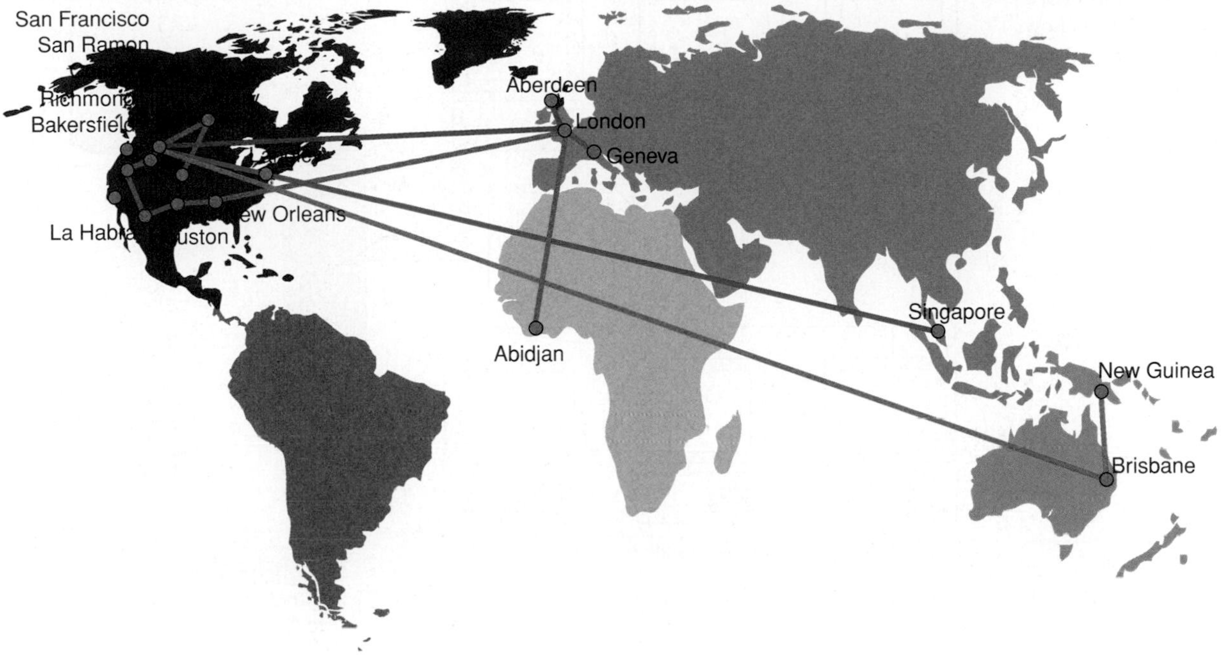

Source: Courtesy of Cisco Systems Inc.

might also be owned and operated as public utilities. Your local cable provider or a local telephone company is probably operating on a MAN. MANs will often provide means for inter-networking of local area networks.

Local Area Networks

Local area networks (LANs) connect computers and other information processing devices within a limited physical area, such as an office, classroom, building, manufacturing plant, or other worksite. LANs have become commonplace in many organizations for providing telecommunications network capabilities that link end users in offices, departments, and other workgroups.

LANs use a variety of telecommunications media, such as ordinary telephone wiring, coaxial cable, or even wireless radio and infrared systems, to interconnect microcomputer workstations and computer peripherals. To communicate over the network, each PC usually has a circuit board called a *network interface card*. Most LANs use a more powerful microcomputer with a large hard disk capacity, called a *file server* or **network server,** that contains a **network operating system** program that controls telecommunications and the use and sharing of network resources. For example, it distributes copies of common data files and software packages to the other microcomputers in the network and controls access to shared laser printers and other network peripherals. See Figure 6.14.

Virtual Private Networks

Many organizations use virtual private networks (VPNs) to establish secure intranets and extranets. A virtual private network is a secure network that uses the Internet as its main *backbone network* but relies on network firewalls, encryption, and other security features of its Internet and intranet connections and those of participating organizations. Thus, for example, VPNs would enable a company to use the Internet to establish secure intranets between its distant branch offices and manufacturing plants and secure extranets between itself and its business customers and suppliers. Figure 6.15 illustrates a VPN in which network routers serve as firewalls to screen Internet traffic between two companies. We will discuss firewalls, encryption, and other network security features in Chapter 13. For the time being, we can think of a VPN as a pipe

FIGURE 6.14

A local area network (LAN). Note how the LAN allows users to share hardware, software, and data resources.

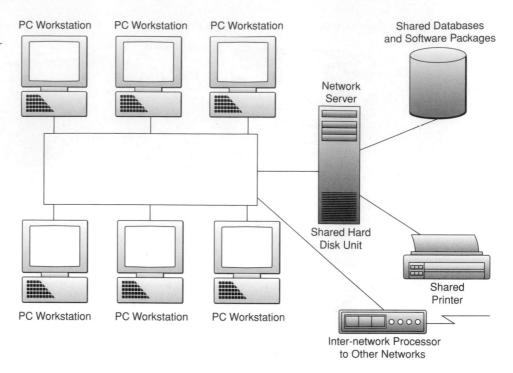

traveling through the Internet. Through this pipe, we can send and receive our data without anyone outside the pipe being able to see or access our transmissions. Using this approach, we can "create" a private network without incurring the high cost of a separate proprietary connection scheme. Let's look at a real-world example about the use of VPN to secure remote and wireless access to sensitive data.

FIGURE 6.15

An example of a virtual private network protected by network firewalls.

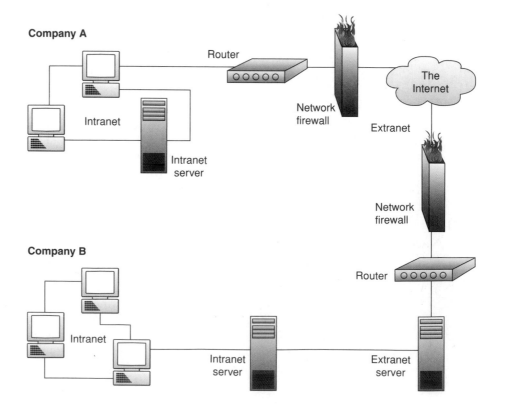

Whole Body Area Network: Human Cellular Towers Maybe?

A team of Irish researchers is studying how humans can become the next wireless infrastructure, by wearing sensors, radios, and gateways linked together in "body-to-body" networks. With redesigned antennas, low-power radios, and new network protocols, potentially huge, constantly shifting body networks could create an "ultra-high-bandwidth mobile infrastructure." Such networks could offload even large file transfers from cellular networks, by making use of parallel transmission and routing through a mesh of body nodes. The body node can link to fixed access points, gateways, or cellular networks when needed. Small sensor nodes would be worn on the head, shoulders, chest, arms, and ankles and a signal collector for them would be worn on the hip.

The work on "body-centric" communications has been a focus of the Institute of Electronics, Communications and Information Technology at Queen's University, Belfast, Northern Ireland. The researchers were awarded a grant in 2010 of about $800,000 from the Royal Academy of Engineering and the Engineering and Physical Research Council. This new work is a five-year exploration of the challenges of body-to-body wireless communications, including how human bodies and movement affect radio signal propagation, according to Dr. Simon Cotton, a research fellow with the Institute.

The concept of body networks is an extension of the work that's being done with wireless medical sensors that are placed on, or implanted in, a patient's body and with battlefield sensors worn or carried by soldiers. The sensors can monitor a wide range of very specific activities and thresholds, collect data, and then transmit the information to a fixed system. The Institute's work looks at creating an on-body network of wireless sensors that can also communicate externally, through some kind of cooperative mesh network infrastructure, according to Cotton.

"The basic idea is that, instead of communicating with a cellular base station 1 to 2 km away, in densely populated areas the information would be transmitted to the nearest available person—using cooperative communications, where all users make a small amount of their bandwidth available for other network users—and so on, until reaching the intended recipient or being relayed on to the cellular network," Cotton writes in an e-mail response to questions. Similar to networks based on the IEEE 802.15.4 standard for wireless sensor networks, body networks could run with "much lower power levels . . . as the signal will be transmitted over distances of tens to hundreds of meters," Cotton says.

Carnegie Mellon University is researching the challenges of getting thousands of wireless sensors to cooperate with each other intelligently. Another benefit is that frequency allocations for such a network can be re-used over much shorter distances, "meaning that the precious radio spectrum is utilized much more fully," Cotton says. A fully functional, reliable body-to-body network could even make at least some cellular base stations in heavily populated areas redundant, Cotton predicts. He envisions such networks being used to transmit even high-definition video content. "The software on the user's device intelligently splits the file into smaller streams and transmits the content to multiple nearby persons, who then forward data to other humans acting as network nodes and so on," he explains. "The file is reassembled when reaching the intended user."

A key element in "wireless body-area networking" is the antenna design. According to the Institute's Web site, "an ideal antenna for WBAN (Whole Body Area Network) use will be low profile or conformal, efficient with minimal power losses in body tissues and won't be adversely affected by the user's movements." The institute has been developing antenna designs, for the 400MHz to 2.4GHz frequencies, to link sensors over the human body, and to also propagate in an omnidirectional coverage pattern for external connectivity. The signal can be affected by the body itself, as anyone can demonstrate just by touching an AM/FM antenna, by the body's motion, including breathing, and the reflection of radio signals (a phenomenon called multipath) in a constantly changing network as the living "nodes" move around and through buildings and streets.

Source: Adapted from John Cox, "Will the Next Wireless Infrastructure Be Humans Wearing Radios?" *Computerworld NZ*, Fairfax New Zealand Ltd., October 30, 2010.

FIGURE 6.16
The functions of the computer systems in client/server networks.

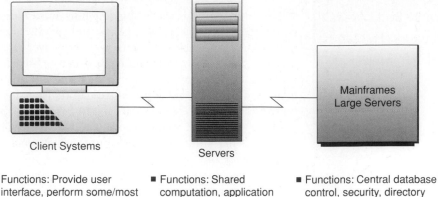

Client Systems

Servers

Mainframes Large Servers

■ Functions: Provide user interface, perform some/most processing on an application.

■ Functions: Shared computation, application control, distributed databases.

■ Functions: Central database control, security, directory management, heavy-duty processing.

Client/Server Networks

Client/server networks have become the predominant information architecture of enterprisewide computing. In a client/server network, end-user PC or NC workstations are the **clients.** They are interconnected by local area networks and share application processing with network **servers,** which also manage the networks. (This arrangement of clients and servers is sometimes called a *two-tier* client/server architecture.) Local area networks (LANs) are also interconnected to other LANs and wide area networks (WANs) of client workstations and servers. Figure 6.16 illustrates the functions of the computer systems that may be in client/server networks, including optional host systems and superservers.

A continuing trend is the **downsizing** of larger computer systems by replacing them with client/server networks. For example, a client/server network of several interconnected local area networks may replace a large mainframe-based network with many end-user terminals. This shift typically involves a complex and costly effort to install new application software that replaces the software of older, traditional mainframe-based business information systems, now called legacy systems. Client/server networks are seen as more economical and flexible than legacy systems in meeting end-user, workgroup, and business unit needs and more adaptable in adjusting to a diverse range of computing workloads.

Network Computing

The growing reliance on the computer hardware, software, and data resources of the Internet, intranets, extranets, and other networks has emphasized that, for many users, "the network is the computer." This network computing or *network-centric* concept views networks as the central computing resource of any computing environment.

Figure 6.17 illustrates that in network computing, **network computers** and other *thin clients* provide a browser-based user interface for processing small application programs called *applets*. Thin clients include network computers, Net PCs, and other low-cost network devices or information appliances. Application and database servers provide the operating system, application software, applets, databases, and database management software needed by the end users in the network. Network computing is sometimes called a *three-tier* client/server model because it consists of thin clients, application servers, and database servers.

Peer-to-Peer Networks

The emergence of peer-to-peer (P2P) networking technologies and applications for the Internet is being hailed as a development that will have a major impact on e-business and e-commerce and the Internet itself. Whatever the merits of such claims, it is clear that peer-to-peer networks are a powerful telecommunications networking tool for many business applications.

FIGURE 6.17
The functions of the
computer systems in
network computing.

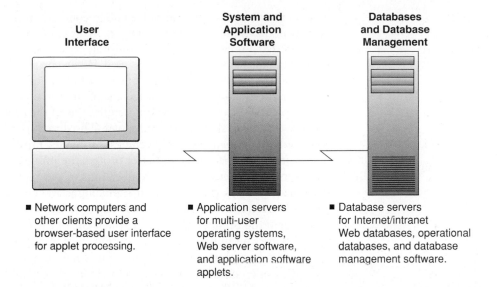

User Interface

System and Application Software

Databases and Database Management

- Network computers and other clients provide a browser-based user interface for applet processing.

- Application servers for multi-user operating systems, Web server software, and application software applets.

- Database servers for Internet/intranet Web databases, operational databases, and database management software.

Figure 6.18 illustrates two major models of **peer-to-peer networking** technology. In the central server architecture, P2P file-sharing software connects your PC to a central server that contains a directory of all of the other users (*peers*) in the network. When you request a file, the software searches the directory for any other users who have that file and are online at that moment. It then sends you a list of user names that are active links to all such users. Clicking on one of these user names prompts the software to connect your PC to that user's PC (making a *peer-to-peer* connection) and automatically transfers the file you want from his or her hard drive to yours.

The *pure* peer-to-peer network architecture has no central directory or server. First, the file-sharing software in the P2P network connects your PC with one of the online

FIGURE 6.18   The two major forms of peer-to-peer networks.

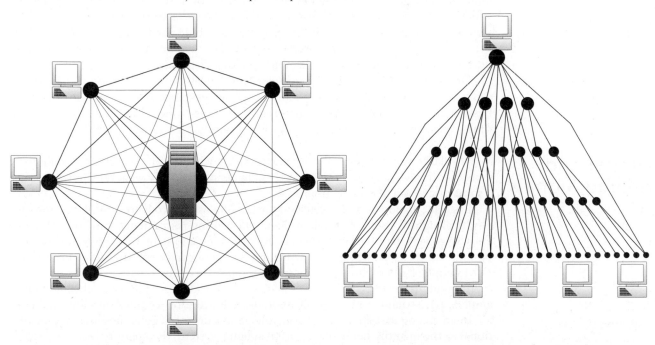

- A peer-to-peer network architecture with a directory of all peers on a central server

- A pure peer-to-peer network architecture with no central directory server users in the network. Then an active link to your user name is transmitted from peer to peer to all the online users in the network that the first user (and the other online users) encountered in previous sessions. In this way, active links to more and more peers spread throughout the network the more it is used. When you request a file, the software searches every online user and sends you a list of active file names related to your request. Clicking on one of these automatically transfers the file from that user's hard drive to yours.

One of the major advantages and limitations of the central server architecture is its reliance on a central directory and server. The directory server can be slowed or overwhelmed by too many users or technical problems. However, it also provides the network with a platform that can better protect the integrity and security of the content and users of the network. Some applications of pure P2P networks, in contrast, have been plagued by slow response times and bogus and corrupted files.

The Internet, as originally conceived in the late 1960s, was a peer-to-peer system. The goal of the original ARPANET (the name of the early version of today's Internet) was to share computing resources around the United States. The challenge for this effort was to integrate different kinds of existing networks, as well as future technologies, with one common network architecture that would allow every host to be an equal player. The first few hosts on the ARPANET (e.g., UCLA and the University of Utah) were already independent computing sites with equal status. The ARPANET connected them together not in a master/slave or client/server relationship, but rather as equal computing peers.

One common use for peer-to-peer networks today is the downloading and trading of files. When the term *peer-to-peer* was used to describe the *Napster* network, it implied that the peer protocol nature was important, but in reality the unique achievement of Napster was the empowerment of the peers (i.e., the fringes of the network) in association with a central index that made it fast and efficient to locate available content. The peer protocol was just a common way to achieve this.

Although much media attention has focused on copyright-infringing uses of file trading networks, there are vast numbers of entirely noninfringing uses. *BitTorrent* was originally designed to keep sites from getting overwhelmed by "flash crowds" and heavy traffic. That makes it very suitable for many situations in which there are massive peaks of demand. Most Linux distributions are released via BitTorrent to help with their bandwidth needs. Another example is *Blizzard Entertainment* (http://www.blizzard.com), which uses a modified version of BitTorrent to distribute patches to its game World of Warcraft (http://www.worldofwarcraft.com). Users have often complained about Bit-Torrent due to a bandwidth cap that almost defeats its purpose.

Other peer-to-peer networks are emerging as well, such as *PeerCast*, which allows someone to broadcast an Internet radio or television station with very little upstream bandwidth due to its distributed nature. Other peer-to-peer broadcast tools, sometimes called *peer-casting*, include the *IceShare* project and *FreeCast*.

Digital and Analog Signals

We regularly hear the words *analog* and *digital* associated with computers, telephones, and other hardware devices. To be sure you understand exactly what these terms mean, a short discussion may be helpful.

Basically, analog or digital refers to the method used to convert information into an electrical signal. Telephones, microphones, measuring instruments, vinyl record players, CD players, tape decks, computers, fax machines, and so on must convert information into an electrical signal in some manner so that it can be transmitted or processed. For example, a microphone must convert the pressure waves that we call *sound* into a corresponding electrical voltage or current, which can be sent down a telephone line, amplified in a sound system, broadcast on the radio, and/or recorded on some medium.

In an analog system, an electrical voltage or current is generated that is proportional to the quantity being observed. In a digital system, the quantity being observed is expressed as a number. This is really all there is to it, but a few details must still be discussed.

For example, in an electronic analog thermometer, if the temperature being measured is 83 degrees, then the analog system would put out, for example, 83 volts. This level could just as well be 8.3 volts or any other voltage proportional to the temperature. Thus, if the temperature doubled to 166 degrees, the output voltage would double to 166 volts (or perhaps 16.6 volts if the instrument were so scaled). The output voltage is, therefore, "analogous" to the temperature—thus the use of the term *analog*.

In the case of an electronic digital thermometer, however, the output would be the number 83 if the temperature were 83 degrees. Hence it is based on "digits." The only thing wrong with this example is that 83 is a decimal number constructed from the 10 symbols 0, 1, 2, . . . , 8, 9. We commonly use 10 symbols in our numbers for historical reasons; it is probably because we have 10 fingers. It is inconvenient, however, to use 10 symbols to express the output as an electrical voltage. It is much more convenient to have only 2 symbols, 0 and 1. In this case, for example, 0 could be represented by 0 volts, and 1 by 5 volts. Recall from Chapter 3 that this system is known as a binary (only two symbols) number system, but the principle is still the same: The output of the digital thermometer is a number, that is, "digits."

For the thermometer example above, 83 is the binary number 1010011. The electronic thermometer would send the sequence 5 volts, 0 volts, 5 volts, 0 volts, 0 volts, 5 volts, and 5 volts to express the number 83 in binary.

A digital system may seem more complicated than an analog system, but it has a number of advantages. The principal advantage is that once the measurement is expressed in digital form, it can be entered into a computer or a microprocessor and manipulated as desired. If we worked with only analog devices, we would eventually have to convert the output of the analog device into digital form if we wanted to input it into a computer. Because computer networks work primarily with digital signals, most of the hardware used by a computer network is digital.

Telecommunications Media

Telecommunications channels make use of a variety of telecommunications media. These include twisted-pair wire, coaxial cables, and fiber-optic cables, all of which physically link the devices in a network. Also included are terrestrial microwave, communications satellites, cellular phone systems, and packet and LAN radio, all of which use microwave and other radio waves. In addition, there are infrared systems, which use infrared light to transmit and receive data. See Figure 6.19.

FIGURE 6.19   Common telecommunications guided media: (a) twisted-pair wire, (b) coaxial cable, and (c) fiber-optic cable.

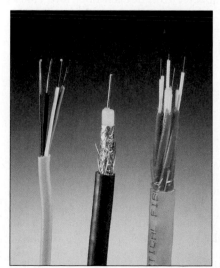

(c)
Source: © Photodisc/PunchStock.

(a)
Source: Phil Degginger/Getty Images.

(b)
Source: © Photodisc/Getty Images.

Wired Technologies

Twisted-Pair Wire

Ordinary telephone wire, consisting of copper wire twisted into pairs (twisted-pair wire), is the most widely used medium for telecommunications. These lines are used in established communications networks throughout the world for both voice and data transmission. Twisted-pair wiring is wrapped or shielded in a variety of forms and used extensively in home and office telephone systems and many local area networks and wide area networks. Transmission speeds can range from 2 million bits per second (unshielded) to 100 million bits per second (shielded).

Coaxial Cable

Coaxial cable consists of a sturdy copper or aluminum wire wrapped with spacers to insulate and protect it. The cable's cover and insulation minimize interference and distortion of the signals the cable carries. Groups of coaxial cables may be bundled together in a big cable for ease of installation. These high-quality lines can be placed underground and laid on the floors of lakes and oceans. They allow high-speed data transmission (from 200 million to more than 500 million bits per second—200–500 Mbps) and are used instead of twisted-pair wire lines in high-service metropolitan areas, for cable television systems, and for short-distance connections of computers and peripheral devices. Coaxial cables are also used in many office buildings and other worksites for local area networks.

Fiber Optics

Fiber optics uses cables consisting of one or more hair-thin filaments of glass fiber wrapped in a protective jacket. They can conduct pulses of visible light elements (*photons*) generated by lasers at transmission rates as high as trillions of bits per second (terabits per second, or Tbps). This speed is hundreds of times faster than coaxial cable and thousands of times better than twisted-pair wire lines. Fiber-optic cables provide substantial size and weight reductions as well as increased speed and greater carrying capacity. A half-inch-diameter fiber-optic cable can carry more than 500,000 channels, compared with about 5,500 channels for a standard coaxial cable.

Fiber-optic cables are not affected by and do not generate electromagnetic radiation; therefore, multiple fibers can be placed in the same cable. Fiber-optic cables have less need for repeaters for signal retransmissions than copper wire media. Fiber optics also has a much lower data error rate than other media and is harder to tap than electrical wire and cable. Fiber-optic cables have already been installed in many parts of the world, and they are expected to replace other communications media in many applications.

New optical technologies such as *dense wave division multiplexing* (DWDM) can split a strand of glass fiber into 40 channels, which enables each strand to carry 5 million calls. In the future, DWDM technology is expected to split each fiber into 1,000 channels, enabling each strand to carry up to 122 million calls. In addition, newly developed *optical routers* will be able to send optical signals up to 2,500 miles without needing regeneration, thus eliminating the need for repeaters every 370 miles to regenerate signals.

The Problem of "The Last Mile"

While on the subject of telecommunication media, we need to understand a pervasive problem in the telecommunications industry: the problem of the last mile. The last-mile problem, although simple to understand, is still one of the greatest challenges faced by telecommunications providers.

The basic problem goes something like this: The telecommunications provider adopts a new, faster, better technology that can provide higher bandwidths and faster telecommunication speeds to consumers. A good example of this type of situation is the invention of fiber-optic cable and its related optical technologies. Fiber can move data at lightning speed and handle a much larger volume of data than the more typical twisted-pair wiring commonly found in households. So the telecommunications provider completely reengineers the network and begins laying fiber instead of copper wire in trenches. The fiber, costing $500,000 to $1 million per mile, begins bringing all of its faster, better, and cheaper benefits to the front door of the consumer. This is where the last-mile problem begins. Out in front of the house lies enough bandwidth to handle more than 100 million telephone calls or download entire movies in a few seconds. The problem is that the house it is connecting to is wired with twisted-pair wiring that just cannot handle the bandwidth provided by fiber. This situation is analogous to hooking up a garden hose to the water volume generated by Niagara Falls. At the end of the day, the amount of water you get is whatever will come out of the garden hose and nothing more. Therefore, the problem is more than just the cost. In many cases, the wiring in a structure cannot be upgraded and the bandwidth right outside the door just cannot be accessed.

Many methods have been offered to solve the last-mile problem. Cable companies are providing a single-wire solution to many modern households. By using sophisticated technologies, they can bring cable television, Internet access, and telephone services into a home using only the coaxial wire originally put there for cable television. Other solutions include bypassing the old wired network completely and providing high-speed services via a satellite or other wireless approach. Regardless of the solution, the problem of the last mile is still very much an issue to consider when designing a telecommunications network.

Although still in the developmental stages, one solution to the last mile problem may be **WiMax.** Defined as *Worldwide Interoperability for Microwave Access,* WiMax is intended to provide high-speed, mobile telecommunications services to diverse Internet connections and locations. There are still many issues to work out regarding WiMax, but it looks like we may be able to solve the problem of last mile connectivity somewhere in the near future.

Wireless Technologies

Wireless telecommunications technologies rely on radio wave, microwave, infrared, and visible light pulses to transport digital communications without wires between communications devices. Wireless technologies include terrestrial microwave, communications satellites, cellular and PCS telephone and pager systems, mobile data radio, wireless LANs, and various wireless Internet technologies. Each technology utilizes specific ranges within the electromagnetic spectrum (in megahertz) of electromagnetic frequencies that are specified by national regulatory agencies to minimize interference and encourage efficient telecommunications. Let's briefly review some of these major wireless communications technologies.

Terrestrial Microwave

Terrestrial microwave involves earthbound microwave systems that transmit high-speed radio signals in a line-of-sight path between relay stations spaced approximately 30 miles apart. Microwave antennas are usually placed on top of buildings, towers, hills, and mountain peaks, and they are a familiar sight in many sections of the country. They are still a popular medium for both long-distance and metropolitan area networks.

Communications Satellites

Communications satellites also use microwave radio as their telecommunications medium. Typically, high-earth orbit (HEO) communications satellites are placed in stationary geosynchronous orbits approximately 22,000 miles above the equator. Satellites are powered by solar panels and can transmit microwave signals at a rate of several hundred million bits per second. They serve as relay stations for communications signals transmitted from earth stations. Earth stations use dish antennas to beam microwave signals to the satellites that amplify and retransmit the signals to other earth stations thousands of miles away.

Whereas communications satellites were used initially for voice and video transmission, they are now also used for high-speed transmission of large volumes of data. Because of time delays caused by the great distances involved, they are not suitable for interactive, real-time processing. Communications satellite systems are operated by several firms, including Comsat, American Mobile Satellite, and Intellsat.

Various other satellite technologies are being implemented to improve global business communications. For example, many companies use networks of small satellite dish antennas known as VSAT (very small aperture terminal) to connect their stores and distant worksites via satellite. Other satellite networks use many low-earth orbit (LEO) satellites orbiting at an altitude of only 500 miles above the earth. Companies like Globalstar offer wireless phone, paging, and messaging services to users anywhere on the globe. Let's look at a real-world example.

View from Space: Satellite Farming for Greener Pastures 	Making the most of natural resources of farms is critical in today's environment, where rainfalls are becoming ever so scarce. Although in Queensland the use of animal recognition technology is being used to conserve water, on the other side of the country in Western Australia, satellite technology is providing farmers with a suite of tools to accurately estimate the amount of feed in their pastures, how quickly their pastures are growing, and the pasture quality. For maximum efficiency on a farm, farmers need to use the pasture when it is at its best. According to Gonzalo Mata, who is in charge of farming systems and Web development for the project, the general rule of thumb is that about only 20 to 30 percent of pasture grown is utilized in many beef and sheep production systems. "Farmers need this information in order to match the animals' nutrient demands for growth and reproduction with the supply of feed which can be very seasonal. If this is not achieved, production is lower or costs increase through the use of supplements to achieve the balance," Mata adds. According to Mata, you can't manage what you can't measure, hence the need to allow farmers to measure how much pasture there is on their farms. The tool uses images from a NASA satellite to create a composite greenness index. The climate data is sourced from the Bureau of Meteorology on a weekly basis, and the two data sources are combined in a pasture growth model. Pastures from Space boasts a 97 percent accuracy and it is possible for farmers with a subscription to have sustainable pasture utilization of more than 50 percent. "Building data over time allows the farmer to do comparisons for specific areas between seasons or between years, which can be a powerful tool to benchmark production and manage risk," says Mata. By going online, the farmer can also look at maps of PGR for their farm, giving them a better understanding of why some parts of the farm are performing better than others. Source: Adapted from Kathryn Edwards, " View from Space: Satellite Farming for Greener Pastures," *Computerworld Australia*, April 29, 2009.

Cellular and PCS Systems

Cellular and PCS telephone and pager systems use several radio communications technologies. However, all of them divide a geographic area into small areas, or *cells*, typically from one to several square miles in area. Each cell has its own low-power transmitter or radio relay antenna device to relay calls from one cell to another. Computers and other communications processors coordinate and control the transmissions to and from mobile users as they move from one area to another.

Cellular phone systems have long used analog communications technologies operating at frequencies in the 800–900 MHz cellular band. Newer cellular systems use digital technologies, which provide greater capacity and security, and additional services such as voice mail, paging, messaging, and caller ID. These capabilities are also available with PCS (personal communications services) phone systems. PCS operates at 1,900 MHz frequencies using digital technologies that are related to digital cellular. However, PCS phone systems cost substantially less to operate and use than cellular systems and have lower power consumption requirements.

Wireless LANs

Wiring an office or a building for a local area network is often a difficult and costly task. Older buildings frequently do not have conduits for coaxial cables or additional twisted-pair wire, and the conduits in newer buildings may not have enough room to pull additional wiring through. Repairing mistakes in and damage to wiring is often difficult and costly, as are major relocations of LAN workstations and other components. One solution to such problems is installing a wireless LAN using one of several wireless technologies. Examples include a high-frequency radio technology similar to digital cellular and a low-frequency radio technology called *spread spectrum.*

The use of wireless LANs is growing rapidly as new high-speed technologies are implemented. A prime example is a new open-standard wireless radio-wave technology technically known as IEEE 802.11b, or more popularly as Wi-Fi (for wireless fidelity). Wi-Fi is faster (11 Mbps) and less expensive than standard Ethernet and other common wire-based LAN technologies. Thus, Wi-Fi wireless LANs enable laptop PCs, PDAs, and other devices with Wi-Fi modems to connect easily to the Internet and other networks in a rapidly increasing number of business, public, and home environments. A faster version (802.11g) with speeds of 54 Mbps promises to make this technology even more widely used. As of December 2009, the newest version, 802.11n, was finalized. This new standard offers speeds of up to 108 Mbps.

Bluetooth

A short-range wireless technology called Bluetooth is rapidly being built into computers and other devices. Bluetooth serves as a cable-free wireless connection to peripheral devices such as computer printers and scanners. Operating at approximately 1 Mbps with an effective range from 10 to 100 meters, Bluetooth promises to change significantly the way we use computers and other telecommunication devices.

To fully appreciate the potential value of Bluetooth, look around the space where you have your computer. You have your keyboard connected to the computer, as well as a printer, pointing device, monitor, and so on. What joins these together are their associated cables. Cables have become the bane of many offices and homes. Many of us have experienced trying to figure out what cable goes where and getting tangled up in the details. Bluetooth essentially aims to fix this; it is a cable-replacement technology.

Conceived initially by Ericsson and later adopted by a myriad of other companies, Bluetooth is a standard for a small, cheap radio chip to be plugged into computers, printers, mobile phones, and so forth. A Bluetooth chip is designed to replace cables by taking the information normally carried by the cable and transmitting it at a special frequency to a receiver Bluetooth chip, which will then give the information received to the computer, telephone, printer, or other Bluetooth device. Given its fairly low cost to implement, Bluetooth is set to revolutionize telecommunications.

The Wireless Web

Wireless access to the Internet, intranets, and extranets is growing as more Web-enabled information appliances proliferate. Smart telephones, pagers, PDAs, and other portable communications devices have become *very thin clients* in wireless networks. Agreement on a standard *wireless application protocol* (WAP) has encouraged the development of many wireless Web applications and services. The telecommunications industry continues to work on *third-generation* (3G) wireless technologies whose goal is to raise wireless transmission speeds to enable streaming video and multimedia applications on mobile devices.

For example, the Smartphone, a PCS phone, can send and receive e-mail and provide Web access via a "Web clipping" technology that generates custom-designed Web pages from many popular financial, securities, travel, sport, entertainment, and e-commerce Web sites. Another example is the Sprint PCS Wireless Web phone, which delivers similar Web content and e-mail services via a Web-enabled PCS phone.

Figure 6.20 illustrates the wireless application protocol that is the foundation of wireless mobile Internet and Web applications. The WAP standard specifies how Web pages in HTML or XML are translated into a *wireless markup language* (WML) by *filter* software and preprocessed by *proxy* software to prepare the Web pages for wireless transmission from a Web server to a Web-enabled wireless device.

FIGURE 6.20 The Wireless Application Protocol (WAP) architecture for wireless Internet services to mobile information appliances.

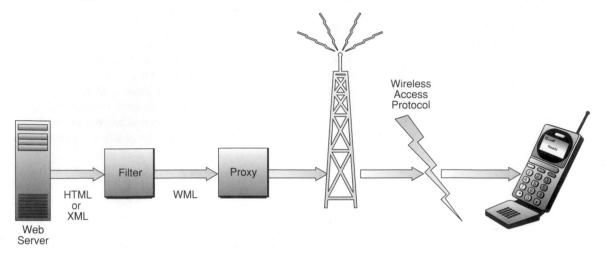

Around the World: Mobile Buying and Banking

In 2009, many U.S. consumers whipped out their smartphones in brick-and-mortar stores to find better deals online, tripling mobile shopping revenue in just one year. The relationship between money and mobile devices, however, varies widely from one part of the world to another. Mobile banking grew significantly in India, while Africa, Latin America, and some other parts of the world appeared ready to bypass banking altogether in favor of payments handled by mobile operators.

"Mobile commerce grew far faster in the U.S. than worldwide, vaulting from US$396 million in 2008 to an estimated $1.2 billion in 2009," says analyst Mark Beccue of ABI Research. Drawing on information from multiple sources, ABI concluded that many smartphone users went shopping in physical stores, looked at products, checked out deals on the same items online and made a purchase without even going home to log onto a computer.

Shopping on the mobile Web has become especially popular in North America, though in Japan, it already accounts for about 20 percent of online purchases, says Beccue. Worldwide, excluding Japan, mobile commerce grew from about $3 billion in 2008 to $4.4 billion in 2009.

Meanwhile, the number of U.S. consumers using mobile banking more than doubled in 2009, from 4 million to 10 million. "That was partly driven by the slumping economy, because many consumers adopt mobile banking to check their balances frequently," says Beccue. In addition, U.S. banks are starting to treat mobile as more than an extension of Web-based banking, with tools such as SMS (Short Message Service).

But mobile banking is most popular in Asia and has made particular gains in India, where much of the country has limited banking infrastructure. Looking to remedy this problem, the Indian government in 2008 started encouraging banks to launch mobile platforms, he says. "They see mobile banking as a way to accelerate the acceptance of personal financial services," Beccue says. More than half of Asia's mobile banking customers in 2009 were in India.

Worldwide, the number of mobile-banking users grew from 24.4 million in 2008 to 52.1 million in 2009.

Half of those users were in the Asia-Pacific region. ABI expects to see 407 million people worldwide use mobile banking by 2015. But by that time, nearly as many people will be handling their money through their phones without ever opening a bank account: By then, approximately 405 million people will be using point-to-point payment systems in which the mobile operator takes in and pays out the cash, Beccue says.

Point-to-point payment systems are becoming an important financial platform in countries where most people have never had access to banks. "In many parts of the developing world, mobile is the most common piece of infrastructure that exists," says Beccue. "In many places, there are more mobile phones than there is running water or electricity."

Source: Adapted from Stephen Lawson, " Mobile Buying Booms in US, Banking in India," *CIO.com*, February 17, 2010.

Telecommunications Processors

Telecommunications processors such as modems, multiplexers, switches, and routers perform a variety of support functions between the computers and other devices in a telecommunications network. Let's take a look at some of these processors and their functions. See Figure 6.21.

Modems

Modems are the most common type of communications processor. They convert the digital signals from a computer or transmission terminal at one end of a communications link into analog frequencies that can be transmitted over ordinary telephone lines. A modem at the other end of the communications line converts the transmitted data back into digital form at a receiving terminal. This process is known as *modulation* and *demodulation*, and the word *modem* is a combined abbreviation of those two words. Modems come in several forms, including small stand-alone units, plug-in circuit boards, and removable modem cards for laptop PCs. Most modems also support a variety of telecommunications functions, such as transmission error control, automatic dialing and answering, and a faxing capability. As shown in Figure 6.21, a modem is used in the private-home setting to accept the data from the Internet provider and convert it to input for a PC.

Modems are used because ordinary telephone networks were first designed to handle continuous analog signals (electromagnetic frequencies), such as those generated by the human voice over the telephone. Because data from computers are in digital form

FIGURE 6.21 Examples of some of the communications processors involved in an Internet connection.

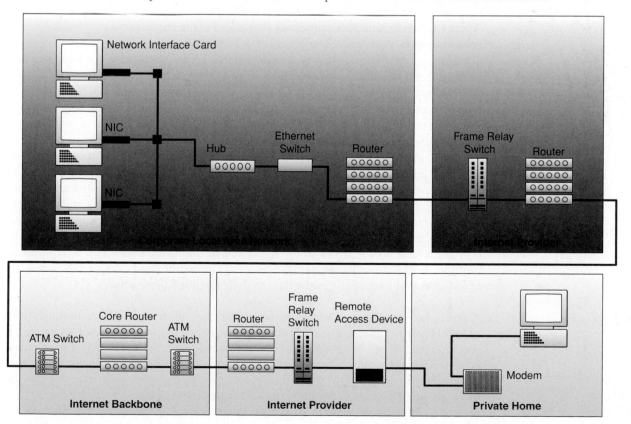

FIGURE 6.22

Comparing modem and telecommunications technologies for Internet and other network access.

Modem (56 Kbps)	DSL (Digital Subscriber Line) Modem
• Receives at 56 Kbps	• Receives at 1.5 Mbps to 5.0 Mbps
• Sends at 33.6 Kbps	• Sends at 128 Kbps to 640 Kbps
• Slowest technology	• Users must be near switching centers
ISDN (Integrated Services Digital Network)	**Cable Modem**
• Sends and receives at 128 Kbps	• Receives at 1.5 Mbps to 20 Mbps
• Users need extra lines	• Sends at 128 Kbps to 2.5 Mbps
• Becoming obsolete	• Speed degrades with many local users
Home Satellite	**Local Microwave**
• Receives at 400 Kbps	• Sends and receives at 512 Kbps to 1.4 Mbps
• Sends via phone modem	• Higher cost
• Slow sending, higher cost	• May require line of sight to base antenna

(voltage pulses), devices are necessary to convert digital signals into appropriate analog transmission frequencies and vice versa. However, digital communications networks that use only digital signals and do not need analog/digital conversion are becoming commonplace. Because most modems also perform a variety of telecommunications support functions, devices called digital modems are still used in digital networks.

Figure 6.22 compares several modem and telecommunications technologies for access to the Internet and other networks by home and business users.

Inter-Network Processors

Telecommunications networks are interconnected by special-purpose communications processors called inter-network processors, such as switches, routers, hubs, and gateways. A *switch* is a communications processor that makes connections between telecommunications circuits in a network. Switches are now available in managed versions with network management capabilities. A bridge is a device that connects two or more local area networks that use the same communications rules or *protocol*. In contrast, a *router* is an intelligent communications processor that interconnects networks based on different rules or *protocols*, so a telecommunications message can be routed to its destination. A *hub* is a port-switching communications processor. Advanced versions of both hubs and switches provide automatic switching among connections called *ports* for shared access to a network's resources. Workstations, servers, printers, and other network resources are typically connected to ports. Networks that use different communications architectures are interconnected by using a communications processor called a *gateway*. All these devices are essential to providing connectivity and easy access between the multiple LANs and wide area networks that are part of the intranets and client/server networks in many organizations.

Again referring to Figure 6.21, we can see examples of all of these elements. The corporate local area network in the upper left of the figure uses a hub to connect its multiple workstations to the network switch. The switch sends the signals to a series of switches and routers to get the data to their intended destination.

Multiplexers

A multiplexer is a communications processor that allows a single communications channel to carry simultaneous data transmissions from many terminals. This process is accomplished in two basic ways. In *frequency division multiplexing* (FDM), a multiplexer effectively divides a high-speed channel into multiple slow-speed channels. In *time division multiplexing* (TDM), the multiplexer divides the time each terminal can use the high-speed line into very short time slots, or time frames.

For example, if we need to have eight telephone numbers for a small business, we could have eight individual lines come into the building—one for each telephone number. Using a digital multiplexer, however, we can have one line handle all eight telephone numbers (assuming we have an eight-channel multiplexer). Multiplexers work to increase the number of transmissions possible without increasing the number of physical data channels.

Telecommunications Software

Telecommunications software is a vital component of all telecommunications networks. Telecommunications and network management software may reside in PCs, servers, mainframes, and communications processors like multiplexers and routers. Network servers and other computers in a network use these programs to manage network performance. Network management programs perform functions such as automatically checking client PCs for input/output activity, assigning priorities to data communications requests from clients and terminals, and detecting and correcting transmission errors and other network problems.

For example, mainframe-based wide area networks frequently use *telecommunications monitors* or *teleprocessing* (TP) monitors. The CICS (Customer Identification Control System) for IBM mainframes is a typical example. Servers in local area and other networks frequently rely on *network operating systems* like Novell NetWare or operating systems like UNIX, Linux, or Microsoft Windows 2008 Servers for network management. Many software vendors also offer telecommunications software as *middleware*, which can help diverse networks communicate with one another.

Telecommunications functions built into Microsoft Windows and other operating systems provide a variety of communications support services. For example, they work with a communications processor (such as a modem) to connect and disconnect communications links and to establish communications parameters such as transmission speed, mode, and direction.

Network Management

Network management packages such as network operating systems and telecommunications monitors determine transmission priorities, route (switch) messages, poll terminals in the network, and form waiting lines (queues) of transmission requests. They also detect and correct transmission errors, log statistics of network activity, and protect network resources from unauthorized access. See Figure 6.23.

FIGURE 6.23

Network management software monitors and manages network performance.

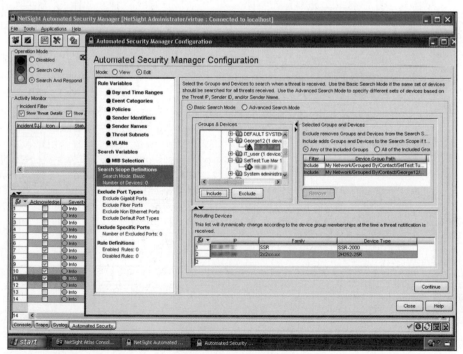

Source: © Enterasys Networks, Inc. All Rights Reserved.

Examples of major **network management** functions include the following:

- **Traffic Management.** Manage network resources and traffic to avoid congestion and optimize telecommunications service levels to users.
- **Security.** Provide security as one of the top concerns of network management today. Telecommunications software must provide authentication, encryption, firewall, and auditing functions, and enforce security policies. Encryption, firewalls, and other network security defenses are covered in Chapter 13.
- **Network Monitoring.** Troubleshoot and watch over the network, informing network administrators of potential problems before they occur.
- **Capacity Planning.** Survey network resources and traffic patterns and users' needs to determine how best to accommodate the needs of the network as it grows and changes.

Network Topologies

There are several basic types of network topologies, or structures, in telecommunications networks. Figure 6.24 illustrates three basic topologies used in wide area and local area telecommunications networks. A *star* network ties end-user computers to a central computer. A *ring* network ties local computer processors together in a ring on a more equal basis. A *bus* network is a network in which local processors share the same bus, or communications channel. A variation of the ring network is the *mesh* network. It uses direct communications lines to connect some or all of the computers in the ring to one another.

Wired networks may use a combination of star, ring, and bus approaches. Obviously, the star network is more centralized, whereas ring and bus networks have a more decentralized approach. However, this is not always the case. For example, the central computer in a star configuration may be acting only as a *switch*, or message-switching computer that handles the data communications between autonomous local

FIGURE 6.24   The ring, star, and bus network topologies.

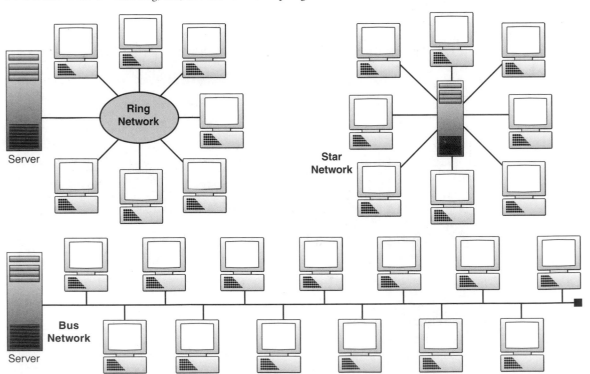

Source: Courtesy of NetSight.

computers. Star, ring, and bus networks differ in their performance, reliability, and cost. A pure star network is considered less reliable than a ring network, because the other computers in the star are heavily dependent on the central host computer. If it fails, there is no backup processing and communications capability, and the local computers are cut off from one another. Therefore, it is essential that the host computer be highly reliable. Having some type of multiprocessor architecture to provide a fault-tolerant capability is a common solution.

Network Architectures and Protocols

Until quite recently, sufficient standards were lacking for the interfaces among the hardware, software, and communications channels of telecommunications networks. This situation hampered the use of telecommunications, increased its costs, and reduced its efficiency and effectiveness. In response, telecommunications manufacturers and national and international organizations have developed standards called *protocols* and master plans called *network architectures* to support the development of advanced data communications networks.

Protocols

A protocol is a standard set of rules and procedures for the control of communications in a network. However, these standards may be limited to just one manufacturer's equipment or just one type of data communications. Part of the goal of communications network architectures is to create more standardization and compatibility among communications protocols. One example of a protocol is a standard for the physical characteristics of the cables and connectors between terminals, computers, modems, and communications lines. Other examples are the protocols that establish the communications control information needed for *handshaking*, which is the process of exchanging predetermined signals and characters to establish a telecommunications session between terminals and computers. Other protocols deal with control of data transmission reception in a network, switching techniques, inter-network connections, and so on.

Network Architectures

The goal of network architectures is to promote an open, simple, flexible, and efficient telecommunications environment, accomplished by the use of standard protocols, standard communications hardware and software interfaces, and the design of a standard multilevel interface between end users and computer systems.

The OSI Model

The Open Systems Interconnection (OSI) model is a standard description or "reference model" for how messages should be transmitted between any two points in a telecommunications network. Its purpose is to guide product implementers so that their products will consistently work with other products. The reference model defines seven layers of functions that take place at each end of a communication. Although OSI is not always strictly adhered to in terms of keeping related functions together in a well-defined layer, many, if not most, products involved in telecommunications make an attempt to describe themselves in relation to the OSI model. It is also valuable as a view of communication that furnishes a common ground for education and discussion.

Developed by representatives of major computer and telecommunication companies beginning in 1983, OSI was originally intended to be a detailed specification of interfaces. Instead, the committee decided to establish a common reference model for which others could develop detailed interfaces that in turn could become standards. OSI was officially adopted as an international standard by the International Organization of Standards (ISO).

The main idea in OSI is that the process of communication between two endpoints in a telecommunication network can be divided into layers, with each layer adding its own set of special, related functions. Each communicating user or program is at a computer equipped with these seven layers of functions. So in a given message between users, there will be a flow of data through each layer at one end down through the layers in that computer; at the other end, when the message arrives, there will be another flow of data up through the layers in the receiving computer and ultimately to the end user or program. The actual programming and hardware that furnishes these seven layers of functions is usually a combination of the computer operating system, applications (e.g., your Web browser), TCP/IP or alternative transport and network protocols, and the software and hardware that enable you to put a signal on one of the lines attached to your computer.

OSI divides telecommunication into seven layers. Figure 6.25 illustrates the functions of the seven layers of the OSI model architecture.

The layers consist of two groups. The upper four layers are used whenever a message passes to or from a user. The lower three layers (up to the network layer) are used when any message passes through the host computer. Messages intended for this computer pass to the upper layers. Messages destined for some other host are not passed to the upper layers but are forwarded to another host. The seven layers are:

- **Layer 1: The physical layer.** This layer conveys the bit stream through the network at the electrical and mechanical level. It provides the hardware means of sending and receiving data on a carrier.

- **Layer 2: The data link layer.** This layer provides synchronization for the physical level and does bit-stuffing for strings of 1's in excess of 5. It furnishes transmission protocol knowledge and management.

- **Layer 3: The network layer.** This layer handles the routing of the data (sending it in the right direction to the right destination on outgoing transmissions and receiving incoming transmissions at the packet level). The network layer does routing and forwarding.

- **Layer 4: The transport layer.** This layer manages the end-to-end control (e.g., determining whether all packets have arrived) and error-checking. It ensures complete data transfer.

FIGURE 6.25 The seven layers of the OSI communications network architecture, and the five layers of the Internet's TCP/IP protocol suite.

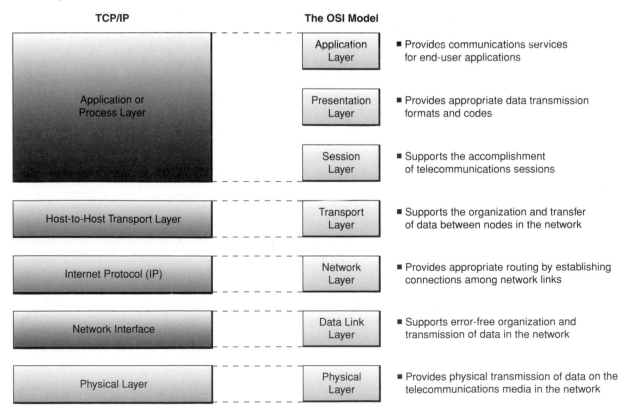

- **Layer 5: The session layer.** This layer sets up, coordinates, and terminates conversations, exchanges, and dialogues between the applications at each end. It deals with session and connection coordination.

- **Layer 6: The presentation layer.** This layer, usually part of an operating system, converts incoming and outgoing data from one presentation format to another (e.g., from a text stream into a pop-up window with the newly arrived text). It's sometimes called the syntax layer.

- **Layer 7: The application layer.** At this layer, communication partners are identified, quality of service is identified, user authentication and privacy are considered, and any constraints on data syntax are identified. (This layer is *not* the application itself, although some applications may perform application layer functions.)

The Internet's TCP/IP

The Internet uses a system of telecommunications protocols that has become so widely used that it is now accepted as a network architecture. The Internet's protocol suite is called **Transmission Control Protocol/Internet Protocol** and is known as TCP/IP. As Figure 6.25 shows, TCP/IP consists of five layers of protocols that can be related to the seven layers of the OSI architecture. TCP/IP is used by the Internet and by all intranets and extranets. Many companies and other organizations are thus converting their client/server and wide area networks to TCP/IP technology, which are now commonly called IP networks.

Although many of the technical aspects of the Internet can appear quite complex, the addressing, routing, and transport protocols, which make sure you get to the right Web site or your e-mail is delivered to the right place, are actually elegantly simple. TCP/IP can be thought of as analogous to how the postal system finds your house and delivers your mail. In this analogy, TCP represents the postal system and the various processes and protocols used to move the mail, while IP represents the zip code and address.

The current IP addressing protocol is called IPv4. When IP was first standardized in September 1981, the specification required that each system attached to the Internet be assigned a unique, 32-bit Internet address value. Systems that have interfaces to more than one network require a unique IP address for each network interface. The first part of an Internet address identifies the network on which the host resides, while the second part identifies the particular host on the given network. Keeping with our postal system analogy, the network address can be thought of as the zip code, and the host address represents the street address. By convention, an IP address is expressed as four decimal numbers separated by periods, such as "127.154.95.6." Valid addresses can range from 0.0.0.0 to 255.255.255.255, creating a total of about 4.3 billion addresses (4,294,967,296 to be exact). Using this two-level addressing hierarchy, any computer connected to the Internet can be located.

IP addressing can identify a specific network connected to the Internet. To provide the flexibility required to support networks of varying sizes, the Internet designers decided that the IP address space should be divided into three address classes—Classes A, B, and C. Each class fixes the boundary between the network prefix and the host number at a different point within the 32-bit address.

Class A networks are defined by the first number in an IP address. The value can range from 000 to 127, creating theoretically 128 unique networks. In reality, however, there are only 126 Class A addresses because both 0.0.0.0 and 127.0.0.0 are reserved for special use. Each Class A network address can support a total of 16,777,214 hosts per network, and they represent 50 percent of the total IPv4 address space. The Class A addresses are normally owned by large Internet service providers or well-established major corporations. For example, General Electric owns 3.0.0.0, IBM owns 9.0.0.0, Ford Motor Co. owns 19.0.0.0, and the U.S. Postal Service owns 56.0.0.0.

Class B network addresses range from 128.0 to 255.254. Using a Class B address, 16,384 networks can be identified with up to 65,534 hosts per network. Because the Class B address allocation contains slightly more than 1 million addresses, it represents

25 percent of the IPv4 address space. Class B addresses are also normally owned by very large service providers and global organizations—AOL uses 205.188.0.0.

Class C addresses range from 192.0.0 to 233.255.255 and represent 12.5 percent of the available IPv4 address space. Slightly less than 2.1 million networks can be identified with a Class C address allowing approximately 537 million hosts. The remaining 12.5 percent of the IPv4 address space is reserved for special use.

You would think that 4.3 billion addresses would be sufficient for quite a while, but the Internet is running out of space. During the early days of the Internet, the seemingly unlimited address space allowed IP addresses to be allocated to an organization based on a simple request rather than on actual need. As a result, addresses were freely assigned to those who asked for them without concerns about the eventual depletion of the IP address space. Now many of the Class A and Class B host addresses are not even in use. To make matters worse, new technologies are extending IP addresses beyond computers to televisions, toasters, and coffeemakers.

This is where IPv6 comes to the rescue. Developed to work with Internet2, IPv6 increases the IP address size from 32 bits to 128 bits to support more levels of the address hierarchy and a much greater number of nodes. IPv6 supports more than 340 trillion trillion trillion addresses, enough for each person in the world to be allocated 1 billion personal IP addresses! That should last for a while.

Voice over IP

One of the newest uses for Internet protocol (IP) is *Internet telephony*—the practice of using an Internet connection to pass voice data using IP instead of using the standard public switched telephone network. Often referred to as **voice over IP** or VoIP, this approach makes use of a packet-based (or switched) network to carry voice calls, instead of the traditional circuit-switched network. In simpler terms, VoIP allows a person to function as if he or she were directly connected to a regular telephone network even when at home or in a remote office. It also skips standard long-distance charges because the only connection is through an ISP. VoIP is being used more and more to keep corporate telephone costs down, as you can just run two network cables to a desk instead of separate network and data cables. VoIP runs right over a standard network infrastructure, but it also demands a very well-configured network to run smoothly.

For those of us who love to talk (and not to pay for it), there is *Skype* (www.skype.com). Skype was founded in 2002 to develop the first peer-to-peer (P2P) telephony network. Today, Skype software allows telephone conversation through a PC and over the Internet instead of a separate phone connection. This proprietary freeware uses a messenger-like client and offers inbound and outbound PSTN (public switched telephone network) facilities.

Skype users can call to any noncomputer-based landline or mobile telephone in the world and call other Skype users for free. The calls made to or received from traditional telephones are charged a fee, as are the voice-mail messages.

Skype software also provides features like voice mail, instant messaging, call forwarding, and conference calling. Skype users are not billed according to the distance between the two countries. Instead, the users are charged according to the prosperity of the country, the volume of calls made to and from the country, and the access charges. The latest statistical figures show that Skype is one of the fastest-growing companies on the Internet:

- Skype has 54 million members in 225 countries and territories, and the number is swelling—just through word-of-mouth marketing by satisfied users!
- Skype is adding approximately 150,000 users a day, and there are 3 million simultaneous users on the network at any given time.
- Skype has been downloaded 163 million times in 225 countries and territories.
- Skype is available in 27 languages.
- Skype has more users and serves more voice minutes than any other Internet voice communications provider.

Skype continues to grow in the consumer sector and is now offering business-specific services designed to reduce business telecommunication costs while offering more flexible alternatives to current landline or mobile approaches. Skype also demonstrates how VoIP is fast becoming part of the telecommunications infrastructure as shown in the following example.

For those of us to love to talk (and want to pay less than the telephone company wants us to pay), there is *Vonage* (www.vonage.com). The name is a play on their motto: Voice-Over-Net-Age—Vonage. Using VoIP technologies, Vonage offers local and long distance telephone service to homes and businesses for a single low monthly price. VoIP has come a long way since Vonage, however. Today, you can find dozens of VoIP providers ranging from basic Internet phone services to complex business PBX services that allow for voice mail, auto-attendant features, call queuing and routing and many, many more features and resources. Most important, business adopting VoIP phone services are saving on the order of 50 percent or more over their previous landline services.

Ottawa Regional Hospital: Lowering Costs while Converting to VoIP 	What started out as an upgrade to the phone system at Ottawa Regional Hospital and Healthcare Center became a badly needed network overhaul that lowered costs and included a conversion to VoIP. The Ottawa, Illinois–based center was running an analog phone system that wouldn't support an IP phone system, let alone the battery of high-bandwidth medical applications that are becoming more and more necessary, says Curt Sesto, director of facilities, construction management, and electronics for the center. When he arrived in 2008, his marching order from the CEO was to get a new phone system right away. "It had been on his radar for a couple of years," he says. One goal was to get rid of the estimated $28,000 per year maintenance cost of the PBXs, for which it was getting increasingly harder to find parts as they grew older. "They could go toes-up at any time," he says. Sesto checked out Siemens, Cisco, and Avaya VoIP systems. The Siemens system was being pushed by PosTrack, which also supplies Siemens medical gear to Ottawa Health. It was the only bidder that urged a data network evaluation as the first step in the process of moving to VoIP, he says. He liked that and also the fact that the Siemens offer was a hosted service. It would take on the task of network monitoring and maintenance, which frees up two to three full-timers who can focus instead on implementing electronic medical records systems, another priority for the center. Voice traffic will run over the same network. The voice system is based on Siemens OpenScape servers located at two separate sites in Chicago for redundancy in case one goes down. It consists of a 30-mile connection over the local Medicacom cable TV network to the state-run Illinois Century Network that is available to hospitals to the Level 3 points of presence. The new phone system can be extended to 15 medical office buildings that are off the Ottawa campus, Sesto says. The old PBXs couldn't handle them, so each had its own small Avaya PBX that is being decommissioned as the central VoIP service rollout reaches each building. The VoIP system has given the center a new voice-mail system that integrates with Outlook so users get e-mail notification of voice messages. They system can also ring more than one phone when an extension is called. So an individual could configure the system to ring the office phone, but also the home phone and mobile. UC features in the system include faxing to e-mails. The network overhaul was more extensive than the CEO had in mind when he asked for a new phone system, but it's more appropriate to the high-bandwidth medical applications the network needs to support, Sesto says. "The old network was like having bicycle tires on an Indy car," he says. Source: Adapted from Tim Greene, "VoIP, Network Overhaul brings Hospital Savings, Unified Communications," *Network World*, November 30, 2009.

Bandwidth Alternatives

The communications speed and capacity of telecommunications networks can be classified by bandwidth. The frequency range of a telecommunications channel, it determines the channel's maximum transmission rate. The speed and capacity of data transmission rates are typically measured in bits per second (bps). This level is sometimes referred to as the *baud* rate, though baud is more correctly a measure of signal changes in a transmission line.

Bandwidth represents the capacity of the connection. The greater the capacity, the more likely that greater performance will follow. Thus, greater bandwidth allows greater amounts of data to move from one point to another with greater speed. Although the relationship among bandwidth, data volume, and speed is theoretically sound, in practice, this is not always the case. A common analogy is to think of bandwidth as a pipe with water in it. The larger the pipe, the more water that can flow through it. If, however, the big pipe is connected to a small pipe, the effective amount of water that can be moved in a given time becomes severely restricted by the small pipe. The same problem occurs with network bandwidth. If a large bandwidth connection tries to move a large amount of data to a network with less bandwidth, the speed of the transmission will be determined by the speed of the smaller bandwidth.

Narrow-band channels typically provide low-speed transmission rates up to 64 Kbps but can now handle up to 2 Mbps. They are usually unshielded twisted-pair lines commonly used for telephone voice communications and for data communications by the modems of PCs and other devices. Medium-speed channels (*medium-band*) use shielded twisted-pair lines for transmission speeds up to 100 Mbps.

Broadband channels provide high-speed transmission rates at intervals from 256 Kbps to several billion bps. Typically, they use microwave, fiber optics, or satellite transmission. Examples are 1.54 Mbps for T1 and 45 Mbps for T3 communications channels, up to 100 Mbps for communications satellite channels, and between 52 Mbps and 10 Gbps for fiber-optic lines. See Figure 6.26.

Switching Alternatives

Regular telephone service relies on *circuit switching*, in which a switch opens a circuit to establish a link between a sender and a receiver; it remains open until the communication session is completed. In message switching, a message is transmitted a block at a time from one switching device to another.

Packet switching involves subdividing communications messages into fixed or variable-length groups called packets. For example, in the X.25 protocol, packets are 128 characters long, while in the *frame relay* technology, they are of variable length. Packet-switching networks are frequently operated by *value-added carriers* who use computers and other communications processors to control the packet-switching process and transmit the packets of various users over their networks.

Early packet-switching networks were X.25 networks. The X.25 protocol is an international set of standards governing the operations of widely used, but relatively slow, packet-switching networks. *Frame relay* is another popular packet-switching protocol and

FIGURE 6.26

Examples of the telecommunications transmission speeds of various network technologies.

Network Technologies	Typical–Maximum bps
Wi-Fi: wireless fidelity	11–54M
Standard Ethernet or token ring	10–16M
High-speed Ethernet	100M–1G
FDDI: fiber distributed data interface	100M
DDN: digital data network	2.4K–2M
PSN: packet switching network–X.25	64K–1.5M
Frame relay network	1.5M–45M
ISDN: integrated services digital network	64K/128K–2M
ATM: asynchronous transfer mode	25/155M–2.4G
SONET: synchronous optical network	45M–40G
Kbps = thousand bps or kilobits per second Mbps = million bps or megabits per second	Gbps = billion bps or gigabits per second

FIGURE 6.27
Why four large retail chains chose different network technologies to connect their stores.

Company	Technology	Why
Sears	Frame relay	Reliable, inexpensive, and accommodates mainframe and Internet protocols
Rack Room	VSAT (very small aperture terminal)	Very inexpensive way to reach small markets and shared satellite dishes at malls
Hannaford	ATM (asynchronous transfer mode)	Very high bandwidth; combines voice, video, and data
7-Eleven	ISDN (integrated services digital network)	Can use multiple channels to partition traffic among different uses

is used by many large companies for their wide area networks. Frame relay is considerably faster than X.25 and is better able to handle the heavy telecommunications traffic of interconnected local area networks within a company's wide area client/server network. ATM (*asynchronous transfer mode*) is an emerging high-capacity *cell switching* technology. An ATM switch breaks voice, video, and other data into fixed cells of 53 bytes (48 bytes of data and 5 bytes of control information) and routes them to their next destination in the network. ATM networks are being developed by many companies needing their fast, high-capacity multimedia capabilities for voice, video, and data communications. See Figure 6.27.

Network Interoperability

Section 256 of the Communications Act, enacted in February 1996, states two key purposes: (1) "to promote nondiscriminatory accessibility by the broadest number of users and vendors of communications products and services to public telecommunications networks used to provide telecommunications service" and (2) "to ensure the ability of users and information providers to seamlessly and transparently transmit and receive information between and across telecommunications networks." To accomplish these purposes, the Federal Communications Commission (FCC) is required to establish procedures to oversee coordinated network planning by providers of telecommunications services. It is also authorized to participate in the development, by appropriate industry standards-setting organizations of public telecommunications, of network interconnectivity standards that promote access.

As you can see, the FCC is a key regulatory agency with regard to telecommunications. Although we tend to think of the FCC as the oversight body for radio and television, it is equally involved in all aspects of data and voice communications. If you reread the first paragraph of this section, it becomes clear that there is an important underlying reason for the FCC to be so involved with telecommunications. The answer lies in the importance of a concept called network interoperability.

This interoperability ensures that anyone anywhere on one network can communicate with anyone anywhere on another network without having to worry about speaking a common language from a telecommunications perspective. All that we have discussed in this chapter with regard to business value would not be possible without complete accessibility, transparency, and seamless interoperability across all networks. Without these things, the Internet would not be possible, nor would e-mail, instant messaging, or even common file sharing.

Fortunately for us, everyone in the telecommunications field understands the importance of network interoperability, and as such, they work together to ensure that all networks remain interoperable.

Summary

● **Telecommunications Trends.** Organizations are becoming networked enterprises that use the Internet, intranets, and other telecommunications networks to support business operations and collaboration within the enterprise and with their customers, suppliers, and other business partners. Telecommunications has entered a deregulated and fiercely competitive environment with many vendors, carriers, and services. Telecommunications technology is moving toward open, inter-networked digital networks for voice, data, video, and multimedia. A major trend is the pervasive use of the Internet and its technologies to build interconnected enterprise and global networks, like intranets and extranets, to support enterprise collaboration, e-commerce, and other e-business applications.

- **The Internet Revolution.** The explosive growth of the Internet and the use of its enabling technologies have revolutionized computing and telecommunications. The Internet has become the key platform for a rapidly expanding list of information and entertainment services and business applications, including enterprise collaboration, electronic commerce, and other e-business systems. Open systems with unrestricted connectivity using Internet technologies are the primary telecommunications technology drivers in e-business systems. Their primary goal is to promote easy and secure access by business professionals and consumers to the resources of the Internet, enterprise intranets, and interorganizational extranets.

- **The Business Value of the Internet.** Companies are deriving strategic business value from the Internet, which enables them to disseminate information globally, communicate and trade interactively with customized information and services for individual customers, and foster collaboration of people and integration of business processes within the enterprise and with business partners. These capabilities allow them to generate cost savings from using Internet technologies, revenue increases from electronic commerce, and better customer service and relationships through better supply chain management and customer relationship management.

- **The Role of Intranets.** Businesses are installing and extending intranets throughout their organizations to (1) improve communications and collaboration among individuals and teams within the enterprise; (2) publish and share valuable business information easily, inexpensively, and effectively via enterprise information portals and intranet Web sites and other intranet services; and

(3) develop and deploy critical applications to support business operations and decision making.

- **The Role of Extranets.** The primary role of extranets is to link the intranet resources of a company to the intranets of its customers, suppliers, and other business partners. Extranets can also provide access to operational company databases and legacy systems to business partners. Thus, extranets provide significant business value by facilitating and strengthening the business relationships of a company with customers and suppliers, improving collaboration with its business partners, and enabling the development of new kinds of Web-based services for its customers, suppliers, and others.

- **Telecommunications Networks.** The major generic components of any telecommunications network are (1) terminals, (2) telecommunications processors, (3) communications channels, (4) computers, and (5) telecommunications software. There are several basic types of telecommunications networks, including wide area networks (WANs) and local area networks (LANs). Most WANs and LANs are interconnected using client/server, network computing, peer-to-peer, and Internet networking technologies.

- **Network Alternatives.** Key telecommunications network alternatives and components are summarized in Figure 6.11 for telecommunications media, processors, software, channels, and network architectures. A basic understanding of these major alternatives will help business end users participate effectively in decisions involving telecommunications issues. Telecommunications processors include modems, multiplexers, inter-network processors, and various devices to help interconnect and enhance the capacity and efficiency of telecommunications channels. Telecommunications networks use such media as twisted-pair wire, coaxial cables, fiber-optic cables, terrestrial microwave, communications satellites, cellular and PCS systems, wireless LANs, and other wireless technologies.

- Telecommunications software, such as network operating systems and telecommunications monitors, controls and manages the communications activity in a telecommunications network.

Key Terms and Concepts

These are the key terms and concepts of this chapter. The page number of their first explanation is in parentheses.

1. Analog (278)
2. Bandwidth (294)
3. Bluetooth (283)
4. Client/server networks (275)
5. Coaxial cable (280)
6. Communications satellites (281)
7. Digital (278)
8. Extranets (266)
9. Fiber optics (280)
10. Internet networking technologies (256)
11. Internet service provider (ISP) (259)
12. Inter-network processors (286)
13. Intranets (263)
14. Legacy systems (276)
15. Local area networks (LAN) (273)
16. Metcalfe's law (252)
17. Middleware (256)
18. Modems (285)
19. Multiplexer (286)
20. Network (252)

21. Network architectures (289)
    a. Open Systems Interconnection (OSI) (289)
    b. TCP/IP (291)
22. Network computing (276)
23. Network interoperability (295)
24. Network topologies (288)
25. Open systems (256)

26. Peer-to-peer networks (277)
27. Protocol (289)
28. Telecommunications (255)
29. Telecommunications media (279)
30. Telecommunications network (269)
31. Telecommunications processors (285)

32. Telecommunications software (287)
33. Virtual private network (VPN) (273)
34. VoIP (292)
35. Wide area networks (WAN) (272)
36. Wireless LAN (283)
37. Wireless technologies (257)

Review Quiz

Match one of the key terms and concepts listed previously with one of the brief examples or definitions that follow. Try to find the best fit for answers that seem to fit more than one term or concept. Defend your choices.

_____ 1. Technique for making telephone calls over the Internet.

_____ 2. The ability for all networks to connect to one another.

_____ 3. An interconnected or interrelated chain, group, or system.

_____ 4. Software that serves to "glue together" separate programs.

_____ 5. The usefulness, or utility, of a network equals the square of the number of users.

_____ 6. Internet-like networks that improve communications and collaboration, publish and share information, and develop applications to support business operations and decision making within an organization.

_____ 7. Provide Internet-like access to a company's operational databases and legacy systems by its customers and suppliers.

_____ 8. Company that provides individuals and organizations access to the Internet.

_____ 9. A communications network covering a large geographic area.

_____ 10. A communications network in an office, a building, or other worksite.

_____ 11. Representation of an electrical signal using binary numbers.

_____ 12. Coaxial cable, microwave, and fiber optics are examples.

_____ 13. A communications medium that uses pulses of laser light in glass fibers.

_____ 14. A short range cable replacement technology for digital devices.

_____ 15. Includes modems, multiplexers, and inter-network processors.

_____ 16. Includes programs such as network operating systems and Web browsers.

_____ 17. A common communications processor for microcomputers.

_____ 18. Helps a communications channel carry simultaneous data transmissions from many terminals.

_____ 19. Star, ring, and bus networks are examples.

_____ 20. Representation of an electrical signal that is analogous to the signal itself.

_____ 21. The communications speed and capacity of telecommunications networks.

_____ 22. Intranets and extranets can use their network firewalls and other security features to establish secure Internet links within an enterprise or its trading partners.

_____ 23. Sturdy cable that provides high bandwidth on a single conductor.

_____ 24. Standard rules or procedures for control of communications in a network.

_____ 25. An international standard, multilevel set of protocols to promote compatibility among telecommunications networks.

_____ 26. The standard suite of protocols used by the Internet, intranets, extranets, and some other networks.

_____ 27. Information systems with common hardware, software, and network standards that provide easy access for end users and their networked computer systems.

_____ 28. Interconnected networks need communications processors such as switches, routers, hubs, and gateways.

_____ 29. Web sites, Web browsers, HTML documents, hypermedia databases, and TCP/IP networks are examples.

_____ 30. Networks in which end-user PCs are tied to network servers to share resources and application processing.

—— 31. Network computers provide a browser-based interface for software and databases provided by servers.

—— 32. End-user computers connect directly with each other to exchange files.

—— 33. Orbiting devices that provide multiple communication channels over a large geographical area.

—— 34. Older, traditional mainframe-based business information systems.

—— 35. Any arrangement in which a sender transmits a message to a receiver over a channel consisting of some type of medium.

—— 36. Provides wireless network access for laptop PCs in business settings.

—— 37. Their goal is to improve the telecommunications environment by fostering standardized protocols, communications hardware and software, and the design of standard interfaces, among other things.

—— 38. A type of communications network consisting of terminals, processors, channels, computers, and control software.

—— 39. Telecommunications technologies that do not rely on physical media such as cables or fiber optics.

Discussion Questions

1. The Internet is the driving force behind developments in telecommunications, networks, and other information technologies. Do you agree or disagree? Why?

2. How is the trend toward open systems, connectivity, and interoperability related to business use of the Internet, intranets, and extranets?

3. Refer to the Real World Case on RFID and personal medical information. Mentioned in the case are implications for both privacy and data security arising from the use of these technologies. Which specific ones could arise as a result, and to what extent do you believe those would inhibit the deployment of these advances?

4. How will wireless information appliances and services affect the business use of the Internet and the Web? Explain.

5. What are some of the business benefits and management challenges of client/server networks? Network computing? Peer-to-peer networks?

6. What is the business value driving so many companies to install and extend intranets rapidly throughout their organizations?

7. What strategic competitive benefits do you see in a company's use of extranets?

8. Refer to the Real World Case on telepresence in the chapter. What seems to be the difference between videoconferencing and telepresence? Given the discussion on the latter in the case, does videoconferencing have a future? Why or why not?

9. Do you think that business use of the Internet, intranets, and extranets has changed what businesspeople expect from information technology in their jobs? Explain.

10. The insatiable demand for everything wireless, video, and Web-enabled everywhere will be the driving force behind developments in telecommunications, networking, and computing technologies for the foreseeable future. Do you agree or disagree? Why?

Analysis Exercises

1. **How many addresses are enough?**
   The Internet Protocol version 4 assigns each connected computer a 4-byte address known as an IP address. Each message, or packet, includes this address so that routers know where to forward it. This is the Internet's version of mailing addresses.

   Each region of the world has been given a range of IP addresses to administer locally, with America taking the largest share. Asia, with a significantly larger population, received a disproportionately small range of numbers and is afraid of running out.

   Anticipating this problem, the Internet Engineering Task Force adopted IPv6, which uses addresses 16 bytes long. Although slow to be adopted, all Internet root servers now support IPv6, and Internet service providers are rolling it out as needed while maintaining backward compatibility for IPv4. The U.S. federal government had mandated the change to IPv6 for all federal agencies by 2008.

   a. Express as a power of 2 the number of nodes that can exist using IPv4.

   b. Express as a power of 2 the number of nodes that can exist using IPv6.

2. **MNO Incorporated Communications Network**
   Calculating Bandwidth
   MNO Incorporated is considering acquiring its own leased lines to handle voice and data communications among its 14 distribution sites in three regions around the country. The peak load of communications for each site is expected to be a function of the number of phone links and the number of computers at that site. Communications data are available below. You have been asked to analyze this information.

   a. Create a database table with an appropriate structure to store the data below. Enter the records shown below and get a printed listing of your table.

b. Survey results suggest that the peak traffic to and from a site will be approximately 2 kilobits per second for each phone line plus 10 kilobits per second for each computer. Create a report showing the estimated peak demand for the telecommunications system at each site in kilobits. Create a second report grouped by region and showing regional subtotals and a total for the system as a whole.

Site Location	Region	Phone Lines	Computers
Boston	East	228	95
New York	East	468	205
Richmond	East	189	84
Atlanta	East	192	88
Detroit	East	243	97
Cincinnati	East	156	62
New Orleans	Central	217	58
Chicago	Central	383	160
Saint Louis	Central	212	91
Houston	Central	238	88
Denver	West	202	77
Los Angeles	West	364	132
San Francisco	West	222	101
Seattle	West	144	54

3. **Wireless Radiation**
   Frying Your Brains?
   Radio waves, microwaves, and infrared all belong to the electromagnetic radiation spectrum. These terms reference ranges of radiation frequencies we use every day in our wireless networking environments. However, the very word *radiation* strikes fear in many people. Cell towers have sprouted from fields all along highways. Tall rooftops harbor many more cell stations in cities. Millions of cell phone users place microwave transmitters/receivers next to their heads each time they make a call. Computer network wireless access points have become ubiquitous. Even McDonald's customers can use their machines to browse the Internet as they eat burgers. With all this radiation zapping about, should we be concerned?

   The electromagnetic spectrum ranges from ultralow frequencies to radio waves, microwaves, infrared, visible light, ultraviolet, X-ray, and up to gamma-ray radiation. Is radiation dangerous? The threat appears to come from two different directions, the frequency and the intensity. A preponderance of research has demonstrated the dangers of radiation at frequencies just higher than those of visible light, even including the ultraviolet light used in tanning beds, X-rays, and gamma-rays. These frequencies are high (the wavelengths are small enough) to penetrate and disrupt molecules and even atoms. The results range from burns to damaged DNA that might lead to cancer or birth defects.

   However, radiation's lower frequencies ranging from visible light (the rainbow colors you can see), infrared, microwave, and radio waves have long waves unable to penetrate molecules. Indeed, microwave wavelengths are so long that microwave ovens employ a simple viewing screen that can block these long waves and yet allow visible light through. As a result, we can watch our popcorn pop without feeling any heat. Keep in mind that visible light consists of radiation frequencies closer to the danger end of the spectrum than microwave light.

   Lower radiation frequencies can cause damage only if the *intensity* is strong enough, and that damage is limited to common burns. Microwave ovens cook food by drawing 800 or more watts and converting them into a very intense (bright) microwave light. Cellular telephones, by comparison, draw a very tiny amount of current from the phone's battery and use the resulting microwaves to transmit a signal. In fact, the heat you feel from the cell phone is not from the microwaves but rather from its discharging battery. It is extremely unlikely that either device can give the user cancer, though a microwave oven could cause serious burns if the operator disables its safety features.

   a. Use an Internet search engine and report on what the World Health Organization (WHO) has had to say about microwave radiation or nonionizing radiation.
   b. Use an Internet search engine to identify the various complaints posed by stakeholders regarding cell phone towers. Write a one-page paper describing an alternative to cell phone towers that would enable cell phone use and yet mitigate all or most of these complaints.

4. **Maximizing Communications**
   Human Networking
   Ms. Sapper, this year's annual partner meeting coordinator for a global accounting firm, faced an interesting challenge. With 400 high-powered partners gathering from all around the world, she wanted to arrange meal seating in a way that maximized diversity at each table. She hoped that this seating would encourage partners to open up new lines of communication and discourage old cliques from re-forming. The banquet facility included 50 tables, each seating eight guests. Sapper had all the necessary partner data, but she found herself stumped about how to maximize diversity at each table. Let's walk her through the process.

   Download and save "partners.xls" from the MIS 10e OLC. Open the file and note that in addition to partners' names, it also contains industry, region, and gender information. The Table No. column has been left blank.

   a. In Excel's menu, select "Data" and then "Sort" and then press the "F1" key for help. Read through each of the topics. How would an *ascending* sort arrange the list "Smith; Jones; Zimmerman"?
   b. What feature allows users to sort month lists so *January* appears before *April?*
   c. Sort the partner data first on Gender, then by Industry, and then by Region, and save the file.
   d. Examine the sorted results from the previous step. Notice that assigning the first eight partners to the *same* table would minimize diversity. This result should also provide a clue about how to *maximize* diversity. Using this insight, assign a table number in the range from 1 to 50 to each partner in your sorted list so to maximize diversity. Save the file as "partners_sorted.xls" and explain your logic.

Metric & Multistandard Components Corp.: The Business Value of a Secure Self-Managed Network for a Small-to-Medium Business

With 22,000 customers, 48,800 cataloged parts, and 150 employees working in five U.S. locations and an office in Germany, the last thing John Bellnier needs is an unreliable network.

Yet that's exactly what he contended with for years as IT manager at Metric & Multistandard Components Corp. (MMCC). MMCC may still be classified as a small business by some standards, but this small-to-medium business (SMB) definitely has been a big-time success story in its industry.

MMCC was founded in 1963 by three Czech immigrants in Yonkers, New York, and has grown into one of the largest U.S. distributors of metric industrial fasteners. In the last 10 years business has doubled, reaching $20 million in sales in 2005, and growing just as fast in 2006. However, the company's growth overwhelmed its telecommunications network, which was managed by an outside telecom network management company. The network crashed frequently, interrupting e-mail communications and leaving customer service representatives unable to fulfill orders promptly.

"We had locked ourselves into a three-year contract with our provider," Bellnier says. "It was a managed system and therefore we didn't have passwords to the routers. I experienced dozens of episodes of spending days on the phone trying to escalate job tickets to get the problems solved. It was a nightmare."

He recalls a particular challenge that occurred when the provider denied that its router had gone down: "Their network was broken, and we had to deal with the downtime consequences on top of spending time trying to convince someone 2,000 miles away that one of their routers needed repair."

Several months before MMCC's contract with the provider was to expire, Bellnier began to seek a better network solution. He outlined five key requirements for a new network for the company:

- **Reliability.** Provide maximum network uptime to sustain business operations.
- **Scalability.** Grow with MMCC's increasing business demands.
- **Security.** Ensure confidentiality and integrity of company data.
- **Economy.** Reduce costs for both initial outlay and ongoing administrative and maintenance overhead.
- **Responsibility.** "I wanted all the hardware from one vendor so when issues come up, I know who to turn to," Bellnier adds.

Bellnier met with MMCC executives in 2004 and told them that he believed he could manage a new companywide network internally, on a limited budget, and he could recoup the upfront investment by lowering operating expenses. Company executives agreed that the current network situation was intolerable and gave Bellnier the go-ahead to research and select an experienced local IT consulting firm that was certified to build telecom networks by one of the top telecom hardware and software vendors.

Bellnier selected Hi-Link Computer Corp., a Cisco Systems Premier Certified Partner that had earned Cisco specializations in wireless local area networks (LANs) and virtual private network (VPN) security. As a first step, Hi-Link audited MMCC's existing network and interviewed management about business goals and requirements. Company management was impressed with Hi-Link and agreed that Bellnier should seek a formal project proposal from the consultants.

Hi-Link's consulting engineers, led by Business Development Manager Jim Gartner, proposed to Bellnier that MMCC build a secure network foundation consisting of virtual private network links between sites. Using Cisco integrated services routers and security appliances, the network blueprint was designed to give Bellnier transparent remote access to all necessary devices, increase his control over the network, and improve network performance. Hi-Link showed Bellnier how a secure network foundation works to automate routine maintenance, monitor the network, and alert IT staff of security or performance issues. Bellnier accepted Hi-Link's network plan and made a formal presentation outlining the proposal to company management.

After discussing the business costs, risks, and benefits of Hi-Link's plan, MMCC executives agreed to the proposal and the following key project objectives:

- **Goal.** Create a business network for MMCC with higher reliability, security, and scalability, but lower costs, than the existing externally managed network.
- **Strategy.** Design an IP (Internet Protocol) network with advanced technologies for high availability and efficient network and security management, which can be operated by a very small IT department.
- **Technology.** Use virtual private network technologies to connect remote offices and users securely and facilitate company expansion.
- **Support.** After designing and quickly implementing a secure network foundation based on Cisco products, Hi-Link will help MMCC with technical support whenever needed.

Once the consulting contract was signed. Hi-Link began working with Cisco and the local telecom company to install the telecommunications lines needed for the new network. When those were in place, it took less than a week to deploy the Cisco routers, switches, and other telecommunications hardware preconfigured by Hi-Link. "Hi-Link made this implementation effortless by working efficiently at the best times for us," Bellnier says. "They handled all the details associated with the local telecom company, Internet providers, and project management."

After the secure, internally managed network was up and running, the following benefits soon became apparent:

- The new network eliminated MMCC's network congestion almost immediately.

- Network bandwidth, reliability, and security were significantly improved.

- The sophisticated network monitoring system greatly improved network management.

- Network downtime was reduced to nearly zero.

- The new network is saving MMCC a significant amount of money.

"The previous network had cost us just under $11,000 a month; the new high-bandwidth telecommunications lines we lease cost $4,400 per month," Bellnier explains. "We've calculated an annual savings of $77,000, which means we got our return on investment in our first six months."

Best of all, the network is transparent and easy to manage. "We can access all our Cisco routers. We can view the errors and logs. All our telecommunications lines are contracted directly with the local exchange carrier, which gives us a direct communications link to resolve troubles," Bellnier says.

Hi-Link's Gartner says of MMCC's network: "Every remote office is configured in exactly the same way, and we can easily duplicate it to bring up any new location. We can easily add extra bandwidth to meet additional demands." Thus, Hi-Link is helping MMCC add wireless capability to all of its warehouses, knowing that additional capacity can be provided if needed.

Gartner emphasizes that as it did for MMCC, a secure network foundation can improve a small company's operational efficiency, secure sensitive data, contain costs, and enhance employee connectivity and customer responsiveness. For example, companies with such network capabilities allow customers to track their orders securely in real time over the Web, empower customer service agents with detailed account information even before they answer the customer's phone call, and provide easy, inexpensive videoconferencing for remote workers, vendors, and customers.

Bellnier offers advice to other IT managers in small companies that may be considering building and managing their own network: "Do not limit company expansion by thinking you cannot support or afford a self-managed system with limited resources," he says.

He adds that MMCC's experience with Hi-Link shows just how quickly an SMB can "recoup the cost and implement a self-managed system with far superior performance and a lot fewer problems."

Source: Adapted from Eric J. Adams, "Creating a Foundation for Growth," *iQ Magazine*, Second Quarter 2006.

CASE STUDY QUESTIONS

1. What were the most important factors contributing to MMCC's success with its new, secure, self-managed network? Explain the reasons for your choices.

2. What are some of the business benefits and challenges of self-managed and externally managed networks?

3. Which type of network management would you advise small-to-medium business firms to use? Explain the reasons for your recommendation.

REAL WORLD ACTIVITIES

1. Use the Internet to discover more about the telecommunications products and services, and the current business performance and prospects, of Cisco Systems and Hi-Link and some of their many competitors in the telecom industry. Which telecom hardware and software company and IT consulting firm would you recommend to a small-to-medium business with which you are familiar? Explain your reasons to the class.

2. In telecommunications network installation and management, as in many other business situations, the choice between "do it yourself" and "let the experts handle it" is a crucial business decision for many companies. Break into small groups with your classmates to debate this choice for small-to-medium businesses. See if you can agree on several key criteria that should be considered in making this decision, and report your conclusions to the class.

REAL WORLD
CASE 4

Starbucks and Others:
The Future of Public Wi-Fi

Public Wi-Fi hot spots have been popular for about eight years. During that time, companies providing the service have been trying to figure out how to monetize it. The dominant model to date has been just to charge for it. Pay us $20 a month, and you can log in at any of our many locations. Recently, however, a kind of tipping point has been reached; now, instead of being rented for a fee, Wi-Fi will increasingly be given away to motivate customers to buy other goods and services. Now Wi-Fi is just like the free toaster that banks used to hand out for opening a new account.

Starbucks is leading a transition from Wi-Fi-for-money to Wi-Fi as a lure to get people to spend money on other things. It probably has to do with the strong competition Starbucks is facing for the morning breakfast crowd from the likes of McDonald's, which is also being more aggressive with Wi-Fi access.

The Starbucks offer may be a stroke of genius. Starbucks and AT&T will give you two hours of free Wi-Fi per day, but only if you use a Starbucks card. If you want more than two hours, you can pay $19.99 per month, which also entitles you to unlimited Wi-Fi offered by AT&T at some 70,000 hot spots in 89 countries. Starbucks not only trumps other sellers of sugar and caffeine by offering free Wi-Fi, but also pushes its lucrative Starbucks card and provides an upgrade path for people eager to hand over money in exchange for unlimited access.

Starbucks cards benefit Starbucks in three ways. First, people with Starbucks cards in their pockets are probably more likely to choose Starbucks when there are other nearby alternatives. Second, by getting millions of customers to pay in advance, Starbucks gets more cash upfront (rather than waiting until people actually get their coffee). Last and best is that cards get lost, stolen, or forgotten. When that happens, Starbucks gets to keep the money without supplying anything.

Like many indie cafes, Seattle's Bauhaus Books and Coffee has long relied on free Wi-Fi to help bring in customers. "In the evenings, the whole bar along the window will be lined with people using their computers," says Grace Heinze, a 13-year manager at Bauhaus, located between downtown Seattle and the trendy neighborhood of Capitol Hill. Bauhaus has thrived despite all of the Starbucks shops that have popped up around it: 15 within half a mile and 38 within one mile.

So is Heinze worried that the fiercely artsy cafe, named for the 1920s German art movement and replete with memorabilia, might lose customers to Starbucks now that it is dumping its high Wi-Fi rate in favor of two free hours of Wi-Fi a day to any customer? Not really.

"People come here because they like our atmosphere and because they like our coffee," Heinze said. "We're not feeling very uptight about this." Wi-Fi hot spots began to emerge around the beginning of the millennium. Propelled by the fast-growing popularity of laptops, Wi-Fi-enabled coffee shops quickly supplanted the older-style cybercafes, which relied on the expensive purchase and upkeep of PCs.

Still, until several years ago, many cafes were granting access to their Wi-Fi hot spots through codes given only to paying customers, according to Jack Kelley, president of Seattle regional chain Caffe Ladro. There was the fear "that if public Wi-Fi was free, you'd fill your place up with 'campers,'" Kelley said, referring to patrons who linger all day without buying anything. But that didn't happen after Ladro's 12 Seattle-area cafes switched to free Wi-Fi several years ago. Nowadays, "we don't even care if you sit in the parking lot and use it," Kelley said. Asked about the impact of Starbucks's move on his business, Kelley retorted, "Wi-Fi is free everywhere these days. Isn't Starbucks a little behind the times?"

As pressure mounts to make more Wi-Fi hot spots free, some operators are turning to Web advertising to offset costs or make money. Those ads are delivered during log-in or at the user's landing page. JiWire serves up ads to more than 8 million users per month on various Wi-Fi networks, including Boingo, at rates far higher than ones on typical Web pages. That kind of advertising "sounds gross" to Ladro's Kelley, though. "It's just like all of those ads in the movie theatre," he said. "I say, enough is enough."

"Many patrons of the smaller coffeehouses will continue to support their local shop due to loyalty, unique surroundings versus corporate giant, community support, convenience of location, etc.," he said. "Any customer losses may also be offset simply because there continues to be so much more demand for Wi-Fi access in general."

Bauhaus's Heinze seconds that. "We're close to two colleges, and we are in a neighborhood with a lot of apartment buildings," she said. Although Bauhaus competes in Starbucks's backyard, according to Heinze, Bauhaus has never "done anything reactive. And isn't that the whole point of being an indie coffeehouse, being your own self? If that happens to be similar to what Starbucks does, that's fine."

Like television, Wi-Fi is increasingly given away in exchange for ads. It's an unproven model; nobody is making huge profits on this approach yet. JiWire's "Ads for Access" program gives some users free Wi-Fi access at hot spots normally paid for by others in exchange for viewing ads over those connections. The company has recently (and wisely) started to target iPhone users. Wi-Fi is free at some airports. One of the largest is Denver International. In addition to advertising, the FreeFi Networks Wi-Fi access is subsidized by Disney-ABC television show rentals, which users can download over the connection. A company called HypeWifi funds its free Wi-Fi access through advertising, but also by doing "market research" for advertisers for a fee. Users logging onto a HypeWifi access point may earn their access by answering a question or two, which is aggregated and presented to the sponsor, along with demographic information about the users.

There's no industry where all players universally provide free Wi-Fi as a matter of course; for example, some hotels offer free Wi-Fi, and some don't. Some airports have it, and some don't. It's also interesting to note that Wi-Fi works as an incentive even when it's not free.

After a few fits and starts, Wi-Fi in the transportation industry is suddenly taking off. A solid majority of major airlines in both the United States and Europe either have or are planning to offer in-flight Wi-Fi. Most will charge for the service. Within two years, all major carriers will offer in-flight Wi-Fi.

Airline Wi-Fi, in turn, has triggered a rush to install Wi-Fi service in trains across Europe. These rail service companies see the airlines as a competitor for the lucrative business traveler market. Commuter trains and even taxis are getting Wi-Fi; in fact, wherever you find a concentration of businesspeople with expense accounts and time to kill, expect to find Wi-Fi there. Everyone wants these customers because they spend money on other things.

Pricing runs the gamut from no-strings-attached free access, to conspicuously overpriced, to creative or selective pricing à la Starbucks or Boingo. Yet the trend is clear: Wi-Fi is transitioning gradually to always free everywhere. There's just no downside to these trends. Everybody loves Wi-Fi—the freer the better.

Some, however, do not think Wi-Fi has a future. "As mobile broadband takes off, Wi-Fi hot spots will become as irrelevant as telephone booths," says Ericsson Telephone Co. chief marketing officer Johan Bergendahl. "Mobile broadband is growing faster than mobile or fixed telephony ever did." In Austria, they are saying that mobile broadband will pass fixed broadband this year. "It's already growing faster, and in Sweden, the most popular phone is a USB modem," says Bergendahl.

As more people start to use mobile broadband, hot spots will no longer be needed. Also, support for high-speed packet access (HSPA), favored by Ericsson, is being built into more and more laptops. Ericsson recently signed a deal to put HSPA technology in some Lenovo notebooks. "In a few years, [HSPA] will be as common as Wi-Fi is today," says Bergendahl.

Challenges still remain. Coverage, availability, and price—especially when someone is roaming on other networks—are all key factors for success. "Industry will have to solve the international roaming issue," Bergendahl says. "Carriers need to work together. It can be as simple as paying 10 per day when you are abroad." Not knowing how high the bill will be after a business trip is not acceptable for professional users. Coverage will also have to improve.

Source: Adapted from Eric Lai, "Indie Coffeehouses Tell Starbucks: Bring on Your Free Wi-Fi," *Computerworld*, February 14, 2008; Mikael Ricknäs, "Ericsson Predicts Demise of Wi-Fi Hotspots," *Computerworld*, March 10, 2008; and Mike Elgan, "Wi-Fi Wants to Be Free," *Computerworld*, February 15, 2008.

CASE STUDY QUESTIONS

1. Do you agree with the plans by Starbucks to offer time-limited free Wi-Fi to customers? Do you think free Wi-Fi would be enough to instill that kind of loyalty? Based on the experiences of the other coffee houses reported above, do you think free access was a critical factor in developing a loyal customer base?

2. Part of the reason for Starbucks's move had to do with increased competition from chains like McDonald's for the morning breakfast crowd. Do you think that free wireless access by such a competitor would have moved a significant portion of Starbucks's customers away? Why or why not?

3. The case notes some companies that offer free Wi-Fi in exchange for viewing advertisements or answering questions for market research studies. Would you be willing to do so in order to get free wireless access, say, at an airport? Would your answer change if you were using a corporate laptop versus your own, because of security concerns?

REAL WORLD ACTIVITIES

1. Johan Bergendahl of Ericsson believes the demise of Wi-Fi is rather imminent and that mobile broadband will replace hot spots for wireless access. Search the Internet for current commercial offerings of mobile broadband and compare their features with Wi-Fi hotspots. Which one would you choose? Which factors would affect your decision?

2. Go online and look at different companies in one of the industries mentioned in the case, noting which companies offer free wireless access and which ones do not. Break into small groups and brainstorm potential explanations for these differences. Do you see any patterns in the type of companies that charge for access versus those that offer it for free?

MODULE III

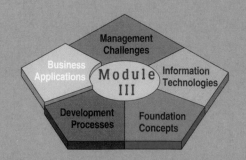

BUSINESS APPLICATIONS

How do internet technologies and other forms of IT support business processes, e-commerce, and business decision making? The four chapters of this module show you how such business applications of information systems are accomplished in today's networked enterprises.

- **Chapter 7: e-Business Systems** describes how information systems integrate and support enterprisewide business processes, as well as the business functions of marketing, manufacturing, human resource management, accounting, and finance.

- **Chapter 8: Enterprise Business Systems** outlines the goals and components of customer relationship management, enterprise resource planning, and supply chain management, and discusses the benefits and challenges of these major enterprise applications.

- **Chapter 9: e-Commerce Systems** introduces the basic process components of e-commerce systems, and discusses important trends, applications, and issues in e-commerce.

- **Chapter 10: Supporting Decision Making** shows how management information systems, decision support systems, executive information systems, expert systems, and artificial intelligence technologies can be applied to decision-making situations faced by business managers and professionals in today's dynamic business environment.

CHAPTER 7

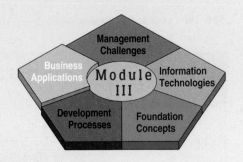

e-BUSINESS SYSTEMS

Chapter Highlights

Learning Objectives

After reading and studying this chapter, you should be able to:

1. Identify the following cross-functional enterprise systems, and give examples of how they can provide significant business value to a company:

    a. Enterprise application integration

    b. Transaction processing systems

    c. Enterprise collaboration systems

2. Give examples of how Internet and other information technologies support business processes within the business functions of accounting, finance, human resource management, marketing, and production and operations management.

SECTION I   e-Business Systems

Introduction

Contrary to popular opinion, e-business is not synonymous with e-commerce. E-business is much broader in scope, going beyond transactions to signify use of the Internet, in combination with other technologies and forms of electronic communication, to enable any type of business activity.

This chapter introduces the fast-changing world of business applications of information technology, which increasingly consists of what is popularly called *e-business* applications. Remember that e-business, a term originally coined by Lou Gerstner, CEO of IBM, is the use of the Internet and other networks and information technologies to support e-commerce, enterprise communications and collaboration, and Web-enabled business processes, both within a networked enterprise and with its customers and business partners. E-business includes *e-commerce*, which involves the buying and selling and marketing and servicing of products, services, and information over the Internet and other networks. We will cover e-commerce in Chapter 9.

In this chapter, we will explore some of the major concepts and applications of e-business. We will begin by focusing in Section I on examples of cross-functional enterprise systems, which serve as a foundation for more in-depth coverage of enterprisewide business systems such as customer relationship management, enterprise resource planning, and supply chain management in Chapter 8. In Section II, we will explore examples of information systems that support essential processes in the functional areas of business.

Read the Real World Case on the next page. We can learn a lot from this case about the challenging work of bringing enterprise solutions into the organization. See Figure 7.1.

Cross-Functional Enterprise Applications

Many companies today are using information technology to develop integrated cross-functional enterprise systems that cross the boundaries of traditional business functions in order to reengineer and improve vital business processes all across the enterprise. These organizations view cross-functional enterprise systems as a strategic way to use IT to share information resources and improve the efficiency and effectiveness of business processes, and develop strategic relationships with customers, suppliers, and business partners. See Figure 7.2, which illustrates a cross-functional business process.

Companies first moved from functional mainframe-based *legacy systems* to integrated cross-functional *client/server* applications. This typically involved installing *enterprise resource planning*, *supply chain management*, or *customer relationship management* software from SAP America, PeopleSoft, Oracle, and others. Instead of focusing on the information processing requirements of business functions, such enterprise software focuses on supporting integrated clusters of business processes involved in the operations of a business.

Now, as we see continually in the Real World Cases in this text, business firms are using Internet technologies to help them reengineer and integrate the flow of information among their internal business processes and their customers and suppliers. Companies all across the globe are using the World Wide Web and their intranets and extranets as a technology platform for their cross-functional and interenterprise information systems.

Enterprise Application Architecture

Figure 7.3 presents an enterprise application architecture, which illustrates the interrelationships of the major cross-functional enterprise applications that many companies have or are installing today. This architecture does not provide a detailed or exhaustive application blueprint, but it provides a conceptual framework to help you

CASE 1

e-Discovery Becomes an Enterprise Solution

When Jonathan Chow, chief information security officer at NBC Universal, found his department's services in increasing demand, that wasn't necessarily a good thing. He says demand for e-discovery services was increasing 30 percent to 50 percent annually in the early and middle parts of the past decade, and he was seeing a dramatic rise in the hours spent supporting e-discovery as his department collected and culled through some of the electronically stored data needed by the company's legal staff.

The information security department, part of corporate IT, owns the e-discovery function and uses it not just for litigation support, Chow explains, but also for merger and acquisition activities and internal investigations generated by human resources (HR) or corporate security, for example. "We used to handle those occasional queries on an ad hoc basis, but as the number of e-discovery requests grew, this became a much larger and much more time-/resource-intensive process to manage," he said via e-mail. "It was obvious that we could more affordably conduct our e-discovery in-house, assuming we could find the best solutions to support our process." So Chow moved e-discovery in-house in 2007.

Discovery is the part of the pretrial process in a lawsuit in which both sides request information, data, and documents

FIGURE 7.1

Enterprise architects create unity out of siloed thinking and disparate applications.

Source: © Corbis/Photolibrary.

from each other as each tries to find, or discover, facts pertinent to the case. Electronic discovery is the part of this long-standing legal process that refers to any information stored electronically. Several factors are driving this trend of bringing the e-discovery function in-house, including an anticipated rise in lawsuits, investigations, and inquiries, as well as the high costs of outsourcing the task. Whatever the drivers, the shift means that IT departments are now implementing and maintaining the systems, and in some cases administering the searches themselves.

"A decade ago, e-discovery was more the exception rather than the norm, so companies did not have to go through it regularly. They weren't familiar with it, they didn't have the staffing, nor did they want the staffing to support it, because it wasn't something that happened frequently," explains Brian Babineau, a senior consulting analyst at ESG. "Now it's become mainstream. Now every litigation or regulatory action is asking for some electronically stored information, and because of that frequency and because it's becoming more of a standard business process, it now makes sense to evaluate whether you should staff it and build some competencies internally," he says.

This shift stems in part from changes to the Federal Rules of Civil Procedure, established in the 1930s to govern civil lawsuits, says Gartner analyst John Bace. The rules were last updated in 2006 to more broadly include electronic records in discovery, the process by which the parties engaged in lawsuits produce information demanded by others involved in the legal action. For his part, NBC Universal's Chow says an analysis of expenses showed that his company, which had used a combination of internal tools and outside help, could be more cost-effective by going in-house. NBC Universal uses Clearwell's e-Discovery Platform to collect the data and perform the initial culling, which allows it to handle 100 percent of the early phases of e-discovery requirements before turning over documents for lawyers to review, Chow says. "Ultimately for my team, the decision to take e-discovery in-house was about efficiency," he adds.

Michael Royer, an IT director at a global entertainment company he declined to name, remembers the early days of electronic discovery, about 10 years ago, when his company's lawyers would "come down to IT asking to find an e-mail." "The standard IT response was, 'We can't do that,'" he says. The systems back then weren't designed to execute searches, he says, nor were policies established to cover such requests. "Every single request became a new dialog with HR or legal or wherever the request was coming from—when could it be done by, what was needed—because everything was a one-off," Royer says.

As a result, Royer's employer often ended up hiring outside vendors to search through electronic records for the required data—an expensive option. By 2005, Royer says, IT realized that it had to take over this service if for no other reason than to reduce what he calls the "ridiculous cost" of outsourcing the e-discovery function.

"We had to find a way to provide a better IT service to reduce the amount of data to hand over, to see how much more of that review cycle we could pull [in-house] with our legal team before they send it out to outside counsel," he says. "It was an IT initiative to say, 'We've got to do this better to cut this cost.'"

Royer says IT's initial implementation focused on giving the company's in-house legal team the technology to search and hold e-mails. A hold keeps the data from being moved into long-term storage. Now, with that done, IT plans to add features so the legal department can perform e-discovery searches and holds on additional data sources and repositories, such as file servers and backup tapes.

Royer could not disclose actual figures, but he says that bringing some of the e-discovery functions in-house immediately reduced the amount of material the company had to send to outside counsel for reviewing. In fact, he says it cut the amount "by well over 75 percent on the next four litigation matters that arose post-implementation. These matters arose within the first six months of go-live, and the cost savings put us into a 300 percent ROI within that same time frame."

The move to bring e-discovery in-house also corresponds with a broadening in how companies define e-discovery, says Jonathan Gossels, president and CEO of SystemExperts Corp., a security consulting firm in Sudbury, Massachusetts. Companies now realize that they need the ability to search electronic records not just in response to legal action, he says. They also need it for regulatory requests and inquiries and for their own internal investigations, such as potential security breaches or personnel violations.

"That's why it makes perfect sense to bring it in-house. It's the recognition that they need it to run their day-to-day business," Gossels says, noting that customers are increasingly defining the function as "discovery and investigations."

In fact, many companies still need to get a good handle on information governance before they can determine how

much of the e-discovery capability they should have under their own purview, adds Gossels. Governance refers to the process, procedures and policies that are in place that dictate what information the company stores, where and how it is stored, and when it should be deleted. Gartner analyst Debra Logan says probably fewer than 10 percent of companies do a really good job at information governance—and even those companies aren't as comprehensive as they could be.

Case in point: Microsoft. Joe Banks, litigation program manager at Microsoft, says the company started to look more closely at litigation costs over the past two years and found that "discovery just leaps off the page. It was exorbitantly expensive, and the trend was just going up. So we wanted to figure out ways to cut costs."

As a result, Banks says, Microsoft invested in e-discovery software. (Banks declines to name the product for publication but says it's not a tool from Microsoft.) He says that although he hasn't seen a product that provides an end-to-end solution, technology improvements in recent years have made bringing e-discovery in-house even more advantageous for companies such as his.

Banks says Microsoft has started to perform pieces of the e-discovery process internally. The company does its own data minimization, which culls through the raw data using specific search parameters; that reduced volume of data can then be handed over to attorneys for review. Banks says he expects Microsoft to increase the percentage of the culling it does internally and, as the technology improves, possibly bringing some of the review process in-house, too.

Advances in technology have helped make it more cost-effective to perform many searches in-house, Banks says, for Microsoft and for just about everyone else. "And when you combine that with the economic factors of the past two years, where people were forced to find ways to cut costs, it was just a natural inflection point for corporations to re-examine the old model."

Source: Adapted from Mary K. Pratt, "e-Discovery Moves In-House," *Computerworld*, Fairfax Media Business Group, October 1, 2010.

CASE STUDY QUESTIONS

1. What does the move from outsourced e-discovery to an enterprise solution mean to the organization? What qualifications or experiences would you think an IT professional should have to create enterprise solutions? Support your answer with examples from the case.

2. Consider the different companies mentioned in the case and their experiences with enterprise architecture. Does this approach seem to work better in certain types of companies or industries than in others? Why or why not?

3. What is the value derived from companies that adopt enterprise-wide solutions? Can you see any disadvantages? Discuss.

REAL WORLD ACTIVITIES

1. e-Discovery is a relatively new approach to litigation. Go online and research the various ways in which it is used. Prepare a report to summarize your work.

2. Have you considered a career as an IT professional? What bundle of courses would you put together to design a major or a track specializing in enterprise solutions? Break into small groups with your classmates to outline the major areas that should be covered.

FIGURE 7.2   The new product development process in a manufacturing company. This is an example of a business process that must be supported by cross-functional systems that cross the boundaries of several business functions.

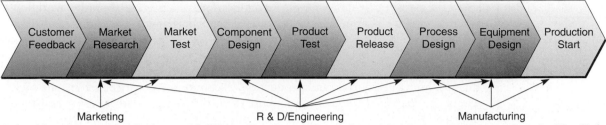

Source: Adapted from Mohan Sawhney and Jeff Zabin, *Seven Steps to Nirvana: Strategic Insights into e-Business Transformation* (New York: McGraw-Hill, 2001), p. 175.

visualize the basic components, processes, and interfaces of these major e-business applications, and their interrelationships to each other. This application architecture also spotlights the roles these business systems play in supporting the customers, suppliers, partners, and employees of a business.

Notice that instead of concentrating on traditional business functions or supporting only the internal business processes of a company, enterprise applications focus on accomplishing fundamental business processes in concert with a company's customer, supplier, partner, and employee stakeholders. Thus, enterprise resource planning (ERP) concentrates on the efficiency of a firm's internal production, distribution, and financial processes. Customer relationship management (CRM) focuses on acquiring and retaining profitable customers via marketing, sales, and service processes. Partner relationship management (PRM) aims to acquire and retain partners who can enhance the sale and distribution of a firm's products and services. Supply chain management (SCM) focuses on developing the most efficient and effective sourcing and procurement processes with suppliers for the products and services that a business needs. Knowledge management (KM) applications provide a firm's employees with tools that support group collaboration and decision support.

We will discuss CRM, ERP, and SCM applications in detail in Chapter 8 and cover KM applications in Chapter 10. Now let's look at a real-world example of some of the challenges involved in rolling out global, cross-functional systems.

FIGURE 7.3

This enterprise application architecture presents an overview of the major cross-functional enterprise applications and their interrelationships.

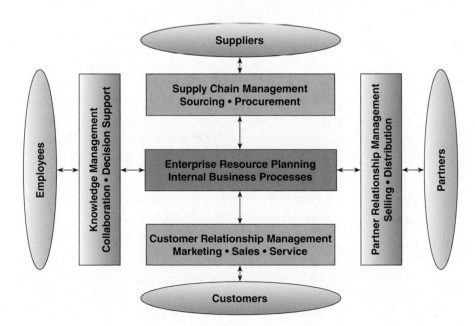

Ogilvy & Mather and MetLife: The Interpersonal Challenges of Implementing Global Applications

Atefeh Riazi's quarter-million frequent-flier miles are testament to the fact that it's not such a small planet after all. As CIO at Ogilvy & Mather Worldwide, Riazi has spent the past years rolling out global applications, such as collaborative workflow systems, creative asset management, knowledge management, messaging, and security for the New York City–based marketing giant. Most recently, Riazi has been trying to convince the Asian, European, and Latin American offices to replace their legacy systems with North America's SAP enterprise resource planning system for finance, human resources, and production. A common enterprise system, she says, would provide Ogilvy's 400 offices in more than 100 countries with access to real-time information so they can make quick decisions, better respond to market changes, and cut costs.

The fact is that globalization adds new dynamics to the workplace, and CIOs who stick to the true-blue American business formula will fail. They must abandon the idea of force-fitting their visions into worldwide offices and move toward a global infrastructure built collaboratively by staff from around the world.

Take the company that rolls out a global system with high-bandwidth requirements. That system might not be feasible for IT directors in the Middle East or parts of Asia, where the cost of bandwidth is higher than in New York. Is the standardized system multilingual? Can it convert different currencies? Can it accommodate complex national tax laws?

For global projects, working virtually is critical, but it's also one of the biggest challenges. "You're dealing with different languages, different cultures, different time zones," says George Savarese, vice president of operations and technology services at New York City–based MetLife. His 6 p.m. Monday meeting, for instance, falls at 8 a.m. in South Korea and 9 p.m. in Brazil. Savarese adds, however, that telephone and e-mail alone won't cut it. "You really have to be there, in their space, understanding where it's at," he says, adding that he spends about half of each month abroad.

"Globalization challenges your people skills every day," says Ogilvy's Riazi. For example, workers in the United Kingdom often rely heavily on qualitative research; they take their time in making decisions, as opposed to Americans, who tend to be action-oriented. So, in a recent attempt to get offices in the United States and the United Kingdom to collaborate on a common system rollout, Riazi hit a wall of resistance because she didn't spend enough time going over analytical arguments with the people in the U.K. office.

Having international teams run global projects goes a long way toward mending fences. Ogilvy, for instance, manages a financial reporting project out of Ireland. "The IT director there has a European point of view, so we're not going to be blindsided by something that isn't a workable solution," she says.

"We have let control go," she says of Ogilvy's New York headquarters. "A lot of global companies cannot let go of that control. They're holding so tight. It's destructive."

Source: Adapted from Melissa Solomon, "Collaboratively Building a Global Infrastructure," *CIO Magazine*, June 1, 2003.

Enterprise Application Integration

How does a business interconnect some of the cross-functional enterprise systems? Enterprise application integration (EAI) software is being used by many companies to connect their major e-business applications. See Figure 7.4. EAI software enables users to model the business processes involved in the interactions that should occur between business applications. EAI also provides *middleware* that performs data conversion and coordination, application communication and messaging services, and access to the application interfaces involved. Recall from Chapter 6 that middleware is any software that serves to glue together or mediate between two separate pieces of

FIGURE 7.4

Enterprise application integration software interconnects front-office and back-office applications.

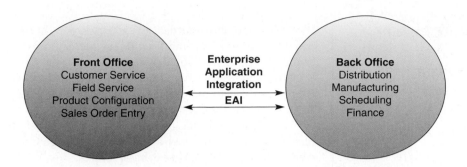

Front Office
Customer Service
Field Service
Product Configuration
Sales Order Entry

Enterprise Application Integration
EAI

Back Office
Distribution
Manufacturing
Scheduling
Finance

software. Thus, EAI software can integrate a variety of enterprise application clusters by letting them exchange data according to rules derived from the business process models developed by users. For example, a typical rule might be:

When an order is complete, have the order application tell the accounting system to send a bill and alert shipping to send out the product.

Thus, as Figure 7.4 illustrates, EAI software can integrate the front-office and back-office applications of a business so they work together in a seamless, integrated way. This is a vital capability that provides real business value to a business enterprise that must respond quickly and effectively to business events and customer demands. For example, the integration of enterprise application clusters has been shown to dramatically improve customer call center responsiveness and effectiveness. That's because EAI integrates access to all of the customer and product data that customer representatives need to quickly serve customers. EAI also streamlines sales order processing so products and services can be delivered faster. Thus, EAI improves customer and supplier experience with the business because of its responsiveness. See Figure 7.5.

FIGURE 7.5

An example of a new customer order process showing how EAI middleware connects several business information systems within a company.

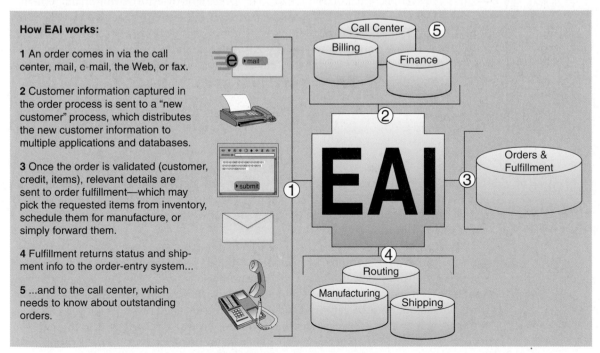

How EAI works:

1 An order comes in via the call center, mail, e-mail, the Web, or fax.

2 Customer information captured in the order process is sent to a "new customer" process, which distributes the new customer information to multiple applications and databases.

3 Once the order is validated (customer, credit, items), relevant details are sent to order fulfillment—which may pick the requested items from inventory, schedule them for manufacture, or simply forward them.

4 Fulfillment returns status and shipment info to the order-entry system...

5 ...and to the call center, which needs to know about outstanding orders.

Coty, Unilever, and iWay: Dealing with Integration Challenges

It's one thing to integrate data across applications in an IT infrastructure. The methods and practices are tried and true. But implementing data integration across a service-oriented architecture poses new challenges.

Coty, the fragrance and personal-care products company, found that the iWay approach was just what it needed to integrate Unilever's cosmetics business, which it acquired in late 2005, in just six months.

Failure to meet that goal would delay the benefits to customers of dealing with one company and product line, and would force Coty to maintain two sales forces, supply chains, and software infrastructures.

Soon after the acquisition, CIO David Berry heard complaints from big customers such as Federated Department Stores that its buyers had to talk to two sales reps after the acquisition or deal with three systems to push one order through.

Orders of Unilever's Chloe or Calvin Klein fragrances had to be sent through a JD Edwards system in Lille, France. Coty's hot-selling Celine Dion or Jennifer Lopez fragrances had to be ordered through its homegrown warehouse management system in Kassel, Germany. Orders for other products went through Oracle Cash-to-Order systems in Coty's North Carolina distribution center.

But connecting JD Edwards to Oracle applications or Oracle apps to SAP is what iWay connectors and adapters do. Berry realized he needed to identify the processes that led to the customer getting, for example, two invoices from Coty, and force them into a single process.

They got iWay's Service Manager to understand the differences between Coty's order entry systems and perform the data transformations between them once a business analyst drew process flow lines on Service Manager's graphical map of the JD Edwards and SAP systems. The Coty order entry system worked in tandem with the Unilever order entry system until their results could be combined to yield one invoice.

The implementation had its share of rough spots. Coty discovered at one point that a day's orders, sent into the iWay system, never emerged at the distribution center. The orders had been improperly formatted so they couldn't be translated into the right destination format, but iWay neglected to inform anyone of the hang-up.

"It was like looking for a needle in a haystack. We needed to improve the visibility into the system," says Gary Gallant, vice president of information management for the Americas at Coty. He found a way to get the system to send a message to administrators when orders were hung up in a "retry" queue.

Berry used this approach to identify customer-facing services, isolate them, and use iWay to translate between them. The result was what appeared to customers to be a fully integrated Unilever/Coty by the six-month deadline.

Source: Adapted from Charles Babcock, "Two Ways to Deal with SOA's Data Integration Challenge," *InformationWeek*, July 9, 2007.

Transaction Processing Systems

Transaction processing systems (TPS) are cross-functional information systems that process data resulting from the occurrence of business transactions. We introduced transaction processing systems in Chapter 1 as one of the major application categories of information systems in business.

Transactions are events that occur as part of doing business, such as sales, purchases, deposits, withdrawals, refunds, and payments. Think, for example, of the data generated whenever a business sells something to a customer on credit, whether in a retail store or at an e-commerce site on the Web. Data about the customer, product, salesperson, store, and so on, must be captured and processed. This need prompts additional transactions, such as credit checks, customer billing, inventory changes, and increases in accounts receivable balances, which generate even more data. Thus, transaction processing activities are needed to capture and process such data, or the operations of a business would grind to a halt. Therefore, transaction processing systems play a vital role in supporting the operations of most companies today.

Online transaction processing systems play a strategic role in Web-enabled businesses. Many firms are using the Internet and other networks that tie them electronically to their customers or suppliers for online transaction processing (OLTP). Such *real-time* systems, which capture and process transactions immediately, can help firms provide superior service to customers and other trading partners. This capability adds value to their products and services, and thus gives them an important way to differentiate themselves from their competitors.

Syntellect's Online Transaction Processing	For example, Figure 7.6 illustrates an online transaction processing system for cable pay-per-view systems developed by Syntellect Interactive Services. Cable TV viewers can select pay-per-view events offered by their cable companies using the phone or the World Wide Web. The pay-per-view order is captured by Syntellect's interactive voice response system or Web server, then transported to Syntellect database application servers. There the order is processed, customer and sales databases are updated, and the approved order is relayed back to the cable company's video server, which transmits the video of the pay-per-view event to the customer. Thus, Syntellect teams with more than 700 cable companies to offer a very popular and very profitable service.

FIGURE 7.6 The Syntellect pay-per-view online transaction processing system.

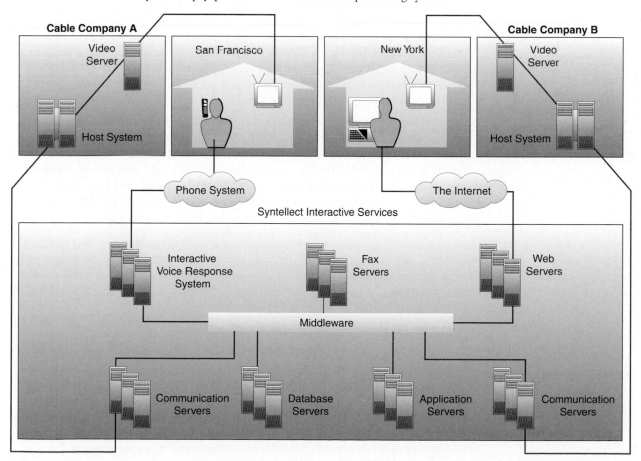

FIGURE 7.7

The transaction processing cycle. Note that transaction processing systems use a five-stage cycle of data entry, transaction processing, database maintenance, document and report generation, and inquiry processing activities

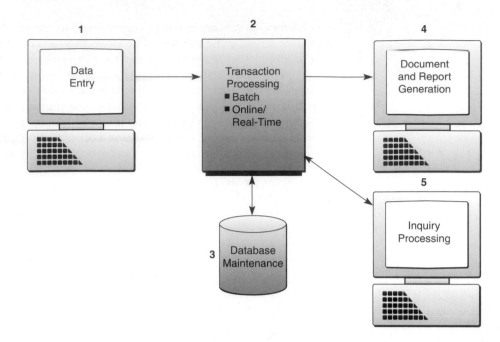

The Transaction Processing Cycle

Transaction processing systems, such as Syntellect's, capture and process data describing business transactions, update organizational databases, and produce a variety of information products. You should understand this as a transaction processing cycle of several basic activities, as illustrated in Figure 7.7.

- **Data Entry.** The first step of the transaction processing cycle is the capture of business data. For example, transaction data may be collected by point-of-sale terminals using optical scanning of bar codes and credit card readers at a retail store or other business. Transaction data can also be captured at an e-commerce Web site on the Internet. The proper recording and editing of data so they are quickly and correctly captured for processing is one of the major design challenges of information systems discussed in Chapter 12.

- **Transaction Processing.** Transaction processing systems process data in two basic ways: (1) batch processing, where transaction data are accumulated over a period of time and processed periodically, and (2) real-time processing (also called online processing), where data are processed immediately after a transaction occurs. All online transaction processing systems incorporate real-time processing capabilities. Many online systems also depend on the capabilities of *fault tolerant* computer systems that can continue to operate even if parts of the system fail. We will discuss this fault tolerant concept in Chapter 13.

- **Database Maintenance.** An organization's databases must be updated by its transaction processing systems so that they are always correct and up-to-date. Therefore, transaction processing systems serve to assist in maintaining the corporate databases of an organization to reflect changes resulting from day-to-day business transactions. For example, credit sales made to customers will cause customer account balances to be increased and the amount of inventory on hand to be decreased. Database maintenance ensures that these and other changes are reflected in the data records stored in the company's databases.

- **Document and Report Generation.** Transaction processing systems produce a variety of documents and reports. Examples of transaction documents include purchase orders, paychecks, sales receipts, invoices, and customer statements. Transaction reports might take the form of a transaction listing such as a payroll register, or edit reports that describe errors detected during processing.

- **Inquiry Processing.** Many transaction processing systems allow you to use the Internet, intranets, extranets, and Web browsers or database management query languages to make inquiries and receive responses concerning the results of transaction processing activity. Typically, responses are displayed in a variety of prespecified formats or screens. For example, you might check on the status of a sales order, the balance in an account, or the amount of stock in inventory and receive immediate responses at your PC.

Enterprise Collaboration Systems

Really difficult business problems always have many aspects. Often a major decision depends on an impromptu search for one or two key pieces of auxiliary information and a quick ad hoc analysis of several possible scenarios. You need software tools that easily combine and recombine data from many sources. You need Internet access for all kinds of research. Widely scattered people need to be able to collaborate and work the data in different ways.

Enterprise collaboration systems (ECS) are cross-functional information systems that enhance communication, coordination, and collaboration among the members of business teams and workgroups. Information technology, especially Internet technologies, provides tools to help us collaborate—to communicate ideas, share resources, and coordinate our cooperative work efforts as members of the many formal and informal process and project teams and workgroups that make up many of today's organizations. Thus, the goal of enterprise collaboration systems is to enable us to work together more easily and effectively by helping us to:

- **Communicate:** Share information with each other.
- **Coordinate:** Organize our individual work efforts and use of resources.
- **Collaborate:** Work together cooperatively on joint projects and assignments.

For example, engineers, business specialists, and external consultants may form a virtual team for a project. The team may rely on intranets and extranets to collaborate via e-mail, videoconferencing, discussion forums, and a multimedia database of work-in-progress information at a project Web site. The enterprise collaboration system may use PC workstations networked to a variety of servers on which project, corporate, and other databases are stored. In addition, network servers may provide a variety of software resources, such as Web browsers, groupware, and application packages, to assist the team's collaboration until the project is completed.

Tools for Enterprise Collaboration

The capabilities and potential of the Internet, as well as intranets and extranets, are driving the demand for better enterprise collaboration tools in business. However, Internet technologies like Web browsers and servers, hypermedia documents and databases, and intranets and extranets provide the hardware, software, data, and network platforms for many of the groupware tools for enterprise collaboration that business users want. Figure 7.8 provides an overview of some of the software tools for electronic communication, electronic conferencing, and collaborative work management.

Electronic communication tools include e-mail, voice mail, faxing, Web publishing, bulletin board systems, paging, and Internet phone systems. These tools enable you to send electronically messages, documents, and files in data, text, voice, or multimedia over computer networks. This helps you share everything from voice and text messages to copies of project documents and data files with your team members, wherever they may be. The ease and efficiency of such communications are major contributors to the collaboration process.

Electronic conferencing tools help people communicate and collaborate as they work together. A variety of conferencing methods enable the members of teams and workgroups at different locations to exchange ideas interactively at the same time, or at different times at their convenience. These include data and voice conferencing,

FIGURE 7.8

Electronic communications, conferencing, and collaborative work software tools enhance enterprise collaboration.

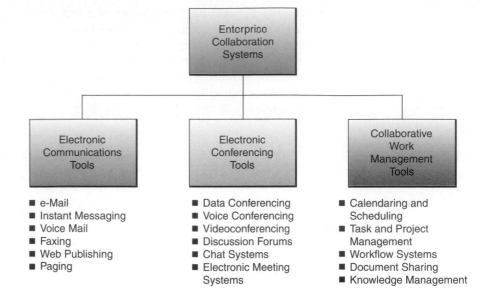

videoconferencing, chat systems, and discussion forums. Electronic conferencing options also include *electronic meeting systems* and other *group support systems* where team members can meet at the same time and place in a *decision room* setting, or use the Internet to work collaboratively anywhere in the world. See Figure 7.9.

FIGURE 7.9

QuickPlace by Lotus Development helps virtual workgroups set up Web-based work spaces for collaborative work assignments.

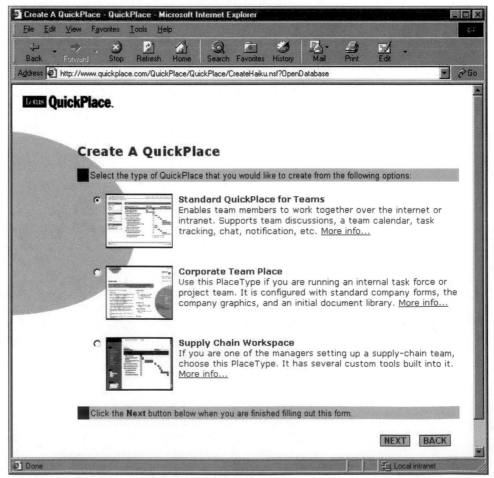

Source: Courtesy of International Business Machines Corporation.

Collaborative work management tools help people accomplish or manage group work activities. This category of software includes calendaring and scheduling tools, task and project management, workflow systems, and knowledge management tools. Other tools for joint work, such as joint document creation, editing, and revision, are found in the software suites discussed in Chapter 4.

Exploring Virtual Worlds as Collaboration Tools	For emergency responders working along Interstate 95, accidents aren't a game; they're a way of life (and death). So it seemed odd to a group of firefighters, cops, and medics when researchers from the University of Maryland suggested that they use a virtual world to collaborate on training for rollovers, multicar pileups, and life-threatening injuries.

The phrase *virtual world* is often associated with Second Life, the much-hyped 3-D environment hosted by Linden Lab that allows users to talk to friends, sell T-shirts, fly around on carpets, and even build amusement parks—in other words, to play. "It wasn't until we started to do elaborate demos that the first responders started to realize the true potential," says Michael Pack, director of research with the University of Maryland's Center for Advanced Transportation Technology, who has since begun rolling out a virtual world pilot project that could accommodate training for hundreds of emergency workers.

Industry analysts and developers of virtual worlds believe that by immersing users in an interactive environment that allows for social interactions, virtual worlds have the potential to succeed where other collaborative technologies, like teleconferencing, have failed. Phone-based meetings begin and end abruptly, at the mercy of the person or service administering it. In a virtual world, conversations between employees can continue within the virtual space—just as they do in company hallways after a meeting ends.

However, businesses must overcome many technical and cultural obstacles before they adopt virtual worlds on a major scale. Perhaps even more important than the technical challenges, companies must tackle the issue of workers' online identities. People's 3-D representations, known as avatars, must be constructed in such a way that allows users of virtual worlds to have faith that they're talking to the right colleague. Security challenges abound; most companies using virtual worlds today do so on a public or externally hosted platform with limited options to protect corporate data.

Pack says training in a virtual world presents a desirable alternative to real-life exercises, which can be pricey and inefficient. "You'd go out in a field and flip a car over and have people act as victims," he says. Trainers couldn't introduce many variables (such as mounting traffic). "It's supposed to be as human as possible, so anything goes," he says. "We've put together lots of scenarios, from fender benders to 20-car pileups. We put [the participants] in dangerous situations to see how they will respond." In virtual worlds, Pack and his team can program multiple scenarios into the software. For example, if a first responder gets out of his car and fails to put on a reflective jacket, the system might respond with a car hitting that person's avatar.

"You want people to be so comfortable in the virtual world that they're not concentrating on how to use them," Pack says. "They can't be worried about how to turn left or talk to someone. They need to be worried about how to do their jobs, just like they would in the real world."

Source: Adapted from C. G. Lynch, "Companies Explore Virtual Worlds as Collaboration Tools," *CIO Magazine*, February 6, 2008. |

SECTION II Functional Business Systems

Introduction

Business managers are moving from a tradition where they could avoid, delegate, or ignore decisions about IT to one where they cannot create a marketing, product, international, organization, or financial plan that does not involve such decisions.

There are as many ways to use information technology in business as there are business activities to be performed, business problems to be solved, and business opportunities to be pursued. As a business professional, you should have a basic understanding and appreciation of the major ways information systems are used to support each of the functions of business that must be accomplished in any company that wants to succeed. Thus, in this section, we will discuss functional business systems, that is, a variety of types of information systems (transaction processing, management information, decision support, and so on) that support the business functions of accounting, finance, marketing, operations management, and human resource management.

Read the Real World Case on the next page. We can learn a lot about the many IT issues involved in unified financial reporting from this case. See Figure 7.10.

IT in Business

As a business professional, it is also important that you have a specific understanding of how information systems affect a particular business function (e.g., marketing) or a particular industry (e.g., banking) that is directly related to your career objectives. For example, someone whose career objective is a marketing position in banking should have a basic understanding of how information systems are used in banking and how they support the marketing activities of banks and other firms.

Figure 7.11 illustrates how information systems can be grouped into business function categories. Thus, information systems in this section will be analyzed according to the business function they support by looking at a few key examples in each functional area. This should give you an appreciation of the variety of functional business systems that both small and large business firms may use.

Marketing Systems

The business function of marketing is concerned with the planning, promotion, and sale of existing products in existing markets, and the development of new products and new markets to better attract and serve present and potential customers. Thus, marketing performs an essential function in the operation of a business enterprise. Business firms have increasingly turned to information technology to help them perform vital marketing functions in the face of the rapid changes of today's environment.

Figure 7.12 illustrates how marketing information systems provide information technologies that support major components of the marketing function. For example, Internet/intranet Web sites and services make an *interactive marketing* process possible where customers can become partners in creating, marketing, purchasing, and improving products and services. *Sales force automation* systems use mobile computing and Internet technologies to automate many information processing activities for sales support and management. Other marketing information systems assist marketing managers in product planning, pricing, and other product management decisions; advertising, sales promotion, and targeted marketing strategies; and market research and forecasting. Finally, enterprisewide systems like customer relationship management (discussed in Chapter 8) link to the portfolio of marketing information systems to provide and obtain data essential to the marketing function. Let's take a closer look at three of these marketing applications.

Interactive Marketing

The term interactive marketing has been coined to describe a customer-focused marketing process that is based on using the Internet, intranets, and extranets to establish two-way transactions between a business and its customers or potential customers.

REAL WORLD CASE 2

Nationwide Insurance: Unified Financial Reporting and "One Version of the Truth"

In a span of three short years, between 2000 and 2002, Nationwide Insurance got a new CEO, CIO, and CFO.

Jerry Jurgensen, elected by Nationwide's board in 2000 to replace the retiring CEO, was hired for his financial acumen and his ability to transform a business's culture. Michael Keller was named the company's first enterprisewide CIO the following year. He had 25 years of IT experience managing big infrastructure and systems integration projects. In 2002, Robert Rosholt replaced the retiring CFO and joined the others in Nationwide's Columbus, Ohio headquarters, bringing along deep experience in all things financial.

The three were old buddies who had worked together at financial giant Bank One. Now they held the reins at Nationwide and their goal was to take its dozens of business units, selling a diverse set of insurance and financial products, to a higher level.

But to get there, Jurgensen needed financial snapshots of how Nationwide was doing at any given moment. And getting them wasn't so easy; in fact, it was almost impossible.

FIGURE 7.10

Companies are deploying technology and reengineering processes in search of "one source of the truth" across the enterprise.

"When you're dealing with 14 general ledger platforms and over 50 applications," Rosholt says, "it was enormous work to get the financials out."

The problem lay knotted in a tangle of systems and applications, and some 240 sources of financial data flowing in and around Nationwide's business units. The units had always run independently, and that's how financial reporting was handled. "There was a variety of [financial reporting] languages," Rosholt says, which affected Nationwide's ability to forecast, budget, and report. "It was difficult," says Rosholt, "to ask 'How are we doing?'" Keller's situation was no better.

"One of the first questions I was asked when I joined was, How much money do we spend, total, on IT?" Keller recalls. "The answer was, we didn't know. It took weeks to put that answer together."

Jurgensen wanted to be able to run Nationwide as if it were one unified enterprise. He wanted, in Rosholt's words, "to do things that are common, and respect the things that are different. And that was a big change."

Indeed, the transformation the company embarked upon in early 2004 was daunting—a master data management makeover that would alter how every Nationwide business reported its financials, how accounting personnel did their jobs, how data were governed and by whom, and how the company's information systems would pull all that together. The goal was simple: one platform; one version of the financial truth. Simple goal, but a difficult challenge.

Good master data governance can happen only when the various constituencies that own the data sources agree on a common set of definitions, rules, and synchronized procedures, all of which requires a degree of political maneuvering that's not for the faint of heart.

Nationwide began its finance transformation program, called Focus, with its eyes wide open. The executive troika of Jurgensen, Rosholt, and Keller had pulled off a similar project at Bank One and thought it knew how to avoid the big mistakes. That, in part, is why Rosholt, who had ultimate say on the project, would not budge on its 24-month time line. "The most important aspect was sticking to discipline and not wavering," he recalls. And that's why the technology piece was, from the outset, the last question to be addressed.

"It wasn't a technology project," insists Lynda Butler, whose position as vice president of performance management was created to oversee Focus (which stands for Faster, Online, Customer-driven, User-friendly, Streamlined). She says that Nationwide approached Focus first and foremost as a business and financial project.

Nationwide considers the project, which made its deadline, a success, although everyone emphasizes that there's more work to be done. Says Keller, "There's a foundation to build on where there wasn't one before."

"Fourteen general ledgers, 12 reporting tools, 17 financial data repositories and 300,000 spreadsheets were used in finance," says Butler. "That's not real conducive to 'one version of the truth.'"

Early in his tenure as CEO, Jurgensen's concerns about the company's financials weren't limited to the timeliness of the data; he was also worried about its integrity and accuracy.

For example, because Nationwide had such a variety of businesses, the company carried a lot of risk—some easily visible, some not. "So, if equity markets went down, we were exposed," notes Butler. "But we didn't realize that until the markets actually went down. We needed some enterprise view of the world."

Executives also knew that common data definitions among all the business units would provide comparable financial data for analysis—which was difficult, if not impossible, without those definitions. "We needed consistent data across the organization," Rosholt says.

"We were looking for one book of record." CFO Rosholt went back to his Bank One roots and recruited Vikas Gopal, who had proven his mettle on similar projects, to lead the IT team.

With no wiggle room on the time line, the team, with Rosholt's encouragement, followed what it refers to as the "80/20" rule. It knew that it wasn't going to get 100 percent of the desired functionality of the new system, so the team decided that if it could get roughly 80 percent of the project up and running in 24 months, it could fix the remaining 20 percent later. "If we went after perfection," says Rosholt, "we'd still be at it."

Keeping in mind that no one would get everything he wanted, the Focus team interviewed key stakeholders in Nationwide's business units to understand where their pain points were. "We went back to basics," says Gopal. "We said, 'Let's talk about your financial systems, how they help your decision making.'"

In other words, people were introduced to the concept of making trade-offs, which allowed the Focus team to target the system's core functionalities and keep control over the project's scope.

It was only after the requirements, definitions, and parameters were mapped out that Gopal's group began to look at technologies. Gopal had two rules to guide them: First, all financial-related systems had to be subscribers to the central book of record. Second, none of the master data in any of the financial applications could ever be out of sync. So the Focus team's final step was to evaluate technologies that would follow and enforce those rules.

His team sought out best-of-breed toolsets from vendors such as Kalido and Teradata that would be able to tie into their existing systems. Gopal wasn't overly "worried about [technology] execution" because he had assembled this type of system before and knew that the technology solutions on the market, even in the most vanilla forms, were robust enough for Nationwide's needs.

What did worry him was Nationwide's legion of financial employees who didn't relish the idea of changing the way they went about their work. At the beginning of the program, Nationwide formed a "One Finance Family" program that tried to unify all the finance folks around Focus. Executives were also able to identify those employees who were most affected through weekly "change meetings" and provide support.

The Focus team had to remain resolute. The overarching theme, that there would be no compromise in data quality and integrity, was repeated early and often, and executives made sure that the gravity of the change was communicated before anyone saw any new software.

Finally, in March 2005, with three waves of planned deployments ahead of it, the team started rolling out the new Focus system. By fall 2005, there was light at the end of the tunnel. The team could see the new business processes and financial data governance mechanisms actually being used by Nationwide employees, and it all was working. "They saw the value they were creating," recalls Butler. "The 'aha' moment came when we finally got a chance to look in the rear-view mirror."

The first benefit of the transformation that Rosholt mentions is something that didn't happen. "You go through a project such as this, in a period of extreme regulatory and accounting oversight, and these things can cough up more issues, such as earnings restatements. We've avoided that," he says. "That doesn't mean we're perfect, but that's one thing everyone's amazed at. We went through all this change and nothing coughed up. Our balance sheet was right."

Source: Adapted from Thomas Wailgum, "How Master Data Management Unified Financial Reporting at Nationwide Insurance," *CIO.com*, December 21, 2007.

CASE STUDY QUESTIONS

1. The project that Nationwide undertook was quite clearly a success. What made this possible? Discuss three different practices that helped Nationwide pull this off. Use examples from the case where necessary.

2. The case notes that Nationwide had in mind a simple goal, but faced a difficult challenge. Why was this so difficult?

3. What is the business value derived from the successful completion of this project? What can executives at Nationwide do now that could not before? Provide some examples.

REAL WORLD ACTIVITIES

1. Technologies and systems involved in financial reporting have received a great deal of attention in the last few years due to renewed regulatory focus on the integrity and reliability of financial information. Go online and research how companies are deploying technology to deal with these issues. Prepare a report to summarize your findings.

2. A number of political and cultural issues were involved in the implementation of the "one source of the truth" approach at Nationwide. Can these obstacles be overcome simply by mandating compliance from top management? What else should companies do to help ease these transitions? Break into small groups with your classmates and brainstorm some possible actions.

FIGURE 7.11 Examples of functional business information systems. Note how they support the major functional areas of business.

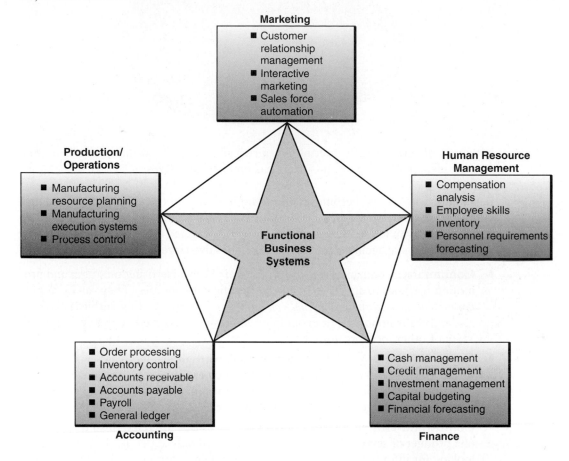

The goal of interactive marketing is to enable a company to use those networks profitably to attract and keep customers who will become partners with the business in creating, purchasing, and improving products and services.

In interactive marketing, customers are not just passive participants who receive media advertising prior to purchase; they are actively engaged in network-enabled proactive and interactive processes. Interactive marketing encourages customers to become involved in product development, delivery, and service issues. This is enabled by various Internet technologies, including chat and discussion groups, Web forms and questionnaires, instant messaging, and e-mail correspondence. Finally, the expected

FIGURE 7.12

Marketing information systems provide information technologies to support major components of the marketing function.

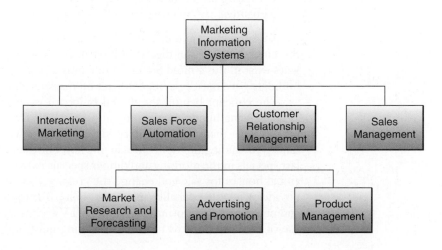

FIGURE 7.13
The five major components of targeted marketing for electronic commerce.

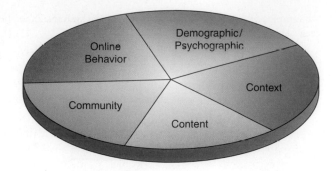

outcomes of interactive marketing are a rich mixture of vital marketing data, new product ideas, volume sales, and strong customer relationships.

Targeted Marketing

Targeted marketing has become an important tool in developing advertising and promotion strategies to strengthen a company's e-commerce initiatives, as well as its traditional business venues. As illustrated in Figure 7.13, targeted marketing is an advertising and promotion management concept that includes five targeting components:

- **Community.** Companies can customize their Web advertising messages and promotion methods to appeal to people in specific communities. They can be *communities of interest*, such as *virtual communities* of online sporting enthusiasts, or arts and crafts hobbyists, or geographic communities formed by the Web sites of a city or other local organization.

- **Content.** Advertising, such as electronic billboards or banners, can be placed on a variety of selected Web sites, in addition to a company's Web site. The content of these messages is aimed at the targeted audience. An ad for a product campaign on the opening page of an Internet search engine is a typical example.

- **Context.** Advertising appears only in Web pages that are relevant to the content of a product or service. So, advertising is targeted only at people who are already looking for information about a subject matter (e.g., vacation travel) that is related to a company's products (e.g., car rental services).

- **Demographic/Psychographic.** Web marketing efforts can be aimed only at specific types or classes of people: for example, unmarried, twenty-something, middle income, male college graduates.

- **Online Behavior.** Advertising and promotion efforts can be tailored to each visit to a site by an individual. This strategy is based on a variety of tracking techniques, such as Web "cookie" files recorded on the visitor's disk drive from previous visits. This enables a company to track a person's online behavior at its Web site so marketing efforts (such as coupons redeemable at retail stores or e-commerce Web sites) can be targeted to that individual at each visit to its Web site.

An interesting and effective marriage between e-business and target marketing is the emergence of the digital billboard. It is estimated that about 450,000 billboard faces exist in the United States. While only a tiny fraction of them are digital, the new billboards are making a huge impact on markets all over the country.

The concept behind the digital billboard is elegantly simple. A billboard is constructed using hundreds of thousands of small LEDs, which are controlled via a computer interface that can be accessed via the Web. Advertisers can change their messages quickly, including multiple times in one day. For example, a restaurant can feature breakfast specials in the morning and dinner specials in the evening. A realtor can feature individual houses for sale and change the creative content when the house sells. Print and broadcast news media alike use digital billboards to deliver headlines, weather updates, and programming information. WCPO-TV credits its meteoric rise in the ratings to the use of digital billboards to deliver breaking news and updates to the nightly newscast.

The television station went from the bottom of the ratings in 2002 to the third largest ABC affiliate in the nation. When the I-35 bridge collapsed in Minneapolis in 2007, a dangerous situation for unsuspecting drivers existed. Within minutes, a digital billboard network in the area switched from showing advertising copy to informing drivers about the collapse. Later that evening, the digital billboards advised motorists to take alternate routes. Target marketing is in the digital arena, with a new way of doing something old.

Sales Force Automation

Increasingly, computers and the Internet are providing the basis for sales force automation. In many companies, the sales force is being outfitted with notebook computers, Web browsers, and sales contact management software that connect them to marketing Web sites on the Internet, extranets, and their company intranets. This not only increases the personal productivity of salespeople, but it dramatically speeds up the capture and analysis of sales data from the field to marketing managers at company headquarters. In return, it allows marketing and sales management to improve the delivery of information and the support they provide to their salespeople. Therefore, many companies are viewing sales force automation as a way to gain a strategic advantage in sales productivity and marketing responsiveness. See Figure 7.14.

For example, salespeople use their PCs to record sales data as they make their calls on customers and prospects during the day. Then each night, sales reps in the field can connect their computers by modem and telephone links to the Internet and extranets, which can access intranet or other network servers at their company. Then, they can upload information on sales orders, sales calls, and other sales statistics, as well as send e-mail messages and access Web site sales support information. In return, the network servers may download product availability data, prospect lists of information on good sales prospects, and e-mail messages.

FIGURE 7.14

This Web-based sales force automation package supports sales lead management of qualified prospects, and management of current customer accounts.

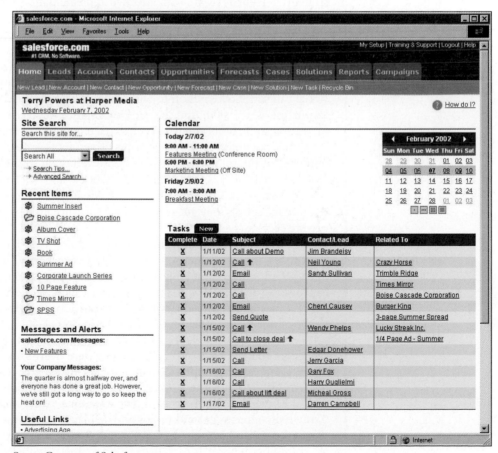

Source: Courtesy of Salesforce.com.

Air Force Extends the Enterprise into Space at Mach 6

Lt. Gen. William Lord, the Air Force's CIO, isn't satisfied with the steps taken thus far to protect the military branch's computer systems and networks. Lord worries that intruders will get past the Air Force's network perimeter defenses—or already have—and he's aggressively trying to prevent it.

Lord compares network firewalls to the fences that surround military bases. They keep out "the honest folks and the dogs," he says, but not your most dangerous enemies. On base, the military employs roving patrols inside the fence line as an added precaution. He wants to do the same thing within the Air Force's IT environment, but with technology in lieu of armed guards.

The critically important job of taking the Air Force's cybersecurity operations to that next level—from "information assurance" to "situational awareness"—is high on Lord's priority list. "The enemy we don't know within the network is the number one thing that keeps me awake," he says.

In mid-2009, Lord was named the Air Force's CIO and chief of warfighting integration. Prior to that, he was commander of Air Force Cyber Command at Barksdale Air Force Base, which helps explain his laser focus on cybersecurity. In late 2010, in a roundtable briefing at the Pentagon, Lord provided an overview on that and his other top priorities.

During the past year, the Air Force has changed the job classification of 30,000 personnel to that of Cyberspace operators and officers, a reflection of new, more stringent skills requirements and training. Lord himself wears the new Cyberspace badge on his uniform. Just last week, the Air Force introduced "cyberspace defense operator" as a career field.

As a next step, Lord is looking to introduce new technologies—packet inspection, network mapping, sensors, and more—as part of an enterprise-wide "layered defense" strategy. That will require both effective implementation and an "operational mindset" focused on cybersecurity, but it will take time, he says.

Lord wants to squeeze inefficiencies from the Air Force's IT operations, not surprising given Defense Secretary Robert Gates's goal of saving $100 billion over five years. Enterprise solutions like data center consolidation, e-mail consolidation, and application consolidation are all on the table. For example, Lord figures the Air Force can save $600 million to $800 million by cutting 9,000 stand-alone apps from its portfolio of 19,000. And the Air Force stands to save tens of millions of dollars by migrating some of its enterprise apps to a cloud computing environment.

Other possibilities include sharing IT services—e-mail, for example—with other branches of the military. Lord says he is even open to the idea of using commercial cloud services such as those offered by Google and Microsoft.

Like other government employees, Air Force leaders are sometimes frustrated that the tech tools they get at work don't measure up to what's widely available in the private sector. (Federal CIO Vivek Kundra calls it the "tech gap" in government.) "We have customers who rightfully demand that they have the same capabilities in our offices, in their vehicles, and when they're airborne," Lord says.

The Air Force is looking to close the gap by offering a range of new tools and capabilities: Windows 7, Macs, in-flight wireless service, 4G wireless, and support for iPhones and Android devices. "I want the rich device experience to be in the hands of our forward-deployed folks," Lord says.

The Air Force is adept at establishing communications on the ground and in space; it's the "aerial layer" in between where there's the most room for improvement, Lord says. Examples of technologies in this area are the Joint Tactical Radio System (JTRS) and the Link 16 over-the-air data network. In a recent demo of JTRS, Lockheed Martin showed that streaming video could be transmitted from an Army helicopter to ground radios and displayed in a Humvee. Impressive but complicated, and it shows why Lord is turning his energies to this area.

Mid-air networking will only get more sophisticated. Lord talks of networking from an F-35 fighter traveling at the speed of sound, and collecting and transmitting ISR (intelligence, surveillance, and reconnaissance) data from unmanned aircraft that bolt through the sky at Mach 6 (six times the speed of sound—4,608 mph or 7,416 kph).

There's much more on the Air Force's IT agenda, including the rollout of Windows 7 to 600,000 PCs, and Lord's interest in conducting an apps-dev competition along the lines of the Apps For Army contest. It's an ambitious set of goals, and none of it will be easy. Nonetheless, it's clear the Air Force is looking more and more like an enterprise every day.

Source: Adapted from John Foley, "Air Force CIO Priorities: Networking at Mach 6," *InformationWeek*, November 8, 2010.

Manufacturing Systems

Manufacturing information systems support the *production/operations* function that includes all activities concerned with the planning and control of the processes producing goods or services. Thus, the production/operations function is concerned with the management of the operational processes and systems of all business firms. Information systems used for operations management and transaction processing support all firms that must plan, monitor, and control inventories, purchases, and the flow of goods and services. Therefore, firms such as transportation companies, wholesalers, retailers, financial institutions, and service companies must use production/operations information systems to plan and control their operations. In this section, we will concentrate on computer-based manufacturing applications to illustrate information systems that support the production/operations function.

Computer-Integrated Manufacturing

Once upon a time, manufacturers operated on a simple build-to-stock model. They built 100 or 100,000 of an item and sold them via distribution networks. They kept track of the stock of inventory and made more of the item once inventory levels dipped below a threshold. Rush jobs were both rare and expensive, and configuration options limited. Things have changed. Concepts like just-in-time inventory, build-to-order (BTO) manufacturing, end-to-end supply chain visibility, the explosion in contract manufacturing, and the development of Web-based e-business tools for collaborative manufacturing have revolutionized plant management.

A variety of manufacturing information systems, many of them Web-enabled, are used to support computer-integrated manufacturing (CIM). See Figure 7.15. CIM is an overall concept that emphasizes that the objectives of computer-based systems in manufacturing must be to:

- **Simplify** (reengineer) production processes, product designs, and factory organization as a vital foundation to automation and integration.
- **Automate** production processes and the business functions that support them with computers, machines, and robots.
- **Integrate** all production and support processes using computer networks, cross-functional business software, and other information technologies.

The overall goal of CIM and such manufacturing information systems is to create flexible, agile, manufacturing processes that efficiently produce products of the highest quality. Thus, CIM supports the concepts of *flexible manufacturing systems*, *agile manufacturing*, and *total quality management*. Implementing such manufacturing concepts enables a company to respond to and fulfill customer requirements quickly with high-quality products and services.

Manufacturing information systems help companies simplify, automate, and integrate many of the activities needed to produce products of all kinds. For example, computers are used to help engineers design better products using both *computer-aided engineering* (CAE) and *computer-aided design* (CAD) systems, and better production processes with *computer-aided process planning*. They are also used to help plan the types of material

FIGURE 7.15
Manufacturing information systems support computer-integrated manufacturing. Note that manufacturing resource planning systems are one of the application clusters in an ERP system.

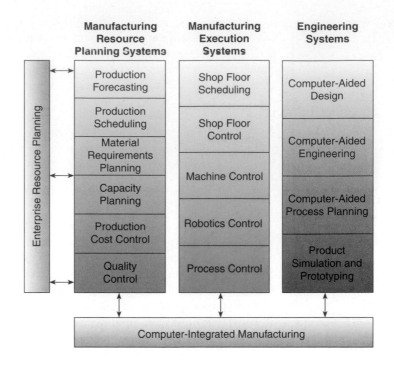

needed in the production process, which is called *material requirements planning* (MRP), and to integrate MRP with production scheduling and shop floor operations, which is known as *manufacturing resource planning.* Many of the processes within manufacturing resource planning systems are included in the manufacturing module of enterprise resource planning (ERP) software, which will be discussed in Chapter 8.

Computer-aided manufacturing (CAM) systems are those that automate the production process. For example, this could be accomplished by monitoring and controlling the production process in a factory (manufacturing execution systems) or by directly controlling a physical process (process control), a machine tool (machine control), or machines with some humanlike work capabilities (robots).

Manufacturing execution systems (MES) are performance-monitoring information systems for factory floor operations. They monitor, track, and control the five essential components involved in a production process: materials, equipment, personnel, instructions and specifications, and production facilities. MES includes shop floor scheduling and control, machine control, robotics control, and process control systems. These manufacturing systems monitor, report, and adjust the status and performance of production components to help a company achieve a flexible, high-quality manufacturing process.

Process control is the use of computers to control an ongoing physical process. Process control computers control physical processes in petroleum refineries, cement plants, steel mills, chemical plants, food product manufacturing plants, pulp and paper mills, electric power plants, and so on. A process control computer system requires the use of special sensing devices that measure physical phenomena such as temperature or pressure changes. These continuous physical measurements are converted to digital form by analog-to-digital converters and relayed to computers for processing.

Machine control is the use of computers to control the actions of machines. This is also popularly called *numerical control.* The computer-based control of machine tools to manufacture products of all kinds is a typical numerical control application used by many factories throughout the world.

Human Resource Systems

The human resource management (HRM) function involves the recruitment, placement, evaluation, compensation, and development of the employees of an organization. The goal of human resource management is the effective and efficient use of the human resources of a company. Thus, human resource information systems (HRIS) are designed to support (1) planning to meet the personnel needs of the business,

FIGURE 7.16 Human resource information systems support the strategic, tactical, and operational use of the human resources of an organization.

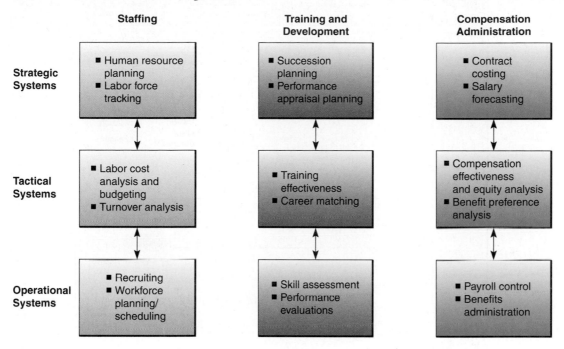

(2) development of employees to their full potential, and (3) control of all personnel policies and programs. Originally, businesses used computer-based information systems to (1) produce paychecks and payroll reports, (2) maintain personnel records, and (3) analyze the use of personnel in business operations. Many firms have gone beyond these traditional *personnel management* functions and have developed human resource information systems that also support (1) recruitment, selection, and hiring; (2) job placement; (3) performance appraisals; (4) employee benefits analysis; (5) training and development; and (6) health, safety, and security. See Figure 7.16.

HRM and the Internet

The Internet has become a major force for change in human resource management. For example, online HRM systems may involve recruiting for employees through recruitment sections of corporate Web sites. Companies are also using commercial recruiting services and databases on the World Wide Web, posting messages in selected Internet newsgroups, and communicating with job applicants via e-mail.

The Internet has a wealth of information and contacts for both employers and job hunters. Top Web sites for job hunters and employers on the World Wide Web include Monster.com, HotJobs.com, and CareerBuilder.com. These Web sites are full of reports, statistics, and other useful HRM information, such as job reports by industry, or listings of the top recruiting markets by industry and profession.

HRM and Corporate Intranets

Intranet technologies allow companies to process most common HRM applications over their corporate intranets. Intranets allow the HRM department to provide around-the-clock services to their customers: the employees. They can also disseminate valuable information faster than through previous company channels. Intranets can collect information online from employees for input to their HRM files, and they can enable managers and other employees to perform HRM tasks with little intervention by the HRM department. See Figure 7.17.

For example, *employee self-service* (ESS) intranet applications allow employees to view benefits, enter travel and expense reports, verify employment and salary information, access and update their personal information, and enter time-sensitive data. Through

FIGURE 7.17

An example of an employee
hiring review system.

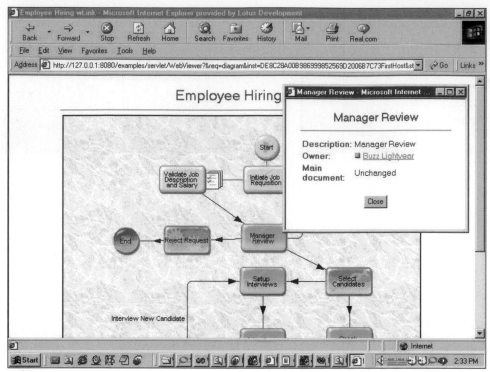

Source: Courtesy of IBM.

this completely electronic process, employees can use their Web browsers to look up individual payroll and benefits information online, right from their desktop PCs, mobile computers, or intranet kiosks located around a work site.

Another benefit of the intranet is that it can serve as a superior training tool. Employees can easily download instructions and processes to get the information or education they need. In addition, employees using new technology can view training videos over the intranet on demand. Thus, the intranet eliminates the need to loan out and track training videos. Employees can also use their corporate intranets to produce automated paysheets, the online alternative to time cards. These electronic forms have made viewing, entering, and adjusting payroll information easy for both employees and HRM professionals.

Chiquita Brands: Finding Out How Many Employees They Have 	It seems like a straightforward and simple question that your typical HR application and corporate ERP system should be able to answer: How many employees are working for our company today? At Chiquita Brands, the Fortune 500 company best known for its blue-stickered bananas, "We couldn't answer that question," recalls Manjit Singh, Chiquita's CIO since September 2006. "It would take us a couple of weeks to get the answer pulled together and by that time, of course, it was all incorrect." Chiquita boasts a global workforce of 23,000 employees in 70 countries on six continents, although most of the workers are predominantly in Central America. Until 2008, the Cincinnati-based food manufacturer had employed a hodgepodge of legacy HR systems that were inadequate at managing the complex demands of its decentralized workforce. Manual, inefficient workarounds (Excel spreadsheets and paper-based processes) were frequently used. When Chiquita hired a new employee, for instance, the HR paper-trail process could contain 20 to 30 steps, Singh notes.

"At any point, if that paper gets lost, things are going to fall through the cracks," he says. "Many times new employees have shown up and haven't had an office, a PC or a phone. Obviously that causes pain to the employee, it doesn't make the employer look good and you've lost productivity from the moment the employee walks through the door."

In October 2008, Chiquita went live on Workday HCM with 5,000 U.S.-based employees and 500 managers across 42 countries. Singh took advantage of customization options Workday offered when necessary. But he and his team tried to minimize customization as much as possible, so that they could shorten implementation time lines as they continue phased rollouts to 18,000 Latin America–based employees and nearly 3,000 employees throughout Europe.

Today, Chiquita's North American operations enjoy the fruits of the new system, including core HR functions such as employee hiring, job changes, compensation tracking and more. "We can see exactly where in the process the employee is, or how the hiring is going, who is holding it up and why it's being held up, so that we can guarantee when an employee walks through the door, they have an office, a phone, a PC, and they've been given access to all of the systems they need to have access to," says Singh.

"That's big, when you talk about the number of employees we hire in a given month," Singh continues. "That drops dollars back down to the bottom line."

Lastly, the new HR system has freed up many of Chiquita's 200 IT staffers to focus on higher-value projects. "I want my folks sitting arm and arm with business folks, talking about process transformation and trying to figure out how to bring products to market even quicker," Singh says, "not keeping the lights on running a system."

Source: Adapted from Thomas Wailgum, "Why Chiquita Said 'No' to Tier 1 ERP Providers and 'Yes' to SaaS Apps from Upstart Workday," *CIO Magazine*, April 7, 2009.

Accounting Systems

Accounting information systems are the oldest and most widely used information systems in business. They record and report business transactions and other economic events. Computer-based accounting systems record and report the flow of funds through an organization on a historical basis and produce important financial statements such as balance sheets and income statements. Such systems also produce forecasts of future conditions such as projected financial statements and financial budgets. A firm's financial performance is measured against such forecasts by other analytical accounting reports.

Operational accounting systems emphasize legal and historical record-keeping and the production of accurate financial statements. Typically, these systems include transaction processing systems such as order processing, inventory control, accounts receivable, accounts payable, payroll, and general ledger systems. Management accounting systems focus on the planning and control of business operations. They emphasize cost accounting reports, the development of financial budgets and projected financial statements, and analytical reports comparing actual to forecasted performance.

Figure 7.18 illustrates the interrelationships of several important accounting information systems commonly computerized by both large and small businesses. Many accounting software packages are available for these applications. Figure 7.19 provides a good summary of the essential purpose of six common, but important, accounting information systems used by both large and small business firms.

Online Accounting Systems

It should come as no surprise that the accounting information systems illustrated in Figures 7.18 and 7.19 are being transformed by Internet technologies. Using the Internet and other networks changes how accounting information systems monitor and track business activity. The interactive nature of online accounting systems calls for

FIGURE 7.18 Important accounting information systems for transaction processing and financial reporting. Note how they are related to each other in terms of input and output flows.

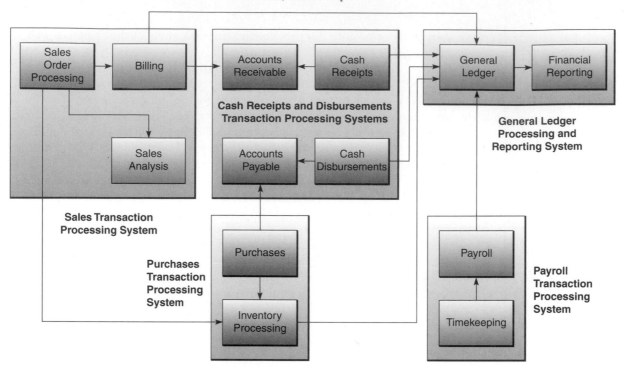

FIGURE 7.19 A summary of six essential accounting information systems used in business.

Common Business Accounting Systems
● **Order Processing** Captures and processes customer orders and produces data for inventory control and accounts receivable.
● **Inventory Control** Processes data reflecting changes in inventory and provides shipping and reorder information.
● **Accounts Receivable** Records amounts owed by customers and produces customer invoices, monthly customer statements, and credit management reports.
● **Accounts Payable** Records purchases from, amounts owed to, and payments to suppliers, and produces cash management reports.
● **Payroll** Records employee work and compensation data and produces paychecks and other payroll documents and reports.
● **General Ledger** Consolidates data from other accounting systems and produces the periodic financial statements and reports of the business.

new forms of transaction documents, procedures, and controls. This particularly applies to systems like order processing, inventory control, accounts receivable, and accounts payable. As outlined in Figure 7.18, these systems are directly involved in the processing of transactions between a business and its customers and suppliers. So naturally, many companies are using Internet and other network links to these trading partners for such online transaction processing systems, as discussed in Section I. Figure 7.20 is an example of an online accounting report.

FIGURE 7.20

An example of an online accounting report.

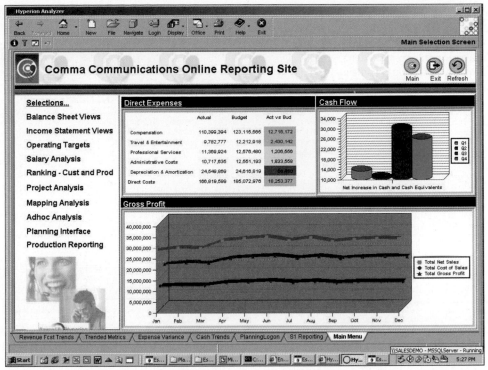

Source: Courtesy of Hyperion.

Financial Management Systems

Computer-based **financial management systems** support business managers and professionals in decisions concerning (1) the financing of a business and (2) the allocation and control of financial resources within a business. Major financial management system categories include cash and investment management, capital budgeting, financial forecasting, and financial planning. See Figure 7.21.

For example, the **capital budgeting** process involves evaluating the profitability and financial impact of proposed capital expenditures. Long-term expenditure proposals for facilities and equipment can be analyzed using a variety of return on investment (ROI) evaluation techniques. This application makes heavy use of spreadsheet models that incorporate present value analysis of expected cash flows and probability analysis of risk to determine the optimum mix of capital projects for a business.

Financial analysts also typically use electronic spreadsheets and other **financial planning** software to evaluate the present and projected financial performance of a business. They also help determine the financing needs of a business and analyze

FIGURE 7.21

Examples of important financial management systems.

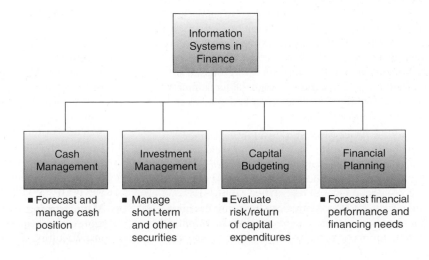

FIGURE 7.22

An example of strategic financial planning using a multiple scenario approach. Note the effect on earnings per share.

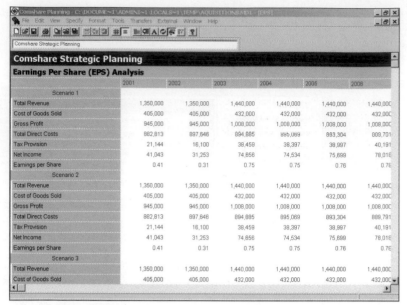

Source: Courtesy of Comshare.

alternative methods of financing. Financial analysts use financial forecasts concerning the economic situation, business operations, types of financing available, interest rates, and stock and bond prices to develop an optimal financing plan for the business. Electronic spreadsheet packages, DSS software, and Web-based groupware can be used to build and manipulate financial models. Answers to what-if and goal-seeking questions can be explored as financial analysts and managers evaluate their financing and investment alternatives. We will discuss such applications further in Chapter 10. See Figure 7.22.

Summary

- **Cross-Functional Enterprise Systems.** Major e-business applications and their interrelationships are summarized in the enterprise application architecture of Figure 7.2. These applications are integrated cross-functional enterprise systems such as enterprise resource planning (ERP), customer relationship management (CRM), and supply chain management (SCM). These applications may be interconnected by enterprise application integration (EAI) systems so that business professionals can more easily access the information resources they need to support the needs of customers, suppliers, and business partners. Enterprise collaboration systems (ECS) are cross-functional systems that support and enhance communication and collaboration among the teams and workgroups in an organization. Refer to Figures 7.4 and 7.8 for summary views of the e-business applications in EAI systems and enterprise collaboration systems.

- **Transaction Processing Systems.** Online transaction processing systems play a vital role in business. Transaction processing involves the basic activities of (1) data entry, (2) transaction processing, (3) database maintenance, (4) document and report generation, and (5) inquiry processing. Many firms are using the Internet, intranets, extranets, and other networks for online transaction processing to provide superior service to

their customers and suppliers. Figure 7.6 illustrates the basic activities of transaction processing systems.

- **Functional Business Systems.** Functional business information systems support the business functions of marketing, production/operations, accounting, finance, and human resource management through a variety of e-business operational and management information systems summarized in Figure 7.11.

- **Marketing.** Marketing information systems support traditional and e-commerce processes and management of the marketing function. Major types of marketing information systems include interactive marketing at e-commerce Web sites, sales force automation, customer relationship management, sales management, product management, targeted marketing, advertising and promotion, and market research. Thus, marketing information systems assist marketing managers in e-commerce product development and customer relationship decisions, as well as in planning advertising and sales promotion strategies and developing the e-commerce potential of new and present products and new channels of distribution.

- **Manufacturing.** Computer-based manufacturing information systems help a company achieve computer-integrated manufacturing (CIM), and thus simplify, automate, and integrate many of the activities needed to quickly produce high-quality products to meet changing customer demands. For example, computer-aided design using collaborative manufacturing networks helps engineers collaborate on the design of new products and processes. Then manufacturing resource planning systems help plan the types of resources needed in the production process. Finally, manufacturing execution systems monitor and control the manufacture of products on the factory floor through shop floor scheduling and control systems, controlling a physical process (process control), a machine tool (numerical control), or machines with some humanlike work capabilities (robotics).

● **Human Resource Management.** Human resource information systems support human resource management in organizations. They include information systems for staffing the organization, training and

development, and compensation administration. HRM Web sites on the Internet or corporate intranets have become important tools for providing HR services to present and prospective employees.

● **Accounting and Finance.** Accounting information systems record, report, and analyze business transactions and events for the management of the business enterprise. Figure 7.19 summarizes six essential accounting systems including order processing, inventory control, accounts receivable, accounts payable, payroll, and general ledger. Information systems in finance support managers in decisions regarding the financing of a business and the allocation of financial resources within a business. Financial information systems include cash management, online investment management, capital budgeting, and financial forecasting and planning.

Key Terms and Concepts

These are the key terms and concepts of this chapter. The page number of their first explanation is in parentheses.

1. Accounting information systems (329)
2. Accounts payable (329)
3. Accounts receivable (329)
4. Batch processing (314)
5. Computer-aided manufacturing (326)
6. Computer-integrated manufacturing (325)
7. Cross-functional enterprise systems (306)
8. E-business (306)
9. Enterprise application architecture (306)
10. Enterprise application integration (310)
11. Enterprise collaboration systems (315)
12. Financial management systems (331)
13. Functional business systems (318)
14. General ledger (329)
15. Human resource information systems (326)
16. Interactive marketing (318)
17. Inventory control (329)
18. Machine control (326)
19. Manufacturing execution systems (326)
20. Manufacturing information systems (325)
21. Marketing information systems (318)
22. Online accounting systems (329)
23. Online HRM systems (327)
24. Online transaction processing systems (313)
25. Order processing (329)
26. Payroll (329)
27. Process control (326)
28. Real-time processing (314)
29. Sales force automation (323)
30. Targeted marketing (322)
31. Transaction processing cycle (314)

Review Quiz

Match one of the key terms and concepts listed previously with one of the brief examples or definitions that follow. Try to find the best fit for the answers that seem to fit more than one term or concept. Defend your choices.

_____ 1. Using the Internet and other networks for e-commerce, enterprise collaboration, and Web-enabled business processes.

_____ 2. Information systems that cross the boundaries of the functional areas of a business in order to integrate and automate business processes.

_____ 3. Information systems that support marketing, production, accounting, finance, and human resource management.

_____ 4. E-business applications fit into a framework of interrelated cross-functional enterprise applications.

_____ 5. Software that interconnects enterprise application systems.

_____ 6. Information systems for customer relationship management, sales management, and promotion management.

_____ 7. Collaborating interactively with customers in creating, purchasing, servicing, and improving products and services.

_____ 8. Using mobile computing networks to support salespeople in the field.

_____ 9. Information systems that support manufacturing operations and management.

_____ 10. A conceptual framework for simplifying and integrating all aspects of manufacturing automation.

_____ 11. Using computers in a variety of ways to help manufacture products.

_____ 12. Use electronic communications, conferencing, and collaborative work tools to support and enhance collaboration among teams and workgroups.

_____ 13. Using computers to operate a petroleum refinery.

_____ 14. Using computers to help operate machine tools.

_____ 15. Information systems to support staffing, training and development, and compensation administration.

_____ 16. Using the Internet for recruitment and job hunting is an example.

_____ 17. Accomplishes legal and historical record-keeping and gathers information for the planning and control of business operations.

_____ 18. An example is using the Internet and extranets to do accounts receivable and accounts payable activities.

_____ 19. Handles sales orders from customers.

_____ 20. Keeps track of items in stock.

_____ 21. Keeps track of amounts owed by customers.

_____ 22. Keeps track of purchases from suppliers.

_____ 23. Produces employee paychecks.

_____ 24. Produces the financial statements of a firm.

_____ 25. Information systems for cash management, investment management, capital budgeting, and financial forecasting.

_____ 26. Performance monitoring and control systems for factory floor operations.

_____ 27. Customizing advertising and promotion methods to fit their intended audience.

_____ 28. Data entry, transaction processing, database maintenance, document and report generation, and inquiry processing.

_____ 29. Collecting and periodically processing transaction data.

_____ 30. Processing transaction data immediately after they are captured.

_____ 31. Systems that immediately capture and process transaction data and update corporate databases.

Discussion Questions

1. Refer to Real World Case 1 on enterprise-wide e-discovery. What are the advantages of a centralized enterprise architecture? What are the advantages of a decentralized approach that leaves these decisions to the operating units? How do you balance both? Discuss.

2. Why is there a trend toward cross-functional integrated enterprise systems in business?

3. Which of the 13 tools for accounting information systems summarized in Figure 7.18 do you feel are essential for any business to have today? Which of them do you feel are optional, depending on the type of business or other factor? Explain.

4. What other solutions could there be for the problem of information systems incompatibility in business besides EAI systems?

5. What are the most important HR applications a company should offer to its employees via a Web-based system? Why?

6. How could sales force automation affect salesperson productivity, marketing management, and competitive advantage?

7. How can Internet technologies be involved in improving a process in one of the functions of business? Choose one example and evaluate its business value.

8. Refer to the Real World Case on Nationwide Insurance in the chapter. Senior management was emphatic about maintaining a 24-month deadline at all cost. Should the scope of the project be adapted to reflect a deadline, or should deadlines reflect the scope of a project? Discuss.

9. What are several e-business applications that you might recommend to a small company to help it survive and succeed in challenging economic times? Why?

10. Refer to the example on virtual worlds in the chapter. How do enterprise collaboration systems contribute to bottom-line profits for a business?

Analysis Exercises

1. **Hybrid Application Service Providers**
   ASP Integrated Applications
   Revenue from desktop application sales ends with the sale. Or does it? Companies like Microsoft provide updates, fixes, and security patches to their software while

developing the next revenue-generating edition. However, they don't make another dime until they release the next edition. But that isn't the only model.

McAfee charges an annual maintenance fee that includes daily application and virus definition updates.

McAfee provides this service free for one year as part of its license. After the first year, license holders may continue to use the software, but they must pay a subscription fee if they want updates. Customers tend to pay for this subscription service in order to protect themselves from new virus threats. Thus, McAfee generates revenue long after the initial sale. In this way, McAfee behaves like an application service provider.

The following questions will help you explore the many ASP-related services that relocate applications, maintenance, and data off your systems and allow you to focus on your mission.

a. AOL offers instant messaging tools for organizations (www.aimatwork.com). Compare business-oriented tools with AIM, AOL's free consumer product.

b. Yahoo and Google are in a heated competition for the same user base. Look up the latest developments for Yahoo at developer.yahoo.com and for Google at labs.google.com. Prepare a table in Word to compare current and beta features for Yahoo and Google. Place "Feature," "Google," and "Yahoo" as column headers. List individual features under "Feature" in the left-hand column. Place the symbol "•" in the cell if it's a current feature for each competitor and the symbol "o" in the cell if it's a beta feature. Leave the cell blank if it isn't available at all. Give the table a professional appearance.

2. **In Search of Talent**
Online Job Matching and Auctions
Many opportunities await those who troll the big job boards, the free-agent sites, the reverse auction services, and the niche sites for specialized jobs and skills. Presented below are a diverse sample of employment–related Web sites.

- eLance.com (www.elance.com)
- Guru.com (www.guru.com)
- Monster.com (www.monster.com)
- vworker (vworker.com)

a. Prepare a review for each job site listed above. Include target employers, target employees, and notable Web site features.

b. Which site did you find most useful? Why?

3. **Integrating Data Capture**
Keys to Better Information
Business systems have long served to automate tasks, facilitate data capture, and enable new opportunities. These processes have crept into virtually all businesses and business processes. RE/MAX real estate agent Rosemary Chiaverini remembers well business 20 years ago and the rather cumbersome process of coordinating key exchanges with fellow agents. "It really limited the number of houses we could show in a day."

A key safe increased productivity by allowing real estate agents to open a key safe at each property. The key locked inside the key safe then provided access to the residence. Showing agents would then leave a business card behind to indicate that they had shown a property, but the listing agent would have to retrieve these cards personally. "I just didn't know for certain who was seeing my homes or what they thought of them."

GE Security's Supra iBox has changed that. Rosemary now uses an electronic, infrared key to open GE's new key safe, and the key records the transaction. When she synchronizes her key online to update her key's codes, this information goes up to GE's database and is shared with the listing agent. With most agents in her area subscribing to this system, Rosemary has Internet access information about who visited one of her listed homes and when. She uses this information to follow up on each visit and gain valuable insights. "Before, I would waste a lot of time calling busy agents who had arranged to show a home but hadn't."

a. Use a search engine to look up the Supra iBox. Describe the product's capabilities.

b. Use a search engine to look up Sprint and the Supra iBox. How has Sprint taken GE's product one step further?

c. Describe the next-generation product you might sell Rosemary once keyless locks become commonplace.

4. **Word's Mail Merge**
Partner Name Tags
Ms. Sapper, this year's annual partner meeting coordinator for a global accounting firm, faced an interesting challenge. She wanted to provide the 400 partners attending the meeting the opportunity to mix, mingle, and network. Most partners only knew a handful of their peers, and Ms. Sapper wanted to make everyone feel as comfortable as possible. With a list of partners in hand, she decided to prepare name tags for each participant. Each tag would include the partner's first name, last name, practice area, and region. Arranging the tags alphabetically by last name at the event's welcome desk would allow each partner to quickly find and use his or her name tag.

Complete the following steps to prepare partner name badges.

a. Download and save "partners.xls" from the MIS 10e OLC.

b. Use Microsoft Word's mail merge feature to generate name tags sorted by last name and then first name. Use a suitable name tag template, and format the name tag as illustrated below. Be sure to include first name, last name, industry, and region. Turn in either the first two pages of the merged names or the merged file, depending on your professor's preference.

Example:

Christoph Aarns
Audit
Asia Pacific

REAL WORLD

CASE 3

Cisco Systems: Telepresence and the Future of Collaboration

If you want to catch a glimpse of the future of knowledge work in the twenty-first century, a good place to start is a small family homestead outside Germantown, Illinois, 40 miles east of St. Louis. That's where Craig Huegens, director of architecture for networks, data centers, and unified communication services at Cisco Systems, lives and works. When Huegens moved there from northern California in December 2000, it was for the most basic of reasons: He wanted his newborn son to grow up around family, who now live just five miles down the road. Nevertheless, it was something of a revolutionary concept because Huegens was Cisco's first full-time IT telecommuter.

Back then, he got by using e-mail and Internet Relay Chat, a primordial form of instant messaging. It took some accommodation on the part of both Huegens and his colleagues back in San Jose, but they made it work. Over the last seven years, Huegens has become the spearpoint for the philosophy and technology at the center of Cisco's biggest strategic shift since the tech bubble burst in 2001—"Cisco 3.0," as CEO and chairman John Chambers likes to call it.

Cisco 1.0 was all about getting people connected by selling truckloads of routers and switches, and it made the company, founded in 1984 by a small group of computer scientists out of Stanford University, one of the fastest-growing in American business history. Cisco 2.0, Chambers says, was centered on business process change—using all that hardware and, of course, a few truckloads of new gear, like information processing telephones—to drive innovation and productivity gains.

Cisco 3.0 employs even more hardware and software to transform business models, and Chambers, with characteristic evangelical fervor, says it will fundamentally change the nature of work, enabling productivity growth to soar back into the realms last seen in the economic surge of the late 1990s. "We believe that productivity can grow not at 1 percent or 2 percent, but 3 percent to 5 percent for the sustainable future," says Chambers in an interview in his office in Cisco's San Jose headquarters.

That's an audacious vision, and it will be driven, Chambers maintains, by the type of collaborative, Web 2.0 technology that now keeps Huegens in touch with his team in San Jose: interactive Web forums like wikis and blogs; IM; interactive "teamspaces" mounted on WebEx (which Cisco acquired in March for $3.2 billion); and above all, videoconferencing and its big brother, telepresence, which is a life-size, high-def, multiple-screen system for face-to-face meetings among users in multiple locations. The question is: Is Cisco's latest initiative just Videoconferencing 2.0, or is it really something revolutionary?

The new emphasis on intensely collaborative technologies at Cisco, a company that epitomizes the catchphrase "eating our own dog food," ups the ante for CIO Rebecca Jacoby. She assumed that post just over a year ago and has been the point person for rolling out telepresence and other new-age tools to the demanding in-house customers at Cisco.

Jacoby, who's been at Cisco for 13 years but is a self-described nontechie (she came up through the manufacturing ranks), takes over at an interesting time. Not only is she Cisco's first female CIO, succeeding the semilegendary Brad Boston, now senior vice president of the Global Government Solutions Group, she is also helping to lead Cisco through a transformation as radical as any in the company's 24-year history. To do so, Jacoby says, Cisco is making itself the test bed for the next generation of collaboration tools. Like many Cisco executives today, Jacoby has a single-screen telepresence unit in a small back room off her office in San Jose. Since it began to roll out the immersive conferencing technology in late 2006, Cisco has deployed telepresence rooms in 160 of its offices worldwide.

When Chambers first talked to Jacoby about taking on the CIO job, she wasn't sure she really wanted the spotlight that goes with being the chief IT executive for one of the world's most powerful and venerated IT companies. The prospect of transforming the entire company, however, "was irresistible to me," she says. Jacoby realized that the conventional role of IT—acquiring and deploying new technologies and educating employees on using them—was now, at least in part, flipped. "When you talk about the collaboration tools out there, they're not necessarily initiated by IT," she says.

Much of what Jacoby talks about is hardly earth-shattering—she has become an enthusiastic user of video blogs, or vlogs, she says—but its pervasive use at a company of Cisco's size and age is probably unusual. With a globalized workforce of highly connected, tech-savvy users, the adoption and learning flow both ways, to and from Cisco's IT group. Jacoby calls it "creating an environment of directed participation," in which the tools already being used by Cisco employees are adapted, refined, and sharpened to drive innovation and growth. "Our biggest challenge," she says, "is just keeping up with where these ideas are going and seeing how we can participate in how they are shaped and focused."

One of the initiatives Jacoby and her team have undertaken is to create an online "communications center of excellence," where new collaboration tools—from wikis to vlogs to telepresence—can be deployed, tested, and refined. Video, she says, is "phenomenally effective," particularly when communicating with employees outside the United States.

Equally powerful has been Cisco's I-Zone wiki, a companywide forum for new business ideas launched not by IT but by the Emerging Technologies Group, headed by Marthin DeBeer. Live for 18 months, the wiki has produced 600 ideas for potential one-billion-dollar-per-annum-size ventures (the minimum level for Cisco to get behind a new business), suggested by the company's more than 61,000 employees.

Reflecting Chambers's mantra that to lead the next phase of the Internet Cisco must constantly reinvent its own processes, the focus on collaboration has also spurred a reorganization of the company's hierarchy. Beginning in the painful 2001 meltdown, when Cisco posted a net loss of $1 billion, Chambers led a shift from the usual product, sales and marketing, and other functional groups toward a more horizontal, less command-and-control structure of "councils, boards, and task forces."

"The councils focus on $10 billion-plus opportunities, the boards on $1 billion opportunities, and the task forces are the implementation of any of the above," Chambers says. It sounds like a somewhat communistic way of reshaping a $35 billion-a-year company, but for Chambers this new structure is key to the company's regeneration. "The first few years were pretty painful," Chambers admits. "It's like anything you do—usually it's not the technology that's your limiting factor, it's people, and getting them to change from, instead of command and control, to collaboration." Cisco, however, makes its living leading technology changes, and the key to Cisco 3.0 will be the most sophisticated and expensive: telepresence.

DeBeer's executive assistant, Margaret Hooshmand, can be found almost every day outside his office in San Jose. Only she's not really there ; she's at the Cisco office in Richardson, Texas, and she bilocates via telepresence to the cubicle adjoining DeBeer's office. You can walk by (in San Jose) and chat with her any time, and if you don't remind yourself, you'll forget to ask her how the weather is in central Texas.

Telepresence was the first new product to emerge from DeBeer's Emerging Technologies Group, and it ramped up in record time, from hiring the first engineer in February 2005 to shipping the first external system in December 2006. Among the design principles, or "Telepresence Rules,"

DeBeer's team devised were: "People will always appear life-size" and "To initiate a meeting you have to do just one thing," for example, press a button on the handset.

If you look behind the curtain, as it were, you'll see that the whole thing runs through a single Ethernet cable. It's a superb piece of technology.

"Cisco is betting on a proprietary approach," says Michelle Damrow, head of product marketing for competitor Polycom's telepresence group. "We think standards-based communications will win eventually." Indeed, Cisco faces strong competition in this nascent market from the likes of HP, which introduced its Halo telepresence system before the Cisco product launched, and from videoconferencing leader Polycom, which offers a high-end telepresence system with merged, seamless displays, as opposed to Cisco's three-separate-screens approach. Damrow notes Polycom is betting on a standards-based system that will interoperate with any standards-based video codex on the market today.

The answer, as you might expect, is that Cisco believes its installed base, its brand power, and its marketing muscle will push enough TelePresence units into the market to allow it to become the de facto standard.

Telepresence itself, says Chambers, will be offered as an on-demand managed service at off-site locations for companies that can't or don't want to invest in their own systems. When interoperability among multiple vendors does come, it will be on Cisco's terms, not industry-imposed.

If that's not quite Web 2.0 enough for you, well, welcome to John Chambers's world. *Cisco 3.0: Coming soon* to a three-screen, high-definition, surround-sound theater near you.

Source: Adapted from Richard Martin, "Cisco's Emerging Collaboration Strategy," *InformationWeek*, January 28, 2008.

CASE STUDY QUESTIONS

1. What are the main business benefits of the collaboration technologies described in the case?

2. How do these go beyond saving on corporate travel? Provide several specific examples.

3. Michelle Damrow of Polycom notes Cisco is betting on a proprietary standard for its TelePresence product, while competitors are going with interoperability. Do you agree with Cisco's strategy? Why or why not? Defend your answer.

4. Think about the I-Zone wiki described in the case, Cisco's forum for new business ideas, and its seeming success in that regard. Why do you think that is the case? Do these technologies foster creativity, provide an opportunity to communicate already existing ideas, or both? Defend your answer.

REAL WORLD ACTIVITIES

1. Go online and search the Internet for commercial offerings that compete with Cisco's TelePresence products, such as those noted in the case. Prepare a report comparing and contrasting their features and specifications, and justify your selection. Would it matter whether the purchasing company was large or small?

2. Put yourself in the place of a newly hired Cisco employee. How comfortable would you feel working on a team distributed across the globe, using the technologies described in the case? What would be the major challenges you would face? Break into small groups with your classmates to discuss these issues, and explore the reasons behind any conflicting viewpoints.

REAL WORLD CASE 4

OHSU, Sony, Novartis, and Others: Strategic Information Systems— It's HR's Turn

"Our people are our most valuable asset." How many times have you heard that company slogan? In recent years, HR departments have focused their technology efforts on driving down costs by automating or outsourcing nonstrategic, transaction-oriented processes such as benefits enrollment and payroll. As a result, many employees can now do a number of things online that used to require the intervention of HR staff, such as viewing pay stubs, changing personal information, or enrolling for benefits.

Increasingly, however, HR is being urged not only to reduce the cost of hiring, retaining, and compensating employees but also to optimize the corporate talent pool. After all, if your workforce is your biggest expense, shouldn't you shape it to support the strategic goals of the business in the best way possible?

Imagine placing an electronic order to hire an employee the same way a factory manager uses ERP software to order more parts for the assembly line. That's roughly what's happening at Oregon Health & Science University (OHSU). "More and more, HR is being called upon to be a strategic partner," says Joe Tonn, manager of HR management systems at OHSU in Portland.

The payoff is significant: The university is filling job openings two weeks faster than it once did and saving at least $1,500 per job now that it's using Oracle Corp.'s iRecruitment software. The iRecruitment application, part of Oracle's e-Business Human Resources Management System (HRMS) suite, enables managers to request a new employee and process applications electronically. The software handles most of the time-consuming administrative work, including routing requisition forms to the appropriate managers and posting the job on the Web site. "We wanted to be able to open a job requisition in the morning and have qualified candidates in the afternoon," says Tonn.

In fact, OHSU now has access to applicants only minutes after a job opening is posted to the university's Web site, and it fills those jobs in just four weeks instead of six or more.

The university also recently added Oracle's Manager Self-Service module for logging changes to employee status (e.g., promotions or use of family leave) and uses the Oracle Employee Self-Service application for benefits management. Tonn expects to add software for performance reviews, succession planning, and learning management over the next couple of years.

Large and midsize organizations such as OHSU are increasingly turning to these new types of employee management applications—commonly called human capital management (HCM) or workforce optimization software—to automate HR processes that used to be done manually, on paper, or by e-mail.

"Human capital management covers the whole discipline of managing the workforce, bringing them in and tracking them over time," says Christa Manning, an analyst at AMR Research Inc. in Boston. AMR forecasts a 10 percent compound annual growth rate through 2010 for the $6 billion HCM market. Much of the market growth can be attributed to the upcoming retirement of baby boomers, which will shrink the pool of available workers. Companies need to automate their systems so they can better identify employees they want to retain and then provide a career path for them.

Sony Computer Entertainment America Inc. uses recruitment software from WorkforceLogic to automate its process for hiring contract workers. Sally Buchanan, director of human resources, says the software is particularly useful for ensuring that hiring managers understand and comply with the legal distinctions between contract and salaried employees.

"When they requisition a contractor, they must answer a series of questions through the WorkforceLogic interface, and the application renders a recommendation on whether the position is best filled by a contractor or by someone on the payroll," says Buchanan.

Employee performance management, career development, and succession planning are all functions that can be automated with HCM applications. For example, Tyco International Ltd. uses Kenexa's CareerTracker to track employee performance and promotions. The software, which is configured with Tyco's performance standards and rating system, can plot employee performance on a graph to identify the top performers, both in terms of job achievement and in meeting Tyco's leadership behavior standards.

Using the database of employee credentials and expertise, Tyco can also locate the best people to fill key job openings and analyze what type of training they'll need. "We can identify who we have and how they fit," says Shaun Zitting, director of organizational development at the Princeton, N.J.–based company.

According to AMR's Manning, most corporate executives like having a tool that helps them evaluate and promote people on purely objective criteria. "They know it's not based on, 'I like Joe because we go to lunch every day.' It brings some real science to the process and allows you to not only identify your top performers but also to know why they're top performers," she says. Career development and succession planning applications have also become more important as baby boomers retire and organizations have to find qualified replacements. Succession planning isn't just for CEOs and other top executives anymore. "It's starting to cascade down into the organization as the collecting and associating of employee information become easier," says Manning.

Managers can associate key characteristics with specific jobs and analyze the traits of successful employees. Employees themselves can use the data to see their most likely career paths in an organization. Compensation management, another function often found in HCM tools, enables organizations to create incentive programs, tie compensation to performance goals, and analyze pay packages and trends.

Scheduling work shifts for 27,000 health care professionals in a wide range of specialties and at multiple locations is a formidable task. At Banner Health, a large hospital system based in Phoenix, however, the implementation of the Kronos scheduling application has automated much of the process. Banner uses the Kronos application to log hours worked and to plan schedules, says Kathy Schultz, director of IT at Banner Health.

Integrating data about hours worked with future scheduling helps to ensure that employees aren't expected to work if they've just put in a lot of overtime. "What hours you work isn't always what you were scheduled to work," notes Schultz. "Having scheduling integrated with live time-and-attendance information is extremely critical."

At pharmaceutical giant Novartis AG, sales and research and development professionals are expected to take various classes to keep them up to date on the latest products and trends. With about 550 Web-based and classroom-based courses available, the old paper- and Excel-based process for administering training had become cumbersome and time-consuming. Yet by using Saba Software Inc.'s Learning Suite, administrative work has been reduced by 50 percent, according to John Talanca, head of learning technologies at Novartis. "It's allowed the administrators to be more efficient and take on other work. In the past, they would spend hours and hours each day managing this," says Talanca.

HR applications often contain a variety of employee data, including salaries, experience, education, performance reviews, and benefits selections. Analysis tools can enable HR managers to leverage those data for strategic decision making. They can, for instance, track employee performance against company benchmarks, forecast the skills that will be needed for future projects, analyze salary increases by geographic region or professional field, or predict trends in benefits selection and costs.

For example, OHSU's Tonn hopes eventually to use analysis tools to evaluate recruiting practices more efficiently.

Honing the school's recruiting campaigns could produce better candidates as well as lower costs. "We can see how many applications a particular source gives us, and whether we ever hire applicants from that source. If we do hire them, do they become successful employees? Running an ad in The Oregonian might produce a thousand applications. But if we didn't hire any of them, then that was a whole lot of administrative work that didn't bear any fruit."

Organizations such as Tyco are increasingly viewing employees as assets, to be acquired, cultivated, and deployed strategically—not unlike product inventory or IT systems. The very name of the software category, human capital management, conveys the notion that a worker is an investment that should be optimized. "Managers want to see how the people they hired are doing," says Manning. "It's taking the organization's people assets and leveraging them to reach business goals, such as increased sales, profitability, and customer satisfaction."

Individually, the various HCM tools are helpful, but to get optimal value, they need to be integrated, with the data stored in a common repository.

Organizational issues may be in the way, such as if the various HCM functions are split between different corporate departments, or if the HCM suite has to be implemented across multiple business units running disparate ERP and HR applications. Changing your HR system from transactional to strategic can take three to five years, but the important thing is to get started. As we move from an industrial to a knowledge economy, it's not what you manufacture but what your people know that gives you competitive advantage.

Source: Adapted from Sue Hildreth, "HR Gets a Dose of Science," *Computerworld*, February 5, 2007; and Mary Brandel, "HR Gets Strategic," *Computerworld*, January 24, 2005.

CASE STUDY QUESTIONS

1. What are some of the business benefits of the technologies described in the case? Provide several examples beyond the mere automation of transaction-oriented processes.

2. Do you think the business value of these strategic HRM applications depends on the type of business a company is in, for instance, consulting, manufacturing, or professional services? Why or why not? Explain.

3. What are some of the challenges and obstacles in developing and implementing HRM systems? Are these unique to this type of system? What strategies would you recommend for companies to meet those challenges? Provide several specific recommendations.

REAL WORLD ACTIVITIES

1. The case refers to a view of employees as "assets, to be acquired, cultivated, and deployed strategically—not unlike product inventory or IT systems." It also mentions that these systems allow managers to evaluate and promote people on objective criteria. Do you believe extensive adoption of these technologies may lead to a depersonalization of the employment relationship? Why or why not? Break into small groups to discuss these issues and then summarize your ideas.

2. What are some of the HR trends that seem to be operating behind this renewed emphasis on strategic applications of technology to this functional area? What new developments have recently arisen in this domain? Search the Internet for innovative applications of IT in HRM, and write a report to summarize your findings.

CHAPTER 8

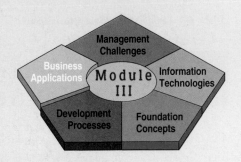

ENTERPRISE BUSINESS SYSTEMS

Learning Objectives

After reading and studying this chapter, you should be able to:

1. Identify and give examples to illustrate the following aspects of customer relationship management, enterprise resource management, and supply chain management systems:

   a. Business processes supported

   b. Customer and business value provided

   c. Potential challenges and trends

2. Understand the importance of managing at the enterprise level to achieve maximum efficiencies and benefits.

SECTION I | Getting All the Geese Lined Up: Managing at the Enterprise Level

Here's a question you probably never expected to find in your information system text: Have you ever noticed how geese fly? They start out as a seemingly chaotic flock of birds but very quickly end up flying in a V-shape or echelon pattern like that shown in Figure 8.1. As you might imagine, this consistency in flying formation is not an accident. By flying in this manner, each bird receives a slight, but measurable, benefit in reduced drag from the bird in front. This makes it easier for all of the birds to fly long distances than if they just took up whatever portion of the sky they happened to find. Of course, the lead bird has the toughest job, but geese have figured out a way to help there, as well. Systematically, one of the birds from the formation will fly up to relieve the current lead bird. In this way, the entire flock shares the load as they all head in the same direction.

Okay, so what does this have to do with information systems? This chapter will focus on systems that span the enterprise and that are intended to support three enterprisewide operations: *customer relationships*, *resource planning*, and *supply chain*. Each operation requires a unique focus and, thus, a unique system to support it, but they all share one common goal: to get the entire organization to line up and head in the same direction, just as the geese do.

We could cover these important enterprise systems in any order, and if we asked three people how to do it, we would likely get three different approaches. For our purposes, we will start with the focus of every business: *the customer*. From there, we will expand our view to the back-office operations and, finally, to systems that manage the movement of raw materials and finished goods. The end result, of course, is that we get all the "geese" in the business to fly in the same direction in as efficient a manner as possible.

FIGURE 8.1

Geese fly in a highly organized and efficient V-shaped formation—much like a well-run business.

Customer Relationship Management: The Business Focus

Introduction

Today, customers are in charge. It is easier than ever for customers to comparison shop and, with a click of the mouse, to switch companies. As a result, customer relationships have become a company's most valued asset. These relationships are worth more than the company's products, stores, factories, Web addresses, and even employees. Every company's strategy should address how to find and retain the most profitable customers possible.

The primary business value of customer relationships today is indisputable. That's why we emphasized in Chapter 2 that becoming a *customer-focused business* was one of the top business strategies that can be supported by information technology. Thus, many companies are implementing *customer relationship management* (CRM) business initiatives and information systems as part of a customer-focused or *customer-centric* strategy to improve their chances for success in today's competitive business environment. In this section, we will explore basic CRM concepts and technologies, as well as examples of the benefits and challenges faced by companies that have implemented CRM systems as part of their customer-focused business strategy. See Figure 8.2.

Let's start with a real-world example. Read the Real World Case on the next page. We can learn a lot about the business benefits (and challenges) of mobile CRM from this example.

What Is CRM?

Managing the full range of the customer relationship involves two related objectives: one, to provide the organization and all of its customer-facing employees with a single, complete view of every customer at every touchpoint and across all channels; and, two, to provide the customer with a single, complete view of the company and its extended channels.

That's why companies are turning to customer relationship management to improve their customer focus. CRM uses information technology to create a cross-functional enterprise system that integrates and automates many of the *customer-serving* processes in sales, marketing, and customer services that interact with a company's customers. CRM systems also create an IT framework of Web-enabled software and databases that integrates these processes with the rest of a company's business operations. CRM systems include a family of software modules that provides the tools that enable a business and its employees to deliver fast, convenient, dependable, and consistent service to its customers. Siebel Systems, Oracle, PeopleSoft, SAP AG, and Epiphany are some of the leading vendors of CRM software. Figure 8.3 illustrates some of the major application components of a CRM system. Let's take a look at each of them.

Contact and Account Management

CRM software helps sales, marketing, and service professionals capture and track relevant data about every past and planned contact with prospects and customers, as well as other business and life cycle events of customers. Information is captured from all customer touchpoints, such as telephone, fax, e-mail, the company's Web site, retail stores, kiosks, and personal contact. CRM systems store the data in a common customer database that integrates all customer account information and makes it available throughout the company via Internet, intranet, or other network links for sales, marketing, service, and other CRM applications.

Sales

A CRM system provides sales representatives with the software tools and company data sources they need to support and manage their sales activities and optimize cross-selling and up-selling. Cross-selling is an approach in which a customer of one product or service, say, auto insurance, might also be interested in purchasing a related product or service, say, homeowner's insurance. By using a cross-selling technique, sales representatives can better serve their customers while simultaneously improving their sales. Up-selling

CASE 1

Dow Corning and DirecTV: CRM Goes Mobile

Chip Reeves knows all about the life of a sales guy. That's because during his nearly 20 years at Dow Corning, a global manufacturer of silicon-based products, he was one. He knows all too well that salespeople ignore any new administrative process or technology unless it allows them to make more sales or use their time more efficiently.

Now, as Dow Corning's director of marketing and sales processes, Reeves is leading the company's convergence of its CRM and e-business efforts, as well as streamlining its compliance and reporting functions. The goal, naturally, is to provide excellent customer service—and to make it easy for Dow Corning sales and marketing staff to use the expansive CRM system. *Real easy.*

Reeves also served as the chairman for the Americas SAP User Group's customer management group, so he knows both the power and limitations of enterprise technologies and the reality of how salespeople use CRM tools on mobile devices such as laptops and smart phones.

Both topics are important if you're to bring mobility to corporate applications. Many companies and CIOs are struggling to determine exactly how best to mobilize critical applications that can bring a measurable payback to the company but also limit the disruption to and administrative headaches in their users' lives. "Salespeople don't want to get on their devices for 30 minutes after a sales call," says Christopher Fletcher, a research director who specializes in mobile applications at AMR Research. "Salespeople by nature are independent, autonomous, and don't always play by corporate rules. It's sometimes tough to get them to use what

seems like administrative functions so that management can have better control."

Reeves says he is always balancing the pushback from the sales folks with the CRM demands of the business. "Heavy involvement with the salespeople has been key, and we're trying to be responsive to them," he notes. "But by no means do we have that balance perfected yet."

A huge part of Reeves' task has been to ensure that Dow Corning's core enterprise applications, which rest on SAP's suite of products, are intact and can be used by all users in Dow Corning's sales and marketing group. "A lot of what we've done in the CRM space has been putting a foundation in to help our people work more effectively and give them more access to information," Reeves says.

While Dow Corning had been smoothing out the back-office infrastructure, however, Reeves and his team also had to ensure that salespeople were being listened to and would want to use the mobile devices and applications. His team approached that by "looking at a day in the life of a salesperson," he says. "Thinking through their information and task needs, what were their priorities, what were their common tasks, what were the process pain points."

One thing became immediately clear to Reeves: When equipping mobile teams (such as the sales force), less is always more. He says that he has preached a "low input, high output" strategy that has guided the entire mobile deployment. Adding dozens and dozens of input fields to salespeople's BlackBerry screens, which forces them to do a ton of extra work, is a recipe for disaster. "We've tried to weed out and simplify the processes: What are we going to need to know and how do we need that information," he says. "There's always a logical explanation for why a field is there. But then the question is: Do we really need it? We're constantly trying to move toward a simpler set of questions."

Since first piloting the devices, Reeves says the mobile team has been working with the salespeople to tweak capabilities and address their ongoing concerns. "We are constantly in change-management mode," he says.

For example, there used to be more than a dozen classifications of customer sales opportunities and two screens full of data to input for each sales opportunity. Now there is one opportunity type that can be filled out—on just one screen. Salespeople can get what Reeves calls "quick links" on SAP CRM data on their BlackBerrys simply by clicking an icon. These quick links show critical data, such as each salesperson's sales by customer, open order statuses, and customer complaints (which is important for a salesperson dropping in on a customer). Before the mobile deployment, when a customer asked to check on order status, the Dow Corning sales rep had to call into Dow Corning customer service operations, Reeves notes. Now the sales rep gets that in seconds on his BlackBerry. For Reeves, it all comes back to: "How much quicker can we get that responsiveness?"

FIGURE 8.2

Mobile CRM increases sales productivity and improves relationships with customers.

Source: © Kablonk! Kablonk!/Photolibrary.

In addition, the sales lead-generation process has been streamlined for salespeople on the BlackBerrys. Again, the quick links allow them to view critical lead information and input data that's tailored specifically to the mobile device's screen size, Reeves says.

Using the SAP Portal technology that lead generation data flows back into Dow Corning's CRM system "without a salesperson having to open up the CRM application," Reeves notes. So far, he estimates that the simplified lead follow-up via the mobile SAP application saves 15 to 30 minutes per lead and increases the likelihood for follow-up.

Satellite TV provider DirecTV ran into similar challenges when implementing their mobile CRM solution. DirecTV works with more than 6,000 independent dealers who resell its service to residential customers.

Directly serving those distributors is a team of nearly 700 area sales managers, who need critical information, such as financial data, active service requests, and activation and cancellation rates, while in the field. For several years, DirecTV has been a satisfied user of Siebel's CRM On Demand system, but it didn't work for field sales managers who couldn't carry around a laptop, says Erik Walters, a program manager for DirecTV's sales and operations arm. "For our guys, that's not mobile enough."

Walters' team faced an increasingly common problem in companies with mobile sales and field employees, such as Dow Corning and many others: *how to mobilize an existing enterprise application.*

DirecTV coupled the back-end CRM application with mobile middleware from Antenna Software. Antenna creates front-end systems that tap into popular enterprise mobility platforms like BlackBerry and Windows Mobile, providing data to mobile users from various databases via a single integrated interface. "DirecTV has 675 employees using Antenna, vastly increasing the productivity of sales managers," Walters says. In the past, an industrious area sales manager would be lucky to see three or four customers a day; now it's closer to 10 or 12.

The move to a mobilized CRM platform is part of a broader shift in the way DirecTV sales managers interact with dealers. The company is changing how it handles calls and requests from dealers, Walters says. "Everybody is looking for that 360-degree view of the dealer customer." To get that view, DirecTV will implement the hosted Call Center On Demand product from Siebel parent Oracle for incoming phone queries from dealers. The success of the mobilized CRM On Demand has given the company confidence to move to a more hosted model for its overall relationship with this critical group of resellers.

Enterprise vendors have certainly realized the importance of mobility and have increased their capabilities and offerings, says Fletcher. Shailesh Rao, vice president of product management at SAP, says, "Customers are demanding that every application vendor provide mobile access." Rao uses Dow Corning's situation as an example of the overall trend that CIOs need to realize. "It's not application-centric anymore; it's more scenario-based information access for mobile workers," he says. "We're not so much talking about the applications. I just want to provide the information the business users want and need the most—irrespective of where the information is coming from."

For any CIO starting out on a mobile endeavor right now, AMR's Fletcher offers these pieces of advice. First, before CIOs start any project, figure out what you want to happen at the end of the project, such as exactly what salespeople will get out of the new system and how long it will take to get payback on the rollout. "Know what your business case is and stick to it," he says.

And second, don't forget the carrot with the stick: "You have to tell salespeople, 'You're going to start using this new CRM system, and you're going to be able to give better quotes to customers.' Or 'we promise to give you 40 new qualified leads every month—but you have to put that critical information into the system,'" he says.

At Dow Corning, Reeves says, his salespeople now have a competitive advantage, but it's still early on in the transformation. "I have a lot of excitement at where we're at today and what's possible looking ahead," Reeves says. "But there's more work to do."

Source: Adapted from Thomas Wailgum, "Mobile CRM: Why Less Is More," *CIO.com*, October 19, 2007; and Richard Martin, "DirecTV Gets Truly Mobile CRM," *InformationWeek*, August 11, 2008.

CASE STUDY QUESTIONS

1. Think about the business benefits of the mobile CRM deployments discussed in the case. How did Dow Corning and DirecTV benefit from these applications? What can they do that was not possible before? What were the effects on productivity?

2. Use examples from the case to illustrate your answer.

3. What are some of the reasons that make it so challenging to mobilize an existing enterprise application? How did the companies featured in the case tackle that challenge?

4. Salespeople are generally known for their independence and emphasis on efficient time management, and not always for their willingness to adopt new technologies pushed by management. What were some of the approaches mentioned in the case that were used to foster adoption? What other alternatives can you think of?

REAL WORLD ACTIVITIES

1. Erik Walters of DirecTV notes that a mobile CRM platform is part of the effort in search of the "360-degree view of the customer." What does he mean by that? Go online and research this concept, other companies that are embracing it, and what technologies they employ. Prepare a report to summarize your findings.

2. Both companies emphasize the many benefits accrued from their mobile CRM deployments. Chip Reeves of Dow Corning states that the application provides their salespeople with a competitive advantage. Do you agree with this statement? Why or why not? Break into small groups with your classmates to discuss whether mobile CRM can provide a lasting competitive advantage.

FIGURE 8.3
The major application
clusters in customer
relationship management.

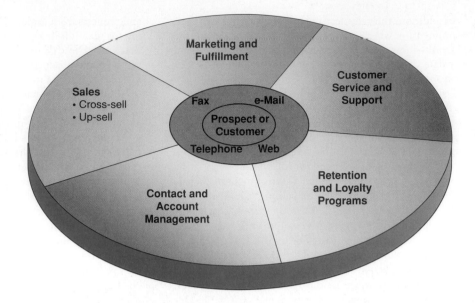

refers to the process of finding ways to sell a new or existing customer a better product than they are currently seeking. Additional examples include sales prospect and product information, product configuration, and sales quote generation capabilities. CRM also provides real-time access to a single common view of the customer, enabling sales representatives to check on all aspects of a customer's account status and history before scheduling their sales calls. For example, a CRM system would alert a bank sales representative to call customers who make large deposits to sell them premier credit or investment services. Or it would alert a salesperson of unresolved service, delivery, or payment problems that could be resolved through a personal contact with a customer.

Marketing and Fulfillment

CRM systems help marketing professionals accomplish direct marketing campaigns by automating such tasks as qualifying leads for targeted marketing, and scheduling and tracking direct marketing mailings. Then the CRM software helps marketing professionals capture and manage prospect and customer response data in the CRM database, and analyze the customer and business value of a company's direct marketing campaigns. CRM also assists in the fulfillment of prospect and customer responses and requests by quickly scheduling sales contacts and providing appropriate information on products and services to them, while capturing relevant information for the CRM database.

Customer Service and Support

A CRM system provides service reps with software tools and real-time access to the common customer database shared by sales and marketing professionals. CRM helps customer service managers create, assign, and manage requests for service by customers. *Call center* software routes calls to customer support agents based on their skills and authority to handle specific kinds of service requests. *Help desk* software helps customer service reps assist customers who are having problems with a product or service by providing relevant service data and suggestions for resolving problems. Web-based self-service enables customers to access personalized support information easily at the company Web site, while it gives them an option to receive further assistance online or by phone from customer service personnel.

Retention and Loyalty Programs

Consider the following:

- It costs six times more to sell to a new customer than to sell to an existing one.
- A typical dissatisfied customer will tell 8 to 10 people about his or her experience.
- A company can boost its profits 85 percent by increasing its annual customer retention by only 5 percent.

FIGURE 8.4   A proposed report format for evaluating the customer retention performance of Charles Schwab & Co.

	Navigation	Performance	Operations	Environment
Customer Retention	Customer retention rate Household retention rate Average customer tenure	Retention rate by customer cohort Retention rate by customer segment Customer loyalty rating	Percentage of customers who are active Web users Percentage of customers who interact via e-mail Decline in customer activity Propensity to defect	Competitors' offers Share of portfolio Comparative retention Comparative customer tenure
Customer Experience	Satisfaction by customer segment Satisfaction by cohort Satisfaction by customer scenario	Customer satisfaction by: ● Task ● Touchpoint ● Channel partner End-to-end performance by scenario Customer satisfaction with quality of information provided	Elapsed time for commonly performed tasks Accuracy of Web search results Percentage of trades executed with price improvement Percentage of e-mails answered accurately in one hour	Comparative satisfaction: Competitors: ● Other online brokers ● Other financial service firms ● All products and services
Customer Spending	Average revenue per customer Average profitability per customer Growth in customer assets Customer lifetime value	Revenues per customer segment Profits per customer segment Growth in customer assets per segment	Daily log-ins at market opening Revenue trades per day Percentage increase in customer assets Cost to serve by touchpoint	Total brokerage assets Growth in brokerage assets

● The odds of selling a product to a new customer are 15 percent, whereas the odds of selling a product to an existing customer are 50 percent.

● Seventy percent of complaining customers will do business with the company again if it takes care of a service problem quickly.

That's why enhancing and optimizing customer retention and loyalty is a major business strategy and primary objective of customer relationship management. CRM systems try to help a company identify, reward, and market to their most loyal and profitable customers. CRM analytical software includes data mining tools and other analytical marketing software, while CRM databases may consist of a customer data warehouse and CRM data marts. These tools are used to identify profitable and loyal customers and to direct and evaluate a company's targeted marketing and relationship marketing programs toward them. Figure 8.4 is an example of part of a proposed Web-based report format for evaluating Charles Schwab & Co.'s customer retention performance.

CRM Is Really Customer Partnership	Businesses that are unwilling to acknowledge the significance of the social computing revolution are "stupid." So says Paul Greenberg, author of *CRM at the Speed of Light* and the president of the 56 Group, a consultancy. Speaking at the Enterprise 2.0 Conference in November 2010, Greenberg did not mince words. The convergence of communication technology and social networking has changed the way that companies relate to customers and customers relate to companies, he insists.

This is not a new trend. It's been accelerating since 2002 or 2003, Greenberg argues. "It's a communications revolution," he said. "This is a social transformation that has impacted businesses."

For Greenberg, customer relationship management, or CRM, has become customer partnership management. The change in the way people communicate, now heavily reliant on social networking tools, demands a new approach to the way businesses interact with customers.

"The customer now controls the business eco-system," he said. "The customer is now in command of the conversations going on out there. . . . The customer can impact your brand, positively or negatively, without your permission. They're operating and communicating in channels that you don't own."

CRM is no longer just a model for managing customers but one for fostering customer engagement, says Greenberg.

Engagement, as described by Greenberg, means listening to customers and allowing them to participate in the product design process. Great customer experiences historically involved a seamless enterprise value chain that functioned efficiently. Nowadays, he says, it's a different story. It's about looking at customers as partners.

As an example of the way businesses should operate, Greenberg points to consumer goods giant Procter & Gamble, which has used feedback from social communities to reengineer its supply chain and solicits product innovation through its Connect + Develop portal.

"We're looking at something dramatic here," concluded Greenberg. "The opportunity is gigantic. Ignore it at your own risk."

Source: Adapted from Thomas Claburn, "Enterprise 2.0: Rethinking Customer Relationship Management," *InformationWeek*, November 10, 2010.

The Three Phases of CRM

Figure 8.5 illustrates another way to think about the customer and business value and components of customer relationship management. We can view CRM as an integrated system of Web-enabled software tools and databases accomplishing a variety of customer-focused business processes that support the three phases of the relationship between a business and its customers.

- **Acquire.** A business relies on CRM software tools and databases to help it acquire new customers by doing a superior job of contact management, sales prospecting, selling, direct marketing, and fulfillment. The goal of these CRM functions is to help customers perceive the value of a superior product offered by an outstanding company.

- **Enhance.** Web-enabled CRM account management and customer service and support tools help keep customers happy by supporting superior service from a responsive networked team of sales and service specialists and business partners. In addition, CRM sales force automation and direct marketing and fulfillment tools help companies cross-sell and up-sell to their customers, thus increasing their profitability to the business. The value the customers perceive is the convenience of one-stop shopping at attractive prices.

- **Retain.** CRM analytical software and databases help a company proactively identify and reward its most loyal and profitable customers to retain and expand their business via targeted marketing and relationship marketing programs. The value the customers perceive is of a rewarding personalized business relationship with "their company."

FIGURE 8.5

How CRM supports the three phases of the relationship between a business and its customers.

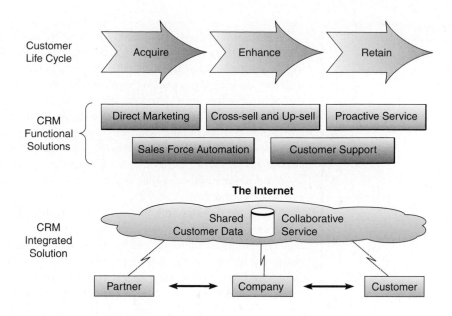

Benefits and Challenges of CRM

The potential business benefits of customer relationship management are many. For example, CRM allows a business to identify and target its best customers—those who are the most profitable to the business—so they can be retained as lifelong customers for greater and more profitable services. It makes possible real-time customization and personalization of products and services based on customer wants, needs, buying habits, and life cycles. CRM can also keep track of when a customer contacts the company, regardless of the contact point. In addition, CRM systems can enable a company to provide a consistent customer experience and superior service and support across all the contact points a customer chooses. All of these benefits would provide strategic business value to a company and major customer value to its customers.

Continental Airlines: Getting to Know Your Customers

Wouldn't it be nice if just once, one of those surly airline employees offered a sincere and unequivocal apology for losing your luggage or for a delayed flight? If you fly first class with Continental Airlines, you may finally get that apology.

Since 2001, the Houston-based carrier has been enhancing the in-flight reports it provides to flight attendants just before takeoff with more detailed information on passengers. For example, in addition to indicating which passengers ordered special meals, the expanded reports flag the airline's high-value customers and detail such things as whether they've had their luggage lost in the recent past or experienced a delayed flight. Armed with this information, flight attendants can now approach these customers during the flight to apologize for the inconveniences.

Such high-touch, personalized service increases customer loyalty, particularly among Continental's most valuable patrons, and that loyalty in turn drives revenue.

Continental breaks customers into different levels of profitability: Since building its new system, the airline reports earning an average of $200 in revenue from each of its 400,000 valuable customers, and an additional $800 in revenue from each of the 35,000 customers it places in its most profitable tier—all because it accords them better service.

Continental's desire to improve its ranking in a competitive industry drove it to build a real-time enterprise data warehouse (EDW). When the EDW was first being developed in 1998, its initial purpose was to bring data from some 27 systems together so that the company could more accurately forecast revenue. Since then, the company has used it to determine whether customer loyalty initiatives really affect revenue. By testing a sample of 30,000 customers who experienced delays, Continental found that those individuals to whom the airline sent a letter of apology and some sort of compensation (either in the form of a free cocktail on their next flight or extra frequent flier miles) forgot the event and didn't hold a grudge. In fact, Continental says that revenue from those passengers who received letters jumped 8 percent.

Using operational and customer data in the EDW, the data warehousing team developed a solution to one of the biggest headaches gate agents face: accommodating passengers inconvenienced by a cancellation or delay. The team created a program that automates the rebooking process. Before the program was developed, gate agents had to figure out on their own how to reroute passengers. Now, when a cancellation or delay occurs, the system does the work for them. For example, when the system identifies a high-value customer whose flight has been cancelled, the gate agent may decide to put that traveler on a competitor's flight just to make the individual happy and to get him on his way as fast as possible.

"Before the data warehouse, the person who yelled the loudest got the best service. Now our most valuable customers get the best service," says Alicia Acebo, Continental's data warehousing director.

Source: Adapted from Meridith Levinson, "Getting to Know Them," *CIO Magazine*, May 9, 2007.

CRM Failures

The business benefits of customer relationship management are not guaranteed and, instead, have proven elusive at many companies. Surveys by industry research groups include a report that more than 50 percent of CRM projects did not produce the results that were promised. In another research report, 20 percent of businesses surveyed reported that CRM implementations had actually damaged long-standing customer relationships. Furthermore, in a survey of senior management satisfaction with 25 management tools, CRM ranked near the bottom in user satisfaction, even though 72 percent expected to have CRM systems implemented shortly.

The common wisdom of why CRM systems fail includes:

- Lack of senior management sponsorship
- Improper change management
- Elongated projects that take on too much, too fast
- Lack of or poor integration between CRM and core business systems
- Lack of end-user incentives leading to poor user adoption rates

Despite the above, research shows that the major reason for CRM failure is a familiar one: lack of understanding and preparation. Too often, business managers rely on a major new application of information technology (like CRM) to solve a business problem without first developing the business process changes and change management programs that are required. For example, in many cases, failed CRM projects were implemented without the participation of the business stakeholders involved. Therefore, employees and customers were not prepared for the new processes or challenges that were part of the new CRM implementation. We will discuss the topic of failures in information technology management, system implementation, and change management further in later chapters.

| Unum Group: The Long Road to CRM | The multiple mergers that formed insurer Unum Group in the late 1990s aggregated billions in revenue, assembled thousands of employees, and created a quagmire of customer data systems that couldn't talk to each other. In all, with Provident, Colonial, Paul Revere, and Unum, there were 34 disconnected policy and claims back-office systems, all loaded with critical customer data. As a result, "it was very difficult to get your hands around the information," understates Bob Dolmovich, Unum Group's vice president of business integration and data architecture. One Unum Group customer's account, for instance, might exist in multiple places within the newly combined company, leading, of course, to a great deal of waste.

For the first couple of years after the mergers, Unum Group used a homegrown data-store solution as a quick fix. But by 2004, the $10 billion disability insurer felt compelled to embark on a new master data management strategy aimed at uniting the company's disparate pockets of customer data, including account activity, premiums, and payments.

Integral to Unum Group's strategy would be a customer data integration (CDI) hub, built on service-oriented architecture, using a standard set of protocols for connecting applications via the Web (in effect, Web services). The project, begun in early 2005, has already improved data quality, soothed the multiple customer records headaches, and created the possibility for a companywide, in-depth customer analysis. But as Dolmovich acknowledges, there's still a long way to go. Of those original 34 systems, he has been able to get rid of only four to date. But he's still optimistic.

Despite the long, slow slog, Dolmovich is hoping that the new CDI approach will ultimately give his company the 360-degree view of the customer that has been promised by vendors since the dawn of CRM. In the late 1990s, enterprise software vendors like Oracle, PeopleSoft, and Siebel sold the single-customer view as CRM's holy grail.

But implementation flameouts and legacy integration nightmares soured many CIOs on these expensive enterprisewide rollouts. A CDI hub differs from a traditional CRM solution in that a CDI hub allows a company to automatically integrate all of its customer data into one database, while ensuring the quality and accuracy of the data before they are sent to the hub's central store for safekeeping.

A stand-alone CRM system can't do that because it can't be integrated with the billing, marketing, ERP, and supply chain systems that house customer data, and it has no way to address inconsistent data across platforms.

Dolmovich says the first data loaded into the CDI hub in late 2005 came from business customers and brokers. With the new system, Dolmovich says, "We are now able to assimilate and display a broker's entire block of business and create some statistics and a profile of our relationship with that broker." Unum Group is now working to create individual profiles of employer customers so that every time a new customer account is created or accessed—perhaps to change an address or add new customer information—all employees of the insurance company, regardless of which system they are using, will see that change at the same time. "The desired end state is a CDI hub that has information about all customers across all products," he says.

Source: Adapted from Thomas Wailgum, "The Quest for Customer Data Integration," *CIO Magazine*, August 1, 2006. |
|---|---|

Trends in CRM

Increasingly, enterprises must create tighter collaborative linkages with partners, suppliers, and customers, squeezing out time and costs while enhancing the customer experience and the total value proposition.

Figure 8.6 outlines four types or categories of CRM that are being implemented by many companies today and summarizes their benefits to a business. These categories may also be viewed as stages or trends in how many companies implement

FIGURE 8.6 Many companies are implementing CRM systems with some or all of these capabilities.

Types of CRM	Business Value
Operational CRM	• Supports customer interaction with greater convenience through a variety of channels, including phone, fax, e-mail, chat, and mobile devices • Synchronizes customer interactions consistently across all channels • Makes your company easier to do business with
Analytical CRM	• Extracts in-depth customer history, preferences, and profitability information from your data warehouse and other databases • Allows you to analyze, predict, and derive customer value and behavior and forecast demand • Lets you approach your customers with relevant information and offers that are tailored to their needs
Collaborative CRM	• Enables easy collaboration with customers, suppliers, and partners • Improves efficiency and integration throughout the supply chain • Allows greater responsiveness to customer needs through sourcing of products and services outside of your enterprise
Portal-Based CRM	• Provides all users with the tools and information that fit their individual roles and preferences • Empowers all employees to respond to customer demands more quickly and become truly customer-focused • Provides the capability to instantly access, link, and use all internal and external customer information

Source: Adapted from mySAP Customer Relationship Management, mySAP.com, 2001, p. 7; and Brian Caulfield, "Toward a More Perfect (and Realistic) e-Business," *Business 2.0*, January 2002, p. 80.

CRM applications, and the figure also outlines some of the capabilities of CRM software products. Most businesses start out with operational CRM systems such as sales force automation and customer service centers. Then analytical CRM applications are implemented using several analytical marketing tools, such as data mining, to extract vital data about customers and prospects for targeted marketing campaigns.

Increasingly, businesses are moving to *collaborative* CRM systems, to involve business partners and customers in collaborative customer services. This includes systems for customer self-service and feedback, as well as **partner relationship management** (PRM) systems. PRM applications apply many of the same tools used in CRM systems to enhance collaboration between a company and its business partners, such as distributors and dealers, to coordinate and optimize sales and service to customers across all marketing channels. Finally, many businesses are building Internet, intranet, and extranet Web-based CRM portals as a common gateway for various levels of access to all customer information, as well as operational, analytical, and collaborative CRM tools for customers, employees, and business partners. Let's look at a real-world example.

Integrated CRM: Hilton's Welcome Mat Starts on the Web	Consider this: A businessman is traveling to Chicago tomorrow. He logs on to Hilton's Web site and decides to stay at Homewood Suites, one of Hilton hotels' nine chains. Next, he goes to the hotel's digital floor plan, takes a look at the rooms available, picks one on the top floor, far from the pool but close to the elevator, and checks in online. When he gets to the hotel the next day, his key is at the front desk, and the desk clerk welcomes him by name. When he gets to his room, he finds feather pillows and the local newspaper, just as he prefers. IT-facilitated customer service is what Hilton is all about. From a do-it-all customer information system to self-service kiosks in hotel lobbies to richly interactive Web sites, its singular goal is to keep customers coming back.

CIO Tim Harvey says Hilton's strong tech portfolio is part of the formula that lets the hotel chain charge more than competitors and still fill up rooms. Revenue per room across Hilton brands is more than 7 percent above the industry average, and as much as 28 percent more at Hampton Inn. "Customers are willing to pay more to stay in our hotels for some reason, and the technology enables that," Harvey says.

Hilton doesn't view technology as a cost center, but rather as an enabler of nearly all business processes. The tech team asks, "What value can I add above and beyond the traditional role of IT?" says Chuck Scoggins, vice president of distribution CRM and pricing technology. Hilton's signature IT project is OnQ, a (mostly) internally developed platform for property management, reservations, e-commerce, and CRM.

OnQ includes 3.5 terabytes of data on 22.5 million guests, and the company is spending $20 million to expand it worldwide.

Harvey credits OnQ with letting Hilton build a reservation system to book large blocks of rooms and conference areas for $10 million and roll it out ahead of schedule. It was Hilton's drive to make sites more interactive that led to the Homewood Suites feature to choose a room by floor plan, the way we can choose airline seats. Homewood, where guests typically stay longer, lagged in online and phone bookings. "People were doing research online, but they just weren't finding what they were looking for," says Scoggins.

Suite Selection lets guests select rooms from floor diagrams, view photos of rooms, and reserve a specific room up to 36 hours before arrival. More than half of those polled by Hilton said Suite Selection improved their travel experience. Homewood now ranks among the top two Hilton properties for online check-ins, with 22 percent of guests doing so.

Whatever the future holds, Hilton can count on one thing: IT will be expected to play a central role in keeping customers happy and coming back.

Source: Adapted from J. Nicholas Hoover, "Hilton's Welcome Mat Starts on the Web," *InformationWeek*, September 15, 2008.

SECTION II Enterprise Resource Planning: The Business Backbone

Introduction

What do Microsoft, Coca-Cola, Cisco, Eli Lilly, Alcoa, and Nokia have in common? Unlike most businesses, which operate on 25-year-old back-office systems, these market leaders reengineered their businesses to run at breakneck speed by implementing a transactional backbone called enterprise resource planning (ERP). These companies credit their ERP systems with having helped them reduce inventories, shorten cycle times, lower costs, and improve overall operations.

Businesses of all kinds have now implemented *enterprise resource planning* (ERP) systems. ERP serves as a cross-functional enterprise backbone that integrates and automates many internal business processes and information systems within the manufacturing, logistics, distribution, accounting, finance, and human resource functions of a company. Large companies throughout the world began to install ERP systems in the 1990s as a conceptual framework and catalyst for reengineering their business processes. ERP also served as the vital software engine needed to integrate and accomplish the cross-functional processes that resulted. Now, ERP is recognized as a necessary ingredient that many companies need in order to gain the efficiency, agility, and responsiveness required to succeed in today's dynamic business environment. See Figure 8.7.

Read the Real World Case on the next page. We can learn a lot about some of the value that can be achieved through ERP from this case.

What Is ERP?

ERP is the technological backbone of e-business, an enterprisewide transaction framework with links into sales order processing, inventory management and control, production and distribution planning, and finance.

Enterprise resource planning is a cross-functional enterprise system driven by an integrated suite of software modules that supports the basic internal business processes of a company. For example, ERP software for a manufacturing company will typically process the data from and track the status of sales, inventory, shipping, and invoicing, as well as forecast raw material and human resource requirements. Figure 8.8 presents the major application components of an ERP system. Figure 8.9 illustrates some of the key cross-functional business processes and supplier and customer information flows supported by ERP systems.

ERP gives a company an integrated real-time view of its core business processes, such as production, order processing, and inventory management, tied together by the ERP application software and a common database maintained by a database management system. ERP systems track business resources (such as cash, raw materials, and production capacity), and the status of commitments made by the business (such as customer orders, purchase orders, and employee payroll), no matter which department (manufacturing, purchasing, sales, accounting, and so on) has entered the data into the system.

ERP software suites typically consist of integrated modules of manufacturing, distribution, sales, accounting, and human resource applications. Examples of manufacturing processes supported are material requirements planning, production planning, and capacity planning. Some of the sales and marketing processes supported by ERP are sales analysis, sales planning, and pricing analysis, while typical distribution applications include order management, purchasing, and logistics planning. ERP systems support many vital human resource processes, from personnel requirements planning to salary and benefits administration, and accomplish most required financial record-keeping and managerial accounting applications. Figure 8.10 illustrates the processes supported by the ERP system that the Colgate-Palmolive Company installed. Let's take a closer look at Colgate's experience with ERP.

REAL WORLD CASE 2

ERP: Smaller in Size But Bigger in Savings

While Enterprise Resource Planning (ERP) software used to be complex and expensive, new technologies and new means of delivery are making ERP both more affordable and more flexible. To Auckland, New Zealand-based furniture and interior design company Matisse International, for instance, cloud-based ERP has been a good investment.

The number-one benefit is reduced costs, says Matisse director, Paul Bertenshaw. He doesn't have to maintain the system or spend money on upgrading software and servers. "Before, every time we needed to upgrade the database we had to pay an external database expert to do it," he says. "Just not having to worry about these things is a great benefit."

Matisse is an ecologically conscious company and its cloud computing solution ties in with that, says Bertenshaw. It helps reduce the number of physical servers needed to run the workplace environment. The ERP inventory management module helps the company control stock levels and avoid overstocking, he says. "We used to have a warehouse and a storage facility in central Auckland. Now, we are down to one warehouse, which saves a huge amount of money."

The reporting ability is also a huge benefit, says Bertenshaw. Before the system was in place he would spend "an awful lot of time" every week exporting data to create sales reports and sales forecasts. "I now have all that information at my fingertips, allowing me to be more productive." Where he can, Bertenshaw uses the processes "out of the box." "We'll change what we do to accommodate the way of the system, rather than the other way around," he says.

Bertenshaw thinks this approach has contributed to the success of the system. It would have been expensive to try to replicate how processes were done in the old system. And now the organization gets the benefits of thousands of other users around the world, requesting enhancements to the system.

While he can't put a figure to the ROI of the system, it has definitely helped reduce costs. "The online store is run completely through NetSuite. Hopefully the revenue from it will cover some of the cost for the system," says Bertenshaw. "The only issue with the system is that it currently doesn't have a payroll module, so this is still run offline."

Iris Enterprise Software, headquartered in the UK but with a local office in Auckland, is seeing an emerging trend of businesses rejecting the traditional vertical industry solutions and adopting flexible ERP systems, says local representative Rupert Ralston.

"To get good ROI from any ERP system implementation, there needs to be a clear understanding of both the total cost of ownership and the expected returns," says Ralston. "Some of the most expensive areas are often overlooked and this can drastically affect the expected ROI." Factors to consider include downtime, data conversion, implementation management, parallel run, staff training and staff re-training.

Ease of use of the system is also an important success factor, especially for organizations with high staff turnover. Businesses are evolving so quickly today that by the time a big, complex implementation goes live, the needs of the business might have changed, adds Ralston.

The University of Canterbury has an enterprise system made up of Oracle's E-Business Suite for financials, PeopleSoft for human resources, Jade student management and Cognos for enterprise reporting. The initial objective for investing in an ERP system was to achieve a "single source of truth" and avoid people keeping their own financial information within their departments, says Lynne O'Donoghue, financial systems and taxation manager at the university.

"Our objective was to get everyone right across the enterprise, using exactly the same system and getting the same information from it. We get ideas from other users across the world which helps us extend the use of the system, in terms of using as much functionality as possible," adds O'Donoghue.

Another benefit is that it is easy to add further Oracle modules, along with in-house applications to the system, she says. "We have added some features to it that it didn't have, for example invoice scanning. We then use Oracle Workflow to route that invoice around the university for approval."

"When we put it in, we considered it to have a life of five years and we have now had it for 10 years. But what we focus more on with the ERP system is total cost of ownership and that is coming down," says O'Donoghue.

FIGURE 8.7

Companies are beginning to see the value of smaller ERP applications and less customization.

Source: Patrice Latron/Corbis.

Mike Lorge, managing director of Sage Business Solutions, Australia and New Zealand, is seeing uptake across the board, irrespective of size of the organization. "If a business has over 10 staff and they are spending more than 30 percent of their time maintaining and updating business information, whether that's in Excel or a legacy accounting package, the business should consider implementing an ERP system," he says.

"Reducing the administrative burden on staff—let's say they are earning on average $50,000 per year—and increasing their productivity by 20 percent, ROI per annum on 10 staff will be $100,000 in gained productivity," he says. "This doesn't include the benefits associated with more streamlined processes, [for example] the ability to respond quicker to customers, maintain more efficient inventory levels, and having more accurate data about the business."

According to Patrick Kouwenhoven, head of software solutions at Gen-i, local companies now put a stronger focus on realizing the benefits of their enterprise solutions. As a result of the recession, companies' view of return on investment has changed. Whereas five years ago CIOs were often looking for ROI over three years, now many want to see that return in six months to a year, says Kouwenhoven.

In many businesses the message is: stop spending money on things that aren't going to add benefits quickly. Partly because of this, Gen-i is seeing increased interest in cloud computing with some of the giants, such as Oracle and SAP, launching lighter software-as-a-service-type (SaaS) offerings.

Kouwenhoven thinks we are going to see a trend where SaaS players have more impact, which, among other things, will reduce the total cost of ownership of ERP systems. The SaaS model opens up ERP to smaller organizations that wouldn't normally look at implementing an ERP system, because of cost and the required change management.

Gen-i sees huge opportunity in on-demand services and is about to launch its own cloud-based solution. The services range from SaaS to infrastructure-as-a-service, with customers paying only for what they use on a monthly basis.

One reason organizations are revisiting their ERP installations is that many initially invested in the late 1990s to deal with the Y2K threat, says TechnologyOne's operating officer Roger Phare.

The strength of these systems was their transaction processing ability that helped streamline supply and manufacturing chains. Their downside was, first, it was hard to get information out and, second, the software was not suited to organizations whose business is primarily managing projects, programs, or activities.

After Y2K, further enabling technologies emerged, among them the web, business intelligence, customer relationship management, and performance planning.

Gen-i's Patrick Kouwenhoven delivers five strategies to get the value out of ERP:

- Make sure you fully understand your business processes before embarking on an ERP implementation. This way you will know what benefits are realistic to expect.
- Use as much of the out-of-the-box functionality as possible.
- Invest in customization of parts of the ERP system to increase competitive advantage.
- Make sensible choices around what to customize. Be open-minded about changing your business processes and workflow instead of heavily customizing the system.
- Invest in a business intelligence tool to help you access the important details from your ERP system.

Source: Adapted from Ulrika Hedquist, "Next Generation of ERP Finds Home in New Zealand," *Computerworld*, Fairfax Media Business Group, May 4, 2010.

CASE STUDY QUESTIONS

1. Why does ERP customization lead to so many headaches when it is time to upgrade?

2. Why are ERP systems getting smaller?

3. Cutting payments outright to ERP vendors may not be possible for smaller companies without the in-house resources that larger organizations have. Are they at the mercy of the software providers? What other alternatives do small companies have? Provide some recommendations.

4. What does Bertenshaw mean when he says Matisee gets the benefit of thousands of users from around the world?

REAL WORLD ACTIVITIES

1. What offerings are available in the ERP marketplace today that were not available when companies first started investing in the technology? What new functionality do these offerings have? Research current ERP alternatives and prepare a report comparing their major features.

2. Should companies scrap their existing ERP implementations and start from scratch again, or should they keep trying to make their existing investments pay off? What are the advantages and disadvantages of each approach? Break into small groups to discuss these issues.

FIGURE 8.8

The major application components of enterprise resource planning demonstrate the cross-functional approach of ERP systems.

FIGURE 8.9 Some of the business process flows and customer and supplier information flows supported by ERP systems.

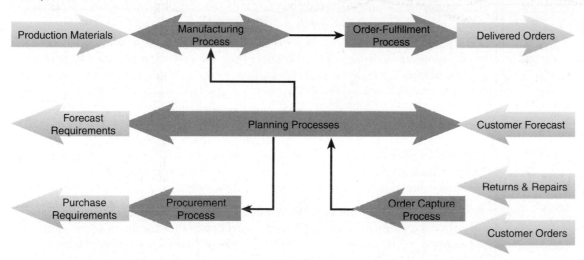

FIGURE 8.10 The business processes and functions supported by the ERP system implemented by the Colgate-Palmolive Company.

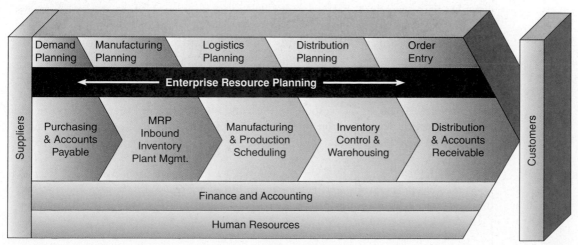

Colgate-Palmolive: The Business Value of ERP	Colgate-Palmolive is a global consumer products company that implemented the SAP R/3 enterprise resource planning system. Colgate embarked on an implementation of SAP R/3 to allow the company to access more timely and accurate data, get the most out of working capital, and reduce manufacturing costs. An important factor for Colgate was whether it could use the software across the entire spectrum of the business. Colgate needed the ability to coordinate globally and act locally. The implementation of SAP across the Colgate supply chain contributed to increased profitability. Now installed in operations that produce most of Colgate's worldwide sales, SAP was expanded to all Colgate divisions worldwide. Global efficiencies in purchasing—combined with product and packaging standardization—also produced large savings.

- Before ERP, it took Colgate U.S. anywhere from one to five days to acquire an order, and another one to two days to process the order. Now, order acquisition and processing combined take four hours, not up to seven days. Distribution planning and picking used to take up to four days; today, they take 14 hours. In total, the order-to-delivery time has been cut in half.

- Before ERP, on-time deliveries used to occur only 91.5 percent of the time, and cases ordered were delivered correctly 97.5 percent of the time. After R/3, the figures are 97.5 percent and 99.0 percent, respectively.

- After ERP, domestic inventories have dropped by one-third, and receivables outstanding have dropped to 22.4 days from 31.4. Working capital as a percentage of sales has plummeted to 6.3 percent from 11.3 percent. Total delivered cost per case has been reduced by nearly 10 percent.

Benefits and Challenges of ERP

As the example of Colgate-Palmolive has just shown, ERP systems can generate significant business benefits for a company. Many other companies have found major business value in their use of ERP in several basic ways:

- **Quality and efficiency.** ERP creates a framework for integrating and improving a company's internal business processes that results in significant improvements in the quality and efficiency of customer service, production, and distribution.

- **Decreased costs.** Many companies report significant reductions in transaction processing costs and hardware, software, and IT support staff compared to the nonintegrated legacy systems that were replaced by their new ERP systems.

- **Decision support.** ERP provides vital cross-functional information on business performance to managers quickly to significantly improve their ability to make better decisions in a timely manner across the entire business enterprise.

- **Enterprise agility.** Implementing ERP systems breaks down many former departmental and functional walls or "silos" of business processes, information systems, and information resources. This results in more flexible organizational structures, managerial responsibilities, and work roles, and therefore a more agile and adaptive organization and workforce that can more easily capitalize on new business opportunities.

The Costs of ERP

An ERP implementation is like the corporate equivalent of a brain transplant. We pulled the plug on every company application and moved to PeopleSoft software. The risk was certainly disruption of business because if you do not do ERP properly, you can kill your company, guaranteed.

FIGURE 8.11

Typical costs of implementing a new ERP system.

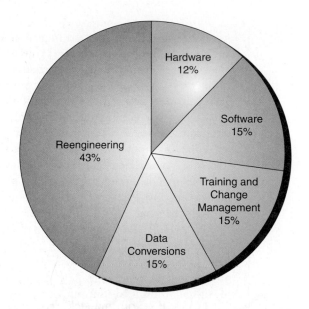

So says Jim Prevo, CIO of Green Mountain Coffee of Vermont, commenting on their successful implementation of an ERP system. Though the benefits of ERP are many, the costs and risks are also considerable, as we will continue to see in some of the real-world cases and examples in the text. Figure 8.11 illustrates the relative size and types of costs of implementing an ERP system in a company. Notice that hardware and software costs are a small part of total costs, and that the costs of developing new business processes (reengineering) and preparing employees for the new system (training and change management) make up the bulk of implementing a new ERP system. Converting data from previous legacy systems to the new cross-functional ERP system is another major category of ERP implementation costs.

The costs and risks of failure in implementing a new ERP system are substantial. Most companies have had successful ERP implementations, but a sizable minority of firms experienced spectacular and costly failures that heavily damaged their overall business. Big losses in revenue, profits, and market share resulted when core business processes and information systems failed or did not work properly. In many cases, orders and shipments were lost, inventory changes were not recorded correctly, and unreliable inventory levels caused major stock-outs to occur for weeks or months. Companies like Hershey Foods, Nike, A-DEC, and Connecticut General sustained losses running into hundreds of millions of dollars in some instances. In the case of FoxMeyer Drugs, a $5 billion pharmaceutical wholesaler, the company had to file for bankruptcy protection and then was bought out by its arch competitor, McKesson Drugs.

The most recent example of ERP failure is Shane Co., the family owned jewelry retailer and one of the 10 largest jewelry retailers in the world. In January 2009, Shane Co. sought bankruptcy protection, attributing the company's decline to delays and cost overruns in their $36 million SAP AG inventory-management system. Shane Co. claimed SAP took almost three years to install and implement the system instead of one year, while costs "ballooned" to $36 million from a projected maximum of $10 million. Shane, based in Centennial, Colorado, became "substantially overstocked with inventory, and with the wrong mix of inventory" when Walldorf, Germany-based SAP finished the system in September 2007, according to the bankruptcy filing. The software "adversely affected sales" through the first nine months of 2008, it said.

American LaFrance: Botched ERP Implementation Leads to Failure (and Bankruptcy)

American LaFrance (ALF), a maker of emergency vehicles such as fire trucks and ambulances, filed for Chapter 11 bankruptcy protection on January 28, 2008; in court papers, it is claiming that their software vendor's work installing and transitioning to a new ERP system contributed to inventory and production problems. Officials at American LaFrance, which has been in business making fire and emergency response equipment since 1832, stated that "this is a legal 'reorganization' process to make the company stronger."

The bankruptcy filing was due to "operational disruptions caused by the installation of a new ERP system," as well as obsolete inventory that American LaFrance's previous owner, Freightliner, did not properly disclose. A New York–based investment company, Patriarch Partners, bought American LaFrance in late 2005 for an undisclosed sum.

"As a result of the unanticipated obsolescence of inventory and the ongoing ERP problems, American LaFrance has incurred approximately $100 million in secured debt since it purchased its business," company officials said in a statement. "These problems have resulted in slowed production, a large unfulfilled backlog, and a lack of sufficient funds to continue operating."

ALF had purchased Freightliner's business in 2005. As part of the purchase agreement, Freightliner had managed inventory, payroll, and manufacturing processes until June 2007, according to news reports. "But American LaFrance, which was preparing to take over those functions by creating its own in-house system, fumbled the changeover," wrote *The Post and Courier* of Charleston, South Carolina.

Citing company statements, the newspaper added: "The two systems were not entirely compatible, and a wide range of financial information was lost in the changeover. Inventory was in disarray, and workers were unable to find the parts they needed." According to U.S. Bankruptcy Court documents, the new system ALF set up with the help of a software vendor had "serious deficiencies" that had "a crippling impact" on the company's operations.

The multitude of business and IT problems "forced American LaFrance to seek protection from its more than 1,000 creditors, who collectively are owed more than $200 million," the paper reported. Results from a recent CIO survey on ERP systems and their importance to twenty-first-century businesses explain how and why technology disasters like American LaFrance's can happen. More than 85 percent of survey respondents agreed or strongly agreed that their ERP systems were essential to the core of their businesses, and that they "could not live without them."

Source: Adapted from Jennifer Zaino, "Modern Workforce: Capital One Puts ERP at Core of Work," *InformationWeek*, July 11, 2005.

Causes of ERP Failures

What have been the major causes of failure in ERP projects? In almost every case, the business managers and IT professionals of these companies underestimated the complexity of the planning, development, and training that were needed to prepare for a new ERP system that would radically change their business processes and information systems. Failure to involve affected employees in the planning and development phases and to change management programs, or trying to do too much too fast in the conversion process were typical causes of failed ERP projects. Insufficient training in the new work tasks required by the ERP system and failure to do enough data conversion and testing were other causes of failure. In many cases, ERP failures were also due to overreliance by company or IT management on the claims of ERP software vendors or on the assistance of prestigious consulting firms hired to lead the implementation. The following experience of a company that did it right gives us a helpful look at what is needed for a successful ERP implementation.

Capital One Financial: Success with ERP Systems

Just a few years ago at Capital One Financial Corp., it took 10 human-resources (HR) specialists to sign off on one change-of-address form. With thousands of employees worldwide, that's a lot of paper-pushing. Today, address changes are done via a self-service application that has freed HR to devote time to strategic staffing, program planning, and change management.

This example illustrates a big change that has taken place at the $2.6 billion-a-year financial services company since it began to roll out PeopleSoft applications. "It's a cultural change that has freed people to not deal with minutiae but to deal with business value," says Gregor Bailar, executive vice president and CIO. "It really has been transformative." Bailar envisions more automation ahead, with financials following in the footsteps of HR's "lean-process" design to deal with the mountain of data requests the financials team receives and processes within the group.

The PeopleSoft ERP system, which serves as Capital One's backbone for financials, HR, asset-management, and supply-chain processes, supports about 18,000 users, including Capital One's 15,000 associates and some business partners. The applications are accessible via a Web portal based on BEA Systems Inc.'s technology.

Capital One is exploring the possibility of partnering with ERP application service providers, now that the hard work of correcting data and linking processes is done. Running the applications may be more of a commodity job at this point, but the applications themselves serve as a pillar for the company's future-of-work initiative. Bailar describes this as "a very mobile, interactive, collaborative environment" designed to support the requirements of the company's biggest asset, its knowledge workers. It's characterized not only by extensive Wi-Fi access, VoIP-enabled laptops, instant messaging, and BlackBerrys, but also by workflows that, for the most part, come to users electronically. Says Bailar, "Everyone's daily life is kind of drawn back to this suite of apps."

Source: Adapted from Jennifer Zaino, "Modern Workforce: Capital One Puts ERP at Core of Work," *InformationWeek*, July 11, 2005.

Trends in ERP

Today, ERP is still evolving—adapting to developments in technology and the demands of the market. Four important trends are shaping ERP's continuing evolution: improvements in integration and flexibility, extensions to e-business applications, a broader reach to new users, and the adoption of Internet technologies.

Figure 8.12 illustrates four major developments and trends that are evolving in ERP applications. First, the ERP software packages that were the mainstay of ERP implementations in the 1990s, and were often criticized for their inflexibility, have gradually been modified into more flexible products. Companies that installed ERP systems pressured software vendors to adopt more open, flexible, standards-based software architectures. This makes the software easier to integrate with other application programs of business users, as well as making it easier to make minor modifications to suit a company's business processes. An example is SAP R/3 Enterprise, released in 2002 by SAP AG as a successor to earlier versions of SAP R/3. Other leading ERP vendors, including Oracle, PeopleSoft, and J.D. Edwards, have also developed more flexible ERP products.

Web-enabling ERP software is a second development in the evolution of ERP. The growth of the Internet and corporate intranets and extranets prompted software companies to use Internet technologies to build Web interfaces and networking capabilities into ERP systems. These features make ERP systems easier to use and connect to other internal applications, as well as to the systems of a company's business partners. This Internet connectivity has led to the development of interenterprise ERP systems that provide Web-enabled links between key business systems (such as inventory

FIGURE 8.12
Trends in the evolution of
ERP applications.

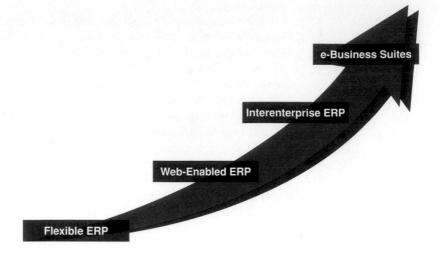

and production) of a company and its customers, suppliers, distributors, and others. These external links signaled a move toward the integration of internal-facing ERP applications with the external-focused applications of supply chain management (SCM) and a company's supply chain partners. We will discuss supply chain management in Section III.

All of these developments have provided the business and technological momentum for the integration of ERP functions into e-business suites. The major ERP software companies have developed modular, Web-enabled software suites that integrate ERP, customer relationship management, supply chain management, procurement, decision support, enterprise portals, health care functionality, and other business applications and functions. Examples include Oracle's e-Business Suite and SAP's mySAP. Some e-business suites disassemble ERP components and integrate them into other modules, while other products keep ERP as a distinct module in the software suite. Of course, the goal of these software suites is to enable companies to run most of their business processes using one Web-enabled system of integrated software and databases, instead of a variety of separate e-business applications. See Figure 8.13. Let's look at a real-world example.

FIGURE 8.13   The application components in Oracle's e-Business Suite software product.

ORACLE E-BUSINESS SUITE

Advanced Planning	Business Intelligence	Contracts
e-Commerce	Enterprise Asset Management	Exchanges
Financials	Human Resources	Interaction Center
Manufacturing	Marketing	Order Fulfillment
Procurement	Product Development	Professional Services Automation
Projects	Sales	Service
Training	Treasury	

Source: Adapted from Oracle Corporation, "E-Business Suite: Manage by Fact with Complete Automation and Complete Information," Oracle.com, 2002.

Visa International: Implementing the e-Business Suite

Despite the innovations brought to global commerce by Visa's sophisticated consumer payments processing system, Visa International had surprisingly outdated systems managing some of its most critical internal business processes. "KPMG did an analysis of our business and found that our internal systems were becoming a risk to our organization," said Gretchen McCoy, senior vice president of Visa International. "We were in the red zone."

McCoy found that Visa's internal systems were unnecessarily complex and utilized few of the advantages that technology can bring to an enterprise. The financial management infrastructure was fragmented, complex, and costly to maintain. Data were not standardized, resulting in many different databases making disparate interpretations of business data. Corporate purchasing, accounts payable, and asset management were managed manually, resulting in time-consuming delays and discrepancies. Fragmented internal systems are not unusual in a company that experiences rapid growth. Visa experienced double-digit growth for 11 consecutive years. Visa chose Oracle e-Business Suite to remedy the problems that come with a complex and inefficient back office.

The resulting implementation turned Visa's cumbersome, outdated desktop procedures into Web-based e-business solutions that met Visa's demands for all roles and processes. For example, Oracle Financials automated Visa's old organization and created a more agile system capable of accounting for the impact of financial activities on a global scale. Accounts payable was transformed from a cumbersome manual process into a streamlined system that automatically checks invoices against outgoing payments and requests review of any discrepancies via e-mail. And Oracle iProcurement helped automate Visa's requisitioning and purchasing system by streamlining the entire purchasing process and implementing a self-service model to increase processing efficiency, said McCoy.

SECTION III Supply Chain Management: The Business Network

Introduction

Starting an e-business takes ideas, capital, and technical savvy. Operating one, however, takes supply chain management (SCM) skills. A successful SCM strategy is based on accurate order processing, just-in-time inventory management, and timely order fulfillment. SCM's increasing importance illustrates how a tool that was a theoretical process 10 years ago is now a hot competitive weapon.

That's why many companies today are making *supply chain management* (SCM) a top strategic objective and major e-business application development initiative. Fundamentally, supply chain management helps a company get the right products to the right place at the right time, in the proper quantity and at an acceptable cost. The goal of SCM is to manage this process efficiently by forecasting demand; controlling inventory; enhancing the network of business relationships a company has with customers, suppliers, distributors, and others; and receiving feedback on the status of every link in the supply chain. To achieve this goal, many companies today are turning to Internet technologies to Web-enable their supply chain processes, decision making, and information flows. Let's take a look at a real-world example.

Read the Real World Case on the next page. We can learn a lot about challenges in supply chain management from this case. See Figure 8.14.

What Is SCM?

Legacy supply chains are clogged with unnecessary steps and redundant stockpiles. For instance, a typical box of breakfast cereal spends an incredible 104 days getting from factory to supermarket, struggling its way through an unbelievable maze of wholesalers, distributors, brokers, and consolidators, each of which has a warehouse. The e-commerce opportunity lies in the fusing of each company's internal systems to those of its suppliers, partners, and customers. This fusion forces companies to better integrate interenterprise supply chain processes to improve manufacturing efficiency and distribution effectiveness.

So **supply chain management** is a cross-functional interenterprise system that uses information technology to help support and manage the links between some of a company's key business processes and those of its suppliers, customers, and business partners. The goal of SCM is to create a fast, efficient, and low-cost network of business relationships, or **supply chain**, to get a company's products from concept to market.

What exactly is a company's supply chain? Let's suppose a company wants to build and sell a product to other businesses. Then it must buy raw materials and a variety of contracted services from other companies. The interrelationships with suppliers, customers, distributors, and other businesses that are needed to design, build, and sell a product make up the network of business entities, relationships, and processes that is called a supply chain. Because each supply chain process should add value to the products or services a company produces, a supply chain is frequently called a *value chain*, a different but related concept that we discussed in Chapter 2. In any event, many companies today are using Internet technologies to create interenterprise e-business systems for supply chain management that help a company streamline its traditional supply chain processes.

Figure 8.15 illustrates the basic business processes in the supply chain life cycle and the functional SCM processes that support them. It also emphasizes how many companies today are reengineering their supply chain processes, aided by Internet technologies and supply chain management software. For example, the demands of today's competitive business environment are pushing manufacturers to use their

REAL WORLD CASE 3

Cisco Systems, Black & Decker, and O'Reilly Auto Parts: Adapting Supply Chains to Tough Times

Whether it's a truck, a tsunami, or an economic downturn, the same general rule applies: You're better off if you can see it coming from a safe distance.

There aren't many companies that understand this notion better than Cisco Systems Inc. White-hot during the 1990s, the company was pummeled after its vaunted inventory forecasting system could not—or did not—predict the dot-com bubble's collapse.

The result of this miscalculation was that sales were halved, the company lost 25 percent of its customers in a matter of weeks, and it ultimately wrote off more than $2 billion in inventory. After that experience, Cisco's supply chain team vowed that it would never get blindsided again.

"There is a huge difference cutting head count between now and 2001," says Karl Braitberg, Cisco's vice president of customer value chain management.

Back then, Cisco's supply chain model was built on a "push" system, where products were made and inventory was built up in anticipation of market demand based on best-guess forecasts. "Then, when demand dropped, the supply chain froze. Nothing happened," Braitberg says. "We knew we had to build a new system that reacts better than just 'push.'"

Every company is tasked with matching its supply to consumer demand. In a normal business cycle, how well that job is accomplished determines whether the company is profitable. But this current economic downturn is anything but normal, and businesses are struggling to simply stay liquid.

There are various strategies to help preserve working capital, including cutting head count, outlets, and manufacturing lines. But for most companies, the key to capital

FIGURE 8.14

Companies are freeing up cash by tightening their supply chain and reducing inventory.

Source: Getty Images.

preservation will be how well they can reduce their inventory levels.

Largely, companies are in survival mode, and they're looking to their supply chain management team to free up precious capital to help them do that. While it may not fall directly on IT executives to make that happen, their role in the equation is very strategic.

With globalization, outsourcing, and increased compliance and security concerns, managing supply chain operations becomes increasingly complex. And shorter, more frequent product cycles targeting more-sophisticated markets create a need to manage more products and parts from remote locations. Add the pressure of shorter cash-to-cash cycles—the time from when a business extends credit to build inventory until the time it gets paid—into the equation, and the need for an intelligent, nimble, and timely flow of information becomes critical.

To have visibility as well as command and control, supply chain operations must be tightly integrated with the IT infrastructure. That isn't the case at many companies, and yet it may be the factor that determines success or failure as they endure and emerge from this downturn.

Like bloodletting, reducing inventory is a delicate matter that most people would prefer to avoid. Inventory can range from materials, to parts, to fully assembled products. Nobody wants to run out. If there's too little, customers won't get orders in a timely manner and market opportunities will be missed. Yet if a company carries too much and demand drops, then the inventory must be "bled down," or reduced in price, until it has a buyer.

During a strong economy and when cash flow is loosened, many companies can get by without rigorous inventory management practices, says Larry Lapide, director of demand management at the MIT Center for Transportation & Logistics in Cambridge, Massachusetts. But during a recession, he adds, "companies had better bleed down inventory to reflect the downturn in sales. If they don't, it just sits there."

Inventory optimization is so critical now because of its impact on available cash, Lapide says. In accounting terms, inventory is an asset. So inventory that is on the books through manufacturing, assembly, and distribution represents credit-funded inventory. With credit at a premium, it's in a company's best interest not only to keep inventory levels tight, but also to sell goods as soon as possible.

Reducing costs and squeezing maximum utility out of fixed assets is nothing new to Black & Decker Corp.'s Hardware and Home Improvement Group in Lake Forest, California. The unit supplies hardware to big-box retailers that have responded to the economic downturn with new low-price strategies. It now falls on Scott Strickland, vice president of IS, to help the group squeeze down its own costs and maintain profit margins.

"We had been loath to drive inventory down to this level," Strickland says.

However, the company had gained invaluable experience by deploying an integrated inventory management system prior to the downturn. The result was that the key decision makers throughout its supply chain were operating with the same information, planners focused only on exceptions, and supplier and material issues were quickly resolved. The system, Strickland says, does the heavy lifting, and as a result, the unit has cut planning cycles from weeks to days and improved forecast accuracy by 10.4 percent.

"If someone had told us nine months ago that we could lower inventory as fast as we could to address a sales decline, we would not have believed it was possible," Strickland says. However, "because of the impetus on freeing up working capital, we have been focused on lowering our inventory and levels. We figured we could do this, and it turned out to not be the bad experience we had imagined."

The effort to lower inventory levels to free up working capital has proved so effective that the Black & Decker unit and its partners are jointly considering making it standard practice even after the economy recovers, Strickland says.

O'Reilly Auto Parts Inc. in Springfield, Missouri, uses inventory as a competitive differentiator, says Greg Beck, vice president of purchasing. One of the largest specialty retailers of automotive aftermarket parts, tools, supplies, and accessories in the United States, O'Reilly is responding to the recession differently than many other companies.

"Business is increasing because of the downturn," Beck says. "People aren't buying new cars but instead are putting more money into fixing old cars."

This isn't to say that O'Reilly lacks supply chain challenges or that it can let down its guard. As the result of an acquisition last year, the company increased its total store count to more than 3,300 and now operates in 38 states. To bolster its competitive advantage, O'Reilly's strategy is to increase customer service levels and replenish inventory on a nightly basis, while at the same time managing an increasing number of products.

The partnership between the supply chain operation and IT was critical to O'Reilly's strategy. The company is using Manhattan Associates Inc.'s replenishment software to collect product data information on the half-hour, while updates from the distribution centers are transmitted nightly. The replenishment system uses this data to determine the forecast for these products. As a result, O'Reilly has increased inventory turns by 44 percent, and it still manages to fulfill 97 percent of customer requests immediately, with 3 percent handled through separate channels. At the same time, the company reduced its inventory levels, freeing up $60 million.

Companies say that driving costs out of the supply chain is an important goal, but the big question is whether—especially during a recession—they can afford to invest in their supply chain IT infrastructures to help make that happen.

Dwight Klappich, an analyst at Gartner Inc., calls that a short-sighted and, in the long term, costly approach. "If this trend continues," Klappich stated in a report, "this myopic focus on short-term tactical issues, while necessary for many businesses, could widen the gap between the best-performing organizations and lower-performing organizations."

Cisco understands this. After the 2001 downturn, it made major system investments to transform its "push-driven," siloed supply chain model into an integrated "pull system" that can extract timely data from suppliers and downstream partners.

This reorder data is sent to Cisco after being triggered by specified parameters and algorithms, to shape "demand signals."

The system doesn't operate in a vacuum. Cisco has optimized its forecasting algorithms by bringing together representatives from its marketing, finance, sales, supply chain, and IT departments, and from key customers. As part of its sales and operations planning process, this group collaborates to create a common view of demand signals. This input drives an agreed-upon plan of action to align manufacturing capacity and inventory deployment and meet customer service levels. In short, they work together with the same data to optimally match supply and demand.

"Now, if there are no pull signals, nothing gets brought into the system," says Cisco's Braitberg.

Manufacturers don't continue to source and build inventory that may sit in some warehouse waiting for customers who may never buy it. Cash is freed up for other purposes.

While Braitberg acknowledges that even past history can't be used as a template for this downturn, Cisco is confident that it has better visibility into market demand when it goes down, and that it will be ready when the green shoots emerge.

"We now have the techniques in place to be hypersensitive to demand changes," Braitberg says, "and we can manage our way through a downturn."

Source: Adapted from William Brandel, "Inventory Optimization Saves Working Capital in Tough Times," *Computerworld*, August 24, 2009.

CASE STUDY QUESTIONS

1. Cisco Systems went from a "push" to a "pull" approach to its supply chain after the dot-com debacle. How are these two approaches different? Does it depend on the state of the economy which one should be used? Why?

2. What are the different elements that need to come together to bring supply chains to the optimal levels needed by these companies? What role does IT play?

3. How are the approaches to inventory management taken by O'Reilly Auto Parts, on one hand, and Cisco Systems and Black & Decker, on the other, different?

REAL WORLD ACTIVITIES

1. The ability to accurately forecast demand is one of the major issues involved in the efforts discussed in the case. Go online and research which technologies companies are employing today to improve this aspect of their supply chains. Prepare a presentation to share your findings with the rest of your class.

2. The case compares short-term tactical needs with long-term strategic investments. How do you make the case, in an economic downturn, for the continued need to invest in technology? Break into small groups and brainstorm some alternatives.

FIGURE 8.15

Supply chain management software and Internet technologies can help companies reengineer and integrate the functional SCM processes that support the supply chain life cycle.

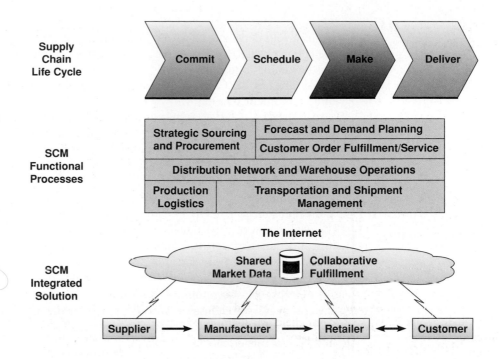

intranets, extranets, and e-commerce Web portals to help them reengineer their relationships with their suppliers, distributors, and retailers. The objective is to significantly reduce costs, increase efficiency, and improve their supply chain cycle times. SCM software can also help to improve interenterprise coordination among supply chain process players. The result is much more effective distribution and channel networks among business partners. The Web initiatives of PC Connection illustrate these developments.

PC Connection: Learning to Stop, Drop, and Ship	

PC Connection has razor-thin margins. To stay healthy, the $1.8 billion-a-year tech reseller has slashed inefficiencies wherever possible in recent years. Yet despite tight financial circumstances, PC Connection invested substantially to overhaul its supply chain, building Web services modules in front of its ERP system to more efficiently integrate with partners and suppliers. The upgrades will help the company take on new business opportunities, such as selling software licenses, that promise higher margins than hardware.

Although the company has grown significantly over the years, the growth hasn't been without pain. While PC Connection now offers goods and services from more than 1,400 manufacturers, its core ERP system hadn't changed much from the days when the company sold directly to customers. "It was built for the days of pick, pack, and ship," Jack Ferguson, PC Connection's treasurer and CFO, says of the company's Oracle JD Edwards ERP system. That became a growing problem as the company over the last several years expanded its catalog and extended its fulfillment network to include more than a dozen external partners to handle increasingly complex drop-ship orders. "We were faced with a growing number of products, and we also had a desire to cut inventory," Ferguson says.

It soon became apparent that the system wasn't built to handle such a multitiered fulfillment network. "Once you move to drop-ship it gets more complicated," says Ferguson, who notes that even basic requirements, like the calculation of sales tax on an order, were affected by the new drop-ship arrangements. Before long, managers from various departments within PC Connection were requesting ad hoc changes to the company's ERP system to meet new requirements as they evolved. But the process was becoming unmanageable.

As a result, PC Connection last year decided to embark on a thorough overhaul of its fulfillment system.

IT staffers looked at numerous off-the-shelf e-commerce packages, but all were found lacking. Instead, the company launched a labor-intensive campaign to internally develop new front-end modules for the existing JD Edwards system. These modules were built using both Web services and traditional EDI to deal with the company's growing web of fulfillment partners.

The first set of enhancements to the JD Edwards system went online recently, and Ferguson says they're already paying off in terms of time and cost savings. "In the past, much of what our buyers did was very manual and time consuming, with lots of order entry across multiple systems," he says. "This takes 90 percent of the manual part out of their day."

Among other things, there are now modules that can automatically determine the quickest, most economical way to fulfill an order, whether directly from one of the company's warehouses or through a partner in a particular geographic location. Still, Ferguson says PC Connection is investing for future growth, and adds that the new system means customer orders will continue to be filled with greater speed and accuracy, even as business picks up.

"It's a customer satisfaction issue," he says. "To stay in the game you have to upgrade your system to handle increased requests."

Source: Adapted from Paul McDougall, "PC Connection Learns to Stop, Drop, and Ship," *InformationWeek*, September 15, 2008.

Electronic Data Interchange

Electronic data interchange (EDI) was one of the earliest uses of information technology for supply chain management. EDI involves the electronic exchange of business transaction documents over the Internet and other networks between supply chain trading partners (organizations and their customers and suppliers). Data representing a variety of business transaction documents (such as purchase orders, invoices, requests for quotations, and shipping notices) are automatically exchanged between computers using standard document message formats. Typically, EDI software is used to convert a company's own document formats into standardized EDI formats as specified by various industry and international protocols. Thus, EDI is an example of the almost complete automation of an e-commerce supply chain process. EDI over the Internet, using secure *virtual private networks*, is a growing B2B e-commerce application.

Formatted transaction data are transmitted over network links directly between computers without paper documents or human intervention. Besides direct network links between the computers of trading partners, third-party services are widely used. Value-added network companies like GE Global Exchange Services and Computer Associates offer a variety of EDI services for relatively high fees, but many EDI service providers now offer secure, lower-cost EDI services over the Internet. Figure 8.16 illustrates a typical EDI system.

EDI is still a popular data-transmission format among major trading partners, primarily to automate repetitive transactions, though it is slowly being replaced by XML-based Web services. EDI automatically tracks inventory changes; triggers orders, invoices, and other documents related to transactions; and schedules and confirms delivery and payment. By digitally integrating the supply chain, EDI streamlines processes, saves time, and increases accuracy. In addition, by using Internet technologies, lower-cost Internet-based EDI services are now available to smaller businesses.

FIGURE 8.16   A typical example of electronic data interchange activities, an important form of business-to-business electronic commerce. EDI over the Internet is a major B2B e-commerce application.

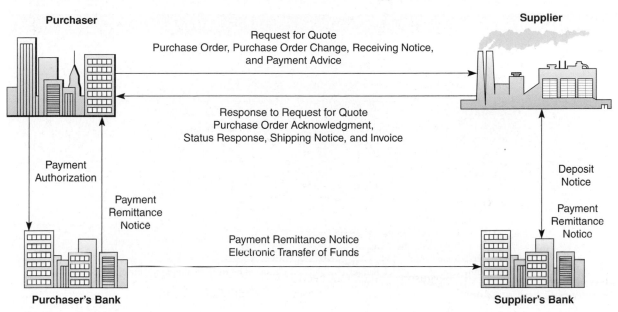

Purchaser

Supplier

Request for Quote
Purchase Order, Purchase Order Change, Receiving Notice, and Payment Advice

Response to Request for Quote
Purchase Order Acknowledgment,
Status Response, Shipping Notice, and Invoice

Payment
Authorization

Payment
Remittance
Notice

Deposit
Notice

Payment
Remittance
Notice

Payment Remittance Notice
Electronic Transfer of Funds

Purchaser's Bank

Supplier's Bank

Telefonica TSAI: Internet EDI	Telefonica is Spain's largest supplier of telecommunications services, serving the Spanish-speaking and Portuguese-speaking world with affiliates in Latin America and the United States. Telefonica Servicios Avanzados de Informacion (TSAI) is a subsidiary of Telefonica that handles 60 percent of Spain's electronic data interchange (EDI) traffic. TSAI's customers are supply chain trading partners—merchants, suppliers, and others involved in business supply chains from design to delivery.

To tap into the sizable market of smaller businesses that can't afford standard EDI services, TSAI offers an Internet EDI service, InfoEDI, based on ECXpert electronic commerce software. InfoEDI allows transactions to be entered and processed on the Internet, so smaller trading partners no longer have to buy and install special connections, dedicated workstations, and proprietary software. Instead, they can access the EDI network through the Internet via TSAI's Web portal.

InfoEDI's forms-based interface lets businesses connect with the InfoEDI simply by using modems and Web browsers. They can then interact with the largest suppliers and retailers to send orders, issue invoices based on orders, send invoice summaries, track status of documents, and receive messages. InfoEDI also provides a product database that lists all details of trading partners' products. Once a trading relationship has been established, each partner has encrypted access to details of its own products. Because those details remain accessible on TSAI's Web server, users need enter only minimal information to create links to those data, which are then plugged in as needed.

The Role of SCM

Figure 8.17 helps us understand the role and activities of supply chain management in business more clearly. The top three levels of Figure 8.17 show the strategic, tactical, and operational objectives and outcomes of SCM planning, which are then accomplished by the business partners in a supply chain at the execution level of SCM. The role of information technology in SCM is to support these objectives with interenterprise information systems that produce many of the outcomes a business needs to manage its supply chain effectively. That's why many companies today are installing SCM software and developing Web-based SCM information systems.

FIGURE 8.17   The objectives and outcomes of supply chain management are accomplished for a business with the help of interenterprise SCM information systems.

SCM Objectives		SCM Outcomes
What? Establish objectives, policies, and operating footprint	**Strategic**	• Objectives • Supply policies (service levels) • Network design
How much? Deploy resources to match supply to demand	**Tactical**	• Demand forecast • Production, procurement, logistics plan • Inventory targets
When? Where? Schedule, monitor, control, and adjust production	**Operational**	• Work center scheduling • Order/inventory tracking
Do Build and transport	**Execution**	• Order cycle • Material movement

Source: Adapted from Keith Oliver, Anne Chung, and Nick Samanach, "Beyond Utopia: The Realist's Guide to Internet-Enabled Supply Chain Management," *Strategy and Business*, Second Quarter, 2001, p. 99.

Until recently, SCM software products have typically been developed for either supply chain planning or execution applications. SCM planning software from vendors such as I2 and Manugistics support a variety of applications for supply and demand forecasting. SCM execution software from vendors such as EXE Technologies and Manhattan Associates support applications like order management, logistics management, and warehouse management. However, big ERP vendors like Oracle and SAP are now offering Web-enabled software suites of e-business applications that include SCM modules. Examples include Oracle's e-Business Suite and SAP AG's mySAP.

Figure 8.18 gives you a good idea of the major planning and execution functions and outcomes that can be provided by SCM software as promised by mySAP's supply chain management module. Now let's look at a real-world example of an SCM system.

Imperial Sugar: Supply Chain Management to the Rescue	It was an otherwise ordinary Thursday night in February 2008 when Imperial Sugar CIO George Muller got the call. "There had been an accident. People were hurt," Muller remembers. Some died. "As more and more of the details started to come out, it was horrific." In the days following the explosion at the company's Port Wentworth, Georgia, refinery, CEO John Sheptor implored his executives to lead with their hearts, not their heads; efforts focused on helping affected employees and their families. But the $522 million sugar refiner—the third largest in the United States—had customer obligations as well. The disaster destroyed approximately 60 percent of its production capacity overnight. It wasn't clear when, or if, the plant would operate again. Imperial Sugar had already weathered some major challenges: bankruptcy, divestiture, and new management. But the Port Wentworth tragedy was the hardest Muller had faced. "Not too many manufacturing companies can withstand that kind of impact to their business and survive," he says. The Georgia refinery remained offline for twenty months. "We didn't have any safety stockpiles," says Muller. "We were scurrying to fulfill as many orders as we could." Some sugar was imported through its joint venture with Mexican refiner Ingenios Santos, but it wasn't enough. "We disappointed many customers," Muller says. He credits supply-chain systems—particularly demand-management software—with helping to make the best of available resources.

FIGURE 8.18 The supply chain management functions and potential benefits offered by the SCM module in the mySAP e-business software suite.

SCM Functions	SCM Outcomes
Planning	
Supply chain design	• Optimize network of suppliers, plants, and distribution centers
Collaborative demand and supply planning	• Develop an accurate forecast of customer demand by sharing demand and supply forecasts instantaneously across multiple tiers • Internet-enable collaborative scenarios, such as collaborative planning, forecasting, and replenishment (CPFR), and vendor-managed inventory
Execution	
Materials management	• Share accurate inventory and procurement order information • Ensure materials required for production are available in the right place at the right time • Reduce raw material spending, procurement costs, safety stocks, and raw material and finished goods inventory
Collaborative manufacturing	• Optimize plans and schedules while considering resource, material, and dependency constraints
Collaborative fulfillment	• Commit to delivery dates in real time • Fulfill orders from all channels on time with order management, transportation planning, and vehicle scheduling • Support the entire logistics process, including picking, packing, shipping, and delivery in foreign countries
Supply chain event management	• Monitor every stage of the supply chain process, from price quotation to the moment the customer receives the product, and receive alerts when problems arise
Supply chain performance management	• Report key measurements in the supply chain, such as filling rates, order cycle times, and capacity utilization

In 1998, Imperial Sugar implemented an all-in-one PeopleSoft ERP system, in lieu of best-of-breed software, to manage 20-odd business processes. After several upgrades, it was clear the demand-management module couldn't handle the complexities of the business. When large beverage and food manufacturers sign an annual contract, Imperial Sugar has to predict how that demand will play out based on seasonal and consumer cycles. "Supply chain is at the heart of our business," says Muller. "For us, it's a differentiator. It's why customers come back."

In 2006, the company added a bolt-on solution from Demand Foresight: Software that essentially learns how demand ebbs and flows over time. The tool allows Imperial Sugar to see the impact of a wide range of factors on demand, react to changes quickly, and track performance.

After the refinery catastrophe. Imperial Sugar needed immediate insight into how many customers it could serve with its available inventory. The software gave them that overview by product line, and its "available to promise" functionality allowed everyone from production to sales to see, in real time, what could be delivered.

Muller won't reveal how much he spent on Demand Foresight, saying only that it was a "drop in the bucket" compared to his last $5.7 million PeopleSoft upgrade and implementation. "It was our saving grace," he says. "It took our demand, our inventory and capacity, and the number of new orders coming in and tied it all together. We couldn't fulfill every order, but we were able to fill more orders than we ever would have had we not had that tool."

Source: Adapted from Stephanie Overby, "Supply Chain Management to the Rescue," *CIO.com*, March 16, 2010.

Benefits and Challenges of SCM

Creating a real-time SCM infrastructure is a daunting and ongoing issue and quite often a point of failure for several reasons. The chief reason is that the planning, selection, and implementation of SCM solutions are becoming more complex as the pace of technological change accelerates and the number of a company's partners increases.

The real world experiences of companies like Cardinal Glass and the promised outcomes that are outlined in Figure 8.18 emphasize the major business benefits that are possible with effective supply chain management systems. Companies know that SCM systems can provide them with key business benefits such as faster, more accurate order processing; reductions in inventory levels; quicker times to market; lower transaction and materials costs; and strategic relationships with their suppliers. All of these benefits of SCM are aimed at helping a company achieve agility and responsiveness in meeting the demands of its customers and the needs of its business partners. Let's look at a recent example.

Emerson Transaction Hub: A Bright Idea That's Paying Off

A couple of years ago, some executives at Emerson asked themselves a question: Why pay to send inventory from one supplier on one ship and goods from a second supplier on another ship, when both deliveries are coming from the same place and could be loaded into a single container?

It was an *aha!* moment that ended up saving millions for the St. Louis manufacturer that regularly ships supplies from Asia to North America and Europe. In late 2005, the company started a pilot program in which a logistics provider that specializes in transportation management for freight carriers worked with two Emerson divisions to consolidate multiple orders into the same shipping container. Not only did the pilot save money, the business units were able to tighten their global supply chains by better tracking shipments and managing inventory.

Naturally, Emerson wanted to expand the program, but here's where things got complicated: Emerson has 70 separate business units that purchase goods from 35,000 suppliers. Each unit communicates with its own suppliers via a combination of e-mail, spreadsheets, faxes, and phone calls. Asking a logistics provider to step into the middle of this tangled transaction web simply wasn't feasible. "It's a brittle system," says Steve Hassell, VP and CIO at Emerson. "If a provider or a business unit makes changes, you have to go and touch tens or hundreds of connections."

Instead, Hassell's team envisioned a single hub that everyone would link to using common communications mechanisms and data formats. It would serve as a unified gateway that Emerson's business units, logistics providers, and suppliers could use to exchange information. Of course, for a single communications hub to work, everyone has to speak the same language. Emerson decided to conduct transactions via two data formats: EDI, using the ANSI ASC X12 format, and OAGIS XML.

Here's how the system works: A business unit initiates a transaction, such as a purchase order, through its ERP system. The order is sent to the transaction hub, which translates the message into OAGIS XML. Providers and suppliers then coordinate shipping, and the providers communicate shipment status to the Emerson division through the hub. The hub is processing about 10,000 transactions per day. Once all business units are on board, Emerson expects to see that number jump to 100,000 transactions.

Hassell estimates that Emerson invested about $500,000 in the hub and has recovered those costs more than several times. Putting 10 suppliers in the same shipping container cuts costs by 35 percent. The company has saved millions in transport costs alone by consolidating shipping. Also, with information such as purchase orders and shipping notices in a common format, Emerson has more visibility into its supply chain, increasing inventory control efficiency by ensuring that materials aren't over- or under-stocked.

FIGURE 8.19

Achieving the goals and objectives of supply chain management is a major challenge for many companies today.

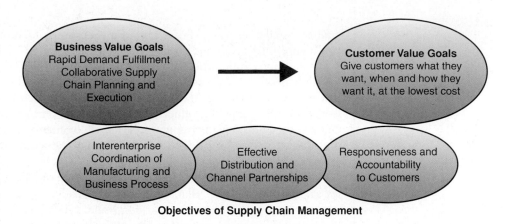

Objectives of Supply Chain Management

Finally, whereas Emerson used to look like 70 smaller businesses to its suppliers, it now looks like one big customer. Suppliers can streamline their business processes through the transaction hub while Emerson gains better leverage to negotiate prices and contracts.

Source: Adapted from Andrew Conry-Murray, "InformationWeek 500: Emerson Transaction Hub: A Bright Idea That's Paying Off in Efficiency, Savings," *InformationWeek*, September 18, 2007.

However, developing effective SCM systems has proven to be a complex and difficult application of information technology to business operations. So achieving the business value and customer value goals and objectives of supply chain management, as illustrated in Figure 8.19, has been a major challenge for most companies.

What are the causes of problems in supply chain management? Several reasons stand out. A lack of proper demand planning knowledge, tools, and guidelines is a major source of SCM failure. Inaccurate or overoptimistic demand forecasts will cause major production, inventory, and other business problems, no matter how efficient the rest of the supply chain management process is constructed. Inaccurate production, inventory, and other business data provided by a company's other information systems are a frequent cause of SCM problems. In addition, lack of adequate collaboration among marketing, production, and inventory management departments within a company, and with suppliers, distributors, and others, will sabotage any SCM system. Many companies that are installing SCM systems consider even the SCM software tools themselves to be immature, incomplete, and hard to implement. These problems are spotlighted in the real-world example of Nike Inc.

Nike Inc.: Failure (and Bouncing Back) with Supply Chain Management

Roland Wolfram, Nike's vice president of global operations and technology, calls the i2 problem a "speed bump." Some speed bump! The i2 problem is a software glitch that cost Nike more than $100 million in lost sales, depressed its stock price by 20 percent, triggered a flurry of class-action lawsuits, and caused Phil Knight, its chairman, president, and CEO, to lament famously, "This is what you get for $400 million, huh?" In the athletic footwear business, only Nike, with a 32 percent worldwide market share (almost double Adidas, its nearest rival) and a market cap that's more than the rest of the manufacturers and retailers in the industry combined, could afford to talk about $100 million like that.

"For the people who follow this sort of thing, we became a poster child for failed implementations," Wolfram says. Yet there was a lesson too for people who do, in fact, follow "this sort of thing," specifically CIOs. The lesson of Nike's failure and subsequent rebound lies in the fact that it had a business plan that was widely understood and accepted at every level of the company. Given that, and the resiliency it afforded the company, the i2 failure ultimately turned out to be, indeed, just a speed bump.

Nike's June 2000 problems with its i2 system reflect the double whammy typical of high-profile enterprise computing failures. First, there's a software problem closely tied to a core business process—in this case, factory orders. Then the glitch sends a ripple through product delivery that grows into a wave crashing on the balance sheet. The wave is big enough that the company must reveal the losses at a quarterly conference call with analysts, or risk the wrath of the Securities and Exchange Commission, shareholders, or both.

Wolfram says Nike's demand-planning strategy was and continues to be a mixture of art and technology. Nike sells too many products (120,000) in too many cycles (four per year) to do things by intuition alone. "We've tuned our system so we do our runs against historical models, and then people look at it to make sure it makes sense," he says. The computer models are trusted more when the product is a reliable seller (that is, just about anything with Michael Jordan's name on it) and the planners' intuition plays a bigger role in new or more volatile products. In this case, says Wolfram, talking with retailers does more good than consulting the system.

So how has Nike's business fared, six years and $500 million later? Wolfram claims that better collaboration with Far East factories has reduced the amount of "prebuilding" of shoes from 30 percent of Nike's total manufacturing units to around 3 percent. The lead time for shoes, he asserts, has gone from nine months to six (in some periods of high demand, seven). Inventory levels have been reduced by cutting Nike's factory order interval time from one month to a week in some cases. So far, the most direct benefits of the system have been typical for ERP: improved financial visibility, cash flow management, revenue forecasting, and an ability to juggle Nike's cash stockpile in different currencies to take advantage of shifting exchange rates—benefits that are enhanced by the single database that holds all the data.

Yet because Nike developed a plan in 1998, and stuck with it, the company claims it can make a coordinated global effort to cut that lead time. The system to make that happen is in place. Given all that has transpired in the past several years, that is rather remarkable.

Source: Adapted from Christopher Koch, "Nike Rebounds: How (and Why) Nike Recovered from its Supply Chain Disaster," *CIO Magazine*, June 15, 2004.

Trends in SCM

The supplier-facing applications arena will see the continued growth of public as well as private networks that transform linear and inflexible supply chains into nonlinear and dynamic fulfillment networks. Supplier-facing applications will also evolve along another dimension: from automation and integration of supply chains to collaborative sourcing, planning, and design across their supplier networks.

Figure 8.20 illustrates the trends in the use of supply chain management today as three possible stages in a company's implementation of SCM systems. In the first stage, a company concentrates on making improvements to its internal supply chain processes and its external processes and relationships with suppliers and customers. Its e-commerce Web site and those of some of its trading partners provide access to online catalogs and useful supply chain information as they support limited online transactions.

In stage two, a company accomplishes substantial supply chain management applications by using selected SCM software programs internally, as well as externally via intranet and extranet links among suppliers, distributors, customers, and other trading partners. Companies in this stage also concentrate on expanding the business network of Web-enabled SCM-capable trading partners in their supply chain to increase its operational efficiency and effectiveness in meeting their strategic business objectives.

FIGURE 8.20   Stages in the use of supply chain management.

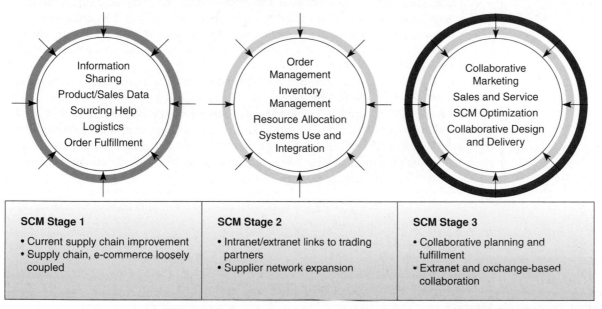

In the third stage, a company begins to develop and implement cutting-edge collaborative supply chain management applications using advanced SCM software, full-service extranet links, and private and public e-commerce exchanges. Examples include collaborative supply chain planning and fulfillment applications like collaborative product design and delivery, and collaborative planning, forecasting, and replenishment (CPFR). In addition, collaborative marketing sales and service applications with trading partners, including customer and partner relationship management systems, may be developed. Companies in this third stage strive to optimize the development and management of their supply chains in order to meet their strategic customer value and business value goals. Let's look at some real-world examples.

CVS, McKesson, and MPT: Web-Based SCM Integration

CVS is a leading drug retail chain, while McKesson is the largest U.S. distributor of pharmaceuticals, health care products, and medical/surgical supplies, with annual sales in excess of $20 billion. Better integration with McKesson is a key strategic move for CVS, as management sees significant potential for improving sales and margins through its enhanced pricing and promotional forecasting systems. Supply chain integration helps the retailer move from pull to push promotions by allowing marketing managers to plan promotions more effectively, using item history taken from historical point-of-sale data on a store-by-store basis. The integration with McKesson substantially reduces the amount of time needed to plan and to stock inventory for individual promotions.

A major objective in the CVS–McKesson chain is to improve business performance through better supply chain integration. This requires much closer cooperation between McKesson and CVS, with McKesson even taking responsibility for CVS stock levels. McKesson monitors CVS's store-level consumption via Web extranet links and replenishes the inventory to meet the agreed-on service levels—true supply chain integration. This cooperative process between supplier and customer is achieved through seamless interenterprise process integration and advanced SCM applications that link CVS directly to McKesson's production department.

Not every supply chain application, however, requires a hefty upfront investment. Modern Plastics Technology (MPT), an injection mold manufacturer in Port Huron,

Michigan, spends just several hundred dollars per month to access the i-Supply Service Web-based supply chain application from SupplySolution Inc. The company had been using electronic data interchange transmissions to fill its orders and was having a tough time keeping up with unscheduled changes in orders, says Doug Archer, vice president of Modern Plastics.

Then a large sealant manufacturer that was one of the company's customers persuaded Modern Plastics to connect with its i-Supply Service application. This Web-based SCM system has enabled Modern Plastics to see what its customers need on a real-time basis. Modern Plastics runs 30 to 40 different products through its presses, and i-Supply now allows management to better plan long production runs or prioritize specific product runs. Additionally, i-Supply helps MPT accomplish more accurate demand forecasting and production scheduling.

Summary

- **Customer Relationship Management: The Business Focus.** Customer relationship management is a cross-functional enterprise system that integrates and automates many of the customer-serving processes in sales, marketing, and customer services that interact with a company's customers. CRM systems use information technology to support the many companies that are re-orienting themselves into customer-focused businesses as a top business strategy. The major application components of CRM include contact and account management; sales, marketing, and fulfillment; customer service and support; and retention and loyalty programs, all aimed at helping a company acquire, enhance, and retain profitable relationships with its customers as a primary business goal. However, many companies have found CRM systems difficult to implement properly due to lack of adequate understanding and preparation by management and affected employees. Finally, many companies are moving toward collaborative CRM systems that support the collaboration of employees, business partners, and the customers themselves in enhancing profitable customer relationships.

- **Enterprise Resource Planning: The Business Backbone.** Enterprise resource planning is a cross-functional enterprise system that integrates and automates many of the internal business processes of a company, particularly those within the manufacturing, logistics, distribution, accounting, finance, and human resource functions of the business. Thus, ERP serves as the vital backbone information system of the enterprise, helping a company achieve the efficiency, agility, and responsiveness required to succeed in a dynamic business environment. ERP software typically consists of integrated modules that give a company a real-time cross-functional view of its core business processes, such as production, order processing, and sales, and its resources, such as cash, raw materials, production capacity, and people. However, properly implementing ERP systems is a difficult and costly process that has caused serious business losses for some companies, which underestimated the planning, development, and training that were necessary to reengineer their business processes to accommodate their new ERP systems. However, continuing developments in ERP software, including Web-enabled modules and e-business software suites, have made ERP more flexible and user friendly, as well as extending it outward to a company's business partners.

- **Supply Chain Management: The Business Network.** Supply chain management is a cross-functional inter-enterprise system that integrates and automates the network of business processes and relationships between a company and its suppliers, customers, distributors, and other business partners. The goal of SCM is to help a company achieve agility and responsiveness in meeting the demands of its customers and needs of its suppliers, by enabling it to design, build, and sell its products using a fast, efficient, and low-cost network of business partners, processes, and relationships, or supply chain. SCM is frequently subdivided into supply chain planning applications, such as demand and supply forecasting, and supply chain execution applications, such as inventory management, logistics management, and warehouse management. Developing effective supply chain systems and achieving the business goals of SCM have proven to be complex and difficult challenges for many firms. But SCM continues to be a major concern and top e-business initiative as companies increase their use of Internet technologies to enhance integration and collaboration with their business partners, and improve the operational efficiency and business effectiveness of their supply chains.

Key Terms and Concepts

These are the key terms and concepts of this chapter. The page number of their first explanation is in parentheses.

1. Customer relationship management (343)
   a. Application components
   b. Business benefits
   c. Challenges
   d. Trends
2. E-business suites (362)

3. Electronic data interchange (368)
4. Enterprise resource planning (354)
   a. Application components
   b. Business benefits
   c. Challenges
   d. Trends

5. Supply chain (364)
6. Supply chain management (364)
   a. Application components
   b. Business benefits
   c. Challenges
   d. Trends

Review Quiz

Match one of the key terms and concepts listed previously with each of the brief examples or definitions that follow. Try to find the best fit for answers that seem to fit more than one term or concept. Defend your choices.

_____ 1. A cross-functional enterprise system that helps a business develop and manage its customer-facing business processes.

_____ 2. A cross-functional enterprise system that helps a business integrate and automate many of its internal business processes and information systems.

_____ 3. A cross-functional interenterprise system that helps a business manage its network of relationships and processes with its business partners.

_____ 4. Includes contact and account management; sales, marketing, and fulfillment; and customer service and support systems.

_____ 5. Includes order management, production planning, accounting, finance, and human resource systems.

_____ 6. Includes demand forecasting, inventory management, logistics management, and warehouse management systems.

_____ 7. Acquiring, enhancing, and retaining profitable relationships with customers.

_____ 8. Improvements in the quality, efficiency, cost, and management of internal business processes.

_____ 9. Development of a fast, efficient, and low-cost network of business partners to get products from concept to market.

_____ 10. Resistance from sales and customer service professionals who are not adequately involved in the development of the system.

_____ 11. Failure of order processing and inventory accounting systems that are reengineered to accommodate a new cross-functional system.

_____ 12. A lack of adequate demand-planning knowledge, tools, and guidelines may cause major overproduction and excess inventory problems.

_____ 13. Toward Web portals and collaborative systems involving business partners as well as customers to coordinate sales and service across all marketing channels.

_____ 14. Toward more flexible, user-friendly, Web-enabled software, integrated into e-business software suites.

_____ 15. Toward the use of Internet technologies to integrate and enhance collaboration with a company's network of business partners.

_____ 16. An integrated system of software modules for customer relationship management, enterprise resource planning, supply chain management, and other business applications.

_____ 17. The automatic exchange of electronic business documents between the networked computers of business partners.

_____ 18. A network of business partners, processes, and relationships that supports the design, manufacture, distribution, and sale of a company's products.

Discussion Questions

1. Should every company become a customer-focused business? Why or why not?

2. Why would systems that enhance a company's relationships with customers have such a high rate of failure?

3. Refer to the Real World Case on Dow Corning and DirecTV in the chapter. Are mobile applications limited to be scaled-down versions of their enterprise counterparts, or will companies start to develop enterprise applications thinking about mobile deployments? Discuss.

4. How could some of the spectacular failures of ERP systems have been avoided?

5. Should companies continue to use EDI systems? Why or why not?

6. Refer to the Real World Case on smaller and less expensive ERP applications in the chapter. Do the examples discussed in the case show that customization and ERPs should never go together? Discuss.

7. How can the problem of overenthusiastic demand forecasts in supply chain planning be avoided?

8. What challenges do you see for a company that wants to implement collaborative SCM systems? How would you meet such challenges?

9. Refer to the Real World Case on Cisco Systems and Others in the chapter. Are supply chains becoming so tightly integrated that resilience against external shocks is minimal? Discuss.

10. Should companies install e-business software suites or "best of breed" e-business software components? Why?

Analysis Exercises

1. **NetSuite's NetSuite**
   Enterprise Systems to Go
   NetSuite by NetSuite Inc. (www.netsuite.com) enables small businesses to develop and deploy ERP, CRM, and e-commerce applications quickly. Their Web site presents detailed information about this software suite. Visit NetSuite's Web site and click on their "NetSuite" product link to see more information about the product's components. Click on the "Customers" link for a list of success stories. Notice the tremendous variety of business types.

   a. Identify and explore NetSuite's components that relate to your business major.
   b. Click on the "Customers" link on NetSuite's home page and select a customer in an industry that interests you (or one assigned by your instructor). Read the customer's success story. What benefits were emphasized?
   c. Would you recommend this suite to a small business owner? Why or why not?

2. **Collaborative CRM**
   Distributed Teams
   A large telecommunications company's real estate holdings include more than 6 million square feet of property. To aid in its more than 400 real estate–related transactions each year, the company contracted the services of a corporate real estate company and a law firm that specialized in corporate real estate. Real estate transactions significantly differ based on type and circumstances unique to each property and property owner. Legal specialists help ensure that each transaction meets its client's risk preferences.

   The telecommunications company wanted an information system using the Lotus Notes/Domino messaging platform to link it with the real estate firm and the law firm in order to:

   ● Capture common transaction information such as property location, transaction type, business unit, "opposing party," and lead contacts.
   ● Record and report what tasks have been completed, when they were completed, and who completed them.
   ● Allow ad hoc posting of additional, transaction-specific information into a common electronic file.

   Team members quickly found that by taking time to update the system they would reduce miscommunications and interruptions and therefore save time overall. Management liked the system because they could track team members' performance, identify processes open to improvement, and identify project delays before they became costly problems.

   a. How do these property transactions differ from commodity supply chain transactions?
   b. What advantage do the real estate company and the law firm gain by adopting their client's technology platform (Lotus Notes/Domino)?
   c. Find a Lotus Notes/Domino product review on the Web, read it, and report your findings to the class. Your presentation should answer the following questions: Who provided the review? What is the reviewer's relationship to the product? What did the reviewer like? What did the reviewer dislike? What competitors were mentioned in the review? How did Lotus Notes/Domino compare?

3. **Enterprise Sales Support**
   Making Up for Missing Features
   Christina Lovan works as an independent agent for Farmers Insurance (www.farmers.com) in O'Fallon, Illinois. As an independent agent, she manages her own office and earns her income entirely from policy sales. Farmers Insurance supports Christina's efforts with training and access to a Web-based suite of applications that help her manage her business. This *extranet* includes contact, customer, and policy management systems, as well as corporate communications. The system also includes a feedback feature agents may use to report software problems or make suggestions regarding future software enhancements.

   Christina enjoys working with people to help them solve their problems. However, to meet these people, Christina needs leads. She purchases leads from Farmers Insurance, Net Quote (www.netquote.com), InsureMe (www.insureme.com), AllQuotes (www.allquotesinsurance.com), and Crisscross (www.criscross.org), a database of local residents and businesses. She asks each client for three referrals at each meeting. She is a member of Business Networking International (www.bni.com), and she is an active member of the local chamber of commerce.

Although the software tools provided by Farmers Insurance allow Christina to track prospective customers, they do not measure information quality. Lead information is expensive to purchase or solicit. Christina needs to know the best way to spend her time and money. Until Farmers provides a system update to accommodate this need, Christina has developed her own data-quality evaluation tools using Microsoft Excel.

With a few basic Excel skills, we can duplicate Christina's efforts. Download and save "Insurance.xls" from the MIS 10e OLC and use it to complete the following exercises. Note that the data providers used in this exercise are real, but the data in this spreadsheet are randomly generated.

a. Pending sales need Christina's immediate attention. Help her spot these opportunities by automatically highlighting them. Select the "Sales Leads" spreadsheet and use Excel's Conditional Formatting feature to set the cell shading color of each *Status* cell (Life, Auto, Home, Health) to green if the status is "Sale" (S) and red if the status is "Pending" (P).

b. Select the "Cover Sheet" spreadsheet. In cell C2, use the COUNTA function to count the total number of sales leads in the Sales Leads sheet. In cells C5 through C8, use the COUNTIF function to count the number of sales made for each type of insurance. In cells D5 through D8, divide the sales made by the number of leads to calculate the percentage of sales. Write these formulas so they calculate the correct answers even when Christina later adds more records to the list. Which product has the highest sales rate?

c. When rating the quality of her information, Christina counts whether or not a lead resulted in at least one sale. Using the IF and the OR functions, write a formula that will display "1" when at least one sale was made to a lead and "0" if the lead generated no sales.

d. Ultimately, Christina needs to know which lead source results in the most sales. Create a pivot table to average the data in the "Sales" for each "Source." Format this result as a percentage. Because a 1 indicates at least one sale and a 0 indicates no sales, the average per source indicates each source's closing rate. Which source had the highest closing rate? Which source had the lowest closing rate?

4. **The Future of Enterprise Systems**
Plug-in ERP
As enterprise systems grow in size to perform ever more operations for an organization, the software system itself becomes increasingly complex and hard to maintain. Add the fact that organizations typically customize these applications and it becomes clear why organizations end up with ever-increasing annual software maintenance budgets.

Is there an alternative model to enterprisewide systems that try to do it all? What if third-party developers produced mutually compatible components or modules for enterprise systems? Such components would plug in to a central system much like a printer, mouse, monitor, and modem plug into a personal computer.

If third parties wrote individual components, they might make them more closely fit the needs of specific types of business. With a better fit, these components would require less customization. Organizations could upgrade or replace components individually and only when needed.

So what is the current state of the art? Visit 20/20 Software Inc.'s Web site (www.2020software.com) and use its "Compare Software" feature to research applications.

a. Identify a system that runs on more than one server operating system.

b. Identify a system that runs on more than one database platform.

c. Describe 20/20 software's revenue model.

REAL WORLD CASE 4

NetSuite Inc., Berlin Packaging, Churchill Downs, and Others: The Secret to CRM Is in the Data

Zach Nelson sits in a Silicon Valley coffeehouse, sipping a latte, nibbling a pastry, and drawing IT architecture diagrams. His mission: to illustrate what he believes is the biggest reason that the software category known as customer relationship management (CRM) has been unable to shake the black marks of too many failed multimillion-dollar deployments.

CRM is easier to implement when a company is young, he says. "The elephant in the room with CRM systems is that there's no customer data native in them," says Nelson, CEO of NetSuite Inc., which sells a suite of Web-based, on-demand business applications, including CRM. "That's why they fail."

When CRM came onto the market in the mid-1990s, driven largely by Siebel Systems, the software typically came bundled with proprietary databases that then had to be populated with customer data housed in disparate enterprise systems. The result? "Customer records are scattered and there's often overlap and inconsistency," Nelson contends.

By the time he's finished with his morning snack, Nelson has also made a convincing case as to why small and midsize companies are primed to get CRM right.

CRM is a lot easier to do early in a company's history than it is later. Also, Web-based subscription software, such as the kind that Nelson's company offers, has given them access to IT applications that in the past might have been too costly or too complex. Designs for Health Inc., a $10 million-a-year maker of prescription nutritional supplements, isn't ready to invest millions in a big CRM package, but it did need a more sophisticated accounting system than Intuit Corp.'s Quick-Books. So, it turned to NetSuite to host a general-ledger application that would let the company automate its accounting processes and easily share the data with other NetSuite applications, such as the CRM module it would add later.

Perhaps the most crucial factor to the CRM success of small and midsize businesses is that most aren't yet paralyzed by data silos and disparate systems, and they've learned from those that have had to spend lots of time and energy bridging the silos. "The biggest problem I have with having disparate systems is determining what is your source of the truth," says Steve Canter, CIO at Berlin Packaging LLC, a $200 million-a-year maker of cans and bottles used to package everything from makeup to jelly. "I have a customer–relationship-management system that has a customer master file. I have an order-management system that has a customer master. If the information between those systems doesn't agree, which one is true? Having a single instance of the customer master, we know what the truth is."

In theory, customer data integration provides a universal view of a customer by resolving discrepancies in names and addresses, as well as summarizing customer interaction data from multiple systems. Customer data in many IT companies remain balkanized as CRM, enterprise resource planning, and supply chain management systems have proliferated. That means the IT behind customer-facing operations such as call centers often can't provide employees with a single view of a customer.

Berlin considered adding a PeopleSoft CRM application to the company's existing PeopleSoft enterprise resource planning and supply chain management system, but it decided that such an effort might prove too distracting. So Berlin opted to use the PeopleTools programming code in the ERP system to build bolt-on applications that convert financial and supply chain management functions into CRM processes. Including housing records on more than 27,000 customers acquired since the mid-1990s, the ERP database now serves as a clearinghouse of customer data that lets any part of the company access definitive and wide-ranging information. The knowledge that there are no other collections of customer data elsewhere in the company provides significant peace of mind.

What's more, Canter not only has accomplished this without absorbing any hard costs, but employees have quickly adopted every tool he's introduced, something that any big-company CIO will tell you is the most elusive part of a CRM deployment. The key, Canter says, has been a combination of incremental changes and interfaces salespeople already are familiar with. "It's not like implementing a CRM system where overnight their lives are changed," he says. "Little by little, they're getting a CRM system without even realizing it."

Creating de facto CRM systems out of other applications isn't for everyone, says Barton Goldenberg, president of CRM consulting firm ISM. Goldenberg is a firm believer that CRM software can provide data intelligence and support for front-end business processes that even the most carefully tweaked ERP system can't match. "Data in its own right [are] useless unless it's put into context," he says. "I can serve data up via pigeons, but it's the CRM application that adds the value."

A CRM deployment that's carefully thought out has done just that for Churchill Downs Inc., the $500 million-a-year operator of six horse-racing tracks, including its namesake, the famed home of the Kentucky Derby. It's also converting its mass-market advertising to a more one-to-one approach.

Before Atique Shah joined the company in late 2003 as vice president of CRM and technology solutions, Churchill Downs had just assumed that the aggregate data culled from its Twin Spires loyalty club could be broken into four distinct buckets of customers.

Shah wasn't so sure. So, he got budget approval to obtain a range of technologies, starting with Epiphany Inc.'s CRM software and supported by SPSS Inc.'s Clementine data-mining tool and IBM's Ascential data-extraction and transformation software. Shah then ran the data through Clementine and discovered that there were actually nine aggregate customer types, which was an indication that its previous marketing efforts probably weren't as useful or relevant as they should have been.

Asked how close he is to achieving a 360-degree view of his customers, he laughs and says, "I believe we're probably at about 190 degrees." Churchill Downs has 27 sources of customer information, and refereeing among them is a constant problem, Shah says.

To reflect the more-detailed profiles that emerged, Shah transitioned from generic labels for the old buckets—platinum, gold, silver, and bronze—to descriptions that hinted at the personalities of each segment. So, a female customer who only visits the track a few times a year and is there more for the social spectacle than for the betting is now known as a "Seldom Sally," and a wealthy man in his fifties who spends more than $100,000 a year at the track and is confident in his racing knowledge is a "Smarty Steve."

Shah published the new intelligence to the company's various tracks and engineered a test campaign with Arlington Park near Chicago. Arlington's staff selected 55,000 households from its database and then broke them into the nine customer segments Clementine had spit out.

Each distinct group of customers then received direct-mail advertisements that reflected its profile, with information and offers that jibed with its attributes. The response rate was impressive, with nearly 10 percent of those who received the mailing coming to the park during the following season. "What was more amazing was that the group of customers they had segmented generated $1.6 million in the first two weeks," Shah says. "A year earlier, the same customers generated $950,000." The success of that campaign underscored the value of the data that Churchill Downs had, in many ways, been sitting on.

However small and midsize companies implement CRM, it's clear that data can translate into increased sales. ISM's Goldenberg reiterates, though, that companies need to make sure data are in order before they launch any major CRM initiative. Even though he believes that in most cases, it's the CRM application, not the data, that's providing the real business value, it's also clear that one can't thrive without the other. "Without accurate, complete, and comprehensive data, any CRM effort will be less than optimal," he says.

Which brings us back to the prediction that NetSuite's Nelson makes: A few years from now, today's small companies will be running circles around their larger competitors, primarily because establishing a master record of customer data will prove to be a less-daunting task for them. The way Nelson sees it, the decision to jump on establishing unified sources of customer data will pay off for the emerging companies that do so. "Once you get your data in place, things that were very complex before become quite trivial, he says.

Maybe not as trivial as sipping coffee and nibbling on a Danish pastry, but wouldn't it be great if it were pretty darn close?

Source: Adapted from Tony Kontzer, " CRM's Secret Is in the Data," *InformationWeek*, August 15, 2005; and Charles Babcock, "Looking for a Clearer View of the Customer," *InformationWeek*, August 8, 2005.

CASE STUDY QUESTIONS

1. What are the business benefits of CRM implementations for organizations such as Berlin Packaging and Churchill Downs? What other uses of CRM would you recommend to the latter? Provide several alternatives.

2. Do you agree with the idea that smaller organizations are better positioned to be more effective users of CRM than larger ones? Why or why not? Justify your answer.

3. One of the main issues noted in the case is the importance of "good" data for the success of CRM implementations. We discussed many of these in Chapter 5, when we compared the file processing and database management approaches to data resource management. Which of the problems discussed there do you see present in this case? How do CRM applications attempt to address them. Use examples from the case to illustrate your answer.

REAL WORLD ACTIVITIES

1. NetSuite Inc. is a leading provider of on-demand enterprise applications, including CRM as featured in the case. Other important players in this market include Salesforce.com and Siebel On Demand. Use the Internet to research all three product offerings and discover how these companies are faring in this increasingly competitive industry. Compare and contrast their product features to understand whether offerings are becoming differentiated or more alike as a result.

2. The CRM implementations in this case highlight the critical importance of information about customers, their preferences and activities, and how to use it to understand and develop better marketing solutions. On the other hand, the degree to which these companies are able to target customers individually may be of concern to some people. Break into small groups with your classmates to discuss these concerns, as well as ways for both companies and their customers to benefit from CRM systems and still protect customer privacy.

CHAPTER 9

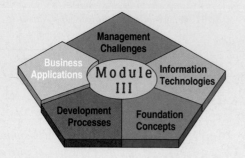

e-COMMERCE SYSTEMS

Chapter Highlights

Learning Objectives

1. Identify the major categories and trends of e-commerce applications.

2. Identify the essential processes of an e-commerce system, and give examples of how it is implemented in e-commerce applications.

3. Identify and give examples of several key factors and Web store requirements needed to succeed in e-commerce.

4. Identify and explain the business value of several types of e-commerce marketplaces.

5. Discuss the benefits and trade-offs of several e-commerce clicks-and-bricks alternatives.

e-Commerce Fundamentals

Introduction to e-Commerce

E-commerce is changing the shape of competition, the speed of action, and the streamlining of interactions, products, and payments from customers to companies and from companies to suppliers.

For most companies today, **electronic commerce** is more than just buying and selling products online. Instead, it encompasses the entire online process of developing, marketing, selling, delivering, servicing, and paying for products and services transacted on inter-networked, global marketplaces of customers, with the support of a worldwide network of business partners. In fact, many consider the term "e-commerce" to be somewhat antiquated. Given that many young businesspeople have grown up in a world in which online commerce has always been available, it may soon be time to eliminate the distinction between e-commerce and e-business and accept that it is all just "business as usual." Until then, we will retain the term "e-commerce" because it allows for a clearer picture of the differences between online and more traditional business transactions.

As we will see in this chapter, e-commerce systems rely on the resources of the Internet and many other information technologies to support every step of this process. We will also see that most companies, large and small, are engaged in some form of e-commerce activities. Therefore, developing an e-commerce capability has become a competitive necessity for most businesses in today's marketplace.

Read the Real World Case on the next page. We can learn a lot about new ways to reach customers using technology from this case. See Figure 9.1.

The Scope of e-Commerce

Figure 9.2 illustrates the range of business processes involved in the marketing, buying, selling, and servicing of products and services in companies that engage in e-commerce. Companies involved in e-commerce as either buyers or sellers rely on Internet-based technologies and e-commerce applications and services to accomplish marketing, discovery, transaction processing, and product and customer service processes. For example, e-commerce can include interactive marketing, ordering, payment, and customer support processes at e-commerce catalog and auction sites on the World Wide Web. However, e-commerce also includes e-business processes such as extranet access of inventory databases by customers and suppliers (transaction processing), intranet access of customer relationship management systems by sales and customer service reps (service and support), and customer collaboration in product development via e-mail exchanges and Internet newsgroups (marketing/discovery).

The advantages of e-commerce allow a business of virtually any size that is located virtually anywhere on the planet to conduct business with just about anyone, anywhere. Imagine a small olive oil manufacturer in a remote village in Italy selling its wares to major department stores and specialty food shops in New York, London, Tokyo, and other large metropolitan markets. The power of e-commerce allows geophysical barriers to disappear, making all consumers and businesses on earth potential customers and suppliers.

e-Commerce Technologies

Which technologies are necessary for e-commerce? The short answer is that most information technologies and Internet technologies that we discuss in this text are, in some form, involved in e-commerce systems. A more specific answer is illustrated in Figure 9.3, which gives an example of the technology resources required by many e-commerce systems. The figure illustrates some of the hardware, software, data, and network components used by FreeMarkets Inc. to provide business-to-business (B2B) online auction e-commerce services.

REAL WORLD CASE 1

Facebook and iPhone May Be the Future of e-Commerce

e-Retailers are cautiously, slowly sorting out how and how much to engage with their customers in social networks such as Facebook and over smartphone apps. Caution, however, may not be a luxury that vendors enjoy. If, for example, their customers are teenage girls and 72 percent of them are on Facebook and 36 percent of them have a smartphone, the luxury of being cautious and taking your dear sweet time simply doesn't exist.

That's the case for the innovative clothing retailer Wet Seal, which is years ahead of most companies in not just learning about online social networking with its customers but getting results. Wet Seal was named the top innovator in the use of wireless technology at the 2010 InformationWeek 500 Conference.

Wet Seal launched a tool in 2008 on its Web site that lets girls create outfits that combine different Wet Seal tops, bottoms, shoes, and accessories. That allows for user-generated content: Girls have created more than a half million outfits on the site, and they provide a stream of new—and credible—content for Wet Seal.

That application got a lot more interesting when, in 2009, Wet Seal embraced its "social merchandising" strategy that blends the Web strategy with Facebook and smartphones, beginning with the iPhone.

In Facebook, Wet Seal's fan page offers a better way to share outfits that girls put together using Wet Seal clothing—sharing them not just with other Wet Seal shoppers, but all of a person's Facebook friends.

On the iPhone, they can view those outfits, including while shopping in stores. They can enter a barcode number of

a shirt into the iPhone app and see what outfits girls have put together around that shirt. Beginning this month, they can beta test an iPhone game that lets them choose what clothes they'd stock if they ran a Wet Seal store. From the WetSeal.com Web site or Facebook page, girls can "shop with friends," connecting their sessions live so they show each other outfits.

The results from Wet Seal's merchandising efforts turned out to be quite impressive! Shoppers using the outfit tool are 40 percent more likely to buy something, and buyers spend 20 percent more. "Shop with friends" users become buyers at 2.5 times Wet Seal's average conversion rate online. The iPhone app generates about 5 percent of Wet Seal's overall Web traffic, and the app has been downloaded more than 65,000 times. Girls look at about 500,000 outfits a week with their iPhones—traffic that spiked to about 750,000 a week the two weeks before back-to-school.

Facebook has become one of the largest marketing bases for store traffic, thanks to coupons and campaigns, and one of the biggest drivers of traffic to WetSeal.com. Just as importantly as those results, Wet Seal's Shawn Keim, the company's director of development, offers some hard-earned wisdom from the past year of marketing on social networks and smartphones. Here are some of the lessons learned:

Be in the Game—or Else: When Wet Seal went to create its Facebook fan page, it found someone already had claimed it. Fortunately, it was one of Wet Seal's own stores, which had done it just for that location. Keim's warning: "The reality was, we needed to get out there. . . . If you don't get out there, someone will fill the gap."

It Can Take Time to Catch On: When the company puts out a new tool, whether on Facebook or the iPhone, it's rarely an overnight sensation. "It typically takes six months to get engagement of one of our initiatives," Keim said. However, you will get feedback quickly from a small group of early adopters, and you need to address it right away. In addition, your infrastructure needs to be ready well before any traffic spikes. Wet Seal first launched iRunway on a single server, since there wasn't a big user base. When that server went down briefly, within a day there were six complaints and the app's ranking went from five stars to two. The application is now split across six servers.

Different Platforms, Different Actions: Girls tend to create content—outfits—on the Web site, but they share those outfits using Facebook. iPhone users generate the most e-mail—20 times more than they generate using the Facebook app—but they don't do a lot of outfit creation or sharing by smartphone. They don't go into the Facebook app via iPhone much. Wet Seal tried its Virtual Runway app in stores, to show the outfits girls made on kiosks, and it wasn't a big hit. On Facebook, it has been a big hit. The lesson is that social, mobile, and e-commerce strategies have to

FIGURE 9.1

Companies are expanding from Web sites and e-mail into new ways of reaching consumers through innovative uses of technology.

complement each other. They'll each do different things for the same customer.

Know Your Audience, Part I: To succeed in this market, Wet Seal needed its executives experimenting with social networks and smartphones. That meant doing a lot of things "IT doesn't like to do," Keim said. Like getting executives iPhones to use, and opening Wet Seal's firewalls to Facebook and Facebook-based online games, like Farmville. Getting execs to use iPhones wasn't hard, but getting them active on Facebook was tougher. The IT team urged executives' daughters to show them how they use Facebook. "While our executives don't use our clothes, their daughters do," Keim said.

Know Your Audience, Part II: When Wet Seal wanted someone to monitor its Facebook fan page, it turned to someone who was doing a lot of posting on the site—and gave her an internship.

Facebook Is a Customer-Support Gold Mine: The intern isn't the only person checking the site. "For customer service, it's one of the primary tools they use to know if there are problems out there," Keim said. Don't expect active social networking types to necessarily call about a problem—they're as likely to just post and vent with friends about it. Wet Seal doesn't erase complaints, but tries to resolve problems in that environment, so people see the issues getting taken care of.

Keep It Current: With its iRunway app, Wet Seal is updating the functionality about every three months, adding some things and dropping others that haven't caught on. When it comes to content, that has to be changing constantly to bring people back. For Wet Seal, the only viable answer for that is user-generated content, like the outfits that girls create. That's cost effective, of course. But it also brings the connection and sharing girls want.

The real issue here is that most of what Wet Seal experienced applies to just about every business on the Internet. Perhaps not as urgently as it does for Wet Seal, with its hyperconnected teen audience. Perhaps. But without a doubt, some element of it will. Just like Amazon and Google shape what people expect on every other Web site, from banks to governments to company intranets, Facebook is shaping how people expect to interact with each other. And companies such as Wet Seal are doing the tricky and sometimes humbling work of figuring out how a new generation of customers expects to use Facebook and other interactive tools to do business with you.

Source: Adapted from Chris Murphy, "Global CIO: How Wet Seal Drives Sales with Facebook, iPhone," *InformationWeek*, September 22, 2010.

CASE STUDY QUESTIONS

1. How did Wet Seal benefit from the innovations discussed in the case? Is it about more efficient transaction processing, better reaching out to customers, or both?

2. Use examples from the case to illustrate your answer.

3. Facebook is a customer-support gold mine. Do you think this is a stretch, or are we in the midst of a turning point in online shopping? Explain your answer.

4. Many of the applications discussed in the case are mostly used by the younger demographic, who grew up around technology. How do online behavior patterns change as they become older, with more responsibilities, and more challenging jobs? Do applications like those discussed in the case become less important? More important?

REAL WORLD ACTIVITIES

1. Consider the examples discussed in the case. Go online and research what other companies or industries are doing in terms of the use of social networking sites and mobile commerce. What other examples can you find? Prepare a report that compares those in your research with the ones described here, highlighting similarities and differences. Can you spot any new trends?

2. How often, if ever, do you shop with your mobile phone? What do you think are some of the roadblocks that prevent the widespread adoption of mobile shopping?

3. What would you suggest companies do to overcome those? Break into small groups with your classmates to develop a few recommendations.

FIGURE 9.2 E-commerce involves accomplishing a range of business processes to support the electronic buying and selling of goods and services.

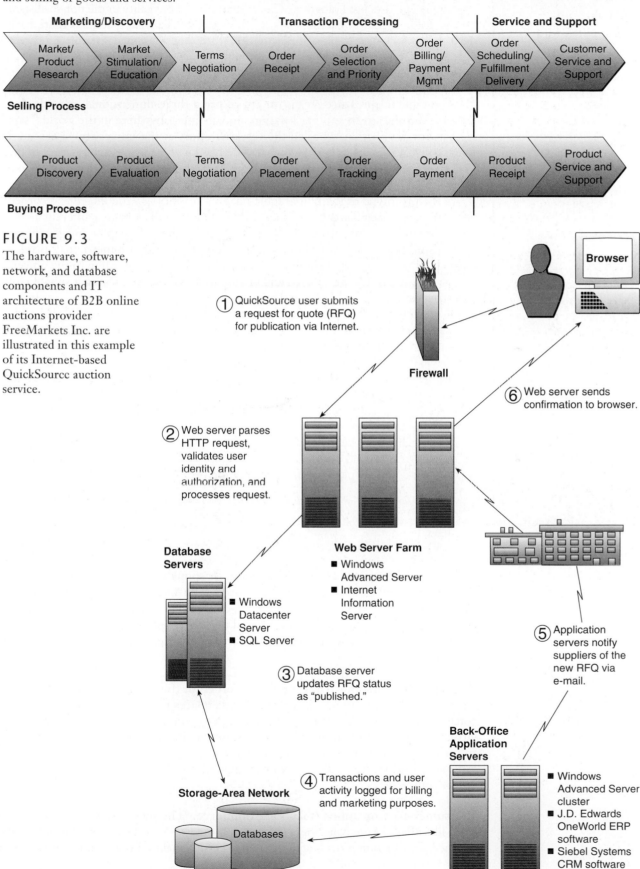

FIGURE 9.3

The hardware, software, network, and database components and IT architecture of B2B online auctions provider FreeMarkets Inc. are illustrated in this example of its Internet-based QuickSource auction service.

Holographs Could Revolutionize Online Shopping

A CEO needs to meet with workers in a remote office, but instead of boarding a plane, she simply employs her hologram. That scenario could be reality in the not-so-distant future, according to researchers at the University of Arizona. Scientists there have developed a new type of holographic telepresence that's designed to project a three-dimensional, full-color, moving image without viewers needing to sport 3-D glasses.

While the technology could be used in TV or movies, it also could be used in advertising, telemedicine, and mapping, as well as in everyday corporate meetings. "Holographic telepresence means we can record a three-dimensional image in one location and show it in another location, in real-time, anywhere in the world," said Nasser Peyghambarian, who led the research effort at the university. "Let's say I want to give a presentation in Shanghai. All I need is an array of cameras here in my Tucson office and a fast Internet connection. At the other end, in China, there would be the 3-D display using our laser system."

In the prototype of the holographic imaging technology, the image is recorded using an array of regular cameras, each one viewing the object from a different angle. The more cameras that are used, the more granular the holographic image will be. Then using fast-pulsed laser beams, a holographic, or three-dimensional, pixel is created. These pixels are the building blocks of the images, according to the university. Everything is fully automated and insensitive to vibration, making it suitable for industrial situations, said Peyghambarian.

Taking holographic imaging from the world of science fiction to the real world could be a significant advancement for business, said Dan Olds, an analyst with the Gabriel Consulting Group. "It can be a game changer in some industries," he added. "There will certainly be plenty of business uses for this technology. The first that come to mind are product demonstrations and giving the ability to actually see a product in 3-D before the money is spent to build it. It also could, for instance, immerse prospective tenants in their new office suite or show hotel mavens the interior decorator's vision for their remodeled rooms." The technology could literally revolutionize online shopping!

If the technology becomes common, it also could greatly decrease the need for business travel. Instead of flying across the country to make a presentation, a business person could simply make the presentation through a hologram.

Source: Adapted from Sharon Gaudin, "Holographs Could Be Game Changer for Business," *ComputerWorld NZ*, Fairfax Media Group, November 5, 2010.

Categories of e-Commerce

Many companies today are participating in or sponsoring four basic categories of e-commerce applications: business-to-consumer, business-to-business, consumer-to-consumer and business-to-government e-commerce. Note: We do not explicitly cover business-to-government (B2G) and *e-government* applications because they are beyond the scope of this text, but many e-commerce concepts apply to such applications.

Business-to-Consumer (B2C) e-Commerce. In this form of e-commerce, businesses must develop attractive electronic marketplaces to sell products and services to consumers. For example, many companies offer e-commerce Web sites that provide virtual storefronts and multimedia catalogs, interactive order processing, secure electronic payment systems, and online customer support. The B2C marketplace is growing like a wildfire but still remains the tip of the iceberg when compared with all online commerce.

Consumer-to-Consumer (C2C) e-Commerce. The huge success of online auctions like eBay, where consumers (as well as businesses) can buy from and sell to one another in an auction process at an auction Web site, makes this e-commerce model an important e-commerce business strategy. Thus, participating in or sponsoring consumer or business auctions is an important e-commerce alternative for B2C, C2B (consumer-to-business), or B2B e-commerce. Electronic personal advertising of products or services to buy or sell by consumers at electronic newspaper sites, consumer e-commerce portals, or personal Web sites is also an important form of C2C e-commerce.

Business-to-Business (B2B) e-Commerce. If B2C activities are the tip of the iceberg, B2B represents the part of the iceberg that is under the water—the biggest part. This category of e-commerce involves both e-business marketplaces and direct market links between businesses. For example, many companies offer secure Internet or extranet e-commerce catalog Web sites for their business customers and suppliers. Also very important are B2B e-commerce portals that provide auction and exchange marketplaces for businesses. Others may rely on electronic data interchange (EDI) via the Internet or extranets for computer-to-computer exchange of e-commerce documents with their larger business customers and suppliers.

Essential e-Commerce Processes

The essential e-commerce processes required for the successful operation and management of e-commerce activities are illustrated in Figure 9.4. This figure outlines the nine key components of an *e-commerce process architecture* that is the foundation of the e-commerce initiatives of many companies today. We concentrate on the role these processes play in e-commerce systems, but you should recognize that many of these components may also be used in internal, noncommerce e-business applications. An example would be an intranet-based human resource system used by a company's employees, which might use all but the catalog management and product payment processes shown in Figure 9.4. Let's take a brief look at each essential process category.

FIGURE 9.4 This e-commerce process architecture highlights nine essential categories of e-commerce processes.

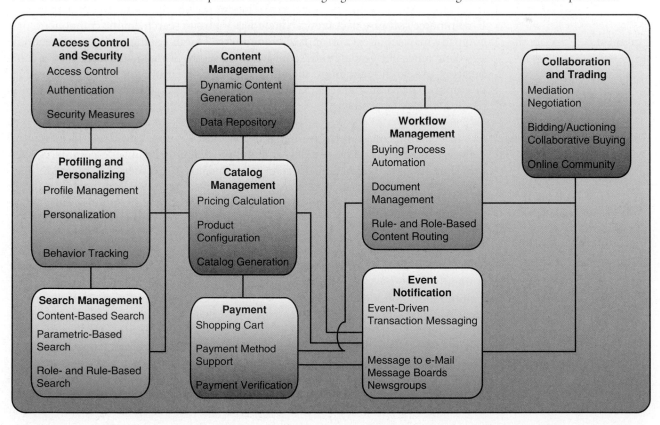

Access Control and Security

E-commerce processes must establish mutual trust and secure access between the parties in an e-commerce transaction by authenticating users, authorizing access, and enforcing security features. For example, these processes establish that a customer and e-commerce site are who they say they are through user names and passwords, encryption keys, or digital certificates and signatures. The e-commerce site must then authorize access to only those parts of the site that an individual user needs to accomplish his or her particular transactions. Thus, you usually will be given access to all resources of an e-commerce site except for other people's accounts, restricted company data, and Web master administration areas. Companies engaged in B2B e-commerce may rely on secure industry exchanges for procuring goods and services or Web trading portals that allow only registered customers to access trading information and applications. Other security processes protect the resources of e-commerce sites from threats such as hacker attacks, theft of passwords or credit card numbers, and system failures. We discuss many of these security threats and features in Chapter 13.

Profiling and Personalizing

Once you have gained access to an e-commerce site, profiling processes can occur that gather data on you and your Web site behavior and choices, as well as build electronic profiles of your characteristics and preferences. User profiles are developed using profiling tools such as user registration, cookie files, Web site behavior tracking software, and user feedback. These profiles are then used to recognize you as an individual user and provide you with a personalized view of the contents of the site, as well as product recommendations and personalized Web advertising as part of a *one-to-one marketing* strategy. Profiling processes are also used to help authenticate your identity for account management and payment purposes and gather data for customer relationship management, marketing planning, and Web site management. Some of the ethical issues in user profiling are discussed in Chapter 13.

Search Management

Efficient and effective search processes provide a top e-commerce Web site capability that helps customers find the specific product or service they want to evaluate or buy. E-commerce software packages can include a Web site search engine component, or a company may acquire a customized e-commerce search engine from search technology companies like Google and Requisite Technology. Search engines may use a combination of search techniques, including searches based on content (e.g., a product description) or parameters (e.g., above, below, or between a range of values for multiple properties of a product).

Content and Catalog Management

Content management software helps e-commerce companies develop, generate, deliver, update, and archive text data and multimedia information at e-commerce Web sites. For example, German media giant Bertelsmann, part owner of BarnesandNoble.com, uses StoryServer content manager software to generate Web page templates that enable online editors from six international offices to easily publish and update book reviews and other product information, which are sold (syndicated) to other e-commerce sites.

E-commerce content frequently takes the form of multimedia catalogs of product information. As such, generating and managing catalog content is a major subset of content management, or catalog management. For example, W.W. Grainger & Co., a multibillion-dollar industrial parts distributor, uses the CenterStage catalog management software suite to retrieve data from more than 2,000 supplier databases, standardize the data, translate it into HTML or XML for Web use, and organize and enhance the data for speedy delivery as multimedia Web pages at its www.grainger.com Web site.

Content and catalog management software works with the profiling tools we mentioned previously to personalize the content of Web pages seen by individual users. For example, Travelocity.com uses OnDisplay content manager software to push personalized promotional information about other travel opportunities to users while they are involved in an online travel-related transaction.

Finally, content and catalog management may be expanded to include *product configuration* processes that support Web-based customer self-service and the *mass customization* of a company's products. Configuration software helps online customers select the optimum feasible set of product features that can be included in a finished product. For example, both Dell Computer and Cisco Systems use configuration software to sell built-to-order computers and network processors to their online customers.

e-Commerce Tools to Close the Deal	Nothing is as heart-wrenching to an e-tailer as watching a customer abandon a full cart just seconds before consummating the deal. To be so close yet so cashless is more than frustrating; it's harmful to an e-tailer's health. A virtual armory of tools are in use to woo, cajole, prompt, and push consumers to make the buy—but are they working, or are they turning even more customers away?

"Most fall woefully short," says Matthew Brown, senior director of e-commerce and interactive marketing at MarketNet. "Instead of focusing on using tools and technologies to help the customer, much more thought and time needs to go into Web site architecture in the first place."

Many theories are being tossed about as to why consumers turn fickle a hair short of the finish line. For each theory, there are a multitude of technological solutions. "Retailers continue to launch and test technologies and features aimed at reducing abandonment or increasing online conversion," says Jessica Ried, a director of retail strategy at Resource Interactive. "In our experience, it is difficult to know for sure if any particular one is going to be effective for a given retailer without testing it with that retailer's customer base, or at least having a solid understanding of existing customer behaviors on the site through site analytics and surveys."

Once an e-tailer understands the true obstacles to closing the deal, there are a range of tools available to clear the way to bigger profits. The most commonly deployed are live chat, pop-up discounts, and follow-up email programs; some are achieved through the standard use of cookies, others via pixel-based triggers. Third-person endorsements are also frequently used. "Hosting consumer-generated content such as ratings and reviews has typically allowed retailers to improve conversions," explains Ried, "as customers are more confident with their selections. That's because they have access to an 'unbiased' opinion, building trust rather than having to rely solely on the marketing copy on the retailer's site."

"We use Liveperson chat extensively. It has been an incredible tool for answering any last-minute doubts during the last few states of the transaction," notes Adrian Salamunovic, cofounder of DNA 11, a multimillion-dollar e-commerce art retailer. "Our average transaction is over US$500, so this is very important to us."

"It pays for itself many times over each month," he adds. "For us, interrupting the client with pop-ups or invitations to chat really doesn't work—in fact, it does the opposite. We've watched customers bounce (exit) quite quickly after being interrupted with pop-ups."

Therein lies the conundrum. No two customers are identical. At least some personalized customization is essential. There is a point, however, at which actions considered helpful by the retailer are perceived as intrusive by the consumer. "Some customers welcome the help; others are unnerved by the Big Brother effect it can suggest," says Resource Interactive's Ried. "Start by considering what is known about consumer behavior in evaluating which technologies, features, and functionalities to explore first."

Source: Adapted from Pam Baker, "Rescuing the e-Commerce Deal When the Customer's Walking Way," *E-Commerce Times*, April 24, 2009.

FIGURE 9.5

The role of catalog/content management and workflow management in a Web-based procurement process: the MS Market system used by Microsoft Corp.

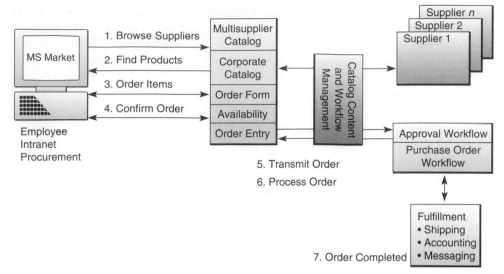

Workflow Management

Many of the business processes in e-commerce applications can be managed and partially automated with the help of workflow management software. E-business workflow systems for enterprise collaboration help employees electronically collaborate to accomplish structured work tasks within knowledge-based business processes. Workflow management in both e-business and e-commerce depends on a *workflow software engine* containing software models of the business processes to be accomplished. The workflow models express the predefined sets of business rules, roles of stakeholders, authorization requirements, routing alternatives, databases used, and sequence of tasks required for each e-commerce process. Thus, workflow systems ensure that the proper transactions, decisions, and work activities are performed, and the correct data and documents are routed to the right employees, customers, suppliers, and other business stakeholders.

As many of you begin your business careers, you will be charged with the responsibility of driving cost out of existing business processes while maintaining or improving the effectiveness of those processes. As you continue to acquire a greater appreciation for, and understanding of, how technology can benefit business, you will explore workflow management as the key to this optimization of cost and effectiveness throughout the business.

For example, Figure 9.5 illustrates the e-commerce procurement processes of the MS Market system of Microsoft Corp. Microsoft employees use its global intranet and the catalog/content management and workflow management software engines built into MS Market to purchase electronically more than $3 billion annually of business supplies and materials from approved suppliers connected to the MS Market system by their corporate extranets.

Microsoft Corporation: e-Commerce Purchasing Processes

MS Market is an internal e-commerce purchasing system that works on Microsoft's intranet. MS Market has drastically reduced the personnel required to manage low-cost requisitions and gives employees a quick, easy way to order materials without being burdened with paperwork and bureaucratic processes. These high-volume, low-dollar transactions represent about 70 percent of total volume but only 3 percent of Microsoft's accounts payable. Employees were wasting time turning requisitions into purchase orders (POs) and trying to follow business rules and processes. Managers wanted to streamline this process, so the decision was made to create a requisitioning tool that would take all the controls and validations used by requisition personnel and push them onto the Web. Employees wanted an easy-to-use online form for ordering supplies that included extranet interfaces to procurement partners, such as Boise Cascade and Marriott.

How does this system work? Let's say a Microsoft employee wants a technical book. He goes to the MS Market site on Microsoft's intranet, and MS Market immediately identifies his preferences and approval code through his log-on ID. The employee selects the Barnes & Noble link, which brings up a catalog, order form, and a list of hundreds of books with titles and prices that have been negotiated between Microsoft buyers and Barnes & Noble. He selects a book, puts it in the order form, and completes the order by verifying his group's cost center number and manager's name.

The order is transmitted immediately to the supplier, cutting down on delivery time, as well as accounting for the payment of the supplies. Upon submission of the order, MS Market generates an order tracking number for reference, sends notification via e-mail to the employee's manager, and transmits the order over the Internet to Barnes & Noble for fulfillment. In this case, since the purchase total is only $40, the manager's specific approval is not required. Two days later, the book arrives at the employee's office. Thus, MS Market lets employees easily order low-cost items in a controlled fashion at a low cost, without going through a complicated PO approval process.

Source: Adapted from Microsoft IT Showcase, "MS Market: Business Case Study," 2002.

Event Notification

Most e-commerce applications are *event-driven* systems that respond to a multitude of events—from a new customer's first Web site access, to payment and delivery processes, to innumerable customer relationship and supply chain management activities. That is why event notification processes play an important role in e-commerce systems; customers, suppliers, employees, and other stakeholders must be notified of all events that might affect their status in a transaction. Event notification software works with workflow management software to monitor all e-commerce processes and record all relevant events, including unexpected changes or problem situations. Then it works with user-profiling software to notify all involved stakeholders automatically of important transaction events using appropriate user-preferred methods of electronic messaging, such as e-mail, newsgroup, pager, and fax communications. This notification includes a company's management, who then can monitor their employees' responsiveness to e-commerce events and customer and supplier feedback.

For example, when you purchase a product at a retail e-commerce Web site like Amazon.com, you automatically receive an e-mail record of your order. Then you may receive e-mail notifications of any change in product availability or shipment status and, finally, an e-mail message notifying you that your order has been shipped and is complete.

Collaboration and Trading

This major category of e-commerce processes consists of those that support the vital collaboration arrangements and trading services needed by customers, suppliers, and other stakeholders to accomplish e-commerce transactions. Thus, in Chapter 2, we discussed how a customer-focused e-business uses tools such as e-mail, chat systems, and discussion groups to nurture online *communities of interest* among employees and customers to enhance customer service and build customer loyalty in e-commerce. The essential collaboration among business trading partners in e-commerce may also be provided by Internet-based trading services. For example, B2B e-commerce Web portals provided by companies like Ariba and Commerce One support matchmaking, negotiation, and mediation processes among business buyers and sellers. In addition, B2B e-commerce is heavily dependent on Internet-based trading platforms and portals that provide online exchange and auctions for e-business enterprises. Therefore, the online auctions and exchanges developed by companies like FreeMarkets are revolutionizing the procurement processes of many major corporations. We will discuss these and other e-commerce applications in Section II.

Electronic Payment Processes

Payment for the products and services purchased is an obvious and vital set of processes in e-commerce transactions. Payment processes, however, are not simple because of the nearly anonymous electronic nature of transactions taking place between the networked computer systems of buyers and sellers and the many security issues involved. E-commerce payment processes are also complex because of the wide variety of debit and credit alternatives, as well as the financial institutions and intermediaries that may be part of the process. Therefore, a variety of electronic payment systems have evolved over time. In addition, new payment systems are being developed and tested to meet the security and technical challenges of e-commerce over the Internet.

Web Payment Processes

Most e-commerce systems on the Web involving businesses and consumers (B2C) depend on credit card payment processes, but many B2B e-commerce systems rely on more complex payment processes based on the use of purchase orders, as was illustrated in Figure 9.5. However, both types of e-commerce typically use an electronic *shopping cart* process, which enables customers to select products from Web site catalog displays and put them temporarily in a virtual shopping basket for later checkout and processing. Figure 9.6 illustrates and summarizes a B2C electronic payment system with several payment alternatives.

Electronic Funds Transfer

Electronic funds transfer (EFT) systems are a major form of electronic payment systems in banking and retailing industries. EFT systems use a variety of information technologies to capture and process money and credit transfers between banks and businesses and their customers. For example, banking networks support teller terminals at all bank offices and automated teller machines (ATMs) at locations throughout the world. Banks, credit card companies, and other businesses may support pay-by-phone services. Very popular also are Web-based payment services, such as PayPal and BillPoint for cash transfers, and CheckFree and Paytrust for automatic bill payment,

FIGURE 9.6

An example of a secure electronic payment system with many payment alternatives.

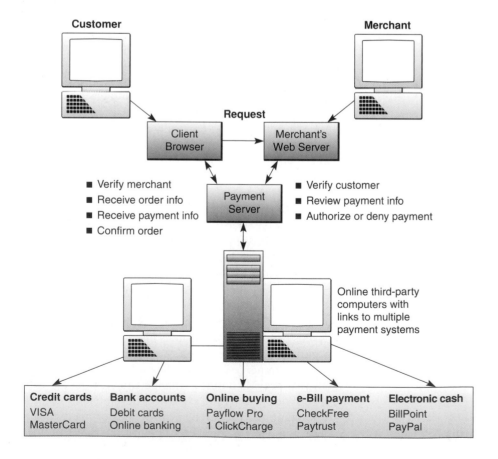

Credit cards	Bank accounts	Online buying	e-Bill payment	Electronic cash
VISA	Debit cards	Payflow Pro	CheckFree	BillPoint
MasterCard	Online banking	1 ClickCharge	Paytrust	PayPal

that enable the customers of banks and other bill payment services to use the Internet to pay bills electronically. In addition, most point-of-sale terminals in retail stores are networked to bank EFT systems, which makes it possible for you to use a credit card or debit card to pay instantly for gas, groceries, or other purchases at participating retail outlets.

Secure Electronic Payments

When you make an online purchase on the Internet, your credit card information is vulnerable to interception by *network sniffers*, software that easily recognizes credit card number formats. Several basic security measures are being used to solve this security problem: (1) encrypt (code and scramble) the data passing between the customer and merchant, (2) encrypt the data passing between the customer and the company authorizing the credit card transaction, or (3) take sensitive information offline. Note: Because encryption and other security issues are discussed in Chapter 13, we will not explain how they work in this section.

For example, many companies use the Secure Socket Layer (SSL) security method developed by Netscape Communications that automatically encrypts data passing between your Web browser and a merchant's server. However, sensitive information is still vulnerable to misuse once it's decrypted (decoded and unscrambled) and stored on a merchant's server, so a digital wallet payment system was developed. In this method, you add security software add-on modules to your Web browser. That enables your browser to encrypt your credit card data in such a way that only the bank that authorizes credit card transactions for the merchant gets to see it. All the merchant is told is whether your credit card transaction is approved or not.

The Secure Electronic Transaction (SET) standard for electronic payment security extends this digital wallet approach. In this method, software encrypts a digital envelope of digital certificates specifying the payment details for each transaction. VISA, MasterCard, IBM, Microsoft, Netscape, and most other industry players have agreed to SET. Therefore, a system like SET may become the standard for secure electronic payments on the Internet. See Figure 9.7.

FIGURE 9.7
VeriSign provides electronic payment, security, and many other e-commerce services.

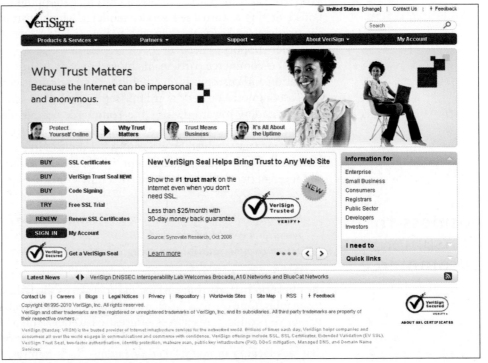

Source: Courtesy of VeriSign Inc.

SECTION II   e-Commerce Applications and Issues

E-commerce is here to stay. The Web and e-commerce are key industry drivers. It's changed how many companies do business. It's created new channels for our customers. Companies are at the e-commerce crossroads, and there are many ways to go.

Thus, e-commerce is changing how companies do business both internally and externally with their customers, suppliers, and other business partners. As managers confront a variety of e-commerce alternatives, the way companies apply e-commerce to their businesses is also subject to change. The applications of e-commerce by many companies have gone through several major stages as e-commerce matures in the world of business. For example, e-commerce between businesses and consumers (B2C) moved from merely offering multimedia company information at corporate Web sites (*brochureware*) to offering products and services at Web storefront sites via electronic catalogs and online sales transactions. B2B e-commerce, in contrast, started with Web site support to help business customers serve themselves, and then moved toward automating intranet and extranet procurement systems. One of the most important things to understand about e-commerce is that by converting a business model from bricks and mortar to an e-commerce approach, the transaction costs (i.e., the costs of doing business with a customer or supplier) drop dramatically. Thus, anything that can be digital will be digital.

Read the Real World Case on the next page. We can learn a lot from this example about the challenges and opportunities faced by companies attempting to conduct online marketing campaigns. See Figure 9.8.

e-Commerce Trends

Figure 9.9 illustrates some of the trends taking place in the e-commerce applications that we introduced at the beginning of this section. Notice how B2C e-commerce moves from simple Web storefronts to interactive marketing capabilities that provide a personalized shopping experience for customers, and then toward a totally integrated Web store that supports a variety of customer shopping experiences. B2C e-commerce is also moving toward a self-service model in which customers configure and customize the products and services they wish to buy, aided by configuration software and online customer support as needed.

B2B e-commerce participants moved quickly from self-service on the Web to configuration and customization capabilities and extranets connecting trading partners. As B2C e-commerce moves toward full-service and wide-selection retail Web portals, B2B is also trending toward the use of e-commerce portals that provide catalog, exchange, and auction markets for business customers within or across industries. Of course, both of these trends are enabled by e-business capabilities like customer relationship management and supply chain management, which are the hallmarks of the customer-focused and inter-networked supply chains of a fully e-business–enabled company.

Business-to-Consumer e-Commerce

E-commerce applications that focus on the consumer share an important goal: to attract potential buyers, transact goods and services, and build customer loyalty through individual courteous treatment and engaging community features.

What does it take to create a successful B2C e-commerce business venture? That's the question that many are asking in the wake of the failures of many pure B2C *dot-com* companies. One obvious answer would be to create a Web business initiative that offers attractive products or services of great customer value, with a business plan based on realistic forecasts of profitability within the first year or two of operation—a condition that was lacking in many failed dot-coms. Such failures, however, have not stemmed the tide of millions of businesses, both large and small, that are moving at least part of

REAL WORLD CASE 2

LinkedIn, Umbria, Mattel, and Others: Driving the "Buzz" on the Web

David Hahn has spotted a trend. As director of advertising for the popular online business networking site LinkedIn, he's being asked pointed questions by large advertisers about his ability to help them find "influentials"—those people within the LinkedIn community who are the most likely to go out and spread the word about a particular product or experience. "Some of them are requesting it specifically, while others are more implying it, but it comes down to the same thing," Hahn says. "Marketers are very interested in the value of online social networks, and how leaders in those networks can be used to drive proactive behaviors in the population."

Hahn isn't alone in his observations.

"The notion of the online influencer is quite the thing today in the marketing world," says Janet Edan-Harris, CEO of Umbria, which monitors chatter in cyberspace communities for corporations wanting to know what's being discussed online about their brands and products. "Companies are incredibly eager to get to those people. Do that—or so the conventional wisdom says—and you'll be in marketing heaven."

But new research, as well as growing business experience, suggests that such thinking may be overly simplistic. The effectiveness of using online word-of-mouth campaigns—or using individuals rather than traditional media advertising to spread the word about products—is increasingly viewed as an effective way to reach consumers.

But the popular notion that frequently accompanies this—that there are special individuals who hold the key to the hearts of entire online communities—is coming under fire.

Dave Balter certainly thinks so. Three years ago, Balter, CEO of BzzAgent, a word-of-mouth marketing firm, had a

FIGURE 9.8

Online opinion leaders may be tapping into underlying trends that are critical to marketers.

Source: © Digital Vision/PunchStock.

revelation: The so-called "influentials," or opinion leaders, in online communities can't be influenced in a way that accelerates the success of a word-of-mouth campaign. "We actually believed in the idea that influentials drove market trends at that point," says Balter. "But upon closer look, we found out it didn't add up. The sales data of our campaigns didn't match the profiles of the opinion leaders we had targeted, and it really caused us to re-evaluate some of our core assumptions." Today, when a client comes in with the goal of influencing the influentials, "we tell them that's fools' gold," says Balter. "It sounds really great, it sounds really sexy, but the results simply don't fly."

This indeed is what Edan-Harris has concluded from her experiences working with online communities. "We say, 'Wait a minute, is this really a correct assumption, that there are individuals on the Internet that have that much influence?'" she says.

Her conclusion: "Not nearly as much as everyone seems to think."

Despite this, companies are putting significant dollars into efforts to find these online opinion leaders, whether they're bloggers, contributors to discussion boards, or members of online social networks. Indeed, a whole cottage industry has sprung up based upon the notion that all marketers need to kick off a successful marketing strategy with a list of Internet opinion leaders. And with the expanding universe of blogs, online communities, and social networks such as MySpace, FaceBook, and LinkedIn, the appeal of this idea has become even more entrenched. There's a growing perception that the increasingly ubiquitous availability of broadband, coupled with the rise in popularity of blogs and online communities, makes influentials even more influential.

It's critical to understand, however, that all of these proponents of opinion leaders as drivers of social and commercial trends aren't talking about media stars or personalities, but about otherwise seemingly ordinary members of a community who, through accumulation of knowledge or number of connections with others, act as catalysts for change. Not surprisingly, marketers of all stripes almost at once began trying to take advantage of this—at first off-line, and now increasingly within the online social networks rising in popularity.

"The largest companies had already established influence-based programs and are now extending that model into the online social networking space," says Matthew Hurst, a scientist at Microsoft LiveLabs who follows online marketing trends. "It's not the notion of influence that's new, it's the technology that is now enabling it to a greater degree." Not surprisingly, a rapidly increasing number of companies have leaped into the fray to help firms identify the influentials in cyberspace.

Buzzlogic is one of them. Launched in 2007, Buzzlogic is dedicated to the idea that opinion leaders in online social networks can be identified, and their influence can be measured.

An early Buzzlogic beta customer is Protuo.com, a Web-based career management portfolio service that provides matchmaking between employers and potential employees. Not having the funds to buy expensive marketing spots in TV, radio, or mainstream print media, Jennifer Gerlach, vice president of marketing, hired Buzzlogic to find the people who are the most influential in the human resource/employee professional space, contact them, and get them to buzz about the product. "We noticed that once one blogger wrote about our service, then suddenly a bunch of other people were writing about it. All at once, there were reviewers everywhere," says Gerlach, who just snagged a major feature in Inc. that she attributes to the online influentials campaign. She says she can map increases in site traffic precisely to blog mentions, and she views the campaign as a huge success.

But despite this apparent triumph, a steadily growing number of online marketing experts would argue that rather than being responsible for the deluge of publicity that Protuo.com is experiencing, the bloggers targeted by Buzzlogic were simply tapping into a sort of zeitgeist waiting to happen—in this case, intense interest in how the Internet could be used to bring employers and candidates together more efficiently than traditional job boards are capable of doing.

Indeed, a growing school of thought is that influentials aren't so much leading trends as acting as mouthpieces for underlying social movements that are either already in progress or lying fallow waiting to be triggered. Thus, successful marketing doesn't depend so much on finding influential people and seeding them with ideas as much as doing the kind of research that exposes embryo trends, and then helping influentials discover them.

This in fact is what Umbria does by focusing on tracking online conversations taking place in discussion boards and social networks as well as blogs. "It's much more important to identify those themes that are gaining momentum than try to find opinion leaders," says Edan-Harris. "You want to ride the wave rather than trying to start one on your own." By listening first to the conversations and being nimble enough to use the Internet to craft campaigns that jump on an existing trend, "you get much better results than attempting to generate your own little epicenter," she says.

Protuo.com's Gerlach agreed with some aspects of that. "There has to be a story around your product, and that story has to resonate in the world for the opinion leader strategy to work," she says.

Herein lies the problem with swallowing the influentials theory whole cloth. Much of the so-called evidence of how the process works is a matter of reverse engineering. Once something happens—if there's a best-selling book coming out of nowhere, or a surprise political upset—you can always go back to the beginning and find the event or person that seems to have triggered it. You can always tell a causal story in retrospect.

Michael Shore, vice president of worldwide consumer insights for Mattel, directs an organization that increasingly monitors blogs, social networks, discussion boards, and forums to figure out what the market might want from toys in general and Mattel products in particular. But unlike many other global consumer-brands companies, Mattel isn't interested in simply smoking out those individuals who are inordinately influential in their online communities and pushing top-down marketing messages onto them.

Despite the fact that this has become the strategy du jour in the online world, Shore's philosophy is a more holistic one.

"We're not just interested in opinion leaders. We'd consider that too narrow a focus," says Shore, who hired MarketTools.com to help him develop and get involved with online communities. Instead, he uses the online universe to do what he calls "cultural assessments" that involve analyzing language, behavioral patterns, and values. Armed with that information, Shore says, Mattel gets valuable information from the Internet that it uses to shape future product development as well as marketing campaigns.

If there's one thing that everyone agrees on, it's that marketers need to invest a great deal more effort into how online social networks and Internet communities actually work with respect to selling products and services at the grassroots level.

"It's an emerging medium, and the rules haven't yet been established," says Umbria's Edan-Harris. "We're still learning what does and doesn't work."

Source: Adapted from Alice LaPlante, "Online Influencers: How the New Opinion Leaders Drive Buzz on the Web," *InformationWeek*, May 5, 2007.

CASE STUDY QUESTIONS

1. How can companies benefit from the "cultural assessments" regularly performed by Mattel? How could the information obtained be used to create business value for those organizations? Provide multiple examples.

2. The case notes that, in spite of disconfirming evidence as to the effectiveness of targeting online opinion leaders, companies are nonetheless increasing their efforts to identify and contact them. Why do you think this is the case?

3. One of the participants in the case states that "you want to ride the wave rather than trying to start one of your own." What does she mean by that? If companies are not starting these "waves," where are they coming from?

REAL WORLD ACTIVITIES

1. A number of technological and cultural developments in recent years has resulted in the emergence of extensive social networks and a large number of avidly followed blogs. Go online to research how companies are tapping into these trends and what new marketing practices have arisen as a result. Prepare a report to summarize your findings.

2. Reflect on your own purchasing behavior. How much do you rely on blogs, feedbacks, and recommendations from past customers to make your own purchase decisions? Why do you (or don't you) rely on these sources of information? Do you believe they are largely unbiased? Break into small groups to discuss these issues with your classmates and compare perspectives on them.

FIGURE 9.9   Trends in B2C and B2B e-commerce, and the business strategies and value driving these trends.

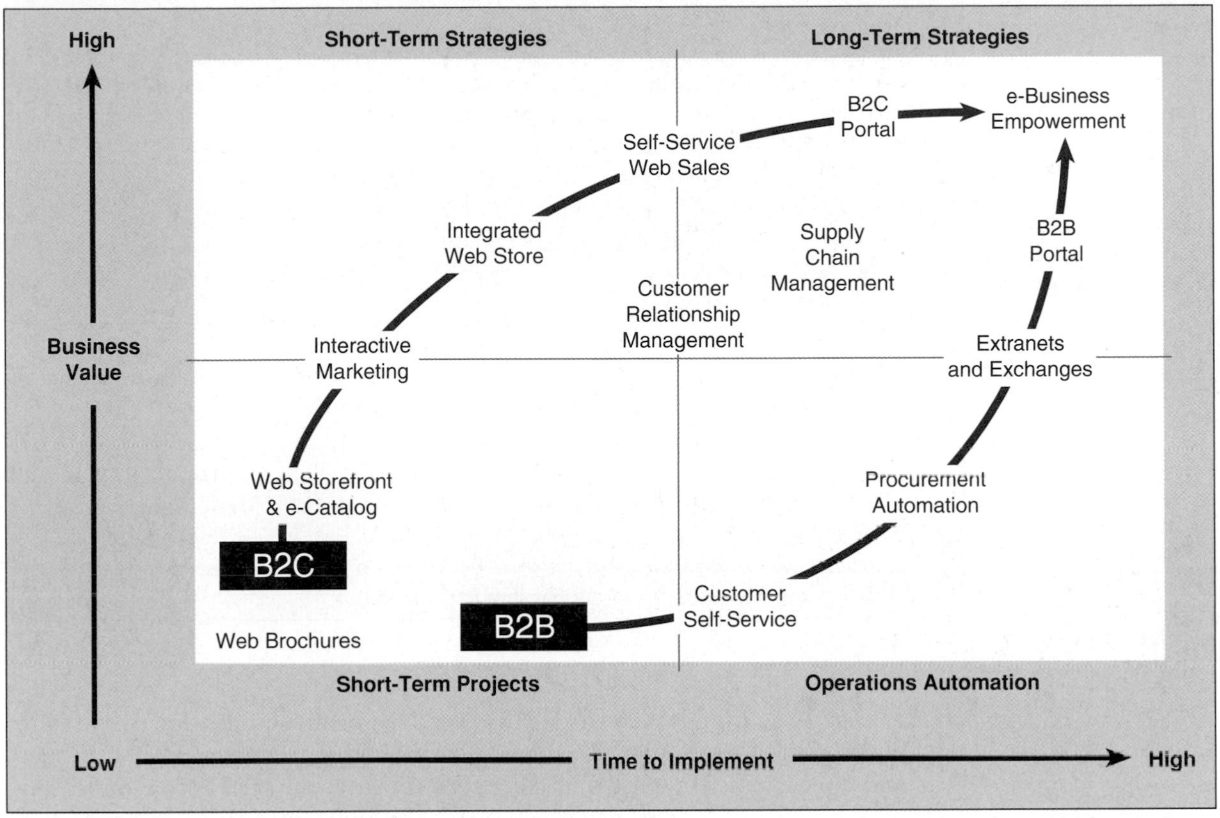

Source: Adapted from Jonathan Rosenoer, Douglas Armstrong, and J. Russell Gates, *The Clickable Corporation: Successful Strategies for Capturing the Internet Advantage* (New York: The Free Press, 1999), p. 24.

their business to the Web. So let's take a look at some essential success factors and Web site capabilities for companies engaged in either B2C or B2B e-commerce. Figure 9.10 provides examples of a few top-rated retail Web companies.

e-Commerce Success Factors

On the Internet, the barriers of time, distance, and form are broken down, and businesses are able to transact the sale of goods and services 24 hours a day, 7 days a week, 365 days a year with consumers all over the world. In certain cases, it is even possible to convert a physical good (CDs, packaged software, a newspaper) to a virtual good (MP3 audio, downloadable software, information in HTML format).

A basic fact of Internet retailing is that all retail Web sites are created equal as far as the "location, location, location" imperative of success in retailing is concerned. No site is any closer to its Web customers, and competitors offering similar goods and services may be only a mouse click away. This scenario makes it vital that businesses find ways to build customer satisfaction, loyalty, and relationships so that customers keep coming back to their Web stores. Thus, the key to e-tail (retail business conducted online) success is to optimize several key factors, such as selection and value, performance and service efficiency, the look and feel of the site, advertising and incentives to purchase, personal attention, community relationships, and security and reliability. Let's briefly examine each of these factors that are essential to the success of a B2C Web business. See Figure 9.11.

Selection and Value.   Obviously, a business must offer Web shoppers a good selection of attractive products and services at competitive prices, or the shoppers will

FIGURE 9.10

Examples of a few top-rated retail Web sites.

Top Retail Web Sites
● **Amazon.com** $19.2B Web sales volume   www.amazon.com Amazon.com is the exception to the rule that consumers prefer to shop "real world" retailers online. The mother of all shopping sites, Amazon features a vast selection of books, videos, DVDs, CDs, toys, kitchen items, electronics, and even home and garden goods sold to millions of loyal customers.
● **Staples, Inc.** $7.7B Web sales volume   www.staples.com Staples tops the "Big 3" office supply giants in terms of Internet sales, although Office Depot and OfficeMax are also members of the top 10 retail Web sites list. Consumers can access the entire catalog online and can have their purchases delivered to their home or office within 24 hours and often within the same business day.
● **Dell, Inc.** $4.8B Web sales volume   www.dell.com Dell has created an online shopping experience for their customers that makes buying and configuring a computer system to meet a specific need almost effortless.
● **Office Depot** $4.8B Web sales volume   www.officedepot.com The Internet has become a transforming force for Office Depot and their Web sales have increased every year since they first launched their Web site. Today, customers can order any product online and can have their purchase delivered directly to their home or business with applicable freight charges or can pick up their purchase at their local Office Depot store with no additional shipping charges.

quickly click away from a Web store. However, a company's prices don't have to be the lowest on the Web if it builds a reputation for high quality, guaranteed satisfaction, and top customer support while shopping and after the sale. For example, top-rated e-tailer REI.com helps you select quality outdoor gear for hiking and other activities with a "How to Choose" section and gives a money-back guarantee on your purchases.

Performance and Service. People don't want to be kept waiting when browsing, selecting, or paying in a Web store. A site must be efficiently designed for ease of

FIGURE 9.11

Some of the key factors for success in e-commerce.

e-Commerce Success Factors
● **Selection and Value.** Attractive product selections, competitive prices, satisfaction guarantees, and customer support after the sale.
● **Performance and Service.** Fast and easy navigation, shopping, and purchasing, and prompt shipping and delivery.
● **Look and Feel.** Attractive Web storefront, Web site shopping areas, multimedia product catalog pages, and shopping features.
● **Advertising and Incentives.** Targeted Web page advertising and e-mail promotions, discounts, and special offers, including advertising at affiliate sites.
● **Personal Attention.** Personal Web pages, personalized product recommendations, Web advertising and e-mail notices, and interactive support for all customers.
● **Community Relationships.** Virtual communities of customers, suppliers, company representatives, and others via newsgroups, chat rooms, and links to related sites.
● **Security and Reliability.** Security of customer information and Web site transactions, trustworthy product information, and reliable order fulfillment.
● **Great Customer Communication.** Easy-to-find contact information, online order status, product support specialists.

access, shopping, and buying, with sufficient server power and network capacity to support Web site traffic. Web shopping and customer service must also be friendly and helpful, as well as quick and easy. In addition, products offered should be available in inventory for prompt shipment to the customer.

Look and Feel. B2C sites can offer customers an attractive Web storefront, shopping areas, and multimedia product catalogs. These could range from an exciting shopping experience with audio, video, and moving graphics to a more simple and comfortable look and feel. Thus, most retail e-commerce sites let customers browse product sections, select products, drop them into a virtual shopping cart, and go to a virtual checkout station when they are ready to pay for their order.

Advertising and Incentives. Some Web stores may advertise in traditional media, but most advertise on the Web with targeted and personalized banner ads and other Web page and e-mail promotions. Most B2C sites also offer shoppers incentives to buy and return. Typically, these incentives mean coupons, discounts, special offers, and vouchers for other Web services, sometimes with other e-tailers at cross-linked Web sites. Many Web stores also increase their market reach by being part of Web banner advertising exchange programs with thousands of other Web retailers. Figure 9.12 compares major marketing communications choices in traditional and e-commerce marketing to support each step of the buying process.

Personal Attention. Personalizing your shopping experience encourages you to buy and make return visits. Thus, e-commerce software can automatically record details of your visits and build user profiles of you and other Web shoppers. Many sites also encourage you to register with them and fill out a personal interest profile. Then, whenever you return, you are welcomed by name or with a personal Web page, greeted with special offers, and guided to those parts of the site in which you are most interested. This *one-to-one marketing* and relationship building power is one of the major advantages of personalized Web retailing.

Community Relationships. Giving online customers with special interests a feeling of belonging to a unique group of like-minded individuals helps build customer loyalty and value. Thus, Web site relationship and affinity marketing programs build and promote virtual communities of customers, suppliers, company representatives, and others via a variety of Web-based collaboration tools. Examples include discussion forums or newsgroups, chat rooms, message board systems, and cross-links to related Web site communities.

Security and Reliability. As a customer of a successful Web store, you must feel confident that your credit card, personal information, and details of your transactions

FIGURE 9.12   How traditional and Web marketing communications differ in supporting each step of the buying process.

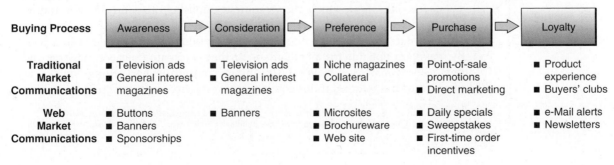

are secure from unauthorized use. You must also feel that you are dealing with a trustworthy business whose products and other Web site information you can trust to be as advertised. Having your orders filled and shipped as you requested, in the time frame promised, and with good customer support are other measures of an e-tailer's reliability.

Great Customer Communications. As more consumers shift their habits from the traditional brick-and-mortar approach to an online shopping experience, one thing becomes even more important than ever: the need for constant and informative communication channels with the customer. Despite the conveniences associated with on-line shopping, consumers still have questions that need to be answered by a human being. Issues ranging from product information to order status or modification are often still handled the "old fashioned way." Land's End, the famous outdoor clothing retailer, provides telephone and chat space access to customer representatives that will even help you pick out your purchases in real time.

Amazon.com: Partnering and Leveraging Infrastructure

Amazon.com has just launched an application on Facebook that enables members of the social network to buy gifts for each other based on wish lists registered with the online retailer. *Amazon Giver* also provides Facebook members with the option of viewing suggested items for friends based on interests listed on their profile pages. A second Facebook application, *Amazon Grapevine*, provides a news feed of friends' activity on Amazon, such as when they update their wish lists, write reviews, or tag products. Both applications only share information between Facebook members who have opted in to the service.

"By combining Amazon's vast selection of products with Facebook's millions of users, we are able to make activities like giftgiving more efficient and rewarding for Facebook users," says Eva Manolis, vice president of Amazon.

By adding the *Amazon Giver* application to their profile, Facebook members get the option of clicking directly to a secure Amazon checkout page. If the recipient has a wish list, then Amazon can ship the item without the buyer entering a shipping address, which would already be on file. In order for people to view a wish list, it would have to be set as "public." With *Amazon Grapevine*, people have the option to choose what type of activity they would be willing to share with friends through the news feed. Activity updates are entirely opt-in.

Amazon.com has also introduced a new way for online merchants to leverage Amazon's infrastructure to ship physical products. "The *Amazon Fulfillment Web Service* (Amazon FWS) allows merchants to tap in to Amazon's network of fulfillment centers and our expertise in logistics," says Amazon Web Services evangelist Jeff Barr. "Merchants can store their own products to our fulfillment centers and then, using a simple Web service interface, fulfill orders for the products."

Amazon FWS is designed to complement *Fulfillment By Amazon* (FBA), the fulfillment service Amazon has offered since 2006, by making the fulfillment process accessible programmatically. Amazon also maintains a separate fulfillment program called *Amazon Advantage*, which allows content publishers to send Amazon music, books, and videos for sale on consignment, with a 55 percent fee.

The idea, Barr explains, is to be able to ship a product with a simple Web service call. By making it possible for merchants to further automate their e-commerce and fulfillment efforts, Amazon is demonstrating its commitment to selling "muck," as CEO Jeff Bezos has referred to his company's e-commerce infrastructure.

Source: Adapted from Antone Gonsalves, "Amazon.com Launches Shopping Apps on Facebook," *InformationWeek*, March 13, 2008; and Thomas Claburn, "Amazon Introduces Fulfillment Web Service," *InformationWeek*, March 20, 2008.

Web Store Requirements

Most business-to-consumer e-commerce ventures take the form of retail business sites on the World Wide Web. Whether a huge retail Web portal like Amazon.com or a small specialty Web retailer, the primary focus of such e-tailers is to develop, operate, and manage their Web sites so they become high-priority destinations for consumers who will repeatedly choose to go there to buy products and services. Thus, these Web sites must be able to demonstrate the key factors for e-commerce success that we have just covered. In this section, let's discuss the essential Web store requirements that you would have to implement to support a successful retail business on the Web, as summarized and illustrated in Figure 9.13.

Developing a Web Store

Before you can launch your own retail store on the Internet, you must build an e-commerce Web site. Many companies use simple Web site design software tools and predesigned templates provided by their Web site hosting service to construct their Web retail store. That includes building your Web storefront and product catalog Web pages, as well as tools to provide shopping cart features, process orders, handle credit card payments, and so forth. Of course, larger companies can use their own software developers or hire an outside Web site development contractor to build a custom-designed e-commerce site. Also, like most companies, you can contract with your ISP (Internet service provider) or a specialized Web hosting company to operate and maintain your B2C Web site.

Once you build your Web site, it must be developed as a retail Web business by marketing it in a variety of ways that attract visitors to your site and transform them into loyal Web customers. So, your Web site should include Web page and e-mail advertising and promotions for Web visitors and customers, as well as Web advertising

FIGURE 9.13 To develop a successful e-commerce business, these Web store requirements must be implemented by a company or its Web site hosting service.

Developing a Web Store		
● **Build**	● **Market**	
Web site design tools	Web page advertising	
Site design templates	E-mail promotions	
Custom design services	Web advertising exchanges with affiliate sites	
Web site hosting	Search engine registrations and optimization	
Serving Your Customers		
● **Serve**	● **Transact**	● **Support**
Personalized Web pages	Flexible order process	Web site online help
Dynamic multimedia catalog	Credit card processing	Customer service e-mail
Catalog search engine	Shipping and tax calculations	Discussion groups and chat rooms
Integrated shopping cart	E-mail order notifications	Links to related sites
Managing a Web Store		
● **Manage**	● **Operate**	● **Protect**
Web site usage statistics	24×7 Web site hosting	User password protection
Sales and inventory reports	Online tech support	Encrypted order processing
Customer account management	Scalable network capacity	Encrypted Web site administration
Links to accounting system	Redundant servers and power	Network firewalls and security monitors

exchange programs with other Web stores. Also, you can register your Web business with its own domain name (e.g., yourstore.com), as well as registering your Web site with the major Web search engines and directories to help Web surfers find your site more easily. In addition, you might consider affiliating as a small business partner with large Web portals like Yahoo! and Netscape, large e-tailers and auction sites like Amazon and eBay, and small business e-commerce portals like Microsoft's Small Business Center.

Spamming Web Searches

A new market for writing has arisen online, and it's targeted at search engines. Content optimized for successful search results ranges from informative articles to incoherent copy stuffed with keywords, a plague that's been labeled search-engine spam. Popular keywords generate significant traffic for Web sites with related content, giving Web site owners a financial incentive to host content that ranks near the top of search results. As traffic rises, ad revenue tends to follow, often through ad-delivery services for Web sites like Google's AdSense.

A cottage industry has formed to help people tailor content for search engines, such as rewriting copy by substituting synonyms for certain words so that text can be repurposed to score well on search engines. The rephrased text looks different to a search engine, contributing to the host site's rank and traffic. Google's Webmaster Guidelines warns against the practice of crafting copy for its search engine: "Make pages for users, not for search engines." But that hasn't stopped many from trying.

Creating content for search engines is one aspect of what's called search-engine optimization or SEO, part of a broader business known as search-engine marketing, or SEM. In sufficient quantity, and absent sufficient quality, SEO content is a form of spam that's aimed at search engines rather than people. And like product-oriented spam, it's controversial.

Chris Winfield, president and cofounder of SEM company 10e20 LLC, says one of the biggest problems for Google, MSN, and Yahoo is search-engine spam. "That spam consists of pages that are created for the search engines or pages that otherwise trick the end user," he says. Ani Kortikar, CEO of SEM company Netramind Technologies Pvt. Ltd., says that while search engines may require businesses to employ certain tactics to show up in search results, the tactics should be used to support good content rather than simply to drive traffic.

But just as legitimate e-mail marketers have felt the backlash against spammers, well-intentioned search-engine marketers—and search engines as well—may suffer if the tricksters continue to thrive. Says Winfield of 10e20, "One of the most important things for any search engine is people having confidence and becoming repeat users."

Source: Adapted from Thomas Claburn, "The Spamming of Web Search," *InformationWeek*, April 1, 2005.

Getting Customers to Find You

Just because your Web store has been launched does not mean customers will come flocking to your cyber front door. Your Web store needs to be discovered by your customers, and this means getting listed in the popular search engines.

You can submit your Web site to search engines such as Yahoo, Google, Live, and others, and each will begin looking at your Web pages and listing you when appropriate search terms are entered. Waiting for your site to show up competitively ranked with all the other similar sites could take weeks and even months. There is a science to search engine ranking and it is an essential element in Web store success.

Search engine optimization (SEO) is considered a subset of search engine marketing, and it focuses on improving the number and/or quality of visitors to a Web site over "natural" (also called "organic" or "algorithmic" search engine) listings. The term SEO can also refer to search engine optimizers, an industry of consultants who carry out optimization projects on behalf of clients.

Search engines display different kinds of listings on a results page, including paid advertising in the form of pay-per-click (PPC) advertisements and paid inclusion listings, as well as unpaid organic search results and keywords specific listings, such as news stories, definitions, map locations, and images. As an Internet marketing strategy, SEO considers how search engines work and what people search for.

Optimizing a Web site primarily involves editing its content and HTML coding to both increase its relevance to specific keywords and to remove barriers to the indexing activities of search engines. Because SEO requires making changes to the source code of a site, it is often most effective when incorporated into the initial development and design of a site, leading to the use of the term "search engine friendly" to describe designs, menus, content management systems, and shopping carts that can be optimized easily and effectively.

A range of strategies and techniques are employed in SEO, including changes to a site's code (referred to as on-page factors) and getting links from other sites (referred to as off-page factors). These techniques include two broad categories: techniques that search engines recommend as part of good design, and those techniques that search engines do not approve of and attempt to minimize the effect of, referred to as spamdexing. Methods such as *link farms*, where a group of Web sites is set up so that all hyperlink to every other Web site in the group, and *keyword stuffing*, where a Web page is loaded with keywords in the meta tags or in content, are examples of techniques considered "black hat" SEO. Such techniques serve only to degrade both the relevance of search results and the user experience of search engines.

SEO, as a marketing strategy, can often generate a good return. However, as the search engines are not paid for the traffic they send from **organic search,** the algorithms used can and do change, and there are many factors that can cause search engine problems when crawling or ranking a site's pages. There are no guarantees of success, either in the short or long term. Because of the lack of guarantees and certainty, SEO is often compared to traditional public relations (PR), with PPC advertising closer to traditional advertising.

Serving Your Customers

Once your retail store is on the Web and receiving visitors, the Web site must help you welcome and serve them personally and efficiently so that they become loyal customers. So most e-tailers use several Web site tools to create user profiles, customer files, and personal Web pages and promotions that help them develop a one-to-one relationship with their customers. This effort includes creating incentives to encourage visitors to register, developing *Web cookie files* to identify returning visitors automatically, or contracting with Web site tracking companies like DoubleClick and others for software to record and analyze the details of the Web site behavior and preferences of Web shoppers automatically.

Of course, your Web site should have the look and feel of an attractive, friendly, and efficient Web store. That means having e-commerce features like a dynamically changing and updated multimedia catalog, a fast catalog search engine, and a convenient shopping cart system that is integrated with Web shopping, promotions, payment, shipping, and customer account information. Your e-commerce order processing software should be fast and able to adjust to personalized promotions and customer options like gift handling, special discounts, credit card or other payments, and shipping and tax alternatives. Also, automatically sending your customers e-mail notices to document when orders are processed and shipped is a top customer service feature of e-tail transaction processing.

Providing customer support for your Web store is an essential Web site capability. Thus, many e-tail sites offer help menus, tutorials, and lists of FAQs (frequently asked questions) to provide self-help features for Web shoppers. Of course, e-mail correspondence with customer service representatives of your Web store offers more personal assistance to customers. Establishing Web site discussion groups and chat rooms for your customers and store personnel to interact helps create a more personal community that can provide invaluable support to customers, as well as build customer loyalty. Providing links to related Web sites from your Web store can help customers find additional information and resources, as well as earning commission income from the affiliate marketing programs of other Web retailers. For example, the Amazon.com affiliate program pays commissions of up to 15 percent for purchases made by Web shoppers clicking to its Web store from your site.

Managing a Web Store

A Web retail store must be managed as both a business and a Web site, and most e-commerce hosting companies offer software and services to help you do just that. For example, companies like FreeMerchant, Prodigy Biz, and Verio provide their hosting clients with a variety of management reports that record and analyze Web store traffic, inventory, and sales results. Other services build customer lists for e-mail and Web page promotions or provide customer relationship management features to help retain Web customers. Also, some e-commerce software includes links to download inventory and sales data into accounting packages like QuickBooks for bookkeeping and preparation of financial statements and reports.

Of course, Web-hosting companies must enable their Web store clients to be available online 24 hours a day and seven days a week all year. This availability requires them to build or contract for sufficient network capacity to handle peak Web traffic loads and redundant network servers and power sources to respond to system or power failures. Most hosting companies provide e-commerce software that uses passwords and encryption to protect Web store transactions and customer records, as well as to employ network firewalls and security monitors to repel hacker attacks and other security threats. Many hosting services also offer their clients 24-hour tech support to help them with any technical problems that arise. We will discuss these and other e-commerce security management issues in Chapter 13.

Global e-Commerce Sees New Highs in India

The Internet has transformed many aspects of life, but perhaps none more so than how we shop for goods and services. More than 8 out of 10 Indian online consumers plan to shop online in the next 12 months and more than a quarter indicate they spend upward of 11 percent of their monthly shopping expenditure on online purchases, according to a recent Nielsen global online shopping report. The report found that Asia-Pacific consumers spend the most on online purchases—as a percentage of total shopping expenditure—compared to any other region globally.

Twenty-three percent of Indians surveyed said that they had never shopped online. Globally, 16 percent of consumers have never shopped online and the percentage is even less in Asia-Pacific, with only 13 percent of consumers indicating that they had never shopped online.

"Low Internet penetration and lack of confidence in using credit card credentials are the biggest challenges for online shopping in India, though high adoption for online travel sites is changing this. The medium to heavy users have always been quite comfortable buying stuff online," says Karthik Nagarajan, director, Online Division at The Nielsen Company.

Shopping through a virtual space calls for trustworthy recommendations to back the products and services for Indians, who trust no one more than family and friends when shopping online. According to the Nielsen report, 71 percent of Indians trust recommendations from family when making an online purchase decision, followed by recommendations from friends at 64 percent and online product reviews at 29 percent.

Online reviews and opinions are most important for Indians when buying consumer electronics (57 percent), software (50 percent), and a car (47 percent). The Nielsen report highlights the importance of online opinions as part of the decision-making process in purchasing products and services. Many Indian consumers went so far as to say they would not buy products or services without considering online reviews, and again this was particularly important in the purchase of consumer electronics (41 percent), a car (38 percent), and software (35 percent).

With online reviews and opinions weighing so heavily in consumers' decision-making processes, it is interesting to note that more than 4 in 10 Indians are more likely to share (post a review/Tweet/review) a negative product or service experience online than they were to share a positive experience. At the country level, this tendency was highest among consumers in China (62 percent), Vietnam (46 percent), and Singapore and India (both 44 percent).

Half of the Indian consumers (50 percent) use social media sites to help them make online purchase decisions. This percentage is higher for the Asia-Pacific region at 60 percent, who use social media sites to help them make purchase decisions (compared to 43 percent globally).

When shopping online, one-third of Indians (33 percent) purchase most frequently from Web sites that allow them to select products from many different stores. Nearly three in 10 (28 percent) prefer online-only retail sites. Nine percent of Indians purchase from Web sites that also have traditional "bricks and mortar" stores and 8 percent buy from sites that also sell their products through catalogues and over the phone.

"There is a bit of a silent social media revolution going on in India at the moment and it is largely mistaken for just social networking. The truth is that discussion boards, forums, and review sites are seeing high growth in terms of conversations, and this is where many shopping decisions are being made," says Nagarajan.

Source: Adapted from The Nielsen Company, "Survey: Indians Rely on Family, Friends for Online Shopping Tips," *Retail in Asia Limited*, September 15, 2010.

Business-to-Business e-Commerce

Business-to-business e-commerce is the wholesale and supply side of the commercial process, where businesses buy, sell, or trade with other businesses. B2B e-commerce relies on many different information technologies, most of which are implemented at e-commerce Web sites on the World Wide Web and corporate intranets and extranets. B2B applications include electronic catalog systems, electronic trading systems such as exchange and auction portals, electronic data interchange, electronic funds transfers, and so on. All of the factors for building a successful retail Web site that we discussed previously also apply to wholesale Web sites for business-to-business e-commerce.

In addition, many businesses are integrating their Web-based e-commerce systems with their e-business systems for supply chain management, customer relationship management, and online transaction processing, as well as with their traditional, or legacy, computer-based accounting and business information systems. This integration ensures that all e-commerce activities are integrated with e-business processes and supported by up-to-date corporate inventory and other databases, which in turn are automatically updated by Web sales activities.

Avnet Tears Up the B2B E-Commerce Playbook

When does a global distributor of electronic components need to start operating more like Amazon.com and other consumer-focused companies? When the market demands that it move in that direction.

At Avnet Inc., they came to just that realization a few years ago as they saw a shift taking place within their electronic components market. While large manufacturers continued to buy large quantities of components for their designs, a growing segment of engineers and smaller companies wanted to buy low volumes (including product samples) online, instead of by phone or face to face. Many of their customers had to either be really patient or simply stubborn to make a successful purchase on the e-commerce site they offered at the time.

Avnet realized the need to shift their B2B e-commerce approach to incorporate a B2C perspective. While they were dealing with business customers, their online purchasing expectations were shaped by their experiences on consumer-friendly Web sites such as Amazon.com and HomeDepot.com. The problem was that the experience and functionality that those kinds of sites provide users isn't easily replicated in a B2B environment, especially within the components industry. For example, Avnet deals with millions of parts, and each part has dozens of technical attributes that must be precisely specified for engineers to determine whether it's the part they need. Additionally, legal and country-specific regulations determine which companies and individuals Avnet can ship certain parts to around the world.

So Avnet went ahead and made a few changes. First, they eliminated the need to register. Previously, all customers had to register to get on the commerce site. To make matters even more complicated, all customers had to qualify for credit before they could search for parts, even if they were purchasing with a credit card. Now anyone can search for part information without having to register and share personal details. Only when customers reach a purchase point does the site then ask them for their information. And if the customer is paying with a credit card, credit checks are out the window.

Previously, customers could search for parts only by entering precise supplier part numbers, which may be up to 50 characters—the equivalent of making a reader search for a book by the unique ISBN number. Furthermore, the search result displayed information on only the part corresponding to the number entered, not on alternative parts that may also meet the customer's requirements. Customers can now search by part number, product name, description, and technical attributes. Returned search results now include similar products that match the engineer's requirements, so the engineer can make informed decisions about alternative parts based on factors such as availability, cost, and manufacturer.

The new e-commerce site, featuring more than 3.5 million electronic components, took two years to develop and deploy, and Avnet keeps on adding functionality based on customer feedback. So far, however, results tell them that customers already like what they see: There has been a 75 percent annual increase in e-commerce revenue and a 50 percent annual increase in site visitors.

Source: Adapted from Steve Phillips and Beth Ely, "Global CIO: Avnet Tears Up the B2B E-Commerce Playbook," *InformationWeek*, June 15, 2009.

e-Commerce Marketplaces

The latest e-commerce transaction systems are scaled and customized to allow buyers and sellers to meet in a variety of high-speed trading platforms: auctions, catalogs, and exchanges.

Businesses of any size can now buy everything from chemicals to electronic components, excess electrical energy, construction materials, or paper products at business-to-business e-commerce marketplaces. Figure 9.14 outlines five major types of e-commerce marketplaces used by businesses today. However, many B2B portals provide several types of marketplaces. Thus, they may offer an electronic

FIGURE 9.14

Types of e-commerce marketplaces.

e-Commerce Marketplaces
● **One to Many.** Sell-side marketplaces. Host one major supplier, who dictates product catalog offerings and prices. Examples: Cisco.com and Dell.com.
● **Many to One.** Buy-side marketplaces. Attract many suppliers that flock to these exchanges to bid on the business of a major buyer like GE or AT&T.
● **Some to Many.** Distribution marketplaces. Unite major suppliers who combine their product catalogs to attract a larger audience of buyers. Examples: VerticalNet and Works.com.
● **Many to Some.** Procurement marketplaces. Unite major buyers who combine their purchasing catalogs to attract more suppliers and thus more competition and lower prices. Examples: the auto industry.
● **Many to Many.** Auction marketplaces used by many buyers and sellers that can create a variety of buyers. Examples: eBay and FreeMarkets.

FIGURE 9.15

An example of a B2B
e-commerce Web portal
that offers exchange,
auction, and reverse auction
electronic markets.

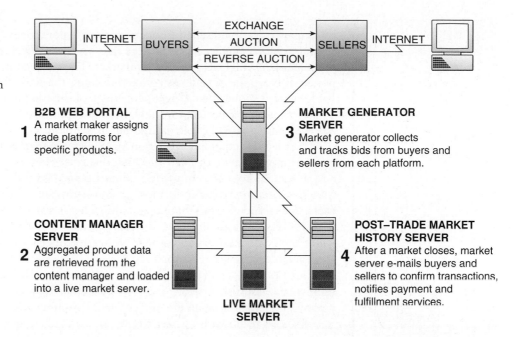

B2B WEB PORTAL
1 A market maker assigns trade platforms for specific products.

MARKET GENERATOR SERVER
3 Market generator collects and tracks bids from buyers and sellers from each platform.

CONTENT MANAGER SERVER
2 Aggregated product data are retrieved from the content manager and loaded into a live market server.

POST–TRADE MARKET HISTORY SERVER
4 After a market closes, market server e-mails buyers and sellers to confirm transactions, notifies payment and fulfillment services.

LIVE MARKET SERVER

catalog shopping and ordering site for products from many suppliers in an industry. Or they may serve as an exchange for buying and selling via a bid-ask process or at negotiated prices. Very popular are electronic auction Web sites for B2B auctions of products and services. Figure 9.15 illustrates a B2B trading system that offers exchange, auction, and reverse auction (where sellers bid for the business of a buyer) electronic markets.

Many of these B2B **e-commerce portals** are developed and hosted by third-party *market-maker* companies who serve as infomediaries that bring buyers and sellers together in catalog, exchange, and auction markets. Infomediaries are companies that serve as intermediaries in e-business and e-commerce transactions. Examples are Ariba, Commerce One, and VerticalNet, to name a few successful companies. All provide e-commerce marketplace software products and services to power business Web portals for e-commerce transactions.

These B2B e-commerce sites make business purchasing decisions faster, simpler, and more cost effective because companies can use Web systems to research and transact with many vendors. Business buyers get one-stop shopping and accurate purchasing information. They also get impartial advice from infomediaries that they can't get from the sites hosted by suppliers and distributors. Thus, companies can negotiate or bid for better prices from a larger pool of vendors. Of course, suppliers benefit from easy access to customers from all over the globe. Now, let's look at a real-world example.

SpecEx.com:
B2B Trading of
Wireless Spectrum

Online marketplaces like Craigslist and Freecycle allow consumers to make low-cost sales—or even exchange goods for free—through sophisticated technological systems that make such transactions efficient.

Some companies are attempting to apply a similar model to online business-to-business marketplaces.

The FCC holds auctions to grant licenses for radio spectrums, and most of these are used by cell phone carriers, or for first responders and their communication gear. But some of these spectrums aren't being used for a variety of reasons.

Spectrum Bridge's Web site, SpecEx.com, aims to create a secondary market for these unused spectrum. The company says the site can provide an easy and effective way to connect buyers and sellers. The market could potentially be large, as public-safety agencies and major wireless carriers like Verizon Wireless and AT&T routinely purchase spectrum on the secondary market. The cable companies could also become potential buyers, especially as some are eyeing the wireless voice space. Spectrum Bridge makes money by taking a percentage of the transaction.

All transfers of spectrum would have to be approved by the FCC, but the agency has been supportive of spectrum trading in the past.

The idea of organizing the secondary spectrum market isn't a new one, but previous attempts have not been successful because they couldn't get enough buyers and sellers. "The spectrum world is almost tribal," says Peter Stanforth, chief technology officer for Spectrum Bridge. "It consists of small groups of people who know each other—and do everything manually." That is not an efficient system for smaller parcels—SpecEx's sweet spot. "By automating a lot of functions and bringing in a wider audience of buyers and sellers, we are making these smaller pieces more liquid and valuable," explains Stanforth.

Rick Rotondo, chief marketing officer of Spectrum Bridge, compares the SpecEx service to Craigslist, a favorite site for consumer bargains. With its launch several years ago, Craigslist made the sale of small consumer items efficient, which is what SpecEx aims to do with respect to the sale of wireless spectrum parcels. "Let's say you had used sunglasses you wanted to sell, for maybe $25. Before online classifieds were introduced, it would not have been cost-efficient to try to sell them to a huge audience in a paper, because the ad probably would have cost you $20." Same thing with wireless spectrum, he says. "Transaction costs are eating up most of the value for small buyers and sellers."

E-commerce technology can standardize much of the process, notes Stanforth. "What we are trying to do is be the eBay of the wireless spectrum world—a one-stop shop where companies can go to monetize excess or idle spectrum, and spectrum seekers can go to find reasonably priced unused spectrums."

Source: Adapted from Erika Morphy, "The Corporate Bargain Hunters' Quest for a Business Model," *E-Commerce Times*, January 20, 2009; and Marin Perez, "Spectrum Bridge Launches Online Secondary Market," *InformationWeek*, September 5, 2008.

Clicks and Bricks in e-Commerce

Companies are recognizing that success will go to those who can execute clicks-and-mortar strategies that bridge the physical and virtual worlds. Different companies will need to follow very different paths when deciding how closely—or loosely—to integrate their Internet initiatives with their traditional operations.

Figure 9.16 illustrates the spectrum of alternatives and benefit trade-offs that e-business enterprises face when choosing an e-commerce clicks-and-bricks strategy. E-business managers must answer this question: Should we integrate our e-commerce virtual business operations with our traditional physical business operations or keep them separate? As Figure 9.16 shows, companies have implemented a range of integration/separation strategies and made key benefit trade-offs in answering that question. Let's take a look at several alternatives.

e-Commerce Integration

The Internet is just another channel that gets plugged into the business architecture.

So says CIO Bill Seltzer of the office supply retailer Office Depot, which fully integrates its OfficeDepot.com e-commerce sales channel into its traditional business operations. Thus, Office Depot is a prime example of why many companies have chosen integrated clicks-and-bricks strategies, where their e-commerce business is integrated in some major ways into the traditional business operations of a company. The business case for such strategies rests on:

FIGURE 9.16   Companies have a spectrum of alternatives and benefit trade-offs when deciding on an integrated or separate e-commerce business.

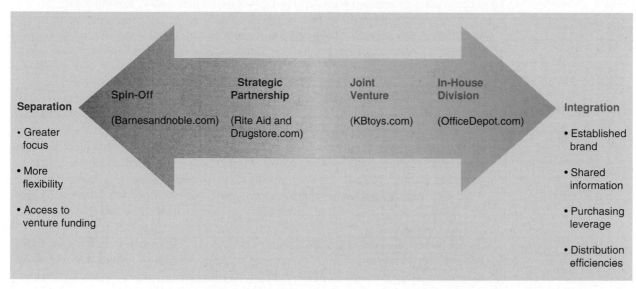

- Capitalizing on any unique strategic capabilities that may exist in a company's traditional business operations that could be used to support an e-commerce business.

- Gaining several strategic benefits of integrating e-commerce into a company's traditional business, such as sharing established brands and key business information, joint buying power, and distribution efficiencies.

For example, Office Depot already had a successful catalog sales business with a professional call center and a fleet of more than 2,000 delivery trucks. Its 1,825 stores and 30 warehouses were networked by a sophisticated information system that provided complete customer, vendor, order, and product inventory data in real time. These business resources made an invaluable foundation for coordinating Office Depot's e-commerce activities and customer services with its catalog business and physical stores. Thus, customers can shop at OfficeDepot.com at their home or business or at in-store kiosks. Then they can choose to pick up their purchases at the stores or have them delivered. In addition, the integration of Web-enabled e-commerce applications within Office Depot's traditional store and catalog operations has helped increase the traffic at their physical stores and improved the catalog operation's productivity and average order size.

| Borders and Amazon.com: Splitting Up Is Never Easy | Borders.com has always been run by Amazon.com. It features Amazon's inventory, site content, fulfillment, and customer service capabilities. The sales even belong to Amazon, with a percentage going to Borders. The new Borders site marks a major juncture in Borders's business and e-commerce strategy and the end of what will be a seven-year relationship with Amazon.com at a time when the Ann Arbor, Michigan–based bookseller is in the midst of a turnaround.

In 2001, when the retailing rivals inked this deal to develop a cobranded Web site, it was mutually beneficial. Amazon.com, which had gone public in 1997, was under pressure to turn its first profit. Extending the e-commerce infrastructure into which it had invested millions of dollars to third parties such as Borders injected much-needed cash into Amazon.com's business. Borders, which like many traditional brick-and-mortar stores at the time, was struggling to make the e-commerce game work for |

them, got a tried and tested, user-friendly e-commerce site powered by a company that consumers trusted. Never mind the fact that Amazon was a competitor.

"The relationship with Amazon.com allowed us at the time to focus on our brick-and-mortar stores while still having an online channel that was branded Borders," says Anne Roman, a spokeswoman for Borders. She notes that the company had its own e-commerce site before it partnered with Amazon but that the costs associated with operating and marketing it outweighed the revenue it generated at the time.

Roman says the existing relationship with Amazon doesn't allow Borders to do all the things it wants to do to move forward to create a more integrated, cross-channel experience for customers, such as give Borders' customers access to author readings and concerts at the company's flagship store in Ann Arbor via online video. Borders also wants customers to be able to earn points toward the Borders Rewards loyalty program when they shop online. Currently, customers can't earn points when they use the cobranded site because it exists as a separate silo of Borders's business. "Once we launch the proprietary site, that loyalty program will be fully integrated into it," says Roman.

However, Borders has to give customers a compelling reason to buy books, movies, and music from Borders.com instead of Amazon.com. That's not going to be easy when Amazon.com has customer loyalty locked up and is so competitive on pricing. Gartner Research analyst Adam Sarner notes that the Web influences 40 percent of commerce in the off-line world. If Borders can take advantage of that dynamic, he adds, they'll be better able to compete with Amazon. "If their site can become a lead management tool that gets more people to visit the store and pick up more books or visit three times instead of two, that might be a better model for them," says Sarner. "Borders has the benefit of the physical stores. That's where they can differentiate themselves from Amazon."

Source: Adapted from Meridith Levinson, "Borders Tries to Open New Chapter with Web Site Relaunch Separate from Amazon.com," *CIO Magazine*, October 2, 2007.

Other Clicks-and-Bricks Strategies

As Figure 9.16 illustrates, other clicks-and-bricks strategies range from partial e-commerce integration using joint ventures and strategic partnerships to complete separation via the spin-off of an independent e-commerce company.

For example, KBtoys.com is an e-commerce joint venture of KB Online Holdings LLC, created by toy retailer KB Toys, and BrainPlay.com, formerly an e-tailer of children's products. The company is 80 percent owned by KB Toys but has independent management teams and separate distribution systems. However, KBtoys.com has successfully capitalized on the shared brand name and buying power of KB Toys, as well as the ability of its customers to return purchases to more than 1,300 KB Toys stores, which also heavily promote the e-commerce site.

The strategic partnership of the Rite Aid retail drugstore chain and Drugstore.com is a good example of a less integrated e-commerce venture. Rite Aid only owns about 25 percent of Drugstore.com, which has an independent management team and a separate business brand. However, both companies share the decreased costs and increased revenue benefits of joint buying power, an integrated distribution center, cobranded pharmacy products, and joint prescription fulfillment at Rite Aid stores.

Finally, let's look at an example of the benefits and challenges of a completely separate clicks-and-bricks strategy. Barnesandnoble.com was created as an independent e-commerce company that was spun off by the Barnes & Noble book retail chain. This status enabled it to gain several hundred million dollars in venture capital funding, create an entrepreneurial culture, attract quality management, maintain a high degree of business flexibility, and accelerate decision making. However, the book e-retailer has done poorly since its founding and failed to gain market share from Amazon.com,

FIGURE 9.17

Key questions for developing an e-commerce channel strategy.

A Checklist for Channel Development
1. What audiences are we attempting to reach?
2. What action do we want those audiences to take? To learn about us, to give us information about themselves, to make an inquiry, to buy something from our site, to buy something through another channel?
3. Who owns the e-commerce channel within the organization?
4. Is the e-commerce channel planned alongside other channels?
5. Do we have a process for generating, approving, releasing, and withdrawing content?
6. Will our brands translate to the new channel or will they require modification?
7. How will we market the channel itself?

its leading competitor. Many business analysts say that the failure of Barnes & Noble to integrate some of the marketing and operations of Barnesandnoble.com within their thousands of bookstores meant it forfeited a key strategic business opportunity.

e-Commerce Channel Choices

Some of the key questions that the management of companies must answer in making a clicks-and-bricks decision and developing the resulting e-commerce channel are outlined in Figure 9.17. An e-commerce channel is the marketing or sales channel created by a company to conduct and manage its chosen e-commerce activities. How this e-commerce channel is integrated with a company's traditional sales channels (e.g., retail/wholesale outlets, catalog sales, and direct sales) is a major consideration in developing its e-commerce strategy.

Thus, the examples in this section emphasize that there is no universal clicks-and-bricks e-commerce strategy or e-commerce channel choice for every company, industry, or type of business. Both e-commerce integration and separation have major business benefits and shortcomings. Deciding on a clicks-and-bricks strategy and e-commerce channel depends heavily on whether a company's unique business operations provide strategic capabilities and resources to support a profitable business model successfully for its e-commerce channel. As these examples show, most companies are implementing some measure of clicks-and-bricks integration because "the benefits of integration are almost always too great to abandon entirely."

REI: Scaling e-Commerce Mountain

When outdoor equipment retailer REI wanted to boost in-store sales, the company looked to its Web site. In June 2003, REI.com launched free in-store pickup for customers who ordered online. The logic behind that thinking: People who visit stores to collect their online purchases might be swayed to spend more money upon seeing the colorful displays of clothing, climbing gear, bikes, and camping equipment.

REI's hunch paid off. "One out of every three people who buy something online will spend an additional $90 in the store when they come to pick something up," says Joan Broughton, REI's vice president of multichannel programs. That tendency translates into a healthy 1 percent increase in store sales.

As Broughton sees it, the mantra for any multichannel retailer should be "a sale is a sale is a sale, whether online, in stores or through catalogs." The Web is simply not an isolated channel with its own operational metrics or exclusive group of customers.

As the Web has matured as a retail channel, consumers have turned to online shopping as an additional place to interact with a retailer rather than a replacement for existing channels such as stores or catalogs.

And to make that strategy as cost-efficient as possible, the company uses the same trucks that restock its stores to fulfill online orders slated for in-store pickup. To make this work, REI had to integrate order information from the Web site and replenishment orders from stores at its distribution warehouse in Washington state.

In and of itself, integrating the two types of order information wasn't complex, says Brad Brown, REI's vice president of information services. What was difficult, however, was coordinating fulfillment of both online and replenishment orders because "orders placed on the Web by customers are nothing like replenishment orders that stores place," he says. Online orders are picked from the warehouse at the time of the order and then put in a queue until the appropriate truck is loaded, whereas store orders are picked by an automated replenishment system that typically picks orders at one time based on either a weekly or biweekly replenishment schedule.

To make in-store pickup a reality, Brown's group wrote a "promise algorithm" that informs customers of a delivery date when they place an online order. Timing can get tricky when orders are placed the day before a truck is scheduled to depart the warehouse with a store-replenishment delivery. For example, if an online order is placed on a Monday night and a truck is scheduled to depart Tuesday morning, the system promises the customer a pickup date of a week later, as if the order would be placed on the following week's truck. However, REI will shoot for fulfilling the order that night; if it can do it, REI (and, ultimately, the customer) is happy because the order arrives sooner than was promised.

Creating effective business-to-consumer retail Web sites entails more than simply calculating sales figures. It's about delivering the functionality that users expect and using the site to drive sales through other channels. And only IT integration can make this happen.

Source: Adapted from Megan Santosus, "Channel Integration—How REI Scaled e-Commerce Mountain," *CIO Magazine*, May 15, 2004.

Summary

- **e-Commerce.** E-commerce encompasses the entire online process of developing, marketing, selling, delivering, servicing, and paying for products and services. The Internet and related technologies and e-commerce Web sites on the World Wide Web and corporate intranets and extranets serve as the business and technology platforms for e-commerce marketplaces for consumers and businesses in the basic categories of business-to-consumer (B2C), business-to-business (B2B), and consumer-to-consumer (C2C) e-commerce. The essential processes that should be implemented in all e-commerce applications—access control and security, personalizing and profiling, search management, content management, catalog management, payment systems, workflow management, event notification, and collaboration and trading—are summarized in Figure 9.4.

- **e-Commerce Issues.** Many e-business enterprises are moving toward offering full-service B2C and B2B e-commerce portals supported by integrated customer-focused processes and inter-networked supply chains, as illustrated in Figure 9.9. In addition, companies must evaluate a variety of e-commerce integration or separation alternatives and benefit trade-offs when choosing a clicks-and-bricks strategy and e-commerce channel, as summarized in Figures 9.16 and 9.17.

- **B2C e-Commerce.** Businesses typically sell products and services to consumers at e-commerce Web sites that provide attractive Web pages, multimedia catalogs, interactive order processing, secure electronic payment systems, and online customer support. However, successful e-tailers build customer satisfaction and loyalty by optimizing factors outlined in Figure 9.11, such as selection and value, performance and service efficiency, the look and feel of the site, advertising and incentives to purchase, personal attention, community relationships, and security and reliability. In addition, a Web store has several key business requirements, including building and marketing a Web business, serving and supporting customers, and managing a Web store, as summarized in Figure 9.13.

- **B2B e-Commerce.** Business-to-business applications of e-commerce involve electronic catalog, exchange, and auction marketplaces that use Internet, intranet, and extranet Web sites and portals to unite buyers and sellers, as summarized in Figure 9.14 and illustrated in Figure 9.15. Many B2B e-commerce portals are developed and operated for a variety of industries by third-party market-maker companies called infomediaries, which may represent consortiums of major corporations.

Key Terms and Concepts

These are the key terms and concepts of this chapter. The page number of their first explanation is in parentheses.

1. Clicks-and-bricks strategy (410)
2. E-commerce channel (413)
3. E-commerce marketplaces (408)
   a. Auction (409)
   b. Catalog (409)
   c. Exchange (409)
   d. Portal (408)
4. E-commerce processes (389)
   a. Access control and security (390)

   b. Collaboration and trading (393)
   c. Content and catalog management (390)
   d. Electronic payment systems (394)
   e. Event notification (393)
   f. Profiling and personalizing (390)
   g. Search management (390)
   h. Workflow management (392)

5. Electronic commerce (384)
   a. Business-to-business (B2B) (388)
   b. Business-to-consumer (B2C) (388)
   c. Consumer-to-consumer (C2C) (388)
6. Electronic funds transfer (EFT) (394)
7. Infomediaries (409)
8. Search engine optimization (404)

Review Quiz

Match one of the key terms and concepts listed previously with each of the brief examples or definitions that follow. Try to find the best fit for the answers that seem to fit more than one term or concept. Defend your choices.

_____ 1. The online process of developing, marketing, selling, delivering, servicing, and paying for products and services.

_____ 2. Business selling to consumers at retail Web stores is an example.

_____ 3. Using an e-commerce portal for auctions by business customers and their suppliers is an example.

_____ 4. Using an e-commerce Web site for auctions among consumers is an example.

_____ 5. E-commerce applications must implement several major categories of interrelated processes, such as search and catalog management, in order to be effective.

_____ 6. Helps to establish mutual trust between you and an e-tailer at an e-commerce site.

_____ 7. Tracks your Web site behavior to provide you with an individualized Web store experience.

_____ 8. Develops, generates, delivers, and updates information to you at a Web site.

_____ 9. Ensures that proper e-commerce transactions, decisions, and activities are performed to serve you more efficiently.

_____ 10. Sends you an e-mail when your e-commerce order has been shipped.

_____ 11. Includes matchmaking, negotiation, and mediation processes among buyers and sellers.

_____ 12. Companies that serve as intermediaries in e-commerce transactions.

_____ 13. A process aimed at improving the volume and/or quality of traffic to a Web site.

_____ 14. An e-commerce marketplace that may provide catalog, exchange, or auction service for businesses or consumers.

_____ 15. Buyers bidding for the business of a seller.

_____ 16. Marketplace for bid (buy) and ask (sell) transactions.

_____ 17. The most widely used type of marketplace in B2C e-commerce.

_____ 18. The marketing or sales channel created by a company to conduct and manage its e-commerce activities.

_____ 19. The processing of money and credit transfers between businesses and financial institutions.

_____ 20. Ways to provide efficient, convenient, and secure payments in e-commerce.

_____ 21. Companies can evaluate and choose from several e-commerce integration alternatives.

_____ 22. Web sites and portals hosted by individual companies, consortiums, or intermediaries that bring together buyers and sellers to accomplish e-commerce transactions.

_____ 23. A component of e-commerce sites that helps customers find what they are looking for.

Discussion Questions

1. Most businesses should engage in e-commerce on the Internet. Do you agree or disagree with this statement? Explain your position.

2. Are you interested in investing in, owning, managing, or working for a business that is primarily engaged in e-commerce on the Internet? Explain your position.

3. Refer to the Real World Case on social networks, mobile commerce, and online shopping in the chapter. Do you think that mobile devices (not just phones anymore) are becoming the major platform for shopping, communication, everything? What are the implications for companies?

4. Why do you think there have been so many business failures among dot-com companies that were devoted only to retail e-commerce?

5. Do the e-commerce success factors listed in Figure 9.11 guarantee success for an e-commerce business venture? Give a few examples of what else could go wrong and how you would confront such challenges.

6. If personalizing a customer's Web site experience is a key success factor, then electronic profiling processes to track visitor Web site behavior are necessary. Do

you agree or disagree with this statement? Explain your position.

7. All corporate procurement should be accomplished in e-commerce auction marketplaces, instead of using B2B Web sites that feature fixed-price catalogs or negotiated prices. Explain your position on this proposal.

8. Refer to the Real World Case on LinkedIn, Umbria, Mattel, and Others in the chapter. What is your take on the debate as to whether these "influential" individuals do really have an effect on others, or they are representative of an underlying cultural trend? How would a company react based on their position on the issue?

9. If you were starting an e-commerce Web store, which of the business requirements summarized in Figure 9.13 would you primarily do yourself, and which would you outsource to a Web development or hosting company? Why?

Analysis Exercises

Complete the following exercises as individual or group projects that apply chapter concepts to real-world business situations.

1. **Small Business e-Commerce Portals**
   On the Internet, small businesses have become big business, and a really big business, Microsoft, wants a piece of the action. The company's Small Business Center (www.microsoft.com/smallbusiness) is one of many sites offering advice and services for small businesses moving online. Most features, whether free or paid, are

   what you'd expect: lots of links and information along the lines established by Prodigy Biz (www.prodigybiz.com) or Entrabase.com. Small Business Center, however, stands out for its affordable advertising and marketing services. See Figure 9.18.

   One program helps businesses create banner ads and places them on a collection of Web sites that it

FIGURE 9.18

Microsoft's Small Business Center is a small business e-commerce portal.

Source: Courtesy of Microsoft®.

claims are visited by 60 percent of the Web surfing community. With its "Banner Network Ads" program, buyers don't pay a huge fee upfront, and they don't run the risk that a huge number of visitors will unexpectedly drive up clickthrough commissions. Instead, this program allows small business to pay a small, fixed fee for a guaranteed number of clickthroughs (people who click on your banner ad to visit your Web site). Small Business Center rotates these banner ads around a network of participating Web sites and removes the ad as soon as it has received the guaranteed number of clickthrough visitors. This action eliminates the guesswork regarding both traffic and fees. The three packages—100, 250, and 1,000 visitors—break down to 50 cents per visitor.

a. Check out Small Business Center and the other e-commerce portals mentioned. Identify several benefits and limitations for a business using these Web sites.

b. Which Web site is your favorite? Why?

c. Which site would you recommend or use to help a small business wanting to get into e-commerce? Why?

2. **e-Commerce Web Sites for Car Buying**
Nowadays new car buyers can configure the car of their dreams on Microsoft's MSN Autos Web site, as well as those of Ford, GM, and other auto giants. Many independent online car purchase and research companies offer similar services. See Figure 9.19. Car buying information provided by manufacturers, brokerage sites, car dealers, financial institutions, and consumer advocate Web sites has exploded in the past few years.

Yet in the age of the Internet, the auto industry remains a steadfast holdout to innovations that might threaten the well-established and well-connected supply chain, the car dealership. American new car buyers simply cannot skip the middleperson and purchase an automobile directly from the manufacturer. That's not just a business decision by the manufacturers; that's the law.

Even so, many car buyers use the Internet as a place to research their purchases. Instead of selling new cars directly, Web sites such as Autobytel.com of Irvine, California, just put consumers in touch with a local dealer where they test-drive a vehicle and negotiate a price. Autobytel.com has been referring buyers to new and used car dealers since 1995. It also offers online financing and insurance.

Online car-buying sites on the Web make consumers less dependent on what cars a dealer has on the lot. At online sites, buyers can customize a car—or van, truck, or sport utility vehicle—by selecting trim, paint, color, and other options before purchase. They can also use Web sites such as CarBuyingTips.com to help prepare for the final negotiating process.

FIGURE 9.19
Table for Problem 2.

Top Car-Buying Web Sites
● **Autobytel.com**　　www.autobytel.com Enter make and model, and a local dealer will contact you with a price offer. Home delivery is an option.
● **AutoNation**　　www.autonation.com Every make and model available, as well as financing and insurance information, home delivery, and test drives.
● **Microsoft MSN Autos**　　www.autos.msn.com Auto reviews, detailed vehicle specifications, safety ratings, and buying services for new and used cars, including customizing your very own Ford.
● **cars.com**　　www.cars.com Research tools include automotive reviews, model reports, dealer locators, and financing information.
● **CarsDirect.com**　　www.carsdirect.com Research price and design, and then order your car. CarsDirect will deliver it to your home. A top-rated site.
● **Edmunds.com**　　www.edmunds.com For an objective opinion, Edmunds.com provides reviews, safety updates, and rebate news for car buyers.
● **FordVehicles.com**　　www.fordvehicles.com Research, configure, price, and order your new Ford car, minivan, truck, or SUV at this Web site.
● **GM BuyPower**　　www.gmbuypower.com With access to nearly 6,000 GM dealerships, car shoppers can get a price quote, schedule a test drive, and buy.

a. Check out several of the Web sites shown in Figure 9.19. Evaluate them based on ease of use, relevance of information provided, and other criteria you feel are important. Don't forget the classic: "Did they make you want to buy?"

b. Which sites would you use or recommend if you or a friend actually wanted to buy a car? Why?

c. Check out the Consumer Federation of America's study on anticompetitive new car-buying state laws or similar studies online. How much does it estimate consumers would save if they could purchase cars directly from manufacturers online?

3. Comparing e-Commerce Sites
In this exercise, you will experiment with electronic shopping and compare alternative e-commerce sites. First, select a category of product widely available on the Web, such as books, CDs, or toys. Second, select five specific products to price on the Internet, for example, five specific CDs you might be interested in buying. Third, search three prominent e-commerce sites selling this type of product and record the price charged for each product by each site.

a. Using a spreadsheet, record a set of information similar to that shown for each product. (Categories describing the product will vary depending on the type of product you select—CDs might require the title of the CD and the performer[s], whereas toys or similar products would require the name of the product and its description.) See Figure 9.20.

b. For each product, rank each company on the basis of the price charged. Give a rating of 1 for the lowest price and 3 for the highest, and split the ratings for ties—two sites tying for the lowest price would each receive a 1.5. If a site does not have one of the products available for sale, give that site a rating of 4 for that product. Add the ratings across your products to produce an overall price/availability rating for each site.

c. Based on your experience with these sites, rate them on their ease of use, completeness of information, and order-filling and shipping options. As in Part (b), give a rating of 1 to the site you feel is best in each category, a 2 to the second best, and a 3 to the poorest site.

d. Prepare a set of PowerPoint slides or similar presentation materials summarizing the key results and including an overall assessment of the sites you compared.

4. e-Commerce: The Dark Side
Anonymous transactions on the Internet can have a dark side. Research each of the terms below on the Web. Prepare a one-page report for each term researched. Your paper should describe the problem and provide examples and illustrations where possible. Conclude each paper with recommendations on how to guard against each type of fraud.

a. Search using the terms "Ponzi Scheme" or "Pyramid Scheme." To find current examples in action, try searching for "plasma TV $50," "cash matrix," "e-books" and "matrix," or "gifting" through a search engine or auction site.

b. Search using the terms "phishing" and "identity." If possible, include a printout of a real-world example that you or an acquaintance may have received via e-mail.

c. Search using the term "third-party escrow." What legitimate function does this serve? Provide an example of a legitimate third-party escrow service for Internet transactions. How has the third-party escrow system been used to commit fraud on the Internet?

d. Prepare a one-page paper describing a type of online fraud not covered in the previous questions. Prepare presentation materials and present your findings to the class. Be sure to include a description of the fraud, how to detect it, and how to avoid it. Use real-world illustrations if possible.

FIGURE 9.20   Table for Problem 3.

Title of Book	Author	Price			Rating		
		Site A	Site B	Site C	A	B	C
The Return of Little Big Man	Berger, T.	15.00	16.95	14.50	2	3	1
Learning Perl/Tk	Walsh, N. & Mui, L.	26.36	25.95	25.95	3	1.5	1.5
Business at the Speed of Thought	Gates, W.	21.00	22.95	21.00	1.5	3	1.5
Murders for the Holidays	Smith, G.		8.25	7.95	4	2	1
Designs for Dullards	Jones	17.95	18.50	18.50	1	2.5	2.5
Sum of ratings (low score represents most favorable rating)					11.5	12	7.5

REAL WORLD CASE 3

Entellium, Digg, Peerflix, Zappos, and Jigsaw: Success for Second Movers in e-Commerce

Anyone who has watched short-track speed skating during the Winter Olympics knows that skating with the lead is no easy task.

The No. 2 skater gets to conserve precious energy by drafting behind the leader. No. 2 watches the frontrunner's every move, gauging when and where to make a bid for the gold. Now corporate America and speed skating have much in common.

There are no safe leads.

For companies that use the Internet as the home base for their businesses, the second-mover advantage seems even more substantial. That's why Paul Johnston is deeply grateful to Marc Benioff.

Johnston's Seattle-based start-up, Entellium, has won hundreds of contracts against Benioff's Salesforce.com and other competitors since it moved from Malaysia in 2004, and its revenues grew fivefold in 2005. What Johnston really likes, though, is not having to sell companies on the concept of letting an outsider host their customer relationship management software.

What makes fast-following the hot strategy of the moment is the relative ease with which founders can get a start-up out on the track and send it chasing the competition. Cheap open-source tools can help you deploy new business software quickly.

Offshore manufacturers can quickly churn out anything from semiconductors to engine parts. The Web connects marketers to a vast pool of beta testers, while angel investors and venture capitalists, flush with new funds, stand at the ready.

Of course, fast-following isn't as simple as saying "Me too." To battle established leaders, you need the right product and strategy, as well as a big dose of savvy. Here's how to show up after the starting gun and still come out on top.

Number 1: Be better, faster, cheaper, and easier

To steal business from Benioff, Johnston knew that Entellium had to offer something different. "This is true for any follower," he says.

It's what Johnston calls the "awesome, awesome, not totally ****-ed up" approach. The first "awesome" is how Entellium's software works. Johnston, formerly an Apple sales executive, aims to bring to the stodgy world of enterprise software the ease of use of consumer-directed offerings like Google Maps and the role-playing game Everquest. He even hired developers from the gaming industry to borrow interface tricks.

After appealing to customers on usability, Johnston hits them with the price: about 40 percent less than the competition. That's the second "awesome." The last part is making Entellium a less risky decision.

Who wants to put their job on the line for a start-up the boss has never heard of? Johnston offers free 24×7 service to make it easier for new customers to stick their necks out.

Number 2: Trip up incumbents with tactics from other fields

Common wisdom would say that the last thing the world needs is another technology news Web site, but Digg founders Jay Adelson and Kevin Rose are uncommonly wise.

A year ago, inspired by social-networking sites like MySpace—whose users rank everything from people to music—Adelson and Rose decided to use the same approach to build a better version of tech news site Slashdot.

Digg lets readers submit news stories and vote for the ones they think are most important. The top 15 vote-getters make it to the front page. The formula is working. Between May and November, the number of monthly unique visitors to Digg surged 284 percent to 404,000, eclipsing Slashdot's 367,000, according to ComScore Media Metrix. In addition, Adelson and Rose recently landed $2.8 million from investors, including eBay founder Pierre Omidyar and Netscape cofounder Marc Andreessen.

Moving forward, Adelson and Rose won't be shy about borrowing even more from seemingly unrelated companies. Soon they'll start tracking what members read and offering story recommendations à la Amazon. Digg is also set to branch out into nontechnology stories, which readers will be able to categorize with Delicious-style social bookmarking tags.

"A lot of companies are afraid to touch their original technology, to reconsider the premise on which they started the business," Adelson notes. "But when you stop doing that, that's when you get lapped [overtaken]."

Number 3: Swipe their business models and start your own race

When Billy McNair and Danny Robinson were hatching the idea for a new DVD company, Netflix handed them part of their business plan. Consumers had already learned that renting by mail was easy. McNair and Robinson believed they could do better than rentals. After all, eBay had shown them how.

By mixing together the best of two worlds, the founders came up with Peerflix, a Web site on which people exchange DVDs for a 99-cent transaction fee. Like eBay, Peerflix sits in the middle, linking movie fans and taking a piece of the action. Eager to avoid going head-to-head with eBay, however, McNair and Robinson are starting with lower-ticket items—those that sell for less than $25—for which auctions may not be worth the hassle.

"We've married the best of online rental services and online secondary markets," McNair claims. Since it launched in September, Peerflix has helped trade nearly 200,000 DVDs, and the founders are now talking about extending the idea to video games and other items.

Number 4: Follow the biggest leader you can find

When he hatched Zappos six years ago, Nick Swinmum put other online shoe sellers in his cross-hairs. Web-based competitors typically carried a limited number of brands and catered to small niches—say, women's dress shoes or men's outdoor boots. Zappos would crush them, Swinmum reasoned, with an online store that offered every conceivable make and model.

That was the right idea, but it focused on the wrong competitors. The online shoe market was so tiny that even if Zappos dominated it, there wouldn't be enough business for the company to thrive. To grow, it had to steal customers from bricks-and-mortar stores. Before 2001, Zappos didn't carry inventory; rather, the company asked distributors to drop-ship directly to consumers.

It was an easy, cheap arrangement, but the problem was that Zappos couldn't guarantee service; 8 percent of the time customers tried to buy shoes, the desired pair was out of stock. In other words, the experience was nothing like walking into a shoe store. "We realized then who our real competition was, and that we had to find a way to make an inventory model work," Swinmum says.

So Zappos began to cozy up to suppliers.

Contrary to industry practice, Swinmum shared data with manufacturers on exactly how well their shoes were selling. "Traditionally the vendor–retail relationship was adversarial," he recognizes. "We thought, 'Instead of trying to hide this information from the brands, let's open everything up. They can help us build the business.'" Did they ever! Grateful shoe reps helped Zappos craft promotions to spur sales.

Since targeting traditional shoe stores, Zappos has thrived. In 2001, the company did $8.6 million in sales; the next year it did $32 million. In 2005, Zappos posted more than $300 million in revenues from an expanding line of shoes, handbags, and other leather goods.

Number 5: Aim for the leader's Achilles' heel

When he was vice president for sales at online marketing shop Digital Impact, Jim Fowler watched his field reps fail with a growing sense of frustration. Their problem? The leading online databases of corporate information, such as Dun & Bradstreet subsidiary Hoover's, didn't offer the deep, up-to-date contact lists that salespeople need to close deals.

Rather than complain about those vendors, Fowler decided to improve on them.

His company, Jigsaw, is a new kind of contact subscription service: All of the names and addresses in Jigsaw's database come from its users. Sales reps pay a minimum of $25 per month to access contacts at thousands of companies, or they pay nothing if they contribute 25 contacts per month themselves. Users police the listings to ensure they're current.

Since Jigsaw's launch in December 2004, its database has surged from 200,000 contacts to more than 2 million; some 38,000 subscribers are adding 10,000 new contacts a day. Through Jigsaw you can find more than 16,000 contacts at Medtronic, for example; Hoover's, meanwhile, offers extensive research on the company but only about 30 contacts. According to Fowler, "It's never too late if you are smarter and better than everyone else."

CASE STUDY QUESTIONS

1. Is the second-mover advantage always a good business strategy? Defend your answer with examples of the companies in this case.

2. What can a front-runner business do to foil the assaults of second movers? Defend your answer using the examples of the front-runner companies in the case.

3. Do second movers always have the advantage in Web-based business success? Why or why not? Evaluate the five strategies given in the case and the companies that used them to help defend your answer.

REAL WORLD ACTIVITIES

1. Use the Internet to research the current business status of all of the many companies in this case. Are the second movers still successfully using their strategies, or have the first movers foiled their attempts? Have new strong players entered the markets of the first and second movers, or have business, economic, or societal developments occurred to change the nature of competition in these markets?

2. Assume you will start an Internet-based business similar to one of those mentioned in this case or another one of your choice. Would you be a first, second, or later mover in the market you select? How would you differentiate yourself from other competitors or prospective new entrants? Break into small groups to share your ideas and attempt to agree on the best Web-based business opportunity of the group.

REAL WORLD CASE 4

KitchenAid and the Royal Bank of Canada: Do You Let Your Brand Go Online All by Itself?

A reputation is a fragile thing—especially on the Internet, where trademarked images are easily borrowed, corporate secrets can be divulged anonymously in chat rooms, and idle speculation and malicious commentary on a blog can affect a company's stock price. Brands are under constant attack, but companies such as BrandProtect, MarkMonitor, and NameProtect (now part of Corporation Services Company) are stepping in to offer companies some artillery in the fight for control of their brands and reputations.

Brian Maynard, director of marketing for KitchenAid, a division of Whirlpool, had a rather unique problem. Like the classic Coke bottle and Disney's Mickey Mouse ears, the silhouette of the KitchenAid mixer, that colorful and distinctively rounded wedding registry staple, is a registered trademark. Although the KitchenAid stand mixer silhouette has been a registered trademark since the mid-1990s, it has been a well-recognized symbol since the current design was introduced in the 1930s. "The KitchenAid mixer is an incredible asset so it is important for us to protect both the name and the image from becoming generic," says Maynard, who reports that the equity of the brand has been estimated to be in the tens of millions of dollars. Any kind of violations that go unnoticed can quickly erode that precious equity.

KitchenAid had experienced some problems on the Web with knockoffs and unauthorized uses of the mixer's image, but getting a handle on the many and varied online trademark infringements seemed daunting. Maynard knew that historically, corporate brands that were not well-protected and policed by their owners had been ruled generic by the courts—aspirin and escalator are two examples. "Throughout history terms like escalator and aspirin have become generic simply because people did not do the work to protect them," says Maynard. "To avoid that fate, you have to show the courts that you have put every effort into protecting your brand. If you don't police your brand, courts will typically rule that the mark is no longer meaningful and has become ubiquitous." So when he received a cold-call from BrandProtect, he was intrigued.

Criminals hijacking online corporate brands and masquerading for profit, however, are ramping up their efforts. Dubbed "brandjacking" by MarkMonitor Inc., a San Francisco–based brand protection service provider, the practice is becoming a major threat to household names. "Not only is the volume of these abuses significant, but abusers are becoming alarmingly savvy marketers," says Frederick Felman, MarkMonitor's chief marketing officer. In its first Brandjacking Index report, Mark-Monitor tracked 25 of the top 100 brands for three weeks by monitoring illegal or unethical tactics that ranged from cyber-squatting to pay-per-click fraud. Media companies made up the greatest percentage of targeted brands.

Cybersquatting, which usually means registering a URL that includes a real brand's name, easily took the prize for the most threats. MarkMonitor tracked more than 286,000 instances in the three-week span. "When I heard about the solution I didn't even realize there was anything like that out there," says Maynard. "I saw right away that it solved a problem I didn't even realize existed."

BrandProtect uses a technology platform that functions like a giant spider, mapping the Web and identifying what's going on in its darkest recesses. The mapping technology is combined with a filter and human analysis component that identifies and returns to its clients actionable data on illicit activities that may adversely affect their corporate identity. Depending on the client's chosen service level, those activities can include any of 22 categories of infractions—from phishing to counterfeiting, misuse of corporate logos and trademarked product images, domain infractions, and employees blogging about corporate trade secrets. Staying ahead of the many ways that a company's brand can be compromised or diluted online is a challenge that Kevin Joy, vice president of marketing for BrandProtect, compares to a never-ending game of Whack-a-Mole.

The challenge of brand protection, however, has grown exponentially for companies operating in the online world. "With the advent of the Internet a few things happened," explains Maynard. "Everyone in the world could now see the mixer so the potential for misuse of our trademark became greater. Because it is so well known, there was more risk of companies creating knock-off products and marketing them under other names. So it was even more important than ever to prove that we were putting every effort into protecting the brand and our trademarks."

Other types of violations also surfaced as KitchenAid's online policing activities grew. Some, such as sites using the logo without permission, were minor and could be easily fixed with a warning letter. Others were not so innocent, such as using the logo to create links to illegal sites. "We spent a lot of time training people and policing online activities," says Maynard.

The many successes have made the relationship worthwhile. Recently, Maynard was impressed by how quickly he was able to resolve a case of domain infraction. A small vendor that works with KitchenAid was experimenting with registering URLs such as shopkitchenaid.com and buykitchenaid.com for marketing purposes. That Friday when Maynard received his report, he noticed the new URLs, recognized the name of the owner, and called his contact at the company to explain that any URLs containing the name KitchenAid had to be owned by the company. Maynard says his contact was shocked by how quickly KitchenAid had gotten on top of the issue. "He didn't even know he couldn't have ownership of that URL and was stunned that we knew about it so quickly."

Given the strategic importance of the KitchenAid brand, Maynard says BD-BrandProtect has played a major role in bringing him peace of mind. "It is my responsibility to protect this brand and I am not going to allow any loss of equity on my watch. In fact, the value of the stand mixer silhouette continues to increase year after year. Before BD-BrandProtect, however, I thought I was out there doing it on my own. Now I know I can leave the brand in better condition than when I started."

As Manager of Brand Standards for the Royal Bank of Canada, Lise Buisson knows that the job of protecting the bank's brand online involves a lot more than finding out when someone has cut and pasted a logo onto their site without permission. "As brands become more valued, any improper use of your brand can become a reputational risk. When someone displays your logo, for example, it becomes a de facto endorsement, whether we have approved it or not. We have to be careful about things like that." Royal Bank of Canada and its subsidiaries operate under the master brand name of RBC. With 70,000 full- and part-time employees serving 15 million clients through offices in North America and 34 countries around the world, RBC is the largest bank in Canada.

"We didn't expect to see what we saw. We were inundated. No one realized how easy it was for someone to come to our site, grab a logo, and put it somewhere else. It forced us to sit down as a group and figure out what we could do," says Buisson. She quickly discovered that a majority of the infractions noted were harmless and did not require a second thought. "In most cases the users were well meaning," she says. "It could be a charity site or mortgage partner using our logo. I would say that 90 percent of these incidents were quite harmless."

"BD-BrandProtect immediately flagged and dealt with a bank in the North Sea region that had used our logo and positioned themselves with another name. When anyone misrepresents themselves as an affiliate of ours, it makes us very nervous," notes Buisson. Where concerns are raised, RBC will take the appropriate measures, from issuing a polite request to the user to cease using their brand to initiating legal action. "In the vast majority of cases a polite letter is enough." Once a year, RBC reviews its branding policies to ensure that the reports continue to reflect their top priorities. It has also established a number of policies to ensure that the appropriate follow-up measures are used when required. "If, for example, we find advertising of our logo on a gambling site, we now have a policy about that," she says.

Buisson says that as Internet activities continue to escalate, she has come to realize that the job of monitoring online brand activities properly would just have been too much for departmental staff to handle. "I'm a big proponent of going to the experts and sitting down and working with them. It's very reassuring to work with a company that's looking out for us. It certainly helps some of us sleep at night."

Source: Adapted from Daintry Duffy, "Brand Aid for a Manufacturer's Online Property," *CIO Magazine*, September 17, 2007; *Royal Bank of Canada Case Study* and *KitchenAid Case Study*, www.bdbrandprotect.com, accessed April 22, 2008; and Gregg Ketzer, "Brandjackers' Make Millions Feeding Off Internet Brand Names," *Computerworld*, April 30, 2007.

CASE STUDY QUESTIONS

1. Consider your own online shopping patterns. How much weight do you place on the presence of a name or logo or other trademark (such as the KitchenAid silhouette) on a Web site when purchasing goods or services? Do you ever stop to consider whether you may have been misled? How could you tell the difference?

2. Brian Maynard of KitchenAid notes that the development of the Internet changed the problem of brand policing. What are some of these changes? What new challenges can you think of that did not exist in the pre-online world? Provide several examples.

3. The companies mentioned in the case (e.g., KitchenAid, RBC, Disney, and Coke) were well established and enjoyed strong brand recognition well before the advent of the Internet. Do you think online-only companies face the same problems as they do? Why or why not? Justify the rationale for your answer.

REAL WORLD ACTIVITIES

1. Online trust providers such as eTrust (www.etrust.org) and others review privacy policies, including information collection and use, sharing and disclosure, and security, and then certify Web sites as meeting their standards. Companies that achieve this can then display a logo to that effect. Search the Internet to discover how these providers prevent unauthorized lifting and use of their certification logos by Web sites that have not gone through the process. Prepare a report to summarize your findings. Have you ever noticed these logos? Does it make any difference to you as a consumer whether a Web site displays them or not?

2. The case features technology developed by BrandProtect (www.brandprotect.com); competitors include MarkMonitor (www.markmonitor.com) and NameProtect (www.cscprotectbrands.com). Visit their Web sites to compare and contrast their offerings. Then break into small groups to compare your findings and discuss new features that you believe are lacking, as well as why you think these vendors should include these features.

CHAPTER 10

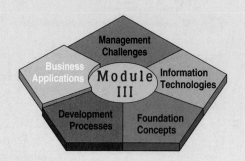

SUPPORTING DECISION MAKING

Chapter Highlights

Learning Objectives

1. Identify the changes taking place in the form and use of decision support in business.

2. Identify the role and reporting alternatives of management information systems.

3. Describe how online analytical processing can meet key information needs of managers.

4. Explain the decision support system concept and how it differs from traditional management information systems.

5. Explain how the following information systems can support the information needs of executives, managers, and business professionals:
   a. Executive information systems
   b. Enterprise information portals
   c. Knowledge management systems

6. Identify how neural networks, fuzzy logic, genetic algorithms, virtual reality, and intelligent agents can be used in business.

7. Give examples of several ways expert systems can be used in business decision-making situations.

SECTION I	# Decision Support in Business

Introduction

As companies migrate toward responsive e-business models, they are investing in new data-driven decision support application frameworks that help them respond rapidly to changing market conditions and customer needs.

To succeed in business today, companies need information systems that can support the diverse information and decision-making needs of their managers and business professionals. In this section, we will explore in more detail how this is accomplished by several types of management information, decision support, and other information systems. We concentrate our attention on how the Internet, intranets, and other Web-enabled information technologies have significantly strengthened the role that information systems play in supporting the decision-making activities of every manager and knowledge worker in business.

Read the Real World Case on the next page. We can learn a lot from this case about new trends in decision making within companies. See Figure 10.1.

Information, Decisions, and Management

Figure 10.2 emphasizes that the type of information required by decision makers in a company is directly related to the **level of management decision making** and the amount of structure in the decision situations they face. It is important to understand that the framework of the classic *managerial pyramid* shown in Figure 10.2 applies even in today's *downsized organizations* and *flattened* or nonhierarchical organizational structures. Levels of management decision making still exist, but their size, shape, and participants continue to change as today's fluid organizational structures evolve. Thus, the levels of managerial decision making that must be supported by information technology in a successful organization are:

- **Strategic Management.** Typically, a board of directors and an executive committee of the CEO and top executives develop overall organizational goals, strategies, policies, and objectives as part of a strategic planning process. They also monitor the strategic performance of the organization and its overall direction in the political, economic, and competitive business environment.

- **Tactical Management.** Increasingly, business professionals in self-directed teams as well as business unit managers develop short- and medium-range plans, schedules, and budgets and specify the policies, procedures, and business objectives for their subunits of the company. They also allocate resources and monitor the performance of their organizational subunits, including departments, divisions, process teams, project teams, and other workgroups.

- **Operational Management.** The members of self-directed teams or operating managers develop short-range plans such as weekly production schedules. They direct the use of resources and the performance of tasks according to procedures and within budgets and schedules they establish for the teams and other workgroups of the organization.

Information Quality

What characteristics of information products make them valuable and useful to you? To answer this important question, we must first examine the characteristics or attributes of **information quality.** Information that is outdated, inaccurate, or hard to understand is not very meaningful, useful, or valuable to you or other business professionals. People need information of high quality, that is, information products whose characteristics, attributes, or qualities make the information more valuable to them. It is useful to think of information as having the three dimensions of time, content, and form. Figure 10.3 summarizes the important attributes of information quality and groups them into these three dimensions.

REAL WORLD CASE 1

Business Intelligence Is Alive and Well in Hong Kong

The upward trend of business intelligence (BI) in Hong Kong is here to stay. BI made it to Gartner's top five for 2010. In Hong Kong, the BI software market is expected to reach US$19.6 million in 2009 and grow 6.4 percent per year over the next five years, according to an IDC report published in 2009.

"From results of a survey we did in 2009, 25 percent of respondents from Hong Kong said they will deploy or will increase current deployment of BI/analytics software during 2010 and 2011," said Sharon Tan, research manager at IDC, a major IT analytics company.

Local users have also ventured into innovative use of BI, said Jason Tang, head of Practices and Solutions, SAS Institute Hong Kong. "Some of the local firms have gone into what we call sentiment analysis," said Tang. "Firms analyze external data and texts from blogs, forums, and social networking sites to learn what customers think about their products and services."

External data provides additional perspectives on targeted campaigns, he added. "Cost reduction was the goal in 2009, but in 2010 differentiation and revenues generation are crucial, and will be facilitated by successful targeted campaigns," said Tang.

Real-time decision making has also become possible for BI users, Tang noted. "For instance, customer service reps can immediately do cross-sale and up sale during phone conversations with customers," said Tang. "BI can also help HR and logistics executives to automate resources allocations and identify available resources real-time."

Predictive analytics will be hot next, said Linda Young, brand manager, Information Management, Software Group,

IBM China/Hong Kong. "Historical data analysis was what BI tools did. This is what we call trend analysis," said Young. "But predictions are what businesses need today." Predictive analytics are rule-based, "what-if?" analyses that help firms estimate inventories, cash flow, turnaround of goods, and profitability, according to Young.

Industry-wise, companies are also using BI for a variety of purposes, including enhancement of green practices. "One of our customers, Cosco, deploys BI-based simulation to help control its CO_2 footprint and operational costs," said Young.

Other uses include complaint management by governments, credit analysis by banks, portfolio ROI prediction by investment banks, and identifying criminals and terrorists by police, Young added.

"Before the credit crunch in 2008, most BI requirements were from retailers, manufacturers, and players in the financial sector," said Young. "But in 2009, inquiries from retail and manufacturing dropped, while most were from insurance and finance."

"Users want to complete deployment and be able to use the tools within two to four weeks rather than several months to a year," said Sinko Choy, sales director, EPM/BI, Oracle Hong Kong. Integration with mobile devices is another capability required. "Because executives are always on-the-go, they need alerts to their mobile phones," Choy noted.

As BI tools come with more capabilities these days, CIOs are increasingly concerned about users' data analysis skills. "That's why you see universities have added BI courses to keep up with the changing workplace," said Young.

"Large organizations tend to have more BI users, therefore they make up a huge proportion of BI users in general," said Tan from IDC. "But as there are cheaper express versions of BI tools, uptake in the SMB (small/medium business) segment is expected while the economy is recovering."

Free analytics tools like Google Analytics helps drive the adoption of BI among SMBs. According to Young, Google Analytics is an example of advanced analytics. "Google Analytics or inexpensive SaaS-based BI that don't require up-front investment in hardware are good ways for SMBs to learn more about the technology," said Young.

"[But] these inexpensive tools don't compete with on-premise BI tools," said Young. "When SMBs grow larger, accumulate more data, and have more stringent data privacy requirements, they will build their own BI platforms."

While agreeing cloud or SaaS is a tech enabler, Tang from SAS said it won't drive BI uptake. "Cloud can make implementation much easier, but ROI and other benefits are the drivers," he noted.

Businesses need to deal with key issues like risk management and compliance, said Tan. "Since BI contains much sensitive data, companies are cautious when it comes to putting them onto the cloud," she concluded.

Business Intelligence tools don't just work for corporations. According to the 1823 Call Center of the Hong

FIGURE 10.1

Business intelligence is replacing gut feeling when it comes to business decisions.

Source: © age fotostock/SuperStock.

Kong SAR Government's Efficiency Unit, the use of a text miner that consolidates information and uncovers hidden relationships through statistical analyses helps improve complaint management.

The Efficiency Unit's implementation of SAS Text Miner started in March 2009 and was completed in September, said WF Yuk, assistant director, Efficiency Unit, Chief Secretary for Administration's Office, the Hong Kong SAR Government.

At a cost of HK$3.3 million, the project isn't just about implementing software, said Yuk. According to him, Chinese unstructured data is hard for text mining because of the structure of Chinese characters. "For instance, Quarry Bay (鰂魚涌) in Chinese is a location in Hong Kong. But while 鰂 and 魚 together is a type of fish, 涌 means a river," said Yuk.

"Another example is the category of construction waste," said Yuk. "We need to let the system know that sand, rubble, concrete, and bricks found in urban areas are related and belong to the category of construction waste. It took us a lot of effort to build a data dictionary."

In 2009, the unit handled more than 2.6 million calls and more than 100,000 text-based messages including e-mails and fax, said Yuk, adding that about 10 percent of the calls are complaints.

Prior to the deployment of text miner and related tools, staffers needed to dig data out from each of the complaint cases to track progress, Yuk noted. "It also took a week to compile reports on key performance indicators such as aban-

doned call rate, customer satisfaction rate, and first-time resolution rate," he said. Now staffers answering calls input incidents reported into the system, said Yuk, adding that calls are recorded so that supervisors can check accuracy. The text mining system is accessed only by business analysts and call center supervisors.

What the text mining system does is to identify the same incidents as reported by different individuals. "For example, a person tells us a location is full of litter while another says there are many unlicensed hawkers," said Yuk. "Yet a third caller tells us that snacks sold at the same location look dirty."

"They seem to be three different incidents, but they are one incident at the same location," said Yuk. "The text mining system is supposed to bring us to attention to this so that we respond in time by notifying the responsible department rather than several departments related to hawker management, public hygiene, and food safety—thus delaying necessary actions."

The text miner also tracks the progress of cases, said Yuk. "The text miner allows us to create performance reports at the click of a mouse through dashboards as all complaints information is consolidated into a single system," said Yuk.

In addition, users can track 'black spots' of different types such as locations where the highest number of dead birds is seen, said Yuk. "This helps us proactively prompt departments to take necessary action."

Source: Adapted from Teresa Leung, "BI Stays Top Priority," *Computerworld Hong Kong*, Questex Media, February 8, 2010.

CASE STUDY QUESTIONS

1. Why are business intelligence and analytics practices becoming so popular with SMBs? Are the information needs of an SMB smaller than that of a large organization? Explain.

2. In what ways have the companies mentioned in the case benefited from their adoption of business analytics? Provide several examples from the case to illustrate your answer.

3. Information quality is central to the approach toward decision making taken by these organizations. What other elements must be present for this approach to be successful (technology, people, culture, and so forth)?

REAL WORLD ACTIVITIES

1. A number of major companies have launched projects geared toward improving their business analytics and decision-making capabilities in the last few years. Go online and research other examples in this trend. What are the similarities with the ones chronicled in the case? What are the differences? Prepare a report that includes a section contrasting your new examples with the ones in the case.

2. If you had to apply the ideas discussed in the case to your academic career, what would be the sources of information? How you would measure whether you are making progress toward attaining your goals? Break into small groups to discuss these issues.

FIGURE 10.2   Information requirements of decision makers. The type of information required by directors, executives, managers, and members of self-directed teams is directly related to the level of management decision making involved and the structure of decision situations they face.

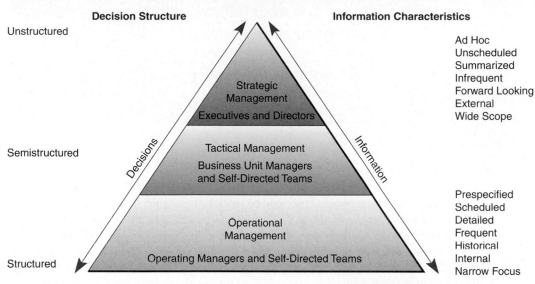

FIGURE 10.3

A summary of the attributes of information quality. This figure outlines the attributes that should be present in high-quality information products.

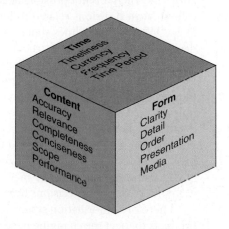

Time Dimension

Timeliness	Information should be provided when it is needed.
Currency	Information should be up-to-date when it is provided.
Frequency	Information should be provided as often as needed.
Time Period	Information can be provided about past, present, and future time periods.

Content Dimension

Accuracy	Information should be free from errors.
Relevance	Information should be related to the information needs of a specific recipient for a specific situation.
Completeness	All the information that is needed should be provided.
Conciseness	Only the information that is needed should be provided.
Scope	Information can have a broad or narrow scope, or an internal or external focus.
Performance	Information can reveal performance by measuring activities accomplished, progress made, or resources accumulated.

Form Dimension

Clarity	Information should be provided in a form that is easy to understand.
Detail	Information can be provided in detail or summary form.
Order	Information can be arranged in a predetermined sequence.
Presentation	Information can be presented in narrative, numeric, graphic, or other forms.
Media	Information can be provided in the form of printed paper documents, video displays, or other media.

FIGURE 10.4   Examples of decisions by the type of decision structure and level of management.

Decision Strategic	Operational Management	Tactical Management	Structure Management
Unstructured	Cash management	Business process reengineering	New e-business initiatives
		Workgroup performance analysis	Company reorganization
Semistructured	Credit management	Employee performance appraisal	Product planning
	Production scheduling	Capital budgeting	Mergers and acquisitions
	Daily work assignment	Program budgeting	Site location
Structured	Inventory control	Program control	

Decision Structure

One way to understand decision making is to look at decision structure. Decisions made at the operational management level tend to be more *structured*, those at the tactical level are more *semistructured*, and those at the strategic management level are more *unstructured*. Structured decisions involve situations in which the procedures to follow, when a decision is needed, can be specified in advance. The inventory reorder decisions that most businesses face are a typical example. Unstructured decisions involve decision situations in which it is not possible to specify in advance most of the decision procedures to follow. Most decisions related to long-term strategy can be thought of as unstructured (e.g., "What product lines should we develop over the next five years?"). Most business decision situations are semistructured; that is, some decision procedures can be prespecified but not enough to lead to a definite recommended decision. For example, decisions involved in starting a new line of e-commerce services or making major changes to employee benefits would probably range from unstructured to semistructured. Finally, decisions that are unstructured are those for which no procedures or rules exist to guide the decision makers toward the correct decision. In these types of decisions, many sources of information must be accessed, and the decision often rests on experience and "gut feeling." One example of an unstructured decision might be the answer to the question, "What business should we be in 10 years from now?" Figure 10.4 provides a variety of examples of business decisions by type of decision structure and level of management.

Therefore, information systems must be designed to produce a variety of information products to meet the changing needs of decision makers throughout an organization. For example, decision makers at the strategic management level may look to *decision support systems* to provide them with more summarized, ad hoc, unscheduled reports, forecasts, and external intelligence to support their more unstructured planning and policymaking responsibilities. Decision makers at the operational management level, in contrast, may depend on *management information systems* to supply more prespecified internal reports emphasizing detailed current and historical data comparisons that support their more structured responsibilities in day-to-day operations. Figure 10.5 compares the information and decision support capabilities of management information systems and decision support systems, which we will explore in this chapter.

Decision Support Trends

The emerging class of applications focuses on personalized decision support, modeling, information retrieval, data warehousing, what-if scenarios, and reporting.

As we discussed in Chapter 1, using information systems to support business decision making has been one of the primary thrusts of the business use of information technology. During the 1990s, however, both academic researchers and business practitioners began to report that the traditional managerial focus originating in classic management information systems (1960s), decision support systems (1970s), and executive information systems (1980s) was expanding. The fast pace of new information technologies like PC hardware and software suites, client/server networks, and networked PC versions of DSS

FIGURE 10.5
Comparing the major differences in the information and decision support capabilities of management information systems and decision support systems.

FIGURE 10.5
Comparing the major differences in the information and decision support capabilities of management information systems and decision support systems.

	Management Information Systems	Decision Support Systems
● Decision support provided	Provide information about the performance of the organization	Provide information and decision support techniques to analyze specific problems or opportunities
● Information form and frequency	Periodic, exception, demand, and push reports and responses	Interactive inquiries and responses
● Information format	Prespecified, fixed format	Ad hoc, flexible, and adaptable format
● Information processing methodology	Information produced by extraction and manipulation of business data	Information produced by analytical modeling of business data

software made decision support available to lower levels of management, as well as to nonmanagerial individuals and self-directed teams of business professionals.

This trend has accelerated with the dramatic growth of the Internet, as well as of intranets and extranets that inter-network with companies and their stakeholders. The e-business and e-commerce initiatives that are being implemented by many companies are also expanding the information and decision support uses and the expectations of a company's employees, managers, customers, suppliers, and other business partners. Figure 10.6 illustrates that all business stakeholders expect easy and instant access to information and Web-enabled self-service data analysis. Today's businesses are responding with a variety of personalized and proactive Web-based analytical techniques to support the decision-making requirements of all of their constituents.

Thus, the growth of corporate intranets and extranets, as well as the Web, has accelerated the development and use of "executive-class" information delivery and decision support software tools by lower levels of management and by individuals and teams of business professionals. In addition, this dramatic expansion has opened the door to the use of such business intelligence (BI) tools by the suppliers, customers, and other business stakeholders of a company for customer relationship management, supply chain management, and other e-business applications.

In 1989, Howard Dresner (later a Gartner Group analyst) proposed BI as an umbrella term to describe "concepts and methods to improve business decision making by using fact-based support systems." It was not until the late 1990s that this usage became widespread. Today, BI is considered a necessary and mission critical element in crafting and executing a firm's strategy. Consider the following findings from a 2009 Gartner Group study:

- Because of lack of information, processes, and tools, through 2012, more than 35 percent of the top 5,000 global companies will regularly fail to make insightful decisions about significant changes in their business and markets.

FIGURE 10.6
A business must meet the information and data analysis requirements of its stakeholders with more personalized and proactive Web-based decision support.

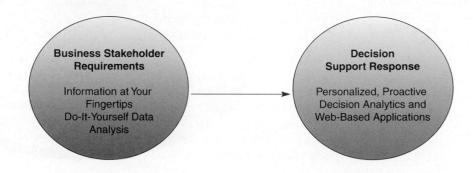

- By 2012, business units will control at least 40 percent of the total budget for business intelligence.

- By 2010, 20 percent of organizations will have an industry-specific analytic application, delivered via software as a service, as a standard component of their business intelligence portfolio.

- In 2009, collaborative decision making will emerge as a new product category that combines social software with business intelligence platform capabilities.

When you consider some of these findings, it becomes easy to see that BI is rapidly becoming the mainstay for business decision making in the modern organization. Before long, it will evolve into a competitive necessity for many industries.

As with all concepts in business-related technologies, business intelligence has evolved from Dresner's original definition focusing on concepts and methods to a more action-oriented approach referred to as *business analytics*. Business analytics (BA) refers to the skills, technologies, applications, and practices applied to a continuous iterative exploration and investigation of a business's historical performance to gain insight and drive the strategic business planning process. Business analytics focuses on developing new insights and understanding of business performance based on data and statistical methods. In contrast, business intelligence traditionally focuses on using a consistent set of metrics to both measure past performance and guide business planning, which is also based on data and statistical methods.

Business analytics makes much more extensive use of data, statistical and quantitative analysis, explanatory and predictive modeling, and fact-based management to drive decision making. Analytics may be used as input for human decisions or may drive fully automated decisions. Business intelligence is more associated with querying, reporting, online analytical processing (OLAP), and "alerts." In other words, querying, reporting, OLAP, and alert tools can answer the questions: *what happened; how many; how often; where; where exactly is the problem;* and *what actions are needed.* Business analytics, in contrast, can answer the questions: *why is this happening; what if these trends continue; what will happen next (that is, predict);* and *what is the best that can happen (that is, optimize).* One of the most common techniques and approaches associated with business analytics is data mining, a concept introduced in Chapter 5 and discussed again later in this chapter.

Figure 10.7 highlights several major information technologies that are being customized, personalized, and Web-enabled to provide key business information and analytical tools for managers, business professionals, and business stakeholders. We highlight the trends toward such business intelligence applications in the various types of information and decision support systems that are discussed in this chapter.

FIGURE 10.7

Business intelligence applications are based on personalized and Web-enabled information analysis, knowledge management, and decision support technologies.

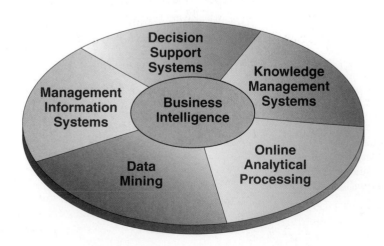

Hyatt Hotels: Dashboards Integrate Financial and Operational Information

A few years ago, executives at Chicago-based Hyatt Hotels decided the company needed a way to consolidate its disparate financial data so that it could more easily forecast future sales and plan its business accordingly. In other words, the company wanted to install a typical financial performance management layer, with dashboards and scorecards for top-level managers. But after some discussion on the matter, the installation grew to be not so typical.

Gebhard Rainer, Hyatt's vice president of hotel finance and systems, wanted to combine these financial elements—budgeting, planning, modeling, and reporting—with operational data from the hotels themselves. The idea was that a complete picture of the company's business, available on a daily basis to executives as well as hotel managers, was not possible without having the two together in the same dashboard.

Motivating the concept was a changing world, with terrorist risks and natural disasters causing an ever-shifting array of business variables. Rainer, in a Middle Eastern country in the aftermath of a terrorist attack several years ago, confronted these issues firsthand—as did the company, which owns hotels in New Orleans and along the hurricane-ravaged Gulf Coast. The first line of business is the safety of hotel guests. But in terms of the big picture, hotel companies must re-forecast their business goals from the ground up based on a set of entirely new metrics dealing with issues from resource allocation to skittish tourists rethinking their travel plans. It wasn't a job for spreadsheets.

Hyatt was among the first of Hyperion's customers to adopt System 9. The company selected Hyperion based on its "integrateability" with its source systems, as well as its user-friendliness. At first, Hyatt wanted a small-scale installation, delivering the System 9 dashboards to about 40 executive users. "This phase was a 'show-me-what-you-can-do' thing," says Sufel Barkat, Hyatt's assistant vice president for financial systems. "We simply wanted to understand the capability of the tools. The next stage will have a much bigger impact." The ultimate plan is to spread the system throughout the Hyatt organization to its many subsidiaries, in the United States and abroad, and to its individual properties—full-blown operational BI. Eventually, hotel managers will have access to dashboards so that everyone is on the same page, and so that local employees can make local decisions based on the same information viewed at headquarters.

Hyatt ended up using a data warehouse from Teradata to cleanse operational information coming from the decentralized ERP systems of Hyatt's individual hotels around the world. The company also uses the warehouse to store and cleanse external marketing data, such as what the competition is up to, or market share in each region.

On the financial side, other sources include the proprietary company's general ledger system and an Oracle database—systems already consolidated and unified through Hyatt's original performance management outlay.

The next step will be to deliver the dashboards to between 500 and 600 users at Hyatt—all the way down to the regional manager level. The full-blown operational BI rollout will target around 3,000 users. So far, in these early stages, Barkat hasn't been able to quantify the results of System 9 with any real figures. But, he says, users have been providing feedback on metrics, which, to him, indicates a strong "cultural and business adaptation" among Hyatt's executive class.

Source: Adapted from Scott Eden, "Hyatt Merges Financial, Ops Data," *InformationWeek*, January 17, 2006.

Decision Support Systems

Decision support systems are computer-based information systems that provide interactive information support to managers and business professionals during the decision-making process. Decision support systems use (1) analytical models, (2) specialized databases, (3) a decision maker's own insights and judgments, and (4) an interactive, computer-based modeling process to support semistructured business decisions.

Example

An example might help at this point. Sales managers typically rely on management information systems to produce sales analysis reports. These reports contain sales performance figures by product line, salesperson, sales region, and so on. A decision support system (DSS), however, would also interactively show a sales manager the effects on sales performance of changes in a variety of factors (e.g., promotion expense and salesperson compensation). The DSS could then use several criteria (e.g., expected gross margin and market share) to evaluate and rank alternative combinations of sales performance factors.

Therefore, DSS are designed to be ad hoc, quick-response systems that are initiated and controlled by business decision makers. Decision support systems are thus able to support directly the specific types of decisions and the personal decision-making styles and needs of individual executives, managers, and business professionals.

DSS Components

Unlike management information systems, decision support systems rely on model bases, as well as databases, as vital system resources. A DSS model base is a software component that consists of models used in computational and analytical routines that mathematically express relationships among variables. For example, a spreadsheet program might contain models that express simple accounting relationships among variables, such as Revenue 2 Expenses 5 Profit. A DSS model base could also include models and analytical techniques used to express much more complex relationships. For example, it might contain linear programming models, multiple regression forecasting models, and capital budgeting present value models. Such models may be stored in the form of spreadsheet models or templates, or statistical and mathematical programs and program modules. See Figure 10.8.

In addition, DSS software packages can combine model components to create integrated models that support specific types of decisions. DSS software typically contains built-in analytical modeling routines and also enables you to build your own models. Many DSS packages are now available in microcomputer and Web-enabled versions. Of course, electronic spreadsheet packages also provide some of the model building (spreadsheet models) and analytical modeling (what-if and goal-seeking analysis) offered by more powerful DSS software. As businesses become more aware of the power of decision support systems, they are using them in ever-increasing areas of the business. See Figure 10.9.

FIGURE 10.8

Components of a Web-enabled marketing decision support system. Note the hardware, software, model, data, and network resources involved.

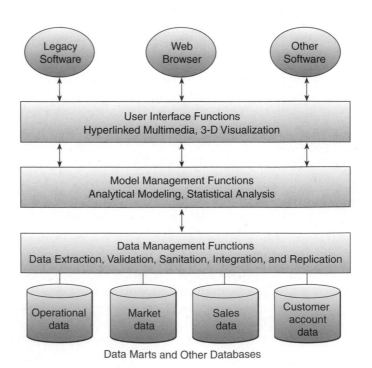

Data Marts and Other Databases

FIGURE 10.9   Many businesses are turning to decision support systems and their underlying models to improve a wide variety of business functions.

Function	Description	Exemplars
	Analytics competitors make expert use of statistics and modeling to improve a wide variety of functions. Here are some common applications:	
Supply chain	Simulate and optimize supply chain flows; reduce inventory and stockouts.	Dell, Walmart, Amazon
Customer selection, loyalty, and service	Identify customers with the greatest profit potential; increase likelihood that they will want the product or service offering; retain their loyalty.	Harrah's, Capital One, Barclays
Pricing	Identify the price that will maximize yield or profit.	Progressive, Marriott
Human capital	Select the best employees for particular tasks or jobs at particular compensation levels.	New England Patriots, Oakland A's, Boston Red Sox
Product and service quality	Detect quality problems early and minimize them.	Honda, Intel
Financial performance	Better understand the drivers of financial performance and the effects of nonfinancial factors.	MCI, Verizon
Research and development	Improve quality, efficacy, and, where applicable, safety of products and services.	Novartis, Amazon, Yahoo

Source: Adapted from Thomas H. Davenport, "Competing on Analytics," *Harvard Business Review*, January 2006.

United Agri Products: Making Better Decisions Using Models and Data

You give employees electronic reports, maybe even a dashboard. But are you helping them make better day-to-day decisions?

Companies can't report their way to great results—though you wouldn't know it from their accumulation of underused reports and dashboards. Companies that get this critical point are moving away from IT-centric business intelligence (BI) programs and toward results-focused performance management. True: BI does more than just generate reports. But add in query and analysis tools, and sophisticated predictive and statistical analytics, and those tools and technologies are overwhelmingly under IT's control.

In contrast, performance management, or PM, is defined by business needs, providing decision makers with the data they need to make the right moves, ones that fit with company strategy.

Most often, companies incorporate performance management into their budgeting and financial processes, in what's called corporate or financial PM. The next step is operational PM, where they apply BI to practical, day-to-day decisions in the supply chain, sales, customer service, and other areas.

That's what's happening at United Agri Products (UAP), a unit of $5 billion-a-year chemical and fertilizer supplier Agrium, which started doing operational PM projects using IBM's Cognos BI platform. "After years of IT preaching the value of BI to business, we reached a point of maturity where the roles started to reverse, and the business started coming to us with ideas," says David Wheat, UAP's director of decision support systems.

UAP's director of operations brought one such project to IT. The CEO had asked him to cut end-of-year inventory by $25 million, a difficult task for an agricultural company given ever-changing weather conditions, crop disease, and insect infestations, all happening across a variety of regions.

"The operations director sketched out exactly what he wanted on a whiteboard," Wheat says. Then he said, "If I can know at any point in time what I have in inventory and can forecast what the consumption will be through the end of the season, I'll know what dollar amount I'll have left and I can go after the high-dollar overages."

With that context, Wheat laid out a model for a PM system that included what data he needed and when he had to have it in order to make decisions. And his model came complete with a financial target.

UAP lacked a sales forecasting application, so Wheat's team developed one by integrating relevant information—current inventory levels, open purchase orders, prior-year purchase histories, and predicted overages or shortages—into a single report. The application includes a daily alert that notifies managers in four regions whenever a purchase order has the potential to create excess season-ending inventory.

"All that data presented in one place, with exceptions highlighted in color, made problems jump right to the top for the director and his regional managers," Wheat says. That information led managers to investigate open, unconfirmed purchase orders to see if they're justified. The result: "Within two weeks, UAP had canceled $2 million worth of POs for products that weren't needed."

Source: Adapted from Dough Henschen, "Decision Time," *InformationWeek*, November 24, 2008.

Management Information Systems

Recall from Chapter 1 that management information systems were the original type of information system developed to support managerial decision making. An MIS produces information products that support many of the day-to-day decision-making needs of managers and business professionals. Reports, displays, and responses produced by management information systems provide information that these decision makers have specified in advance as adequately meeting their information needs. Such predefined information products satisfy the information needs of decision makers at the operational and tactical levels of the organization who are faced with more structured types of decision situations. For example, sales managers rely heavily on sales analysis reports to evaluate differences in performance among salespeople who sell the same types of products to the same types of customers. They have a pretty good idea of the kinds of information about sales results (by product line, sales territory, customer, salesperson, and so on) that they need to manage sales performance effectively.

Managers and other decision makers use an MIS to request information at their networked workstations that supports their decision-making activities. This information takes the form of periodic, exception, and demand reports and immediate responses to inquiries. Web browsers, application programs, and database management software provide access to information in the intranet and other operational databases of the organization. Remember, operational databases are maintained by transaction processing systems. Data about the business environment are obtained from Internet or extranet databases when necessary.

Management Reporting Alternatives

Management information systems provide a variety of information products to managers. Four major **reporting alternatives** are provided by such systems.

- **Periodic Scheduled Reports.** This traditional form of providing information to managers uses a prespecified format designed to provide managers with information on a regular basis. Typical examples of such periodic scheduled reports are daily or weekly sales analysis reports and monthly financial statements.

- **Exception Reports.** In some cases, reports are produced only when exceptional conditions occur. In other cases, reports are produced periodically but contain information only about these exceptional conditions. For example, a credit manager can be provided with a report that contains only information on customers who have exceeded their credit limits. Exception reporting reduces *information overload* instead of overwhelming decision makers with periodic detailed reports of business activity.

- **Demand Reports and Responses.** Information is available whenever a manager demands it. For example, Web browsers, DBMS query languages, and report generators enable managers at PC workstations to get immediate responses or to find and obtain customized reports as a result of their requests for the information they need. Thus, managers do not have to wait for periodic reports to arrive as scheduled.

- **Push Reporting.** Information is *pushed* to a manager's networked workstation. Thus, many companies are using Webcasting software to broadcast selectively reports and other information to the networked PCs of managers and specialists over their corporate intranets. See Figure 10.10.

FIGURE 10.10 An example of the components in a marketing intelligence system that uses the Internet and a corporate intranet system to "push" information to employees.

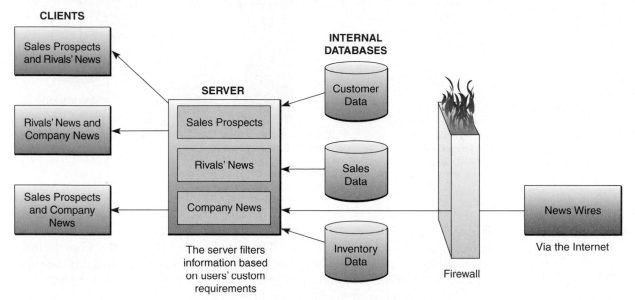

Online Analytical Processing

At a stockholder meeting, the former CEO of PepsiCo, D. Wayne Calloway, said: "Ten years ago I could have told you how Doritos were selling west of the Mississippi. Today, not only can I tell you how well Doritos sell west of the Mississippi, I can also tell you how well they are selling in California, in Orange County, in the town of Irvine, in the local Vons supermarket, in the special promotion, at the end of Aisle 4, on Thursdays."

The competitive and dynamic nature of today's global business environment is driving demands by business managers and analysts for information systems that can provide fast answers to complex business queries. The IS industry has responded to these demands with developments like analytical databases, data marts, data warehouses, data mining techniques, and multidimensional database structures (discussed in Chapter 5), and with specialized servers and Web-enabled software products that support online analytical processing (OLAP).

Online analytical processing enables managers and analysts to interactively examine and manipulate large amounts of detailed and consolidated data from many perspectives. OLAP involves analyzing complex relationships among thousands or even millions of data items stored in data marts, data warehouses, and other multidimensional databases to discover patterns, trends, and exception conditions. An OLAP session takes place online in real time, with rapid responses to a manager's or analyst's queries, so that the analytical or decision-making process is undisturbed. See Figure 10.11.

Online analytical processing involves several basic analytical operations, including consolidation, "drill-down," and "slicing and dicing." See Figure 10.12.

- **Consolidation.** Consolidation involves the aggregation of data, which can involve simple roll-ups or complex groupings involving interrelated data. For example, data about sales offices can be rolled up to the district level, and the district-level data can be rolled up to provide a regional-level perspective.

- **Drill-down.** OLAP can also go in the reverse direction and automatically display detailed data that comprise consolidated data. This process is called drill-down. For example, the sales by individual products or sales reps that make up a region's sales totals could be easily accessed.

- **Slicing and Dicing.** Slicing and dicing refers to the ability to look at the database from different viewpoints. One slice of the sales database might show all sales of a product type within regions. Another slice might show all sales by sales channel within each product type. Slicing and dicing is often performed along a time axis to analyze trends and find time-based patterns in the data.

FIGURE 10.11

Online analytical processing may involve the use of specialized servers and multidimensional databases. OLAP provides fast answers to complex queries posed by managers and analysts using traditional and Web-enabled OLAP software.

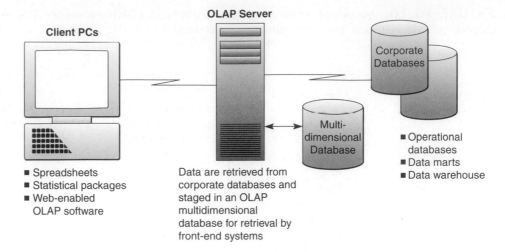

OLAP Examples

Probably the best way to understand the power of OLAP fully is to look at common business applications of the technique. The real power of OLAP comes from the marriage of data and models on a large scale. Through this marriage, managers can solve a variety of problems that previously would be considered too complex to tackle effectively. Common business areas where OLAP can solve complex problems include:

• Marketing and sales analysis

• Clickstream data

• Database marketing

• Budgeting

• Financial reporting and consolidation

• Profitability analysis

• Quality analysis

Let's look at one or two examples of how OLAP can be used in the modern business setting.

FIGURE 10.12

Comshare's Management Planning and Control software enables business professionals to use Microsoft Excel as their user interface for Web-enabled online analytical processing.

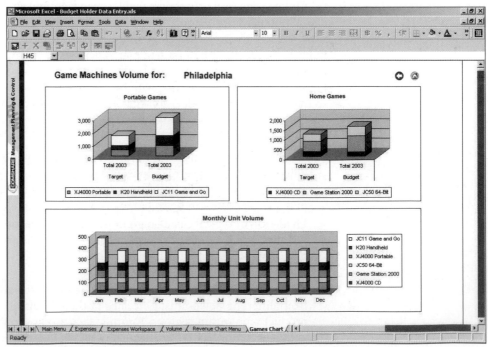

Source: Used with permission from Microsoft®.

It is near the end of a business quarter, and senior management is worried about the market acceptance of several new products. A marketing analyst is asked to provide an update to senior management. The problem is that the update must be delivered in less than an hour due to a last-minute request from the CEO. The analyst really only has a few minutes to analyze the market acceptance of several new products, so she decides to group 20 products that were introduced between six and nine months ago and compare their sales with a comparable group of 50 products introduced between two and three years ago. The analyst just defines two new, on-the-fly, product groupings and creates a ratio of the new group to the older group. She can then track this ratio of sales revenue or volume by any level of location, over time, by customer sector or by sales group. Defining the new groupings and the ratio takes a couple of minutes, and any of the analyses take a matter of a few seconds to generate, even though the database has tens of thousands of products and hundreds of locations. It takes no more than a total of 15 minutes to spot that some regions have not accepted the new products as fast as others.

Then, the analyst investigates whether this was because of inadequate promotion, unsuitability of the new products, lack of briefings of the sales force in the slow areas, or whether some areas always accept new products more slowly than others. Looking at other new product introductions by creating new groupings of products of different ages, she finds that the same areas are always conservative when introducing expensive new products. She then uses this information to see if the growth in the slow areas is in line with history and finds that some areas have taken off even more slowly than previously. Given the results of this analysis, senior management decides it is premature in its concern and tables further discussion until the next quarterly sales data can be assessed.

In another example, let's consider a general merchandise retailer who has joined the e-tailing ranks, wants the company Web site to be as "sticky" as possible, and has begun to analyze clickstream data to surmise why customers might leave the site prematurely. The company sharpened its analysis to determine the value of abandoned shopping carts. When a customer leaves the site in the middle of a shopping trip, for whatever reason, the company looks to see what products were in the abandoned cart. The data are then compared with similar data from other carts to examine:

- How much revenue the abandoned carts represented (in other words, the amount of revenue that was lost because of the customer's early departure).

- Whether the products in the cart were high-profit items or loss leaders.

- Whether the same products were found in other abandoned carts.

- The volume of products and the number of different product categories in the cart.

- Whether the total bill for the abandoned carts consistently fell within a certain dollar range.

- How the average and total bills for abandoned carts compared with unabandoned carts (those that made it through the checkout process).

The results of using OLAP to conduct this analysis trigger some interesting theories. For instance, it is possible that none of the products in the cart was appealing enough to a particular customer to keep that customer shopping. The customer might have been annoyed by frequent inquiries, such as "Are you ready to check out?" At a particular dollar total, the customer might have changed his or her mind about the entire shopping trip and left. It's also possible that a number or mix of products in a cart reminded the customer of another site that might offer a steeper discount for similar purchases.

Admittedly, some of these theories are mere guesses. After all, maybe the customer's Internet connection was on the fritz, or the site had a bug that abruptly booted the user. When examined regularly and with consistent metrics, however, clickstreams can reveal interesting patterns. After several analyses, the e-tailer decides to make some changes to the Web site.

First, the e-tailer tweaks the site to show a rolling total as items are added to the cart, thereby allowing the customer to see the total charge during the shopping time and to check out once the magic budget limit is reached. In addition, rather than requiring the customer to go to another page for specific product information, the site now invites the customer to see pop-up product information with a click of the right mouse button, keeping the buy mode alive. Finally, the vendor decides to integrate the clickstream data with more specific customer behavior information, including information from the CRM system.

Rather than just examining a customer's navigation patterns and guessing about which actions to take, the e-tailer can combine those patterns with more specific customer data (such as previous purchases in that product category, key demographic and psychographic data, or lifetime value score) to provide a complete view of that customer's value and interests. That kind of analysis will show you whether the lost customer was a one-time-only shopper or a high-value customer. A tailored e-mail message or electronic coupon—perhaps targeting one of the products left behind on a prior trip—could make all the difference the next time that high-value customer logs on.

Here's a real-world example of how OLAP can help solve complex business problems.

BI Is About Talk, Not Tech	Research firm Gartner has warned organizations against splurging on technology for Business Intelligence (BI) projects.

Speaking of the discipline of BI, rather than the technology, Gartner global BI manager Ian Bertram says organizations will fail if they "throw products at the problem" and do not invest in training or acquire business support.

The BI discipline involves analysis of raw data through data mining and online analytical processing, which companies can use, for example, to find malfunctioning machines, improve manufacturing processors and cut costs. The sticking points, Bertram says, are as much about improving poor communication and BI skills, as sifting useful data from the rubbish.

"Organizations tend to throw technology at BI problems. You could have the right tool, but it could be doomed to failure because of political and cultural issues, an absence of executive support so the message doesn't get out, and poor communication and training," Bertram says. "It provides transparency through all levels of business right down to the forklift driver and can help business to react fast to competition and change."

Gartner says BI is top of mind for CIOs, along with enterprise information and content management, data management and integration, and social software and collaboration. It has remained in the top spot for three years in the firm's annual Executive Programs survey, while the firm predicts BI vendor revenue in the Asia Pacific region will increase by a CAGR (compound annual growth rate) of 15.5 percent by 2011, thanks in part to emerging green field developments.

Bertram says many organizations struggle to find benchmarks and metrics, and do not know where to define objectives. "Having a standard set of enterprise metrics sounds easy, but can be quite complex. We've come across organizations with a 1000 metrics, but [which] follow the old Kaplan and Norton balanced scorecard and focus on 'visionary' metrics at the top," he says. Subsequent metrics gathered from all levels of an organization should assist with achieving the "visionary" objectives.

Gartner endorses the concept of the BI competency center (BICC). A BICC is a centralized hub within an organization, devoted to BI. Representatives from each unit chair the center and are tasked with deciding how BI can best serve their field of work, including defining governance, appropriate metrics and architecture, and staff training.

Bertram, who recently discussed the BI competency center at a Sydney Summit, says businesses of all sizes can make money from a well-planned BI process. "Sydney Water saved millions when it found [through BI] one of its turbines was running all the time. They were able to balance the load across other turbines," he says.

"You could pick a number of organizations from every sector and find those that haven't managed [BI] projects well. They realize the BI technology is not a silver bullet and that it is intrinsically linked to business process and management of applications and data," he says.

Source: Adapted from Darren Pauli, "The Key to BI is Talk, Not Tech: Gartner," *Computerworld*, Fairfax Media Business Group, March 2, 2009.

FIGURE 10.13

Geographic information systems facilitate the mining and visualization of data associated with a geophysical location.

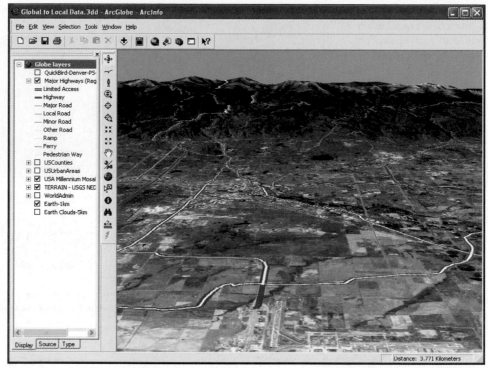

Source: Courtesy of Rockware Inc.

Geographic Information and Data Visualization Systems

Geographic information systems (GIS) and data visualization systems (DVS) are special categories of DSS that integrate computer graphics with other DSS features. A geographic information system is a DSS that uses *geographic databases* to construct and display maps, as well as other graphics displays that support decisions affecting the geographic distribution of people and other resources. Many companies are using GIS technology along with *global positioning system* (GPS) devices to help them choose new retail store locations, optimize distribution routes, or analyze the demographics of their target audiences. For example, companies like Levi Strauss, Arby's, Consolidated Rail, and Federal Express use GIS packages to integrate maps, graphics, and other geographic data with business data from spreadsheets and statistical packages. GIS software such as MapInfo and Atlas GIS is used for most business GIS applications. See Figure 10.13.

Data visualization systems represent complex data using interactive, three-dimensional, graphical forms such as charts, graphs, and maps. DVS tools help users interactively sort, subdivide, combine, and organize data while the data are in their graphical form. This assistance helps users discover patterns, links, and anomalies in business or scientific data in an interactive knowledge discovery and decision support process. Business applications like data mining typically use interactive graphs that let users drill down in real time and manipulate the underlying data of a business model to help clarify their meaning for business decision making. Figure 10.14 is an example of airline flight analysis by a data visualization system.

The concept of the geographic information system and data visualization is not a new one. One of the first recorded uses of the concept occurred in September 1854. During a 10-day period, 500 people, all from the same section of London, England, died of cholera. Dr. John Snow, a local physician, had been studying this cholera epidemic for some time. In trying to determine the source of the cholera, Dr. Snow located every cholera death in the Soho district of London by marking the location of the home of each victim with a dot on a map he had drawn. Figure 10.15 contains a replica of his original map.

As can be seen on the map, Dr. Snow marked the deaths with dots, and the 11 *X*s represent water pumps. By examining the scattering and clustering of the dots, Dr. Snow observed that the victims of the cholera shared one common attribute: They all lived

FIGURE 10.14

Using a data visualization system to analyze airplane flights by segment and average delay, with drill-down to details.

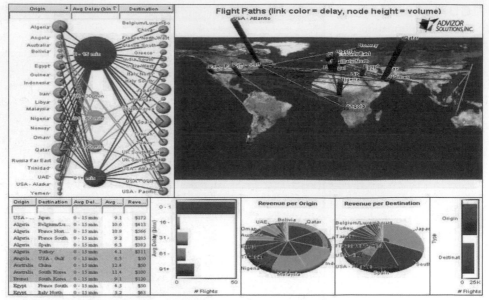

Source: Courtesy of ADVIZOR Solutions, Inc. www.advisorsolutions.com.

FIGURE 10.15

Replica of Dr. John Snow's cholera epidemic map.

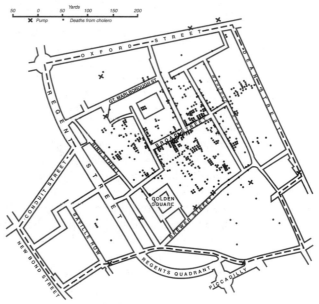

Source: E.R. Tufte, *The Visual Display of Quantitative Information,* 2nd ed. (Cheshire, Connecticut; Graphics Press, 2001), p. 24.

near—and drank from—the Broad Street water pump. To test his hypothesis, Dr. Snow requested that the handle of the pump be removed, thus rendering it inoperable. Within a very short time, the cholera epidemic, which claimed more than 500 lives, was over.

| JPMorgan and Panopticon: Data Visualization Helps Fixed Income Traders | Visualizing and understanding vast quantities of credit market data can be overwhelming using traditional techniques such as charts and tables. Navigating through this data to find specific reports and analytical information can also prove daunting, and traditional information delivery mechanisms have tended to provide unruly volumes of data.

The Internet is today the obvious delivery mechanism for such market data and proprietary analyses, yet the providers of such services must deliver more intuitive visualization and navigation to provide better value to their customers. |

Fixed income research and analytics providers are looking at new means of visualizing data to provide more valuable and intuitive services to their users by going beyond simple online tables, charts, and document repositories.

JPMorgan created their CreditMap application using Panopticon Developer in order to provide their customers with a graphical representation of real-time activity in the corporate bond market. JPMorgan blurred the lines between providing informative research and valuable analytics, which has enabled them to win the Euromoney award for "Best Online Fixed Income Research."

JPMorgan was able to provide their users with quicker access to their existing online information using new visualization and navigation tools. To do this, they implemented Panopticon's interactive treemap visualization as a presentation layer and navigation system that provides a bird's-eye view of the data, at the same time allowing the user to drill down to specific reports and analytics.

JPMorgan's CreditMap allows users to visualize information through the use of color, size, and proximity in any way they desire with an easily customizable interface. This interface acts as a catalyst, enabling users to recognize patterns, analyze information, and make decisions more quickly and more accurately than ever before. Before CreditMap, the brokerage firm's customers could read text reports on the corporate bond market and view various tables of statistical information. But the market is so extensive that it could be difficult to keep things in perspective or to be aware of many of the investment opportunities.

CreditMap presents the corporate bond universe as a quilt of rectangles on a computer screen. The quilt is divided into industry sectors, and the rectangles within each sector represent bond issues. The size of the rectangle indicates the size of the issue, and the color indicates the issue's performance. So at a glance, investors can see which sectors and which individual issues are hot, and whether an issue's size fits their investment needs. Clicking on a rectangle opens a window that gives basic information on the issue—including its ratings and the name and phone number of the analyst who covers the issue—along with a drop-down menu offering detailed research.

"Panopticon treemaps have greatly enhanced our users' ability to visualize the credit markets and utilize analytics—it was an important contributing factor to us winning the Euromoney award," says Lee McGinty, head of European Portfolio & Index Strategy at JPMorgan.

Source: Adapted from *Case Study: JPMorgan CreditMap*, www.panopticon.com, March 2008.

Using Decision Support Systems

A decision support system involves an interactive analytical modeling process. For example, using a DSS software package for decision support may result in a series of displays in response to alternative what-if changes entered by a manager. This differs from the demand responses of management information systems because decision makers are not demanding prespecified information; rather, they are exploring possible alternatives. Thus, they do not have to specify their information needs in advance. Instead, they use the DSS to find the information they need to help them make a decision. This is the essence of the decision support system concept.

Four basic types of analytical modeling activities are involved in using a decision support system: (1) what-if analysis, (2) sensitivity analysis, (3) goal-seeking analysis, and (4) optimization analysis. Let's briefly look at each type of analytical modeling that can be used for decision support. See Figure 10.16.

What-If Analysis

In what-if analysis, a user makes changes to variables, or relationships among variables, and observes the resulting changes in the values of other variables. For example, if you were using a spreadsheet, you might change a revenue amount (a variable) or a tax rate formula (a relationship among variables) in a simple financial spreadsheet model. Then you could command the spreadsheet program to recalculate all affected variables in the

FIGURE 10.16
Activities and examples of the major types of analytical modeling.

Type of Analytical Modeling	Activities and Examples
What-if analysis	Observing how changes to selected variables affect other variables. *Example:* What if we cut advertising by 10 percent? What would happen to sales?
Sensitivity analysis	Observing how repeated changes to a single variable affect other variables. *Example:* Let's cut advertising by $100 repeatedly so we can see its relationship to sales.
Goal-seeking analysis	Making repeated changes to selected variables until a chosen variable reaches a target value. *Example:* Let's try increases in advertising until sales reach $1 million.
Optimization analysis	Finding an optimum value for selected variables, given certain constraints. *Example:* What's the best amount of advertising to have, given our budget and choice of media?

spreadsheet instantly. A managerial user would be able to observe and evaluate any changes that occurred to the values in the spreadsheet, especially to a variable such as net profit after taxes. To many managers, net profit after taxes is an example of the *bottom line*, that is, a key factor in making many types of decisions. This type of analysis would be repeated until the manager was satisfied with what the results revealed about the effects of various possible decisions. Figure 10.17 is an example of what-if analysis.

Sensitivity Analysis

Sensitivity analysis is a special case of what-if analysis. Typically, the value of only one variable is changed repeatedly, and the resulting changes on other variables are observed. As such, sensitivity analysis is really a case of what-if analysis that involves repeated changes to only one variable at a time. Some DSS packages automatically make

FIGURE 10.17
This what-if analysis, performed by @RISK for Excel, involves the evaluation of probability distributions of net income and net present value (NPV) generated by changes to values for sales, competitors, product development, and capital expenses.

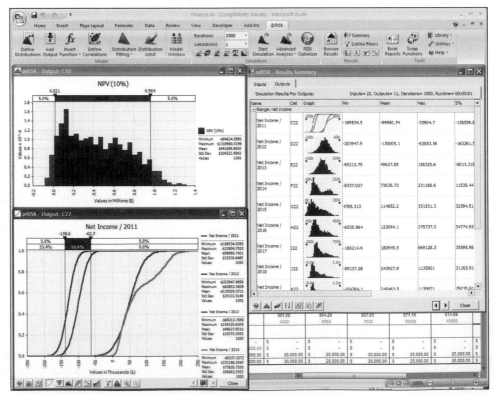

Source: @RISK software. Image courtesy of Palisade Corporation.

repeated small changes to a variable when asked to perform sensitivity analysis. Typically, decision makers use sensitivity analysis when they are uncertain about the assumptions made in estimating the value of certain key variables. In our previous spreadsheet example, the value of revenue could be changed repeatedly in small increments, and the effects on other spreadsheet variables observed and evaluated. This process would help a manager understand the impact of various revenue levels on other factors involved in decisions being considered. A typical example might be determining at what point the interest rate on a loan makes a project no longer feasible. By varying the interest rate used in a net present value calcuation, for example, a manager can determine the range of acceptable interest rates under which a project can move forward. Approaching the problem this way allows the manager to make decisions about a forthcoming project without knowing the actual cost of the money being borrowed.

Goal-Seeking Analysis

Goal-seeking analysis reverses the direction of the analysis done in what-if and sensitivity analyses. Instead of observing how changes in a variable affect other variables, goal-seeking analysis (also called *how-can* analysis) sets a target value (goal) for a variable and then repeatedly changes other variables until the target value is achieved. For example, you could specify a target value (goal) of $2 million in net profit after taxes for a business venture. Then you could repeatedly change the value of revenue or expenses in a spreadsheet model until you achieve a result of $2 million. Thus, you would discover the amount of revenue or level of expenses the business venture needs to reach the goal of $2 million in after-tax profits. Therefore, this form of analytical modeling would help answer the question, "How can we achieve $2 million in net profit after taxes?" instead of the question, "What happens if we change revenue or expenses?" So, goal-seeking analysis is another important method of decision support.

Optimization Analysis

Optimization analysis is a more complex extension of goal-seeking analysis. Instead of setting a specific target value for a variable, the goal is to find the optimum value for one or more target variables, given certain constraints. Then one or more other variables are changed repeatedly, subject to the specified constraints, until you discover the best values for the target variables. For example, you could try to determine the highest possible level of profits that could be achieved by varying the values for selected revenue sources and expense categories. Changes to such variables could be subject to constraints, such as the limited capacity of a production process or limits to available financing. Optimization typically is accomplished using software like the Solver tool in Microsoft Excel and other software packages for optimization techniques, such as linear programming.

Casual Male Retail Group: On-Demand Business Intelligence

Ask Dennis Hernreich, COO and CFO of Casual Male Retail Group, what his life was like before he switched to an on-demand business intelligence reporting application, and he remembers the frustration all too easily.

Casual Male Retail Group, a specialty retailer of big and tall men's apparel with $464 million in annual sales, was using a legacy on-premise reporting application for its catalog operations. (The company also has 520 retail outlets and e-commerce operations.) Yet the reporting features built into the system were "extremely poor," as Hernreich describes them: "Visibility to the business? Terrible. Real-time information? Doesn't exist. How are we doing with certain styles by size? Don't know."

"It was unacceptable," Hernreich says. In addition, you could only view those "canned" reports (which lacked features such as exception reporting) by making a trip to the printer for a stack of printouts. "It was hundreds of pages," he recalls. "That's just not how you operate today."

It's not as though Casual Male didn't have all this information; it just didn't have an intuitive and easy way to see the sales and inventory trends for its catalog business in real time. That changed in 2004, when Casual Male began to use a on-demand BI tool from vendor Oco (www.oco-inc.com), which takes all of Casual Male's data, builds and maintains a data warehouse for it off-site, and creates "responsive, real-time reporting dashboards that give us and our business users information at their fingertips," Hernreich says.

Today, Hernreich and Casual Male's merchandise planners and buyers have access to easy-to-consume dashboards full of catalog data: "What styles are selling today? How much inventory are we selling today? Where are we short? Where do we need to order? How are we selling by size? What are we out of stock in?" he says. "All of these basic questions, in terms of running the business—that's what we're learning every day from these reports."

Best of all, those annoying trips to the printer have ended.

Source: Adapted from Thomas Wailgum, "Business Intelligence and On-Demand: The Perfect Marriage?" *CIO Magazine*, March 27, 2008.

Data Mining for Decision Support

We discussed data mining and data warehouses in Chapter 5 as vital tools for organizing and exploiting the data resources of a company. Thus, data mining's main purpose is to provide decision support to managers and business professionals through a process referred to as *knowledge discovery*. Data mining software analyzes the vast stores of historical business data that have been prepared for analysis in corporate data warehouses and tries to discover patterns, trends, and correlations hidden in the data that can help a company improve its business performance.

Data mining software may perform regression, decision tree, neural network, cluster detection, or market basket analysis for a business. See Figure 10.18. The data mining process can highlight buying patterns, reveal customer tendencies, cut redundant costs, or uncover unseen profitable relationships and opportunities. For example, many companies use data mining to find more profitable ways to perform successful direct mailings, including e-mailings, or discover better ways to display products in a store,

FIGURE 10.18

Data mining software helps discover patterns in business data, like this analysis of customer demographic information.

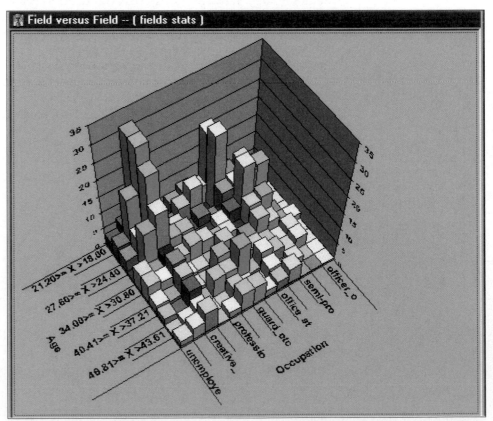

Source: Courtesy of XpertRule Software.

design a better e-commerce Web site, reach untapped profitable customers, or recognize customers or products that are unprofitable or marginal.

Market basket analysis (MBA) is one of the most common and useful types of data mining for marketing and is a key technique in business analytics. The purpose of market basket analysis is to determine which products customers purchase together with other products. MBA takes its name from the concept of customers throwing all of their purchases into a shopping cart (a market basket) during grocery shopping. It can be very helpful for a retailer or any other company to know which products people purchase as a group. A store could use this information to place products frequently sold together into the same area, and a catalog or World Wide Web merchant could use it to determine the layouts of a catalog and order form. Direct marketers could use the basket analysis results to determine which new products to offer their prior customers.

In some cases, the fact that items are sold together is obvious; every fast-food restaurant asks its customers "Would you like fries with that?" whenever a customer orders a sandwich. Sometimes, however, the fact that certain items would be sold together is far from obvious. A well-known example is the relationship between beer and diapers. A supermarket performing a basket analysis discovered that diapers and beer sell well together on Thursdays. Although the result makes some sense—couples stock up on supplies for themselves and for their children before the weekend starts— it's far from intuitive. The strength of market basket analysis is as follows: By using computer data mining tools, it's not necessary for a person to think of which products consumers would logically buy together; instead, the customers' sales data speak for themselves. This is a good example of data-driven marketing.

Consider some of the typical applications of MBA:

- **Cross Selling.** Offer the associated items when customer buys any items from your store.

- **Product Placement.** Items that are associated (such as bread and butter, tissues and cold medicine, potato chips and beer) can be put near each other. If the customers see them, it has higher probability that they will purchase them together.

- **Affinity Promotion.** Design the promotional events based on associated products.

- **Survey Analysis.** The fact that both independent and dependent variables of market basket analysis are nominal (categorical) data type makes MBA very useful to analyze questionnaire data.

- **Fraud Detection.** Based on credit card usage data, we may be able to detect certain purchase behaviors that can be associated with fraud.

- **Customer Behavior.** Associating purchase with demographic, and socioeconomic data (such as age, gender, and preference) may produce very useful results for marketing.

Once it is known that customers who buy one product are likely to buy another, it is possible for a company to market the products together or make the purchasers of one product target prospects for another. If customers who purchase diapers are already likely to purchase beer, they'll be even more likely to buy beer if there happens to be a beer display just outside the diaper aisle. Likewise, if it's known that customers who buy a sweater from a certain mail-order catalog have a propensity toward buying a jacket from the same catalog, sales of jackets can be increased by having the telephone representatives describe and offer the jacket to anyone who calls in to order the sweater. By targeting customers who are already known to be likely buyers, the effectiveness of a given marketing effort is significantly increased—regardless of whether the marketing takes the form of in-store displays, catalog layout design, or direct offers to customers.

Boston Celtics: Using Data Analytics to Price Tickets

Boston Celtics executives are taking advantage of a data analytics tool in their annual January task of setting prices for the 18,600 seats in TD Banknorth Garden. The NBA team installed the StratBridge.net tool from StratBridge Inc. to monitor consumer demand through real-time displays of sold and available seats in its home arena. Now team officials are also using the tool during the month-long project to set base ticket prices for the next season.

The new tool has helped the organization quickly develop promotions and sales strategies to fill available seats and to analyze revenue based on long-term sales trends, says Daryl Morey, senior vice president of operations and information for the Celtics. "Until we had this tool, it was very difficult to create dynamic packages because our ticket providers didn't have a rapid way to see which seats were open," Morey says. "Now we can actually see in real time every single seat and how much it is sold for."

The basketball team has already seen a "seven figure" return on investment fueled by five-figure revenue boosts every one to two weeks since it began to use StratBridge.net in 2006, according to Morey. Before using data analytics, sales executives used Excel spreadsheets to adjust pricing. In that system, pricing could be adjusted only for all the seats within each of 12 large sections in the arena. "It was a leap of faith looking at the data at that level," says Morey.

Using the analytics tool, for example, planners found that ticket buyers tended to favor aisle seating in certain sections; as a result, the team now focuses on marketing the inner seats. Now, in the ticket office, group- and individual-ticket sellers can see an image of the arena seating chart on a plasma TV screen with different color blocks indicating real-time availability and revenue for home games. Sales executives can access this information from their desktops to study buying trends and design new promotions.

StratBridge.net extracts data from internal and external sources and displays it visually in Internet browsers and Microsoft Office applications. The analysis can be presented to users in Word, Excel, PowerPoint, and Adobe PDF files. Bill Hostmann, an analyst at Gartner Inc., said companies trying to market "perishable" products like basketball games, hotel rooms, or live television broadcasts are beginning to turn to this type of data analysis, which was first perfected in the airline industry. "You're seeing more and more of this kind of analytical functionality being embedded in the application itself as a part of the process, as opposed to being done on a quarterly or weekly basis," Hostmann said. "The ROI is very fast on these types of applications."

Source: Adapted from Heather Havenstein, "Celtics Turn to Data Analytics Tool for Help Pricing Tickets," *Computerworld*, January 6, 2006.

Executive Information Systems

Executive information systems (EIS) are information systems that combine many of the features of management information systems and decision support systems. When they were first developed, their focus was on meeting the strategic information needs of top management. Thus, the first goal of executive information systems was to provide top executives with immediate and easy access to information about a firm's *critical success factors* (CSFs), that is, key factors that are critical to accomplishing an organization's strategic objectives. For example, the executives of a retail store chain would probably consider factors such as its e-commerce versus traditional sales results or its product line mix to be critical to its survival and success.

Yet managers, analysts, and other knowledge workers use executive information systems so widely that they are sometimes humorously called "everyone's information systems." More popular alternative names are enterprise information systems (EIS) and executive support systems (ESS). These names also reflect the fact that more features, such as Web browsing, e-mail, groupware tools, and DSS and expert system capabilities, are being added to many systems to make them more useful to managers and business professionals.

Features of an EIS

In an EIS, information is presented in forms tailored to the preferences of the executives using the system. For example, most executive information systems emphasize the use of a graphical user interface, as well as graphics displays that can be customized to

FIGURE 10.19

This Web-based executive information system provides managers and business professionals with a variety of personalized information and analytical tools for decision support.

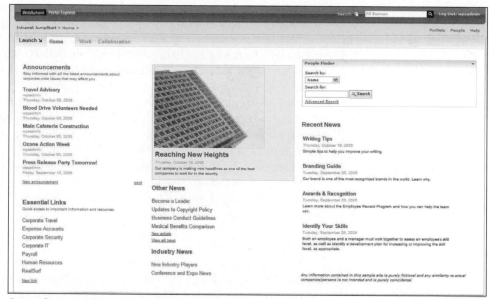

Source: Courtesy of International Business Machines Corporation.

the information preferences of executives using the EIS. Other information presentation methods used by an EIS include exception reporting and trend analysis. The ability to *drill down*, which allows executives to retrieve displays of related information quickly at lower levels of detail, is another important capability.

Figure 10.19 shows one of the displays provided by the Web-enabled Hyperion executive information system. Notice that this display is simple and brief, and note how it provides users of the system with the ability to drill down quickly to lower levels of detail in areas of particular interest to them. In addition to the drill-down capability, the Hyperion EIS emphasizes trend analysis and exception reporting. Thus, a business user can quickly discover the direction in which key factors are heading and the extent to which critical factors are deviating from expected results.

Executive information systems have spread into the ranks of middle management and business professionals as their feasibility and benefits have been recognized and as less expensive systems for client/server networks and corporate intranets became available. For example, one popular EIS software package reports that only 3 percent of its users are top executives.

PureSense and Farming: Watering Plans Based on Minute-by-Minute Data	Derk VanKonynenburg used to think the information he got from measuring the soil moisture every 15 minutes on his 1,500-acre fruit and almond orchard was as precise as he could possibly need. He gets the data from probes that measure moisture in the soil and send readings over a wireless link to a collection station. From there, it's relayed to a data center, and VanKonynenburg accesses the data online from a PC, helping him decide when and how much to water the trees.

Once VanKonynenburg and his partners got accustomed to the feed, however, they wanted even more data, and they wanted it better. "We decided we needed a measurement every minute," he says.

That's right. On this one midsize farm around Modesto, California, a farmer is measuring the soil moisture every single minute of the day to make irrigation decisions.

Understand that VanKonynenburg isn't looking at that moisture count minute-by-minute like a stock ticker, waiting to hit the water switch. He looks about once a day to create an irrigation plan. But because the farm irrigates in bursts—say, seven minutes on and 14 minutes off—collecting readings every 15 minutes wasn't accurate enough. With better understanding of moisture needs, "We think it may allow us to lower our water use another 10 percent," says VanKonynenburg, "and 10 percent is a huge number."

PureSense was founded by a team of technologists and farmers determined to give farmers a better sense of what's going on in the ground on their farms, beyond just giving them weather data and related calculations. Farmers have been "running blind for years," says John Williamson, cofounder and chief operating officer of PureSense, which says it has about 200 customers, mostly in California.

VanKonynenburg is also looking for more uses for the data he's collecting on soil moisture, temperature, and sunshine. He'd like to use the dashboard he gets from PureSense, which is focused on irrigation decisions, to determine risks for certain pests, fungus, and bacteria to determine the best time to spray for them. Like any busy executive, he wants one decision-making dashboard.

Irrigation, like most elements of farming, won't become automated. Soil moisture provides insight into what's happening in the fields and allows more informed decisions, but there are still critical judgments to be made. "You need data and then you need smart people with enough experience to interpret that," VanKonynenburg says. "A lot of those decisions are subjective."

Although he could access his moisture sensor data on an iPhone, he laughs off the idea. "I'm 69 years old," he says, adding that checking data once a day on the computer is fine. Then, a moment later, VanKonynenburg can't help but confess: "I suspect that a year from now, I will be carrying one."

Source: Adapted from Chris Murphy, "Make Every Drop Count," *InformationWeek*, November 16, 2009.

Enterprise Portals and Decision Support

Don't confuse portals with the executive information systems that have been used in some industries for many years. Portals are for everyone in the company, and not just for executives. You want people on the front lines making decisions using browsers and portals rather than just executives using specialized executive information system software.

We mentioned previously in this chapter that major changes and expansions are taking place in traditional MIS, DSS, and EIS tools for providing the information and modeling managers need to support their decision making. Decision support in business is changing, driven by rapid developments in end-user computing and networking; Internet and Web technologies; and Web-enabled business applications. One of the key changes taking place in management information and decision support systems in business is the rapid growth of enterprise information portals.

Enterprise Information Portals

A user checks his e-mail, looks up the current company stock price, checks his available vacation days, and receives an order from a customer—all from the browser on his desktop. That is the next-generation intranet, also known as a corporate or enterprise information portal. With it, the browser becomes the dashboard to daily business tasks.

An enterprise information portal (EIP) is a Web-based interface and integration of MIS, DSS, EIS, and other technologies that give all intranet users and selected extranet users access to a variety of internal and external business applications and services. For example, internal applications might include access to e-mail, project Web sites, and discussion groups; human resources Web self-services; customer, inventory, and other corporate databases; decision support systems; and knowledge management systems. External applications might include industry, financial, and other Internet news services; links to industry discussion groups; and links to customer and supplier Internet and extranet Web sites. Enterprise information portals are typically tailored or personalized to the needs of individual business users or groups of users, giving them a personalized *digital dashboard* of information sources and applications. See Figure 10.20.

The business benefits of enterprise information portals include providing more specific and selective information to business users, providing easy access to key corporate intranet Web site resources, delivering industry and business news, and providing better access to company data for selected customers, suppliers, or business partners. Enterprise information portals can also help avoid excessive surfing by employees across company

FIGURE 10.20

An enterprise information portal can provide a business professional with a personalized workplace of information sources, administrative and analytical tools, and relevant business applications.

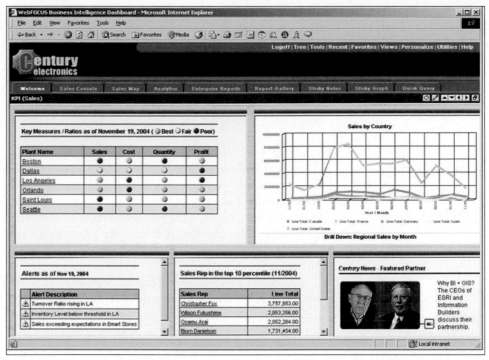

Source: Courtesy of Information Builders.

and Internet Web sites by making it easier for them to receive or find the information and services they need, thus improving the productivity of a company's workforce.

Figure 10.21 illustrates how companies are developing enterprise information portals as a way to provide Web-enabled information, knowledge, and decision

FIGURE 10.21

The components of this enterprise information portal identify it as a Web-enabled decision support system that can be personalized for executives, managers, employees, suppliers, customers, and other business partners.

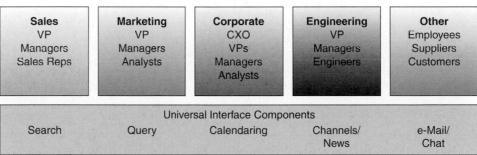

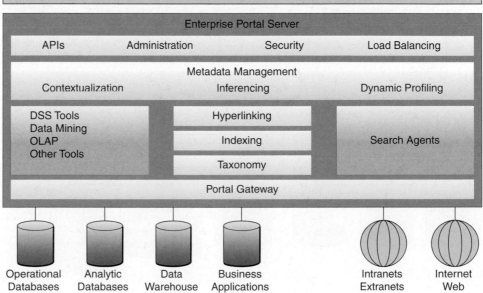

support to their executives, managers, employees, suppliers, customers, and other business partners. The enterprise information portal is a customized and personalized Web-based interface for corporate intranets, which gives users easy access to a variety of internal and external business applications, databases, and services. For example, the EIP in Figure 10.20 might give a qualified user secure access to DSS, data mining, and OLAP tools; the Internet and the Web; the corporate intranet; supplier or customer extranets; operational and analytical databases; a data warehouse; and a variety of business applications.

Knowledge Management Systems

We introduced knowledge management systems in Chapter 2 as the use of information technology to help gather, organize, and share business knowledge within an organization. In many organizations, hypermedia databases at corporate intranet Web sites have become the *knowledge bases* for storage and dissemination of business knowledge. This knowledge frequently takes the form of best practices, policies, and business solutions at the project, team, business unit, and enterprise levels of the company.

For many companies, enterprise information portals are the entry to corporate intranets that serve as their knowledge management systems. That's why such portals are called enterprise knowledge portals by their vendors. Thus, enterprise knowledge portals play an essential role in helping companies use their intranets as knowledge management systems to share and disseminate knowledge in support of business decision making by managers and business professionals. See Figure 10.22. Now let's look at an example of a knowledge management system in business.

FIGURE 10.22 This example of the capabilities and components of an enterprise knowledge portal emphasizes its use as a Web-based knowledge management system.

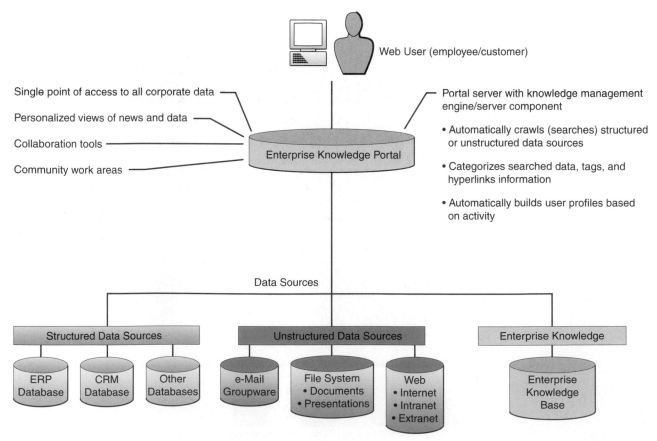

You Might Have to Torture the Data to Learn

Although an enterprise resource planning (ERP) system is great for integrating data across a large organization, this type of software is not well suited for producing predictive analytics, said a SAS data expert at a recent lecture at the Richard Ivey School of Business in Toronto.

As the amount of data produced by businesses has expanded, the traditional response has been to produce more reports. But according to Mark Moorman, data expert and advisor to Office of the CTO at the US-based SAS Institute, there "is way too much data and not enough information about that data."

Reports tend to conceal important factors like economics, geography, and meteorology, he said. But predictive analytics (along with an assessment of how accurate it is) can add needed value to an organization and help it make better business decisions. Furthermore, not everyone within an organization wants to be made into an analyst by having to go through a plethora of reports that an ERP system produces, said Moorman. "What they really want is the answer."

But before a business can begin to reap the benefits of predictive analytics, some buy-in may be required. Getting commitment from the executive level could be a challenge, especially if the organization has always based decisions on intuition, said Moorman.

But the IT department could be another hurdle considering the tradition of controlling, managing, and keeping data intact and "now we are asking them to be a little more free, and be a little more loose, and allow us to torture that data a little." Once IT and business are merged, "you'll get a more streamlined understanding of what technology can do and the business applications you can apply them to," said Moorman.

The other speaker at the lecture was Ian Ayres, Yale professor and author of Super Crunchers: Why Thinking-By-Numbers is the New Way to be Smart. Super crunching, explained Ayres, is performing analytics on large amounts of data sets and "is data-driven decision making, it's having impact on decisions with the speed and scale we haven't seen before".

Techniques—regression and randomization—used in super crunching have been used for decades, said Ayres. The former is the mining of historical data to make predictions. The latter approach is data mined from observing groups impacted by different variables as in medical research when a drug is administered to one group and a placebo to another. Ayres thinks that e-commerce businesses not engaged in these tools are "really making a big mistake."

But accepting super crunching as a business tool may not be simple. Regression analysis is little understood and "ends up being trust me statistics." Randomization trials, on the other hand, have transparency and therefore garner more trust. "One of the ways to get organizations moving toward becoming super crunching predictive analytics organizations is to use randomized trials as a starter drug," said Ayres.

Although ERP systems can solve many problems, they are historical databases with little ability to formulate predictions on the data. The issue is they have been erroneously marketed and sold "as a panacea, a silver bullet," said Moorman.

But the use of predictive analytics is probably more conducive to some industries than others. Financial services have been using predictive analytics because that is the nature of their business, said Moorman. But "laggards," like many retailers, are no longer perceiving themselves as merely "dollar-based" transactional businesses, and are increasingly turning to super crunching techniques.

Super crunching, said Ayres, doesn't mean the death of intuition in the business. "But increasingly the best decision makers have to be willing to put their intuitions to the test."

Source: Adapted from Kathleen Lau, "Why You Might Need to Torture Data," *Computerworld* Hong Kong, Questex Media, July 8, 2008.

SECTION II Artificial Intelligence Technologies in Business

Business and AI

Artificial intelligence (AI) technologies are being used in a variety of ways to improve the decision support provided to managers and business professionals in many companies. See Figure 10.23. For example:

> *AI-enabled applications are at work in information distribution and retrieval, database mining, product design, manufacturing, inspection, training, user support, surgical planning, resource scheduling, and complex resource management.*
>
> *Indeed, for anyone who schedules, plans, allocates resources, designs new products, uses the Internet, develops software, is responsible for product quality, is an investment professional, heads up IT, uses IT, or operates in any of a score of other capacities and arenas, AI technologies already may be in place and providing competitive advantage.*

Read the Real World Case on the next page. We can learn a lot about innovative uses of virtual reality in business from this example.

An Overview of Artificial Intelligence

What is artificial intelligence? Artificial intelligence (AI) is a field of science and technology based on disciplines such as computer science, biology, psychology, linguistics, mathematics, and engineering. The goal of AI is to develop computers that can simulate the ability to think, as well as see, hear, walk, talk, and feel. A major thrust of artificial intelligence is the simulation of computer functions normally associated with human intelligence, such as reasoning, learning, and problem solving, as summarized in Figure 10.24.

Debate has raged about artificial intelligence since serious work in the field began in the 1950s. Technological, moral, and philosophical questions about the possibility of intelligent, thinking machines are numerous. For example, British AI pioneer Alan Turing in 1950 proposed a test to determine whether machines could think. According to the Turing test, a computer could demonstrate intelligence if a human interviewer, conversing with an unseen human and an unseen computer, could not tell which was which. Although much work has been done in many of the subgroups that fall under the AI umbrella, critics believe that no computer can truly pass the Turing test. They claim that it is just not possible to develop intelligence to impart true humanlike capabilities to computers, but progress continues. Only time will tell whether we will achieve the ambitious goals of artificial intelligence and equal the popular images found in science fiction.

One derivative of the Turing test that is providing real value to the online community is a CAPTCHA. A **CAPTCHA** (Completely Automated Public Turing test to tell Computers and Humans Apart) is a type of challenge-response test used in a wide variety of computing applications to determine that the user is really a human and not a computer posing as one. A CAPTCHA is sometimes described as a reverse Turing test because it is administered by a machine and targeted to a human, in contrast to the standard Turing test that is typically administered by a human and targeted to a machine. The process involves one computer (such as a server for a retail Web site) asking a user to complete a simple test that the computer is able to generate and grade. Because other computers are unable to solve the CAPTCHA, any user entering a correct solution is presumed to be human. A common type of CAPTCHA requires that the user type the letters of a distorted image, sometimes with the addition of an obscured sequence of letters or digits that appears on the screen. No doubt you have seen this when registering for a new account with a merchant or checking out from an online purchase. Figure 10.25 shows several common examples of CAPTCHA patterns.

REAL WORLD
CASE 2

Kimberly-Clark Corp.: Shopping for Virtual Products in Virtual Stores

Using a new tool developed by Kimberly-Clark Corp., a woman stood surrounded by three screens showing a store aisle, a retina-tracking device recording her every glance. At Kimberly-Clark, innovation doesn't stop with developing more-absorbent diapers or stronger paper towels. The consumer-goods maker also is using IT to help retailers market and sell products—and not just the ones made by Kimberly-Clark.

Virtual reality technology has found its footing in many industries and applications, including health care, automotive, and aerospace. Now, consumer goods manufacturer Kimberly-Clark has incorporated proprietary virtual reality technology into its new Innovation Design Studio, and it expects big payback from its technological leap.

Asked by a Kimberly-Clark researcher to find a big box of Huggies Natural Fit diapers in size three, the woman pushed forward on a handle like that of a shopping cart, and the video simulated her progress down the aisle. Spotting the distinctive red packages of Huggies, she turned the handle to the right to face a dizzying array of diapers. After pushing a button to get a kneeling view of the shelves, she reached forward and tapped the screen to put the box she wanted in her virtual cart.

Kimberly-Clark hopes these virtual shopping aisles will help it better understand consumer behavior and make the testing of new products faster, more convenient, and more precise.

The mobile testing unit is usually based in a new high-tech studio that Kimberly-Clark completed in the basement of a nondescript office building in Appleton, Wisconsin. The cavernous room also features a U-shaped floor-to-ceiling screen that re-creates in vivid detail interiors of the big retailers that sell the company's products—a tool that the company will use in presentations to executives in bids to win shelf space. A separate area is reserved for real replicas of store interiors, which can be customized to match the flooring, light fixtures, and shelves of retailers such as Target Corp. and Walmart Stores Inc.

As the fragmented television market raises doubts about the effectiveness of traditional ads and competition for shelf space increases, manufacturers and retailers are intensifying their focus on ways to get consumers' attention while they are in the store.

The efforts go well beyond the usual cardboard displays and sample handouts. A group including manufacturers Procter & Gamble Co., Coca-Cola Co., and General Mills Inc., and retailers Kroger Co. and Walmart announced the results of a test that tracked shoppers' movement in stores using a combination of infrared beams and human observation.

Nielsen Co. plans to syndicate such data and sell it to clients, much as it does with television ratings.

"By engaging ourselves and our customers in this virtual world, we can spark better ideas to improve the shopping experience and collaborate on new product concepts and innovations," says Ramin Elvaz, Kimberly-Clark vice president of North Atlantic Insight, Strategy and Growth.

Kimberly-Clark says its studio allows researchers and designers to get a fast read on new product designs and displays without having to stage real-life tests in the early stages of development. Doing the research in a windowless basement, rather than an actual test market, also avoids tipping off competitors early in the development process.

"We're trying to test ideas faster, cheaper, and better," says Ramin Eivaz, a vice president at Kimberly-Clark focusing on strategy.

Before, new product testing typically took eight months to two years. Now, that time is cut in half, he says. Projects that test well with the virtual-reality tools will be fast-tracked to real-store trials, Mr. Eivaz says.

Once product design options have been determined, Kimberly-Clark brings retail executives into the studio so they can see how the new product would actually look on the shelf and fit in with the existing assortment—an important factor in decisions the retailers make on space.

The company declined to reveal how much it spent to build the Appleton studio. "We made a significant investment in the studio and expect it will yield a positive return with our customers in the future," a spokesman says.

The battle for shelf space is accelerating as consumer-products companies have introduced more and more new products. Meanwhile, retailers are churning out more of their own private-label products. The rate of new-product launches has grown steadily since 2000, with more than 40,000 new packaged-goods introductions in 2007, says Tom

FIGURE 10.23

Virtual reality technologies enable companies to develop and test new products without actually making them.

Source: © Toru Hanai/Reuters/Landov.

Vierhile, director of Productscan Online, market research firm Datamonitor's database of new products.

However, Kimberly-Clark is particularly enthusiastic about how the design center can help its retail partners improve their in-store designs and merchandising. For example, using the virtual reality technology and K-C SmartStation, the manufacturer can create store models, allowing retailers to envision hypothetical store designs and merchandising concepts. Likewise, eye-tracking technology in the high-tech kiosk allows the study of consumers' reactions in simulated shopping settings to determine how different environments or packaging affect buying decisions.

Inside the center's virtual reality theater, visitors are surrounded by screens on which rear-projection equipment displays virtual images powered by applications running on eight Hewlett-Packard high-end rack-mount PCs. The system's 3-D capabilities were developed with RedDotSquare. Sensors embedded in the walls, ceilings, and floor detect the visitors' movements, track their locations, and can even tell exactly what they're looking at, says Kurt Schweitzer, director, IT business partner for marketing, strategy, and innovation. This allows the system to further immerse visitors by making things happen around them, such as opening a door near where they're standing or changing their perspective on what's going on, he says.

The center lets store managers use "multiple senses and not just visualization" to assess product display effectiveness, Schweitzer says. The front screen of the immersion center is more than 20 feet wide and is flanked by two side screens that rest at 45-degree angles, creating a wraparound effect.

The wings can move inward to 90-degree angles, forming a three-sided box. "When you step into that 8-foot-high physical space, the word immersive takes on a whole new meaning," Schweitzer says.

To sell retailers on new products, manufacturers are revealing more about their product pipelines to drum up interest early on. Over the past several months, Kimberly-Clark says it has brought in executives from major chains, including Target, Walmart and Kroger, to see the Appleton facility. Kimberly-Clark uses the data from its virtual-reality tests with consumers to tout how products in development perform.

"It no longer works to show up on a retailer's doorstep with your new product and say, 'Isn't this pretty?'" Mr. Eivaz

says. "We need to be an indispensable partner to our retailers and show we can do more for them."

When grocery chain Safeway Inc. asked its major manufacturers for display suggestions to lift traffic through its center aisles in late 2005, Kimberly-Clark used an early version of the virtual-reality modeling technology it was developing for the new studio to pitch for more room for its Huggies diapers and other baby products. The company created three-dimensional models of a store display that resembled a nursery, complete with a giant, colorful bathtub.

The company had consumers navigate the store virtually, testing how easily they could find certain items in the area.

"We hadn't seen that type of technology applied to that type of traditional merchandising and store decor before," says Michael Minasi, Safeway's president of marketing. When it tested the display inside its stores, sales of items in that section increased. Nevertheless, in the end, reality set limits. "Some of the decor and decoration components were easier to do virtually than they were to do in the real world, mostly from a cost and implementation standpoint," Minasi says. However, a version of Kimberly-Clark's concept was put in place at a handful of Safeway stores.

In the store-model section of its new studio, Kimberly-Clark goes to elaborate lengths with its re-creations aimed to impress retail executives. Once, the company readied the studio for visitors from Target. The store's branded shopping carts were lined up at the doorway, next to a stand holding recent Target sales fliers and a faux ATM. Standing behind a pharmacy counter was a Kimberly-Clark employee outfitted in a lab coat with a Target logo. Target's standard white tiles covered the floor, its beige light fixtures hung above, and Target store shelves were fully stocked with diapers and other baby products made by Kimberly-Clark and its competitors.

"What if you just spent a lot of money on a package's shade of red but it doesn't look good in their store?" says Don Quigley, president of Kimberly-Clark's consumer sales and customer development, North America. "This is where you can spot that, before you ship a single case of product."

Source: Adapted from Ellen Byron, "A Virtual View of the Store Aisle," *Wall Street Journal*, October 3, 2007; Jill Jusko, "Kimberly-Clark Embraces Virtual Reality," *IndustryWeek*, December 1, 2007; and Marianne Kolbasuk McGee, "InformationWeek 500: Kimberly-Clark's Virtual Product Demo Center Yields Real Ideas on How to Sell More Products," *InformationWeek*, September 17, 2007.

CASE STUDY QUESTIONS

1. What are the business benefits derived from the technology implementation described in the case? Also discuss benefits other than those explicitly mentioned in the case.

2. Are virtual stores like this one just an incremental innovation on the way marketing tests new product designs? Or do they have the potential to radically reinvent the way these companies work? Explain your reasons.

3. What other industries could benefit from deployments of virtual reality like the one discussed in the case? Leaving aside the cost of the technology, what new products or services could you envision within those industries? Provide several examples.

REAL WORLD ACTIVITIES

1. What is the current cutting-edge technology in virtual reality, and how are companies using it? Go online to research this topic and prepare a presentation to share your work.

2. With technologies like these, will consumers entirely do away with retailers sometime in the future, shopping only through virtual representations of a retail store? Will consumers even want it to look like a retail store? Break into small groups to propose arguments for and against these questions.

FIGURE 10.24

Some of the attributes of intelligent behavior. AI is attempting to duplicate these capabilities in computer-based systems.

Attributes of Intelligent Behavior
● Think and reason.
● Use reason to solve problems.
● Learn or understand from experience.
● Acquire and apply knowledge.
● Exhibit creativity and imagination.
● Deal with complex or perplexing situations.
● Respond quickly and successfully to new situations.
● Recognize the relative importance of elements in a situation.
● Handle ambiguous, incomplete, or erroneous information.

The Domains of Artificial Intelligence

Figure 10.26 illustrates the major **domains** of AI research and development. Note that AI **applications** can be grouped under three major areas—cognitive science, robotics, and natural interfaces—though these classifications do overlap, and other classifications can be used. Also note that expert systems are just one of many important AI applications. Let's briefly review each of these major areas of AI and some of their current technologies. Figure 10.27 outlines some of the latest developments in commercial applications of artificial intelligence.

Cognitive Science. This area of artificial intelligence is based on research in biology, neurology, psychology, mathematics, and many allied disciplines. It focuses on researching how the human brain works and how humans think and learn. The results of such research in *human information processing* are the basis for the development of a variety of computer-based applications in artificial intelligence.

Applications in the cognitive science area of AI include the development of *expert systems* and other *knowledge-based systems* that add a knowledge base and some reasoning capability to information systems. Also included are *adaptive learning systems* that can modify their behaviors on the basis of information they acquire as they operate. Chess-playing systems are primitive examples of such applications, though many more applications are being implemented. *Fuzzy logic* systems can process data that are incomplete or ambiguous, that is, *fuzzy data*. Thus, they can solve semistructured

FIGURE 10.25

Examples of typical CAPTCHA patterns that can be easily solved by humans but prove difficult to detect by a computer.

FIGURE 10.26
The major application areas of artificial intelligence. Note that the many applications of AI can be grouped into the three major areas of cognitive science, robotics, and natural interfaces.

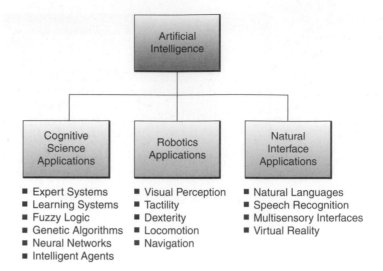

problems with incomplete knowledge by developing approximate inferences and answers, as humans do. *Neural network* software can learn by processing sample problems and their solutions. As neural nets start to recognize patterns, they can begin to program themselves to solve such problems on their own. *Genetic algorithm* software uses Darwinian (survival of the fittest), randomizing, and other mathematics functions

FIGURE 10.27
Examples of some of the latest commercial applications of AI.

Commercial Applications of AI

Decision Support

- Intelligent work environment that will help you capture the *why* as well as the *what* of engineered design and decision making.

- Intelligent human–computer interface (HCI) systems that can understand spoken language and gestures, and facilitate problem solving by supporting organizationwide collaborations to solve particular problems.

- Situation assessment and resource allocation software for uses that range from airlines and airports to logistics centers.

Information Retrieval

- AI-based intranet and Internet systems that distill tidal waves of information into simple presentations.

- Natural language technology to retrieve any sort of online information, from text to pictures, videos, maps, and audio clips, in response to English questions.

- Database mining for marketing trend analysis, financial forecasting, maintenance cost reduction, and more.

Virtual Reality

- X-ray–like vision enabled by enhanced-reality visualization that allows brain surgeons to "see through" intervening tissue to operate, monitor, and evaluate disease progression.

- Automated animation interfaces that allow users to interact with virtual objects via touch (e.g., medical students can "feel" what it's like to suture severed aortas).

Robotics

- Machine-vision inspections systems for gauging, guiding, identifying, and inspecting products and providing competitive advantage in manufacturing.

- Cutting-edge robotics systems, from microrobots and hands and legs to cognitive robotic and trainable modular vision systems.

to simulate evolutionary processes that can generate increasingly better solutions to problems. In addition, *intelligent agents* use expert system and other AI technologies to serve as software surrogates for a variety of end-user applications.

Robotics. AI, engineering, and physiology are the basic disciplines of robotics. This technology produces robot machines with computer intelligence and computer-controlled, humanlike physical capabilities. This area thus includes applications designed to give robots the powers of sight, or visual perception; touch, or tactile capabilities; dexterity, or skill in handling and manipulation; locomotion, or the physical ability to move over any terrain; and navigation, or the intelligence to find one's way to a destination.

Natural Interfaces. The development of natural interfaces is considered a major area of AI applications and is essential to the natural use of computers by humans. For example, the development of *natural languages* and speech recognition are major thrusts of this area of AI. Being able to talk to computers and robots in conversational human languages and have them "understand" us as easily as we understand each other is a goal of AI research. This goal involves research and development in linguistics, psychology, computer science, and other disciplines. Other natural interface research applications include the development of multisensory devices that use a variety of body movements to operate computers, which is related to the emerging application area of *virtual reality*. Virtual reality involves using multisensory human–computer interfaces that enable human users to experience computer-simulated objects, spaces, activities, and "worlds" as if they actually exist. Now, let's look at some examples of how AI is becoming increasingly more relevant in the business world.

| Artificial Intelligence Gets Down to Business | Today, AI systems can perform useful work in "a very large and complex world," says Eric Horvitz, an AI researcher at Microsoft Research (MSR). "Because these small software agents don't have a complete representation of the world, they are uncertain about their actions. So they learn to understand the probabilities of various things happening, they learn the preferences of users and costs of outcomes and, perhaps most important, they are becoming self-aware."

These abilities derive from something called machine learning, which is at the heart of many modern AI applications. In essence, a programmer starts with a crude model of the problem he's trying to solve but builds in the ability for the software to adapt and improve with experience.

Speech recognition software gets better as it learns the nuances of your voice, for example, and over time Amazon.com more accurately predicts your preferences as you shop online. Machine learning is enabled by clever algorithms, of course, but what has driven it to prominence in recent years is the availability of huge amounts of data, both from the Internet and, more recently, from a proliferation of physical sensors.

For instance, Microsoft Research has combined sensors, machine learning, and analysis of human behavior in a road traffic prediction model. Predicting traffic bottlenecks would seem to be an obvious and not very difficult application of sensors and computer forecasting. But MSR realized that most drivers hardly need to be warned that the interstate heading out of town will be jammed at 5 p.m. on Monday. What they really need to know is where and when anomalies, or "surprises," are occurring and, perhaps more important, where they will occur. So MSR built a "surprise forecasting" model that learns from traffic history to predict surprises 30 minutes in advance based on actual traffic flows captured by sensors. In tests, it has been able to predict about 50 percent of the surprises on roads in the Seattle area, and it is in use now by several thousand drivers who receive alerts on their Windows Mobile devices.

Few organizations need to make sense of as much data as do search engine companies. For example, if a user searches Google for "toy car" and then clicks on a Walmart ad that appears at the top of the results, what's that worth to Walmart, and how much should Google charge for that click? The answers lie in an AI specialty that employs "digital trading agents," which companies like Walmart and Google use in automated online auctions.

Michael Wellman, a University of Michigan professor and an expert in these markets, explains: "There are millions of keywords, and one advertiser may be interested in hundreds or thousands of them. They have to monitor the prices of the keywords and decide how to allocate their budget, and it's too hard for Google or Yahoo to figure out what a certain keyword is worth. They let the market decide that through an auction process."

When the "toy car" query is submitted, in a fraction of a second Google looks up which advertisers are interested in those keywords, then looks at their bids and decides whose ads to display and where to put them on the page. "The problem I'm especially interested in," Wellman says, "is how should an advertiser decide which keywords to bid on, how much to bid and how to learn over time—based on how effective their ads are—how much competition there is for each keyword."

Source: Adapted from Gary Anthes, "Future Watch: A.I. Comes of Age," *Computerworld*, January 26, 2009.

Expert Systems

One of the most practical and widely implemented applications of artificial intelligence in business is the development of expert systems and other knowledge-based information systems. A knowledge-based information system (KBIS) adds a knowledge base to the major components found in other types of computer-based information systems. An **expert system (ES)** is a knowledge-based information system that uses its knowledge about a specific, complex application area to act as an expert consultant to end users. Expert systems provide answers to questions in a very specific problem area by making humanlike inferences about knowledge contained in a specialized knowledge base. They must also be able to explain their reasoning process and conclusions to a user, so expert systems can provide decision support to end users in the form of advice from an expert consultant in a specific problem area.

Components of an Expert System

The components of an expert system include a knowledge base and software modules that perform inferences on the knowledge in the knowledge base and communicate answers to a user's questions. Figure 10.28 illustrates the interrelated components of an expert system. Note the following components:

FIGURE 10.28
A summary of four ways that knowledge can be represented in an expert system's knowledge base.

Methods of Knowledge Representation
● **Case-Based Reasoning.** Representing knowledge in an expert system's knowledge base in the form of cases, that is, examples of past performance, occurrences, and experiences.
● **Frame-Based Knowledge.** Knowledge represented in the form of a hierarchy or network of *frames*. A frame is a collection of knowledge about an entity consisting of a complex package of data values describing its attributes.
● **Object-Based Knowledge.** Knowledge represented as a network of objects. An object is a data element that includes both data and the methods or processes that act on those data.
● **Rule-Based Knowledge.** Knowledge represented in the form of rules and statements of fact. Rules are statements that typically take the form of a premise and a conclusion, such as If (condition), Then (conclusion).

FIGURE 10.29 Components of an expert system. The software modules perform inferences on a knowledge base built by an expert and/or knowledge engineer. This provides expert answers to an end user's questions in an interactive process.

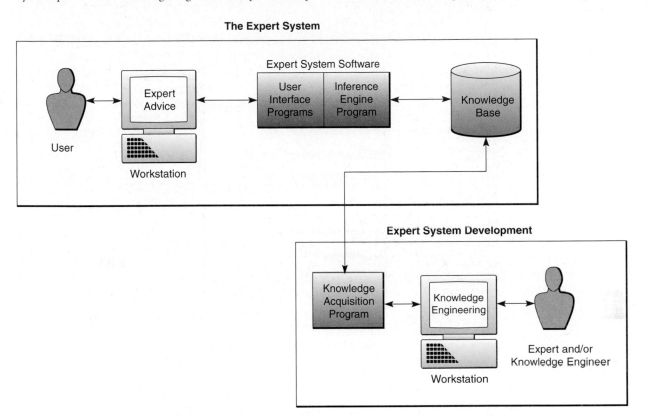

- **Knowledge Base.** The knowledge base of an expert system contains (1) facts about a specific subject area (e.g., *John is an analyst*) and (2) heuristics (rules of thumb) that express the reasoning procedures of an expert on the subject (e.g., *IF John is an analyst, THEN he needs a workstation*). There are many ways that such knowledge is represented in expert systems. Examples are *rule-based*, *frame-based*, *object-based*, and *case-based* methods of knowledge representation. See Figure 10.29.

- **Software Resources.** An expert system software package contains an inference engine and other programs for refining knowledge and communicating with users. The inference engine program processes the knowledge (such as rules and facts) related to a specific problem. It then makes associations and inferences resulting in recommended courses of action for a user. User interface programs for communicating with end users are also needed, including an explanation program to explain the reasoning process to a user if requested. Knowledge acquisition programs are not part of an expert system but are software tools for knowledge base development, as are *expert system shells*, which are used for developing expert systems.

Expert System Applications

Using an expert system involves an interactive computer-based session in which the solution to a problem is explored, with the expert system acting as a consultant to an end user. The expert system asks questions of the user, searches its knowledge base for facts and rules or other knowledge, explains its reasoning process when asked, and gives expert advice to the user in the subject area being explored. For example, Figure 10.30 illustrates an expert system application.

Expert systems are being used for many different types of applications, and the variety of applications is expected to continue to increase. You should realize, however,

FIGURE 10.30

Tivoli Business Systems Manager by IBM automatically monitors and manages the computers in a network with proactive expert system software components based on IBM's extensive mainframe systems management expertise.

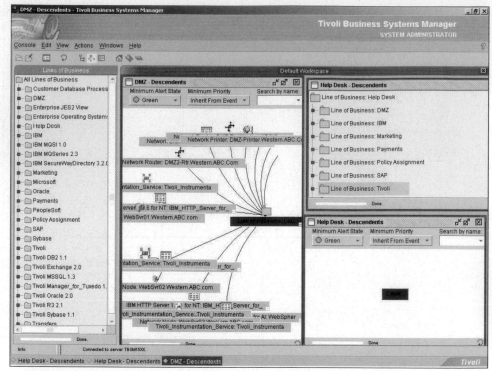

Source: Courtesy of International Business Machines Corporation.

that expert systems typically accomplish one or more generic uses. Figure 10.31 outlines five generic categories of expert system activities, with specific examples of actual expert system applications. As you can see, expert systems are being used in many different fields, including medicine, engineering, the physical sciences, and business. Expert systems now help diagnose illnesses, search for minerals, analyze compounds, recommend repairs, and do financial planning. So from a strategic business standpoint, expert systems can be and are being used to improve every step of the product cycle of a business, from finding customers to shipping products to providing customer service.

Benefits of Expert Systems

An expert system captures the expertise of an expert or group of experts in a computer-based information system. Thus, it can outperform a single human expert in many problem situations. That's because an expert system is faster and more consistent, can have the knowledge of several experts, and does not get tired or distracted by over-work or stress. Expert systems also help preserve and reproduce the knowledge of experts. They allow a company to preserve the expertise of an expert before she leaves the organization. This expertise can then be shared by reproducing the software and knowledge base of the expert system.

Limitations of Expert Systems

The major limitations of expert systems arise from their limited focus, inability to learn, maintenance problems, and developmental cost. Expert systems excel only in solving specific types of problems in a limited domain of knowledge. They fail miserably in solving problems requiring a broad knowledge base and subjective problem solving. They do well with specific types of operational or analytical tasks but falter at subjective managerial decision making.

Expert systems may also be difficult and costly to develop and maintain. The costs of knowledge engineers, lost expert time, and hardware and software resources may be too high to offset the benefits expected from some applications. Also, expert systems

FIGURE 10.31

Major application categories and examples of typical expert systems. Note the variety of applications that can be supported by such systems.

Application Categories of Expert Systems

• **Decision Management.** Systems that appraise situations or consider alternatives and make recommendations based on criteria supplied during the discovery process:
    Loan portfolio analysis
    Employee performance evaluation
    Insurance underwriting
    Demographic forecasts

• **Diagnostic/Troubleshooting.** Systems that infer underlying causes from reported symptoms and history:
    Equipment calibration
    Help desk operations
    Software debugging
    Medical diagnosis

• **Design/Configuration.** Systems that help configure equipment components, given existing constraints:
    Computer option installation
    Manufacturability studies
    Communications networks
    Optimum assembly plan

• **Selection/Classification.** Systems that help users choose products or processes, often from among large or complex sets of alternatives:
    Material selection
    Delinquent account identification
    Information classification
    Suspect identification

• **Process Monitoring/Control.** Systems that monitor and control procedures or processes:
    Machine control (including robotics)
    Inventory control
    Production monitoring
    Chemical testing

can't maintain themselves; that is, they can't learn from experience but instead must be taught new knowledge and modified as new expertise is needed to match developments in their subject areas.

Although there are practical applications for expert systems, applications have been limited and specific because, as discussed, expert systems are narrow in their domain of knowledge. An amusing example of this is the user who used an expert system designed to diagnose skin diseases to conclude that his rusty old car had likely developed measles. In addition, once some of the novelty had worn off, most programmers and developers realized that common expert systems were just more elaborate versions of the same decision logic used in most computer programs. Today, many of the techniques used to develop expert systems can now be found in most complex programs without any fuss about them.

I Now Pronounce You Man and Robot

Researchers in the U.K. are working on a robot that will develop emotions as it interacts with people. Scientists at the University of Hertfordshire announced in late 2010 that they've finalized a prototype of a robot capable of learning how to express emotions. According to the university, the robot is designed to form attachments, interact with people, and show emotions through bodily expressions.

So far the robot's range of emotions include happiness, sadness, fear, excitement, and pride. "This behavior is modeled on what a young child does," said Lola Caamero, lead researcher on the project. "This is also very similar to the way chimpanzees and other non-human primates develop effective bonds with their caregivers."

The robots, according to the university, are designed to learn how to respond to humans, feeding off facial expressions and other social cues, much as young children learn to interact socially.

There has been increasing discussion of robotic companions hitting the market in the not-so-distant future. A New Jersey-based company, TrueCompanion.com, announced early this year that it was taking the wraps off its talking robotic girlfriend. Roxxxy the Robot is no inanimate doll. It's designed with artificial intelligence and the ability to carry on a conversation.

These kinds of robotic advances won't come as a shock to David Levy, a British artificial intelligence researcher, who nearly three years ago predicted that robotics were about to begin making such dramatic advances that humans will be marrying robots by the year 2050.

Robots, Levy said, will lose their industrial look and jerky movements to become human-like machines that people use as aids, consider friends, fall in love with, and even take as spouses.

In the work being done today on the robots with emotions, the robots not only learn to adapt to the moods and actions of their human companions but they also are able to form attachments to particular people. "The more they interact, and are given the appropriate feedback and level of engagement from the human caregiver, the stronger the bond developed and the amount learned," the university noted. Researchers are hoping the robots can one day become companions and caregivers for sick children.

Source: Adapted from Sharon Gaudin, "Scientists Build Robot that Can Learn Emotions," *Computerworld*, Fairfax Media Group, August 17, 2010.

Developing Expert Systems

What types of problems are most suitable to expert system solutions? One way to answer this question is to look at examples of the applications of current expert systems, including the generic tasks they can accomplish, as were summarized in Figure 10.31. Another way is to identify criteria that make a problem situation suitable for an expert system. Figure 10.32 outlines some important criteria.

Figure 10.32 emphasizes that many real-world situations do not fit the suitability criteria for expert system solutions. Hundreds of rules may be required to capture the assumptions, facts, and reasoning that are involved in even simple problem situations. For example, a task that might take an expert a few minutes to accomplish might require an expert system with hundreds of rules and take several months to develop.

The easiest way to develop an expert system is to use an expert system shell as a developmental tool. An expert system shell is a software package consisting of an expert system without its kernel, that is, its knowledge base. This leaves a *shell* of software (the inference engine and user interface programs) with generic inferencing and user interface capabilities. Other development tools (e.g., rule editors, user interface generators) are added in making the shell a powerful expert system development tool.

Expert system shells are now available as relatively low-cost software packages that help users develop their own expert systems on microcomputers. They allow trained users to develop the knowledge base for a specific expert system application.

FIGURE 10.32

Criteria for applications that are suitable for expert systems development.

Suitability Criteria for Expert Systems
● **Domain.** The domain, or subject area, of the problem is relatively small and limited to a well-defined problem area.
● **Expertise.** Solutions to the problem require the efforts of an expert. That is, a body of knowledge, techniques, and intuition is needed that only a few people possess.
● **Complexity.** Solution of the problem is a complex task that requires logical inference processing, which would not be handled as well by conventional information processing.
● **Structure.** The solution process must be able to cope with ill-structured, uncertain, missing, and conflicting data, and a problem situation that changes with the passage of time.
● **Availability.** An expert exists who is articulate and cooperative, and who has the support of the management and end users involved in the development of the proposed system.

For example, one shell uses a spreadsheet format to help end users develop IF–THEN rules, automatically generating rules based on examples furnished by a user. Once a knowledge base is constructed, it is used with the shell's inference engine and user interface modules as a complete expert system on a specific subject area. Other software tools may require an IT specialist to develop expert systems. See Figure 10.33.

Knowledge Engineering

A knowledge engineer is a professional who works with experts to capture the knowledge (facts and rules of thumb) they possess. The knowledge engineer then builds the knowledge base (and the rest of the expert system if necessary), using an iterative, prototyping process until the expert system is acceptable. Thus, knowledge engineers perform a role similar to that of systems analysts in conventional information systems development.

Once the decision is made to develop an expert system, a team of one or more domain experts and a knowledge engineer may be formed. Experts skilled in the use of

FIGURE 10.33

Using the Visual Rule Studio and Visual Basic to develop rules for a credit management expert system.

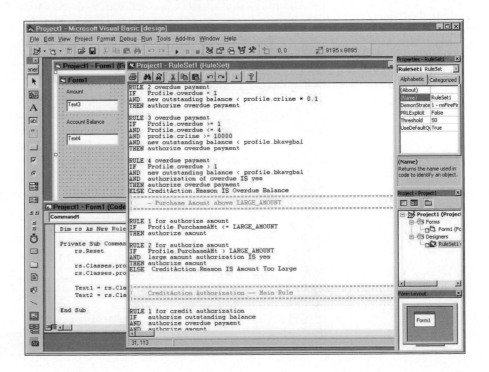

expert system shells could also develop their own expert systems. If a shell is used, facts and rules of thumb about a specific domain can be defined and entered into a knowledge base with the help of a rule editor or other knowledge acquisition tool. A limited working prototype of the knowledge base is then constructed, tested, and evaluated using the inference engine and user interface programs of the shell. The knowledge engineer and domain experts can modify the knowledge base, and then retest the system and evaluate the results. This process is repeated until the knowledge base and the shell result in an acceptable expert system.

Neural Networks

Neural networks are computing systems modeled after the brain's meshlike network of interconnected processing elements, called *neurons*. Of course, neural networks are a lot simpler in architecture (the human brain is estimated to have more than 100 billion neuron brain cells!). Like the brain, however, the interconnected processors in a neural network operate in parallel and interact dynamically. This interaction enables the network to "learn" from data it processes. That is, it learns to recognize patterns and relationships in these data. The more data examples it receives as input, the better it can learn to duplicate the results of the examples it processes. Thus, the neural network will change the strengths of the interconnections between the processing elements in response to changing patterns in the data it receives and the results that occur. See Figure 10.34.

| Modern Neurosurgery: Neural Nets Help Save Lives | Neurosurgery, surgery performed on the brain and spinal cord, has advanced to extraordinary levels of skill and success in just the last decade. One of the most common applications of neurosurgical techniques is the removal of brain tumors. Currently, surgeons search for tumors manually using a metal biopsy needle inserted into the brain. Guided by ultrasound and modern imaging techniques such as MRI/CT scans, they primarily use tactile feedback to localize the tumor. This method, however, can be imprecise, as the tumors can easily shift during surgery, causing |

FIGURE 10.34
Evaluating the training status of a neural network application.

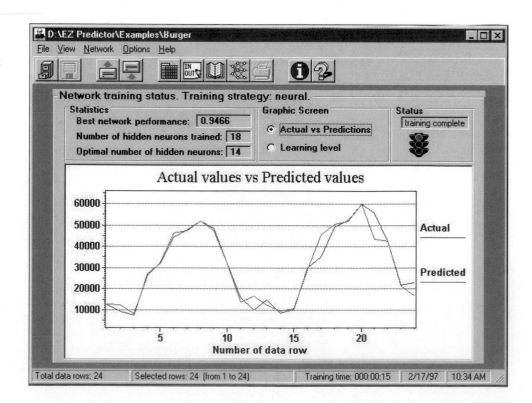

healthy tissue to be mistakenly treated as tumorous tissue. This inaccuracy can increase the risk of a stroke should a needle accidentally sever an artery.

A new technique, which is a combination of hardware and software, has been developed that gives neurosurgeons the ability to find their way through the brain while doing less damage as they operate. The primary piece of the hardware is a robotic probe that has on its tip several miniature sensors: an endoscope that transmits images and instruments that measure tissue density and blood flow. This probe is inserted into the brain and guided through it by a robotic mechanism that is more precise and accurate than human hands.

The real power in this miracle technique, however, is the sophisticated, adaptable neural network software that provides an instant in-depth analysis of the data gathered by the probe. Surgeons are able to look at a computer screen in the operating room and see a vast array of useful real-time information about what is going on in the patient's brain, such as whether the probe is encountering healthy tissue, blood vessels, or a tumor. The neural net software is adaptable in that it learns from experience the difference between normal tissue and tumorous tissue. Laboratory biopsy test results are used to validate the data used for training the neural net software. Once trained, the neural net can be used to identify in real time abnormal tissues encountered during surgical operations. Once learned, the probe is robotically advanced and stops immediately when it detects a signature significantly different from what was learned to be normal tissue. At this point, tissue identification is performed automatically, and the results presented to the surgeon. The surgeon can then treat the abnormal tissue appropriately and without delay.

This new technique gives surgeons finer control of surgical instruments during delicate brain operations. Overall, the new technique will increase the safety, accuracy, and efficiency of surgical procedures.

Source: Adapted from Bioluminate Inc., Press Release, "Bioluminate to Develop 'Smart Probe' for Early Breast Cancer Detection," December 5, 2002; and "NASA Ames Research Center Report," Smart Surgical Probe, Bioluminate Inc., 2003.

For example, a neural network can be trained to learn which credit characteristics result in good or bad loans. Developers of a credit evaluation neural network could provide it with data from many examples of credit applications and loan results to process, with opportunities to adjust the signal strengths between its neurons. The neural network would continue to be trained until it demonstrated a high degree of accuracy in correctly duplicating the results of recent cases. At that point, it would be trained enough to begin making credit evaluations of its own.

Fuzzy Logic Systems

In spite of their funny name, fuzzy logic systems represent a small, but serious, application of AI in business. Fuzzy logic is a method of reasoning that resembles human reasoning, in that it allows for approximate values and inferences (fuzzy logic) and incomplete or ambiguous data (fuzzy data) instead of relying only on *crisp data*, such as binary (yes/no) choices. For example, Figure 10.35 illustrates a partial set of rules (fuzzy rules) and a fuzzy SQL query for analyzing and extracting credit risk information on businesses that are being evaluated for selection as investments.

Notice how fuzzy logic uses terminology that is deliberately imprecise, such as *very high, increasing, somewhat decreased, reasonable*, and *very low*. This language enables fuzzy systems to process incomplete data and quickly provide approximate, but acceptable, solutions to problems that are difficult for other methods to solve. Thus, fuzzy logic queries of a database, such as the SQL query shown in Figure 10.35, promise to improve the extraction of data from business databases. It is important to note that fuzzy logic isn't fuzzy or imprecise thinking. Fuzzy logic actually brings precision to decision scenarios where it previously didn't exist.

FIGURE 10.35 An example of fuzzy logic rules and a fuzzy logic SQL query in a credit risk analysis application.

```
Fuzzy Logic Rules

Risk should be acceptable
If debt-equity is very high
   then risk is positively increased
If income is increasing
   then risk is somewhat decreased
If cash reserves are low to very low
   then risk is very increased
If PE ratio is good
   then risk is generally decreased
```

```
Fuzzy Logic SQL Query

Select companies
   from financials
      where revenues are very large
      and pe_ratio is acceptable
      and profits are high to very high
      and (income/employee_tot) is reasonable
```

Fuzzy Logic in Business

Examples of applications of fuzzy logic are numerous in Japan but rare in the United States. The United States has preferred to use AI solutions like expert systems or neural networks, but Japan has implemented many fuzzy logic applications, especially the use of special-purpose fuzzy logic microprocessor chips, called fuzzy process controllers. Thus, the Japanese ride on subway trains, use elevators, and drive cars that are guided or supported by fuzzy process controllers made by Hitachi and Toshiba. Many models of Japanese-made products also feature fuzzy logic microprocessors. The list is growing and includes autofocus cameras, autostabilizing camcorders, energy-efficient air conditioners, self-adjusting washing machines, and automatic transmissions.

Genetic Algorithms

The use of genetic algorithms is a growing application of artificial intelligence. Genetic algorithm software uses Darwinian (survival of the fittest), randomizing, and other mathematical functions to simulate an evolutionary process that can yield increasingly better solutions to a problem. Genetic algorithms were first used to simulate millions of years in biological, geological, and ecosystem evolution in just a few minutes on a computer. Genetic algorithm software is being used to model a variety of scientific, technical, and business processes.

Genetic algorithms are especially useful for situations in which thousands of solutions are possible and must be evaluated to produce an optimal solution. Genetic algorithm software uses sets of mathematical process rules (*algorithms*) that specify how combinations of process components or steps are to be formed. This process may involve trying random process combinations (*mutation*), combining parts of several good processes (*crossover*), and selecting good sets of processes and discarding poor ones (*selection*) to generate increasingly better solutions. Figure 10.36 illustrates a business use of genetic algorithm software.

United Distillers: Moving Casks Around with Genetic Algorithms

United Distillers (now part of Diageo PLC) is the largest and most profitable spirits company in the world. United Distillers' two grain distilleries account for more than one-third of total grain whiskey production, and the company's Johnnie Walker brand is the world's top whiskey, achieving sales of up to 120 million bottles a year.

Nevertheless, Christine Wright, Inventory and Supply Manager at United Distillers, points out that some parts of the business attract less attention than others: "Each week, 20,000 casks are moved in and out of our 49 warehouses throughout Scotland to provide the whiskey needed for the blending program. Warehousing is a physical and laborious process and has tended to be the forgotten side of the business." The introduction of genetic algorithm computer technology, however, during the past year has given a fillip to the blend selection process at United Distillers.

"We want to maximize our operational efficiency without compromising the quality," states Christine Wright. United Distillers' Blackgrange warehouse site alone houses approximately 3 million casks, indicating the scale of the challenge. Of the 20,000 casks that are moved each week, 10,000 are not used but are moved only to allow access to those identified by the selection process. "Although we had 100 percent accurate positional information about all the stock, casks had to be selected numerically. Given the practical challenges involved in warehouse management, casks are seldom stored numerically."

Information held on the system about recipes, site constraints, and the blending program is given to the XpertRule package, which works out the best combinations of stocks to produce the blends. This information is supplemented with positional information about the casks. The system then optimizes the selection of required casks, keeping to a minimum the number of "doors" (warehouse sections) from which the casks must be taken and the number of casks that need to be moved to clear the way. Other constraints must be satisfied, such as the current working capacity of each warehouse and the maintenance and restocking work that may be in progress. Lancashire-based expert systems specialist XpertRule Software Limited has worked closely with United Distillers to develop the software application using XpertRule. The system is based on the use of genetic algorithms and adopts the Darwinian principle of natural selection to optimize the selection process.

"The incidence of non-productive cask movements has plummeted from a high of around 50 percent to a negligible level of around 4 percent and our cask handling rates have almost doubled." She adds: "The new technology enables staff to concentrate on what they want to achieve, rather than the mechanism of how to go about it. They can concentrate on the constraints that they wish to impose and get the system to do the leg work of finding the best scenario within those constraints. It means that the business can be driven by primary objectives." "Not only does the lack of wasted effort allow warehouse staff to get on with their work, but it enables them to plan ahead and organize long-term maintenance programs. It encourages a mind-set that is strategic, rather than reactive, and empowers managers to manage their own sites."

Source: Adapted from XpertRule Case Study, "A Break from Tradition in Blend Selection at United Distillers & Vintners," http://www.xpertrule.com/pages/case_ud.htm, accessed April 23, 2008.

FIGURE 10.36

Risk Optimizer software combines genetic algorithms with a risk simulation function in this airline yield optimization application.

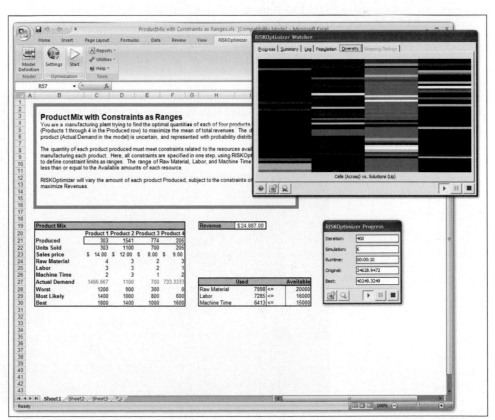

Source: RISKOptimizer software. Image courtesy of Palisade Corporation.

Virtual Reality

Virtual reality (VR) is computer-simulated reality. Virtual reality is a fast-growing area of artificial intelligence that had its origins in efforts to build more natural, realistic, multisensory human–computer interfaces. So virtual reality relies on multisensory input/output devices such as a tracking headset with video goggles and stereo earphones, a *data glove* or jumpsuit with fiber-optic sensors that track your body movements, and a *walker* that monitors the movement of your feet. Then you can experience computer-simulated "virtual worlds" three-dimensionally through sight, sound, and touch. Virtual reality is also called *telepresence*. For example, you can enter a computer-generated virtual world, look around and observe its contents, pick up and move objects, and move around in it at will. Thus, virtual reality allows you to interact with computer-simulated objects, entities, and environments as if they actually exist. See Figure 10.37.

VR Applications

Current applications of virtual reality are wide-ranging and include computer-aided design (CAD), medical diagnostics and treatment, scientific experimentation in many physical and biological sciences, flight simulation for training pilots and astronauts, product demonstrations, employee training, and entertainment, especially 3-D video arcade games. CAD is the most widely used industrial VR application. It enables architects and other designers to design and test electronic 3-D models of products and structures by entering the models themselves and examining, touching, and manipulating sections and parts from all angles. This scientific-visualization capability is also used by pharmaceutical and biotechnology firms to develop and observe the behavior of computerized models of new drugs and materials and by medical researchers to develop ways for physicians to enter and examine a virtual reality of a patient's body.

VR becomes *telepresence* when users, who can be anywhere in the world, use VR systems to work alone or together at a remote site. Typically, this involves using a VR system to enhance the sight and touch of a human who is remotely manipulating equipment to accomplish a task. Examples range from virtual surgery, where surgeon and patient may be on either side of the globe, to the remote use of equipment in hazardous environments such as chemical plants or nuclear reactors.

The hottest VR application today is Linden Lab's *Second Life*. Here, users can create avatars to represent them, teleport to any of the thousands of locations in *Second Life*, build personal domains, "buy" land, and live out their wildest fantasies. *Second Life* has grown to enormous proportions, although actual statistics regarding size and

FIGURE 10.37

This landscape architect uses a virtual reality system to view and move through the design of the Seattle Commons, an urban design proposal for downtown Seattle.

Source: © George Steinmetz/Corbis.

number of users are constantly in dispute. Today, *Second Life* is home to individuals, commercial organizations, universities, governments (the Maldives was the first country to open an embassy in *Second Life*), churches, sports entertainment, art exhibits, live music, and theater. Just about anything goes in *Second Life* and, as technologies advance, the lines between your first life and your second one may begin to blur—stay tuned.

There has been increasing interest in the potential social impact of new virtual reality technologies. It is believed by many that virtual reality will lead to a number of important changes in human life and activity. For example:

- Virtual reality will be integrated into daily life and activity and will be used in various human ways.

- Techniques will be developed to influence human behavior, interpersonal communication, and cognition (i.e., virtual genetics).

- As we spend more and more time in virtual space, there will be a gradual "migration to virtual space," resulting in important changes in economics, worldview, and culture.

- The design of virtual environments may be used to extend basic human rights into virtual space, to promote human freedom and well-being or to promote social stability as we move from one stage in sociopolitical development to the next.

- Virtual reality will soon engage all of the senses including smell, taste, and touch.

Norsk Hydro: Drilling Decisions Made in a Virtual Oil Field

Norsk Hydro, based in Oslo, Norway, is a *Fortune* 500 energy and aluminum supplier operating in more than 40 countries worldwide. It is a leading offshore producer of oil and gas, the world's third-largest aluminum supplier, and a leader in the development of renewable energy sources. Norsk Hydro is also an innovator in the use of virtual reality technology. It uses VR to make decisions that, if wrong, could cost the company millions in lost revenues and, more important, could harm the environment. One example of its successful use of VR is the Troll Oil Field project.

The Troll Oil Field is located in the North Sea. The eastern part of the field has an oil column only 39–46 feet wide, but with in-place reserves of approximately 2.2 billion barrels. The oil is produced by horizontal wells located 1.5–5 feet above the point where the oil and seawater make contact.

During one drilling of a horizontal well, the drill bit was in sand of relatively low quality. No further good-quality reservoir sands were predicted from the geological model along the planned well track. Approximately 820 feet remained to the planned total depth, so a major decision to terminate the well required confirmation. If the decision to terminate the well was the right decision, the cost of drilling to that date would be lost, but no further loss or damage to the environment would occur. If, however, the decision to terminate the well was the wrong decision, valuable oil reserves would be lost forever.

Virtual reality technology was fundamental in deciding whether to terminate the well. All relevant data were loaded into the system for review. During a virtual reality session, the well team discovered a mismatch between the seismic data and the geological model. Based on this observation, they made a quick reinterpretation of some key seismic horizons and updated the geological model locally around the well.

The updated model changed the prognosis for the remaining section of the well from poor-quality sand to high-quality sand. It was decided to continue drilling, and the new prognosis was proven correct. As a result, 175 meters of extra-high-quality sand with an estimated production volume of 100,000 standard cubic meters of oil were drilled in the last section of the well.

Source: Adapted from Norsk Hydro Corporate Background, www.hydro.com, 2004; and Schlumberger Information Solutions, "Norsk Hydro Makes a Valuable Drilling Decision," Schlumberger Technical Report GMP-5911, 2002.

FIGURE 10.38

Examples of different types of intelligent agents.

Types of Intelligent Agents
User Interface Agents
● **Interface Tutors.** Observe user computer operations, correct user mistakes, and provide hints and advice on efficient software use.
● **Presentation Agents.** Show information in a variety of reporting and presentation forms and media based on user preferences.
● **Network Navigation Agents.** Discover paths to information and provide ways to view information that are preferred by a user.
● **Role-Playing Agents.** Play what-if games and other roles to help users understand information and make better decisions.
Information Management Agents
● **Search Agents.** Help users find files and databases, search for desired information, and suggest and find new types of information products, media, and resources.
● **Information Brokers.** Provide commercial services to discover and develop information resources that fit the business or personal needs of a user.
● **Information Filters.** Receive, find, filter, discard, save, forward, and notify users about products received or desired, including e-mail, voice mail, and all other information media.

Intelligent Agents

Intelligent agents are growing in popularity as a way to use artificial intelligence routines in software to help users accomplish many kinds of tasks in e-business and e-commerce. An intelligent agent is a *software surrogate* for an end user or a process that fulfills a stated need or activity. An intelligent agent uses its built-in and learned knowledge base about a person or process to make decisions and accomplish tasks in a way that fulfills the intentions of a user. Sometimes an intelligent agent is given a graphic representation or persona, such as Einstein for a science advisor, Sherlock Holmes for an information search agent, and so on. Thus, intelligent agents (also called *software robots* or "bots") are special-purpose, knowledge-based information systems that accomplish specific tasks for users. Figure 10.38 summarizes major types of intelligent agents.

The wizards found in Microsoft Office and other software suites are among the most well-known examples of intelligent agents. These wizards are built-in capabilities

FIGURE 10.39

Intelligent agent software such as Copernic can help you access information from a variety of categories and form a variety of sources.

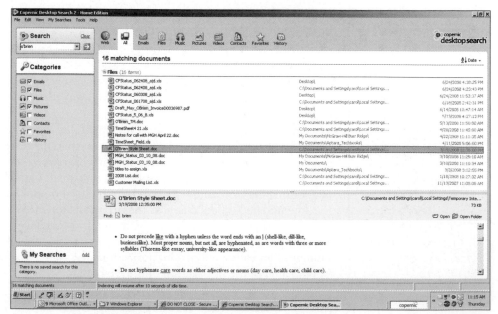

Source: Courtesy of Copernic.

that can analyze how an end user is using a software package and offer suggestions on how to complete various tasks. Thus, wizards might help you change document margins, format spreadsheet cells, query a database, or construct a graph. Wizards and other software agents are also designed to adjust to your way of using a software package so that they can anticipate when you will need their assistance. See Figure 10.39.

The use of intelligent agents is growing rapidly as a way to simplify software use, search Web sites on the Internet and corporate intranets, and help customers do comparison shopping among the many e-commerce sites on the Web. Intelligent agents are becoming necessary as software packages become more sophisticated and powerful, as the Internet and the World Wide Web become more vast and complex, and as information sources and e-commerce alternatives proliferate exponentially. In fact, some commentators forecast that much of the future of computing will consist of intelligent agents performing their work for users.

| Security Uses of Intelligent Software Agents | In 2002, the Army began to use intelligent software agents instead of people to route the background files of soldiers who required security clearance to the proper authorities for review. *The result*: A process that once took days now takes 24 hours. The Army reduced its year-long backlog, and the Army Central Clearance Facility in Fort Meade, Maryland, can now handle 30 percent more requests a year. The intelligent agent retrieves the necessary background information from existing records and builds an electronic folder for each case. It then examines the file to determine whether it's a clean case or there are warning signs, such as financial problems, arrests, or anything to indicate that a person might be susceptible to improper influence. Human investigators take closer looks at the tough cases.

Intelligent agents are semiautonomous, proactive, and adaptive software systems that can act on a user's behalf. Give an intelligent agent a goal, such as to help a U.S. ambassador pick a safe evacuation route following a terrorist attack in a foreign country, and it creates the best plan after gathering weather information, news reports, airplane schedules, road information, and police reports.

Such agents can also help investigators identify unusual patterns of activity, says Henry Lieberman, research scientist and leader of the Software Agents Group at the MIT Media Lab in Cambridge, Massachusetts. "Law enforcement can say to an intelligent agent, 'Let me know when any person arrived from a sensitive Middle Eastern country that was recently involved in a large bank transfer.' Or government agencies like the Securities and Exchange Commission can use them to monitor financial statements for fraud. Maybe they could have caught the whole Enron thing earlier."

Nevertheless, the issue of trust may deter their widespread adoption in business. "People just aren't used to using these kinds of things yet," says Lieberman. "When you first start using one of these agents, you have to watch it closely to make sure it's doing what you want. But performance improves over time. And the agent just makes a proposal. Then it's up to you."

Source: Adapted from Stephanie Overby, "Security Strategy Includes Intelligent Software Agents," *CIO Magazine*, January 1, 2003. |

Summary

- **Information, Decisions, and Management.** Information systems can support a variety of management decision-making levels and decisions. These include the three levels of management activity (strategic, tactical, and operational decision making) and three types of decision structures (structured, semistructured, and

unstructured). Information systems provide a wide range of information products to support these types of decisions at all levels of the organization.

- **Decision Support Trends.** Major changes are taking place in traditional MIS, DSS, and EIS tools for providing the information, and modeling managers need to support their decision making. Decision support in business is changing, driven by rapid developments in end-user computing and networking; Internet and Web technologies; and Web-enabled business applications. The growth of corporate intranets and extranets, as well as the Web, has accelerated the development of "executive-class" interfaces like enterprise information portals and Web-enabled business intelligence software tools, as well as their use by lower levels of management and individuals and teams of business professionals. In addition, the growth of e-commerce and e-business applications has expanded the use of enterprise portals and DSS tools by the suppliers, customers, and other business stakeholders of a company.

- **Management Information Systems.** Management information systems provide prespecified reports and responses to managers on a periodic, exception, demand, or push reporting basis to meet their need for information to support decision making.

- **OLAP and Data Mining.** Online analytical processing interactively analyzes complex relationships among large amounts of data stored in multidimensional databases. Data mining analyzes the vast amounts of historical data that have been prepared for analysis in data warehouses. Both technologies discover patterns, trends, and exception conditions in a company's data that support business analysis and decision making.

- **Decision Support Systems.** Decision support systems are interactive, computer-based information systems that use DSS software and a model base and database to provide information tailored to support semistructured and unstructured decisions faced by individual managers. They are designed to use a decision maker's own insights and judgments in an ad hoc, interactive, analytical modeling process leading to a specific decision.

- **Executive Information Systems.** Executive information systems are information systems originally designed to support the strategic information needs of top management; however, their use is spreading to lower levels of management and business professionals. EIS are easy to use and enable executives to retrieve information tailored to their needs and preferences. Thus, EIS can provide information about a company's critical success factors to executives to support their planning and control responsibilities.

- **Enterprise Information and Knowledge Portals.** Enterprise information portals provide a customized and personalized Web-based interface for corporate intranets to give their users easy access to a variety of internal and external business applications, databases, and information services that are tailored to their individual preferences and information needs. Thus, an EIP can supply personalized Web-enabled information, knowledge, and decision support to executives, managers, and business professionals, as well as to customers, suppliers, and other business partners. An enterprise knowledge portal is a corporate intranet portal that extends the use of an EIP to include knowledge management functions and knowledge base resources so that it becomes a major form of knowledge management system for a company.

- **Artificial Intelligence.** The major application domains of artificial intelligence (AI) include a variety of applications in cognitive science, robotics, and natural interfaces. The goal of AI is the development of computer functions normally associated with human physical and mental capabilities, such as robots that see, hear, talk, feel, and move, and software capable of reasoning, learning, and problem solving. Thus, AI is being applied to many applications in business operations and managerial decision making, as well as in many other fields.

- **AI Technologies.** The many application areas of AI are summarized in Figure 10.26, including neural networks, fuzzy logic, genetic algorithms, virtual reality, and intelligent agents. Neural nets are hardware or software systems based on simple models of the brain's neuron structure that can learn to recognize patterns in data. Fuzzy logic systems use rules of approximate reasoning to solve problems when data are incomplete or ambiguous. Genetic algorithms use selection, randomizing, and other mathematic functions to simulate an evolutionary process that can yield increasingly better solutions to problems. Virtual reality systems are multisensory systems that enable human users to experience computer-simulated environments as if they actually existed. Intelligent agents are knowledge-based software surrogates for a user or process in the accomplishment of selected tasks.

- **Expert Systems.** Expert systems are knowledge-based information systems that use software and a knowledge base about a specific, complex application area to act as expert consultants to users in many business and technical applications. Software includes an inference engine program that makes inferences based on the facts and rules stored in the knowledge base. A knowledge base consists of facts about a specific subject area and heuristics (rules of thumb) that express the reasoning procedures of an expert. The benefits of expert systems (such as preservation and replication of expertise) must be balanced with their limited applicability in many problem situations.

Key Terms and Concepts

These are the key terms and concepts of this chapter. The page number of their first explanation is in parentheses.

1. Analytical modeling (441)
   a. Goal-seeking analysis (443)
   b. Optimization analysis (443)
   c. Sensitivity analysis (442)
   d. What-if analysis (441)
2. Artificial intelligence (AI) (452)
3. Business intelligence (BI) (429)
4. Data mining (444)
5. Data visualization system (DVS) (439)

6. Decision structure (428)

7. Decision support system (431)

8. Enterprise information portal (EIP) (448)

9. Enterprise knowledge portal (450)

10. Executive information system (EIS) (446)

11. Expert system (ES) (458)

12. Expert system shell (462)

13. Fuzzy logic (465)

14. Genetic algorithms (466)

15. Geographic information system (GIS) (439)

16. Inference engine (459)

17. Intelligent agent (470)

18. Knowledge base (459)

19. Knowledge engineer (463)

20. Knowledge management system (450)

21. Management information system (434)

22. Model base (432)

23. Neural network (464)

24. Online analytical processing (OLAP) (435)

25. Robotics (457)

26. Virtual reality (VR) (468)

Review Quiz

Match one of the key terms and concepts listed previously with one of the brief examples or definitions that follow. Try to find the best fit for answers that seem to fit more than one term or concept. Defend your choices.

_____ 1. Decision-making procedures cannot be specified in advance for some complex decision situations.

_____ 2. Information systems for the strategic information needs of top and middle managers.

_____ 3. Systems that produce predefined reports for management.

_____ 4. Provide an interactive modeling capability tailored to the specific information needs of managers.

_____ 5. Provides business information and analytical tools for managers, business professionals, and business stakeholders.

_____ 6. A collection of mathematical models and analytical techniques.

_____ 7. Analyzing the effect of changing variables and relationships and manipulating a mathematical model.

_____ 8. Changing revenues and tax rates to see the effect on net profit after taxes.

_____ 9. Changing revenues in many small increments to see revenue's effect on net profit after taxes.

_____ 10. Changing revenues and expenses to find how you could achieve a specific amount of net profit after taxes.

_____ 11. Changing revenues and expenses subject to certain constraints to achieve the highest profit after taxes.

_____ 12. Real-time analysis of complex business data.

_____ 13. Attempts to find patterns hidden in business data in a data warehouse.

_____ 14. Represents complex data using three-dimensional graphical forms.

_____ 15. A customized and personalized Web interface to internal and external information resources available through a corporate intranet.

_____ 16. Using intranets to gather, store, and share a company's best practices among employees.

_____ 17. An enterprise information portal that can access knowledge management functions and company knowledge bases.

_____ 18. Information technology that focuses on the development of computer functions normally associated with human physical and mental capabilities.

_____ 19. Development of computer-based machines that possess capabilities such as sight, hearing, dexterity, and movement.

_____ 20. Computers that can provide you with computer-simulated experiences.

_____ 21. An information system that integrates computer graphics, geographic databases, and DSS capabilities.

_____ 22. A knowledge-based information system that acts as an expert consultant to users in a specific application area.

_____ 23. A collection of facts and reasoning procedures in a specific subject area.

_____ 24. A software package that manipulates a knowledge base and makes associations and inferences leading to a recommended course of action.

_____ 25. A software package consisting of an inference engine and user interface programs used as an expert system development tool.

_____ 26. An analyst who interviews experts to develop a knowledge base about a specific application area.

_____ 27. AI systems that use neuron structures to recognize patterns in data.

_____ 28. AI systems that use approximate reasoning to process ambiguous data.

_____ 29. Knowledge-based software surrogates that do things for you.

_____ 30. Software that uses mathematical functions to simulate an evolutionary process.

Discussion Questions

1. Are the form and use of information and decision support systems for managers and business professionals changing and expanding? Why or why not?

2. Has the growth of self-directed teams to manage work in organizations changed the need for strategic, tactical, and operational decision making in business?

3. What is the difference between the ability of a manager to retrieve information instantly on demand using an MIS and the capabilities provided by a DSS?

4. Refer to the Real World Case on business intelligence in Hong Kong in the chapter. Information is one part (albeit a very important one) of decision making, with managers being the other. What experiences and qualifications are important in preparing managers for "fact-based" decision making? How are those obtained?

5. In what ways does using an electronic spreadsheet package provide you with the capabilities of a decision support system?

6. Are enterprise information portals making executive information systems unnecessary? Explain your reasoning.

7. Refer to the Real World Case on Kimberly-Clark and virtual reality in the chapter. Is the company fixing something that was not broken? Explain.

8. Can computers think? Will they ever be able to? Explain why or why not.

9. Which applications of AI have the most potential value for use in the operations and management of a business? Defend your choices.

10. What are some of the limitations or dangers you see in the use of AI technologies such as expert systems, virtual reality, and intelligent agents? What could be done to minimize such effects?

Analysis Exercises

1. **e-Commerce Web Site Reviews**
BizRate.com
BizRate (www.bizrate.com) instantly provides information about hundreds of online stores. Supported product lines include books, music, electronics, clothes, hardware, gifts, and more. Customer reviews help shoppers select products and retailers with confidence. BizRate also features a "Smart Choice" tag that balances retailer reviews, price, and other variables to recommend a "best buy."

   a. Use BizRate.com to check out a product of interest. How thorough, valid, and valuable were the product and retailer reviews to you? Explain.

   b. How could nonretail businesses use a similar Web-enabled review system? Give an example.

   c. How is BizRate's Web site functionality similar to a decision support system (DSS)?

2. **Enterprise Application Integration**
Digital Desktops
Information coming from a variety of business systems can appear on the executive desktop as a consolidated whole. Often referred to as a digital dashboard, the information contained in such a view might include the executive's schedule, current e-mail, a brief list of production delays, major accounts past due, current sales summaries, and a financial market summary. Although it isn't possible to fit all of an organization's information on a single screen, it is possible to summarize data in ways specified by the executive and then act as a launching point or portal for further point-and-click enquiries.

How might such a system look? Portals such as my.Excite.com, my.MSN.com, iGoogle (www.google.com/ig), and my.Yahoo.com make good general-purpose information portals. These Web sites contain characteristics in common with their business-oriented brethren. They provide information from many different sources such as e-mail, instant messages, calendars, tasks lists, stock quotes, weather, and news. They allow users to determine what information sources they see; for example, a user may choose to list only business-related news and omit sports, lottery results, and horoscopes. They also allow users to filter the information they see; for example, a user may choose to view only local weather, news containing specific key words, or market results only for stocks the user owns. They allow users to arrange their own information space so that information a user finds most important appears in the right place. Finally, they allow users to drill down into the information they find important to receive more detail.

Once a user has set up an account and identified his or her preferences, these public portals remember the user's preferences and deliver only what the user has requested. Users may change their preferences as often as they wish, and the controls to make these changes require only point-and-click programming skills.

   a. Visit one of the portal sites listed above. Configure the site to meet your own information needs. Provide a printout of the result.

   b. Look up Digital Dashboard on the 20/20 Software Web site (www.2020software), read about products with this feature, and describe these products in your own words.

3. Case-Based Marketing
Selling on Amazon.com
A case-based reasoning system is a type of expert system. It attempts to match the facts on hand to a database of prior cases. When a case-based reasoning system finds one or more cases in its database that closely match the facts at hand, it then evaluates and reports the most common outcomes. Given enough cases, such a system can prove very useful. Even better, if a case-based system automatically captures cases as they occur, then it will become a powerful tool that continually fine-tunes its results as it gains "experience."

Amazon.com relies on just such a system to refer books to its customers. Like many e-commerce sites, Amazon allows visitors to search for, buy, and review books. Amazon.com takes its database interactivity a step further. Given a particular book title, its case-based reasoning engine examines all past sales of that book to see if the customers who bought that book shared other book purchases in common. It then produces a short list and presents that list to the user. The overall effect approaches that of a sales clerk who says, "Oh! If you like this book, then you'll really like reading these as well." Amazon's system has the experience of hundreds of millions more transactions than even the most wizened and well-read sales clerk.

Equipped with this information, customers may consider purchasing additional books, or the information may increase customers' confidence that they have selected the right book. Better information increases customers' confidence in their purchases and encourages additional sales.

a. What is the source of expertise behind Amazon's online book recommendations?
b. How do you feel about online merchants tracking your purchases and using this information to recommend additional purchases?
c. What measures protect consumers from the government's obtaining their personal shopping histories maintained by Amazon?
d. Although Amazon doesn't share personal information, it still capitalizes on its customers' shopping data. Is this ethical? Should Amazon offer its customers the right to opt out of this information-gathering?

4. Palm City Police Department
Goal Seeking
The Palm City Police Department has eight defined precincts. The police station in each precinct has primary responsibility for all activities in its precinct area. The table lists the current population of each precinct, the number of violent crimes committed in each precinct, and the number of officers assigned to each precinct. The department has established a goal of equalizing access to police services. Ratios of population per police officer and violent crimes per police officer should be calculated for each precinct. These ratios for the city as a whole are shown at right.

a. Build a spreadsheet to perform this analysis and print it out.
b. Currently, no funds are available to hire additional officers. On the basis of the citywide ratios, the department has decided to develop a plan to shift resources as needed to ensure that no precinct has more than 1,100 residents per police officer and no precinct has more than seven violent crimes per police officer. The department will transfer officers from precincts that easily meet these goals to precincts that violate one or both of these ratios. Use "goal seeking" on your spreadsheet to move police officers between precincts until the goals are met. You can use the goal-seek tool to see how many officers would be required to bring each precinct into compliance and then judgmentally reduce officers in precincts that are substantially within the criteria. Print out a set of results that allow the departments to comply with these ratios and a memorandum to your instructor summarizing your results and the process you used to develop them.

Precinct	Population	Violent Crimes	Police Officers
Shea Blvd.	96,552	318	85
Lakeland Heights	99,223	582	108
Sunnydale	68,432	206	77
Old Town	47,732	496	55
Mountainview	101,233	359	82
Financial District	58,102	511	70
Riverdale	78,903	537	70
Cole Memorial	75,801	306	82
Total	**625,978**	**3,315**	**629**
Per Officer	**995.196**	**5.270**	

REAL WORLD CASE 3

Goodyear, JEA, OSUMC, and Monsanto: Cool Technologies Driving Competitive Advantage

If necessity is the mother of invention, then capitalism is surely the mother of innovation. Companies are being driven to develop unique applications of undeniably cool technologies by the drive to create a sustainable competitive advantage. "At the end of the day, as cool as this thing we've developed is, it's a tool," says Stephanie Wernet, Goodyear's CIO. "It is meant to serve a business end. In our case, this tool lets us put out new, more innovative products faster than the competition."

Working with Sandia National Labs, Goodyear's IT department developed software to design and test tires virtually. In the past, the company built physical prototypes and tested them by driving thousands of miles on tracks. Using a mathematical model, the software simulates tire behavior in different driving conditions so that the designer can see how the tire gets pushed, pulled, and stretched as it rolls down a road, hits bumps, turns corners, screeches to a halt, and grips the road in wet, dry, and icy conditions. Goodyear wanted to shorten that time to get its products to market more quickly.

Three research and development employees advanced the idea of testing prototypes using computer simulations, which could do the job faster.

The company had never done simulations but figured initial investments and subsequent maintenance costs were worth the payoff. Goodyear's cost of goods sold, as well as its sales, decreased by 2.6 percent from 2003 to 2004, the year its first fully simulated tires hit the market. Meanwhile, the research and development (R&D) budget for tire testing and design decreased by 25 percent.

Custom-built software runs on hundreds of processors on hundreds of Linux computers in a massively parallel computing environment. Goodyear invested more than $6 million to build this high-powered computing environment. It plans to expand and upgrade its Linux clusters to meet business demands for new tires and to improve the fidelity of its virtual tests. The company believes it is the first tire maker to use computers to design and test its wheels. Although the auto industry has done computer-assisted design work since the 1980s, the technology had not been applied to tires because their malleable materials made simulation difficult.

Designers can perform 10 times more tests, reducing a new tire's time to market from two years to as little as nine months. Goodyear attributes its sales growth from $15 billion in 2003 to $20 billion in 2005 to new products introduced as a result of this change.

Public utility JEA uses neural network technology to create an artificial intelligence system it has recently implemented. The system automatically determines the optimal combinations of oil and natural gas the utility's boilers need to produce electricity cost-effectively, given fuel prices and the amount of electricity required. It also ensures that the amount of nitrous oxide (N2O) emitted during the generation process does not exceed government regulations.

JEA needed to decrease operating expenses, in particular fuel costs, as oil and gas prices began their precipitous ascent in 2002. Forty percent of JEA's $1.3 billion budget goes to the purchase of oil and gas to power its boilers, so a small change in the way electricity is produced could add millions of dollars to the bottom line. Neural network technology models the process of producing electricity. Optimization software from NeuCo determines the right combinations of oil and gas to produce electricity at low cost while minimizing emissions.

JEA, which serves more than 360,000 customers in Jacksonville and three neighboring Florida counties, is the first utility in the world to apply neural network technology to the production of electricity in circulating fluidized-bed boilers. It built a system that makes decisions based on historical operating data and as many as 100 inputs associated with the combustion process, including air flows and megawatt outputs. The system learns which fuel combinations are optimal by making adjustments to the boiler in real time; it also forecasts what to do in the future based on specific fuel cost assumptions. "We had issues with oil prices. At the same time, gas prices went from $4 a BTU to over $14. We need to use gas because it decreases emissions. This solution helped us balance all of those items," says Wanyonyi Kendrick, JEA's CIO.

The project, which IT drove, cost $800,000 and paid for itself in eight weeks. The system reduced the quantity of natural gas that is used to control N_2O emissions by 15 percent, an estimated annual savings of $4.8 million. With natural gas prices at $11 per BTU, JEA expects to save $13 million on fuel in 2006. What's more, JEA has discovered it can use the new technology applications for its water business.

The Ohio State University Medical Center (OSUMC) replaced its overhead rail transport system with 46 self-guided robotic vehicles to move linens, meals, trash, and medical supplies throughout the 1,000-bed hospital. The robots do not interact with patients; they carry out routine tasks that hospital staff used to do. Faced with declining revenue and rising costs, OSUMC needed to save money while improving patient care. A steering committee comprising IT, other hospital departments, consultants, and vendors drove this project. They convinced medical staff of its value by demonstrating the technology and communicating how it improved working conditions and patient care. Materials transport was identified as a place to cut costs since the hospital needed to upgrade the existing system.

The robots, made by FMC Technologies, are guided by a wireless infrared network from Cisco Systems. The network is embedded in corridor walls and elevators designed for the robots' use. Three Windows servers linked to the network maintain a database of robot jobs and traffic patterns. OSUMC is the first hospital in the United States to implement an infrared-guided automated system for transporting materials.

Hospital staff use a touch-screen computer connected to a server to call a robot when, for example a linen cart needs to go to the laundry room. To get from point A to point B, the robots rely on a digital map of the medical center programmed into their memory; they also track their movements against the number of times their wheels rotate in a full circle. So if it takes a robot 1,000 wheel revolutions to get from a building's kitchen to the sixth floor, and its wheels have moved in 500 revolutions, the robot knows it is halfway there. If a robot loses network contact, it shuts down.

The $18 million system is expected to save the hospital approximately $1 million a year over the next 25 years. Since it went live in 2004, OSUMC has saved $27,375 annually on linen delivery alone. OSUMC's CIO Detlev Smaltz says the system improves patient care by freeing up personnel: "If we can take mundane jobs like taking out the trash off of our employees and give them more time to do the things they came into the health-care profession to do, then that's an added benefit of the system."

Monsanto's IT department created software to identify genes that indicate a plant's resistance to drought, herbicides, and pests; those genetic traits are used to predict which plants breeders should reproduce to yield the healthiest, most bountiful crops.

The software crunches data from breeders worldwide and presents them in a colorful, easy-to-comprehend fashion. By pinpointing the best breeding stock, it increases breeders' odds of finding a commercially viable combination of genetic traits from one in a trillion to one in five. Monsanto's global breeding organization drove the project.

When the patent expired for Roundup, Monsanto's signature weed killer, the St. Louis company invested in growing its business involving seeds and genetic traits, which comprises more than half of its $6.3 billion revenue and $255 million profits in 2005. Monsanto believes it can sell more corn, soybean, and cotton seeds if farmers know its seeds will produce heartier crops and require fewer sprays of insecticide and herbicide, thus reducing costs.

Monsanto's scientists use the software to engineer seeds that effectively resist drought and pests and to produce plants that are healthier for humans and animals to eat. They do it by implanting those seeds with the genetic material that makes a plant resist insects or produce more protein. What would Gregor Mendel, the father of genetics, think of this? "This is really different from the way breeders bred their crops," says Monsanto CIO Mark Showers. "They didn't have this level of molecular detail to determine and select plants they wanted to move forward from year to year."

Monsanto reaps the benefit of its software but wouldn't reveal development costs. Earnings per share (EPS) on an ongoing basis grew from $1.59 to $2.08, or 30 percent, from 2004 to 2005. Its EPS is expected to grow by 20 percent more in 2006. "In the last four or five years, we've had a marked improvement in taking market share from our competition. We've grown our share at a couple of points per year," says Showers.

Source: Adapted from Meridith Levinson, "IT Innovation: Robots, Supercomputers, AI and More," *CIO Magazine*, August 15, 2006.

CASE STUDY QUESTIONS

1. Consider the outcomes of the projects discussed in the case. In all of them, the payoffs are both larger and achieved more rapidly than in more traditional system implementations. Why do you think this is the case? How are these projects different from others you have come across in the past? What are those differences? Provide several examples.

2. How do these technologies create business value for the implementing organizations? In which ways are these implementations similar in how they accomplish this, and how are they different? Use examples from the case to support your answer.

3. In all of these examples, companies had an urgent need that prompted them to investigate these radical, new technologies. Do you think the story would have been different had the companies been performing well already? Why or why not? To what extent are these innovations dependent on the presence of a problem or crisis?

REAL WORLD ACTIVITIES

1. Choose one of the companies introduced in the case and search the Internet to update the current status of their project. Also take a look at their competitors, and discover how they have responded to the introduction of the developments mentioned in the case. Have they attempted to imitate them?

2. As these technologies go beyond the capacity and abilities of human beings, what is the role of people in the processes they affect? Do you think these technologies empower us by allowing us to overcome our limitations and expand our range of possibilities? Instead, do they relegate people to the role of uncritically accepting the outcomes of these processes? Break into small groups to discuss these issues, and note which arguments that support one or the other position arise as a result.

CASE 4

Hillman Group, Avnet, and Quaker Chemical: Process Transformation through Business Intelligence Deployments

Jim Honerkamp, CIO of Hillman Group, is proud of his new business intelligence (BI) system. Why not? It's much better than what came before. In the bad old days, executives looking for sales information, for example, had to ask one of Honerkamp's programmers to make a manual database query to pull the numbers from the company's legacy systems. The lag time made the charts "stale the minute they came out," according to Honerkamp, whose company is a $380 million manufacturer and distributor of engraving technologies and hardware, such as keys and signs.

With Hillman Group's new BI system, curious business executives can query the system themselves and get instant answers about such critical questions as the number of unfilled customer orders, which is tracked by the system in real time. There's just one problem: The new system hasn't made the business better—at least not yet—only better informed.

That's generally the problem with BI, the umbrella term that refers to a variety of software applications used to analyze an organization's raw data (e.g., sales transactions) and extract useful insights from them. Most CIOs still think of it as a reporting and decision support tool. Although the tools haven't changed much recently, there is a small revolution going on in the ways BI tools are being deployed by some CIOs. Done right, BI projects can transform business processes—and the businesses that depend on those processes—into lean, mean machines.

It isn't easy to take BI to the next level; it requires a change in thinking about the value of information inside organizations from the CEO down. Information is power, and some people don't like to share it. Yet sharing is vital to this new vision of BI because everyone involved in the process must have full access to information to be able to change the ways that they work.

The other major impediment to using BI to transform business processes is that most companies don't understand their business processes well enough to determine how to improve them. Companies also need to be careful about the processes they choose. If the process does not have a direct impact on revenue, or the business isn't behind standardizing the process across the company, the entire BI effort could disintegrate. Companies need to understand all the activities that make up a particular business process, how information and data flow across various processes, how data are passed between business users, and how people use it to execute their particular part of the process. They need to understand all this before they start a BI project—if they hope to improve how people do their jobs.

The new, greater scope of these BI projects gives CIOs a strong justification for working with the business to study processes and determine how these tools and the insights they provide can support and improve them. Companies that use BI to uncover flawed business processes are in a much better position to successfully compete than those companies that use BI merely to monitor what's happening. Indeed, CIOs who don't use BI to transform business operations put their companies at a disadvantage. For CIOs who have carried out this difficult strategy successfully, there is no looking back.

Avnet, a computer systems, component, and embedded subsystems manufacturer, took the new process-oriented BI strategy directly to the processes that matter most: selling and serving customers. The company has put together a system from three BI vendors—Informatica, Business Objects, and InfoBurst—to generate reports on orders, shipment schedules, and dates by which Avnet will no longer manufacture certain products. Reports, however, were just the beginning. To transform the sales and customer service processes, CIO Steve Phillips rolled out the system to 2,000 salespeople so that they could actively incorporate that information into their day-to-day workflows and interactions with customers.

Employees use the information to modify their individual and teamwork practices, which leads to improved performance among the sales teams. When sales executives see a big difference in performance from one team to another, they work to bring the laggard teams up to the level of the leaders. "We try to identify, using our reporting tools, where best practices exist inside our work teams and then extend those best practices across the company," says Phillips.

One of those best practices is to alert customers if a product they have purchased in the past is about to be discontinued. Salespeople can ensure that customers have ordered enough for all of their future needs or identify a new component to replace the one that's being phased out. Those kinds of conversations boost sales and convince customers that Avnet's salespeople are looking out for their needs and interests.

It helps that Avnet's sales team is flexible and willing to adapt to the information. "Because our sales team is so flexible, they'll take this information from BI reports and change processes when they see a benefit to it," says Phillips.

Sometimes, they don't even realize they are changing the ways they work—a kind of organic reengineering. Indeed, salespeople benefit so directly from better information and have such a big impact on revenue that they can be the best advocates for transformative BI in the company.

Yet this kind of effortless link between information and processes doesn't happen by magic. Phillips says his company has been able to use BI effectively because IT and business users have worked closely and steadily. "We needed to know how things really happen day to day, over and above the documented processes so that we could anticipate some of the business's information needs as we built out the warehouse," says Phillips.

Now that the BI system matches up with the way the company conducts its business, improving those processes and sharing the improvements are that much easier. "This is not just about reporting," says Phillips. "It's about using BI to make us smarter."

Quaker Chemical used its BI system to change completely the way it manages accounts receivable. In the past, the process of keeping track of whether customers paid their bills, and if they paid them on time, was primarily the purview of employees in the accounting department. Collection managers used the company's accounting system to identify which accounts were overdue, but they had limited information about the details of overdue balances. As a result, they had visibility only into glaring payment problems—customers who hadn't paid their bills at all in 60 days or more—and couldn't proactively identify which customers were at risk for not paying in full. Occasionally, they asked a sales manager to get involved, but the whole process for identifying which customers weren't paying and why they weren't paying and putting salespeople on the case was ad hoc.

To improve accounts receivable, Quaker Chemical decided in early 2005 that salespeople needed to play a larger, more formal role in the collections process. After all, they were the ones who had the primary relationship with the customers and had opportunities to speak with them more often, more proactively, and more sympathetically about their outstanding payments.

To get the salespeople involved, the IT department created a data mart that extracted accounts receivable information from transaction systems: It analyzed historical payments and historical balances by customer and by transaction and then loaded it into the data warehouse. By using its BI tools from SAS to analyze factors such as the amount of time it took Quaker Chemical to collect payment from a customer on a given invoice, as well as the number of times

a customer paid part, but not all, of what he or she owed, the company was able to identify which customers were consistently paying late and which customers weren't paying at all. The IT department programmed the data warehouse to run reports automatically on which customers still owed money to Quaker Chemical. The system would then send those reports directly to the sales manager in charge of those accounts several times a month so that they could follow up with those customers. Collections managers no longer have to keep tabs on this information manually.

Quaker CIO Irving Tyler says this business process change was successful in part because IT was careful to deliver only the most specific, relevant information in these reports to salespeople. "If you don't focus the information and deliver it intelligently, people won't understand how to incorporate it into their workflows," says Tyler. This kind of dramatic change in process needs to be linked to the overall business strategy, according to Tyler. "Information doesn't necessarily change anything. You have to have a strategy to drive any change," he says.

Avnet and Quaker Chemical demonstrate that BI is about more than decision support. As a result of improvements in the technology and the way CIOs are implementing it, BI now has the potential to transform organizations. CIOs like Avnet's Phillips and Quaker Chemical's Tyler who successfully use BI to improve business processes contribute to their organizations in more far-reaching ways than by implementing basic reporting tools. "Our BI system provides information that helps us seek out greater efficiency," says Avnet's Phillips.

Source: Adapted from Meridith Levinson, "Business Intelligence: Not Just for Bosses Anymore," *CIO Magazine*, January 15, 2006; and Diann Daniel, "Five Ways to Get Your Employees Better Information More Quickly," *CIO Magazine*, January 10, 2008.

CASE STUDY QUESTIONS

1. What are the business benefits of BI deployments such as those implemented by Avnet and Quaker Chemical? What roles do data and business processes play in achieving those benefits?

2. What are the main challenges to the change of mindset required to extend BI tools beyond mere reporting? What can companies do to overcome them? Use examples from the case to illustrate your answer.

3. Both Avnet and Quaker Chemical implemented systems and processes that affect the practices of their salespeople. In which ways did the latter benefit from these new implementations? How important was their buy-in to the success of these projects? Discuss alternative strategies for companies to foster adoption of new systems like these.

REAL WORLD ACTIVITIES

1. Search the Internet for other examples of both "mere reporting" and transformational implementations of business intelligence tools. In which ways are these similar to the ones discussed in the case? In which ways are these different? What seems to be the main distinction between reporting and process-transformation BI rollouts? Prepare a report to summarize your findings.

2. How do you think the possession or access to certain information shapes the political dynamics of organizations? Do you believe companies should be open about widespread access to information, or will they be better off by restricting it? Why? Break into small groups with your classmates to discuss these issues, and take turns advocating the two alternative positions.

MODULE IV

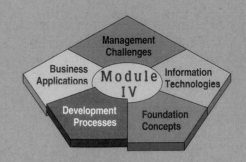

DEVELOPMENT PROCESSES

How can business professionals plan, develop, and implement strategies and solutions that use information technologies to help meet the challenges and opportunities faced in today's business environment? Answering that question is the goal of the chapters of this module, which concentrate on the processes for planning, developing, and implementing IT-based business strategies and applications.

- **Chapter 11: Developing Business/IT Strategies** emphasizes the importance of the planning process in developing IT/business strategies and the implementation challenges that arise when introducing new IT-based business strategies and applications into an organization.

- **Chapter 12: Developing Business/IT Solutions** introduces the traditional, prototyping, and end-user approaches to the development of information systems and discusses the processes and managerial issues in the implementation of new business applications of information technology.

CHAPTER 11

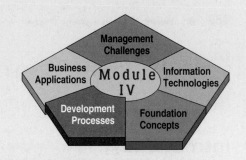

DEVELOPING BUSINESS/IT STRATEGIES

Chapter Highlights

Learning Objectives

After reading and studying this chapter, you should be able to:

1. Discuss the role of planning in the business use of information technology, using the scenario approach, and planning for competitive advantage as examples.

2. Discuss the role of planning and business models in the development of business/IT strategies, architectures, and applications.

3. Identify several change management solutions for end-user resistance to the implementation of new IT-based business strategies and applications.

SECTION I # Planning Fundamentals

Introduction

Imagine taking a caravan of thousands of people on a journey with no map, no plan, no one in charge, no logistical support, no way to keep everyone informed, no scouting reports to assess and update progress, and no navigational instruments. It would be sheer madness, yet that's how most companies are handling the transition to e-business.

Information technology has created a seismic shift in the way companies do business. Just knowing the importance and structure of e-business is not enough. You need to create and implement an action plan that allows you to make the transition from an old business design to a new e-business design.

That is why you need to learn some fundamental planning concepts, which is the goal of this section. We will first discuss several strategic planning concepts and then talk more specifically about developing IT-based business strategies and other planning issues. In Section II, we will discuss the process of implementing IT-based business plans and the challenges that arise when introducing new IT strategies and applications within a company.

Read the Real World Case on the next page. We can learn a lot about recent development trends and issues. See Figure 11.1.

Organizational Planning

Figure 11.2 illustrates the components of an organizational planning process. This fundamental planning process consists of (1) team building, modeling, and consensus; (2) evaluating what an organization has accomplished and the resources they have acquired; (3) analyzing their business, economic, political, and societal environments; (4) anticipating and evaluating the impact of future developments; (5) building a shared vision and deciding on what goals they want to achieve; and (6) deciding which actions to take to achieve their goals.

The result of this process is what we call a *plan*, which formally articulates the actions we feel are necessary to achieve our goals. Thus, a plan is an action statement. Plans lead to actions, actions produce results, and part of planning is learning from results. In this context, the planning process is followed by implementation, which is monitored by control measures, which provide feedback for planning.

Strategic planning deals with the development of an organization's mission, goals, strategies, and policies. Corporations may begin the process by developing a shared vision using a variety of techniques, including team building, scenario modeling, and consensus-creating exercises. Team planning sessions frequently include answering *strategic visioning* questions such as those shown in Figure 11.3. *Tactical planning* involves the setting of objectives and the development of procedures, rules, schedules, and budgets. *Operational planning* is done on a short-term basis to implement and control day-to-day operations. Typical examples are project planning and production scheduling.

Many organizational planning methodologies are used in business today. In this section, let's concentrate on two of the most popular methodologies: the scenario approach and planning for competitive advantage.

The Scenario Approach

Planning and budgeting processes are notorious for their rigidity and irrelevance to management action. Strict adherence to a process of rapid or efficient completion may only make the process less relevant to the true management agenda.

Managers and planners continually try different approaches to make planning easier, more accurate, and more relevant to the dynamic, real world of business.

REAL WORLD CASE 1

Planning for Cloud Applications Must Include the Developers

CIOs and IT managers know they must address concerns like security, compliance, service levels and end-user resistance when moving to cloud-based enterprise software, but they must not overlook a critical area: the feelings of their IT staffers.

When companies decide to unplug on-premise servers, ditch the applications housed on them, and adopt vendor-hosted software in the cloud, the IT staffers in charge of supporting and maintaining those discarded in-house systems are bound to get nervous.

High-level IT executives may have all the "i"s dotted and all the "t"s crossed in their research and planning process, but if the switch to the cloud causes ill will among their IT troops, the initiative could well be doomed, because buy-in from the IT rank and file is key.

It's the IT department's foot soldiers who will be in charge of training and supporting end users on the new cloud-based software, which often requires adjusting to, or developing, an interface that is different. These staffers may also have to build links between the new and existing systems, develop customized applications and tools, monitor the cloud vendor's performance, and keep tabs on end-user activities.

If IT staffers feel left out of the conversation and used as expendable pawns bound to go the way of the on-premise systems they used to maintain, their aversion to cloud-based software could spread to the organization at large.

IT staffers raised concerns about job security quickly and directly at the advertising and event marketing agency Momentum Worldwide, with offices in New York, London,

FIGURE 11.1

The development staff must be a part of all strategic moves—including moving to a cloud.

Source: © Punchstock.

and Sydney, as soon as they were informed the company planned to move its enterprise portal to a cloud, software-as-a-service model offered by Palo Alto-based enterprise collaboration vendor Socialtext.

"As we talked this through with the IT group, they were very concerned about: 'What are we going to do? If we're not managing as many servers, if we're not supporting infrastructure, where does that leave us?'" said Momentum Global IT director Doug Pierce.

About 8 of the IT department's 28 staffers saw their roles change when Momentum turned off its data center servers. "Our IT employees had a lot of questions. They flat-out asked: 'What does this mean for me and my job?'" Pierce said.

IT leaders better be ready to have an honest and informed conversation with their staffers. The path to success begins with explaining to them clearly the rationale for the move. "Being upfront about it, not hiding it, keeping it very open, and making sure IT employees understood was very helpful to our department's successful transition," Pierce said.

That's what IT leaders also did at worldwide electronic manufacturing services provider Sanmina-SCI when it decided to move 16,000 employees from an on-premise Microsoft Outlook-Exchange system to Google Apps, a communication and collaboration suite hosted by Google.

"The starting point is laying the context of what one is trying to do and where IT organizations in general are headed to over the next several years. That helps to frame the discussion," said Manesh Patel, CIO of Sanmina-SCI, which has about 700 IT staffers. "Setting that context is the first thing that CIOs need to do," he added.

At Sanmina-SCI, IT leaders told their team that with cloud computing, IT departments can shift grunt, hands-on system maintenance to hosted vendors, freeing up the IT department to provide value with more custom work tailored to their business.

"My view is that IT is becoming more of a service-oriented organization, providing more value-added services, with less emphasis on [maintaining in-house] systems, networks, and architectures," Patel said. "You still need some of that, but not as much."

When making the pitch to IT staffers, CIOs shouldn't focus exclusively on the issue of cutting costs. "If you look at it from a pure cost standpoint, you run the risk of creating a lot of negative reaction," Patel said.

As for most organizations, cost was an important element and initial driver for Sanmina-SCI, but the company was also seeking a longer-term value in making employees more productive and more effective when working with customers and suppliers.

"Make sure you communicate those things and provide the vision of what that means. Sometimes IT organizations are very cost-centric, and that's the only message," Patel added.

"IT leadership wanted software products that could move as fast as our business, and with this framework we can pull software in or out of our portal literally overnight," Pierce said.

In some cases, IT staffers quickly embrace the switch, like at Duralee Fabrics, a worldwide company with showrooms all over Europe and Asia, which ditched an on-premise, overtaxed, and creaky e-mail system that crashed frequently and replaced it with Google Apps for its 200 users. This lifted a heavy burden off of its six-person IT staff. "They were thrilled when we got rid of it and everything moved to the cloud," said Bill Kelly, Duralee's CIO.

There is no sugar-coating the fact that some roles will need to change, especially for employees directly tasked with supporting and maintaining the on-premise software and infrastructure being decommissioned. Those employees are often valuable and efficient, and with some retraining they can jump into new roles in the IT department that they may find more rewarding than their previous tasks. But IT leaders need to offer direction and resources to make that happen.

"IT management has to provide leadership, guidance, and assistance in helping employees make that transition. At the end of the day, not everyone makes it, but it's a trend over the next several years and those who embrace it will be more successful," Patel said.

Sanmina-SCI actively worked with impacted IT staffers to help them, and overall the transition went pretty smoothly, although there isn't much a company can do about employees who resist change.

"Sometimes you have people who want to do a very specific thing and they may not be a fit going forward," Patel said. "They may decide to pursue other opportunities elsewhere, or you may have to make that decision for them. In our experience, that's an exception. For the most part, we've been able to redirect our resources to more value-added activities."

Momentum managed to get all of its impacted IT employees on board with the switch. "It was a discussion early on that your roles are going to change, your skills are going to change, and we're going to work with you to get those skills up to speed in a cloud offering," Pierce said.

"We let them know that, hey, we're going into new technologies that are at the forefront of innovation and you're going to be right there with us, so they're very excited. We took the time to explain the vision and rally the troops around it," he said.

With an increase in this type of more creative, custom work often comes higher recognition for the IT department from the business units, the sort that infrastructure support work rarely prompts. "If we did a perfect job maintaining the in-house service for e-mail, no one is going to run into the IT department to high-five us on the great job we're doing. But if it goes down for five minutes, they'll be at the door with knives and pitchforks," Kelly said.

Source: Adapted from Juan Carlos Perez, "Cloud Apps Adoption Can Lead to IT Staff Unrest," *Computerworld*, Questex Media, May 17, 2010.

CASE STUDY QUESTIONS

1. How does the role of the developer change when moving applications to the cloud? Do you agree with this new development? Why or why not?

2. Why would there be internal resistance to moving applications to a cloud? Does this present a threat to developers in other areas of their work?

3. How do companies benefit from having their CIO meet with developers regarding strategic initiatives? Provide a few examples.

REAL WORLD ACTIVITIES

1. The IT function is notorious for being dynamic, and its leaders are no exception. Go online to research recent trends affecting the traditional roles of senior IT executives and how those roles are changing. Prepare a presentation to share your findings with the rest of the class.

2. "In the future, the prevalence of IT in product offerings will blur the distinction between IT and other areas of the company, to the extent that the IT function will cease to exist as a separate entity." Do you agree with this statement? Why? Break into small groups with your classmates to see if you can reach a consensus on the issue.

FIGURE 11.2 The components of an organizational planning process.

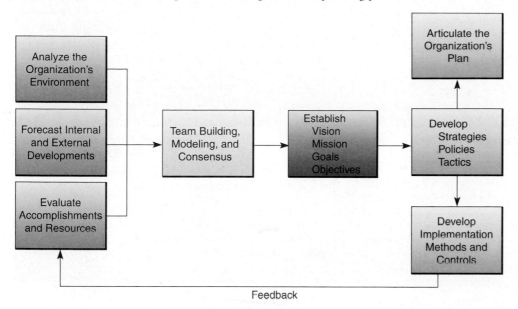

The **scenario approach to planning** has gained in popularity as a less formal, but more realistic, strategic planning methodology for use by business professionals.

In the scenario approach, teams of managers and other planners participate in what management author Peter Senge calls *microworld*, or *virtual world*, exercises. A microworld is a simulation exercise that is a microcosm of the real world. In a microworld exercise, managers can safely create, experience, and evaluate a variety of scenarios of what might be happening, or what might happen in the real world.

> *When a work team goes white water rafting or engages in some other outdoor team-building exercise, the team members are creating a microworld to reflect on and improve the way they work together. When personnel staff create a role-playing exercise to be used in a supervisory training, they are creating a microworld. Many team retreats serve as microworlds.*

Thus, in the scenario approach to strategic IS planning, teams of business and IS managers create and evaluate a variety of business scenarios. For example, they make assumptions about what a business will be like three to five years or more into the future, and the role that information technology can or will play in those future scenarios.

FIGURE 11.3 Examples of strategic visioning questions in planning for e-business initiatives.

Strategic Business Visioning	
● **Understanding the Customer**	Who are our customers? How are our customers' priorities shifting? Who should be our target customers? How will an e-business help reach our target customer segments?
● **Customer Value**	How can we add value for the customer with e-business services? How can we become the customer's first choice?
● **Competition**	Who are our real competitors? What is our toughest competitor's business model? What are they doing in e-business and e-commerce? Are our competitors potential partners, suppliers, or customers in an e-business venture?
● **Value Chain**	How would we design a value chain if we were just starting an e-business? Who would be our supply chain partners? What roles should we play: e-commerce Web site, B2C portal, B2B marketplace, or partner in an e-commerce alliance?

FIGURE 11.4   Converging business, political, and technological trends that are shaping strategic business/IT planning.

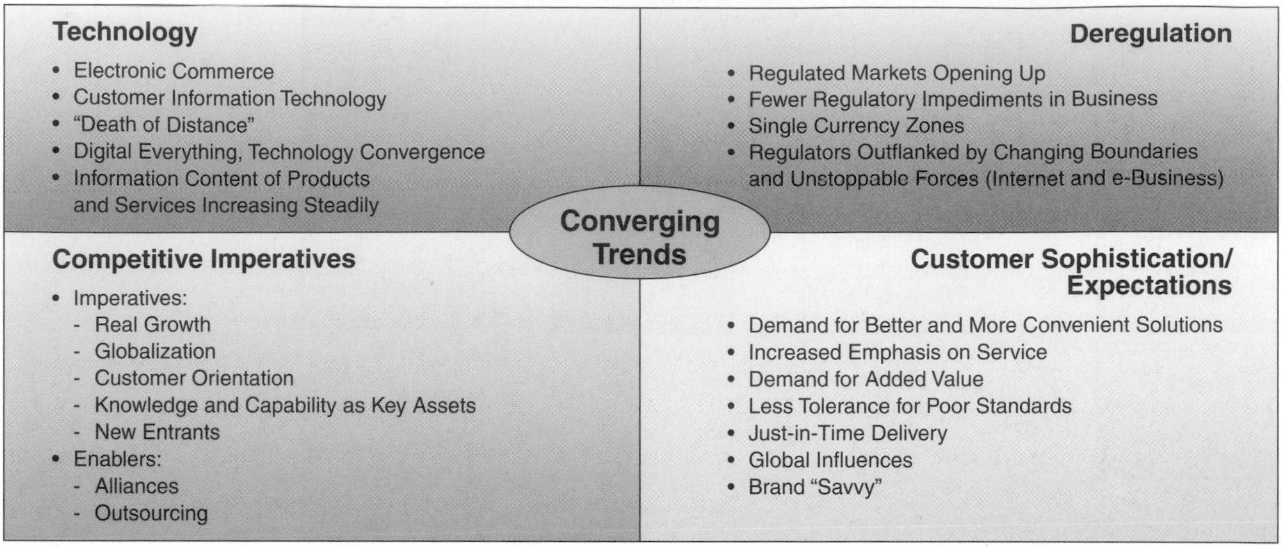

Technology
- Electronic Commerce
- Customer Information Technology
- "Death of Distance"
- Digital Everything, Technology Convergence
- Information Content of Products and Services Increasing Steadily

Deregulation
- Regulated Markets Opening Up
- Fewer Regulatory Impediments in Business
- Single Currency Zones
- Regulators Outflanked by Changing Boundaries and Unstoppable Forces (Internet and e-Business)

Converging Trends

Competitive Imperatives
- Imperatives:
  - Real Growth
  - Globalization
  - Customer Orientation
  - Knowledge and Capability as Key Assets
  - New Entrants
- Enablers:
  - Alliances
  - Outsourcing

Customer Sophistication/ Expectations
- Demand for Better and More Convenient Solutions
- Increased Emphasis on Service
- Demand for Added Value
- Less Tolerance for Poor Standards
- Just-in-Time Delivery
- Global Influences
- Brand "Savvy"

Alternative scenarios are created by the teams or by business simulation software, based on combining a variety of developments, trends, and environmental factors, including political, social, business, and technological changes that might occur. For example, Figure 11.4 outlines key business, political, and technological trends that could help guide business/IT planning.

Risk Assessment and Mitigation

CIOs are frequently asked, "What are our IT risks?" Unfortunately, this question is too generic because there are multiple kinds of risk. Before starting any risk assessment, IT needs to understand both the concern prompting the request and which risks need to be assessed. Moreover, everyone needs to understand that nearly all risks that affect an IT organization affect the entire business. Risks fall into four categories that require different mitigation tools:

Business operations risk. An assessment determines the risks involved in addressing or ignoring a particular competitive threat. Analyzing competitive threats helps the company decide whether to invest the resources necessary to combat the threat. Determining appropriate responses to competitive threats from nontraditional sources can be particularly difficult. The appropriate mitigation tool is a good business case that evaluates all associated risks. For new business opportunities, a thorough risk assessment may be as important to success as accurate financial projections.

Program risk. For approved or existing programs, management concerns focus on whether the program or project will be delivered on time, within budget, and with high quality. Effective project management and regular monitoring mitigate risk.

Business interruption risk. This type of risk affects the company's ability to continue operating under difficult circumstances. Scenarios run the gamut from a failed server to a destroyed building. In most cases, a failed server causes minor problems for certain people. In contrast, a destroyed building can bring all company operations to a halt. A continuity-of-operations plan that describes how the business will function in the event of various difficulties mitigates risk.

Market risk. This category is divided into geopolitical and industry-specific risks. Geopolitical risks include war, terrorism, and epidemics, as well as nationalization and import restrictions. These risks vary depending on the country, the complexity of the corporate supply chain, and the importance of the industry to political leadership. Industry-specific risks also vary. Scenario planning mitigates risk by developing responses to various unlikely events. Most important, it attempts to discover previously unknown risks because the most dangerous risk is often the one you don't identify.

Before embarking on any risk assessment, clarify which types of risk are of concern to your executive management; then select the appropriate mitigation tools to address potential difficulties. Depending on the financial consequences, risk insurance may be warranted. Thorough risk assessments leverage creative thinking into constructive preparations for addressing potential threats, and they're essential to success. As the old adage goes, "Forewarned is forearmed."

Source: Adapted from Bart Perkins, "Know Which Risks Matter," *Computerworld*, December 17, 2007.

Planning for Competitive Advantage

Betting on new IT innovations can mean betting the future of the company. Leading-edge firms are sometimes said to be on the "bleeding edge." Almost any business executive is aware of disastrous projects that had to be written off, often after large cost overruns, because the promised new system just did not work.

Planning for competitive advantage is especially important in today's competitive business arena and complex information technology environment. So, strategic business/IT planning involves an evaluation of the potential benefits and risks a company faces when using IT-based strategies and technologies for competitive advantage. In Chapter 2, we introduced a model of *competitive forces* (competitors, customers, suppliers, new entrants, and substitutes) and *competitive strategies* (cost leadership, differentiation, growth, innovation, and alliances), as well as a value chain model of basic business activities. These models can be used in a strategic planning process to help generate ideas for the strategic use of information technologies to support new e-business initiatives.

Also popular in strategic business/IT planning is the use of a *strategic opportunities matrix* to evaluate the strategic potential of proposed business/IT opportunities, as measured by their risk/payoff probabilities. See Figure 11.5.

SWOT Analysis

SWOT analysis (strengths, weaknesses, opportunities, and threats) is used to evaluate the impact that each possible strategic opportunity can have on a company and its use of information technology. A company's strengths are its core competencies and resources in which it is one of the market or industry leaders. Weaknesses are areas of substandard business performance compared to others in the industry or market segments. Opportunities are the potential for new business markets or innovative breakthroughs that might greatly expand present markets. Threats are the potential for

FIGURE 11.5

A strategic opportunities matrix helps to evaluate the strategic risk/payoff potential of proposed business/IT opportunities.

TABLE 11.1 Example of a SWOT Analysis by a Human Resources Consulting Firm

Strengths	Weaknesses	Opportunities	Threats
Market reputation	Shortage of trained consultants at the operating level	Well-established market niche	Large consultancies operating at a minor market level
Partner-level expertise in HRM	Lack of ability to manage multidisciplinary assignments	New market opportunities for consulting in areas other than HRM	Many small consultancies looking to invade the marketplace

business and market losses posed by the actions of competitors and other competitive forces, changes in government policies, disruptive new technologies, and so on.

An example of SWOT analysis might come from a marketing problem. In competitor analysis, marketers build detailed profiles of each competitor in the market, focusing especially on their relative competitive strengths and weaknesses. Marketing managers may examine each competitor's cost structure; sources of profits, resources, and competencies; competitive positioning and product differentiation; degree of vertical integration; historical responses to industry developments; and other factors.

Marketing management often finds it necessary to invest in research to collect the data required to perform accurate marketing analysis. As such, they often conduct market research to obtain this information; although marketers use a variety of techniques, some of the more common methods include:

- Qualitative marketing research, such as focus groups.
- Quantitative marketing research, such as statistical surveys.
- Experimental techniques, such as test markets.
- Observational techniques, such as ethnographic (on-site) observation.
- Marketing managers may also design and oversee various environmental scanning and competitive intelligence processes to help identify trends and inform the company's marketing analysis.

Table 11.1 shows the content of a typical SWOT analysis. Now let's look at a real-world example of how a company used technology to support SWOT analyses, and much more.

Bristow Helicopters: Technology-Supported SWOT, and Much More 	When Bristow Helicopters Ltd. started losing market share in the 1990s, executives moved to improve business processes across the Redhill, England-based company. "We needed to change facilities and maintenance processes, improve the efficiencies of the staff, improve the interface between sales and clients," says John Cloggie, technical director at the European business unit of Houston-based Bristow Group Inc., which provides helicopter services to the oil and gas industry. A key goal of this reengineering effort was to cut several million dollars from the operating budget of Bristow Helicopters. The company managed the project using MindGenius, "mind-mapping" software from East Kilbride, Scotland-based Gael Ltd. The product enabled it to conduct a SWOT analysis (an assessment of its strengths, weaknesses, opportunities, and threats), carve out various process reengineering tasks, and delegate them to appropriate groups. Each team then took the high-level version of the map and created its own subcategories, tasks, and deadlines for its designated work segment. Since beginning the project in 2004, says Cloggie, the company has managed to cut $6 million from its operating budget. "Mind mapping, of course, didn't directly create our $6 million savings, but it did allow us to control the project while it was being delivered," he says. "The speed with which you can map processes and capture knowledge is a huge return."

Mind mapping has been around for centuries, but it didn't garner much attention until psychologist Tony Buzan began to promote information visualization techniques in the 1970s. A mind map is a diagram that radially arranges words and images around a central theme. It's based on the cognitive theory that many people learn and recall information more easily through graphical representations. Mind mapping—increasingly called business mapping as it makes inroads into corporate settings—is used for a range of problem-solving and brainstorming activities, including managing projects, mapping business processes, creating workflows, planning events, and programming software.

At Bristow Helicopters, mind mapping is used for "virtually all business strategy projects," says Cloggie. Bristow has also used MindGenius for managing employee-retention efforts, and the company always uses it when introducing new aircraft types. "We have a [mind map] template that's 90 percent usable for any aircraft type. It's not just a checklist; it's a tool to help the engineer understand the processes by which he'll bring the aircraft in," says Cloggie. "Through it, he understands the interface with manufacturing, among different departments within the company, and with the Civil Aviation Authority."

As key business strategies are developed around mind maps, the technology will need to move beyond its status as a desktop product to better facilitate collaboration, say users. In fact, Cloggie was recently invited, along with other mind-map software users from various industries, to speak on this need before the Scottish Parliament.

"We talked about the need to take mind maps from being a personal tool to a cross-departmental business tool; you can't extract their true, cross business abilities if you can't work on maps simultaneously," says Cloggie. "With real-time collaboration, you can have experts develop templates and facilitators work with different teams to create maps, with the business as a whole sharing them."

Source: Adapted from Kym Gilhooly, "Business on the Map," *Computerworld*, July 3, 2006.

Business Models and Planning

"Business model" was one of the great buzzwords of the Internet boom, routinely invoked, as the writer Michael Lewis put it, "to invoke all manner of half-baked plans." A good business model, however, remains essential to every successful organization, whether it's a new venture or an established player.

A business model is a conceptual framework that expresses the underlying economic logic and system that prove how a business can deliver value to customers at an appropriate cost and make money. A business model answers vital questions about the fundamental components of a business, such as: Who are our customers? What do our customers value? How much will it cost to deliver that value to our customers? How do we make money in this business?

A business model specifies what value to offer customers, which customers should receive this value, which products and services will be supplied, and what the price will be. It also specifies how the business will organize and operate to have the capability to provide this value and sustain any advantage from providing this value to its customers. Figure 11.6 outlines more specific questions about the components of a business that all business models must answer. Figure 11.7 lists questions that illustrate the essential components of e-business models.

A business model is a valuable planning tool because it focuses attention on how all the essential components of a business fit into a complete system. Done properly, it forces entrepreneurs and managers to think rigorously and systemically about the value and viability of the business initiatives they are planning. Then the strategic planning process can be used to develop unique business strategies that capitalize on a firm's business model to help it gain competitive advantages in its industry and the markets it wants to dominate.

FIGURE 11.6

Questions that illustrate the components of all business models. A good business model effectively answers these questions.

Component of Business Model	Questions for All Business Models
Customer value	Is the firm offering its customers something distinctive or at a lower cost than its competitors?
Scope	To which customers (demographic and geographic) is the firm offering this value? What is the range of products/services offered that embody this value?
Pricing	How does the firm price the value?
Revenue source	Where do the dollars come from? Who pays for what value and when? What are the margins in each market and what drives them? What drives value in eachsource?
Connected activities	What set of activities does the firm have to perform to offer this value and when? How connected (in cross section and time) are these activities?
Implementation	What organizational structure, systems, people, and environment does the firm need to carry out these activities? What is the fit between them?
Capabilities	What are the firm's capabilities and capabilities gaps that need to be filled? How does a firm fill these capabilities gaps? Is there something distinctive about these capabilities that allows the firm to offer the value better than other firms and that makes them difficult to imitate? What are the sources of these capabilities?
Sustainability	What is it about the firm that makes it difficult for other firms to imitate it? How does the firm keep making money? How does the firm sustain its competitive advantage?

FIGURE 11.7

Questions that illustrate the components of e-business models that can be developed as part of the strategic business/IT planning process.

Component of Business Model	Questions Specific to e-Business Models
Customer value	What is it about Internet technologies that allows your firm to offer its customers something distinctive? Can Internet technologies allow you to solve a new set of problems for customers?
Scope	What is the scope of customers that Internet technologies enable your firm to reach? Does the Internet alter the product or service mix that embodies the firm's products?
Pricing	How does the Internet make pricing different?
Revenue source	Are revenue sources different with the Internet? What is new?
Connected activities	How many new activities must be performed as a result of the Internet? How much better can Internet technologies help you to perform existing activities?
Implementation	How do Internet technologies affect the strategy, structure, systems, people, and environment of your firm?
Capabilities	What new capabilities do you need? What is the impact of Internet technologies on existing capabilities?
Sustainability	Do Internet technologies make sustainability easier or more difficult? How can your firm take advantage of it?

Iridium Satellite: Finding the Right Business Model	Left for dead by many observers in the IT and telecommunications worlds just a few years ago, the reborn Iridium Satellite LLC, which provides satellite-based communications services, is showing new signs of life. Nowhere near the revenue and customer numbers posted by huge wireless telecommunications companies such as

Verizon Wireless and AT&T, it's definite progress for a company that was brought out of bankruptcy in 2000 and remodeled with a new focus and direction.

The first Iridium marketed itself as a consumer satellite telephone service, but its original phone was too bulky and its service too expensive for general adoption. There were also some service quirks consumers wouldn't accept, such as the need for line-of-sight connection to a satellite, which precluded using the phones indoors. After the buyout, the company recreated itself as a telecommunications provider that could offer reliable service in remote areas where cellular phones and landlines won't work, such as barren deserts, the Earth's poles, deep wilderness, disaster areas, and other isolated and harsh environments.

"Originally Iridium was focused on the wrong business, on the mass-market consumer business selling directly to customers," says Matt Desch, the company's CEO and chairman. Since its rebirth in 2001, the company has worked with more than 150 partner companies to find new business uses and niches for Iridium service in industries from mining to manufacturing to oil and gas exploration to forestry to emergency response needs. "We've developed an ecosystem around ourselves," Desch said. "That's a big difference."

Not all of Iridium's service is provided using handsets. An increasing part of its business is in machine-to-machine communications, using a sensor device about the size of a deck of playing cards that is attached to a ship, truck, container, or similar item. The device can send and receive short bursts of communications data to a satellite wherever it is on Earth. Some of these sensors are even located on buoys in the ocean, where weather agencies can monitor wave heights, winds, and other storm data in real time to provide warnings for onrushing storms. "That's the real fast part of our growth," Desch said of the short-burst data communications segment.

Max Engel, an analyst with Frost & Sullivan in Palo Alto, California, said that although Iridium's original idea to be a satellite phone service for the masses "was an obvious example of stupid failure," the change in business plan raises the service's prospects. "What the new management did when they bought it was it took the assets that originally cost billions, but were now freed of those expectations," Engel said. "They then asked, 'what can we do with this' and enlisted many partners" to create a more workable business model. "Yes, they're very nichy, but as long as you've got bunches of niches, who cares?" says Engel. "They've redesigned their business to suit their assets instead of creating an asset to do business."

"We're obviously hitting our stride," says Desch. "We're a lifeline where no other device can be used."

Source: Adapted from Todd Weiss, "Defying Naysayers, Iridium Satellite Finds a Business Model," *Computerworld*, July 27, 2007.

Business/IT Architecture Planning

Figure 11.8 illustrates the business/IT planning process, which focuses on discovering innovative approaches to satisfying a company's customer value and business value goals. This planning process leads to development of strategies and business models for new e-business and e-commerce platforms, processes, products, and services. Then a company can develop IT strategies and an IT architecture that supports building and implementing its newly planned business applications.

Both the CEO and the chief information officer (CIO) of a company must manage the development of complementary business and IT strategies to meet its customer value and business value vision. This *coadaptation* process is necessary because, as we have seen so often in this text, information technologies are a fast-changing but vital component in many strategic business initiatives. The business/IT planning process has three major components:

- **Strategic Development.** Developing business strategies that support a company's business vision, for example, using information technology to create innovative

FIGURE 11.8 The business/IT planning process emphasizes a customer and business value focus for developing business strategies and models, and an IT architecture for business applications.

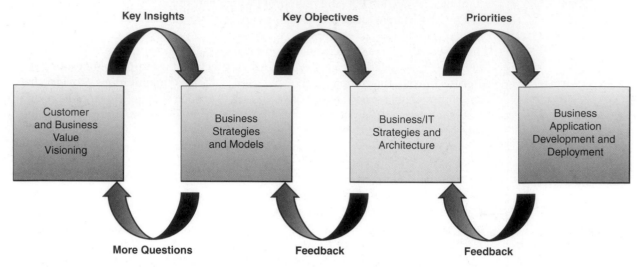

e-business systems that focus on customer and business value. We will discuss this process in more detail shortly.

- **Resource Management.** Developing strategic plans for managing or outsourcing a company's IT resources, including IS personnel, hardware, software, data, and network resources.

- **Technology Architecture.** Making strategic IT choices that reflect an information technology architecture designed to support a company's e-business and other business/IT initiatives.

Information Technology Architecture

The information technology architecture that is created by the strategic business/IT planning process is a conceptual design, or blueprint, that includes the following major components:

- **Technology Platform.** The Internet, intranets, extranets, and other networks, computer systems, system software, and integrated enterprise application software provide a computing and communications infrastructure, or platform, that supports the strategic use of information technology for e-business, e-commerce, and other business/IT applications.

- **Data Resources.** Many types of operational and specialized databases, including data warehouses and Internet/intranet databases (as reviewed in Chapter 5) store and provide data and information for business processes and decision support.

- **Applications Architecture.** Business applications of information technology are designed as an integrated architecture of enterprise systems that support strategic business initiatives, as well as cross-functional business processes. For example, an applications architecture should include support for developing and maintaining inter-enterprise supply chain applications, as well as integrated enterprise resource planning and customer relationship management applications as we discussed in Chapter 8.

- **IT Organization.** The organizational structure of the IS function within a company and the distribution of IS specialists are designed to meet the changing strategies of a business. The form of the IT organization depends on the managerial philosophy and business/IT strategies formulated during the strategic planning process. We will discuss the IT organization in Chapter 14.

Balanced Scorecard

In 1992, Robert S. Kaplan and David Norton introduced the **balanced scorecard** (BSC), a method for measuring a company's activities in terms of its vision and strategies.

It gives managers a comprehensive view of the performance of a business and has become a popular business and IT planning tool.

BSC is a strategic management system that forces managers to focus on the important performance metrics that drive success. It balances a financial perspective with customer, internal process, and learning and growth perspectives. The system consists of four processes: (1) translating the vision into operational goals; (2) communicating the vision and linking it to individual performance; (3) business planning; (4) feedback and learning, and then adjusting the strategy accordingly.

The **scorecard** seeks to measure a business from the following perspectives:

- **Financial Perspective.** This measures reflecting financial performance; for example, number of debtors, cash flow, or return on investment. The financial performance of an organization is fundamental to its success. Even **nonprofit organizations** must make the books balance. Financial figures suffer from two major drawbacks:
    - They tell us what has happened to the organization historically, but they may not tell us what is currently happening or be a good indicator of future performance.
    - It is common for the current market value of an organization to exceed the market value of its assets. Tobin's q measures the ratio of the value of a company's assets to its market value. The excess value can be thought of as intangible assets. These figures are not measured by normal financial reporting.
- **Customer Perspective.** This measures having a direct impact on customers; for example, time taken to process a phone call, results of customer surveys, number of complaints, or competitive rankings.
- **Business Process Perspective.** This measures reflecting the performance of key business processes; for example, time spent prospecting, number of units that required rework, or process cost.
- **Learning and Growth Perspective.** This measures describing the company's learning curve; for example, number of employee suggestions or total hours spent on staff training.

The balanced scorecard approach is not without its detractors, however. A major criticism of the balanced scorecard is that the scores are not based on any proven economic or financial theory and have no basis in the decision sciences. The process is entirely subjective and makes no provision to assess quantities like risk and economic value in a way that is actuarially or economically well-founded. The BSC does not provide a bottom-line score or a unified view with clear recommendations; rather, it is only a list of metrics. Positive responses from users of BSC may merely be a type of placebo effect, as there are no empirical studies linking the use of balanced scorecard to better decision making or improved financial performance of companies.

Despite these criticisms, BSC can be found in many organizations and is a common strategic planning tool. Figure 11.9 shows an example of a balanced scorecard analysis.

Identifying Business/IT Strategies

Companies need a strategic framework that can bridge the gap between simply connecting to the Internet and harnessing its power for competitive advantage. The most valuable Internet applications allow companies to transcend communication barriers and establish connections that will enhance productivity, stimulate innovative development, and improve customer relations.

Internet technologies and e-business and e-commerce applications can be used strategically for competitive advantage, as this text repeatedly demonstrates. However, in order to optimize this strategic impact, a company must continually assess the strategic value of such applications. Figure 11.10 is a strategic positioning matrix that can help a company identify where to concentrate its strategic use of Internet technologies to gain a competitive advantage. Let's take a look at the strategies that each quadrant of this matrix represents.

FIGURE 11.9

An example of a balanced scorecard analysis.

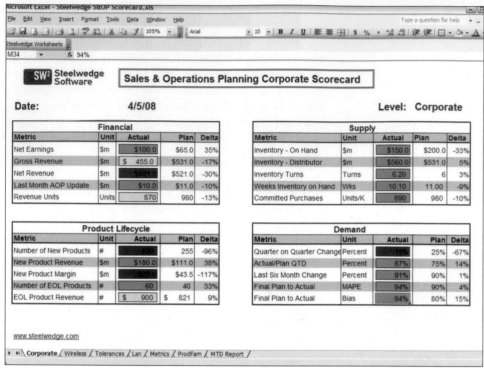

Source: Courtesy of Steelwedge Software, Inc.

- **Cost and Efficiency Improvements.** This quadrant represents a low amount of internal company, customer, and competitor connectivity and use of IT via the Internet and other networks. One recommended strategy would be to focus on improving efficiency and lowering costs by using the Internet and the World Wide Web as a fast, low-cost way to communicate and interact with customers, suppliers, and business partners. The use of e-mail, chat systems, discussion groups, and a company Web site are typical examples.

FIGURE 11.10

A strategic positioning matrix helps a company optimize the strategic impact of Internet technologies for e-business and e-commerce applications.

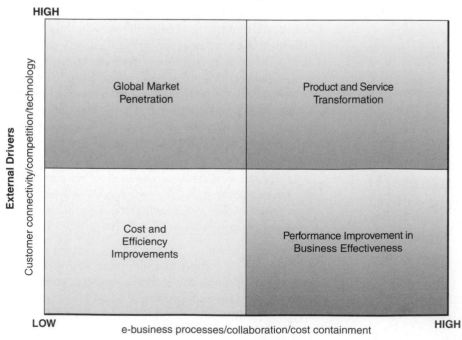

- **Performance Improvement in Business Effectiveness.** Here a company has a high degree of internal connectivity and pressures to improve its business processes substantially, but external connectivity by customers and competitors is still low. A strategy of making major improvements in business effectiveness is recommended. For example, widespread internal use of Internet-based technologies like intranets and extranets can substantially improve information sharing and collaboration within the business and with its trading partners.

- **Global Market Penetration.** A company that enters this quadrant of the matrix must capitalize on a high degree of customer and competitor connectivity and use of IT. Developing e-business and e-commerce applications to optimize interaction with customers and build market share is recommended. For example, e-commerce Web sites with value-added information services and extensive online customer support would be one way to implement such a strategy.

- **Product and Service Transformation.** Here a company and its customers, suppliers, and competitors are extensively networked. Internet-based technologies, including e-commerce Web sites and e-business intranets and extranets, must now be implemented throughout the company's operations and business relationships. This enables a company to develop and deploy new Internet-based products and services that strategically reposition it in the marketplace. Using the Internet for e-commerce transaction processing with customers at company Web sites and e-commerce auctions and exchanges for suppliers are typical examples of such strategic e-business applications. Let's look at more specific examples.

e-Business Strategy Examples	**Market creator.** Use the Internet to define a new market by identifying a unique customer need. This model requires you to be among the first to market and to remain ahead of competition by continuously innovating. Examples: Amazon.com and E*TRADE.

Market creator. Use the Internet to define a new market by identifying a unique customer need. This model requires you to be among the first to market and to remain ahead of competition by continuously innovating. Examples: Amazon.com and E*TRADE.

Channel reconfiguration. Use the Internet as a new channel to access customers, make sales, and fulfill orders directly. This model supplements, rather than replaces, physical distribution and marketing channels. Example: Cisco and Dell.

Transaction intermediary. Use the Internet to process purchases. This transactional model includes the end-to-end process of searching, comparing, selecting, and paying online. Examples: Microsoft Expedia and eBay.

Infomediary. Use the Internet to reduce the search cost. Offer the customer a unified process for collecting information necessary to make a large purchase. Examples: HomeAdvisor and Auto-By-Tel.

Self-service innovator. Use the Internet to provide a comprehensive suite of services that the customer's employees can use directly. Self-service affords employees a direct, personalized relationship. Examples: Employease and Healtheon.

Supply chain innovator. Use the Internet to streamline the interactions among all parties in the supply chain to improve operating efficiency. Examples: McKesson and Ingram Micro.

Channel mastery. Use the Internet as a sales and service channel. This model supplements, rather than replaces, the existing physical business offices and call centers. Example: Charles Schwab.

Source: Adapted from Joan Magretta, "Why Business Models Matter," *Harvard Business Review*, May 2002.

Business Application Planning

The business application planning process begins after the strategic phase of business/IT planning has occurred. Figure 11.11 shows that the application planning process includes the evaluation of proposals made by the IT management of a company for using information technology to accomplish the strategic business priorities developed earlier in the planning process, as was illustrated in Figure 11.8. Then, company

FIGURE 11.11

A business application planning process includes consideration of IT proposals for addressing the strategic business priorities of a company and planning for application development and implementation.

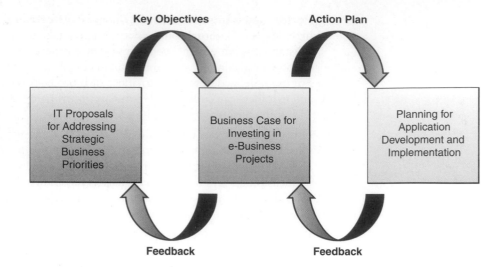

executives and business unit managers evaluate the business case for investing in proposed e-business development projects based on the strategic business priorities that they decide are most desirable or necessary at that point in time. Finally, business application planning involves developing and implementing business applications of IT, as well as managing their development projects. We will cover the application development and implementation process in Chapter 12. Now, let's examine a real world example.

Avnet Marshall: e-Business Planning

Figure 11.12 outlines Avnet Marshall's planning process for e-business initiatives and compares it to conventional IT planning approaches. Avnet Marshall weaves both e-business and IT strategic planning together *coadaptively* under the guidance of the CEO and the CIO, instead of developing IT strategy by just tracking and supporting business strategies. Avnet Marshall also locates IT application development projects within the business units that are involved in an e-business initiative to form centers of business/IT expertise throughout the company. Finally, Avnet Marshall uses an application development process with rapid deployment of e-business applications, instead of a traditional systems development approach. This application development strategy trades the risk of implementing incomplete applications with the benefits of gaining competitive advantages from early deployment of e-business services to employees, customers, and other stakeholders. It also involves them in the fine-tuning phase of application development.

Source: Adapted from Omar El Sawy, Arvind Malhotra, Sanjay Gosain and Kerry Young, "IT-Intensive Value Innovation in the Electronic Economy: Insights from Marshall Industries," *MIS Quarterly*, December 1997.

FIGURE 11.12

Comparing conventional and e-business strategic and application planning approaches.

Conventional IT Planning	Avnet Marshall's e-Business Planning
• Strategic alignment: IT strategy tracks specified enterprise strategy	• Strategic improvisation: IT strategy and enterprise business strategy coadaptively unfold based on the clear guidance of a focus on customer value
• CEO endorses IT vision shaped through CIO	• CEO proactively shapes IT vision jointly with CIO as part of e-business strategy
• IT application development projects functionally organized as technological solutions to business issues	• IT application development projects co-located with e-business initiatives to form centers of IT-intensive business expertise
• Phased application development based on learning from pilot projects	• Perpetual application development based on continuous learning from rapid deployment with incomplete functionality and end-user involvement

FIGURE 11.13   E-business architecture planning integrates business strategy development and business process engineering to produce e-business and e-commerce applications using the resources of the IT architecture, component development technologies, and a repository of business models and application components.

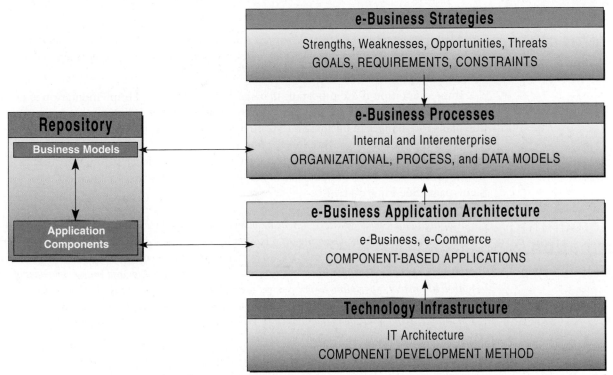

Source: Adapted from Peter Fingar, Harsha Kumar, and Tarun Sharma, *Enterprise E-Commerce: The Software Component Breakthrough for Business to Business Commerce* (Tampa, FL: Meghan-Kiffer Press, 2000), p. 68.

Business/IT Architecture Planning

Another way to look at the business/IT planning process, which is growing in acceptance and use in industry, is shown in Figure 11.13. E-business architecture planning combines contemporary strategic planning methods (for example, SWOT analysis and alternative planning scenarios) with more recent business modeling and application development methodologies (for example, component-based development). As illustrated in Figure 11.13, strategic e-business initiatives, including strategic goals, constraints, and requirements, are developed based on SWOT analysis and other planning methods. Application developers then use business process engineering methods to define how strategic business requirements are to be implemented; they use organizational, process, and data models to create new internal and interenterprise e-business processes among a company's customers, suppliers, and other business partners.

Component-based e-business and e-commerce applications are then developed to implement the new business processes using application software and data components stored in a *repository* of reusable business models and application components. Of course, the business process engineering and component-based application development activities are supported by a company's technology infrastructure; this includes all the resources of its IT architecture, as well as the necessary component development technologies. So, e-business architecture planning links strategy development to business modeling and component development methodologies in order to produce the strategic e-business applications needed by a company.

SECTION II   Implementation Challenges

Implementation

Many companies plan really well, yet few translate strategy into action, even though senior management consistently identifies e-business as an area of great opportunity and one in which the company needs stronger capabilities.

Implementation is an important managerial responsibility. Implementation is doing what you planned to do. You can view implementation as a process that carries out the plans for changes in business/IT strategies and applications that were developed in the planning process we covered in Section I.

Read the Real World Case on the next page. We can learn a lot from this case about some of the ways companies can bring everybody involved in a project onto the same page. See Figure 11.14.

Implementing Information Technology

Moving to an e-business environment involves a major organizational change. For many large, global companies, becoming an e-business is the fourth or fifth major organizational change they have undergone since the early 1980s. Many companies have gone through one or more rounds of business process reengineering (BPR); installation and major upgrades of an ERP system; upgrading legacy systems to be Y2K compliant; creating shared service centers; implementing just-in-time (JIT) manufacturing; automating the sales force; contract manufacturing; and the major challenges related to the introduction of euro currency.

Implementation of new e-business strategies and applications is only the latest catalyst for major organizational changes enabled by information technology. Figure 11.15 illustrates the impact and the levels and scope of business changes that applications of information technology introduce into an organization. For example, implementing an application such as online transaction processing brings efficiency to single-function or core business processes. Yet, implementing e-business applications such as enterprise resource management or customer relationship management requires a reengineering of core business processes internally and with supply chain partners, thus forcing a company to model and implement business practices by leading firms in their industry. Of course, any major new business initiatives can enable a company to redefine its core lines of business and precipitate dramatic changes within the entire interenterprise value chain of a business.

As we will see in this section, implementing new business/IT strategies requires managing the effects of major changes in key organizational dimensions such as business processes, organizational structures, managerial roles, employee work assignments, and stakeholder relationships that arise from the deployment of new business information systems. For example, Figure 11.16 emphasizes the variety and extent of the challenges reported by 100 companies that developed and implemented new enterprise information portals and ERP systems.

End-User Resistance and Involvement

Any new way of doing things generates some resistance from the people affected. For example, the implementation of new work support technologies can generate employees' fear and resistance to change. Let's look at a real-world example that demonstrates the challenges of implementing major business/IT strategies and applications, the change management challenges that confront management. Customer relationship management (CRM) is a prime example of a key e-business application for many companies today. It is designed to implement a business strategy of using IT to support a total customer care focus for all areas of a company. Yet CRM projects have a history of a high rate of failure in meeting their objectives. For example, according to a report from Meta Group, a staggering 55 percent to 75 percent of CRM projects fail to meet their objectives, often as a result of sales-force automation problems and "unaddressed cultural issues"—sales staffs that are often resistant to, or even fearful of, using CRM systems.

REAL WORLD
CASE 2

Centene, Flowserve, and Shaw Industries: Relationships, Collaboration, and Project Success

Managed care provider Centene has just finished deploying a new financial system. CIO Don Imholz says the project, which involved multiple PeopleSoft modules as well as financial planning and reporting software from Hyperion, was completed "very quickly"—in 12 months—and on budget.

Imholz believes the project was successful for a number of reasons, including that the company implemented proven technology and hired a systems integrator to help who was experienced with PeopleSoft. Most importantly, Imholz says the project was successful because of "good teaming between the IT organization, the finance organization and the systems integration resources."

In other words, much of the project's success came down to people skills.

The constructive relationship between IT and finance—and in particular, between Imholz and Centene's CFO, William Scheffel—ultimately kept the project on track when the going got tough.

And it did get tough.

For example, at one point, the project team was having trouble setting up the technical environment needed to deploy a Hyperion module that a third-party was going to host. The difficulties that IT encountered put the project's schedule at risk, says Imholz.

Had the relationship between IT and finance been acrimonious, the organizations would have pointed fingers at each other—a counterproductive move that would have further delayed the project. Instead, says Imholz, they worked together to recover the lost time and keep the implementation on schedule.

"We could have blamed each other and told each other we can't help," says the CIO. "But there's no value in doing that. It delays getting to the solution. If IT or finance tried

FIGURE 11.14

Fostering relationships between IT and business partners has a major impact on project success.

Source: © Manchan/Getty Images.

to recover the schedule alone it wouldn't have happened. We had to do it together."

Good relationships—between IT and business partners, project managers and IT staff, and project managers and stakeholders—keep IT projects on track, say IT leaders and project management experts.

Bad relationships, however, are a leading cause of project failure.

Faced with mounting operational and regulatory pressures, Linda Jojo, Flowserve's CIO, knew it was time to simplify the company's entire IT infrastructure—an endeavor that would bring about sweeping changes across an enterprise spanning more than 56 countries.

At Flowserve, a world leader in the supplying of pumps, valves, seals, automation, and services to the power, oil, gas, chemical, and other industries, Jojo's assignment was heavy on IT change as the company sought to update processes and systems: establishing a common IT infrastructure, introducing global help desk capabilities, and cutting dozens of disparate ERP systems. But that didn't stop her from taking a decidedly business approach to simplifying Flowserve's IT footprint.

"The first step was making sure that this wasn't viewed as an IT project," says Jojo. "From our CEO, our leadership team and our board of directors on down, we've made sure that this project is something we talk about in terms of its business impact."

It's a tactic that helped set the scope for a project that could have otherwise become unwieldy. For starters, Jojo helped assemble 35 divisional representatives from across the globe at the company's world headquarters. Here, holed up in a conference room for 17 weeks, these divisional representatives pored over disparate systems and processes, deciding what was—and wasn't—worthy of improvement.

Throughout this period, Flowserve also called on internal subject-matter experts, from engineers to sales representatives, to offer their in-the-trenches take on the company's shortcomings.

The result: a blueprint for business standards, the design of a common financial chart of accounts, and the creation of a set of data standards for customers and suppliers. In addition to creating project perimeters, Jojo says that by involving business leaders in the critical design phase, she was able to garner widespread support for a companywide strategic business initiative costing more than $60 million over four years.

"I've seen projects that should have been successful fail purely because of relationship issues," says Greg Livingston, director of IS planning and system development at Shaw Industries, a flooring manufacturer.

On the other hand, when mutual trust exists between IT project managers and stakeholders, "IT project managers are more likely to discuss problems that could threaten the project as they arise," says Imholz. If bad blood exists between the two groups, project managers may not be inclined to point out those issues, or they may try to cover them up.

"If you look at projects that fail, invariably someone on those projects knew things were going bad," says Imholz. "If you don't have relationships and trust, those things don't surface. And when you don't do something about problems in a timely manner, those problems invariably get bigger. In many cases, minor problems become more serious because they're not addressed in a timely manner. A culture of openness is absolutely essential to good project performance."

Furthermore, when something does go wrong with a project, business partners are less likely to place the sole blame for them on IT if they respect IT, says Shaw Industries's Livingston. In fact, they're more likely to give IT some leeway with the project schedule, he says.

"It doesn't matter what technology you're using, how talented your technology staff is and how knowledgeable the business partners are on process and business improvement: Every system initiative will have issues," says Livingston. "If you don't have a relationship, you resort to pointing fingers as opposed to being transparent and admitting 'we messed up' or 'we didn't test that as well.' If you have a good relationship, you'll sit down and find a way to make it work."

Decisions affecting the project also get made more promptly when everyone involved gets along. "Fast and good decisions are crucial to keeping projects on track," says Imholz. "The failure of senior people to make decisions means decisions are made at lower levels of the organization. If you have a software developer who's waiting for a decision on a business requirement, there's three things that can happen: He can guess what to do and guess right. He can wait for a decision and while he's waiting he's not as productive. Third, he can guess and guess wrong. If those are equal possibilities, two-thirds of the time it will be detrimental to the project. And if you stack enough of those decisions on top of each other, it will negatively impact the project."

Despite the positive impact good relationships have on project management, IT project managers rely more heavily on software and methodologies than on building relations when they need to improve their delivery. It's no wonder: Compared with the time it takes to build relationships, software seems like a quick fix. IT project managers are also most comfortable with tools.

Shaw Industries's Livingston is using Scrum, an agile software development practice, to improve relationships between IT and business partners and ensure project success. With Scrum, says Livingston, business partners meet with IT during a four- to eight-hour planning meeting to look at all the projects in the backlog and to jointly determine which one will bring the greatest value to Shaw Industries. IT then divides the project into sprints—30-day increments of work. When IT completes a sprint, business partners assess IT's progress and suggest any necessary changes.

"The agile development methodology, just by design, promotes better relationships," says Livingston. "Scrum and Agile force interaction on a more frequent basis. By doing so, IT delivers solutions on an incremental basis to the business, as opposed to the waterfall method, where it's a year and a half before the business sees the fruits of an initiative."

Livingston says it's not necessary for IT and other business functions to get along swimmingly for Agile to work effectively. Agile can work even if there's initial tension between the groups, he says. "We've had groups with troubled relationships, and certainly initial meetings are not always effective out of the gate," he says. "But at least we can agree that we're going to focus on 15 key items in the next 30 days, and at the end of the 30 days, we'll get back to you."

The process forces IT and business partners to prioritize projects together and agree on the 15 items IT will complete in 30 days. Scrum also then drives IT's behavior. At the end of that 30 days, IT has to show something for its work. Scrum makes IT accountable to the business.

When business partners see IT making tangible progress every 30 days, their confidence in IT grows. Says Livingston, "If the business partner sees results more frequently than they used to, relationships can get better. Agile promotes better relationships just by forcing a process, forcing interaction."

Between the structure that Scrum imposes and the relationships that grow out of it, project delivery improves. Livingston says Shaw Industries is seeing this happen: "Better collaboration results in better value for the business," he says.

Source: Adapted from Meridith Levinson, "Project Management: How IT and Business Relationships Shape Success," *CIO.com*, September 16, 2009; and Cindy Waxer, "Using IT to Transform the Business: Three Keys to Success," *CIO.com*, August 6, 2007.

CASE STUDY QUESTIONS

1. Why do you think the practices described in the case led to success for these companies?
2. How do they change the structure of projects so that the likelihood of a positive outcome increases?
3. In the case of Shaw Industries, how did Scrum help?
4. Provide three specific examples from the case, and explain where and how those activities helped the company move their projects along.
5. Using examples from the case and your own understanding of how those worked, can you distill a set of recommendations that companies should follow when managing technology-based projects? Would these be universal, or would you add any limitations to their applicability?

REAL WORLD ACTIVITIES

1. The Scrum approach to project management has become quite popular in recent years. Go online and research other companies that are using it to organize their projects. Have those experiences been positive as well? What can you tell about how the approach works from your research? Prepare a report to summarize your findings.
2. Would the issues discussed in the case be solved by making a business executive the head of any projects involving IT? Why or why not? Break into small groups with your classmates and develop a justification for both alternatives.

FIGURE 11.15   The impact and the levels and scope of business change introduced by implementations of information technology.

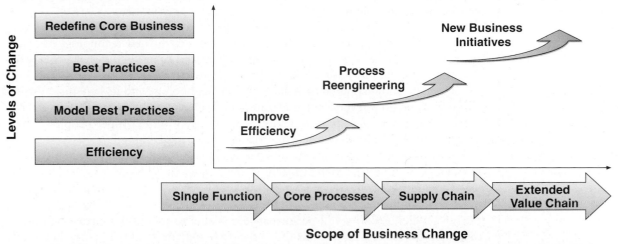

Source: Adapted from Craig Fellenstein and Ron Wood, *Exploring E-Commerce, Global E-Business and E-Societies* (Upper Saddle River, NJ: Prentice Hall, 2000), p. 97.

FIGURE 11.16

The 10 greatest challenges of developing and implementing intranet enterprise portals and enterprise resource planning systems reported by 100 companies.

Intranet Enterprise Portal Challenges	Enterprise Resource Planning Challenges
• Security, security, security	• Getting end-user buy-in
• Defining the scope and purpose of the portal	• Scheduling/planning
• Finding the time and the money	• Integrating legacy systems/data
• Ensuring consistent data quality	• Getting management buy-in
• Getting employees to use it	• Dealing with multiple/international sites and partners
• Organizing the data	• Changing culture/mind-sets
• Finding technical expertise	• IT training
• Integrating the pieces	• Getting, keeping IT staff
• Making it easy to use	• Moving to a new platform
• Providing all users with access	• Performance/system upgrades

Société de Transport de Montréal: Smooth Ride after a Bumpy Start

Suburban sprawl might make a great business case for a transit agency, but when it came to servers, Canada's Société de Transport de Montréal (STM) drew the line. Mike Stefanakis, senior systems engineer at STM, says that the main reason he started looking at virtualization technology was to prevent server sprawl. He wanted consolidation, particularly for development servers at the agency, which provides more than 360 million bus and metro rides each year.

"We crunched the numbers and realized that our growth was going to cause a few problems in the near future," he says. If things kept going as they had, the agency would need an additional 20 to 30 servers each year, on top of its existing base of 180 primarily Wintel machines. "Too many servers were going to be needed to feed the needs of our users and clients," Stefanakis says.

But even though staffers were convinced of virtualization's benefits pretty early on, the agency's end users didn't necessarily feel the same way. Several factors contributed to the initial resistance. For starters, there was a fear of the unknown. There were questions like "How stable is this new technology?" and "What do you mean I will be sharing my resources with other servers?" Potential users thought the new technology might slow them down.

To help users get over their fears, Stefanakis focused on giving people the information they needed, while explaining the advantages of the new technology. Among them: great response time for business applications and baked-in disaster recovery. If anything does fail, restoration is just a quickly restored image away.

Stefanakis and his staff kept "talking up" the technology and its benefits. "Virtualization came up in every budget, strategy and development meeting we had," he recalls. "We made sure the information was conveyed to the proper people so that everyone in our department knew that virtualization was coming."

STM has been staging production servers in its virtual environment since December 2005. The first virtual machine was staged in STM's testing center as a means of quickly recovering a downed production server. Once the first few applications were implemented, user resistance quickly became history. "After people see the advantages, stability and performance available to them on a virtual platform, they tend to lose any inhibitions they previously may have had. The psychological barrier for virtualization has been broken," Stefanakis says, "and now users will ask for a new server as if they are ordering a coffee and danish."

Source: Adapted from Mary Ryan Garcia, "After Bumpy Start, Transit Agency Finds Virtualization a Smooth Ride," *Computerworld*, March 8, 2007.

One of the keys to solving problems of end-user resistance to new information technologies is proper education and training. Even more important is end-user involvement in organizational changes and in the development of new information systems. Organizations have a variety of strategies to help manage business change, and one basic requirement is the involvement and commitment of top management and all business stakeholders affected by the planning processes that we described in Section I.

Direct end-user participation in business planning, as well as application development projects before a new system is implemented, is especially important in reducing the potential for end-user resistance. That's why end users frequently are members of systems development teams or do their own development work. Such involvement helps ensure that end users assume ownership of a system and that its design meets their needs. Systems that tend to inconvenience or frustrate users cannot be effective systems, no matter how technically elegant they are and how efficiently they process data. For example, Figure 11.17 illustrates some of the major obstacles to knowledge management systems in business. Notice that end-user resistance to sharing knowledge is the biggest obstacle to the implementation of knowledge management applications. Let's look at a real-world example that spotlights end-user resistance and what one company did about it.

FIGURE 11.17

Obstacles to knowledge management systems. Note that end-user resistance to knowledge sharing is the biggest obstacle.

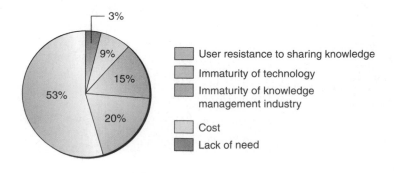

Implementation and Change Management Are Key Issues for Consultants to Avoid Problems

California's Marin County has sued Deloitte Consulting for US$30 million over a botched SAP Enterprise Resource Planning (ERP) project. The lawsuit, filed in Marin County Superior Court in mid-2010, accuses Deloitte of misrepresenting its skills and capabilities when originally pitching for the project back in 2004.

The 38-page complaint alleges that Deloitte was lying when the company promised to assemble a team of its "best resources" for the project and when it claimed to have "deep SAP and public sector knowledge" when marketing itself to the county.

Deloitte's misrepresentation of facts resulted in a defectively designed and deficiently implemented project that resulted in the county having to pay millions of dollars to remedy, the lawsuit alleged.

Meanwhile, Deloitte is claiming that it fulfilled all of its obligations under the contract. The company filed an administrative claim shortly after the suit was filed with the Marin County Board of Supervisors seeking more than $444,000 in unpaid dues, and an additional $111,000 in late charges.

"To be clear, the SAP software was working properly when we completed our work in November 2007," a company spokesman said by e-mail.

"Although we are confident that we will prevail in court, it remains our belief that this dispute can and should be resolved in a more logical fashion that benefits the county and its taxpayers," the statement said.

According to Marin County's complaint, the county hired Deloitte to replace its aging financial management, payroll, and HR systems because the county did not have the skills to accomplish the task in-house.

At the time it was hired, Deloitte knew that the county would depend exclusively on Deloitte's resources and on its recommendations for the project, the complaint noted.

"Throughout the months-long selection process county officials stressed to Deloitte that county officials did not have experience working on projects," such as the SAP implementation, the complaint said.

Deloitte knew that its consultants were the only ones with SAP knowledge on the project and that it would be the "lead party" on the entire effort.

Deloitte was selected from a pool of 13 vendors, based on its claims about its skills, its integration testing processes, and its change management abilities. The company's failure to deliver on any of these fronts resulted in a SAP system that was full of errors and substantially worse than the legacy system it was meant to replace. For instance, the error rate on the new payroll system was about five times higher compared to the legacy system, forcing the county to limit its use of the system and turn to manual processes instead, the complaint noted.

The problems became so bad that the county fired Deloitte in late 2007 and instituted a "Get Well" project to stabilize the system. Deloitte treated Marin County as little more than a "trial-and-error public sector training ground" for its inexperienced consultants, the lawsuit claimed. Much of the system had to be redesigned, retested, and reimplemented over the past few years at substantial taxpayer cost, the complaint alleged.

Deloitte did not have the ability or intention to provide the skilled resources needed for the project, but it claimed otherwise, just to secure the county's "lucrative" contract, the complaint noted, while asking the court to order Deloitte to pay back the $30 million the county has spent so far on the project.

In its administrative complaint, Deloitte noted that Marin County officials had not informed it of any deficiencies nor of any breach of contract, and neither had it withheld any payments even though the agreement between the two parties clearly allowed for action.

If the county had any issues with Deloitte, it never made them known until after a specific change order was placed in June 2007, shortly before the company was fired. "We fulfilled each and every one of our obligations under the contract, as evidenced three years ago when all of our work was approved by the county officials responsible for the project," the company noted.

Numerous lawsuits have been filed over the past several years in connection with failed ERP implementations. The only difference with Marin County's lawsuit is that it targets the systems integrator rather than the ERP vendor. Almost all other cases have involved customers suing ERP vendors directly for botched implementations.

Earlier in 2010 for instance, a lawsuit between SAP and one of its customers, Waste Management, was quietly settled for an undisclosed amount. Waste Management had earlier sued SAP for fraud after incurring what it said were significant damages from a $100 million ERP project that it said had turned out to be a complete disaster. Similarly, last August, Public Health Foundation Enterprises sued Lawson Software over a failed ERP implementation.

Source: Adapted from Jaikumar Vijayan, "Deloitte Hit with $30M Lawsuit Over Failed ERP Project," *Computerworld*, Hong Kong, Questex Media, June 7, 2010.

Change Management

Figure 11.18 illustrates some of the key dimensions of change management and the level of difficulty and business impact involved. Notice some of the people, process, and technology factors involved in the implementation of business/IT strategies and applications, or other changes caused by introducing new information technologies into a company. Some of the technical factors listed, such as systems integrators and outsourcing, will be discussed in more detail in the next few chapters. For example, systems integrators are consulting firms or other outside contractors who may be paid to assume the responsibility for developing and implementing a new e-business application, including designing and leading its change management activities. In addition, notice that people factors have the highest level of difficulty and longest time to resolve of any dimension of change management.

Thus, people are a major focus of organizational change management. This includes activities such as developing innovative ways to measure, motivate, and reward performance. It is important to design programs to recruit and train employees in the core competencies required in a changing workplace. Change management also involves analyzing and defining all changes facing the organization, as well as developing programs to

FIGURE 11.18 Some of the key dimensions of change management. Examples of the people, process, and technology factors involved in managing the implementation of IT-based changes to an organization.

	Technology	Process	People
Strategic	• Enterprise Architecture • Supplier Partnership • Systems Integrators • Outsourcing	• Ownership • Design • Enterprisewide Processes • Interenterprise Processes	• Change Leaders • Loose/Tight Controls • Executive Sponsorship and Support • Aligning on Conditions of Satisfaction
Operational	• Technology Selection • Technology Support • Installation Requirements	• Change Control • Implementation Management • Support Processes	• Recruitment • Retention • Training • Knowledge Transfer

Impact on Business — High / Low

Level of Difficulty/Time to Resolve — Low / High

Source: Adapted from Grant Norris, James Hurley, Kenneth Hartley, John Dunleavy, and John Balls, *E-Business and ERP: Transforming the Enterprise*, p. 120. Copyright © 2000 by John Wiley & Sons, Inc. Reprinted by permission.

reduce the risks and costs and to maximize the benefits of change. For example, implementing a new e-business application such as customer relationship management might involve developing a *change action plan*, assigning selected managers as *change sponsors*, developing employee *change teams*, and encouraging open communications and feedback about organizational changes. Some key tactics that change experts recommend include:

- Involve as many people as possible in e-business planning and application development.
- Make constant change an expected part of the culture.
- Tell everyone as much as possible about everything as often as possible, preferably in person.
- Make liberal use of financial incentives and recognition.
- Work within the company culture, not around it.

DHL Express: The Challenges of Global Change

Depending on the business pressure *du jour*, large IT shops tend to swing back and forth from one organizational model to another. Need to save money and promote technology standards across the organization? Centralize. Need to respond more quickly to local market demands and better align with the business? Decentralize. "It's a constant tension between the two extremes of the pendulum," says Ron Kifer, senior vice president and CIO for the United States and Canada at DHL Express.

The global transportation and logistics services giant began to centralize and consolidate IT infrastructure and services six years ago, building a massive computing supercenter in Kuala Lumpur to manage IT for most of its operations in the Asia-Pacific and emerging markets, Kifer says. Two years ago, DHL opened a supercenter in Scottsdale, Arizona, to consolidate IT for the United States, Canada, and parts of Central and South America; and this year, the company set up a supercenter in Prague to condense IT for most of Europe and the Mediterranean.

Although centralization drove down costs, it did make it harder for business units to ensure that IT spending was in sync with business strategy. "It was difficult to get the right people from the business together with the right people from IT to define project requirements in a manner that was suitable for design and specification," Kifer says. Multiple iterations of project requirement specs were continually shifting between the business and IT (because of their remoteness to each other), adding cost and time to project life cycles, he says.

DHL has now embarked on an IT transformation that aims to give it the best of both worlds. The arrangement separates the supply side of DHL's IT organization from the demand side, and it puts IT demand management under the business's control. "Demand CIOs" report to regional CEOs and manage the region's IT budget, Kifer says, to align IT spending more closely with business strategy. The demand management function—Express Business IT (EbIT)—is staffed by IT employees who were previously focused on demand management aspects of IT. Under the new model, Kifer says, DHL will be able to reap the cost savings of its centralized computing supercenters, as well as the alignment benefits of having IT closely tied to regional operations. All regions of DHL are adopting this organizational model. Regional teams are in charge of implementing the EbIT functions within their regions, Kifer says, but a "thin global group" under a single CIO is coordinating to ensure a consistent approach, standards, processes, and tools from region to region. DHL also has a global corporate transformation office supporting this initiative.

For many employees, the reorganization means a dramatic change in roles, reporting relationships, and processes, Kifer says. DHL's change management plan emphasizes education and training to help employees understand the benefits of these changes to the company as a whole—and to them personally.

Source: Adapted from "Case Study: DHL's Global Change Management Plan," *CIO Magazine*, November 1, 2005.

A Change Management Process

An eight-level process of change management for organizations is illustrated in Figure 11.19. This change management model is only one of many that could be applied to manage organizational changes caused by new business/IT strategies and applications and other changes in business processes. For example, this model suggests that the business vision created in the strategic planning phase should be communicated in a compelling *change story* to the people in the organization. Evaluating the readiness for changes within an organization and then developing change strategies and choosing and training change leaders and champions based on that assessment could be the next steps in the process.

These change leaders are the change agents that would then be able to lead change teams of employees and other business stakeholders in building a business case for changes in technology, business processes, job content, and organizational structures. They could also communicate the benefits of these changes and lead training programs on the details of new business applications. Of course, many change management models include methods for performance measurement and rewards to provide financial incentives for employees and stakeholders to cooperate with changes that may be required. In addition, fostering a new e-business culture within an organization by establishing communities of interest for employees and

FIGURE 11.19 A process of change management. Examples of the activities involved in successfully managing organizational change caused by the implementation of new business processes.

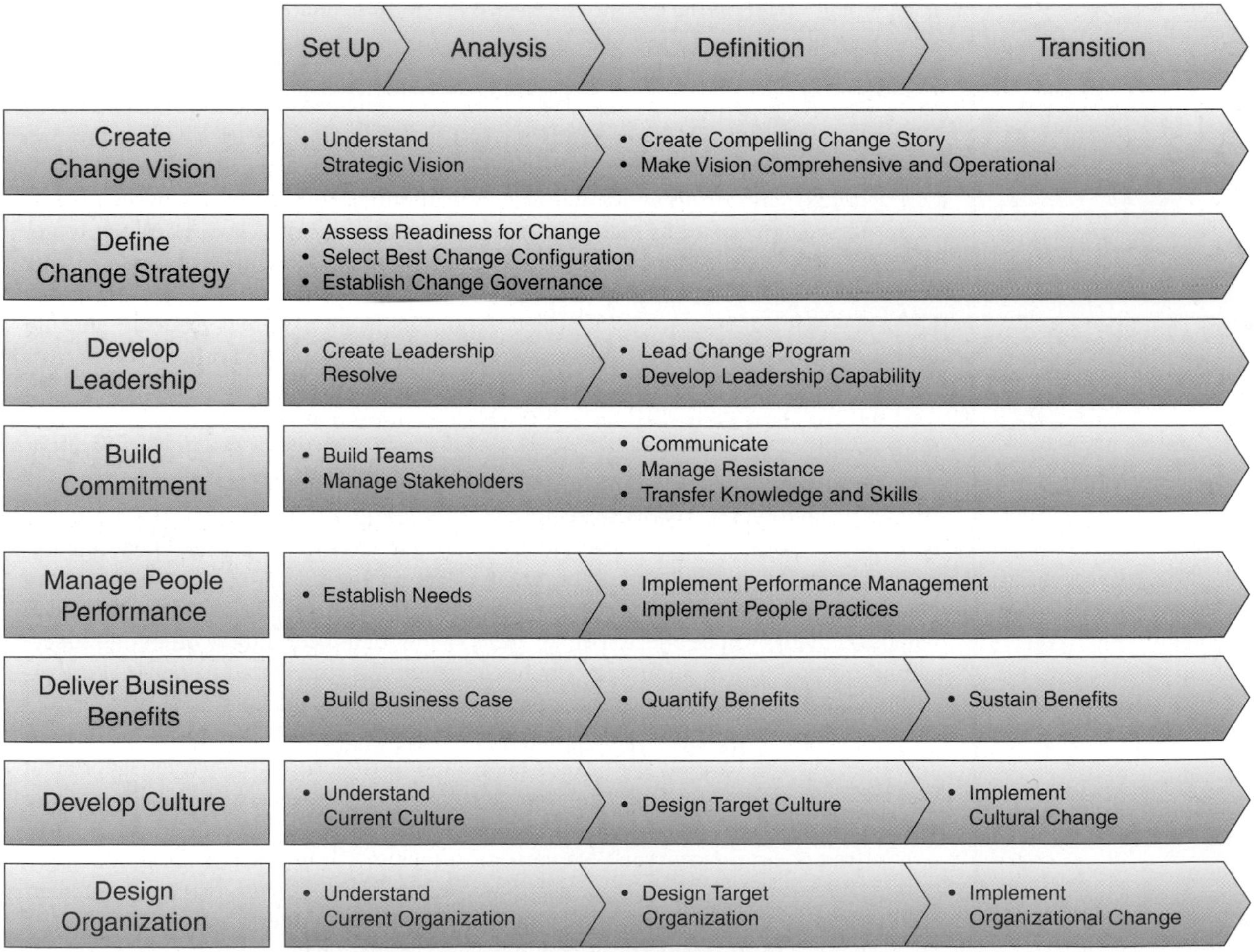

Source: Adapted from Martin Diese, Conrad Nowikow, Patric King, and Amy Wright, *Executive's Guide to E-Business: From Tactics to Strategy*, p. 190. Copyright © 2000 by John Wiley & Sons, Inc. Reprinted by permission.

FIGURE 11.20 Avnet Marshall moved through several stages of organizational transformation as it implemented various e-business and e-commerce applications, driven by the customer value focus of its Free.Perfect.Now business model.

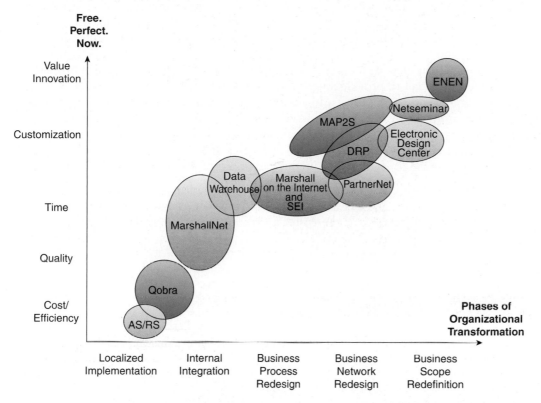

other business stakeholders via Internet, intranet, and extranet discussion groups could also be a valuable change management strategy. Such groups would encourage stakeholder involvement and buy-in for the changes brought about by implementing new e-business applications of information technology.

Avnet Marshall: Organizational Transformation

Figure 11.20 illustrates how a company like Avnet Marshall can transform itself via information technology. Notice how Avnet Marshall moved through several stages of organizational transformation as it implemented various e-business and e-commerce applications.

First, Avnet Marshall implemented an automated shipping and receiving system (AS/RS) and a quality order booking, resell application (Qobra) as it focused on achieving customer value through cost savings generated by the efficiencies of automating these core business processes. Then it focused on achieving interconnectivity internally and building a platform for enterprise collaboration and knowledge management by implementing its AvNet intranet and a data warehouse. The second step was building an Avnet Marshall Web site on the Internet to offer customers 24/7 online e-commerce transactions and customer support services. In addition, the company built a customized Web site for customers of its European partner SEI.

Next, Avnet Marshall connected with its suppliers by building a PartnerNet extranet and the Distribution Resource Planner (DRP) system, a supply chain management application that enables the company and its suppliers to help manage a customer's purchases and inventories. Avnet Marshall also implemented a customer relationship management and market intelligence system known as the Manufacturing Account Profile Planner (MAPP), which integrates and uses all the customer information from other systems to target its marketing activities more efficiently and manage its customer contacts. As Figure 11.20 illustrates, Avnet Marshall's other innovative e-business applications help its customers (1) simulate online and design custom special-purpose microprocessor chips (Electronic Design Center); (2) design new products online with suppliers, as well as take online training classes using real-time streaming video and audio and online chat (Netseminar); and (3) offer online seminars and push broadcasts to their own employees and customers—the Education News and Entertainment Network (ENEN).

All of the new technologies and applications we have mentioned now enable Avnet Marshall to provide more value to its customers with fast delivery of high-quality customized products. In addition, all of these initiatives created many new interenterprise business links between Avnet Marshall and its customers and business partners. These major technological and business changes required the organizational change phases noted in Figure 11.20. In a little over five years, Avnet Marshall had transformed itself into a premier example of an inter-networked, customer value–focused business.

Source: Adapted from Omar El Sawy, Arvind Malhotra, Sanjay Gosain, and Kerry Young, "IT-Intensive Value Innovation in the Electronic Economy: Insights from Marshall Industries," *MIS Quarterly*, December 1997.

Summary

- **Organizational Planning.** Managing information technology requires planning for changes in business goals, processes, structures, and technologies. Planning is a vital organizational process that uses methods like the scenario approach and planning for competitive advantage to evaluate an organization's internal and external environments; forecast new developments; establish an organization's vision, mission, goals, and objectives; develop strategies, tactics, and policies to implement its goals; and articulate plans for the organization to act upon. A good planning process helps organizations learn about themselves and promotes organizational change and renewal.

- **Business/IT Planning.** Strategic business/IT planning involves aligning investment in information technology with a company's business vision and strategic goals such as reengineering business processes or gaining competitive

advantages. It results in a strategic plan that outlines a company's business/IT strategies and technology architecture. The technology architecture is a conceptual blueprint that specifies a company's technology platform, data resources, applications architecture, and IT organization.

- **Implementing Business Change.** Implementation activities include managing the introduction and implementation of changes in business processes, organizational structures, job assignments, and work relationships resulting from business/IT strategies and applications such as e-business initiatives, reengineering projects, supply chain alliances, and the introduction of new technologies. Companies use change management tactics such as user involvement in business/IT planning and development to reduce end-user resistance and maximize acceptance of business changes by all stakeholders.

Key Terms and Concepts

These are the key terms and concepts of this chapter. The page number of their first explanation is in parentheses.

1. Business model (489)
2. Business/IT planning (490)
   a. Business application planning (495)
   b. E-business architecture planning (497)
   c. Strategic planning (482)
3. Change management (504)
4. End-user involvement (502)
5. End-user resistance (502)
6. Implementation (498)
7. Information technology architecture (492)
8. Organizational planning (482)
9. Planning for competitive advantage (487)
10. Scenario approach to planning (485)
11. SWOT analysis (487)

Review Quiz

Match one of the key terms and concepts listed previously with each of the brief examples or definitions that follow. Try to find the best fit for answers that seem to fit more than one term or concept. Defend your choices.

_____ 1. An organization should create a shared business vision and mission, and plan how it will achieve its strategic goals and objectives.

_____ 2. Outlines a business vision, business/IT strategies, and technical architecture for a company.

_____ 3. A blueprint for information technology in a company that specifies a technology platform, applications architecture, data resources, and IT organization structure.

_____ 4. Evaluating strategic business/IT opportunities based on their risk/payoff potential for a company.

_____ 5. Planning teams simulate the role of information technology in various hypothetical business situations.

_____ 6. Evaluating IT proposals for new business application development projects.

_____ 7. Evaluating strategic business opportunities based on a company's capabilities and the competitive environment.

_____ 8. Accomplishing the strategies and applications developed during organizational planning.

_____ 9. Managing the introduction of new technologies and IT-based strategies in organizations.

_____ 10. End users frequently resist the introduction of new technology.

_____ 11. End users should be part of planning for organizational change and business/IT project teams.

_____ 12. Expresses how a business can deliver value to customers and make money.

_____ 13. Identifying and developing e-business strategies for a company would be an example.

_____ 14. A combination of traditional planning methods with business modeling and application development.

Discussion Questions

1. "Planning is a useless endeavor because developments in e-business and e-commerce and in the political, economic, and societal environments are moving too quickly nowadays." Do you agree or disagree with this statement? Why?

2. "Planning and budgeting processes are notorious for their rigidity and irrelevance to management action." How can planning be made relevant to the challenges facing a business?

3. Refer to the Real World Case on developer feelings and application changes. Does it seem reasonable that developers should be worried about moving applications to a cloud environment? Discuss.

4. What planning methods would you use to develop business/IT strategies and applications for your own business? Explain your choices.

5. What are several e-business and e-commerce strategies and applications that should be developed and implemented by many companies today? Explain your reasoning.

6. Refer to the Real World Case on Centene, Flowserve, and Shaw Industries in the chapter. Where is the value in the approach taken by Flowserve to reaching consensus on their massive project? Discuss.

7. How can a company use change management to minimize the resistance and maximize the acceptance of changes in business and technology? Give several examples.

8. "Many companies plan really well, yet few translate strategy into action." Do you think this statement is true? Why or why not?

9. Review the real-world examples on user resistance and involvement in the chapter. What else would you recommend to encourage user acceptance in both cases? Explain your recommendations.

10. What major business changes beyond e-business and e-commerce do you think most companies should be planning for in the next 10 years? Explain your choices.

Analysis Exercises

1. **Business on the Fly**
   Remote Point of Sales in Mexico
   Melissa and "Rook" Nelson, co-owners of Skydive Chicago, shut down their northern operations in mid-December each year. With heavy cloud cover and frigid

temperatures, they just cannot find enough skydivers willing to jump over the frozen Chicago landscape. Without customers, valued staff members would migrate to southern drop zones, and more than a million dollars in aircraft assets would sit in a hangar. Some northern drop zone owners turn to hauling freight. Others lease their aircraft to southern drop zones. Melissa and Rook, world-champion skydivers themselves, developed other plans.

Each winter, Skydive Chicago moves their operations to sunny Ixtapa, Mexico. By moving south, Skydive Chicago keeps its aircraft in operation, provides year-round employment for valued staff members, gives its northern customers a sunny winter holiday destination, and introduces skydiving to crowds of tourists seeking to enjoy the beach from a new angle.

When Skydive Chicago relocates to Ixtapa, they take their computers with them. "We use them for everything," said Rook. "Everything" includes Web site updates, newsletters, video editing, photo printing, jump manifesting, e-mail, customer account management, and credit card processing. With three computers, a credit card reader, a router, an Internet connection through Telmex, and credit card clearing through Authorize.Net, business continues in a much more hospitable climate.

a. Research credit card readers. What are the popular brands? What features do they offer? How much do they cost?

b. Research mobile point-of-sale devices. What are the popular brands? What features do they offer? How much do they cost?

c. Look up "Authorize.Net" and explore the Web site as a prospective retail merchant. Read and summarize a retail merchant case study.

2. **Online University Degrees**
Distance Learning
"Distance learning" is a growth business with an increasing number of accredited universities adding new online degrees to their offerings every year. However, prospective employers often value these degrees little more than the "mail-order degree" variety. University administrators would like to bring in additional revenue but without compromising their degree's integrity or cannibalizing their traditional student base.

a. Use news.google.com to find and read three articles about successful online degree programs. What are the key elements for success mentioned in the articles?

b. Prepare a SWOT analysis describing this business opportunity for your university's administration.

c. What sorts of concerns might the faculty have about an online degree program? What steps would you recommend the administration take in order to make an online degree initiative attractive to the faculty, whose help is required to make the endeavor a success?

3. **Strategic Opportunities Matrix**
Planning Tool
The strategic opportunities matrix described in this chapter provides a simple analysis tool for strategic planning groups. It places all plans in direct competition with each other and so participants can quickly identify the most promising plans to evaluate in greater detail.

Use the Internet and your own experience to evaluate each of the following opportunities and place them appropriately on a strategic opportunities matrix. Explain how you assessed each decision.

a. Online sale and distribution of digital college textbooks.

b. Customized news alerts by topic, industry, region, business function, or other key word.

c. Online college degrees from accredited universities.

d. Brainstorm opportunities that might fit both the "High Ability to Deliver with IT" and the "High Strategic Business Potential" categories. Present your best idea to the class and explain how it fits both classifications.

4. **Practical Change Management**
A Practical Exercise
"Culture" evolves from and sets boundaries for interactions between people in an environment defined by rules, rule enforcement, and the example set by leadership. Conversely, culture can have a significant impact on which rule changes leadership can impose, as well as on the cost of these changes.

New software systems invariably mean change. As a minimum, new software will require new procedures. In many cases, new systems herald significant organizational change. Managers responsible for implementing these systems must take an organization's culture into consideration when planning implementation.

To see these challenges for yourself, find an example of a proposed rule change within your student government organization or any other group you belong to. Read about or monitor the debate, and interview representatives from each side of the issue.

a. Briefly describe the proposed change.

b. What group or groups oppose the change? What motivates them?

c. What group or groups benefit from the change? What motivates them?

d. Apply the change management principles outlined in this chapter to describe the steps you think leadership could take to ensure success at the lowest reasonable cost.

REAL WORLD CASE 3

Forrester, NMSU, Exante Financial Services, and Others: Getting Real about Strategic Planning

It must be nice to be the CIO of a FedEx, or a GE, or a Credit Suisse, where IT and the business are so tightly aligned you can barely tell the two apart. In such companies, corporate leaders understand that IT is a strategic asset and support it as such. These are places where the CIO is encouraged to spend the majority of his time on the Big Picture. If one works in that kind of IT Wonderland, getting a good strategic plan down on paper is probably a snap.

The vast majority of CIOs, however, work in places where the business itself may not have a clearly articulated strategy. In such companies, corporate leaders don't care too much for IT, much less value it strategically. These are places where the CIO's time is devoured by day-to-day operations and there's little time left to look beyond the next few months. If one lives with that kind of tactical IT reality, getting a good strategic plan down on paper is practically impossible.

For most CIOs, putting together an IT strategic plan—that annual road map to guide IT through the next 12 months and beyond—is dauntingly hard. Although the odds may be stacked against the average CIO, the truth is that those IT leaders who don't master the art of strategic planning won't last long. "The purpose of the IT strategic plan is to improve the business-IT relationship. A CIO needs it to communicate with the business, to tell them that he understands the company's needs and to set expectations," says Alex Cullen, Forrester Research vice president and research director.

"A CIO can't succeed without it." Michael Jones, CIO of the National Marrow Donor Program, calls it "the business case for IT."

The cardinal rule in developing an IT strategy is to connect it to the business strategy. "The business should have desired outcomes—market share gains, higher customer satisfaction levels, shortened cycle times," says independent IT analyst Laurie Orlov. "IT has to figure out where they factor into that." Yet for all the whining CIOs have had to endure about how IT needs to be more strategic, the businesses they support are often in even more dire strategic straits. "Businesses very often don't have a strategy. Or they do, but it's very high-level and vague. Or they reserve the right to change it. Or they have some strategies, but they don't apply to all the business activities taking place," says Forrester's Cullen.

So, CIOs who operate in strategy-free organizations are off the hook, right? Wrong. "It's the ultimate cop-out for CIOs to say they can't do an IT strategy because the business doesn't have an articulated strategy," says Orlov. Fuzzy business goals present a challenge, but smart CIOs should see that as an opportunity. "People in the business are very focused on operations or other minutiae," says Dave Aron, vice president and research director for Gartner Executive Programs. "IT can help the business articulate what will help it win and how IT fits into that. Then you go from just being an order taker to actually influencing overall strategy."

Michael Hites knew the lack of vision at New Mexico State University (NMSU) would be a challenge. "If you don't have the highest level plan in place, even the best IT strategic plan won't work," explains Hites.

"I've seen it; I've lived it." When he became CIO in 2003, NMSU's plan was no different from any other school's. So Hites's first IT strategic plan was standard and risk-averse. IT plodded along doing good work but nothing particularly strategic. In the absence of a more ambitious university plan, there was nothing to anchor a real IT strategy, says Hites. "If you stick your neck out [in that environment], the university may or may not be behind you," he notes.

Then a funny thing happened. After several years of bugging people about the lack of a strategic plan for the university, Hites was put in charge of strategic planning for the entire university and named vice president of planning and technology.

Hites and his team have lots of great ideas—about $15 million worth of them, he says—but his organization is "funded to the tune of half a million a year." The question he's faced with each year is "how to spend that little bit to do something strategic. If the university has the 'mom-and-apple-pie' strategy of 'helping students succeed' or 'increasing research,' anything you do is going to foster those objectives. And you can never be sure you're making the right choices. But if a university steps out on a limb and says, 'We will have best online education program in criminal justice in world,' then that becomes the strategic focus," says Hites.

"It can be appropriate for the CIO to help push business along in terms of strategy," says Forrester vice president and principal analyst Bobby Cameron. That doesn't necessarily mean the CIO takes on a second full-time job.

When Kelly Clark joined Exante Financial Services, a financial services provider for the health care industry, he wanted to change the IT strategic planning process.

"Generally, it's done at the end of the year," explains Clark. "You look at the budget, see you have X number of dollars, and figure out what you can do. It's reactive." Clark wanted a proactive process, a "business overlay that said, 'here's what the market is looking for, here's what we have, here's what we need.'" Exante had a business road-mapping process but no business and systems strategy, so Clark told his CEO and CFO they needed one—and they bought it. "So off we went," says Clark. "We created an enterprise strategic plan and IT became a piece of that."

Bethesda Lutheran Homes and Services (BLHS), a faith-based provider of services for individuals with developmental disabilities, was a couple of years into a five-year organizational strategic plan when Brian Tennant became its CIO. The plan, however, was strategic in name only. "It was generic: Be the best and grow by this amount," recalls Tennant. "But it was unclear why they picked the growth number or how they would measure it. And they hadn't paid much attention to whether it was on track. Nothing was grounded in reality." Frankly, that didn't matter much to Tennant at first. BLHS had acquired Good Shepherd Communities, based in Orange County, California, in 2005. It increased its size by two-thirds, and there was a "whole pile of modernization to do," recalls Tennant, including adjusting the core ERP system. Even with an overarching business strategy, IT's mission was clear: Integrate and upgrade.

Now that all that work is wrapping up, Tennant knows it's time to create a plan to guide his department of 10 through the next three to five years. But Tennant is not waiting for the 105-year-old organization to come up with a new five-year plan specific enough to guide IT; he's helping shape it. "I see myself as a member of the senior management team who just happens to be in charge of IT," says Tennant. "So I'm taking the opportunity to weigh in early and weigh in on all disciplines, not just my own."

Senior leaders, Tennant included, are vetting the new plan with the board, operating divisions, donors, and families of those to whom they provide aid. The goal is to create what they're calling "strategic positioning statements," such as attracting a younger demographic as donors or expanding services or creating financial stability. "I'm already starting to think about how IT will fit into those goals," says Tennant.

Exante's Clark says that if strategic planning is important, IT needs to put its money where its mouth is. "Often the problem is financial," Clark says. "Everything is focused on capital expenses." Clark says he has invested in people

and processes to make sure the IT strategic plan remains a priority. "You need a dedicated team," he says. "Most organizations don't assign IT strategic planning to someone as a full-time job. Hence it doesn't become a discipline; it becomes a burden." Clark made strategic planning the full-time responsibility of his directors. "Once the positions were open," he says, "we found people were itching to do it."

"Someone in IT should be thinking about IT strategy most of the time," agrees Orlov. "And their job the rest of the time should be making sure they're connected to everything that's going on in the business."

If an IT leader can set aside extra time now, the theory is that strategic planning will become an organic part of the company's life and interactions. It will no longer be like a series of appointments that you'd just as soon cancel—and it will get easier.

"If you did a strategic plan for the first time last year, you'll find that this year it takes less time. And next year will be even better," says Cullen. "You can focus more time on discussions with people and less time on the mechanics of putting it together. It could even become the part you like best about your job because that's where you can talk about what you want to do and why it matters to the organization."

It could be fun—which is why strategic planning isn't really like a root canal. Root canals have no fun parts.

Source: Adapted from Stephanie Overby, "How to Get Real About Strategic Planning," *CIO Magazine*, January 28, 2008.

CASE STUDY QUESTIONS

1. Consider statements made in the case about business often not having an overarching business strategy that can serve as guidance for the development of a strategy for IT.

2. How is it possible that companies get by without some sort of stable and clear direction? What does this tell you about the business and industry environment in which they operate?

3. Dave Aron of Gartner notes that in some cases the lack of clear business strategy provides an opportunity for IT leaders to step in and help articulate it and the role IT will play in the new strategy. This sounds like a good thing for IT people. What is the downside of being in this situation?

4. Why do you think IT's success is dependent on the overall business strategy of an organization? Why must they be tied together? Provide several reasons.

REAL WORLD ACTIVITIES

1. Go online and follow up on some of the organizations featured in the case (note that Exante Financial Services has recently merged with OptumHealth). How have these organizations been doing lately? Research what the news media and their own financial reports say, if anything, about the role of their IT investments and practices on their current status. How does that relate to what you read about them in the case?

2. One of the organizations featured in the case is New Mexico State University (NMSU). Think about how IT can be of strategic importance to universities and educational institutions. Break into small groups with your classmates to discuss some possibilities and how these apply to your educational experience. What suggestions would you have for improving its performance?

REAL WORLD CASE 4

Blue Cross and Blue Shield, and Others: Understanding the Science behind Change

Kevin Sparks has been trying to get his staff to change the way it monitors and supports the data center for the past year, but he hasn't been getting anywhere.

Not that he's getting resistance—at least not overtly. His staffers at Blue Cross and Blue Shield of Kansas City agree that installing automated monitoring software, along with a centralized control room and a set of standard processes for responding to problems, would be more efficient than the way they deal with things now, which is mostly through ad hoc heroism.

"Logic always prevails and everyone will agree—at the intellectual level—that we need to change things," says Sparks, who is vice president and CIO. Then he finds himself surrounded by empty chairs at meetings while the people who should be sitting there are off fighting the latest fire.

"I tell them I need them at the meetings and if we changed things they'd have the time to be there. But things always break down when we talk about taking monitoring out of their hands through automation," Sparks says.

To help his staff accept the new processes, Sparks says he's taken layoffs off the table, even though the proposed automation and process efficiencies could reduce the need for bodies. The change is part of a larger effort to implement the IT Infrastructure Library (ITIL) process framework to improve overall productivity. "I don't want fewer people; I want the ones I have to do more things," he says, sighing with frustration.

In other words, Sparks's staff doesn't seem to have any logical reason for resisting the changes; but before you dismiss them as a bunch of inflexible, fearful losers, know this: They are just like you.

Maybe your resistance to change manifests itself in a different way or in a different setting; for example, it might be a refusal to throw away that old slide rule, to look while the nurse draws your blood, or to dance at weddings. We all refuse to change our ways. This happens for reasons that are often hard to articulate, until you begin to look at it from a scientific perspective. In the past few years, improvements in brain analysis technology have allowed researchers to track the energy of a thought coursing through the brain in much the same way that they can track blood flowing through the circulatory system.

These advances are bringing a much-needed hard foundation of science to a leadership challenge that to CIOs has long seemed hopelessly soft and poorly defined: change management. Pictures of the brain show that our responses to change are predictable and universal. From a neurological perspective, we all respond to change in the same way: We try to avoid it. Yet understanding the brain's chemistry and mechanics has led to insights that can help CIOs ameliorate the pain of change and improve people's abilities to adapt to new ways of doing things.

Change hurts. Not the boo-hoo, woe-is-me kind of hurt that executives tend to dismiss as an affliction of the weak and sentimental, but actual physical and psychological discomfort.

The brain pictures actually prove it. Change lights up an area of the brain, the prefrontal cortex, which is like RAM memory in a PC. The prefrontal cortex is fast and agile, able to hold multiple threads of logic at once to enable quick calculations. Like RAM, the prefrontal cortex's capacity is finite; it can deal comfortably with only a handful of concepts before bumping up against limits. That bump generates a palpable sense of discomfort, producing fatigue and even anger.

Resistance to change is not inevitable. The prefrontal cortex has its limitations, but it is also capable of insight and self-control. The ability to be aware of our habitual impulses and do something about them is what makes us human.

"The prefrontal cortex is extremely influential in our behavior, but it does not have to be completely determinative," says Jeffrey M. Schwartz, research psychiatrist at the School of Medicine at the University of California at Los Angeles. "We can make decisions about how much we want to be influenced by our animal biology."

Unfortunately, traditional change management tactics are based more in animal training than in human psychology. Leaders promise bonuses and promotions to those who go along with the change (the carrot), and they punish those who don't with less important work and the potential loss of their jobs (the stick). "The carrot-and-stick approach works at the systemwide level—offering cash bonuses to the sales department to increase the number of customers in Latin America will get you more customers there, for example—but at a personal level it doesn't work," says David Rock, founder and CEO of Results Coaching Systems, a consulting firm. "Our personal motivations are too complex, and you can only offer so many raises."

Patience is critical, says Rock. "You have to paint a broad picture of change and resist the urge to fill in all the gaps for people," he says.

"They have to fill them in on their own. If you get too detailed, it prevents people from making the connections on their own." Leaving holes in any plan is especially hard for CIOs, who tend to be ambitious and process-oriented, which means they have thought out all the details involved in a strategy or systems change and believe they know all the steps required to get there. In general, they're bursting with the need to tell everyone exactly how to do it.

"When I put out change proposals, it's obvious to me why we should be changing, so when people resist I tend to get more aggressive in trying to convince them," says Matt Miszewski, CIO of the state of Wisconsin. "But we lose people in that situation. The more we try to explain things, the more dug in they get."

To try to focus people's attention on personal insight and change their behavior, Rock uses the same technique that psychoanalysts have used since the profession began: He asks questions. "When you ask someone questions, you are getting them to focus on an idea," he says. "When you pay more attention to something, you make more connections in the brain." Rock also says that asking questions gets people to voice their ideas. "The best way to get people to change is to lay out the objective in basic terms and then ask them how they would go about getting there," Rock says.

One of the biggest mistakes that leaders, like CIOs, make in trying to win over the skeptical middle is assuming that everyone is motivated by ambition, as many CIOs are. Many people, especially IT professionals, are motivated as much or more by the work they do (for example, the craft of software development) as they are by the opportunity to move up in the hierarchy. "There are a lot of people who don't want to be king or queen," says Michael Wakefield, senior enterprise associate at the Center for Creative Leadership, a consulting firm. "That's difficult for people to reveal because they fear their bosses will start to question their courage and commitment." If these people don't see an opportunity to maintain their allegiance to the work they love as part of a change, they won't see the benefit of going along. They will remain skeptical or, worse, move into the camp of active resisters.

One of the best ways to bring the skeptics around is through learning.

At the New York State Workers' Compensation Board, a change readiness survey of employees at the beginning of an effort to shift compensation cases from paper folders to electronic files found that employees' number-one demand was for training. "They wanted reassurance that we weren't going to ask them to do something new without giving them the support they needed to do it," says Nancy Mulholland, who is deputy executive director and CIO of the Workers' Compensation Board.

Change management is time-consuming and hard to quantify for process-oriented CIOs. Yet avoiding the challenge leads to failure. "Anybody can stick $2,000 in someone's face to get them to finish a job, but it's the people who can inspire others to follow them that are the most successful in the long run," says Richard Toole, who is CIO for PharMerica, a pharmacy services company. "The soft stuff is important," but inspiring others to change isn't a matter of charisma or charm, say the experts.

Sparks's latest tactic for engaging his staff's prefrontal cortexes was to bring in an outside consultant to discuss the IT Infrastructure Library program and to field concerns. "We had an outstanding instructor, and she was able to address many of the questions people had," recalls Sparks. "I could begin to see the lights come on in some of the skeptics. After a long meeting, one of my people stood up and said, 'You know, we should have started working on this [automated monitoring] six months ago.'"

Source: Adapted from Christopher Koch, "Change Management—Understanding the Science of Change," *CIO Magazine*, September 15, 2006.

CASE STUDY QUESTIONS

1. Although a very detailed change proposal may prevent people from making their own connections, as discussed in the case, it may lead others to consider the proposal to be vague and unfinished. How do you balance these two concerns? What guidelines would you use to ensure that you are not veering too far off in either direction?

2. Kevin Sparks of Blue Cross and Blue Shield of Kansas City had a difficult time convincing his people of the need for change. What would you have suggested he do before you read the case? What about afterwards? How did your recommendations change as a result?

3. Organizational change goes beyond promotions and the threat of layoffs. What ways other than those discussed in the case would you use to entice people to embrace proposed changes? Provide several suggestions and justify their rationale.

REAL WORLD ACTIVITIES

1. Search the Internet for examples of recent successful and failed IT implementations. What was the role of employee involvement and resistance in each one of those? What strategies did companies use to manage the change process, and how much success did they have in doing so?

2. Prepare a report to share your findings with the class.

3. Break into small groups to discuss what change management strategies and tactics you would use to ensure a smooth transition, either at a company you are familiar with or at one you know about from previous research for this or another class. How would you achieve a good balance between positive and negative consequences, as well as involvement in the process? Choose one of your group members to share your insights with the rest of the class.

CHAPTER 12

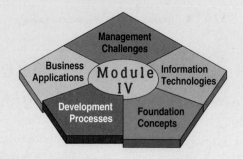

DEVELOPING BUSINESS/IT SOLUTIONS

Chapter Highlights

Learning Objectives

After reading and studying this chapter, you should be able to:

1. Use the systems development process outlined in this chapter and the model of IS components from Chapter 1 as problem-solving frameworks to help you propose information systems solutions to simple business problems.

2. Describe and give examples to illustrate how you might use each of the steps of the information systems development life cycle to develop and implement a business information system.

3. Explain how prototyping can be used as an effective technique to improve the process of systems development for end users and IS specialists.

4. Understand the basics of project management and their importance to a successful system development effort.

5. Identify the activities involved in the implementation of new information systems.

6. Compare and contrast the four basic system conversion strategies.

7. Describe several evaluation factors that should be considered in evaluating the acquisition of hardware, software, and IS services.

SECTION I Developing Business Systems

IS Development

Suppose the chief executive of the company where you work asks you to find a Web-enabled way to get information to and from the salespeople in your company. How would you start? What would you do? Would you just plunge ahead and hope you could come up with a reasonable solution? How would you know whether your solution was a good one for your company? Do you think there might be a systematic way to help you develop a good solution to the CEO's request? There is a way, and it's a problem-solving process called *the systems approach.*

When the systems approach to problem solving is applied to the development of information systems solutions to business problems, it is called *information systems development* or *application development.* This section will show you how the systems approach can be used to develop business systems and applications that meet the business needs of a company, as well as its employees and stakeholders.

Refer to the Real World Case on the next page. We can learn a lot about the importance of careful software development and testing from this example. See Figure 12.1.

The Systems Approach

The systems approach to problem solving uses a systems orientation to define problems and opportunities and then develop appropriate, feasible solutions in response. Analyzing a problem and formulating a solution involve the following interrelated activities:

1. Recognize and define a problem or opportunity using *systems thinking.*
2. Develop and evaluate alternative system solutions.
3. Select the system solution that best meets your requirements.
4. Design the selected system solution.
5. Implement and evaluate the success of the designed system.

Systems Thinking

Using systems thinking to understand a problem or opportunity is one of the most important aspects of the systems approach. Management consultant and author Peter Senge calls systems thinking *the fifth discipline.* Senge argues that mastering systems thinking (along with the disciplines of personal mastery, mental models, shared vision, and team learning) is vital to personal fulfillment and business success in a world of constant change. The essence of the discipline of systems thinking is "seeing the forest *and* the trees" in any situation by:

- Seeing *interrelationships* among *systems* rather than linear cause-and-effect chains whenever events occur.
- Seeing *processes* of change among *systems* rather than discrete "snapshots" of change, whenever changes occur.

One way of practicing systems thinking is to try to find systems, subsystems, and components of systems in any situation you are studying. This is also known as using a *systems context,* or having a *systemic view* of a situation. For example, the business organization or business process in which a problem or opportunity arises could be viewed as a system of input, processing, output, feedback, and control components. Then to understand a problem and solve it, you would determine whether these basic systems functions are being properly performed. See Figure 12.2.

Example. The sales process of a business can be viewed as a system. You could then ask: Is poor sales performance (output) caused by inadequate selling effort (input),

REAL WORLD
CASE 1

The Bugs Will Always Show Themselves, But Often Too Late

The programmer of large-scale organizational software applications carries a large responsibility. The millions of lines of program code that are generated by a programming team must not only perform the tasks intended but must do so with 100 percent error-free accuracy. A single hyphen out of place can spell disaster for the end-user beneficiaries of the software as well as the developers. Failure to find that one tiny error in the code when the error is made can cost millions, if not billions, later down the road when it finally decides to reveal itself. Consider these examples:

On January 15, 1990, around 60,000 AT&T long-distance customers tried to place long-distance calls as usual—and got nothing. Behind the scenes, the company's long-distance switches, all 114 of them, kept rebooting in sequence. AT&T assumed it was being hacked, and for nine hours, the company and law enforcement tried to work out what was happening. In the end, AT&T uncovered the culprit: an obscure fault in its new software.

The month before the crash, AT&T tweaked the code to speed up the process. The trouble was, things were too fast. The first server to overload sent two messages, one of which hit the second server just as it was resetting. The second server assumed that there was a fault in its internal logic and reset itself. It put up its own "do not disturb" sign and passed the problem on to a third switch and so the problem cascaded through the whole system. All 114 switches in the system kept resetting themselves, until engineers reduced the message load on the whole system and the wave of resets finally broke.

FIGURE 12.1

Taking time to thoroughly test the software is the only way to avoid possibly deadly errors.

Source: © Ryan McVay/Getty Images.

In the meantime, AT&T lost an estimated $60 million in long-distance charges from calls that didn't go through. The company took a further financial hit a few weeks later when it knocked a third off its regular long-distance rates on Valentine's Day to make amends with customers. Lesson learned: Test the "tweaked code" before releasing it.

Introduced in 2006, Windows Genuine Advantage (WGA) was never a popular initiative with Microsoft's customers. It did nothing to help the security or stability of a legitimate Windows installation. All it did was help Microsoft root out software piracy. In that task, it was as vigilant as, well, a vigilante. In fact, in late August 2007, it found piracy everywhere it looked—even among thousands of legitimate Windows customers.

Someone on the WGA team accidentally installed bug-filled preproduction software on the WGA servers. The team quickly rolled back to a tested release of the software, but they didn't check that their fix actually addressed the problem. It didn't. So for 19 hours the server flagged thousands of WGA clients across the globe as illegal. Windows XP customers were told they were running pirated software. Windows Vista customers had features turned off, including the eye candy Aero theme and support for ReadyBoost virtual RAM drives.

The first official response to complaints didn't help much: Disgruntled patrons were advised to try to revalidate on Tuesday. But even when the problem was fixed, Vista clients still had to revalidate their Windows installations before they could ReadyBoost their way back into Aero.

OK, so this was a relatively mild issue in engineering terms, and strictly speaking, it was caused by human error. But the error in question was deploying buggy, untested software, and when you factor in the number of people affected, the level of anger induced, and the knock-on effect of bad publicity, it was more severe than it seems at first glance.

Not all software bugs can be laughed off, however. Some of them are fatal. Medical and military software can be especially dangerous when not properly tested. During the first Persian Gulf War, Iraqi-fired Scud missiles were the most threatening airborne enemies to U.S. troops. Once one of these speeding death rockets launched, the U.S.'s best defense was to intercept it with an antiballistic Patriot missile. The Patriot worked a bit like a shotgun, getting within range of an oncoming missile before blasting out a cloud of 1,000 pellets to detonate its warhead.

A Patriot needed to deploy its pellets between 5 and 10 meters from an oncoming missile for the best results. This requires split-second timing, which is always tricky with two objects moving very fast toward each other. Even the Patriot's most prominent booster, then-President George H.W. Bush, conceded that one Scud (out of 42 fired) got past the Patriot. The single failure the president acknowledged was at a U.S. base in Dhahran, Saudi Arabia, on February 25,

1991, and it cost 28 soldiers their lives. The fault was traced to a software error.

The Patriot's trajectory calculations revolved around the timing of radar pulses, and they had to be modified to deal with the high speed of modern missiles. A subroutine was introduced to convert clock time more accurately into floating-point figures for calculation. It was a neat little fix, but the programmers did not put the call to the subroutine everywhere it was needed.

Apparently, the issue was known, and a temporary fix was in place: Reboot the system every so often to reset the clocks. Unfortunately, the term "every so often" wasn't defined, and that was the problem in late February at Dhahran. The system had been running for 100 hours, and the clocks were off by about a third of a second. A Scud travels half a kilometer in that time, so there was no chance the Patriot could have intercepted it. Lesson learned: Precise definitions of instructions for use of an application are essential.

Radiation therapy is a handy tool in the fight against some contained forms of cancer: Beams of electrons zap the bad stuff, and the body disposes of the dead matter. It has a strong success rate, but it depends on accurate aim and focus. That's something that the medical world leaves to machinery. Unfortunately for six patients between 1985 and 1986, the Therac-25 was the machine in question.

The Therac-25 handled two types of therapy: a low-powered direct electron beam and a megavolt X-ray mode, which required shielding and filters and an ion chamber to keep the dangerous beams safely on target. The trouble was that the software that powered the unit was repurposed from the previous model, and it wasn't adequately tested.

If the operators changed the mode of the device too quickly, a race condition occurred: Two sets of instructions were sent, and the first one to arrive set the mode. In six documented cases, this meant that megavolt X-rays were sent, unfiltered and unshielded, toward patients requiring direct electron therapy. At least two of them screamed in pain and tried to run from the room. All of them suffered radiation poisoning, which claimed several lives.

The Therac-25, which was recalled in 1987, has become an object lesson in what can go wrong with powerful medical machinery. The code didn't cause overdoses in earlier Therac models because hardware constraints prevented them. Lesson learned: Reusing code on a new system without thorough testing is a programming no-no, with good reason.

The process of software testing takes time and money and generally occurs in an environment where getting the application done and in the hands of those who need it is a constant pressure. Remembering that the bugs will eventually, and always, find themselves should be enough motivation to get it right the first time. But, often it is not.

Source: Adapted from Matt Lake, "Epic Failures: 11 Infamous Software Bugs," *Computerworld Hong Kong*, Questex Media, September 17, 2010.

CASE STUDY QUESTIONS

1. Why does it seem that thorough software testing is so objectionable?

2. In software development and testing, are there times when complete error checking is not necessary? Why?

3. What are the business benefits of implementing a mandated error-checking plan in software development? Classify them into those that enhance the effectiveness and the efficiency of the development and testing process.

REAL WORLD ACTIVITIES

1. Go online and research issues surrounding error-prevention techniques (backup and disaster recovery included). Prepare a report to summarize your findings.

2. If software continues to be more and more complex, will we ever find a way to eliminate all the coding and logic errors in modern software? Break into small groups to discuss this issue.

FIGURE 12.2

An example of systems thinking. You can better understand a sales problem or opportunity by identifying and evaluating the components of a sales system.

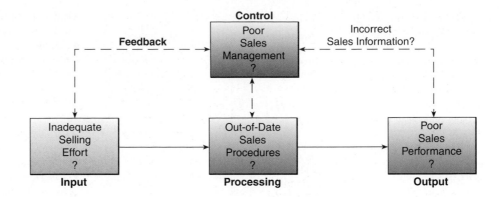

out-of-date sales procedures (processing), incorrect sales information (feedback), or inadequate sales management (control)? Figure 12.2 illustrates this concept.

Systems Analysis and Design

The overall process by which information systems are designed and implemented within organizations is referred to as systems analysis and design (SA&D). Within this process are contained activities that include the identification of business problems; the proposed solution, in the form of an information system (IS), to one or more of the problems identified; and the design and implementation of that proposed solution to achieve the desired and stated goals of the organization.

Today, there are many approaches to SA&D. The two most common approaches are **object-oriented analysis and design** and the **life cycle approach.** Although each has its advantages and disadvantages, and the two approaches differ in many respects, both are concerned with the analysis and design of a successful information system. In most cases, the choice will depend upon the type of system under study and the degree to which users are able to specify their needs and requirements clearly. A thorough discussion of both approaches is beyond the scope of this text, so we will focus on the most common method: the life cycle approach.

The Systems Development Life Cycle

One method of using the systems approach to develop information system solutions, and the most prevalent one in organization systems analysis and design, can be viewed as a multistep, iterative process called the systems development life cycle (SDLC). Figure 12.3 illustrates what goes on in each stage of this process: (1) investigation, (2) analysis, (3) design, (4) implementation, and (5) maintenance.

It is important to realize, however, that all of the activities involved in the SDLC are highly related and interdependent. In actual practice, therefore, several developmental activities may be occurring at the same time, while certain activities within a given step may be repeated. This means both users and systems analysts may repeat previous activities at any time to modify and improve a system under development. We will discuss the activities and products of each step of the systems development cycle in this chapter.

Starting the Systems Development Process

Do we have business opportunities? What are our business priorities? How can information technologies provide information system solutions that address our business priorities? These are the questions that have to be answered in the **systems investigation stage,** which is the first step in the systems development process. This stage may involve consideration of proposals generated by a business/IT planning process, which we will discuss in detail in Chapter 14. The investigation stage also includes the preliminary feasibility study of proposed information system solutions to meet a company's business priorities and opportunities as identified in a planning process.

FIGURE 12.3

The traditional information systems development life cycle. Note how the five steps of the cycle are based on the stages of the systems approach. Also note the products that result from each step in the cycle, and that you can recycle back to any previous step if more work is needed.

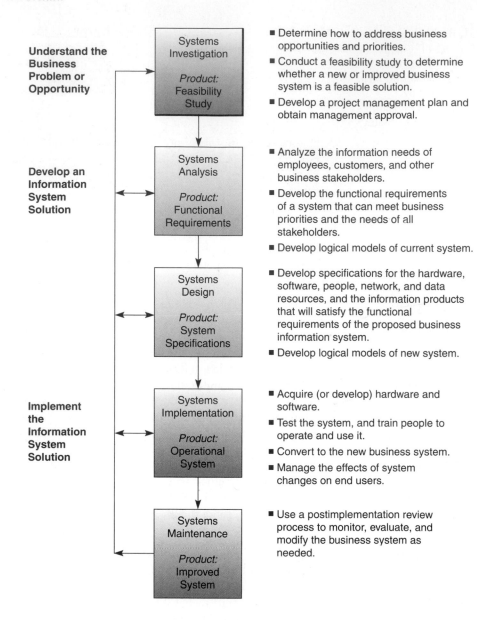

Understand the Business Problem or Opportunity

Systems Investigation

Product: Feasibility Study

- Determine how to address business opportunities and priorities.
- Conduct a feasibility study to determine whether a new or improved business system is a feasible solution.
- Develop a project management plan and obtain management approval.

Develop an Information System Solution

Systems Analysis

Product: Functional Requirements

- Analyze the information needs of employees, customers, and other business stakeholders.
- Develop the functional requirements of a system that can meet business priorities and the needs of all stakeholders.
- Develop logical models of current system.

Systems Design

Product: System Specifications

- Develop specifications for the hardware, software, people, network, and data resources, and the information products that will satisfy the functional requirements of the proposed business information system.
- Develop logical models of new system.

Implement the Information System Solution

Systems Implementation

Product: Operational System

- Acquire (or develop) hardware and software.
- Test the system, and train people to operate and use it.
- Convert to the new business system.
- Manage the effects of system changes on end users.

Systems Maintenance

Product: Improved System

- Use a postimplementation review process to monitor, evaluate, and modify the business system as needed.

Feasibility Studies

Because the process of development can be costly, the systems investigation stage typically requires the development of a feasibility study. At this stage, this is a preliminary study where the information needs of prospective users and the resource requirements, costs, benefits, and feasibility of a proposed project are determined. A team of business professionals and IS specialists might then formalize the findings of this study in a written report that includes preliminary specifications and a developmental plan for a proposed business application. If the management of the company approves the recommendations of the feasibility study, the development process can continue.

By design, the preliminary feasibility study of a project is a very rough analysis of its viability that must be continually refined over time. It is, nonetheless, a necessary first step in making the final commitment of organizational resources to the development of the proposed system. In some cases, however, the preliminary feasibility assessment is unnecessary. For extremely small or obvious projects, it may actually represent a waste of valuable time. Also, certain changes in the business environment may dictate the need for change, regardless of the assessed feasibility of such change. If the government changes the tax structure for employee income, an organization has no choice but to make the necessary changes to their payroll system. If a critical program has a major bug in it, the organization has no choice but to address and resolve it. In other words, there is little point in assessing the feasibility of a problem that must be solved. In these cases, the feasibility assessment may be better directed to the analysis of alternative approaches to the solution rather than the problem itself. Nevertheless, a thorough preliminary feasibility study should be the default standard in the organization, and a decision to eliminate this first step in the process should always be carefully scrutinized and justified.

Thus, the goal of the preliminary feasibility study is to evaluate alternative system solutions and to propose the most feasible and desirable business application for development. The feasibility of a proposed business system can be evaluated in terms of five major categories, as illustrated in Figure 12.4.

Operational Feasibility

The operational feasibility assessment focuses on the degree to which the proposed development project fits in with the existing business environment and objectives with regard to development schedule, delivery date, corporate culture, and existing business processes. Further, this assessment also determines the degree to which the project meets the specific business objectives set forth during the proposal phase. In the early stages of operational feasibility assessment, we are primarily interested in determining whether the identified problem is worth solving or the proposed solution actually solves the problem at hand. Additionally, we must concern ourselves with an initial assessment of **schedule feasibility:** Can we identify and solve the problem at hand within a reasonable time period? In the latter stages of operational feasibility assessment, such as during the physical design phase of the SDLC, we shift our focus to one of strategic fit and organizational impact, such as determining to what degree the proposed physical system will require changes in our organizational structure, or what changes in the current spans of authority need to be made to accommodate the new system.

Economic Feasibility

The purpose of the economic feasibility assessment is to determine the extent to which the proposed system will provide positive economic benefits to the organization. This determination involves the identification, and quantification, of all benefits expected

FIGURE 12.4

Operational, economic, technical, human, and legal/political factors. Note that there is more to feasibility than cost savings or the availability of hardware and software.

Operational Feasibility	Economic Feasibility
• How well the proposed system supports the business priorities of the organization. • How well the proposed system will solve the identified problem. • How well the proposed system will fit with the existing organizational structure.	• Cost savings. • Increased revenue. • Decreased investment requirements. • Increased profits. • Cost/benefit analysis.
Technical Feasibility	**Human Factors Feasibility**
• Hardware, software, and network capability, reliability, and availability.	• Employee, customer, supplier acceptance. • Management support. • Determining the right people for the various new or revised roles.
Legal/Political Feasibility	
• Patent, copyright, and licensing. • Governmental restrictions. • Affected stakeholders and reporting authority.	

from the system, as well as the explicit identification of all expected costs of the project. In the early stages of the project, defining and assessing all of the benefits and costs associated with the new system is impossible. Thus, the economic feasibility assessment is an ongoing process in which the definable short-term costs are constantly being weighed against the definable long-term benefits. If a project cannot be accurately judged as economically feasible using hard costs, then the project should not proceed, regardless of the other assessment category outcomes.

The assessment of economic feasibility typically involves the preparation of a cost/benefit analysis. If costs and benefits can be quantified with a high degree of certainty, they are referred to as *tangible*; if not, they are called *intangible*. Examples of tangible costs are the costs of hardware and software, employee salaries, and other quantifiable costs needed to develop and implement an IS solution. Intangible costs are difficult to quantify; they include the loss of customer goodwill or employee morale caused by errors and disruptions arising from the installation of a new system.

Tangible benefits are favorable results, such as the decrease in payroll costs caused by a reduction in personnel or a decrease in inventory carrying costs caused by reduction in inventory. Intangible benefits are harder to estimate. Such benefits as better customer service or faster and more accurate information for management fall into this category. Figure 12.5 lists typical tangible and intangible benefits with examples. Possible tangible and intangible costs would be the opposite of each benefit shown.

Technical Feasibility

The assessment of technical feasibility is focused on gaining an understanding of the present technical resources of the organization and their applicability to the expected needs of the proposed system. The analyst must assess the degree to which the current technical resources, including hardware, software, and operating environments, can be upgraded or added to such that the needs of the proposed system can be met. If the current technology is deemed sufficient, then the technical feasibility of the project is clear. If this is not the case, however, the analyst must determine whether the technology necessary to meet the stated specifications exists. The danger is that the project may require technology that does not yet exist in a stable form. Despite the claims of vendors that they can supply whatever is required, the analyst must be able to assess accurately the degree to which the needed technology exists in a form suitable for the proposed project. See Figure 12.6.

FIGURE 12.5

Possible benefits of new information systems, with examples. Note that an opposite result for each of these benefits would be a cost or disadvantage of new systems.

Tangible Benefits	Example
● Increase in sales or profits.	● Development of IT-based products.
● Decrease in information processing costs.	● Elimination of unnecessary documents.
● Decrease in operating costs.	● Reduction in inventory carrying costs.
● Decrease in required investment.	● Decrease in inventory investment required.
● Increased operational efficiency.	● Less spoilage, waste, and idle time.

Intangible Benefits	Example
● Improved information availability.	● More timely and accurate information.
● Improved abilities in analysis.	● OLAP and data mining.
● Improved customer service.	● More timely service response.
● Improved employee morale.	● Elimination of burdensome job tasks.
● Improved management decision making.	● Better information and decision analysis.
● Improved competitive position.	● Systems that lock in customers.
● Improved business image.	● Progressive image as perceived by customers, suppliers, and investors.

FIGURE 12.6

Examples of how a feasibility study might measure the feasibility of a proposed e-commerce system for a business.

Operational Feasibility	Economic Feasibility
● How well a proposed e-commerce system fits the company's plans for developing Web-based sales, marketing, and financial systems.	● Savings in labor costs. ● Increased sales revenue. ● Decreased investment in inventory. ● Increased profits. ● Acceptable return on investment.
Technical Feasibility	**Human Factors Feasibility**
● Capability, reliability, and availability of Web store hardware, software, and management services.	● Acceptance of employees. ● Management support. ● Customer and supplier acceptance. ● Staff developers have necessary skills.
Legal/Political Feasibility	
● No patent or copyright violations. ● Software licensing for developer side only. ● No governmental restrictions. ● No changes to existing reporting authority.	

Human Factors Feasibility

It is one thing to assess the degree to which a proposed system can work and quite another to evaluate whether the system will work. The human factors feasibility assessment focuses on the most important components of a successful system implementation: the managers and end users. No matter how elegant the technology, the system will not work if the end users and managers do not perceive it to be relevant and, therefore, do not support it. In this category, we assess the degree of resistance to the proposed system, the perceived role of the end users in the development process, the degree of change to the end users' working environment as a result of the new system, and the current state of human resources available to conduct the project and to manage and use the system on completion.

Legal/Political Feasibility

This category of assessment is often overlooked during the early stages of project initiation and analysis. The legal and political feasibility of a proposed project includes a thorough analysis of any potential legal ramifications resulting from the construction and implementation of the new system. Such legal issues include copyright or patent infringements, violation of existing antitrust laws (such as in the antitrust suit brought against Microsoft Corporation over Windows and Internet Explorer by the U.S. Justice Department in 1998), foreign trade restrictions, or any existing contractual obligations of the organization.

The political side of the assessment focuses on understanding who the key stakeholders within the organization are and the degree to which the proposed system may positively or negatively affect the distribution of power. Such distribution can have major political repercussions and may cause disruption or failure of an otherwise relevant development effort.

Systems Analysis

What is **systems analysis?** Whether you want to develop a new application quickly or are involved in a long-term project, you will need to perform several basic activities of systems analysis. Many of these activities are an extension of those used in conducting a feasibility study. Systems analysis is not a preliminary study; however, it is an in-depth study of end-user information needs that produces *functional requirements* that are used as the basis for the design of a new information system. Systems analysis traditionally involves a detailed study of:

- The information needs of a company and end users like yourself.
- The activities, resources, and products of one or more of the present information systems being used.
- The information system capabilities required to meet your information needs, and those of other business stakeholders that may use the system.

Organizational Analysis

An **organizational analysis** is an important first step in systems analysis. How can people improve an information system if they know very little about the organizational environment in which that system is located? They can't. That's why the members of a development team have to know something about the organization, its management structure, its people, its business activities, the environmental systems it must deal with, and its current information systems. Someone on the team must know this information in more detail for the specific business units or end-user workgroups that will be affected by the new or improved information system being proposed. For example, a new inventory control system for a chain of department stores cannot be designed unless someone on a development team understands a great deal about the company and the types of business activities that affect its inventory. That's why business end users are frequently added to systems development teams.

Analysis of the Present System

Before you design a new system, it is important to study the system that will be improved or replaced (assuming there is one). You need to analyze how this system uses hardware, software, network, and people resources to convert data resources, such as transactions data, into information products, such as reports and displays. Then you should document how the information system activities of input, processing, output, storage, and control are accomplished.

For example, you might evaluate the format, timing, volume, and quality of input and output activities. Such *user interface* activities are vital to effective interaction between end users and a computer-based system. Then, in the systems design stage, you can specify what the resources, products, and activities should be to support the user interface in the system you are designing.

Walmart and Others: Stress-Testing Web Sites for the Holiday Season

What if, in the days leading up to Christmas, a crush of shoppers forced a retailer to lock its doors during peak business hours? Unimaginable—but that's exactly what happened in varying degrees at the Web stores for Walmart, Macy's, and other retailers as the 2006 holiday season got off to a blazing start.

Walmart's failure on Black Friday, the day after Thanksgiving, was the most stunning. Walmart.com was down for a total of about 10 hours that day, according to Internet monitoring firm Keynote Systems, forcing it to greet shoppers at times with a "come back later" notice. "I'm afraid it was too much of a good thing on Friday," a Walmart spokesman said. Walmart expected order activity to be double the level of the previous year's Black Friday, but it came in at seven times the previous year's volume. Walmart had set big online goals for that holiday season, having spent 13 months adding faster checkouts and an interactive toy section, the kind of features it hoped would lure about 300 million visitors.

Not if the door is closed.

Macy's site performed poorly for about nine hours on that Black Friday, according to Keynote, and was down for about an hour that day and then again part of the following Tuesday. The sites for Zappos and Foot Locker also had some performance problems. Keynote says most sites, including Walmart's, recovered Monday and didn't have major problems that day.

With the Web bringing in increasingly significant sales, why would retailers drop the ball on site performance? In most cases, they aren't. Many conduct load testing, forecasting, and monitoring using tools from companies such as Keynote and Gomez, and they use content distribution networks to speed performance. They build their e-commerce infrastructures with an eye on performance, with redundancy at common failure points. But sites can still fail.

One reason is that the various teams—marketing, site designers, QA testers—too often aren't watching or sharing the same metrics, says Matthew Poepsel, vice president of professional services at Gomez.

If groups worry only about their metrics—marketing pushes a promotion, for instance, without being sure site design and capacity can handle it—you have "individual success but collective failure," he says. When a problem hits, Poepsel says, 80 percent of the recovery time is spent identifying the problem. "Once you know what the problem is, you can get it fixed pretty quickly, unless it's a sheer bandwidth issue and you need to cut a new contract," he says.

Customers are ruthlessly unforgiving of poor performance. In a Gomez survey of 1,173 online shoppers, 53 percent say they'll switch to a competitor if a site takes too long to load, and 21 percent will call customer service. When testing their systems for load capacity in preparation for Black Friday, retailers typically used twice the capacity their sites had on the same day last year, says Keynote, which equates that level to a 600 percent increase over an average shopping day outside of the holidays.

Stores that kept their sites up did blockbuster business. However, when a major competitor's site fails, other sites pick up a rush of new customers, which can overwhelm their sites. There's less time than ever to react to shifts in traffic, too.

Source: Adapted from Mary Hayes Weier, "Opening Holiday Weeks Show Uptime Isn't Easy for Online Retailers," *InformationWeek*, December 4, 2006.

Logical Analysis

One of the primary activities that occur during the analysis phase is the construction of a logical model of the current system. The logical model can be thought of as a blueprint of the current system that displays only *what* the current system does without regard for *how* it does it. By constructing and analyzing a logical model of the current system, a systems analyst can more easily understand the various processes, functions, and data associated with the system without getting bogged down with all the issues surrounding the hardware or the software. Also, by creating a logical model, the various noncomputer components of a system can be incorporated, analyzed, and understood. For example, in the physical version of a system, a person's inbox may be the location where new orders are stored until they have been entered into the computer. In the logical model, that inbox is treated just like a computer hard drive or other electronic storage media. In a logical sense, it is just another place to store data.

Logical and physical models are not limited to use in the design of an information system. They are commonly used in a variety of situations with which you are familiar. Take, for example, the remodeling of your house.

Let's say you want to knock out a wall to expand two small bedrooms into one big one. You also want to add a second bathroom for your guests. One way to approach this would be to call in the contractor and have him start tearing out the wall and adding the plumbing. The problem with this approach is that you have no blueprint for what you are trying to accomplish. You may find that the wall you want removed also holds up part of the second floor. Tearing it out would make for a bad day. Using this approach, you are proceeding with the redesign of the physical model without analyzing the logical model.

A better approach would be to have an architect look at the blueprints to see the feasibility of accomplishing your goals. If it is discovered that the wall cannot be removed, no harm is done. Then, alternative designs—say, putting in an archway between the two rooms—can be easily tested without any costly mistakes. Once the logical model

FIGURE 12.7

Examples of functional requirements for a proposed e-commerce system for a business.

Examples of Functional Requirements
● **User Interface Requirements** Automatic entry of product data and easy-to-use data entry screens for Web customers.
● **Processing Requirements** Fast, automatic calculation of sales totals and shipping costs.
● **Storage Requirements** Fast retrieval and update of data from product, pricing, and customer databases.
● **Control Requirements** Signals for data entry errors and quick e-mail confirmation for customers.

of the remodeling project has been determined to be sound, the physical model can be redone with the expected, and desired, positive consequences. The same approach is used when designing or redesigning information systems.

Functional Requirements Analysis and Determination

This step of systems analysis is one of the most difficult. You may need to work as a team with IS analysts and other end users to determine your specific business information needs. For example, first you need to determine what type of information each business activity requires; what its format, volume, and frequency should be; and what response times are necessary. Second, you must try to determine the information processing capabilities required for each system activity (input, processing, output, storage, control) to meet these information needs. *As with the construction of the logical model, your main goal is to identify what should be done, not how to do it.*

When this step of the life cycle is complete, a set of functional requirements for the proposed new system will exist. Functional requirements are end-user information requirements that are not tied to the hardware, software, network, data, and people resources that end users presently use or might use in the new system. That is left to the design stage to determine. For example, Figure 12.7 shows examples of functional requirements for a proposed e-commerce application for a business.

Systems Design

Once the analysis portion of the life cycle is complete, the process of **systems design** can begin. Here is where the logical model of the current system is modified until it represents the blueprint for the new system. This version of the logical model represents what the new system will do. During the **physical** design portion of this step, users and analysts will focus on determining *how* the system will accomplish its objectives. This is where issues related to hardware, software, networking, data storage, security, and many others will be discussed and determined. As such, systems design consists of design activities that ultimately produce physical system specifications satisfying the functional requirements that were developed in the systems analysis process.

A useful way to look at systems design is illustrated in Figure 12.8. This concept focuses on three major products, or *deliverables*, that should result from the design

FIGURE 12.8   Systems design can be viewed as the design of user interfaces, data, and processes.

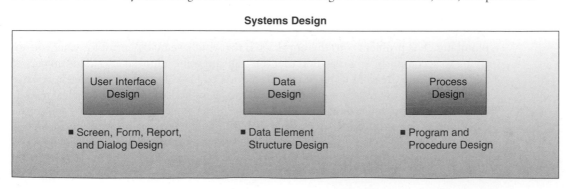

stage. In this framework, systems design consists of three activities: user interface, data, and process design. This results in specifications for user interface methods and products, database structures, and processing and control procedures.

Prototyping

During the design phase, the development process frequently takes the form of, or includes, a *prototyping* approach. Prototyping is the rapid development and testing of working models, or **prototypes,** of new applications in an interactive, iterative process that can be used by both IS specialists and business professionals. Prototyping, as a development tool, makes the development process faster and easier, especially for projects where end-user requirements are hard to define. Prototyping has also opened up the application development process to end users because it simplifies and accelerates systems design. Thus, prototyping has enlarged the role of the business stakeholders affected by a proposed system and helps make possible a quicker and more responsive development process called *agile systems development* (ASD). See Figure 12.9.

The Prototyping Process

Prototyping can be used for both large and small applications. Typically, large business systems still require using a traditional systems development approach, but parts of such systems can frequently be prototyped. A prototype of a business application needed by an end user is developed quickly using a variety of application development software tools. The prototype system is then repeatedly refined until it is acceptable.

As Figure 12.9 illustrates, prototyping is an iterative, interactive process. End users with sufficient experience with application development tools can do prototyping themselves. Alternatively, you could work with an IS specialist to develop a prototype system in a series of interactive sessions. For example, you could develop, test, and refine prototypes of management reports, data entry screens, or output displays.

Usually, a prototype is modified several times before end users find it acceptable. Program modules are then generated by application development software using

FIGURE 12.9

Application development using prototyping. Note how prototyping combines the steps of the systems development life cycle and changes the traditional roles of IS specialists and end users.

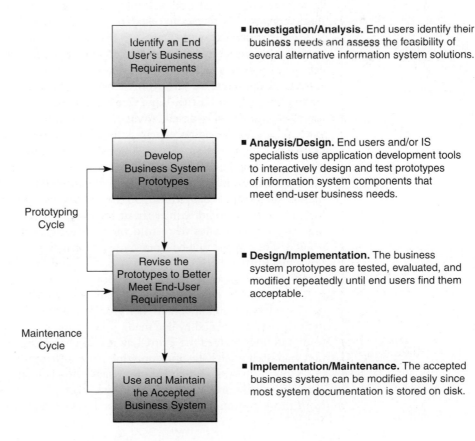

- **Investigation/Analysis.** End users identify their business needs and assess the feasibility of several alternative information system solutions.

- **Analysis/Design.** End users and/or IS specialists use application development tools to interactively design and test prototypes of information system components that meet end-user business needs.

- **Design/Implementation.** The business system prototypes are tested, evaluated, and modified repeatedly until end users find them acceptable.

- **Implementation/Maintenance.** The accepted business system can be modified easily since most system documentation is stored on disk.

FIGURE 12.10

An example of a typical application of prototyping during a software development project.

Example of Prototyping Development
● **Team.** A few end users and IS developers form a team to develop a business application.
● **Schematic.** The initial prototype schematic design is developed.
● **Prototype.** The schematic is converted into a simple point-and-click prototype using prototyping tools.
● **Presentation.** A few screens and routine linkages are presented to users.
● **Feedback.** After the team gets feedback from users, the prototype is reiterated.
● **Reiteration.** Further presentations and reiterations are made.
● **Consultation.** Consultations are held with IT consultants to identify potential improvements and conformance to existing standards.
● **Completion.** The prototype is used as a model to create a finished application.
● **Acceptance.** Users review and sign off on their acceptance of the new business system.
● **Installation.** The new business software is installed on network servers.

conventional programming languages. The final version of the application system is then turned over to its end users for operational use. While prototyping is a useful method of allowing an end user to develop small software applications, its real power is as a development tool, within a life cycle project, to help analysts and users finalize the various interfaces and functions of a large business system. Figure 12.10 outlines a typical prototyping-based systems development process for a business application.

Frito-Lay Inc.: Failure and Success in Systems Development

Frito-Lay created national sales teams to focus on top customers such as supermarket chains, but the teams, used to working regionally, found nationwide collaboration difficult. Although Frito-Lay had rich stores of market research and other pertinent customer information housed in databases at its headquarters, there was no easy way for team members to find what they needed. Frustration rose, performance suffered, and sales team turnover reached 25 percent.

So Mike Marino, Frito-Lay's vice president for category and customer development, engaged Dallas-based Navigator Systems to help. Navigator consultants envisioned a Web-based enterprise knowledge portal that would combine tools for knowledge management and collaboration, enabling the team to better serve the customer while helping reduce frustration and turnover.

A portal development project team was formed to work with the national supermarket sales team because they had the most centralized and demanding customers. "We knew if we could deliver there, we could satisfy any customer," Marino says. The supermarket sales team told the project team what kind of knowledge they needed. The request ranged from simple information, such as why Frito-Lay products Lays and Ruffles were in one part of a store and Doritos were in another, to more complex research on what motivates shoppers as they move through a store.

A few months later, the project team presented a working prototype they had developed to a group of beta users from the supermarket sales team only to find that, in the quest for speed, they had made a classic and crippling error. Because the project team had not involved the Frito-Lay team in the design of the prototype, the portal they had built wasn't specific enough for the supermarket sales team.

"Conceptually, it was a great idea," says Frito-Lay sales team leader Joe Ackerman. "But when folks are not on the front line, their view of what is valuable is different from those running 100 miles an hour in the field." The project team needed to backtrack and plug in the missing features, but they also had to win back the sales force, who now suspected that even a revised tool would be a waste of time.

The project team then spent the next four months working with salespeople to evolve the prototype into a system they would embrace. For example, a call-reporting feature was added. "So many people want to know what happened on a sales call, the account manager involved can be on the phone for days," Ackerman explains. "Now, we're able to post that to a Web site. It frees up the account manager to document the call once and move on."

Other changes included enabling users to analyze and manipulate data rather than just viewing data, and developing reports tailored to customers' needs. "The original reports were very general," Ackerman says, so users would have had to spend lots of time reformatting them for customer presentations. Ackerman was also enlisted for the official rollout of the portal.

Now Ackerman says that better collaboration with the portal has helped to reduce turnover significantly, while improved access to knowledge-based data has enabled account managers to present themselves to customers as consultants with important data to share.

Source: Adapted from Kathleen Melymuka, "Profiting from Mistakes," *Computerworld*, April 20, 2001.

User Interface Design

Let's take a closer look at user interface design, since it is the system component closest to business end users and the one they will most likely help design. The user interface design activity focuses on supporting the interactions between end users and their computer-based applications. Designers concentrate on the design of attractive and efficient forms of user input and output, such as easy-to-use Internet or intranet Web pages.

As we mentioned earlier, user interface design is frequently a *prototyping* process, where working models or prototypes of user interface methods are designed and modified several times with feedback from end users. The user interface design process produces detailed design specifications for information products such as display screens, interactive user/computer dialogues (including the sequence or flow of dialogue), audio responses, forms, documents, and reports. Figure 12.11 gives examples of user interface design elements and other guidelines suggested for the multimedia Web pages of e-commerce Web sites. Figure 12.12 presents actual before-and-after screen displays of the user interface design process for a work scheduling application of State Farm Insurance Company.

FIGURE 12.11 Useful guidelines for the design of business Web sites.

Checklist for Corporate Web sites

- **Remember the Customer:** Successful Web sites are built solely for the customer, not to make company vice presidents happy.

- **Aesthetics:** Successful designs combine fast-loading graphics and simple color palettes for pages that are easy to read.

- **Broadband Content:** The Web's coolest stuff can't be accessed by most Web surfers. Including a little streaming video isn't bad, but don't make it the focus of your site.

- **Easy to Navigate:** Make sure it's easy to get from one part of your site to another. Providing a site map, accessible from every page, helps.

- **Searchability:** Many sites have their own search engines; very few are actually useful. Make sure yours is.

- **Incompatibilities:** A site that looks great on a PC using Internet Explorer can often look miserable on an iBook running Netscape.

- **Registration Forms:** Registration forms are a useful way to gather customer data. But make your customers fill out a three-page form, and watch them flee.

- **Dead Links:** Dead links are the bane of all Web surfers—be sure to keep your links updated. Many Web-design software tools can now do this for you.

FIGURE 12.12   An example of the user interface design process. State Farm developers changed this work scheduling and assignment application's interface after usability testing showed that end users working with the old interface (at left) didn't realize that they had to follow a six-step process. If users jumped to a new page out of order, they would lose their work. The new interface (at right) made it clearer that a process had to be followed.

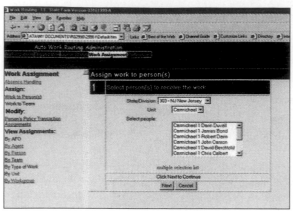
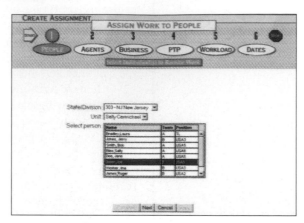

Source: Courtesy of the Usability Lab of State Farm.

Listen to the Users: It's All About the Interface

Four years after its debut, the "ribbon" interface in Microsoft's Office suite still gives businesses the shudders, a research firm said recently.

The interface first appeared in Office 2007 to catcalls as users struggled with the massive redesign, which substituted a wide ribbon-like display at the top for the traditional drop-down menus, small icons, and toolbars that epitomized Windows applications' look-and-feel for decades.

Months after the release of Office 2010, which also relies on the ribbon, enterprise IT professionals still think the interface is a headache, said Diane Hagglund, a senior analyst at Dimensional Research.

After polling more than 950 business IT executives, managers, and staffers, Hagglund found that the ribbon and its impact on worker training led all worries about deploying Office 2010. Nearly half of the IT pros—45 percent—pegged user training on the ribbon as a concern, more than double that of worries about the new software's stability and reliability, and significantly higher than the next-most expressed anxieties, including nonribbon training issues and add-in compatibility problems.

In the past, Microsoft has argued that training problems stemming from the ribbon interface have been overblown. Users, however, have continued to knock the ribbon, whether in Office on Windows or in the just-shipped Office for Mac 2011, which features a variant on the interface.

Dimensional also noted a slow uptake of Office 2010 so far, with just 20 percent of organizations polled having rolled out the suite to any PCs outside test scenarios. But 2011 should be a barn burner for Microsoft. Forty-two percent of the polled IT professionals said their organizations would broadly deploy Office 2010 in 2011, more than twice the 18 percent who said the same about 2010.

Two weeks ago, Microsoft touted a 15 percent year-over-year increase in Office sales revenues for the third quarter, the boost coming from 2010's June launch. The company also announced that sales of Office 2010 were 20 percent higher than for Office 2007 during its early months. At the same time, Microsoft said consumer sales of Office—the bulk of which would be the lowest-priced Home & Student edition, historically the biggest retail seller—were "outstanding," but said nothing similar about how the suite is selling to businesses.

Hagglund had a hunch why enterprises are hesitant to jump on Office 2010. "What was really interesting was hearing [from IT professionals] about the increased complexity of the desktop," she said, ticking off factors ranging from multiple versions of

Windows—including the nearly-decade-old XP—and multiple editions of Office to Windows 7 migration plans that are only now getting into swing.

"I really feel for the front line IT people today," she said. "It's just getting tougher and tougher." The most surprising result of the survey, said Hagglund, was the large number of IT professionals who said that their organizations are running Office alternatives as well as Microsoft's suite.

Source: Adapted from Gregg Keizer, "IT Pros: Office Ribbon Interface Still a Headache," *Computerworld Hong Kong*, Questex Media, November 4, 2010.

FIGURE 12.13
Examples of system specifications for a new e-commerce system for a business.

Examples of System Specifications
● **User Interface Specifications**   Use personalized screens that welcome repeat Web customers and that make product recommendations.
● **Database Specifications**   Develop databases that use object/relational database management software to organize access to all customer and inventory data and to multimedia product information.
● **Software Specifications**   Acquire an e-commerce software engine to process all e-commerce transactions with fast responses, i.e., retrieve necessary product data and compute all sales amounts in less than one second.
● **Hardware and Network Specifications**   Install redundant networked Web servers and sufficient high-bandwidth telecommunications lines to host the company e-commerce Web site.
● **Personnel Specifications**   Hire an e-commerce manager and specialists and a Webmaster and Web designer to plan, develop, and manage e-commerce operations.

System Specifications

System specifications formalize the design of an application's user interface methods and products, database structures, and processing and control procedures. Therefore, systems designers will frequently develop hardware, software, network, data, and personnel specifications for a proposed system. Figure 12.13 shows examples of system specifications that could be developed for an e-commerce system of a company.

End-User Development

In a traditional systems development cycle, your role as a business end user is similar to that of a customer or a client. Typically, you make a request for a new or improved system, answer questions about your specific information needs and information processing problems, and provide background information on your existing business systems. IS professionals work with you to analyze your problem and suggest alternative solutions. When you approve the best alternative, it is designed and implemented. Here again, you may be involved in a prototyping design process or be on an implementation team with IS specialists.

In end-user development, however, IS professionals play a consulting role while you do your own application development. Sometimes, user consultants may be available to help you and other end users with your application development efforts. This may include training in the use of application packages; selection of hardware and software; assistance in gaining access to organization databases; and, of course, assistance in analysis, design, and implementation of the business application of IT that you need.

Focus on IS Activities

It is important to remember that end-user development should focus on the fundamental activities of any information system: input, processing, output, storage, and control, as we described in Chapter 1. Figure 12.14 illustrates these system components and the questions they address.

FIGURE 12.14   End-user development should focus on the basic information processing activity components of an information system.

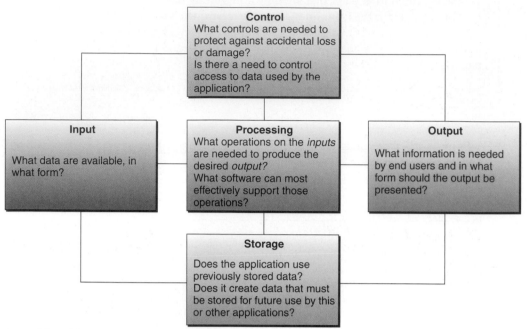

Source: Adapted from James N. Morgan, *Application Cases in MIS*, 4th ed. (New York: Irwin/McGraw-Hill, 2002), p. 31.

When analyzing a potential application, you should first focus on the *output* to be produced by the application. What information is needed and in what form should it be presented? Next, look at the *input* data to be supplied to the application. What data are available? From what sources? In what form? Then you should examine the *processing* requirements. What operations or transformation processes will be required to convert the available inputs into the desired output? Among software packages the developer is able to use, which package can best perform the operations required?

You may find that the desired output cannot be produced from the inputs that are available. If this is the case, you must either make adjustments to the output expected, or find additional sources of input data, including data stored in files and databases from external sources. The *storage* component will vary in importance in end-user applications. For example, some applications require extensive use of stored data or the creation of data that must be stored for future use. These are better suited for database management development projects than for spreadsheet applications.

Necessary *control* measures for end-user applications vary greatly depending upon the scope and duration of the application, the number and nature of the users of the application, and the nature of the data involved. For example, control measures are needed to protect against accidental loss or damage to end-user files. The most basic protection against this type of loss is to make backup copies of application files on a frequent and systematic basis. Another example is the cell protection feature of spreadsheets that protects key cells from accidental erasure by users.

Doing End-User Development

In end-user development, you and other business professionals can develop new or improved ways to perform your jobs without the direct involvement of IS specialists. The application development capabilities built into a variety of end-user software packages have made it easier for many users to develop their own computer-based

FIGURE 12.15

Microsoft FrontPage is an example of an easy-to-use end-user Web site development tool.

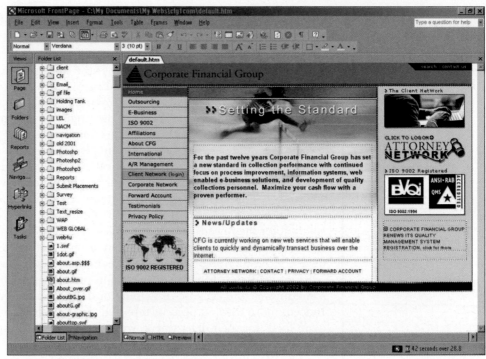

Source: Courtesy of the Corporate Financial Group.

solutions. For example, Figure 12.15 illustrates a Web site development tool you could use to help you develop, update, and manage an intranet Web site for your business unit. You might choose instead to use an electronic spreadsheet package as a tool to develop an easy way to analyze weekly sales results for the sales managers in a company. You could also use a Web site development package to design Web pages for a small business Web store or a departmental intranet Web site. See Figure 12.16.

FIGURE 12.16

How companies are encouraging and managing intranet Web site development by business end users.

Encouraging End-User Web Development
● **Look for Tools That Make Sense.**   Some Web development tools may be more powerful and more costly than what your business end users really need.
● **Spur Creativity.**   Consider a competition among business departments for the best Web site, to help spur users to more creative uses of their intranet sites.
● **Set Some Limits.**   Yes, you have to keep some control. Consider putting limits on exactly which parts of a Web page users can change and who can change which pages. You still want some consistency across the organization.
● **Give Managers Responsibility.**   Make business unit managers sign off on who will be Web publishing from their groups, and make the managers personally responsible for the content that goes on their Web sites. That will help prevent the publishing of inappropriate content by some users.
● **Make Users Comfortable.**   Training users well on the tools will help users become confident in their ability to properly manage and update their sites—and save IT the trouble of fixing problems later on or providing continuous support for minor problems.

Blue Prism: "Shadow" IT Is Becoming More Pervasive

Businesses increasingly accept the existence of a "shadow" IT culture, in which end users install uncontrolled rogue technology to make good the shortcomings of over-stretched IT departments. Rogue IT includes users who install software or tamper with existing software or macros without the IT department's consent, according to a survey by integration specialist Blue Prism. Budget and resource constraints often lead to elements of rogue behavior, reported by 67 percent of respondents to the survey. Twenty-four percent believed that rogue IT isn't used in their organizations, and 10 percent admitted that they didn't know.

These systems are not necessarily simple variations on the Excel spreadsheet. On the contrary, they can be very sophisticated—rivaling and even exceeding any technological solution produced by IT departments. Such systems range from consumer solutions like Google Apps to highly tailored ones. It seems that end users are increasingly aware nowadays that their IT department cannot always deliver a practical solution for their needs, which can lead to the creation of a shadow IT culture within an organization, whereby users actively install their own applications or find their own work-around solutions in order to do their day-to-day job.

This is often because IT departments have to manage business-critical projects, sometimes at the expense of helping business users with tactical change requests. Indeed, more than 52 percent reported that working on strategic projects was the main focus for their department, with 40 percent saying that delivering day-to-day business change requests was their priority.

The Blue Prism survey, however, also challenges the traditional perception that IT departments frown upon rogue behavior by users. The survey concludes that many IT departments fully understand why pockets of rogue behavior exist, and it reveals that these departments were equally pragmatic when asked for the best way of dealing with it.

With this change in the relationship between end users and technology, the IT department's singular claim to technology knowledge is disappearing, and with it, its position of power. The more technologists try to counter this effect by enforcing the old ways, the more defunct and isolated they will become; their decisions will be ignored and their solutions will be unused. One of the primary reasons shadow systems succeed is that people at the front lines of organizations need them.

They know that when they have a problem and when they find a solution that works well for them, their needs are met. IT departments, on the other hand, focus too strongly on the technology to solve a problem rather than on the problem itself—to the extent that when end users do not use officially sanctioned solutions, IT may proceed on radical search-and-destroy missions of user-created systems. In doing so, it ignores why the user did not use its solutions in the first place and, in effect, it destroys one of the few sources of IT strategic and competitive advantage an organization has.

Source: Adapted from Tom Jowitt, "'Shadow IT Culture on the Rise for Businesses," *CIO Magazine*, July 5, 2007; and Sandy Behrens, "Time to Rethink Your Relationship with End Users," *CIO Magazine*, July 24, 2007.

Technical Note: Overview of Object-Oriented Analysis and Design

As stated at the beginning of the chapter, there are two common approaches to analysis and design: SDLC and object-oriented. Whereas the SDLC remains the predominant approach to software development, the object-oriented approach is gaining favor, particularly among programmers focusing on complex systems that require handling a wide variety of complex data structures, such as audio, video, images, documents, Web pages, and other types of data.

We introduced the concepts of objects and object oriented databases in Chapter 5. Thorough coverage of the object-oriented approach to analysis and design is beyond the scope of this text, but a brief overview is presented here. Let's begin with a simple definition of anything object-oriented.

An **object-oriented system** is composed of *objects*. An object can be anything a programmer wants to manage or manipulate—cars, people, animals, savings accounts, food products, business units, organizations, customers—literally anything. Once an object is defined by a programmer, its characteristics can be used to allow one object to interact with another object or pass information to another object. The behavior of an object-oriented system entails collaboration between these objects, and the state of the system is the combined state of all the object in it.

Collaboration between objects requires them to send messages or information to one another. The exact semantics of message sending between objects varies, depending on the kind of system being modeled. In some systems, "sending a message" is the same as "invoking a method." In others, "sending a message" might involve sending data using a pre-prescribed media. The three areas of interest to us in an object-oriented system are object-oriented programming, object-oriented analysis, and object-oriented design.

Object-oriented programming (OOP) is the programming paradigm that uses "objects" to design applications and computer programs. It employs several techniques from previously established paradigms, including:

- **Inheritance.** The ability of one object to inherit the characteristics of a higher-order object. For example, all cars have wheels; therefore, an object defined as a *sports car* and as a special type of the object *cars* must also have wheels.

- **Modularity.** The extent to which a program is designed as a series of interlinked yet stand-alone modules.

- **Polymorphism.** The ability of an object to behave differently depending on the conditions in which its behavior is invoked. For example, two objects that inherit the behavior *speak* from an object class *animal* might be a dog object and a cat object. Both have a behavior defined as *speak*. When the dog object is commanded to speak, it will *bark*, whereas when the cat object is commanded to speak, it will *meow*.

- **Encapsulation.** Concealing all of the characteristics associated with a particular object inside the object itself. This paradigm allows objects to inherit characteristics simply by defining a subobject. For example, the object *airplane* contains all of the characteristics of an airplane: wings, tail, rudder, pilot, speed, altitude, and so forth.

Even though it originated in the 1960s, OOP was not commonly used in mainstream software application development until the 1990s. Today, many popular programming languages (e.g., ActionScript, Ada95/2005, C+, C++, Delphi, Java, JavaScript, Lisp, Objective-C, Perl, PHP, Python, RealBasic, Ruby, Squeak, VB.Net, Visual FoxPro, and Visual Prolog) support OOP.

Object-oriented analysis (OOA) aims to model the *problem domain*, that is, the problem we want to solve, by developing an object-oreinted (OO) system. The source of the analysis is a set of written requirements statements and/or diagrams that illustrate the statements.

Similar to the SDLC-developed model, an object-oriented analysis model does not take into account implementation constraints, such as concurrency, distribution, persistence, or inheritance, nor how the system will be built. Because object-oriented systems are modular, the model of the system can be divided into multiple domains, each of which are separately analyzed and represent separate business, technological, or conceptual areas of interest. The result of object-oriented analysis is a description of what is to be built, using concepts and relationships between concepts, often expressed as a conceptual model. Any other documentation needed to describe what is to be built is also included in the results of the analysis.

Object-oriented design (OOD) describes the activity when designers look for logical solutions to solve a problem using objects. Object-oriented design takes the

536 ● Module IV / Development Processes

conceptual model that results from the object-oriented analysis and adds implementation constraints imposed by the environment, the programming language, and the chosen tools, as well as architectural assumptions chosen as the basis of the design.

The concepts in the conceptual model are mapped to concrete classes, abstract interfaces, and roles that the objects take in various situations. The interfaces and their implementations for stable concepts can be made available as reusable services. Concepts identified as unstable in OOA will form the basis for policy classes that make decisions and implement environment or situation-specific logics or algorithms. The result of OOD is a detailed description of how the system can be built, using objects.

Thus, the object-oriented world bears many similarities to the more conventional SDLC approach. This approach simply takes a different view of the programming domain and thus approaches the problem-solving activities inherent in system development from a different direction.

In the next section, we will continue to look at systems development by changing our focus from design to implementation.

SECTION II · Implementing Business Systems

Implementation

Once a new information system has been designed, it must be implemented as a working system and maintained to keep it operating properly. The implementation process we will cover in this section follows the investigation, analysis, and design stages of the systems development life cycle we discussed in Section I. Implementation is a vital step in the deployment of information technology to support the employees, customers, and other business stakeholders of a company.

Read the Real World Case on the next page. We can learn a lot from this case about the challenges of upgrading enterprise applications from this case. See Figure 12.17.

Implementing New Systems

Figure 12.18 illustrates that the systems implementation stage involves hardware and software acquisition, software development, testing of programs and procedures, conversion of data resources, and a variety of conversion alternatives. It also involves the education and training of end users and specialists who will operate a new system.

Implementation can be a difficult and time-consuming process; however, it is vital in ensuring the success of any newly developed system. Even a well-designed system will fail if it is not properly implemented, which is why the implementation process typically requires a **project management** effort on the part of IT and business unit managers. They must enforce a project plan, which includes job responsibilities, timetables for major stages of development, and financial budgets. This is necessary if a project is to be completed on time and within its established budget, while still meeting its design objectives. Figure 12.19 illustrates the activities and timetables that might be required to implement an intranet for a new employee benefits system in the human resource department of a company.

Project Portfolio Management: Shoot the Bad Projects, Keep the Good Ones

IT departments are either the darlings or the despised of corporate America, and some practitioners would debate which extreme causes the most pain. Let's face it; nowadays the reward for doing a great job is more work. Once an IT group earns the trust of business units, it must then survive the onslaught of new projects. Good organizations, like good bosses, don't want you to take on more than you can handle and collapse in the process.

Smart organizations have a grip on project portfolio management (PPM) and are willing to prioritize and, when needed, end projects when they turn bad. Like risk management, PPM is nothing new for mature disciplines. "We've picked up where construction and engineers have been for years," says John Nahm, an IT project manager for the state of Virginia.

The highest performers in the IT world, as defined in a recent study by the IT Process Institute, are those most likely to cancel projects—at a rate double that of their lower-performing counterparts, in fact. "It's counterintuitive until you think about it," says Kurt Milne, managing director of the institute. The business world is accustomed to trying new initiatives but being willing to move on if they don't work. But, as Milne points out, in IT there's value in stability, so we're hesitant to pull the trigger. "I don't know that that's a skill that IT folks think they need to have, but logically, it makes sense to shoot your bad projects and move on."

Line-of-business executives understand capacity planning and prioritization, Milne says, but they expect these choices to be presented in business language. What they don't understand is when IT overpromises and then underdelivers, failing to

(text continues on page 540)

REAL WORLD CASE 2

JetBlue Airways, WestJet Airlines, and Others: The Difficult Path to Software Upgrades

Few things in the airline business are more daunting than upgrading to a new reservations system. Do it well and customers are none the wiser; mess it up and a carrier risks losing customers and tarnishing its brand. Discount carriers JetBlue Airways Corp. and WestJet Airlines Ltd. both recently switched reservations systems. The differing outcomes are a reminder of how the implementation of new technology can be just as crucial as the technology itself.

Despite months of planning, when WestJet flipped the switch on its new system, its Web site crashed repeatedly and its call center was overwhelmed. It took months to resolve all the issues. JetBlue, which later upgraded to the same software, smoothed its transition by building a backup Web site and hiring 500 temporary call-center workers.

Reservations are at the heart of a customer's relationship with an airline. So messing with the reservations system "is certainly not for the faint of heart," says Rick Zeni, a vice president of JetBlue who led the Forest Hills, N.Y., carrier through its transition.

Both WestJet and JetBlue previously used a system designed for start-up airlines with simpler needs. As the carriers grew, they needed more processing power to deal with increasing numbers of customers.

FIGURE 12.17

Major software upgrades can become make-or-break scenarios for companies today.

Source: © Ryan McVay/Getty Images.

They also wanted additional functions, such as the ability to link their prices and seat inventories to other airlines with whom they might wish to cooperate.

After studying alternatives, WestJet and JetBlue independently selected a system offered by Sabre Holdings Corp., a provider of such technology to 300 airlines and owner of Travelocity and other online travel agencies. JetBlue says the new system cost about $40 million, including $25 million in capital spending and $15 million in one-time operating expenses. WestJet did not disclose its costs.

The system sells seats and collects passenger payments but it also controls much of the passenger experience: shopping on the airline's Web site; interacting with reservation agents; using airport kiosks; selecting seats; checking bags; boarding at the gate; rebooking and getting refunds for cancellations. "It has a very big circle of influence and has to integrate with other systems in the airline," says Steve Clampett, an executive at Sabre Airline Solutions division. "It's as visible a technology upgrade as in almost any industry."

WestJet, which has 88 planes and is Canada's second-largest airline, switched to Sabre in October 2009 after it had shifted to a lighter winter schedule and canceled some flights. A big challenge was the overnight transition of 840,000 files—transactions of customers who already had purchased flights—from WestJet's old reservations server in Calgary to Sabre's servers in Tulsa, Oklahoma. It didn't go well, says Bob Cummings, WestJet's executive vice president of marketing and sales, because the migration required WestJet agents to go through complex steps to process the data.

Making matters worse, WestJet didn't reduce the number of passengers on the flights operating after the cutover, nor did it tell customers of its upgrade plans until the day of the switch. "We didn't want to telegraph dates so a competitor would put on a big fare sale," Mr. Cummings says. WestJet's customer loyalty scores tumbled as a result of long waits and booking difficulties. The airline sent apology letters, offered flight credits to some customers, and a month later bolstered its call center with temporary staffers in India.

"We were in pretty good shape in mid-January from a service perspective," Mr. Cummings says. "But this is a three- to six-month recovery process." He says WestJet remains enthusiastic about the new system's potential, which will allow the airline to fulfill its plans to begin cooperating with U.S. and international airlines.

JetBlue, which has 151 aircraft, had the benefit of observing WestJet's transition, at WestJet's invitation. JetBlue decided to make its switch on a Friday night because Saturday traffic tends to be low. It trimmed its schedule that January weekend and sold abnormally low numbers of seats on remaining flights. With WestJet's crashing Web site in mind, JetBlue developed a backup site that it used twice for a few hours.

JetBlue also contracted for 500 outside reservations agents. After the switch, in which 900,000 passenger records were moved to Tulsa from Minneapolis, JetBlue routed basic calls to the temporary workers, leaving its own call staff to tackle more complex tasks. The extra agents stayed in place for two months, "one of the wisest investments we made," Zeni says.

There were still glitches. Call wait times increased, and not all of the airport kiosks and ticket printers came online right away. JetBlue still must add some booking functions in the future. But having Sabre, says JetBlue CEO Dave Barger, was an important factor in the airline's recent decision to co-operate on some routes in and out of Boston and New York with AMR Corp.'s American Airlines.

The word "upgrade" has long been a virtual bogeyman for SAP customers, given the historical pain, time, and cost of moving to a new version of the vendor's ERP software. For some time, SAP has been trying to entice users onto the modern ECC 6.0 through its "enhancement pack" program, which promises to let users add new features without the pain of a full technical upgrade. Customers can't take advantage of the packs until they move to 6.0.

For legacy customers who don't yet wish to upgrade, this means an increase in cost for vendor support, a jump to a third-party maintenance provider—which has its own uncertainties, given ongoing high-profile lawsuits—or a decision to go with no paid support at all. The pack strategy is therefore crucial for SAP, which needs to preserve lucrative maintenance revenue while making life easier on customers and stemming defections to other options, particularly SaaS (software as a service) applications, where upgrades are handled by the vendor.

SAP's strategy with the packs "makes a lot of sense," says Tim Ferguson, CIO at Northern Kentucky University. "Relatively speaking, compared to previous ways that SAP did this, they're very easy to install." NKU has served as a beta tester for the packs, which helped the school influence SAP to add key features it desired.

While NKU's core SAP functions for billing, payroll, and other areas are fairly stable, the systems that touch students each day must evolve regularly, Ferguson says. One of the packs provided a new Web service that allows students to register for classes through their iPhones, for example. "The students that are coming out this generation, they expect different types of services. We have to change to meet those needs," says Ferguson.

SAP's pack strategy is apparently pleasing some customers. But it still involves some work. "I've mostly heard good things," says Jon Reed, an independent analyst who closely tracks SAP. "But they're not quite as painless as SAP's marketing sometimes presented it."

System testing remains a crucial factor, Reed says. "Things break during an on-premise implementation and there's a preferred method of handling that, including sandboxing and testing, so when you pull that lever there are no problems. Customers still need to anticipate how it might break their system."

But SourceGas, a U.S. natural gas utility, had only one issue when installing the enhancement packs, specifically a problem with the "flexible real estate" functionality in SAP, says Michael Catterall, director of enterprise solutions. The company uses that module to manage information regarding the many property easements and rights-of-way it maintains for its infrastructure around the country.

"When we brought up enhancement pack 4, because of how we had it configured, we kind of broke it a little bit," he says.

SourceGas plans to "keep watching the enhancement packs as they are coming out," Catterall says. "First, we're looking at where we can improve and get more out of modules we put in."

Meanwhile, there is the substantial task of getting to ECC 6.0 in the first place.

Upgrade expenses can amount to 50 to 85 percent of the original implementation costs, with the price tag varying, depending on factors like the number of integration points and customizations, according to analyst Ray Wang, partner with Altimeter Group.

"Ultimately, upgrading makes sense for R/3 customers who are still committed to SAP and want new functionality provided in the packs," says Wang. But those customers potentially have other options these days, in the form of third-party maintenance from companies such as Rimini Street, as well as SaaS applications. Meanwhile, on-demand products from vendors such as Workday, which makes human-resources software, and CRM (customer relationship management) specialist Salesforce.com are being used by some legacy SAP customers, who are finding that integrating them back to the core ERP system isn't overly difficult, Wang says.

Source: Adapted from Susan Carey, "Two Paths to Software Upgrade," *Wall Street Journal*, April 13, 2010; and Chris Kanaracus, "SAP Users: Upgrading Has Its Benefits," *CIO.com*, April 9, 2010.

CASE STUDY QUESTIONS

1. In the case, both airlines upgraded to the same application but approached the upgrade process differently. What were those differences, and how much impact did they have on the outcome of the project?

2. What precautions did the organizations in the case take to prevent software upgrade problems? To what extent do you believe those helped?

3. SAP customers have the choice between upgrading to the most recent version of the application suite or integrating third-party products into their existing infrastructure. What are the advantages and disadvantages of each alternative?

REAL WORLD ACTIVITIES

1. Why are ERP upgrades so complex and expensive? What role does ERP customization, if any, play in this process? Go online and research other examples discussing ERP upgrades. Can you discern a pattern in what seems to be the major cost drivers of the upgrade process?

2. Place yourself in the position of a WestJet or JetBlue customer while the upgrading was being implemented. What, if anything, would you have done differently had the companies told you that a major software upgrade would be happening soon? Should they have told you? Break into small groups with your classmates and discuss these questions.

meet deadlines or not completing a project. Unless IT becomes skilled at PPM, we'll never close this credibility gap.

Once you put a process in place, the other P-word—politics—will inevitably appear. The magic behind PPM is that, when you do it right, it becomes clear why a given project shouldn't get done in the context of your overall IT governance strategy. Consider the following situation: Your portfolio management process comes up with a "not now" or a "no" for a business unit's project, but the business unit (which has its own budget and a degree of autonomy) moves ahead without IT's approval; this rogue project then creates urgent unplanned work for IT as the improperly planned technology spirals out of control or fails to integrate with enterprise systems. What do you do in this case?

ITPI's Milne answers this question with a question: "How do you handle it when your corporate strategy says, 'We're not going into the Latin America market,' and a line business does it anyway?" If your PPM process is sufficiently integrated into executive corporate strategy, units that are totally out of line will not need to be nailed by IT; the organization will rein them in, with or without IT's participation.

Source: Adapted from Jonathan Feldman, "Project Management Keeps IT from Being a Victim of Success," *InformationWeek*, April 5, 2008.

FIGURE 12.18   An overview of the implementation process. Implementation activities are needed to transform a newly developed information system into an operational system for end users.

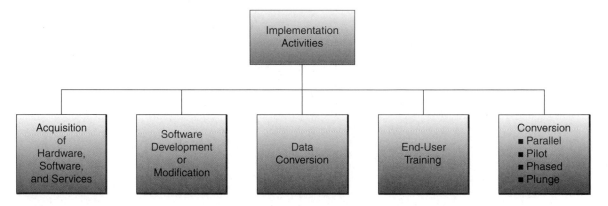

FIGURE 12.19

An example of the implementation process activities and timetables for a company installing an intranet-based employee benefits system in its human resource management department.

Intranet Implementation Activities	Month 1	Month 2	Month 3	Month 4
Acquire and install server hardware and software	■			
Train administrators	■			
Acquire and install browser software	■	■		
Acquire and install publishing software	■			
Train benefits employees on publishing software	■			
Convert benefits manuals and add revisions	■	■		
Create Web-based tutorials for the intranet		■		
Hold rollout meetings				■

Project Management

Any discussion of information systems design and development would be incomplete without including a discussion of basic project management concepts, techniques, and tools. Before we progress any further in our discussion of implementation, we need to understand how our project, which we hope is on time and within budget, got to this point. Although a thorough discussion of project management is far beyond the scope of this text, we can, nonetheless, look at the big picture and acquaint ourselves with the necessary steps in the process. It is important to note that the skills and knowledge necessary to be a good project manager will translate into virtually any project environment, and most organizations regularly seek people who have acquired these skills.

What Is a Project?

A **project** is a special set of activities with a clear beginning and end. Every project has a set of *goals*, *objectives*, and *tasks*. Every project must also deal with a set of *limitations* or *constraints*. Finally, although the content can vary from one project to the next, there are many important similarities in the process. The first, and probably the greatest, contribution of the modern project management approach is to identify the project as a series of steps or phases. The SDLC is a project management approach tailored toward the design and development of information systems. Before we return our focus to a specific project management approach such as the SDLC, let's look at a more generic picture of project management and see how it compares. No matter what the project, three elements will be necessary to manage it effectively and efficiently: *process*, *tools*, and *techniques*.

The Process of Project Management

The modern project management approach has identified five phases in the process. Figure 12.20 illustrates the five phases.

FIGURE 12.20

The five phases of project management.

Project Management Phase	Example Activities
Initiating/Defining	• State the problem(s)/goal(s). • Identify the objectives. • Secure resources. • Explore costs/benefits in feasibility study.
Planning	• Identify and sequence activities. • Identify the "critical path." • Estimate time and resources needed for completion. • Write a detailed project plan.
Executing	• Commit resources to specific tasks. • Add additional resources/personnel if necessary. • Initiate project work.
Controlling	• Establish reporting obligations. • Create reporting tools. • Compare actual progress with baseline. • Initiate control interventions if necessary.
Closing	• Install all deliverables. • Finalize all obligations/commitments. • Meet with stakeholders. • Release project resources. • Document the project. • Issue final report.

Initiating and Defining. The first phase of the project management process serves as a foundation for all that follows. The most important objective to achieve during this phase is the clear and succinct statement of the problem that the project is to solve or the goals that the project is to achieve. Any ambiguity at this point often spells doom for even the best-executed projects. Also during this phase, it is necessary to identify and secure the resources necessary to execute the project, explore the costs and benefits, and identify any risks. As you have probably recognized, this is exactly what happens during the systems investigation phase of the SDLC.

Planning. The next phase in the project management process involves planning the project. Here every project objective and every activity associated with that objective must be identified and sequenced. Several tools have been created to assist in the sequencing of these activities including simple *dependence diagrams, program evaluation and review* (PERT), *critical path method* (CPM), and a commonly used timeline diagram known as a *Gantt chart*. Although all of these tools have a particular use in project management, their common use is to help plan and sequence activities associated with the objectives of the project so that nothing is left out, performed out of logical sequence, or done twice. These same tools also help the project manager determine how long each activity will take and, thus, how long the project will take. Later in the project process, the tools will help determine whether the project is on schedule and, if not, where the delays occurred and what can be done to remedy the delay.

Executing. Once all of the activities in the planning phase are complete and all detailed plans have been created and approved, the execution phase of the project can begin. It is here that all of the plans are put into motion. Resources, tasks, and schedules are brought together, and the necessary work teams are created and set forth on their assigned paths. In many respects, this is the most exciting part of the project management process. The phases of systems analysis and system design are the primary phases associated with project execution in the SDLC.

Controlling. Some project management experts suggest that controlling is just an integral part of the execution phase of project management; others suggest it must be viewed as a separate set of activities that, admittedly, occur simultaneous to the execution phase. In either case, it is important to give sufficient attention to the controlling activities to ensure that the project objectives and deadlines are met.

Probably the single most important tool for project control is the report. Three common types of reports are generated to assist with project control. The *variance report* contains information related to the difference between actual and planned project progress. It helps identify when a project is off track but provides little evidence as to what is causing the delay.

The second and third types of reports are more helpful in determining the cause of delays and the appropriate corrections. The *status report* is an open-ended report that details the process that led to the current project state. By analyzing this report, a project manager can pinpoint where the delay began and can create a plan to get past it and possibly make up for lost time. This is where the *resource allocation* report becomes useful. This report identifies the various resources (people, equipment, and so on) that are being applied to specific project activities, as well as where currently unused, or *slack*, resources may be available.

Closing. This last phase of the project management process focuses on bringing a project to a successful end. The beginning of the end of a project is the implementation and installation of all of the project deliverables. The next step is the formal release of the project resources so they can be redeployed into other projects or job roles. The final step in this phase is to review the final documentation and publish the final project report. This is where the good and bad news concerning the project are documented, and the elements necessary for a postproject review are identified.

Many airline pilots (and passengers, for that matter) identify the final approach and landing as one of the most critical elements of any flight. It is during those remaining moments that even the smoothest of flights can come to an undesirable conclusion. Projects are quite similar in this regard. The most beautifully planned, executed, and controlled project can be deemed a failure if it is poorly implemented. As such, we must turn our attention back to the issues of systems implementation; we hope that this time it will be with a clearer understanding of how we arrived at this point and the process we will follow to do it again in another project.

Evaluating Hardware, Software, and Services

A major activity during the implementation phase of the SDLC is the acquisition of the hardware and software necessary to implement the new system. How do companies evaluate and select hardware, software, and IT services, such as those shown in Figure 12.21? Large companies may require suppliers to present bids and proposals based on system specifications developed during the design stage of systems development. Minimum acceptable physical and performance characteristics for all hardware and software requirements are established. Most large business firms and all government agencies formalize these requirements by listing them in a document called an RFP (request for proposal) or RFQ (request for quotation). Then they send the RFP or RFQ to appropriate vendors, who use it as the basis for preparing a proposed purchase agreement.

Companies may use a *scoring* system of evaluation when there are several competing proposals for a hardware or software acquisition. They give each **evaluation factor** a certain number of maximum possible points. Then they assign each competing proposal points for each factor, depending on how well it meets the user's specifications. Scoring evaluation factors for several proposals helps organize and document the evaluation process. It also spotlights the strengths and weaknesses of each proposal.

Whatever the claims of hardware manufacturers and software suppliers, the performance of hardware and software must be demonstrated and evaluated. Independent hardware and software information services (such as Datapro and Auerbach) may be used to gain detailed specification information and evaluations. Other users are frequently the best source of information needed to evaluate the claims of manufacturers

FIGURE 12.21

Examples from the IBM Corporation of the kinds of hardware, software, and IS services that many companies are evaluating and acquiring to support their e-commerce initiatives.

Hardware
Full range of offerings, including xSeries servers, iSeries midrange servers for small and midsize businesses, RS/6000 servers for UNIX customers, and z900 mainframes for large enterprises. Also has full range of storage options.

Software
Web server: Lotus DominoGo Web server.
Storefront: WebSphere Commerce Suite (formerly known as Net.Commerce) for storefront and catalog creation, relationship marketing, and order management. Can add Commerce Integrator to integrate with back-end systems and Catalog Architect for content management.
Middleware/transaction services: WebSphere application server manages transactions. MQ Series queues messages and manages connections. CICS processes transactions.
Database: DB2 Universal Database.
Tools: WebSphere Studio includes set of predefined templates and common business logic.
Other applications include: IBM Payment Suite for handling credit cards and managing digital certificates.

Services
IBM Global Services, which includes groups organized by each major industry, including retail and financial. Can design, build, and host e-commerce applications.

and suppliers. That's why Internet newsgroups and Weblogs established to exchange information about specific software or hardware vendors and their products have become one of the best sources for obtaining up-to-date information about the experiences of users of the products.

Large companies frequently evaluate proposed hardware and software by requiring the processing of special *benchmark* test programs and test data. Benchmarking simulates the processing of typical jobs on several computers and evaluates their performances. Users can then evaluate test results to determine which hardware device or software package displayed the best performance characteristics.

Hardware Evaluation Factors

When you evaluate the hardware needed by a new business application, you should investigate specific physical and performance characteristics for each computer system or peripheral component to be acquired. Specific questions must be answered concerning many important factors. Ten of these **hardware evaluation factors** and questions are summarized in Figure 12.22.

Notice that there is much more to evaluating hardware than determining the fastest and cheapest computing device. For example, the question of obsolescence must be addressed by making a technology evaluation. The factor of ergonomics is also very important. Ergonomic factors ensure that computer hardware and software are user-friendly, that is, safe, comfortable, and easy to use. Connectivity is another important evaluation factor because so many network technologies and bandwidth alternatives are available to connect computer systems to the Internet, intranet, and extranet networks.

FIGURE 12.22

A summary of 10 major hardware evaluation factors. Notice how you can use this to evaluate a computer system or a peripheral device.

Hardware Evaluation Factors	Rating
Performance What is its speed, capacity, and throughput?	
Cost What is its lease or purchase price? What will be its cost of operation and maintenance?	
Reliability What are the risk of malfunction and its maintenance requirements? What are its error control and diagnostic features?	
Compatibility Is it compatible with existing hardware and software? Is it compatible with hardware and software provided by competing suppliers?	
Technology In what year of its product life cycle is it? Does it use a new untested technology, or does it run the risk of obsolescence?	
Ergonomics Has it been "human factors engineered" with the user in mind? Is it user-friendly, designed to be safe, comfortable, and easy to use?	
Connectivity Can it be easily connected to wide area and local area networks that use different types of network technologies and bandwidth alternatives?	
Scalability Can it handle the processing demands of a wide range of end users, transactions, queries, and other information processing requirements?	
Software Are system and application software available that can best use this hardware?	
Support Are the services required to support and maintain it available?	
Overall Rating	

FIGURE 12.23

A summary of selected software evaluation factors. Note that most of the hardware evaluation factors in Figure 12.22 can also be used to evaluate software packages.

Software Evaluation Factors	Rating
Quality Is it bug-free, or does it have many errors in its program code?	
Efficiency Is the software a well-developed system of program code that does not use much CPU time, memory capacity, or disk space?	
Flexibility Can it handle our business processes easily, without major modification?	
Security Does it provide control procedures for errors, malfunctions, and improper use?	
Connectivity Is it *Web-enabled* so it can easily access the Internet, intranets, and extranets, on its own, or by working with Web browsers or other network software?	
Maintenance Will new features and bug fixes be easily implemented by our own software developers?	
Documentation Is the software well documented? Does it include help screens and helpful software agents?	
Hardware Does existing hardware have the features required to best use this software?	
Other Factors What are its performance, cost, reliability, availability, compatibility, modularity, technology, ergonomics, scalability, and support characteristics? (Use the hardware evaluation factor questions in Figure 12.22.)	
Overall Rating	

Software Evaluation Factors

You should evaluate software according to many factors that are similar to those used for hardware evaluation. Thus, the factors of performance, cost, reliability, availability, compatibility, modularity, technology, ergonomics, and support should be used to evaluate proposed software acquisitions. In addition, however, the **software evaluation factors** summarized in Figure 12.23 must also be considered. You should answer the questions they generate in order to evaluate software purchases properly. For example, some software packages are notoriously slow, hard to use, bug-filled, or poorly documented. They are not a good choice, even if offered at attractive prices.

Evaluating IS Services

Most suppliers of hardware and software products and many other firms offer a variety of **IS services** to end users and organizations. Examples include assistance in developing a company Web site; installation or conversion of new hardware and software; employee training; and hardware maintenance. Some of these services are provided without cost by hardware manufacturers and software suppliers.

Other types of IS services needed by a business can be outsourced to an outside company for a negotiated price. For example, *systems integrators* take over complete responsibility for an organization's computer facilities when an organization outsources its computer operations. They may also assume responsibility for developing and implementing large systems development projects that involve many vendors and subcontractors. Value-added resellers (VARs) specialize in providing industry-specific hardware, software, and services from selected manufacturers. Many other services are available to end users, including systems design, contract programming, and consulting services. Evaluation factors and questions for IS services are summarized in Figure 12.24.

FIGURE 12.24

Evaluation factors for IS services. These factors focus on the quality of support services business users may need.

Evaluation Factors for IS Services	Rating
Performance What has been their past performance in view of their past promises?	
Systems Development Are Web site and other e-business developers available? What are their quality and cost?	
Maintenance Is equipment maintenance provided? What are its quality and cost?	
Conversion What systems development and installation services will they provide during the conversion period?	
Training Is the necessary training of personnel provided? What are its quality and cost?	
Backup Are similar computer facilities available nearby for emergency backup purposes?	
Accessibility Does the vendor provide local or regional sites that offer sales, systems development, and hardware maintenance services? Is a customer support center at the vendor's Web site available? Is a customer hotline provided?	
Business Position Is the vendor financially strong, with good industry market prospects?	
Hardware Do they provide a wide selection of compatible hardware devices and accessories?	
Software Do they offer a variety of useful e-business software and application packages?	
Overall Rating	

Other Implementation Activities

Testing, data conversion, documentation, and training are keys to successful implementation of a new business system.

Testing

System testing may involve testing and debugging software, testing Web site performance, and testing new hardware. An important part of testing is the review of prototypes of displays, reports, and other output. Prototypes should be reviewed by end users of the proposed systems for possible errors. Of course, testing should not occur only during the system's implementation stage, but throughout the system's development process. For example, you might examine and critique prototypes of input documents, screen displays, and processing procedures during the systems design stage. Immediate end-user testing is one of the benefits of a prototyping process.

Data Conversion

Implementing new information systems for many organizations today frequently involves replacing a previous system and its software and databases. One of the most important implementation activities required when installing new software in such cases is called data conversion. For example, installing new software packages may require converting the data elements in databases that are affected by a new application into new data formats. Other data conversion activities that are typically required include correcting incorrect data, filtering out unwanted data, consolidating data from several databases, and organizing data into new data subsets, such as databases, data marts, and data warehouses. A good data conversion process is essential because improperly organized and formatted data are frequently reported to be one of the major causes of failures in implementing new systems.

During the design phase, the analysts created a data dictionary that not only describes the various data elements contained in the new system but also specifies any necessary conversions from the old system. In some cases, only the name of the data element is changed, as in the old system field CUST_ID becoming CLIENT_ID in the new system. In other cases, the actual format of the data is changed, thus requiring some conversion application to be written to filter the old data and put them into the new format. An example of this might be the creation of a new CUSTOMER_ID format to allow for expansion or to make two merged systems compatible with one another. This type of data element conversion requires additional time to occur because each element must be passed through the conversion filter before being written into the new data files.

Yet another issue is the time necessary to transfer the data from the old data files into the files for the new system. Although it is possible that the new system may have been designed to use the existing data files, this is not normally the case, especially in situations where a new system is replacing a legacy system that is fairly old. The time necessary to transfer the old data can have a material impact on the conversion process and on the strategy that is ultimately selected. Consider the following situation.

Suppose the conversion to the new system requires the transfer of data from 10 different data files. The average record length across the 10 files is 1,780 bytes, and the total number of records contained in the 10 files is 120 million. With this information and an estimate of the transfer time in bytes per minute, the total transfer time can be easily calculated as follows: Assume a transfer rate of 10.5 megabytes per second (Mbps) (Fast Ethernet) with no conversion algorithm.

$$1,780 \text{ bytes} \times 120 \text{ million records} = 213,600,000,000 \text{ bytes}.$$

$$213,600,000,000 \text{ bytes}/10.5 \text{ Mbps} = 20,343 \text{ seconds}.$$

$$20,343 \text{ seconds} = 5.65 \text{ hours}.$$

Although the preceding calculations appear to be such that the conversion process does not take an inordinate amount of time, we must also be aware that they assume an error-free transfer, no format conversion, and 100 percent use of available network bandwidth. If the transfer is done using a slower communication medium, say 1.25 Mbps, the time jumps to 47.47 hours (just under two days).

The important consideration here is not just the time necessary to effect the transfer but the preservation of the integrity of the current system data files during the process. If the transfer turns out to be about 4.5 hours, then it could theoretically occur after business hours and be easily accomplished by the opening of the next day's business. If, however, the process takes two full days, then it would need to begin at the close of business on Friday and would not be complete until late Sunday afternoon. Should any glitches show up in the process, either the transfer would have to wait a week to be rerun, or the possibility of disrupting daily operations or losing new data would be very real. As you can see, careful thought to the logistics associated with data transfer must be given when recommending the most appropriate conversion strategy for the new system.

Documentation

Developing good user documentation is an important part of the implementation process. Sample data entry display screens, forms, and reports are good examples of documentation. When *computer-aided systems engineering* methods are used, documentation can be created and changed easily because it is stored and accessible on disk in a *system repository*. Documentation serves as a method of communication among the people responsible for developing, implementing, and maintaining a computer-based system. Installing and operating a newly designed system or modifying an established application requires a detailed record of that system's design. Documentation is extremely important in diagnosing errors and making changes, especially if the end users or systems analysts who developed a system are no longer with the organization.

FIGURE 12.25 How one company developed training programs for the implementation of an e-commerce Web site and intranet access for its employees.

| **Training** | *Training* is a vital implementation activity. IS personnel, such as user consultants, must be sure that end users are trained to operate a new business system or its implementation will fail. Training may involve only activities like data entry, or it may also involve all aspects of the proper use of a new system. In addition, managers and end users must be educated in how the new technology affects the company's business operations and management. This knowledge should be supplemented by training programs for any new hardware devices, software packages, and their use for specific work activities. Figure 12.25 illustrates how one business coordinated its end-user training program with each stage of its implementation process for developing intranet and Internet access within the company. |

System Conversion Strategies

The initial operation of a new business system can be a difficult task. This typically requires a conversion process from the use of a present system to the operation of a new or improved application. Conversion methods can soften the impact of introducing new information technologies into an organization. Four major forms of system conversion are illustrated in Figure 12.26. They include:

- Parallel conversion
- Phased conversion
- Pilot conversion
- Direct conversion

Direct Conversion

The simplest conversion strategy, and probably the most disruptive to the organization, is the **direct cutover** approach. This method, sometimes referred to as the **slam dunk** or **cold-turkey strategy,** is as abrupt as its name implies. Using this approach,

FIGURE 12.26

The four major forms of conversion to a new system.

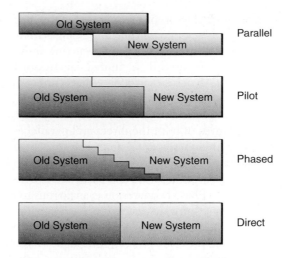

the old system is just turned off, and the new system is turned on in its place. Although this method is the least expensive of all available strategies and may be the only viable solution in situations where activating the new system is an emergency or when the two systems cannot coexist under any conditions, it is also the one that poses the greatest risk of failure. Once the new system becomes operational, the end users must cope with any errors or dysfunctions, and depending on the severity of the problem, this approach can have a significant effect on the quality of the work performed. Direct conversion should be considered only in extreme circumstances where no other conversion strategy is viable.

Parallel Conversion

At the opposite end of the risk spectrum is the **parallel conversion** strategy. Here, the old and new systems are run simultaneously until the end users and project coordinators are fully satisfied that the new system is functioning correctly and the old system is no longer necessary. Using this approach, a parallel conversion can be effected with either a **single cutover,** where a predetermined date for stopping the parallel operation is set, or a **phased cutover,** where some predetermined method of phasing in each piece of the new system and turning off a similar piece of the old system is employed.

Although clearly having the advantage of low risk, the parallel approach also brings with it the highest cost. To execute a parallel approach properly, the end users must literally perform all daily functions with both systems, thus creating a massive redundancy in activities and literally double the work. In fact, unless the operational costs of the new system are significantly less than the old system, the cost of parallel operation can be as much as three to four times greater than the old system alone. During a parallel conversion, all outputs from both systems are compared for concurrency and accuracy, until it is determined that the new system is functioning at least as well as the one it is replacing. Parallel conversion may be the best choice in situations where an automated system is replacing a manual one. In certain circumstances where end users cannot cope with the often-confusing redundancy of two systems, the parallel conversion strategy may not be viable. Also, parallel conversion may not be possible if the organization does not have the available computing resources to operate two systems at the same time.

Pilot Conversion

In some situations, the new system may be installed in multiple locations, such as a series of bank branches or retail outlets. In other cases, the conversion may be able to be planned from a geographic perspective. When these types of scenarios exist, the possibility of using a **pilot conversion** strategy exists. This approach allows for the conversion to the new system, using either a direct or parallel method, at a single location. The advantage to this approach is that a location can be selected that best represents the conditions across the organization but also may be less risky in terms of any loss of time or delays in processing. Once the installation is complete at the pilot site, the process can be evaluated and any changes to the system made to prevent problems encountered at the pilot site from reoccurring at the remaining installations. This approach may also be required if the individual sites or locations have certain unique characteristics or idiosyncrasies making either a direct or parallel approach infeasible.

Phased Conversion

A **phased** or **gradual conversion** strategy attempts to take advantage of the best features of both the direct and parallel approaches, while minimizing the risks involved. This incremental approach to conversion allows for the new system to be brought online as a series of functional components that are logically ordered to minimize disruption to the end users and the flow of business.

Phased conversion is analogous to the release of multiple versions of an application by a software developer. Each version of the software should correct any known bugs and should allow for 100 percent compatibility with data entered into or processed by the previous version. Although it has the advantage of lower risk, the phased approach takes the most time and, thus, creates the most disruption to the organization over time.

Postimplementation Activities

When all is said and done, the single most costly activity occurs after the system implementation is complete: the **postimplementation maintenance phase.** The primary objectives associated with systems maintenance are to correct errors or faults in the system, provide changes to effect performance improvement, or adapt the system to changes in the operating or business environment. In a typical organization, more programmers and analysts are assigned to application maintenance activities than to application development. Further, although a new system can take several months or years to design and build and can cost hundreds of thousands or millions of dollars, the resulting system can operate around the clock and last for 5 to 10 years, or longer. One major activity in postimplementation involves making changes to the system after the users have finally had an opportunity to use it. These are called **change requests.** Such requests can range from fixing a software bug not found during testing to designing an enhancement to an existing process or function.

Systems Maintenance

Managing and implementing change requests is only one aspect of the systems maintenance phase activities. In some ways, once the maintenance phase begins, the life cycle starts over again. New requirements are articulated, analyzed, designed, checked for feasibility, tested, and implemented. Although the range and nature of specific maintenance requests vary from system to system, four basic categories of maintenance can be identified: (1) corrective, (2) adaptive, (3) perfective, and (4) preventive.

The activities associated with **corrective maintenance** are focused on fixing bugs and logic errors not detected during the implementation testing period. **Adaptive maintenance** refers to those activities associated with modifying existing functions or adding new functionality to accommodate changes in the business or operating environments. **Perfective maintenance** activities involve changes made to an existing system that are intended to improve the performance of a function or interface. The final category of maintenance activities, **preventive maintenance,** involves those activities intended to reduce the chances of a system failure or extend the capacity of a current system's useful life. Although often the lowest-priority maintenance activity, preventive maintenance is, nonetheless, a high-value-adding function and is vital to an organization realizing the full value of its investment in the system.

Postimplementation Review

The maintenance activity also includes a postimplementation review process to ensure that newly implemented systems meet the business objectives established for them. Errors in the development or use of a system must be corrected by the maintenance process. This includes a periodic review or audit of a system to ensure that it is operating properly and meeting its objectives. This audit is in addition to continually monitoring a new system for potential problems or necessary changes.

| Project Success (or Failure): What We Know but Choose to Ignore | There is no mystery as to why most projects succeed or fail; people have been writing about effective project management for millennia. More than 2,000 years ago, Sun Tzu described how to organize a successful, highly complex project (a military campaign) in *The Art of War*. Fred Brooks's classic book, *The Mythical Man-Month*, offers management advice targeted at running large IT projects. The U.K. National Audit Office recently published an excellent guide to delivering successful IT-enabled business change. Over the past 10 years, virtually every major IT publication has printed articles on why large projects succeed or fail.

Despite all the excellent advice available, more than half of the major projects undertaken by IT departments still fail or get canceled. We know what works. We just don't do it.

An ineffective executive sponsor. A weak or, even worse, nonexistent executive sponsor almost guarantees business project failure. Under weak executive leadership, all projects become IT projects rather than business initiatives with IT components.

A poor business case. An incomplete business case allows incorrect expectations to be set—and missed.

The business case is no longer valid. Marketplace changes frequently invalidate original business assumptions, but teams often become so invested in a project that they ignore warning signs and continue as planned.

The project is too big. Bigger projects require more discipline.

A lack of dedicated resources. Large projects require concentration and dedication for the duration. But key people are frequently required to support critical projects while continuing to perform their existing full-time jobs.

Out of sight, out of mind. If your suppliers fail, you fail, and you own it. Don't take your eyes off them.

Unnecessary complexity. Projects that attempt to be all things to all people usually result in systems that are difficult to use, and they eventually fail.

Cultural conflict. Projects that violate cultural norms of the organization seldom have a chance.

No contingency. Stuff happens. Projects need flexibility to address the inevitable surprises.

Too long without deliverables. Most organizations expect visible progress in six to nine months.

Long projects without intermediate products risk losing executive interest, support, and resources.

Betting on a new, unproven technology. Enough said.

An arbitrary release date. Date-driven projects have little chance of success. Companies should learn to plan the project before picking a release date, not the other way around.

Anything here that doesn't make sense? *That's exactly the point.*

Source: Adapted from Bart Perkins, "12 Things You Know About Projects but Choose to Ignore," *Computerworld*, March 12, 2007. |
|---|---|

Summary

● **The Systems Development Life Cycle.** Business end users and IS specialists may use a systems approach to help them develop information system solutions to meet business opportunities. This frequently involves a systems development life cycle where IS specialists and end users conceive, design, and implement business systems. The stages, activities, and products of the information systems development life cycle are summarized in Figure 12.3.

● **Prototyping.** Prototyping is a major alternative methodology to the traditional information systems development life cycle. It includes the use of prototyping

FIGURE 12.27

An overview of the implementation process. Implementation activities are needed to transform a newly developed information system into an operational system for end users.

Implementing New Systems
● **Acquisition** Evaluate and acquire necessary hardware and software resources and information system services. Screen vendor proposals.
● **Software Development** Develop any software that will not be acquired externally as software packages. Make any necessary modifications to software packages that are acquired.
● **Data Conversion** Convert data in company databases to new data formats and subsets required by newly installed software.
● **Training** Educate and train management, end users, customers, and other business stakeholders. Use consultants or training programs to develop user competencies.
● **Testing** Test and make necessary corrections to the programs, procedures, and hardware used by a new system.
● **Documentation** Record and communicate detailed system specifications, including procedures for end users and IS personnel and examples of input screens and output displays and reports.
● **Conversion** Convert from the use of a present system to the operation of a new or improved system. This may involve operating both new and old systems in *parallel* for a trial period, operation of a *pilot* system on a trial basis at one location, *phasing* in the new system one location at a time, or a *direct cutover* to the new system.

tools and methodologies, which promote an iterative, interactive process that develops prototypes of user interfaces and other information system components. See Figure 12.9.

● **End-User Development.** The application development capabilities built into many end-user software packages have made it easier for end users to develop their own business applications. End users should focus their development efforts on the system components of business processes that can benefit from the use of information technology, as summarized in Figure 12.14.

● **Implementing IS.** The implementation process for information system projects is summarized in Figure 12.27. Implementation involves acquisition, testing, documen-

tation, training, installation, and conversion activities that transform a newly designed business system into an operational system for end users.

● **Evaluating Hardware, Software, and Services.** Business professionals should know how to evaluate the acquisition of information system resources. IT vendors' proposals should be based on specifications developed during the design stage of systems development. A formal evaluation process reduces the possibility of incorrect or unnecessary purchases of hardware or software. Several major evaluation factors, summarized in Figures 12.22, 12.23, and 12.24, can be used to evaluate hardware, software, and IS services.

Key Terms and Concepts

These are the key terms and concepts of this chapter. The page number of their first explanation is in parentheses.

1. Conversion (548)
2. Cost/benefit analysis (522)
3. Data conversion (546)
4. Documentation (547)
5. Economic feasibility (521)

6. End-user development (531)
7. Feasibility study (520)
8. Functional requirements (526)
9. Human factors feasibility (523)
10. Implementation process (537)

11. Intangible (522)
    a. Benefits (522)
    b. Costs (522)
12. Legal/political feasibility (523)
13. Logical model (525)

14. Operational feasibility (521)
15. Organizational analysis (524)
16. Postimplementation review (550)
17. Project management (541)
18. Prototyping (527)
19. Systems analysis and design (519)

20. Systems approach (516)
21. Systems development life cycle (519)
22. Systems implementation (537)
23. Systems maintenance (550)
24. System specifications (531)
25. Systems thinking (516)

26. System testing (546)
27. Tangible (522)
   a. Benefits (522)
   b. Costs (522)
28. Technical feasibility (522)
29. User interface design (529)

Review Quiz

Match one of the key terms and concepts listed previously with each of the brief examples or definitions that follow. Try to find the best fit for answers that seem to fit more than one term or concept. Defend your choices.

_____ 1. Using an organized sequence of activities to study a problem or opportunity using systems thinking.

_____ 2. Trying to recognize systems and the new inter-relationships and components of systems in any situation.

_____ 3. Evaluating the success of a solution after it has been implemented.

_____ 4. Your evaluation shows that benefits outweigh costs for a proposed system.

_____ 5. The costs of acquiring computer hardware, software, and specialists.

_____ 6. Loss of customer goodwill caused by errors in a new system.

_____ 7. Increases in profits caused by a new system.

_____ 8. Improved employee morale caused by efficiency and effectiveness of a new system.

_____ 9. A multistep process to conceive, design, and implement an information system.

_____ 10. A diagram or blueprint of a system that shows what it does without regard to how it does it.

_____ 11. Determines the organizational, economic, technical, and operational feasibility of a proposed information system.

_____ 12. The goal of this feasibility analysis category is to determine whether the proposed system will provide positive economic benefits.

_____ 13. Reliable hardware and software are available to implement a proposed system.

_____ 14. Determining whether or not any copyright or patent infringements may exist as the result of a new system.

_____ 15. Do we have the right people to operate the new system?

_____ 16. A multistage process for studying in detail the information needs of users and any information systems presently used, and then developing a system to correct a problem or improve operations.

_____ 17. A detailed description of user information needs and the input, processing, output, storage, and control capabilities required to meet those needs.

_____ 18. Systems design should focus on developing user-friendly input and output methods for a system.

_____ 19. A detailed description of the hardware, software, people, network, and data resources and information products required by a proposed system.

_____ 20. Acquiring hardware and software, testing and documenting a proposed system, and training people to use it.

_____ 21. Making improvements to an operational system.

_____ 22. An interactive and iterative process of developing and refining information system prototypes.

_____ 23. Managers and business specialists can develop their own e-business applications.

_____ 24. Correcting, converting, filtering, consolidating, and organizing data when replacing an old system.

_____ 25. Operate in parallel with the old system, use a test site, switch in stages, or cut over immediately to a new system.

_____ 26. Checking whether hardware and software work properly for end users.

_____ 27. A user manual communicates the design and operating procedures of a system.

_____ 28. Keeping an IS project on time and within its budget would be a major goal.

_____ 29. Cost and benefits that can be quantified with a high degree of certainty.

_____ 30. The degree to which a proposed system fits with the business environment and organizational objectives.

_____ 31. Costs and benefits of a new system that are hard to quantify.

_____ 32. A phase within systems analysis focused on understanding the organization and its environment.

_____ 33. The process by which a system goes from designs and blueprints to becoming a working system.

Discussion Questions

1. Why has prototyping become a popular way to develop business applications? What are prototyping's advantages and disadvantages?

2. Refer to the Real World Case on software programming errors in the chapter. Does the ability of technology to provide developers with multiple combinations of operating systems and applications mean that companies should be required, or expected, to support all possible ones? Discuss.

3. Review the real-world example about Walmart and Others in the chapter. How could these companies prepare for the unexpected changes in demand that brought down their Web sites? Explain your reasoning.

4. What are the three most important factors you would use in evaluating computer hardware? Computer software? Explain why.

5. Assume that in your first week on a new job you are asked to use a type of business software that you have never used before. What kind of user training should your company provide to you before you start?

6. Refer to the Real World Case on WestJet, JetBlue, and Others in the chapter. In general, is it a good idea for companies to make major software upgrades public beforehand? What are the advantages and disadvantages of doing so? Do they have an ethical responsibility to tell their customers? Discuss.

7. What is the difference between the parallel, direct, phased, and pilot forms of IS conversion? Which conversion strategy is best? Explain why.

8. Review the Microsoft real-world example in the chapter. How might you change the user interface of Microsoft's ribbon in Word and those of some of its other products? Defend your proposals.

9. Review the real-world example discussing the factors involved in project failure in the chapter. If these are well-known, why would companies choose to ignore them over and over again? What could be the reasons behind such behavior?

10. Pick a business task you would like to computerize. How could you use the steps of the information systems development life cycle as illustrated in Figure 12.3 to help you? Use examples to illustrate your answer.

Analysis Exercises

1. **SDLC in Practice**
   Community Action
   The systems development life cycle (SDLC) provides a structured problem-solving software development methodology. What works for information system–related problems, however, also works for many business problems, too. The SDLC provides a framework that requires adherents to follow a logical sequence. This sequence promotes careful analysis and helps ensure that you are doing the right thing as well as doing the thing right.

   You can use the SDLC to address many business problems. Think about a problem in your community. Your community may include your campus, your work, or your neighborhood. Your instructor may provide additional guidelines. Select a problem, complete each step in turn, and prepare a report detailing each step. Due to the location-specific nature of this exercise, expect to conduct firsthand research and interviews.

   a. Select a problem and quantify its effects.
   b. Identify the cause or causes of the problem.
   c. Describe various solutions to this problem. Include estimated costs and benefits for each solution.
   d. Select a solution and prepare a plan for its implementation.
   e. Identify the parties responsible for monitoring and maintaining the solution. What metrics should they use to monitor the results?

2. **Planning for Success**
   Project Planning
   Projects have many dependencies, any of which could become points of failure. Without the cooperation or input from even one vital resource, a project may fail to meet its objectives. Effective project planning helps project managers think through a project before it starts and prepare communication strategies in advance.

   a. Read the article "How to Create a Clear Project Plan," *Darwin Magazine*, August 2004 (http://tinyurl.com/24oub5a), and summarize its main points.
   b. Read through the "SDLC in Practice" exercise above, and select a problem as directed by your professor.
   c. Prepare a project plan for the problem you selected above.
   d. Present your project plan to your class. Solicit your peers' suggestions for improvement.

3. **Americans with Disabilities Act**
   Enabling Technologies
   The Americans with Disabilities Act prohibits discrimination on the basis of disability in regard to public accommodations and commercial facilities. This act has been interpreted to include certain information systems as well. All information systems development

projects should take ADA issues into consideration during development. Accommodating employees and customers with disabilities must never become an afterthought.

Even if you do not presently have physical limitations, you may either have limitations in the future or have employees under your supervision who require special tools to enable access to information systems. Research information systems access solutions. Be sure to include a detailed description of the hardware or software solution, solution provider, and cost of accommodating each limitation listed below.

a. Partial visual impairment
b. Total visual impairment
c. Manual dexterity impairment

4. **Central London Congestion Charging Scheme Conversion Strategies**
The city of London has been well known for its many historic sites, live theater, and heavy traffic. In spite of a sophisticated underground subway system known locally as the "tube," traffic delays, car exhaust, noise pollution, and vehicle-pedestrian accidents have plagued Londoners for decades. After long deliberation, London's city government adopted the Central London Congestion Charging Scheme. This plan involved establishing a toll perimeter around London's center. Rather than stopping cars to collect tolls, however, London set up video cameras at each toll zone crossing. These cameras link to a billing system that charges each vehicle's registered owner a one-day access toll with same-day reentrance privileges. The steep toll, about $8, discourages vehicle traffic into London's city center.

Londoners who live within the toll zone receive a special discount, as do residents living near the toll zone boundary, certain government workers, and businesses operating fleets of vehicles. Tolls remain in effect during working hours on workdays. Car owners have until the end of the day to pay their toll through e-mail, SMS messaging, telephone, Web site, or kiosk.

The tolls have resulted in a significant decrease in automobile traffic, increased use of mass transit, fewer accidents, and faster driving times. The tolls have had a negligible effect on business operations and most residents. They have also generated significant revenue that London uses to maintain the system and to enhance public transportation.

Consider the massive work involved in educating the public, marking all streets entering the toll zone, setting up cameras, and building the information systems. The information systems alone must process the raw images, match license plates to a payment database, receive payments, send out nonpayment notices, and process appeals. Police also use the system's databases for a variety of law enforcement–related work.

a. Briefly describe the advantages and disadvantages of each conversion strategy (parallel, pilot, phased, and plunge) as they apply to the Central London Congestion Charging Scheme project.
b. Which conversion strategy would you recommend for this project?
c. Defend your recommendation in detail.

CASE 3

PayPal: Going Global All Languages at a Time

When you're a global company that keeps expanding into new countries, how do you keep all of your consumer sites updated in the local language—without spending a ton of time and money?

PayPal realized five years ago that if it didn't solve this problem it would hinder the e-commerce payment company's ability to grow, says Matthew Mengerink, the company's vice president of core technologies; his IT responsibilities include PayPal's architecture and payment system infrastructure. Today, PayPal has re-architected the software code for its site to allow simultaneous refreshes for 15 locales ranging from France to Poland. In the development community, they call this unusual achievement "polylingual simultaneous shipping" or "SimShip."

"This is a big problem that's been around a long time," says Ron Rogowski, a principal analyst for Forrester Research, who specializes in globalization issues. "For the most part, companies really do a poor job localizing content," he says, noting that technology solutions in this area aren't plentiful, and companies also must conquer organizational battles over who controls what content. "Companies would like to manage their translations better," Rogowski says, "to realize internal and external cost savings. But the real benefit is the potential for revenue growth, the ability to roll into markets quickly."

That ability today translates into a large portion of PayPal's bottom line: For PayPal, international business now represents 44 percent of net revenue, which was $582 million for the first quarter of 2008, a 32 percent increase year-over-year. As of late 2007, PayPal handled about $1,806 in payment volume per second; the company's re-architected code played a key role in this increase.

PayPal, now part of online auction giant eBay, had to go global to support customer desire, Mengerink says. People outside of the United States were demanding that eBay let them use PayPal (the primary purchase mechanism on eBay) and that PayPal be presented to them as seamlessly as it had been presented in English, he says. The company had to do more than present a stilted translation of English into, say, French or German, he adds.

"Imagine you're going into a bank and you want to speak French," Mengerink says. "The teller can speak French. But that's not enough. You want to feel you're in France. You want to see the French flag on the wall. Especially in the banking industry, it was very important to express something that people trust in such a way that it is natural and native for them," he says.

Traditionally, companies solve the localization issue by working with third-party translation companies, whose staffers convert an English-based site into multiple languages, says Mengerink. The problem: "If you can't send them the smallest amount of text, it gets fantastically expensive," Mengerink says. "Here at PayPal you have a full site experience, you have to translate it, and we're an Internet company; we update the site every six weeks. How do you not slow the company down with the process of translation?"

PayPal's decision to custom-develop a solution is unusual and interesting. Few software vendors compete in the translation tools arena. Also, many companies can't even overcome the organizational hurdles related to translation. "There's a whole organizational issue that has to be looked at who's in charge of what," says Rogowski.

For example, he notes, a consumer electronics company may not even have similar-looking content, never mind identical content, on Web sites in multiple countries. "A lot of times Web content springs up without any plan for centralization," he says. "Before your company can translate all of its sites efficiently, you may get embroiled in organizational messes," Rogowski warns, which is why some companies are tackling the problem silo by silo.

Not Paypal. Five years ago, Mengerink and a team of localization experts inside of IT began their project to fix the problem in a very centralized way. Often, Mengerink says, companies facing this problem try to cut and paste code, and then translate it into different languages; this can lead to trouble because it's not simple to keep compressing and unifying the code. "It's far easier to manipulate text than code, he says.

PayPal decided that it had to re-architect its code to accommodate the language localization issue—purely for reasons of business speed. He says, "If you get the architecture right, you can get into new countries faster." No commercial tools existed that fit the bill, Mengerink says, so all the development was done in-house with a small IT team; PayPal will not disclose the exact size of the team or the cost metrics.

"There's this notion of a country code and a language code," Mengerink says. "Your software has to understand two things: *What country am I in and what language is being read?* This is extremely important because there are countries outside the United States where customers cannot imagine not having multiple languages, Canada, for example. The first thing we said is put both codes everywhere," Mengerink says. Then his developers had to create a code base with much more flexibility than the original; it had to convince the software, for instance, that strings of information such as e-mail addresses, customer support phone numbers, and time of day would change depending on the country code.

The second key to the project's success for PayPal: Ghassan Haddad, PayPal's director of localization, and the development team created a tool that color codes text in the software code base to note newly added strings of text that will need translating. "People just program as if it's in English, Mengerink says. "At the same time, the software extracts the new pieces." Then PayPal can send only the new pieces, instead of whole paragraphs, to the translation house. "This can take 5, 10 days depending on the size of the release," Mengerink says. "Then off we go to the races, releasing simultaneously in all locales."

So what's the next challenge for Mengerink and his developer team at PayPal? "We got very good at managing content with engineering," he says. "Now the question is, how we put that content management in the hands of business. They want to change it themselves without an intermediary. The business folks are saying 'we respect you but pretty please can we do it ourselves?' That's a challenge, he says, given that the development toolset will continue to grow.

By the way, PayPal isn't looking to license the technology it developed. "Our tools are built for PayPal, Mengerink says. "We're encouraging others to build it for themselves." Although his team worked primarily in HTML, the programming language is not the important choice, he says. "Think about the methodology. That's a really critical part. We built custom tools and they literally change every six months. This is a nascent industry. When you start looking at the publishing tools and content tools, most are appropriate for preview and publish," he says.

That's a simpler model than what PayPal does, for example, frequently linking new content with new features, he notes. "There was a lot of fear, a lot of people saying, 'Why aren't we being industry standard?' Leverage what you can, but you have to be good at creating your own tools. In the beginning, there was a lot of healthy skepticism, even internally,"

Mengerink says. "Some of your execs and developers will note that their last company tried to do simultaneous shipping and failed," he says. "Some people in the developer community still don't think it's possible," he adds. "Once it was done, we saw that it's not just manageable, it's a core advantage."

The sooner your company can start working on a SimShip project, the better: "Once you get too big, you can't afford the interrupt to the cycle," he notes.

"Very early on, you have to create the generic structures for the code," he says. "Build every next thing correct."

What's the bottom line for PayPal from Mengerink's team's work? "Today, we have 15 languages, 17 currencies, 190 markets," he says. "Our code base has grown a lot. All of the new code is being built using the right structure. You have to build internationalized." PayPal's re-architected code base now keeps e-commerce humming as the company continues to expand: PayPal's net total payment volume for 2007, the total value of transactions, was $47 billion, a gain of 33 percent over the previous year.

To put that in context, PayPal's net total payment volume for fourth quarter 2007, $14 billion, represented almost 12 percent of U.S. e-commerce, and almost 8 percent of global e-commerce.

Source: Adapted from Laurianne McLaughlin, "How PayPal Keeps E-Commerce Humming in 15 Languages at Once," *CIO Magazine*, March 14, 2008.

CASE STUDY QUESTIONS

1. One of the challenges that PayPal faces now that it has managed to overcome the polylingual obstacle is finding the best way to put this functionality in the hands of the business, so that they do not have to go through IT each time. How do you balance this need for responsiveness and flexibility versus IT's need to keep some degree of control to make sure everything keeps working with everything else? Provide some recommendations to managers who find themselves in this situation.

2. PayPal opted to deviate from industry standards and build its own custom technology that would better suit its needs. When is it a good idea for companies to take this alternative? What issues factor into that decision. Provide a discussion and some examples.

3. Although the new system has been quite successful, PayPal has chosen not to license this technology to others, forgoing a potentially important revenue stream given the lack of good solutions to this problem. Why do you think PayPal chose not to sell this technology? Do you really think this can be made into a strategic advantage over their competitors? How easy would it be for their competitors to imitate this accomplishment?

REAL WORLD ACTIVITIES

1. Choose two or three companies with global operations that interest you and visit their Web sites for countries other than the United States. Even if you are not familiar with the language, do the Web sites have the same look and feel of the U.S. site? In which ways are they similar, and in which ways are they different? If you did not know, would you have guessed it was the same company? Prepare a presentation with screenshots to share your findings with the rest of the class.

2. Although PayPal opted for a centralized approach to keep consistency across Web site appearance and content, other companies let both of these vary for each of the countries in which they operate. When would you use one or the other approach? Would it depend on the company, products offered, markets, countries, or on another factor? Break into small groups with your classmates to discuss these issues.

CASE 4

Queen's Medical Center, National Public Radio, Worldspan, and Others: Your IT Project Has Been Backlogged

Everyone at The Queen's Medical Center in Honolulu wants some shiny new piece of technology. Doctors and nurses who have seen a new pharmacy management system demonstrated at a recent conference think the hospital should have it. An administrator wants his department to have PDAs for wireless access to e-mail. Someone else wants a hospitalwide dietary management system but doesn't have the budget to fund it. All of these people want CIO and vice president of IT Ken Kudla to get it all for them.

Yet before he even thinks about eking new systems out of his $13 million annual operating budget, Kudla has to contend with the 30 projects he has going on right now. He's in the middle of upgrading the hospital's network and deploying an antispam management system. He's due to replace the seven different systems that make up his hospital information system. Meanwhile, he's trying to finish a document imaging project begun back in 2002, for which funding has been scarce. "CIOs are being bombarded," he says. "There's a pent-up demand for things."

Kudla isn't alone. According to "The State of the CIO 2006," an annual survey by CIO Magazine, demand for IT is back with a vengeance. It's almost like the late 1990s, except that what's missing now is the money, staff, and late-night takeout to deal with today's demand. In turn, the requests for IT projects are piling up. CIOs say that managing this application backlog is the number-one barrier to their job effectiveness today, regardless of industry or company size.

How CIOs manage this burgeoning demand has a direct impact on whether or not business leaders view IT as responsive to their needs. "Any CIO who sets an expectation that something will get done—and it doesn't—will be committing career suicide," says Bob Holstein, CIO at National Public Radio. The challenge for CIOs, then, is to ensure that projects already in the queue are aligned with ever-changing business priorities, to manage business-side expectations, and to control new sources of application demand from today's more sophisticated users. "One way you can interpret this problem is that users have a lot more appreciation of what's possible," says Holstein, "Or that the technology world has moved very quickly, and those business units want more, and they want it faster."

Whatever the source of the application backlog, CIOs should follow this cardinal rule. Don't complain; nobody—especially your CEO—likes a whiner. "I tell my staff, 'You can't be a victim,'" says Susan Powers, CIO of Worldspan. "I don't accept the victim mentality."

To some extent, backlogs have always been around because users have always cried for the latest applications. Ten years ago, during the Internet buildout, everyone got what they wanted. Then Y2K put the brakes on many less-critical projects. "Perhaps that started some of the backlog," Kudla says. Then came the dot.com bust, 9/11, and bad times for many companies.

Still, application demand remained. There may have been less development during the years when companies were focused on survival and keeping costs down, but users "still had their wish lists," says Stephen Rood, CIO of Strategic Technology, an IT consulting firm that advises small and midsize companies. Now, those needs are out in the open again, fueling CIOs' concerns about project backlogs.

How one defines and deals with any backlog boils down to two factors: the source of the demand and the project's stage of development. Holstein identifies two different types of backlogs: a backlog of desire (applications that users are yearning for) and a backlog of commitment (projects that are approved but not started). CIOs need to pay attention to both. If internal customers can't get an IT project on a CIO's radar screen, "they perceive there's a backlog because the IT shop can't do what they want,. Holstein says.

When projects have been promised but not delivered, he says, "expectations have been set and not fulfilled." It may be that an IT organization hasn't planned properly, or that managers aren't tracking projects well, or that developers are taking time to assess the ins and outs of a project. Whatever the reason, users have not gotten what they were promised.

One way to look at the backlog is to consider the whole spectrum of projects that IT is currently working on but has not finished, in addition to the ones ready to go. Powers has a list of 100 projects at Worldspan that have funding and that IT has started. Outside the top 100 are projects that are on deck. "When you finish [project] three, you bring in [project] 101," she explains. If she doesn't have the right staff with the right skills available for the next project on the list, she may skip to another. "We tend to have a backlog of about one year's worth of work. But because we prioritize every two weeks, some items never make it to the active list," Powers says.

No matter how good CIOs are at keeping a grip on their backlog, ever-shifting business priorities always threaten to shake up the IT agenda. One of the toughest tasks for CIOs is to align the jumble of projects vying for resources with the company's strategic needs. In a fast-paced business climate, new projects—especially those that come from the top floor—scream for attention. "They can also come about quite innocently," Holstein says, due to external factors that cause the business climate to shift. "What was a top priority becomes priority number 10."

A major contributor to the application backlog has been compliance-related projects, such as investments for Sarbanes-Oxley and HIPAA regulations. IT has to complete those projects by set dates, and in many cases, these infrastructure projects require substantial IT resources. Invariably, notes Holstein, implementing compliance projects pushes others farther down the to-do list. At Worldspan, Powers says, compliance-related projects trumped even a project that aimed to improve how the company prioritizes its IT projects.

The backlog generated by a new corporate agenda is worse for the CIO, who has to scramble to execute a decision she wasn't consulted about. Rood has seen it happen: A CEO and COO decide that they want a CRM system. When the CEO tells the CIO about it, the CIO is clueless as to why the project is necessary. The new project sends the IT department scrambling to jump-start the CRM project and pushes everything else to the side. "That will upset what the priorities are in terms of technology needs for the entire organization," observes Rood.

At The Queen's Medical Center, Kudla wages a constant battle to ensure that all of his constituents know that every IT project has to be in sync with the center's strategic initiatives. As a member of the senior management team, he considers it his most important task to make sure his peers are aware of and agree to the center's priorities. Everyone, from senior executives on down, should know that a pharmacy management system is important for the hospital; they should also understand that rolling out the wireless PDAs for e-mail is "low on my food chain."

Rood, who's been in the IT field for 26 years, says he learned this lesson early in his career. "When you're new, everyone wants to shake your hand, welcome you on board, take you out to lunch, and at the end of the day you've got 50 things from everyone to do," he recalls. "It all adds up to a backlog, and then you're going to be crying to the CEO: 'I can't do this.'" At that point, he says, CIOs either have to

take the hit and not deliver what they promised (which could get them fired), "enter a crash mode, where they push their staff to the point of exhaustion to complete a project," or spend extra on contract labor to meet a deadline. "In any case, it becomes a no-win situation," he says.

Powers gets around the problem of not wanting to say no by sending the message that IT is a resource to be managed like any other; her organization can do anything given enough time and money. Then the onus is on users to justify and manage their requests through Worldspan's project justification process.

Kudla of The Queen's Medical Center expects that once he upgrades the hospital's seven major systems, new demand will surface. "Once the system is stabilized and users realize the potential of the new system, I anticipate a demand for new functionality," he says.

Kudla anticipates requests for, among other things, automating the capture of data from patient monitors and expansion of wireless access on the hospital campus. In other words, the application backlog isn't a problem one solves, it's a condition one lives with as technology matures and expands into new areas of the business, enabling growth and greater efficiency.

"Of course, working harder and more funding help," concludes Worldspan's Powers.

Source: Adapted from Thomas Wailgum, "The Number-One Problem of CIOs: The Project Backlog," *CIO Magazine*, December 11, 2007.

CASE STUDY QUESTIONS

1. The case notes that a changing environment or business priorities can render an ongoing project obsolete even before it has been completed. What alternatives do CIOs who find themselves in this situation have with respect to dealing with the troubled project? Would you go ahead and finish it, or scrap it altogether? How would you justify either position?

2. Do you agree with the statement: "Application backlog is not a problem one solves; it's a condition one lives with"? Why or why not? To the extent that it is true, how can IT executives manage things differently to make this situation more approachable? Provide some specific suggestions.

3. Susan Powers at Worldspan says she addresses the backlog problem by positioning her IT organization as a resource that should be used and managed in the most effective manner, like any other resource a company may have. What do you think of this approach? Is IT really like any other resource?

4. In which way is IT different from other areas of a company like marketing or finance?

REAL WORLD ACTIVITIES

1. Go online and search the Internet to discover how typical the experiences reported in the case are for other companies in different industries. How are the ones you discover addressing these issues? How similar or different are those strategies with the ones discussed in the case? Prepare a report to summarize your findings.

2. Which of the following strategies do you think IT executives should adopt to improve their current situation: reject new projects, attempt to increase staff and funding, prioritize often, or all of the above? Break into small groups with your classmates to discuss these and other strategies you may have thought of; compare and contrast advantages and disadvantages of each.

MODULE V

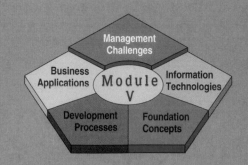

MANAGEMENT CHALLENGES

What managerial challenges do information systems pose for today's business enterprises? The two chapters of this module emphasize how managers and business professionals can manage the successful use of information technologies in a global economy.

- **Chapter 13: Security and Ethical Challenges** discusses the threats against and defenses needed for the performance and security of business information systems, as well as societal impact and ethical implications of information technology.

- **Chapter 14: Enterprise and Global Management of Information Technology** discusses the major challenges that information technology presents to business managers, the components of information systems management, and the managerial implications of the use of information technology in global business.

CHAPTER 13

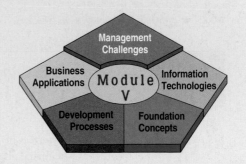

SECURITY AND ETHICAL CHALLENGES

Chapter Highlights

Learning Objectives

1. Identify several ethical issues regarding how the use of information technologies in business affects employment, individuality, working conditions, privacy, crime, health, and solutions to societal problems.

2. Identify several types of security management strategies and defenses and explain how they can be used to ensure the security of business applications of information technology.

3. Propose several ways that business managers and professionals can help lessen the harmful effects and increase the beneficial effects of the use of information technology.

SECTION I	Security, Ethical, and Societal Challenges of IT

Introduction

There is no question that the use of information technology in business presents major security challenges, poses serious ethical questions, and affects society in significant ways. Therefore, in this section, we explore the threats to businesses and individuals as a result of many types of computer crime and unethical behavior. In Section II, we will examine a variety of methods that companies use to manage the security and integrity of their business systems. Now let's look at a real-world example.

Read the Real World Case on the next page. We can learn a lot from this case about the security issues that result from the pervasive use of IT in organizations and society today. See Figure 13.1.

Business/IT Security, Ethics, and Society

The use of information technologies in business has had a major impact on society and thus raises ethical issues in the areas of crime, privacy, individuality, employment, health, and working conditions. See Figure 13.2.

It is important to understand that information technology has had beneficial results, as well as detrimental effects, on society and people in each of these areas. For example, computerizing a manufacturing process may have the beneficial result of improving working conditions and producing products of higher quality at lower cost, but it also has the adverse effect of eliminating people's jobs. So your job as a manager or business professional should involve managing your work activities and those of others to minimize the detrimental effects of business applications of information technology and optimize their beneficial effects. That would represent an ethically responsible use of information technology.

Ethical Responsibility of Business Professionals

As a business professional, you have a responsibility to promote ethical uses of information technology in the workplace. Whether or not you have managerial responsibilities, you should accept the ethical responsibilities that come with your work activities. That includes properly performing your role as a vital human resource in the business systems you help develop and use in your organization. As a manager or business professional, it will be your responsibility to make decisions about business activities and the use of information technologies that may have an ethical dimension that must be considered.

For example, should you electronically monitor your employees' work activities and e-mail? Should you let employees use their work computers for private business or take home copies of software for their personal use? Should you electronically access your employees' personnel records or workstation files? Should you sell customer information extracted from transaction processing systems to other companies? These are a few examples of the types of decisions you will have to make that have an ethical dimension. So let's take a closer look at several ethical foundations in business and information technology.

Business Ethics

Business ethics is concerned with the numerous ethical questions that managers must confront as part of their daily business decision making. For example, Figure 13.3 outlines some of the basic categories of ethical issues and specific business practices that have serious ethical consequences. Notice that the issues of intellectual property rights, customer and employee privacy, security of company records, and workplace safety are highlighted because they have been major areas of ethical controversy in information technology.

How can managers make ethical decisions when confronted with business issues such as those listed in Figure 13.3? Several important alternatives based on theories of corporate social responsibility can be used. For example, in business ethics, the *stockholder theory* holds that managers are agents of the stockholders, and their only ethical responsibility is to increase the profits of the business without violating the law or engaging in fraudulent practices.

REAL WORLD CASE 1

Don't Let the Data Escape Right Under Your Nose

Cyber criminals are increasingly becoming more sophisticated in their methods of attack. Often we can equate this to the methods of data exfiltration as well. Exfiltration, or exportation, of data is usually accomplished by copying the data from the system via a network channel, although removable media or physical theft can also be utilized.

In 2009, the SpiderLabs team at Trustwave investigated over 200 data breaches in 24 different countries. While the methods used by cyber criminals to exfiltrate data from a compromised environment varied, the method of entry into an environment was often via the remote access application being utilized by the target organization.

In the SpiderLabs investigations, 45 percent of compromises occurred by attackers gaining access to a system through a remote access application. These were not complex application flaws, and the attacks looked no different to the IT staff than, for example, the CEO connecting from London while on a business trip. The attackers also didn't need to brute-force the accounts they used. SpiderLabs found that 90 percent of these attacks were successful because of vendor-default or easily guessed passwords, like "temp:temp" or "admin:nimda."

Once a foothold is established, attackers often launch network enumeration tools. Network enumeration tools are often used by the attacker to discover additional targets within the environment and retrieve system information, such as usernames, group privileges, network shares, and available services. The noise generated by enumeration tools can indicate a prelude to an attack. Unfortunately, most entities are not properly monitoring their systems and therefore fail to observe these indicators.

It was these types of tools that led attackers to the systems of additional hotel properties through trusted private circuits. The internal connections were subsequently exploited, resulting in the breach of data from physically dispersed sites. Without the existence of these connections, breaches within the hospitality sector would likely have been contained to only a few properties.

Once attackers gained access to the target environment, they harvested data using either manual or automated methods. Using manual processes, potentially valuable databases and documents were located, and searches of the operating system were conducted using specific keywords to further identify data.

The automated method was custom written malware that took advantage of a flaw found in the security controls of the applications being used to process confidential data. Generally, many application security designs do not apply more controls and alerting capabilities over components that process data in the clear.

A target system that receives encrypted data and stores encrypted data but transmits data to an upstream host is susceptible to a data breach while the data is processed by the target system. This occurs because data processed by a system must be decrypted in RAM (random access memory—see Chapter 3) for the application to understand it. During this process, cyber criminals in 2009 frequently employed RAM parsers—67 percent of SpiderLabs' investigations involving malware concluded that automated tools were used to harvest data out of RAM while the system was using the data in some capacity.

The average time the cyber criminals were able to access the target systems and data was 156 days. For that period of time, attackers entered the environment, set up their tools to remove data, and also harvested the data before a single IT or security department reacted to their activities. Some 2009 investigations showed recurring activity from the same cyber criminals over the course of three years. Long times to detection were typical in 2009 and, seemingly armed with this knowledge, cyber criminals are not practicing stealth in their activities.

In 38 cases, cyber criminals used the remote access application previously utilized for initial entry to extract data. Other existing services, such as native FTP and HTTP client functionality, were also frequently leveraged for data extraction.

Specifically, when malware was utilized for data extraction, FTP and SMTP functionality were regularly observed.

FIGURE 13.1

The pervasive use of information technology in organizations and society presents individuals with new ethical challenges and dilemmas.

Source: © Punchstock.

(In reverse analysis of custom malware, binaries would disclose the existence of FTP functionality including hard-coded IP addresses and credentials.) With off-the-shelf malware, such as keystroke loggers, attackers most often used built-in FTP and e-mail capabilities to exfiltrate data. When e-mail services were employed for extraction, the attackers often opted to install a malicious SMTP server directly on the compromised system to ensure the data was properly routed.

Only a single case contained the use of an encrypted channel for data extraction, further suggesting that criminals are rarely concerned with raising alarm. Due to natively available network services, lack of proper egress filtering and poor system monitoring practices, criminals are using available network services or choosing to install their own basic services.

It is clear that in all of these cases sensitive data was sent out of a target environment. During this time, the IT security teams did not detect the loss.

When looking for signs of an attack, IT security teams seem to expect something complex. However, attacks are usually very simple, not "noisy," and likely appear benign in a routine log review. It is not until the data has left the target environment and shows up in some other capacity that the breach is detected. Paying close attention to the behaviors of "normal" activity against "standard" systems is the key to identifying a problem before it is too late. Every anomaly should be viewed with a degree of suspicion and addressed through internal investigation or, if necessary, review by an outside expert.

Source: Adapted from Nicholas J. Percoco, "Data Exfiltration: How Data Gets Out," *Computerworld Hong Kong*, Questex Media, March 19, 2010.

CASE STUDY QUESTIONS

1. Why is "data exfiltration" such an important problem? Is this another form of hacking? Explain.

2. How does IT provide more opportunities for difficult security issues to arise? How does IT help address those?

3. Use examples from the case to justify your answer.

4. Should organizations pursue high security standards regardless (or in spite of) their bottom-line impact? Or should they limit themselves to those scenarios where only the big risks are managed?

REAL WORLD ACTIVITIES

1. The passage of the Sarbanes-Oxley Act in the United States has greatly increased the compliance obligations of publicly traded companies. Go online to research how this landmark legislation affected the obligations of IT departments, and the way in which they develop and implement new technologies. Prepare a presentation to synthesize your findings.

2. Should an IT department closely monitor all the day-to-day accesses to their system? Is this a productive use of their time? What do you think? Break into small groups with your classmates to discuss your positions. Can you reach a consensus on this issue?

FIGURE 13.2

Important aspects of the security, ethical, and societal dimensions of the use of information technology in business. Remember that information technologies can support both beneficial and detrimental effects on society in each of the areas shown.

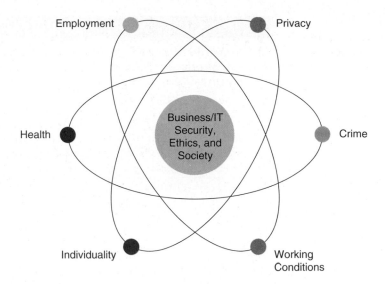

However, the *social contract theory* states that companies have ethical responsibilities to all members of society, which allows corporations to exist according to a social contract. The first condition of the contract requires companies to enhance the economic satisfaction of consumers and employees. They must do that without polluting the environment or depleting natural resources, misusing political power, or subjecting their employees to dehumanizing working conditions. The second condition requires companies to avoid fraudulent practices, show respect for their employees as human beings, and avoid practices that systematically worsen the position of any group in society.

The *stakeholder theory* of business ethics maintains that managers have an ethical responsibility to manage a firm for the benefit of all its stakeholders, that is, all individuals and groups that have a stake in, or claim on, a company. These stakeholders usually include the corporation's stockholders, employees, customers, suppliers, and the local community. Sometimes the term is broadened to include all groups who can affect or be affected by the corporation, such as competitors, government agencies, and special-interest groups. Balancing the claims of conflicting stakeholders is obviously not an easy task for managers.

Technology Ethics

Another important ethical dimension deals specifically with the ethics of the use of any form of technology. For example, Figure 13.4 outlines four principles of technology ethics. These principles can serve as basic ethical requirements that companies should meet to help ensure the ethical implementation of information technologies and information systems in business.

FIGURE 13.3   Basic categories of ethical business issues. Information technology has caused ethical controversy in the areas of intellectual property rights, customer and employee privacy, security of company information, and workplace safety.

Equity	Rights	Honesty	Exercise of Corporate Power
Executive salaries	Corporate due process	Employee conflicts	Product safety
Comparable worth	Employee health	of interest	Environmental issues
Product pricing	screening	**Security of company**	Disinvestment
Intellectual	**Customer privacy**	**information**	Corporate contributions
property rights	**Employee privacy**	Inappropriate gifts	Social issues raised by
Noncompetitive	Sexual harassment	Advertising content	religious organizations
agreements	Affirmative action	Government contract issues	Plant/facility closures and
	Equal employment	Financial and cash	downsizing
	opportunity	management procedures	Political action committees
	Shareholder interests	Questionable business	**Workplace safety**
	Employment at will	practices in foreign	
	Whistle-blowing	countries	

FIGURE 13.4

Ethical principles to help evaluate the potential harms or risks of the use of new technologies.

Principles of Technology Ethics
● **Proportionality.** The good achieved by the technology must outweigh the harm or risk. Moreover, there must be no alternative that achieves the same or comparable benefits with less harm or risk.
● **Informed Consent.** Those affected by the technology should understand and accept the risks.
● **Justice.** The benefits and burdens of the technology should be distributed fairly. Those who benefit should bear their fair share of the risks, and those who do not benefit should not suffer a significant increase in risk.
● **Minimized Risk.** Even if judged acceptable by the other three guidelines, the technology must be implemented so as to avoid all unnecessary risk.

One common example of technology ethics involves some of the health risks of using computer workstations for extended periods in high-volume data entry job positions. Many organizations display ethical behavior by scheduling work breaks and limiting the exposure of data entry workers to staring at a computer monitor to minimize their risk of developing a variety of work-related health disorders, such as hand or eye injuries. The health impact of information technology is discussed later in this chapter.

Ethical Guidelines

We have outlined a few ethical principles that can serve as the basis for ethical conduct by managers, end users, and IS professionals. But what more specific guidelines might help your ethical use of information technology? Many companies and organizations answer that question today with detailed policies for ethical computer and Internet usage by their employees. For example, most policies specify that company computer workstations and networks are company resources that must be used only for work-related uses, whether using internal networks or the Internet.

Another way to answer this question is to examine statements of responsibilities contained in codes of professional conduct for IS professionals. A good example is the code of professional conduct of the Association of Information Technology Professionals (AITP), an organization of professionals in the computing field. Its code of conduct outlines the ethical considerations inherent in the major responsibilities of an IS professional. Figure 13.5 is a portion of the AITP code of conduct.

FIGURE 13.5

Part of the AITP standards of professional conduct. This code can serve as a model for ethical conduct by business end users as well as IS professionals.

AITP Standards of Professional Conduct
In recognition of my obligation to my employer I shall:
● Avoid conflicts of interest and ensure that my employer is aware of any potential conflicts.
● Protect the privacy and confidentiality of all information entrusted to me.
● Not misrepresent or withhold information that is germane to the situation.
● Not attempt to use the resources of my employer for personal gain or for any purpose without proper approval.
● Not exploit the weakness of a computer system for personal gain or personal satisfaction.
In recognition of my obligation to society I shall:
● Use my skill and knowledge to inform the public in all areas of my expertise.
● To the best of my ability, ensure that the products of my work are used in a socially responsible way.
● Support, respect, and abide by the appropriate local, state, provincial, and federal laws.
● Never misrepresent or withhold information that is germane to a problem or a situation of public concern, nor will I allow any such known information to remain unchallenged.
● Not use knowledge of a confidential or personal nature in any unauthorized manner to achieve personal gain.

Source: 2007 PricewaterhouseCoopers Global Security Survey.

Business and IS professionals can live up to their ethical responsibilities by voluntarily following such guidelines. For example, you can be a **responsible professional** by (1) acting with integrity, (2) increasing your professional competence, (3) setting high standards of personal performance, (4) accepting responsibility for your work, and (5) advancing the health, privacy, and general welfare of the public. Then you would be demonstrating ethical conduct, avoiding computer crime, and increasing the security of any information system you develop or use.

Enron Corporation: Failure in Business Ethics

Much has been said about the driven, cultlike ethos of the organization that styled itself "the world's leading company." Truth be told, for all its razzle-dazzle use of Internet technology, a lot of the things Enron did weren't so very exceptional: paying insanely large bonuses to executives, for example, often in the form of stock options (a practice that not only hid true compensation costs but also encouraged managers to keep the stock price up by any means necessary); promising outlandish growth, year after year, and making absurdly confident predictions about every new market it entered, however untested; scarcely ever admitting a weakness to the outside world; and showing scant interest in the questions or doubts of some in its own ranks about its questionable, unethical, and even illegal business and accounting practices.

Credibility comes hard in business. You earn it slowly by conducting yourself with integrity year in and year out, or by showing exceptional leadership in exceptional circumstances, such as on September 11, 2001. The surest way to lose it, short of being caught in an outright lie, is to promise much and deliver little. Those, at least, are two conclusions suggested by an exclusive survey of executives that Clark, Martire, and Bartolomeo conducted for *Business 2.0*.

Executives rated Enron Chairman and CEO Ken Lay least credible of the business figures in the survey. Perhaps it had something to do with statements like:

- "Our performance has never been stronger; our business model has never been more robust; our growth has never been more certain . . . I have never felt better about the prospects for the company."—E-mail to employees, August 14, 2001
- "The company is probably in the strongest and best shape that it has ever been in."—Interview in *BusinessWeek*, August 24, 2001
- "Our 26 percent increase in [profits] shows the very strong results of our core wholesale and retail energy businesses and our natural gas pipelines."—Press release, October 16, 2001

Yet three weeks later, Enron admitted that it had overstated earnings by $586 million since 1997. Within a few more weeks, Enron also disclosed a stunning $638 million third-quarter loss and then filed for Chapter 13 bankruptcy.

Dick Hudson, former CIO of Houston-based oil drilling company Global Marine Inc. and now president of Hudson & Associates, an executive IT consulting firm in Katy, Texas, thinks Enron started with a good business strategy and that if it hadn't pushed the envelope, it could well have been a successful Fortune 1000 firm. Instead, it aimed for the Fortune 10, so it got into markets such as broadband, which is a tough nut to crack even for the industry's leaders. "Those good old boys in Houston, they had to walk with the big dogs," accuses Hudson. "They are a textbook case of greed and mismanagement."

On May 25, 2006, Kenneth Lay was convicted on six counts of securities and wire fraud and faced a total of 45 years in prison. Lay died on July 5, 2006, before sentencing could be passed. His protege, Jeffrey K. Skilling, was convicted of 19 of 28 counts, and was sentenced to 24 years in prison. Andrew S. Fastow, the former chief financial officer, was sentenced to six years in prison for his role in the conspiracy that led to the collapse of Enron. His former lieutenant, Michael Kopper, received a reduced sentence of 37 months for cooperating with the investigation.

Source: Adapted from Melissa Solomon and Michael Meehan, "Enron Lesson: Tech Is for Support," *Computerworld*, February 18, 2002.

Computer Crime

Cyber-crime is becoming one of the Net's growth businesses. Today, criminals are doing everything from stealing intellectual property and committing fraud to unleashing viruses and committing acts of cyberterrorism.

Computer crime, a growing threat to society, is caused by the criminal or irresponsible actions of individuals who are taking advantage of the widespread use and vulnerability of computers and the Internet and other networks. It presents a major challenge to the ethical use of information technologies. Computer crime also poses serious threats to the integrity, safety, and survival of most business systems and thus makes the development of effective security methods a top priority. See Figure 13.6.

Computer crime is defined by the Association of Information Technology Professionals (AITP) as including (1) the unauthorized use, access, modification, and destruction of hardware, software, data, or network resources; (2) the unauthorized release of information; (3) the unauthorized copying of software; (4) denying an end user access to his or her own hardware, software, data, or network resources; and (5) using or conspiring to use computer or network resources to obtain information or tangible property illegally. This definition was promoted by the AITP in a Model Computer Crime Act and is reflected in many computer crime laws.

The Online Crusade against Phishing	Until just a few years ago, Gary Warner did not have the kind of day job you'd expect from an antiphishing crusader. He didn't work for a security vendor or a bank, or any kind of company you'd expect to care about phishing. Warner's career as a cybersleuth began on Halloween 2000. That's when his company's Web site was defaced by an entity named Pimpshiz as part of a pro-Napster Internet graffiti campaign.
	"My boss came to me and said, 'Find out who did this and put them in jail,'" said Warner, who was at the time an IT staffer with Energen, a Birmingham, Alabama, oil and gas company. It was an eye-opening experience. "I called the police and they were like, 'What do you want us to do?'" he said. Months later, when Pimpshiz struck servers at NASA, Warner reached out, calling staff there and saying "Hey, we know who this guy is. Here's his name and address."
	Since then, Warner has quietly become one of the most-respected authorities on phishing in the United States—the kind of guy that federal agents and banking IT

FIGURE 13.6

How large companies are protecting themselves from cyber-crime.

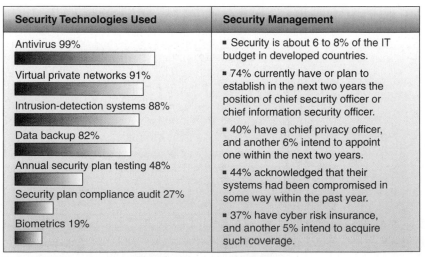

Security Technologies Used	Security Management
Antivirus 99%	■ Security is about 6 to 8% of the IT budget in developed countries.
Virtual private networks 91%	■ 74% currently have or plan to establish in the next two years the position of chief security officer or chief information security officer.
Intrusion-detection systems 88%	
Data backup 82%	■ 40% have a chief privacy officer, and another 6% intend to appoint one within the next two years.
Annual security plan testing 48%	
Security plan compliance audit 27%	■ 44% acknowledged that their systems had been compromised in some way within the past year.
Biometrics 19%	■ 37% have cyber risk insurance, and another 5% intend to acquire such coverage.

Source: 2007 PricewaterhouseCoopers Global Security Survey.

staff call when they want to know how to catch the bad guys and shut down their credit-card-stealing Web sites.

With Warner's help, authorities eventually arrested Pimpshiz, whose real name is Robert Lyttle, in connection with the defacements.

Warner said that the Pimpshiz case was formative, underlining how hard it is for law enforcement to catch the bad guys on the Internet. "The experience showed me that it's not that they don't care," Warner said. "Their hands are tied by the legal process."

In July of 2007, with recommendations from FBI and Secret Service agents, Warner took a job as Director of Research in Computer Forensics with the University of Alabama at Birmingham (UAB). He also began working with law enforcement, not only educating FBI and Secret Service agents on how crimes were committed, but also helping to track down the criminals and helping with takedowns.

For Warner, the work isn't so much a job, as it is his moral responsibility as a computer scientist. "One of the things that really bothered me from the very beginning was people who were using my field to attack other people," he said. "The way I see it, this is our Internet. I'm going to stand at the end of my driveway and protect what's mine."

Warner is now focusing on fighting cyber-crime full-time and on training a new generation of network forensics investigators.

"You wouldn't believe the looks on their eyes the first time they got an e-mail back from a Webmaster saying, 'Thanks for letting me know. I just shut that down.'" Five days after final exams at the University of Alabama at Birmingham and though it would have no effect on their grades, four students were still coming into the labs to help shut down phishers.

"That idea that as a private citizen, you can help, that's the kind of thing we're trying to inspire," he says.

Source: Adapted from Robert McMillan, "Crime and Punishment: The White Knight of Phish-Busting," *Computerworld*, December 31, 2007.

Hacking and Cracking

Cyber-thieves have at their fingertips a dozen dangerous tools, from "scans" that ferret out weaknesses in Web site software programs to "sniffers" that snatch passwords.

Hacking, in computerese, is the obsessive use of computers or the unauthorized access and use of networked computer systems. Hackers can be outsiders or company employees who use the Internet and other networks to steal or damage data and programs. One of the issues in hacking is what to do about a hacker who commits only *electronic breaking and entering*, that is, gets access to a computer system and reads some files but neither steals nor damages anything. This situation is common in computer crime cases that are prosecuted. In most cases, courts have found that the typical computer crime statute language prohibiting malicious access to a computer system did apply to anyone gaining unauthorized access to another's computer networks. See Figure 13.7.

Hackers can monitor e-mail, Web server access, or file transfers to extract passwords, steal network files, or plant data that will cause a system to welcome intruders. A hacker may also use remote services that allow one computer on a network to execute programs on another computer to gain privileged access within a network. Telnet, an Internet tool for interactive use of remote computers, can help hackers discover information to plan other attacks. Hackers have used Telnet to access a computer's e-mail port, for example, to monitor e-mail messages for passwords and other information about privileged user accounts and network resources. These are just some of the typical types of computer crimes that hackers commit on the Internet on a regular basis. That's why Internet security measures like encryption and firewalls, as discussed in the next section, are so vital to the success of e-commerce and other e-business applications.

The hacking community is quick to make the distinction between hacking and cracking. A cracker (also called a black hat or darkside hacker) is a malicious or criminal

FIGURE 13.7

Examples of common hacking tactics to assault companies through the Internet and other networks.

Common Hacking Tactics

Denial of Service. This is becoming a common networking prank. By hammering a Web site's equipment with too many requests for information, an attacker can effectively clog the system, slowing performance or even crashing the site. This method of overloading computers is sometimes used to cover up an attack.

Scans. Widespread probes of the Internet to determine types of computers, services, and connections. That way the bad guys can take advantage of weaknesses in a particular make of computer or software program.

Sniffer. Programs that covertly search individual packets of data as they pass through the Internet, capturing passwords or the entire contents.

Spoofing. Faking an e-mail address or Web page to trick users into passing along critical information like passwords or credit card numbers.

Trojan Horse. A program that, unknown to the user, contains instructions that exploit a known vulnerability in some software.

Back Doors. In case the original entry point has been detected, having a few hidden ways back makes reentry easy—and difficult to detect.

Malicious Applets. Tiny programs, sometimes written in the popular Java computer language, that misuse your computer's resources, modify files on the hard disk, send fake e-mail, or steal passwords.

War Dialing. Programs that automatically dial thousands of telephone numbers in search of a way in through a modem connection.

Logic Bombs. An instruction in a computer program that triggers a malicious act.

Buffer Overflow. A technique for crashing or gaining control of a computer by sending too much data to the buffer in a computer's memory.

Password Crackers. Software that can guess passwords.

Social Engineering. A tactic used to gain access to computer systems by talking unsuspecting company employees out of valuable information such as passwords.

Dumpster Diving. Sifting through a company's garbage to find information to help break into their computers. Sometimes the information is used to make a stab at social engineering more credible.

hacker. This term is seldom used outside of the security industry and by some modern programmers. The general public uses the term *hacker* to refer to the same thing. In computer jargon, the meaning of *hacker* can be much more broad. The name comes from the opposite of white hat hackers.

Usually a cracker is a person who maintains knowledge of the vulnerabilities he or she finds and exploits them for private advantage, not revealing them to either the general public or the manufacturer for correction. Many crackers promote individual freedom and accessibility over privacy and security. Crackers may seek to expand holes in systems; any attempts made to patch software are generally to prevent others from also compromising a system over which they have already obtained secure control. In the most extreme cases, a cracker may work to cause damage maliciously or make threats to do so for blackmail purposes.

The term *cracker* was coined by Richard Stallman to provide an alternative to abusing the existing word *hacker* for this meaning. This term's use is limited (as is "black hat") mostly to some areas of the computer and security field and, even there, is considered controversial. One group that refers to themselves as hackers consists of skilled computer enthusiasts. The other, and more common usage, refers to people who attempt to gain unauthorized access to computer systems. Many members of the first group attempt to convince people that intruders should be called crackers rather than hackers, but the common usage remains ingrained.

Cyber-Theft

Many computer crimes involve the theft of money. In the majority of cases, they are inside jobs that involve unauthorized network entry and fraudulent alteration of computer databases to cover the tracks of the employees involved. Of course, many computer crimes involve the use of the Internet. One early example was the theft of $11 million from Citibank in late 1994. Russian hacker Vladimir Levin and his accomplices in St. Petersburg used the Internet for an electronic break-in of Citibank's mainframe systems in New York. They then succeeded in transferring the funds from several Citibank accounts to their own accounts at banks in Finland, Israel, and California.

In most cases, the scope of such financial losses is much larger than the incidents reported. Companies don't usually reveal that they have been targets or victims of computer crime. They fear scaring customers and provoking complaints by shareholders. In fact, several British banks, including the Bank of London, paid hackers more than a half million dollars not to reveal information about electronic break-ins.

Cyberterrorism

Cyberterrorism is the leveraging of an organization's or government's computers and information, particularly via the Internet, to cause physical, real-world harm or severe disruption of infrastructure. There are some that argue cyberterrorism is really a form of hacking or information warfare. They disagree with labeling it terrorism because of the unlikelihood of the creation of fear, significant physical harm, or death in a population using electronic means, considering current attack and protective technologies.

The National Conference of State Legislatures (NCSL) puts a much finer point on the definition of the term:

> the use of information technology by terrorist groups and individuals to further their agenda. This can include use of information technology to organize and execute attacks against networks, computer systems and telecommunications infrastructures, or for exchanging information or making threats electronically.

Cyberterrorism can have a serious large-scale influence on significant numbers of people. It can significantly weaken a country's economy, thereby denying it access to vital resources and making it more vulnerable to military attack. Cyberterror can also affect Internet-based businesses. Like bricks and mortar retailers and service providers, most Web sites that produce income (whether by advertising, monetary exchange for goods, or paid services) could stand to lose money in the event of downtime created by cyber-criminals. As Internet businesses have increasing economic importance to countries, what is normally cyber-crime becomes more political and therefore "terror" related.

To date, there have been no reported cyber-attacks on the United States. There have, however, been several large-scale examples of cyberterrorism in other countries. One such example occurred in Romania when cyberterrorists illegally gained access to the computers controlling the life-support systems at an Antarctic research station, endangering the 58 scientists involved. However, the culprits were stopped before damage actually occurred. Mostly nonpolitical acts of sabotage have caused financial and other damage, as in a case where a disgruntled employee caused the release of untreated sewage into water in Maroochy Shire, Australia. Computer viruses have degraded or shut down some nonessential systems in nuclear power plants, but this is not believed to have been a deliberate attack.

More recently, in May 2007, Estonia was subjected to a mass cyber-attack in the wake of the removal of a Russian World War II war memorial from downtown Talinn. The attack was a distributed denial of service attack in which selected sites were bombarded with traffic in order to force them off-line; nearly all Estonian government ministry networks, as well as two major Estonian bank networks, were knocked off-line; in addition, the political party Web site of Estonia's current Prime Minister Andrus Ansip featured a counterfeit letter of apology from Ansip for removing the memorial statue. Despite speculation that the attack had been coordinated by the Russian government, Estonia's defense minister admitted he had no evidence linking cyber attacks to Russian authorities. Russia called accusations of its involvement "unfounded," and neither NATO nor European Commission experts were able to find any proof of official Russian government participation. In January 2008, a man from Estonia was convicted for launching the attacks against the Estonian Reform Party Web site and fined.

**Cyber-Crimes in
Africa: Companies
Are Easy Prey**

Growth in African connectivity and poor investment in security on the part of businesses and government has spurred the rise of hackers, both malicious and constructive, across the continent. Increasingly, government and corporate Web sites and databases are being attacked, with vital information stolen. Meanwhile there has been a rise in the number of "white hat" security experts who have worked with site and business owners to alert them of security threats and gaps.

"The availability of super fast affordable Internet has allowed many people to rush to technology but without focus on threat of cybercrime; the hacking space in East Africa is now rising at an alarming rate with many hackers being lured into it by the fast cash," said Fredrick Wahome, managing director of Secunets Technologies in Kenya.

The connectivity growth has allowed banks to offer online banking services, but they often do not seal security holes. This has allowed young, tech savvy employees to exploit online customers. Some local techies have said they resorted to publicly exposing businesses' security vulnerabilities after their efforts to get the attention of management proved futile.

The lack of attention on the part of management has led to hackers seeking to engage with "white hat" security experts and hopefully raise awareness of the need for security and penetration testing.

"We will identify the vulnerabilities and try to report them both publicly and privately depending on severity, receptiveness without causing bad press for black hat," said Douglas Onyango, CTO of Delta IT Solutions in Uganda.

At the same time, hacking events such as Random Hacks of Kindness have been organized in the region to raise awareness and develop applications that can be used in times of disaster.

"Random Hacks of Kindness brought together software developers to respond to challenges facing humanity in the area of natural disaster by building software solutions that make a difference on the ground," said Linda Kamau, a developer with Ushahidi and the coordinator of the event.

The first hacker event was organized in mid-2010 as part of a global coordinated event but the developers have been organizing monthly overnight hacker events that have yielded important applications.

"Developers have come up with important apps; person-finder technology that includes a database scheme to synchronize multiple databases; a 'need help' mobile application to receive emergency messages; and a website to register emergencies and forward text messages to a mobile number," added Kamau.

The Random Hacks of Kindness event is usually held at the Innovation Hub in Nairobi and developers participating have been invited to test sites and tech installations before launch or track malicious hackers.

"Hacking costs time and money to organizations and many have realized, after we alert them, of the bugs," said Marie Githinji, a developer and participant in Random Hacks. "During the launch of one of the e-commerce sites, we were invited to test and track any attacks."

The financial costs of security have sometimes put off companies from engaging security professionals, but multinational corporations in telecommunications and banking have been breached.

"About 90 percent of the Fortune 500 operating in Kenya have been successfully attacked; in these companies you will find 70 percent of the IT administrators are non-technical and are expected to protect company perimeter," added Secunets' Wahome.

To tackle issues of cyber-crime and malicious attacks, governments in the region have started developing cyber-crime policies even though they are yet to be passed into law.

Source: Adapted from Rebecca Wanjiku, "Connectivity Growth Spurs Hacker Growth in Africa," *Computerworld*, Questex Media, October 22, 2010.

FIGURE 13.8

Internet abuses in the workplace.

Internet Abuses	Activity
General E-mail Abuses	Include spamming, harassments, chain letters, solicitations, spoofing, propagations of viruses/worms, and defamatory statements.
Unauthorized Usage and Access	Sharing of passwords and access into networks without permission.
Copyright Infringement/ Plagiarism	Using illegal or pirated software that costs organizations millions of dollars because of copyright infringements. Copying of Web sites and copyrighted logos.
Newsgroup Postings	Posting of messages on various non-work–related topics from sex to lawn care advice.
Transmission of Confidential Data	Using the Internet to display or transmit trade secrets.
Pornography	Accessing sexually explicit sites from workplace as well as the display, distribution, and surfing of these offensive sites.
Hacking	Hacking of Web sites, ranging from denial of service attacks to accessing organizational databases.
Non-Work–Related Download/Upload	Propagation of software that ties up office bandwidth. Use of programs that allow the transmission of movies, music, and graphical materials.
Leisure Use of the Internet	Loafing around the Internet, which includes shopping, sending e-cards and personal e-mail, gambling online, chatting, game playing, auctioning, stock trading, and doing other personal activities.
Usage of External ISPs	Using an external ISP to connect to the Internet to avoid detection.
Moonlighting	Using office resources such as networks and computers to organize and conduct personal business (side jobs).

Source: Adapted from Keng Siau, Fiona Fui-Hoon Nah, and Limei Teng, "Acceptable Internet Use Policy," *Communications of the ACM*, January 2002, p. 76.

Unauthorized Use at Work

The unauthorized use of computer systems and networks can be called *time and resource theft*. A common example is unauthorized use of company-owned computer networks by employees. This use may range from doing private consulting or personal finances to playing video games to unauthorized use of the Internet on company networks. Network monitoring software, called *sniffers*, is frequently used to monitor network traffic to evaluate network capacity, as well as to reveal evidence of improper use. See Figure 13.8.

According to one survey, 90 percent of U.S. workers admit to surfing recreational sites during office hours, and 84 percent say they send personal e-mail from work. So this kind of activity alone may not get you fired from your job; however, other Internet activities at work can bring instant dismissal. For example, *The New York Times* fired 23 workers because they were distributing racist and sexually offensive jokes on the company's e-mail system.

Xerox Corp. fired more than 40 workers for spending up to eight hours a day on pornography sites on the Web. Several employees even downloaded pornographic videos, which took so much network bandwidth that it choked the company network and prevented coworkers from sending or receiving e-mail. Xerox instituted an eight-member SWAT team on computer abuse that uses software to review every Web site its 40,000 computer users view each day. Other companies clamp down even harder by installing software like SurfWatch, which enables them to block and monitor access to off-limit Web sites.

| Survey: E-mail and Internet Abuse Can Get You Fired | Think you can get away with using e-mail and the Internet in violation of company policy? *Think again*. A new survey found that more than one-quarter of employers have fired workers for misusing e-mail, and one-third have fired workers for misusing the Internet on the job. The study, conducted by the American Management Association and the ePolicy Institute, surveyed 304 U.S. companies of all sizes. |

The vast majority of bosses who fired workers for Internet misuse, 84 percent, said the employee was accessing porn or other inappropriate content. Although it is obviously wrong to look at inappropriate content on company time, a surprising number of people were fired just for surfing the Web. As many as 34 percent of managers in the study said they let go of workers for excessive personal use of the Internet, according to the survey.

Among managers who fired workers for e-mail misuse, 64 percent did so because the employee violated company policy and 62 percent said the workers' e-mail contained inappropriate or offensive language. More than a quarter of bosses said they fired workers for excessive personal use of e-mail, and 22 percent said their workers were fired for breaching confidentiality rules in e-mail.

Companies are worried about the inappropriate use of the Internet, and so 66 percent of those in the study said they monitor Internet connections. As many as 65 percent of them use software to block inappropriate Web sites. Eighteen percent of the companies block URLs (uniform resource locators) to prevent workers from visiting external blogs.

Companies use different methods to monitor workers' computers, with 45 percent of those participating in the survey tracking content, keystrokes, and time spent at the keyboard. An additional 43 percent store and review computer files. Twelve percent monitor blogs to track content about the company, and 10 percent monitor social-networking sites.

The researchers found that even though only two states require companies to notify their workers that they're monitoring them, most tell employees of their monitoring activities. Of the companies that monitor workers in the survey, 83 percent said they tell employees that they are monitoring content, keystrokes, and time spent at the keyboard. As many as 84 percent tell employees that they review computer activity, and 71 percent alert workers that they monitor their e-mails.

Source: Adapted from Nancy Gohring, "Over 50% of Companies Fire Workers for E-Mail, 'Net Abuse," *CIO Magazine*, February 28, 2008.

Software Piracy

Computer programs are valuable property and thus the subject of theft from computer systems. However, unauthorized copying of software, or software piracy, is also a major form of software theft. Software piracy by company employees is widespread, which has resulted in lawsuits by the Software Publishers Association, an industry association of software developers, against major corporations that allowed unauthorized copying of their programs.

Unauthorized copying is illegal because software is intellectual property that is protected by copyright law and user licensing agreements. For example, in the United States, commercial software packages are protected by the Computer Software Piracy and Counterfeiting Amendment to the Federal Copyright Act. In most cases, the purchase of a commercial software package is really a payment to license its fair use by an individual end user. Therefore, many companies sign *site licenses* that legally allow them to make a certain number of copies for use by their employees at a particular location. Other alternatives are *shareware*, which allows you to make copies of software for others, and *public domain software*, which is not copyrighted.

The most recent study by the Business Software Alliance, an antipiracy group whose members include Apple Computer, IBM, Intel, and Microsoft, shows that in 2007, pirated software accounts for 38 percent of software in use worldwide. Reported losses from software piracy in 2007 were almost $48 billion—up $8 billion from the year before. "That's over a third of the industry's revenue," says Bob Kruger, the group's vice president for enforcement. According to the findings, only $50 billion of the $100 billion in software purchased in 2007 was legally acquired. In other words, for every dollar spent on software purchased legitimately worldwide, there was 50 cents' worth of software that was obtained illegally.

For example, Carol Bartz, the president and chairman of Autodesk, Inc. (www.autodesk.com) reports that one of their flagship products, AutoCAD, has 90 percent of the computer-aided design (CAD) market in China, yet sales are virtually negligible due to the widespread acceptance of software piracy. Bartz also states that many software companies are reluctant to pursue the educational market due to concerns that several copies of purchased software may lead to millions of copies of illegal software, produced "in the name of educating children."

Theft of Intellectual Property

Software is not the only property that is subject to computer-based piracy. Other intellectual property theft occurs in the form of infringements of copyrighted material, such as music, videos, images, articles, books, and other written works, which most courts have deemed illegal. Digitized versions can easily be captured by computer systems and made available for people to access or download at Internet Web sites or can be readily disseminated by e-mail as file attachments. The development of peer-to-peer (P2P) networking technologies (discussed in Chapter 6) has made digital versions of copyrighted material even more vulnerable to unauthorized use. For example, P2P file-sharing software enables direct MP3 audio file transfers of specified tracks of music between your PC and those of other users on the Internet. Thus, such software creates a *peer-to-peer network* of millions of Internet users who electronically trade digital versions of copyrighted or public domain music stored on their PC's hard drives. More recently, music publishers and manufacturers are offering legal, and relatively inexpensive, methods to access online music in a variety of formats. Because of this proactive posture, the music industry reports that illegal downloading of music and video properties is down and continuing to drop significantly. Let's look at the ongoing debate in this controversial area more closely with a real-world example that emphasizes the threat of developments in IT to intellectual property rights.

Music Piracy: The Long War

"Canadian pirates" is what the music dealers call publishing houses across the line who are flooding this country, they say, with spurious editions of the latest copyrighted popular songs. They use the mails [sic] to reach purchasers, so members of the American Music Publishers' Association assert, and as a result the legitimate music publishing business of the United States has fallen off 50 percent in the past twelve months. Their investigation has revealed that all of the most popular pieces have been counterfeited, despite the fact that they are copyrighted, and by unknown publishers are sold at from 2 cents to 5 cents per copy, though the original compositions sell at from 20 to 40 cents per copy.

Sounds somewhat familiar? You may be a little too young to remember, but it was published in *The New York Times* sometime ago—June 13, 1897 to be exact. As you can see, music piracy is hardly a recent phenomenon. It has, however, reached staggering proportions in the last two decades or so, from Napster to torrents, and including the less sophisticated but widely available CD burners.

However, only a few years after Napster's launch, online song-swapping took a big hit from a dogged legal campaign by the Recording Industry Association of America (RIAA) to shut down the top services, Napster and Audiogalaxy. Others—like Kazaa and Morpheus—went on the run, as their users were being sued by the RIAA.

Other networks, like Gnutella, had been built to withstand legal assault. By avoiding centralized servers and spreading the goods around the globe, the free-music hackers hoped their networks would be impossible to shut down. Too bad they also became impossible to use. Shawn Fanning (the creator of Napster) had a hit because Napster provided quick and easy access to a huge trove of music. His deservedly nameless imitators required far more work to find far fewer tunes.

At times, the attention moved to the pirating and copying of physical CDs. Look at the numbers: Industry estimates say that more than 6 billion blank CDs were sold worldwide in 2003—that's one for every person alive today—along with 44 million drives on which to burn them. By 2004, worldwide sales of CD-Audio, CD-ROM, and CD-R all together surpassed 30 billion units. In addition, millions of people now own writable drives—far more than the most optimistic membership claims made by Napster or any of its heirs. "You'll find one on nearly every consumer PC," cites Gartner analyst Mary Craig, one of the more bearish forecasters in the business. "They're not using them for backups."

Today, peer-to-peer (P2P) torrent clients have spread broadly. LimeWire, a grizzled veteran of the peer-to-peer (P2P) file-sharing scene, remains the most popular software for exchanging music, video, and software—much of it pirated—through the Internet, with μTorrent a not-too-close second. LimeWire was used on 17.8 percent of PCs in September of 2007, according to a Digital Media Desktop Report. Since about half of surveyed PCs have at least one peer-to-peer sharing application installed, that gives LimeWire a 36.4 percent share—more than three times the 11.3 percent share of the next-most-popular client, μTorrent.

Source: Adapted from Paul Boutin, "Burn Baby Burn," *Wired*, December 2002; and Eric Lai, "Study: LimeWire Remains Top P2P Software; μTorrent Fast-Rising No. 2," *Computerworld*, April 17, 2008.

Computer Viruses and Worms

One of the most destructive examples of computer crime involves the creation of a **computer virus** or *worm*. *Virus* is the more popular term, but technically, a virus is a program code that cannot work without being inserted into another program. A worm is a distinct program that can run unaided. In either case, these programs copy annoying or destructive routines into the networked computer systems of anyone who accesses computers infected with the virus or who uses copies of magnetic disks taken from infected computers. Thus, a computer virus or worm can spread destruction among many users. Although they sometimes display only humorous messages, they more often destroy the contents of memory, hard disks, and other storage devices. See Figure 13.9.

Computer viruses typically enter a computer system through e-mail and file attachments via the Internet and online services or through illegal or borrowed copies of software. Copies of *shareware* software downloaded from the Internet can be another source of viruses. A virus usually copies itself into the files of a computer's operating system. Then the virus spreads to the main memory and copies itself onto the computer's hard disk and any inserted floppy disks. The virus spreads to other computers through e-mail, file transfers, other telecommunications activities, or floppy disks from infected computers. Thus, as a good practice, you should avoid using software from questionable sources without checking for viruses. You should also regularly use *antivirus programs* that can help diagnose and remove computer viruses from infected files on your hard disk. We will discuss defense against viruses further in Section II.

Oldies but Goodies: Old Threats That Just Won't Go Away

Worried about the virulent Storm worm that has been buffeting the Internet with mass mailings? Symantec Corp. researchers said that the "Storm Trojan," aka "Peacomm," is now spreading via AOL Instant Messenger (AIM), Google Talk, and Yahoo Messenger.

An alert to some Symantec customers pegged the new infection vector as "insidious" because the message—such as the cryptic "LOL;)"—and the included URL can be dynamically updated by the attacker. Even worse, according to Alfred Huger, senior director of Symantec's security response team, "it injects a message

(text continues on page 578)

FIGURE 13.9 The top five virus families of all time. Note that three of the five occurred during 2004.

Top Five Virus Families of All Time

MyDoom　　　　　　**First Discovered: 1/26/2004**

- Spreads both by e-mail and over the Kazaa file-sharing network. It appears to install some form of backdoor component on compromised machines, as well as effecting a denial of service attack on the SCO Group's Web site.
- The e-mail poses either as a returned message, or as a Unicode message that can't be rendered properly, and urges the target to click on the attachment to see the message.
- This worm also has a backdoor component, which opens up two TCP ports that stay open even after the worm's termination date (February 12, 2004).
- Upon executing the virus, a copy of Notepad is opened, filled with lots of nonsense characters.

Netsky　　　　　　**First Discovered: 3/3/2004**

- A mass-mailing worm that spreads by e-mailing itself to all e-mail addresses found in files on all local and mapped network drives.
- It also tries to spread via peer-to-peer file-sharing applications by copying itself into the shared folder used by the file-sharing applications (it searches for folders whose name contains the string "share" or "sharing"), renaming itself to pose as one of 26 other common files along the way.

SoBig　　　　　　**First Discovered: 6/25/2003**

- A mass-mailing e-mail worm that arrives in the form of an e-mail attachment named either "Movie_0074.mpeg.pif," "Document003.pif," "Untitled1.pif," or "Sample.pif." The message subject title will read either "Re: Movies," "Re: Sample," "Re: Document," or "Re: Here is that sample," and it will appear to originate from big@boss.com.
- The worm will scan all .WAB, .DBX, .HTML, .HTM, .EML, and .TXT files on the victim's machine looking for e-mail addresses to which it can send itself and attempts to spread over the local network.
- It will also attempt to download updates for itself.

Klez　　　　　　**First Discovered: 4/17/2002**

- A mass-mailing e-mail worm that arrives in the form of an e-mail attachment with a random file name. The worm exploits a known vulnerability in MS Outlook to autoexecute on unpatched clients. Once run, the worm will try to disable a selection of security applications—specifically virus scanners—and tries to copy itself to all local and networked drives, renaming itself with a random file name.
- Virus has a very damaging payload: It drops the W32/Elkern virus, which will delete all files it can find on the infected machine and any mapped network drives on the 13th of all even-numbered months.

Sasser　　　　　　**First Discovered: 8/24/2004**

- Spreads by exploiting a recent Microsoft vulnerability, spreading from machine to machine with no user intervention required.
- The worm spawns multiple threads, some of which scan the local class A subnet, others the class B subnet, and others completely random subnets. The worm scans public ranges like 10.0.0.0 and 192.168.0.0 only if they are part of the local subnet.

The Cost of All This . . .

- Nearly 115 million computers across 200 countries were infected at one time or another in 2004 by rapidly proliferating software agents including Trojans, viruses, and worms.
- As many as 11 million computers worldwide—mostly within homes and small organizations—are now believed to be permanently infected and are used by criminal syndicates or malevolents to send out spam; mount distributed denial of service (DDoS) attacks; carry out extortion, identity theft, and phishing scams; or disseminate new viruses.
- The total economic damage worldwide from virus proliferation—with an additional 480 new species in 2004 alone—is now estimated to be between $166 billion and $202 billion for 2004 by the mi2g Intelligence Unit.
- With an installed base of around 600 million Windows-based computers worldwide, average damage per installed machine is between $277 and $336.

Source: Mi2g.com, "2004: Year of the Global Malware Epidemic—Top Ten Lesson," November 21, 2004.

and URL only into already open windows. It's not just some random message that pops up, but it appears only to people you are already talking to. That makes the approach very effective."

Well, you should be concerned about the Storm worm, but Gunter Ollmann, director of security strategy at IBM's Internet Security Systems, says the most common malware attack today is coming from the Slammer worm. *No, you didn't misread that last sentence.* The Slammer worm, which hit in January 2003, is still working its way around the Internet and within corporate networks, according to Ollmann. And it's still spreading in a big way. Slammer isn't the only piece of old-time malware that is still wreaking havoc.

"The stuff malware authors wrote a while ago is still out there and still propagating and still infecting machines," he said. "Some have more infections now than they did when they were headline news. All those old vulnerabilities haven't all gone away." Slammer, the worm that brought many networks to their knees by attacking Microsoft's SQL Server, is at the top of Ollmann's list of current malware problems.

"When we hear about the latest worm and zero-day, Slammer still beats them by a long shot," he added. "Slammer is still out there on a large number of infected hosts and it's still sending out malicious network traffic—malicious packets. . . . When people restore data after a crash, it probably is from an old system and it may not have the patches so it can easily be re-infected."

Another problem is that some users just don't do the patching they should, while other users aren't even aware that Microsoft SQL Server is running on their desktop because it's common to several other applications. If they don't know it's there, they don't know to take care of it.

"All these old viruses are never going to go away," said Ollmann.

Source: Adapted from Sharon Gaudin, "Oldies but Goodies: Slammer Worm Still Attacking," *InformationWeek*, August 24, 2007; and Gregg Keizer, "'Storm Trojan' Ignites Worm War," *Computerworld*, February 12, 2007.

Adware and Spyware

Two more recent entries into the computer vulnerabilities arena are adware and spyware. By definition, adware is software that, while purporting to serve some useful function and often fulfilling that function, also allows Internet advertisers to display advertisements as banners and pop-up ads without the consent of the computer user. In the extreme, adware can also collect information about the user of its host computer and send it over the Internet to its owner. This special class of adware is called **spyware** and is defined as any software that employs users' Internet connection in the background without their knowledge or explicit permission. Spyware programs collect specific information about you, ranging from general demographics like name, address, and Internet surfing habits to credit card, Social Security number, user names, passwords, or other personal information. It is important to understand that not all adware programs are spyware. Proper adware represents a viable, albeit sometimes irritating, revenue model for many software companies that allows you to get products for free and, when used correctly, does not pose any significant privacy threat. In contrast, spyware is and should be considered a clear threat to your privacy.

Whereas proper adware generally allows the computer user to opt in to its use in exchange for free use of a piece of software, spyware operates under a rather bizarre ethical model. Consider the following:

- You illegally enter a bank's computer system and place a stealth piece of software in their system. If you are detected or caught, you might be prosecuted and may go to jail.

- You write a worm or virus and spread it around the Internet or other networks. If you are detected or caught, you might be prosecuted and may go to jail.

- You write a program that spreads a spyware agent across computer systems connected to the Internet that steals the private information of the users it infects, manipulates their Internet experience, and uses other people's Web sites and browsers to display your advertising. If you are detected or caught, you may get rich, you don't go to jail, and the computer users are left with possibly rebuilding their computer system to get rid of your spyware.

Spyware has a variety of characteristics, beyond its potential for stealing valuable private information, which make it undesirable to most computer users. At the very least, it plagues the user of the infected machine with unwanted advertising. More often, it watches everything a user does online and sends that information back to the marketing company that created the spyware. Often, spyware applications add advertising links to Web pages owned by other people, for which the Web page owner does not get paid, and may even redirect the payments from legitimate affiliate-fee advertisers to the makers of the spyware. Other undesirable characteristics include setting an infected system's browser home page and search settings to point to the spyware owner's Web sites (generally loaded with advertising), often in a manner that prevents you from changing back the settings (referred to as home-page hijacking). In the extremes, spyware can make a dial-up modem continually call premium-rate phone numbers, thus causing large telephone charges (and usually fees to the spyware owner) or leave security holes in an infected system allowing the makers of the spyware—or, in particularly bad cases, anyone at all—to download and run software on the infected machine (such downloads are called *Trojans*). In almost all cases, spyware severely degrades system performance. As you can see, spyware doesn't have any redeeming features except for the benefits to its owner. Its use is pervasive, and failing to protect against it virtually ensures that your system will eventually become infected.

Protecting against adware and spyware generally requires the purchase and installation of one of a variety of programs designed to prevent the software from being downloaded and installed. Once a computer is infected, however, removal programs are often not completely successful in eliminating the nuisance.

| Commtouch: Trends in Virus, Spam, and Phishing | Commtouch, a developer of technology for real-time antispam and virus protection, reports on a variety of spam and computer virus statistics on a periodic basis. Although new threats arise daily by the hundreds (if not thousands), just looking at a single quarter will provide you with an idea of what is constantly going on in this world. So here are some of the highlights from the first quarter of 2010:

A glitch in SpamAssassin, the most widely used free antispam software, at the beginning of 2010 resulted in false positives and rejection of legitimate mail. SpamAssassin is widely used by organizations, universities, and also vendors who integrate it into their own detection engines. The buggy parameter in the rule, clearly created many years ago, stated that messages from 2010 were "from the far future," and thus raising the false-positive ratio by as much as 20 percent.

During the first quarter of 2010, Commtouch analyzed which categories of Web sites were most likely to be compromised with malware or phishing. As expected and in line with the last several quarters, pornographic and sexually explicit sites ranked highest in the categories infected with malware. On the list of Web categories likely to be hosting hidden phishing pages, sites related to sex education ranked highest. These are followed by socially oriented sites such as games, chat, and social networking, which are easier targets for posting hidden phishing pages.

The lifespan of zombies (computers connected to the Internet that have been compromised by a hacker, a computer virus, or a trojan horse) is very short, and |

according to Commtouch Labs, the first quarter saw an average turnover of 305,000 zombies each day that were newly activated for malicious activity, like sending malware and spam. Brazil continued to produce the most zombies with 14 percent of the overall count.

As part of Commtouch's analysis of spam trends, Commtouch Labs monitors the domains that are used by spammers in the "from" field of the spam e-mails. Naturally, the addresses are typically faked in order to fool antispam systems and to give the impression of a reputable, genuine source. Occasionally spammers will use a company name, for example, UPS—particularly when sending malware disguised as "UPS delivery information." The domain that is most often faked, however, is gmail.com.

Spam levels averaged 83 percent of all e-mail traffic throughout the quarter, peaking at nearly 92 percent near the end of March and bottoming out at 75 percent at the start of the year. Assuming worldwide e-mail traffic of about 220 billion e-mails per day, this would equate to an average of about 183 billion spam messages per day. The following table shows the most popular spam topics in the first quarter of 2010:

Category of Spam	% of Spam
Pharmacy	81.0
Replicas	5.4
Enhancers	2.3
Phishing	2.3
Degrees	1.3
Casino	1.0
Weight Loss	0.4
Other	6.3

Source: Commtouch, "Q1 2010 Internet Threats Trend Report," http://www.commtouch.com.

Privacy Issues

Information technology makes it technically and economically feasible to collect, store, integrate, interchange, and retrieve data and information quickly and easily. This characteristic has an important beneficial effect on the efficiency and effectiveness of computer-based information systems. The power of information technology to store and retrieve information, however, can have a negative effect on the **right to privacy** of every individual. For example, confidential e-mail messages by employees are monitored by many companies. Personal information is being collected about individuals every time someone visits a site on the World Wide Web. Confidential information on individuals contained in centralized computer databases by credit bureaus, government agencies, and private business firms has been stolen or misused, resulting in the invasion of privacy, fraud, and other injustices. The unauthorized use of such information has badly damaged the privacy of individuals. Errors in such databases could seriously hurt the credit standing or reputation of an individual.

Governments around the world, but none more than in the United States, are debating privacy issues and considering various forms of legislation. With regard to the Internet, opt-in versus opt-out is central to the debate over privacy legislation. Consumer protection groups typically endorse an opt-in standard, making privacy the default. An opt-in system automatically protects consumers who do not specifically allow data to be compiled about them. Most business interests back opt-out, arguing it doesn't disrupt the flow of e-commerce. Interestingly, current laws in this regard differ between the

United States and Europe. In the United States, opt-out is the default position, whereas in Europe, consumers must opt-in or their information cannot be used.

Additional privacy issues under debate include:

- Accessing private e-mail conversations and computer records and collecting and sharing information about individuals gained from their visits to Internet Web sites and newsgroups (violation of privacy).

- Always knowing where a person is, especially as mobile and paging services become more closely associated with people rather than places (computer monitoring).

- Using customer information gained from many sources to market additional business services (computer matching).

- Collecting telephone numbers, e-mail addresses, credit card numbers, and other personal information to build individual customer profiles (unauthorized personal files).

Privacy on the Internet

If you don't take the proper precautions, any time you send an e-mail, access a Web site, post a message to a newsgroup, or use the Internet for banking and shopping . . . whether you're online for business or pleasure, you're vulnerable to anyone bent on collecting data about you without your knowledge. Fortunately, by using tools like encryption and anonymous remailers—and by being selective about the sites you visit and the information you provide—you can minimize, if not completely eliminate, the risk of your privacy being violated.

The Internet is notorious for giving its users a feeling of anonymity when in reality they are highly visible and open to violations of their privacy. Most of the Internet and its World Wide Web, e-mail, chat, and newsgroups are still a wide open, unsecured electronic frontier, with no tough rules on what information is personal and private. Information about Internet users is captured legitimately and automatically each time you visit a Web site or newsgroup and is recorded as a "cookie file" on your hard disk. Then the Web site owners or online auditing services like DoubleClick may sell the information from cookie files and other records of your Internet use to third parties. To make matters worse, much of the Net and Web is an easy target for the interception or theft by hackers of private information furnished to Web sites by Internet users.

Of course, you can protect your privacy in several ways. For example, sensitive e-mail can be protected by encryption, if both e-mail parties use compatible encryption software built into their e-mail programs. Newsgroup postings can be made privately by sending them through *anonymous remailers* that protect your identity when you add your comments to a discussion. You can ask your Internet service provider not to sell your name and personal information to mailing list providers and other marketers. Finally, you can decline to reveal personal data and interests on online service and Web site user profiles to limit your exposure to electronic snooping.

Identity Theft: As Easy as Stealing a Check

Frank W. Abagnale Jr. was a check forger for five years in the 1960s. Currently he runs Abagnale and Associates, a financial fraud consultancy company. His life story provided the inspiration for the feature film *Catch Me If You Can*, starring Leonardo DiCaprio as Frank Abagnale Jr., as well as Tom Hanks.

Forty years ago, few people could have predicted that identity theft would become as big an epidemic as it is today. Few could have imagined that protecting your identity would mean taking mail to the post office instead of leaving it in our mailboxes for pickup, shredding documents before throwing them in the trash, or that a $2 pen could help prevent a crime.

"We need to find ways to protect ourselves before identity theft strikes. We can make drastic improvements toward diminishing this crime, but it will never disappear altogether. If you haven't been a victim of identity theft, it is because thieves haven't gotten to you yet. If things fail to change, your turn will come. Prevention is not simply a matter of following a checklist of tips, it is about education—the primary factor in protecting ourselves," says Frank W. Abagnale Jr.—and he should know.

Although more and more people are using online banking, America's 78 million baby boomers, who make up 15 percent of the U.S. population, continue to be a paper-driven majority. This group also accounts for 30 percent of fraud victims, as estimated by Consumer Action, a consumer-advocacy group.

"A check holds all of the information needed to steal your identity: name, address, bank account, routing number. If written with a ball point pen, information can easily be removed by a process called check washing, a common form of identity theft. It is the process of taking a check or document that has already been filled out, removing the ink with a regular household chemical, then re-writing in a new dollar amount and recipient," says Abagnale. If you are careless, your personal check could contribute to the 1.2 million fraudulent checks written every day. That's more than 13 per second.

The American Bankers Association states that check fraud is growing 25 percent per year. To slow this growth, it is important to understand how it works. "I know firsthand how easy it is to perform check fraud. About 40 years ago, I cashed $2.5 million in fraudulent checks in every state and 26 foreign countries over a five-year period. I was involved in a high-stakes game of stolen identities. And to know how easy it can be to perform, I know it is just as easy to prevent," he notes.

Criminals rely on our mistakes to make their job easier. Taking a few precautions will make you less attractive to predators. Don't leave mail in your mailbox overnight or over the weekend. When writing checks and filling out important documents, use a gel pen, so thieves can't remove the ink and change the information. In addition, shred or tear up unwanted documents that contain personal information before discarding them. The cost of a high-quality shredder is far less than the cost of having your identity stolen.

"Let's face it; we can't always control what is happening in our world, so we must take steps to control what we can. Technology is here to stay, but there are still simple and inexpensive ways to prevent identity theft when writing checks. Remember that a crook always looks for the easiest route to riches. Don't hand him a map. Be proactive and start protecting yourself today," says Abagnale.

Source: Adapted from Frank Abagnale, "Abagnale: Top Tips to Prevent Identity Theft and Fraud," *CIO Magazine*, May 24, 2007.

Computer Matching

Computer profiling and mistakes in the computer matching of personal data are other controversial threats to privacy. Individuals have been mistakenly arrested and jailed and people have been denied credit because their physical profiles or personal data have been used by profiling software to match them incorrectly or improperly with the wrong individuals. Another threat is the unauthorized matching of computerized information about you extracted from the databases of sales transaction processing systems and sold to information brokers or other companies. A more recent threat is the unauthorized matching and sale of information about you collected from Internet Web sites and newsgroups you visit, as we discussed previously. You are then subjected to a barrage of unsolicited promotional material and sales contacts as well as having your privacy violated.

Privacy Laws

Many countries strictly regulate the collection and use of personal data by business corporations and government agencies. Many government *privacy laws* attempt to enforce the privacy of computer-based files and communications. For example, in the

United States, the Electronic Communications Privacy Act and the Computer Fraud and Abuse Act prohibit intercepting data communications messages, stealing or destroying data, or trespassing in federal-related computer systems. Because the Internet includes federal-related computer systems, privacy attorneys argue that the laws also require notifying employees if a company intends to monitor Internet usage. Another example is the U.S. Computer Matching and Privacy Act, which regulates the matching of data held in federal agency files to verify eligibility for federal programs.

More recently, new legislation intended to protect individual privacy has created some new challenges for organizations. Sarbanes-Oxley, the Health Insurance Portability and Accountability Act (HIPAA), Gramm-Leach-Bliley, the USA PATRIOT Act, the California Security Breach Law, and Securities and Exchange Commission rule 17a-4 are but a few of the compliance challenges facing organizations. In an effort to comply with these new privacy laws, it is estimated that a typical company will spend 3–4 percent of its IT budget on compliance applications and projects.

HIPAA. The Health Insurance Portability and Accountability Act (HIPAA) was enacted by the U.S. Congress in 1996. It is a broad piece of legislation intended to address a wide variety of issues related to individual health insurance. Two important sections of HIPAA include the privacy rules and the security rules. Both of these portions of the law are intended to create safeguards against the unauthorized use, disclosure, or distribution of an individual's health-related information without their specific consent or authorization. While the privacy rules pertain to all Protected Health Information (PHI) including paper and electronic, the security rules deal specifically with Electronic Protected Health Information (EPHI). These rules lay out three types of security safeguards required for compliance: *administrative, physical,* and *technical.* For each of these types, the rules identify various security standards, and for each standard, name both required and addressable implementation specifications. Required specifications must be adopted and administered as dictated by the HIPAA regulation. Addressable specifications are more flexible. Individual covered entities can evaluate their own situation and determine the best way to implement addressable specifications.

Sarbanes-Oxley. The Sarbanes-Oxley Act of 2002, also known as the Public Company Accounting Reform and Investor Protection Act of 2002 and commonly called Sarbanes-Oxley, Sarbox, or SOX, is a U.S. federal law enacted on July 30, 2002, as a reaction to a number of major corporate and accounting scandals, including those affecting Enron, Tyco International, Adelphia, Peregrine Systems, and WorldCom. These scandals, which cost investors billions of dollars when the share prices of affected companies collapsed, shook public confidence in the nation's securities markets. Named after sponsors U.S. Senator Paul Sarbanes and U.S. Representative Michael G. Oxley, the act was approved by the House by a vote of 334-90 and by the Senate 99-0. President George W. Bush signed it into law, stating it included "the most far-reaching reforms of American business practices since the time of Franklin D. Roosevelt."

The legislation set new or enhanced standards for all U.S. public company boards, management, and public accounting firms. It does not, however, apply to privately held companies. The act contains 11 sections, ranging from additional corporate board responsibilities to criminal penalties, and requires the Securities and Exchange Commission (SEC) to implement rulings on requirements to comply with the new law.

Debate continues over the perceived benefits and costs of SOX. Supporters contend the legislation was necessary and has played a useful role in restoring public confidence in the nation's capital markets by, among other things, strengthening corporate accounting controls. Opponents of the bill claim it has reduced America's international competitive edge against foreign financial service providers, saying SOX has introduced an overly complex and regulatory environment into U.S. financial markets.

Computer Libel and Censorship

The opposite side of the privacy debate is the right of people to know about matters others may want to keep private (freedom of information), the right of people to express their opinions about such matters (freedom of speech), and the right of people to publish those opinions (freedom of the press). Some of the biggest battlegrounds in the debate are the bulletin boards, e-mail boxes, and online files of the Internet and public information networks such as America Online and the Microsoft Network. The weapons being used in this battle include *spamming*, *flame mail*, libel laws, and censorship.

Spamming is the indiscriminate sending of unsolicited e-mail messages (*spam*) to many Internet users. Spamming is the favorite tactic of mass mailers of unsolicited advertisements, or *junk e-mail*. Spamming has also been used by cyber-criminals to spread computer viruses or infiltrate many computer systems.

Flaming is the practice of sending extremely critical, derogatory, and often vulgar e-mail messages (*flame mail*) or newsgroup postings to other users on the Internet or online services. Flaming is especially prevalent on some of the Internet's special-interest newsgroups.

There have been many incidents of racist or defamatory messages on the Web that have led to calls for censorship and lawsuits for libel. In addition, the presence of sexually explicit material at many World Wide Web locations has triggered lawsuits and censorship actions by various groups and governments.

The Current State of Cyber Law

Cyber law is the term used to describe laws intended to regulate activities over the Internet or via the use of electronic data communications. Cyber law encompasses a wide variety of legal and political issues related to the Internet and other communications technologies, including intellectual property, privacy, freedom of expression, and jurisdiction.

The intersection of technology and the law is often controversial. Some feel that the Internet should not (or possibly cannot) be regulated in any form. Furthermore, the development of sophisticated technologies, such as encryption and cryptography, make traditional forms of regulation extremely difficult. Finally, the fundamental end-to-end nature of the Internet means that if one mode of communication is regulated or shut down, another method will be devised and spring up in its place. In the words of John Gilmore, founder of the Electronic Frontier Foundation, "the Internet treats censorship as damage and simply routes around it."

One example of advancements in cyber law is found in the Federal Trade Commission's (FTC) Consumer Sentinel Project. Consumer Sentinel is a unique investigative cyber-tool that provides members of the Consumer Sentinel Network with access to data from millions of consumer complaints. Consumer Sentinel includes complaints about identity theft, do-not-call registry violations, computers, the Internet, and online auctions, telemarketing scams, advance-fee loans, and credit scams, sweepstakes, lotteries, and prizes, business opportunities and work-at-home schemes, health and weight loss products, debt collection, credit reports, and other financial matters.

Consumer Sentinel is based on the premise that sharing information can make law enforcement even more effective. To that end, the Consumer Sentinel Network provides law-enforcement members with access to complaints provided directly to the Federal Trade Commission by consumers, as well as providing members with access to complaints shared by data contributors.

According to the FTC Sentinel Report for 2007, more than 800,000 complaints were processed through Sentinel with Internet-related offenses representing 11 percent of the total complaints, and computer-related identity theft representing 23 percent. While many of these complaints are difficult, if not impossible to prosecute, we are beginning to see more resources being committed to addressing cyber-related crime.

Cyber law is a new phenomenon, having emerged after the onset of the Internet. As we know, the Internet grew in a relatively unplanned and unregulated manner. Even the early pioneers of the Internet could not have anticipated the scope and far-reaching consequences of the cyberspace of today and tomorrow. Although major legal disputes related to cyber activities certainly arose in the early 1990s, it was not until 1996 and 1997 that an actual body of law began to emerge. The area, clearly in its infancy, remains largely unsettled. The debate continues regarding the applicability of analogous legal principles derived from prior controversies that had nothing to do with cyberspace. As we progress in our understanding of the complex issues in cyberspace, new and better laws, regulations, and policies will likely be adopted and enacted.

Other Challenges

Let's now explore some other important challenges that arise from the use of information technologies in business, as illustrated in Figure 13.2. These challenges include the potential ethical and societal impact of business applications of IT in the areas of employment, individuality, working conditions, and health.

Employment Challenges

The impact of information technologies on employment is a major ethical concern that is directly related to the use of computers to achieve automation of work activities. There can be no doubt that the use of information technologies has created new jobs and increased productivity while also causing a significant reduction in some types of job opportunities. For example, when computers are used for accounting systems or the automated control of machine tools, they are accomplishing tasks formerly performed by many clerks and machinists. Also, jobs created by information technology may require different types of skills and education than do the jobs that are eliminated. Therefore, people may become unemployed unless they can be retrained for new positions or new responsibilities.

However, there can be no doubt that Internet technologies have created a host of new job opportunities. Many new jobs, including Internet Web masters, e-commerce directors, systems analysts, and user consultants, have been created to support e-business and e-commerce applications. Additional jobs have been created because information technologies make possible the production of complex industrial and technical goods and services that would otherwise be impossible to produce. Thus, jobs have been created by activities that are heavily dependent on information technology, in such areas as space exploration, microelectronic technology, and telecommunications.

Computer Monitoring

One of the most explosive ethical issues concerning workplace privacy and the quality of working conditions in business is computer monitoring. That is, computers are being used to monitor the productivity and behavior of millions of employees while they work. Supposedly, computer monitoring occurs so employers can collect productivity data about their employees to increase the efficiency and quality of service. However, computer monitoring has been criticized as unethical because it monitors individuals, not just work, and is done continually, which violates workers' privacy and personal freedom. For example, when you call to make a reservation, an airline reservation agent may be timed on the exact number of seconds he or she took per caller, the time between calls, and the number and length of breaks taken. In addition, your conversation may be monitored. See Figure 13.10.

Computer monitoring has been criticized as an invasion of the privacy of employees because, in many cases, they do not know that they are being monitored or don't know how the information is being used. Critics also say that an employee's right of due process may be harmed by the improper use of collected data to make personnel decisions. Because computer monitoring increases the stress on employees who must work under constant electronic surveillance, it has also been blamed for causing health problems among monitored workers. Finally, computer monitoring has been blamed for robbing workers of the dignity of their work. In its extremes, computer monitoring can create an "electronic sweatshop," in which workers are forced to work at a hectic pace under poor working conditions.

FIGURE 13.10
Computer monitoring can be used to record the productivity and behavior of people while they work.

Source: © LWA-JDC/Corbis.

Political pressure is building to outlaw or regulate computer monitoring in the workplace. For example, public advocacy groups, labor unions, and many legislators are pushing for action at the state and federal level in the United States. The proposed laws would regulate computer monitoring and protect the worker's right to know and right to privacy. In the meantime, lawsuits by monitored workers against employers are increasing. So computer monitoring of workers is one ethical issue in business that won't go away.

Challenges in Working Conditions

Information technology has eliminated monotonous or obnoxious tasks in the office and the factory that formerly had to be performed by people. For example, word processing and desktop publishing make producing office documents a lot easier to do, and robots have taken over repetitive welding and spray painting jobs in the automotive industry. In many instances, this shift allows people to concentrate on more challenging and interesting assignments, upgrades the skill level of the work to be performed, and creates challenging jobs requiring highly developed skills in the computer industry and computer-using organizations. Thus, information technology can be said to upgrade the quality of work because it can upgrade the quality of working conditions and the content of work activities.

Of course, some jobs in information technology—data entry, for example—are quite repetitive and routine. Also, to the extent that computers are used in some types of automation, IT must take some responsibility for the criticism of assembly-line operations that require the continual repetition of elementary tasks, thus forcing a worker to work like a machine instead of like a skilled craftsperson. Many automated operations are also criticized for relegating people to a "do-nothing" standby role, where workers spend most of their time waiting for infrequent opportunities to push some buttons. Such effects do have a detrimental effect on the quality of work, but they must be compared against the less burdensome and more creative jobs created by information technology.

Challenges of Individuality

A frequent criticism of information systems centers on their negative effect on the individuality of people. Computer-based systems are criticized as impersonal systems that dehumanize and depersonalize activities that have been computerized because they eliminate the human relationships present in noncomputer systems.

Another aspect of the loss of individuality is the regimentation that seems required by some computer-based systems. These systems do not appear to possess any flexibility. They demand strict adherence to detailed procedures if the system is to work. The negative impact of IT on individuality is reinforced by horror stories that describe how inflexible and uncaring some organizations with computer-based processes are when it comes to rectifying their own mistakes. Many of us are familiar with stories of how computerized customer billing and accounting systems continued to demand payment and send warning notices to a customer whose account had already been paid, despite repeated attempts by the customer to have the error corrected.

However, many business applications of IT are designed to minimize depersonalization and regimentation. For example, many e-commerce systems stress personalization and community features to encourage repeated visits to e-commerce Web sites. Thus, the widespread use of personal computers and the Internet has dramatically improved the development of people-oriented and personalized information systems.

Health Issues

The use of information technology in the workplace raises a variety of health issues. Heavy use of computers is reportedly causing health problems like job stress, damaged arm and neck muscles, eyestrain, radiation exposure, and even death by computer-caused accidents. For example, computer monitoring is blamed as a major cause of computer-related job stress. Workers, unions, and government officials criticize computer monitoring as putting so much stress on employees that it leads to health problems.

People who sit at PC workstations or visual display terminals (VDTs) in fast-paced, repetitive keystroke jobs can suffer a variety of health problems known collectively as *cumulative trauma disorders* (CTDs). Their fingers, wrists, arms, necks, and backs may become so weak and painful that they cannot work. Strained muscles, back pain, and nerve damage may result. In particular, some computer workers may suffer from *carpal tunnel syndrome*, a painful, crippling ailment of the hand and wrist that typically requires surgery to cure.

Prolonged viewing of video displays causes eyestrain and other health problems in employees who must do this all day. Radiation caused by the cathode ray tubes (CRTs) that produce video displays is another health concern. CRTs produce an electromagnetic field that may cause harmful radiation of employees who work too close for too long in front of video monitors. Some pregnant workers have reported miscarriages and fetal deformities due to prolonged exposure to CRTs at work. Studies have failed to find conclusive evidence concerning this problem; still, several organizations recommend that female workers minimize their use of CRTs during pregnancy.

Ergonomics

Solutions to some of these health problems are based on the science of ergonomics, sometimes called *human factors engineering*. See Figure 13.11. The goal of ergonomics is to design healthy work environments that are safe, comfortable, and pleasant for people to work in, thus increasing employee morale and productivity. Ergonomics emphasizes the healthy design of the workplace, workstations, computers and other machines, and even software packages. Other health issues may require ergonomic solutions emphasizing job design rather than workplace design. For example, this approach may require policies providing for work breaks from heavy video monitor use every few hours, while limiting the CRT exposure of pregnant workers. Ergonomic job design can also provide more variety in job tasks for those workers who spend most of their workday at computer workstations.

Societal Solutions

As we noted at the beginning of the chapter, the Internet and other information technologies can have many beneficial effects on society. We can use information technologies to solve human and social problems through societal solutions such as medical diagnosis, computer-assisted instruction, governmental program planning, environmental quality control, and law enforcement. For example, computers can help diagnose an illness,

FIGURE 13.11
Ergonomic factors in the workplace. Note that good ergonomic design considers tools, tasks, the workstation, and the environment.

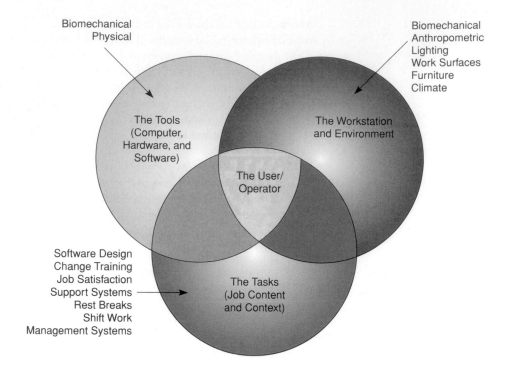

prescribe necessary treatment, and monitor the progress of hospital patients. Computer-assisted instruction (CAI) and computer-based training (CBT) enable interactive instruction tailored to the needs of students. Distance learning is supported by tele-communications networks, videoconferencing, e-mail, and other technologies.

Information technologies can be used for crime control through various law-enforcement applications. For example, computerized alarm systems allow police to identify and respond quickly to evidence of criminal activity. Computers have been used to monitor the level of pollution in the air and in bodies of water, detect the sources of pollution, and issue early warnings when dangerous levels are reached. Computers are also used for the program planning of many government agencies in such areas as urban planning, population density and land use studies, highway planning, and urban transit studies. Computers are being used in job placement systems to help match unemployed persons with available jobs. These and other applications illustrate that information technology can be used to help solve the problems of society.

Obviously, individuals or organizations that do not accept ethical responsibility for their actions cause many of the detrimental effects of information technology. Like other powerful technologies, information technology possesses the potential for great harm or great good for all humankind. If managers, business professionals, and IS specialists accept their ethical responsibilities, then information technology can help improve living and working conditions for all of society.

SECTION II   Security Management of Information Technology

Introduction

With Internet access proliferating rapidly, one might think that the biggest obstacle to e-commerce would be bandwidth. But it's not; the number one problem is security. And part of the problem is that the Internet was developed for interoperability, not impenetrability.

As we saw in Section I, there are many significant threats to the security of information systems in business. That's why this section is dedicated to exploring the methods that companies can use to manage their security. Business managers and professionals alike are responsible for the security, quality, and performance of the business information systems in their business units. Like any other vital business assets, hardware, software, networks, and data resources need to be protected by a variety of security measures to ensure their quality and beneficial use. That's the business value of security management.

Read the Real World Case on the next page. We can learn a lot about why IT managers are increasingly concerned about securing the user end of their networks, and how they are facing this challenge. See Figure 13.12.

Tools of Security Management

The goal of security management is the accuracy, integrity, and safety of all information system processes and resources. Thus, effective security management can minimize errors, fraud, and losses in the information systems that interconnect today's companies and their customers, suppliers, and other stakeholders. As Figure 13.13 illustrates, security management is a complex task. As you can see, security managers must acquire and integrate a variety of security tools and methods to protect a company's information system resources. We discuss many of these security measures in this section.

Top Executives Agree: Information Security Is a Top Priority

What do chief executive officers and other business leaders really think about information security? A recent survey and interviews conducted by *InformationWeek* reveal that they're more aligned with "infosec" (information security) teams than you might think—when comes to information security, non-IT executives just might get it. The results suggest that C-level executives not only recognize the importance of information security, but actively support the efforts of their IT organizations to protect corporate assets and reduce risk.

At times, that comes as a surprise. The rants from IT pros about stingy executives who are ignorant of critical security issues and regard security as an impediment to doing business are quite common. Indeed, conflicts between executives and IT organizations are still common. Moneymaking opportunities that present considerable security risks still go forward over the objections of information security teams. Conversely, security teams don't always appreciate that risk can't be entirely eliminated, or that some security measures go so far as to make information and technology too cumbersome to be useful.

Among the more security-minded executives is William McNabb, chief executive officer of investment firm Vanguard Group. He sums up his company's information security responsibility this way: "We manage more than a trillion dollars of other people's money. That's important trust they've placed with us, and we have to do everything in our power to protect it." Seventy-five percent of survey respondents say information security is among the highest of corporate priorities.

There are four major reasons for this high level of executive support. First is the rise of high-volume theft of credit card information, Social Security numbers, and other personal data. Such attacks began to make headlines in 2005, when DSW Shoe Warehouse and ChoicePoint were hit. In the DSW case, thieves stole 1.4 million

(text continues on page 592)

REAL WORLD CASE 2

Wyoming Medical Center, Los Angeles County, and Raymond James: Endpoint Security Gets Complicated

Users say protecting network end points is becoming more difficult as the type of endpoint devices—desktops, laptops, smartphones—grows, making security a complex moving target. The problem is compounded by the range of what groups within corporations do on these devices, which translates into different levels of protection for classes of users on myriad devices.

"Deciding the appropriate device defense becomes the No. 1 job of endpoint security specialists," says Jennifer Jabbush, CISO of Carolina Advanced Digital consultancy. Depending on the device and the user's role, end points need to be locked down to a greater or lesser degree.

For instance, Wyoming Medical Center in Casper, Wyoming, has four classifications of PCs: "open PCs in hallways for staff use; PCs at nursing stations; PCs in offices; and PCs on wheels that move between patient rooms and handle very specific, limited applications," says Rob Pettigrew, manager of technical systems and help desk for the center.

Pettigrew is deploying Novell ZenWorks to 850 of the center's 900 PCs in order to make sure each class has the right software. With 110 applications and 40 major medical software systems, that makes a huge matrix of machine types and restrictions to contend with, he says.

In addition, physicians in affiliated clinics can access via SSL VPN (a kind of VPN that is accessible over Web browsers), but they are limited to reaching Web servers in a physician's portal, which is protected from the hospital data network. Some Citrix thin clients are also used to protect

FIGURE 13.12

The proliferation of end-user devices is making endpoint security more important than ever.

Source: © Bloomberg/Getty Images.

data from leaving the network but overall the strategy for unmanaged machines is a work in progress, Pettigrew says. "We're hoping to get more help desk to deal with the external physicians," he says.

One concern that can be addressed by endpoint security is data privacy, which is paramount for the Los Angeles County Department of Health Services in California, says Don Zimmer, information security officer for the department. He supports about 18,000 desktops and laptops and operates under the restrictions of Health Insurance Portability and Accountability Act (HIPAA) regulations. "That means disk encryption," he says.

"If it's not encrypted and there is a breach, then we have to start calling people," he says. To avoid violating patients' privacy and a loss of public trust, the department encrypts the drives of all the PC end points with software from PointSec.

Equally important is keeping sensitive information off movable media that can plug into USB ports. The department uses Safend's USB Port Protector product that either denies access to sensitive documents or requires that they be encrypted and password-protected before being placed on the removable device.

Everyone's talking about the insider threat. But protecting data can't supersede the requirement to give users the access they need to do their jobs—otherwise, soon you'll have neither business data nor employees to worry about.

Striking a balance between access and protection isn't easy, however. In an *InformationWeek* Analytics/DarkReading.com endpoint security survey of 384 business technology pros, 43 percent classify their organizations as "trusting," allowing data to be copied to USB drives or other devices with no restrictions or protective measures.

Still, IT is aware of the need to move from a stance of securing end points to assuming that laptops and smartphones will be lost, good employees will go bad, and virtual machines will be compromised. Instead of focusing on end points, let fortifications follow the data: Decide what must be protected, find out everywhere it lives, and lock it down against both inside and outside threats, whether via encryption, multitiered security suites, or new technologies like data loss prevention (DLP).

DLP suites combine network scanning and host-based tools to collect, categorize, and protect corporate intellectual property. These products can maintain an archive of data and documents, along with associated permissions by group, individual, and other policies.

They then actively scan internal networks and external connections looking for anomalies. This takes data protection beyond perimeter or endpoint protection; DLP facilitates internal safety checks, allowing "eyes-only" data to remain eyes only and minimizing the risk that sensitive data will be viewed by the wrong folks, even in-house.

Zimmer says he is looking into DLP software as well that can restrict the access individual devices have to data.

Although the technology can be effective, it also requires that businesses locate and classify their data so they can set policies surrounding it—a job that can seem insurmountable, depending on how data have been stored.

For Pettigrew, this means finding the 5 percent of sensitive data stored outside the medical center's electronic medical records system.

Rather than deal with many vendors for specific endpoint protection products, some businesses opt for endpoint security suites, such as those that evolved from the antivirus roots of vendors, including McAfee and Symantec.

Sam Ghelfi, chief security officer at financial firm Raymond James, opted for Sophos's Endpoint Protection and Data Security Suite, which offers firewall, antivirus, data loss prevention, antispyware, encryption, and network access control (NAC). The company wants tight control over the Web content that is available to users to minimize the malware coming in via basic Web browsing. The company uses a Sophos Web proxy that filters sites based on reputation, but also the content that sites return.

Mobile devices that could contain confidential company information are disk encrypted, again using Sophos agents. If a device is lost or stolen, the encryption key is wiped out, making it impossible to decrypt the contents of the hard drive.

Ghelfi says he believes in personal firewalls on individual machines because they can stop groups of devices from talking to other groups. "Centrally managed, they can reveal network traffic patterns," he says.

He doesn't use all of the features of the Sophos suite, though. For instance, he is just getting around to implementing NAC to let unmanaged guest machines get on the network but still minimize risk that they are infected.

That will clear them based on authentication, access method and type of machine, but for contractors that require access to the main network, he also insists that they install the Sophos suite. Other unmanaged machines, such as those of guests, are allowed access only through a dedicated wireless network that leads to a limited set of servers in a network segment flanked by firewalls, he says.

"Such endpoint security suites can be attractive financially," Jabbusch says, "because customers can wind up with reduced agent, license and support fees and less management overhead." There may be a certain amount of convenience if customers decide to layer on more applications within a suite.

The newest class of devices—smartphones—is presenting ongoing challenges as organizations figure out how to deal with them. Particularly dicey is whether to allow employees to use their personally owned devices for business and to access the business network.

The jury is still out, at least among state government chief information officers. A recent survey by the National Association of State Chief Information Officers says that of 36 states responding to a survey, 39 percent say they allow personal smartphones if they are protected by state security measures. Twenty-seven percent say they don't allow personal smartphones on their networks, 17 percent say they are reviewing state policy, and 17 percent say they don't have statewide control—each agency sets its own policies.

A separate Forrester Research survey says that 73 percent of businesses surveyed are at least somewhat concerned about smartphones being authorized for business use. According to DeviceLock, its survey of more than 1000 IT professionals found that fewer than 40 percent of respondents said yes to the question: "Have you taken any steps to secure your business against the security threat posed by iPhones? "Analyzing the responses by region, researchers found that only 25 percent of respondents in North America and Western Europe said yes to the question, suggesting this is a "back burner" security issue, says the endpoint data leak-prevention specialist.

Jabbush says the type of smartphone is a factor. "I can't imagine allowing an iPhone," she says. "A BlackBerry is somewhat better" because BlackBerries have a management infrastructure and the devices can be locked down to corporate policies.

Mobile device security is one of those areas that should get more attention. However, it is likely that this topic will remain buried—until a lost or stolen iPhone leads to a visible and costly security breach.

Source: Adapted from Tim Greene, "Endpoint Security Gets Complicated," *Network World*, April 1, 2010; and Joe Hernick, "InformationWeek Analytics: Endpoint Security and DLP," *InformationWeek*, April 27, 2009.

CASE STUDY QUESTIONS

1. What is the underlying issue behind endpoint security, and why is it becoming even more difficult for companies to address it? Define the problem in your own words using examples from the case.

2. What are the different approaches taken by the organizations in the case to address this issue? What are the advantages and disadvantages of each? Provide at least two examples for each alternative.

3. A majority of respondents to a survey discussed in the case described their company as "trusting." What does this mean? What is the upside of a company being "trusting"? What is the downside? Provide some examples to illustrate your answers.

REAL WORLD ACTIVITIES

1. Data loss prevention (DLP) was a technology mentioned in the case, and one that is garnering more and more attention from corporate security departments. Go online and research what DLP involves, and look for examples of its application to actual problems, and their outcomes. Prepare a report to summarize your work.

2. Whether to allow employees to use their own smartphones (or other devices yet to be invented) on corporate networks is quickly becoming a contested issue. What do companies stand to gain, or lose, in either case? What about employees? Break into small groups with your classmates to discuss these questions.

FIGURE 13.13

Examples of important security measures that are part of the security management of information systems.

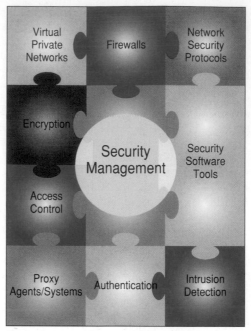

Source: Courtesy of Wang Global.

credit card numbers from stores in 25 states. Meanwhile, poor controls at Choice-Point enabled scam artists posing as legitimate businesses to access consumer records and perpetrate identity theft. Since then, a string of larger information thefts from the likes of the Hannaford Bros, grocery chain, job site Monster.com, retailer TJX, and, most recently, Heartland Payment systems has put executives on notice: Such breaches can no longer be dismissed as merely isolated incidents.

Second, the high-profile thefts have triggered a number of state breach-disclosure laws, which compel companies to publicize the theft or loss of personally identifiable information. Companies also face industry data-protection standards, the most prominent of which is the Payment Card Industry Data Security Standard, which requires a variety of security measures for businesses that accept and process credit cards.

The third trend changing executives' attitudes about security is the rising cost of information breaches.

From lawsuit payouts to fines to the expense of setting up credit-monitoring services for victimized customers, executives can see exactly how much a security failure costs. U.S. companies paid an average of $202 per exposed record in 2008, up from $197 in 2007, according to a report by the Ponemon Institute, a privacy management researcher. The report also says the average total cost per breach for each company was $6.6 million in 2008, up from $6.3 million in 2007 and $4.7 million in 2006.

The fourth major trend is the damage to a company's brand and reputation. While it's hard to put a price on the loss of customer trust or efforts to repair a brand, no CEO wants to have to try to do that math.

Source: Adapted from Andrew Conry-Murray, "A Unified Front," *InformationWeek*, February 16, 2009.

Inter-Networked Security Defenses

Few professionals today face greater challenges than those IT managers who are developing Internet security policies for rapidly changing network infrastructures. How can they balance the need for Internet security and Internet access? Are the budgets for Internet security adequate? What impact will intranet, extranet, and Web application development have on security architectures? How can they come up with best practices for developing Internet security policy?

The security of today's networked business enterprises is a major management challenge. Many companies are still in the process of getting fully connected to the Web and the Internet for e-commerce and are reengineering their internal business processes with intranets, e-business software, and extranet links to customers, suppliers, and other business partners. Vital network links and business flows need to be protected from external attack by cyber-criminals and from subversion by the criminal or irresponsible acts of insiders. This protection requires a variety of security tools and defensive measures and a coordinated security management program. Let's take a look at some of these important security defenses.

Encryption

Encryption of data has become an important way to protect data and other computer network resources, especially on the Internet, intranets, and extranets. Passwords, messages, files, and other data can be transmitted in scrambled form and unscrambled by computer systems for authorized users only. Encryption involves using special mathematical algorithms, or keys, to transform digital data into a scrambled code before they are transmitted, and then to decode the data when they are received. The most widely used encryption method uses a pair of public and private keys unique to each individual. For example, e-mail could be scrambled and encoded using a unique *public key* for the recipient that is known to the sender. After the e-mail is transmitted, only the recipient's secret *private key* could unscramble the message. See Figure 13.14.

Encryption programs are sold as separate products or built into other software used for the encryption process. There are several competing software encryption standards, but the top two are RSA (by RSA Data Security) and PGP (which stands for "pretty good privacy"), a popular encryption program available on the Internet. Software products including Microsoft Windows XP, Novell NetWare, and Lotus Notes offer encryption features using RSA software.

FIGURE 13.14   How public key/private key encryption works.

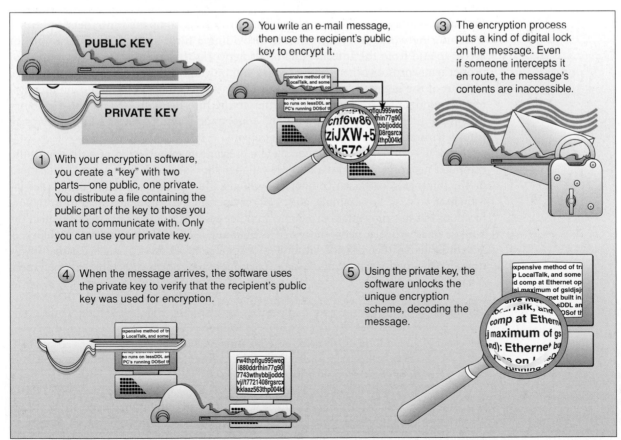

FIGURE 13.15   An example of the Internet and intranet firewalls in a company's networks.

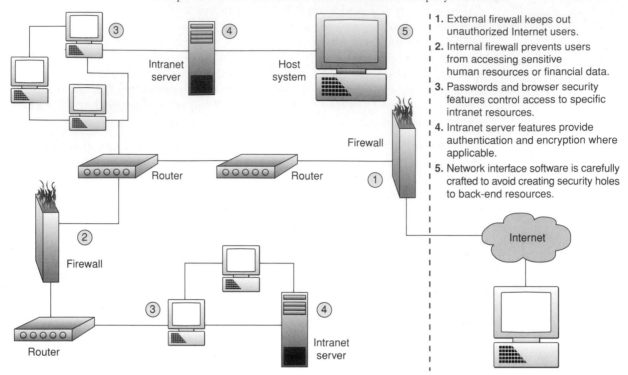

1. External firewall keeps out unauthorized Internet users.
2. Internal firewall prevents users from accessing sensitive human resources or financial data.
3. Passwords and browser security features control access to specific intranet resources.
4. Intranet server features provide authentication and encryption where applicable.
5. Network interface software is carefully crafted to avoid creating security holes to back-end resources.

Firewalls

Another important method for control and security on the Internet and other networks is the use of firewall computers and software. A network firewall can be a communications processor, typically a *router*, or a dedicated server, along with firewall software. A firewall serves as a gatekeeper system that protects a company's intranets and other computer networks from intrusion by providing a filter and safe transfer point for access to and from the Internet and other networks. It screens all network traffic for proper passwords or other security codes and only allows authorized transmissions in and out of the network. Firewall software has also become an essential computer system component for individuals connecting to the Internet with DSL or cable modems because of their vulnerable, "always-on" connection status. Figure 13.15 illustrates an Internet/intranet firewall system for a company.

Firewalls can deter, but not completely prevent, unauthorized access (hacking) into computer networks. In some cases, a firewall may allow access only from trusted locations on the Internet to particular computers inside the firewall, or it may allow only "safe" information to pass. For example, a firewall may permit users to read e-mail from remote locations but not run certain programs. In other cases, it is impossible to distinguish the safe use of a particular network service from unsafe use, so all requests must be blocked. The firewall may then provide substitutes for some network services (such as e-mail or file transfers) that perform most of the same functions but are not as vulnerable to penetration.

WhiteHat Security: "Black Box Testing" Mimics Hackers to Discover Vulnerabilities

Jeremiah Grossman wants you to know that firewalls and SSL encryption won't prevent a hacker from breaking into your e-commerce Web site, compromising your customers' data, and possibly stealing your money. That's because most Web site attacks these days exploit bugs in the Web application itself, rather than in the operating system on which the application is running.

Grossman is the founder and chief technology officer of WhiteHat Security, a Silicon Valley firm that offers an outsourced Web site vulnerability management service. Using a combination of proprietary scanning and so-called ethical hacking, WhiteHat assesses the security of its clients' Web sites, looking for exploitable vulnerabilities.

WhiteHat does its scanning without access to the client's source code and from outside the client's firewall using the standard HTTP Web protocol. This approach is sometimes called "black box testing" because the Web site's contents are opaque to the security assessors. The problem with black box testing, of course, is that it is sure to miss many vulnerabilities and back doors that are hidden in the source code. Black box testing can only find vulnerabilities that are visible to someone who is using your Web site, but the advantage of this approach is that it precisely mimics how a hacker would most likely conduct his reconnaissance and break-in.

From his vantage point at WhiteHat, Grossman has seen several organizations migrate Web sites from Microsoft's original ASP to ASP.NET. "ASP classic, the first generation of ASP websites, are generally riddled with vulnerabilities," he says. Yet when these organizations rewrote their applications using ASP.NET, suddenly their applications improved tremendously security-wise. "Same developers, two different frameworks. It wasn't an education problem; it was a technology problem."

At another company—a financial institution—WhiteHat discovered an easily exploited vulnerability that would have let customers steal money. WhiteHat called up the company, and the problem was hot-fixed within 24 hours. A few months later, the vulnerability came back. "The developers were working on the next release, set to come out in two to three months. Some developer did not back-port the hot-fix from the production server to the development server. So when the push occurred three months later, they pushed the vulnerability again." Ugh!

You may not be a big fan of this approach to security, but if you talk to Grossman for a couple of hours, he will convince you that it's a necessary part of today's e-commerce Web sites. Yes, it would be nice to eliminate these well-known bugs with better coding practices, but we live in the real world. It's better to look for the bugs and fix them than to just cross your fingers and hope that they aren't there.

Source: Adapted from Simson Garfinkel, "An Introduction to the Murky Science of Web Application Security," *CIO Magazine*, May 11, 2007.

Denial of Service Attacks

Major attacks against e-commerce and corporate Web sites in the past few years have demonstrated that the Internet is extremely vulnerable to a variety of assaults by criminal hackers, especially distributed denial of service (DDOS) attacks. Figure 13.16 outlines the steps organizations can take to protect themselves from DDOS attacks.

Denial of service assaults via the Internet depend on three layers of networked computer systems: (1) the victim's Web site, (2) the victim's Internet service provider (ISP), and (3) the sites of "zombie" or slave computers that the cyber-criminals commandeered. For example, in early 2000, hackers broke into hundreds of servers, mostly poorly protected servers at universities, and planted Trojan horse.exe programs, which were then used to launch a barrage of service requests in a concerted attack on e-commerce Web sites like Yahoo! and eBay.

As Figure 13.16 shows, defensive measures and security precautions must be taken at all three levels of the computer networks involved. These are the basic steps

FIGURE 13.16
How to defend against denial of service attacks.

Defending against Denial of Service
● **At the zombie machines:** Set and enforce security policies. Scan regularly for Trojan horse programs and vulnerabilities. Close unused ports. Remind users not to open .exe mail attachments.
● **At the ISP:** Monitor and block traffic spikes. Filter spoofed IP addresses. Coordinate security with network providers.
● **At the victim's Web site:** Create backup servers and network connections. Limit connections to each server. Install multiple intrusion-detection systems and multiple routers for incoming traffic to reduce choke points.

companies and other organizations can take to protect their Web sites from denial of service and other hacking attacks. Now let's take a look at a real-world example of a more sophisticated defense technology.

As If Phishing Wasn't Enough: Denial of Service Attacks

Kevin Dougherty has seen his share of spam and phishing scams, as has any IT leader in the financial services industry. But the sender's name on this particular e-mail sent a shudder down his spine: It was from one of his board members at the Central Florida Educators' Federal Credit Union (CFEFCU). The e-mail claimed in convincing detail that there was a problem with the migration to a new Visa credit card that the board member was promoting to the credit union's customers. The fraudulent message urged customers to click on a link—to a phony Web site set up by criminals—and enter their account information to fix the problem.

But what happened later that Friday afternoon—after Dougherty, who is senior vice president of IT and marketing, had wiped the credit card migration information off the Web site and put up an alert warning customers of the scam—really scared him.

Around 2 p.m., the site suddenly went dark, like someone had hit it with a baseball bat. That's when Dougherty realized that he was dealing with something he hadn't seen before. And he couldn't describe it with conventional terms like phishing or spamming. This was an organized criminal conspiracy targeting his bank. "This wasn't random," he says. "They saw what we were doing with the credit card and came at us hard."

Dougherty's Web site lay in a coma from a devastating distributed denial of service (DDOS) attack that, at its peak, shot more than 600,000 packets per second of bogus service requests at his servers from a coordinated firing squad of compromised computers around the globe. That the criminals had the skill and foresight to launch a two-pronged attack against Dougherty and his customers was a clear indication of how far online crime, which is now a $2.8 billion business according to research company Gartner, has come in the past few years.

Obviously, the first thing Dougherty had to do was stop the attack. He had to hurriedly assemble a coalition of vendors and consultants to help him, and then he had to convince his CEO that drastic steps were needed—steps that would temporarily cut off customers from any possibility of getting to their accounts online until the problems were completely eradicated. Dougherty wanted to have the site temporarily blacklisted with his telecom provider, BellSouth, to deflect the attack, thereby reducing pressure on the site and giving him the time and flexibility to make protective changes. But his CEO resisted—as might anyone who has not experienced an attack. "He wanted to keep it up so we could service the members," says Dougherty.

At 11 p.m., after a long night of battling the attackers and plotting strategy, Dougherty finally convinced his CEO to have the site blacklisted and to take a break until morning.

Continuing in a tired and emotional state would have played into the attackers' hands. "It's a mind game," says Dougherty.

By Saturday morning, Dougherty had RSA, a security vendor he called in when the attacks began, working to set up a "takedown" service that seeks out and dispatches criminal Web sites (in this case, more than 30) with its own cyber baseball bat. Meanwhile, BellSouth began beefing up security around the credit union site to try to thwart attacks.

The site was back up by Saturday evening. In the end, 22 customers gave up their information to the thieves and the total losses were "less than five figures," says Dougherty. Though the credit union had averted disaster, "it was a rude awakening," he says.

Source: Adapted from Nancy Weil, "Your Plan to Fight Cyber Crime," *CIO Magazine*, June 15, 2007.

E-mail Monitoring

Spot checks just aren't good enough anymore. The tide is turning toward systematic monitoring of corporate e-mail traffic using content-monitoring software that scans for troublesome words that might compromise corporate security. The reason: Users of monitoring software said they're concerned about protecting their intellectual property and guarding themselves against litigation.

As we mentioned in Section I, Internet and other online e-mail systems are one of the favorite avenues of attack by hackers for spreading computer viruses or breaking into networked computers. E-mail is also the battleground for attempts by companies to enforce policies against illegal, personal, or damaging messages by employees versus the demands of some employees and others who see such policies as violations of privacy rights.

Employee Monitoring: Who's Watching Now?

Just the mention of employee monitoring raises concerns about Big Brother and privacy, as well as issues of trust, loyalty, and respect. Yet monitoring employee use of e-mail, the Internet, and telephones in the workplace has become more common than gatherings at the office watercooler. Ten years ago, employee monitoring meant that the supervisor would walk the floor and watch the activities of workers. Today, businesses increasingly use automated tools to ensure that workers are completing tasks, not wasting resources, and complying with a growing list of government regulations.

A report by the Privacy Rights Clearinghouse says there's little that employees can do to limit monitoring by their employers. Bosses have the right to listen to workers' phone calls in most instances, obtain records of those calls, use software to see what's being displayed on computer screens, check what information is stored on hard disks, and track and record e-mail. Some companies have little choice but to monitor employees.

Presidio Financial Partners provides investment consulting services, controlling approximately $3 billion in assets for 150 clients. It falls under the scrutiny of the Securities and Exchange Commission and the National Association of Securities Dealers, and it must provide regulators with access to e-mail and other correspondence between the company and its clients, as well as maintain an archive of the information.

"We have to have this information at our disposal," says Jeff Zlot, managing director for Presidio. "But our clients are high-profile individuals, and the last thing we need is information getting into the wrong hands."

Presidio began to use Fortiva Supervision software from Fortiva to monitor, track, and archive the e-mail of its consultants, and it was pleased that Fortiva keeps archived material encrypted. Fortiva Supervision is used to track e-mail between Presidio salespeople and clients, specifically looking for keywords that could pose problems. "We can show the regulators that we set up guidelines and that we are enforcing those guidelines from a sales supervision standpoint," Zlot says.

Phrases that will be flagged by the software include such things as guaranteed return or guaranteed performance, or any time the word *complaint* is used. If the keywords are spotted, supervisors must review the e-mail. As many as 50 e-mails a day get queued for review. "This forces the sales supervisors to look and approve the work the employees are doing," Zlot says.

The growing number of automated monitoring tools makes it easier for employers to keep an eye on what employees are doing than in the old days—when you really had to keep an eye on them.

Source: Adapted from Darrell Dunn, "Who's Watching Now?" *InformationWeek*, February 27, 2006.

Virus Defenses

Is your PC protected from the latest viruses, worms, Trojan horses, and other malicious programs that can wreak havoc on your PC? Chances are it is, if it's periodically linked to the corporate network. These days, corporate antivirus protection is a centralized function of information technology. Someone installs it for you on your PC and notebook or, increasingly, distributes it over the network. The antivirus software runs in the background, popping up every so often to reassure you. The trend right now is to automate the process entirely.

FIGURE 13.17

An example of security suite PC software that includes antivirus and firewall protection.

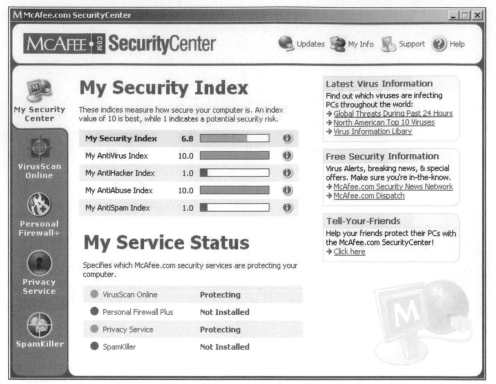

Source: Courtesy of McAfee.

Many companies are building defenses against the spread of viruses by centralizing the distribution and updating of antivirus software as a responsibility of their IS departments. Other companies are outsourcing the virus protection responsibility to their Internet service providers or telecommunications or security management companies.

One reason for this trend is that the major antivirus software companies like McAfee (VirusScan) and Symantec (Norton Antivirus) have developed network versions of their programs, which they are marketing to ISPs and others as a service they should offer to all their customers. The antivirus companies are also marketing *security suites* of software that integrate virus protection with firewalls, Web security, and content-blocking features. See Figure 13.17.

Privacy Refined: Don't Forget Your Digital Trail	People are willing to adjust their ideas about privacy if they can benefit from revealing more of their personal information, the CEO of Infosys Technologies said.

"You allow that privacy to be compromised for a benefit," CEO Kris Gopalakrishnan said during a talk at MIT's Emerging Technologies conference. The definition of privacy must now take into account whether personal information is "properly used to give additional benefits," he said.

His remarks came in a speech about how most everyday items, from appliances to roadways, will contain processors and connect to the Internet. This pervasive network will carry data that generates real-time traffic reports from sensors embedded in roadways or allows a doctor to monitor a patient's blood pressure remotely, he said.

Gopalakrishnan, whose company is one of India's largest IT outsourcing providers, estimates that 50 to 60 billion devices will be connected to the Internet in the coming decades as processor prices decrease. "That is an incredible expansion of the network," he said. "These devices will have intelligence, but most intelligence will rely on the network."

While some will argue whether such a ubiquitous network sacrifices privacy, Gopalakrishnan contends that technology has already changed the word's meaning. "In the digital world you are leaving trails all over the place," he said.

Simple acts like using a cell phone and buying an airline ticket leave digital "fingerprints," and closed-circuit cameras are scattered throughout cities like New York and London. But there are positive trade-offs for sharing personal information, he argued. Mobile phones and the Web have made life far more convenient, and closed-circuit cameras can prevent crime and help fight terrorism.

Social networking is a great example of our willingness to give up some of our privacy for what people see as a benefit—being part of an online community of friends.

For the Internet of Things to come about, though, all the legacy devices will need to be gradually upgraded. "The big issue is the legacy problem," Gopalakrishnan said, "appliances that don't have sensors because they're old."

But he implied that sensor networks will help save money, and there are ways to get around the shortage of sensor-enabled equipment. Infosys developed a power strip, he said, into which devices that lack sensors can be plugged. By controlling devices plugged into the strip, Infosys was able to cut the electricity use in an office 10 percent.

Smart networks will be used for a wide range of things and will lead to changes in data storage and parsing, he said. "This will happen over 20 to 30 years. We will need to develop new databases and analytical tools to use the data."

Source: Adapted from Fred O'Connor, "Infosys CEO: People Trade Privacy for Benefits," *Computerworld Hong Kong*, Questex Media, September 28, 2010.

Other Security Measures

Let's now briefly examine a variety of security measures that are commonly used to protect business systems and networks. These include both hardware and software tools, like fault-tolerant computers and security monitors, and security policies and procedures, like passwords and backup files. All are part of an integrated security management effort at many companies today.

Security Codes

Typically, a multilevel **password** system is used for security management. First, an end user logs on to the computer system by entering his or her unique identification code, or user ID. Second, the end user is asked to enter a password to gain access into the system. (Passwords should be changed frequently and consist of unusual combinations of upper- and lowercase letters and numbers.) Third, to access an individual file, a unique file name must be entered. In some systems, the password to read the contents of a file is different from that required to write to a file (change its contents). This feature adds another level of protection to stored data resources. For even stricter security, however, passwords can be scrambled, or *encrypted*, to avoid their theft or improper use, as we will discuss shortly. In addition, *smart cards*, which contain microprocessors that generate random numbers to add to an end user's password, are used in some secure systems.

Backup Files

Backup files, which are duplicate files of data or programs, are another important security measure. Files can also be protected by *file retention* measures that involve storing copies of files from previous periods. If current files are destroyed, the files from previous periods can be used to reconstruct new current files. Sometimes, several generations of files are kept for control purposes. Thus, master files from several recent periods of

FIGURE 13.18

The eTrust security monitor manages a variety of security functions for major corporate networks, including monitoring the status of Web-based applications throughout a network.

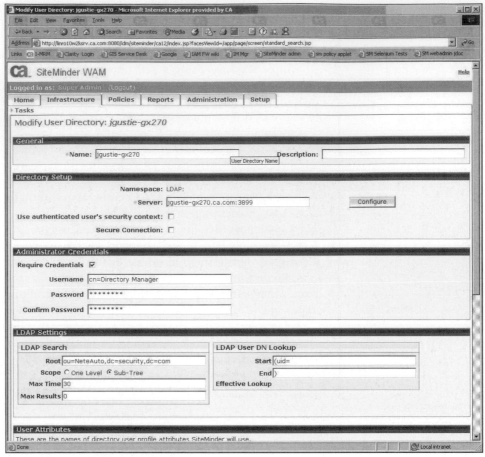

Source: Courtesy of Site Minder.

processing (known as *child*, *parent*, and *grandparent* files) may be kept for backup purposes. Such files may be stored off-premises, that is, in a location away from a company's data center, sometimes in special storage vaults in remote locations.

Security Monitors

Security of a network may be provided by specialized system software packages known as **system security monitors**. See Figure 13.18. System security monitors are programs that monitor the use of computer systems and networks and protect them from unauthorized use, fraud, and destruction. Such programs provide the security measures needed to allow only authorized users to access the networks. For example, identification codes and passwords are frequently used for this purpose. Security monitors also control the use of the hardware, software, and data resources of a computer system. For example, even authorized users may be restricted to the use of certain devices, programs, and data files. In addition, security programs monitor the use of computer networks and collect statistics on any attempts at improper use. They then produce reports to assist in maintaining the security of the network.

Biometric Security

Biometric security is a fast-growing area of computer security. These are security measures provided by computer devices that measure physical traits that make each individual unique, such as voice verification, fingerprints, hand geometry, signature dynamics, keystroke analysis, retina scanning, face recognition, and genetic pattern analysis. Biometric control devices use special-purpose sensors to measure and digitize a biometric profile of a person's fingerprints, voice, or other physical trait. The digitized signal is processed and compared to a previously processed profile of the individual stored on

FIGURE 13.19

An evaluation of common biometric security techniques based on user requirements, accuracy, and cost.

Evaluation of Biometric Techniques				
	User Criteria		System Criteria	
	Intrusiveness	Effort	Accuracy	Cost
Dynamic signature verification	Excellent	Fair	Fair	Excellent
Face geometry	Good	Good	Fair	Good
Finger scan	Fair	Good	Good	Good
Hand geometry	Fair	Good	Fair	Fair
Passive iris scan	Poor	Excellent	Excellent	Poor
Retina scan	Poor	Poor	Very good	Fair
Voice print	Very good	Poor	Fair	Very good

magnetic disk. If the profiles match, the individual is allowed entry into a computer network and given access to secure system resources. See Figure 13.19.

Notice that the examples of biometric security listed in Figure 13.19 are rated according to the degree of intrusiveness (how much the technique interrupts a user) and the relative amount of effort required by the user to authenticate. Also, the relative accuracy and cost of each are assessed. As you can see, trade-offs in these four areas exist in every example. Whereas face geometry is judged easy on the user in terms of intrusiveness and effort, its accuracy is not considered as high as that of other methods. Biometrics is still in its infancy, and many new technologies are being developed to improve on accuracy while minimizing user effort.

Computer Failure Controls

"Sorry, our computer systems are down" is a well-known phrase to many end users. A variety of controls can prevent such computer failure or minimize its effects. Computer systems fail for several reasons—power failures, electronic circuitry malfunctions, telecommunications network problems, hidden programming errors, computer viruses, computer operator errors, and electronic vandalism. For example, computers are available with automatic and remote maintenance capabilities. Programs of preventive maintenance of hardware and management of software updates are commonplace. A backup computer system capability can be arranged with *disaster recovery organizations*. Major hardware or software changes are usually carefully scheduled and implemented to avoid problems. Finally, highly trained data center personnel and the use of performance and security management software help keep a company's computer system and networks working properly.

Fault-Tolerant Systems

Many firms also use fault-tolerant computer systems that have redundant processors, peripherals, and software that provide a *fail-over* capability to back up components in the event of system failure. This system may provide a *fail-safe* capability so that the computer system continues to operate at the same level even if there is a major hardware or software failure. Many fault-tolerant computer systems, however, offer a *fail-soft* capability so that the computer system can continue to operate at a reduced but acceptable level in the event of a major system failure. Figure 13.20 outlines some of the fault-tolerant capabilities used in many computer systems and networks.

What If the Internet Went Down . . . and Didn't Come Back Up?

Yes. We know we all rely on the Internet. But how much?

Imagine, if you will, a world with no Internet. No e-mail. No e-commerce. And no BlackBerrys. E-mail would be supplanted by snail mail; cell phones by land lines.

Now imagine what the future would look like. Futurists say virtual business services of all sorts, accounting, payroll and even sales would come to a halt, as would many companies.

If the Internet were to cease functioning today, the effect would be similar for many people. Increasingly, we are growing up with ubiquitous communication, information at our fingertips, and shopping at the click of a mouse. Many businesses would also come to a crashing halt. Customer lists consisting solely of e-mail addresses are singularly useless without e-mail, and online brochures and catalogs are simply computer wallpaper without the wherewithal to allow potential customers to browse them. And for software developers and others who rely on customer downloads and online credit card payments, the business world would come to an end until they completely rebuilt their business model.

Yes, the corporate landscape would certainly have a very different look, and a lot of businesses would definitely not be able to adjust. Amazon.com? Forget it. E-Bay—gone. E-Trade—bye-bye. In fact, any online shopping would be toast, unless it was conducted through a proprietary service using its dedicated lines (at considerably higher cost). So would payment systems that depend on Internet connections, payroll services, online banking, and Web-based backup services and customer support.

And a lot of media outlets that have moved most of their operations online would scramble madly to resurrect hard copy and its associated advertising revenues.

And don't even think about the blind panic of last-minute Christmas shopping without all those e-tailers promising next-day delivery!

On the plus side, we'd be forever rid of those infernal "male member enhancement" e-mail messages and the kind offers of millions of dollars from strangers on foreign shores that clutter up our inboxes. "One of the things which would disappear with the Internet would be machine-made fame. Modern mass communications have created centripetal attention structures that bottle celebrity, and celebrities, for sale," says futurist Thornton May. "Our adoration of princesses, movie stars, and basketball players would come to an end. This is not necessarily a bad thing."

Could we really go back to the pre-Internet days over time? "We wouldn't do that. We'd recreate the Internet," says May. He adds, "Would Net2 that would be erected to replace Net1 be better? And how long would it take to get Net2 up?"

And then how long would it take us to catch up with our e-mail?

Source: Adapted from Lynn Greiner, "What If the Internet Went Down . . . and Didn't Come Back Up?" *CIO*, January 15, 2008.

FIGURE 13.20

Methods of fault tolerance in computer-based information systems.

Layer	Threats	Fault-Tolerant Methods
Applications	Environment, hardware, and software faults	Application-specific redundancy and rollback to previous checkpoint
Systems	Outages	System isolation, data security, system integrity
Databases	Data errors	Separation of transactions and safe updates, complete transaction histories, backup files
Networks	Transmission errors	Reliable controllers; safe asynchrony and handshaking; alternative routing; error-detecting and error-correcting codes
Processes	Hardware and software faults	Alternative computations, rollback to checkpoints
Files	Media errors	Replication of critical data on different media and sites; archiving, backup, retrieval
Processors	Hardware faults	Instruction retry; error-correcting codes in memory and processing; replication; multiple processors and memories

Disaster Recovery

Natural and human-made disasters do happen. Hurricanes, earthquakes, fires, floods, criminal and terrorist acts, and human error can all severely damage an organization's computing resources and thus the health of the organization itself. Many companies, especially online e-commerce retailers and wholesalers, airlines, banks, and Internet service providers, for example, are crippled by losing even a few hours of computing power. Many firms could survive only a few days without computing facilities. That's why organizations develop disaster recovery procedures and formalize them in a *disaster recovery plan*. It specifies which employees will participate in disaster recovery and what their duties will be; what hardware, software, and facilities will be used; and the priority of applications that will be processed. Arrangements with other companies for use of alternative facilities as a disaster recovery site and off-site storage of an organization's databases are also part of an effective disaster recovery effort.

System Controls and Audits

Two final security management requirements that need to be mentioned are the development of information system controls and auditing business systems. Let's take a brief look at these two security measures.

Information System Controls

Information system controls are methods and devices that attempt to ensure the accuracy, validity, and propriety of information system activities. Information system (IS) controls must be developed to ensure proper data entry, processing techniques, storage methods, and information output. Thus, IS controls are designed to monitor and maintain the quality and security of the input, processing, output, and storage activities of any information system. See Figure 13.21.

For example, IS controls are needed to ensure the proper entry of data into a business system and thus avoid the garbage in, garbage out (GIGO) syndrome. Examples include passwords and other security codes, formatted data entry screens, and audible error signals. Computer software can include instructions to identify incorrect, invalid, or improper input data as it enters the computer system. For example, a data entry program can check for invalid codes, data fields, and transactions, and conduct "reasonableness checks" to determine if input data exceed specified limits or are out of sequence.

FIGURE 13.21

Examples of information system controls. Note that they are designed to monitor and maintain the quality and security of the input, processing, output, and storage activities of an information system.

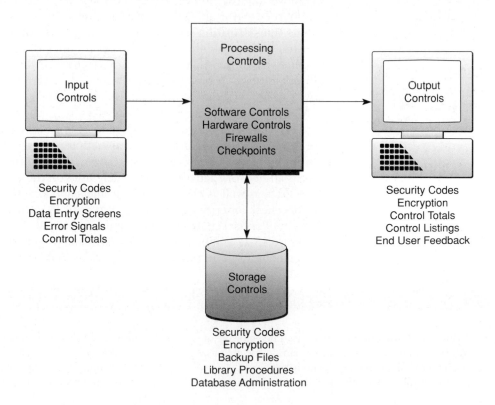

Input Controls

Security Codes
Encryption
Data Entry Screens
Error Signals
Control Totals

Processing Controls

Software Controls
Hardware Controls
Firewalls
Checkpoints

Output Controls

Security Codes
Encryption
Control Totals
Control Listings
End User Feedback

Storage Controls

Security Codes
Encryption
Backup Files
Library Procedures
Database Administration

FIGURE 13.22

How to protect yourself from cyber-crime and other computer security threats.

Security Management for Internet Users	
1. Use antivirus and firewall software and update it often to keep destructive programs off your computer.	6. Use the most up-to-date version of your Web browser, e-mail software, and other programs.
2. Don't allow online merchants to store your credit card information for future purchases.	7. Send credit card numbers only to secure sites; look for a padlock or key icons at the bottom of the browser.
3. Use a hard-to-guess password that contains a mix of numbers and letters, and change it frequently.	8. Use a security program that gives you control over "cookies" that send information back to Web sites.
4. Use different passwords for different Web sites and applications to keep hackers guessing.	9. Install firewall software to screen traffic if you use DSL or a cable modem to connect to the Net.
5. Install all operating system patches and upgrades.	10. Don't open e-mail attachments unless you know the source of the incoming message.

Auditing IT Security

IT security management should be periodically examined, or audited, by a company's internal auditing staff or external auditors from professional accounting firms. Such audits review and evaluate whether proper and adequate security measures and management policies have been developed and implemented. This process typically involves verifying the accuracy and integrity of the software used, as well as the input of data and output produced by business applications. Some firms employ special computer security auditors for this assignment. They may use special test data to check processing accuracy and the control procedures built into the software. The auditors may develop special test programs or use audit software packages.

Another important objective of business system audits is testing the integrity of an application's *audit trail*. An audit trail can be defined as the presence of documentation that allows a transaction to be traced through all stages of its information processing. This journey may begin with a transaction's appearance on a source document and end with its transformation into information in a final output document or report. The audit trail of manual information systems is quite visible and easy to trace. However, computer-based information systems have changed the form of the audit trail. Now auditors must know how to search electronically through disk and tape files of past activity to follow the audit trail of today's networked computer systems.

Many times, this *electronic audit trail* takes the form of *control logs* that automatically record all computer network activity on magnetic disk or tape devices. This audit feature can be found on many online transaction processing systems, performance and security monitors, operating systems, and network control programs. Software that records all network activity is also widely used on the Internet, especially the World Wide Web, as well as on corporate intranets and extranets. Such an audit trail helps auditors check for errors or fraud, but also helps IS security specialists trace and evaluate the trail of hacker attacks on computer networks.

Figure 13.22 summarizes 10 security management steps you can take to protect your computer system resources from hacking and other forms of cyber-crime.

Summary

- **Ethical and Societal Dimensions.** The vital role of information technologies and systems in society raises serious ethical and societal issues in terms of their impact on employment, individuality, working conditions, privacy, health, and computer crime, as illustrated in Figure 13.2.

  Employment issues include the loss of jobs—a result of computerization and automation of work—versus the jobs created to supply and support new information technologies and the business applications they make possible. The impact on working conditions involves the issues of computer monitoring of employees and the quality of the working conditions of the jobs that use information technologies heavily. The effect of IT on individuality addresses the issues of the depersonalization, regimentation, and inflexibility of some computerized business systems.

Employees' heavy use of computer workstations for long periods raises issues about and may cause work-related health disorders. The use of IT to access or collect private information without authorization, as well as for computer profiling, computer matching, computer monitoring, and computer libel and censorship, raises serious privacy issues. Computer crime issues surround activities such as hacking, computer viruses and worms, cyber-theft, unauthorized use at work, software piracy, and piracy of intellectual property.

Managers, business professionals, and IS specialists can help solve the problems of improper use of IT by assuming their ethical responsibilities for the ergonomic design, beneficial use, and enlightened management of information technologies in our society.

● **Ethical Responsibility in Business.** Business and IT activities involve many ethical considerations. Basic principles of technology and business ethics can serve as guidelines for business professionals when dealing with ethical business issues that may arise in the widespread use of information technology in business and society. Examples include theories of corporate social responsibility, which outline the ethical responsibility of management and employees to a company's stockholders, stakeholders, and society, and the four principles of technology ethics summarized in Figure 13.4.

● **Security Management.** One of the most important responsibilities of the management of a company is to ensure the security and quality of its IT-enabled business activities. Security management tools and policies can ensure the accuracy, integrity, and safety of the information systems and resources of a company and thus minimize errors, fraud, and security losses in its business activities. Examples mentioned in the chapter include the use of encryption of confidential business data, firewalls, e-mail monitoring, antivirus software, security codes, backup files, security monitors, biometric security measures, computer failure controls, fault-tolerant systems, disaster recovery measures, information system controls, and security audits of business systems.

Key Terms and Concepts

These are the key terms and concepts of this chapter. The page number of their first explanation is in parentheses.

1. Antivirus software (598)
2. Audit trail (604)
3. Backup files (599)
4. Biometric security (600)
5. Business ethics (562)
6. Computer crime (568)
7. Computer matching (582)
8. Computer monitoring (585)
9. Computer virus (576)
10. Cyber law (584)
11. Disaster recovery (603)
12. Distributed denial of service (DDOS) (595)
13. Encryption (593)
14. Ergonomics (587)
15. Ethical foundations (562)
16. Fault tolerant (601)
17. Firewall (594)
18. Flaming (584)
19. Hacking (569)
20. Information system controls (603)
21. Intellectual property theft (575)
22. Opt-in/Opt-out (580)
23. Passwords (599)
24. Security management (589)
25. Societal solutions (587)
26. Software piracy (574)
27. Spamming (584)
28. Spyware/Adware (578)
29. System security monitor (600)
30. Unauthorized use (573)

Review Quiz

Match one of the key terms and concepts listed previously with one of the brief examples or definitions that follow. Try to find the best fit for the answers that seem to fit more than one term or concept. Defend your choices.

_____ 1. Ensuring the accuracy, integrity, and safety of business/IT activities and resources.

_____ 2. Control totals, error signals, backup files, and security codes are examples.

_____ 3. Software that can control access and use of a computer system.

_____ 4. A computer system can continue to operate even after a major system failure if it has this capability.

_____ 5. A computer system that serves as a filter for access to and from other networks by a company's networked computers.

_____ 6. Laws and regulations focused on issues related to the Internet and other forms of networked communications.

_____ 7. The presence of documentation that allows a transaction to be traced through all stages of information processing.

_____ 8. Using your voice or fingerprints to identify yourself electronically.

_____ 9. A plan to continue IS operations during an emergency.

_____ 10. Scrambling data during its transmission.

_____ 11. Ethical choices may result from decision-making processes, cultural values, or behavioral stages.

_____ 12. Managers must confront numerous ethical questions in their businesses.

_____ 13. Sending unsolicited e-mail indiscriminately.

_____ 14. Software that can infect a machine and transmit private information back to its owner.

_____ 15. Two different perspectives on the use of private information.

_____ 16. Using computers to identify individuals that fit a certain profile.

_____ 17. Using computers to monitor the activities of workers.

_____ 18. Overwhelming a Web site with requests for service from captive computers.

_____ 19. Using computers and networks to steal money, services, software, or data.

_____ 20. Using company computers to access the Internet during work hours for personal business.

_____ 21. Unauthorized copying of software.

_____ 22. Unauthorized copying of copyrighted material.

_____ 23. Electronic breaking and entering into a computer system.

_____ 24. A program that makes copies of itself and destroys data and programs.

_____ 25. Finds and eliminates computer viruses.

_____ 26. Sending extremely critical, derogatory, and vulgar e-mail messages.

_____ 27. Designing computer hardware, software, and workstations that are safe, comfortable, and easy to use.

_____ 28. Applications of information technology that have beneficial effects for society at large.

_____ 29. Duplicate files of programs or data that are periodically copied and stored elsewhere in case the original is damaged and needs to be restored.

_____ 30. A piece of data, known only to an authorized user, that is used to gain access to a system.

Discussion Questions

1. What can be done to improve the security of business uses of the Internet? Give several examples of security measures and technologies you would use.

2. What potential security problems do you see in the increasing use of intranets and extranets in business? What might be done to solve such problems? Give several examples.

3. Refer to the real-world example about copying CDs and music downloading in the chapter. Is copying music CDs an ethical practice? How about Internet music downloading? Explain.

4. What are your major concerns about computer crime and privacy on the Internet? What can you do about it? Explain.

5. What is disaster recovery? How could it be implemented at your school or work?

6. Refer to the Real World Case on data exfiltration. Most or all companies have a security and compliance program of some sort, but not all of them "live" by it.

What does it take for a company to take this next step? What is the role of IT in that scenario?

7. Is there an ethical crisis in business today? What role does information technology play in unethical business practices?

8. What are several business decisions that you will have to make as a manager that have both ethical and IT dimensions? Give examples to illustrate your answer.

9. Refer to the Real World Case on endpoint security in the chapter. How do companies strike a balance between providing users with access to the information they need in the form that is most useful to them, while at the same time enforcing adequate security? What issues should organizations consider when making this decision?

10. What would be examples of one positive and one negative effect of the use of information technologies in each of the ethical and societal dimensions illustrated in Figure 13.2? Explain several of your choices.

Analysis Exercises

1. Problems with Passwords
Authentication

Network and application managers need to know who is accessing their systems to determine appropriate access levels. Typically, they require that users create secret passwords. A secret password, known only to the user, allows an administrator to feel confident that a user is who the user says he or she is. Systems administrators even have the authority to determine the characteristics of passwords. For example, they may set a minimum length and require that a password include numbers, symbols, or mixed letter case. They may also require that a user change his or her password every few weeks or months. These approaches have numerous problems:

- Users often forget complicated or frequently changing passwords, resulting in frequent calls to a help desk. The help-desk employee then faces the burden of identifying the employee by some other means and resetting the password. This process takes time and is subject to social engineering.

- Users may write down their passwords. However, this leaves passwords subject to discovery and theft.

- Users often pick the same password for many different accounts, which means that someone who discovers one of these passwords then has the "keys" to all the accounts.

- Users may pick an easy-to-remember password, which is easy to anticipate and therefore easy to guess. Password-cracking programs cycle through entire dictionaries of English language words and common word/number combinations such as "smart1" or "2smart4U."

- Users may give away their passwords over the phone (social engineering) or via e-mail (phishing, a type of social engineering) to individuals representing themselves as a system administrator. Perhaps you have already received e-mails purportedly from a financial institution claiming identity or account difficulties and asking you to "reconfirm" your account information on their authentic-looking Web site.

As you can see, using passwords to identify a person is fraught with problems. Here are some alternatives to explore. Look up each authentication approach listed below on the Internet, describe the method in your own words (be sure to cite your sources), and briefly list the advantages and disadvantages.

a. Biometrics (biological measuring)
b. Smart cards
c. Biochips

2. Your Internet Job Rights
Three Ethical Scenarios

Whether you're an employer or an employee, you should know what your rights are when it comes to Internet use in the workplace. Mark Grossman, a Florida attorney who specializes in computer and Internet law, gives answers to some basic questions.

- **Scenario 1:** Nobody told you that your Internet use in the office was being monitored. Now you've been warned you'll be fired if you use the Internet for recreational surfing again. What are your rights?

  Bottom line: When you're using your office computer, you essentially have no rights. You'd have a tough time convincing a court that the boss invaded your privacy by monitoring your use of the company PC on company time. You should probably be grateful you got a warning.

- **Scenario 2:** Your employees are abusing their Internet privileges, but you don't have an Internet usage policy. What do you do?

  Bottom line: Although the law isn't fully developed in this area, courts are taking a straightforward approach: If it's a company computer, the company can control the way it's used. You don't need an Internet usage policy to prevent inappropriate use of your company computers. To protect yourself in the future, distribute an Internet policy to your employees as soon as possible.

- **Scenario 3:** Employee John Doe downloads adult material to his PC at work, and employee Jane Smith sees it. Smith then proceeds to sue the company for sexual harassment. As the employer, are you liable?

  Bottom line: Whether it comes from the Internet or from a magazine, adult material has no place in the office. So Smith could certainly sue the company for allowing a sexually hostile environment. The best defense is for the company to have an Internet usage policy that prohibits visits to adult sites. Of course, you have to follow through. If someone is looking at adult material in the office, you must at least send the offending employee a written reprimand. If the company lacks a strict Internet policy, though, Smith could prevail in court.

a. Do you agree with the advice of attorney Mark Grossman in each of the scenarios? Why or why not?
b. What would your advice be? Explain your positions.
c. Identify any ethical principles you may be using to explain your position in each of the scenarios.

3. Exploiting Security Weaknesses
Social Engineering

An employee who needs permission to access an electronic workspace, database, or other information systems resource typically fills in a request form and obtains approval from the responsible manager. The manager then routes the request to one of the system's administrators.

Highly trusted and well-trained systems administrators spend a significant amount of time doing nothing more technical than adding or removing names from access control lists. In large organizations, it's not unusual for systems administrators to have never met any of the people involved in a specific request. The administrators may not even work in the same office.

Hackers have learned to take advantage of this approach to access authorization. They begin by probing an organization. The hacker doesn't expect to compromise the system during this initial probe. He or she just starts by making a few phone calls to learn who is responsible for granting access and how to apply. A little more probing helps the hacker learn who's who within the organization's structure. Some organizations even post this information online in the form of employee directories. With this information in hand, the hacker knows whom to talk to, what to ask for, and what names to use to sound convincing. The hacker is now ready to try to impersonate an employee and trick a systems administrator into revealing a password and unwittingly granting unauthorized access.

Organizations determine who needs access to which applications. They also need a system through which they can authenticate the identity of an individual making a request. Finally, they need to manage this process both effectively and inexpensively.

a. Describe the business problems that this exercise presents.
b. Suggest several ways to reduce an organization's exposure to social engineering.
c. Prepare an orientation memo to new hires in your IT department describing "social engineering." Suggest several ways employees can avoid being tricked by hackers.

4. Privacy Statements
The Spyware Problem
Web surfers may feel anonymous as they use the Internet, but that feeling isn't always justified. IP addresses, cookies, site log-in procedures, and credit card purchases all help track how often users visit a site and what pages they view. Some companies go further.

Some free screensaver software and peer-to-peer file sharing come with "spyware" embedded within their applications. Once loaded, these applications run in the background. What they actually track depends on the specific software. To stay on the "right side" of U.S. law, these companies outline their software's functions in general terms and include this information in the small print within their end-user licensing agreement (EULA) and/or privacy policy. In fact, these agreements may even include a stipulation that users not disable any part of their software as a condition for free use.

Because most users don't read these policies, they have no idea what privacy rights they may have given up. They indeed get their free file-sharing program or screen saver, but they may be getting a lot more. Some spyware programs even remain on hard drives and stay active after users have uninstalled their "free" software.

a. Use a search engine to search for "spyware," "spyware removal," "adware," or other related terms. Prepare a one-page summary of your results. Include URLs for online sources.
b. Select three of your favorite Web sites and print out their privacy policies. What do they share in common? How do they differ?
c. Write your own Web site privacy policy, striking a balance between customer and business needs.

REAL WORLD CASE 3

Ethics, Moral Dilemmas, and Tough Decisions: The Many Challenges of Working in IT

What Bryan found on an executive's computer six years ago still weighs heavily on his mind. He's particularly troubled that the man he discovered using a company PC to view pornography of Asian women and of children was subsequently promoted and moved to China to run a manufacturing plant. "To this day, I regret not taking that stuff to the FBI." It happened when Bryan, who asked that his last name not be published, was IT director at the U.S. division of a $500 million multinational corporation based in Germany.

The company's Internet usage policy, which Bryan helped develop with input from senior management, prohibited the use of company computers to access pornographic or adult-content Web sites. One of Bryan's duties was to use products from SurfControl PLC to monitor employee Web surfing and to report any violations to management.

Bryan knew that the executive, who was a level above him in another department, was popular within both the U.S. division and the German parent. Yet when the tools turned up dozens of pornographic Web sites visited by the executive's computer, Bryan followed the policy.

"That's what it's there for. I wasn't going to get into trouble for following the policy," he reasoned.

Bryan's case is a good example of the ethical dilemmas that IT workers may encounter on the job. IT employees have privileged access to digital information, both personal and professional, throughout the company, and they have the technical prowess to manipulate that information. That gives them both the power and responsibility to monitor and report employees who break company rules. IT professionals may also uncover evidence that a coworker is, say, embezzling funds, or they could be tempted to peek at private salary information or personal e-mails. There's little guidance, however, on what to do in these uncomfortable situations.

In the case of the porn-viewing executive, Bryan didn't get into trouble, but neither did the executive, who came up with "a pretty outlandish explanation" that the company accepted, Bryan says. He considered going to the FBI, but the Internet bubble had just burst and jobs were hard to come by. "It was a tough choice," Bryan says. "But I had a family to feed."

Perhaps it would ease Bryan's conscience to know that he did just what labor attorney Linn Hynds, a senior partner at Honigman Miller Schwartz and Cohn LLP, would have advised in his case. "Let the company handle it," she says. "Make sure you report violations to the right person in your company, and show them the evidence. After that, leave it to the people who are supposed to be making that decision." Ideally, corporate policy takes over where the law stops, governing workplace ethics to clear up gray areas and remove personal judgment from the equation as much as possible.

"If you don't set out your policy and your guidelines, if you don't make sure that people know what they are and understand them, you're in no position to hold workers accountable," says John Reece, a former chief information officer at the Internal Revenue Service and Time Warner Inc.

Having clear ethical guidelines also lets employees off the hook emotionally if the person they discover breaking the policy is a friend, someone who reports to them directly, or a supervisor, says Reece, who is now head of consultancy at John C. Reece and Associates LLC. Organizations that have policies in place often focus on areas where they had trouble in the past or emphasize whatever they are most worried about. When Reece was at the IRS, for example, the biggest emphasis was on protecting the confidentiality of taxpayer information.

At the U.S. Department of Defense, policies usually emphasize procurement rules, notes Stephen Northcutt, president of the SANS Technology Institute and author of *IT Ethics Handbook: Right and Wrong for IT Professionals*. Adding to the complexity, an organization that depends on highly skilled workers might be more lenient. When Northcutt worked in IT security at the Naval Surface Warfare Center in Virginia, it was a rarefied atmosphere of highly sought-after PhDs. "I was told pretty clearly that if I made a whole lot of PhDs very unhappy so that they left, the organization wouldn't need me anymore," says Northcutt.

Of course, that wasn't written in any policy manual, so Northcutt had to read between the lines. "The way I interpreted it was: Child pornography, turn that in," he says. "But if the leading mathematician wants to download some pictures of naked girls, they didn't want to hear from me."

Northcutt says that he did find child porn on two occasions and that both events led to prosecution. As for other offensive photos that he encountered, Northcutt pointed out to his superiors that there might be a legal liability, citing a Supreme Court decision that found that similar pictures at a military installation indicated a pervasive atmosphere of sexual harassment. That did the trick. "Once they saw that law was involved, they were more willing to change culture and policy," Northcutt says.

When policies aren't clear, ethical decisions are left to the judgment of IT employees, which varies by person and the particular circumstances. For example, Gary, a director of technology at a nonprofit organization in the Midwest, flat-out refused when the assistant chief executive officer wanted to use a mailing list that a new employee had stolen from her former employer. Yet Gary, who asked that his last name not be used, didn't stop his boss from installing unlicensed software on PCs for a short time, although he refused to do it himself. "The question is, how much was it really going to hurt anybody? We were still going to have 99.5 percent compliant software. I was OK with that."

He says he uninstalled it, with his boss's approval, as soon as he could, which was about a week later.

Northcutt argues that the IT profession should have two things that professions such as law or accounting have had for years: a code of ethics and standards of practice. That way, when company policy is nonexistent or unclear, IT professionals still have standards to follow.

That might be useful for Tim, a systems administrator who works at a Fortune 500 agricultural business. When Tim, who asked that his last name not be published, happened across an unencrypted spreadsheet of salary information on a manager's PC, he copied it. He didn't share the information with anyone or use it to his advantage. It was an impulsive act, he admits, that stemmed from frustration with his employer. "I didn't take it for nefarious reasons; I just took it to prove that I could," he says.

Tim's actions point to a disturbing trend: IT workers are justifying their ethically questionable behavior. That path can end in criminal activity, says fraud investigator Chuck Martell. "We started seeing a few cases about seven or eight years ago," says Martell, managing director of investigative services at Veritas Global LLC, a security firm in Southfield, Michigan. "Now we're investigating a tremendous amount of them."

Whole Foods Market Chairman and CEO John Mackey spent years earning a positive reputation as a corporate leader who was not afraid to take a stand on ethics issues. Before other companies figured out that it pays to be environmentally friendly, Whole Foods led by setting standards for humane animal treatment. In 2006, Mackey took the bold step of reducing his own annual salary to one dollar, pledging money instead for an emergency fund for his staff. Not shy about expressing his views, Mackey challenged leading thinkers, like Nobel Prize–winner Milton Friedman, on business ethics issues. Like many leaders, Mackey seemed to relish the public spotlight.

On July 20, 2007, however, Mackey got more than he bargained for in terms of publicity. *The Wall Street Journal* reported that Mackey had long used the pseudonym "Rahodeb" to make postings in Yahoo Finance forums that flattered his own company and leveled criticisms against the competition. Serious financial and possibly legal repercussions continue to unfold from this incident, and the final consequences may not be known for some time.

Amid the furor that followed this disclosure of Mackey's secret online alias, it is vital that we not lose sight of the critical issues it raises about ethics and leadership in a rapidly evolving business world. There is no question that the current climate has prompted many more companies to tackle ethics issues.

By now, "business ethics" is an established part of doing business, not just in the United States, but also increasingly around the world. People no longer joke that "business ethics is an oxymoron," as society has come not merely to expect, but to demand, that business conduct itself according to basic rules of ethics and integrity. Business will always need to pay attention to ethics and leadership, but these lessons are continually challenged by new developments, including technological advances that promote new kinds of communication online. Business leaders cannot afford to overlook these challenges, as even a single misstep can be enough to undo a reputation for ethical leadership.

Source: Adapted from Tam Harbert, "Ethics in IT: Dark Secrets, Ugly Truths—and Little Guidance," *Computerworld*, October 29, 2007; and David Schmidt, "What Is the Moral Responsibility of a Business Leader?" *CIO Magazine*, September 12, 2007.

CASE STUDY QUESTIONS

1. Companies are developing ethical policies and guidelines for legal reasons, but also to clarify what is acceptable and what is not. Do you think any of the issues raised in the case required clarification? Would you take exception to any of them being classified as inappropriate behavior? Why do you think these things happen anyway?

2. In the first example (Bryan's), it is apparent that he did not believe justice had been ultimately served by the decision his company made. Should he have taken the issue to the authorities? Or was it enough that he reported the problem through the proper channels and let the organization handle it, as was the recommendation of Linn Hynds? Provide a rationale for the position you are willing to take on this matter.

3. In the case, Gary chose not to stop his boss from installing unlicensed software, although he refused to do it himself. If installing unlicensed software is wrong, is there any difference between refusing to do it versus not stopping somebody else? Do you buy his argument that it was not really going to hurt anybody? Why or why not?

REAL WORLD ACTIVITIES

1. Go online to follow up on John Mackey's story and search for other instances of debatable behavior where IT has been an important factor. Are the ones featured in the case exceptions, or are these occurrences becoming more and more common? How do organizations seem to be coping with these issues? What type of responses did you find? Prepare a report to summarize your findings.

2. The case features many examples of what is arguably unethical behavior, including child pornography, accessing adult content on company-owned equipment, installing unlicensed software, and so on. Are some of these practices "more wrong" than others? Is there any one that you would not consider problematic? Break into small groups to discuss these questions, and make a list of other ethical problems involving IT that were not mentioned in the case.

REAL WORLD CASE 4

Raymond James Financial, BCD Travel, Houston Texans, and Others: Worrying about What Goes Out, Not What Comes In

It's not what's coming into the corporate network that concerns Gene Fredriksen; it's what's going out. For the chief security officer at securities brokerage Raymond James Financial Inc. in St. Petersburg, Florida, leakage of sensitive customer data or proprietary information is the new priority. The problem isn't just content within e-mail messages, but the explosion of alternative communication mechanisms that employees are using, including instant messaging, blogs, FTP transfers, Web mail, and message boards. It's not enough to just monitor e-mail, Fredriksen says. "We have to evolve and change at the same pace as the business," he explains. "Things are coming much faster."

So Fredriksen is rolling out a network-based outbound content monitoring and control system. The software, from San Francisco–based Vontu Inc., sits on the network and monitors traffic in much the same way that a network-based intrusion-detection system would. Rather than focusing on inbound traffic, however, Vontu monitors the network activity that originates from Raymond James's 16,000 users. It examines the contents of each network packet in real time and issues alerts when policy violations are found.

Network-based systems do more than just rule-based scanning for Social Security numbers and other easily identifiable content. They typically analyze sensitive documents and content types and generate a unique fingerprint for each. Administrators then establish policies that relate to that content, and the system uses linguistic analysis to identify sensitive data and enforce those policies as information moves across the corporate LAN. The systems can detect both complete documents and "derivative documents," such as an IM exchange in which a user has pasted a document fragment.

When BCD Travel began to investigate what it would take to get Payment Card Industry (PCI) certification for handling customer credit card data, Brian Flynn, senior vice president of technology, realized that he didn't really know how his employees were handling such information. Not only could PCI certification be denied, but the travel agency's reputation and business could also be harmed. At the National Football League's Houston Texans, IT Director Nick Ignatiev came to the same realization as he investigated PCI certification.

In both cases, vendors they'd been working with suggested a new technology: outbound content management tools that look for proprietary information that might be leaving the company via e-mail, instant messaging, or other avenues. Flynn started to use Reconnex's iGuard network appliance, with vivid results. "It was a shock to see what was going out, and that gave us the insight to take action," he says. After Ignatiev examined his message flow using Palisade Systems's PacketSure appliance, he too realized that his employees needed to do a better job protecting critical data, including customer credit cards, scouting reports, and team rosters.

How does the technology work? Basically, the tools filter outgoing communication across a variety of channels, such as e-mail and IM, to identify sensitive information. They're based on some of the same technologies—like pattern matching and contextual text search—that help antivirus and antispam tools block incoming threats.

Tools typically come with basic patterns already defined for personally identifiable information, such as Social Security and credit card numbers, as well as templates for commonly private information, such as legal filings, personnel data, and product testing results.

Companies typically look for three types of information using these tools, notes Paul Kocher, president of the Cryptography Research consultancy. The first, and easiest, type is personally identifiable information, such as Social Security numbers and credit card information. The second type is confidential company information, such as product specifications, payroll information, legal files, or supplier contracts. Although this information is harder to identify, most tools can uncover patterns of language and presentation when given enough samples, Kocher notes. The third category is inappropriate use of company resources, such as potentially offensive communications involving race.

The traditional security methods may restrict sensitive data to legitimate users, but Flynn and Ignatiev found that even legitimate users were putting the data, and their companies, at risk. At BCD Travel, a corporate travel service, nearly 80 percent of its 10,000 employees work in call centers and thus have legitimate access to sensitive customer information. BCD and the Texans did not find malicious activity; instead, they found people who were unaware of security risks, such as sending a customer's credit card number by e-mail to book a flight or room from a vendor that didn't have an online reservations system.

Fidelity Bancshares Inc. in West Palm Beach, Florida, is using the message-blocking feature in PortAuthority from PortAuthority Technologies Inc. in Palo Alto, California. Outbound e-mail messages that contain Social Security numbers, account numbers, loan numbers, or other personal financial data are intercepted and returned to the user, along with instructions on how to send the e-mail securely.

Joe Cormier, vice president of network services, says he also uses PortAuthority to catch careless replies. Customers often send in questions and include their account information. "The customer service rep would reply back without modifying the e-mail," he says.

"The challenge with any system like this is they're only as valuable as the mitigation procedures you have on the back end," notes Fredriksen. Another key to success is educating users about monitoring to avoid "Big Brother" implications. "We are making sure that the users understand why we implement systems like this and what they're being used for, he says.

Mark Rizzo, vice president of operations and platform engineering at Perpetual Entertainment Inc. in San Francisco, learned in a previous job the consequences of not protecting intellectual property. "I have been on the side of things disappearing and showing up at competitors," he says. The start-up online game developer deployed Tablus's Content Alarm to remedy the problem. Rizzo uses it to look for suspicious activity, such as large files that are moving outside the corporate LAN. Now that the basic policies and rules have been set, the system doesn't require much ongoing maintenance, he says. Still, Rizzo doesn't use blocking because he would need to spend significant amounts of time to create more policies in order to avoid false positives.

Although companies in highly regulated industries can justify investing in outbound content monitoring and blocking tools, other organizations may have to sharpen their pencils to justify the cost. These are very expensive solutions to deploy. Fredriksen, who built a system to support 16,000 users, says that for a setup with about 20,000 users, "you're in the $200,000 range, easily."

With outbound content management tools, "you can build very sophisticated concept filters," says Cliff Shnier, vice president for the financial advisory and litigation practice at Aon Consulting. Typically, the tools come with templates for types of data that most enterprises want to filter, and they can analyze contents of servers and databases to derive filters for company-specific information, he says.

(Consulting firms can improve these filters using linguists and subject matter experts.)

As any user of an antispam tool knows, no filter is perfect. "A big mistake is to have too much faith in the tools. They can't replace trust and education," says consultant Kocher. They also won't stop a determined thief, he says.

Even when appropriately deployed, these tools don't create an ironclad perimeter around the enterprise. For example, they can't detect information that flows through Skype voice over IP (VoIP) service or SSL (Secure Sockets Layer) connections, Kocher notes. They can also flood logs with false positives, which makes it hard for IT security staff to identify real problems.

That's why chief information officers should look at outbound content management as a supplemental tool to limit accidental or unknowing communication of sensitive data, not as the primary defense. Fredriksen says that although Vontu is important, it's still just one piece of a larger strategy that includes an overlapping set of controls that Raymond James uses to combat insider threats. "This augments the intrusion–detection and firewall systems we have that control and block specific ports," he says. "It's just a piece. It's not the Holy Grail."

Source: Adapted from Galen Gruman, "Boost Security with Outbound Content Management," *CIO Magazine*, April 9, 2007; and Robert Mitchell, "Border Patrol: Content Monitoring Systems Inspect Outbound Communications," *Computerworld*, March 6, 2006.

CASE STUDY QUESTIONS

1. Barring illegal activities, why do you think that employees in the organizations featured in the case do not realize themselves the dangers of loosely managing proprietary and sensitive information? Would you have thought of these issues?

2. How should organizations strike the right balance between monitoring and invading their employees' privacy, even if it would be legal for them to do so? Why is it important that companies achieve this balance? What would be the consequences of being too biased to one side?

3. The IT executives in the case all note that outbound monitoring and management technologies are only part of an overall strategy, and not their primary defense. What should be the other components of this strategy? How much weight would you give to human and technological factors? Why?

REAL WORLD ACTIVITIES

1. Technologies such as VoIP used by Skype and similar products make it more difficult to monitor outgoing information. Search the Internet to help you understand these technologies and why these problems arise. Other than banning them, what alternatives would you suggest to companies facing this problem? Prepare a presentation to deliver your recommendations.

2. As a customer of many of the companies noted in the case, or others in the same industries, what is your expectation about the measures and safeguards that these organizations have implemented to protect inappropriate leaking of your personal information? After reading the case, has your expectation changed? Break into small groups with your classmates to discuss these issues.

CHAPTER 14

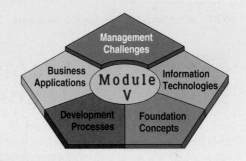

ENTERPRISE AND GLOBAL MANAGEMENT OF INFORMATION TECHNOLOGY

Chapter Highlights

Learning Objectives

1. Identify each of the three components of IT management and use examples to illustrate how they might be implemented in a business.

2. Explain how failures in IT management can be reduced by the involvement of business managers in IT planning and management.

3. Identify several cultural, political, and geoeconomic challenges that confront managers in the management of global information technologies.

4. Explain the effect on global business/IT strategy of the trend toward a transnational business strategy by international business organizations.

5. Identify several considerations that affect the choice of IT applications, IT platforms, data access policies, and systems development methods by a global business enterprise.

6. Understand the fundamental concepts of outsourcing and offshoring, as well as the primary reasons for selecting such an approach to IS/IT management.

| **SECTION I** | # Managing Information Technology |

Business and IT

The strategic and operational importance of information technology in business is no longer questioned. As the 21st century unfolds, many companies throughout the world are intent on transforming themselves into global business powerhouses through major investments in global e-business, e-commerce, and other IT initiatives. Thus, there is a real need for business managers and professionals to understand how to manage this vital organizational function. In this section, we explore how the IS function can be organized and managed, and we emphasize the importance of a customer and business value focus for the management of information technologies. Whether you plan to be an entrepreneur and run your own business, a manager in a corporation, or a business professional, managing information systems and technologies will be one of your major responsibilities. See Figure 14.1.

Read the Real World Case on the next page. We can learn a lot from this case about the many challenges faced by major multinational companies trying to save money and streamline IT budgets.

Managing Information Technology

As we have seen throughout this text, information technology is an essential component of business success for companies today; however, information technology is also a vital business resource that must be properly managed. Thus, we have also seen many real-world examples in which the management of information technologies plays a pivotal role in ensuring the success or contributing to the failure of a company's strategic business initiatives. Therefore, managing the information systems and technologies that support the modern business processes of companies today is a major challenge for both business and IT managers and professionals.

How should information technology be managed? Figure 14.2 illustrates one popular approach to managing information technology in a large company. This managerial approach has three major components:

- **Managing the Joint Development and Implementation of Business/IT Strategies.** Led by the CEO (chief executive officer) and CIO (chief information officer), proposals are developed by business and IT managers and professionals regarding the use of IT to support the strategic business priorities of the company. This business/IT planning process *aligns* IT with strategic business goals. The process also includes evaluating the business case for investing in the development and implementation of each proposed business/IT project.

- **Managing the Development and Implementation of New Business/IT Applications and Technologies.** This step is the primary responsibility of the CIO and CTO (chief technology officer). This area of IT management involves managing the processes for information systems development and implementation we discussed in Chapter 12, as well as the responsibility for research into the strategic business uses of new information technologies.

- **Managing the IT Organization and the IT Infrastructure.** The CIO and IT managers share responsibility for managing the work of IT professionals who are typically organized into a variety of project teams and other organizational subunits. In addition, they are responsible for managing the IT infrastructure of hardware, software, databases, telecommunications networks, and other IT resources, which must be acquired, operated, monitored, and maintained.

Let's look at a real-world example.

REAL WORLD CASE 1

Wasting Money at the Speed of Light

Even in these lean times, where tech budgets are trimmed to the bone, money gets wasted. Companies routinely overspend on software licenses and service-level agreements. It's possible to have too much bandwidth at your disposal and to store too much e-mail on company servers, not to mention the billions of dollars still wasted on paper and ink. These things are dragging your precious IT resources down the drain.

It doesn't have to be this way. Though there's no one-click solution to any of these money wasters, there are ways companies can stop the flow of wasted dollars and use it on the items that will make their IT organization shine. Here are the secrets.

IT's Biggest Money Waster No. 1: Dusty Software Licenses

Collectively, US companies are paying billions for shelfware—whether it's software that was never adopted or for employees they no longer have, and often at prices that are higher than what is actually needed. A 2010 IDC survey of midsize and large businesses found that well over half of enterprise applications are underutilized, with anywhere from 25 percent to more than 75 percent of licenses paid for but unused, noted IDC analyst Amy Konar.

"Organizations typically use less than 50 percent of an installed ERP system and are paying significant licensing and maintenance fees for modules and functionality that are not providing value to the business," said Kathryn Douglass, managing partner of IT consultants WillowTree Advisors.

FIGURE 14.1

E-mail is one of the largest cost centers in IT.

Source: Doug Menuez/Getty Images

"They need to review their named-user licenses and renegotiate agreements to remove unused or duplicate users from licenses. The difference between a 2,000-named-user license and a 1,500-named-user license can easily be $500,000."

Every company should start by collecting information on the software they are paying for and what they actually use, said Schmidt. Asset tracking and license optimization need to account for such details as downgrade rights and second-machine use rights. Global companies may have concurrent agreements that allow them to use one license 24/7, shifting from one physical location to another as the day progresses. Even users of cloud apps need to closely monitor their usage levels—which can be hard to do manually.

For large enterprises, the amount of money left on the table is far from trivial. Procter & Gamble used Flexera's FlexNet Manager Suite to eliminate unnecessary licenses for its Oracle and SAP products, trimming more than $30 million from its annual software budget.

IT's Biggest Money Waster No. 2: The Paper Chase

Despite the influx of digital technology over the past 30 years, U.S. office workers still consume an average of 10,000 pages per person every year—about $80 worth—according to the Lawrence Berkeley National Laboratory. Nearly half of that paper ends up as trash before the day is out.

U.S. corporations spend $120 billion per year on paper forms alone, notes a Xerox study. But the costs don't end at paper. Ounce for ounce, the ink inside a typical printer cartridge is 15 times more expensive than Dom Perignon champagne, according to Chronicle Research. Filing that paper, copying it, mailing it, storing it, and finding it again can add up to more than 30 times the original cost of printing, per a 2005 study by the Minnesota Office of Environmental Assistance.

Get rid of forms that need to be processed by hand, said Paula Selvidge, VP of user experience at PerfectForms, a business process automation company. Simply converting required forms from paper to digital instantly saved $10,000 for one school in Fremont, California, Selvidge said.

Get employees to stop needlessly printing all or parts of e-mails, Web pages, or other electronic documents that don't really need to be on paper, said Kent Dunn, VP of sales and business development for GreenPrint. GreenPrint claims an enterprise with 5,000 PCs will avoid printing some 6.3 million pages, saving nearly $400,000 annually.

Even moving from cutting paper checks to using electronic deposits will save one pound of paper per employee each year, saving employers an average of $176 per head, according to a study conducted by Javelin Research and sponsored by PayItGreen, a coalition of electronic payments vendors.

IT's Biggest Money Waster No. 3: Gold-Plated Service-Level Agreements

Whether it's for help desk services, Web hosting, or server uptime guarantees, too many IT organizations are paying for Lexus-level service when a Toyota Camry SLA is more than adequate.

"Most sourcing agreements for IT services include amazingly high service levels," said Matthew H. Podowitz, independent IT consultant and author of The IT Value Challenge blog. "But how many businesses really require 99.999 uptime 24 hours a day, 7 days a week?"

That five-nines uptime agreement may mean your site or servers will only be unavailable for perhaps 15 minutes per year, he added. "But if you paid for only 98.5 percent uptime, and your systems went down for maybe a dozen hours a year, so what?"

Unless that downtime puts you at a competitive disadvantage or causes revenue to slip through the cracks, it probably won't make a difference, he said. There are exceptions, of course. If you're a county government, you don't want to reduce the uptime for your 911 emergency service, but your accounting data probably doesn't need to be accessible 24/7/365.

The hardest part said Baschab? Deciding what services are essential and which are merely optional. "The most difficult part is separating the needed services vs. the 'fat' that can creep in over time," he added. "This requires careful analysis and considerable experience in benchmarking, IT demand management, service-level setting, and governance."

IT's Biggest Money Waster No. 4: The E-mail Monster

It's widely understood that e-mail is a productivity drain, but it also drains money out of an organization in terms of storage, maintenance, software licenses, server upkeep, and the constant battle against spam, malware, and data leaks. It's a problem that will only get worse.

Netizens sent 247 billion e-mails a day in 2009, per the Radicati Group, with enterprise e-mail accounting for roughly a quarter of that total. By 2013, e-mail volume will double—creating a massive storage headache for enterprises.

"Resources consumed by e-mail messages and their attachments are a major concern for many companies," said WillowTree's Douglass. "A 10,000-user organization without mailbox policies consumes an average of 30GB of storage per day from e-mail messages alone."

Using software configurations or an enterprise e-mail management tool in conjunction with an e-mail archive policy can cut storage costs by managing retention, enforcing limits on the size of file attachments, and redirecting users to third-party collaboration tools like SharePoint, where large files can be shared more efficiently, said Douglass. But others argue that the proper place for e-mail is the cloud, where the rising storage, maintenance, and security concerns are somebody else's problem.

IT's Biggest Money Waster No. 5: Excess Bandwidth

You can't have too much bandwidth at your disposal—at least, that's the common belief. But many companies are wasting their money on bandwidth they don't really need instead of doing a better job managing the bandwidth they already have, said Andrew Rubin, CEO of network visibility/optimization provider Cymtec. If a problem arises anywhere on the network, IT's first response is almost always to throw more bandwidth at it, he said.

"If you've got a T1 line, then it's time for a T3. Still too slow? Then go for a 100Mb pipe. But when they look at their actual bandwidth usage they find out they've got a 100Mb pipe but are only using 1 percent of it."

"Deep down, ambitious executives believe they will be the next eBay, and that's a good thing," Woods said. "So when it comes time to build, small companies buy expensive servers or managed hosting ('to grow into') when Amazon's cloud will serve them surpassingly well. Medium-sized companies buy elaborate blade infrastructure and Tier 1 bandwidth in major markets like New York or San Francisco, when they only need downmarket hardware and more affordable hosting solutions. And they will never meet a salesperson who doesn't agree."

Source: Adapted from Dan Tynan, "Biggest Money Wasters in IT," *Computerworld Hong Kong*, Questex Media, November 16, 2010.

CASE STUDY QUESTIONS

1. The case notes one of the hardest parts to adjusting service-level costs is deciding which services are essential and which ones are optional. How would you go about this?

2. How can an organization get control of employees printing unnecessarily? Is it even feasible?

3. Most people would argue that e-mail is an essential part of their workflow and communications, yet it is a huge cost drain. What is the answer?

REAL WORLD ACTIVITIES

1. Go online and research the IT budgets of various companies. Prepare a report and compare different budgets for similar companies.

2. The case mentions five big money wasters in IT. Can you think of more? Can you find solutions?

FIGURE 14.2

The major components of information technology management. Note the executives with primary responsibilities in each area.

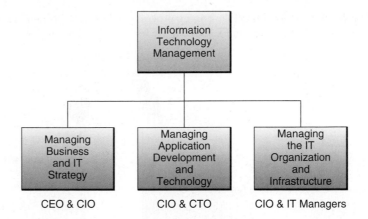

Avnet Marshall: Managing IT

Figure 14.3 contrasts how Avnet Marshall's information technology management differs from conventional IT management. Notice that it uses the model of IT management illustrated in Figure 14.2. For example, in technology management, Avnet Marshall uses a best-of-breed approach that supports business needs instead of enforcing a standardized and homogeneous choice of hardware, software, database, and networking technologies. In managing its IT organization, Avnet Marshall hires IS professionals who can integrate IT with business. These IS professionals are organized in workgroups around business/IT initiatives that focus on building IT-enabled business services for customers.

Business/IT Planning

Figure 14.4 illustrates the business/IT planning process, which focuses on discovering innovative approaches to satisfying a company's customer value and business value goals. This planning process leads to the development of strategies and business models for new business applications, processes, products, and services. Then a company can

FIGURE 14.3

Comparing conventional and e-business-driven IT management approaches.

IT Management	Conventional Practices	Avnet Marshall's Business/IT Practices
Technology Management	• Approach to IT infrastructure may sacrifice match with business needs for vendor homogeneity and technology platform choices.	• Best-of-breed approach to IT infrastructure in which effective match with business needs takes precedence over commitment to technology platform choices and vendor homogeneity.
Managing the IT Organization	• Hire "best by position" who can bring specific IT expertise.	• Hire "best athletes" IS professionals who can flexibly integrate new IT and business competencies.
	• Departments organized around IT expertise with business liaisons and explicit delegation of tasks.	• Evolving workgroups organized around emerging IT-intensive business initiatives with little explicit delegation of tasks.
	• IT projects have separable cost/value considerations. Funding typically allocated within constraints of yearly budget for IT function.	• IT funding typically based on value proposition around business opportunity related to building services for customers. IT project inseparable part of business initiative.

Source: Adapted from Omar El Sawy, Arvind Malhotra, Sanjay Gosain, and Kerry Young, "IT-Intensive Value Innovation in the Electronic Economy: Insights from Marshall Industries," *MIS Quarterly*, September 1999.

FIGURE 14.4 The business/IT planning process emphasizes a customer and business value focus for developing business strategies and models and an IT architecture for business applications.

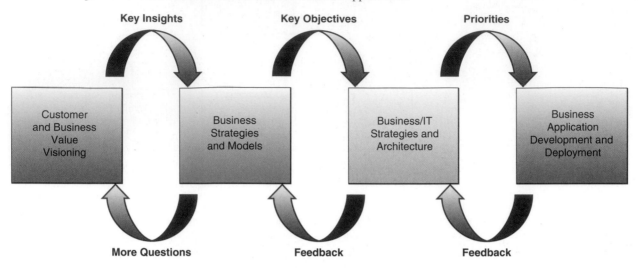

develop IT strategies and an IT architecture that supports building and implementing its newly planned business applications.

Both the CEO and the CIO of a company must manage the development of complementary business and IT strategies to meet its customer value and business value vision. This *coadaptation* process is necessary because, as we have seen so often in this text, information technologies are a fast-changing but vital component in many strategic business initiatives. The business/IT planning process has three major components:

- **Strategy Development.** Developing business strategies that support a company's business vision. For example, using information technology to create innovative e-business systems that focus on customer and business value. We will discuss this process in more detail shortly.

- **Resource Management.** Developing strategic plans for managing or outsourcing a company's IT resources, including IS personnel, hardware, software, data, and network resources.

- **Technology Architecture.** Making strategic IT choices that reflect an information technology architecture designed to support a company's business/IT initiatives.

Information Technology Architecture

The IT architecture created by the strategic business/IT planning process is a conceptual design, or blueprint, that includes the following major components:

- **Technology Platform.** The Internet, intranets, extranets, and other networks, computer systems, system software, and integrated enterprise application software provide a computing and communications infrastructure, or platform, that supports the strategic use of information technology for e-business, e-commerce, and other business/IT applications.

- **Data Resources.** Many types of operational and specialized databases, including data warehouses and Internet/intranet databases (as reviewed in Chapter 5), store and provide data and information for business processes and decision support.

- **Applications Architecture.** Business applications of information technology are designed as an integrated architecture *or portfolio* of enterprise systems that support strategic business initiatives, as well as cross-functional business processes. For example, an applications architecture should include support for developing and maintaining the interenterprise supply chain applications and integrated

FIGURE 14.5
Comparing business/IT strategic and application planning approaches.

Conventional IT Planning	Avnet Marshall's Business/IT Planning
● Strategic alignment: IT strategy tracks specified enterprise strategy.	● Strategic improvisation: IT strategy and enterprise business strategy coadaptively unfold based on the clear guidance of a focus on customer value.
● CEO endorses IT vision shaped through CIO.	● CEO proactively shapes IT vision jointly with CIO as part of e-business strategy.
● IT application development projects functionally organized as technological solutions to business issues.	● IT application development projects co-located with e-business initiatives to form centers of IT-intensive business expertise.
● Phased application development based on learning from pilot projects.	● Perpetual application development based on continuous learning from rapid deployment and prototyping with end-user involvement.

enterprise resource planning and customer relationship management applications discussed in Chapters 7 and 9.

● **IT Organization.** The organizational structure of the IS function within a company and the distribution of IS specialists are designed to meet the changing strategies of a business. The form of the IT organization depends on the managerial philosophy and business/IT strategies formulated during the strategic planning process.

Avnet Marshall: Business/IT Planning

Figure 14.5 outlines Avnet Marshall's planning process for business/IT initiatives and compares it with conventional IT planning approaches. Avnet Marshall weaves both business and IT strategic planning together *coadaptively* under the guidance of the CEO and the CIO, instead of developing IT strategy by just tracking and supporting business strategies. Avnet Marshall also locates IT application development projects within the business units that are involved in an e-business initiative to form centers of business/IT expertise throughout the company. Finally, Avnet Marshall uses a prototyping application development process with rapid deployment of new business applications instead of a traditional systems development approach. This application development strategy trades the risk of implementing incomplete applications with the benefits of gaining competitive advantages from early deployment of new e-business services to employees, customers, and other stakeholders and of involving them in the "fine-tuning" phase of application development.

Source: Adapted from Omar El Sawy, Arvind Malhotra, Sanjay Gosain, and Kerry Young, "IT-Intensive Value Innovation in the Electronic Economy: Insights from Marshall Industries," *MIS Quarterly*, September 1999.

Managing the IT Function

A radical shift is occurring in corporate computing—think of it as the recentralization of management. It's a step back toward the 1970s, when a data processing manager could sit at a console and track all the technology assets of the corporation. Then came the 1980s and early 1990s. Departments got their own PCs and software; client/server networks sprang up all across companies.

Three things have happened in the past few years: The Internet boom inspired businesses to connect all those networks; companies put on their intranets essential applications without which their businesses could not function; and it became apparent that maintaining PCs on a network is very, very expensive. Such changes create an urgent need for centralization.

Organizing IT

In the early years of computing, the development of large mainframe computers and telecommunications networks and terminals caused a centralization of computer hardware and software, databases, and information specialists at the corporate level of organizations. Next, the development of minicomputers and microcomputers accelerated a downsizing trend, which prompted a move back toward decentralization by many business firms. Distributed client/server networks at the corporate, department, workgroup, and team levels came into being, which promoted a shift of databases and information specialists to some departments and the creation of *information centers* to support end-user and workgroup computing.

Lately, the trend is to establish more centralized control over the management of the IT resources of a company while still serving the strategic needs of its business units, especially their e-business and e-commerce initiatives. This trend has resulted in the development of hybrid structures with both centralized and decentralized components. See Figure 14.6. For example, the IT function at Avnet Marshall is organized into several business-focused development groups, as well as operations management and planning groups.

Some companies spin off their information systems function into IS *subsidiaries* that offer IS services to external organizations, as well as to their parent company. Other companies create or spin off their e-commerce and Internet-related business units or IT groups into separate companies or business units. Corporations also **outsource,** that is, turn over all or parts of their IS operations to outside contractors known as *systems integrators.* In addition, some companies are outsourcing software procurement and support to *application service providers* (ASPs), which provide and support business application and other software via the Internet and intranets to all of a company's employee workstations. We will discuss outsourcing in greater detail later in this section. In the meantime, let's take a few minutes to review, and expand on, what we know about managing the various functions and activities in IS.

Managing Application Development

Application development management involves managing activities such as systems analysis and design, prototyping, applications programming, project management, quality assurance, and system maintenance for all major business/IT development projects. Managing application development requires managing the activities of teams of systems analysts, software developers, and other IS professionals working on a variety of information systems development projects. Thus, project management is a key IT management responsibility if business/IT projects are to be completed on time, within their budgets, and meet their design objectives. In addition, some systems

FIGURE 14.6

The organizational components of the IT function at Avnet Marshall.

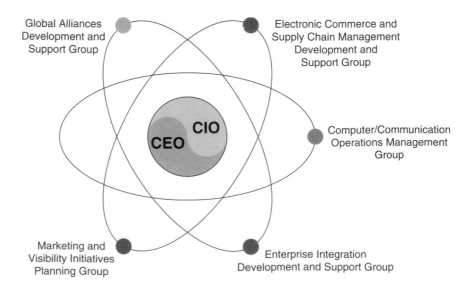

development groups have established *development centers* staffed with IS professionals. Their role is to evaluate new application development tools and help information systems specialists use them to improve their application development efforts.

Managing IS Operations

IS operations management is concerned with the use of hardware, software, network, and personnel resources in the corporate or business unit data centers (computer centers) of an organization. Operational activities that must be managed include computer system operations, network management, production control, and production support.

Most operations management activities are being automated by the use of software packages for computer system performance management. These system performance monitors look after the processing of computer jobs, help develop a planned schedule of computer operations that can optimize computer system performance, and produce detailed statistics that are invaluable for effective planning and control of computing capacity. Such information evaluates computer system utilization, costs, and performance. This evaluation provides information for capacity planning, production planning and control, and hardware/software acquisition planning. It is also used in quality assurance programs, which emphasize the quality of services to business end users. See Figure 14.7.

System performance monitors also supply information needed by chargeback systems that allocate costs to users on the basis of the information services rendered. All costs incurred are recorded, reported, allocated, and charged back to specific end-user business units, depending on their use of system resources. When companies use this arrangement, the information services department becomes a service center whose costs are charged directly to business units rather than being lumped with other administrative service costs and treated as overhead costs.

Many performance monitors also feature **process control** capabilities. Such packages not only monitor but also automatically control computer operations at large data centers. Some use built-in expert system modules that are based on knowledge gleaned from experts in the operations of specific computer systems and operating systems. These performance monitors provide more efficient computer operations than human-operated systems. They also enable "lights out" data centers at some companies, where computer systems are operated unattended, especially after normal business hours.

FIGURE 14.7

The CA-Unicenter TNG system performance monitor includes an Enterprise Management Portal module that helps IT specialists monitor and manage a variety of networked computer systems and operating systems.

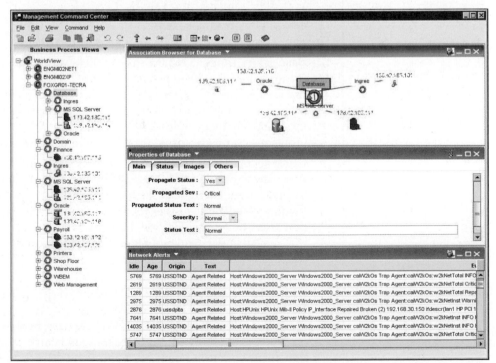

Source: Courtesy of Computer Associates.

IT Staff Planning

The success or failure of an information services organization rests primarily on the quality of its people. Many firms consider IT staff planning, or recruiting, training, and retaining qualified IS personnel, as one of their greatest challenges. Managing information services functions involves the management of managerial, technical, and clerical personnel. One of the most important jobs of information services managers is to recruit qualified personnel and develop, organize, and direct the capabilities of existing personnel. Employees must be continually trained to keep up with the latest developments in a fast-moving and highly technical field. Employee job performances must be continually evaluated, and outstanding performances must be rewarded with salary increases or promotions. Salary and wage levels must be set, and career paths must be designed so that individuals can move to new jobs through promotion and transfer as they gain seniority and expertise.

The CIO and Other IT Executives

The chief information officer (CIO) oversees all use of information technology in many companies and brings it into alignment with strategic business goals. Thus, all traditional computer services, Internet technology, telecommunications network services, and other IS technology support services are the responsibility of this executive. The CIO does not direct day-to-day information services activities; instead, CIOs concentrate on business/IT planning and strategy. They also work with the CEO and other top executives to develop strategic uses of information technology in e-business and e-commerce that help make the firm more competitive in the marketplace. Many companies have also filled the CIO position with executives from the business functions or units outside the IS field. Such CIOs emphasize that the chief role of information technology is to help a company meet its strategic business objectives.

Top IT Jobs: Requirements and Compensation

- **Chief information officer**
  Base salary range: $194,000–$303,000+; varies by location
  Bonus range: Up to 40 percent of salary
  The top position in IT isn't all about technology. To land this job, you need to be a Business Technologist with a big "B" and a big "T." If you understand the business, the organization's strategy, and the broad spectrum of technologies, systems, applications, and people necessary to execute it, you will be in great demand by organizations.

- **Chief technology officer**
  Base salary range: $162,000–$245,000+; varies by location
  Bonus range: Up to 40 percent of salary
  If you're second-in-command to the CIO or chief technology officer and you have years of applications development experience, your next move should be into the chief technology officer's spot. To land this job, you'll need to be a passionate problem solver with a demonstrated record of reducing development time.

- **Chief security officer**
  Base salary range: $142,000–$205,000+; varies by location
  Bonus range: Up to 40 percent of salary
  If you understand the issues related to securing the data resources and information assets of the organization, then this is the job for you. Strong candidates with a deep understanding of both the technical and managerial sides of the field are in great demand.

- **E-commerce architect**
  Base salary range: $115,000–$170,000+; varies by location
  Bonus range: Up to 15 percent of salary
  If you know Java, Perl, C++, and Web services; have experience in systems architecture; and can design an Internet solution from concept through implementation, many companies want you to plan and develop their e-commerce sites.

- **Technical team leader**
  Base salary range: $75,000–$100,000+; varies by location
  Bonus range: Up to 20 percent of salary
  Senior technical team leaders with good communication, project management, and leadership skills, as well as knowledge of Web languages and databases, are still in great demand.

- **Practice manager**
  Base salary range: $70,000–$100,000+; varies by location
  Bonus range: Up to 20 percent of salary
  If you've got a background in IT assessment and a pedigree in business development (MBA preferred), you can land a job as a point person for big projects. You'll need skills in IT operations and software assessment, as well as in marketing, staffing, budgeting, and building customer relationships.

- **Systems analyst**
  Base salary range: $56,000–$100,000+; varies by location
  Bonus range: Up to 25 percent of salary
  If you have problem-solving skills and a degree in information systems (BS or MBA), you can be assured of finding a good job as a systems analyst. You'll need to have excellent interpersonal skills, good technical skills, and an ability to apply your problem-solving and critical-thinking skills to the design of new systems.

Source: www.salary.com.

Technology Management

The management of rapidly changing technology is important to any organization. Changes in information technology, like the rise of the PC, client/server networks, and the Internet and intranets, have come swiftly and dramatically and are expected to continue into the future. Developments in information systems technology have had, and will continue to have, a major impact on the operations, costs, management work environment, and competitive position of many organizations.

Thus, all information technologies must be managed as a technology platform for integrating internally focused or externally facing business applications. Such technologies include the Internet, intranets, and a variety of e-commerce and collaboration technologies, as well as integrated enterprise software for customer relationship management, enterprise resource planning, and supply chain management. In many companies, technology management is the primary responsibility of a chief technology officer (CTO), who is in charge of all information technology planning and deployment.

Managing User Services

Teams and workgroups of business professionals commonly use PC workstations, software packages, and the Internet, intranets, and other networks to develop and apply information technology to their work activities. Thus, many companies have responded by creating user services, or *client services*, functions to support and manage end-user and workgroup computing.

End-user services provide both opportunities and problems for business unit managers. For example, some firms create an *information center* group staffed with user liaison specialists or Web-enabled intranet help desks. IS specialists with titles such as user consultant, account executive, or business analyst may also be assigned to end-user workgroups. These specialists perform a vital role by troubleshooting problems, gathering and communicating information, coordinating educational efforts, and helping business professionals with application development.

In addition to these measures, most organizations still establish and enforce policies for the acquisition of hardware and software by end users and business units. This process ensures their compatibility with company standards for hardware, software, and network connectivity. Also important is the development of applications with proper security and quality controls to promote correct performance and safeguard the integrity of corporate and departmental networks and databases.

Outsourcing and Offshoring IT and IS

An increasingly popular approach to managing the IS and IT functions of the organization is to adopt an outsourcing strategy. Outsourcing, in broad terms, is the purchase of goods or services that were previously provided internally from third-party partners. Outsourcing is a generic term used for a broad range of information technology functions that are selectively contracted to an external service provider.

Outsourcing

A commonly outsourced IS function is software application development. This process includes contracting (or subcontracting) with an external organization for the development of complete or partial software products/projects, the purchase of packaged or customized package software products, or activities and/or resources that aid in the software development life cycle. Figure 14.8 lists the functions typically outsourced, the reasons behind the decision to outsource, and several aspects associated with successful vendor selection and a successful outsourcing effort.

Although companies can, theoretically, choose to outsource any organization function for any reason, there are five main reasons behind a decision to outsource:

FIGURE 14.8 Outsourcing's Top 10. Notice, despite all of the media coverage, application development is No. 3.

Top 10 Reasons Companies Outsource	Top 10 Factors in Vendor Selection
1. Reduce and control operating costs	1. Commitment to quality
2. Improve company focus	2. Price
3. Gain access to world-class capabilities	3. References/reputation
4. Free internal resources for other purposes	4. Flexible contract terms
5. Necessary resources are not available internally	5. Scope of resources
6. Accelerate reengineering benefits	6. Additional value-added capability
7. Function is difficult to manage internally or is out of control	7. Cultural match
8. Make capital funds available	8. Existing relationship
9. Share risks	9. Location
10. Cash infusion	10. Other

Top 10 Factors for Successful Outsourcing	Top 10 IT Areas Being Outsourced
1. Understand company goals and objectives	1. Maintenance and repair
2. A strategic vision and plan	2. Training
3. Select the right vendor	3. Applications development
4. Ongoing management of the relationships	4. Consulting and reengineering
5. A properly structured contract	5. Mainframe data centers
6. Open communication with affected individuals/groups	6. Client/server services and administration
7. Senior executive support and involvement	7. Network administration
8. Careful attention to personnel issues	8. Desktop services
9. Near-term financial justification	9. End-user support
10. Use of outside expertise	10. Total IT outsourcing

Source: The Outsourcing Institute.

Save Money—Achieve Greater Return on Investment (ROI)

- Outsourcing IS/IT functions to skilled service providers is often a strategic approach to stretching strained budgets. Companies that take a well-managed approach to outsourcing can gain cost savings of upwards of 40–80 percent.

Focus on Core Competencies

- Outsourced professionals allow an organization and its employees to focus on the business they are in rather than a business in which they are not. By using an outsourcing strategy for application development, an organization can focus its IS professionals on identifying and solving business problems rather than on programming and prototyping new applications.

Achieve Flexible Staffing Levels

- Strategic use of an outsourcing approach to IS/IT functions can result in business growth without increasing overhead. Outsourcing provides a pool of qualified professionals available for unique, niche, or overflow projects. If the unique skill set required by an organization is difficult to find or expensive to maintain in-house, outsourcing can allow for the acquisition of the needed expertise.

Gain Access to Global Resources

- The Outsourcing Institute asserts that the rules for successfully growing a business have changed: "It's no longer about what you own or build. . . . [Instead] success is hinged to resources and talent you can access." Using global expertise allows an organization to gain the advantage of skilled labor, regardless of location, and significantly increase the quality of its deliverables. As such, outsourcing can create opportunities for smaller businesses that might not otherwise be possible due to costs or geophysical constraints.

Decrease Time to Market

- Outsourcing extends the traditional small business benefits of flexibility and responsiveness, allowing smaller organizations to compete effectively against bigger firms. Supplementing an existing workforce with offshore support could allow for productivity 24 hours a day. Having access to resources able to work on key projects even while local employees are asleep can serve to accelerate time to market and provide a key competitive advantage.

Offshoring

Although often confused with outsourcing, offshoring is also increasingly becoming part of a strategic approach to IS/IT management. Offshoring can be defined as a relocation of an organization's business processes (including production/manufacturing) to a lower-cost location, usually overseas. Offshoring can be considered in the context of either *production* offshoring or *services* offshoring. After its accession to the World Trade Organization (WTO), China emerged as a prominent destination for production offshoring. After technical progress in telecommunications improved the possibilities of trade in services, India became a country that chose to focus on this domain.

The growth of services offshoring in information systems is linked to the availability of large amounts of reliable and affordable communication infrastructure following the telecom bust of the late 1990s. Coupled with the digitization of many services, it became possible to shift the actual delivery location of services to low-cost locations in a manner theoretically transparent to end users.

India, the Philippines, Ireland, and Eastern European countries benefited greatly from this trend due to their large pool of English-speaking and technically qualified workers. India's offshoring industry took root in IT functions in the 1990s and has since moved to back-office processes, such as call centers and transaction processing, as well as high-end jobs such as application development.

Offshoring is often enabled by the transfer of valuable information to the offshore site. Such information and training allows the remote workers to produce results of comparable value previously produced by internal employees. When such transfer includes proprietary materials, such as confidential documents and trade secrets, protected by nondisclosure agreements, then intellectual property has been transferred or exported. The documentation and valuation of such exports is quite difficult but should be considered because it comprises items that may be regulated or taxable.

Offshoring has been a controversial issue with heated debates. On one hand, it is seen as benefiting both the origin and destination country through free trade. On the other hand, job losses in developed countries have sparked opposition to offshoring. Some critics agree that both sides will benefit in terms of overall production and numbers of jobs created but that the subjective quality of the new jobs will be less than the previous ones. While this debate continues, companies continue to use offshoring as a viable IS/IT management approach. Let's look at a real-world example of global outsourcing.

Royal Dutch Shell: Multisupplier Global Outsourcing Deal 	Royal Dutch Shell has signed a five-year, $4 billion outsourcing deal with three global IT and telecommunications suppliers. The value of the contracts for the three suppliers is $1.6 billion with AT&T, $1 billion for EDS, and $1.6 billion with T-Systems. Shell announced that it has contracted T-Systems, AT&T, and EDS under a master service agreement (MSA), for "significant improvements" to its efficiency and productivity that will see an axing of some tech jobs and a transfer of 3,000 IT staff to the service providers. Under the MSA, Shell will outsource its IT infrastructure in three service bundles: "AT&T for network and telecommunications, T-Systems for hosting and storage, and EDS for end user computing services and for integration of the infrastructure services." The suppliers will provide integrated services to more than 1,500 sites worldwide. "Shell's approach combines all the advantages of decentralised service provision with the benefits and efficiency of a centralised governance structure," says Elesh Khakhar, a partner at consultant firm TPI, which is an advisor to Shell. Khakar added that the multisupplier deal has been designed to "encourage collaborative behavior" between suppliers, while it allows Shell to "retain full control of strategy and service integration. In addition to all of the usual business benefits, Shell will be able to exploit emerging commoditized services designed for the consumer market, such as email or internet phone services, and integrate them within their services when they become robust enough for commercial use." Shell CIO Alan Matula said: "This deal is a major strategic choice for Shell. Partnering with EDS, T-Systems and AT&T gives us greater ability to respond to the growing demands of our businesses. It allows Shell IT to focus on Information Technology that drives competitive position in the oil and gas market, whilst suppliers focus on improving essential IT capability." Source: Adapted from Siobhan Chapman, "Shell Signs $4 Billion, Multi-Supplier Outsourcing Deal," *CIO Magazine*, April 3, 2008.

Trends in Outsourcing and Offshoring

While in the past much of the motivation to outsource and offshore various portions of the IT/IS operation of a firm were driven primarily by cost, a more recent and troubling trend is the increasing motivation to find highly qualified IT/IS talent. Jobs are plentiful in the United States for today's IS graduate, but enrollments in United States's IS programs remain down. This results in a decreasing supply of qualified labor for the best paying jobs in the field. To combat this, firms are looking at the science and engineering graduate of other countries to fill their needs. As we discussed in Chapter 2, the jobs that were outsourced and offshored in the late 1990s and early 2000 were not the ones typically benchmarked by university-level IS programs. As such, no real job opportunities were lost to qualified graduates. Today, however, the lack of qualified IS graduates means companies have to turn elsewhere to fill these jobs. The jobs are staying here, but the labor is being imported. The single most effective method to counter this trend is for more young people to seek a career in the information systems field. IS/IT is one of the hottest fields on the planet for job opportunities, and the word needs to get out. Many organizations are focusing on outreach programs that extend down to the pre-high school levels to begin educating, or reeducating, the public with regard to these vast opportunities.

Failures in IT Management

Managing information technology is not an easy task. The information systems function often has performance problems in many organizations. The promised benefits of information technology have not occurred in many documented cases. Studies by management consulting firms and university researchers have shown that many businesses have not been successful in managing their use of information technology. Thus, it is evident that in many organizations, information technology is not being used effectively and efficiently, and there have been **failures in IT management.** For example:

- Information technology is not being used *effectively* by companies that use IT primarily to computerize traditional business processes instead of developing innovative e-business processes involving customers, suppliers, and other business partners, e-commerce, and Web-enabled decision support.

- Information technology is not being used *efficiently* by information systems that provide poor response times and frequent downtimes, or by IS professionals and consultants who do not properly manage application development projects.

Let's look more closely, using a real-world example.

Risk without Reward: Weak IT Controls at Société Générale

It's a lethal combination of process oversights and system failures that is the stuff of CIO nightmares: An investigation into rogue trader Jerome Kerviel's fraudulent actions at Société Générale bank uncovered an apparent breakdown in financial and internal IT controls, subverted by an employee with IT know-how and authorized systems access. IT experts say the case should serve as a warning that businesses can do better to manage IT-related risk.

"Much time is spent on protecting the external threat," says J.R. Reagan, managing director and global solution leader for risk, compliance and security at Bearing-Point. "But the internal threat can be even larger in terms of risk to the company." In the case of Société Générale, not only were IT security controls insufficient, but the bank's staff did not fully investigate red flags that arose. Recent research by the Ponemon Institute concludes that "insider threats represent one of the most significant information security risks." In a survey of 700 IT practitioners, 78 percent said they believe individuals have too much access to information that isn't pertinent to their jobs, while 59 percent said such access presents business risks. What's more, IT professionals see a disconnect with business leaders: 74 percent said senior management does not view governance of access to information as a strategic issue.

One of Société Générale's primary business lines is derivatives—financial instruments that allow traders to make contracts on a wide range of assets (such as equities, bonds, or commodities) and attempts to reduce (or hedge) the financial risk for one party in the deal. Trading derivatives, however, necessitates some aggressiveness and can be fraught with risk.

Reagan observes that in the case of Société Générale, "their activities deal with high volume, high velocity and quick tempo trading of stock," and it's likely business leaders "wouldn't put up with" security measures that would slow them down. For example, Société Générale employed single-factor authentication (using one method, such as passwords, to grant access to its systems) rather than stronger dual-factor authentication (requiring that individuals employ two methods of identifying themselves to gain access). "The security team needs to explain the risk exposure and the possibility of losing billions in fraudulent trades if security is not adequately addressed," Reagan says. "But most security guys aren't well enough in tune with the business to be able to articulate a business case like that."

That disconnect can be enormously destructive, as the Société Générale incident shows. "The Société Générale case brings to the fore the fact that business risk can be directly exposed through IT," says Scott Crawford, a security expert and research director at Enterprise Management Associates. "Kerviel allegedly manipulated the IT controls on the business systems based on his midoffice experience and back-office knowledge and expertise."

"Businesses are just now beginning to awaken to the controls within the IT environment," Crawford says. "If you're betting the farm and strategy on the IT controls, it behooves the organization to ensure that those controls are reasonably resistant to subversion."

Source: Adapted from Nancy Weil, "Risk without Reward," *CIO Magazine*, May 1, 2008.

Management Involvement

What is the solution to failures in the information systems function? There are no quick and easy answers. However, the experiences of successful organizations reveal that extensive and meaningful managerial and end-user involvement is the key ingredient of high-quality information systems performance. Involving business managers in the governance of the IS function and business professionals in the development of IS applications should thus shape the response of management to the challenge of improving the business value of information technology. See Figure 14.9.

Involving managers in the management of IT (from the CEO to the managers of business units) requires the development of *governance structures* (e.g., executive councils, steering committees) that encourage their active participation in planning and controlling the business uses of IT. Thus, many organizations have policies that require managers to be involved in IT decisions that affect their business units. This requirement helps managers avoid IS performance problems in their business units and development projects. With this high degree of involvement, managers can improve the strategic business value of information technology. Also, as we noted in Chapter 12, only direct end-user participation in system development projects can solve the problems of employee resistance and poor user interface design. Overseeing such involvement is another vital management task.

IT Governance

Information technology governance (ITG) is a subset discipline of corporate governance focused on the information technologies (IT), information systems (IS), their performance, use, and associated risks. The rising interest in IT governance is due, in part, to governmental compliance initiatives such as Sarbanes-Oxley in the United States and its counterpart in Europe, Basel II. Additional motivation comes from the acknowledgment that IT projects can easily get out of control and profoundly affect the performance of an organization.

A characteristic theme of IT governance discussions is that the IT capability can no longer be thought of as a mythical black box, the contents of which are known only to the IT personnel. This traditional handling of IT management by board-level executives is due to limited technical experience and the perceived complexity of IT. Historically, key

FIGURE 14.9   Senior management needs to be involved in critical business/IT decisions to optimize the business value and performance of the IT function.

IT Decision	Senior Management's Role	Consequences of Abdicating the Decision
● **How much should we spend on IT?**	Define the strategic role that IT will play in the company, and then determine the level of funding needed to achieve that objective.	The company fails to develop an IT platform that furthers its strategy, despite high IT spending.
● **Which business processes should receive our IT dollars?**	Make clear decisions about which IT initiatives will and will not be funded.	A lack of focus overwhelms the IT unit, which tries to deliver many projects that may have little companywide value or can't be implemented well simultaneously.
● **Which IT capabilities need to be companywide?**	Decide which IT capabilities should be provided centrally and which should be developed by individual businesses.	Excessive technical and process standardization limit the flexibility of business units, or frequent exceptions to the standards increase costs and limit business synergies.
● **How good do our IT services really need to be?**	Decide which features—for example, enhanced reliability or response time—are needed on the basis of their costs and benefits.	The company may pay for service options that, given its priorities, aren't worth their costs.
● **What security and privacy risks will we accept?**	Lead the decision making on the trade-offs between security and privacy on one hand and convenience on the other.	An overemphasis on security and privacy may inconvenience customers, employees, and suppliers; an underemphasis may make data vulnerable.
● **Whom do we blame if an IT initiative fails?**	Assign a business executive to be accountable for every IT project; monitor business metrics.	The business value of systems is never realized.

Source: Jeanne W. Ross and Peter Weill, "Six IT Decisions Your IT People Shouldn't Make," *Harvard Business Review*, November 2002, p. 87.

decisions were often deferred to IT professionals. IT governance implies a system in which all stakeholders, including the board, internal customers, and related areas such as finance, have the necessary input into the decision-making process. This prevents a single stakeholder, typically IT, from being blamed for poor decisions. It also prevents users from later complaining that the system does not behave or perform as expected.

The focus of ITG is specifying decision inputs and rights along with an accountability framework such that desirable behaviors toward and in the use of IT are developed. It highlights the importance of IT-related matters in contemporary organizations and ensures that strategic IT decisions are owned by the corporate board, rather than by the CIO or other IT managers. The primary goals for information technology governance are to (1) assure that the significant organizational investments in IT and IS generate their maximum business value and (2) mitigate the risks that are associated with IT. This is accomplished by implementing an organizational structure with well-defined roles for the responsibility of the decisions related to the management and use of IT such as infrastructure, architecture, investment, and use.

One very popular approach to IT governance is COBIT (Control Objectives for Information and related Technology). COBIT is a framework of best practices for IT management created by the Information Systems Audit and Control Association (ISACA) and the IT Governance Institute (ITGI). COBIT provides all members of the organization with a set of generally accepted measures, indicators, processes, and best practices to help them maximize the benefits derived through the use of information technology and in developing appropriate IT governance and control structures in a company.

COBIT has 34 high-level processes covering 210 control objectives categorized in four domains: (1) Planning and Organization, (2) Acquisition and Implementation,

(3) Delivery and Support, and (4) Monitoring. Managers benefit from COBIT because it provides them with a foundation upon which IT-related decisions and investments can be based. Decision making is more effective because COBIT helps management define a strategic IT plan, define the information architecture, acquire the necessary IT hardware and software to execute an IT strategy, ensure continuous service, and monitor the performance of the IT system. IT users benefit from COBIT because of the assurance provided to them by COBIT's defined controls, security, and process governance. COBIT also benefits auditors because it helps them identify IT control issues within a company's IT infrastructure, and it helps them corroborate their audit findings. Figure 14.10 illustrates the relationships between the four domains in COBIT and categorizes both the high-level processes and control objectives associated with them.

Let's look at a real-world example of COBIT in action.

FIGURE 14.10   COBIT is a popular IT governance approach that focuses on all aspects of the IT function throughout the organization.

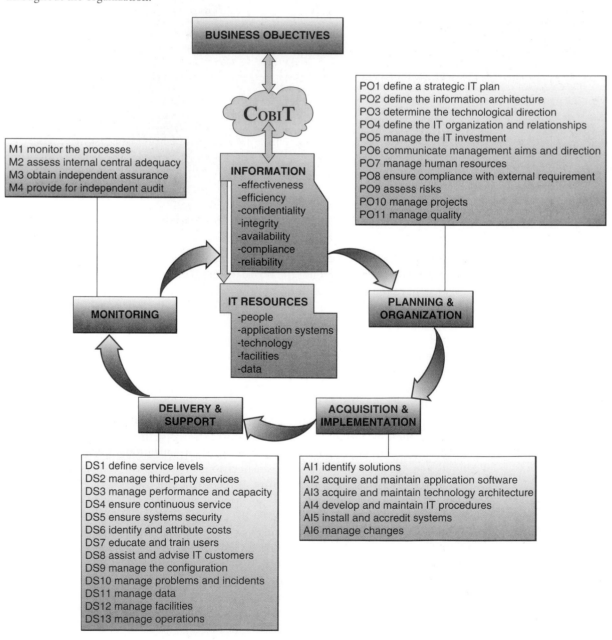

COBIT May Not Be the Answer

Companies managing their ICT assets well turn in consistently higher profitability than their peers and command a premium on the sharemarket, studies suggest.

A presentation and discussion organized by the NZ (New Zealand) Computer Society in late 2008 in Wellington, New Zealand, considered this equation, and particularly the role of governance frameworks such as COBIT in delivering business benefits.

"Do good governance and prudent management necessarily go together?" asked principal presenter Matthew Nicho, of AUT University; or are there other factors involved in good management, which arise from the same mindset that produces good governance?

A similarly misleading relationship could exist between good governance in general and good governance in ICT, said one participant; the latter could be an effect rather than a cause, with good general governance producing the benefits.

The studies in question are ageing, Nicho admits. One series cited, from PricewaterhouseCoopers, produced encouraging figures from 2003 and 2005 together with some indications of how the situation might be improved; but he has yet to analyze the 2007 figures fully.

Nevertheless, participants in the discussion agreed that the same factors still hold today and are probably more relevant in straitened economic times.

Nicho's figures indicate that comparatively few local companies have adopted COBIT and many of those that have done so have no satisfactory measurement of whether it is leading to good management.

Disinclination to adopt COBIT and measure its impact could be an outcome of the smaller size of New Zealand companies, some suggested; the cost of implementation looms larger in small companies, which also lack the organizational structures implied by such frameworks.

When managers and staffers wear "half-a-dozen hats," the framework is distorted, one participant said.

In the absence of objective measurement, there is a danger for compliance with a framework to become an end in itself, some said.

Source: Adapted from Stephen Bell, "Governance, Management and Business Success," *Computerworld New Zealand*, Fairfax Media Business Group, December 18, 2008.

SECTION II Managing Global IT

The International Dimension

Whether they are in Berlin or Bombay, Kuala Lumpur or Kansas, San Francisco or Seoul, companies around the globe are developing new models to operate competitively in a digital economy. These models are structured, yet agile; global, yet local; and they concentrate on maximizing the risk-adjusted return from both knowledge and technology assets.

International dimensions have become a vital part of managing a business enterprise in the inter-networked global economies and markets of today. Whether you become a manager in a large corporation or the owner of a small business, you will be affected by international business developments and deal in some way with people, products, or services whose origin is not your home country.

Read the Real World Case on the next page. We can learn a lot about the challenges facing senior IT executives who operate in a globalized world. See Figure 14.11.

Global IT Management

Figure 14.12 illustrates the major dimensions of the job of managing global information technology that we cover in this section. Notice that all global IT activities must be adjusted to take into account the cultural, political, and geoeconomic challenges that exist in the international business community. Developing appropriate business and IT strategies for the global marketplace should be the first step in global information technology management. Once that is done, end users and IS managers can move on to developing the portfolio of business applications needed to support business/IT strategies; the hardware, software, and Internet-based technology platforms to support those applications; the data resource management methods to provide necessary databases; and finally the systems development projects that will produce the global information systems required.

Global Teams: It's Still a Small World

We seem to have reached a point where virtually every CIO is a global CIO—a leader whose sphere of influence (and headaches) spans continents. The global CIO's most common challenge, according to CIO Executive Council members, is managing global virtual teams. In an ideal world, HR policies across the global IT team should be consistent, fair, and responsive. Titles and reporting structures (if not compensation) should be equalized.

The council's European members, representing Royal Dutch Shell, Galderma, Olympus, and others, commissioned a globalization playbook that collects and codifies best practices in this and other globalization challenges.

Obtain local HR expertise. Companies must have a local HR person in each country to deal with local laws. "Hiring, firing, and training obligations must be managed very differently in each location, and you need someone with local expertise on the laws and processes," says Michael Pilkington, former chief information officer of Euroclear, the Brussels-based provider of domestic and cross-border settlement for bond, equity, and fund transactions.

Create job grade consistency across regions. Euroclear is moving toward a job evaluation methodology that organizes job types into vertical categories, such as managing people/process, product development, business support, and project management. This provides a basis for comparing and managing roles and people across locations. Grade level is not the same thing as a title; people's titles are much more subject to local conventions.

(text continues on page 635)

Cadbury, Forrester Research, A.T. Kearney, and Others: IT Leaders Face New Challenges in a Globalized World

Wayne Shurts had no experience overseeing IT operations in emerging markets when Cadbury CEO Todd Stitzer appointed him global CIO the summer of 2009. The geographic parameters of Shurts's responsibilities at the sweets maker—with a presence everywhere from Pakistan to Palau—multiplied overnight. The former CIO for North America now spends most of his time globe-trotting from his home base in Parsippany, New Jersey, to London headquarters to operations on six continents.

Shurts also had to shift his thinking. The $7.8 billion company has made a concerted effort to expand in the developing world, giving it the biggest and most dispersed emerging markets business in the confectionery industry. In fact, Cadbury's business in rapidly developing markets was a major driver in Kraft's $19.5 billion takeover bid for the British candy maker. Last year, 60 percent of the company's growth came from emerging markets.

"That means that my world as CIO does not solely revolve around big economies of North America, Europe, Australia and New Zealand," explains Shurts.

"Emerging markets are not afterthoughts to me. They demand—and get—a lot of my attention." Shurts isn't alone. In industries ranging from consumer goods and agriculture to banking and electronics, multinationals are investing more in the Middle East, Asia, Eastern Europe, Africa, and South America. Now imagine developing a single system that manages reinsurance business processes for numerous offices around the world—offices whose staffs speak different languages, are in different time zones, and just might be stuck in their ways as to how they manage their business. It's a challenge that could overwhelm you if you tried to tackle it all at once instead of breaking it into small pieces.

"Companies are going to tap those markets as mature markets stagnate or decline," says Bob Haas, a partner and vice president with A.T. Kearney who leads the consultancy's strategic IT practice for North America. "And CIOs are gaining more and more responsibility for those emerging markets since IT is one of the most globally integrated corporate functions."

The work amounts to much more than just bringing some distant locations into the IT fold. Setting up shop in Bogotá or in Bursa, Turkey, is clearly a different proposition than supporting a new office in Boise, Idaho, or Brussels. Infrastructure limitations, local talent supply, unfamiliar business and cultural norms, limited vendor support, and restricted budgets require creative solutions. At the same time, there is pressure to integrate these often one-off extensions of the company into the global infrastructure.

Bobby Cameron, vice president and principal analyst with Forrester Research, got a call recently from the chief information officer of a U.S.-based agribusiness building a new manufacturing plant in a tiny Peruvian fishing village. "It's 250 miles away from Lima. There's no water. There's no electricity. There's nothing there," Cameron says. "What's that about?"

It's about having an ideal port for moving goods throughout South America. All the chief information officer has to do is figure out how to build something from nothing without many of the support structures—vendors, a trained workforce, infrastructure—he'd have in a mature market. "And once you get through all of that," says Cameron," then you have to figure out how to connect it to the global infrastructure."

It's an extreme example, but supporting business in developing regions rarely lends itself to cookie-cutter IT. Moreover, the importance of emerging markets today means IT leaders can't fob off secondhand technology to non-Western locations.

"The strategy of many corporations was basically to develop things in major markets then hand down those solutions to the emerging markets," Shurts says. "Hey, this laptop is two years old, maybe we pass that down, too."

That's not the case at Cadbury, explains Shurts. "I have to deliver strategies that address the specific needs of emerging markets. It requires some creativity and new thinking."

Understanding your company's business model for developing markets is critical. "Will there be manufacturing? Will you distribute from this market? How will your salesforce engage customers and what is their role while engaged?" says Ed Holmes, vice president of Global IT for Stiefel, an $812 million dollar skin care company, acquired by GlaxoSmithKline, that operates in 28 countries.

You may end up providing technology and services similar to those you supply in established markets, Holmes adds, "but you must challenge the baseline assumptions in order to ensure that your solution will fit the market both economically and culturally."

FIGURE 14.11

Emerging economies are increasingly demanding—and getting—IT executives' attention.

Obstacles vary by location. Many developing markets face disadvantages after decades of having closed economies, including limited exposure to global business practices. But two overriding—and sometimes conflicting—considerations for global CIOs are cost structure and scalability. "From an IT perspective, these markets need to grow at an investment rate that makes sense for them," Shurts explains. "What they need today may not be what they need tomorrow. And tomorrow might actually mean tomorrow."

In its early days, an operation in an emerging market country may not need, nor could it support, the complexity and cost of a full-fledged ERP system. "Then, suddenly, through organic growth and an acquisition, everything changes and you do need the disciplines and features that an ERP system provides," Shurts says.

For instance, there's little support for emerging market needs among IT vendors, which means global CIOs and their teams go it alone, for the most part. Traditional solutions from IT vendors can be "too heavy and expensive for emerging markets," says Shurts. "It is very easy and neat and comfortable to walk around with that developed market mind-set. There's a whole industry of people who would love for you to do that—hardware, software companies that have built their businesses focused on the developed market," Shurts says. "It's much harder to get out of that comfort zone."

Typical of global CIOs, Shurts finds that exciting. "Many of them enjoy starting from scratch," says Forrester's Cameron. "They can't turn to IBM or SAP and have them solve all of their problems."

Cadbury does try to take advantage of corporate-level IT investments where possible. "We can leverage some systems from our developed markets and adapt that to emerging markets at a much lower cost," Shurts says.

SAP instances, for example, where 80 percent of the investment has been made in a more established market, may be used in a developing market, even if that new market can't support all the same capabilities, has different legal or regulatory needs, or requires unique functionality. The Australia instance has been leveraged in parts of Asia; the Britain/Ireland instance has been reused in South Africa; and the initial instance in Brazil is being recycled for use throughout Latin America.

Other IT priorities just don't apply. In the United States, Canada, and Australia, Cadbury IT is laser-focused on trade promotion management. Sophisticated tools are used to analyze the amount of money Cadbury spends and types of corporate programs it uses to promote its products.

None of that will do a lick of good in South America or India, where the mom-and-pop shop still rules, and there are no big promotions to manage with Wal-Mart. Rather, the focus is on lower-end tools to determine the right delivery routes, make sales calls, and take orders. The good news is that there are similarities across the company's locations. "Route-to-market tools, salesforce automation and supply chain planning are important to all emerging markets," Shurts says.

Every country has its own particular problems. In some, the concept of urgency—embedded in the workplace culture of established markets—is foreign. In others, it is about infrastructure, or lack thereof. For instance, notes Shurts, most countries in Africa still struggle with broadband access. This problem will be alleviated somewhat by submarine cable projects on either side of the continent, scheduled to go live this fall, but "that's the most frustrating thing for us," Shurts says. "We do a lot of satellite in Africa and with our global applications—HR, finance. You'll notice slower response rates and latency."

Importing hardware and software may be the best way to go in Dubai and Abu Dhabi. But CIOs managing IT in Brazil—including Shurts and Holmes—know that heavy tariffs there mean it's cheaper to buy everything in-country. "Our standard procurement solution doesn't really work there," says Holmes. "The only way you learn about these country-specific challenges is by engaging with other CIOs, talking to your HR leads in those locations and paying attention to previous challenges in other business functions."

"You have the ability to completely rethink the norms. This lets you create new solutions that would not have otherwise been viable," says Holmes. "The best opportunity is learning something that can then be translated back to a larger, more costly country." Less-developed regions of the world can also serve as testing grounds for new technologies or processes, says Haas, because the IT environment is less complex.

It's a big job, but lots of CIOs are going to have to do it, says Haas, who thinks developing markets experience is becoming a rite of passage for tomorrow's multinational CIOs. "Because we're a business with a very big presence in emerging markets, I am faced with the challenges of supporting IT in developing markets more than my peers," says Shurts. "But for others, it's coming. It's absolutely coming."

Source: Adapted from Stephanie Overby, "Globalization: New Management Challenges Facing IT leaders," *CIO.com*, November 12, 2009.

CASE STUDY QUESTIONS

1. What are the challenges faced by the CIOs mentioned in the case? Group them into categories and use examples from the case to define each.

2. The case mentions that the traditional approach toward emerging countries had been to develop technology in the corporate offices and then hand them down to satellite operations. How has that changed, as discussed in the case?

3. "IT is one of the most globally integrated corporate functions." How is IT different from other business areas when it comes to global integration? Why do you think this is the case?

REAL WORLD ACTIVITIES

1. Go online and search for other examples of large multinational organizations facing similar challenges. Summarize your findings and compare them to the ones chronicled in the case. Can you find any new ones not mentioned here?

2. Do you think some form of international experience is key to your long-term career success? Have you ever considered taking a position abroad? Why or why not? Break into small groups with your classmates to discuss the advantages and disadvantages of moving abroad to gain these experiences.

FIGURE 14.12

The major dimensions of global e-business technology management.

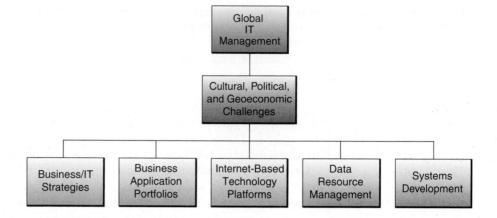

Manage dispersed staff as portfolio teams. ON Semiconductor has IT staff that support sales in Slovakia, where ON has a factory; in Hong Kong, where ON has a major sales office; in Shenzhen, China, where a customer service center is located; and in Kuala Lumpur, Malaysia, at its regional development center. ON overcomes potential disconnects by having a single sales IT portfolio owner, based at headquarters in Phoenix, who sets objectives and distributes work to the members of that team no matter where they reside.

Make the work meaningful. To keep morale high and turnover low, be sure that each remote location contributes to important projects. Don't send remote workers a steady diet of maintenance. Pilkington suggests building a center of excellence in each remote location.

Clearly defining the roles of remote groups can also help knit them together. For example, global company leaders can hold meetings at all levels to discuss the distinct purposes of corporate headquarters, the regions, and the local units. Knowing what their roles are in the larger picture and what they can expect from others "creates a sense of identity and purpose," says Nariman Karimi, senior vice president and chief information officer of DHL Asia Pacific.

Bring remote staff to headquarters. ON Semiconductor brings its foreign-based employees to the United States to work on key initiatives and interact with other business units at corporate headquarters. This may not be a monetary reward, but in many cultures it represents an endorsement and source of pride.

Foster communication across regional boundaries. Videoconferencing is an obvious tool to enhance global team communication, but it's important to have in-person meetings as well. At DHL, Karimi, together with the regional board members, visits one of the top 10 sites around the Asia Pacific region each month; each gets at least one personal visit a year. The visits include time for the local unit to showcase itself, and there is also unstructured time for informal and personal interaction.

Source: Adapted from Richard Pastore, "Global Team Management: It's a Small World After All," *CIO Magazine*, January 23, 2008.

Cultural, Political, and Geoeconomic Challenges

"Business as usual" is not good enough in global business operations. The same holds true for global e-business technology management. There are too many cultural, political, and geoeconomic (geographic and economic) realities that must be confronted for a business to succeed in global markets. As we have just mentioned, global information technology management must focus on developing global business IT strategies and managing global e-business application portfolios, Internet technologies, platforms, databases, and systems development projects. Managers, however, must also accomplish this task from a perspective and through methods that take into account the cultural, political, and geoeconomic differences that exist when doing business internationally.

For example, a major **political challenge** is that many countries have rules regulating or prohibiting transfer of data across their national boundaries (transborder data flows), especially personal information such as personnel records. Others severely restrict, tax, or prohibit imports of hardware and software. Still others have local content laws that specify the portion of the value of a product that must be added in that country if it is to be sold there. Some countries have reciprocal trade agreements that require a business to spend part of the revenue it earns in a country in that nation's economy.

Geoeconomic challenges in global business and IT refer to the effects of geography on the economic realities of international business activities. The sheer physical distances involved are still a major problem, even in this day of Internet telecommunications and jet travel. For example, it may still take too long to fly in specialists when IT problems occur in a remote site. It is still difficult to communicate in real time across the world's 24 time zones. It is still difficult to get good-quality telephone and telecommunications service in many countries. There are still problems finding the job skills required in some countries or enticing specialists from other countries to live and work there. Finally, there are still problems (and opportunities) in the great differences in the cost of living and labor costs in various countries. All of these geoeconomic challenges must be addressed when developing a company's global business and IT strategies.

Cultural challenges facing global business and IT managers include differences in languages, cultural interests, religions, customs, social attitudes, and political philosophies. Obviously, global IT managers must be trained and sensitized to such cultural differences before they are sent abroad or brought into a corporation's home country. Other cultural challenges include differences in work styles and business relationships. For example, should you take your time to avoid mistakes or hurry to get something done early? Should you go it alone or work cooperatively? Should the most experienced person lead, or should leadership be shared? The answers to such questions depend on the culture you are in and highlight the cultural differences that might exist in the global workplace. Let's take a look at a real-world example about what it takes to be global.

Global CIOs: What Does It Take to Become One?

Let's take the glamorous title of "Global CIO" and break it down into some of the job realities. What do multinational CIOs have to do that their domestic counterparts don't?

First, overcome language and cultural barriers. Then rethink "normal" business practices while coping with IT skill shortages and inexperienced labor pools. Next, build something from nothing. Now connect it to the global corporate infrastructure. Finally, leap tall buildings in a single bound.

That last one might just be the easiest task on the to-do list for IT executives in emerging global markets. "It requires some creativity and new thinking," says Cadbury CIO Wayne Shurts, in a vastly modest understatement of the challenges he and his international colleagues face.

At the same time, fresh approaches from less-developed corners of the world can become testing grounds for new technologies that scale back up to the corporate parent. The emerging markets teams at Cadbury, for example, came up with a sales-force automation tool for smartphones that could end up as part of the candymaker's global applications set. As CIO Shurts notes, the innovative IT mind-set springing up in these green-field markets can be a valuable upgrade for the company's entire global organization.

Because there are more programmers being trained every day in developing parts of the world, IT professionals in the United States are now competing in the global talent pool, as well. Although many U.S. companies today are still hiring globally only when their need is short-lived, or when skills are scarce or too high-priced in the local or domestic labor pool, some are going global just to find the best of the best, no matter where they're located.

And as many executive recruiters will tell you, CIOs who "go global" somewhere along their career paths develop business muscles their domestic colleagues can't match. The sheer variety of experiences in dealing with developing markets ultimately forges an IT chief who thinks very differently about the world of business.

Will a global tour of duty become a necessity for CIO success in the future?

Source: Adapted from Maryfran Johnson, "The Global CIO Job Description," *CIO*, November 12, 2009; and Mary Brandel, "Swimming in the Global Talent Pool," *Computerworld*, January 15, 2007.

Global Business/IT Strategies

Businesses are moving away from *international* strategies in which foreign subsidiaries are autonomous but depend on headquarters for new processes, products, and ideas; or from *global* strategies, in which a company's worldwide operations are closely managed by corporate headquarters. Instead, companies are moving toward a transnational strategy, where the company's business depends heavily on its information systems and Internet technologies to help it integrate its global business activities. Instead of having independent IS units at its subsidiaries, or even a centralized IS operation directed from its headquarters, a transnational business tries to develop an integrated and cooperative worldwide hardware, software, and Internet-based architecture for its IT platform. Figure 14.13 compares the three approaches to global business/IT strategy. Figure 14.14 illustrates how transnational business and IT strategies have been implemented by global companies.

FIGURE 14.13 Companies operating internationally are moving toward transnational business and IT strategies. Note some of the chief differences among international, global, and transnational business and IT strategies.

Comparing Global Business/IT Strategies		
International	**Global**	**Transnational**
• Autonomous operations • Region specific • Vertical integration • Specific customers • Captive manufacturing • Customer segmentation and dedication by region and plant	• Global sourcing • Multiregional • Horizontal integration • Some transparency of customers and production • Some cross regionalization	• Virtual business operations via global alliances • World markets and mass customization • Global e-commerce and customer service • Transparent manufacturing • Global supply chain and logistics • Dynamic resource management
Information Technology Characteristics		
• Stand-alone systems • Decentralized/no standards • Heavy reliance on interfaces • Multiple systems, high redundancy, and duplication of services and operations • Lack of common systems and data	• Regional decentralization • Interface dependent • Some consolidation of applications and use of common systems • Reduced duplication of operations • Some worldwide IT standards	• Logically consolidated, physically distributed, Internet connected • Common global data resources • Integrated global enterprise systems • Internet, intranet, extranet, and Web-based applications • Transnational IT policies and standards

FIGURE 14.14   Examples of how transnational business and IT strategies were implemented by global companies.

Tactic	Global Alliances	Global Sourcing and Logistics	Global Customer Service
Examples	British Airways/US Airways KLM/Northwest Qantas/American	Benetton	American Express
IT Environment	Global network (online reservation system).	Global network, EPOS terminals in 4,000 stores, CAD/CAM in central manufacturing, robots and laser scanner in automated warehouse.	Global network linked from local branches and local merchants to the customer database and medical or legal referrals database.
Results	• Coordination of schedules • Code sharing • Coordination of flights • Co-ownership	• Produce 2,000 sweaters per hour using CAD/CAM • Quick response (in stores in 10 days) • Reduced inventories (just-in-time)	• Worldwide access to funds • "Global Assist" hotline • Emergency credit card replacement • 24-hour customer service

Global Business/IT Applications

The applications of information technology developed by global companies depend on their **global business/IT strategies** and their expertise and experience in IT. Their IT applications, however, also depend on a variety of global business drivers, that is, business requirements caused by the nature of the industry and its competitive or environmental forces. One example would be companies like airlines or hotel chains that have global customers who travel widely or have global operations. Such companies need global IT capabilities for online transaction processing so that they can provide fast, convenient service to their customers—or face losing them to their competitors. The economies of scale provided by global business operations are other business drivers that require the support of global IT applications. Figure 14.15 summarizes some of the business requirements that make global IT a competitive necessity.

Of course, many global IT applications, particularly finance, accounting, and office applications, have been in operation for many years. For example, most multinational

FIGURE 14.15

Some of the business reasons driving global business applications.

Business Drivers of Global IT
• **Global Customers.** Customers are people who may travel anywhere or companies with global operations. Global IT can help provide fast, convenient service.
• **Global Products.** Products are the same throughout the world or are assembled by subsidiaries throughout the world. Global IT can help manage worldwide marketing and quality control.
• **Global Operations.** Parts of a production or assembly process are assigned to subsidiaries based on changing economic or other conditions. Only global IT can support such geographic flexibility.
• **Global Resources.** The use and cost of common equipment, facilities, and people are shared by subsidiaries of a global company. Global IT can keep track of such shared resources.
• **Global Collaboration.** The knowledge and expertise of colleagues in a global company can be quickly accessed, shared, and organized to support individual or group efforts. Only global IT can support such enterprise collaboration.

companies have global financial budgeting, cash management systems, and office automation applications such as fax and e-mail systems. As global operations expand and global competition heats up, however, there is increasing pressure for companies to install global e-commerce and e-business applications for their customers and suppliers. Examples include global e-commerce Web sites and customer service systems for customers, and global supply chain management systems for suppliers. In the past, such systems relied almost exclusively on privately constructed or government-owned telecommunications networks; now the explosive business use of the Internet, intranets, and extranets for e-commerce has made such applications much more feasible for global companies.

Omnicom Group Drives Global ERP Deployment

Omnicom Group Inc. is a strategic holding company that manages a portfolio of leading advertising and marketing services agencies. Omnicom has more than 60,000 employees worldwide and reported annual revenue of $13 billion in 2008.

Many of Omnicom's agencies needed more capable and efficient enterprise resource planning (ERP) and accounting systems to meet the increasing client demands for more detailed information and the financial reporting deadlines that the parent company sets.

Zimmerman Advertising, an Omnicom subsidiary that AdWeek ranks as the 14th-largest advertising firm in the United States, was saddled with a cumbersome financial management application. "Our system had not been updated or enhanced in many years—it was in maintenance mode," says Joe Weiner, vice president and corporate controller at Zimmerman. "We were left with few options in terms of improving the existing system. As a result, our financial reporting capabilities were limited and we had minimal ability to reengineer processes and to import and export data."

To improve financial management at its agencies and corporate reporting, Omnicom made the strategic decision to standardize on Microsoft Dynamics AX. "We needed to implement best-in-class financial management software that would allow our agencies to report in faster time frames and meet the varying client demands for information," says Wayne Wilson, global program manager for Omnicom. "Additionally, Microsoft Dynamics AX had the scalability and localization capabilities—both language and statutory—that we required as a global organization."

Omnicom created a template for Microsoft Dynamics AX that would streamline deployments across locations, set standards needed for reporting, and make it easier to customize the solution at the local level to meet the unique needs of individual agencies. For quick and easy access to information, Omnicom implemented Enterprise Portal for Microsoft Dynamics AX, which provides Web-based access to key information.

At Zimmerman, the efficiencies gained with the new system have been dramatic. "Microsoft Dynamics AX offers a multidimensional chart of accounts that vastly improves our revenue and expense reporting," says Chuck Miller, financial systems manager at Zimmerman. "We're also seeing many other efficiencies in our processes.

We save 80 hours each month with our new process for importing transactions, and our ability to capture more detailed information is better as well. We're also using the online document-handling function to save and retrieve documents electronically, and we have established automatic workflows."

"As a global company, we had to ensure we had alignment between our strategic goals at the corporate level and the individual implementations that were occurring throughout the agencies," explains Wilson. "We aligned the Microsoft product, our corporate goals, and the agencies' local requirements. The coordinated efforts of the consulting and development teams made it so that knowledge gained in one area of the program was incorporated into other areas of the program."

Source: Adapted from *Microsoft Case Study*, "Omnicom Group Drives Global ERP Deployment with Strategy and Development Support," January 29, 2010.

Global IT Platforms

The management of technology platforms (also called the technology infrastructure) is another major dimension of global IT management—that is, managing the hardware, software, data resources, telecommunications networks, and computing facilities that support global business operations. The management of a global IT platform not only is technically complex but also has major political and cultural implications.

For example, hardware choices are difficult in some countries because of high prices, high tariffs, import restrictions, long lead times for government approvals, lack of local service or spare parts, and lack of documentation tailored to local conditions. Software choices can also present unique problems. Software packages developed in Europe may be incompatible with American or Asian versions, even when purchased from the same hardware vendor. Well-known U.S. software packages may be unavailable because there is no local distributor or because the software publisher refuses to supply markets that disregard software licensing and copyright agreements.

Managing international data communications networks, including Internet, intranet, extranet, and other networks, is a key global IT challenge. Figure 14.16 outlines the top 10 international data communications issues as reported by IS executives at 300 Fortune 500 multinational companies. Notice how political issues dominate the top 10 listing over technology issues, clearly emphasizing their importance in the management of global telecommunications.

Establishing computing facilities internationally is another global challenge. Companies with global business operations usually establish or contract with systems integrators for additional data centers in their subsidiaries in other countries. These data centers meet local and regional computing needs and even help balance global computing workloads through communications satellite links. Offshore data centers, however, can pose major problems in headquarters' support, hardware and software acquisition, maintenance, and security. That's why many global companies turn to application service providers or systems integrators like EDS or IBM to manage their overseas operations.

FIGURE 14.16

The top 10 issues in managing international data communications.

International Data Communications Issues
Network Management Issues
● Improving the operational efficiency of networks
● Dealing with different networks
● Controlling data communication security
Regulatory Issues
● Dealing with transborder data flow restrictions
● Managing international telecommunication regulations
● Handling international politics
Technology Issues
● Managing network infrastructure across countries
● Managing international integration of technologies
Country-Oriented Issues
● Reconciling national differences
● Dealing with international tariff structures

Source: Adapted from Vincent S. Lai and Wingyan Chung, "Managing International Data Communications," *Communications of the ACM*, March 2002, p. 91.

Orbitz.com: Toward an Integrated Global Platform

Originally established through a partnership of major airlines, and subsequently owned by various entities, Orbitz.com—the flagship brand of Orbitz Worldwide—has been in operation since 2001. Now it's undertaking a major upgrade to improve its online platform and enhance its ability to do business worldwide. All of this has to happen without disrupting Orbitz's ongoing operations.

Orbitz must interface with an array of systems to conduct business: It still has ties into the reservation systems of its original airline owners and those of other airlines it has partnered with along the way. It also must tap into the global distribution systems that still account for a great deal of the airline reservation business. And Orbitz isn't only about airline tickets. The real action and the real profits in the travel industry these days are in hotel rooms, car rentals, train trips, luxury cruises, bus tours, event tickets, and all of that rolled up into vacation packages.

Orbitz was left without a CIO after the departure of Bahman Koohestani. "I certainly understand enough about IT to run this organization," says Mike Nelson, chief operations officer, who has a background in financial planning and operations, not technology.

Jack Staehler, group vice president of technology, isn't worried about the lack of a CIO title. "The global platform, that's my charter," he says.

Code-named Austin, Orbitz's new online platform is a component-based system that uses a great deal of the Java code underpinning Orbitz's current platform.

What's different is that it can support multiple Web sites, both internal and external to Orbitz. It features standards-based user-interface technology able to incorporate dynamic updates and accessible from a range of devices. The idea is to be able to plug in data feeds from Orbitz's systems, like CheapTickets.com, and those of its partners and potential partners. It's multilingual and multicurrency, yet location specific.

For example, it understands what a domestic flight is wherever it's being accessed; previously, "domestic" was hardwired into the Orbitz system as referring to the United States.

Orbitz began rolling out Austin in 2008, starting with the Ebookers site in England. "The new Web site aims to make booking decisions easier through simpler navigation and more product choice," the company said in a release. Hooking into the Orbitz system, for instance, tripled hotel inventory available to Ebookers customers.

One reason Orbitz is in such a hurry is that the online travel industry isn't standing still. Travel search engines like Kayak.com, which can operate across platforms, threaten online travel sites with some of the same disintermediation that travel sites brought to travel agencies years ago. And some observers wonder when, not if, the 800-pound Internet gorilla, Google, will enter the online travel market.

"We're trying to accelerate this as much as possible, but it's a huge task," Nelson says. "You can only throw bodies at it so much, and that doesn't mean it's going to happen any faster."

Source: Adapted from John Soat, "Orbitz's Long, Strange Trip to a New Online Platform," *InformationWeek*, February 9, 2008.

The Internet as a Global IT Platform

What makes the Internet and the World Wide Web so important for international business? This interconnected matrix of computers, information, and networks that reaches tens of millions of users in over one hundred countries is a business environment free of traditional boundaries and limits. Linking to an online global infrastructure offers companies unprecedented potential for expanding markets, reducing costs, and improving profit margins at a price that is typically a small percentage of the corporate communications budget. The Internet provides an interactive channel for direct communication and data exchange with customers, suppliers, distributors, manufacturers, product developers, financial backers, information providers—in fact, with all parties involved in a given business venture.

So the Internet and the World Wide Web have now become vital components in international business and commerce. Within a few years, the Internet, with its

FIGURE 14.17
Key questions for
companies establishing
global Internet Web sites.

Key Questions
• Will you have to develop a new navigational logic to accommodate cultural preferences?
• What content will you translate, and what content will you create from scratch to address regional competitors or products that differ from those in the United States?
• Should your multilingual effort be an adjunct to your main site, or will you make it a separate site, perhaps with a country-specific domain name?
• What kinds of traditional and new media advertising will you have to do in each country to draw traffic to your site?
• Will your site get so many hits that you'll need to set up a server in a local country?
• What are the legal ramifications of having your Web site targeted at a particular country, such as laws on competitive behavior, treatment of children, or privacy?

interconnected network of thousands of networks of computers and databases, has established itself as a technology platform free of many traditional international boundaries and limits. By connecting their businesses to this online global infrastructure, companies can expand their markets, reduce communications and distribution costs, and improve their profit margins without massive cost outlays for new telecommunications facilities. Figure 14.17 outlines key considerations for global e-commerce Web sites.

The Internet, along with its related intranet and extranet technologies, provides a low-cost interactive channel for communications and data exchange with employees, customers, suppliers, distributors, manufacturers, product developers, financial backers, information providers, and so on. In fact, all parties involved can use the Internet and other related networks to communicate and collaborate to bring a business venture to its successful completion. As Figure 14.18 illustrates, amazing growth has occurred worldwide with regard to the Internet; however, much work needs to be done to bring secure Internet access and e-commerce to more people in more countries. Nonetheless, the trend is clearly toward continued expansion of the Internet as it becomes a pervasive IT platform for global business.

Global Data Access Issues

Global data access issues have been a subject of political controversy and technology barriers in global business operations for many years but have become more visible with the growth of the Internet and the pressures of e-commerce. A major example is the issue of

FIGURE 14.18 Current numbers of Internet users by world region. Note: Internet usage and population statistics, updated on December 31, 2009.

World Regions	Population (2009 Est.)	Population (% of World)	Internet Usage, Latest Data	Usage Growth 2000–2009 (%)	Penetration (% Population)	World Users (%)
Africa	991,002,342	14.0	86,217,900	1,809.8	8.7	4.8
Asia	3,808,070,503	56.3	764,435,900	568.8	20.1	42.4
Europe	803,850,808	11.4	425,773,571	305.1	53.0	23.6
Middle East	202,687,005	4.0	58,309,546	1,675.1	28.8	3.2
North America	340,831,831	5.1	259,561,000	140.1	76.2	14.4
Latin America/Caribbean	586,662,468	8.5	186,922,050	934.5	31.9	10.4
Oceania/Australia	34,700,201	0.5	186,922,050	177.0	60.8	1.2
WORLD TOTAL	6,767,805,208	100.0	1,802,330,457	399.3	26.6	100.0

Source: www.internetworldstats.com.

FIGURE 14.19

Key data privacy provisions of the agreement to protect the privacy of consumers in e-commerce transactions between the United States and the European Union.

U.S.–E.U. Data Privacy Requirements
● Notice of purpose and use of data collected
● Ability to opt out of third-party distribution of data
● Access for consumers to their information
● Adequate security, data integrity, and enforcement provisions

transborder data flows (TDF), in which business data flow across international borders over the telecommunications networks of global information systems. Many countries view TDF as a violation of their national sovereignty because these data flows avoid customs duties and regulations for the import or export of goods and services. Others view TDF as a violation of their laws to protect the local IT industry from competition or their labor regulations for protecting local jobs. In many cases, the data flow business issues that seem especially politically sensitive are those that affect the movement out of a country of personal data in e-commerce and human resource applications.

Many countries, especially those in the European Union (E.U.), may view transborder data flows as a violation of their privacy legislation because, in many cases, data about individuals are being moved out of the country without stringent privacy safeguards. For example, Figure 14.19 outlines the key provisions of a data privacy agreement between the United States and the European Union. The agreement exempts U.S. companies engaging in international e-commerce from E.U. data privacy sanctions if they join a self-regulatory program that provides E.U. consumers with basic information about, and control over, how their personal data are used. Thus, the agreement is said to provide a "safe harbor" for such companies from the requirements of the E.U.'s Data Privacy Directive, which bans the transfer of personal information on E.U. citizens to countries that do not have adequate data privacy protection.

Europe: Tighter Laws Worry Security Professionals

Moves by several European countries to tighten laws against computer hacking worry security professionals who often use the same tools as hackers but for legitimate purposes. The United Kingdom and Germany are among the countries that are considering revisions to their computer crime laws in line with the 2001 Convention on Cybercrime, a Europe-wide treaty, and with a similar E.U. measure passed in early 2005.

But security professionals are scrutinizing those revisions out of concern for how prosecutors and judges could apply the laws. Security professionals are especially concerned about cases where the revisions apply to programs that could be used for bad or good. Companies often use hacking programs to test the mettle of their own systems.

"One useful utility in the wrong hands is a potentially malicious hacking tool," says Graham Cluley, senior technology consultant at Sophos in Abingdon, England. The proposed revisions would make it illegal to create or supply a tool to someone who intends to use it for unauthorized computer access or modification. Likewise, the proposed changes to German law would also criminalize making and distributing hacking tools. The German government said the changes will bring it into compliance with the 2001 Convention on Cybercrime. Several German security companies are planning to lobby against the law, as they fear it could hamper those who test security systems, says Alexander Kornbrust, founder and chief executive officer of Red-Database-Security in Neunkirchen, Germany. For example, tools to check the strength of passwords, often freely distributed, could also be used by malicious hackers, he says.

"The security community is very unhappy with this approach," Kornbrust says. "The concern is that the usage and possession of so-called hacker tools will become illegal."

The United Kingdom and Germany are trying to align their laws with Article 6 of the convention, which bans the creation of computer programs for the purpose of committing cyber-crime. So far, 43 countries have signed the convention, which indicates their willingness to revise their laws to comply. Fifteen have ratified the convention. After a country changes its laws, it can ratify the convention and put it into force.

Source: Adapted from Dave Gradijan, "Euro Computer Crime Laws Have Security Pros Worried," *CSO Magazine*, September 29, 2006.

Internet Access Issues

The Paris-based organization Reporters Without Borders (RSF) reports that there are 45 countries that "restrict their citizens' access to the Internet." At its most fundamental, the struggle between Internet censorship and openness at the national level revolves around three main means: controlling the conduits, filtering the flows, and punishing the purveyors. In countries such as Burma, Libya, North Korea, Syria, and the countries of Central Asia and the Caucasus, Internet access is either banned or subject to tight limitations through government-controlled ISPs, says the RSF.

Figure 14.20 outlines the restrictions to public **Internet access** by the governments of the countries deemed most restrictive by the Paris-based Reporters Without Borders (RSF). See their Web site at www.rsf.fr.

As an example, Internet censorship in the People's Republic of China is conducted under a wide variety of laws and administrative regulations. In accordance with these laws, more than sixty Internet regulations have been made by the People's Republic of China (PRC) government, and censorship systems are vigorously implemented by provincial branches of state-owned ISPs, business companies, and organizations. Most national laws of the People's Republic of China do not apply to the Special Administrative Regions of Hong Kong or Macau. There are no known cases of the PRC authorities censoring critical political or religious content in those areas.

The escalation of the government's effort to neutralize critical online opinion comes after a series of large anti-Japanese, anti-pollution and anti-corruption protests, many of which were organized or publicized using instant messaging services, chat rooms, and text messages. The size of the Internet police is estimated at more than 30,000. Critical comments appearing on Internet forums, blogs, and major portals such as Sohu and Sina usually are erased within minutes.

The apparatus of the PRC's Internet repression is considered more extensive and more advanced than in any other country in the world. The regime not only blocks Web site content but also monitors the internet access of individuals. Amnesty International notes that China "has the largest recorded number of imprisoned journalists and cyber-dissidents in the world." The offenses of which they are accused include communicating with groups abroad, opposing the persecution of the Falun Gong, signing online petitions, and calling for reform and an end to corruption.

FIGURE 14.20

Countries that restrict or forbid Internet access by their citizens.

Global Government Restrictions on Internet Access
● **High Government Access Fees** Kazakhstan, Kyrgyzstan
● **Government-Monitored Access** China, Iran, Saudi Arabia, Azerbaijan, Uzbekistan
● **Government-Filtered Access** Belarus, Cuba, Iraq, Tunisia, Sierra Leone, Tajikistan, Turkmenistan, Vietnam
● **No Public Access Allowed** Burma, Libya, North Korea

So the Internet has become a global battleground over public access to data and information at business and private sites on the World Wide Web. Of course, this becomes a business issue because restrictive access policies severely inhibit the growth of e-commerce with such countries. Most of the rest of the world has decided that restricting Internet access is not a viable policy but in fact would hurt their countries' opportunities for economic growth and prosperity. Instead, national and international efforts are being made to rate and filter Internet content deemed inappropriate or criminal, such as Web sites for child pornography or terrorism. In any event, countries that significantly restrict Internet access are also choosing to restrict their participation in the growth of e-commerce.

To RSF and others, these countries' rulers face a losing battle against the Information Age. By denying or limiting Internet access, they stymie a major engine of economic growth. By easing access, however, they expose their citizenry to ideas that potentially might destabilize to the status quo. Either way, many people will get access to the electronic information they want. "In Syria, for example, people go to Lebanon for the weekend to retrieve their e-mail," says Virginie Locussol, RSF's desk officer for the Middle East and North Africa.

Global Systems Development

Just imagine the challenges of developing efficient, effective, and responsive applications for business end users domestically. Then, multiply that by the number of countries and cultures that may use a global e-business system. That's the challenge of managing global systems development. Naturally, there are conflicts over local versus global system requirements, as well as difficulties agreeing on common system features, such as multilingual user interfaces and flexible design standards. All of this effort must take place in an environment that promotes involvement and "ownership" of a system by local end users.

Other systems development issues arise from disturbances caused by systems implementation and maintenance activities. For example, "An interruption during a third shift in New York City will present midday service interruptions in Tokyo." Another major development issue relates to the trade-offs between developing one system that can run on multiple computer and operating system platforms or letting each local site customize the software for its own platform.

Other important global systems development issues are concerned with global standardization of data definitions. Common data definitions are necessary for sharing data among the parts of an international business. Differences in language, culture, and technology platforms can make global data standardization quite difficult. For example, a sale may be called an "order booked" in the United Kingdom, an "order scheduled" in Germany, and an "order produced" in France. Yet, businesses are moving ahead to standardize data definitions and structures. By moving their subsidiaries into data modeling and database design, they hope to develop a global data architecture that supports their global business objectives.

Systems Development Strategies

Several strategies can be used to solve some of the systems development problems that arise in global IT. The first strategy is to transform an application used in the home office into a global application. Often, the system that has the best version of an application will be chosen for global use. Another approach is to set up a *multinational development team* with key people from several subsidiaries to ensure that the system design meets the needs of local sites, as well as corporate headquarters.

A third approach is called *parallel development*. That's because parts of the system are assigned to different subsidiaries and the home office to develop at the same time, based on the expertise and experience at each site. Another approach is the concept of *centers of excellence*. In this approach, an entire system may be assigned for development to a particular subsidiary based on its expertise in the business or technical dimensions needed for successful development. A final approach that has rapidly become a major

FIGURE 14.21 An example of Internet-enabled collaboration in global IT systems development. Note the roles played by the client company, off-shore outsource developer, global open-source community, and just-in-time development team.

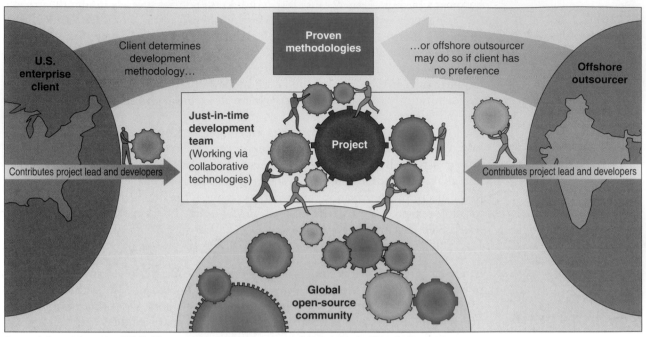

Source: Adapted from Jon Udell, "Leveraging a Global Advantage," *Infoworld*, April 21, 2003, p. 35.

development option is to outsource the development work to global or *offshore* development companies that have the skills and experience required to develop global business/IT applications. Obviously, all of these approaches require development team collaboration and managerial oversight to meet the global needs of a business. So, global systems development teams are making heavy use of the Internet, intranets, groupware, and other electronic collaboration technologies. See Figure 14.21.

| Invensys PLC: Drawing Talent from Around the World for Software Development

  | It's great being able to draw upon your best programmers from throughout the world. SimSci-Esscor, the industrial process simulation and control unit of Invensys PLC, will assign personnel from any of its offices to assemble the right team. "Our development projects operate in a virtual mode and gather people from multiple sites based on project needs," says Joe Ayers, director of development services at SimSci-Esscor in Lake Forest, California. "It is common for projects to utilize developers from three different time zones in a 'follow the sun' development mode."

 The approach allows Invensys to find the right talent for the project, and work is done in an efficient way. But managing those far-flung developers can be a nightmare. "Invensys had brought together multiple companies with different cultures and processes," Ayers explains. "Some of the issues we have had to address include duplication of source code, multiple tools and processes in use, and limited network connectivity and reliability."

 To tackle these issues, Invensys created a virtual development infrastructure for 135 developers in five locations. To facilitate communication, it incorporated desktop-sharing tools, instant messaging, conference calling, and voice-over-IP technology.

 For working on the code itself, the company deployed three products from Telelogic AB in Malmo, Sweden: Synergy/CM for controlling project configuration items, Synergy/Change for controlling change requests, and Synergy/Distributed CM for synchronizing change requests and source code between databases at multiple |

sites. It also implemented a wide-area file-sharing system from Availl Inc. in Andover, Massachusetts, for other documents. "With this development structure, we have the ability to add or remove changes to software builds at the last minute, with no project-delivery slips attributed to distributed development complexity over the last year," says Ayers. "We've been able to lower project start-up time and project costs."

Experts say managing distributed development teams requires a mix of processes and tools. "Rarely is it a problem with the technology, though that used to be a major hurdle in the past," says Dale Karolak, vice president of product development at Intier Automotive Inc. in Novi, Michigan, and author of *Global Software Development: Managing Virtual Teams and Environments.* "Most problems now are with communications, documentation and alignment." Karolak says managers need to exert more discipline when it comes to scheduling and holding meetings and tracking project targets, and spend more time visiting off-site locations for face-to-face meetings. Proper management also requires a greater awareness of potential problems.

"Jump on problems right away. Don't wait," Karolak says. "Longer distances will cause longer delays in solving the issues if they are not addressed quickly."

Source: Adapted from Drew Robb, "Global Workgroups," *Computerworld*, August 15, 2005.

Summary

- **Managing Information Technology.** This can be viewed as managing three major components: (1) the joint development and implementation of e-business and IT strategies, (2) the development of e-business applications and the research and implementation of new information technologies, and (3) IT processes, professionals, and subunits within a company's IT organization and IS function.

- **Failures in IT Management.** Information systems are not being used effectively or efficiently by many organizations. The experiences of successful organizations reveal that the basic ingredient of high-quality information system performance is extensive and meaningful management, as well as user involvement in the governance and development of IT applications. Thus, managers may serve on executive IT groups and create IS management functions within their business units.

- **Managing Global IT.** The international dimensions of managing global information technologies include dealing with cultural, political, and geoeconomic challenges posed by various countries; developing appropriate business and IT strategies for the global marketplace; and developing a portfolio of global e-business

and e-commerce applications and an Internet-based technology platform to support them. In addition, data access methods have to be developed and systems development projects managed to produce the global e-business applications that are required to compete successfully in the global marketplace.

- **Global Business and IT Strategies and Issues.** Many businesses are becoming global companies and moving toward transnational business strategies in which they integrate the global business activities of their subsidiaries and headquarters. This transition requires that they develop a global IT platform—that is, an integrated worldwide hardware, software, and Internet-based network architecture. Global companies are increasingly using the Internet and related technologies as a major component of this IT platform to develop and deliver global IT applications that meet their unique global business requirements. Global IT and end-user managers must deal with limitations to the availability of hardware and software; restrictions on transborder data flows, Internet access, and movement of personal data; and difficulties with developing common data definitions and system requirements.

Key Terms and Concepts

These are the key terms and concepts of this chapter. The page number of their first explanation is in parentheses.

1. Application development management (620)

2. Business/IT planning process (617)

3. Centralization or decentralization of IT (620)

4. Chargeback systems (621)

5. Chief information officer (CIO) (622)

6. Chief technology officer (CTO) (623)

● *Module V / Management Challenges*

7. Data center (621)

8. Downsizing (620)

9. Global business drivers (638)

10. Global information technology management (632)

    a. Data access issues (642)

    b. Systems development issues (645)

11. IS operations management (621)

12. IT architecture (618)

13. IT staff planning (622)

14. Management and end-user involvement (628)

15. Managing information technology (614)

16. Offshoring (625)

17. Outsourcing (624)

18. System performance monitor (621)

19. Technology management (623)

20. Transborder data flows (TDF) (643)

21. Transnational strategy (637)

22. User services (623)

Review Quiz

Match one of the key terms and concepts listed previously with one of the brief examples or definitions that follow. Try to find the best answer, even though some seem to fit more than one term or concept. Defend your choices.

_____ 1. Focuses on discovering innovative approaches to satisfying a company's customer value and business value goals with the support of IT.

_____ 2. Concerned with the use of hardware, software, network, and IS personnel resources within the corporate or business unit.

_____ 3. Managing business/IT planning and the IS function within a company.

_____ 4. A conceptual design, or blueprint, of an organization's IS/IT functions, hardware, and software created by a strategic business/IT planning process.

_____ 5. Many organizations have both centralized and decentralized IT units.

_____ 6. Managing the creation and implementation of new business applications.

_____ 7. End users need liaison, consulting, and training services.

_____ 8. Involves recruiting, training, and retaining qualified IS personnel.

_____ 9. Corporate locations for computer system operations.

_____ 10. Rapidly changing technological developments must be anticipated, identified, and implemented.

_____ 11. A relocation of an organization's business processes (including production/manufacturing) to a lower-cost location, usually overseas.

_____ 12. The executive responsible for strategic business/IT planning and IT management.

_____ 13. The executive in charge of researching and implementing new information technologies.

_____ 14. Software that helps monitor and control computer systems in a data center.

_____ 15. The cost of IS services may be allocated back to end users.

_____ 16. Many business firms are replacing their mainframe systems with networked PCs and servers.

_____ 17. The purchase of goods or services from third-party partners that were previously provided internally.

_____ 18. Managing IT to support a company's international business operations.

_____ 19. A business depends heavily on its information systems and Internet technologies to help it integrate its global business activities.

_____ 20. Global customers, products, operations, resources, and collaboration.

_____ 21. Global telecommunications networks like the Internet move data across national boundaries.

_____ 22. Agreement is needed on common user interfaces and Web site design features in global IT.

_____ 23. Security requirements for personal information in corporate databases within a host country are a top concern.

_____ 24. Business managers should oversee IT decision making and projects that are critical to their business units' success.

Discussion Questions

1. What has been the impact of information technologies on the work relationships, activities, and resources of managers?

2. What can business unit managers do about performance problems in the use of information technology

and the development and operation of information systems in their business units?

3. Refer to the Real World Case on IT money wasters in the chapter. IT may hold the key to large savings

throughout the organization. What does it take to be successful in this regard?

4. How are Internet technologies affecting the structure and work roles of modern organizations? For example, will middle management wither away? Will companies consist primarily of self-directed project teams of knowledge workers? Explain your answers.

5. Should the IS function in a business be centralized or decentralized? Use the Internet to find recent developments to support your answer.

6. Refer to the Real World Case on the globalization challenges faced by CIOs in the chapter. All those mentioned are CIOs from headquarters who went abroad, but there is no mention of CIOs from emerging countries taking over the global helm. Why do you think this is the case?

7. How might cultural, political, or geoeconomic challenges affect a global company's use of the Internet? Give several examples.

8. Will the increasing use of the Internet by firms with global business operations change their move toward a transnational business strategy? Explain.

9. How might the Internet, intranets, and extranets affect the business drivers or requirements responsible for a company's use of global IT, as shown in Figure 14.13? Give several examples to illustrate your answer.

Analysis Exercises

1. **Top-Rated Web Sites for Executives**
   CEO Express
   Check out CEO Express (www.ceoexpress.com), a top-rated Web portal for busy executives. See Figure 14.22. The site provides links to top U.S. and international newspapers, business and technology magazines, and news services. Hundreds of links to business and technology research sources and references are provided, as well as travel services, online shopping, and recreational Web sites. Premium services include e-mail, contact management, calendaring and scheduling, community networking, and powerful information organizing and sharing tools.

   a. Evaluate the CEO Express Web site as a source of useful links to business and technology news, analysis, and research sources for business executives and professionals.

   b. Compare CEO Express with Google News (news.google.com) and Google IG (www.google.com/ig). What advantages does CEO Express provide?

   c. Select the featured article from the "Editor's Corner." What was the source? Summarize the article. Was it useful to you?

FIGURE 14.22
The CEO Express Web site.

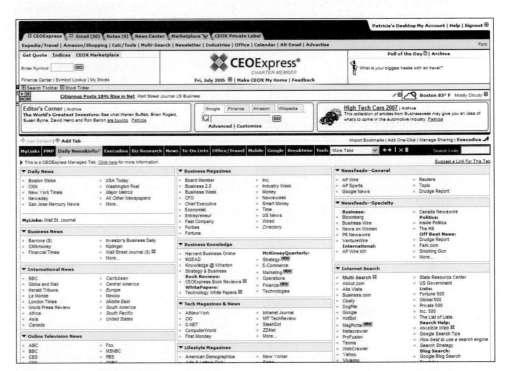

Source: Courtesy of CEO Express.

2. Information and Communications for Development
Assessing Global Capabilities
More than one billion people take their electrical and telecommunications systems for granted. However, for billions more, the service-on-demand mentality remains a distant dream and Internet access only a rumor. Recognizing the need to promote global information and communications technologies (GICT), the World Bank has undertaken numerous technology infrastructure assessment and development projects.

  a. What is the World Bank (www.worldbank.org) doing to address third-world computer literacy needs?
  b. What is MIT (www.mit.edu) doing to help increase global computer literacy?

3. Overseas Assignments
Incompatible Electricity?
Business travelers who need to remain connected face special challenges outside their home country, especially those who work out of their hotel rooms. Electricity varies by voltage, cycles, and electric-plug shape. Likewise, telephone jacks may vary from country to country and, for the most part, American cell phones work only in America.

If you find yourself on an overseas assignment, how will you keep your laptop computer charged? How will you access the Internet? Can you free yourself from expensive hotel telephone surcharges?

Pick a country to "visit" (your professor may assign one instead), and report on specific solutions to each question. Be sure to include the manufacturer and model number of any hardware you may require. Cite all your sources.

  a. What do you need to bring with you to keep your laptop computer charged?
  b. What do you need to bring with you to connect your laptop's modem to the local telephone network?
  c. What will you use in place of your handy cell phone?
  d. Use a collaboration-enabled system such as Blackboard, Web CT, Dreamweaver, or Front Page to merge, organize, and publish your results with the rest of your class to create an online resource.

4. Knowledge Work on the Move
Business Process Outsourcing
As a result of the location independence of knowledge work, many organizations seek to lower their labor costs by moving their digital operations overseas. When managers evaluate such opportunities, they must consider the following regional attributes:

  • Political and regulatory environment
  • Infrastructure (electrical, telecommunications)
  • Professionally skilled labor force
  • Information systems skilled labor force

All prospective locations must have a supportive political and regulatory environment; however, variations within the other three attributes will pose special limitations. For example, India has millions of well-educated workers but notoriously unreliable telecommunications and electrical grids. Organizations that set up outsourcing operations in India build their own islands of stability with backup power and satellite telecommunications systems. A region with a shortage of professionally skilled labor may offer labor-intensive activities such as call centers or data entry instead, yet even these jobs require basic computer literacy.

The value of services provided depends primarily on the expertise or creativity involved in its performance. List suitable job titles for each work characteristic below. Rank each item in order of the value provided.

  a. Digitize: Convert data or information into a digital form.
  b. Distribute: Process information in one direction or another based on strict rules and nondigital inputs (if the inputs were digital, a computer could probably do the job).
  c. Analyze: Process information based on human expertise.
  d. Create: Create new information or products based on human expertise.

REAL WORLD CASE 3

Toyota, Procter & Gamble, Hess Corporation, and Others: Retiring CIOs and the Need for Succession Planning

Barbra Cooper started as a CIO when the position was still called "vice president of information services." In her more than 30 years in IT, she's seen the role become ever more strategic. Until now, the CIO is in the unique position of being the C-level officer who can "see across the entire enterprise."

As the CIO for Toyota Motor Sales USA, Cooper thinks tomorrow's CIOs will be even more strategic and influential, but she also worries about the future business and technology changes they face. "The next 10 to 20 years are going to be challenging," she says. As she talks about the challenges that lie ahead, the question arises: Where will the IT leaders come from to tackle them?

It's a question more and more IT executives are asking themselves. CIOs are moving up and out. The first full-career CIO generation is beginning to retire. Others are increasingly taking on broader responsibilities or moving out of IT and into other business leadership roles as the position evolves beyond its technology roots. In fact, CIO's 2008 State of the CIO report found that 56 percent of CIOs surveyed say long-term strategic thinking and planning is the executive leadership skill most critical in their current role, followed by collaboration and influence (47 percent), and expertise running IT (39 percent). At the same time, many CIOs don't know who would lead IT if they left tomorrow. When you consider that just 17 percent of respondents to the State of the CIO survey cited people development as a critical leadership competency, that's not surprising.

The skills to be CIO have also changed as the role has shifted from technologist to business strategist. It used to be that "we could afford to let the business tell us what they wanted us to do, be good at delivering it and keep our jobs," says Cooper. "Now, the physics and velocity of business and its demands mean you can't afford to wait until something happens."

Indeed, CEOs now look to the CIO to act more as a strategic business leader and less as a function head. TAC Worldwide CEO Robert Badavas says he seldom speaks about technology with his CIO; instead, the two talk about "shaping the business value to our clients," he says. To be successful, he notes, the CIO needs to understand the value proposition of the business. "By staying in the silo of technology, HR, accounting or any other," says Badavas, "you're not going to be as valuable to the business." Or to the CEO.

With all that in mind, CIOs today must groom not only competent replacements for themselves but also next-generation IT leaders who are "business ready" and able to succeed in a more IT-intense and integral business environment. The shift in business expectations means that CIOs have better job security than in the past.

It also takes longer to find good ones with the right mix of business and technical know-how. For example, Pete Walton is in his second stint as CIO at Hess Corp. The petroleum products company coaxed him out of retirement in 2005 when its CIO at that time left. Hess wanted someone who could take its Information Services "to the next level," says Walton.

"CEOs want someone who's business savvy and can figure out how you can use technology for the business. Trying to find that hybrid person is hard," says Diane S. Wallace, chief information officer for the state of Connecticut. It will only get harder to find them, just for demographic reasons. "We have this triple threat of labor shortage: The Boomers are retiring, young people are not going into IT and fewer people are getting degrees," says Robert D. Scott, who in February retired as Procter & Gamble's vice president of global business services. Scott says he noticed a drop in IT interest during the technology bubble of the late 1990s.

Then the rush to outsourcing created a cloud around U.S. IT jobs. That pall persists despite strong job growth in IT, which is expected to add more than 200,000 jobs by 2016, according to the Bureau of Labor Statistics.

Procter & Gamble (P&G) is a case in point. It outsourced about half of its IT staff in 2003, but IT employment is now back to the level it was five years ago. Scott says that this is because the company outsourced its commodity IT, and "internal IT moved up the food chain, and is creating more and more business value."

Scott says P&G continues to attract strong candidates for IT jobs, but the hiring pool is not as deep as in years past. Plus, P&G believes strongly in promoting people steeped in its culture. It worries about keeping its Generation Y employees. The triple threat is already creating an IT brain drain. Wallace says 40 percent of her staff of 518 will be eligible for retirement in the next two to three years. Barbara A. White, chief information officer and associate provost at the University of Georgia, says that when three staff members retired in April, she lost their combined 90 years of experience, and she has a lot of staff likely to retire in the next 10 years.

Toyota's Cooper is dedicating time to prepare her organization for the future, which includes being as proactive as possible and staying ahead of the business needs. It also means a commitment to active succession planning. Two years ago, Cooper sat down for 90 minutes with 27 team members who reported either directly to her or directly to another team member. Each meeting was an open coaching session structured around her ideas of what IT leaders will need to be in 10 years. She then crafted a three- to four-page letter for each team member, detailing the capabilities she wanted them to develop and a plan for showing how they were achieving them. Those who reported directly to her received a summary of what she sent to their team members.

Procter & Gamble has a corporate culture that promotes from within. It saw, however, that good technical talent was getting harder to keep, and it also understood that

Generation Y employees expect to change companies frequently. To combat both challenges, it blazed a new, faster IT career path for its younger workers.

IT leadership adopted an accelerated development program, as a part of the career path, says Scott. It would place a new set of top performers in a Career Executive Development Program, designed to provide them exposure to high-level IT executives and assignments to help accelerate their growth. It comes with one caveat: If you don't perform, you'll be looking for another employer. It's a modified version of what's in place in the company's fabled brand management department.

"We wanted to signal that we were very serious about growing people, and were willing to invest extra time and energy" in them, he says. The program is only two years old and is too new to have clear results (no one, for instance, has been asked to leave yet).

P&G also created what it calls "The CIO Circle," which rewards long-time IT people who have mastered an area of technical expertise. This "master's" designation allows P&G to acknowledge their status as knowledge leaders even if they are not on the management track. Rewards programs encourage employee loyalty, says Laurie Orlov, a consultant and principal of LMO Insight. Fast-track development in particular should help companies cultivate Generation Y leaders. With so much training and management exposure, they have every reason to stay, she says.

Chief information officers who are serious about developing leaders in their group have to be willing to invest time in their people and to give them opportunities to grow, even

if that means sometimes letting them fail. It might also mean getting out of their way when the time comes. Hess Corp.'s Walton says that his goal at all of his jobs has been to identify and develop replacements for himself. "You do that by creating opportunities for them, you make them look like leadership heroes in the eyes of their business and let them take all the glory," says Walton, who is 63 and retired from Hess for the second time last month after the company named Jeff Steinhorn, who served under Walton, as its new CIO.

Like most chief information officers who aim to develop their staff, Walton has used a multipronged strategy for helping people along: He mentors, he provides role models, he moves staff into new opportunities, and he invests heavily in education. In fact, he sent selected top managers to a Harvard Business School executive program, and IT has two memberships to the BSG Concours Group, a strategy and executive education firm.

Walton sees the coming leadership challenge as a plus, not a minus. "There is a gap, but it's an exciting one to fill," he says. For one thing, Walton thinks the blend of experience and technical savvy available when you mix Baby Boomers and Generation Y is a powerful one for companies that work to bring these generations together.

He is talking with Hess about how to do it, and he may want to take on such a role in the future. Now that a new IT leader is in place at Hess, however, Walton can relax for a bit. "I'm going to get my [golf] handicap down," he says.

Source: Adapted from Michael Fitzgerald, "How to Develop the Next Generation of IT Leaders," *CIO Magazine*, May 2, 2008.

CASE STUDY QUESTIONS

1. Several comments in the case note that chief information officers are in a unique position for companywide leadership, extending beyond their primary technological concerns. Why do you think this is the case? How are CIOs different in this regard from other chief officers, for example, in finance, HR, or marketing?

2. After reading the case, what do you think are the most important competencies for the successful CIO of tomorrow? How do you rate yourself in those? Have you considered the importance of these skills and abilities before?

3. How can chief information officers prepare their successors for an uncertain future that will most likely require skills different from those possessed by the successful CIOs of today? Which key competencies are enduring, and which ones are a function of the current technological environment? How can chief information officers prepare for the latter?

REAL WORLD ACTIVITIES

1. Go online to research the topic of executive succession planning and the different approaches in use by companies today. Are there any differences for those in information technology, as opposed to other functional areas, because of the dynamics of technology change and evolution? Which competencies are being targeted for IT executives? Prepare a report to summarize your findings.

2. The case mentions several strategies used by companies to mentor and develop their next generation of IT leaders: career planning, leadership development exercises, coaching, and so on. As a Generation Y member discussed in the chapter, how do these fit in with your expectations for the future? Break into small groups with your classmates to discuss these issues; in particular, to what extent you believe these approaches match well with your culture and personality?

REAL WORLD CASE 4

Reinsurance Group of America and Fonterra: Going for Unified Global Operations

The reinsurance industry isn't for the faint of heart. The business processes that enable reinsurance firms to form agreements with other insurance companies to accept all or part of their risk can get mighty complex, mighty quickly.

Now imagine developing a single system that manages reinsurance business processes for numerous offices around the world—offices whose staffs speak different languages, are in different time zones, and just might be stuck in their ways as to how they manage their business. It's a challenge that could overwhelm you if you tried to tackle it all at once instead of breaking it into small pieces.

When workers in the global software group at Reinsurance Group of America Inc. (RGA) in Chesterfield, Missouri, first took on this mammoth project, they would have been the first to tell you they were unprepared for the obstacles that lay ahead.

"This whole system required so much communication and teamwork, and I'm not sure we understood at first what we needed to contribute to make it a success," says Mike Ring, project manager at RGA. Yet by engaging the business and adapting its own practices to the demands of the situation, the group is successfully rolling out an integrated, multicurrency, multilanguage life reinsurance administration system, dubbed CybeRe, for its international division.

Before CybeRe, workers in RGA's global offices mainly relied on a mix of spreadsheets and databases to manage clients. Now, with information stored in one location, workers can analyze data by client, contract, and product and find client errors more easily. "People can stop worrying about, 'If I sell this business, how am I going to manage it?'" says Azam Mirza, vice president of global software and head of the CybeRe effort.

The system also strengthens data validation and data quality, Ring adds, which will enable better risk analysis and retention analysis, resulting in better profitability. Ultimately, return on investment will reach more than 15 percent, "which compares very favorably to the average ROI for RGA's products, which are normally in the range of 12 percent to 15 percent," Mirza says.

The picture wasn't always this rosy. When the project began six years ago, IT began to gather business requirements from the global offices, planning to emerge a couple of years later with a full-blown system. By late 2001, however, it became apparent that a phased approach was more practical. "The different units all do things slightly differently, and getting everyone to agree became very contentious," explains Kam Chan, chief architect of CybeRe. So the group embarked on a plan to build a pilot system in one office (South Africa) and gradually implement it in the remaining ones, with as few customizations as possible.

It wasn't always smooth sailing. For one thing, converting all the historical data and loading it into the CybeRe system required a significant data cleansing and migration effort. Other factors, such as differences in the terminologies used in various offices, also caused delays. For example, while it gathered requirements, IT asked whether the South African office used compound benefits. Although it said it did not, it turned out that the office just used a different term: acceleration of benefits.

"The change in scope delayed us four or five months," Mirza says. Probably the biggest challenge—which continues today—is getting people to accept common practices as defined by the system. "That's where we're the bad guys," Mirza says. "If they really need it, they have to prove it. We challenge everything. We don't want to create a product that's convoluted because it tries to be everything to everybody."

Despite the local customizations, RGA still maintains just one version of CybeRe. Local units can just "turn on" the options or customizations that are relevant to their businesses. "Not maintaining 13 different versions is very important," Mirza says. "It's critical to our success."

"Given the life reinsurance market's consolidation of recent years, CybeRe should provide RGA with an important competitive weapon. RGA aims to 'reinvent reinsurance.' That is an ambitious goal. CybeRe is an important step along the way."

Greg James is chief information officer and general manager of global business processes at Fonterra. It is a unique role, instrumental in ensuring that the only silos at the dairy group are of the giant stainless steel variety. James was on sabbatical following a year-long assignment in Europe with the New Zealand Dairy Board when he was offered to head what he describes as a "small business initiative" called Jedi. The call came from an executive of Fonterra, which had just been formed, and the job was director of the dairy group's biggest business transformation program to date.

Jedi, which was rolled out in 2.5 years, entailed moving Fonterra's commodity business to a common ERP platform and "a single global way of doing things." James says the Jedi program aimed to look at the supply chain of the dairy giant "from cow to manufacturing to storage to happy customers."

The change involved was massive, for Fonterra's supply chain covers four million cows that produce 20 billion liters of milk each year. It has offices in 70 countries and employs nearly 19,000 staff. Fonterra, says James, would be recognized as New Zealand's largest company if it were listed in the Stock Exchange. In order to implement the new environment, "We had to reinvent ourselves; analyze every part of the business, all processes, all organizational structure," says James.

In effect, the Jedi program dismantled traditional silos in the organization and standardized global processes. "It has enabled us to effectively bring all components that previously existed in each group, in other business units, bring them all together and get commonality in terms of the way we do things. It has driven consistency of processes, and has enabled us to draw consistency in approaching framework in terms of how we operate."

Today, he notes, "We do the things the same way in Germany, Mexico and New Zealand." As James explains, Fonterra was set up in 2000 as an amalgamation of the old dairy industry, with self-contained business functions. Fonterra consolidated its back-office functions globally within New Zealand, into a business transactional services activity based in Hamilton. James says the Hamilton operations fared well when benchmarked against BPO organizations locally and overseas. "Our model is better than most international models." Instead of having disparate sales offices for various business units, a customer service center was set up at the Auckland's Princes Street headquarters. This center operates around the clock, providing multilingual support for customers across the globe.

For Fonterra's 200-member IS team, the new system means being exposed to areas of the business they traditionally would not have been. "If they worked in this part of the business under the old structure, they tended to stay in that part of the business.

But now we pool the resources together so it means they could be working on X, Y, or Z within any given period. They are given a lot more flexibility and ability to learn the various parts of the business in the new model."

He believes this setup also helps in staff retention. "It does give us the ability to retain staff as opposed to having staff leave to go to other organizations to experience different types of skill sets." If there is another thing James is empathic about, it is that these days at Fonterra, "There is no such thing as an IT project by itself."

"We sit down with the business in terms of our planning, and we align our plans to their plans." He says there is now an "enterprise road map" that consists of all the activities the business wants to undertake over the next 18 months up to three years.

What is his primary advice for IT professionals who wish to move on to chief information officer and other C-level roles? "Make sure that you understand the business that you work with." He adds, "Keep a watchful eye on very, very competent people that you might need to hire one day to be part of a bigger team." They could be people in your current organization or people you meet outside, in industry functions.

Lastly, he says, "Never ever fear hiring someone in your organization that is smarter than you. You actually need a lot of smart people working around you."

Source: Adapted from Mary Brandel, "Reinsurance Group Simplifies on Global Scale with Administration System," *Computerworld*, March 14, 2005; and Divina Paredes, "Unifying Global Operations," *CIO Magazine*, March 27, 2007.

CASE STUDY QUESTIONS

1. What is the business value of these global system developments for the companies mentioned in the case? How did they achieve these benefits? What were the major obstacles they had to overcome?

2. What are the advantages and disadvantages of a full-blown versus a phased approach for system implementations in general, and global ones in particular? How do you make the decision on which road to take?

3. How important is it that all units in global organization speak the same business language, and use the same functions and business processes? How do you balance the competing needs for flexibility and consistency across operations?

REAL WORLD ACTIVITIES

1. Both organizations featured in the case have been quite successful with their global rollouts. Search the Internet for examples of less-than-thriving global or international system implementations. How do they compare to the ones in the case? What differences in the approaches taken by the successful and unsuccessful cases do you think could account for the differences in outcome? Prepare a report and a presentation to share your findings with the rest of the class.

2. Implementing major systems in global organizations, particularly when development is concentrated in headquarters or a powerful country subsidiary, can cause a lot of resentment and frustration for the other units in the organization. Break into small groups with your classmates to discuss which approaches companies can take to ease these issues and incorporate all of their units into the process.

Review Quiz Answers

Chapter 1

Foundations of Information Systems in Business

1. 19	8. 22*b*	15. 3	22. 24	29. 16*d*	36. 11	43. 22*a*
2. 23	9. 8	16. 14	23. 24*a*	30. 16*e*	37. 7	44. 4
3. 23*a*	10. 9	17. 16	24. 24*b*	31. 26	38. 26*d*	45. 26*f*
4. 23*b*	11. 10	18. 17	25. 22	32. 26*c*	39. 5	46. 20
5. 23*c*	12. 25	19. 13	26. 16*a*	33. 26*b*	40. 6	47. 26*e*
6. 15	13. 12	20. 13*a*	27. 16*b*	34. 26*a*	41. 14*a*	48. 26*g*
7. 1	14. 2	21. 13*b*	28. 16*c*	35. 18	42. 21	

Competing with Information Technology

1. 3	4. 11	7. 6	10. 2	13. 8
2. 4	5. 5	8. 14	11. 1	14. 9
3. 12	6. 13	9. 10	12. 15	15. 7

Computer Hardware

1. 3	9. 21	17. 9*c*	25. 15	33. 34*c*	41. 36	49. 28*d*
2. 2	10. 1	18. 20	26. 12	34. 4	42. 6	50. 34*b*
3. 5	11. 7	19. 19	27. 16	35. 34	43. 32	51. 29
4. 8	12. 13	20. 35	28. 17	36. 37	44. 31	52. 34*d*
5. 27	13. 14	21. 10	29. 33	37. 34*a*	45. 9	53. 34*g*
6. 30	14. 9*a*	22. 28*c*	30. 24	38. 34*f*	46. 11	
7. 25	15. 9*b*	23. 34*e*	31. 28	39. 31*b*	47. 23	
8. 22	16. 18	24. 26	32. 28*a*	40. 31*a*	48. 28*b*	

Chapter 4

Computer Software

1. 5	7. 32	13. 33	19. 37	25. 20	31. 28	37. 16
2. 2	8. 6	14. 12	20. 8	26. 3	32. 15	38. 36
3. 31	9. 34	15. 11	21. 26	27. 14	33. 38	
4. 1	10. 22	16. 35	22. 17	28. 10	34. 18	
5. 4	11. 27	17. 9	23. 29	29. 24	35. 25	
6. 7	12. 19	18. 30	24. 13	30. 23	36. 21	

Chapter 5

Data Resource Management

1. 11	7. 12	13. 6	19. 13*a*	25. 1	31. 16*a*	37. 16
2. 3	8. 20*b*	14. 16*e*	20. 13*e*	26. 13	32. 20	
3. 9	9. 13*d*	15. 16*g*	21. 13*b*	27. 16*b*	33. 7	
4. 19	10. 20*d*	16. 16*f*	22. 20*e*	28. 18	34. 14	
5. 2	11. 8	17. 16*c*	23. 20*a*	29. 4	35. 16*d*	
6. 10	12. 5	18. 15	24. 20*c*	30. 17	36. 13*c*	

Chapter 6

Telecommunications and Networks

1. 34	7. 8	13. 9	19. 24	25. 21*a*	31. 22	37. 21
2. 23	8. 11	14. 3	20. 1	26. 21*b*	32. 26	38. 30
3. 20	9. 35	15. 31	21. 2	27. 25	33. 6	39. 37
4. 17	10. 15	16. 32	22. 33	28. 12	34. 14	
5. 16	11. 7	17. 18	23. 5	29. 10	35. 28	
6. 13	12. 29	18. 19	24. 27	30. 4	36. 36	

Chapter 7

e-Business Systems

1. 8	6. 21	11. 5	16. 23	21. 3	26. 19	31. 24
2. 7	7. 16	12. 11	17. 1	22. 2	27. 30	
3. 13	8. 29	13. 27	18. 22	23. 26	28. 31	
4. 9	9. 20	14. 18	19. 25	24. 14	29. 4	
5. 10	10. 6	15. 15	20. 17	25. 12	30. 28	

Chapter 8

Enterprise Business Systems

1. 1	5. 4*a*	9. 6*b*	13. 1*d*	17. 3
2. 4	6. 6*a*	10. 1*c*	14. 4*d*	18. 5
3. 6	7. 1*b*	11. 4*c*	15. 6*d*	
4. 1*a*	8. 4*b*	12. 6*c*	16. 2	

Chapter 9

e-Commerce Systems

1. 5	6. 4*a*	11. 4*b*	16. 3*c*	21. 1
2. 5*b*	7. 4*f*	12. 7	17. 3*b*	22. 3
3. 5*a*	8. 4*c*	13. 8	18. 2	23. 4*g*
4. 5*c*	9. 4*h*	14. 3*d*	19. 6	
5. 4	10. 4*e*	15. 3*a*	20. 4*d*	

Chapter 10

Supporting Decision Making

1. 6	7. 1	13. 4	19. 25	25. 12
2. 10	8. 1*d*	14. 5	20. 26	26. 19
3. 21	9. 1*c*	15. 8	21. 15	27. 23
4. 7	10. 1*a*	16. 20	22. 11	28. 13
5. 3	11. 1*b*	17. 9	23. 18	29. 17
6. 22	12. 24	18. 2	24. 16	30. 14

Chapter 11

Developing Business/IT Strategies

1. 8	4. 9	7. 11	10. 5	13. 2*c*
2. 2	5. 10	8. 6	11. 4	14. 2*b*
3. 7	6. 2*a*	9. 3	12. 1	

Chapter 12

Developing Business/IT Solutions

1. 19	7. 27*a*	13. 28	19. 24	25. 1	30. 14
2. 25	8. 11*a*	14. 12	20. 22	26. 26	31. 11
3. 16	9. 20	15. 9	21. 23	27. 4	32. 15
4. 2	10. 13	16. 21	22. 18	28. 17	33. 10
5. 27*b*	11. 7	17. 8	23. 6	29. 27	
6. 11*b*	12. 5	18. 29	24. 3		

Chapter 13

Security and Ethical Challenges

1. 24	6. 10	11. 15	16. 7	21. 26	26. 18
2. 20	7. 2	12. 5	17. 8	22. 21	27. 14
3. 29	8. 4	13. 27	18. 12	23. 19	28. 25
4. 16	9. 11	14. 28	19. 6	24. 9	29. 3
5. 17	10. 13	15. 22	20. 30	25. 1	30. 23

Chapter 14

Enterprise and Global Management of Information Technology

1. 2	6. 1	11. 16	16. 8	21. 20
2. 11	7. 22	12. 5	17. 17	22. 10*b*
3. 15	8. 13	13. 6	18. 10	23. 10*a*
4. 12	9. 7	14. 18	19. 21	24. 14
5. 3	10. 19	15. 4	20. 9	

Selected References

Preface

Sawhney, Mohan, and Jeff Zabin. *The Seven Steps to Nirvana: Strategic Insights into e-Business Transformation*. New York: McGraw-Hill, 2001.

Chapter 1—Foundations of Information Systems in Business

Barlas, D. "Accessing Suppliers," *LINE56.com*, article ID=3810, 2002.

Central Intelligence Agency. *CIA Factbook*. August 2003.

"Citibank E-Mail Hoax and Webpage Scam," http://www.millersmiles.co.uk/identitytheft/citibank-email-verification-hoax.htm, November 2003.

Institute for Development Policy and Management. http://www.egov4dev.org/home.htm and http://www.e-devexchange.org/eGov/home.htm, March 2004.

Kalakota, Ravi, and Marcia Robinson. *E-Business 2.0: Roadmap for Success*. Reading, MA: Addison-Wesley, 2001.

Lee, Allen. "Inaugural Editor's Comments." *MIS Quarterly*, March 1999.

Leinfuss, Emily. "Making the Cut." *Computerworld*, September 20, 1999.

Norris, Grant; James Hurley; Kenneth Hartley; John Dunleavy; and John Balls. *E-Business and ERP: Transforming the Enterprise*. New York: John Wiley & Sons, 2000.

Radcliff, Deborah. "Aligning Marriott." *Computerworld*, April 20, 2000.

Rosencrance, L. "Citibank Customers Hit with E-Mail Scam." *Computerworld*, October 24, 2003.

Steadman, Craig. "Failed ERP Gamble Haunts Hershey." *Computerworld*, November 1, 1999.

Vijayan, Jaikumar. "E-Procurement Talks Back." *Computerworld*, Premiere 100 Best in Class supplement, March 11, 2002.

Weiss, Todd. "Hershey Upgrades R/3 ERP System without Hitches." *Computerworld*, September 9, 2002.

Chapter 2—Competing with Information Technology

"Agilent Technologies ERP Information for Customers," http://www.tmintl.agilent.com/model/index.shtml, n.d.

Applegate, Lynda; Robert D. Austin; and F. Warren McFarlan. *Corporate Information Systems Management: Text and Cases*. 6th ed. Burr Ridge, IL: Irwin/McGraw-Hill, 2003.

Bowles, Jerry. "Best Practices for Global Competitiveness." *Fortune*, Special Advertising Section, November 24, 1997.

Caron, J. Raymond; Sirkka Jarvenpaa; and Donna Stoddard. "Business Reengineering at CIGNA Corporation: Experiences and Lessons from the First Five Years." *MIS Quarterly*, September 1994.

Christensen, Clayton. *The Innovators Dilemma: When New Technologies Cause Great Firms to Fail*. Boston: Harvard Business School Press, 1997.

Cronin, Mary. *The Internet Strategy Handbook*. Boston: Harvard Business School Press, 1996.

Davenport, Thomas H. *Process Innovation: Reengineering Work through Information Technology*. Boston: Harvard Business School Press, 1993.

El Sawy, Omar, and Gene Bowles. "Redesigning the Customer Support Process for the Electronic Economy: Insights from Storage Dimensions." *MIS Quarterly*, December 1997.

El Sawy, Omar; Arvind Malhotra; Sanjay Gosain; and Kerry Young. "IT-Intensive Value Innovation in the Electronic Economy: Insights from Marshall Industries." *MIS Quarterly*, September 1999.

Frye, Colleen. "Imaging Proves Catalyst for Reengineering." *Client/Server Computing*, November 1994.

Garner, Rochelle. "Please Don't Call IT Knowledge Management!" *Computerworld*, August 9, 1999.

Goldman, Steven; Roger Nagel; and Kenneth Preis. *Agile Competitors and Virtual Organizations: Strategies for Enriching the Customer*. New York: Van Nostrand Reinhold, 1995.

Grover, Varun, and Pradipkumar Ramanlal. "Six Myths of Information and Markets: Information Technology Networks, Electronic Commerce, and the Battle for Consumer Surplus." *MIS Quarterly*, December 1999.

Hamm, Steve, and Marcia Stepaneck. "From Reengineering to E-Engineering." *BusinessWeek e.biz*, March 22, 1999.

Hoffman, T. "In the Know: Knowledge Management Case Study Pays Off for BAE Systems." *Computerworld*, October 14, 2002.

"Intel Telecom Case Studies, Best Known Call Center Practices," http://www.intel.com/network/csp/resources/case_studies/enterprise/7867web.htm, n.d.

Kalakota, Ravi, and Marcia Robinson. *E-Business 2.0: Roadmap for Success.* Reading, MA: Addison-Wesley, 2001.

Kettinger, William; Varun Grover; and Albert Segars. "Do Strategic Systems Really Pay Off? An Analysis of Classic Strategic IT Cases." *Information Systems Management*, Winter 1995.

Kettinger, William; James Teng; and Subashish Guha. "Business Process Change: A Study of Methodologies, Techniques, and Tools." *MIS Quarterly*, March 1997.

"New Wal-Mart Fulfillment Distribution Center to Provide Service to Wal-Mart.com," Walmartstores.com, August 2, 2000.

Nonaka, Ikujiro. "The Knowledge Creating Company." *Harvard Business Review*, November–December 1991.

Porter, Michael, and Victor Millar. "How Information Gives You Competitive Advantage." *Harvard Business Review*, July–August 1985.

Prokesch, Steven. "Unleashing the Power of Learning: An Interview with British Petroleum's John Browne." *Harvard Business Review*, September–October 1997.

Sambamurthy, V.; Anandhi Bharadwaj; and Varun Grover. "Shaping Agility through Digital Options: Reconceptualizing the Role of Information Technology in Contemporary Firms." *MIS Quarterly*, June 2003.

Seybold, Patricia. *Customers.com: How to Create a Profitable Business Strategy for the Internet and Beyond.* New York: Times Books, 1998.

Shapiro, Carl, and Hal Varian. *Information Rules: A Strategic Guide to the Network Economy.* Boston: Harvard Business School Press, 1999.

Siekman, Philip. "Why Infotech Loves Its Giant Job Shops." *Fortune*, May 12, 1997.

Songini, Marc. "ERP Effort Sinks Agilent Revenue." *Computerworld*, August 26, 2002.

Strategy Works. "Retrieval Is the Key to the New Economy," http://www.thestrategyworks.com/articles/knowledge2.htm, August 31, 2000.

Weill, Peter, and Michael Vitale. *Place to Space: Migrating to E-Business Models.* Boston: Harvard Business School Press, 2001.

Chapter 3—Computer Hardware

Computerworld, PC Week, PC Magazine, and *PC World* are just a few examples of many good magazines for current information on computer systems hardware and its use in end-user and enterprise applications.

The World Wide Web sites of computer manufacturers such as Apple Computer, Dell Computer, Gateway, IBM, Hewlett-Packard, Compaq, and Sun Microsystems are good sources of information on computer hardware developments.

Alexander, Steve. "Speech Recognition." *Computerworld*, November 8, 1999.

"Computing in the New Millennium." *Fortune*, Technology Buyers Guide, Winter 2000.

Guyon, Janet. "Smart Plastic." *Fortune*, October 13, 1997.

"Hardware." *Fortune*, Technology Buyer's Guide, Winter 1999.

Hecht, Jeff. "Casino Chips to Carry RFID Tags." *New Scientist*, January 2004.

Joch, Alan. "Fewer Servers, Better Service." *Computerworld*, June 4, 2001.

Kennedy, Ken, et al. "A Nationwide Parallel Computing Environment." *Communications of the ACM*, November 1997.

Messerschmitt, David. *Networked Applications: A Guide to the New Computing Infrastructure.* San Francisco: Morgan Kaufmann, 1999.

Ouellette, Tim. "Goodbye to the Glass House." *Computerworld*, May 26, 1997.

Ouellette, Tim. "Tape Storage Put to New Enterprise Uses." *Computerworld*, November 10, 1997.

Reimers, Barbara. "Blades Spin ROI Potential." *Computerworld*, February 11, 2002.

Simpson, David. "The Datamation 100." *Datamation*, July 1997.

"Top 500 Supercomputer Sites: ASCII White," www.top500.org, May 18, 2003.

Chapter 4—Computer Software

Examples of many good magazines for current information and reviews of computer software for business applications can be found at ZD Net, the Web site for ZD Publications (www.zdnet.com), including *PC Magazine, PC Week, PC Computing, Macworld, Inter@ctive Week,* and *Computer Shopper.*

The Web sites of companies like Microsoft, Sun Microsystems, Lotus, IBM, Apple Computer, and Oracle are good sources of information on computer software developments.

Ascent Solutions Inc. http://www.ascentsolutionsus.com/erp.htm.

Citrix i-Business Report. "Achieving Business Transformation through Application Service Providers." *Business Communications Review*, May 3, 2002.

Gonsalves, A. "At Orbitz, Linux Delivers Double the Performance at One-Tenth the Cost." *InternetWeek.com*, July 1, 2003.

Iyer, Bala; Jim Freedman; Mark Gaynor; and George Wyner. "Web Services: Enabling Dynamic Business Networks." *Communications of the Association for Information Systems*, Volume 11, 2003.

Mearian, Lucas. "Fidelity Makes Big XML Conversion." *Computerworld*, October 1, 2001.

Microsoft Corporation. "Introducing the Windows 2003 Family," http://www.microsoft.com, July 1, 2003.

Oracle Corporation. "Visa to Save Millions a Year by Automating Back-Office Processes with Oracle

E-Business Suite," Customer Profile, www.oracle.com, September 13, 2002.

Orbitz Corporate. http://www.orbitz.com/App/about/about.jsp?z=63z0&r=42.

Sliwa, Carol. ".Net vs. Java." *Computerworld*, May 20, 2002.

Smith, T. "How Web Services Help Wells Fargo Customers." *InternetWeek*, May 13, 2003.

Transchannel, LLC. "Transchannel Announces ie2 for People-Soft," http://www.prnewswire.com/, 2002.

Vogelstein, Fred. "Servers with a Smile." *Fortune*, September 30, 2002.

Wainewright, Ivan. "An Introduction to Application Service Providers (ASPs)." *TechSoup*, May 1, 2000.

Chapter 5—Data Resource Management

Amato-McCoy, D. "Enterprise Data Solution Finds a Home at BofA." *Financial Technology Network*, http://www.financetech.com/story/BNK/BNK20021210S0030, December 10, 2002.

Fox, Pimm. "Extracting Dollars from Data." *Computerworld*, April 15, 2002.

IBM Case Study Series. "Kingslake Connects Customers in Sri Lanka with DB2 Everywhere," http://www.306.ibm.com/software/success/cssdb.nsf/cs/NAVO4VPV97?OpenDocument&Site=indwireless, n.d.

IBM Corporation. "DB2 Business Intelligence," www.ibm.com, July 27, 2003.

Jacobsen, Ivar; Maria Ericsson; and Ageneta Jacobsen. *The Object Advantage: Business Process Reengineering with Object Technology*. New York: ACM Press, 1995.

Kalakota, Ravi, and Marcia Robinson. *E-Business 2.0: Roadmap for Success*. Reading, MA: Addison-Wesley, 2002.

Kingslake International Press Release. "Kingslake Helps Sri Lankan Manufacturers Profit and Grow." 2003.

Lorents, Alden, and James Morgan. *Database Systems: Concepts, Management and Applications*. Fort Worth, TX; Dryden Press, 1998.

MacSweeney, G. "Aetna Mines Ethnic Health Data." *InsuranceTech*, April 1, 2003.

Mannino, Michael. *Database Application Development and Design*. New York: McGraw-Hill/Irwin, 2001.

Nance, Barry. "Managing Tons of Data." *Computerworld*, April 23, 2001.

Teradata Corporation Case Report. "State of Iowa: Closing the Tax Gap in Iowa," http://www.teradata.com/t/pdf.aspx?a=83673&b=87463, 2002.

Whiting, R. "The Data Warehousing Advantage, Part II." *Information Week*, July 28, 2003.

Chapter 6—Telecommunications and Networks

Armor, Daniel. *The E-Business (R)Evolution: Living and Working in an Interconnected World*. Upper Saddle River, NJ: Prentice Hall, 2000.

Barksdale, Jim. "The Next Step: Extranets." *Netscape Columns: The Main Thing*, December 3, 1996.

"Boeing 777: A Case Study," http://www.eweek.org/2002/nbm/collaborate/collab01.html, n.d.

Bresnick, Alan. "Verizon Turns Up Heat in Online Data Wars." *Cable Datacom News*, June 1, 2003.

"Cable Modem Info Center," www.cabledatacomnews.com, July 26, 2003.

Caputo, L. "JHI Online Directory Up and Running for Student Users." *The Johns Hopkins Newsletter*, January 28, 1999.

Chatterjee, Samir. "Requirements for Success in Gigabit Networking." *Communications of the ACM*, July 1997.

"Countrywide Home Loans Uses Netscape Platform to Develop Extensive Internet and Intranet Solutions." Netscape Corporate Public Relations Press Release, August 15, 1996.

Cronin, Mary. *Doing More Business on the Internet*. New York: Van Nostrand Reinhold, 1995.

CyberAtlas Inc. "The Big Picture: Geographics: Population Explosion!" www.cyberatlas.internet.com, June 23, 2003.

"Holiday Autos," http://www.itcasestudies.com/case/ser30.html, n.d.

Housel, Thomas, and Eric Skopec. *Global Telecommunications Revolution: The Business Perspective*. New York: McGraw-Hill/Irwin, 2001.

"Johns Hopkins International: Bridging the Communication Gap among Remote Office Employees, "*Intranets.com Case Study*, http://www.intranets.com/ProductInfo/CaseStudies/Johns_Hopkins.asp, 2004.

Kalakota, Ravi, and Marcia Robinson. *E-Business 2.0: Roadmap for Success*. Reading, MA: Addison-Wesley, 2001.

Lais, Sami. "Satellites Link Bob Evans Farms." *Computerworld*, July 2, 2001.

Messerschmitt, David. *Network Applications: A Guide to the New Computing Infrastructure*. San Francisco: Morgan Kaufmann, 1999.

Murphy, Kate. "Cruising the Net in Hyperdrive." *BusinessWeek*, January 24, 2000.

Norris, G. "Boeing's Seventh Wonder," *IEEE Spectrum*, http://www.spectrum.ieee.org/publicaccess/1095b777.html, 1995.

O'Brien, Atiye. "Friday Intranet Focus." *Upside.com: Hot Private Companies*. Upside, 1996.

Orenstein, David. "Price, Speed, Location All Part of Broadband Choice." *Computerworld*, July 26, 1999.

Papows, Jeff. "Endquotes." *NetReady Adviser*, Winter 1997.

Schultz, B. "User Excellence Award Honorable Mentions." *Network World*, November 13, 2000.

"Snap-On Tools Company Uses Netscape Software for Extranet Solution." Netscape Corporate Public Relations Press Release, March 6, 1997.

Stuart, Anne. "Cutting the Cord." *Inc. Tech*, March 2001.

UPS corporate Web site. "About UPS," http://www.ups.com/content/us/en/about/index.html, n.d.

Chapter 7—e-Business Systems

Afuah, Allan, and Christopher Tucci. *Internet Business Models and Strategies*. New York: McGraw-Hill/Irwin, 2001.

"Baker Tanks Leverages salesforce.com's Wireless Access to Extend Range of Customer Service." Salesforce.com, 2002.

Clark, Charles; Nancy Cavanaugh; Carol Brown; and V. Sambamurthy. "Building Change-Readiness Capabilities in the IS Organization: Insights from the Bell Atlantic Experience." *MIS Quarterly*, December 1997.

Cole-Gomolski, Barb. "Users Loath to Share Their Know-How." *Computerworld*, November 17, 1997.

Collett, S. "SAP: Whirlpool's Rush to Go Live Leads to Shipping Snafus." *Computerworld*, November 4, 1999.

"Communications Leader Becomes Customer-Focused E-Business," *Siebel.com*, March 12, 2001.

Cronin, Mary. *The Internet Strategy Handbook*. Boston: Harvard Business School Press, 1996.

Cross, John; Michael Earl; and Jeffrey Sampler. "Transformation of the IT Function at British Petroleum." *MIS Quarterly*, December 1997.

Das, Sidhartha; Shaker Zahra; and Merrill Warkentin. "Integrating the Content and Process of Strategic MIS Planning with Competitive Strategy." *Decision Sciences Journal*, November–December 1991.

De Geus, Arie. "Planning as Learning." *Harvard Business Review*, March–April 1988.

Earl, Michael. "Experiences in Strategic Information Systems Planning." *MIS Quarterly*, March 1993.

El Sawy, Omar, and Gene Bowles. "Redesigning the Customer Support Process for the Electronic Economy: Insights from Storage Dimensions." *MIS Quarterly*, December 1997.

Gates, Bill. *Business @ the Speed of Thought*. New York: Warner Books, 1999.

Grover, Varun; James Teng; and Kirk Fiedler. "IS Investment Priorities in Contemporary Organizations." *Communications of the ACM*, February 1998.

Hawson, James, and Jesse Beeler. "Effects of User Participation in Systems Development: A Longitudinal Field Experiment." *MIS Quarterly*, December 1997.

Hoffman, Thomas. "Intranet Helps Workers Navigate Corporate Maze." *Computerworld*, June 4, 2001.

Kalakota, Ravi, and Marcia Robinson. *E-Business 2.0: Roadmap for Success*. Reading, MA: Addison-Wesley, 2001.

Keen, Peter, and Craigg Ballance. *Online Profits: A Manager's Guide to Electronic Commerce*. Boston: Harvard Business School Press, 1997.

Kettinger, William; James Teng; and Subashish Guha. "Business Process Change: A Study of Methodologies, Techniques, and Tools." *MIS Quarterly*, March 1997.

Koudsi, Suzanne. "Actually, It Is Like Brain Surgery." *Fortune*, March 20, 2000.

KPMG Case Study. "Think Different: Apple Americas Transforms Its US Business with SAP/R3 in Just Twelve Months." 1999.

Levinson, M. "Cleared for Takeoff." *CIO*, April 1, 2002.

Martin, Chuck. *The Digital Estate: Strategies for Competing, Surviving, and Thriving in an Internetworked World*. New York: McGraw-Hill, 1997.

Orenstein, David. "Enterprise Application Integration." *Computerworld*, October 4, 1999.

Robb, Drew. "Rediscovering Efficiency." *Computerworld*, July 16, 2001.

Sawhney, Mohan, and Jeff Zabin. *The Seven Steps to Nirvana: Strategic Insights into e-Business Transformation*. New York: McGraw-Hill, 2001.

Chapter 8—Enterprise Business Systems

Afuah, Allan, and Christopher Tucci. *Internet Business Models and Strategies.* New York: McGraw-Hill/Irwin, 2001.

Clark, Charles; Nancy Cavanaugh; Carol Brown; and V. Sambamurthy. "Building Change-Readiness Capabilities in the IS Organization: Insights from the Bell Atlantic Experience." *MIS Quarterly,* December 1997.

Cole-Gomolski, Barb. "Users Loath to Share Their Know-How." *Computerworld,* November 17, 1997.

Collett, S. "SAP: Whirlpool's Rush to Go Live Leads to Shipping Snafus." *Computerworld,* November 4, 1999.

Collett Stacy. "SWOT Analysis." *Computerworld,* July 19, 1999.

Cronin, Mary. *The Internet Strategy Handbook.* Boston: Harvard Business School Press, 1996.

Cross, John; Michael Earl; and Jeffrey Sampler. "Transformation of the IT Function at British Petroleum." *MIS Quarterly,* December 1997.

Das, Sidhartha; Shaker Zahra; and Merrill Warkentin. "Integrating the Content and Process of Strategic MIS Planning with Competitive Strategy." *Decision Sciences Journal,* November–December 1991.

De Geus, Arie. "Planning as Learning." *Harvard Business Review,* March–April 1988.

De Geus, Arie. "The Living Company." *Harvard Business Review,* March–April 1997.

Deise, Martin; Conrad Nowikow; Patrick King; and Amy Wright. *Executive's Guide to E-Business: From Tactics to Strategy.* New York: John Wiley & Sons, 2000.

Earl, Michael. "Experiences in Strategic Information Systems Planning." *MIS Quarterly,* March 1993.

El Sawy, Omar, and Gene Bowles. "Redesigning the Customer Support Process for the Electronic Economy: Insights from Storage Dimensions." *MIS Quarterly,* December 1997.

El Sawy, Omar; Arvind Malhotra; Sanjay Gosain; and Kerry Young. "IT-Intensive Value Innovation in the Electronic Economy: Insights from Marshall Industries." *MIS Quarterly,* September 1999.

Fingar, Peter; Harsha Kumar; and Tarun Sharma. *Enterprise E-Commerce: The Software Component Breakthrough for Business to Business Commerce.* Tampa, FL: Meghan-Kiffer Press, 2000.

Grover, Varun; James Teng; and Kirk Fiedler. "IS Investment Priorities in Contemporary Organizations." *Communications of the ACM,* February 1998.

Hawson, James, and Jesse Beeler. "Effects of User Participation in Systems Development: A Longitudinal Field Experiment." *MIS Quarterly,* December 1997.

Hills, Melanie. *Intranet Business Strategies.* New York: John Wiley & Sons, 1997.

Kalakota, Ravi, and Marcia Robinson. *E-Business: Roadmap for Success.* Reading, MA: Addison-Wesley, 1999.

Keen, Peter G. W. *Shaping the Future: Business Design through Information Technology.* Boston: Harvard Business School Press, 1991.

Kettinger, William; James Teng; and Subashish Guha. "Business Process Change: A Study of Methodologies, Techniques, and Tools." *MIS Quarterly,* March 1997.

Koudsi, Suzanne. "Actually, It Is Like Brain Surgery." *Fortune,* March 20, 2000.

Levinson, M. "Cleared for Takeoff." *CIO,* April 1, 2002.

Maglitta, Joseph. "Rocks in the Gears: Reengineering the Workplace." *Computerworld,* October 3, 1994.

Magretta, Joan. "Why Business Models Matter." *Harvard Business Review,* May 2002.

Norris, Grant; James Hurley; Kenneth Hartley; John Dunleavy; and John Balls. *E-Business and ERP: Transforming the Enterprise.* New York: John Wiley & Sons, 2000.

Peppers & Rogers Group. "Honeywell Aerospace Trains a New Breed of Sales Force on CRM." SearchCRM.com, http://searchcrm.techtarget.com/originalContent/0%2C289142%2Csid11_gci859703%2C00.html, October 29, 2002.

Prokesch, Steven. "Unleashing the Power of Learning: An Interview with British Petroleum's John Browne." *Harvard Business Review,* September–October 1997.

Senge, Peter. *The Fifth Discipline: The Art and Practice of the Learning Organization.* New York: Currency Doubleday, 1994.

Whirlpool Corporation corporate Web site. http://www.whirlpoolcorp.com/about/default.asp, n.d.

Chapter 9—e-Commerce Systems

Armor, Daniel. *The E-Business (R)Evolution: Living and Working in an Interconnected World.* Upper Saddle River, NJ: Prentice Hall, 2000.

Cross, Kim. "Need Options? Go Configure." *Business 2.0,* February 2000.

Davis, Jeffrey. "How IT Works." *Business 2.0,* February 2000.

Davis, Jeffrey. "Mall Rats." *Business 2.0,* January 1999.

Enterasys Company Info. http://www.enterasys.com/corporate, n.d.

Essex, David. "Betting on Win 2K." *Computerworld,* February 26, 2001.

Fellenstein, Craig, and Ron Wood. *Exploring E-Commerce, Global E-Business, and E-Societies.* Upper Saddle River, NJ: Prentice Hall, 2000.

Fingar, Peter; Harsha Kumar; and Tarun Sharma. *Enterprise E-Commerce*. Tampa, FL: Meghan-Kiffer Press, 2000.

Georgia, Bonnie. "Give Your E-Store an Edge." *Smart Business*, October 2001.

Gulati, Ranjay, and Jason Garino. "Get the Right Mix of Clicks and Bricks." *Harvard Business Review*, May–June 2000.

Hoque, Faisal. *E-Enterprise: Business Models, Architecture and Components*. Cambridge, UK: Cambridge University Press, 2000.

Kalakota, Ravi, and Marcia Robinson. *E-Business 2.0: Roadmap for Success*. Reading, MA: Addison-Wesley, 2001.

Kalakota, Ravi, and Andrew Whinston. *Electronic Commerce: A Manager's Guide*. Reading, MA: Addison-Wesley, 1997.

Keenan, Faith, and Timothy Mullaney. "Let's Get Back to Basics." *BusinessWeek e.biz*, October 29, 2001.

Leon, Mark. "Trading Spaces." *Business 2.0*, February 2000.

May, Paul. *The Business of E-Commerce: From Corporate Strategy to Technology*. Cambridge, UK: Cambridge University Press, 2001.

Microsoft IT Showcase. "MS Market: Business Case Study," http://download.microsoft.com/download/6/5/9/659955d7-0cb7-42b6-8e78-daf1e9c49a75/MSMarketBCS.doc, 2002.

Morgan, Cynthia. "Dead Set against SET?" *Computerworld*, March 29, 1999.

Nesdore, P. "Customer Relationship Management: Getting Personal," e-commerceIQ.com, http://www.ecommerceiq.com/special_interests/crm/80-eCommerceIQ_crm.html, 2003.

"Pay-Per-Click Marketing," http://www.pay-per-click-adwords.com/pay-per-click-adwords.html, n.d.

Rayport, Jeffrey, and Bernard Jaworski. *Introduction to e-Commerce*. New York: McGraw-Hill/Irwin, 2001.

Riley, M.; S. Laiken; and J. Williams. "Digital Business Designs in Financial Services," Mercer Management Consulting Commentary, http://www.mercermc.com/Perspectives/WhitePapers/Commentaries/Comm00DBDinFinancialServices.pdf, 2002.

Rosenoer, Jonathan; Douglas Armstrong; and J. Russell Gates. *The Clickable Corporation: Successful Strategies for Capturing the Internet Advantage*. New York: The Free Press, 1999.

"Servers with a Smile." *Fortune*, Technology Buyers Guide, Summer 2000.

Seybold, Patricia, with Ronnie Marshak. *Customers.Com: How to Create a Profitable Business Strategy for the Internet and Beyond*. New York: Times Business, 1998.

Sliwa, Carol. "Users Cling to EDI for Critical Transactions." *Computerworld*, March 15, 1999.

"Tech Lifestyles: Shopping." *Fortune*, Technology Buyers Guide, Winter 2001.

"Telefónica Servicios Avanzados De Informació Leads Spain's Retail Industry into Global Electronic Commerce," www.netscape.com/solutions/business/profiles, March 1999.

Young, Eric. "Web Marketplaces That Really Work." *Fortune/CNET Tech Review*, Winter 2002.

Chapter 10—Supporting Decision Making

"AmeriKing," Customer Profile, Plumtree.com, October 25, 2002.

Ashline, Peter, and Vincent Lai. "Virtual Reality: An Emerging User-Interface Technology." *Information Systems Management*, Winter 1995.

Beacon Analytics Case Study. "Analyzing Key Measures in a Retail Environment," http://www.beaconus.com/downloads/Beacon%20Case%20Study-The%20GAP.pdf, 2003.

Begley, Sharon. "Software au Naturel." *Newsweek*, May 8, 1995.

Belcher, Lloyd, and Hugh Watson. "Assessing the Value of Conoco's EIS." *MIS Quarterly*, September 1993.

Bioluminate Inc. press release. "Bioluminate to Develop 'Smart Probe' for Early Breast Cancer Detection," http://www.bioluminate.com/press_rel1.html, December 5, 2000.

Bose, Ranjit, and Vijayan Sugumaran. "Application of Intelligent Agent Technology for Managerial Data Analysis and Mining." *The Data Base for Advances in Information Systems*, Winter 1999.

Botchner, Ed. "Data Mining: Plumbing the Depths of Corporate Databases." *Computerworld*, Special Advertising Supplement, April 21, 1997.

Brown, Eryn. "Slow Road to Fast Data." *Fortune*, March 18, 2002.

Brown, Stuart. "Making Decisions in a Flood of Data." *Fortune*, August 13, 2001.

Bylinsky, Gene. "The e-Factory Catches On." *Fortune*, August 13, 2001.

Cox, Earl. "Relational Database Queries Using Fuzzy Logic." *AI Expert*, January 1995.

Darling, Charles. "Ease Implementation Woes with Packaged Datamarts." *Datamation*, March 1997.

Deck, Stewart. "Data Visualization." *Computerworld*, October 11, 1999.

Deck, Stewart. "Data Warehouse Project Starts Simply." *Computerworld*, February 15, 1999.

Deck, Stewart. "Early Users Give Nod to Analysis Package." *Computerworld*, February 22, 1999.

Freeman, Eva. "Desktop Reporting Tools." *Datamation*, June 1997.

Gantz, John. "The New World of Enterprise Reporting Is Here." *Computerworld*, February 1, 1999.

"GAP, Inc. at a Glance," http://www.gapinc.com/about/At_A_Glance.pdf, Summer 2004.

Glode, M. "Scans: Most Valuable Player." *Wired Magazine*, July 22, 1997.

Goldberg, David. "Genetic and Evolutionary Algorithms Come of Age." *Communications of the ACM*, March 1994.

Gorry, G. Anthony, and Michael Scott Morton. "A Framework for Management Information Systems." *Sloan Management Review*, Fall 1971; republished Spring 1989.

Hall, Mark. "Get Real." *Computerworld*, April 1, 2002.

Hall, Mark. "Supercomputing: From R&D to P&L." *Computerworld*, December 13, 1999.

Hoffman, Thomas. "In the Know." *Computerworld*, October 14, 2002.

Jablonowski, Mark. "Fuzzy Risk Analysis: Using AI Systems." *AI Expert*, December 1994.

Kalakota, Ravi, and Marcia Robinson. *E-Business 2.0: Roadmap for Success*. Reading, MA: Addison-Wesley, 2001.

Kalakota, Ravi, and Andrew Whinston. *Electronic Commerce: A Manager's Guide*. Reading, MA: Addison-Wesley, 1997.

King, Julia. "Sharing GIS Talent with the World." *Computerworld*, October 6, 1997.

Kurszweil, Raymond. *The Age of Intelligent Machines*. Cambridge, MA: MIT Press, 1992.

Lundquist, Christopher. "Personalization in E-Commerce." *Computerworld*, March 22, 1999.

Machlis, Sharon. "Agent Technology." *Computerworld*, March 22, 1999.

Mailoux, Jacquiline. "New Menu at PepsiCo." *Computerworld*, May 6, 1996.

McNeill, F. Martin, and Ellen Thro. *Fuzzy Logic: A Practical Approach*. Boston: AP Professional, 1994.

Mitchell, Lori. "Enterprise Knowledge Portals Wise Up Your Business." *Infoworld.com*, December 2000.

Murray, Gerry. "Making Connections with Enterprise Knowledge Portals." White Paper. *Computerworld*, September 6, 1999.

"NASA Ames Research Center Report," Smart Surgical Probe, Bioluminate Inc., http://technology.arc.nasa.gov/success/probe.html, 2003.

Norsk Hydro Corporate Background. http://www.hydro.com/en/about/index.html, 2004.

Orenstein, David. "Corporate Portals." *Computerworld*, June 28, 1999.

Ouellette, Tim. "Opening Your Own Portal," *Computerworld*, August 9, 1999.

Pimentel, Ken, and Kevin Teixeira. *Virtual Reality through the New Looking Glass*. 2nd ed. New York: Intel/McGraw-Hill, 1995.

Rosenberg, Marc. *e-Learning: Strategies for Delivering Knowledge in the Digital Age*. New York: McGraw-Hill, 2001.

Schlumberger Information Solutions. "Norsk Hydro Makes a Valuable Drilling Decision," Schlumberger Technical Report GMP-5911, http://www.sis.slb.com/media/software/success/ir_drillingdecision.pdf, 2002.

Shay, S. "Trendlines." *CIO Magazine*, February 1, 1998.

Turban, Efraim, and Jay Aronson. *Decision Support Systems and Intelligent Systems*. Upper Saddle River, NJ: Prentice Hall, 1998.

Vandenbosch, Betty, and Sid Huff. "Searching and Scanning: How Executives Obtain Information from Executive Information Systems." *MIS Quarterly*, March 1997.

Wagner, Mitch. "Reality Check." *Computerworld*, February 26, 1997.

Watson, Hugh, and John Satzinger. "Guidelines for Designing EIS Interfaces." *Information Systems Management*, Fall 1994.

Watterson, Karen. "Parallel Tracks." *Datamation*, May 1997.

Winston, Patrick. "Rethinking Artificial Intelligence." Program Announcement, Massachusetts Institute of Technology, September 1997.

Wreden, Nick. "Enterprise Portals: Integrating Information to Drive Productivity." *Beyond Computing*, March 2000.

Chapter 11—Developing Business/IT Strategies

Afuah, Allan, and Christopher Tucci. *Internet Business Models and Strategies*. New York: McGraw-Hill/Irwin, 2001.

Clark, Charles; Nancy Cavanaugh; Carol Brown; and V. Sambamurthy. "Building Change-Readiness Capabilities in the IS Organization: Insights from the Bell Atlantic Experience." *MIS Quarterly*, December 1997.

Cole-Gomolski, Barb. "Users Loath to Share Their Know-How." *Computerworld*, November 17, 1997.

Collett Stacy. "SWOT Analysis." *Computerworld*, July 19, 1999.

Cronin, Mary. *The Internet Strategy Handbook*. Boston: Harvard Business School Press, 1996.

Cross, John; Michael Earl; and Jeffrey Sampler. "Transformation of the IT Function at British Petroleum." *MIS Quarterly*, December 1997.

Das, Sidhartha; Shaker Zahra; and Merrill Warkentin. "Integrating the Content and Process of Strategic MIS Planning with Competitive Strategy." *Decision Sciences Journal*, November–December 1991.

De Geus, Arie. "Planning as Learning." *Harvard Business Review*, March–April 1988.

De Geus, Arie. "The Living Company." *Harvard Business Review*, March–April 1997.

Deise, Martin; Conrad Nowikow; Patrick King; and Amy Wright. *Executive's Guide to E-Business: From Tactics to Strategy*. New York: John Wiley & Sons, 2000.

Earl, Michael. "Experiences in Strategic Information Systems Planning." *MIS Quarterly*, March 1993.

El Sawy, Omar, and Gene Bowles. "Redesigning the Customer Support Process for the Electronic Economy: Insights from Storage Dimensions." *MIS Quarterly*, December 1997.

El Sawy, Omar; Arvind Malhotra; Sanjay Gosain; and Kerry Young. "IT-Intensive Value Innovation in the Electronic Economy: Insights from Marshall Industries." *MIS Quarterly*, September 1999.

Fingar, Peter; Harsha Kumar; and Tarun Sharma. *Enterprise E-Commerce: The Software Component Breakthrough for Business to Business Commerce*. Tampa, FL: Meghan-Kiffer Press, 2000.

Grover, Varun; James Teng; and Kirk Fiedler. "IS Investment Priorities in Contemporary Organizations." *Communications of the ACM*, February 1998.

Hawson, James, and Jesse Beeler. "Effects of User Participation in Systems Development: A Longitudinal Field Experiment." *MIS Quarterly*, December 1997.

Hills, Melanie. *Intranet Business Strategies*. New York: John Wiley & Sons, 1997.

Kalakota, Ravi, and Marcia Robinson. *E-Business: Roadmap for Success*. Reading, MA: Addison-Wesley, 1999.

Keen, Peter G. W. *Shaping the Future: Business Design through Information Technology*. Boston: Harvard Business School Press, 1991.

Kettinger, William; James Teng; and Subashish Guha. "Business Process Change: A Study of Methodologies, Techniques, and Tools." *MIS Quarterly*, March 1997.

Koudsi, Suzanne. "Actually, It Is Like Brain Surgery." *Fortune*, March 20, 2000.

Maglitta, Joseph. "Rocks in the Gears: Reengineering the Workplace." *Computerworld*, October 3, 1994.

Magretta, Joan. "Why Business Models Matter." *Harvard Business Review*, May 2002.

Norris, Grant; James Hurley; Kenneth Hartley; John Dunleavy; and John Balls. *E-Business and ERP: Transforming the Enterprise*. New York: John Wiley & Sons, 2000.

Prokesch, Steven. "Unleashing the Power of Learning: An Interview with British Petroleum's John Browne." *Harvard Business Review*, September–October 1997.

Senge, Peter. *The Fifth Discipline: The Art and Practice of the Learning Organization*. New York: Currency Doubleday, 1994.

Chapter 12—Developing Business/IT Solutions

Anthes, Gary. "The Quest for IT E-Quality." *Computerworld*, December 13, 1999.

Clark, Charles; Nancy Cavanaugh; Carol Brown; and V. Sambamurthy. "Building Change-Readiness Capabilities in the IS Organization: Insights from the Bell Atlantic Experience." *MIS Quarterly*, December 1997.

Cole-Gomolski, Barbara. "Companies Turn to Web for ERP Training." *Computerworld*, February 8, 1999.

Cole-Gomolski, Barbara. "Users Loath to Share Their Know-How." *Computerworld*, November 17, 1997.

Cronin, Mary. *The Internet Strategy Handbook*. Boston: Harvard Business School Press, 1996.

Deise, Martin; Conrad Nowikow; Patrick King; and Amy Wright. *Executive's Guide to E-Business: From Tactics to Strategy*. New York: John Wiley & Sons, 2000.

"Design Matters." *Fortune*, Technology Buyers Guide, Winter 2001.

E-Government for Development Information Exchange. "Failed Electronic Voter Registration in Uganda," http://www.egov4dev.org/iecuganda.htm#title, 2002.

Hawson, James, and Jesse Beeler. "Effects of User Participation in Systems Development: A Longitudinal Field Experiment." *MIS Quarterly*, December 1997.

Hills, Melanie. *Intranet Business Strategies*. New York: John Wiley & Sons, 1997.

Kalakota, Ravi, and Marcia Robinson. *E-Business 2.0: Roadmap for Success*. Reading, MA: Addison-Wesley, 2001.

King, Julia. "Back to Basics." *Computerworld*, April 22, 2002.

Lazar, Jonathan. *User-Centered Web Development*. Sudbury, MA: Jones and Bartlett, 2001.

McDonnel, Sharon. "Putting CRM to Work." *Computerworld*, March 12, 2001.

Melymuka, Kathleen. "An Expanding Universe." *Computerworld*, September 14, 1998.

Melymuka, Kathleen. "Energizing the Company." *Computerworld*, August 13, 2001.

Melymuka, Kathleen. "Profiting from Mistakes." *Computerworld*, April 20, 2001.

Morgan, James N. *Application Cases in MIS*. 4th ed. New York: Irwin/McGraw-Hill, 2002.

Neilsen, Jakob. "Better Data Brings Better Sales." *Business 2.0*, May 15, 2001.

Nielsen, Jakob. "Design for Process, Not for Products." *Business 2.0*, July 10, 2001.

Orenstein, David. "Software Is Too Hard to Use." *Computerworld*, August 23, 1999.

Ouellette, Tim. "Giving Users the Key to Their Web Content." *Computerworld*, July 26, 1999.

Ouellette, Tim. "Opening Your Own Portal." *Computerworld*, August 9, 1999.

Panko, R. "Application Development: Finding Spreadsheet Errors." *InformationWeek*, May 29, 1995.

Panko, R. "What We Know about Spreadsheet Errors." *Journal of End-User Computing*, 10:2, 1998, pp. 15–21.

Schwartz, Matthew. "Time for a Makeover." *Computerworld*, August 19, 2002.

Senge, Peter. *The Fifth Discipline: The Art and Practice of the Learning Organization*. New York: Currency Doubleday, 1994.

Sliwa, Carol. "E-Commerce Solutions: How Real?" *Computerworld*, February 28, 2000.

Solomon, Melissa. "Filtering Out the Noise." *Computerworld*, February 25, 2002.

Songini, Marc. "GM Locomotive Unit Puts ERP Roll-out Back on Track." *Computerworld*, February 11, 2002.

"Uganda," U.S. Library of Congress Country Study, http://lcweb2.loc.gov/cgi-bin/query/r?frd/cstdy: (DOCID+ug0000), 2000.

Whitten, Jeffrey, and Lonnie Bentley. *Systems Analysis and Design Methods*. 5th ed. New York: McGraw-Hill/Irwin, 2000.

Chapter 13—Security and Ethical Challenges

Alexander, Steve, and Matt Hamblen. "Top-Flight Technology." *Computerworld*, September 23, 2002.

Anthes, Gary. "Biometrics." *Computerworld*, October 12, 1998.

Anthes, Gary. "When Five 9s Aren't Enough." *Computerworld*, October 8, 2001.

Berniker, M. "Study: ID Theft Often Goes Unrecognized," *Internetnews.com*, http://www.internetnews.com/ec-news/article.php/3081881, 2003.

Boutin, Paul. "Burn Baby Burn." *Wired*, December 2002.

Deckmyn, Dominique. "More Managers Monitor E-Mail." *Computerworld*, October 18, 1999.

Dejoie, Roy; George Fowler; and David Paradice, eds. *Ethical Issues in Information Systems*. Boston: Boyd & Fraser, 1991.

Donaldson, Thomas. "Values in Tension: Ethics Away from Home." *Harvard Business Review*, September–October 1996.

Dunlop, Charles, and Rob Kling, eds. *Computerization and Controversy: Value Conflicts and Social Choices*. San Diego: Academic Press, 1991.

Elias, Paul. "Paid Informant." *Red Herring*, January 16, 2001.

Harrison, Ann. "Virus Scanning Moving to ISPs." *Computerworld*, September 20, 1999.

"In Depth: Security." *Computerworld*, July 9, 2001.

Johnson, Deborah. "Ethics Online." *Communications of the ACM*, January 1997.

Joy, Bill. "Report from the Cyberfront." *Newsweek*, February 21, 2000.

Lardner, James. "Why Should Anyone Believe You?" *Business 2.0*, March 2002.

Levy, Stephen, and Brad Stone. "Hunting the Hackers." *Newsweek*, February 21, 2000.

Madsen, Peter, and Jay Shafritz. *Essentials of Business Ethics*. New York: Meridian, 1990.

McCarthy, Michael. "Keystroke Cops." *The Wall Street Journal*, March 7, 2000.

Nance, Barry. "Sending Firewalls Home." *Computerworld*, May 28, 2001.

Naughton, Keith. "CyberSlacking." *Newsweek*, November 29, 1999.

Neumann, Peter. *Computer-Related Risks*. New York: ACM Press, 1995.

Phillips, Robert. *Stakeholder Theory and Organizational Ethics*. San Francisco: Berrett-Koehler, 2003.

Radcliff, Deborah. "Cybersleuthing Solves the Case." *Computerworld*, January 14, 2002.

Robinson, Lori. "How It Works: Viruses." *Smart Computing*, March 2000.

Rothfeder, Jeffrey. "Hacked! Are Your Company Files Safe?" *PC World*, November 1996.

Rothfeder, Jeffrey. "No Privacy on the Net." *PC World*, February 1997.

Sager, Ira; Steve Hamm; Neil Gross; John Carey; and Robert Hoff. "Cyber Crime." *BusinessWeek*, February 21, 2000.

Schoepke, P., and G. Milner, "Phishing Scams Increase 180% in April Alone!" *BankersOnline.com*, http://www.bankersonline.com/technology/tech_phishing052404.html, 2004.

Smith, H. Jefferson, and John Hasnas. "Debating the Stakeholder Theory." *Beyond Computing*, March–April 1994.

Smith, H. Jefferson, and John Hasnas. "Establishing an Ethical Framework." *Beyond Computing*, January–February 1994.

Solomon, Melissa, and Michael Meehan. "Enron Lesson: Tech Is for Support." *Computerworld*, February 18, 2002.

Spinello, Richard. *Cyberethics: Morality and Law in Cyberspace*. 2nd ed. Sudbury, MA: Jones and Bartlett, 2003.

Sullivan, B. "ID Theft Victims Face Tough Bank Fights," MSNBC.com, http://msnbc.msn.com/id/4264051/, 2004.

VanScoy, Kayte. "What Your Workers Are Really Up To." *Ziff Davis Smart Business*, September 2001.

Verton, Dan. "Insider Monitoring Seen as Next Wave in IT Security." *Computerworld*, March 19, 2001.

Vijayan, Jaikumar. "Nimda Needs Harsh Disinfectant." *Computerworld*, September 24, 2001.

Vijayan, Jaikumar. "Securing the Center." *Computerworld*, May 13, 2002.

Willard, Nancy. *The Cyberethics Reader*. Burr Ridge, IL: Irwin/McGraw-Hill, 1997.

York, Thomas. "Invasion of Privacy? E-Mail Monitoring Is on the Rise." *InformationWeek Online*, February 21, 2000.

Youl, T. "Phishing Scams: Understanding the Latest Trends." *FraudWatch International*, White Paper, 2004.

Chapter 14—Enterprise and Global Management of Information Technology

Bryan, Lowell; Jane Fraser; Jeremy Oppenheim; and Wilhelm Rall. *Race for the World: Strategies to Build a Great Global Firm.* Boston: Harvard Business School Press, 1999.

Christensen, Clayton. *The Innovators Dilemma: When New Technologies Cause Great Firms to Fail.* Boston: Harvard Business School Press, 1997.

Cronin, Mary. *Global Advantage on the Internet.* New York: Van Nostrand Reinhold, 1996.

"Delta Signs Offshore Call Center Agreement." *South Florida Business Journal*, October 7, 2002.

El Sawy, Omar; Arvind Malhotra; Sanjay Gosain; and Kerry Young. "IT-Intensive Value Innovation in the Electronic Economy: Insights from Marshall Industries." *MIS Quarterly*, September 1999.

Gilhooly, Kym. "The Staff That Never Sleeps." *Computerworld*, June 25, 2001.

Grover, Varun; James Teng; and Kirk Fiedler. "IS Investment Opportunities in Contemporary Organizations." *Communications of the ACM*, February 1998.

Hall, Mark. "Service Providers Give Users More IT Options." *Computerworld*, February 7, 2000.

Ives, Blake, and Sirkka Jarvenpaa. "Applications of Global Information Technology: Key Issues for Management." *MIS Quarterly*, March 1991.

Kalakota, Ravi, and Marcia Robinson. *E-Business 2.0: Roadmap for Success.* Reading, MA: Addison-Wesley, 2001.

Kalin, Sari. "The Importance of Being Multiculturally Correct." Global Innovators Series, *Computerworld*, October 6, 1997.

Kirkpatrick, David. "Back to the Future with Centralized Computing." *Fortune*, November 10, 1997.

LaPlante, Alice. "Global Boundaries.com." Global Innovators Series, *Computerworld*, October 6, 1997.

Leinfuss, Emily. "Blend It, Mix It, Unify It." *Computerworld*, March 26, 2001.

McDougall, P. "Opportunity on the Line." *InformationWeek*, October 20, 2003.

Mearian, Lucas. "Citibank Overhauls Overseas Systems." *Computerworld*, February 4, 2002.

Mische, Michael. "Transnational Architecture: A Reengineering Approach." *Information Systems Management*, Winter 1995.

Palvia, Prashant; Shailendra Palvia; and Edward Roche, eds. *Global Information Technology and Systems Management.* Marietta, GA: Ivy League, 1996.

Radcliff, Deborah. "Playing by Europe's Rules." *Computerworld*, July 9, 2001.

Ross, Jeanne, and Peter Weill. "Six IT Decisions Your IT People Shouldn't Make." *Harvard Business Review*, November 2002.

Songini, Marc, and Kim Nash. "Try, Try Again." *Computerworld*, February 18, 2002.

Thibodeau, Patrick. "Europe and U.S. Agree on Data Rules." *Computerworld*, March 20, 2000.

Vitalari, Nicholas, and James Wetherbe. "Emerging Best Practices in Global Systems Development." In *Global Information Technology and Systems Management*, ed. Prashant Palvia et al. Marietta, GA: Ivy League, 1996.

West, Lawrence, and Walter Bogumil. "Immigration and the Global IT Workforce." *Communications of the ACM*, July 2001.

Accounting Information Systems Information systems that record and report business transactions and the flow of funds through an organization, and then produce financial statements. These statements provide information for the planning and control of business operations, as well as for legal and historical recordkeeping.

Accounts Payable Those accounts that represent what a business owes to others.

Accounts Receivable Those accounts that represent what others owe to a business.

Ada A programming language named after Augusta Ada Byron, considered the world's first computer programmer. Developed for the U.S. Department of Defense as a standard high-order language.

Ad Hoc Inquiries Unique, unscheduled, situation-specific information requests.

Adware Software that pushes advertising to a particular machine. Adware is usually not considered to be malicious, as it is often incorporated with a useful piece of software desired by a user.

Agile Company A company that employs agile manufacturing practices. Also, a company that has converted to a primarily software-based business model and is more quickly able to respond to changing market conditions.

Agile Competition The ability of a company to operate profitably in a competitive environment of continual and unpredictable changes in customer preferences, market conditions, and business opportunities.

Algorithm A set of well-defined rules or processes for solving a problem in a finite number of steps.

Analog Computer A computer that operates on data by measuring changes in continuous physical variables such as voltage, resistance, and rotation. Contrast with Digital Computer.

Analytical Database A database of data extracted from operational and external databases to provide data tailored to online analytical processing, decision support, and executive information systems.

Analytical Modeling Interactive use of computer-based mathematical models to explore decision alternatives using what-if analysis, sensitivity analysis, goal-seeking analysis, and optimization analysis.

Anti-Virus Software Software specifically intended to protect a particular machine or network from the intrusion of software-based viruses.

Applet A small, limited-purpose application program or small, independent module of a larger application program.

Application Development See Systems Development.

Application Development Mangement The process by which an organization manages the in-house development of software applications.

Application Generator A software package that supports the development of an application through an interactive terminal dialogue, where the programmer/analyst defines screens, reports, computations, and data structures.

Application Portfolio A planning tool used to evaluate present and proposed information systems applications in terms of the amount of revenue or assets invested in information systems that support major business functions and processes.

Applications Architecture A conceptual planning framework in which business applications of information technology are designed as an integrated architecture of enterprise systems that support strategic business initiatives and cross-functional business processes.

Application Server System software that provides a middleware interface between an operating system and the application programs of users.

Application Service Provider (ASP) A company that specializes in providing turnkey services for various software applications such that an organization can avoid the administration associated with licensing and updates of common software platforms used throughout the company.

Application Software Programs that specify the information processing activities required for the completion of specific tasks of computer users. Examples are electronic spreadsheet and word processing programs or inventory or payroll programs.

Application-Specific Programs Application software packages that support specific applications of end users in business, science and engineering, and other areas.

Arithmetic-Logic Unit (ALU) The unit of a computing system containing the circuits that perform arithmetic and logical operations.

Artificial Intelligence (AI) A science and technology whose goal is to develop computers that can think, as well as see, hear, walk, talk, and feel. A major thrust is the development of computer functions normally associated with human intelligence, for example, reasoning, inference, learning, and problem solving.

ASCII: American Standard Code for Information Interchange A standard code used for information interchange among data processing systems, communication systems, and associated equipment.

Assembler A computer program that translates an assembler language into machine language.

Assembler Language A programming language that utilizes symbols to represent operation codes and storage locations.

Asynchronous A sequence of operations without a regular or predictable time relationship. Thus, operations do not happen at regular timed intervals, but an operation will begin only after a previous operation is completed. The data transmission involves the use of start and stop bits with each character to indicate the beginning and end of the character being transmitted. Contrast with Synchronous.

Audit Trail The presence of media and procedures that allow a transaction to be traced through all stages of information processing, beginning with its appearance on a source document and ending with its transformation into information in a final output document.

Automated Teller Machine (ATM) A special-purpose transaction terminal used to provide remote banking services.

Back-End Processor Typically, a smaller, general-purpose computer dedicated to database processing using a database management system (DBMS). Also called a database machine or server.

Background Processing The automatic execution of lower-priority computer programs when higher-priority programs are not using the resources of the computer system. Contrast with Foreground Processing.

Backup Files Files that have been copied and stored via a backup process to protect against damage or loss of the original files.

Backward-Chaining An inference process that justifies a proposed conclusion by determining if it will result when rules are applied to the facts in a given situation.

Bandwidth The frequency range of a telecommunications channel, which determines its maximum transmission rate. The speed and capacity of transmission rates are typically measured in bits per second (bps). Bandwidth is a function of the telecommunications hardware, software, and media used by the telecommunications channel.

Bar Codes Vertical marks or bars placed on merchandise tags or packaging that can be sensed and read by optical character-reading devices. The width and combination of vertical lines are used to represent data.

Barriers to Entry Technological, financial, or legal requirements that deter firms from entering an industry.

BASIC: Beginner's All-Purpose Symbolic Instruction Code A programming language developed at Dartmouth College and designed for programming by end users.

Batch Processing A category of data processing in which data are accumulated into batches and processed periodically. Contrast with Real-Time Processing.

Baud A unit of measurement used to specify data transmission speeds. It is a unit of signaling speed equal to the number of discrete conditions or signal events per second. In many data communications applications, it represents one bit per second.

Binary Pertaining to a characteristic or property involving a selection, choice, or condition in which there are two possibilities, or pertaining to the number system that utilizes a base of 2.

Biometric Controls Computer-based security methods that measure physical traits and characteristics such as fingerprints, voice prints, and retina scans. Also called Biometric Security.

Bit A contraction of "binary digit." It can have the value of either 0 or 1.

Block A grouping of contiguous data records or other data elements that are handled as a unit.

Bluetooth A method by which two or more devices can wirelessly connect to each other while in close proximity.

Branch A transfer of control from one instruction to another in a computer program that is not part of the normal sequential execution of the instructions of the program.

Browser See Web Browser.

Buffer Temporary storage used when transmitting data from one device to another to compensate for a difference in rate of flow of data or time of occurrence of events.

Bug A mistake or malfunction.

Bulletin Board System (BBS) A service of online computer networks in which electronic messages, data files, or programs can be stored for other subscribers to read or copy.

Bundling The inclusion of software, maintenance, training, and other products or services in the price of a computer system.

Bus A set of conducting paths for movement of data and instructions that interconnects the various components of the CPU.

Business Ethics An area of philosophy concerned with developing ethical principles and promoting ethical behavior and practices in the accomplishment of business tasks and decision making.

Business Intelligence (BI) A term primarily used in industry that incorporates a range of analytical and decision support applications in business including data mining, decision support systems, knowledge management systems, and online analytical processing.

Business/IT Planning The process of developing a company's business vision, strategies, and goals, as well as how they will be supported by the company's information technology architecture and implemented by its business application development process.

Business Process Reengineering (BPR) Restructuring and transforming a business process by a fundamental rethinking and redesign to achieve dramatic improvements in cost, quality, speed, and so on.

Byte A sequence of adjacent binary digits operated on as a unit and usually shorter than a computer word. In many computer systems, a byte is a grouping of eight bits that can represent one alphabetic or special character or that can be packed with two decimal digits.

C A low-level structured programming language that resembles a machine-independent assembler language.

C++ An object-oriented version of C that is widely used for software package development.

Cache Memory A high-speed temporary storage area in the CPU for storing parts of a program or data during processing.

Capacity Management The use of planning and control methods to forecast and control information processing job loads, hardware and software usage, and other computer system resource requirements.

CASE Tools Specialized software applications intended to support the development of software. CASE is an acronym for computer-based software engineering.

Case-Based Reasoning Representing knowledge in an expert system's knowledge base in the form of cases, that is, examples of past performance, occurrences, and experiences.

Cathode Ray Tube (CRT) An electronic vacuum tube (television picture tube) that displays the output of a computer system.

CD-ROM An optical disk technology for microcomputers featuring compact disks with a storage capacity of over 500 megabytes.

Cellular Phone Systems A radio communications technology that divides a metropolitan area into a honeycomb of cells to greatly increase the number of frequencies and thus the users that can take advantage of mobile phone service.

Central Processing Unit (CPU) The unit of a computer system that includes the circuits that control the interpretation and execution of instructions. In many computer systems, the CPU includes the arithmetic-logic unit, the control unit, and the primary storage unit.

Change Management Managing the process of implementing major changes in information technology, business processes, organizational structures, and job assignments to reduce the risks and costs of change and optimize its benefits.

Channel (1) A path along which signals can be sent. (2) A small special-purpose processor that controls the movement of data between the CPU and input/output devices.

Chargeback Systems Methods of allocating costs to end-user departments on the basis of the information services rendered and information system resources utilized.

Chat Systems Software that enables two or more users at networked PCs to carry on online, real-time text conversations.

Check Bit A binary check digit: for example, a parity bit.

Check Digit A digit in a data field that is utilized to check for errors or loss of characters in the data field as a result of data transfer operations.

Checkpoint A place in a program where a check or a recording of data for restart purposes is performed.

Chief Information Officer A senior management position that oversees all information technology for a firm concentrating on long-range information system planning and strategy.

Clicks-and-Bricks Strategy A business model that combines both a bricks-and-mortar approach and an online presence.

Client (1) An end user. (2) The end user's networked microcomputer in client/server networks. (3) The version of a software package designed to run on an end user's networked microcomputer, such as a Web browser client and a groupware client.

Client/Server Network A computer network where end-user workstations (clients) are connected via telecommunications links to network servers and possibly to mainframe superservers.

Clock A device that generates periodic signals utilized to control the timing of a computer. Also, a register whose contents change at regular intervals in such a way as to measure time.

Cloud Computing A method of computing in which an individual or an organization makes use of another organizations excess computing power or data storage capacity.

Coaxial Cable A sturdy copper or aluminum wire wrapped with spacers to insulate and protect it. Groups of coaxial cables may also be bundled together in a bigger cable for ease of installation.

COBOL: Common Business Oriented Language A widely used business data processing programming language.

Code Computer instructions.

Cognitive Science An area of artificial intelligence that focuses on researching how the human brain works, and how humans think and learn, to apply such findings to the design of computer-based systems.

Cognitive Styles Basic patterns in how people handle information and confront problems.

Cognitive Theory Theories about how the human brain works and how humans think and learn.

Collaborative Work Management Tools Software that helps people accomplish or manage joint work activities.

Communications Satellite Earth satellites placed in stationary orbits above the equator that serve as relay stations for communications signals transmitted from earth stations.

Competitive Advantage Developing products, services, processes, or capabilities that give a company a superior business position relative to its competitors and other competitive forces.

Competitive Forces A firm must confront (1) rivalry of competitors within its industry, (2) threats of new entrants, (3) threats of substitutes, (4) the bargaining power of customers, and (5) the bargaining power of suppliers.

Competitive Strategies A firm can develop cost leadership, product differentiation, and business innovation strategies to confront its competitive forces.

Compiler A program that translates a high-level programming language into a machine-language program.

Computer A device that has the ability to accept data; internally store and execute a program of instructions; perform mathematical, logical, and manipulative operations on data; and report the results.

Computer-Aided Design (CAD) The use of computers and advanced graphics hardware and software to provide interactive design assistance for engineering and architectural design.

Computer-Aided Engineering (CAE) The use of computers to simulate, analyze, and evaluate models of product designs and production processes developed using computer-aided design methods.

Computer-Aided Manufacturing (CAM) The use of computers to automate the production process and operations of a manufacturing plant. Also called factory automation.

Computer-Aided Planning (CAP) The use of software packages as tools to support the planning process.

Computer-Aided Software Engineering (CASE) Same as Computer-Aided Systems Engineering, but emphasizing the importance of software development.

Computer-Aided Systems Engineering (CASE) Using software packages to accomplish and automate many of the activities of information systems development, including software development or programming.

Computer Application The use of a computer to solve a specific problem or accomplish a particular job for an end user. For example, common business computer applications include sales order processing, inventory control, and payroll.

Computer-Assisted Instruction (CAI) The use of computers to provide drills, practice exercises, and tutorial sequences to students.

Computer-Based Information System An information system that uses computer hardware and software to perform its information processing activities.

Computer Crime Criminal actions accomplished through the use of computer systems, especially with intent to defraud, destroy, or make unauthorized use of computer system resources.

Computer Ethics A system of principles governing the legal, professional, social, and moral responsibilities of computer specialists and end users.

Computer Generations Major stages in the historical development of computing.

Computer Graphics Using computer-generated images to analyze and interpret data, present information, and create computer-aided design and art.

Computer Industry The industry composed of firms that supply computer hardware, software, and services.

Computer-Integrated Manufacturing (CIM) An overall concept that stresses that the goals of computer use in factory automation should be to simplify, automate, and integrate production processes and other aspects of manufacturing.

Computer Matching Using computers to screen and match data about individual characteristics provided by a variety of computer-based information systems and databases to identify individuals for business, government, or other purposes.

Computer Monitoring Using computers to monitor the behavior and productivity of workers on the job and in the workplace.

Computer Program A series of instructions or statements in a form acceptable to a computer, prepared to achieve a certain result.

Computer System Computer hardware as a system of input, processing, output, storage, and control components. Thus, a computer system consists of input and output devices, primary and secondary storage devices, the central processing unit, the control unit within the CPU, and other peripheral devices.

Computer Terminal Any input/output device connected by telecommunications links to a computer.

Computer Virus or Worm Program code that copies its destructive program routines into the computer systems of anyone who accesses computer systems that have used the program, or anyone who uses copies of data or programs taken from such computers. This spreads the destruction of data and programs among many computer users. Technically, a virus will not run unaided but must be inserted into another program, whereas a worm is a distinct program that can run unaided.

Concurrent Processing The generic term for the capability of computers to work on several tasks at the same time, that is, concurrently. This may involve specific capabilities such as overlapped processing, multiprocessing, multiprogramming, multitasking, and parallel processing.

Connectivity The degree to which hardware, software, and databases can be easily linked together in a telecommunications network.

Control (1) The systems component that evaluates feedback to determine whether the system is moving toward the achievement of its goal and then makes any necessary adjustments to the input and processing components of the system to ensure that proper output is produced. (2) A management function that involves observing and measuring organizational performance and environmental activities and modifying the plans and activities of the organization when necessary.

Control Listing A detailed report that describes each transaction occurring during a period.

Control Totals Accumulating totals of data at multiple points in an information system to ensure correct information processing.

Control Unit A subunit of the central processing unit that controls and directs the operations of the computer system. The control unit retrieves computer instructions in proper sequence, interprets each instruction, and then directs the other parts of the computer system in their implementation.

Conversion The process in which the hardware, software, people, network, and data resources of an old information system must be converted to the requirements of a new information system. This usually involves a parallel, phased, pilot, or plunge conversion process from the old to the new system.

Cooperative Processing Information processing that allows the computers in a distributed processing network to share the processing of parts of an end user's application.

Cost/Benefit Analysis Identifying the advantages or benefits and the disadvantages or costs of a proposed solution.

Critical Success Factors A small number of key factors that executives consider critical to the success of the enterprise. These are key areas in which successful performance will assure the success of the organization and attainment of its goals.

Cross-Functional Information Systems Information systems that are integrated combinations of business information systems, thus sharing information resources across the functional units of an organization.

Cursor A movable point of light displayed on most video display screens to assist the user in the input of data.

Customer Relationship Management (CRM) A cross-functional e-business application that integrates and automates many customer-serving processes in sales, direct marketing, account and order management, and customer service and support.

Cybernetic System A system that uses feedback and control components to achieve a self-regulating capability.

Cylinder An imaginary vertical cylinder consisting of the vertical alignment of tracks on each surface of magnetic disks that are accessed simultaneously by the read/write heads of a disk drive.

Data Facts or observations about physical phenomena or business transactions. More specifically, data are objective measurements of the attributes (characteristics) of entities such as people, places, things, and events.

Data Administration A data resource management function that involves the establishment and enforcement of policies and procedures for managing data as a strategic corporate resource.

Database An integrated collection of logically related data elements. A database consolidates many records previously stored in separate files so that a common pool of data serves many applications.

Database Administration   A data resource management function that includes responsibility for developing and maintaining the organization's data dictionary, designing and monitoring the performance of databases, and enforcing standards for database use and security.

Database Administrator (DBA)   A specialist responsible for maintaining standards for the development, maintenance, and security of an organization's databases.

Database Maintenance   The activity of keeping a database up to date by adding, changing, or deleting data.

Database Management Approach   An approach to the storage and processing of data in which independent files are consolidated into a common pool, or database, of records available to different application programs and end users for processing and data retrieval.

Database Management System (DBMS)   A set of computer programs that controls the creation, maintenance, and utilization of the databases of an organization.

Database Processing   Utilizing a database for data processing activities such as maintenance, information retrieval, or report generation.

Data Center   An organizational unit that uses centralized computing resources to perform information processing activities for an organization. Also known as a computer center.

Data Conferencing   Users at networked PCs can view, mark up, revise, and save changes to a shared whiteboard of drawings, documents, and other material.

Data Conversion   Converting data into new data formats required by a new business application and its software and databases. Also includes correcting incorrect data, filtering out unwanted data, and consolidating data into new databases and other data subsets.

Data Design   The design of the logical structure of databases and files to be used by a proposed information system. This design produces detailed descriptions of the entities, relationships, data elements, and integrity rules for system files and databases.

Data Dictionary   A software module and database containing descriptions and definitions concerning the structure, data elements, interrelationships, and other characteristics of a database.

Data Entry   The process of converting data into a form suitable for entry into a computer system. Also called data capture or input preparation.

Data Flow Diagram   A graphic diagramming tool that uses a few simple symbols to illustrate the flow of data among external entities, processing activities, and data storage elements.

Data Management   Control program functions that provide access to data sets, enforce data storage conventions, and regulate the use of input/output devices.

Data Mining   Using special-purpose software to analyze data from a data warehouse to find hidden patterns and trends.

Data Model   A conceptual framework that defines the logical relationships among the data elements needed to support a basic business or other process.

Data Modeling   A process in which the relationships between data elements are identified and defined to develop data models.

Data Planning   A corporate planning and analysis function that focuses on data resource management. It includes the responsibility for developing an overall information policy and data architecture for the firm's data resources.

Data Processing   The execution of a systematic sequence of operations performed on data to transform them into information.

Data Redundancy   The storage of a particular data element or elements in more than one physical location or form.

Data Resource Management   A managerial activity that applies information systems technology and management tools to the task of managing an organization's data resources. Its three major components are database administration, data administration, and data planning.

Data Warehouse   An integrated collection of data extracted from operational, historical, and external databases and cleaned, transformed, and cataloged for retrieval and analysis (*data mining*) to provide business intelligence for business decision making.

Debug   To detect, locate, and remove errors from a program or malfunctions from a computer.

Decision Support System (DSS)   An information system that utilizes decision models, a database, and a decision maker's own insights in an ad hoc, interactive analytical modeling process to reach a specific decision by a specific decision maker.

Demand Reports and Responses   Information provided whenever a manager or end user demands it.

Desktop Publishing   The use of microcomputers, laser printers, and page makeup software to produce a variety of printed materials that were formerly produced only by professional printers.

Desktop Videoconferencing   The use of end-user computer workstations to conduct two-way interactive video conferences.

Development Centers   Systems development consultant groups formed to serve as consultants to the professional programmers and systems analysts of an organization to improve their application development efforts.

Digital Computer   A computer that operates on digital data by performing arithmetic and logical operations on the data. Contrast with Analog Computer.

Digitizer   A device that is used to convert drawings and other graphic images on paper or other materials into digital data that are entered into a computer system.

Direct Access   A method of storage in which each storage position has a unique address and can be individually accessed in approximately the same period without having to search through other storage positions. Same as Random Access. Contrast with Sequential Access.

Direct Access Storage Device (DASD)   A storage device that can directly access data to be stored or retrieved, for example, a magnetic disk unit.

Direct Data Organization   A method of data organization in which logical data elements are distributed randomly on or within the physical data medium. For example, logical data records distributed randomly on the surfaces of a magnetic disk file. Also called direct organization.

Direct Input/Output   Methods such as keyboard entry, voice input/output, and video displays that allow data to be input into or output from a computer system without the use of machine-readable media.

Disaster Recovery   Methods for ensuring that an organization recovers from natural and human-caused disasters that have affected its computer-based operations.

Discussion Forum   An online network discussion platform to encourage and manage online text discussions over a period among members of special-interest groups or project teams.

Distributed Databases   The concept of distributing databases or portions of a database at remote sites where the data are most frequently referenced. Sharing of data is made possible through a network that interconnects the distributed databases.

Distributed Denial of Service   A malicious attack on a computer system by using a wide distribution of computers to simultaneously and continuously send requests to a single computer or website thus making legitimate requests almost impossible to accomodate.

Distributed Processing   A form of decentralization of information processing made possible by a network of computers dispersed throughout an organization. Processing of user applications is accomplished by several computers interconnected by a telecommunications network, rather than relying on one large centralized computer facility or on the decentralized operation of several independent computers.

Document   (1) A medium on which data have been recorded for human use, such as a report or invoice. (2) In word processing, a generic term for text material such as letters, memos, and reports.

Documentation   A collection of documents or information that describes a computer program, information system, or required data processing operations.

Downsizing   Moving to smaller computing platforms, such as from mainframe systems to networks of personal computers and servers.

Downtime   The time interval during which a device is malfunctioning or inoperative.

DSS Generator   A software package for a decision support system that contains modules for database, model, and dialogue management.

Duplex   In communications, pertains to a simultaneous two-way independent transmission in both directions.

EBCDIC: Extended Binary Coded Decimal Interchange Code   An eight-bit code that is widely used by mainframe computers.

Echo Check   A method of checking the accuracy of data transmission in which the received data are returned to the sending device for comparison with the original data.

e-Commerce Marketplaces   Internet, intranet, and extranet Web sites and portals hosted by individual companies, consortiums of organizations, or third-party intermediaries providing electronic catalog, exchange, and auction markets to unite buyers and sellers to accomplish e-commerce transactions.

Economic Feasibility   Whether expected cost savings, increased revenue, increased profits, and reductions in required investment exceed the costs of developing and operating a proposed system.

EDI: Electronic Data Interchange   The automatic electronic exchange of business documents between the computers of different organizations.

Edit   To modify the form or format of data. For example, to insert or delete characters such as page numbers or decimal points.

Edit Report   A report that describes errors detected during processing.

Electronic Business (e-Business)   The use of Internet technologies to inter-network and empower business processes, electronic commerce, and enterprise communication and collaboration within a company and with its customers, suppliers, and other business stakeholders.

Electronic Commerce (e-Commerce)   The buying and selling, marketing and servicing, and delivery and payment of products, services, and information over the Internet, intranets, extranets, and other networks, between an inter-networked enterprise and its prospects, customers, suppliers, and other business partners. Includes business-to-consumer (B2C), business-to-business (B2B), and consumer-to-consumer (C2C) e-commerce.

Electronic Communications Tools   Software that helps communicate and collaborate with others by electronically sending messages, documents, and files in data, text, voice, or multimedia over the Internet, intranets, extranets, and other computer networks.

Electronic Conferencing Tools   Software that helps networked computer users share information and collaborate while working together on joint assignments, no matter where they are located.

Electronic Data Processing (EDP)   The use of electronic computers to process data automatically.

Electronic Document Management   An image-processing technology in which an electronic document may consist of digitized voice notes and electronic graphics images, as well as digitized images of traditional documents.

Electronic Funds Transfer (EFT)   The development of banking and payment systems that transfer funds electronically instead of using cash or paper documents such as checks.

Electronic Mail (e-mail)   Sending and receiving text messages between networked PCs over telecommunications networks. E-mail can also include data files, software, and multimedia messages and documents as attachments.

Electronic Meeting Systems (EMS)   Using a meeting room with networked PCs, a large-screen projector, and EMS software to facilitate communication, collaboration, and group decision making in business meetings.

Electronic Payment Systems   Alternative cash or credit payment methods using various electronic technologies to pay for products and services in electronic commerce.

Electronic Spreadsheet Package   An application program used as a computerized tool for analysis, planning, and modeling that allows users to enter and manipulate data into an electronic worksheet of rows and columns.

Emulation   To imitate one system with another so that the imitating system accepts the same data, executes the same programs, and achieves the same results as the imitated system.

Encryption   To scramble data or convert them, prior to transmission, to a secret code that masks the meaning of the data to unauthorized recipients. Similar to enciphering.

End User Anyone who uses an information system or the information it produces.

End-User Computing Systems Computer-based information systems that directly support both the operational and managerial applications of end users.

End-User Development The process by which the end user of a software application is also the primary developer of the software.

End-User Involvement The process and activities associated with involving the end user or end user representative in the various phases of complex software development. User involvement is considered a necessary but not sufficient condition for software success.

Enterprise Application Integration (EAI) A cross-functional e-business application that integrates front-office applications like customer relationship management with back-office applications like enterprise resource management.

Enterprise Collaboration Systems The use of groupware tools and the Internet, intranets, extranets, and other computer networks to support and enhance communication, coordination, collaboration, and resource sharing among teams and workgroups in an inter-networked enterprise.

Enterprise Information Portal A customized and personalized Web-based interface for corporate intranets and extranets that gives qualified users access to a variety of internal and external e-business and e-commerce applications, databases, software tools, and information services.

Enterprise Knowledge Portal An enterprise information portal that serves as a knowledge management system by providing users with access to enterprise knowledge bases.

Enterprise Model A conceptual framework that defines the structures and relationships of business processes and data elements, as well as other planning structures, such as critical success factors and organizational units.

Enterprise Resource Planning (ERP) Integrated cross-functional software that reengineers manufacturing, distribution, finance, human resources, and other basic business processes of a company to improve its efficiency, agility, and profitability.

Entity Relationship Diagram (ERD) A data planning and systems development diagramming tool that models the relationships among the entities in a business process.

Entropy The tendency of a system to lose a relatively stable state of equilibrium.

Ergonomics The science and technology emphasizing the safety, comfort, and ease of use of human-operated machines such as computers. The goal of ergonomics is to produce systems that are user-friendly: safe, comfortable, and easy to use. Ergonomics is also called human factors engineering.

Exception Reports Reports produced only when exceptional conditions occur, or reports produced periodically that contain information only about exceptional conditions.

Executive Information System (EIS) An information system that provides strategic information tailored to the needs of executives and other decision makers.

Executive Support System (ESS) An executive information system with additional capabilities, including data analysis, decision support, electronic mail, and personal productivity tools.

Expert System (ES) A computer-based information system that uses its knowledge about a specific complex application area to act as an expert consultant to users. The system consists of a knowledge base and software modules that perform inferences on the knowledge and communicate answers to a user's questions.

Extranet A network that links selected resources of a company with its customers, suppliers, and other business partners, using the Internet or private networks to link the organizations' intranets.

Facilities Management The use of an external service organization to operate and manage the information processing facilities of an organization.

Fault Tolerant Systems Computers that have multiple central processors, peripherals, and system software and that are able to continue operations even if there is a major hardware or software failure.

Faxing (Facsimile) Transmitting and receiving images of documents over the telephone or computer networks using PCs or fax machines.

Feasibility Study A preliminary study that investigates the information needs of end users and the objectives, constraints, basic resource requirements, cost/benefits, and feasibility of proposed projects.

Feedback (1) Data or information concerning the components and operations of a system. (2) The use of part of the output of a system as input to the system.

Fiber Optics The technology that uses cables consisting of very thin filaments of glass fibers that can conduct the light generated by lasers for high-speed telecommunications.

Field A data element that consists of a grouping of characters that describe a particular attribute of an entity. For example, the name field or salary field of an employee.

Fifth Generation The next generation of computers. Major advances in parallel processing, user interfaces, and artificial intelligence may provide computers that will be able to see, hear, talk, and think.

File A collection of related data records treated as a unit. Sometimes called a data set.

File Management Controlling the creation, deletion, access, and use of files of data and programs.

File Processing Organizing data into specialized files of data records designed for processing only by specific application programs. Contrast with Database Management Approach.

Financial Management Systems Information systems that support financial managers in the financing of a business and the allocation and control of financial resources. These include cash and securities management, capital budgeting, financial forecasting, and financial planning.

Firewall Computers, communications processors, and software that protect computer networks from intrusion by screening all network traffic and serving as a safe transfer point for access to and from other networks.

Firmware The use of microprogrammed read-only memory circuits in place of hard-wired logic circuitry. See also Microprogramming.

Floating Point Pertaining to a number representation system in which each number is represented by two sets of digits. One set represents the significant digits or fixed-point "base" of the number, while the other set of digits represents the "exponent," which indicates the precision of the number.

Floppy Disk   A small plastic disk coated with iron oxide that resembles a small phonograph record enclosed in a protective envelope. It is a widely used form of magnetic disk media that provides a direct access storage capability for microcomputer systems.

Flowchart   A graphical representation in which symbols are used to represent operations, data, flow, logic, equipment, and so on. A program flowchart illustrates the structure and sequence of operations of a program, whereas a system flowchart illustrates the components and flows of information systems.

Foreground Processing   The automatic execution of the computer programs that have been designed to preempt the use of computing facilities. Contrast with Background Processing.

Format   The arrangement of data on a medium.

FORTRAN: FORmula TRANslation   A high-level programming language widely utilized to develop computer programs that perform mathematical computations for scientific, engineering, and selected business applications.

Forward Chaining   An inference strategy that reaches a conclusion by applying rules to facts to determine if any facts satisfy a rule's conditions in a particular situation.

Fourth-Generation Languages (4GL)   Programming languages that are easier to use than high-level languages such as BASIC, COBOL, or FORTRAN. They are also known as nonprocedural, natural, or very high-level languages.

Frame   A collection of knowledge about an entity or other concept consisting of a complex package of slots, that is, data values describing the characteristics or attributes of an entity.

Frame-Based Knowledge   Knowledge represented in the form of a hierarchy or network of frames.

Front-End Processor   Typically a smaller, general-purpose computer that is dedicated to handling data communications control functions in a communications network, thus relieving the host computer of these functions.

Functional Business Systems   Information systems within a business organization that support one of the traditional functions of business such as marketing, finance, or production. Functional business systems can be either operations or management information systems.

Functional Requirements   The information system capabilities required to meet the information needs of end users. Also called system requirements.

Fuzzy Logic Systems   Computer-based systems that can process data that are incomplete or only partially correct, that is, fuzzy data. Such systems can solve unstructured problems with incomplete knowledge, as humans do.

General-Purpose Application Programs   Programs that can perform information processing jobs for users from all application areas. For example, word processing programs, electronic spreadsheet programs, and graphics programs can be used by individuals for home, education, business, scientific, and many other purposes.

General-Purpose Computer   A computer that is designed to handle a wide variety of problems. Contrast with Special-Purpose Computer.

Generate   To produce a machine-language program for performing a specific data processing task based on parameters supplied by a programmer or user.

Genetic Algorithm   An application of artificial intelligence software that uses Darwinian (survival of the fittest) randomizing and other functions to simulate an evolutionary process that can yield increasingly better solutions to a problem.

Gigabyte   One billion bytes. More accurately, 2 to the 30th power, or 1,073,741,824 in decimal notation.

GIGO   An acronym of "Garbage In, Garbage Out," which emphasizes that information systems will produce erroneous and invalid output when provided with erroneous and invalid input data or instructions.

Global Company   A business that is driven by a global strategy so that all of its activities are planned and implemented in the context of a whole-world system.

Global e-Business Technology Management   Managing information technologies in a global e-business enterprise, amid the cultural, political, and geoeconomic challenges involved in developing e-business/IT strategies, global e-business and e-commerce applications portfolios, Internet-based technology platforms, and global data resource management policies.

Global Information Technology   The use of computer-based information systems and telecommunications networks using a variety of information technologies to support global business operations and management.

Globalization   Becoming a global enterprise by expanding into global markets, using global production facilities, forming alliances with global partners, and so on.

Goal-Seeking Analysis   Making repeated changes to selected variables until a chosen variable reaches a target value.

Graphical User Interface   A software interface that relies on icons, bars, buttons, boxes, and other images to initiate computer-based tasks for users.

Graphics   Pertaining to symbolic input or output from a computer system, such as lines, curves, and geometric shapes, using video display units or graphics plotters and printers.

Graphics Pen and Tablet   A device that allows an end user to draw or write on a pressure-sensitive tablet and have the handwriting or graphics digitized by the computer and accepted as input.

Graphics Software   A program that helps users generate graphics displays.

Group Decision Making   Decisions made by groups of people coming to an agreement on a particular issue.

Group Decision Support System (GDSS)   A decision support system that provides support for decision making by groups of people.

Group Support Systems (GSS)   An information system that enhances communication, coordination, collaboration, decision making, and group work activities of teams and workgroups.

Groupware   Software to support and enhance the communication, coordination, and collaboration among networked teams and workgroups, including software tools for electronic communications, electronic conferencing, and cooperative work management.

Hacking (1) Obsessive use of a computer. (2) The unauthorized access and use of computer systems.

Handshaking Exchange of predetermined signals when a connection is established between two communications terminals.

Hard Copy A data medium or data record that has a degree of permanence and that can be read by people or machines.

Hardware (1) Machines and media. (2) Physical equipment, as opposed to computer programs or methods of use. (3) Mechanical, magnetic, electrical, electronic, or optical devices. Contrast with Software.

Hash Total The sum of numbers in a data field that are not normally added, such as account numbers or other identification numbers. It is utilized as a control total, especially during input/output operations of batch processing systems.

Header Label A machine-readable record at the beginning of a file containing data for file identification and control.

Heuristic Pertaining to exploratory methods of problem solving in which solutions are discovered by evaluation of the progress made toward the final result. It is an exploratory trial-and-error approach guided by rules of thumb. Opposite of algorithmic.

Hierarchical Data Structure A logical data structure in which the relationships between records form a hierarchy or tree structure. The relationships among records are one to many, because each data element is related only to one element above it.

High-Level Language A programming language that utilizes macro instructions and statements that closely resemble human language or mathematical notation to describe the problem to be solved or the procedure to be used. Also called a compiler language.

Homeostasis A relatively stable state of equilibrium of a system.

Host Computer Typically a larger central computer that performs the major data processing tasks in a computer network.

HTML See Hypertext Markup Language.

Human Factors Hardware and software capabilities that can affect the comfort, safety, ease of use, and user customization of computer-based information systems.

Human Information Processing A conceptual framework about the human cognitive process that uses an information processing context to explain how humans capture, process, and use information.

Human Resource Information Systems (HRIS) Information systems that support human resource management activities such as recruitment, selection and hiring, job placement and performance appraisals, and training and development.

Hybrid AI Systems Systems that integrate several AI technologies, such as expert systems and neural networks.

Hypermedia Documents containing multiple forms of media, including text, graphics, video, and sound, that can be interactively searched, like Hypertext.

Hypertext Text in electronic form that has been indexed and linked (hyperlinks) by software in a variety of ways so that it can be randomly and interactively searched by a user.

Hypertext Markup Language (HTML) A popular page description language for creating hypertext and hypermedia documents for World Wide Web and intranet Web sites.

Icon A small figure on a video display that looks like a familiar office or other device, such as a file folder (for storing a file) or a wastebasket (for deleting a file).

Image Processing A computer-based technology that allows end users to electronically capture, store, process, and retrieve images that may include numeric data, text, handwriting, graphics, documents, and photographs. Image processing makes heavy use of optical scanning and optical disk technologies.

Impact Printers Printers that form images on paper through the pressing of a printing element and an inked ribbon or roller against the face of a sheet of paper.

Implementation Process The process and activities associated with installing a software application and preparing it for actual use.

Index An ordered reference list of the contents of a file or document, together with keys or reference notations for identification or location of those contents.

Index Sequential A method of data organization in which records are organized in sequential order and also referenced by an index. When utilized with direct access file devices, it is known as index sequential access method, or ISAM.

Inference Engine The software component of an expert system, which processes the rules and facts related to a specific problem and makes associations and inferences resulting in recommended courses of action.

Infomediaries Third-party market-maker companies that serve as intermediaries to bring buyers and sellers together by developing and hosting electronic catalog, exchange, and auction markets to accomplish e-commerce transactions.

Information Data placed in a meaningful and useful context for an end user.

Information Appliances Small Web-enabled microcomputer devices with specialized functions, such as handheld PDAs, TV set-top boxes, game consoles, cellular and PCS phones, wired telephone appliances, and other Web-enabled home appliances.

Information Architecture A conceptual framework that defines the basic structure, content, and relationships of the organizational databases that provide the data needed to support the basic business processes of an organization.

Information Center A support facility for the end users of an organization. It allows users to learn to develop their own application programs and accomplish their own information processing tasks. End users are provided with hardware support, software support, and people support (trained user consultants).

Information Float The time that a document is in transit between the sender and receiver and thus unavailable for any action or response.

Information Processing A concept that covers both the traditional concept of processing numeric and alphabetic data and the processing of text, images, and voices. It emphasizes that the production of information products for users should be the focus of processing activities.

Information Quality   The degree to which information has content, form, and time characteristics that give it value for specific end users.

Information Resource Management (IRM)   A management concept that views data, information, and computer resources (computer hardware, software, networks, and personnel) as valuable organizational resources that should be efficiently, economically, and effectively managed for the benefit of the entire organization.

Information Retrieval   The methods and procedures for recovering specific information from stored data.

Information Superhighway   An advanced high-speed Internet-like network that connects individuals, households, businesses, government agencies, libraries, schools, universities, and other institutions with interactive voice, video, data, and multimedia communications.

Information System   (1) A set of people, procedures, and resources that collects, transforms, and disseminates information in an organization. (2) A system that accepts data resources as input and processes them into information products as output.

Information System Model   A conceptual framework that views an information system as a system that uses the resources of hardware (machines and media), software (programs and procedures), people (users and specialists), and networks (communications media and network support) to perform input, processing, output, storage, and control activities that transform data resources (databases and knowledge bases) into information products.

Information Systems Development   See Systems Development.

Information System Specialist   A person whose occupation is related to the providing of information system services, for example, a systems analyst, programmer, or computer operator.

Information Technology (IT)   Hardware, software, telecommunications, database management, and other information processing technologies used in computer-based information systems.

Information Technology Architecture   A conceptual blueprint that specifies the components and interrelationships of a company's technology infrastructure, data resources, applications architecture, and IT organization.

Information Technology Management   Managing information technologies by (1) the joint development and implementation of business and IT strategies by business and IT executives, (2) managing the research and implementation of new information technologies and the development of business applications, and (3) managing the IT processes, professionals, subunits, and infrastructure within a company.

Information Theory   The branch of learning concerned with the likelihood of accurate transmission or communication of messages subject to transmission failure, distortion, and noise.

Input   Pertaining to a device, process, or channel involved in the insertion of data into a data processing system. Opposite of Output.

Input/Output (I/O)   Pertaining to either input or output, or both.

Input/Output Interface Hardware   Devices such as I/O ports, I/O buses, buffers, channels, and I/O control units, which assist the CPU in its input/output assignments. These devices make it possible for modern computer systems to perform input, output, and processing functions simultaneously.

Inquiry Processing   Computer processing that supports the real-time interrogation of online files and databases by end users.

Instruction   A grouping of characters that specifies the computer operation to be performed.

Intangible Benefits and Costs   The nonquantifiable benefits and costs of a proposed solution or system.

Integrated Circuit   A complex microelectronic circuit consisting of interconnected circuit elements that cannot be disassembled because they are placed on or within a "continuous substrate" such as a silicon chip.

Integrated Packages   Software that combines the ability to do several general-purpose applications (such as word processing, electronic spreadsheet, and graphics) into one program.

Intelligent Agent   A special-purpose knowledge-based system that serves as a software surrogate to accomplish specific tasks for end users.

Intelligent Terminal   A terminal with the capabilities of a microcomputer that can thus perform many data processing and other functions without accessing a larger computer.

Interactive Marketing   A dynamic collaborative process of creating, purchasing, and improving products and services that builds close relationships between a business and its customers, using a variety of services on the Internet, intranets, and extranets.

Interactive Processing   A type of real-time processing in which users can interact with a computer on a real-time basis.

Interactive Video   Computer-based systems that integrate image processing with text, audio, and video processing technologies, which makes interactive multimedia presentations possible.

Interface   A shared boundary, such as the boundary between two systems. For example, the boundary between a computer and its peripheral devices.

Internet   A rapidly growing computer network of millions of business, educational, and governmental networks connecting hundreds of millions of computers and their users in over 200 countries.

Inter-Network Processor   Communications processors used by local area networks to interconnect them with other local area and wide area networks. Examples include switches, routers, hubs, and gateways.

Inter-Networks   Interconnected local area and wide area networks.

Interoperability   Being able to accomplish end-user applications using different types of computer systems, operating systems, and application software, interconnected by different types of local and wide area networks.

Interorganizational Information Systems   Information systems that interconnect an organization with other organizations, such as a business and its customers and suppliers.

Interpreter   A computer program that translates and executes each source language statement before translating and executing the next one.

Interrupt A condition that causes an interruption in a processing operation during which another task is performed. At the conclusion of this new assignment, control may be transferred back to the point at which the original processing operation was interrupted or to other tasks with a higher priority.

Intranet An Internet-like network within an organization. Web browser software provides easy access to internal Web sites established by business units, teams, and individuals, and other network resources and applications.

Inverted File A file that references entities by their attributes.

IT Architecture A conceptual design for the implementation of information technology in an organization, including its hardware, software, and network technology platforms, data resources, application portfolio, and IS organization.

Iterative Pertaining to the repeated execution of a series of steps.

Java An object-oriented programming language designed for programming real-time, interactive, Web-based applications in the form of applets for use on clients and servers on the Internet, intranets, and extranets.

Job A specified group of tasks prescribed as a unit of work for a computer.

Job Control Language (JCL) A language for communicating with the operating system of a computer to identify a job and describe its requirements.

Joystick A small lever set in a box used to move the cursor on the computer's display screen.

K An abbreviation for the prefix *kilo*, which is 1,000 in decimal notation. When referring to storage capacity, it is equivalent to 2 to the 10th power, or 1,024 in decimal notation.

Key One or more fields within a data record that are used to identify it or control its use.

Keyboarding Using the keyboard of a microcomputer or computer terminal.

Knowledge Base A computer-accessible collection of knowledge about a subject in a variety of forms, such as facts and rules of inference, frames, and objects.

Knowledge-Based Information System An information system that adds a knowledge base to the database and other components found in other types of computer-based information systems.

Knowledge Engineer A specialist who works with experts to capture the knowledge they possess to develop a knowledge base for expert systems and other knowledge-based systems.

Knowledge Management Organizing and sharing the diverse forms of business information created within an organization. Includes managing project and enterprise document libraries, discussion databases, intranet Web site databases, and other types of knowledge bases.

Knowledge Workers People whose primary work activities include creating, using, and distributing information.

Language Translator Program A program that converts the programming language instructions in a computer program into machine language code. Major types include assemblers, compilers, and interpreters.

Large-Scale Integration (LSI) A method of constructing electronic circuits in which thousands of circuits can be placed on a single semiconductor chip.

Legacy Systems The older, traditional, mainframe-based business information systems of an organization.

Light Pen A photoelectronic device that allows data to be entered or altered on the face of a video display terminal.

Liquid Crystal Displays (LCDs) Electronic visual displays that form characters by applying an electrical charge to selected silicon crystals.

List Organization A method of data organization that uses indexes and pointers to allow for nonsequential retrieval.

List Processing A method of processing data in the form of lists.

Local Area Network (LAN) A communications network that typically connects computers, terminals, and other computerized devices within a limited physical area such as an office, building, manufacturing plant, or other work site.

Locking In Customers and Suppliers Building valuable relationships with customers and suppliers that deter them from abandoning a firm for its competitors or intimidating it into accepting less profitable relationships.

Logical Data Elements Data elements that are independent of the physical data media on which they are recorded.

Logical System Design Developing general specifications for how basic information systems activities can meet end-user requirements.

Loop A sequence of instructions in a computer program that is executed repeatedly until a terminal condition prevails.

Machine Cycle The timing of a basic CPU operation as determined by a fixed number of electrical pulses emitted by the CPU's timing circuitry or internal clock.

Machine Language A programming language in which instructions are expressed in the binary code of the computer.

Macro Instruction An instruction in a source language that is equivalent to a specified sequence of machine instructions.

Magnetic Disk A flat, circular plate with a magnetic surface on which data can be stored by selective magnetization of portions of the curved surface.

Magnetic Ink An ink that contains particles of iron oxide that can be magnetized and detected by magnetic sensors.

Magnetic Ink Character Recognition (MICR) The machine recognition of characters printed with magnetic ink. Primarily used for check processing by the banking industry.

Magnetic Tape A plastic tape with a magnetic surface on which data can be stored by selective magnetization of portions of the surface.

Mag Stripe Card A plastic, wallet-size card with a strip of magnetic tape on one surface; widely used for credit/debit cards.

Mainframe A larger computer system, typically with a separate central processing unit, as distinguished from microcomputer and minicomputer systems.

Management Information System (MIS) A management support system that produces prespecified reports, displays, and responses on a **periodic, exception, demand, or push reporting basis.**

Management Support System (MSS)   An information system that provides information to support managerial decision making. More specifically, an information-reporting system, executive information system, or decision support system.

Managerial End User   A manager, entrepreneur, or managerial-level professional who personally uses information systems. Also, the manager of the department or other organizational unit that relies on information systems.

Managerial Roles   Management of the performance of a variety of interpersonal, information, and decision roles.

Manual Data Processing   Data processing that requires continual human operation and intervention and that utilizes simple data processing tools such as paper forms, pencils, and filing cabinets.

Manufacturing Information Systems   Information systems that support the planning, control, and accomplishment of manufacturing processes. This includes concepts such as computer-integrated manufacturing (CIM) and technologies such as computer-aided manufacturing (CAM) or computeraided design (CAD).

Marketing Information Systems   Information systems that support the planning, control, and transaction processing required for the accomplishment of marketing activities, such as sales management, advertising, and promotion.

Mass Storage   Secondary storage devices with extra-large storage capacities, such as magnetic or optical disks.

Master File   A data file containing relatively permanent information that is utilized as an authoritative reference and is usually updated periodically. Contrast with Transaction File.

Mathematical Model   A mathematical representation of a process, device, or concept.

Media   All tangible objects on which data are recorded.

Megabyte   One million bytes. More accurately, 2 to the 20th power, or 1,048,576 in decimal notation.

Memory   See Storage.

Menu   A displayed list of items (usually the names of alternative applications, files, or activities) from which an end user makes a selection.

Menu Driven   A characteristic of interactive computing systems that provides menu displays and operator prompting to assist an end user in performing a particular job.

Metadata   Data about data; data describing the structure, data elements, interrelationships, and other characteristics of a database.

Metcalfe's Law   A theory advanced by Robert Metcalfe that suggests that the value of a given network will double with the additional of each successive connection or node.

Microcomputer   A very small computer, ranging in size from a "computer on a chip" to handheld, laptop, and desktop units, and servers.

Micrographics   The use of microfilm, microfiche, and other microforms to record data in greatly reduced form.

Microprocessor   A microcomputer central processing unit (CPU) on a chip. Without input/output or primary storage capabilities in most types.

Microprogram   A small set of elementary control instructions called microinstructions or microcode.

Microprogramming   The use of special software (microprograms) to perform the functions of special hardware (electronic control circuitry). Microprograms stored in a read-only storage module of the control unit interpret the machine language instructions of a computer program and decode them into elementary microinstructions, which are then executed.

Microsecond   A millionth of a second.

Middleware   Software that helps diverse software programs and networked computer systems work together, thus promoting their interoperability.

Midrange Computer   A computer category between microcomputers and mainframes. Examples include minicomputers, network servers, and technical workstations.

Millisecond   A thousandth of a second.

Minicomputer   A type of midrange computer.

Model Base   An organized software collection of conceptual, mathematical, and logical models that express business relationships, computational routines, or analytical techniques.

Modem   (MOdulator-DEModulator) A device that converts the digital signals from input/output devices into appropriate frequencies at a transmission terminal and converts them back into digital signals at a receiving terminal.

Monitor   Software or hardware that observes, supervises, controls, or verifies the operations of a system.

Moore's Law   A theory advanced by Gordon Moore that suggests that computing power will double every 18 to 24 months at a given price point.

Mouse   A small device that is electronically connected to a computer and is moved by hand on a flat surface to move the cursor on a video screen in the same direction. Buttons on the mouse allow users to issue commands and make responses or selections.

Multidimensional Structure   A database model that uses multidimensional structures (such as cubes or cubes within cubes) to store data and relationships between data.

Multimedia Presentations   Providing information using a variety of media, including text and graphics displays, voice and other audio, photographs, and video segments.

Multiplex   To interleave or simultaneously transmit two or more messages on a single channel.

Multiplexer   An electronic device that allows a single communications channel to carry simultaneous data transmissions from many terminals.

Multiprocessing   Pertaining to the simultaneous execution of two or more instructions by a computer or computer network.

Multiprocessor Computer Systems   Computer systems that use a multiprocessor architecture in the design of their central processing units. This includes the use of support microprocessors and multiple instruction processors, including parallel processor designs.

Multiprogramming   Pertaining to the concurrent execution of two or more programs by a computer by interleaving their execution.

Multitasking   The concurrent use of the same computer to accomplish several different information processing tasks. Each task may require the use of a different program or the concurrent use of the same copy of a program by several users.

Nanosecond   One billionth of a second.

Natural Language   A programming language that is very close to human language. Also called very high-level language.

Network   An interconnected system of computers, terminals, and communications channels and devices.

Network Architecture   A master plan designed to promote an open, simple, flexible, and efficient telecommunications environment through the use of standard protocols, standard communications hardware and software interfaces, and the design of a standard multilevel telecommunications interface between end users and computer systems.

Network Computer   A low-cost networked microcomputer with no or minimal disk storage, which depends on Internet or intranet servers for its operating system and Web browser, Java-enabled application software, and data access and storage.

Network Computing   A network-centric view of computing in which "the network is the computer," that is, the view that computer networks are the central computing resource of any computing environment.

Network Data Structure   A logical data structure that allows many-to-many relationships among data records. It allows entry into a database at multiple points, because any data element or record can be related to many other data elements.

Network Topologies   The various configurations by which computers can be networked and connected together.

Neural Networks   Computer processors or software whose architecture is based on the human brain's meshlike neuron structure. Neural networks can process many pieces of information simultaneously and learn to recognize patterns and programs to solve related problems on their own.

Node   A terminal point in a communications network.

Nonprocedural Languages   Programming languages that allow users and professional programmers to specify the results they want without specifying how to solve the problem.

Numerical Control   Automatic control of a machine process by a computer that makes use of numerical data, generally introduced as the operation is in process. Also called machine control.

Object   A data element that includes both data and the methods or processes that act on those data.

Object-Based Knowledge   Knowledge represented as a network of objects.

Object-Oriented Language   An object-oriented programming (OOP) language used to develop programs that create and use objects to perform information processing tasks.

Object Program   A compiled or assembled program composed of executable machine instructions. Contrast with Source Program.

OEM: Original Equipment Manufacturer   A firm that manufactures and sells computers by assembling components produced by other hardware manufacturers.

Office Automation (OA)   The use of computer-based information systems that collect, process, store, and transmit electronic messages, documents, and other forms of office communications among individuals, workgroups, and organizations.

Off-line   Pertaining to equipment or devices not under control of the central processing unit.

Offshoring   A relocation of an organization's business processes to a lower cost location overseas.

Online   Pertaining to equipment or devices under control of the central processing unit.

Online Analytical Processing (OLAP)   A capability of some management, decision support, and executive information systems that supports interactive examination and manipulation of large amounts of data from many perspectives.

Online Transaction Processing (OLTP)   A real-time transaction processing system.

Open Systems   Information systems that use common standards for hardware, software, applications, and networking to create a computing environment that allows easy access by end users and their networked computer systems.

Operand   That which is operated upon. That part of a computer instruction that is identified by the address part of the instruction.

Operating Environment   Software packages or modules that add a graphics-based interface among end users, the operating system, and their application programs and that may also provide multitasking capability.

Operating System   The main control program of a computer system. It is a system of programs that controls the execution of computer programs and may provide scheduling, debugging, input/output control, system accounting, compilation, storage assignment, data management, and related services.

Operational Feasibility   The willingness and ability of management, employees, customers, and suppliers to operate, use, and support a proposed system.

Operation Code   A code that represents specific operations to be performed upon the operands in a computer instruction.

Operations Support System (OSS)   An information system that collects, processes, and stores data generated by the operations systems of an organization and produces data and information for input into a management information system or for the control of an operations system.

Operations System   A basic subsystem of the business firm that constitutes its input, processing, and output components. Also called a physical system.

Optical Character Recognition (OCR)   The machine identification of printed characters through the use of light-sensitive devices.

Optical Disks   A secondary storage medium using CD (compact disk) and DVD (digital versatile disk) technologies to read tiny spots on plastic disks. The disks are currently capable of storing billions of characters of information.

Optical Scanner   A device that optically scans characters or images and generates their digital representations.

Optimization Analysis Finding an optimum value for selected variables in a mathematical model, given certain constraints.

Organizational Feasibility How well a proposed information system supports the objectives of an organization's strategic plan for information systems.

Output Pertaining to a device, process, or channel involved with the transfer of data or information out of an information processing system. Opposite of Input.

Outsourcing Turning over all or part of an organization's information systems operation to outside contractors, known as systems integrators or service providers.

Packet A group of data and control information in a specified format that is transmitted as an entity.

Packet Switching A data transmission process that transmits addressed packets such that a channel is occupied only for the duration of transmission of the packet.

Page A segment of a program or data, usually of fixed length.

Paging A process that automatically and continually transfers pages of programs and data between primary storage and direct access storage devices. It provides computers with multiprogramming and virtual memory capabilities.

Parallel Processing Executing many instructions at the same time, that is, in parallel. Performed by advanced computers using many instruction processors organized in clusters or networks.

Parity Bit A check bit appended to an array of binary digits to make the sum of all the binary digits, including the check bit, always odd or always even.

Pascal A high-level, general-purpose, structured programming language named after Blaise Pascal. It was developed by Niklaus Wirth of Zurich in 1968.

Pattern Recognition The identification of shapes, forms, or configurations by automatic means.

PCM: Plug-Compatible Manufacturer A firm that manufactures computer equipment that can be plugged into existing computer systems without requiring additional hardware or software interfaces.

Peer-to-Peer Network (P2P) A computing environment in which end-user computers connect, communicate, and collaborate directly with one another via the Internet or other telecommunications network links.

Pen-Based Computers Tablet-style microcomputers that recognize handwriting and hand drawing done by a pen-shaped device on their pressure-sensitive display screens.

Performance Monitor A software package that monitors the processing of computer system jobs, helps develop a planned schedule of computer operations that can optimize computer system performance, and produces detailed statistics that are used for computer system capacity planning and control.

Periodic Reports Providing information to managers using a prespecified format designed to provide information on a regularly scheduled basis.

Peripheral Devices In a computer system, any unit of equipment, distinct from the central processing unit, that provides the system with input, output, or storage capabilities.

Personal Digital Assistant (PDA) Handheld microcomputer devices that enable you to manage information such as appointments, to-do lists, and sales contacts, send and receive e-mail, access the Web, and exchange such information with your desktop PC or network server.

Personal Information Manager (PIM) A software package that helps end users store, organize, and retrieve text and numerical data in the form of notes, lists, memos, and a variety of other forms.

Physical System Design Design of the user interface methods and products, database structures, and processing and control procedures for a proposed information system, including hardware, software, and personnel specifications.

Picosecond One trillionth of a second.

Plasma Display Output devices that generate a visual display with electrically charged particles of gas trapped between glass plates.

Plotter A hard-copy output device that produces drawings and graphical displays on paper or other materials.

Pointer A data element associated with an index, a record, or other set of data that contains the address of a related record.

Pointing Devices Devices that allow end users to issue commands or make choices by moving a cursor on the display screen.

Pointing Stick A small buttonlike device on a keyboard that moves the cursor on the screen in the direction of the pressure placed upon it.

Point-of-Sale (POS) Terminal A computer terminal used in retail stores that serves the function of a cash register as well as collecting sales data and performing other data processing functions.

Port (1) Electronic circuitry that provides a connection point between the CPU and input/output devices. (2) A connection point for a communications line on a CPU or other front-end device.

Postimplementation Review Monitoring and evaluating the results of an implemented solution or system.

Presentation Graphics Using computer-generated graphics to enhance the information presented in reports and other types of presentations.

Prespecified Reports Reports whose format is specified in advance to provide managers with information periodically, on an exception basis, or on demand.

Private Branch Exchange (PBX) A switching device that serves as an interface between the many telephone lines within a work area and the local telephone company's main telephone lines or trunks. Computerized PBXs can handle the switching of both voices and data.

Procedure-Oriented Language A programming language designed for the convenient expression of procedures used in the solution of a wide class of problems.

Procedures Sets of instructions used by people to complete a task.

Process Control The use of a computer to control an ongoing physical process, such as petrochemical production.

Process Design The design of the programs and procedures needed by a proposed information system, including detailed program specifications and procedures.

Processor A hardware device or software system capable of performing operations on data.

Program A set of instructions that causes a computer to perform a particular task.

Programmed Decision A decision that can be automated by basing it on a decision rule that outlines the steps to take when confronted with the need for a specific decision.

Programmer A person mainly involved in designing, writing, and testing computer programs.

Programming The designing, writing, and testing of a program.

Programming Language A language used to develop the instructions in computer programs.

Programming Tools Software packages or modules that provide editing and diagnostic capabilities and other support facilities to assist the programming process.

Project Management Managing the accomplishment of an information system development project according to a specific project plan, so a project is completed on time, is within its budget, and meets its design objectives.

Prompt Messages that assist a user in performing a particular job. This would include error messages, correction suggestions, questions, and other messages that guide an end user.

Protocol A set of rules and procedures for the control of communications in a communications network.

Prototype A working model. In particular, a working model of an information system that includes tentative versions of user input and output, databases and files, control methods, and processing routines.

Prototyping The rapid development and testing of working models, or prototypes, of new information system applications in an interactive, iterative process involving both systems analysts and end users.

Pseudocode An informal design language of structured programming that expresses the processing logic of a program module in ordinary human language phrases.

Pull Marketing Marketing methods that rely on the use of Web browsers by end users to access marketing materials and resources at Internet, intranet, and extranet Web sites.

Push Marketing Marketing methods that rely on Web broadcasting software to push marketing information and other marketing materials to end users' computers.

Quality Assurance Methods for ensuring that information systems are free from errors and fraud and provide information products of high quality.

Query Language A high-level, humanlike language provided by a database management system that enables users to easily extract data and information from a database.

Queue (1) A waiting line formed by items in a system waiting for service. (2) To arrange in or form a queue.

RAID Redundant array of independent disks. Magnetic disk units that house many interconnected microcomputer hard disk drives, thus providing large, fault-tolerant storage capacities.

Random Access Same as Direct Access. Contrast with Sequential Access.

Random-Access Memory (RAM) One of the basic types of semiconductor memory used for temporary storage of data or programs during processing. Each memory position can be directly sensed (read) or changed (written) in the same length of time, regardless of its location on the storage medium.

Reach and Range Analysis A planning framework that contrasts a firm's ability to use its IT platform to reach its stakeholders with the range of information products and services that can be provided or shared through IT.

Read-Only Memory (ROM) A basic type of semiconductor memory used for permanent storage. Can only be read, not "written," that is, changed. Variations are Programmable Read-Only Memory (PROM) and Erasable Programmable Read-Only Memory (EPROM).

Real Time Pertaining to the performance of data processing during the actual time a business or physical process transpires, in order that results of the data processing can be used to support the completion of the process.

Real-Time Processing Data processing in which data are processed immediately rather than periodically. Also called online processing. Contrast with Batch Processing.

Record A collection of related data fields treated as a unit.

Reduced Instruction Set Computer (RISC) A CPU architecture that optimizes processing speed by the use of a smaller number of basic machine instructions than traditional CPU designs.

Redundancy In information processing, the repetition of part or all of a message to increase the chance that the correct information will be understood by the recipient.

Register A device capable of storing a specified amount of data, such as one word.

Relational Data Structure A logical data structure in which all data elements within the database are viewed as being stored in the form of simple tables. DBMS packages based on the relational model can link data elements from various tables as long as the tables share common data elements.

Remote Access Pertaining to communication with the data processing facility by one or more stations that are distant from that facility.

Remote Job Entry (RJE) Entering jobs into a batch processing system from a remote facility.

Report Generator A feature of database management system packages that allows an end user to quickly specify a report format for the display of information retrieved from a database.

Reprographics Copying and duplicating technology and methods.

Resource Management An operating system function that controls the use of computer system resources such as primary storage, secondary storage, CPU processing time, and input/output devices by other system software and application software packages.

Robotics The technology of building machines (robots) with computer intelligence and humanlike physical capabilities.

Routine An ordered set of instructions that may have some general or frequent use.

RPG: Report Program Generator A problem-oriented language that utilizes a generator to construct programs that produce reports and perform other data processing tasks.

Rule Statements that typically take the form of a premise and a conclusion, such as if–then rules: If (condition), Then (conclusion).

Rule-Based Knowledge Knowledge represented in the form of rules and statements of fact.

Scalability The ability of hardware or software to handle the processing demands of a wide range of end users, transactions, queries, and other information processing requirements.

Scenario Approach A planning approach in which managers, employees, and planners create scenarios of what an organization will be like three to five years or more into the future and identify the role IT can play in those scenarios.

Schema An overall conceptual or logical view of the relationships between the data in a database.

Scientific Method An analytical methodology that involves (1) recognizing phenomena, (2) formulating a hypothesis about the causes or effects of the phenomena, (3) testing the hypothesis through experimentation, (4) evaluating the results of such experiments, and (5) drawing conclusions about the hypothesis.

Search Engine Optimization A process by which a website can advance the likelihood that it will be listed for a particular website query.

Secondary Storage Storage that supplements the primary storage of a computer. Synonymous with auxiliary storage.

Sector A subdivision of a track on a magnetic disk surface.

Security Codes Passwords, identification codes, account codes, and other codes that limit the access and use of computer-based system resources to authorized users.

Security Management Protecting the accuracy, integrity, and safety of the processes and resources of an inter-networked e-business enterprise against computer crime, accidental or malicious destruction, and natural disasters, using security measures such as encryption, firewalls, antivirus software, fault tolerant computers, and security monitors.

Security Monitor A software package that monitors the use of a computer system and protects its resources from unauthorized use, fraud, and vandalism.

Semiconductor Memory Microelectronic storage circuitry etched on tiny chips of silicon or other semiconducting material. The primary storage of most modern computers consists of microelectronic semiconductor storage chips for random-access memory (RAM) and read-only memory (ROM).

Semistructured Decisions Decisions involving procedures that can be partially prespecified but not enough to lead to a definite recommended decision.

Sensitivity Analysis Observing how repeated changes to a single variable affect other variables in a mathematical model.

Sequential Access A sequential method of storing and retrieving data from a file. Contrast with Random Access and Direct Access.

Sequential Data Organization Organizing logical data elements according to a prescribed sequence.

Serial Pertaining to the sequential or consecutive occurrence of two or more related activities in a single device or channel.

Server (1) A computer that supports applications and telecommunications in a network, as well as the sharing of peripheral devices, software, and databases among the workstations in the network. (2) Versions of software for installation on network servers designed to control and support applications on client microcomputers in client/server networks. Examples include multiuser network operating systems and specialized software for running Internet, intranet, and extranet Web applications, such as electronic commerce and enterprise collaboration.

Service Bureau A firm offering computer and data processing services. Also called a computer service center.

Smart Products Industrial and consumer products, with "intelligence" provided by built-in microcomputers or microprocessors that significantly improve the performance and capabilities of such products.

Software Computer programs and procedures concerned with the operation of an information system. Contrast with Hardware.

Software Package A computer program supplied by computer manufacturers, independent software companies, or other computer users. Also known as canned programs, proprietary software, or packaged programs.

Software Piracy Unauthorized copying of software.

Software Suites A combination of individual software packages that share a common graphical user interface and are designed for easy transfer of data between applications.

Solid State Pertaining to devices such as transistors and diodes whose operation depends on the control of electric or magnetic phenomena in solid materials.

Source Data Automation The use of automated methods of data entry that attempt to reduce or eliminate many of the activities, people, and data media required by traditional data entry methods.

Source Document A document that is the original formal record of a transaction, such as a purchase order or sales invoice.

Source Program A computer program written in a language that is subject to a translation process. Contrast with Object Program.

Spamming A process in which a single advertiser sends thousands of messages to computer users without their permission. The computer version of junk mail.

Special-Purpose Computer A computer designed to handle a restricted class of problems. Contrast with General-Purpose Computer.

Speech Recognition Direct conversion of spoken data into electronic form suitable for entry into a computer system. Also called voice data entry.

Spooling Simultaneous peripheral operation online. Storing input data from low-speed devices temporarily on high-speed secondary storage units, which can be quickly accessed by the CPU. Also, writing output data at high speeds onto magnetic tape or disk units from which it can be transferred to slow-speed devices such as a printer.

Spyware Also called Adware.

Stage Analysis A planning process in which the information system's needs of an organization are based on an analysis of its current stage in the growth cycle of the organization and its use of information systems technology.

Standards Measures of performance developed to evaluate the progress of a system toward its objectives.

Storage Pertaining to a device into which data can be entered, in which they can be held, and from which they can be retrieved at a later time. Same as Memory.

Strategic Information Systems Information systems that provide a firm with competitive products and services that give it a strategic advantage over its competitors in the marketplace. Also, information systems that promote business innovation, improve business processes, and build strategic information resources for a firm.

Strategic Opportunities Matrix A planning framework that uses a matrix to help identify opportunities with strategic business potential, as well as a firm's ability to exploit such opportunities with IT.

Structure Chart A design and documentation technique to show the purpose and relationships of the various modules in a program.

Structured Decisions Decisions that are structured by the decision procedures or decision rules developed for them. They involve situations in which the procedures to follow when a decision is needed can be specified in advance.

Structured Programming A programming methodology that uses a top-down program design and a limited number of control structures in a program to create highly structured modules of program code.

Structured Query Language (SQL) A query language that is becoming a standard for advanced database management system packages. A query's basic form is SELECT . . . FROM . . . WHERE.

Subroutine A routine that can be part of another program routine.

Subschema A subset or transformation of the logical view of the database schema that is required by a particular user application program.

Subsystem A system that is a component of a larger system.

Supercomputer A special category of large computer systems that are the most powerful available. They are designed to solve massive computational problems.

Superconductor Materials that can conduct electricity with almost no resistance. This allows the development of extremely fast and small electronic circuits. Formerly only possible at supercold temperatures near absolute zero. Recent developments promise superconducting materials near room temperature.

Supply Chain The network of business processes and interrelationships among businesses that are needed to build, sell, and deliver a product to its final customer.

Supply Chain Management Integrating management practices and information technology to optimize information and product flows among the processes and business partners within a supply chain.

Switch (1) A device or programming technique for making a selection. (2) A computer that controls message switching among the computers and terminals in a telecommunications network.

Switching Costs The costs in time, money, effort, and inconvenience that it would take a customer or supplier to switch its business to a firm's competitors.

SWOT Analysis A business planning process in which various aspects of a business situation are analyzed and compared. SWOT is an acronym for Strengths, Weaknesses, Opportunities, and Threats.

Synchronous A characteristic in which each event, or the performance of any basic operation, is constrained to start on, and usually to keep in step with, signals from a timing clock. Contrast with Asynchronous.

System (1) A group of interrelated or interacting elements forming a unified whole. (2) A group of interrelated components working together toward a common goal by accepting inputs and producing outputs in an organized transformation process. (3) An assembly of methods, procedures, or techniques unified by regulated interaction to form an organized whole. (4) An organized collection of people, machines, and methods required to accomplish a set of specific functions.

System Flowchart A graphic diagramming tool used to show the flow of information processing activities as data are processed by people and devices.

Systems Analysis (1) Analyzing in detail the components and requirements of a system. (2) Analyzing in detail the information needs of an organization, the characteristics and components of presently utilized information systems, and the functional requirements of proposed information systems.

Systems Approach A systematic process of problem solving that defines problems and opportunities in a systems context. Data are gathered describing the problem or opportunity, and alternative solutions are identified and evaluated. Then the best solution is selected and implemented, and its success is evaluated.

Systems Design Deciding how a proposed information system will meet the information needs of end users. Includes logical and physical design activities and user interface, data, and process design activities that produce system specifications that satisfy the system requirements developed in the systems analysis stage.

Systems Development (1) Conceiving, designing, and implementing a system. (2) Developing information systems by a process of investigation, analysis, design, implementation, and maintenance. Also called the systems development life cycle (SDLC), information systems development, or application development.

Systems Development Tools Graphical, textual, and computer-aided tools and techniques used to help analyze, design, and document the development of an information system. Typically used to represent (1) the components and flows of a system, (2) the user interface, (3) data attributes and relationships, and (4) detailed system processes.

Systems Implementation The stage of systems development in which hardware and software are acquired, developed, and installed; the system is tested and documented; people are trained to operate and use the system; and an organization converts to the use of a newly developed system.

Systems Investigation The screening, selection, and preliminary study of a proposed information system solution to a business problem.

Systems Maintenance The monitoring, evaluating, and modifying of a system to make desirable or necessary improvements.

System Software Programs that control and support operations of a computer system. System software includes a variety of programs, such as operating systems, database management systems, communications control programs, service and utility programs, and programming language translators.

System Specifications The product of the systems design stage. It consists of specifications for the hardware, software, facilities, personnel, databases, and the user interface of a proposed information system.

Systems Thinking Recognizing systems, subsystems, components of systems, and system interrelationships in a situation. Also known as a systems context or a systemic view of a situation.

System Support Programs Programs that support the operations, management, and users of a computer system by providing a variety of support services. Examples are system utilities and performance monitors.

Tangible Benefits and Costs The quantifiable benefits and costs of a proposed solution or system.

Task and Project Management Managing team and workgroup projects by scheduling, tracking, and charting the completion status of tasks within a project.

Task Management A basic operating system function that manages the accomplishment of the computing tasks of users by a computer system.

TCP/IP Transmission control protocol/Internet protocol. A suite of telecommunications network protocols used by the Internet, intranets, and extranets that has become a de facto network architecture standard for many companies.

Technical Feasibility Whether reliable hardware and software capable of meeting the needs of a proposed system can be acquired or developed by an organization in the required time.

Technology Management The organizational responsibility to identify, introduce, and monitor the assimilation of new information system technologies into organizations.

Telecommunications Pertaining to the transmission of signals over long distances, including not only data communications but also the transmission of images and voices using radio, television, and other communications technologies.

Telecommunications Channel The part of a telecommunications network that connects the message source with the message receiver. It includes the hardware, software, and media used to connect one network location to another for the purpose of transmitting and receiving information.

Telecommunications Controller A data communications interface device (frequently a special-purpose mini- or microcomputer) that can control a telecommunications network containing many terminals.

Telecommunications Control Program A computer program that controls and supports the communications between the computers and terminals in a telecommunications network.

Telecommunications Monitors Computer programs that control and support the communications between the computers and terminals in a telecommunications network.

Telecommunications Processors Inter-network processors such as switches and routers and other devices such as multiplexers and communications controllers that allow a communications channel to carry simultaneous data transmissions from many terminals. They may also perform error monitoring, diagnostics and correction, modulation-demodulation, data compression, data coding and decoding, message switching, port contention, and buffer storage.

Telecommuting The use of telecommunications to replace commuting to work from one's home.

Teleconferencing The use of video communications to allow business conferences to be held with participants who are scattered across a country, continent, or the world.

Telephone Tag The process that occurs when two people who wish to contact each other by telephone repeatedly miss each other's phone calls.

Teleprocessing Using telecommunications for computer-based information processing.

Terabyte One trillion bytes. More accurately, 2 to the 40th power, or 1,009,511,627,776 in decimal notation.

Text Data Words, phrases, sentences, and paragraphs used in documents and other forms of communication.

Throughput The total amount of useful work performed by a data processing system during a given period.

Time Sharing Providing computer services to many users simultaneously while providing rapid responses to each.

Total Quality Management Planning and implementing programs of continuous quality improvement, where quality is defined as meeting or exceeding the requirements and expectations of customers for a product or service.

Touch-Sensitive Screen An input device that accepts data input by the placement of a finger on or close to the CRT screen.

Track The portion of a moving storage medium, such as a drum, tape, or disk, that is accessible to a given reading head position.

Trackball A rollerball device set in a case used to move the cursor on a computer's display screen.

Transaction An event that occurs as part of doing business, such as a sale, purchase, deposit, withdrawal, refund, transfer, or payment.

Transaction Document A document produced as part of a business transaction, for example, a purchase order, paycheck, sales receipt, or customer invoice.

Transaction File A data file containing relatively transient data to be processed in combination with a master file. Contrast with Master File.

Transaction Processing Cycle A cycle of basic transaction processing activities including data entry, transaction processing, database maintenance, document and report generation, and inquiry processing.

Transaction Processing System (TPS) An information system that processes data arising from the occurrence of business transactions.

Transaction Terminals Terminals used in banks, retail stores, factories, and other work sites to capture transaction data at their point of origin. Examples are point-of-sale (POS) terminals and automated teller machines (ATMs).

Transborder Data Flows (TDF) The flow of business data over telecommunications networks across international borders.

Transform Algorithm Performing an arithmetic computation on a record key and using the result of the calculation as an address for that record. Also known as key transformation or hashing.

Transnational Strategy A management approach in which an organization integrates its global business activities through close cooperation and interdependence among its headquarters, operations, and international subsidiaries and its use of appropriate global information technologies.

Turnaround Document Output of a computer system (such as customer invoices and statements) that is designed to be returned to the organization as machine-readable input.

Turnaround Time The elapsed time between submission of a job to a computing center and the return of the results.

Turnkey Systems Computer systems in which all of the hardware, software, and systems development needed by a user are provided.

Unbundling The separate pricing of hardware, software, and other related services.

Uniform Resource Locator (URL) An access code (such as http://www.sun.com) for identifying and locating hypermedia document files, databases, and other resources at Web sites and other locations on the Internet, intranets, and extranets.

Universal Product Code (UPC) A standard identification code using bar coding printed on products that can be read by optical scanners such as those found at a supermarket checkout.

Unstructured Decisions Decisions that must be made in situations in which it is not possible to specify in advance most of the decision procedures to follow.

User Friendly A characteristic of human-operated equipment and systems that makes them safe, comfortable, and easy to use.

User Interface That part of an operating system or other program that allows users to communicate with it to load programs, access files, and accomplish other computing tasks.

User Interface Design Designing the interactions between end users and computer systems, including input/output methods and the conversion of data between human-readable and machine-readable forms.

Utility Program A standard set of routines that assists in the operation of a computer system by performing some frequently required process such as copying, sorting, or merging.

Value-Added Carriers Third-party vendors who lease telecommunications lines from common carriers and offer a variety of telecommunications services to customers.

Value-Added Resellers (VARs) Companies that provide industry-specific software for use with the computer systems of selected manufacturers.

Value Chain Viewing a firm as a series, chain, or network of basic activities that adds value to its products and services and thus adds a margin of value to the firm.

Videoconferencing Real-time video and audio conferencing (1) among users at networked PCs (desktop videoconferencing) or (2) among participants in conference rooms or auditoriums in different locations (teleconferencing). Videoconferencing can also include whiteboarding and document sharing.

Virtual Communities Groups of people with similar interests who meet and share ideas on the Internet and online services and develop a feeling of belonging to a community.

Virtual Company A form of organization that uses telecommunications networks and other information technologies to link the people, assets, and ideas of a variety of business partners, no matter where they may be, to exploit a business opportunity.

Virtual Machine Pertaining to the simulation of one type of computer system by another computer system.

Virtual Mall An online multimedia simulation of a shopping mall with many different interlinked retail Web sites.

Virtual Memory The use of secondary storage devices as an extension of the primary storage of the computer, thus giving the appearance of a larger main memory than actually exists.

Virtual Private Network A secure network that uses the Internet as its main backbone network to connect the intranets of a company's different locations or to establish extranet links between a company and its customers, suppliers, or other business partners.

Virtual Reality The use of multisensory human/computer interfaces that enable human users to experience computer-simulated objects, entities, spaces, and "worlds" as if they actually existed.

Virtual Storefront An online multimedia simulation of a retail store shopping experience on the Web.

Virtual Team A team whose members use the Internet, intranets, extranets, and other networks to communicate, coordinate, and collaborate with one another on tasks and projects, even though they may work in different geographic locations and for different organizations.

VLSI: Very-Large-Scale Integration Semiconductor chips containing hundreds of thousands of circuits.

Voice Conferencing Telephone conversations shared among several participants via speaker phones or networked PCs with Internet telephone software.

Voice Mail Unanswered telephone messages that are digitized, stored, and played back to the recipient by a voice messaging computer.

Voice over IP (VoIP) A process where the Internet is used as the network carrier for telephone or voice communication.

Volatile Memory Memory (such as electronic semiconductor memory) that loses its contents when electrical power is interrupted.

Wand A handheld optical character recognition device used for data entry by many transaction terminals.

Web Browser A software package that provides the user interface for accessing Internet, intranet, and extranet Web sites. Browsers are becoming multifunction universal clients for sending and receiving e-mail, downloading files, accessing Java applets, participating in discussion groups, developing Web pages, and other Internet, intranet, and extranet applications.

Web Publishing   Creating, converting, and storing hyperlinked documents and other material on Internet or intranet Web servers so that they can be easily shared via Web browsers with teams, workgroups, or the enterprise.

Web Services   A collection of Web and object-oriented technologies for linking Web-based applications running on different hardware, software, database, or network platforms. For example, Web services could link key business functions within the applications a business shares with its customers, suppliers, and business partners.

What-If Analysis   Observing how changes to selected variables affect other variables in a mathematical model.

Whiteboarding   See Data Conferencing.

Wide Area Network (WAN)   A data communications network covering a large geographic area.

Window   One section of a computer's multiple-section display screen, each section of which can have a different display.

Wireless LANs   Using radio or infrared transmissions to link devices in a local area network.

Wireless Technologies   Using radio wave, microwave, infrared, and laser technologies to transport digital communications without wires between communications devices. Examples include terrestrial microwave, communications satellites, cellular and PCS phone and pager systems, mobile data radio, and various wireless Internet technologies.

Word   (1) A string of characters considered as unit. (2) An ordered set of bits (usually larger than a byte) handled as a unit by the central processing unit.

Word Processing   The automation of the transformation of ideas and information into a readable form of communication. It involves the use of computers to manipulate text data to produce office communications in the form of documents.

Workgroup Computing   Members of a networked workgroup may use groupware tools to communicate, coordinate, and collaborate and to share hardware, software, and databases to accomplish group assignments.

Workstation   (1) A computer system designed to support the work of one person. (2) A high-powered computer to support the work of professionals in engineering, science, and other areas that require extensive computing power and graphics capabilities.

World Wide Web (WWW)   A global network of multimedia Internet sites for information, education, entertainment, e-business, and e-commerce.

XML (Extensible Markup Language)   A Web document content description language that describes the content of Web pages by applying hidden identifying tags or contextual labels to the data in Web documents. By categorizing and classifying Web data this way, XML makes Web content easier to identify, search, analyze, and selectively exchange between computers.

Name Index

Company Index

Subject Index

Information technology management
  approaches, 614, 617
  challenges, 50–59, 585–587, 615–616
  changes, 619–620
  components, 617
  cost savings, 615–616
  failures, 627–631
  global dimensions, 632–647
  offshoring, 625–627
  operations, 621
  outsourcing, 624–625
  staff planning, 622, 625
  technology management, 623
  user services, 623–624
Information technology organization
  architectures, 492, 619, 620
  impact of cloud computing, 483–484
  international, 632, 635
  management issues, 585–586
  relations with business partners, 499–500
  staff planning, 622, 625
  top jobs, 622–623
Information technology planning, 482–497
  approaches, 617–618, 619
  architectures, 618–619
  backlogs, 558–559
  business application planning, 495–497
  cloud computing, 483–484
  e-business architecture planning, 497
  in global organizations, 637–638
  process, 491–492, 617–619
  strategy development, 491–492, 618
Inkjet printers, 140–141
Innovation strategies, 84, 85
Input
  to computer systems, 60, 127, 131–140
  data, 69, 314
Input technologies, 69, 131–140
  magnetic stripe technology, 139
  pen-based computing, 134–135
  pointing devices, 131, 134
  scanners, 134, 137–139
  touch screens, 134, 160–161
  wands, 138
Inquiry processing, 315
Instant messaging, 171
Intangible benefits, 522
Integrated packages, 170
Intellectual property theft, 574–576
Intelligent agents, 470–471
Intelligent terminals, 119
Interactive marketing, 318, 321–322
Interenterprise information systems, 98
Interface, 63
Internet; *see also* e-business; e-commerce; Web
  access, 125–126, 644–645
  advertising, 302
  applications, 260
  business value, 262–263
  cloud computing, 179, 213
  dependence, 601–602
  e-mail
    monitoring, 597
    software, 171, 175
    spam, 580, 584
    volumes, 616
  file sharing, 278
  as global platform, 641–642
  growth, 255, 259, 642
  history, 278
  IP addresses, 291, 298
  mobile access, 283–285
  number of users, 255, 259, 642
  privacy issues, 580–581, 584, 598–599
  search engines, 81–82, 231, 260, 404, 405–406

  structure, 259
  TCP/IP, 290, 291–292
Internet networking technologies, 256
Internet service providers (ISPs), 259–260, 291
Internet telephony, 292
Internet2, 257–258
Inter-network processors, 286
Interpreters, 201
Intranets, 46
  business value, 264–266
  defined, 263–264
  human resources systems, 326–328
Inventory control systems, 329, 330
IS; *see* Information systems
ISPs; *see* Internet service providers
IT; *see* Information technology
ITG; *see* Information technology governance

Java, 198, 199, 201
Join operations, 219

Kilobytes, 143
KMS; *see* Knowledge management systems
Knowledge-based systems, 45
Knowledge bases, 459
Knowledge-creating companies, 100–101
Knowledge discovery, 444
Knowledge engineering, 463–464
Knowledge engineers, 463–464
Knowledge management systems (KMS), 49,
    100–101, 309, 450
Knowledge workers, 66

Language processors, 201
Language translators, 201
LANs; *see* Local area networks
Laser printers, 140–141
Legacy systems, 276
Legal feasibility, 521, 523
Legal issues, 584–585; *see also* Computer crime
Leveraging investment, 86
Libel, 584
Licensing, software, 179–180, 615
Linux, 187, 287
Liquid crystal displays, 135, 140
Local area networks (LANs), 273, 283
Logical data elements, 212, 215
Logical models, 525–526
Loyalty programs, 346–347

Mac OS X, 188–189
Machine control, 326
Machine languages, 191–192
Machine learning, 457–458
Machines, 66–67; *see also* Computers; Hardware
Magnetic disks, 146–147
Magnetic ink character recognition (MICR), 139
Magnetic stripe technology, 139
Magnetic tape, 147
Mainframe computer systems, 117, 123–124, 126
Malware, 576–580
Management; *see also* Information technology
    management
  careers, 57
  challenges, 560–654
Management information systems (MIS), 44, 49,
    434–435
Management involvement, 628, 629
Management reporting, 434–435
Management support systems, 48–49
MANs; *see* Metropolitan area networks

Manufacturing execution systems (MES), 326
Manufacturing information systems, 325–326
Market-maker companies, 409
Marketing information systems, 318–324; *see also*
    Customer relationship management
  interactive marketing, 318, 321–322
  sales force automation, 323–324
  targeted marketing, 322–323
Media; *see also* Storage
  communications, 68
  data storage, 67
  hyper-, 231–232, 265, 279
  telecommunications, 279
Medicine
  e-health records, 132, 133
  hospitals, 132–133, 228–229, 293
  imaging technology, 158–159
  information technology, 228–229
  neurosurgery, 464–465
  RFID implants, 270–271
  voice recognition systems, 132–133
Megabytes, 143
Memory; *see also* Storage
  cache, 127
  random-access, 144
  read-only, 144–145
  virtual, 184
MES; *see* Manufacturing execution systems
Metadata, 222–223, 233
Metcalfe's law, 252, 255
Metropolitan area networks (MANs), 272–273
MICR; *see* Magnetic ink character recognition
Microcomputer systems, 117–121
  connectivity, 119
  corporate criteria, 119
  network computers, 120
  operating systems, 119
  security-equipped, 119
Microcomputers, 117
Microsoft Windows, 119, 160, 181, 185–186,
    530–531
Microsoft Windows NT, 185
Microsoft Windows Server 2008, 185–186
Microsoft Windows XP, 185
Middleware, 191, 256–257, 287
Midrange systems, 117, 121–122
Million instructions per second (MIPS), 128
Milliseconds, 128
Mind mapping, 488–489
Minicomputers, 122
Minisupercomputers, 124, 126
MIPS; *see* Million instructions per second
MIS; *see* Management information systems
Mobile phones; *see* Cellular telephones
Model bases, 432
Modems, 285–286
Modularity, 535
Monitors, 134
Moore's law, 128–130, 152
Mouse, 131
Multidimensional databases, 217, 219, 220
Multiplexers, 286–287
Multiprogramming, 185
Multitasking, 185

Nanoseconds, 128
Nanotechnology, 113
Natural interfaces, 457
Natural languages, 193, 242
Natural queries, 242
NCs; *see* Network computers
.NET, 186, 198–199
Network architectures, 289–291
Network computers (NCs), 120, 276, 277